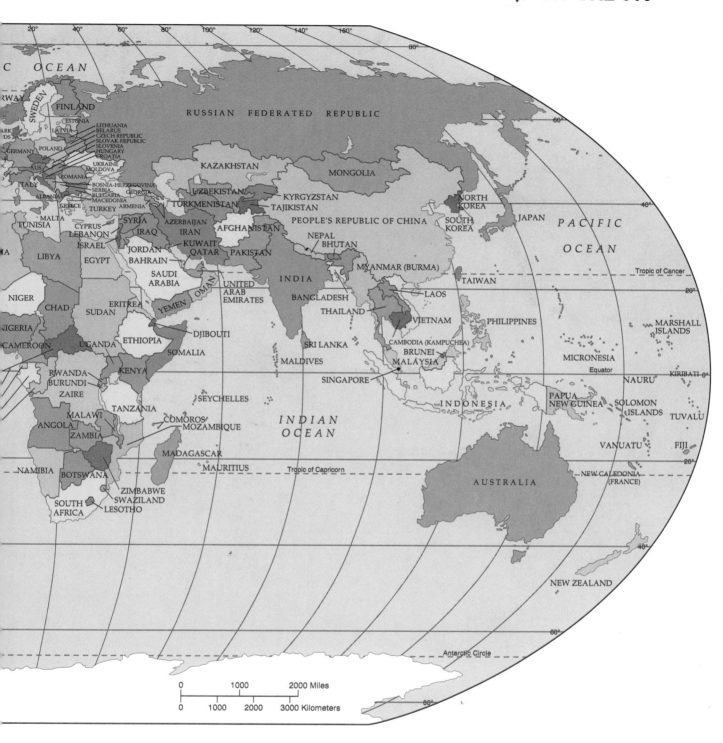

C OCEAN

RWAY
SWEDEN
FINLAND

ESTONIA
LITHUANIA
BELARUS
CZECH REPUBLIC
SLOVAK REPUBLIC
SLOVENIA
HUNGARY
CROATIA
UKRAINE
MOLDOVA
ROMANIA
BOSNIA-HERZEGOVINA
SERBIA
BULGARIA
MACEDONIA
ALBANIA
GREECE
TURKEY

ARK
DS
GERMANY
POLAND
AUS.
ITALY

LATVIA

ARMENIA

GEORGIA

RUSSIAN FEDERATED REPUBLIC

KAZAKHSTAN

MONGOLIA

NORTH
KOREA

SOUTH
KOREA

JAPAN

PACIFIC

OCEAN

UZBEKISTAN
TURKMENISTAN
TAJIKISTAN
KYRGYZSTAN

PEOPLE'S REPUBLIC OF CHINA

MALTA
TUNISIA

CYPRUS
LEBANON
ISRAEL

SYRIA
IRAQ

AZERBAIJAN
IRAN

AFGHANISTAN

LIBYA
EGYPT

JORDAN
BAHRAIN

KUWAIT
QATAR

NEPAL
BHUTAN

PAKISTAN

SAUDI
ARABIA

MYANMAR (BURMA)

TAIWAN

Tropic of Cancer

NIGER
CHAD
ERITREA
SUDAN

YEMEN

OMAN

UNITED
ARAB
EMIRATES

INDIA

BANGLADESH

LAOS

NIGERIA
CAMEROON
UGANDA

ETHIOPIA
DJIBOUTI
SOMALIA

THAILAND

VIETNAM

PHILIPPINES

MARSHALL
ISLANDS

SRI LANKA
MALDIVES

CAMBODIA (KAMPUCHEA)
BRUNEI
MALAYSIA

MICRONESIA

RWANDA
BURUNDI
ZAIRE

KENYA

SINGAPORE

Equator

NAURU

KIRIBATI 0°

SEYCHELLES

INDIAN
OCEAN

INDONESIA

PAPUA
NEW GUINEA

SOLOMON
ISLANDS

TUVALU

MALAWI
TANZANIA

ANGOLA
ZAMBIA

COMOROS
MOZAMBIQUE

MADAGASCAR

VANUATU

FIJI

NAMIBIA
BOTSWANA

ZIMBABWE
SWAZILAND

MAURITIUS

Tropic of Capricorn

NEW CALEDONIA
(FRANCE)

AUSTRALIA

SOUTH
AFRICA

LESOTHO

NEW ZEALAND

Antarctic Circle

0   1000   2000 Miles

0   1000   2000   3000 Kilometers

OUT OF MANY

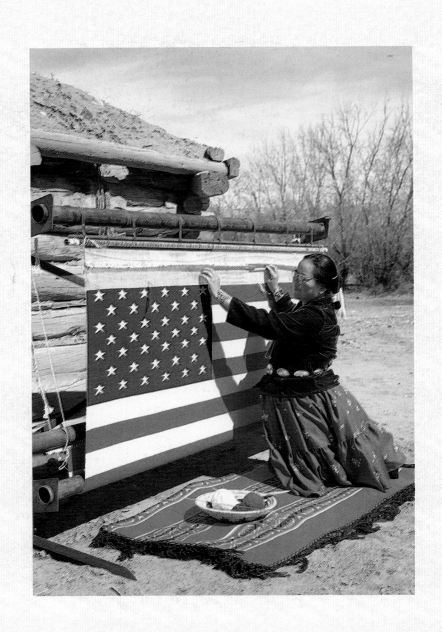

Combined Edition

OUT OF MANY

A HISTORY
OF THE
AMERICAN PEOPLE

JOHN MACK FARAGHER
Yale University

MARI JO BUHLE
Brown University

DANIEL CZITROM
Mount Holyoke College

SUSAN H. ARMITAGE
Washington State University

 Prentice Hall Englewood Cliffs, New Jersey 07632

Out of many : a history of the American people / John Mack Faragher.
. . . [et al.].— Combined ed.
    p.   cm.
Includes bibliographical references and index.
ISBN 0-13-556599-5
  1. United States--History.   I. Faragher, John Mack.
E178.1.0935   1994b   93-11738
1973 — dc 20   CIP

To our students, our sisters, and our brothers

Acquisitions Editor: Stephen Dalphin
Development Editor: Susanna Lesan
Production Editor: Marianne Peters
Art Director: Anne T. Bonanno
Editor-in-Chief: Charlyce Jones Owen
Marketing Manager: Roland Hernandez
Supplements Development: Jane Ritter
Interior and Cover Designer: Lydia Gershey
Cover Art: Original Weaving © Donna P. Simons, 1993
              Photograph © Stuart J. Simons, 1993

Prepress Buyer: Kelly Behr
Manufacturing Buyer: Mary Ann Gloriande
Photo Researcher: Linda Sykes/Photosearch
Photo Editor: Lorinda Morris-Nantz
Copy Editor: Bruce Fulton
Editorial Assistant: Caffie Risher

© 1994 by Prentice-Hall, Inc.
A Paramount Communications Company
Englewood Cliffs, New Jersey 07632

Printed in the United States of America
10 9 8 7 6 5 4 3 2 1

ISBN 0-13-556599-5

Prentice-Hall International (UK) Limited, *London*
Prentice-Hall of Australia Pty. Limited, *Sydney*
Prentice-Hall Canada Inc., *Toronto*
Prentice-Hall Hispanoamericana, S.A., *Mexico*
Prentice-Hall of India Private Limited, *New Delhi*
Prentice-Hall of Japan, Inc., *Tokyo*
Simon & Schuster Asia Pte. Ltd., *Singapore*
Editora Prentice-Hall do Brasil, Ltda., *Rio de Janeiro*

About the Weaving

The cover image was designed by Donna Pinkowitz Simons and created with a variety of textures and motifs to represent various times and places in American History. The artist used hand-made, hand-dyed yarns, as well as other media: leather, beads, lace, twigs, feathers, film, and more. Ms. Simons has designed for major corporate, advertising, and publishing clients. Her work includes textile design and illustration in a variety of media. Ms. Simons lives with her husband and three daughters in Essex County, New Jersey.

BRIEF CONTENTS

CONTENTS

29   WAR ABROAD, WAR AT HOME, 1965–1974   925

30   THE OVEREXTENDED SOCIETY, 1974–1980   961

MAPS

CHARTS, GRAPHS, AND TABLES

PREFACE

OUT OF MANY

Out of Many: A History of the American People recounts the story of our country by focusing on the experiences of diverse communities of Americans. One of the most characteristic features of this country has always been its astounding variety. The American people include the descendants of native Indians, colonial Europeans, Africans, and migrants from virtually every country and continent. Indeed, as we approach a new century, a tide of immigrants from Latin America and Asia rivals the great migration from eastern and southern Europe a hundred years ago. Moreover, the United States is one of the world's largest nations, incorporating more than 3.6 million square miles of territory. With climates ranging from the tropical jungles of southern Florida to the frozen tundra of arctic Alaska, from the arid deserts of the Southwest to the lush forests of the Great Lakes, regional societies have understandably developed important distinctions and differences. The struggle to make a nation out of our many communities is what much of American history is all about.

Communities are made up of people whose lives are woven into a fabric of relationships and values. Networks of kinship and friendship, and connections across generations and among families, establish the bonds essential to community life. Shared feelings about values and history establish the basis for common identity. In communities, people find the power to act collectively in their own interest.

But American communities frequently took shape as the result of serious conflicts among groups, and within communities there often has been significant fighting between competing groups or classes. And despite consistent laments about the loss of community in modern America, community has not passed away but rather has been reinvented. Once primarily defined by neighborhood or homeland, communities today may be composed of people living in widely distant locations but connected together by means of modern communication.

The title for our book was suggested by the Latin phrase selected by John Adams, Benjamin Franklin, and Thomas Jefferson for the Great Seal of the United States: *E Pluribus Unum*—"Out of Many Comes Unity." National unity, the founders of the nation understood, could not be imposed by a powerful central authority but had to develop out of mutual respect for Americans of different backgrounds. The revolutionary leadership expressed the hope that such respect could grow on the basis of a remarkable proposition: "We hold these truths to be self-evident, that all men are created equal; that they are endowed by their Creator with certain unalienable rights; that among these, are life, liberty, and the pursuit of happiness." The national government of the United States would preserve local and state authority but would guarantee individual rights. The nation would be strengthened by guarantees of difference.

Out of Many—it is the promise of America, and the premise of this book. The underlying dialectic of American history, we believe, is that we find our *unity* in the *differences* among ourselves, and that these differences can be our strengths as long as we affirm the promise of the Declaration. Protecting the "right to be different," in other words, is absolutely fundamental to the continued existence of democracy, and that right is best protected by the existence of strong communities. We are bound together as a nation by the ideal of local and cultural differences protected by our common committment to the values of our revolution.

Today—with the many social and cultural conflicts that abound in the United States—some Americans have lost faith in that vision. But our history shows that the promise of American unity always has been problematic. Centrifugal forces have been powerful in the American past, and at times the country has seemed about to fracture into its component parts. Our transformation from a collection of groups and regions into a nation has been marked by painful and often violent struggles. Our past is filled with conflicts between Indians and colonists, masters and slaves, Patriots and Loyalists, Northerners and Southerners, Easterners and Westerners, capitalists and workers, and sometimes the government and the people. Americans often appear to be little more than a contentious collection of peoples with conflicting interests, divided by region and background, race and class.

We have not always lived up to the American promise, and there is a dark side to our history. It took the bloodiest war in American history to secure the human rights of African Americans, and the struggle for full equality continues more than a century later. During the great influx of immigrants in the early twentieth century fears led to movements to "Americanize" the foreign born by forcing them, in the words of one leader, "to give up the languages, customs, and methods of life which they have brought with them across the ocean, and adopt instead the language, habits, and customs of this country, and the general standards and ways of American living." Similar thinking motivated Congress to bar the immigration of Asians and other ethnic groups into the country, and to force assimilation on American Indians by denying them the freedom to practice their religion or even speak their own language.

But other Americans argued for a more idealistic version of "Americanization." "What is the American, this new man?" asked the French immigrant Michel Crevecoeur in 1782. "A strange mixture of blood which you will find in no other country," he answered; in America, "individuals of all nations are melted into a new race of men." A century later Crevecoeur was echoed by historian Frederick Jackson Turner, who believed that "in the crucible of the frontier, the immigrants were Americanized, liberated, and fused into a mixed race, English in neither nationality nor characteristics. The process has gone on from the early days to our own."

This process of "acculturation" — to use a sociological term — has been one of the most fundamental aspects of our history. It did not occur, however, because of compulsory "Americanization" programs, but rather because of the influence of free public education, the appeal of popular participation in democratic politics, and the impact of popular culture. Contemporary America does have a common culture: most of us laugh at the same television sitcoms and share the same aspiration to own a home and send our children to college — all unique American traits.

To a degree that too few Americans appreciate, this common culture resulted from a complicated process of mutual discovery that took place when different ethnic and regional groups encountered one another. Consider just one small and unique aspect of our culture, the barbecue. Americans have been barbecuing since before the beginning of written history. Early settlers adopted this technique of cooking from the Indians — the word itself comes from a native term for a framework of sticks over a fire on which meat was slowly cooked. Colonists typically barbecued pork, fed on Indian corn. African

slaves lent their own touch by introducing the use of spicy sauces. Thus the ritual that is a part of nearly every American family's Fourth of July celebrates the heritage of diversity that went into making our common culture.

Or consider the Navajo Indians of the Southwest. Conquered by the American army and herded onto a barren reservation in the middle of the nineteenth century, they nearly perished as a people. But eventually regaining their homeland, they rose to become the largest and one of the most influential Indian tribes in twentieth-century America. Much of their success came from their ability to learn from their neighbors. Originally nomadic hunters, they were inspired to settle down by the example of the farming Pueblos who taught them to weave cotton cloth. Many of the Navajo then took to raising sheep, something they learned from neighboring Hispanic ranchers, and by the late nineteenth century they had transformed themselves into a nation of shepherds. From American traders they learned to weave their wool for export, and soon fine Navajo rugs were being sought by collectors from around the world. The process of acculturation (beautifully symbolized in the photograph that opens this book) has helped the Navajos to survive and prosper as a people.

But as the Navajo suggest, the process of "Americanization" and acculturation has not erased the differences among us. We continue to be a nation of diverse communities. Acculturation has not meant that Americans have given up the sense of pluralistic identity. The American educator John Dewey recognized this important fact early in this century. "The genuine American, the typical American is himself a hyphenated character," he declared, "international and interracial in his make-up." When the student "recognizes all the factors which have gone into our being, he will continue to prize and reverence that coming from his own past, but he will think of it as honored in being simply one factor in forming a whole nobler than itself." The point about our "hyphenated character," Dewey declared, "is to see to it that the hyphen *connects* instead of separates."

We the authors of *Out of Many* share Dewey's perspective on American history. "Creation comes from the impact of diversity," wrote the American philosopher Horace Kallen. We also endorse his vision of the American promise: "A democracy of nationalities, cooperating voluntarily and autonomously through common institutions, . . . a multiplicity in a unity, an orchestration of mankind."

THE PLAN OF THE BOOK

In *Out of Many* each chapter opens with a description of a representative community. Some present contending American communities struggling with one another: African slaves and English masters on the rice plantations of colonial Georgia, Tejanos and Americans during the Texas war of independence, anti-war and pro-war factions in Milwaukee during World War I. Other chapters open with portraits of communities facing social change: the feminists of Seneca Falls, New York, in 1848, the sitdown strikers of Flint, Michigan in 1934, the African Americans of Montgomery, Alabama in 1955. As the story unfolds we find communities growing to include ever larger groups of Americans: during the Revolution Continental soldiers from every colony forging a national patriotic army at Valley Forge; the transformation of Washington, D.C. from a Southern town to a national capital in the midst of the Civil War; and in the 1920s the creation of a national moviegoing community that dreamed a collective dream of material prosperity and upward mobility.

Out of Many is also continental in its approach. Selecting examples from all regions of the country, we encourage students to see America as the enormous nation it is. The founding of the first European settlements in the New World, for example, we illustrate with a vignette of seventeenth-century Santa Fe, New Mexico. We present territorial expansion into the American West from the point of view of the Mandan villagers of the upper Missouri River of North Dakota. The policies of the Reconstruction era we introduce through the experience of African Americans in Hale County, Alabama. We illustrate some of the ironies of World War II with the story of the "Zoot Suit Riots" of Los Angeles. With community introductions from New England to the South, the Midwest to the Far West, *Out of Many* is the only textbook that adopts a truly continental perspective.

In these ways *Out of Many* breaks new ground. We continue to believe, however, that the traditional turning points of the American past remain critically important. The Revolution and the struggle over the Constitution, the Civil War and Reconstruction, the Great Depression and World War II are watershed periods for us. In *Out of Many* we seek to *integrate* the narrative of national history with the story of our many communities. The Revolutionary and Constitutional period, tried the ability of local communities to forge a new unity, and success depended upon the ability to build a nation without compromising local identity. The Civil War and Reconstruction formed a second great test of the balance between the national ideals of the revolution and the power of local and sectional communities. The Depression and the New Deal demonstrated the impotence of local communities and the growing power of national institutions during the greatest economic challenge in our history. Rather than telling two stories — one of the people, the other of the nation — the community focus of *Out of Many* weaves them into a single compelling narrative.

Although we share joint responsibility for the entire book, the chapters were individually authored: John Mack Faragher wrote chapters 1–8; Mari Jo Buhle wrote chapters 18–20, 25–26, 29–30; Daniel Czitrom wrote chapters 17, 21–24, 27–28, 31; and Susan H. Armitage wrote chapters 9–16.

SPECIAL FEATURES

Out of Many combines the best of the traditional American history textbooks with a new approach. Each chapter includes features that aid the student and offer an exciting new look.

- Outlines at the opening of each chapter summarize all the important topics and at a glance tell students what they can expect from the chapter.
- Abundant illustrations and photographs include many never before used in an American history text. There are *no* anachronistic graphics — each one dates from the historical period under discussion. The extensive captions treat the graphics as visual evidence of the American past, providing full documentation and an explanation of their significance.
- Maps — more than any competing American history text — use bold new projections that cover the entire continent and provide students a world image with which they are familiar.
- Chronologies at the conclusion of each chapter provide students with a quick review of the main points and dates.
- A short list of additional readings at the end of the chapter is designed to be accessible to the interested introductory student. Extensive bibliographies on all the topics at the back of the book provide complete lists of current American historical scholarship.

CLASSROOM ASSISTANCE PACKAGE

In classrooms across the country, most instructors come up against students who perceive history as merely a jumble of names, dates, and events. The key to bringing dimension to our dynamic past for students is a scholarship-laden, pedagogically rich text accompanied with a multimedia classroom assistance package that brings the 1600s through the 1990s alive with the help of state-of-the-art laser discs, satellite-view maps, and authentic historical documents.

Instructor's Resource Manual
Prepared by Bill Cecil-Fronsman, Washburn University of Topeka. A true time-saver in developing and preparing lecture presentations, this indispensable guide contains chapter outlines, detailed chapter overviews, out-of-class activities, discussion questions, readings, and audio-visual aids.

Test Item File
Prepared by Marilyn Rhinehart of North Harris College, assisted by Elizabeth Neumeyer of Kellogg Community College. The Test Item File (TIF) offers a menu of over 1500 multiple-choice, identification, matching, short answer, and essay test questions. Objective questions are classified as to question type: factual and conceptual. The Test Item File also includes 10–15 questions per chapter, prepared by Robert Tomes of St. Johns University, on maps found in the chapter.

Prentice Hall Test Manager
IBM 5.25″, IBM 3.5″, Macintosh.
With Test Manager, instructors can select items from the Test Item File and use them to design their own exams.

Transparency Pack
Prepared by Robert Tomes of St. Johns University Transparency acetates in full color of all maps in the text. Each map is accompanied by a page of descriptive material and discussion questions.

Blank Maps
This collection of blank maps can be photocopied and used by the instructor for map testing purposes (see the Test Item File) or for other class exercises. A set will be provided free to the instructor upon adoption.

Study Guides, Volumes I and II
Prepared by Elizabeth Neumeyer of Kellogg Community College and designed according to a SQ3r (Survey-Questions-Read-Recite-Review) methodology, the Study Guides include for each text chapter a brief overview, a list of chapter objectives, an extensive questioning technique applied to chapter topics, study skills exercises, identification of terms, multiple choice, fill-in-the-blank, matching, short answer, and essay questions. In addition, each chapter includes two-to-three pages of specific map questions and exercises. The map reviews have been prepared by Robert Tomes, who has also prepared the map test items and other map-related material in the supplements.

Understanding and Answering Essay Questions
This brief supplement, authored by Mary L. Kelley of San Antonio College and free to students upon adoption, suggests helpful study techniques, as well as specific analytical tools for understanding different types of essay questions and precise guidelines for preparing well-crafted essay answers.

Documents Set to Accompany Out of Many, Volumes I and II
Selected and edited by John Mack Faragher and Daniel Czitrom. For collateral reading, we have gathered and carefully edited over 300 documents that relate directly to the themes and content presented in *Out of Many*. Organized in the same manner as the text, each chapter contains approximately 10 documents falling into five general categories: community-related; social history; government; cultural; and political. Each document (approximately two pages in length) includes a brief introduction as well as a number of questions following it to encourage critical analysis of the reading and to relate it to the content of the textbook. The documents are available free to the instructor and at a nominal fee to the student with the purchase of the textbook.

Themes of the Times

The New York Times and Prentice Hall are sponsoring *Themes of the Times,* a program designed to enhance student access to current information of relevance in the classroom. Through this program, the core subject matter provided in the text is supplemented by a collection of current articles from one of the world's most distinguished newspapers, *The New York Times*. Articles include the 150th anniversary of the Oregon Trail, discovering an African American cemetery of the 1790s in New York City, and deciphering the language of the early American tribes. These articles demonstrate the vital, ongoing connection between what is learned in the classroom and what is happening in the world around us. To enjoy the wealth of information of *The New York Times* daily, a reduced subscription rate is available. For information, call toll-free: 1-800-631-1222.

Prentice Hall and *The New York Times* are proud to co-sponsor *Themes of the Times*. We hope it will make the reading of both textbooks and newspapers a more dynamic, involving process.

The American History Videodisc

Produced by the Instructional Resources Corporation and containing nearly 2500 still images as well as 68 motion picture sequences, *The American History Videodisc* provides an extensive library of visual images to enhance your lectures. Available in both level I (no computer needed) and level III (computer-assisted) formats, the videodisc is extremely easy to use, and is supported by a 342-page guidebook that includes an index to the images and a caption describing each image. Available free to qualified adopters. Contact your Prentice Hall representative for details.

ACKNOWLEDGEMENTS

In the five years it has taken to take *Out of Many* from idea to reality, we have often been reminded that although writing history sometimes feels like isolated work, it actually involves a collective effort. We want to thank the many people whose efforts have made the publication of this book possible.

Historians around the country greatly assisted us by reading and commenting on our chapters. For the commitment of their valuable time we want to thank:

Donald Abbe, Texas Tech University
William L. Barney, University of North Carolina
Alwyn Barr, Texas Tech University
Peter V. Bergstrom, Illinois State University
William C. Billingsley, South Plains College
Bill Cecil-Fronsman, Washburn University of Topeka
Victor W. Chen, Chabot College
Matthew Coulter, Collin County Community College
Kenneth Goings, Florida Atlantic University
Fred R. van Hartesveldt, Fort Valley State College
Raymond M. Hyser, James Madison University
John Inscoe, University of Georgia
John C. Kesler, Lakeland Community College
Frank Lambert, Purdue University
Susan Rimby Leighow, Millersville University
Janice M. Leone, Middle Tennessee University
George Lipsitz, University of California, San Diego
Judy Barrett Litoff, Bryant College
Jesus Luna, California State University
M. Delores McBroome, Humboldt State University
Dr. Larry Madaras, Howard Community College
Robert L. Matheny, Eastern New Mexico University
Warren Metcalf, Arizona State University
M. Catherine Miller, Texas State University
Gregory H. Nobles, Georgia Institute of Technology
Dale Odom, University of Texas at Denton
Christie Farnham Pope, Iowa State University
Susan Porter-Benson, University of Missouri
Marilyn D. Rhinehart, North Harris College
Neal Salisbury, Smith College
Steven Schuster, Brookhaven Community College
John David Smith, North Carolina State University
Mark W. Summers, University of Kentucky
John D. Tanner Jr., Palomar College
Robert R. Tomes, St. John's University
John Trickel, Richland Community College
Robert C. Vitz, Northern Kentucky University
Charles Reagan Wilson, University of Mississippi
William Woodward, Seattle Pacific University
Loretta E. Zimmerman, University of Florida

At Prentice Hall, Steve Dalphin, Executive Editor, oversaw the entire project, and we came to count on his candor and good humor to see us through the process. Susanna Lesan, Development Editor, worked with us on literally every aspect of this book, not only the text itself but the illustrations, maps, charts, and captions as well. Her discerning eye and good sense saved us from many errors of style and substance, and it is fair to say that without her efforts this book would never have been published. Marianne Peters, Production Editor, worked long hours to keep the project on schedule and to accommodate our last-minute changes, particularly on the maps! Her enthusiasm for the project kept us all going. And, of course, our marketing campaign has been placed in the able hands of Roland Hernandez. Among our many other friends at Prentice Hall we also want to thank Caffie Risher, Editorial Assistant; Bruce Fulton, Copy Editor; Anne T. Bonanno, Art Director; Charlyce Jones Owen, Editor in Chief; Phil Miller, Publisher; and Will Ethridge, Editorial Director.

Each of us depended upon a great deal of support and assistance with the research and writing that went into this book. We want to thank: Kathryn Abbott, Nan Boyd, Krista Comer, Matthew Crocker, Crista DeLuzio, Keith Edgerton, Carol Frost, Margaret Hannigan, Jesse Hoffnung Garskof, Jane Gerhard, Todd Gernes, Melani McAlister, Christiane Mitchell, J. C. Mutchler, Tricia Rose, and Jessica Shubow.

Our families and close friends were supportive and ever so patient as this project slowly made its way to completion. But we want especially to thank Paul Buhle, Bob Greene, and Michele Hoffnung.

ABOUT THE AUTHORS

JOHN MACK FARAGHER is the Arthur Unobskey Professor of American History at Yale University. Born in Arizona and raised in southern California, he received his B.A. at the University of California, Riverside, and his Ph.D. at Yale University. He is the author of *Women and Men on the Overland Trail* (1979), which won the Frederick Jackson Turner Award of the Organization of American Historians, *Sugar Creek: Life on the Illinois Prairie* (1986), and *Daniel Boone: The Life and Legend of an American Pioneer* (1992).

Chris Freitag

MARI JO BUHLE is Professor of American Civilization and History at Brown University, specializing in American women's history. She is the author of *Women and American Socialism, 1820–1920* (1981) and coeditor of *The Concise History of Woman Suffrage* (1978) and *Encyclopedia of the American Left* (1990). She currently serves as an editor of a series of books on women and American history for the University of Illinois Press and is also a member of the editorial board of the *Journal of American History*. Professor Buhle holds a fellowship (1991–1996) from the John D. and Catherine T. MacArthur Foundation.

DANIEL CZITROM is Associate Professor of History at Mount Holyoke College. He received his B.A. from the State University of New York at Binghamton and his M.A. and Ph.D. from the University of Wisconsin, Madison. He is the author of *Media and the American Mind: From Morse to McLuhan* (1982), which won the First Books Award of the American Historical Association. His scholarly articles and essays have appeared in the *Journal of American History, American Quarterly, The Massachusetts Review,* and *The Atlantic.* He is currently completing *Mysteries of the City: Culture, Politics, and the Underworld in New York, 1870–1920.*

SUSAN H. ARMITAGE is Professor of History at Washington State University, where she directs the American Studies Program and teaches women's history. She earned her Ph.D. from the London School of Economics and Political Science. Among her many publications on western women's history are two coedited books, *The Women's West (1987)* and *So Much To Be Done: Women on the Mining and Ranching Frontier* (1991). She is currently working on a history of a community in the Northwest and on a coedited study of multicultural western women.

1 A CONTINENT OF VILLAGES,
TO 1500

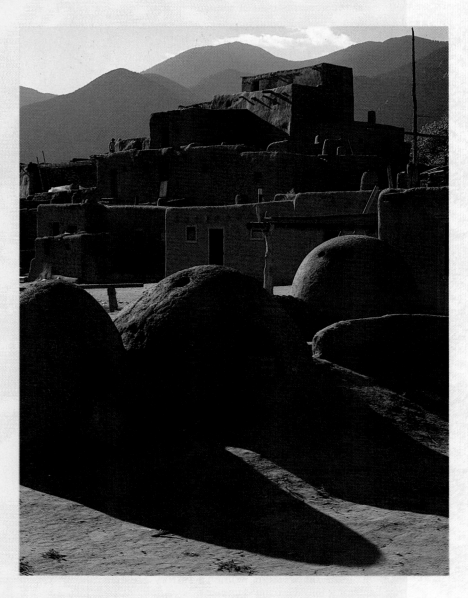

AMERICAN COMMUNITIES

• CAHOKIA ON THE MISSISSIPPI

As the sun rose over the river bottom, people walked down the narrow city streets to their places of work. Some hurried to shops where they manufactured tools, crafted pottery, worked metal, or fashioned ornamental jewelry — goods destined to be exchanged in the distant corners of the continent. Others left their densely populated neighborhoods for the outlying countryside, where in the humid summer heat they worked the seemingly endless fields that fed the city. From almost anywhere people could see, rising from the city center, the great temple where priests in splendid costumes acted out public rituals of death and renewal.

This scene describes life not in preindustrial Europe but in thirteenth-century North America. These people lived and worked on the alluvial soil of the Mississippi River, across from present-day St. Louis, at a place archaeologists have named Cahokia. In its heyday, in the mid-1200s, Cahokia was an urban cluster of perhaps 30,000 people. Its farm fields were thick with corn, beans, and pumpkins, crops no European had ever seen. The temple, a huge earthwork pyramid, covered fifteen acres at its base and rose as high as a ten-story building. On top were the sacred residences of chiefs and priests, who dressed in elaborate headdresses made from the plumage of tropical New World birds.

THIRTEENTH-CENTURY INDIAN PEOPLE BUILD A CIVILIZATION IN THE HEARTLAND

Cahokia thrived, then withered and died in the fourteenth century, as did dozens of other urban clusters along the banks of North America's vast inland river system. The rise and collapse of city-states and empires has been a recurrent feature of human history. But the evidence of Cahokia's existence has been less accessible, for its people left us no written records. Instead, the central mound and dozens of smaller ones in the surrounding area, as well as hundreds more throughout the Mississippi Valley, remained to puzzle the European immigrants who resettled the valley in the eighteenth and nineteenth centuries. Treasure seekers plundered them, and later the mounds were dynamited and plowed under for farmland. It was one of the worst archaeological disasters in American history. A few mounds were saved because their grounds were used as parks or estates. Cahokia's central mound survived because its summit became the site for a monastery.

This seated figure thought to be a worshiping man (ca. 1500) and the bottle in the shape of a nursing mother (ca. 1300) were found at Mississippian sites like Cahokia. The Mississippians were master maize farmers who lived in permanent villages and cities with residential neighborhoods and central plazas marked by huge platform temples. Without written records, we can only speculate about the thoughts and feelings of the people of Cahokia, but such works of art are testimonials to the universal human emotions of religious awe and maternal affection.

The objects in these mounds convinced excavators that they had found the ruins of a vanished civilization. The first comprehensive study of Cahokia, published in 1848 by the Smithsonian Institution, noted that "the mound-builders were an agricultural people, considerably advanced in arts, manners, habits, and religion." But, the report concluded, since "Indians were hunters averse to labor, and not known to have constructed any works approaching in skillfulness of design or in magnitude those under notice," surely these wonders must have been constructed by a "lost race." There may always be a market for such theories. Not long ago it was fashionable to credit the marvels of ancient America to "interterrestrials."

But thanks to modern archaeology, we now know that the vast urban complex of Cahokia, stretching six miles along the Mississippi from the tenth to the fourteenth centuries, was constructed by the ancestors of contemporary Indian people. We know its residents were not nomadic hunters but farmers. These agricultural people, whom archaeologists call the Mississippians, developed a highly intensive system of farming that supported densely settled urban centers. At Cahokia, hundreds of acres of crops fed the most populated urban community north of the Valley of Mexico. Mississippian farmers constructed ingenious raised plots of land on which they heaped compost in wide ridges, facilitating drainage and providing protection against unseasonable frosts. The farmers attached pens to their little square houses of wood and mud in which they kept flocks of domesticated turkeys, and perhaps small herds of young deer which they slaughtered for meat and hides. We also know that the city of Cahokia included large numbers of specialized artisans, and that it was renowned for the manufacture of high-quality flint hoes, exported throughout the Mississippi valley. Cahokia was at the center of a long-distance trading system that linked together hundreds of the Indian towns of the continent. Copper came from Lake Superior, mica from the southern Appalachians, conch shells from the Atlantic coast.

We know that the temple mounds and other monumental public works at Cahokia were aspects of a society dominated by an elite class of priests and rulers. From the pyramids of the ancient Egyptians to the Acropolis of the ancient Greeks, urban societies characteristicly build such awe-inspiring public works—symbols of power, perhaps. The great Cahokia mound was a human-constructed acropolis, from which the elite could look down on their subjects from their adobe palaces. High on the imposing mound, these structures must have inspired awe in the people of the city. In Cahokia, then, we see the beginnings of the modern state, supported by tribute. There is not indication, however, that the Mississippians had yet developed a system of writing, without which it is impossible to record the tax accounts of a true state system. We know that the Cahokians lived in a sophisticated community, the product of thousands of years of history, but without written documents we cannot know their own version of that history.

Every human society is made up of communities. A community is a set of relationships that link men, women, and their families into a coherent social whole, more than the sum of its parts. In a community people develop the capacity for unified action. They learn, often through trial and error, how to adapt to their environment. The sentiment that binds the members of a community together is the origin of group identity and ethnic pride. The term "community" is frequently employed to convey a sense of harmony and social peace, but the social process through which communities are defined, governed, and directed often included a great deal of conflict. In the making of history, communities are far more important than even the greatest of leaders, for the community is the institution most capable of passing a distinctive historical tradition to future generations. Communities of people—whose lives are bound together in multiple ways—range in size from local neighborhoods to nations. This book examines American history from the perspective of community life—an ever widening frame that has included larger and larger groups of Americans.

Although nineteenth- and twentieth-century stereotypes would emphasize the image of the isolated Indian hunter, all Indian peoples, in fact, lived in strong, vibrant communities, whether small hunting bands or large agricultural cities such as Cahokia. Before the coming of the Europeans, North America was, as one historian phrases it, "a continent of villages," a landscape of thousands of local communities. Over many centuries the Indian peoples of North America developed a variety of community types, each with its own system of family and social organization, each having a unique relationship to the environment. The wonders of Cahokia were but one aspect of the little-understood history of the Indians of the Americas.

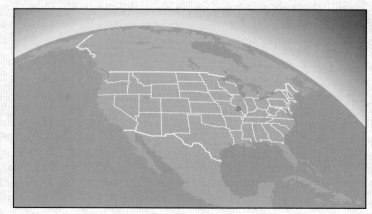

Settling the Continent

"Why do you call us Indians?" a Massachusetts native complained to Puritan missionary John Eliot in 1646. Christopher Columbus, who mistook the Arawaks of the Caribbean for the people of the East Indies, called them *Indios.* By the middle of the sixteenth century this Spanish word had passed into English as *Indians,* and was commonly used to refer to all the native peoples of the Americas. Today anthropologists often use the term *Amerindians,* and many people prefer *Native American.* But most indigenous Americans refer to themselves as Indian people.

Who Are the Indian People?

At the time of the first European contacts at the beginning of the sixteenth century, the native inhabitants of the Western Hemisphere represented over 2,000 cultures, spoke hundreds of different languages, and made their livings in scores of fundamentally different environments. They had no general term for themselves but used group names based on ethnic identity. The people of the mid-Atlantic coast, for example, called themselves Lenni Lenape, meaning "true men"; those of the northern Great Plains were Lakota, or "the allies"; the hunters of the Southwest used the name Dine (pronounced "dee-nay"), meaning simply "the people." Europeans knew these three groups by different names: Delawares, from the principal river of their region, and Sioux and Apache, both meaning "enemy" in the language of their neighbors. Just as the term *European* includes the English, French, and Spanish, so *Indian* covers an enormous diversity among the peoples of the Americas.

Once informed Europeans realized that the Americas were in fact a "New World" rather than part of the Asian continent, they began debating how people had moved there from Europe and Asia, where biblical events were believed to have transpired. Over the following centuries elaborate theories of transoceanic migrations were proposed, linking native Americans to ancient Greeks, Carthaginians, Tartars, Chinese, Welsh, and even the survivors of mythical Atlantis. Common to all these theories was a belief that the Americas had been populated for a few thousand years at most, and that native American societies were the degenerate offspring of a far superior Old World culture.

A number of Spanish observers thoroughly thought through the problem of Indian origins. In 1590 Joseph de Acosta reasoned that since Old World animals were present in the Americas, they must have crossed over by a land bridge, which could have been used by humans as well. A few years later, Enrico Martin speculated that since no such land passage had been found between the Americas and Europe, it must exist in the unexplored far northwest of the continent, and the people using it must thus have been Asians. In the 1650s Bernabe Cobo, who had lived most of his life in the Caribbean, argued that Indian people had to have been in America for centuries, because of the great variety of native languages. But, he continued, their physical similarities suggested "it was doubtless one nation or family of men which passed to people this land." Here were the principal elements of the migration hypothesis: Indian people were descended from a common stock of Asian migrants, had arrived by way of a northwestern land passage, and had experienced a long and independent history in the Americas.

Certainly no single physical type characterizes all the native peoples of the Americas. Despite being called "yellow men" or "redskins" by colonists and frontiersmen of the eighteenth and nineteenth centuries, few fit those descriptions. The color of their skin ranged from mahogany to light brown, and most had straight, black hair, and dark, almond-shaped eyes. But only when Europeans compared them with other continental groups, such as Africans, did they seem similar enough to be classified as a group. Modern laboratory analysis of blood samples reveals that the most distinctive marker of Native American populations is blood type: the vast majority have type O blood, and a few type A, but unlike Old World peoples, almost none have type B.

Migration from Asia

Scientific analysis suggests the Asian origins of the American Indians. The most ancient human fossils in the Americas share a common dental pattern with fossils found in northeastern Asia. Since modern Asian populations include all three blood groups, however, migrations to the New World must have occurred before the evolution of the modern Asian type, which scientists date at about 30,000 years ago. Studies of genetic evolution suggest that it took at least 20,000 years to evolve the variety of physical traits found among native American populations today; linguists estimate it would require about 25,000 years for the development from a common base of the nearly 500 distinct languages of the Americas. The evidence, then, points to a move to the Americas from Asia 25,000 to 30,000 years ago—about the time that Scandinavia and Japan were being settled.

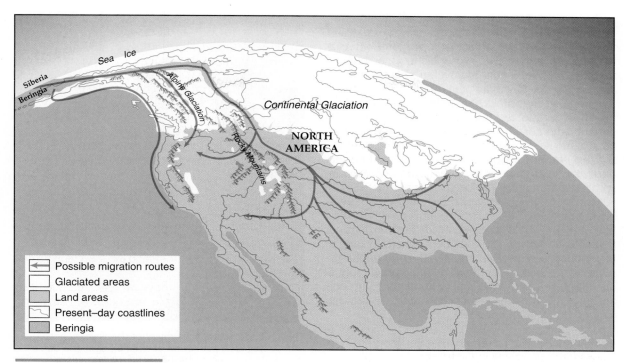

Beringia Migration Routes

During the Ice Age, Asia and North America were joined where the Bering Straits are today, forming a migration route for hunting peoples. Either by boat along the coast, or through a narrow corridor between the huge northern glaciers, these migrants made their way to the heartland of the continent.

At the time of the migrations from Asia to the Americas the Northern Hemisphere was experiencing the final ice age, which characterized the geological epoch known as the Pleistocene. Huge glaciers locked up massive volumes of water, and sea levels were as much as 300 feet lower than they are today. Asia and North America were joined by a huge subcontinent of ice-free, treeless grassland, 750 miles wide from north to south. Geologists have named this area Beringia, from the Bering Straits. Summers there were warm, winters cold, dry, and almost snow-free. This was a perfect environment for the large mammals known as *megafauna*—mammoth and mastadon, bison, horse, reindeer, camel, and saiga (a goatlike antelope).

Beringia also attracted Stone Age hunter-gatherers who lived in small, nomadic bands and subsisted almost entirely on these megafauna. The animals provided them not only with food, but with hides for clothing and shelter, dung for fuel, and bones for tools and weapons. Hunting bands were driven to expand by the powerful force of their own population growth and the pressure it placed on local resources. At an annual growth rate of only 0.5 percent — typical of today's remaining hunting-and-gathering peoples — population doubles every 140 years. Ancient Asian hunters had open country into which they could move, so it is likely that their growth rates were high and their colonization of new territory correspondingly rapid. Following the big game, and accompanied by a husky-like species of dog, hunting bands gradually expanded through Beringia, moving as far east as the Yukon River basin of northern Canada.

Archaeologists disagree about the dating of these earliest migrations. Field excavations in the Yukon basin in 1966 recovered fossilized bone tools estimated to be 27,000 years old — the earliest evidence of the human occupation of the Americas. Fieldworkers found that these tools fit perfectly into their hands and had worn edges exactly where one would expect them to be. Later digs produced the jawbones of several dogs estimated to be at least 30,000 years old. Other archaeologists remain skeptical about this evidence, however. They continue to believe that the migration took place much later, perhaps around 15,000 B.C. Because much of Beringia was later submerged beneath rising seas, definitive archaeological evidence of migration from Asia may be difficult to find. No specimens of human fossils have yet been uncovered, but Beringian archaeology is only in its beginnings.

Huge glaciers blocked southern movement during most of the last ice age, but occasionally a narrow land corridor opened up along the eastern base of the Rocky Mountains. Hunting bands following this corridor south could have emerged on the northern Great Plains — a hunter's paradise teeming with megafauna of great variety — as early as 25,000 years ago. Migrants may also have moved south in boats, following the Pacific coastline. Rapid population growth would have enabled these groups to populate the entire Western Hemisphere in only a few thousand years. Remarkably, the oral traditions of many Indian peoples depict a long journey from a distant place of origin to a new homeland. Europeans have recorded the Pima people of the Southwest singing this "Emergence Song":

> This is the White Land; we arrive singing,
> Headdresses waving in the breeze.
> We have come! We have come!
> The land trembles with our dancing and singing.

Clovis: The First American Technology

The tools found at the earliest North American archaeological sites consist of crude stone or bone choppers and scrapers, similar to artifacts from the same period found in Europe or Asia. About 12,000 years ago, however, there seems to have developed a much more sophisticated style of toolmaking, named after the site of its discovery in 1932 near Clovis, New Mexico. The Clovis tradition was a powerful new technology, unlike anything found in the archaeology of the Old World. In the years since the initial discovery, archaeologists have unearthed Clovis artifacts at sites ranging from Montana to Mexico, Nova Scotia to Arizona. All of these finds date back to within one or two thousand years of one another, suggesting that Clovis spread quickly throughout the continent. This has led in turn to speculation that the settlement of North America might then have been entering its final phase, as the continent filled with people. To feed their expanding populations, communities now had to find a more efficient way to hunt, which they did by adopting this greatly improved technology.

Clovis bands were mobile communities numbering perhaps thirty to fifty individuals from several interrelated families. They returned to the same

These Clovis points are typical of thousands that archaeologists have found at sites all over the continent, dating from a period about 12,000 years ago. When inserted in a spear shaft, these three- to six-inch fluted points made effective weapons for hunting mammoth and other big game. Clovis points are usually found at what appear to have been ancient camp sites, along with other stone tools such as choppers, scrappers, and knives used in the processing of meat and hide.

hunting camps year after year, pursuing seasonal migration within territories of several hundred square miles. Near Delbert, Nova Scotia, archaeologists discovered the floors of ten tents arranged in a semicircle, their doors opening south to avoid the prevailing northerly winds. Both this camp and others found throughout the continent overlooked watering places that would attract game. Clovis blades were excavated amid the remains of mammoth, camel, horse, giant armadillo, and sloth. Hunters apparently drove these animals into shallow bogs, killed them with spears, and butchered them on the spot.

THE BEGINNING OF REGIONAL CULTURES

About 15,000 years ago a global warming trend began to alter the North American climate. The giant continental glaciers began to melt, a shift so pronounced by 8000 B.C. that it marks the passing of the

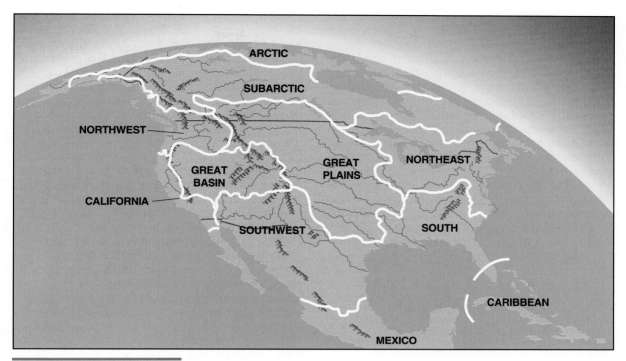

The Regions of North America
For the last 10,000 years regions have played an important role in the history of the continent.
The Indian peoples of North America were first to develop regionally distinct cultures.

Pleistocene epoch. As the glaciers retreated, the northern latitudes were colonized by plants, animals, and humans. Meltwater created the lake and river systems of today and raised the level of the surrounding seas, flooding Beringia as well as vast stretches of the Atlantic and Gulf coasts and creating fertile tidal pools and offshore fishing banks. These monumental transformations produced new patterns of wind, rainfall, and temperature, reshaping the ecology of the entire continent. The result was the distinct North American regions of today. The great integrating force of a single continental climate faded, and with its passing a continental Clovis culture fragmented into many different regional patterns.

Regions have always played an important role in American history. Occupying more than a third of the continent, the United States is alone among the world's nations in encompassing all five general classes of global climate: tropical jungles, arid deserts and grasslands, temperate woodlands, subarctic forests, and frozen polar tundra. It also contains some of the world's largest lakes, most extensive grasslands, and mightiest rivers. These variations in climate and geography combine to form the distinct regions of America: Northeast, South, Great Plains, Great Basin, Southwest, Northwest, and California. Within these regions, human communities have had to adapt to nature, developing their own ways of life. Indian peoples were the first in North America to embark on the long journey toward regionally distinct cultures, developing a wide variety of food sources to support their growing populations. Just as regions shaped the life ways and history of Indian peoples, so too they would nurture the development of regional American cultures after the coming of the Europeans.

Hunting Traditions of the Plains and Forests

One of the most important effects of this massive climatological shift was the stress it placed on the megafauna, animals suited best to an ice age environment. The archaeological record details the extinction of thirty-two classes of large New World animals, including not only the mammoth and mastodon but the horse and camel, both of which evolved in America, then migrated to Asia across Beringia. There is a good deal of controversy over the role humans played in these extinctions. Whatever the exact sequence of events, it seems likely that lowered reproduction and survival rates of the megafauna forced hunting bands to intensify their efforts, and that the combined effects of warmer climate and greater hunting eventually led to what some archaeologists have called the "Pleistocene Overkill."

As the megafauna declined, hunters on the Great Plains turned to the herds of American bison, more commonly called buffalo. In archaeological sites dating to about 10,000 years ago, a new style of tools is found in association with animal remains.

When in 1927 archaeologists at Folsom, New Mexico, uncovered this dramatic example of a projectile point embedded in the ribs of long-extinct species of bison it was the first proof that Indians had been in North America for many thousands of years. Folsom points, dating from about 8,000 B.C., are smaller and more delicate than those of the previous Clovis tradition, making them more effective for hunters on the run, surrounding herd animals.

This technology, seemingly based on the Clovis tradition, features more delicate but deadlier points. Archaeologists have given this new tradition the name Folsom, after the site of the first major excavation in New Mexico. In one dramatic find, a Folsom point was discovered embedded between the fossilized ribs of a buffalo. Attached to lances, these points were probably used with wooden spear throwers that enabled hunters to launch their weapons with great accuracy and velocity over distances of a hundred yards. Somewhat later, after this technology had evolved into a tradition that archaeologists call Plano, the points are found with grinding tools for vegetable foods, demonstrating the development of a varied diet on the Great Plains.

Archaeological finds also suggest the growing complexity of early Indian communities. Folsom and Plano hunters frequently stampeded herds of bison or other animals into canyon traps or over cliffs. At one such kill site in southeastern Colorado, estimated to be 8,500 years old, archaeologists uncovered the remains of nearly 200 bison that had been slaughtered and then systematically butchered on a single occasion. This job would have required at least 150 men and women and a sophisticated division of labor, which in turn probably involved the cooperation of a number of communities. Taking food in such quantities indicates a knowledge of basic preservation techniques: these people must have been among the first to make jerky, or dried strips of meat, and pemmican, a mixture of dried meat, animal fat, and berries that can keep into the winter when stored in hide containers. These characteristic products of the Great Plains would become the staple food items of the European fur trade in the West.

The passing of the Pleistocene was followed by a final wave of Beringia migrants — the Athapascans, or Na-Dene people. After entering North America they moved southeast from Alaska, following the wake of the melting western glacier. From 7,000 to 4,000 years ago, they settled the boreal forests in the northwest of the continent. Although they eventually adopted a technology similar to that of neighboring peoples, the Na-Dene maintained a separate cultural and linguistic identity. Athapascan-speakers later migrated from their northern homeland, journeying across the Great Plains to the Southwest. In a final migration from Asia that took place about 5,000 years ago, the Inuits (or Eskimos) and Aleuts, other hunting peoples, crossed the flooded Bering Straits by boat. The Inuits colonized the polar coasts of the Arctic, the Aleuts the Aleutian Islands (which are named for them) and the southern coast of Alaska.

Desert Culture in Western America

In addition to intensified hunting and foraging, the retreat of the glaciers led to new subsistence traditions in other regions: desert foraging in the arid Great Basin, fishing along the northwest coast of the Pacific, and hunting and gathering in the forests of the humid eastern half of the continent. These developments took place roughly 10,000 to 2,500 years ago during the Archaic period, a time that corresponds to what archaeologists in Europe, Asia, and Africa call the Mesolithic, or Middle Stone Age.

In the Great Basin of present-day Utah and Nevada — a huge sink surrounded by mountains — the warming trend associated with the end of the ice age created a desert where once there had been enormous inland seas. Here, Indian people developed the Desert Culture, a way of life based on the pursuit of small game and the intensified foraging of plant foods. Small mobile communities or bands of desert foragers migrated within rather small territories. They collected seeds, fiber, and prickly pear from the yucca one season, then moved to highland mesas to gather grass seed, acorns, juniper berries, and piñon nuts, and next to mountain streams to spear and net fish. This strategy required considerable skill in handicrafts: fiber baskets for collecting, pitch-lined baskets for cooking, nets and traps, stone grinders for processing seeds and nuts, as well as stone knives, hammers, and mauls.

Desert foragers lived in caves and rock shelters, where archaeologists today find their artifacts. In addition to stone tools there are objects of wood, hide, and fiber, wonderfully preserved for thousands of years in the dry climate. Danger Cave, Utah, for example, has yielded twine and rope made of plant fiber and animal fur, the oldest baskets in North America, and even a carefully tied bundle of sticks used in gambling games. Other caves have produced hide and fiber sandals and marvelous decoys for luring ducks and geese on the receding lakes. The Desert Culture persisted into the nineteenth century among modern Shoshoni and Ute communities. Once scornfully called Diggers because of their practice of gathering edible roots, and ridiculed for their "primitive" life ways, these peoples can now be appreciated for their very sophisticated adjustments to a harsh environment and their receptiveness to innovation.

Descriptions of the culture of the modern Shoshonis suggest that the force of community was strong among the people of the desert. Strong emphasis on sharing and gift giving, condemnation of hoarding, and the limits on possessions necessitated by a nomadic lifestyle prevented excess accumulation of goods by individuals or families. Thus, desert communities were characterized by general social equality. Decisions were made by consensus among the adults of the community, and leadership tended to be informal, based on proven achievement and reputation. The men of foraging bands generally married women from other bands, and wives came to live with the people of their husbands, creating important linkages between groups that contributed to the sense of shared ethnic identity.

The innovative practices of the Desert Culture gradually spread from the Great Basin to the Great Plains, where foraging techniques began to supplement intensive hunting, and to the Southwest, where they provided the foundation for what would become another distinctive regional culture. About 6,000 years ago, archaeologists estimate, colonists from the Great Basin carried the Desert Culture farther west to California. There, in the natural abundance of the valleys and coasts, Indians developed an economy capable of supporting some of the densest populations and the first permanently settled communities in North America. Another dynamic center in the West developed along the northwest Pacific coast, where Indian communities developed a way of life based on the exploitation of abundant fish and sea mammals. This Old Cordilleran Culture became the basis for the historic cultures of the Plateau and Northwest, which also included sedentary communities with large, dense populations.

Forest Efficiency

There were similar trends east of the Mississippi. Before the massive deforestation undertaken by European settlers during the eighteenth and nineteenth centuries, the whole of eastern North America was a vast forest. Hardwoods grew north of the thirty-fifth parallel, southern pine to the south. The Winnebagos of the Great Lakes region sang of these forests:

> Pleasant it looked,
> this newly created world.
> Along the entire length and breadth
> of the earth, our grandmother
> extended the green reflection
> of her covering
> and the escaping odors
> were pleasant to inhale.

Archaic forest communities achieved a comfortable and secure life based on their sophisticated knowledge of the rich and diverse available resources — a principle that archaeologists have termed *forest efficiency.* Archaic Indian communities of the forest hunted small game and gathered seeds, nuts, roots, and other wild plant foods. They also developed the practice of burning the woodlands and prairies to produce a *climax growth* of berries, fruits, and edible roots. These burns provided both harvestable food and an attractive environment for grazing animals, which were hunted for their meat and hides. Another important resource was the abundant fish of the rivers.

Archaeological sites in the East suggest growing populations and increasingly permanent community settlements during the late Archaic period — evidence of the viability of forest efficiency. Archaeologists have excavated elaborate weirs, such as the one at Boylston Street in Boston. Dating to about 2500 B.C. it consisted of some 65,000 stakes with brush inserted among them to trap fish. Its use would have required a large, well-organized work force. Different economic roles for the sexes are reflected in the goods buried in the graves of these people: axes, fishhooks, and animal bones for men; nut-cracking stones, beads, and pestles for women.

Two variations of the Eastern Archaic deserve special notice. On the shores of the western Great Lakes about 5,000 years ago, a people belonging to the Old Copper Culture developed impressive techniques of heating and hammering raw copper into beautiful tools and ornaments. At about the same time, along the North Atlantic coast, a group known as the Red Paint People (because of their practice of lining graves with red ocher) became skilled marine hunters and boatmen — the eastern equivalent of the fishers of the Pacific Northwest. They crafted impressive specimens of wood, bone, and antler, and created an elaborate cult that included burial mounds. Goods and ideas from these two cultures circulated throughout the eastern part of the continent. The burial cult of the Red Paint People is thought to have been the origin for later and much more elaborate mound building. Interregional exchanges would grow increasingly important in the centuries to come.

THE DEVELOPMENT OF FARMING

The exploitation of a wide variety of food sources during the Archaic period eventually led many Indian people to develop and adopt the practice of farming. The dynamic center of this development in North America was the highlands of Mexico, from where the new technology spread north and east.

Mexico

During the late stages of the Archaic or Mesolithic period, people in four different areas of the world developed farming systems. Each system was based on the cultivation of an important food source: rice in Southeast Asia, wheat in the Near East, potatoes in the Andean highlands of South America, and maize (or Indian corn) in Mexico. In each of these centers, a number of additional domesticated plants supplemented the staple crop, but the greatest variety were developed in Mexico: along with maize, beans and squash were the basic foods (together known throughout America as *"the three sisters"*); other well-known Mexican cultivated plants included tomatoes, peppers, avocados, cocoa (chocolate), and vanilla. Today the major carbohydrate sources from America — maize and potatoes — contribute more to the world's supply of staple foods than do wheat and rice; these "miracle crops" fueled the expansion of European human and livestock populations in the three centuries after 1650. Without these, and other New World crops such as tobacco, American cotton, and rubber — each of which became the basis for important new industries and markets — the history of the modern world would have been far different.

Archaeological evidence suggests that plant cultivation in the highlands of central Mexico began about 9,000 years ago. Scientific analyses of fossilized human feces discovered in the caves of Mexico document a gradual shift in diet from meat to vegetable foods. These new food sources were cultivated rather than gathered. By crossbreeding varieties of plants, at first by chance and later, perhaps, by design, ancient Mexicans developed crops that responded well to human care and produced larger quantities of food in a limited space than plants occurring naturally. Maize was particularly productive; over time it was adapted to a wide range of American climates, and farming spread throughout the temperate regions of North America.

As farming became increasingly important, it radically reshaped social life. Greater productivity spurred population growth to even higher levels. Farming systems could support large and densely settled communities like Cahokia on the banks of the Mississippi. Societies fully committed to farming possessed what demographers call the *carrying capacity* to support as many as 100 persons per square mile; foraging societies required nearly 100 square miles of territory to feed that same number. Larger populations such as Cahokia were much more settled. People remained near their cultivated

This Maya wall mural suggests the elaborate class system that developed in the complex agricultural societies of Mesoamerica. During the first millennium A.D., when Maya urban civilization was at its height, the kingdom of Tikal in present Guatemala counted a population of 500,000, and its achievements in architecture, art, science, and literature rivaled those of ancient Egypt, Greece, or China. Maya power was based on the abundant exports of its productive agricultural system, the most important of which was cacao or chocolate.

fields throughout the growing season — the first step in the development of villages with permanent architecture. Autumn harvests had to be stored during winter months, creating the necessity for the management of surplus food. In turn, these food stores made possible a new division of labor, including specialized occupations, political officers, and religious priests. Ultimately, unequal access to wealth resulted in the creation of classes.

Archaeological evidence suggests that by 1000 B.C., urban communities governed by permanent bureaucracies had begun to form in Mexico. By A.D. 650, a highly productive form of irrigation farming was supporting an urban civilization of more than 200,000 people in the high valley where Mexico City stands today. This was the capital of the Toltec people. An elite class of leaders controlled an elaborate trading system that stretched from present-day Arizona south to Central America. This network may have included coastal shipping connections with the Inca civilization of Peru, which developed at about the same time. Urban communities had a highly specialized division of labor. Artisans manufactured tools and produced clothing, stoneware, pottery, obsidian blades, and more. The bureaucratic elite collected taxes and tribute to maintain this vast urban structure. They had armies

of workers construct monumental edifices such as the Pyramids of the Sun and Moon, the ruins of which remind us today of the marvels of that ancient world.

City-states developed throughout Mexico and Central America, dominating the farmers of the countryside and waging war against one another. The rulers displayed their power through terrifying public rituals of human sacrifice and even cannibalism atop their grand pyramids. With fabulous art and architecture, highly developed math and science, and several systems of glyphic writing, the Indians of Mexico and Central America had developed a civilization with all the traits of the classic European varieties. Eventually, the Toltecs were overthrown by invaders from northern Mexico known as the Aztecs. (For a discussion of the Aztecs, see Chapter 2.)

The Resisted Revolution

Historians once described the development of farming as the "Neolithic Revolution." They believed that agricultural communities offered such obvious advantages that their neighbors must have rushed to adopt this way of life. Societies that remained without a farming tradition must simply have been too "primitive" to achieve this breakthrough; vulnerability to fickle nature was the penalty for their ignorance. This interpretation was part of a scheme of social evolution whose proponents viewed human history as the story of technological progress, with savage hunters gradually developing into civilized farmers.

But there is very little evidence to support this notion of a "revolution" occurring during a short, critical period. The adoption of farming was a gradual process, one that required hundreds, even thousands of years. Moreover, ignorance of cultivation was never the reason that cultures failed to take up farming, for all hunter-gatherer peoples understand a great deal about plant reproduction. The Menomini Indians of the northern forests of Wisconsin, for example, when gathering wild rice, purposely allowed some of it to fall back into the water to ensure a crop for the next season. Desert Paiutes of the Great Basin irrigated stands of their favorite wild food sources. And Californians deposited their feces in a common location so that the seeds passing through their digestive systems would grow to create natural gardens of their favorite foods.

The way today's remaining hunter-gatherers view the farming way of life is instructive. Foragers generally look upon their own way of getting food as vastly superior to any other. The food sources of desert gatherers, for example, are considerably more varied and higher in protein than those of desert farmers, whose diets concentrate on grains, far less preferred on the forager menu. Because foragers took advantage of natural diversity, they were also less vulnerable to climatological stress; although gathering communities frequently experienced periods of hunger and fasting, unlike farming societies, they were rarely devastated by famine. Foragers also complain that farming requires much more work. Why sweat all day in the fields producing tasteless corn, they argue, when in an hour or two one could gather enough sweet prickly pear to last a week? Indeed, rather than freeing men and women from the tyranny of nature, farming tied people to a work discipline unlike anything previously known in human history. Finally, foragers consider their migratory ways far more interesting than village life, which they claim is dull and monotonous, and preferable only for those whose possessions are too cumbersome to move.

Like the development of more sophisticated traditions of tool manufacture, farming represented another stage in the economic intensifications that kept populations and available resources in balance. As this new technology became available, cultures in different regions assessed its advantages and limitations. In regions such as California and the Pacific Northwest, acorn gathering or salmon fishing made cultivation seem a waste of time. In the Great Basin, several peoples attempted to implement a farming system, but ultimately failed. Before the invention of modern irrigation systems, which require sophisticated engineering, only Archaic Desert Culture could prevail in this harsh environment. In the neighboring Southwest, however, farming resolved certain ecological dilemmas and transformed the way of life. It seems that where climate favored cultivation, people tended to adopt farming as a prominent or supplemental form of production, thus continuing the Archaic tradition of diversity in the production of food. In a few areas, repeated increases in cultivation pushed in the direction of an urban civilization like that of central Mexico.

Increasing Social Complexity

Most hunting and foraging societies remained relatively simple in their social organization and their distribution of material goods and possessions. Farming created the basis for much greater social complexity within Indian communities. Most important were significantly more elaborate systems of kinship. Greater population density prompted families to group themselves into clans. Often, different clans became responsible for different social, political, or ritual functions. Clans became an important mechanism for binding together the people of several communities into a tribe. Tribes, based on ethnic, linguistic, and territorial unity, were led by leaders or chiefs from honored clans, who were often advised by councils of elders. The city of Cahokia would have been governed by such a system of chiefs. This council sometimes arbitrated disputes between individuals or families, but most crimes — theft, adultery, rape, murder — were avenged by the aggrieved kinship group itself.

The primary function of chiefs was the supervision of the economy, the collection and storage of the harvest, and the distribution of food to the clans. Differences in wealth, though small by the standards of modern societies, might develop between the families of a farming tribe. But these inequalities were kept in check by redistribution according to principles of sharing similar to those operating in foraging communities. Nowhere in North America did Indian cultures develop a concept of private ownership of land or other resources, which were invariably considered the common property of the people and were worked collectively.

Indian communities practiced a rather strict sexual division of labor that in its details varied tremendously from culture to culture. Among foraging peoples, hunting was generally assigned to men, while the gathering of food and the maintenance of home-base camps was the responsibility of women. This pattern probably originated during the long Paleolithic era. But the development of farming called these patterns into question. In Mexico, where communities became almost totally dependent upon their crops, both sexes worked in the fields. Where hunting remained important, the older division of labor remained, with women responsible for field work. Nearly always, however, Indian patterns would contrast in important details with the norms of colonizing Europeans, and thus they became the basis for a good deal of misunderstanding. When they saw Indian women working in the cornfields, English colonists thought them greatly oppressed; Indians, on the other hand, thought colonial men who labored in the fields were performing "women's work."

In most North American Indian farming communities, women and men belonged to separate social groupings with their own rituals and lore. Membership in these societies was one of the most important elements of a person's identity. Marriage ties, on the other hand, were relatively weak, and in most Indian communities divorce was usually simple: The couple separated without a great deal of ceremony, the children almost always remaining with the mother. All Indian women controlled their own bodies, were free to determine the timing of reproduction, free to use secret herbs to prevent pregnancy, induce abortion, and ease the pains of childbirth. All this was strikingly different from European patterns, in which the rule of men over women and fathers over households was thought to be the social ideal.

Farming communities were thus far more complex than foraging communities. But they were also less stable, for growing populations demanded increasingly large surpluses of food, and this need frequently led to social conflict and warfare. Moreover, farming systems were especially vulnerable to climatological disruptions such as drought, as well as ecological crises of their own creation, such as soil depletion or erosion.

The Religion of Foragers and Farmers

In the era just preceding and coinciding with European colonization, the religion of Indian peoples was shaped primarily by the two great traditions of foraging and farming. The first, rooted deep in the Paleolithic past, is sometimes called the Hunting Tradition. This complex of beliefs centered in the relationship of hunters and prey, and celebrated the existence of a "Master of Animals," often portrayed as the sacred bear. Associated with this tradition was the vision quest, whereby young adults sought out personal protective spirits by isolating themselves in the wilderness, exposing themselves to the elements, fasting, and inducing hallucinations and dreams. An individual who developed a special sensitivity to spiritual forces might become a shaman — "medicine" man or woman — of the community. This tradition was practiced throughout the continent, but was strongest in the northern latitudes, where hunting played the most important role in the economy.

With the northward spread of maize farming came a second religious force — the Agrarian Tradition. It focused on the concept of fertility, celebrated in ritual festivals marking the annual change of seasons. Because it was associated with the greater social complexity required by farming, this tradition generally included organized cult societies and priesthoods, rather than individualistic shamans. At its most elaborate, it featured a war–sacrifice–cannibalism complex glorifying violence and including the ritual consumption of enemy flesh, a set of beliefs that may have originated in the awe-inspiring displays of the Mexican city-states. The archaeological evidence suggests that this was the religion practiced in the city of Cahokia.

Although religious beliefs were often as distinctive as the local communities that held them, some combination of these two traditions characterized most of the Indian cultures of North America. Natural and supernatural forces were thought to be inseparable, a system of belief called *pantheism;* men and women were thought to share a basic kinship with animals, plants, inanimate objects, and natural forces. Although a number of native cultures promoted the existence of a paramount spiritual force, native religion was generally polytheistic, embracing numerous gods and spirits.

Farmers of the Southwest

During the late Archaic period, from 5,000 to 3,000 years ago, the southwest region of the continent experienced increased levels of rainfall and more abundant local resources. As a result, human populations proliferated. Mexican cultivated plants first appeared in the area during this period, and their casual cultivation became a supplement to gather-

The creation of man and woman depicted on a pot (dated about 1000 A.D.) from the ancient villages of the Mimbres River of southwestern New Mexico, the area of Mogollon culture. The Mogollons were the first farmers north of Mexico, and their spirited pottery is world renowned for its artistry. Such artifacts were usually intended as grave goods, to honor the dead.

Human figures dance on this characteristic piece of red-on-buff pottery of the Hohokam (dated about 1000 A.D.). The Hohokam, located on the floodplain of the Gila River near present-day Phoenix, Arizona, were the first irrigation farmers of North America. The Pima and Papago people of Arizona may be descended from them.

ing and hunting. At Bat Cave, New Mexico, archaeologists have found inch-long ears of maize that are about four thousand years old, along with early varieties of beans and squash — the earliest evidence of cultivation north of Mexico.

But about three thousand years ago, in one of the periodic shifts that punctuate the history of climate, drier conditions suddenly threatened the balance between population and resources. It seems to have been in this context that systematic farming was first adopted by the Mogollon. This group, named for the area along the southern Arizona–New Mexico border where they thrived, cultivated maize, beans, and squash with digging sticks until the thirteenth century A.D. Living in permanent villages near mountain streams and along ridges, these people devised ingenious pit houses, well suited to the temperature extremes common to the region. Called *kivas* by their Pueblo descendants, these subterranean rooms also served as storehouses for crops and as the centers for religious ceremony. Also uncovered at these sites are examples of the first woven cotton cloth and the first fired pottery north of Mexico.

Sometime after the establishment of these Mogollon villages, a colony was established along the floodplain of the Salt and Gila rivers in southern Arizona by an emigrant group from Mexico called the Hohokam ("those who are gone" in the language of the modern Pimas and Papagos of the area). One of the Hohokam's many community sites has been thoroughly excavated, a place the Pimas of today call Skoaquik, or Snaketown. Located near present-day Phoenix, the site includes the remains of a hundred pit houses spread over 300 acres. The Hohokam built and maintained the first irrigation system in America, channeling river water many miles to desert fields of maize, beans, squash, tobacco, and cotton. The number and variety of Mexican goods uncovered at Snaketown — rubber balls, mirrors of pyrite mosaics, copper bells, and fashionable ear ornaments — suggest that this was a community of Mexican merchants, where locally mined turquoise was traded for manufactured goods. The Hohokam even developed a process for etching shells with animal designs. With platform mounds for religious ceremonies and large courts for ball-playing, theirs was a sophisticated desert outpost of classic Mexican civilization.

The Anasazi

The best-known farming culture of the Southwest developed several hundred miles to the north in the Four Corners area, where Arizona, New Mexico, Utah, and Colorado meet on the plateau of the Colorado River. Called the Anasazi ("ancient outsiders'' in the Navajo language), this culture first took shape when growing populations made a transition from nomadic gathering to village cultivation during the first century A.D. In the eighth century a pronounced shift to a drier climate presented the Anasazi with the choice of either reverting to nomadism or finding ways of adapting and improving their farming systems. Like most cultures confronted with such a dilemma, they chose to intensify their productive system.

The classic period of Anasazi culture followed. In terraced fields irrigated by canals flowing from mountain catchment basins, they grew high-yield varieties of maize. This they supplemented with the meat of animals hunted with the highly effective bow and arrow, which first appeared in the region about A.D. 500. The Anasazi are admired for their fine basketry and exquisite painted pottery, but it is their urban architecture that most awes visitors to the region today. Anasazi communities lived in multistoried apartments — later called *pueblos* by Spanish invaders — clustered about central plazas; kivas were used for storage and religious ceremonies. Among the most spectacular of their ruins are those at Chaco Canyon, where Pueblo Bonito, completed in the twelfth century, contains over 650 interconnected rooms. It memorializes the Golden Age of the Anasazi.

Anasazi culture extended over an area larger than California. The sites of over 25,000 Anasazi communities are known in New Mexico alone. Only a few have been excavated, so there is much that archaeologists do not yet understand. Recent field work has revealed hundreds of miles of arrow-straight roads connecting community sites, and there are suggestions of an interpueblo communication system consisting of mountaintop signaling stations. By the time of their greatest strength, the Anasazi had erected an immense urban network that distributed food and other resources through a region prone to drought.

But during the thirteenth century, drought in the Southwest worsened. Growing Anasazi populations continued to intensify their production methods, building increasingly complex irrigation canals, check dams, and terraced fields; many large fields were mulched with small stones to better retain moisture. But a devastating drought from 1276 to 1293 (precisely dated with the aid of tree-ring analysis) resulted in repeated crop failures and eventual famine.

The Anasazi were confronted with an additional difficulty — the arrival of bands of Athapascan migrants who for a thousand years or more had been gradually moving south from subarctic regions. These people were the immediate ancestors of the

The spectacular ruins of the cliff-dwelling community of Mesa Verde, in southern Colorado, contains 200 rooms on three stories. It was built in the 12th century A.D. during the ''golden age'' of the Anasazi, an agricultural people who created a complex urban civilization amid the arid landscape of the Colorado plateau. Defensive sites like this may have protected the inhabitants against the raids of nomads such as the Athapascans.

Navajos and the Apaches, and judging by their descendants, they must have been fierce fighters. By the fourteenth and fifteenth centuries, the Athapascans were raiding Anasazi farming communities, taking food, goods, and possibly slaves. The dramatic Anasazi cliff dwellings at Mesa Verde, Colorado, constructed at about this time, may have been built as a defense against these raiders. Gradually the Anasazi abandoned the Four Corners altogether. Their movements have not yet been fully traced, but most of the migrants seem to have resettled in communities along the Rio Grande, joining with local residents to form the Pueblo people of modern times.

Farmers of the Eastern Woodlands

Outside the Southwest, farming became most important east of the Mississippi. Archaeologists date the beginning of the farming culture known as Woodland from the first appearances of pottery in the East about 3,000 years ago. Woodland was based on a sophisticated way of life that combined gathering and hunting with the cultivation of a few crops. Pipes, which appear at about the same time in archaeological digs, suggest the early local production of tobacco, whose cultivation spread north from the Caribbean region, where it had first been domesticated. Sunflowers were one of a variety of locally domesticated plants. Eastern peoples lived most of the year at permanent community sites, but moved seasonally to take advantage of the resources at different locations.

Even before maize was adapted to these colder northern latitudes, there were movements toward an increasingly settled existence and more complex social organization. The first of these, beginning about 3,000 years ago and extending through the first two centuries A.D., is called the Adena tradition, after an archaeological site near the center of Adena influence on the upper Ohio River. The Adena people lived in permanent villages and built elaborate burial mounds, the most famous of which is the Great Serpent Mound of southern Ohio, the largest effigy earthwork in the world. Archaeologists were provided a remarkable glimpse of the Adena diet when they discovered the naturally mummified bodies of several individuals in a Kentucky salt cave.

The Great Serpent Mound in southern Ohio, the shape of an uncoiling snake more than 1,300 feet long, is the largest effigy earthwork in the world. Monumental public works like these suggest the high degree of social organization of the Adena people, one of the first cultures of eastern North America to settle down in permanent villages. They were primarily gatherers and hunters, but had begun to farm native crops like sunflowers, pumpkins, and tobacco.

This mica sheet cut in the shape of a human hand was crafted by a northeastern Indian of the Hopewell tradition around the 5th century A.D. To honor the dead, Hopewellians produced a marvelous array of grave furnishings in representational and abstract styles that represent a high point of artistic achievement.

Analysis of the digested food preserved in their stomachs showed that just before their deaths they had eaten the seeds of sunflower, pigweed, lamb's quarters, and marsh elder — all probably cultivated species — as well as hickory nuts, acorns, wild lily and iris bulbs, fish, and game. Apparently they washed it all down with a mild laxative prepared from a mineral mined from the cave walls.

Following Adena, and perhaps building upon its patterns, was the Hopewell tradition of the first to the seventh centuries A.D., which extended over the entire Mississippi–Ohio Valley. The Hopewell people were devoted to *mortuary cults*. Local communities honored the dead through ceremony, display, and the construction of elaborate burial mounds. In support of this cult, Hopewellian chiefs mobilized an elaborate trade network that included obsidian from the Rocky Mountains, copper from the Great Lakes, mica from the Appalachians, and shells from the Gulf Coast. These materials were used in the production of grave goods that represent a high point of artistic expression.

Mississippian Society

Both the Adena and the Hopewell traditions flourished and then collapsed, victims perhaps of shifting patterns of climate. Local communities continued to practice their late Archaic subsistence strategies, but lowered productivity made it impossible for them to continue the expensive cultural displays demanded by their mortuary cults. Following the collapse of Hopewell, however, several important innovations appeared in the East. The bow and arrow, developed on the Great Plains, appeared east of the Mississippi about the seventh century, greatly increasing the efficiency of hunting. About the same time, a new variety of maize called Northern Flint became available; it had larger cobs and more kernels, yet matured in a shorter time, and so was perfect for northern temperate latitudes. Also about this time a shift from digging sticks to flint hoes took place, further increasing the productive potential of maize farming. There arose, on the basis of these innovations, a powerful new culture known as Mississippian, because its influence was greatest in the river valley.

The Mississippians were master maize farmers who lived in permanent villages along the river bottoms. At key sites, clusters of villages grew into dense urban centers with residential neighborhoods and central plazas marked by huge platform mounds. A sophisticated division of labor included artisans, priests, and an elite class of rulers. The most important of these cities was Cahokia on the Mississippi, the urban heart of Mississippian America. Other regional centers with thousands of residents were located on the Arkansas River near Spiro, Oklahoma, on the Black Warrior River at Moundville, Alabama, at Hiwassee Island on the Tennessee, and along the Etowah and Ocmulgee rivers in Georgia.

These centers, linked by a vast water transportation system, became the earliest city-states in North America, hierarchical chiefdoms that extended their control over the farmers of the surrounding countryside. With continued population growth, these cities engaged in vigorous and probably violent competition for the limited space along the river bottoms. It may have been the need for more orderly ways of allocating territories that stimulated the evolution of political hierarchies. The

Indian Trade Networks of the West
Long before the era of colonization, trade connected Indian peoples of different communities and even different regions. Through artifacts, archaeologists have been able to reconstruct the Indian trading networks of the pre-colonial West.

tasks of preventing local conflict, storing large food surpluses, and redistributing foodstuffs from farmers to artisans and elites required a leadership class with the power to command. Mound building and the use of tribute labor in the construction of other public works testified to the power of chiefs, who lived in sumptuous quarters atop the mounds.

Mississippian culture reached its height between the eleventh and thirteenth centuries A.D., the same period in which the Anasazi constructed their desert cities. Both groups adapted to their own environment the technology spreading northward from Mexico. Both developed impressive artistic traditions, and their feats of engineering reflect the beginnings of science. They were complex societies characterized by urbanism, social stratification, craft specialization, and regional trade — except for the absence of a writing system, all the traits of European civilization.

Warfare and Violence

The late thirteenth century marked the end of several hundred years of weather very favorable to maize farming, and the beginning of a century and a half of cool, dry conditions. Although the changes in climate in the Mississippi Valley were not as severe as those that devastated the Anasazi of the Southwest, over the long term they significantly lowered the potential of farming to support growing urban populations. Some archaeologists have suggested that one consequence of this extended drought may have been greatly increased violence and social disorder.

Warfare among Indian peoples certainly predated the colonial era. Organized violence was probably rare among hunting bands, who seldom could muster the manpower for more than a small raid against an enemy. Certain hunting peoples, though, such as the southward-moving Athapascans, must have engaged in systematic raiding of settled farming communities. Warfare was common among farming confederacies fighting to gain additional lands for cultivation. The first Europeans to enter the South described highly organized combat among large tribal armies. The bow and arrow was a deadly weapon of war, and the practice of scalping seems to have originated among warring tribes, who believed one could capture a warrior's spirit by taking his scalp lock. (During the colonial period,

Europeans warring with Indians placed bounties on scalps, encouraging an increase in the practice, and it spread widely among the tribes of other regions.) Sculpted images of human sacrifice found at Mississippian sites suggest that the inhabitants practiced a war–sacrifice–cannibalism complex similar to those of Mexico.

The archaeological remains of Cahokia reveal that during the thirteenth and fourteenth centuries the people of that great city surrounded the central sections of their city with a heavy log stockade. There must have been a great deal of violent warfare with other nearby communities. Also during this period, numerous towns formed throughout the river valleys of the Mississippi, each based on the domination of farming countrysides by metropolitan centers. The fourteenth century may have been a period of intense conflict and war between these competing city-states. Eventually conditions in the upper Mississippi Valley deteriorated so badly that Cahokia and many other sites were abandoned altogether, and as the cities collapsed, people relocated in smaller, decentralized communities. Among the peoples of the South, however, Mississippian patterns continued into the period of colonization.

NORTH AMERICA ON THE EVE OF COLONIZATION

The first Europeans to arrive in North America found a continent populated by more than 350 native societies speaking nearly as many distinct languages. Anthropologists of the early twentieth century estimated that the population of the entire area north of Mexico was little more than a million. Recently, however, historians have substantially revised this figure.

The Indian Population of America

In determining the precolonial population of the Americas, today's historical demographers consider a number of factors — the carrying capacity of different technological and economic systems, the archaeological evidence, the very earliest European accounts, and the estimated impact of epidemic diseases (for a discussion of epidemics among

Indian Population Density in 1500

Indian population density in the fifteenth century, before the era of European colonization. Population was highest in farming societies or in coastal areas with marine resources, and lowest in extreme environments like the Great Basin.

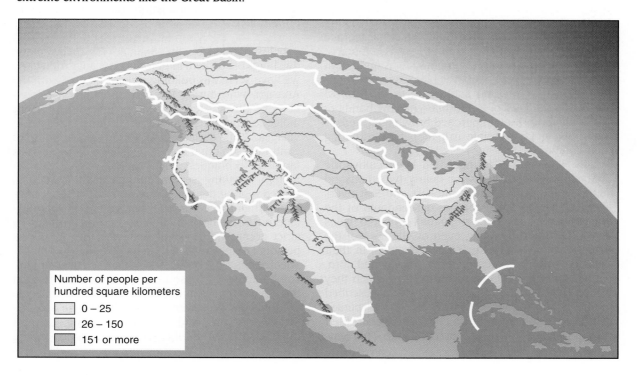

Number of people per hundred square kilometers

- 0 – 25
- 26 – 150
- 151 or more

Indian peoples, see Chapter 2). Although estimates vary, most historians now believe that the population of America north of Mexico in the early sixteenth century numbered between 7 and 12 million. Another 25 million were concentrated in the complex societies of the Mexican highlands. And the population of the Western Hemisphere as a whole was 60 to 70 million, comparable to Europe's population at the time.

Population density in North America varied widely according to ways of life. Scattered bands populated the Great Basin, the Great Plains, and subarctic regions, while the foraging peoples of the Northwest and California were densely settled because of the high productivity of their fishing and gathering economies. The Southwest, South, and Northeast contained the largest populations, and these were the areas where European explorers, conquerors, and colonists first concentrated their efforts.

The Southwest

It was only after the United States conquered the northern third of Mexico during the Mexican War (1846–48) that Americans began to refer to this region as the Southwest. To the Aztecs, who left this land when they emigrated south into central Mexico, it was known as Aztlan. When in the nearly nineteenth century it became the northern frontier of the young Mexican nation, people thought of it as "El Norte." But by any name, the single overwhelming fact of life there is aridity. Summer rains average only ten to twenty inches annually, and on much of the dry desert cultivation is impossible. A number of rivers, however, flow out of the pine-covered mountain plateaus. Trending southward to the Gulf of Mexico or the Gulf of California — narrow bands of green winding through parched browns and reds — they have made possible irrigation farming along their course.

By 1500 Indian farmers had been cultivating their southwestern fields for nearly two thousand years. In the flood plain of the Gila and Salt rivers lived the Pimas and Papagos, descendants of the ancient Hohokam. Working small irrigated fields along the Colorado River, even on the floor of the Grand Canyon, were the Yuman peoples. In their oasis communities, desert farmers cultivated corn, beans, squash, sunflowers, and cotton, which they traded throughout the Southwest. Often described as individualists, desert farmers lived in dispersed settlements that the Spanish called *rancherias,* their dwellings separated by as much as a mile. That way,

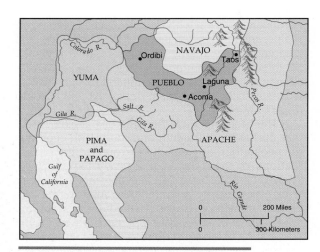

Indian Groups on the Eve of Colonization: Southwest

The Southwest was populated by desert farmers like the Pimas, Papagos, Yumans, and Pueblos, as well as by nomadic hunters and raiders like the Apaches and Navajos.

say the Pimas, people avoid getting on each other's nerves. Rancherias were governed by councils of adult men whose decisions required unanimous consent, although a headman was chosen to manage the irrigation works. Ceremonialism focused appropriately on rainmaking; one ritual required everyone to drink cactus wine until thoroughly drunk, a state of purification that was thought to bring rain.

East of the Grand Canyon lived the Pueblo peoples, named by the Spanish for their unique dwellings of stacked, interconnected apartments. As we have seen, this building style originated with the Anasazi, who during the great population relocations of the fourteenth century joined with other indigenous groups to form the numerous Pueblo villages. This architectural inheritance points to continuities in other areas of Pueblo culture, such as farming techniques and religious practices. Although speaking several languages, the Pueblos shared a great deal in common, most notably their commitment to communal village life. In this they differed from the individualistic desert farmers. A strict communal code of behavior that regulated personal conduct was enforced by a maze of matrilineal clans and secret religious societies; unique combinations of these clans and societies formed the governing systems of different Pueblo villages. Seasonal public ceremonies in the village squares included singing and chanting, dancing, colorful impersonations of the ancestral spirits called

The community of Walpi, high on what is called First Mesa, is situated at the center of the Hopi homeland in northeastern Arizona. Founded in the thirteenth century A.D., Walpi is among the oldest continuously-occupied towns in the United States. This late-nineteenth century photograph was taken by William H. Jackson, one of the most famous of western photographers.

kachinas, and the comic antics of "clowns" who mimicked in slapstick style those who did not conform to the communal ideal.

The Pueblos inhabit the oldest continuously occupied towns in the United States. The village of Oraibi dates from the twelfth century, when the Hopis ("peaceful ones" in their Uto-Aztecan language) founded it in the isolated western mesas of the Colorado Plateau. Using dry-farming methods and drought-resistant plants, they produced rich harvests of corn and squash amid shifting sand dunes. On a mesa top about fifty miles southwest of present-day Albuquerque, Anasazi immigrants from Mesa Verde built Acoma, the "sky city," in the late thirteenth century. The Pueblo people established approximately seventy other villages during the next two hundred years, of which two dozen survive today, including the large Indian towns of Laguna, Isleta, Santo Domingo, Jemez, San Felipe, and Taos.

In the arid deserts and mountains surrounding these towns were bands of nomadic hunters, some of whom had lived in the region thousands of years. But there were also more recent immigrants, the Athapascans. They hunted and foraged, traded meat and medicinal herbs with farmers, and frequently raided and plundered these same villages and rancherias. Gradually, some of the Athapascan people surrounding the Pueblo villages adopted their neighbors' farming and handicraft skills; these people became known as the Navajos. Others, more heavily influenced by the hunting and gathering traditions of the Great Basin and Great Plains, continued their hunting and raiding ways, and were given the name Apaches.

The South

The South enjoys a mild, moist climate with short winters and long summers, ideal for farming. From the Atlantic and Gulf coasts, a broad fertile plain extends inland to the Piedmont, a plateau separating the coastal plains from the Appalachian Mountains. The transition between plateau and coastal plain is marked by the Fall Line, an area of rapids and waterfalls on the descending rivers. The upper courses of the waterways originating in the Appalachian highlands offered ample rich bottom land for farming. The extensive forests, mostly of yellow pine, offered abundant animal resources. In the sixteenth century, large populations of Indian peoples farmed this rich land, fishing or hunting local fauna to supplement their diets. They lived in communities ranging from villages of twenty or so dwellings to large towns of a thousand or more inhabitants.

Mississippian cultural patterns continued among the peoples of the South. They were organized into confederacies of farming towns, the most powerful living along the Gulf coast and the river bottoms. Because most of these groups were quickly decimated in the first years of colonization, they are poorly documented. We know the most about the Natchez, farmers of the rich flood plains of the lower Mississippi delta who survived into the eighteenth century before being destroyed in a war with the French. Overseeing the Natchez was a ruler known as the Great Sun, who lived in royal splendor on a ceremonial mound in his village capital. When out among his subjects he was carried on a litter, the

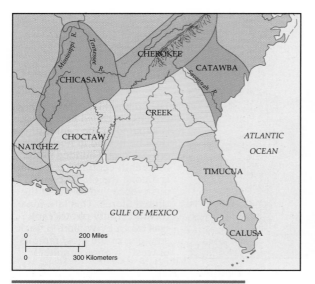

Indian Groups on the Eve of Colonization: South

On the eve of colonization the Indian societies of the South all shared many of the traits of the complex Mississippian farming culture.

path before him swept by his retinue of servants and wives. Natchez society was class-based. Noble families were represented on the Great Sun's council of advisers and appointed village peace and war chiefs. Persistent territorial conflict with other confederacies elevated warfare to an honored status among the Natchez, and public torture and human sacrifice of enemies were commonplace. The Natchez give us our best glimpse at what life would have been like in the community of Cahokia.

The earliest chronicles of the Spanish conquistadors suggest that the tribes of Florida were also sophisticated chiefdoms with classes, monarchs, and priests. Archaeological evidence implies that central towns dominated farmers in the countryside, extracting from them large quantities of maize, squash, and other cultivated plants grown on fields large enough to support populations numbering in the tens of thousands. Like the Natchez villages and the city of Cahokia, these Florida towns focused on ceremonial mounds, on which resided the ruling families. Honored clans lived in the plaza below, and ordinary people dwelled on the fringes of town and in the countryside.

These societies proved highly vulnerable to conquest. The looser confederacies of the interior were considerably more resilient. Among the most prominent of the interior "tribes" or "nations," as the Europeans called them, were the Choctaws in present-day Mississippi and Alabama, the Chickasaws in western Tennessee, and the Creeks in Georgia, each numbering several dozen towns. On the mountain plateaus lived the Cherokees, the single largest confederacy, which included more than sixty towns. Farming was somewhat less important in the highlands than along the coast, hunting somewhat more so. There were no ruling classes or kings, and leaders included women as well as men. Most peoples reckoned their descent matrilineally (back through generations of mothers), and after marriage husbands left the homes of their mothers to reside with the families of their wives. Women controlled household and village life, and were influential as well in the matrilineal clans that linked communities together. Councils of elderly men governed the confederacies, but were joined by clan matrons for annual meetings at the central council house. These gatherings could last days or even weeks, since everyone, male or female, was given the opportunity to speak.

The peoples of the South farmed the same crops, hunted in the same kind of piney woods, and lived in similar villages. They celebrated a common round of agricultural festivals that brought clans together from surrounding communities. At the harvest festival, for example, people thoroughly cleaned their homes and villages. They fasted and purified themselves by consuming the "black drink," a libation that induced visions. They extinguished the old fires and lit new ones, then celebrated the new crop of sweet corn with dancing and other festivities. During the following days, villages, clans, and groups of men and women competed against each other in the ancient stick-and-ball game that the French named lacrosse; in the evenings men and women played chunkey, a gambling game. The peoples of the South had much in common, but their tribal confederacies were frequently at war with one another.

The Northeast

The Northeast, the colder sector of the eastern woodlands, has a varied geography of coastal plains and mountain highlands, great rivers, lakes, and valleys. After A.D. 500, cultivation became the main support of the Indian economy in those places where the growing season was long enough to bring a crop of corn to maturity. In such areas of the Northeast — along the coasts and in the river valleys — the populations of Indian peoples were large and dense.

The Iroquois of present-day Ontario and upstate New York have lived in the region for at least 4,500 years. They were among the first northeastern peoples to adopt cultivation. The archaeological evidence suggests that as they shifted from primary reliance on fishing and hunting to maize farming, they relocated their villages from river bottoms to hilltops. There Iroquois women produced crops of corn, beans, squash, and sunflowers sufficient to support fifty *longhouses,* each occupied by a large matrilineal extended family. Some of those houses were truly long; archaeologists have excavated the foundations of some that extended 400 feet and would have housed dozens of families. Typically, these villages were surrounded by substantial palisades, clear evidence of intergroup conflict and warfare.

Indian Groups on the Eve of Colonization: Northeast

The Indian peoples of the Northeast were divided into two prominent language families, Iroquoian and Algonquian. Most were village peoples, although the Mohawk, Oneida, Onondaga, Cayuga, and Seneca forged the Iroquois Confederacy in the fifteenth century.

Population growth and the resulting intensification of farming in Iroquoia stimulated the development of chiefdoms there as elsewhere. By the fifteenth century several centers of population, each in a separate watershed, had coalesced from east to west across upstate New York. These were the five Iroquois chiefdoms or "nations": the Mohawks, Oneidas, Onondagas, Cayugas, and Senecas. Iroquois oral histories collected during the nineteenth century recall this as a period of persistent violence, possibly the consequence of conflicts over territory.

Historians believe that the Iroquois founded a confederacy to control this violence. The confederacy outlawed warfare among the member nations and established regulated forms of gift exchange and payment to replace revenge. Iroquois oral history refers to the founder of the confederacy, chief Deganawida the lawgiver, "blocking out the sun" as a demonstration of his powers, suggesting that these events might have taken place during the full solar eclipse that was visible in the Northeast in 1451. As a model, the confederacy used the powerful metaphor of the longhouse; each nation, it was said, occupied a separate hearth but acknowledged descent from a common mother. As in the longhouse, women played important roles in choosing male leaders who would represent their lineages and chiefdom on the Iroquois council. The confederacy suppressed violence among its members, but did not hesitate to encourage war against outside groups such as the neighboring Huron or the Erie, who constructed defensive confederacies of their own at about the same time. The Iroquois Confederacy would become one of the most powerful forces during the colonial period.

The other major language group of the Northeast was Algonquian, which included at least fifty distinct cultures. North of the Great Lakes and in northern New England the Algonquians were hunters and foragers, organized into bands with loose ethnic affiliations. Several of these peoples, including the Micmacs, Crees, Montagnais, and Ojibwas (also known as Chippewas), would become the first producers in the early fur trade. Among the Algonquians of the Atlantic coast, from present-day Massachusetts south to Virginia, as well as among those in the Ohio Valley, farming led to the development of settlements as densely populated as those of the Iroquois — though the abundance of coastal and riverine resources made the bow and arrow and the fishing spear as important to these

CHRONOLOGY

25,000 B.C.	Oldest fossil evidence for humans in the Americas
13,000 B.C.	Global warming trend begins
10,000 B.C.	Clovis technology
8,000 B.C.	Beginning of the Archaic period
7,000 B.C.	First cultivation of plants in the Mexican highlands
5,000 B.C.	Athapascan migrations to America begin
4,000 B.C.	First settled communities along the Pacific coast
3,000 B.C.	Inuit and Aleut migrations begin
2,000 B.C.	Mexican crops introduced into the Southwest
1,000 B.C.	Beginning of Mogollon, Hohokam, and Adena cultures
A.D. 500	High point of Hopewell culture
A.D. 650	Bow and arrow, flint corn, and hoes in the Northeast
A.D. 1000	Tobacco in use throughout North America
A.D. 1150	Founding of Hopi village of Oraibi, oldest town in America
A.D. 1250	High point of Mississippian and Anasazi culture
A.D. 1276	Severe drought begins in the Southwest
A.D. 1300	Arrival of Athapascans in the Southwest
A.D. 1451	Founding of Iroquois confederacy

people as the hoe. In contrast with the Iroquois, most of the Algonquians were patrilineal. They lived in less extensive dwellings in smaller villages, often lacking palisade fortifications. Local communities were relatively autonomous, but central confederacies nevertheless took shape during the fifteenth and sixteenth centuries. Among these groupings were the tribes or nations of the early colonial era, including the Massachusets, Narragansets, and Pequots of New England, the Delawares and the peoples of Powhatan's confederacy on the mid-Atlantic coast, and the Shawnees, Miamis, Kickapoos, and Potawatomis of the Ohio Valley.

CONCLUSION

The history of the Indian peoples of North America was linked to the physical development of the continent, and in response to their various regional environments they created ways of life that contin-

ued to shape North America during the colonial era. Exaggerated tales of fabulous wealth in the Pueblo towns lured the Spanish conquistadors northward. Colonists remained to farm the land, something they could not have done without learning much from the Pueblos about the arid Southwest. The first European colonists in the South depended upon the Indians to supply them with rich harvests from their extensive fields, the legacy of the Mississippian period of North American history. This mild and fertile region became the prime location for the first productive plantation economy of the English colonies, which grew Indian tobacco for export. Along the northeast coast, English colonists settled the former village sites of Algonquians, planting Indian corn in the same fields and fishing in the same waters. In short, it is impossible to imagine European colonial societies without the prior existence of Indian communities.

"Columbus did not discover a new world," wrote the historian J. H. Perry. "He established contact between two worlds, both already old." Likewise, the world of North America did not suddenly change with the arrival of Europeans in the sixteenth century. In the first encounters, Indian peoples were generally wary, but curious and ready to trade. The European colonists who came to settle faced thousands of Indian communities with deep roots and vibrant traditions. It would be more than two centuries before colonists outnumbered Indians. Indian communities viewed these colonists as invaders, and called upon their traditions and their gods in defending their communal homelands.

Additional Readings

BRIAN M. FAGAN, *The Great Journey: The Peopling of Ancient America* (1987). An account of the Asian migration to the Americas, told through the study of archaeology. For new discoveries — which keep pushing the dating further back — see recent issues of *National Geographic* and *Scientific American.*

STUART J. FIEDEL, *Prehistory of the Americas* (1987). The best introduction for the nonspecialist, covering the first migrations, the development of technologies, and the spread of farming.

ALVIN JOSEPHY, editor, *America in 1492* (1992). Important essays by the leading scholars of the North American Indian experience. Includes a beautiful collection of illustrations and maps as well as an excellent bibliography.

ALICE B. KEHOE, *North American Indians: A Comprehensive Account* (1992). The best general anthropological survey of the history and culture of the Indians of North America. Organized by culture areas, the new edition covers all the peoples of the continent and includes the most recent scholarship.

ROBERT SILVERBERG, *Mound Builders of Ancient America:* *The Archaeology of a Myth* (1968). A brilliant history of opinion and theory about the mound builders, combined with a review of the best archaeological evidence available at the time.

WILLIAM C. STURTEVANT, general editor, *Handbook of North American Indians,* 20 vol. (1978–). The most comprehensive collection of the best current scholarship. When complete, there will be a volume for each of the culture regions of North America; volumes on origins, Indian–white relations, languages, and art; a biographical dictionary; and a general index.

RUSSELL THORNTON, *American Indian Holocaust and Survival: A Population History Since 1492* (1987). The best introduction to the historical demography of North America. In a field of great controversy, it provides a judicious review of all the evidence.

CARL WALDMAN, *Atlas of the North American Indian* (1985). A collection of essential maps, from the first migrations to the present. More than simply an atlas, however, it is a comprehensive introduction to the Indian history of North America. Contains an excellent bibliography.

2 WHEN WORLDS COLLIDE, 1492–1590

It was late August 1590 when the English ships sailed through Hatteras Inlet into Pamlico Sound, off the coast of present-day North Carolina, and made their way north through rough seas to Roanoke Island. Governor John White had returned to relieve the first English community transplanted to the shores of North America. That group included some sixty-five single men and twenty families, including White's daughter, son-in-law, and granddaughter. The last of these, Virginia Dare, was the first English baby born in America.

Upon reaching the island one of the sailors blew "many familiar English tunes" on a trumpet and "called to them friendly," White wrote, "but we had no answer." Anxiously he went ashore to the little fortified settlement, but "we found the houses taken down" with many possessions "spoiled and

THE ENGLISH AND THE ALGONQUIANS MEET

scattered about." Suddenly he spied near the entrance to the fort some writing on a tree trunk: "in fair capital letters was graven CROATOAN." White had instructed the colonists to leave such a message if they had to move, and, if there was trouble, to mark it with a cross. White noted with relief that this carving was "without any cross or sign of distress." Croatoan was a friendly Indian village fifty miles south. Sure that his people awaited him there, White left the island for his ship.

The Roanoke settlement was sponsored by Walter Raleigh, a wealthy adventurer who sought profit and prestige by planting an English colony in the New World. His first expedition to the area, in 1584, reported that the coastal region was densely populated by a "very handsome and goodly people." These Indians, the most southerly of the Algonquian coastal peoples, enjoyed a prosperous livelihood farming, fishing, and hunting from their small villages of one or two dozen long-houses. At "an island which they called Roanoke," the English were "entertained with all love and kindness" by a chief named Wingina. Wingina was the "big man" of several surrounding villages, and he viewed these visitors as potential allies in his struggle to extend his authority over still others. So when the English asked his permission to establish a settlement on the island, he readily granted it. Wingina sent two of his own men back with them to England, to make preparations for the colonizing expedition.

Raleigh's first colony in this land, which he christened Virginia in honor of Elizabeth I, the virgin queen, was a dismal failure. Manteo and Wanchese, the Indian emissaries, were extremely helpful in helping prepare the "scientific" component of the mission, led by Thomas Harriot, a scholar from

In July, 1585, John White visited the coastal Algonquian village of Secoton, where he painted this composite scene including many fascinating details: the Indians' bark-covered houses, their manner of sitting to eat, one of their fertility dances, and in the lower left a mortuary temple ("the Tombe of their Herounds"). Note also the three crops of corn made possible by the mild climate, as well as the man assigned to sit on a platform amid the ripening crop to keep away the birds.

Oxford University, and John White, a trained artist. These four men worked at learning one another's language, and there seems to have been a good deal of mutual respect among them. But when the two Indians returned with the English to Roanoke late in the summer of 1585, they had very different messages for their people. Manteo, from the village of Croatoan, was fascinated with the English, and argued that their technology and weaponry would make them powerful allies. Wanchese of Roanoke, however, offered disturbing reports of the savage inequalities of English society, and warned of the brutality of the soldiers who composed the majority of the colonists. Indeed, Raleigh had directed the mission's commander to "proceed with extremity" should the Indians prove difficult, and "bring them all in subjection to civility." He had several hopes: a lucrative trade in furs; a flourishing plantation agriculture. But most of all, he and the other investors in the expedition hoped to discover gold or silver. In any case, bringing the Indians to "civility" was essential, for they would become the serfs of the English masters. "The English would act just as the Spanish had done in creating their empire," writes the historian Carl Sauer; they had "naked imperial objectives."

A colony such as this one — some 100 soldiers and adventurers with plunder foremost in their minds — was incapable of supporting itself. After building a rough fort on the island, the English went to Wingina for supplies of food. With the harvest in the storage pits, with fish running in the streams and game flocking the woods, Wingina did the hospitable thing. It was, after all, the duty of a chief to distribute presents and incur obligations. But as fall turned to winter, and the stores declined, the constant English demands began to tax the resources of the Indians. Rather than hunt or fish, the colonists were out exploring for precious metals. They attacked several outlying villages, burned longhouses and cornfields, and kidnapped women. By the spring — traditionally the "starving season" for the Indians, before the crops were up and the game fat — Wingina and his people had had enough. But the English caught wind of the Indians' rising hostility, and in May of 1586 they surprised the

Roanoke villagers, killing several of the leading men and beheading Wingina. Soon thereafter the colonists returned to England, leaving a legacy of violence and hatred in their wake.

John White and Thomas Harriot, who had spent their time exploring the physical and human world of the coast and recording their findings in notes and sketches, were appalled by this turn of events. To Raleigh, Harriot argued that the attack came "upon causes that on our part might easily enough have been borne." White put forth a new plan for a colony of real settlers, a group of English families who could form a community that could live in association with the Indians. "There is good hope," wrote Harriot, that "through discreet dealing" the Indians may "honor, obey, fear and love us." Harriot and White clearly thought English civilization was superior to the civilization of the Indians, but their vision differed from that of the plunderers.

In 1587 Raleigh arranged for White to return as governor of a new family colony to be planted on the Chesapeake, north of Roanoke. When White and the other settlers arrived at Roanoke to pick up some heavy equipment left there, however, the ship's captain abandoned them so that he might be free to attack rich Spanish ships in the Caribbean. Despite their good intentions, these colonists had to live with the reputation left by the former expedition. Within a month one of their number was shot full of arrows as he fished for crabs. The attackers were led by Wanchese, who after Wingina's death became the most militant opponent of the English among the Roanoke Indians. Manteo, baptized a Christian, remained White's friend and supporter.

White retaliated by attacking Wanchese's village, but the Indians fled into the forest with few casualties. Knowing that their entire mission hung in the balance, but without a ship large enough to carry them all back to England, the colonists begged White to sail home in the one small seaworthy ship they had, to press Raleigh for support. With great reluctance he left, arriving to find war threatening between England and Spain. Three years of frustrating delay passed before White was able to return to Roanoke with supplies and additional men in August of 1590.

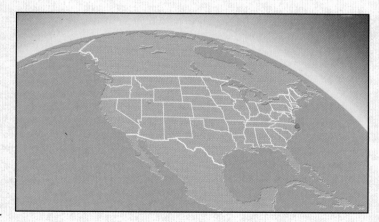

Anxious to speed southward to Croatoan, White and his men reboarded their ship. But the seas were heavy, and a storm was blowing up. "We drove fast into the shore," White wrote, and all hands feared imminent shipwreck. Several times they dropped anchor, but each time the cable broke. Finally, left with one last anchor, White and the captain agreed that they would have to leave the sound for deeper waters. Tossed home on a stormy sea, White would never again return to America. The English settlers of Roanoke became known as the Lost Colony, their disappearance and ultimate fate one of the enduring mysteries of colonial history.

Today, many historians believe that those English men and women probably went with Manteo to Croatoan, and lived out the rest of their lives beside the Algonquian villagers. When Virginia Dare and the other children grew up, they must have married into Indian families—an ironic end to Raleigh's vision of conquest, a fulfillment of White and Harriot's vision of a colonial community. But the endurance of the Roanoke settlers provides one of the first examples of the importance of community in the settlement of North America.

The Expansion of Europe

There may have been numerous unrecorded contacts between the peoples of America and the Old World before the fifteenth century. Archaeological excavations at L'Anse aux Meadows on the fog-bound Newfoundland coast provide evidence for a Norse landing in North America in the tenth or eleventh century. Scandinavian sagas told how these settlers were forced out of their encampments by native hunters, but by the fifteenth century these tales were scarcely remembered in Europe.

By contrast, the contact with the Americas established in 1492 by Christopher Columbus had earthshaking consequences. Columbus wrote an account of his voyage that was immediately published in Latin, and editions in many other languages circulated throughout Europe before 1500. By that time, hundreds of Spaniards had begun a sustained campaign of colonization on the islands of the Caribbean. Within a generation, continental exchanges of peoples, crops, animals, and germs had reshaped the Atlantic world. The key to understanding these remarkable events is the transformation of Europe during the several centuries preceding the voyage of Columbus.

European Communities

Western Europe was an agricultural society, the majority of its people peasant farmers. Farming and livestock raising had been practiced in Europe for thousands of years, but great advances in the technology of farming took place during the late Middle Ages. Water mills, iron plows, improved devices for harnessing ox and horse power, and systems of crop rotation greatly increased productivity. Over several centuries farmers more than doubled the quantity of European land in cultivation. The increased supply of food helped the population of western Europe nearly triple between the eleventh and fourteenth centuries.

Most Europeans were village people, living in family households. Men performed the basic field work; women were responsible for child care, livestock, and food preparation. In the European pattern, daughters usually left the home and village of their families to take up residence among their husband's people. Women were furnished with dowries, but generally excluded from inheritance. Divorce was almost unknown.

Europe was a world of social contrasts. Most land was owned by a powerful group of landlords who claimed a disproportionate share of wealth and power. These feudal lords commanded labor service

A French peasant labors in the field before a spectacular Catholic cathedral in a page taken from the illuminated manuscript *Tres Riches Heures,* made in the fifteenth century for the Duc de Berry. In 1580 the essayist Montaigne talked with several American Indians at the French court who "noticed among us some men gorged to the full with things of every sort while their other halves were beggars at their doors, emaciated with hunger and poverty," and "found it strange that these poverty-striken halves should suffer such injustice, and that they did not take the others by the throat or set fire to their houses."

from peasants and tribute in the form of crops. The landlords were the main beneficiaries of medieval economic expansion, accumulating great estates and building castles. A relatively small class of freehold farmers also benefited from the rebuilding of Europe, but the majority of peasants experienced little improvement in their standard of living.

Europeans were Christians, united under the authority of the Roman Catholic Church, whose complex organization spanned thousands of local communities with a hierarchy that extended from parish priests all the way to the pope in Rome. At the core of Christian belief was a set of communal values: love of God the father, loving treatment of neighbors, and the fellowship of all believers. Yet the Catholic Church itself was one of the most powerful landowners in Europe, and it devoted its considerable resources to awe-inspiring display rather than the amelioration of poverty and suffering. It insisted on its dogmas and actively persecuted heretics, nonbelievers, and believers in older, "pagan" religions, who were branded "witches." The church legitimized the power relationships of Europe and counseled the poor and downtrodden to place their hopes in heavenly rewards.

For the great majority of Europeans, living conditions were harsh. Most rural people survived on bread and porridge, supplemented with seasonal vegetables and an occasional piece of meat or fish. Infectious diseases abounded; perhaps a third of all children died before their fifth birthday, and only half the population reached adulthood. Famines periodically ravaged the countryside. In the fourteenth century, for example, a series of crop failures resulted in widespread starvation and death. This episode prepared the way for Black Death, a widespread epidemic of bubonic plague that swept in from Asia and wiped out a third of Europe's population between 1347 and 1353.

But Europe soon recovered from the devastation of the Black Death. Its agricultural economy, strengthened by the technological breakthroughs of the Middle Ages, provided the basis for renewed growth, and by 1500 the population of western Europe had nearly returned to its former peak of about 30 million. Although Europe's social structure was hierarchical and authoritarian, its agricultural systems had the capacity for far greater growth than the farming economy of the Americas.

The Merchant Class and the Renaissance

The economic growth of the late Middle Ages was accompanied by the expansion of commerce, especially trade in basic goods such as cereals and timber, minerals and salt, wine, fish, and wool. Commercial expansion stimulated the growth of markets and towns. In England, for example, over a hundred towns were founded in the twelfth century alone. The Low Countries — today's Holland and Belgium — were northern centers of this flourishing commerce. But the heart of this dynamic European commercialism lay in the city-states of Italy.

During the late Middle Ages, the cities of Venice,

Western Europe in the Fifteenth Century
During the fifteenth century the monarchs of western Europe unified their realms and began the construction of royal bureaucracies and standing armies and navies. These states sponsored the voyages that inaugurated the era of European colonization.

Genoa, and Pisa launched armed, commercial fleets that seized control of the trade of the Mediterranean. Their merchants became the principal outfitters of the Crusades, a series of great military expeditions promoted by the Catholic Church to recover Palestine from the Muslims. The conquest of the Holy Land by Crusaders at the end of the eleventh century delivered into the hands of the Italian merchants the silk and spice trades of Asia. Tropical spices — cloves, cinnamon, nutmeg, and pepper — were in great demand, for they made the European diet far less monotonous for the lords who could afford them. Asian civilization also supplied a number of technical innovations that further propelled European economic growth. The compass, gunpowder, and the art of printing with movable type — "the three greatest inventions known to man," in the opinion of the sixteenth-century English philosopher Francis Bacon — each came from China, along with other innovations such as the water mill and the mechanical clock.

Another benefit of European contact with Muslim civilization was a reintroduction to the learning of Greece and Rome. Many of the most important ancient texts had been lost in Europe, but Muslim scholars had preserved them in the great libraries of Alexandria (Egypt) and Baghdad (in what is now Iraq). A revival of interest in classical antiquity sparked the period of intellectual and artistic flowering during the fourteenth and fifteenth centuries known as the Renaissance. The revolution in publishing (made possible by the perfection of the printing press and movable type), the beginning of regular postal service, and the growth of universities helped to spread this movement throughout the elite circles of Europe.

In art, as in literature and philosophy, the Renaissance celebrated human possibility. The Gothic style of medieval cathedrals, whose soaring forms were intended to take human thoughts heavenward, gradually gave way to the use of measured classical styles, encouraging rational reflection. In painting and sculpture there was a new focus on the human body. Artists modeled muscles with light and shadow to produce heroic images of men and women. These were aspects of what became known as *humanism,* a revolt against religious authority in which the secular took precedence over the purely religious. The Renaissance outlook was a critical component of the spirit that motivated the exploration of the Americas.

The New Monarchies

The Renaissance flowered amid the ruins of the plague-ridden fourteenth century. Famine and disease led to violence, as groups fought for shares of a shrinking economy. In Flanders during the 1320s, peasants rose against both nobility and church, beginning a series of rebellions that culminated in the great English Peasants' Revolt of 1381. "We are made men in the likeness of Christ," one rebel cried out, "but you treat us like savage beasts." Meanwhile, civil and international warfare among the nobility decimated the landed classes and greatly reduced their power, and the Catholic Church was seriously weakened by an internal struggle between French and Italian factions.

During this period of social and political chaos, the monarchs of Western Europe emerged as the new centers of power, building their legitimacy by promising internal order as they unified their realms. They began the construction of royal bureaucracies and standing armies and navies. In many cases, these new monarchs found support among the merchant class, which in return sought lucrative royal contracts and trading monopolies. The alliance between commercial interests and the new states was another of the important developments that prepared the way for European expansion.

Portuguese Explorations

Portugal, a narrow land along the western coast of the Iberian Peninsula with a long tradition of seafaring, became the first of these new kingdoms to explore distant lands. Lisbon, the principle port on the sea route between the Mediterranean and north-

Wat Tyler and John Ball, the leaders of the English Peasants' Revolt of 1381, join their forces in Canterbury during the march on London. Tyler urged his followers to kill "all lawyers and servants of the King," while Ball, a priest, preached radical doctrines of equality. In the new England, he declared, "there shall be neither vassals nor lords. . . . Are we not all descended from the same parents, Adam and Eve?" The rebels attacked the capital, burning and killing, before being crushed by an armed force of lords. "Villeins ye are," King Richard II told the peasants, "and villeins ye shall remain"

western Europe, was a bustling, cosmopolitan city with large enclaves of Italian merchants. By 1385 local merchants had grown powerful enough to place their own favorite, Joao I, on the throne, and he laid ambitious plans to establish a Portugese trading empire.

A central figure in this development was the son of the king, Prince Henry, known to later generations as "the Navigator." In the spirit of Renaissance learning, he established an academy of eminent geographers, instrument makers, shipbuilders, and seamen at his institute on Sagres Point, the southwestern tip of Portugal. By the mid-fifteenth century, as a result of their efforts, all educated Europeans knew the world was "round." The men of Sagres studied the seafaring techniques of Asia and the Muslim world. Incorporating these with European designs, they developed a new ship called the caravel, a faster, more maneuverable, and more seaworthy vessel than any previously known in Europe.

Using these ships, the Portuguese plied the Atlantic coast of northwestern Africa for direct access to the lucrative gold and slave trades of that continent. By the time of Prince Henry's death in 1460, they had colonized the Atlantic islands of the Azores and the Madeiras, and founded bases along the West African Gold Coast. In 1488 the Portuguese captain Bartholomew Diaz rounded the southern tip of the continent, and ten years later Vasco da Gama, with the aid of Arab pilots, reached India. The Portuguese eventually erected strategic trading forts along the coasts of Africa, India, and China, the first and longest-lasting outposts of European world colonization, and gained control of much of the Asian spice trade. Most important for the history of the Americas, they established the Atlantic slave trade. (For a full discussion of slavery, see Chapter 4.)

Columbus Reaches the Americas

In 1476, Christopher Columbus, a young Genoan merchant, was shipwrecked off Sagres Point in Portugal. Making his way to Lisbon, he joined his brother, a chart maker in the Italian community there. Over the next ten years Columbus worked as a seafaring merchant, visiting ports from Iceland in the north Atlantic to the Gold Coast in the south. He married and settled on the Portuguese island colony of Madeira in the Atlantic, and it was there that he developed the idea of opening a new route to Asia by sailing west across the ocean. Such a venture would require royal backing, but when he approached the various monarchs of Europe with his idea, their advisers laughed at his geographic ignorance, pointing out that his calculation of the distance to Asia was much too short. They were right, Columbus was wrong, but it turned out to be an error of monumental good fortune.

Columbus finally sold his idea to the monarchs of Castille and Aragon, Isabella and Ferdinand. These two had just conquered the southern Iberian province of Grenada from the Moors of North Africa, and through marriage had joined their kingdoms to form the state of Spain. This completed the *Reconquista,* a centuries-long struggle between Catholics and Moslems, and finally ended Muslim rule in Iberia. Through these many generations of warfare, the Spanish had developed a military tradition that thrived on conquest. Military service was the avenue by which ordinary men could rise into the ranks of the nobility. The Spanish had already tested their military system in the mid-fifteenth century against the Guanches, the native inhabitants of the Canary Islands in the Atlantic; after several decades of struggle, the Guanches were defeated and enslaved, and eventually extinguished as a people.

Now the Catholic monarchs of Spain needed new lands to conquer. Observing the successful Portuguese push to the south, they also became interested in opening lucrative trade routes of their own with Asia. Columbus's title for his expedition, "the Enterprise of the Indies," suggests its commercial motive. Columbus's expedition symbolized hopes of both trade and conquest. There was no vision here of a colonial community. Like the first English colony of Roanoke, the Spanish had only "naked imperial objectives" in mind.

His ships left Spain in August of 1492, pushed west across the Atlantic by the prevailing trade winds. By October flocks of birds and bits of driftwood announced the ships' approach to land. They arrived at a small, flat island somewhere in the Bahamas. Although scholars disagree on the precise location, many believe it to be a spot now known as Samana Cay. Columbus, however, believed he was somewhere near the Asian mainland. He explored the northern coasts of Cuba and Hispaniola before heading home, fortuitously catching the westerly winds that blow from the American coast toward Europe north of the tropics. One of Columbus's most important contributions was the discovery of the clockwise circulation of the Atlantic winds and currents that would carry thousands of European ships back and forth to the Americas.

Leading Columbus's triumphal procession to the royal court were a number of kidnapped Taino Indians from the Bahamas, dressed in bright feathers with ornaments of gold. The natives, Columbus noted, were "of a very acute intelligence," but had "no iron or steel weapons." A conflict between the

Samana Cay, a small, flat island among the Bahamas, may have been the site of Columbus's landing in 1492. His three ships anchored at the furthest point in this photograph, then entered the small bay in rowboats. "Presently they saw naked people," reads Columbus's journal. He landed, and "with the royal standard unfurled" took possession for the king and queen of Spain. Many of the native inhabitants gathered, and from them Columbus learned that they called the island Guanahani, land of the iguanas. He rechristened it San Salvador, "our savior."

Tainos and several armed Spaniards had ended quickly with the deaths of two natives. "Should your majesties command it," Columbus announced, "all the inhabitants could be made slaves." Moreover, he reported that "there are many spices and great mines of gold and of other metals." In fact, none of the spices familiar to Europeans grew in the Caribbean and there were only small quantities of precious metals in the riverbeds of the islands. But the sight of the little gold ornaments worn by the Indians had infected Columbus with a bad case of gold fever. On his return, he left a small force behind in a rough fort on Hispaniola — the first European foothold in the Americas.

The initial violence, kidnapping, and lust for gold were ominous signs for the native peoples of the Caribbean. But the monarchs, enthusiastic about Columbus's report, financed a convoy of seventeen ships and fifteen hundred men that left in late 1493 to begin the colonization of the islands Columbus described as "rich for planting and sowing, for breeding cattle of every kind, for building towns and villages." But on his return to Hispaniola he found his fort in ruins, his men killed by Indians who had lost patience with continuing Spanish outrages. It was much like the situation John White found on his return to Roanoke. Columbus destroyed the nearby native villages, enslaving the Tainos and demanding tribute from them in gold. He sent boatloads of slaves back to Spain, but most soon sickened and died, and the supply of gold quickly ran out. By 1496 the Spanish monarchs had become so dissatisfied

with these results that they ordered Columbus home in leg irons.

Columbus made two additional trips to the Caribbean, both characterized by the same violent slave raiding and obsessive searching for gold. He died in Spain in 1506, still convinced that he had opened the way to Asia. This belief persisted among many Europeans well into the sixteenth century. But others had already begun to see the discoveries from a different perspective. Amerigo Vespucci of Florence, who voyaged to the Caribbean in 1499, was the first European to describe the lands as *Mundus Novus,* a New World. When European geographers finally named these continents in the sixteenth century, they called them America, after Vespucci.

THE SPANISH IN THE AMERICAS

A century after Columbus's death, before the English had planted a single New World colony of their own, the Spanish had created a huge and wealthy empire in the Americas. In theory, all law and policy for the empire came from Spain; in practice, the isolation of the settlements led to a good deal of local autonomy. The Spanish created a caste system, in which a small minority of settlers and their offspring controlled the lives and labor of millions of Indian and African workers. But it was also a society in which colonists, Indians, and Africans mixed to form a new people.

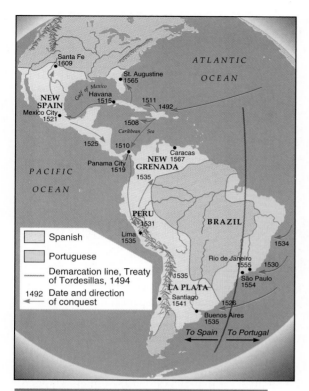

The Spanish and Portuguese Empires in 1610
The Spanish conquest of the Americas was a series of invasions, each new one building upon the last. By the early seventeenth century the Spanish New World empire stretched from Santa Fe, New Mexico in the north to Santiago, Chile in the south.

The Invasion of America

The first stages of the Spanish invasion of America included scenes of frightful violence. Armies marched across the Caribbean islands, plundering villages, slaughtering men, and capturing women. Columbus and his successors established an institution known as the *encomienda,* in which Indians were compelled to labor in the service of Spanish lords. Rather than work, one conquistador noted, many Indians took poison, "and others hanged themselves. . . ." Faced with labor shortages, slavers raided what King Ferdinand labeled the "useless islands" of the Bahamas, and soon had entirely depopulated them. The depletion of gold on Hispaniola led to the invasion of the islands of Puerto Rico and Jamaica in 1508, then Cuba in 1511. Meanwhile, rumors of wealthy societies to the west

led to scores of probing expeditions. The Spanish invasion of Central America began in 1511, and two years later Vasco Nunez de Balboa crossed the Isthmus of Panama to the "South Sea," the Pacific Ocean. In 1517 Spainards landed on the coast of Mexico, and within a year they had made contact with the Aztec empire.

The Aztecs had migrated to the Valley of Mexico from the harsh deserts of the American Southwest in the thirteenth century, just as the Toltec empire was in the last stage of collapse. (For a discussion of the development of Mexico, see Chapter 1.) The warlike Aztecs settled the marshy lake district of the valley and built the city of Tenochtitlán. By the early fifteenth century they had come to dominate the peoples of the highlands, in the process building a powerful state. Tribute flowed into Tenochtitlán from all over Mexico and Central America. In public rituals designed to appease their gods, Aztec priests brutally sacrificed captives atop the grand pyramids. By 1519 the population of the Aztec capital numbered approximately 300,000; the city was five times the size of the largest city in Spain.

Hernando Cortes, a veteran of the conquest of Cuba, landed on the Mexican coast with armed troops in 1519. Within two years he overthrew the Aztec empire, a spectacular military accomplishment that has no parallel in the annals of conquest. The Spanish had superior arms and horses. The Indians found the latter terrifying, mistaking mounted men for four-legged monsters. But these were not the principal causes of the Spanish success. Aztec resistance was impeded by a rigid bureaucracy that was fatally late in responding to the crisis. Cortes skillfully exploited the resentments of the many native peoples who lived under Aztec oppression, forging Spanish–Indian alliances that would become a model for the subsequent European colonization of the Americas. In the aftermath of conquest, the Spanish unmercifully plundered Aztec society, providing the Catholic monarchs with wealth beyond their wildest imagining. Later, the discovery of rich silver mines and the exploitation of Mexican labor through the encomienda system turned Spain into the mightiest state in Europe. The wealth that Spain gained from the New World encouraged men like Raleigh to go looking for the same thing.

The Destruction of the Indies

The Indian peoples of the Americas resisted Spanish conquest, but most proved a poor match for mounted warriors with steel swords and vicious

"The Cruelties used by the Spaniards on the Indians," from a 1599 English edition of *The Destruction of the Indies* by Bartolome de las Casas. Las Casas passionately denounced the Spanish conquest and defended the rights of the Indians. But his work was used by other European powers to condemn Spain as a means of covering up their own dismal colonial records. These images were copied from a series of engravings produced by Theodore de Bry that accompanied Las Casas's original edition.

bloodhounds. The record of the conquest, however, includes many brave Indian leaders and thousands of martyrs. Some native defenders were more successful than others. The Carib people (for which the Caribbean takes its name) successfully defended the outermost islands until the end of the sixteenth century, and in the arid lands of northern Mexico the nomadic tribes known collectively as the Chichimecs proved equally difficult to subdue.

Some Europeans protested the horrors of the conquest. Principal among them was Bartolomé de las Casas, a Spanish Catholic priest who had participated in the plunder of Cuba in 1511, but who several years later suffered a crisis of conscience and began to denounce the conquest. The Christian mission in the New World was to convert the Indians, he argued, and "the means to effect this end are not to rob, to scandalize, to capture or destroy them, or to lay waste their lands." Long before the world recognized the concept of universal human rights, Las Casas was proclaiming that "the entire human race is one," which earned him a reputation as one of the towering moral figures in the early history of the Americas. Las Casas had powerful supporters at court who made repeated but unsuccessful attempts to reform the treatment of Indians.

In his brilliant history of the conquest, *The Destruction of the Indies* (1552), Las Casas blamed the Spanish for millions of deaths — in effect, genocide. Translated into several languages and widely circulated throughout Europe, Las Casas's book was used by other European powers to condemn Spain as a means of covering up their own dismal colonial records. Later scholars, doubting Las Casas's estimates of huge population losses, criticized his work as part of a "Black Legend" of the Spanish conquest. Las Casas himself anticipated these doubts. "Who of those born in future centuries will believe this?" he wrote; "I myself, who am writing this and saw it, and know most about it, can hardly believe that such was possible." But many of today's historians find Las Casas to be more believable. Demographic studies suggest that the native people of Hispaniola numbered in the millions when Columbus arrived; fifty years later they had been reduced no more than a few hundred, and soon the Tainos had disappeared from the face of the earth. In Mexico, the 1519 population of 25 million plummeted to only a million a century later.

Las Casas was incorrect, however, in attributing most of these losses to warfare. To be sure, thousands of lives were lost in battle, but these deaths were but a small proportion of the overall population decline. Thousands more starved because their economies were destroyed or their food stores taken by conquering armies. Even more important, native birth rates fell drastically after the conquest. Indian women were so "worn out with work," one Spaniard wrote, that they avoided conception, induced abortion, and even "killed their children with their own hands so that they shall not have to endure the same hardships."

By far the greatest loss of life resulted from the introduction of Old World diseases. Pre-Columbian America seems to have had no virulent epidemic diseases, and because of this Indian peoples lacked the antibodies necessary to protect them from European germs and viruses. A shipload of colonists carried smallpox to Hispaniola in 1516, causing an epidemic in the Caribbean that had crossed into Mexico by 1520, eventually spreading along the trading network through both continents. After conquest, the Aztecs sang of an earlier time:

> There was then no sickness.
> They had then no aching bones.
> They had then no high fever.
> They had then no smallpox.
> They had then no burning chest.
> They had then no abdominal pains.
> They had then no consumption.
> They had then no headache.
> At that time the course of humanity was orderly.
> The foreigners made it otherwise when they arrived here.

Smallpox devastated Peru in 1524, strategically weakening the Inca empire eight years before it was conquered by the Spanish conquistador Francisco Pizarro. Spanish chroniclers wrote that this single epidemic killed half of the native Americans it touched. Disease was the secret weapon of the Spanish, and it helps explain their almost unbelievable success in the conquest.

Areas spared in one epidemic were affected in later ones. At least three dozen massive epidemics of smallpox ravaged Indian America over the next three centuries. Other virulent diseases followed the same course. Measles, the second greatest killer, first swept through the Americas in 1531–1533; bubonic plague invaded in 1545, followed by influenza in 1559, typhus in 1586, diphtheria in 1601, and scarlet fever in 1637. Combined with warfare, famine, and lowered birth rates, epidemic disease knocked Indian populations into a downward spiral from which they did not recover until the twentieth century. Overall, Indian population fell by 90 percent, the greatest demographic disaster in world history. The outstanding difference between the European colonial experience in the Americas and elsewhere — Africa and Asia, for example — was this radical reduction in the native population.

It is possible that the New World sent one disease back across the Atlantic. On the basis of considerable evidence, archaeologists have concluded that syphilis was present in ancient America, but not the Old World. (Recent findings, though, may alter these conclusions.) The first recorded epidemic of venereal syphilis in Europe took place in Spain in

This drawing of victims of the smallpox epidemic that struck the Aztec capital of Tenochititlan in 1520 is taken from the Florentine Codex, a post-conquest history written and illustrated by Aztec scribes. "There came amongst us a great sickness, a general plague," reads the account, "killing vast numbers of people. It covered many all over with sores: on the face, on the head, on the chest, everywhere. . . . The sores were so terrible that the victims could not lie face down, nor on their backs, nor move from one side to the other. And when they tried to move even a little, they cried out in agony."

1493, and many historians think it may have been carried home by the sailors on Columbus's ships. By 1495 the disease was spreading rapidly among Europe's armies, and by the sixteenth century it had found its way to Asia and Africa. The passage of diseases between the Old and New Worlds was one part of the large-scale continental exchange that marks the beginning of the modern era of world history.

Continental Exchange

The most obvious exchange was the vast influx into Europe of the precious metals plundered from the Aztec and Incan empires of the New World. "The best thing in the world is gold," Columbus wrote. "It can even send souls to heaven." In a moment of reflection Cortes confided that "we Spaniards suffer from a disease of the heart, the specific remedy for which is gold." Most of the booty was melted down, destroying forever thousands of priceless Indian artifacts. Even more important were the silver mines the Spanish discovered and operated in Mexico and Peru. Between 1500 and 1550 the amount of silver coin circulating in Europe tripled, then tripled again before 1600. The result was runaway inflation, which stimulated commerce and raised profits but lowered the standard of living for the majority. Rising prices during the sixteenth century, for example, depressed the value of European wages by more than 50 percent.

But of even greater long-term importance were the New World crops brought to Europe. Maize (Indian corn) from Mexico — the staff of life for most North Americans — became a staple human crop in Mediterranean countries, the dominant feed for

Continental Exchange

The exchange between continents of crops and animals, microbes and men, marks the beginning of the modern era of world history.

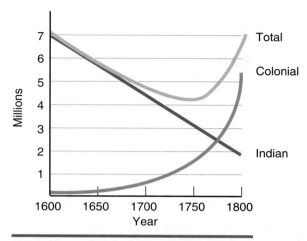

The Indian and Colonial Population of North America

Epidemic disease was the primary factor in the drastic reduction of native population. Colonial population overtook and passed the Indian population of the continent in the eighteenth century.

Source: *Historical Statistics of the United States* (Washington, D.C.: Government Printing Office, 1976), 8, 1168; Russell Thornton, *American Indian Holocaust and Survival* (Norman: University of Oklahoma Press, 1987), 32.

livestock elsewhere in Europe, and the primary provision for the slave ships of Africa. Over the next few centuries, potatoes from Peru provided the margin between famine and subsistence for the peasant peoples of northern Europe and Ireland. These "miracle crops" provided abundant food sources that, for the most part, finally eliminated the persistent problem of famine in Europe.

Although the Spanish failed to locate valuable spices such as black pepper or cloves in the New World, new tropical crops more than compensated. Tobacco was prescribed as an antidote against disease when it first appeared in Europe about 1550, but was soon in wide use as an intoxicant. American vanilla and chocolate both became highly valued. American cotton proved superior to Asian varieties for the production of cheap textiles. Each of these native plants, along with tropical transplants from the Old World to the New — sugar, rice, and coffee, among the most important — supplied the basis for important new industries and markets that altered the course of world history.

Columbus introduced domesticated animals into Hispaniola and Cuba, and livestock were later transported to Mexico. The movement of Spanish settlement into northern Mexico was greatly aided by an advancing wave of livestock, for grazing

animals seriously disrupted native fields and forests. Horses, used by Spanish stockmen to tend their cattle, also spread northward. Eventually they reached the Great Plains of North America, where they would transform the lives of the nomadic hunting Indians.

The First Europeans in North America

Ponce de Leon, governor of Puerto Rico, was the first conquistador to attempt to extend the Spanish conquest to North America. In 1513 he landed on the southern Atlantic coast, which he named in honor of the Easter season — *pascua florida. Florida* thus became the oldest European place name in the United States. Ponce encountered warriors from some of the powerful Indian chiefdoms of the South, who beat back his attempts to take slaves, and finally killed him in battle in 1521. Seven years later another Spanish attempt to colonize Florida, under the command of Panfilo de Naravez, ended in disaster. Most of Naravez's troops were lost in a shipwreck, but a small group of them survived, living and wandering for several years among the Indian peoples of the Gulf coast and Southwest until finally rescued in 1536 by Spanish slave hunters in northern Mexico. One of these men, Cabeza de Vaca, published an account of his adventures in which he told of a North American empire known as Cibola, with golden cities "larger than the city of Mexico."

Cabeza de Vaca's report inspired two attempts to penetrate the mystery of North America. The first was mounted by Hernando de Soto, a veteran of the conquest of Peru. After landing in Florida in 1539 with a Cuban army of over 700 men and thousands of hogs and cattle, he commandeered food and slaves from the Mississippian Indian towns in his path as he pushed hundreds of miles through the heavily populated South. He failed, though, to locate another Aztec empire. In present-day Alabama, thousands of Choctaw warriors beseiged his army, and a few months later the Chickasaws chewed the Spaniards apart. Their numbers depleted by half, de Soto desperately drove his men westward, crossing the Mississippi and marching deep into present Arkansas before returning to the banks of the great river, where the conquistador finally died in 1541. Some 300 of de Soto's dispirited survivors eventually reached Mexico on rafts in 1543. The native peoples of the South had successfully turned back Spanish invasion, and they remained in control of their country for another 250 years. If this were the

This first European attempt to picture an American buffalo (1557) drew on the accounts of those who had seen them. A bull stood about seven feet tall at the shoulder and could weigh up to a ton. In the sixteenth century there may have been as many as forty million buffalo on the Great Plains. Although many Indians hunted them for food, the heyday of the buffalo-hunting nomads would come after their acquisition of the horse.

ºend of the story, it would barely deserve mentioning. But de Soto's army introduced epidemic diseases to the South that drastically depopulated and undermined the societies there. When Europeans finally returned to colonize the region in the seventeenth century, they found the descendants of the Mississippian chiefdoms living in much simpler tribal confederacies.

The same year of the de Soto expedition, 1539, Spanish officials in Mexico launched the second *entrada de conquista* of North America, this one aimed at the Southwest. Francisco Vasquez de Coronado led 300 mounted men and infantry and 800 Indian porters north along well-marked Indian trading paths, passing through the settlements of Piman Indians near the present border of the United States and Mexico and finally reaching the Pueblo villages along the Rio Grande. The initial resistance of the Pueblo people was quickly quashed. But Coronado was deeply disappointed by these towns "of stone and mud, rudely fashioned," and sent out expeditions in all directions in search of the cities of Cibola. They brought back word of the Colorado River and the Grand Canyon, the isolated Hopis, and the town of Acoma high "on the world's strongest rock," but nothing matching the rumors of Cibola. Coronado himself took his army as far north as the Great Plains, where he observed great herds of "shaggy cows" (buffalo) and made contact with

nomadic hunting peoples, but returned without gold. For the next fifty years Spain lost all interest in the Southwest.

The Spanish New World Empire

Despite these setbacks in North America, by the late sixteenth century the Spanish had control of a powerful empire in the Americas. A century after Columbus, some 200,000 European immigrants, most of them Spaniards, had settled in the Americas. Another 125,000 Africans had been forcibly resettled on the Spanish plantations of the Caribbean, as well as on the plantations of Brazil (see Chapter 4). The Portuguese had colonized Brazil under the terms of the Treaty of Tordesillas, a 1494 agreement dividing the Americas between Spain and Portugal. Most of the Spanish settlers resided in the more than two hundred urban communities founded during the conquest, including cities such as Santo Domingo in Hispaniola; Havana, Cuba; Mexico City, built atop

The Ethnic Composition of the Population of the Americas

In the five hundred years since the colonial invasion of the Americas, the population has included varying proportions of native, European, and African peoples, as well as large numbers of persons with mixed ancestry.

Source: Colin McEvedy and Richard Jones, *Atlas of World Population History* (New York: Penguin, 1978), 280.

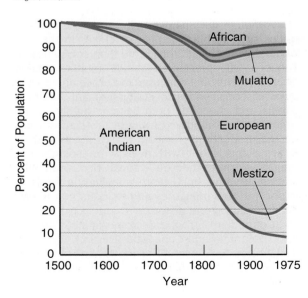

the ruins of Tenochtitlan; and Quito, Peru, at the center of the conquered empire of the Incas. Only a small number of Spaniards and their offspring lived in the countryside. There they supervised Indian or African workers in mining, ranching, or agriculture. Because European women constituted only about 10 percent of the immigrants, from the beginning male colonists married or simply lived with African or Indian women. The result was the growth of large mixed-ancestry groups known respectively as mulattoes and mestizos. The Spanish established what has been called a "frontier of inclusion," their communities characterized by a great deal of marriage and sexual mixing between male colonists and native women. Hundreds of thousands of Indians died, but Indian genes were passed on to generations of mestizo peoples, who became the majority population in the mainland Spanish American empire; in the Caribbean, Africans were prominent in the mixing process. The coming of the Spanish to the Americas marked the death of many peoples, but also the birth of several new ones.

Populated by Indians, Africans, Spanish colonists, and their mixed offspring, the New World colonies of Spain made up one of the largest empires in the history of the world. The Council of the Indies, composed of the principal advisers of the Spanish king, and acting in his name, made all the principal laws and regulations for the empire and approved all the clerical and secular appointments to positions of authority. The council oversaw the work of the *Casa de Contratacion,* the imperial board of trade that authorized all colonial commerce, collected custom duties, and enforced trade regulations from its headquarters in the principal Spanish port of Seville. The viceroyalties of New Spain and Peru were the principal administrative districts of the empire. Under them was a descending structure of authority, from the *audiencias*— such as that of Mexico — to the *presidencias,* the captaincies general, and finally the civil governments of the towns.

The empire thus operated in theory as a highly centralized and bureaucratic system. But the deliberations of the Council of the Indies on the one hand and the administration of local affairs on the other were separated by a tremendous distance; what looked in the abstract to be a centrally administered empire often proved to tolerate significant local autonomy. Passive resistance and sometimes outright defiance of central authority were commonplace in this system. This was reflected in the well-known phrase of local officials: "I obey but I do not execute."

NORTHERN EXPLORATIONS AND ENCOUNTERS

With the Spanish empire at the height of its power in the sixteenth century, the merchants and monarchs of other important European seafaring states looked across the Atlantic for opportunities of their own. France was first to sponsor intensive expeditions to the New World in the early sixteenth century. At first the French attempted to plant settlements on the coasts of Brazil and Florida, but Spanish opposition ultimately persuaded them to concentrate on the North Atlantic. It was the second half of the sixteenth century before England developed its own plans to colonize North America. With the Spanish in Florida and the French establishing close ties with coastal tribes as far south as present-day Maine, the English focused on the middle latitudes.

The Reformation

The religious revolt against Catholicism known as the Reformation was an essential ingredient in the expansion of the northern European peoples. The first sparks of this revolt were produced by Renaissance humanism, which implicitly questioned the authority of religious dogma. The Reformation formally began, however, when the German priest Martin Luther publicized his differences with Rome in 1517. Eternal salvation was a gift from God, Luther declared, not something earned by good works or service to the Roman Catholic Church. He also emphasized the importance of individual Bible study — which underlined the impact of the revolution in printing and literacy — thereby undercutting the authority of priests. Luther had attacked the Catholic hierarchy, and they in turn excommunicated him in 1521. His ideas fit into a climate of widespread dissatisfaction with the power and prosperity of the Catholic Church. Adding to their impact was the adoption of Luther's movement by German princes who wished to strengthen their independence from Rome. The controversy thus became political, inaugurating a series of bloody religious wars that dominated Europe for the next century.

There was considerable enthusiasm for Luther's protests — or *Protestantism*— in France. Catholic persecution of Protestants in the 1520s caused one of the most prominent leaders to flee across the border to Switzerland. This was John Calvin, a reformer even more radical than Luther. Calvin

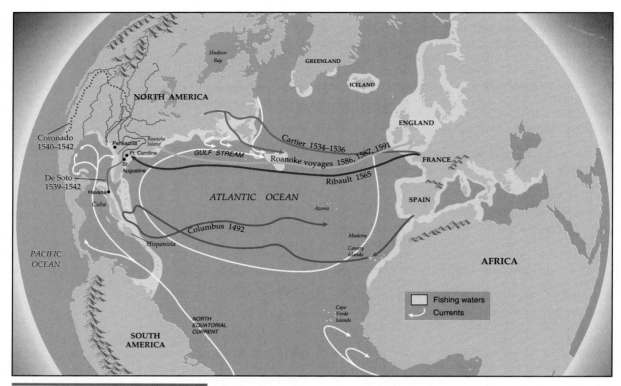

European Exploration, 1492–1587
The voyages across the Atlantic utilized the clockwise circulation of winds and currents. By the mid sixteenth century Europeans had explored most of the Atlantic coast of North America, and had penetrated into the interior in the disasterous expeditions of De Soto and Coronado.

organized a model Christian community that by the 1530s controlled the city-state of Geneva. A former lawyer, Calvin became the most systematic of the early Protestant theologians. In his doctrine of predestination, he declared that God had chosen a small number of men and women for "election," or salvation, while condemning the vast majority to eternal damnation. Calvinists were encouraged to examine themselves closely for "signs of election," and work to demonstrate thrift, industry, sobriety, and personal responsibility, which Calvin argued were essential to the Christian life. These ideas proved powerful in the growth of the spirit of enterprise that characterized early European capitalism.

Sixteenth-century England became deeply involved in struggles to reform the Catholic Church. At first King Henry VIII of England (reigned 1509–47) supported the church against the Protestants. But in England too there was great public resentment of the ostentatious display of the church and the drain of tax money to Rome. When the pope refused to grant Henry an annulment of his marriage to Catherine of Aragon, daughter of Ferdinand and Isabella of Spain, the king exploited this popular mood. Taking up the cause of reform in 1534, he declared himself head of a separate Church of England. He later took over the English estates of the Catholic Church — about a quarter of the country's land — and used their revenues to begin constructing a powerful English state system, including a standing army and navy. Working through Parliament, Henry carefully enlisted the support of the merchants and landed gentry for his program, parceling out a measure of royal prosperity in the form of titles, offices, lands, and commercial favors. By the mid-sixteenth century he had forged a solid alliance with the wealthy merchant class.

The Protestant movement also took root in France, but with a very different outcome. Calvin's French followers — known as the Huguenots — were concentrated among merchants and the middle class, but also included many of the nobility. In 1560 a group of Huguenot nobles were defeated in an attempt to sieze power in the French state, and this began nearly forty years of religious struggle. In 1572 the French crown directed the murder of more than 3,000 Huguenots in Paris, and many more throughout the country. This bloodshed, known as the St. Bartholomew's Day Massacre, made France infamous as the enemy of Protestantism, which was growing in popularity in England. In 1589 the Huguenot Henry IV became king of France, but found it impossible to govern until he converted to Catholicism four years later. His Edict of Nantes of 1598 established the rights of Huguenots to their views, but made Roman Catholicism the official religion of France. Thus England and France moved in very different directions during the Reformation.

The First French Colonies

The first French attempt to establish colonies in North America culminated efforts by Huguenot leaders who dreamed of a Protestant refuge for French men and women in the New World. In 1562, under the authority of Caspard de Coligny, an influential Huguenot Admiral of the Realm, Jean Ribault and 150 Protestants from Normandy landed on Parris Island, near present-day Beaufort, South Carolina. The party began constructing a fort and crude mud huts. Ribault soon returned to France for supplies, where he was caught up in the religious wars. Meanwhile the colonists nearly starved, finally resorting to cannibalism before being rescued by a passing British ship. In 1564 another French expedition under Ribault established the Huguenot colony of Fort Caroline on the St. Johns River of Florida, south of present Jacksonville.

Nearby were villages of the Timucua Indians. Ribault provided a detailed description of Timucua farming, including the cultivation of "a grain they call Mahiz, whereof they make their meal," and the care of their gardens of beans, squash, and root crops. They took fish in elaborate weirs, he wrote, "made in the water with great reeds so well and cunningly set together, after the fashion of a labyrinth or maze, with so many turns or crooks . . ." He was amazed at the abundance of game in the forests, including turkeys and "wild swine." The latter were hogs that had escaped from de Soto's expedition twenty-five years before. Supplementing Ribault's report were the drawings of Jacques le Moyne, later engraved and circulated throughout Europe. Together they provide one of the best ethnographic descriptions we have of the Timucuas, who disappeared as the result of warfare and disease over the next two centuries. Ribault reported that the Indians were friendly and hospitable, welcoming the Frenchmen into their homes and honoring them with food and drink. It is likely that the natives viewed the French as potential allies against the Spanish, who had plundered the coast many times in pursuit of slaves.

Indeed, the Spanish had already established a foothold along the Atlantic coast of Florida. They were not interested in settlement, but wished rather to protect their fleets riding the off-shore Gulf Stream home to Spain. Fort Caroline was manned not only by Frenchmen but by French Protestants — deadly

This imposing fortress, Castillo de San Marcos, was built between 1672 and 1695 to defend the town of Saint Augustine, making it the oldest masonry fort in the United States. Saint Augustine itself is the oldest continuously occupied European city in the country, founded by the Spanish in 1565 to guard the Gulf Stream route to Europe used by the galleons loaded with New World treasure.

enemies of the Catholic monarchs of Spain. "We are compelled to pass in front of their port," wrote one official of New Spain, "and with the greatest ease they can sally out with their armadas to seek us." In 1565 the Spanish crown sent Don Pedro Menendez de Aviles, captain general of the Indies, to crush the Huguenots. He established the Spanish fort of St. Augustine on the coast, south of the French, then marched overland through the swamps to surprise them with an attack from the rear. "I put Jean Ribaut and all the rest of them to the knife," Menendez wrote triumphantly to the king, "judging it to be necessary to the service of the Lord Our God and of Your Majesty." St. Augustine remained to become the oldest continuously occupied European city in North America. But more than 500 Frenchmen lay dead on the beaches of Florida; the French attempt to plant a colony along the South Atlantic coast had ended in disaster.

Fish and Furs

Of far more lasting significance for the French overseas empire was the entrance of French fishermen into the waters of the North Atlantic. It is possible that fishing ships from England, France, Spain, and Portugal had discovered the great northern fishing grounds long before Columbus's voyages. In the Grand Banks, the waters teemed with "so great multitudes of certain big fishes," in the words of one early seaman, "that they sometimes stayed my ships." By 1500, hundreds of ships and thousands of sailors were regularly fishing the coastal waters of the North Atlantic, many making landfall to take on wood and fuel and to dry their catch. The contacts between Europeans and natives took a different form along the North Atlantic coast than in the tropics: relationships were based on trade rather than conquest. They contrasted dramatically with patterns in the Spanish New World empire — and with later English colonization.

The first official voyages of exploration in the North Atlantic used the talents of experienced European sailors and fishermen. With a crew from Bristol, England, the Genovese John Cabot reached Labrador in 1497, and in 1524 the Tuscan captain Giovanni da Verrazano sailed with a crew from France, exploring the North American coast from Cape Fear (in today's North Carolina) to the Penobscot River (Maine). Anxious to locate empires to conquer or a passage to the spice trade of Asia, the French king commissioned the experienced captain Jacques Cartier. In 1534, 1535, and 1541, Cartier reconnoitered the St. Lawrence River, which led deep into the continental interior, and established France's imperial claim to the lands of Canada.

Northern Europeans thus discovered the northern Indians, and the Indians in turn discovered them. Native tales told of seeing the approach of floating islands (ships) with many tall trees (masts) and hairy bears (sailors) running about in the branches. Beards "held an ugly fascination for them," one Frenchman noted. To northern Indian women, a beard was "a monstrosity," a mark of weak intelligence and limited sex appeal, "the greatest disfigurement that a face can have." When one Huron of the St. Lawrence wanted to insult another, he called him *sascoinronte* or "bearded-one."

But the Indians immediately appreciated the usefulness of textiles, glass, copper, and ironware. Seeing Cartier's approach, the Micmacs waved him ashore. "The savages showed marvelous great pleasure in possessing and obtaining iron wares and other commodities," he noted in his report. For his part, Cartier was interested in the fur coats of the Indians. Europeans, like Indians, used furs for winter clothing. But the growing population of the late Middle Ages had so depleted the wild game of Europe that the price of furs had risen beyond the reach of most people. The North American fur trade thus filled an important demand and produced high profits.

By no means were Indians simply the victims of European traders. Indian traders had a sharp eye for quality, and because of the unbridled competition among the Europeans, they could demand good exchange rates. But the trade also had negative consequences for Indian people. Epidemic European diseases soon began to ravage their communities. Intense rivalry broke out between tribes over hunting territories, resulting in deadly warfare. By the 1580s, disease and violence had turned the St. Lawrence Valley into a virtual no-man's land. Moreover, as European manufactured goods, such as metal knives, kettles, and firearms, became essential to their way of life, the Indians became dependent upon European suppliers. Ultimately, the fur trade was stacked in favor of Europeans.

By the end of the sixteenth century over a thousand ships per year were trading for furs along the northern coast. The trade between Indians and Europeans of many nations, both along the coast and at the annual summer trade fair at the St. Lawrence village of Tadoussac, grew increasingly

In his sketch of this "Captaine" of the Illinois nation (drawn about 1700), the French artist Charles Becard de Granville carefully noted the tattooing of the warrior's face and body, his distinctive costume and feather headdress, his spear and tobacco pipe. Like this chief, Indian men were almost always clean shaven. Indian women believed beards to be "the greatest disfigurement that a face can have."

social change at home. Perhaps most important were changes in the economy. As the prices of goods rose steeply—the result of New World inflation—English landlords, their rents fixed by custom, sought ways to increase their incomes. Seeking profits in the woolen trade, many converted the common pasturage used by tenants into grazing land for sheep, with the result that large numbers of farmers were dislocated. Between 1500 and 1650 a third of all the common lands in England were "enclosed" in this way. In a phrase of the day, "sheep ate men." Deprived of their traditional livelihoods, thousands of families sought employment in the cities. The population of London grew from 60,000 to 200,000 over the sixteenth century, and other urban areas expanded similarly. It was a time of great disruption and poverty for common folk, but increasing prosperity for landlords and merchants.

Henry VIII of England died in 1547. He was succeeded by his young and sickly son Edward VI, who soon died, then by his Catholic daughter Mary, who attempted to reverse her father's Reformation from the top. She added her own chapter to the century's many religious wars, martyring hundreds of English Protestants and gaining the title of "Bloody Mary." But upon Mary's death in 1558, her half sister Elizabeth I (reigned 1558–1603) came to the throne. Elizabeth sought to end the religious turmoil by tolerating a variety of views within the English church. Criticized by radical Protestants for not going far enough, and condemned by Catholics for her "pretended title to the kingdom," Elizabeth nevertheless gained popularity among the English people with her moderate approach. The Spanish monarchy, the head of the most powerful empire in the world, declared itself the defender of the Catholic faith, and vowed to overthrow her. England and Spain now became the two principal rivals of the Catholic–Protestant confrontation.

Early English Efforts in the Americas

It was during Elizabeth's reign that England first turned toward the New World. Its first ventures were aimed at breaking the Spanish trading monopoly with tropical America. In 1562 John Hawkins inaugurated English participation in the slave trade, violating Spanish regulations by transporting African slaves to the Caribbean and bringing back valuable tropical goods. In 1567 the Spanish attacked Hawkins, an event English privateers such as Francis Drake used as an excuse for launching a

important as the century progressed. Among these European traders, the French were probably the most numerous, and in the early seventeenth century they would move to consolidate their hold by planting colonies along the St. Lawrence.

Sixteenth-Century England

Like the first colonial efforts of the French, the English movement across the Atlantic was tied to

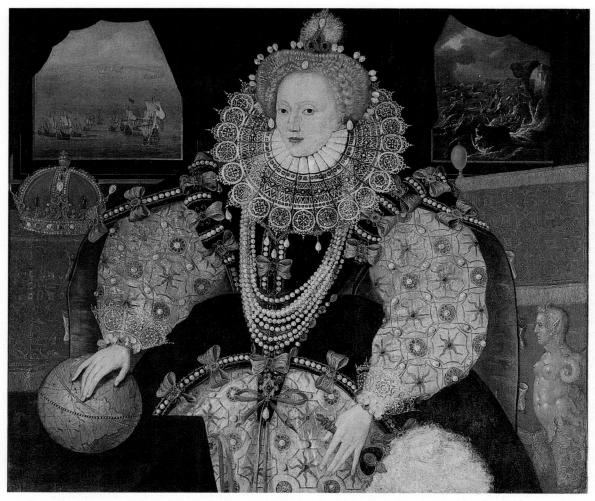

The Armada Portrait of Elizabeth I, painted by an unknown artist in 1648. Dressed in her royal finery and surrounded by nautical images and symbols, the queen places her hand on the globe, symbolizing the rising seapower of England. Through the open windows we see the battle against the Spanish Armada in 1588 and the destruction of the Spanish ships in a providential storm, interpreted by the Queen as an act of divine intervention.

series of devastating and lucrative raids against Spanish New World ports and fleets. The voyages of these English "Sea Dogs" greatly enriched their investors, including Elizabeth herself. From a voyage that cost several thousand pounds, Drake was said to have returned with booty valued in the millions. The English thus began their American adventures by slaving and plundering.

A consensus soon developed among Elizabeth's closest advisers that the time had come to enter the competition for America. In a state paper written for the queen, Richard Hakluyt summarized the advantages that would come from colonies: they could provide bases from which to raid the Spanish in the Caribbean, outposts for an Indian market for English goods, and plantations for growing tropical products, freeing the nation from a reliance on the long-distance trade with Asia. These colonies could be populated by the "multitudes of loiterers and idle vagabonds" of England, who could support the enterprise by farming the American soil. He urged Elizabeth to establish such colonies "upon the mouths of the great navigable rivers" from Florida to the St. Lawrence. Hakluyt's plan for English colonization was not exactly a vision of colonial community. It would contrast dramatically with later English colonies in Virginia and New England.

Although Elizabeth refused to commit the state to Hakluyt's plan, she authorized several private attempts at exploration and colonization, and even invested in these ventures herself. In the late 1570s Martin Frobisher conducted three voyages of exploration to the lands of "Meta Incognita" beyond the North Atlantic; he brought back an Eskimo man, woman, and child, and samples of worthless ores. Walter Raleigh and his half brother Humphrey Gilbert, soldiers and adventurers, planned the first colonizing venture in 1578, but it failed to get off the ground. Then in 1583 Gilbert sailed with a flotilla of ships from Plymouth; he landed at St. John's Bay, Newfoundland, where he encountered fishermen from several other nations but nevertheless claimed the territory for his queen. Gilbert's ship was lost on the return voyage.

Raleigh followed up his brother's efforts with plans to establish a colony southward, in the more hospitable climate of the mid-Atlantic coast. Although the Roanoke enterprise of 1584–87 seemed far more likely to succeed than Gilbert's, it too eventually failed. The greatest legacy of the expedition was the scientific work of Thomas Harriot and John White, who mapped the area, surveyed its commercial potential, and studied the Indian residents. Harriot's *A Briefe and True Report of the Newfound Land of Virginia* (1588) was addressed mainly to the problem of identifying the "merchantable commodities" that would support the settlement, for without products a colonial system was impossible. A later edition of this book included engravings based on White's watercolors of the people and landscape of Virginia. Together, the work of these men provided the most accurate and sensitive description of North American Indians made at the moment of their contact with Europeans.

King Philip II of Spain was outraged at the English incursions into territory reserved by the pope for Catholics. He had authorized the destruction of the French colony in Florida, and now he committed himself to smashing England. In 1588 he sent a fleet of 130 ships carrying 30,000 men to invade the British Isles. Countered by captains such as Drake and Hawkins, who commanded smaller

The care that John White brought to his painting is evident in this watercolor of an Algonquian mother and daughter (1585). The woman's fringed deerskin skirt is edged with white beads, and the decoration on her face and upper arms seem to be tattooed. The little wooden doll in the girl's hand was a gift from White. All the Indian girls, wrote Thomas Harriot, "are greatly delighted with puppetts and babes which were brought out of England."

and more maneuverable ships, and frustrated by an ill-timed storm that the English chose to interpret as an act of divine intervention, the Spanish Armada floundered. Half the ships were destroyed, their crews killed or captured. The war would continue until 1604, but the Spanish monopoly of the New World had been broken in the English Channel.

CHRONOLOGY

1347–53	Black Death in Europe
1381	English Peasants' Revolt
1488	Diaz sails around the African continent
1492	Columbus first arrives in the Caribbean
1494	Treaty of Tordesillas
1500	High point of the Renaissance
1508	Spanish invade Puerto Rico
1513	Ponce de Leon lands in Florida
1514	Las Casas begins preaching against the conquest
1516	Smallpox introduced to the New World
1517	Martin Luther breaks with the Roman Catholic Church
1519	Cortez lands in Mexico
1534	Cartier first explores the St. Lawrence River
1539	De Soto and Coronado expeditions
1550	Tobacco introduced to Europe
1552	Las Casas's *Destruction of the Indies* published
1558	Elizabeth I of England begins her reign
1562	Huguenot colony planted along the mid-Atlantic coast
1565	St. Augustine founded
1572	St. Bartholomew's Day Massacre in France
1583	Gilbert attempts to plant a colony in Newfoundland
1585–87	Raleigh's colony on Roanoke Island
1588	English defeat the Spanish Armada
1590	John White returns to find Roanoke colony abandoned

CONCLUSION

The Spanish opened the era of European colonization in the Americas with Columbus's voyage in 1492. The consequences for the Indian peoples of the Americas were disastrous. The Spanish succeeded in constructing the world's most powerful empire on the backs of Indian and African labor. The New World colonies of Spain were characterized by a great deal of mixing between the mostly male colonists and native women; in this sense they were communities of "inclusion." Inspired by the Spanish success, both the French and the English had begun to make feeble attempts to colonize the coast of North America. By the end of the sixteenth century, however, they had not succeeded in establishing any colonial communities of their own. The colonists of Roanoke had themselves become part of an Indian community. In the next century, the English would adopt another model of colonization, the transplantation of complete communities of families across the Atlantic.

Additional Readings

ALFRED W. CROSBY, JR., *The Columbian Exchange: Biological and Cultural Consequences of 1492* (1972). This is the pathbreaking account of the intersection of the biospheres of the Old and New Worlds.

CHARLES GIBSON, *Spain in America* (1966). The best introductory history of the Spanish American empire.

LEWIS HANKE, *The Spanish Struggle for Justice in the Conquest of America* (1949; reprint, 1965). The classic account of Las Casas's attempts to rectify the wrongs against the Indians.

MIGUEL LEON-PORTILLA, *The Broken Spears: The Aztec Account of the Conquest of Mexico* (1962). The history of the Spanish conquest as told by the Aztecs, drawn from manuscripts dating as early as 1528, only seven years after the fall of Tenochtitlán.

SAMUEL ELIOT MORISON, *The European Discovery of America: The Northern Voyages, A.D. 500–1600* (1971) and *The Southern Voyages, A.D. 1492–1616* (1974). The most detailed treatment of all the important European explorations of the Americas.

J. H. PARRY, *The Age of Reconnaissance* (1963). This readable book illuminates the background of European expansion.

DAVID BEERS QUINN, *Set Fair for Roanoke: Voyages and Colonies, 1584–1606* (1985). The story of Roanoke — the Indian village, the English settlement, and the Lost Colony. It includes the latest ethnographic and archaeological findings.

KIRKPATRICK SALE, *The Conquest of Paradise: Christopher Columbus and the Columbian Legacy* (1990). Despite its harsh view of Columbus, this biography provides important information on the world of the Caribbean and the disastrous effects of the encounter with Europeans.

CARL ORTWIN SAUER, *Sixteenth Century North America: The Land and the People as Seen by the Europeans* (1971). An excellent source for the explorations of the continent, providing abundant descriptions of the Indians.

DAVID E. STANNARD, *American Holocaust: Columbus and the Conquest of the New World* (1992). Argues that the Spanish inaugurated a genocidal policy that continued into the twentieth century.

3 PLANTING COLONIES IN NORTH AMERICA, 1588–1701

It was a hot August day in 1680 when the frantic messengers rode into the small mission outpost of El Paso with the news: the Pueblo Indians to the north had risen in revolt, and the corpses of more than 400 colonists lay bleeding in the dust. Two thousand Spanish survivors huddled inside the Palace of Governors in Santa Fe, surrounded by 3,000 angry warriors. The Pueblo leaders had sent two crosses inside the palace — one white, the other red. Which would it be, surrender or death?

Spanish colonists had been in New Mexico for nearly a century. Franciscan priests came first, then a military expedition from Mexico in search of precious metals. High in the picturesque foothills of the Sangre de Cristo Mountains in 1609

THE PUEBLOS AND THE
SPANISH FIND AN
ACCOMMODATION

the colonial authorities founded La Villa Real de la Santa Fe de San Francisco — "the royal town of the holy faith of St. Francis" — soon known simply as Santa Fe. The colonization program included the conversion of the Indians to Christianity, their subjection to the king of Spain, and their employment as workers for the colonial elite who lived in the ranchos scattered around the edge of the town.

In the face of overwhelming Spanish power — the same military might that had retaken Spain from the Moors of North Africa and conquered the great American civilizations of the Aztecs and Incas — the Pueblos adopted a flexibile attitude. Twenty thousand of them converted to Christianity, but most of these thought of the new religion as simply an appendage to their complex culture. The Christian God was but a minor addition to their numerous dieties; church holidays were included in their own religious calendar and celebrated with native dances and rituals.

Most ethnographers agree that the Pueblos were a sexually spirited people. Many of their public dances included erotic displays and sometimes ended in spectacles of public intercourse. Fornication was their symbol of the powerful force that brought the separate worlds of men and women together, and thus was their symbol for community. The sexual celibacy of the Franciscan priests not only astounded the Pueblos but horrified them, for it marked the priests as only half-persons. And they found the Franciscan practice of subjecting themselves to prolonged fasts and tortures like self-flagellation completely inexplicable. "You Christians are crazy," one

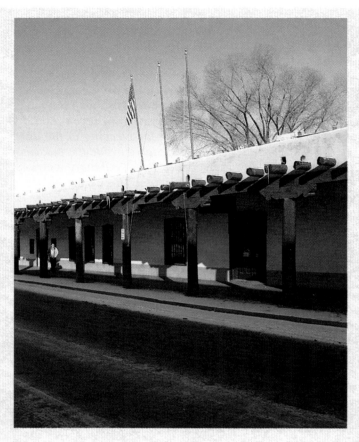

Now a museum, the Palace of the Governors, facing the plaza in Santa Fe, served as the official seat of government for the colony of New Mexico throughout the colonial period. First erected by Pueblo Indians under Spanish supervision in 1609–1614, and rebuilt numerous times thereafter, it represents a fusion of Indian and Spanish building techniques and styles. Following the Pueblo Revolt, on the elegant inlaid stone floors where the governor had held court, Pueblo women ground their corn.

Pueblo chief told a priest. "You go through the streets in groups, flagellating yourselves, and it is not well that the people of this pueblo should be encouraged to commit such madness." The missionaries, on the other hand, outraged by what they considered Pueblo sacrileges, invaded underground kivas and destroyed sacred Indian artifacts, publicly humiliated holy men, and compelled whole villages to perform penance by working in irrigation ditches and fields.

Such violations of the deepest traditions of Pueblo community life eventually led to the revolt of 1680. In New Mexico, several years before, the Spanish governor had executed three Pueblo priests and publicly whipped dozens more for secretly practicing their religion. One of those priests, Popé of San Juan Pueblo, vowed to overthrow the regime, and during the next several years he carefully organized a conspiracy among more than twenty Indian towns.

There were plenty of local grievances. The Hopi people who live in the isolated mesas of northern Arizona still tell stories of a missionary who "was always figuring what he could do to harm them." The ultimate outrage came when he ordered that all the young women of the village be brought to live with him. The revolt came off with remarkable precision throughout the colony. The Hopis surrounded the missionary's house. "I have come to kill you," the chief announced. "You can't kill me," the priest cried from behind his locked door. "I will come to life and wipe out your whole tribe." "My gods have more power than you have," the chief shouted back. He and his men broke down the door, overpowered the missionary, hung him from the beams, and kindled a fire beneath his feet.

From throughout the province, the colonists fled to the protection of the Palace of Governors in Santa Fe. When the Indians demanded their surrender, the Spanish sent back the red cross, signaling defiance. But after a siege lasting five days the Pueblos agreed to allow most of them to flee south to El Paso, "the poor women and children on foot and unshod,'' in the words of one account, and ''of such a hue that they looked like dead people.'' The Indians then ransacked the missions and churches, desecrating the holy furnishings with human excrement, leaving the mutilated bodies of priests lying upon their altars. They transformed the governor's chapel into a traditional kiva, his palace into a communal dwelling. On the elegant inlaid stone floors where the governor had held court, Pueblo women now ground their corn.

Santa Fe became the capital of a Pueblo confederacy led by Popé. He forced Christian Indians to the river to scrub away the taint of baptism. Then he ordered the destruction of everything Spanish. But this the Pueblos could not do. The colonists had introduced horses and sheep, fruit trees and wheat, new tools and new crafts — all of which the Indians found useful. Although they looked forward to a world without Jesus, they could not imagine a world without peaches. Moreover, the Spanish had supported the Pueblos in their struggle against their traditional enemies, the nomadic Navajos and Apaches. Equipped with stolen horses and weapons, the nomads had become considerably more dangerous, and their raids on the unprotected Pueblo villages became much more destructive after the colonists fled. With chaos mounting, Popé was deposed in 1690, and many of the Indians found themselves thinking the unthinkable: If only the Spanish would come back!

Come back they did, beginning in 1692, and after six years of fighting succeeded in reestablishing Spanish authority. But both sides had learned a lesson, and over the next generation the colonists and the Indians reached an implicit understanding. Pueblos dutifully observed Catholicism in the missionary chapels, while missionaries tolerated the practice of traditional religion in the Indians' underground kivas. Royal officials guaranteed the inviolability of Indian lands, and Pueblos pledged loyalty to the Spanish monarch. Pueblos voluntarily turned out for service on colonial lands, and colonists abandoned the system of forced labor. Together the Spanish and the Pueblos held off the nomadic tribes for the next 150 years. Colonist and Indian communities remained autonomous, but they learned to live with one another.

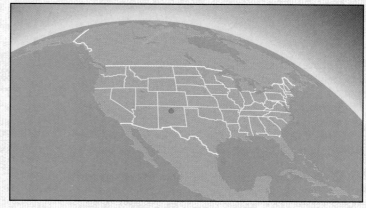

In planting their colonies, Europeans had to give careful consideration not only to the physical environment but to the human environment as well, for North America was home to a great variety of peoples. For their part, Indians were not simply victims of colonization; they also acted out of interests of their own. Everywhere, violence was a part of colonization, but so was an exchange of material goods, of ideas, and of peoples. From the beginning, the colonial communities of North America thus took a variety of forms. New Mexico illustrates one of the many complex ways in which colonialism developed during the first century of the European invasion of North America.

THE SPANISH AND FRENCH IN NORTH AMERICA

At the end of the sixteenth century the Spanish and the French were the only European powers directly involved in North America. The Spanish had built a series of forts along the Florida coast to protect the Gulf Stream sea lanes used by the convoys carrying wealth from their New World colonies. The French were deeply involved in the fur trade of the St. Lawrence River. Early in the seventeenth century both would be drawn into planting far more substantial colonies — New Mexico and New France — in North America. Because neither France nor Spain was willing or able to transport large numbers of its citizens to populate these colonies, both relied on a policy of converting Indians into subjects, and in both New Mexico and New France there was a good deal of cultural and sexual mixing between colonists and natives. These areas became "frontiers of inclusion," where native peoples were included in colonial society, and they would contrast dramatically with the patterns established by the English.

New Mexico

After the expedition of Francisco Vasquez de Coronado in 1539 failed to turn up Indian empires to conquer in the northern Mexican deserts, the Spanish interest in the Southwest faded. But while the densely settled farming communities of the Pueblos may not have offered wealth to plunder, they did offer a harvest of souls. This spiritual treasure was too good to forgo, and by the 1580s Franciscan missionaries had entered the area. Soon rumors drifted back to Mexico City of rich mines along the Rio Grande. The name that Spanish officials bestowed on the region at this time — Nuevo Mexico — registered their hopes of discovering a new Aztec empire there. Juan de Onate, a member of a wealthy mining family, financed a colonizing expedition with the dual purpose of mining gold and souls. In 1598 he led 130 predominantly Indian and mestizo soldiers and their families, along with some 20 missionaries, north into New Mexico.

Reaching the valley of the Rio Grande, Onate advanced from town to town, announcing the establishment of Spanish authority. The reaction of the Pueblos ranged from skepticism to hostility. Encountering the most resistance at Acoma, Onate lay seige to the pueblo on the rock. Indian warriors killed dozens of Spaniards with their arrows, and women and even children bombarded the attackers with stones. But in the end, the Spanish succeeded in climbing the rock walls and laying waste to the town, killing eight hundred men, women, and children. All surviving warriors had one of their feet severed, and more than five hundred persons were carried off into slavery. Why had they resisted? Onate asked one of the Acoma chiefs. "Some . . . wanted to make peace," he replied, "but others did not, and because they could not agree, they would not submit."

The conquest of the Pueblos included many such horrible scenes. "I know for certain that the soldiers have violated Indian women," one priest wrote to his superiors. "Let us go to the pueblos to fornicate with Indian women," he quoted the troops. Since these were hard-boiled soldiers, he probably tempered their language. The Franciscans were also critical of Onate, who, they said, lived in sin with Indian women, exploited Indian men, and subverted the Christian cause. "If you who are Christians cause so much harm and violence," a Pueblo asked one of the priests, "why should we become Christians?" To the Spanish authorities in Mexico, however, it was Onate's failure to locate the storied mines that caused displeasure. He was recalled in 1606.

The Spanish were about to abandon the colony, but after publicizing a surge in Christian conversions

---

New Mexico in the Seventeenth Century
By the end of the seventeenth century New Mexico contained 3,000 colonial settlers in several towns, surrounded by an estimated 50,000 Pueblo Indians living in some fifty farming villages.

among the Indians, the church convinced the monarchy to subsidize New Mexico as a special missionary colony. In 1609 the new governor, Don Pedro de Peralta, founded the capital of Santa Fe, and from this base the Franciscans penetrated all the surrounding Indian villages. They had their greatest success among the youth, many of whom were taken from their families and raised by the priests. Pueblo religious leaders called these converts "wetheads," because of the Christian practice of baptism. The Pueblos who most resisted Christianity — the Acomas, the Zunis, and the isolated Hopis — retained their old customs, including their matrilineal kinship system. But acculturation dramatically affected many others, who often adopted the Spanish kinship pattern of reckoning descent through both the male and female lines. As one Pueblo tale put it, "When Padre Jesus came, the Corn Mothers went away."

The colonial economy of New Mexico — based on small-scale agriculture and sheep raising — was never very prosperous. The Indians were forced to labor for colonists and priests. As one Spanish official put it, "One comes to the Indies not to plow and sow, but only to eat and loaf." After the initial conquest, few new colonists came up the dusty road from Mexico. Population growth was almost entirely the result of natural increase deriving from unions between colonial men and Indian women. By the late seventeenth century this northernmost outpost of the far-flung Spanish American empire contained some 3,000 mostly mestizo settlers in a few towns along the Rio Grande, surrounded by an estimated 50,000 Pueblo Indians in some fifty villages.

The First Communities of New France

In the early seventeenth century the French devised a strategy to capture a monopoly of the northern fur trade. Samuel de Champlain, an agent of the royal Canadian Company who had helped establish the outpost of Port Royal on the Bay of Fundy in 1605, founded the town of Quebec three years later at a site where he could intercept the traffic in furs to the Atlantic. He forged an alliance with the Hurons, who controlled access to the rich fur grounds of the Great Lakes, and joined them in making war on their traditional enemies, the Five Nation Iroquois Confederacy. In his diplomacy, Champlain relied on the tradition of commercial relations that had developed between Europeans and Indians during the sixteenth century. He sent agents and traders to live among the Indians, where they learned native languages and customs, and directed the flow of furs to Quebec.

The early French colonial system, based on commerce rather than conquest, thus differed considerably from the Spanish. Moreover, the fur trade led to the dispersion of Frenchmen among Indian communities. The Spaniards, in contrast, had concentrated in towns. Jesuit missionaries often accompanied these French traders, and sometimes led the way. First arriving in New France in 1625, the Jesuits were few in number. But they were notably successful. Unlike Spanish missionaries, who insisted that conversion be linked to the acceptance of European cultural norms, the Jesuits introduced Christianity as a supplement to the Indian way of life. There was an important similarity between the French and Span-

This illustration, taken from Samuel de Champlain's 1613 account of the founding of New France, depicts him joining the Huron attack on the Iroquois in 1609. The French and the Huron Indians allied to control access to the great fur grounds of the West. The Iroquois then formed an alliance of their own with the Dutch, who had founded a trading colony on the Hudson River. The palm trees and hammocks in the background of this drawing suggest that it was not executed by an eyewitness, but rather by an illustrator more familiar with South American scenes.

ish colonial systems, however. Since the fur trade required only small numbers of French colonists, and because most of those who came were men, New France also became a frontier of inclusion, with a good deal of sexual mixing.

French authorities worried a great deal about this mixing, and they encouraged more colonists, especially families with women, to settle the narrow belt of fertile land along the St. Lawrence. These communities became the heart of New France. Small clusters of riverbank farmers known as *habitants* lived on the lands of *seigneurs*. These communities, with their manor houses, Catholic churches, and perhaps a public building or two, resembled European villages. Although the growing season was short, by employing Indian farming techniques *habitants* were able to produce subsistence crops, and eventually they developed a modest export economy. But these communities looked west toward the continental interior rather than east across the Atlantic. It was typical for the sons of *habitants* to take to the woods in their youth, working as agents for the fur companies or as independent traders. Most returned to take up farming, but others remained in Indian villages, where they married Indian women and raised families. Such French traders were living on the Great Lakes as early as the 1620s, and from the late 1660s to the 1680s the French established outposts at each of the strategic points on the lakes. By the 1670s French fur traders and missionaries were exploring the reaches of the upper Mississippi River. In 1681, fur trade commandant Robert Sieur de La Salle navigated the mighty river to its mouth on the Gulf of Mexico and claimed its entire watershed—a great inland empire—for France.

The population of New France grew through the seventeenth century, but was still only 15,000 by 1700. Quebec City, the administrative capital, was small by Spanish colonial standards, and Montreal, founded in 1642 as a missionary and trading center, remained little more than a frontier outpost. The strength of New France lay in the extent of its trading system.

ENGLAND IN AMERICA

England first attempted to plant colonies in North America during the 1580s, in Newfoundland and at Roanoke in present-day North Carolina. Both attempts were failures. The war with Spain, lasting from 1588 to 1604, suspended colonization efforts, but thereafter the English once again turned to the Americas. In contrast to the Spanish and French colonies, based on the inclusion of Indian people, the English transplanted complete communities made up of families, establishing "frontiers of exclusion." They pushed Indians to the periphery rather than incorporating them within colonial communities.

Jamestown and the Powhatan Confederacy

Early in his reign, King James I (reigned 1603–25) issued royal charters for the colonization of the mid-Atlantic region known as Virginia to English joint-stock companies, which raised capital by selling shares. These companies hoped to reap profits from the conquest of unknown Indian empires, from rich gold or silver mines, or from plantation agriculture. One company attempted a settlement called

New France in the Seventeenth Century
The heart of New France was the communities stretching along the Saint Lawrence River between the towns of Quebec and Montreal.

Two scenes from John Smith's memoirs (1624) engraved by the artist Robert Vaughan. Pocahontas, the daughter of chief Powhatan, intervenes to save Smith from execution. And seizing chief Opechancanough by the scalplock, Smith attempts to obtain needed supplies from the Indians. Pocahontas later married a leading colonist and died on a visit to England. Opechancanough suceeded his brother Powhatan, and ruled the Chesapeake Algonquian confederacy for a quarter century.

King Powhatan comands C:Smith to be slaine, daughter Pokahontas begs his life his thankfulln and how he subiected 39 of their kings. reade

C:Smith taketh the King of Pamavnkee prisoner 1608

Sagadahoc on the coast of Maine, but ineffective leadership and poor relations with Indians who were trading partners of the French led to its abandonment within a year. In 1607 a London group of investors known as the Virginia Company sent ships to the more temperate latitudes of Chesapeake Bay, where a hundred men built a fort they named Jamestown, in honor of the king. It was destined to become the first permanent English settlement in North America.

The Chesapeake was already home to an estimated 20,000 Algonquian people. The English colonists were immediately confronted by Powhatan, the powerful *werowance,* or leader, of an Indian confederacy. Powhatan had mixed feelings about the English. The Spanish had already attempted to plant a base nearby, bringing conflict and disease to his region. But he looked forward to valuable trade with the English, as well as their support for his struggle to extend his confederacy over outlying tribes. As was the case in Mexico and along the St. Lawrence, Indians used Europeans to pursue ends of their own.

The English saw themselves as latter-day conquistadors. Abhorring the idea of physical labor, they survived the first year only with Powhatan's material assistance. Like the first Roanoke colonists (see Chapter 2), they were unable to support themselves. "In our extremity the Indians brought us corn," wrote John Smith, the colony's military leader, "when we rather expected they would destroy us." Jamestown grew so dependent upon Algonquian stores that in 1609 Smith and his men began to plunder food from surrounding tribes. In retaliation, Powhatan decided to starve the colonists out. He now realized, he declared to Smith, that the English had come "not for trade, but to invade my people and possess my country" — the approach not of the French but of the Spanish. During the terrible winter of 1609–10 scores of colonists starved and a number resorted to cannibalism. By spring only 60 remained of the more than 900 colonists sent to Virginia.

Determined to prevail, the Virginia Company sent out a large additional force of men, women, and livestock, committing themselves to a protracted war against the Indians. By 1613 the colonists firmly controlled the territory between the James and York rivers. Worn down by warfare and disease, Powhatan accepted a treaty of peace in 1614. "I am old and ere long must die," he declared; "I know it is better to eat good meat, lie well, and sleep with my women and children, laugh and be merry than to be forced to flee and be hunted." He sent his daughter Pocahontas, fluent in English, on a diplomatic mission to Jamestown. She converted to Christianity and married John Rolfe, a leading settler. Their relationship was the best known of many intimate connections between Indians and Englishmen during those early years. Like that of the Spanish and the French, early English colonization included social and cultural mixing. But Pocahontas died of disease while visiting England in 1617. Crushed by the news of her death, her father abdicated in favor of his brother Opechancanough. Powhatan died the following year.

Tobacco, Expansion, and Warfare

Tobacco provided the Virginia colonists with the "merchantable commodity" for which Thomas Harriot, the scientist who accompanied the Roanoke expedition, had searched (see Chapter 2). In 1613 John Rolfe developed a hybrid of hearty North American and mild West Indian varieties, and soon the first commercial shipments of cured Virginia leaf reached England. Tobacco had been introduced to English consumers by Francis Drake in the 1580s, and despite King James's description of the habit as "loathsome to the eye, hateful to the nose, harmful to the brain, dangerous to the lungs," the smoking craze had created strong consumer demand by the 1610s. Tobacco provided the Virginia Company with the first returns on its investment. Its cultivation, however, quickly exhausted the soil, creating pressures for further expansion into Indian territory. Because tobacco also required a great deal of hand labor, the company instituted headright grants — awards of large plantations to men on the condition that they transport workers from England at their own cost. Between 1619 and 1624 more than 4,500 English settlers arrived, many with families. High rates of mortality, however, kept the total population at just over a thousand. In populating their colony with families, the English had chosen a policy quite different from the Spanish and French practice.

With no need to incorporate Indians into the population, the English moved in the direction of exclusion.

As the English pressed for additional lands, Opechancanough prepared the Chesapeake Algonquians for a final assault on the invaders. He encouraged a cultural revival under the guidance of the prophet Nemattanew, who instructed his followers to reject the English and their ways but to learn the use of firearms. This would be the first of many Indian resistance movements led jointly by strong political and religious figures. The uprising, which began on Good Friday, March 22, 1622, completely surprised the English. Nearly 350 people, a quarter of the settlers, were killed before Jamestown could mobilize its forces. Yet the colony managed to hang on, and the attack stretched into a ten-year war of attrition. Horrors were committed by both sides, but English officials saw advantages in open warfare. As one wrote, "We may now by right of war, and law of nations, invade the country and destroy them who sought to destroy us, whereby we shall enjoy their cultivated places." Indian territory might now be obtained under the conventions of a "just war."

Lasting until 1632, the war bankrupted the Virginia Company. In 1624 the king converted Virginia into a royal colony, and the representative assembly organized by the company in 1619 now met under the authority of an appointed royal governor. Although disease, famine, and warfare took a heavy toll, the booming economy led to a doubling of the English colonial population every five years from 1625 to 1640, by which time it numbered approximately 10,000. Opechancanough emerged from the turmoil as undisputed leader of the Algonquians, but other tribes, decimated by casualties and disease, were forced to accept English domination. By 1640 the native population of the Chesapeake had declined to about 10,000.

Numerical strength thus shifted in favor of the English. In 1644, Opechancanough's community, the Pamunkeys, organized a final desperate revolt in which over 500 colonists were killed. But the Virginians crushed the Algonquians in 1645, capturing and executing their leader. The colonists then signed a formal treaty with the Indians, who were granted small reserved territories. By the 1670s, when the English population of Virginia numbered over 40,000, only a dozen tribes and about 2,000 Algonquians remained from the 20,000 who inhabited the area when Jamestown was founded. Today some 1,500 people claiming Algonquian identity live in Chesapeake Indian communities that trace their roots to Powhatan's confederacy. They attend their own churches and schools, and some work at fishing, hunting, and farming while others commute to work in metropolitan Richmond or Washington, D.C.

Maryland

In 1632, King Charles I (reigned 1625–49) granted ten million acres at the northern end of Chesapeake Bay to the Calvert family, the Lords Baltimore, important supporters of the monarchy. They named their colony Maryland, in honor of the king's wife. The first party of colonists founded the settlement of St. Marys near the mouth of the Potomac River in 1634. Two features distinguished Maryland from Virginia. First, the Calverts were sole owners of all the land, which they planned to carve into feudal manors providing them with annual rents. And since the proprietors were Catholics, they encouraged settlement by their coreligionists, a persecuted minority in seventeenth-century England. Maryland would be the only English colony in North America with a substantial Catholic minority. Wealthy Catholic landlords were appointed to the governing council, and they came to dominate Maryland's House of Delegates, founded in 1635.

Despite these differences, Maryland quickly assumed the character of neighboring Virginia. Its tobacco plantation economy created pressures for labor and expansion that could not be met under the Calverts' original feudal plans. In 1640 the colony adopted the system of headright grants developed in Virginia, and settlements of independent planters quickly spread out on both sides of the bay. By the 1670s Maryland's English population numbered over 15,000.

Indentured Servants

At least three-quarters of the English migrants to the Chesapeake came as indentured servants. In exchange for the cost of their transportation, they contracted to labor for a master for a fixed term. A minority were convicts or vagabonds bound into service by English courts for as long as fourteen years. Most, however, were young, unskilled males, who served for two to seven years. Indentured servants also included skilled craftsmen, women, and even children, who were expected to serve until they reached the age of twenty-one.

Masters were obliged to feed, clothe, and house these servants adequately. But work in the tobacco fields was backbreaking, and records include complaints of inadequate care. One Virginia ballad chronicled these complaints:

William Buckland, seen here in a portrait by the artist Charles Willson Peale, was a skilled English carpenter who indentured himself to the Virginia planter George Mason. Few indentured servants could command terms as attractive as Buckland's. Indeed, for most of the indentured immigrants of the colonial period, bound labor was not a little unlike slavery.

Come all you young fellows wherever you be,
Come listen awhile and I will tell thee,
Concerning the hardships that we undergo,
When we get lagg'd to Virginia

Now in Virginia I lay like a hog,
Our pillow at night is a brick or a log,
We dress and undress like some other sea dog,
How hard is my fate in Virginia.

Many servants tried to escape, but capture could mean a doubling of their terms. Servants enjoyed little personal freedom: They could not travel, marry, or own property. Women who bore illegitimate children had their term lengthened to compensate for time lost in childbirth and infant care. But on reaching the end of their service, servants were eligible for "freedom dues": clothing, tools, a gun, a spinning wheel, or perhaps food—something to help them get started on their own. Some masters granted freed servants a plot of land. But most former servants headed west, where they risked the danger of Indian attacks in the hope of starting a farm in the backcountry.

Reliance on indentured labor was unique to the English colonies. New France had little need for a systematic resort to servitude, and the Spanish depended upon the labor of Indians or enslaved Africans. Africans were first introduced to the Chesapeake in 1619, but slaves were more expensive than servants, and as late as 1680 they made up less than 7 percent of the Chesapeake population. For many servants, however, the distinction between slavery and servitude may have seemed academic. Extremely high rates of mortality—the result of malaria, influenza, typhoid fever, and dysentery—meant that approximately two of every five servants failed to survive their term. In the hard-driving climate of the Chesapeake, many masters treated servants cruelly, and women especially were vulnerable to sexual exploitation. The harsh system of indentured labor prepared the tobacco masters of the Chesapeake for the transition to slavery accomplished during the second half of the seventeenth century. (For a complete discussion of slavery, see Chapter 4.)

Community Life in the Chesapeake

Most migrants were men, and male servants surviving their term of indenture had a difficult time finding a wife. Tobacco masters commonly received numerous offers from men to pay off the indenture of a prospective wife, and free unmarried women often married as soon as they arrived in the Chesapeake. English men seemed to suffer a higher rate of mortality than women in the disease-ridden environment of the early Chesapeake, and widows remarried quickly, sometimes within days. Their scarcity value provided women with certain advantages. Shrewd widows bargained for remarriage agreements that provided for larger shares of the estate upon the death of their husband. So notable was the concentration of wealth in the hands of these widows that one historian has suggested that early Virginia was a "matriarchy." Because of the high mortality, however, family size was smaller than in England. Kinship bonds, one of the most important components of community, were fragile and weak.

Visitors from England frequently remarked on the crude conditions of community life. Prosperous planters, investing everything in tobacco production, lived in rough wooden dwellings. Fifty miles inland, on the western edge of the settlements, freed servants lived with their families in shacks, huts, or even caves. Colonists spread across the countryside in search of new tobacco lands, creating dispersed rather than clustered patterns of settlement. The numerous navigable rivers flowing into Chesapeake Bay provided ships with direct access to most plantations, and thus few towns or central settlements developed. Before 1650 there were relatively few community institutions such as schools and churches. The settlements of the Chesapeake, the site of England's premier colony in North America, looked like temporary society. Meanwhile, the Spanish in the Caribbean and Mexico were building communities that grew into great cities with permanent institutions.

In contrast to the colonists of New France, who were developing a distinctive American identity, the colonial population of the Chesapeake maintained close emotional ties to England. Most property-owning men could participate in the selection of delegates to the colonial assemblies of Virginia and Maryland. But colonial politics were shaped by the continuing close relationship with the mother country rather than by local developments. There was little movement toward a distinctively American point of view in the seventeenth-century Chesapeake.

NEW ENGLAND

Both in climate and in geography, the northern coast of North America was far different from the Chesapeake. "Merchantable commodities" such as tobacco could not be produced there, and thus it was a far less favored region for investment and settlement. Instead, the region became a haven for Protestant dissenters from England, who gave the colonies of the north a distinctive character.

Puritanism

Most English men and women continued to practice a Christianity little different from traditional Catholicism. But the English followers of John Calvin, known as Puritans because they wished to purify and reform the English church from within, grew increasingly influential during the last years of Elizabeth's reign. Their emphasis on enterprise meant that the Puritans appealed to those groups — merchants, entrepreneurs, and commercial farmers — most responsible for the rapid economic and social transformation of England. But they were the most vocal critics of the disruptive effects of these changes, condemning the decline of the traditional rural community and the growing number of "idle and masterless men." They argued for reviving communities by placing reformed Christian congregations at their core to monitor the behavior of individuals. Puritanism was thus as much a set of social and political values as religious ones, a way of managing change in troubling times. By the early

seventeenth century Puritans were in control of many congregations, and had become an influential force at the universities in Oxford and Cambridge, training centers for the future English ministry.

King James I, who assumed the throne after Elizabeth's death, abandoned the policy of religious tolerance, vowing to root Puritans out of the English church. But this persecution merely stiffened the Puritans' resolve and turned them toward overt political opposition. An increasingly vocal Puritan minority in Parliament complained that the Church of England was too "Catholic." These Puritans criticized King Charles I (reigned 1625–49), James's son and sucessor, for supporting High Church policies — which emphasized the authority of the church and its traditional forms of worship — as well as for marrying a Catholic princess. In 1629, determined to rule without these troublesome opponents, Charles adjourned Parliament and launched a campaign of repression against the Puritans. "I am verily persuaded God will bring some heavy affliction upon this land," the Puritan leader John Winthrop despaired. This political turmoil provided the context for the migration of thousands of English Protestants to New England.

Early Contacts in New England

The northern Atlantic coast seemed an unlikely spot for English colonies, for the region was dominated by French and Dutch traders. In the early seventeenth century Samuel de Champlain established trading contacts with coastal Algonquians as far south as Cape Cod. The Dutch, following the explorations of Henry Hudson for the United Provinces of the Netherlands, established settlements and a lucrative fur trade on the Hudson River. In 1613 the English, desperate to keep their colonial options open, dispatched a fleet from Jamestown that destroyed the French post at Port Royal on the northern coast and harassed the Dutch on the Hudson. The following year John Smith explored the northern coastline and christened the region New England. The region was "so planted with Gardens and Corne fields," he wrote, that "I would rather live here than any where." But Smith's plans for a New England colony were aborted when he was captured and held captive by the French.

Then a twist of fate transformed English fortunes. From 1616 to 1618 bubonic plague ravaged the native peoples of the northern coast. Whole villages disappeared, and the trade system of the French and the Dutch was seriously disrupted. Indians perished so quickly and in such numbers that few remained to bury the dead. The scattered

A Puritan attempts to drive away Father Christmas, but a friendlier man welcomes him in this English cartoon of 1653. The Puritans considered Christmas a pagan festival. On Christmas Day 1621, when Governor William Bradford of Plymouth found a group of settlers celebrating in the streets he ordered them to cease, and he was proud of the fact that as long as he ruled the colony "nothing hath been attempted that way, at least openly."

"bones and skulls made such a spectacle," wrote a visitor, "it seemed to me a new found Golgotha." Modern estimates confirm the testimony of a surviving Indian that his people "had been melted down by this disease, whereof nine-tenths of them have died." The native population of New England as a whole dropped from an estimated 120,000 to less than 70,000. So crippled were the surviving coastal societies that they could not provide effective resistance to the planting of English colonies.

Plymouth Colony

The first English colony in New England was founded by a group of religious dissenters known to later generations as the Pilgrims. They were called Separatists, who believed the English church was so corrupt that they must establish their own independent congregations. The Separatists first moved to Holland in 1609, but, fearful that Dutch society was seducing their children, a group of them soon began exploring the idea of emigrating to North America. Backed by the Virginia Company of London, 102 persons, a majority of them women and children traveling with other family members, sailed from Plymouth, England, on the *Mayflower* in September 1620.

The agreement with the Virginia Company called for the Pilgrims to settle near the Chesapeake. But they arrived instead in New England and selected a site on Massachusetts Bay at an abandoned Indian village called Patuxet, a place John Smith had named Plymouth. About a third of the emigrants were "strangers," men hired by the investors. Since the expedition now found itself outside the jurisdiction of the Virginia Company, these men began to grumble about Pilgrim authority. To preserve order, the Pilgrim leader, William Bradford, drafted the Mayflower Compact, and in November the men did "covenant and combine [themselves] together into a civil body politic." It was the first document of self-government in North America.

Landing at Plymouth, the Pilgrims thanked God for "sweeping away great multitudes of natives" to "make room for us." But they had been weakened by scurvy and malnutrition, and over the winter nearly half of them perished. Like the settlers of Jamestown, the Pilgrims were rescued by Indians. Massasoit, the *sachem* (leader) of the Pokanokets, offered food and advice to them in the early months of 1621. He was anxious to establish an alliance with the newcomers against the Narragansetts, a powerful neighboring tribe to his immediate west who had been spared the ravages of the plague.

The interpreter in these negotiations was an Indian named Squanto. A former resident of Patuxet village, he had been kidnapped in 1614 by the captain of one English ship and had returned to New England five years later as guide on another. It was then he made the horrifying discovery that plague had wiped out his village. Knowledgeable in the ways of the Europeans, Squanto became an adviser to Massasoit. With the arrival of the Pilgrims, this last survivor of the Patuxets now resumed his former residence, but as guide and interpreter for the English. Squanto secured seed corn for the colonists and instructed them on its cultivation.

Deeply in debt to its investors, always struggling to meet its payments through the Indian trade, fishing, and lumbering, the Plymouth colony was never a financial success. Most families practiced self-sufficient farming. By their own standards, however, the Pilgrims succeeded during the first two or three decades in establishing the community they desired. So strong was their communal agreement that the annual meeting of property-owning men reelected William Bradford to thirty consecutive one-year terms as governor. By midcentury, however, the Plymouth population had dispersed into eleven separate communities, and diversity had begun to disrupt this separatist retreat.

The Massachusetts Bay Colony

In England, the Puritan movement continued its struggle to reform the national church. The political climate of the late 1620s, however, convinced a number of influential Puritans that the only way to protect their congregations was emigration. Some went to Ireland, others to the Netherlands or the West Indies, but many decided on New England, where they could establish, in the words of John Winthrop, "a city on a hill," a model of reform for England. In 1629 a royal charter was granted to a group of wealthy Puritans who called their enterprise the Massachusetts Bay Company. As a song of the day put it:

Stay not among the wicked,
Lest that with them you perish,
But let us to New England go,
And the pagan people cherish.

They were given exclusive rights to settlement and trade, as well as to "religiously, peaceably and civilly" govern the territory and the native people between the Merrimack and Charles rivers, from the Atlantic "to the south sea on the west part." An advance force of two hundred settlers soon left for the fishing settlement of Naumkeag on Massachusetts Bay, which they renamed Salem.

The Puritan emigration to Massachusetts became known as the Great Migration, a phrase that would be repeated many times in American history. Between 1629 and 1643 some 20,000 persons relocated to New England. Boston, founded in 1630, was their central settlement; within five years it was ringed by towns as far as thirty miles inland. By 1640 settlements had spread seventy-five miles west, into the Connecticut River valley.

Most colonists arrived in groups from long-established communities in the east of England and were frequently led by men with extensive experience in local English government. It was therefore easy for these groups to transfer their customs and social patterns. Taking advantage of a loophole in their charter, the Puritan leaders transferred company operations to America in 1629, and within a few years they had transformed the company into a civil government. The original charter established a General Court composed of a governor and his deputy, a board of magistrates (advisers), and the members of the corporation, known as *freemen*. In 1632 Governor Winthrop and his advisers declared all male heads of household who were also church members to be freemen. Two years later the free-

men established their right to select delegates to represent the towns in drafting the laws of the colony. These delegates and the magistrates later separated into two legislative houses. Thus a joint-stock company provided the beginnings for democratic suffrage and the bicameral division of legislative authority in America.

Indians and Puritans

The Algonquian Indians of southern New England found these Europeans considerably different from the French and Dutch traders who had preceded them. The principal concern of the English was not commerce — although the fur trade remained an important part of their economy — but the acquisition of Indian land for their growing settlements. Massasoit attempted to use the colonists to his own advantage. But he soon found that when the English attacked his enemies, their true motive was expansion. In 1623, on Massasoit's urging, the Pilgrim military commander Miles Standish attacked a group of Massachusetts Indians north of Plymouth. When Standish brought back the sachem's head and placed it on a pike outside the settlement's gates, the meaning of the gesture was not lost on the Pokanokets. If we are allies, one Pokanoket man asked, "how cometh it to pass that when we come

The first map printed in the English colonies, this view of New England was published in Boston in 1677. With north oriented to the right, it looks west from Massachusetts Bay, the two vertical black lines indicating the approximate boundaries of the Commonwealth of Massachusetts. The territory west of Rhode Island is noted as an Indian stronghold, the homelands of the Narragansett, Pequot, and Nipmuck peoples.

to Patuxet you stand upon your guard, with the mouths of your pieces [guns] presented to us?'' Even the Pokanokets were soon calling their English allies *wotowquenange,* or ''cutthroats.''

Ravaged by disease, the Pokanokets' northern neighbors, the Massachusetts, were ill prepared for the Puritan landings that took place after 1629. The English believed they had the right to take ''unused'' lands, and depopulated Massachusetts' villages became prime targets. As one colonist wrote: ''Their land is spacious and void, and there are few and [they] do but run over the grass, as do also the foxes and wild beasts.'' Conflicts between settlers over title, however, made it necessary to obtain deeds from Indians, and the English used a variety of tactics to pressure them into signing quitclaims. They allowed their livestock to graze native fields, making them useless for cultivation; they fined Indians for violations of English law, such as working on the Sabbath, then demanded land as payment; and they made deals with fraudulent sachems. For giving up the land that became Charlestown, for example, the ''Squaw Sachem'' of the Pawtuckets received twenty-one coats, nineteen fathoms of wampum, and three bushels of corn. Disorganized and demoralized, many of the coastal Algonquians soon placed themselves under the protection of the English.

Indian peoples to the west, however, remained a formidable presence. They blocked Puritan expansion until they were devastated in 1633–34 by an epidemic of smallpox that spread from the St. Lawrence south to Long Island Sound. This occurred at the same time that hundreds of English migrants were crowding into coastal towns. ''Without this remarkable and terrible stroke of God upon the natives,'' recorded a town scribe, ''we would with much more difficulty have found room, and at far greater charge have obtained and purchased land.'' In the aftermath of the epidemic, colonists established many new inland towns.

By the late 1630s the most powerful tribes in the vicinity of the Puritans were the Narragansets of present-day Rhode Island and their traditional enemies the Pequots, principal trading partners of the Dutch. The Pequots lived on Long Island Sound near the mouth of the Connecticut River, where they controlled the production of wampum, woven belts of sea shells used as a medium of exchange in the Indian trade. In 1637 the Narragansetts, in alliance with the English, who were looking for an excuse to smash the Dutch, went to war against the Pequots. Narragansett warriors and English troops attacked the main Pequot village, killing most of its slumber-ing residents, including women and children. Unaccustomed to such tactics, the shocked Narragansetts cried out to the English: ''It is too furious, it slays too many men.'' A band of Pequots escaped the carnage and fled west, but were captured by the Mohawks and their leader killed. After the Pequot War it would be four decades before there was another serious Indian conflict in New England.

New England Communities

Back in England, the conflict between King Charles and Parliament broke into armed conflict in 1642. Several years of violent confrontation led to the execution of the king in 1649 and the proclamation of an English ''Commonwealth,'' headed by the Puritan leader Oliver Cromwell. Because the Puritans played an active role in the English Civil War, they no longer had the same incentive to leave the country, and in fact many Puritans returned from New England to participate in the war.

New England's economy had depended upon the sale of supplies and land to arriving emigrants, but the importance of this ''newcomer market'' declined with slackening migration in the 1640s. Lacking a single exportable commodity like tobacco, New Englanders were forced to diversify into a variety of enterprises, including farming, fishing, and lumbering. Merchants began construction of what would become, by the end of the century, the most sizable shipping fleet in the colonies, and became active in the carrying trade between the Caribbean and Chesapeake colonies and Europe. The development of a diversified economy would provide New England with considerable long-term strength.

The communities of New England were quite distinct from those of the Chesapeake, because the vast majority of the Puritans had come in family groups with relatively few servants. Farming, which occupied the vast majority of the colonists, was a family affair. Indeed, the family provided the Puritans with a model for society as a whole. Like kings or governors, parents were expected to control their children. ''Surely there is in all children a stubbornness, and stoutness of mind arising from natural pride,'' one Puritan declared, ''which must be broken and beaten down.'' Parents often participated in the choice of mates for their offspring, and children typically married in the order of their births, younger siblings waiting until arrangements had been made for their elders.

It is mistaken, however, to regard the Puritans as ''puritanical.'' Although adultery was a capital crime in New England, Puritans accepted sexual expression within marriage. Couples were expected to be in love when they married. Thus Puritan parents had to walk a fine line between arranging marriages and allowing their courting children the freedom to express themselves. The practice of "bundling" helped to resolve this tension. The loving couple was allowed to lie in bed together, with their lower bodies wrapped in an apron and separated by a "bundling board"; within these limits they were free to caress and pet. In the words of an old ballad:

> She is modest, also chaste
> While only bare from neck to waist,
> And he of boasted freedom sings,
> Of all above her apron strings.

The family economy operated through the combined efforts of husband and wife. Men were generally responsible for field work, women for the work of the household, which included gardening, tending to the dairy and henhouse, and providing fuel and water. Women managed a rich array of tasks, and some housewives independently traded garden products, milk, and eggs. "I meddle not with the geese nor turkeys," one New England man noted, "for they are hers for she hath been and is a good wife to me." But the cultural ideal was the subordination of women to men. "I am but a wife, and therefore it is sufficient for me to follow my husband," wrote Lucy Winthrop Downing, and her brother John Winthrop declared that "a true wife accounts her subjection her honor and freedom." Married women could neither make contracts nor own property, neither vote nor hold office. The extraordinarily high birth rate of Puritan women was another evidence of their "subjection." A typical woman, marrying in her early twenties and surviving through her forties, could expect to bear eight children. After the premature deaths of her first two babies, the poet Jane Colman Turell wrote:

> And now O gracious Savior lend thine ear,
> To this my earnest cry and humble prayer,
> That when the hour arrives with painful throes,
> Which shall my burden to the world disclose;
> I may deliverance have, and joy to see
> A living child, to dedicate to Thee.

Yet there were many loving Puritan households with contented husbands and wives. "Women are creatures without which there is no comfortable living for man," wrote the Puritan minister John

Mrs. Freake and Baby Mary, by an unknown Boston artist in 1674. The mother wears the standard Puritan costume for women, although her decorative banding, lacework, and jewelry mark her taste as rather sumptuous by New England standards. One young Puritan woman who wore lace garments to the meetinghouse wrote that "the elders with others entreated me to leave them off, for they gave great offense." The baby is clothed very much in the manner of her mother, reflecting the view that children were simply miniature adults.
(Unknown artist. *Mrs. Elizabeth Freake and Baby Mary.* 1671–74. Oil on canvas. 108 × 93.4 cm. Worcester Art Museum, Worcester, MA. Gift of Mr. and Mrs. Albert W. Rice.)

Cotton, although he added that "it is true of them what is said of governments, that bad ones are better than none." Anne Bradstreet, a Massachusetts wife and mother, and the first published poet of New England, made a more sensitive conveyance of feeling when she wrote about her husband and marriage:

> If ever two are one, then surely we.
> If ever man were lov'd by wife, then thee;
> If ever wife was happy in a man,
> Compare with me ye women if you can.

The Puritans stressed the importance of well-ordered communities as well as families. Colonists often emigrated in kin groups that made up the core of the new towns. This was a considerably different pattern from the colonists of New Mexico, for example, who consisted almost entirely of single men, who took native women for wives. The Massachusetts General Court granted townships to proprietors representing the congregation, who then distributed fields, pasture, and woodlands in quantities proportional to the recipient's social status, so that wealthy families received more than humble ones. Settlers clustered their dwellings at the town center, near the meeting house that served as both church and civic center. Some towns, particularly those along the coast such as Boston, soon became centers of shipping. These clustered settlements and strong, vital communities made seventeenth-century New England quite different from Chesapeake society.

The Puritans also built an impressive educational system. In 1647 Massachusetts required that towns with 50 families or more support a public school; those with 100 families were to establish a "grammar" school that taught Latin, knowledge of which was required for admission to Harvard College, founded in 1636. Connecticut enacted similar requirements. Literacy was higher in New England than elsewhere in the colonies, or even much of Europe, though far fewer New England women than men could read and write because of the exclusion of girls from the grammar schools. By 1639 a printing press operated in Boston, the first one in the English colonies, and the next year it published the first American English publication, *The Bay Psalm Book*. The first American newspaper was also published in Boston, but its criticism of local authorities led to its suppression. In keeping with the dominant Protestant character of the colonies, most seventeenth-century colonial publications were ministers' sermons and tracts.

Dissent and New Communities

The Puritans emigrated in order to practice their variety of Christianity, but they had little tolerance for other religious points of view. Religious disagreement among the colonists soon provoked the founding of three new colonies. Thomas Hooker, minister of the congregation at Cambridge, disagreed with the policy of restricting the suffrage to male church members. In 1636 he led his followers west to the Connecticut River, where they founded the town of Hartford. Hooker helped write the Fundamental Orders that marked the beginning of the Connecticut colony. In 1637 a group of London

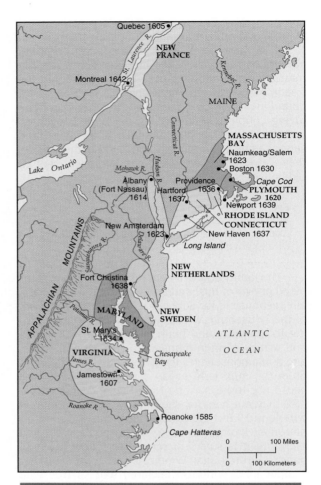

European Colonies of the Atlantic Coast, 1607–39
Virginia on Chesapeake Bay was the first English colony in North America, but by the mid-seventeenth century Virginia was joined by settlements of Scandanavians on the Delaware River, and Dutch on the Hudson River, as well as English religious dissenters in New England. The territories indicated here reflect the vague boundaries of the early colonies.

Puritans holding even stricter beliefs than the colonists of Massachusetts established the colony of New Haven on Long Island Sound. Connecticut absorbed New Haven upon receiving a royal charter in 1662.

Another dissenter was the minister Roger Williams, who came to New England in 1631 to take up duties for the congregation in Salem. Williams believed in the separation of church and state. He preached, moreover, that the colonists had no absolute right to Indian land, but must bargain for it in good faith. These were dangerous ideas, and Williams was banished from the colony in 1636. With a group of his followers, he emigrated to the Narragansett country, where he purchased land from the Indians and founded the town of Providence.

The next year Boston shook with another religious controversy. Anne Hutchinson, the wife of a Puritan merchant who arrived in New England in 1634, was a brilliant woman who led religious discussion groups that criticized various Boston ministers for a lack of piety. The concentration of attention on good works, she argued, led people to believe that they could earn their way to heaven, a "popish" or Catholic heresy in the eyes of Calvinists. Hutchinson was called before the General Court, where the Puritan leaders made it clear that they would not tolerate a woman who publicly criticized men. Although she handled herself very skillfully, Hutchinson made the mistake of claiming that she had received a direct "revelation" from God, and so was excommunicated and banished. She and her followers moved to Roger Williams's settlement, where they established another community in 1638.

A third group of dissenters, Samuel Gorton and his followers, were similarly banished and likewise relocated to the Narragansett haven. In 1644, Roger Williams received a charter creating the colony of Rhode Island, named for the principal island in Narragansett Bay, as a protection for these several dissenting communities. A new royal charter of 1663 guaranteed self-government and complete religious liberty, and strengthened the colony's territorial claims for its approximately two thousand inhabitants.

In 1643, Massachusetts Bay led the other New England colonies in forming a Confederation of United Colonies in opposition to Rhode Island. By the 1670s Massachusetts's population had grown to over 40,000, most of it concentrated in and around Boston. There were communities as far west as the Connecticut River valley and in the northern regions known as Maine (not separated from Massachusetts until 1820), and New Hampshire, set off as a royal colony in 1680. Next in size was Connecticut, its population numbering about 17,000. Plymouth had only 6,000 inhabitants; it would be absorbed by Massachusetts in 1691.

THE RESTORATION COLONIES

The Puritan Commonwealth established after the execution of King Charles attempted to provide a measure of central control with the passage in 1651

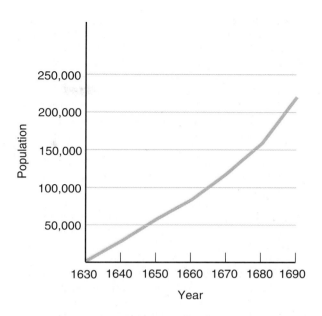

Population Growth of the British Colonies in the Seventeenth Century

British colonial population grew steadily through the century, then increased sharply in the closing decade as a result of the new settlements of the Restoration Colonies.

of a set of Navigation Acts regulating colonial commerce. But the regime was preoccupied with English domestic affairs and left the colonies largely to their own devices. Cromwell ruled as Lord Protector of the Commonwealth, but the new order failed to survive his death in 1658. Desperate for political stability, after nearly two decades of Civil War and political strife, Parliament restored the Stuart monarchy in 1660, placing Charles II, son of the former king, on the throne. At the same time, Parliament retained for itself certain significant powers of state. During his reign, King Charles II created several new proprietary colonies, on the model of Maryland.

Early Carolina

In 1663 the king issued the first of the "restoration" charters, for a territory called Carolina that stretched from Virginia south to Spanish Florida. Virginians had already begun moving into the northern parts of this territory, and in 1664 the Carolina proprietors

The Restoration Colonies
After the restoration of the Stuart monarchy in 1660, King Charles II of England created several new proprietary colonies along the Atlantic coast.

distinctly West Indian character to the colony. By the end of the seventeenth century South Carolina's population included 6,000 settlers, some 2,500 of them enslaved Africans. (For a discussion of slavery in the English Caribbean and Lower South, see Chapter 4.)

From New Netherland to New York

In 1664 Charles created another new colony by granting to his brother James, the duke of York, a vast territory from Maine south to the Delaware River. Its boundaries conflicted with the Dutch colony of New Netherland on the Hudson River. Long a center of European commerce, the Netherlands rose to become the greatest merchant and naval power of the Atlantic world in the seventeenth century. Launching attacks on the Portuguese empire, the Dutch seized a number of strategic locations and created their own far-flung empire. They controlled trading posts in India, Indonesia, and China; sugar plantations in Brazil; as well as the fur trading and farming colony of New Netherland, extending from Manhattan (established 1623) upriver to Albany (established 1614). The Dutch also succeeded in overwhelming the small colony of Swedes on the lower Delaware River, incorporating that region into their sphere of influence in the 1640s.

The Dutch established an alliance with the Iroquois Confederacy. Equipped with arms and ammunition, the Iroquois began a series of military expeditions known as the Beaver Wars. They invaded the territory of neighboring peoples, and in the late 1640s attacked and dispersed the Hurons, who had long controlled the flow of furs from the Great Lakes to the French in Montreal. The Indian nation that held this critical middleman position was assured enormous gains, since it received a percentage of the entire volume of the trade. Sitting in a strategic position between the coast and the interior, the Iroquois sought to channel all furs through their hands, extending the Dutch trading system deep into the continent. Meanwhile, persistent conflict with coastal Algonquians erupted in a series of brutal wars. By the 1660s most of these Indians had withdrawn into the interior.

The English began to challenge the Dutch in the mid-seventeenth century. The two powers fought an inconclusive naval war in the English Channel during the early 1650s, then, a decade later, clashed along the West African coast. In 1664 an English fleet sailed into Manhattan harbor and forced the surrender of New Amsterdam without a shot. The

appointed a governor for the settlements in the area of Albermarle Sound and created a popularly elected assembly. By 1675, North Carolina, as it became known, was home to 5,000 small farmers and large tobacco planters.

Settlement farther south began in 1670 with the founding of coastal Charleston. Most South Carolina settlers came from Barbados, a Caribbean colony the English had founded in 1627, which had grown rich from the production and sale of sugar. By the 1670s the island had become overpopulated with English settlers and Africans. The latter, imported as slaves to work the plantations, made up a majority of the population. Hundreds of Barbadians, both free and slave, relocated to South Carolina, lending a

This is the earliest known view of New Amsterdam, printed in 1651. Like the French, the Dutch intended to construct a fur trade network that extended far into the continent. Thus the prominent position given to the Indians shown arriving with their goods. They paddle a dugout canoe of distinctive design known to have been produced by the Algonquian peoples in the vicinity of Long Island Sound. Twenty-five years after its founding, the Dutch settlement still occupies only the lower tip of Manhattan island.

next year, England declared war on the United Provinces, a conflict that lasted until 1667. Only five years of peace transpired before a third and final war broke out. These Anglo-Dutch Wars marked the decline of the Dutch and the ascendance of the English to dominance of the Atlantic.

New Netherland was renamed New York in honor of the duke of York. Otherwise little was done to disturb the existing order, the English preferring to reap the benefits of this profitable and dynamic colony. Ethnically and linguistically diversified, accommodating a wide range of religious sects, New York had become the most heterogeneous colony in North America. In 1674 the colonists were granted the status of English subjects, and in 1683, after persistent appeals, the duke approved the creation of a representative assembly. The communities of the Delaware Valley became the proprietary colony of New Jersey in 1665, but continued to be governed by New York until the 1680s. By the 1670s the combined population of these settlements numbered over 10,000, with more than 1,500 people clustered in the governmental and commercial center of New York City.

The Founding of Pennsylvania

In 1676, proprietary rights to the western portion of New Jersey were sold to a group of English Quakers including William Penn, who intended to make the area a religious haven for Quakers. Members of the Society of Friends, a dissenting sect, Quakers were committed to religious toleration and pacifism. Penn himself had been imprisoned four times for publicly expressing these views. But he was the son of the wealthy and influential English admiral Sir William Penn, a close adviser of the king. In 1681, to settle a large debt owed to Sir William, King Charles granted the younger Penn a huge territory west of the Delaware River. The next year Penn supervised the laying out of his capital of Philadelphia.

Penn wanted this colony to be a "holy experiment." In his first Frame of Government, drafted in 1682, he included guarantees of religious freedom, civil liberties, and elected representation. He also attempted to deal fairly with the Algonquian Indians, not permitting colonization until settlement rights were negotiated and lands purchased. In 1682 and 1683, he made an agreement with the sachem Tammany of the Delaware tribe at the Indian town of Shackamaxon on the Delaware River. In subsequent years Chief Tammany appeared in many popular stories and myths among the peoples of the mid-Atlantic region. By the time of the Revolution, his name had become emblematic of the American spirit of independence and was adopted as the name of a New York political club. Although Pennsylvania's relations with the Indians later soured, during Penn's lifetime his reputation for fair dealing led a number of Indian groups to resettle in the Quaker colony.

During the first decade of Pennsylvania's settle-

The Delawares presented William Penn with this wampum belt after the Shacka-maxon treaty of 1682. In friendship a Quaker in distinctive hat clasps the hand of an Indian. The diagonal stripes on either side of the figures convey information about the territorial terms of the agreement. Wampum belts like this one, made from strings of white and purple shells, were used to commemorate treaties throughout the colonial period, and during the seventeenth century were the most widely accepted form of money in the northeastern colonies.

ment over 10,000 colonists arrived from England, and agricultural communities were soon spreading from the Delaware into the fertile interior valleys. In 1704 Penn approved the creation of a separate government for the area formerly controlled by the Scandanavians and Dutch, which became the colony of Delaware. In the eighteenth century, Pennsylvania would be known as America's breadbasket, and Philadelphia would become the most important colonial port in late-eighteenth-century North America.

CONFLICT AND WAR

Pennsylvania's peaceful relations with the Indians proved the great exception, for the last quarter of the seventeenth century was a time of great violence throughout all the colonial regions of the continent. Much of this warfare was between colonists and Indians, but intertribal warfare and intercolonial rivalry greatly contributed to the violence. It extended from Santa Fe — where the revolt of the Pueblos, recounted in the chapter introduction, was the single most effective instance of Indian resistance to colonization — to the shores of Hudson's Bay where French and English traders fought for access to the rich fur region of the north.

King Philip's War

During the nearly forty years of relative peace that followed the Pequot War of 1637, the Algonquian and English peoples of New England lived in close, if tense, contact. Several Puritan ministers, including John Eliot and Thomas Mayhew, began to preach to the Indians, and several hundred Algonquian converts eventually relocated in Christian Indian communities called "praying towns." Outside the colonial boundaries, however, there remained a number of independent Indian tribes, including the Pokanokets and the Narragansetts of Rhode Island and the Abenakis of northern New England. The extraordinary expansion of the Puritan population, and their hunger for land, created pressures for further expansion into those territories.

This would be a conflict not only between the English and the Algonquians, but between the United Colonies and Rhode Island. The Pokanokets and Narragansetts had permitted dissenters from Puritan rule to settle in their homelands, and moves against their territory were in part intended to constrict the growth of the dissenting colony. In 1671 the Pokanokets were forced by their Pilgrim allies to concede authority over their homeland territory. This humiliation convinced the Pokanoket sachem, Metacomet, the English-educated son of Massasoit, that his people must break their half-century alliance with Plymouth and take up armed resistance. The Puritan colonies, meanwhile, prepared for a war of conquest.

In the spring of 1675 three Pokanoket men were arrested by the Plymouth authorities and executed for the murder of a Christian Indian. Fearing the moment of confrontation had arrived, Metacomet appealed to the Narragansetts for a defensive alliance. The United Colonies and New York — each

Metacomet, or King Philip, in a mid-eighteenth century engraving by Paul Revere of Boston. Like his father Massassoit, Metacomet tried to cooperate with English colonists, but finally had to fight to maintain his own authority. For many years after the war, the authorities at Plymouth kept his severed head on display. Because his remains never received an honored burial, say the descendants of the Pokanokets, Metacomet's ghost still rises and walks about his homeland.

hoping for territorial gain — took this as the moment to send armed forces into Narragansett country, attacking and burning a number of villages. Despite English claims that the war had been started by an Indian conspiracy, the natives seem to have been drawn into war by these early attacks. Metacomet, who was given the name "King Philip" by his English teachers, escaped from his Pokanoket homeland into the interior with a guerrilla army. What became known as King Philip's War soon engulfed New England.

Things at first went well for the Indians. They forced the abandonment of English settlements on the Connecticut River, and torched a number of towns less than twenty miles from Boston. By the beginning of 1676, however, their campaign was in collapse. A combined colonial army invaded Narragansett country, where it burned villages, killing women and children, and defeated a large Indian force in a battle known as the Great Swamp Fight. In western New England, Metacomet appealed to the Iroquois for supplies and support, but instead they attacked and defeated his forces. Metacomet retreated back to his homeland, where the colonists annihilated his army in August 1676. The victors killed Metacomet, mutilated his body, and triumphantly marched his head on a pike through their towns. The colonists then sold his wife and son, among hundreds of other captives, into West Indian slavery.

In their attack on Metacomet's army, the Iroquois were motivated by interests of their own. Casting themselves in the role of powerful intermediaries between other tribes and the English colonies, the Iroquois wanted to subjugate all rival trading systems. In a series of negotiations conducted at Albany in 1677, the Iroquois Confederacy and the colony of New York created an alliance known as the Covenant Chain, which sought to establish Iroquois dominance over all other tribes as well as New York dominance over all other colonies. During the 1680s the Iroquois pressed their claims as far west as the Illinois country, fighting the western Algonquians allied with the French trading system.

At the conclusion of King Philip's War some four thousand Algonquians and two thousand English colonists were dead, and dozens of English and Indian towns lay in smoking ruins. Measured against the size of the population, it was one of the most destructive wars in American history. Fearing attack from Indians close at hand, colonists attacked and killed the Christian Indian residents of the praying towns. The war marked the end of organized Indian resistance in New England. Yet a number of the praying towns, such as Mashpee on Cape Cod, as well as communities of Narragansetts, Pequots, and other tribal groups, survived into the twentieth century. Their several thousand residents have an alternative perspective on the history of New England.

Bacon's Rebellion

At the same time as King Philip's War, another English–Indian confrontation took place in the Chesapeake. In the 1670s the Susquehannocks of the upper Potomac River came into conflict with planters expanding from Virginia. Violent raids in 1675, led by the wealthy backcountry planter Nathaniel Bacon, included the indiscriminate murder of Indians. These raids precipitated the Susquehanna War. The efforts of Virginia governor William Berkeley to suppress these unauthorized military expeditions so infuriated Bacon and his followers that in the spring of 1676 they turned their fury against the colonial capital of Jamestown itself. Berkeley fled across the Chesapeake while Bacon pillaged and burned the capital. Soon thereafter Bacon died of dysentery, a common fate of the day, and his rebellion collapsed. The next year Virginia signed a treaty ending hostilities with the Indians, but most of the Susquehannocks had already returned to New York, where they joined the Covenant Chain of the Iroquois.

This brief but violent clash marked an important change of direction for Virginia. During his reign as "General of Virginia," Bacon had issued a manifesto demanding not only the death or removal of all Indians from the colony, but also an end to the rule of aristocratic "grandees" and "parasites." The rebellion thus signaled a developing conflict between tidewater and backcountry regions. In 1677, in a replay of Virginia events known as Culpeper's Rebellion, backcountry men in the Albermarle region of North Carolina overthrew the proprietary government and established a government of their own before being suppressed by English authorities. Little practical political change resulted from the two rebellions. But in the aftermath of these rebellions, Virginia and North Carolina authorities began to favor armed expansion into Indian territory, hoping to gain the support of backcountry men by enlarging

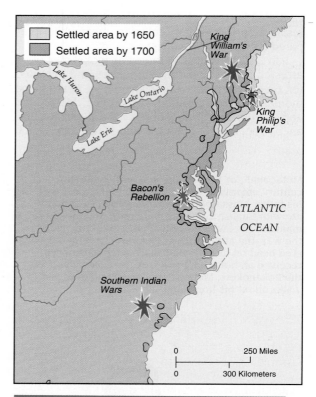

The Spread of Settlement in the British Colonies, 1650–1700

The spread of settlement in the English colonies between 1650 and 1700 created the conditions for the violent conflicts of the late seventeenth century.

the stock of available colonial land. Moreover, planters' fears of disorder among former servants encouraged them to accelerate the transition to slave labor.

Wars in the South

Intercolonial and inter-Indian rivalry also combined to cause massive violence in South Carolina during the 1670s, as colonists there began the operation of a large-scale Indian slave trade. Charleston merchants encouraged Yamasees, Creeks, Cherokees, and Chickasaws to wage war and take captives among Indians allied to rival colonial powers: the mission Indians of Spanish Florida, the Choctaw allies of the French, and the Tuscaroras, trading partners of the Virginians.

This vicious slave trade extended well into the eighteenth century, and thousands of southern Indians were sold into captivity. Most of the Indian men were shipped from Charleston to West Indian or northern colonies; the Indian women remained in South Carolina, where many eventually formed relationships and had children with male African slaves. Those hardest hit were the mission Indians of northern Florida. By 1710 some 12,000 of them had been captured and sold, thousands of others had been killed or dispersed, and the Spanish mission system there, in operation for more than a century, lay in ruins.

The Glorious Revolution in America

Upon Charles II's death in 1685, his brother and sucessor, James II, began a concerted effort to strengthen royal control over the colonies. He abolished the assembly of New York and placed all power in the hands of the royal governor. Colonial assemblies continued to operate in the other colonies, but many became involved in bitter disputes with their governors. In his most dramatic action, the king abolished altogether the charter governments of the New England, New York, and New Jersey colonies, combining them into what he called the Dominion of New England. Edmund Andros, the royal governor of this dominion, attempted to enforce the Navigation Acts, encouraged the imposition of Anglican forms of worship in Puritan areas, and violated traditions of local autonomy. In England, the same imperious style on the part of King James alienated Parliament, and in a bloodless transition, afterward known as the Glorious Revolution, Parliament deposed the king in 1688 and replaced him with his daughter and Dutch son-in-law, Mary and William of Orange.

In the colonies, the Glorious Revolution resulted in a series of rebellions against the authorities set in place by King James II. In the spring of 1689, a Boston mob, inflamed by rumors that the governor was a closet Catholic, captured Andros and deported him to England. Puritan officials then reestablished the colonial charter government. When news of the Boston revolt arrived in New York, it inspired an uprising there. Led by the German merchant Jacob Leisler, a group including prominent Dutch merchants seized control of the city and called for the formation of a new legislature. In Maryland, rumors of a Catholic plot led to the overthrow of the proprietary rule of the Calvert family by an insurgent group called the Protestant Association. The government of England did not fully reestablish its authority in these colonies until 1691–92, when Massachusetts, New York, and Maryland all were declared royal colonies. In New York, Leisler was tried and executed.

King William's War

The year 1689 also marked the beginning of nearly seventy-five years of armed conflict between English and French forces for control of the North American interior. The Iroquois–English Covenant Chain challenged New France to press even harder in search of commercial opportunities in the interior. In the far north, the English countered French dominance with the establishment of Hudson's Bay Company, a royal fur-trade monopoly that in 1670 was given exclusive rights to Rupert's Land, the watershed of the great northern bay.

Hostilities began with English–Iroquois attacks on Montreal, and violence between rival French and English traders on Hudson's Bay. These skirmishes were part of a larger conflict between England and France called the War of the League of Augsburg in Europe and King William's War in the North American colonies. In 1690 the French and their Algonquian allies counterattacked, burning frontier settlements in New York, New Hampshire, and Maine and pressing the attack against the towns of the Iroquois. The same year, a Massachusetts fleet briefly captured the strategic French harbor at Port Royal, but a combined English colonial force failed in its attempt to conquer the French settlements along the Saint Lawrence. This inconclusive war was ended by the Treaty of Ryswick of 1697, which established an equally inconclusive peace. War between England and France would resume only five years later.

The persistent violence of these years concerned English authorities, who began to fear the loss of their North American possessions, either from outside attack or from internal disorder. To shore up central control, in 1701 the English Board of Trade recommended making all charter and proprietary governments into royal colonies. After a brief period under royal rule, William Penn regained private control of his domain, but Pennsylvania was

CHRONOLOGY

1598	Juan de Onate leads Spanish into New Mexico
1607	English found Jamestown
1608	French found Quebec
1609	Spanish found Santa Fe
1620	Pilgrim emigration
1622	Indian uprising in Virginia
1625	Jesuit missionaries arrive in New France
1629	Puritans begin settlement of Massachusetts Bay
1649	Execution of Charles I
1660	Stuart monarchy restored, Charles II becomes king
1675	King Philip's War
1676	Bacon's Rebellion
1680	The Pueblo Revolt
1681	La Salle explores the Mississippi
1688	The Glorious Revolution
1689–97	King William's War
1698	Reconquest of the Pueblos completed
1701	English impose royal governments on all their colonies

the last remaining proprietary colony. Among the charter colonies, only Rhode Island and Connecticut retained their original governments. The result of this quarter-century of violence was the tightening of the imperial reins.

CONCLUSION

At the beginning of the seventeenth century the European presence north of Mexico was extremely limited: two Spanish bases in Florida, a few Franciscan missionaries among the Pueblos, and fishermen along the North Atlantic coast. By 1700 the human landscape of the Southwest, the South, and the Northeast had been transformed. A total of 275,000 Europeans and Africans had moved into these three regions, the vast majority to the British colonies. Indian societies had been disrupted, depopulated, in some cases destroyed, but beyond the colonial boundaries Indians still greatly outnumbered colonists. The Spanish and French colonies were characterized by the inclusion of Indians into the social and economic life of the community. But along the Atlantic coast the English had established communities of exclusion, whose implications for the future of colonist–Indian relations were ominous.

Additional Readings

James Axtell, *The European and the Indian: Essays in the Ethnohistory of Colonial America* (1981). A readable introduction to the dynamics of mutual discovery between natives and colonizers.

Carl Bridenbaugh, *Vexed and Troubled Englishmen, 1590–1642* (1968). A social history of the English people on the eve of colonization, emphasizing their religious and economic problems.

W. J. Eccles, *France in America* (1972). The most comprehensive introduction to the history of New France.

Edmund S. Morgan, *American Slavery, American Freedom* (1975). A classic interpretation of early Virginia. Morgan argues that early American ideas of freedom for some were based on the reality of slavery for others.

Neal Salisbury, *Manitou and Providence: Indians, Europeans, and the Making of New England* (1982). One of the best examples of the new ethnohistory of Indians; a provocative intercultural approach to the history of the Northeast.

David J. Weber, *The Spanish Frontier in North America* (1992). A powerful new overview that includes the history of New Mexico and Florida.

4 SLAVERY AND EMPIRE, 1441–1770

• PLANTATIONS OF COASTAL GEORGIA

Africans labored in the steamy heat of the coastal Georgia rice fields, the breeches of the men rolled up over their knees, the sack skirts of the women gathered and tied about their hips, leaving them, in the words of one shocked observer, "two thirds naked." Standing on the banks of canals that channeled water to the fields, African slave drivers, whips at the ready, supervised the work. Upriver, groups cut away cypress and gum trees and cleared the swampland's jungle maze of undergrowth; others constructed levees, preparing to bring more land under cultivation. An English overseer or plantation master could be seen here and there, but overwhelmingly it was a country populated by Africans.

These plantations were southern extensions of the South Carolina rice belt. Although slavery had been prohibited by Georgia's original colonial charter of 1732, the restriction was lifted when Georgia became a royal colony two decades later. By 1770 15,000 African Americans lived on several hundred coastal plantations, and the population of the region was 80 percent African. The rice plantations were owned by a small elite, dominated by a tight circle of crown officials and their relatives and associates. Georgia's royal governor and lieutenant governor, for example, owned more than a dozen plantations with over fifty thousand acres and eight hundred slaves. Plantations with names such as Mulberry Grove, New Settlement, and Walnut Hill were among the most recent, and most profitable, additions to the British New World empire.

*AFRICAN SLAVES
MAKE A COMMUNITY
OF THEIR OWN
IN THE NEW WORLD*

Rice had become one of the most valuable commodities produced in mainland North America, surpassed in value only by tobacco and wheat. The growth of rice production in the Lower South was matched by an enormous expansion in the Atlantic slave trade. Having no experience in rice cultivation, planters pressed slave traders to supply them with Africans from rice-growing regions such as the Windward Coast of West Africa. In its work force, its methods, and even its tools, southern rice culture was patterned on an African model.

Although the number of North American slaves who were "country born" (native to America) grew steadily in the eighteenth century, the majority on the rice plantations continued to be what were known as "salt water" Africans. These men and women had endured the shock of enslavement.

A RICE FIELD

Slave men and women labor under the direction of an overseer on a rice plantation of the Ogeechee River, near the Georgia coast, in an engraving of the nineteenth century. Lacking experience in the production of rice, English planters depended upon the experience of people from the Windward Coast of Africa, where rice cultivation was a tradition. In the economy of the eighteenth century rice was a valuable commodity, and over the history of the slave trade at least 100,000 Africans disembarked at Charleston, South Carolina on their way to coastal rice plantations.

Ripped from their homeland communities in West Africa by slave raiders, they were brutally marched to coastal forts. There they were imprisoned, subjected to humiliating inspections of their bodies, and branded on the buttocks like animals. Packed into the holds of stinking ships, they were forced into the nightmare of the Middle Passage across the Atlantic Ocean. When finally unloaded on a strange continent, they were sold at auctions held on American docks, then once again marched overland, this time to the isolated coastal frontier of Georgia. On the rice plantations they suffered from overwork and numerous physical ailments that resulted from improper diet, inadequate clothing, and poor housing. Mortality rates were exceptionally high, especially for infants. Colonial laws permitted masters to discipline and punish slaves indiscriminately. They were whipped, confined in irons, branded, castrated, or sold away, with little regard for their connections or relations.

Africans struggled to make a place for themselves in this inhospitable world. Putting their knowledge of rice production to advantage, they compelled their masters to accept the familiar work routines and rhythms of West Africa. Low-country plantations operated according to the task system: once slaves finished their specific jobs, they could use their remaining time to hunt, fish, or cultivate family gardens. Masters frequently complained that "tasking" did not produce the same level of profit as the gang labor system of the sugar plantations, but African rice hands refused to work any other way.

Many ran away. Readers of Savannah newspapers were urged to look out for fugitives: Statira, a woman of the "Gold Coast Country" with tribal markings upon her temples, or "a negro fellow named Mingo, about 40 years old, and his wife Quante, a sensible wench about 20 with her child, a boy about 3 years old, all this country born." Some fled in groups, heading for the Creek Indian settlements in northern Florida, or toward St. Augustine, where the Spanish promised them safe haven. Some struck out violently at their masters, as did a group of nine Africans from a Savannah plantation in 1759. They killed their master and stole a boat, planning to head upriver, but were apprehended as they lay in wait to murder their hated overseers.

But the most important act of resistance took place among the vast majority who remained: the construction of African-American communities that could provide a haven in the heartless world of slavery. On the plantations, they married, raised children, and over time constructed kinship networks. They passed on African names and traditions, created new ones, and buried their dead in cemeteries separate from those of the master class. These links between individuals and families formed the basis for reestablished communities. African American communities combined elements of both African languages and English to form dialects that allowed newly arrived people from many different African ethnic groups as well as American-born slaves to communicate with one another. Neither individuals nor families alone can make a language; that is something only a community can do. The common African heritage and a common status as slaves supplied the basis for the African American community. Communities provided newly arrived Africans and the American-born with the opportunity to build relationships. Without African American communities there could have been no African American culture.

Traveling through the low country during the 1740s, an English missionary heard a clamor in the woods along the road. As he peered through the trees he was startled to see a group of slaves "dancing round the fire." The African community was refitting dance, song, and story to New World circumstances, just as it was reestablishing traditional African arts such as woodworking, iron making, and weaving. Through their culture, the slaves shared a powerful awareness of their common oppression. They told or sang dialect tales of mistreatment, as in this song of Quow, the punished slave:

Was matter Buddy Quow?
I ble Obesha bang you . . . .
Dah Backrow Man go wrong you, Buddy
    Quow,
Dah Backrow Man go wrong you, Buddy
    Quow.

[What's the matter Brother Quow?
I believe the overseer's beat you . . . .
The white man's wronged you, Brother
    Quow,
The white man's wronged you, Brother
    Quow.]

Just as European settlers planted colonial communities, so Africans, the most populous of the peoples to come to North America during the colonial era, constructed distinctive communities of their own. The history of African Americans includes the story of the Atlantic slave trade and the Middle Passage, the plunder of Africa and the profit of the empire. But it is also a story of achievement under the most difficult of circumstances, the making of families, kin networks, and communities. They "labor together and converse almost wholly among themselves," a minister wrote of low-country slaves. "They are, as 'twere, a nation within a nation."

THE BEGINNINGS OF AFRICAN SLAVERY

Household slaves had long been a part of the world of Mediterranean Europe. War captives were sold to wealthy families, who put them to work as servants or artisans. In the fifteenth century, Venetian and Genoese merchants led the traffic in captured Muslims, Africans, and especially Slavic peoples (the term *slave* derives from *Slav*). Many Europeans, however, were disturbed by the moral implications of enslaving Christians, and in the early fifteenth century the pope excommunicated a number of merchants engaged in selling such captives. Africans and Muslims, however, were sufficiently different in culture and appearance to quiet those concerns.

Portugal and Africa

One of the goals of Portuguese expansion in the fifteenth century was access to the lucrative West African trade dominated by the Moors of northern Africa — the ancestors of the Algerians, Libyans, and Moroccans of today. The pope awarded the Portuguese a monopoly on African coastal trade, and they constructed a series of coastal bases, most prominently the fortress of Elmina on the Gold Coast. Soon their ships were returning with gold, wrought iron, ivory, tortoise shell, African textiles, and slaves. The first African slaves to arrive in Lisbon were twelve men kidnapped by a Portuguese captain in 1441; three years later another Portuguese crew seized twenty-nine men and women off Cape Blanco and shipped them home. Traders soon found it considerably more efficient to leave the kidnapping to Africans who were willing to sell slaves in exchange for European commodities. By the 1450s a small but regular slave trade was in place.

The greatest market for these slaves was the large sugar plantations the Portuguese established on their island colony of Madeira, off the coast of northern Africa. Portuguese masters brutally exploited these Africans, working many of them to death, since profits were high and costs of replacement low. Sugar and slaves had gone together since Italian merchants set up the first modern sugar plantations on the islands of the Mediterranean. To obtain sugar, Europeans were willing to subject Africans to slavery. One of modern history's great ironies is the connection between the sweetness of sugar and the suffering of slavery.

Sugar and Slaves

The use of Africans as slaves thus came to the Americas along with the spread of sugar production.

Spain hoped to duplicate the success of the Portuguese, and one of the first products Columbus introduced to the New World was sugar cane. Sugar plantations were soon operating on the island of Hispaniola. At first the Spanish tried to use the native peoples of the Caribbean as a slave labor force. But because of the rapid and massive depopulation of the native peoples through disease and warfare, the Spanish soon turned to the Africans, who were already working in Spain. Bartolomé de las Casas, champion of the Indians, was one of the first to promote the use of Africans as a slave labor force instead of native peoples of the Caribbean. He later came to see the error of his way, concluding "that black slavery was as unjust as Indian slavery and was no remedy at all." The introduction of horse-powered sugar mills around 1510 so increased the demand for labor that in 1518 Spain granted Portuguese slavers an *asiento* (license) to bring slaves directly from Africa. In 1535 a Spanish official in Hispaniola declared that "as a result of the sugar factories, the land seems an . . . image of Ethiopia itself."

Slave Colonies of the Seventeenth and Eighteenth Centuries

By the eighteenth century the system of slavery had created societies with large African populations throughout the Caribbean and along the southern coast of North America.

The Portuguese sent even more Africans to the sugar plantations they established in northeast Brazil. Short of capital, they turned to Dutch financiers to provision these plantations, which became a model of efficient and brutal exploitation. Brazil was soon the center of world sugar production. By 1600 some 25,000 enslaved Africans labored on the plantations of these two sugar regions of the New World.

Utilizing their experience in Brazil, the Dutch became responsible for the next extension of slavery in the Americas. As part of their worldwide offensive against the Portuguese empire (see Chapter 3) the Dutch seized Brazil in 1630, and for over twenty years they controlled this lucrative colony. Skilled at finance and commerce, they greatly expanded the European market for sugar, converting it from a luxury item for the rich to a staple for European workers. Along with other addictive tropical commodities such as tobacco, coffee, and tea, sugar became what one historian has called a "proletarian hunger-killer," helping to sustain people through increasingly long working days. As the market for sugar expanded, the Dutch expanded their sugar operations throughout the tropics.

It was the Dutch, for example, who introduced sugar cultivation in Barbados. As a result, that small island became the most valuable of England's colonies. Once the profitability of sugar had been demonstrated, the English expanded their Caribbean holdings, seizing the island of Jamaica from the Spanish in 1655 and making it over in the image of Barbados. Jamaica would become the most valuable portion of Britain's eighteenth-century empire. The French repeated the process. They first developed sugar plantations on the small island of Martinique, then seized the eastern half of Hispaniola from the Spanish and created a sugar colony called St. Domingue (today's Haiti). Caribbean sugar and slaves had become the centerpiece of the European colonial system.

West Africans

The men and women whose labor made these tropical colonies so profitable came from the long-established societies and local communities of West Africa. In the sixteenth century more than a hundred different peoples lived along the coast of West Africa, from Cape Verde south to Angola. In the north were groups such as the Wolof, Mandingo, Hausa, Ashanti, and Yoruba; to the south the Ibo, Seke, Bakongo, and Mbundu.

The most important institution in these societies was the local community, which was organized by kinship. Decisions about production, storage, and distribution were generally made by clan leaders and village chiefs; local courts arbitrated disputes. Men frequently took a second or third wife. This marriage system, known as *polygyny*, produced very large composite families with complex internal relationships. Because of restrictions on sexual relations, however, West African women bore fewer children than the typical European woman, and many enjoyed considerable social and economic independence as tradeswomen.

West African societies were based on sophisticated farming systems many thousands of years old. Farmers cultivated millet, sorghum, and rice on grassy savannas and in river valleys, fruits, root crops, and other vegetables in the tropical forests that straddled the equator. Having mastered the art of iron making and bronze casting, West Africans produced an impressive array of artistic work, housewares, tools, and weapons. But because their soils were rather thin and poor, iron plows were not useful. Rather, like the farmers of native North America, Africans practiced "shifting cultivation": they cleared land by burning, used hoes or digging sticks to cultivate fields, and after several years moved on to other plots while the cleared land lay fallow. Men worked at clearing the land, women at

This image of Mansa Musa (1312–1337), the ruler of the Moslem kingdom of Mali in west Africa, is taken from the Catalan Atlas, a magnificent map presented to the king of France in 1381 by his cousin, the king of Aragon. In the words of the Catalan inscription, Musa was "the richest, the most noble lord in all this region on account of the abundance of gold that is gathered in his land." He holds what was thought to be the world's largest gold nugget. Under Musa's reign, Timbuktu became a capital of world renown.

The Africa Slave Trade

The enslaved men, women, and children transported to the Americas came from west Africa, the majority from the lower Niger River (called the Slave Coast), and the region of the Congo and Angola.

cultivation and the sale of surpluses in the lively West African markets.

Farming sustained large populations and thriving networks of commerce, and in some areas kingdoms and states developed. Along the upper Niger River, where the grassland gradually turns to desert, towns such as Timbuktu developed into trading centers. These towns sent West African metal goods, gold, ivory, and textiles to the Mediterranean via trans-Saharan caravans of Moors and other Muslim traders. A series of military empires rose and fell while attempting to control the wealth of such towns. When the Portuguese first arrived in the fifteenth century, the most important state in this region was the powerful Muslim kingdom of Songhai, noted for the cavalry and army with which it controlled the flow of trade. There were a number of lesser states and kingdoms along the coast, and it was with these that the Portuguese first bargained for Africans who could be sold as slaves.

West Africans were accustomed to regular agricultural labor. This was important, because it proved to be practically impossible to convert large numbers of foraging or nomadic peoples into efficient plantation workers. Moreover, varieties of household slavery were commonplace in West African societies. Slaves there were often treated more as members of the family than as mere possessions. The West African familiarity with "unfree" labor made it possible for African and European traders to begin the trade in human merchandise.

THE AFRICAN SLAVE TRADE

Africans made up the largest group of people to cross the Atlantic to the Americas before the nineteenth century, outnumbering European immigrants by the astounding ratio of six to one. This was the

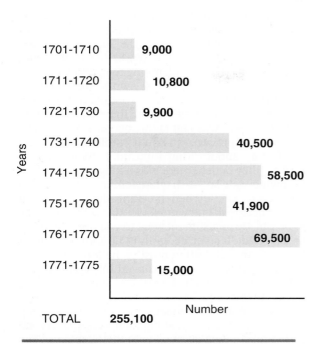

Years	Number
1701-1710	9,000
1711-1720	10,800
1721-1730	9,900
1731-1740	40,500
1741-1750	58,500
1751-1760	41,900
1761-1770	69,500
1771-1775	15,000
TOTAL	255,100

Estimated Number of Africans Imported to British North America, 1701–1775

With the exception of the 1750s — when the British colonies were engulfed by the Seven Years War — the slave trade continued to rise in importance in the decades before the Revolution.

Source: R. C. Simmons, *The American Colonies: From Settlement to Independence* (London: Longman, 1976), 186.

largest forced migration in world history. The Atlantic slave trade, which began with the Portuguese in the fifteenth century and did not end in the United States until 1807 (and continued elsewhere in the Americas until the 1870s) is a brutal chapter in the making of America.

The Demography of the Slave Trade

Scholars today estimate that slavers transported 10 to 12 million Africans to the Americas during the four-century history of the trade. Seventy-six percent arrived from 1701 to 1810 — the peak period of colonial demand for labor, when tens of thousands of individuals were shipped from Africa each year. Of this vast multitude, about half were delivered to Dutch, French, or British sugar plantations in the Caribbean, a third to Portuguese Brazil, and 10 percent to Spanish America. A much smaller proportion — about one in twenty, or an estimated 596,000 men, women, and children — were transported to the British colonies of North America.

Among the Africans brought to the Americas, men generally outnumbered women two to one. Since most Africans were destined for field work, this ratio probably reflected the preferences of plantation owners. The majority of captured and transported Africans were young people, between the ages of fifteen and thirty. Nearly every ethnic group in West Africa was represented.

Slavers of All Nations

All the nations of western Europe participated in the slave trade. Dutch slavers began challenging Portuguese control at the end of the sixteenth century. After several decades of stiff competition and conflict, the Dutch West India Company captured the Portuguese Gold Coast fortress of Elmina in 1637. During the sugar boom of the seventeenth century Holland became the most prominent slave-trading nation. The English also entered the trade in the sixteenth century, beginning with the African voyages of John Hawkins. But the Royal African Company, a slave-trading enterprise based in London, was not organized until 1672. During the Anglo-Dutch Wars of this period, the two commercial superpowers battled each other so destructively along the African coast that they finally agreed to allow free slave trading in the region. In 1698 England ended the monopoly enjoyed by the Royal African Company and threw open the trade to independent merchants. Soon hundreds of ships from Bristol and Liverpool were competing with those from London. As a result, the number of slaves shipped to North America skyrocketed. The Dutch and Portuguese, however, continued to play important roles, alongside slave traders from France, Sweden, and a number of German duchies.

For the most part the European presence in Africa was confined to outposts, although the Portuguese established a colony in Angola. Trading companies constructed forts on the model of Elmina along the West African coast. Sometimes called castles, because of their resemblance to medieval fortresses, these forts were designed for defense against coastal attack by rival traders. By the early eighteenth century more than two dozen trading castles dotted the 220 miles of the Gold Coast alone.

As the slave trade peaked in the middle of the century, however, independent traders invaded the former preserves of the great companies, and the forts became less important. More common were small coastal clusters of huts where European factors or native merchants set up operations with the cooperation of local headmen or chiefs.

This informal manner of trading offered opportunities for small operators, such as the New England slavers who entered the trade in the early eighteenth century. Often bartering rum or salt fish for men and women, these Yankees earned a reputation for unscrupulous dealings. They came by it honestly: "Water your rum as much as possible," one New England merchant instructed his captain, "and sell as much by the short measure as you can." At first, most New England slavers sailed principally from Massachusetts, but after 1750 the center shifted to Rhode Island; slavers based in Philadelphia or Charleston accounted for only 7 percent of the business in the eighteenth century. Many great New England fortunes were built from profits in the slave trade.

The Shock of Enslavement

The slave trade was a collaboration between European and African traders. The Europeans were dependent upon the favor of local rulers. Many of the former lived permanently in coastal forts and married African women, reinforcing their commercial ties with family relations. In many areas a mixed-ancestry group became prominent in the coastal slave trade. Europeans rarely participated in slave raiding, leaving this grim business to the Africans themselves. African traders usually received about half the price the European trader could command in the New World. Slaves were not at all reticent about condemning the participation of their fellow Africans. "I must own to the shame of my own countrymen," wrote Ottobah Cugoano, who was sold into slavery in the mid-eighteenth century, "that I was first kidnapped and betrayed by my own complexion." In South Carolina, slaves told a folk tale about "King Buzzard." "Way back in Africa," they began, there was a king who betrayed his own people so "dem white folks could ketch 'em and chain 'em." When the king died, "de Great Master decide dat he were lower dan all other mens or beasts. He punishment were to wander for eternal time over de face er de earth in de form of a great buzzard, an' dat carrion must be he food."

Most Africans were enslaved through warfare. Large armies launched massive attacks, burning whole towns and taking hundreds of prisoners. More common were smaller raids in which a group of armed men attacked at nightfall, seized everyone within reach, then escaped with their captives. One English trader, visiting the base camp of a raiding party, knew that a new group of captives was about to arrive when he observed the glow of burning villages on the distant horizon. Kidnapping, called *panyaring* in the jargon of the slave trade, was also common. One seaman, ashore while his slave ship awaited its cargo, amused himself by peeking at a young African woman bathing. Suddenly two raiders jumped from the bushes and dragged her off. He later saw them carry her on board and sell her to the

A slave coffle in an eighteenth-century print. As the demand for slaves increased, raids extended deeper and deeper into the African interior. Tied together with forked logs or bark rope, men, women, and children were marched hundreds of miles toward the coast, where their African captors traded them to European traders.

captain, no questions asked. Captured African children sometimes played games of panyaring while waiting to be taken aboard the slave ships.

As the demand for slaves increased in the eighteenth century with the expansion of the plantation system in the Americas, raids extended deeper and deeper into the African interior. Raiders marched large groups of captives, sometimes numbering in the hundreds, several hundred miles to the coast. An English trader stationed in Senegambia observed 2,000 slaves brought in by Mandingo traders, "tied by the neck with leather-thongs, at about a yard distance from each other, 30 or 40 in a string." Such a march was filled with terrors. One account describes a two-month trip in which numerous captives died of hunger, thirst, or exhaustion, several attempted suicide, and the whole party was forced to hide to avoid capture by a rival band of raiders. The captives finally arrived on the coast, where they were sold to an American vessel bound for South Carolina.

Enslavement was an unparalleled shock. Venture Smith, an African born in Guinea in 1729, was eight years old when he was captured. After many years in North American slavery, he still vividly recalled the attack on his village, the torture and murder of his father, and the long march of his people to the coast. "The shocking scene is to this day fresh in my mind," he wrote, "and I have often been overcome while thinking on it." The horror was captured in a song mournfully chanted by captives from the interior kingdom of Bornu on their march to the Slave Coast, a song remembered by African Americans:

> Where are we going? Where are we going?
> Where are we going, Rubee?
> Hear us, save us, make us free,
> Send our Arka down from thee!
> Here the Ghiblee wind is blowing,
> Strange and large the world is growing!
> Tell us, Rubee, where are we going?
> Where are we going, Rubee?

> Bornu! Bornu! Where is Bornu!
> Where are we going, Rubee?
> Bornu-land was rich and good,
> Wells of water, fields of food;
> Bornu-land we see no longer,
> Here we thirst, and here we hunger,
> Here the Moor man smites in anger;
> Where are we going, Rubee?

> Where are we going? Where are we going?
> Hear us, save us, Rubee!
> Moons of marches from our eyes,
> Bornu-land behind us lies;

Portrait of Olaudah Equiano, by an unknown English artist, ca. 1780. Captured in Nigeria in 1756 when he was eleven years old, Equiano was transported to America and eventually purchased by an English sea captain. After ten years a slave, he succeeded in buying his own freedom and dedicated himself to the antislavery cause. His book, *The Interesting Narrative of the Life of Olaudah Equiano* (1789), was published in numerous editions, translated into several languages, and became the prototype for dozens of other slave narratives in the nineteenth century.

> Hot the desert wind is blowing,
> Wild the waves of sand are flowing!
> Hear us! Tell us, where are we going?
> Where are we going, Rubee?

On the coast, European traders and African raiders assembled their captives. Prisoners waited in dark dungeons or in open pens called *barracoons*. Traders split up families and ethnic groups to lessen the possibility of collective resistance. Captains carefully inspected each man and woman, and those selected for transport were branded on the back or buttocks with the mark of the buyer. Olaudah Equiano, an Ibo captured in 1756 when he was a boy of eleven, remembered that "those white men with horrible looks, red faces, and long hair, looked and acted . . . in so savage a manner; . . . I had never seen among any people such instances of brutal cruelty.'' Equiano's narrative, written during the 1780s, after he had secured his freedom, is one of the few that provide an African account of enslavement. He and his fellow captives became convinced that they ''had got into a world of bad spirits,'' and were about to be eaten by cannibals. A French trader wrote that many prisoners were ''positively prepossessed with the opinion that we transport them into our country in order to kill and eat them.''

The Middle Passage

From coastal forts and barracoons, crews rowed small groups of slaves out to the waiting ships and packed them into shelves below deck only six feet long by two and a half feet high. ''Rammed like

herring in a barrel,'' wrote one observer, slaves were ''chained to each other hand and foot, and stowed so close, that they were not allowed above a foot and a half for each in breadth.'' With scarcely room to turn over, people were forced to sleep ''spoon fashion,'' and the tossing of the ship knocked them about so violently that the skin over their elbows sometimes was worn to the bone from scraping on the planks. Slavers debated the merits of various packing strategies. One camp argued that additional room lessened mortality and thus increased profits. But the great demand and the price for slaves in the mid-eighteenth century gave the upper hand to the ''tight packers,'' those willing to risk life in order to carry as many men and women as possible. One ship designed to carry 450 slaves regularly crossed the Atlantic with more than 600.

Their holds filled with human cargo, the ships headed toward Cape Verde to catch the trade winds blowing towards America. In the eighteenth century English sailors christened the voyage the Middle Passage, the middle part of a triangle from England to Africa, Africa to America, and America back to England. A favorable voyage from Senegambia to Barbados might be accomplished in as little as three weeks, but a ship from Guinea or Angola becalmed in the doldrums or driven back by storms might take as much as three months.

The voyage was marked by a daily routine. In the morning the crewmen opened the hatch and brought the captives on deck. After attaching their leg irons to a great chain running the length of the bulwarks, they issued a meal of beans. After breakfast came a ritual known as ''dancing the slave'':

Slaves on the deck of a French slave ship of the eighteenth century, and below deck on a Spanish slaver, a sketch made when the vessel was captured by a British warship in the early nineteenth century. Slaves were ''stowed so close, that they were not allowed above a foot and a half for each in breadth,'' wrote one observer. The close quarters and unsanitary conditions created a stench so bad that Atlantic sailors said you could ''smell a slaver five miles down wind.''

while an African thumped an upturned kettle or plucked a banjo, the crew commanded men and women to jump up and down in a bizarre session of aerobic exercise. A day spent chained on deck was concluded by a second bland meal and then the stowing away. During the night, according to one seaman, there issued from below "a howling melancholy noise, expressive of extreme anguish." Down in the hold, the groans of the dying, the shrieks of women and children, the suffocating heat and stench were, in the words of Olaudah Equiano, "a scene of horror almost inconceivable." In the words of a slave song from South Carolina:

Here wey de wail an' moan
Of Af'ica sound,
Wuss dan de cry
Of Af'ica chillun.

Such scenes marked the transition of Africans to America.

Among the worst of the horrors was the absence of adequate sanitation. There were "necessary tubs" set below deck, but Africans, "endeavoring to get to them, tumble over their companions," one eighteenth-century ship's surgeon wrote, "and as the necessities of nature are not to be resisted, they ease themselves as they lie." Efficient captains ordered crews to scrape and swab the holds daily, but so sickening was the task that on many ships it was rarely performed and Africans were left to wallow in their filth. When first taken below deck, the boy Equiano remembered, "I received such a salutation in my nostrils as I had never experienced in my life," and "became so sick and low that I was not able to eat." Atlantic sailors said you could "smell a slaver five miles down wind." Many sickened and died in these conditions. Many others contracted dysentery, known as the "flux." Frequent shipboard epidemics of smallpox, measles, and yellow fever added to the misery. Historians estimate that during the Middle Passage of the eighteenth century a minimum of one in every five or six Africans perished.

There was plenty of resistance. While ships were still within sight of the African coast, hope remained alive and the danger of revolt was great. One historian has found references to fifty-five slave revolts on British and American ships from 1699 to 1845. On the open sea, however, resistance took more desperate form. The sight of the disappearing coast of Africa "left me abandoned to despair," wrote Equiano; "I now saw myself deprived of all chance of returning to my native country, or even the least glimpse of hope of gaining the shore." He witnessed several Africans jump overboard and drown, "and I believe many more would very soon have done the same if they had not been prevented by the ship's crew." Captains took the precaution of spreading netting along the sides of their ships. "Could I have got over the nettings," Equiano declared, "I would have jumped over the side."

On every voyage a number of Africans refused to eat. When he could not force himself to take a bite, Equiano was thrown across the windlass and flogged. Others had red-hot coals held to their lips. If this failed to open their mouths, the ship's surgeon would hammer a screw vise between their teeth, crank it open, and insert a funnel through which food was poured down their throats. Some people went berserk, others lapsed into a state of shock or coma. The crewmen might flog these victims to bring them to their senses, but failing this, they clubbed and threw them overboard so to prevent them from influencing the others. Equiano was struck by the irony of men and women being "flogged unmercifully for thus attempting to prefer death to slavery."

Arrival in the New World

As the ship approached its destination the crew prepared the human cargo for market. If supplies permitted, Africans might benefit from increased rations of food, and perhaps rum. All but the most rebellious were freed from their chains and allowed to wash themselves and move about the deck. Once the ship was docked, shoreside agents sent African assistants on board to reassure the captives that the worst was over, and that once off the ship they would be treated with kindness. Captains did what they could to get their Africans into presentable condition. In one case, those exhibiting the bloody discharge characteristic of the flux were plugged with clumps of hemp fiber by the ship's surgeon. To impress buyers, slavers might parade Africans off the ship to the tune of an accordion or the beat of a drum. But the toll of the Middle Passage was difficult to disguise. One observer described a disembarking group as "walking skeletons covered over with a piece of tanned leather."

Some cargoes were destined for a single wealthy planter, or consigned to a merchant who sold the captives in return for a commission; in other cases the captain himself was responsible. Buyers painstakingly examined the Africans, who once again suffered the indignity of probing eyes and poking fingers. This caused "much dread and trembling among us," wrote Equiano, "and nothing but bitter cries." In ports such as Charleston, sale might take place by auction, or by a method known as the

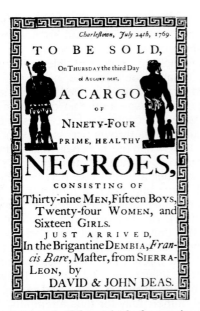

TO BE SOLD,

On Thursday the third Day of August next,

A CARGO

OF

NINETY-FOUR

PRIME, HEALTHY

NEGROES,

CONSISTING OF

Thirty-nine Men, Fifteen Boys, Twenty-four Women, and Sixteen Girls.

JUST ARRIVED,

In the Brigantine Dembia, *Francis Bare,* Maſter, from Sierra-Leon, by

DAVID & JOHN DEAS.

The announcement of the arrival of a consignment of slaves in Charleston, South Carolina, in 1769, where the most common method of sale was by auction. Men and women alike were subjected to intimate inspection before the bidding began. Buyers were quite interested in the ethnic origins of slaves, but gave little concern to keeping family members together.

scramble. In that event, standard prices were set in advance for men, women, boys, and girls. The Africans were then driven into a corral, and at a signal the buyers rushed among them, grabbing their pick of the lot. The noise, clamor, and eagerness of the buyers, Equiano remembered, renewed all the terrible apprehensions of the Africans. "In this manner, without scruple, are relations and friends separated, most of them never to see each other again." Bought by a Virginian, Equiano was taken to an isolated tobacco plantation where he found himself unable to communicate with any of his fellow slaves, who came from other ethnic groups. "In this state," he wrote, "I was constantly grieving and pining, and wishing for death, rather than anything else."

The Effects on Africa

Africa began the sixteenth century with genuine independence. But as surely as Europe and America grew stronger as a result of the trade and the labor of slaves, so Africa grew weaker by their loss. In the short term, slave-trading kingdoms on the coast increased their power at the expense of interior kings. Thus the interior West African state of Songhai gave way to the Gold Coast state of Akwamu. In the Niger delta the slaving states of Nembe, Bonny, and Kalabari arose, and to the south the kingdom of Imbangala drew slaves from central Africa. But these coastal states found that the slave trade was a viper that could easily strike back at them. "Merchants daily seize our own subjects, sons of the land and sons of our noblemen, they grab them and cause them to be sold," King Dom Affonso of the Kongo wrote to the Portuguese monarch in the sixteenth century; "and so great, Sir, is their corruption and licentiousness that our country is being utterly depopulated."

But despite the loss of millions of men and women over the centuries, depopulation was not the worst result of the slave trade. Some regions suffered a net loss, but most of West Africa continued to grow in population, though at a slower rate. More serious was the long-term stagnation of the West African economy. Labor was drawn away from farming and other productive activities, and imported consumer goods such as textiles and metalwares stifled local manufacturing. Iron smelting was abandoned altogether. African traders were expert at driving a hard bargain, and over several centuries they gained an increasing price for slaves—the result of rising demand and increased competition among European slavers. But even when they appeared to get the best of the exchange, the ultimate advantage lay with the Europeans, who received wealth-producing workers in return for mere consumer goods.

For every man or woman taken captive, as many as two more died in the chronic slave raiding. Many West African states became little more than machines for supplying captives, and a "gun–slave cycle" pushed neighboring kingdoms into a destructive arms race. The resulting political and cultural demoralization prepared the way for the European conquest of Africa in the nineteenth century. The leaders of West Africa during the centuries of slave trading, writes the Nigerian poet Chinweizu, "had been too busy organizing our continent for the exploitative advantage of Europe, had been too busy with slaving raids upon one another, too busy decorating themselves with trinkets imported from Europe, too busy impoverishing and disorganizing the land, to take thought and long-range action to protect our sovereignty."

THE DEVELOPMENT OF NORTH AMERICAN SLAVE SOCIETIES

New World slavery was nearly two centuries old before it became an important system of labor in North America. There were slaves in each of the

British colonies during the seventeenth century, but in 1700 they were only 11 percent of the colonial population. During the eighteenth century slavery greatly expanded, and by 1770 Africans and African Americans numbered 460,000, or more than 20 percent of the colonial population.

Slavery Comes to North America

The first Africans in Virginia arrived in 1619 when a Dutch slave trader exchanged "20 and odd Negroes" for badly needed provisions. But since slaves generally cost twice as much as indentured servants, yet held forth the same appallingly short life expectancy, they offered planters little economic benefit. Consequently, only a relatively small number were brought to Virginia over the next several decades. In fact, there are indications that those Africans who worked in the tobacco fields were not slaves at all, but servants. Although there surely were slaves among the population in the early years, the first recorded instances of slavery date from around 1640. An interesting case illustrates the ambiguous status of black Virginians. In 1654 the African John Castor told a local court that "he came unto Virginia for seven or eight years of indenture, yet Anthony Johnson his Master had kept him his servant seven years longer than he should or ought." Johnson claimed that "he had the Negro for his life." The court decided in the master's favor. Strange to say, Johnson himself was an African. He had arrived in 1621 as an indentured servant, but achieved his freedom and became a landowner. Property records reveal that other Africans acquired farms and servants or slaves of their own. Moreover, sexual mixing between Africans and Europeans had produced by the end of the seventeenth century a sizable group of free people of mixed ancestry—*mulattoes*. The presumption that dark skin inevitably meant slavery did not yet exist.

In the last quarter of the seventeenth century, however, a number of developments encouraged the expansion of true slavery. In colonies such as Pennsylvania, European immigrants discovered better opportunities as free farmers, and it became increasingly difficult to recruit them as indentured servants. Moreover, after Bacon's Rebellion and the other social conflicts of the 1670s, a number of colonial leaders became concerned about potential rebellions among former indentured servants. Underlying their concern was the fact that people were living longer, possibly the result of being better fed and more resistant to disease. Consequently, more servants were surviving their indentures. But these improvements in living conditions also affected Africans, increasing their rates of survival, and planters began to see more advantage in the purchase of slaves. During these same years, the supply of slaves in North America increased when the Royal African Company inaugurated direct shipments from West Africa to the mainland.

Thus the work force of indentured servants was gradually replaced by a work force of slaves. By 1700 the number of African slaves had probably surpassed the number of indentured servants. There were some 19,000 Africans in Maryland and Virginia, about 22 percent of the population. In South Carolina, where indentured servants had never been an important part of the labor force, Africans constituted over 40 percent of the settler population by the end of the seventeenth century.

As its importance rose, slavery was written into law, a process best observed in the case of Virginia. In 1662 colonial officials declared that children inherited the status of their slave mothers, five years later they added that baptism could no longer alter conditions of servitude. Two important avenues to freedom were thus closed. The colony then placed life-threatening violence in the hands of masters,

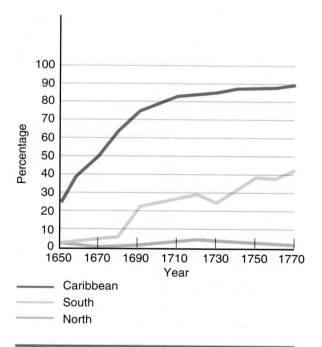

Africans as a Percentage of Total Population of the British Colonies, 1650–1770.

Although the proportion of Africans and African Americans was never as high in the South as in the Caribbean, the ethnic structure of the South diverged radically from the North during the eighteenth century.

Source: Robert W. Fogel and Stanley L. Engerman, *Time on the Cross* (Boston: Little, Brown, 1974), 21.

declaring in 1669 that the death of a slave during punishment "shall not be accounted felony." At the end of the century the colonial legislature extended this principle to include the dismemberment or private execution of runaways. Such regulations accumulated piecemeal until 1705, when Virginia gathered them into a comprehensive slave code that became a model for other colonies.

The institution of slavery was thus strengthened just as the Atlantic slave trade reached flood tide in the eighteenth century. During that century's first decade, more Africans were imported into North America than the total number for the previous ninety-three years of colonial history. The English colonies were primed for an unprecedented growth of plantation slavery.

The Chesapeake

During the eighteenth century the European demand for tobacco increased more than tenfold. This demand was largely supplied by increased production in the Chesapeake. Tobacco exports rose by an average of 2 percent annually through the century, exceeding 100 million pounds a year by the early 1770s. Tobacco plantations spread through all sections of the tidewater country, from Delaware south along the coast into the Albemarle Sound region of North Carolina. Planters eventually extended their operations into the Piedmont, above the fall line of Atlantic-flowing rivers. Tobacco was far and away the single most important commodity produced in North America, accounting for more than a quarter of the value of all colonial exports.

The expansion of tobacco production could not have taken place without an enormous growth in the size of the slave labor force. Unlike sugar, tobacco did not require large plantations and could be produced successfully on relatively small farms. But it was a heavily labor-intensive crop, and from the beginnings of Chesapeake colonization its cultivation had been the responsibility of indentured servants and slaves. As tobacco farming grew, slaveholding became widespread. By midcentury slaves were included in a majority of upcountry households and as many as three-quarters of the households in the tidewater. Tobacco farms varied in size, from small establishments where farmers worked side by side with one or two slaves, to large, self-sufficient plantations having dozens of slaves. By 1770 more than a quarter million slaves labored in the colonies of the Upper South, and because of the exploding market for tobacco, their numbers were expanding at something like double the rate of the general population.

Arriving at the Chesapeake during the summer, many slave ships unloaded their cargoes for sale at Baltimore. But most dispersed their slaves in small groups of three or four at the wharves of individual planters along the numerous rivers of the bay. From 1700 to 1770 a total of perhaps 80,000 Africans were imported into the Chesapeake colonies.

Shipments from Africa thus accounted for part of the growth of the slave population, but natural increase was much more important. In this regard, the slave colonies of the Chesapeake were unique in the Western Hemisphere. In the Caribbean and Brazil, the tropical climate allowed year-round cultivation, and there was no winter season of reduced toil. Because sugar profits were so high, many sugar planters preferred to work their slaves to death, replenishing them with a constant stream of new arrivals from Africa. They calculated that they could make greater profits through extreme exploitation of the labor force than by creating the better living and working conditions that would allow the Africans to reproduce at normal rates. In Virginia, however, lower rates of profit may have caused tobacco planters to pay more attention to the health of their labor force, establishing work routines that were not so deadly. Food supplies were also more plentiful in North America than in the Caribbean, where nearly every morsel had to be imported, and the better-fed

Tobacco Exported to England
(thousands of pounds)

	Chesapeake	Total
1700	37,166	37,840
1725	20,968	21,046
1750	50,785	51,339
1775	54,458	55,968

Source: *Historical Statistics of the United States* (Washington, D.C.: GPO, 1976), 1189–90, 1193.

Rice Exported to England
(hundreds of pounds)

	Carolina	Georgia	Total
1700	3,079	—	3,037
1725	52,268	—	53,670
1750	164,378	1,783	166,672
1775	452,822	110,020	576,916

Source: *Historical Statistics of the United States* (Washington, D.C.: GPO, 1976), 1189–90, 1193.

An Overseer Doing His Duty, a watercolor sketch made by Benjamin Henry Latrobe during a trip to Virginia in 1798. The majority of masters in the tobacco region owned only one or two slaves, and worked with them in the fields. In his portrayal of this overseer, relaxing as he supervises his workers, Latrobe clearly expressed his disgust for slavery.

Chesapeake populations of Africans were more resistant to disease. Historians continue to debate these important differences. But whatever the causes, self-sustained population growth among Chesapeake slaves had begun by the 1730s, and by the 1770s the majority were "country-born."

The Lower South

For fifty years after the founding of the South Carolina colony in 1670, the area outside the immediate region of Charleston remained a rough and dangerous frontier. English settlers raised cattle, often using Africans who had experience in the pastoral economies of West Africa. Others engaged in the deerskin trade, bartering English goods with the numerous Indian people of the backcountry. But the most valuable part of the early Carolina economy was the Indian slave trade. Practicing a strategy of divide and conquer, using Indian tribes to fight one another, Carolinians enslaved tens of thousands of Indians before the 1730s. In the Tuscarora War of 1712–13, the colonists themselves went to war against this tribe, killing at least a thousand warriors. They shipped another thousand women and children to slave markets in the Caribbean. Native peoples of the region were so enraged that three years later they staged a general uprising. Led by the Yamasees, they nearly defeated the colonial forces. Only by enlisting the aid of the Cherokees was South Carolina able to turn the tide at the last minute.

By the time of the Yamasee War, however, rice production had become the most dynamic sector of the South Carolina economy. As in the case of cattle grazing, the cultivation of rice depended upon the expertise of West Africans. Another important crop was added in the 1740s, when a young South Carolina woman by the name of Elizabeth Lucas Pickney successfully adapted West Indian indigo to the lowcountry climate. It is likely that here as well, the assistance of West Indian slaves skilled in indigo culture was crucial. The indigo plant, native to India, produced a deep blue dye important in textile manufacture. Rice grew in the lowlands, but indigo could be cultivated on the high ground. And since they had different seasonal growing patterns, the two crops harmonized perfectly. Rice and indigo production rose steadily over the next thirty years. By the 1770s they were among the most valuable commodities exported from the mainland colonies of North America.

Like tobacco, the expansion of rice and indigo production depended upon the growth of African slavery. Because Indian slaves were dangerous as long as they were near their homelands, most were shipped off to other colonies. They were replaced by thousands of Africans. By the 1730s the annual rate of importation had risen to a thousand or more each year. At the height of the trade in the early 1770s, more than 4,000 Africans arrived annually. Before the international slave trade to the United States was ended in 1807, at least 100,000 Africans arrived at Charleston. One of every five ancestors of today's African Americans passed through Charleston on his or her way to the rice and indigo fields.

By the 1740s many of the arriving Africans were being taken to Georgia, a colony created by an act of the English Parliament in 1732. Its leader, James Edward Oglethorpe, hoped to establish a buffer against Spanish invasion from Florida and make it a haven for poor British farmers, who could then sell their products in the markets of South Carolina. Under his influence, Parliament agreed to prohibit slavery there. Soon, however, Georgia's coastal regions were being colonized by South Carolina planters with their slaves. In 1752 Oglethorpe and Georgia's trustees abandoned their experiment, and the colony was opened to slavery under royal authority. The Georgia coast had already become an extension of the Carolina lowcountry slave system.

By 1770 there were nearly 90,000 African Americans in the Lower South, about 60 percent of the population of South Carolina and Georgia. In the coastal areas where they were concentrated, however, they constituted more like 80 percent. The slave economy of the Lower South was dominated by large plantations, which had between fifty and seventy-five slaves. English overseers and African drivers directed their labor, and the work was hard. But because of the task system that African rice workers insisted upon, slaves exercised a measure of control over their own lives. The African American communities of the Lower South, like those of the Chesapeake, achieved self-sustained growth by the middle of the eighteenth century.

Slavery in the Spanish Colonies

Slavery was basic to the Spanish colonial labor system, yet doubts about the enslavement of Africans were raised by both church and the crown. The papacy denounced slavery numerous times as a violation of Christian principles, and although the Catholic Church in Spanish America owned slaves and profited from their labor, numerous priests preached against the institution. The Spanish monarchy was perpetually troubled about the question of slavery. In 1693, for example, the king instructed the captain general of Cuba to caution masters not to increase the "sorrow" of slaves with "distempered rigor." During the early eighteenth century, many Spanish slaves were freed by their masters; others purchased their freedom from their own earnings. But the institution of slavery remained intact, and later in the eighteenth century, when sugar production expanded in Cuba, the slave system there was as brutal as any in the history of the Americas.

The character of slavery, then, varied with local conditions. One of the most benign forms operated in Spanish Florida. Africans were among the sixteenth-century Spanish settlers there, and slaves were initially engaged in cattle raising and farming. But the colony was intended primarily as a protective buffer against the English. In 1699 the Spanish declared Florida a refuge for escaped slaves from the English colonies, offering free land to any fugitives who would help defend the colony. Over the next half century, refugee Indians and fugitive Africans established numerous communities in the countryside surrounding St. Augustine. North of the city, Fort Moosa was manned by Negro troops commanded by their own officers. Slaves could be found in many Florida communities, but in a form more like the household slavery of the Mediterranean and Africa than the plantation slavery of the British colonies.

In New Mexico, the Spanish established a very different form of slavery. Although very few Africans accompanied the Spanish colonists there, Indian slavery quickly became established. In the sixteenth century the colonial governor sent Indian slaves to the mines of Mexico. The enslavement of Indians was one of the causes of the Pueblo Revolt (see Chapter 3), which some historians have suggested was as much a slave rebellion as an Indian uprising. During the eighteenth century, the Spanish were much more cautious in their treatment of the Pueblos, who were officially considered Catholics. But they captured and enslaved "infidel Indians" such as the Apaches or nomads from the Great Plains, using them as house servants and field workers.

Slavery in French Louisiana

Slavery was also important in Louisiana, the colony founded by the French in the lower Mississippi Valley in the early eighteenth century. After La Salle's descent of the Mississippi River in 1682, the French planned a colony there to anchor their New World empire. In the early eighteenth century French Canadians established bases at Biloxi and Mobile on the Gulf of Mexico, but it was not until 1718 that they laid out the city of New Orleans on the Mississippi. Upriver, colonists established an alliance with the powerful Choctaw nation, and with their assistance defeated an opposing confederacy of Chickasaw and Natchez Indians during the 1720s and 1730s.

By 1750 several thousand French colonists, many from New France and the Caribbean, had established farms and plantations on the Gulf Coast and in a narrow strip of settlement along the Mississippi River. Soon they were exporting rice, indigo, and tobacco, in addition to furs and skins from the Indian trade of the backcountry. As with the

Spanish in St. Augustine, however, the French were primarily interested not in exporting but in defending their access to the Mississippi against Spanish and English threats. Consequently, African slaves amounted to no more than a third of the colonial population of 10,000. Only at the end of the eighteenth century would the colony of Louisiana become an important North American slave society.

Slavery in the North

North of the Chesapeake, slavery was much less important. Slaves worked on some farms, but almost never in groups. In the port cities, however, slavery was considerably more important. Although slaves were first shipped to Philadelphia in the 1680s, their numbers remained small until the expansion of the slave trade in the eighteenth century. "We have negroes flocking in upon us," a Quaker complained in the 1730s. A visitor to the city in 1750 noted that slaves were bought "by almost everyone who could afford it," and that Quakers had "as many negroes as other people." In 1770 about 500 masters owned about a thousand slaves, mostly one or two apiece. The largest slaveholder employed thirteen slaves in the manufacture of rope. Slaves, together with a small group of free blacks, made up about 9 percent of the city's population.

It was the Quakers, however, who voiced the first antislavery sentiment in the colonies. In *Considerations on the Keeping of Negroes* (1754), John Woolman pointed to the Bible's declaration that all peoples were of one blood. He urged his readers to imagine themselves in the place of the African people. Suppose, he wrote,

> that our ancestors and we had been exposed to constant servitude in the more servile and inferior employments of life; that we had been destitute of the help of reading and good company; that amongst ourselves we had had few wise and pious instructors; that the religious amongst our superiors seldom took notice of us; that while others in ease have plentifully heaped up the fruit of our labour, we had received barely enough to relieve nature, and being wholly at the command of others had generally been treated as a contemptible, ignorant part of mankind. Should we, in that case, be less abject than they now are?

It was not until the Revolution, however, that antislavery sentiment became more widespread.

In New York slavery was somewhat more important. Perhaps as many as 7,000 Africans entered through the port between 1700 and 1770. The majority remained in the city or the greater Hudson Valley, where they worked on farms and dairies. By 1770, New York and New Jersey were home to some 27,000 African Americans, about 10 percent of the population. Black people were concentrated even more highly in New York City. A British naval officer stationed in the port during the 1750s observed that "the laborious people in general are Guinea negroes," and as early as 1690 artisans and laborers complained that slave competition "so much impoverished them, that they cannot by their labours get a competency for the maintenance of themselves and families." In 1770, 3,000 slaves and 100 free blacks, about 17 percent of the population, lived in the city.

The most important center of slavery in the North was Newport, Rhode Island. In 1760 African Americans there made up about 20 percent of the population, a concentration resulting from that port's dominance of the midcentury slave trade. Moreover, the area was unique for the large slave gangs used in cattle and dairy operations in the Narragansett country, some of which were as large as Virginia plantations. Elsewhere in New England there were slaves in all the port towns. Boston, where slaves made up about 5 percent of the residents, was probably typical. In the countryside a few slaves were scattered among the farms.

BECOMING AFRICAN AMERICAN

In 1774 a group of enslaved Massachusetts Africans spoke for tens of thousands of others when they petitioned the British authorities for their freedom. "We were unjustly dragged by the cruel hand of power from our dearest friends," they wrote, "and some of us stolen from the bosoms of our tender parents and from a populous, pleasant and plentiful country, and brought hither to be made slaves for life in a Christian land." Men and women from dozens of ethnic groups, representing many different languages, religions, and customs, had been transported across the Atlantic without any of their cultural possessions. In America they were subjected to the control of masters intent on maximizing their work and minimizing their liberty. Yet African Americans carved out lives of their own with a degree of independence. Their African heritage was not erased; it provided them with a fundamental outlook, the basis for a common identity.

The majority of Africans transported to North America arrived during the eighteenth century. They were met by a rapidly growing population of country-born slaves, or *creoles,* a term first used by slaves in Brazil to distinguish their children, born in the New World, from newly arrived Africans. The perspective of creoles was shaped by their having grown up under slavery, and that perspective helped them to determine which elements of African culture were incorporated into the emerging culture of the African American community. That community was formed out of the relationship between creoles and Africans, and between slaves and their European masters.

The Daily Life of Slaves

Slaves were agricultural workers. Because they made up the overwhelming majority of the labor force that made the plantation colonies so profitable, it is fair to say that Africans built the South. As an agricultural people, Africans were accustomed to the routines of rural labor. Even African women had extensive experience in the fields, and it was put to use on the plantations. Most Africans were field hands, and even domestic servants labored in the fields when necessary. As crop production expanded during the eighteenth century, and plantations became larger and more extensive, labor specialization took place. On the eighteenth-century Virginia plantation of George Mason, for example, slaves worked as carpenters, coopers, sawyers, blacksmiths, tanners, curriers, shoemakers, spinners, weavers and knitters, and even distillers.

Masters clothed their workers in rude clothing, sufficient in the summer but nearly always inadequate in the winter. Increasingly the plantations were supplied by cheap goods from the new industrial looms of England. Stiff shoes were a necessity in the cold months, but they so cramped the feet that everyone looked forward to shedding them in the spring and going barefoot all summer and fall. Hand-me-down clothes from the master's family offered slaves an opportunity to brighten their costumes, and many of them dressed in a crazy quilt of styles and colors. Similarly, they relieved the monotony of their rations of corn and pork with vegetables from their small gardens, game and fish from field and stream, and wild plant foods from the forests. On the whole, their diet must have been sufficient, for they not only survived but rapidly reproduced during the eighteenth century.

The growing African population, and larger plantations on which larger numbers lived and worked together, created the "critical mass" necessary for the emergence of African American communities and African American culture. The typical slave served on a plantation having a work force of ten or more. On small farms, Africans might work side by side with their owners and, depending on the character of the master, might enjoy living conditions not too different from those of other family members. But plantations offered possibilities for a more autonomous cultural life.

Families and Communities

The family was the most important institution for the development of community and culture. Slave codes did not provide for legal slave marriages, for that would have contradicted the master's freedom to dispose of his property as he saw fit. "The endearing ties of husband and wife are strangers to us," declared the Massachusetts slaves who petitioned for their freedom in 1774, "for we are no longer man and wife than our masters or mistresses think

View of Mulberry House and Grounds, by Thomas Coram, ca. 1770. The slave quarters are front and center in this painting of a rice plantation near Charleston, South Carolina. The steep roofs of the slave cabins was an African architectural feature that slave builders introduced in America, allowing the heat to dissipate in the rafters above the living quarters.
(Thomas Coram. View of Mulberry Plantation. 1770. Oil on paper, 10 × 17.6 cm. Gibbes Museum of Art.)

proper." How, they asked, "can a slave perform the duties of a husband to a wife or parent to his child? How can a husband leave master to work and cleave to his wife? How can the wife submit themselves to their husbands in all things? How can the child obey their parents in all things?" The creation and maintenance of slave family life was essential not only for reproduction, but for the development of African American culture.

Despite the barriers, however, by the 1730s Africans in both the Chesapeake and the Lower South had created stable families. On large plantations throughout the southern colonies, travelers found Africans living in nuclear-family households. In many cases men and women lived together in the slave quarters, and this was clearly the ideal. But on smaller plantations, men frequently married women from neighboring farms, and with the permission of both owners visited their families in the evenings or on Sundays. Indeed, some historians have noted that Africans seemed to prefer to marry outside their own plantations. This may have been a continuation of an African pattern known as *exogamy*, which required husband and wife to come from different villages. By contrast, English men and women throughout the colonies tended toward *endogamy*, choosing mates from those close at hand. Frequently they married cousins, something the slaves scrupulously avoided.

Many observers noted that premarital pregnancy was relatively common. This too may have been a continuation of African customs permitting premarital sexual relations among young people. (Premarital pregnancy was common among many eighteenth-century white colonists as well.) Generally, when a slave woman became pregnant, she and the potential father married. "Their marriages are generally performed amongst themselves," one visitor to North Carolina wrote of the Africans he observed in the 1730s; "the man makes the woman a present, such as a brass ring or some other toy, which she accepts of, becomes his wife." Common throughout the South was the postnuptial ritual in which the couple jumped over a broomstick together, declaring their relationship to the rest of the community. This custom may have originated in Africa, although versions of it were practiced in medieval Europe as well.

Recent studies of naming practices among eighteenth-century African Americans illustrate their commitment to establishing a system of kinship. Frequently sons were named for their fathers, perhaps a way of strengthening the paternal bonds of men forced to live away from their families. Children of both sexes were named for grandparents and other kin. African names were common; names such as Cudjo (Monday), Quow (Thursday), or Coffee (Friday) continued the African tradition of "weekday" names. Later in the century Anglo names became more general. Margery and Moody, slaves of Francis Jerdone of Louisa County, Virginia, named their six children Sam, Rose, Sukey, Mingo, Maria, and Comba, mixing both African and English traditions. Many Africans carried names known only within their community, and these were often African. In the sea island region of the Lower South, such names were common until the twentieth century.

Slave owners generally knew their slaves only by their first names, but many slaves seem to have had surnames. During the Revolution, when many African Americans fled to the British in search of freedom, their names were written down, and these lists generally include full names. Moreover, three of every five black men had surnames different from the owners from whom they had fled. Two male slaves boarding British ships belonged to the Virginia planter George Washington, but only one, Harry Washington, carried his name; the other, Daniel Payne, carried a name that linked him to the place where his parents or grandparents had first labored in America.

Emotional ties to particular places, connections between the generations, and relations of kinship and friendship linking neighboring plantations and farms were the foundation stones of African American community life. Kinship was especially important. African American parents encouraged their children to use family terms in addressing unrelated persons: *auntie* or *uncle* became a respectful way of addressing older men and women, *brother* and *sister* affectionate terms for age mates. *Fictive kinship* may have been one of the first devices enslaved Africans used to humanize the world of slavery; during the Middle Passage, it was common for children to call their elders aunt and uncle, for adults to address all children as son or daughter.

African American Culture

The eighteenth century was the formative period in the development of the African American community, for it was then that the high birth rate and the growing numbers of country-born provided the necessary stability for the evolution of culture. During this period, men and women from dozens of African ethnic groups molded themselves into a new people. Distinctive patterns in music and dance, religion, and oral tradition illustrate the resilience of the human spirit under bondage as well as the successful struggle of African Americans to create a spiritually sustaining culture of their own.

The reluctance of eighteenth-century masters to Christianize their slaves facilitated the adaptation of the African outlook to American conditions. Slave owners feared that baptism would open the way to claims of freedom, or give Africans dangerous notions of universal brotherhood and equality with masters. One frustrated missionary was told by a planter that a slave was "ten times worse when a Christian than in his state of paganism." Because of this attitude, a Protestant minister wrote from South Carolina in the 1770s, most slaves "are to this day as great strangers to Christianity, and as much under the influence of pagan darkness, idolatry and superstition, as they were at their first arrival from Africa." One man's superstition, of course, is another man's religion, and the majority of black southerners before the American Revolution practiced some form of African religion. Large numbers of African Americans were not converted to Christianity until the Great Awakening, which swept across the South after the 1760s (see Chapter 5).

One of the most crucial areas of religious practice concerned the rituals of death and burial. African Americans kept separate graveyards, often decorating them with distinctive markers of African design. The African custom of covering graves with shells and pottery was continued in the colonies. African Americans generally believed that the spirits of their dead would return to Africa. "Some destroy themselves through despair and from a persuasion they fondly entertain, that after death they will return to their beloved friends and native country," wrote one South Carolinian.

The burial ceremony was perhaps the most important of their rituals. They often held it at night to keep it from masters, who objected to the continuation of African traditions. Historical knowledge of these secret proceedings comes from the accounts of a few white observers, from the stories and recollections of slaves, and from the reconstructions of twentieth-century anthropologists. The deceased was laid out, and around the body men and women would shuffle counterclockwise in a slow dance step while singing ancestral songs. The pace gradually increased, finally reaching a frenzied but joyful conclusion. Dance was a form of worship, a kind of prayer, a means of achieving union with the ancestors and the gods. The circle dance was a widespread custom in West Africa, and in America it became known as the *ring shout*. As slaves from different backgrounds joined together in the circle, they were beginning the process of cultural unification.

Music and dance may have formed the foundation of African American culture, coming even before a common language. Many eighteenth-century observers commented on the musical and rhythmic gifts of Africans. Thomas Jefferson, raised on a Virginia plantation, wrote that blacks "are more generally gifted than the whites, with accurate ears for tune and time." And Olaudah Equiano remembered his people, the Ibos, as "a nation of dancers, musicians, and poets." Many Africans were

An African stringed instrument called "mbanza" in America evolved into the "banjo": an animal skin stretched across a gourd with an unfretted wooden neck. The "dirty" sound of the instrument and the style in which it was played echoed the tonic and rhythmic complexity associated with African music. Introduced by slave musicians, by the nineteenth century the banjo had become an American folk instrument used by black and white alike.

accomplished players of stringed instruments and drums, and their style featured improvisation and rhythmic complexity — elements that would become prominent in African American music. In America, slaves re-created African instruments, as in the case of the banjo, and mastered the art of the European violin and guitar. Fearing that slaves might communicate by code, authorities frequently outlawed drums. But using bones, spoons, or sticks or simply "patting juba" (slapping their thighs), slaves produced elaborate multi-rhythmic patterns.

Africans fused these traditions to those of Europe, creating a hybrid musical culture with a strong African foundation. Masters encouraged work songs, since they seemed to increase productivity. Festivals at harvest time, holidays, or on Saturday nights were a favorite amusement of masters and their families, who especially enjoyed the energetic dancing. In the North, where African Americans were more isolated from one another, festivals offered a time to come together. In eighteenth-century New England, blacks held festivals on election day. Country folk came to town to vote, and those with slaves brought them along. In the larger towns, blacks assembled on the common to elect a "governor" of their own. In New York this occasion was known as the Pinkster festival, "the carnival of the African race."

One of the most important developments of the eighteenth century was the invention of an African American language. An English traveler during the 1770s complained he could not understand Virginia slaves, who spoke "a mixed dialect between the Guinea and English." But such a language made it possible for country-born and "salt-water" Africans to communicate. The two most important dialects were Gullah and Geeche, named after two of the African peoples most prominent in the Carolina and Georgia low country, the Golas and Gizzis of the Windward Coast. These creole languages were a transitional phenomenon, gradually giving way to distinctive forms of black English — although in certain isolated areas, such as the sea islands of the Carolinas and Georgia, they persisted into the twentieth century. Modern studies of Gullah and Geeche demonstrate that they included more than 4,000 words from at least twenty-one African dialects and languages.

A common language made it possible to preserve some of the oral traditions of West Africa. Scholars have traced versions of many African American stories directly to African origins. There were many types of stories; perhaps most notable were the trickster tales, in which the weak triumph over the strong by using their wits. The African American tales of Brer (brother) Rabbit were related to stories told among the Ewe people of West Africa. In one, Fox and Bear capture Brer Rabbit by setting out a doll made of tar. When the "tar baby" refuses to answer Rabbit's hello, he gets angry and kicks it, thus entangling himself. But then he tricks Fox and Bear into throwing him into the "terrible" briar patch, and he escapes. Slaves must have identified with Rabbit, but they did not try to romanticize his plight; he had acted rashly in the first place by kicking the tar baby.

The Africanization of the South

The African American community often looked to recently arrived Africans for religious leadership. Ancestor worship, divination, and magic were strengthened by constant African infusions through the eighteenth century. Many of these beliefs and practices had much in common with European folklore, especially magic and medicinal lore. In 1729 the governor of Virginia agreed to free one of his elderly slaves, "who has performed many wonderful cures of diseases," after the man revealed the secret formulas of his medical magic. Throughout the South, many whites had as much faith in slave conjurers and herb doctors as the slaves themselves did. This was but one of many ways in which white and black southerners came to share a common culture. Acculturation was by no means a one-way street; English men and women in the South were also being Africanized.

Slaves worked in the kitchens of their masters, and thus introduced an African style of cooking into colonial diets already transformed by the addition of Indian crops. African American culinary arts are responsible for such southern perennials as barbecue, fried chicken, black-eyed peas, and collard greens. And the liberal African use of red pepper, sesame seeds, and other sharp flavors established the southern preference for highly spiced foods. In Louisiana, a combination of African, French, and Indian elements produced a most distinguished American regional cuisine, exemplified by gumbos and jambalayas.

Mutual acculturation is also evident in many aspects of material culture. Southern basket weaving used Indian techniques and African designs. There was a good deal of woodcarving featuring African motifs. African architectural designs featuring high, peaked roofs (to drain off the heat) and broad, shady porches gradually became part of a distinctive southern style. The West African iron working tradition was evident throughout the South, especially in the ornamentation of the homes of Charleston and New Orleans.

Even more important were less tangible aspects of culture. Slave mothers nursed white children as well as their own. As one English observer wrote, "each child has its [black] Momma, whose gestures and accent it will necessarily copy, for children, we all know, are imitative beings." Thus did many Africanisms pass into the English language of the South: *goober* (peanut), *yam, banjo, okay, tote.* Some linguists have argued that the Southern "drawl," evident among both black and white speakers, derived from the incorporation of African intonations of words and syllables.

African American music and dance also deeply affected white culture. These art forms offer a good example of mutual aculturation. At eighteenth-century plantation dances, the music was usually provided by Africans playing mostly European instruments but also their own instruments, such as the banjo. African American fiddlers were common throughout the South by the time of the Revolution, but the banjo also became the characteristic folk instrument of the white South. Towards the end of the evening, the musicians were often told to play-

some "Negro jigs," and servants were asked to demonstrate the African manner of dancing. They sometimes parodied the elegant and rigid dances of their masters, while whites in turn attempted to imitate African rhythmic dance styles. In such a back-and-forth fashion the traditions of both groups were gradually transformed.

Violence and Resistance

Slavery was a system based on the use of force and violence. Fear underlay the daily life of both masters and slaves. Owners could be humane, but slaves had no guarantees of benevolent treatment, and the kindest master could be mean. Even the most cultured masters of the eighteenth century thought nothing about floggings of fifty or seventy-five lashes. "Der prayer was answered," sang the Africans of South Carolina, "wid de song of a whip." Although the typical planter punished slaves with extra work, public humiliation, or solitary confinement, the threat of the lash was omnipresent. There were also sadistic masters who branded, stabbed, burned, maimed, mutilated, raped, or castrated their slaves.

Yet African Americans demonstrated a resisting

Fugitive slaves flee through the swamps in Thomas Moran's *The Slave Hunt* (1862). Many slaves ran away from their masters, and colonial newspapers included notices urging readers to be on the lookout for them. Some fled in groups or collected together in isolated communities called "maroons," located in inaccessible swamps and woods.

spirit. "You would really be surprised at their per-serverance," one English traveler of the 1740s re-marked, "either from obstinacy or, which I am more apt to suppose, from greatness of soul." In their day-to-day existence they often refused to cooper-ate: they malingered, they mistreated tools and animals, they destroyed the master's property. Flight was also an option, and judging from the advertise-ments placed by masters in colonial newspapers, even the most trusted Africans ran away. "That this slave should run away and attempt getting his liberty, is very alarming," read the notice of one Maryland master in 1755; "he has always been too kindly used," and was "one in whom his master has put great confidence, and depended on him to overlook the rest of the slaves, and he had no kind of provocation to go off." A South Carolinian noted that his absent slave "may possibly have a ticket that I gave him, mentioning he was in quest of a runaway, [and] as I did not mention when he was to return, he may endeavour to pass by that." An analysis of hundreds of eighteenth-century adver-tisements for runaways reveals that 80 percent of them were men, most in their twenties and presum-ably unattached.

Runaways sometimes collected together in semipermanent communities called *maroons,* from the Spanish *cimarron,* meaning wild and untamed. The African communities in Spanish Florida were often referred to as maroons. Indeed, as a whole these mixed African and Creek Indian Florida peo-ples called themselves Seminoles, a name deriving from their pronunciation of *cimarron.* Maroons also settled in the backcountry of the Lower South. In 1771, Georgia's governor warned that north of Savannah "a great number of fugitive Negroes had committed many robberies and insults," and he sent a detachment of militia to destroy their camps. The "black Indian" violence continued, however, and reached catastrophic proportions during the Revo-lution. Although maroons were less common in the Upper South, a number of fugitive communities existed in the Great Dismal Swamp between Virginia and North Carolina. In the 1730s a group of escaped Africans built a community of grass houses and set up a tribal government there, but they were soon dispersed by the authorities.

The most direct form of resistance was revolt. A number of uprisings took place in the Lower South, where slaves were a majority of the population. Three whites were killed in a 1720 insurrection. Ten years later, authorities uncovered a plot in which slaves planned to gather in Charleston, under the pretense of a dance, seize arms, and begin a war on the planter elite. During the subsequent years, as rice production boomed and thousands of Africans were imported to work the fields, tensions ran high. The year 1738 witnessed a series of small uprisings throughout South Carolina and Georgia. Then in September 1739, the largest slave rebellion of the colonial period took place when a group of twenty Angolans sacked the armory in Stono, South Caro-lina. They armed themselves and began a march toward Florida and freedom. Beating drums to attract other slaves to their cause, they grew to nearly one hundred. They plundered a number of planters' homes along the way and killed some thirty colonists. Pausing in a field to celebrate their victory with dance and song, they were overtaken by the militia and destroyed in a pitched battle. That same year there was an uprising in Georgia, proba-bly inspired by the Stono Rebellion. Another took place in South Carolina the following year. As a result of these episodes, the slave trade to Charles-ton was practically cut off for the next ten years.

The second most notable slave uprising oc-curred in New York City. In 1712, twenty-three Africans took an oath of secrecy, which they sealed by sucking each other's blood, and rubbed them-selves with a conjurer's powder to make themselves invisible. Then, in revenge for what they called the "hard usage" of their masters, they armed them-selves with guns, swords, daggers, and hatchets, killed nine colonists, and burned several buildings before being surrounded by the militia. Six of the conspirators committed suicide rather than surren-der. Those captured were hanged, burned at the stake, or broken on the wheel. In 1741 New York authorities uncovered what they thought was an-other conspiracy. Thirteen black leaders were burned alive, eighteen hanged, and eighty sold and shipped off to the West Indies. A family of colonists and a Catholic priest, accused of providing weapons, were also executed.

Wherever masters held slaves there were per-sistent fears of uprisings. But compared with such slave colonies as Jamaica, Guiana, or Brazil, there were few slave revolts in North America. The con-ditions favoring revolt — large African majorities, brutal exploitation with correspondingly low sur-vival rates and little acculturation, and geographic isolation — prevailed only in some areas of the Lower South. Indeed, the very success of African Americans at establishing families, communities, and a culture of their own inevitably made them less likely to take the risks that rebellions required.

The Structure of Empire

Slavery contributed enormously to the economic growth and development of Europe during the colonial era, especially Great Britain just before the industrial revolution of the eighteenth century. Slavery was the most dynamic force in the Atlantic economy during that century, creating the conditions for industrialization. The slave colonies themselves, however, partook little of the economic diversification that characterized industrialization, because planters single-mindedly committed their resources to the expansion and extension of the plantation system.

Slavery the Mainspring

The slave colonies—the sugar islands of the West Indies and the colonies of the South—were responsible for 95 percent of the exports of the British colonies in the Americas during the eighteenth century. Although the slave colonies of the South constituted considerably less than half the population of Britain's mainland North American possessions, they accounted for better than 80 percent of the value of their exports. Moreover, there was the prime economic importance of the slave trade itself, which one economist of the day described as the "foundation" of the British economy, "the mainspring of the machine which sets every wheel in motion." Slavery was, in the words of another Englishman, "the strength and sinews of this western world." Slavery was the most dynamic force in the British empire in the Americas.

The profits of individual investors in the slave system varied widely, of course. Slave traders expected a return of 30 percent or more, but many ventures ended in financial disaster. Profits in sugar production during the boom of the seventeenth century easily exceeded 20 percent, but returns fell during the succeeding century. As late as 1776, however, the British economist Adam Smith wrote that "the profits of a sugar plantation in any of our West Indian colonies are generally much greater than those of any other cultivation that is known either in Europe or America." Economic historians estimate that annual profits during the eighteenth century averaged 15 percent of invested capital in the slave trade, 10 percent in plantation agriculture. Some of the first of England's great modern fortunes were accumulated as a result of slavery's miseries.

But it was slavery's impact on economic development that was most important. The most obvious and direct effect was on the growth of transport: in

The New England artist John Greenwood painted this amusing view of New England sea captains in Surinam in 1757. By the early eighteenth century New England merchant traders like these had become important participants in the traffic in slaves and sugar to and from the West Indies. Northern ports thus became important pivots in the expanding commercial network linking slave plantations with Atlantic markets.

John Greenwood Sea Captains Carousing in Surinam. *Oil on bed ticking. 95.9 × 191.2 cm. The Saint Louis Art Museum, Museum Purchase.*

the eighteenth century better than 10 percent of all English shipping was devoted to the African and American trades. These ships had to be outfitted and provisioned, trade goods had to be manufactured, and the commodities produced on slave plantations had to be processed. The multiplier effects of these activities are best seen in the growth of English cities such as Liverpool and Bristol. There the African and American trades provided employment for an army of ships' crews, dockmen, construction workers, traders, shopkeepers, lawyers, clerks, factory workers, and officials of all ranks down to the humblest employees of the custom house. It was said of Bristol that "there is not a brick in the city but what is cemented with the blood of a slave."

The profits of the slave trade and slave production resulted in huge accumulations of capital, much of it invested in enterprises in these same cities. One historian estimates that during the eighteenth century the slave system generated more than three hundred million pounds in Great Britain alone. This capital funded the first modern banks and insurance companies, and eventually found its way into a wide range of economic activities. In the countryside surrounding Liverpool, capital acquired through slavery was invested in the cotton textile industry. Later, the demand for raw cotton to supply cotton textile factories led to the further expansion of American plantation slavery. The connections between slavery and the growth of industry were clear and dramatic.

Mercantilism

When imperial officials argued that colonies existed solely for the benefit of the mother country, they principally had in mind the great wealth produced by slavery. To insure that this wealth benefited the nation-state, Great Britain and the other European imperial powers created a system of regulations that later became known as *mercantilism*. The essence of mercantilism was the control of the economy by the nation-state. Just as the monarchs of western Europe had extended their control over the political affairs of their nations, so they also sought to control the national and colonial economy. Such a nationalist program was applied most successfully in England, where the monarchy and Parliament undertook to establish a uniform monetary system, to regulate workers and the poor, to encourage agriculture and manufacturing, and to protect themselves with tariff barriers from foreign competition. The state also sought to organize and control colonial trade to the maximum advantage of its own shippers, merchants, manufacturers, and bureaucrats.

The basic assumption of the mercantilists, as an English proponent put it, was that "there is but a certain proportion of trade in the world." They imagined a "zero-sum" world economy, in which total economic gains were equal to total losses. Profits were thought to result from successful speculation, crafty dealing, or simple plunder — all forms of stealing wealth. The institution of slavery confirmed the theory, for it was nothing more than a highly developed system by which some stole the labor of others. The essence of the competition between nation-states, the mercantilists argued, was the struggle to acquire and hoard the fixed amount of wealth that existed in the world. The nation that accumulated the largest treasure would be the most powerful.

Wars for Empire

The mercantilist era was thus a period of intense and violent competition among European nation-states. Wars usually began in the Old World, spilling over into the New, but they also originated in conflicts over the colonies themselves. In the Anglo–Dutch Wars of the 1650s and 1660s, England replaced Holland as the dominant Atlantic power. Then, beginning with King William's War (1689–97), England and France opened a long struggle for colonial supremacy in North America that was not concluded until 1763. (For further discussion of these two conflicts, see Chapter 3.) British wars with the French and Spanish empires in North America filled much of the first half of the eighteenth century. The fighting took place principally at the peripheries of empire, on the frontiers separating Spanish Florida from the Lower South and New France from New England.

In the southern region, these wars had everything to do with slavery. The first fighting of the eighteenth century took place during Queen Anne's War (known in Europe as the War of the Spanish Succession), a conflict that pitted Great Britain and its allies against France and Spain. In 1702 troops from South Carolina invaded Florida, plundering and burning St. Augustine in an attempt to destroy the refuge for fugitive slaves there. Four years later a combined French and Spanish fleet took revenge by bombarding Charleston. The British finally emerged victorious, and in 1713, as part of the Peace of Utrecht, Spain ceded to the English the exclusive right to supply slaves to its American colonies.

The entrance of British slavers into Spanish

ports provided an opportunity for illicit trade, and sporadic fighting between the two empires broke out a number of times over the next two decades. Robert Walpole, British prime minister from 1722 to 1748, wished to avoid the outbreak of full-scale war, but a faction in the House of Commons that wanted to bring even more slave colonies into the British orbit looked forward to smashing the Spanish in the Caribbean. In 1739, at the urging of these men, a certain Captain Jenkins testified before the Commons to the indignities suffered by British merchant sailors at the hands of the Spanish. In a dramatic flourish he produced a dried and withered ear, which he said they had cut from his head. The public outrage that followed this absurd event stirred up an enthusiasm for vengeance, forcing Walpole to finally agree to a war of Caribbean conquest recorded in history as the War of Jenkins' Ear.

The consequences, however, were far from ridiculous. English troops allied with Creek Indians invaded Florida once again, laying waste to the last of the old mission stations but failing to capture St. Augustine. In response, the Spanish, including several companies of African Americans, invaded Georgia. Although the Spanish were defeated seventy-five miles south of Savannah, the campaign resulted in an agreement on the boundary between Georgia and Florida, which was established at its present location. Elsewhere the British were not so lucky: in the Caribbean the imperial fleet suffered disaster at the hands of the Spanish.

In the northern region the principal focus of the struggle was control of the Indian trade. In 1704, during Queen Anne's War, the French and their Algonquian Indian allies raided New England frontier towns such as Deerfield, Massachusetts, dragging men, women, and children into captivity in Canada. In turn, the English mounted a series of expeditions against the strategic French fortress of Port Royal, which they captured in 1710. At the war's conclusion in 1713, France was forced to cede Acadia, Newfoundland, and Hudson's Bay to Great Britain in exchange for guarantees of security for the French-speaking residents of those provinces. Nearly thirty years of peace followed, but from 1740 to 1748 England again went to war against France and Spain. During King George's War (known in Europe as the War of the Austrian Succession), the French attacked the British in Nova Scotia, Indian and Canadian raids again devastated the border towns of New England and New York, and hundreds of British subjects were killed or captured.

The French, allied with the Spanish and Germans, were equally successful in Europe. What finally turned the tide of this war was the capture in 1745 of the French fortress of Louisburg, at the entrance to the Gulf of the St. Lawrence, by an expedition of Massachusetts troops in conjunction with the royal navy. Deprived of the most strategic of its American ports, and fearful of losing the wealth of their sugar islands, France agreed to a negotiated settlement in 1748. Since the outcome was essentially a stalemate, the treaty restored the prewar status quo, returning Louisburg to France. This disgusted the merchants of New England, who wanted to expand their commercial influence in the maritime colonies. Although the treaty left the North American conflict between France and Britain still simmering, it was the first time that the concluding battle of a European war had been fought in North America. Conflict between French and British colonists would begin the next war.

British Colonial Regulation

Mercantilists used means other than war to win the wealth of the world. In the sixteenth century the Spanish monarchy became the first to create a state trading monopoly — the Casa de Contracion — to manage the commerce of its empire. It limited colonial trade to prescribed ports such as Seville or Vera Cruz, protected it from attack and plunder, and established a system of great convoys that crossed the oceans under the protection of well-armed galleons. Lacking the same extensive overseas empire, other European states attempted in the seventeenth century to break into the international contest by chartering large trading monopolies. The East India Company (spices and tea), the Hudson's Bay Company (furs), and the Royal African Company (slaves) were each British state trading monopolies, and all of the major powers had similar organizations.

English manufacturers complained that the merchant-dominated trading monopolies paid too little attention to the export of their products to colonial markets. Reacting to these charges, Parliament passed a series of Navigation Acts from 1660 to 1696. These measures created the legal and institutional structure of Britain's eighteenth-century colonial system. They defined the colonies as both suppliers of raw materials and markets for English manufactured goods. Merchants from other nations were expressly forbidden to trade in the colonies, and all trade had to be conducted in British vessels, including ships built in the colonies themselves. The regulations specified a list of *enumerated goods,* colonial products that could be shipped only to England. These included the products of the southern slave colonies (sugar, molasses, rum, tobacco, rice, and indigo), those of the northern Indian trade (furs and skins), as well as the products essential for supplying the shipping industry (masts, tar, pitch, resin, and turpentine). The bulk of these products were not destined for English consumption, but were reexported elsewhere, to the great profit of English merchants.

England also placed limitations on colonial enterprises that might compete with those at home. A series of enactments — including the Wool Act of 1699, the Hat Act of 1732, and the Iron Act of 1750 — restricted the development of colonial manufactures. Moreover, colonial assemblies were forbidden to impose tariffs on English imports as a way to protect colonial industries. Banking was disallowed, local coinage prohibited, and the export of coin from England forbidden. Badly in need of a circulating medium, Massachusetts illegally minted copper coin, and several colonies issued paper currency, forcing Parliament to explicitly legislate against the practice. The colonists depended mostly upon "commodity money" (furs, skins, or hogsheads of tobacco) and the circulation of foreign currency. The most common form of the latter was the Spanish silver peso, usually called a *dollar* (a transliteration of the German *thaler,* another large silver coin). Official rates of exchange between commodity money, colonial paper, foreign currency, and English pounds allowed this chaotic system to operate without too much difficulty.

Certain British interests pressed for even more stringent restrictions. But as the colonies grew more populated, and as the trade in colonial products increased, the British came to agree that it made little sense to tamper with such a prosperous system. Between 1700 and 1760 the quantity of goods exported from the colonies to the mother country rose 165 percent, while imports from Britain to North America increased by more than 400 percent. Especially important was the size of the North American market for English goods, which by the 1720s exceeded the demand of the West Indian market. Prime Minister Walpole pursued a policy later characterized as *salutory neglect,* in which colonial rules and regulations were not enforced, to the detriment of overall trade and commerce. During the first half of the eighteenth century, the colonists complained very little about the operation of the mercantilist system, in large part because of the lax enforcement.

The Colonial Economy

The colonists were content with the system for another reason: for the most part it operated to their benefit. Despite being restricted to English markets, southern slave owners made healthy profits on the sale of their commodities. They enjoyed a protected market, in which competing goods from outside the empire were heavily taxed. Moreover, agricultural products more than held their value against the price of manufactures, and planters found themselves with steadily increasing purchasing power.

Pennsylvania, New York, and New England, and increasingly the Chesapeake as well, produced grain and flour, meat and dairy products. None of these was included in the list of enumerated goods, and they could thus be sold freely abroad. They found their most ready market in the Caribbean and the Lower South, where food production was slighted in

British Colonial Trade in the Americas (in 1000s of £)				
	Exports to Britain		Imports from Britain	
	£	%	£	%
British West Indies	96,808	64.0	41,653	38.8
Southern Mainland Colonies	47,192	31.2	27,561	25.7
Other Mainland Colonies	7,160	4.7	37,939	35.4
Total	151,160	99.9	107,153	99.9

Source: Eric Williams, *Capitalism and Slavery,* pp. 225–226.

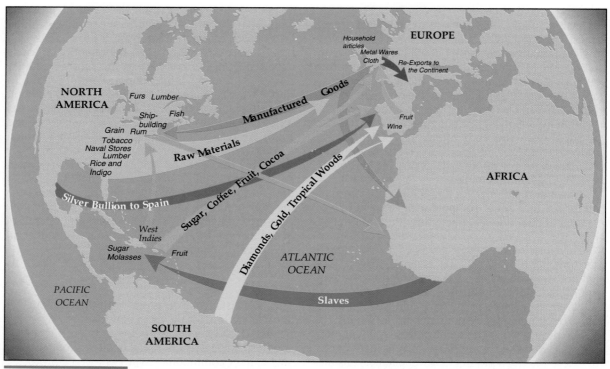

Atlantic Trade Routes

The pattern of commerce between Europe, Africa, and the Americas became known as the "triangular trade." Sailors called the voyage of slave ships from Africa to America the "middle passage" because it formed the crucial middle section of this trading triangle.

favor of sugar and rice. Most of this trade was carried in New England ships. Indeed, the New England shipbuilding industry was greatly stimulated by the allowance under the Navigation Acts for ships built and manned in the colonies. So many ships were built for English buyers that by midcentury nearly a third of all British tonnage was American-made.

The greatest benefits for the port cities of the North came from their commercial relationship to the slave colonies. New England merchants had become important players in the slave trade by the early eighteenth century, and soon thereafter they began to make inroads as well into the export trade of the West Indian colonies. It was in the Caribbean that northern merchants most blatantly ignored mercantilist regulations. In violation of Spanish, French, and Dutch rules, they traded foodstuffs for sugar in foreign colonies, then illegally sent it to England. The Molasses Act of 1733, which Parliament enacted under pressure from English West Indian planters, placed a prohibitive duty on sugar products brought from foreign colonies to North America. Had these regulations been strictly applied, they surely would have caused conflict with the colonists, but in fact enforcement was lax. By 1750, more than sixty distilleries in Massachusetts Bay were exporting over 2 million gallons of rum, most of it produced from illegally obtained sugar. The benefits of the British system (in which British colonial rules and regulations were not enforced) to the North American colonies are clearly shown by such growth and prosperity among the merchants and manufacturers of the port cities.

As early as 1715, the West Indian trade accounted for more than half of the tonnage passing through the port of Boston. The volume of the Caribbean trade remained steady over the next half century, but Boston merchants greatly increased

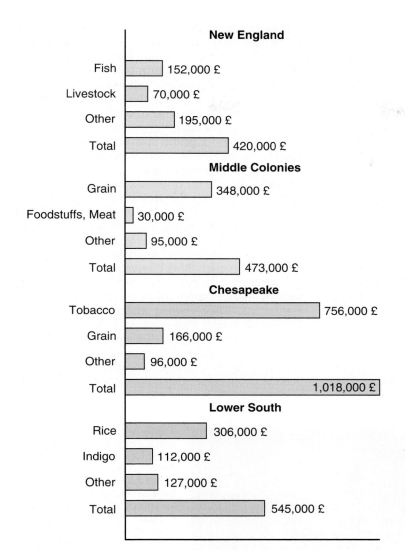

New England
- Fish — 152,000 £
- Livestock — 70,000 £
- Other — 195,000 £
- Total — 420,000 £

Middle Colonies
- Grain — 348,000 £
- Foodstuffs, Meat — 30,000 £
- Other — 95,000 £
- Total — 473,000 £

Chesapeake
- Tobacco — 756,000 £
- Grain — 166,000 £
- Other — 96,000 £
- Total — 1,018,000 £

Lower South
- Rice — 306,000 £
- Indigo — 112,000 £
- Other — 127,000 £
- Total — 545,000 £

Value of Colonial Exports by Region, Annual Average, 1768–1772

With tobacco, rice, and indigo, the Chesapeake and the Lower South were the most valuable exporting regions, although the Middle Colonies were becoming major exporters of grain.

Source: James F. Shepherd and Gary M. Walton, *Shipping, Maritime Trade and the Economic Development of Colonial America* (Cambridge, England: Cambridge University Press, 1972), 211–227.

their commerce with the slave colonies of the Chesapeake and Lower South. A similar pattern is evident in the statistics of other northern ports. The carrying trade in slave products made it possible for the northern and middle colonies to purchase British imports despite the relative absence of valuable products from their own regions. Gradually, the commercial economies of the Northeast and the South were becoming integrated. From the 1730s to the 1770s, for example, while the volume of trade between Great Britain and Charleston doubled, the trade between Charleston and northern ports grew sevenfold. The same happened in Virginia. Mer-

chants in Boston, Newport, New York, and Philadelphia increasingly provided southern planters not only with shipping services, but with credit and insurance. Like London, Liverpool, and Bristol — though on a smaller scale — the port cities of the North became pivots in the expanding trade network linking slave plantations with Atlantic markets. This trade provided northern merchants with the capital that financed commercial growth and development in their cities and the surrounding countryside. Slavery thus contributed to the growth of a score of northern port cities, forming an indirect but essential part of their economies.

SLAVERY AND FREEDOM

The prosperity of the eighteenth-century plantation economy thus improved the living conditions for the residents of northern cities as well as for a large segment of the population of the South, providing them with the opportunity for a kind of freedom unknown in the previous century. The price of prosperity and freedom was the oppression and exploitation of millions of Africans and African Americans. Freedom for white men based on the slavery of African Americans is the greatest paradox of American history.

The Social Structure of the Slave Colonies

At the summit of southern colonial society stood a small elite of wealthy planters, in contrast with the mass of unfree men and women who formed the working population. Slavery had produced a society in which property was concentrated in the hands of a wealthy few. The richest 10 percent of colonists owned more than half the cultivated land and over 60 percent of the wealth. Although there was no colonial aristocracy, no noble titles or royal appointments, the landed elite of the slave colonies came very close to constituting one.

Among the hundred wealthiest Virginians of the 1770s, for example, more than 80 percent had inherited their wealth from their fathers, and a number were third- or fourth-generation colonials. Less than 10 percent were "self-made," and most of these men had acquired their fortunes through commerce or the law. The typical wealthy Virginia planter lived in a tidewater county; owned several thousand acres of prime farmland and more than 100 slaves; resided in a luxurious plantation mansion, built perhaps in the fashionable Georgian style; and had an estate valued at more than 10,000 pounds. Elected to the House of Burgesses, and forming the group from which the magistrates and counselors of the colony were chosen, these "first families of Virginia" — the Carters, Harrisons, Lees, Fitzhughs, Washingtons, Randolphs, and others — were a self-perpetuating governing class.

A similar elite ruled the Lower South, although wealthy masters spent relatively little time on their plantations. They resided instead in fashionable Charleston, where they made up a close-knit group who controlled the colonial government. To be elected to the legislature, a man needed a minimum estate of 2,000 pounds; only the wealthiest 10 percent could claim such a distinction. A number of

Alexander Spotswood Payne and his brother John Robert Dandridge Payne with their African American nurse, painted by an unknown Virginia artist, ca. 1790. White and black southerners lived in intimate contact. White children were breastfed by African nannies, and interracial sex was very much a part of plantation life. But whiteness was the universal badge of freedom, blackness a mark of bondage. Despite their close association, said Thomas Jefferson, the two peoples were divided by "deep rooted prejudices entertained by the whites" and "ten thousand recollections, by the blacks, of the injuries they have sustained."
(Alexander Spotswood Payne and his Brother, John Robert Dandridge Payne, with Their Nurse. 1790–1800. Oil on canvas. 56" H × 69" W (142.2 × 175.2 cm). Virginia Museum of Fine Arts, Gift of Miss Dorothy Payne.

men held considerably more property. When William Elliot, a wealthy Charleston planter, died in the 1770s, he left a home in the city, several plantations with over 420 slaves, and an estate valued at 24,000 pounds. "They live in as high a style here, I believe, as any part of the world," wrote a visitor to Charleston.

A considerable distance separated this slave-owning elite from typical southern landowners. About half the adult white males were small planters and farmers. But while the gap between rich and middling colonists grew larger during the eighteenth century, the prosperity of the plantation economy created generally favorable conditions for this large landed class. Slave ownership, for example, became widespread among this group during the eighteenth century. In Virginia at midcentury, 45 percent of heads of household held one to four slaves. A typical small planter in South Carolina died leaving an estate valued at about 300 pounds. This could include about a hundred acres, eight slaves, seven horses, twenty-four cattle, and a tobacco crop still in the field. Poorer farmers kept a slave or two, who perhaps slept in the loft or the barn.

Despite the prosperity of slavery in the eighteenth century, however, a substantial portion of colonists owned no land or slaves at all. Some rented land or worked as tenant farmers, some hired out as overseers or farm workers, and still others were indentured servants. Throughout the plantation region, landless men constituted about 40 percent of the population. A New England visitor found a "much greater disparity between the rich and poor in Virginia" than at home.

White Skin Privilege

But all the white colonists of eighteenth-century North America shared the privileged status of their skin color. In the early seventeenth century there had been more diversity in views about race. For some, black skin was thought to be a sign of God's curse. "The blackness of the Negroes," one Englishman argued, "proceedeth of some natural infection." But not everyone shared those views. "I can't think there is any intrinsic value in one colour more than another," a second Englishman remarked, "nor that white is better than black, only we think it so because we are so." As slavery became increasingly important, however, Virginia officials took considerable care to create legal distinctions between the status of colonists and that of Africans. Beginning in 1670, free Africans were prohibited from owning Christian servants. Ten years later,

another law declared that any African, free or slave, who struck a Christian would receive thirty lashes on his bare back. One of the most important measures was designed to suppress intimate interracial contacts. Although there were many cases of masters forcing themselves on African women, most of the "mixing" took place between white servants and enslaved Africans. A 1691 act "for prevention of that abominable mixture and spurious issue which hereafter may encrease in this dominion" established severe penalties for interracial sexual relationships. Colonial policy thus deliberately encouraged the growth of racism.

In the Chesapeake, relationships between indentured servants and African slaves had by 1700 produced a rather large group of mulattoes. Although the majority of them, born of African mothers, were slaves, a minority, the children of European women and African men, were free. According to a Maryland census of 1755 — the only one taken during the colonial period that counted mulattoes separately — over 60 percent of mulattoes were slaves. But Maryland mulattoes also made up three-quarters of a small free African American population. This group, numbering about 4,000 in the 1770s, was denied the right to vote, to hold office, or to testify in court — all on the basis of racial background. Denied the status of citizenship enjoyed by even the poorest of white men, free blacks were a pariah group who raised the status of white colonials by contrast.

Racial distinctions thus served as a constant reminder of the common freedom of white colonists, and the common debasement of all blacks, slave or free. Racism set up a wall of contempt between colonists and African Americans. By the final quarter of the eighteenth century, when Thomas Jefferson reflected on what he called "the real distinctions which nature has made" between the races, the ideology of racism was fully developed. "In memory they are equal to the whites," Jefferson wrote of the slaves, but "in reason much inferior," while "in imagination they are dull, tasteless, and anomalous." Jefferson gave no real consideration to the argument of the freed slave Olaudah Equiano that "slavery debases the mind." But he was on firmer ground, perhaps, when he argued that the two peoples were divided by "deep rooted prejudices entertained by the whites" and "ten thousand recollections, by the blacks, of the injuries they have sustained." "I tremble for my country when I reflect that God is just," he concluded in a deservedly famous passage, and "[remember] that his justice cannot sleep forever."

CHRONOLOGY

1441	African slaves first brought to Portugal
1518	Spain grants license to Portuguese slavers
1535	Africans constitute a majority on Hispaniola
1619	First Africans brought to Virginia
1655	English seize Jamaica
1662	Virginia law makes slavery hereditary
1670	South Carolina founded
1672	Royal African Company organized
1691	Virginia prohibits interracial sexual contact
1698	Britain opens the slave trade to all its merchants
1699	Spanish declare Florida a refuge for escaped slaves
1702	South Carolinians burn St. Augustine
1705	Virginia Slave Code established
1706	French and Spanish navies bombard Charleston
1710	English capture Port Royal
1712	Slave uprising in New York City
1713	Peace of Utrecht
1722–48	Robert Walpole leads British cabinet
1733	Molasses Act
1739	Stono Rebellion War of Jenkins' Ear
1740–48	King George's War
1741	Africans executed in New York for conspiracy
1752	Georgia officially opened to slavery
1770s	Peak period of the English colonies' slave trade
1807	International slave trade ended in the United States

CONCLUSION

During the eighteenth century nearly half a million Africans were kidnapped from their homes, marched to the African coast, and packed into ships for up to three months. Eventually they arrived in a confusing New World, where they provided the labor that made colonialism pay. Southern planters, northern merchants, and especially British traders and capitalists benefited greatly from the commerce in slave-produced crops, and that prosperity filtered down to affect many of the colonists of British North America. Slavery was fundamental to the operation of the British empire in North America. Although African Americans received little in return, their labor helped build the greatest accumulation of capital that Europe had ever seen. But despite enormous hardship and suffering, African Americans survived by forming new communities in the colonies, rebuilding families, restructuring language, reforming culture. African American culture added important components of African knowledge and experience to colonial agriculture, art, music, and cuisine. The African Americans of the English colonies lived better lives than the slaves worked to death on Caribbean sugar plantations, but never so good as the men they were forced to serve. As the slaves sang on the Georgia coast: "Dah Backrow Man go wrong you, Buddy Quow."

Additional Readings

MICHAEL CRATON, *Sinews of Empire: A Short History of British Slavery* (1974). An introduction to the British mercantile empire that emphasizes the importance of slavery. Includes a comparison of the mainland colonies with the Caribbean.

PHILIP D. CURTIN, *The African Slave Trade: A Census* (1969). The pioneer work in the quantitative history of the slave trade. All subsequent histories of the slave trade are indebted to Curtin.

HERBERT G. GUTMAN, *The Black Family in Slavery and Freedom, 1750–1925* (1976). A path-breaking history of the development of the African American community in North America. The sections on the eighteenth century provide evidence of the development of multi-generational family and kin networks.

WINTHROP D. JORDAN, *White over Black: American Attitudes toward the Negro, 1550–1812* (1968). Remains the best and most comprehensive history of racial values and attitudes. A searching examination of British and American literature, folklore, and history.

ROBERT W. JULY, *A History of the African People* (1992). A comprehensive history that covers Africa from the ancient world to the industrial present. Discusses the different cultures of West Africa and the effects of the slave trade and European colonization.

DANIEL P. MANNIX AND MALCOLM COWLEY, *Black Cargoes: A History of the Atlantic Slave Trade* (1962). An overview of the slave trade with a focus on the Middle Passage. Rich with horrifying historical testimony.

GERALD W. MULLIN, *Flight and Rebellion: Slave Resistance in Eighteenth-Century Virginia* (1972). Details how the acculturation of Africans in America made resistance possible. Evidence is drawn from colonial manuscripts and newspapers.

HOWARD H. PECKHAM, *The Colonial Wars, 1689–1762* (1964). A lively survey of the wars among Great Britain, France, and Spain in North America, from King Wiliam's War to the French and Indian War.

WALTER RODNEY, *How Europe Underdeveloped Africa* (1974). This highly influential book traces the relationship between Europe and Africa from the fifteenth to the twentieth century, and demonstrates how Europe's industrialization became Africa's impoverishment.

MECHAL SOBEL, *The World They Made Together: Black and White Values in Eighteenth-Century Virginia* (1987). Demonstrates the ways in which both Africans and Europeans shaped the formation of American values, perceptions, and identities.

STERLING STUCKEY, *Slave Culture: Nationalist Theory and the Foundations of Black America* (1987). By concentrating on folklore, the author illuminates the African origins of African American culture. Includes important evidence on African American religion in the era before Christianization.

PETER H. WOOD, *Black Majority: Negroes in Colonial South Carolina from 1670 through the Stono Rebellion* (1974). The classic study of the Lower South in the colonial period. Wood argues that the region was shaped by the interaction of Africans and Europeans.

5 THE CULTURES OF COLONIAL NORTH AMERICA, 1701–1780

● NORTHAMPTON, MASSACHUSETTS

Jonathan Edwards, minister of the Puritan church in Northampton, a rural town on the Connecticut River in western Massachusetts, rose before his congregation and began to preach. His words were frightening. "God will crush you under his feet without mercy, He will crush out your blood and make it fly, and it shall be sprinkled on His garments." Such torments would continue for "millions of millions of ages," and for most people, there could be no hope of relief from hell's fires. "It would be no wonder if some persons, that now sit here in some seats of this meeting house in health, quiet and secure, should be there before tomorrow morning." Edwards believed that the people needed to "have their hearts touched," and he was gratified by the response of the community. "It was in the latter part of December, 1734," he wrote, "that the Spirit of God began extraordinarily to set in, and wonderfully to work among us."

THE PURITANS REVIVE THEIR COMMUNITY

"Before the sermon was done," remembered one Northampton parishioner, "there was a great moaning and crying through the whole house—What shall I do to be saved?—Oh I am going to Hell!—Oh what shall I do for Christ?" Sarah Edwards, the minister's wife, lost "all ability to stand or speak"; occasionally her body would twitch. At the height of her ecstasy, her husband wrote, her "soul dwelt on high, and was lost in God, and seemed almost to leave the body." According to another observer, "the minister was obliged to desist—the shrieks and cries were piercing and amazing." But church membership increased with this style of preaching, and religious fervor swept through the community. Edwards was one of the originators of the American tradition of emotional preaching. But there must have been more to the Northampton revival than the power of one man, for it soon became a movement, spreading to other communities throughout the Connecticut Valley. A few years later an even greater revival, the Great Awakening, swept through all the colonies and plunged Northampton into turmoil once again. There must have been important issues preparing a common ground for these religious revivals.

Founded in 1654 on the site of an Algonquian Indian village, Northampton had grown from its original 50 households to more than 200 by the time of the 1734 revival. The last of the community's land had been parceled out to its farmers. Barred from the north by the French and Indians, and with

The interior of the West Parish Congregational Church of Barnstable, Massachusetts, built in the early eighteenth century, is typical of the meeting houses of New England. Puritan congregations assigned seats according to "estate, office, and age." In 1729 the church in Northampton, Massachusetts, scrapped their old seating plan in which people were sorted by age and sex for a new one ranking family groups according to wealth.

New York to the west, young men had little opportunity to move to new territory, and few could afford to buy land at the high market prices, so they had to rely on gifts or bequests from their fathers. Meanwhile, a small elite of well-to-do families controlled a disproportionately large share of local real estate. From their ranks came the majority of the officials of local and county government, as well as the ministers and elders of the Puritan congregations.

By the time Edwards became pastor in 1729, the authority and influence of the church had declined greatly. In the early days church and community had been one, but as the leaders of the community devoted their energies to the pursuit of wealth, the fire seemed to go out of religion. The congregation adopted rules allowing church membership without evidence of a conversion experience, and some families simply fell away from the church.

When a new meeting house was built to replace the old ramshackle one, a controversy broke out over seating arrangements. The former meeting house had benches on either side of a central passage, with adult men on one side — arranged in order of their ages — and their wives on corresponding seats across the aisle. But after much debate, priority seating in the pews of the new meeting house was given to the town's richest men, and they were allowed to sit with their wives and children. It was an important symbol of change. Edwards wrote that the Northampton community had been divided into "two parties," the rich and the envious.

Many of the town's young people were faced with a bleak future. Because the farm household was the most important economic unit in New England, couples could not marry until young men accumulated land. By the 1730s the typical man was forced to postpone his wedding until he was nearly thirty, all the time living with his parents. One can imagine the frustrations this produced, and there were growing discipline problems at home.

Restless youths began to congregate together, away from the supervision of their parents. "Young people of both sexes [are] getting together in the night," pastor Edwards warned the parents, staging events they called "frolics," that included drinking, dancing, and even "different sexes lying in bed together." Some of the adults made light of their minister's warning; if their young people did not socialize, they said, they would "be ignorant how to behave themselves in company." But according to Edwards, the practice of frolicking "has been one main thing that has led to that growth of uncleanness that has been in the land."

This group of disaffected young people became Edwards's special constituency. The revival began during services he directed at them. Everywhere it was the young people who played the most important role in the movement to restore religious passion. Typical converts were in their early twenties. Moreover, reversing a tendency for women to be more active in the church, young men predominated among the reborn. Edwards and other revival preachers called for a return to the traditions of thePuritan faith. They criticized the worldliness of their communities, joining young people in questioning the order of the world into which they had been born. The Awakening reflected the tensions that had arisen in the maturing communities of the colonies, in which frontier opportunity had given way to the inequities of class.

The revival of religion that shook communities throughout the British colonies was one of the first "national" events in American history. Thousands of people experienced conversion, new sects and churches sprang up, and many old ones split into opposing factions, causing great disruption. The followers of one enthusiastic preacher burned their wigs, jewelry, and fine clothes in a bonfire. Then they marched around the fire, chanting curses at their opponents, whose religious writings were next to go into the flames. In the town of South Hadley, near Northampton, the congregation voted to dismiss their minister, who lacked the emotional fire they wanted in a preacher. When he refused to vacate his pulpit, they pulled him down, roughed him up, and threw him out the church door. Such episodes spoke clearly of the popular passions aroused during the Awakening. According to one minister, "Multitudes were seriously, soberly, and solemnly out of their wits."

The disaffection of young people with the social and economic conditions of the mid-eighteenth century may have prepared the way, but the Great Awakening remained a religious event. Though the social order in Northampton was challenged, it remained intact. After the fervor died down, as it inevitably did, the leading families of the community, who had always been uncomfortable with the implications of Edwards's message, voted their preacher out of the pulpit. He had begun to produce some of the most creative religious and theological writings of the colonial period, works in which he struggled to harmonize sixteenth-century Calvinism with the eighteenth-century philosophy of the Enlightenment. But this meant little to men and women seeking to reestablish tranquility in their community. Edwards spent several years ministering to a congregation of Indians in the Berkshire hills. Then he was called to become president of the new Presbyterian College of New Jersey (later Princeton), but he died soon after assuming office.

The turmoil in Northampton was part of the community tension associated with the maturation of colonial societies

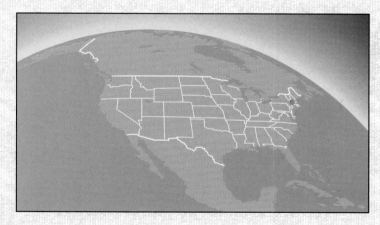

in North America. There were other troubles elsewhere. Like those in Northampton, these subsided, but potential conflicts remained. They would surface once again during the political struggles of the American Revolution.

NORTH AMERICAN REGIONS

By the second quarter of the eighteenth century a half dozen distinct European colonial regions had been established in North America. The British provinces of the Atlantic coastal plain stretched from Newfoundland in the north to Georgia in the south. French communities filled the valley of the St. Lawrence River and were scattered through the continental interior from the Great Lakes down the Mississippi to the Gulf of Mexico. And the Spanish defended the northern borderlands of their Caribbean and Mexican empires with colonies from Florida in the east to Texas and New Mexico in the west.

Population Growth

All the colonial regions of the continent experienced rapid population growth in the eighteenth century. From about 290,000 colonists north of Mexico in 1700, the population expanded to approximately 1.3 million fifty years later. "Our people must at least be doubled every twenty years," Benjamin Franklin wrote of the British colonial population in 1751. And indeed, at an average annual growth rate of 3 percent, the colonial population in the British,

French, and Spanish colonies doubled every generation. The growth rates of preindustrial populations are typically less than 1 percent per year, approximately the rate of Europe's growth in the eighteenth century. But North American colonists experienced what English economist Thomas Malthus, writing at the end of the eighteenth century, described as "a rapidity of increase probably without parallel in history."

High fertility played an important role in this extraordinary growth. In the English colonies, for example, it was common for women to bear seven or more children, and women in the French and Spanish colonies were equally fecund. The Quakers of Pennsylvania, who held very negative views of sexuality, limited their family size through abstinence, but elsewhere in North America fertility approached the biological maximum. Though systematic statistics are not available, the average annual birthrate in all colonial regions was probably better than 50 live births for every 1,000 persons — nearly four times the rate of the late-twentieth-century United States.

More unusual, however, these high birthrates were combined with low death rates. In most colonial areas there were less than 30 deaths for every 1,000 persons; this was 15 or 20 percent lower

Estimated Total Population of the British North American Colonies, 1700–1780

With an annual growth rate of about 3 percent, the population of the British colonies doubled every generation.

Source: Historical Statistics of the United States (Washington, D.C.: Government Publishing Office, 1976), 1168.

than the mortality rates of Europe. (Compare the death rate in the United States today, which is about 9 per 1,000.) Preindustrial populations in Europe suffered dramatic periodic losses, as during a series of bad harvests between 1740 and 1743, when death rates in some localities rose as high as several hundred per thousand. But blessed with fertile lands and the effectiveness of Indian agricultural techniques, North America simply had no famines. Disease continued to ravage Indian communities, but for colonists, most of whom avoided the congestion of cities and lived in the open air of the countryside, North America was a remarkably healthy environment. Most important for the growth of population was the relatively low level of infant mortality and the extraordinary number of people who survived to reproductive age.

The combination of high fertility and low mortality accounts for most of the growth of the North American colonial population. The expanding population comprised a number of distinctive colonial regions in North America, each with its characteristic forms of community life. These regions would dramatically shape the history of the continent.

The Spanish Borderlands

The most populous Spanish colony in North America continued to be New Mexico. Its population in 1750 stood at approximately 10,000 colonists — two-thirds of them living in the four principal towns of Santa Fe, Santa Cruz, Albuquerque, and El Paso — and 20,000 Pueblo Indians, their numbers decimated by disease. New Mexicans spread out from their original communities along the Rio Grande to establish new farming and ranching settlements to the east and north. There were also new colonial outposts along the northern borders of New Spain. Concerned about French movement into the lower Mississippi River valley, the Spanish established a number of presidios (military posts) on the fringes of Louisiana, and in 1716 began constructing a string of Franciscan missions among the Indian peoples of Texas. By 1750 the settlement at San Antonio de Bexar, which included the mission later known as the Alamo, had become the center of this developing frontier province. Ranching and farming communities also spread along the lower Rio Grande valley. In present-day Arizona, west of New Mexico, Jesuit missionaries led by Father Eusebio Kino moved into the lower Colorado and Gila River valleys in the 1690s, founding missions among the desert Indians. One of these, San Xavier del Bac, near Tucson, is

acclaimed the most striking example of Spanish colonial architecture in the United States. The missionaries introduced a ranching system that dominated the region's economy for the next 200 years.

Midcentury found the Spanish considering new outposts along the California coast. Juan Cabrillo, an associate of Hernando Cortes, had first explored the coastal waters in 1542, discovering the fine harbor at San Diego. In 1603 the explorer Sebastián Vizcaíno had come upon Monterey Bay. But the Spanish did little to follow up on these finds. Finally, in 1769, acting on royal fears of Russian expansion from the north (for a discussion of Russian America, see Chapter 9), officials in Mexico City ordered Gaspar de Portolá, governor of Baja California, to march north. With him were Franciscan missionaries led by Junípero Serra, *presidente* of the missions in Baja. At San Diego, Portolá and Serra founded the first mission and pueblo complex in present-day California. Portolá then proceeded overland, becoming the first European to explore the interior valleys and mountains of California, and in 1770 he and Serra established their headquarters at Monterey. Two years later Juan Bautista de Anza established an overland route from southern Arizona across the blistering deserts to California, and in 1776 he led a colonizing expedition that founded the pueblo of San Francisco. Over the next fifty years the number of California settlements grew to include twenty-one missions and a half dozen presidios and pueblos, including the town of Los Angeles. Founded in 1781 by a group of mestizo settlers from Sinaloa, Mexico, Los Angeles by the end of the century had become the largest town in California, with a population of 300.

The communities of the Spanish borderlands were situated on the far north of the empire, linked to more prosperous Mexico by tenuous overland or ocean connections. Isolated, experiencing relatively little in-migration, the colonial population was native-born within a generation. Most were farmers or ranchers who had their own small homesteads but shared grazing, timber, and water rights with others in their communities. As population grew, the pressure on available resources increased, much like the situation in colonial Northampton. These scarce resources were overseen by local councils of elder men, who appointed local managers. But there were also echoes of European feudalism. Many common people owed labor service or rents to the landlord class. Situated as they were, however, in the backwater of empire, these lords lacked the means of acquiring great wealth. While the *ricos* — the dons and doñas — lived a life of elegance compared with

The church of San Xavier del Bac, constructed in the late eighteenth century, is located a few miles south of the city of Tucson, where Jesuit Father Eusebio Kino founded a mission among the Pima Indians in 1700. Known as the White Dove of the Desert, it is acclaimed as the most striking example of Spanish colonial architecture in the United States.

the peons, all the people of the borderlands shared in the relative poverty of their region.

Most colonists were mestizos, although the acquisition of property could "whiten" one's ancestry, and the *ricos* usually claimed pure Spanish heritage. One of the preoccupations of the elite was making sure daughters married men who could claim Spanish descent. Among wealthy and aspiring families, therefore, young women were sheltered and isolated from society. Spanish law, though, granted married women impressive rights to property, allowing them far greater autonomy than that enjoyed by the women of the British colonies. Among the common people, mixture with Indians continued. The powerful assimilation of cultures that took place throughout the Spanish borderlands is evident in the blend of European and native styles in the adobe architecture of the Southwest.

A distinguishing mark of these colonial communities was their close association with the mission system. Conquest meant conversion, and conversion, it was hoped, led Indians toward "civilization." The plan was to transform Indians into Christians and loyal subjects by educating them and, more important, putting them to work raising cattle and crops. The most extensive mission system was that of California. Indian labor, directed by the mission priests, produced a flourishing local economy based on extensive herds of horses, cattle, and sheep as well as irrigated farming. One of the most prosper-

ous missions was San Gabriel, whose large vineyards and orchards produced fine wines and brandies. Indians also constructed the adobe and stone churches, built on Spanish and Moorish patterns, whose ruins have become the symbol of colonial California.

Often forgotten in nostalgia about the missions, however, is the force required to keep the system functioning. The harsh discipline included shackles, solitary confinement, and whipping posts. There was resistance from the very beginning. At Mission Santa Cruz, a priest who thrashed the Indians too often was murdered. In 1775 the villagers around San Diego rose up and killed several priests. The history of many missions was punctuated by revolts. But the arms and organization of Spanish soldiers were usually sufficient to suppress uprisings. Another form of protest was flight; sometimes whole villages fled to the inaccessible mountains. Observers noted the despondency of mission Indians. "I have never seen any of them laugh," one European visitor wrote. "I have never seen a single one look anyone in the face. They have the air of taking no interest in anything." Disease and a plummeting birthrate led to a dramatic population decline. At the beginning of the nineteenth century the mission population numbered about 20,000 Indians. This represented a decline of about a third in thirty years or less. By that time, many of the "neophytes" had grown up at the missions and knew no other way of life, and the Spanish stood a reasonable chance of building a solid native colonial population.

Thus did the Catholic Church play a dominant role in the community life of the borderlands, just as the Puritan Church did in New England communities. In the eighteenth century, religion was no private affair. It was a deadly serious business dividing nations into warring camps, and the Spanish were the special protectors of the traditions of Rome. The object of colonization, one colonial promoter wrote, was "enlarging the glorious gospel of Christ, and leading the infinite multitudes of these simple people that are in error into the right and perfect way of salvation." These words were written by the English imperialist Richard Hakluyt in 1584, but they could as easily have come from Eusebio Kino or Junípero Serra. In the Spanish colonies, Catholicism was part of the organized apparatus of empire, and religious dissent was not allowed. Certain of the truth of their "right and perfect way," the Spanish could see no reason for tolerating the errors of others.

The French Crescent

In France, as in Spain, church and state were interwoven. During the seventeenth century the kings' prime ministers, Cardinal Richelieu and Cardinal Mazarin, laid out a fundamentally Catholic imperial policy, and thus did the French construct a second Catholic empire in North America. In 1674, church and state collaborated in the establishment of the bishopric of Quebec. Under aggressive leadership that office founded local seminaries, oversaw the appointment and review of priests, and laid the foundation of the resolutely Catholic culture of New France. Meanwhile, Jesuits missionaries continued to carry Catholicism deep into the continent. The eighteenth-century struggle between the British and French empires in North America was perceived to be a continuation of the European religious wars.

The number of French colonists rose from less than 15,000 in 1700 to more than 70,000 at midcentury, an impressive rate of growth. Wishing to dominate the heart of the continent and block British westward expansion, the French used their trade network and alliances with the Indians to establish a great crescent of military posts and settlements. These fortifications extended from the mouth of the St. Lawrence, through the Great Lakes, and down the Mississippi River from Illinois to the Gulf of Mexico. The entrance to the Gulf of the St. Lawrence was protected by the garrison town of Louisburg, on Cape Breton Island; the city of New Orleans guarded the other end of the crescent at the mouth of the Mississippi. The French thus laid a thin colonial cover over a vast territory, and with it the basis for what they hoped would be further development. True, British colonists far outnumbered the French, observed a military officer of New France, but numbers were not of first importance, for "the Canadians are brave, much inured to war, and untiring in travel. Two thousand of them will at all times and in all places thrash the people of New England."

The heart of the French empire in North America were the farming communities of *habitants* along the banks of the St. Lawrence from above Quebec City to below Montreal, and on the Bay of Fundy in Acadia. There were also farming communities in the Illinois country, which shipped wheat down the Mississippi to supply the sugar plantations of Louisiana. By the mid-eighteenth century, it was these Louisiana plantations — extending along the river from Natchez and Baton Rouge to New Orleans — that constituted the most profitable French colony in North America.

Throughout French America, colonists recreated the *long-lot* pattern of the St. Lawrence; it was the distinctive French stamp on the landscape. Aerial photographs of the Mississippi reveal the persistence of this pattern, and characteristic French colonial houses survive in locations such as Ste. Genevieve, Missouri. The long-lot pattern was also transplanted along the upper Mississippi, at places such as Kaskaskia and Prairie du Chien and at the strategic passages of the Great Lakes — Mackinac, Sault Ste. Marie, and Detroit. In 1750 Detroit was a fort community with a small administrative center, several stores, a Catholic church, and 100 households of mestizo, or, to use the French term, *métis,* families. French and métis farmers worked the land along the river, and nearby were villages inhabited by more than 6,000 Ottawa, Potawatomi, and Huron Indians.

Such communities combined French and Indian elements. Detroit looked like "an old French village," said one observer, except that its houses were "mostly covered with bark," in Indian style. "It is not uncommon to see a Frenchman with Indian shoes and stockings, without breeches, wearing a strip of woolen cloth to cover what decency requires him to conceal," wrote another; "yet at the same time he wears a fine ruffled shirt and a laced waistcoat, with a fine handkerchief on his head."

Family and kinship were also cast in the Indian pattern. Households frequently consisted of several related families, but wives limited their fertility and bore an average of only two or three children. There were arranged marriages and occasional polygamy,

The persistence of French colonial long lots in the pattern of modern landholding is clear in this enhanced satellite photograph of the Mississippi River near New Orleans. Long lots, the characteristic form of property holding in New France, were designed to offer as many settlers as possible a share of good bottom land as well as a frontage on the waterways, which served as the basic transportation network.

but women had easy access to divorce and enjoyed property rights. Yet the people focused their activities on commerce, and identified themselves overwhelmingly as Catholic. Choosing a path of mutual accommodation, the French and Indians established some of the most interesting and distinct communities in North America. They contrasted dramatically with the completely English communities of New England, like the one in Northampton.

Colonial Government

The administration of both the Spanish and French colonies was highly centralized. New France was ruled by a superior council including the royal governor and intendant, as well as the bishop of Quebec. In New Spain, the Council of the Indies and the royal viceroy had direct executive authority over all political affairs. Thus the far-flung communities of the French crescent and the Spanish borderlands developed few representative institutions of self-government.

The situation in the British colonies was quite different. During the early eighteenth century the British government of Prime Minister Robert Walpole worked on the assumption that a decentralized administration would best accomplish the nation's economic goals. Contented colonies, Walpole argued, would present far fewer problems. "One would not strain any point where it can be of no service to our King or country," a British official advised the governor of South Carolina in 1722; "the government should be as easy and mild as possible." The Board of Trade, empowered by Parliament to manage the colonies, played a coordinating rather than an executive function. Armed with royal charters guaranteeing a measure of independence and self-government, the British colonies acted like separate provinces. They argued and contested with each other as well as with the mother country.

Each of the British colonies was administered by royally appointed governors and constituent assemblies. Because property holding was relatively widespread, the proportion of adult white men enjoying the right to vote for representatives to the assembly was 50 percent or higher in all the British colonies.

By proportion, this was the largest electorate in the world. In contrast, because of restrictions on the franchise, two-thirds of the political boroughs of eighteenth-century England, each with populations in the tens of thousands, had electorates of 500 or fewer voters.

A large electorate, however, did not mean that colonial politics were democratic. The world view of the British was founded on the principle of deference to authority. The well-ordered family — in which children were to be strictly governed by their parents and wives by their husbands — was the model for civil order. The occupant of each rung on the social ladder was entitled to the deference of those below. Members of subordinate groups, which in some colonies amounted to nine of every ten adults in the population, were denied the right to vote and hold public office. This was a world of hierarchies, of lesser born and better born, slaves and servants, as well as racial and ethnic ranks in which Africans, Indians, and other groups were considered social inferiors to Englishmen. In the words of Britain's eighteenth-century imperial battle song:

Rule, Britannia, rule the waves;
Britons never will be slaves.

This ideology of deference demanded that leadership be entrusted to men of merit, a quality closely associated with social position and wealth. Thus, at all levels British colonial government was dominated by an elite. In New England towns, such as Northampton, John Adams remembered after the Revolution, "you will find that the office of justice of the peace, and even the place of representative, which has ever depended only on the freest election of the people, have generally descended from generation to generation, in three or four families at most." Likewise, large landowners and planters were most likely to be elected to serve on the county court, the most important institution of local government outside of New England. Provincial councils and assemblies were also controlled by the elite of planters, merchants, and professionals.

The important political developments in eighteenth-century British North America, then, had little to do with democracy. To educated British colonists, the word *democracy* implied rule by the mob, the normal order of the world turned upside down. Over the century, however, there was an important movement toward stronger institutions of representative government. By midcentury most colonial assemblies had achieved considerable power over provincial affairs, and enjoyed parity with governors and imperial authorities. They collected local revenues and allocated funds for government programs, asserted the right to audit the accounts of public officers, and in some cases even acquired the power to approve the appointment of provincial officials. Royal governors sometimes balked at such claims of power, but because the assemblies controlled the purse strings, most governors were unable to resist this trend.

The potential power of the assemblies was compromised somewhat by competition among elite families for patronage and government contracts. The royal governors who were most successful at realizing their agendas were those who became adept at playing off one provincial faction against another. Nevertheless, all this conflict had the important effect of schooling the colonial elite in the art of politics. It was not democratic politics, but it nevertheless held important implications for the development of American institutions.

New England

In New England, Puritan congregations governed local communities. Just as New Spain and New France had their official church, so did New England, except that its was Puritan rather than Roman Catholic. Under the New England plan, the local church of a community such as Northampton, in Massachusetts, was free to run its own affairs under the guidance of the General Court. The Puritan colonies allotted each congregation a small tract of land. Members divided this land among themselves on the basis of status and seniority, laying out central villages and building churches (called *meeting houses*) that were maintained through taxation. All adult male church members constituted the *freemen* of the town, and thus there was very little distinction between religious and secular authority. At the town meeting the freemen chose their minister, voted on his salary and support, and elected local men to offices ranging from constable to town clerk to fence viewer. Thus the Puritan tradition emphasized the importance of autonomous community life.

The establishment of Puritanism, however, came at the price of repression. The Puritans left England not to create a society where religion could be freely practiced, but to establish their own version of the "right and perfect way." Their notion of liberty was consistent with severe restraints upon individuals. The General Court, for example, passed a statute threatening that "if any man shall exceed the bounds of moderation, we shall punish him severely." Specifics were left to the imagination. Not only did the Puritans exile dissidents such as Roger Williams and Anne Hutchinson (see Chapter 3); they banned Anglicans and Baptists, and they jailed, tortured, and even executed Quakers, using a gallows set up on Boston Common. In *The Bloudy Tenent of Persecution,* published in London in 1644, Roger Williams, the leader of dissenting Rhode Island, made one of the first formal arguments for religious toleration, writing that "forced worship stinks in God's nostrils." After the excesses of the English Civil War, the restored king, Charles II, declared that "the sad experience" of religious strife during that period demonstrated "that there is very little fruit of all these forcible courses," and ordered a stop to the persecution of Quakers in Massachusetts.

The new climate of opinion was best expressed by the English philosopher John Locke in his *Letter on Tolerance* of 1688. Churches were voluntary societies, he argued, and could work only through persuasion. Repression of dissent in these churches only insured that men and women went through the motions of official religious practice without really believing in it, and thus bred hypocrisy. Moreover, the fact that a religion was sanctioned by the state was no evidence of its truth, since different nations had different official religions. Consequently, the state had no legitimate concern with religious belief. There were religious matters, Locke admitted, that could not be tolerated; he argued for continuing to withhold tolerance from Catholics, because he considered their allegiance to the pope a form of treason, and from atheists, because he believed a man who did not believe in God could not be trusted to take a valid oath. Locke's ideas were embodied in the Toleration Act, passed by Parliament in 1689. Protestant dissenters were allowed to practice their religion in authorized places, although the Church of England continued to enjoy tax support.

New England at first resisted the implications of the Toleration Act. But under pressure from English authorities, Massachusetts and Connecticut reluctantly allowed other Protestant denominations to begin practicing their religion openly in 1700, although Congregationalism remained officially sup-

---

North American Cultural Regions

By the middle of the eighteenth century, a number of distinctive colonial regions had been established in North America.

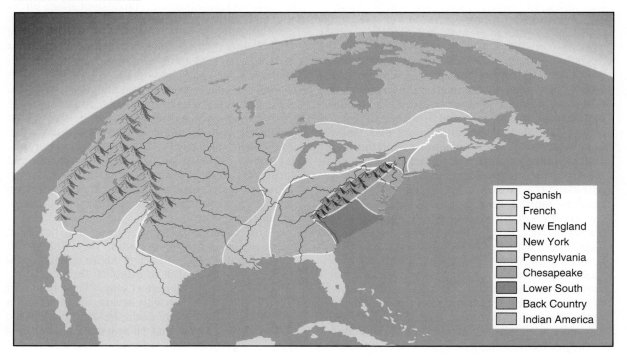

☐	Spanish
☐	French
☐	New England
☐	New York
☐	Pennsylvania
☐	Chesapeake
☐	Lower South
☐	Back Country
☐	Indian America

ported through taxation. The Society for the Propagation of the Gospel, which the Church of England organized in 1701 as its missionary agency in North America, founded a large number of Anglican churches in the colonies over the next half century, many of them in New England. By midcentury, there were Anglican, Baptist, and Presbyterian congregations in many New England towns. But in New England, the Congregational Church was not "disestablished" until well after the Revolution, and not until 1833 in Massachusetts.

The system of town and church government was well suited to population growth. Largely because of natural increase, the 90,000 people of 1700 had grown to 360,000 fifty years later. As towns grew too large for the available land, groups of residents left together, "hiving off" to form new towns elsewhere. During the eighteenth century, as the Congregationalists lost their position of absolute dominance, a pattern of family migration gradually overtook this unique tradition of group settlement. But the cohesive forces of church and town remained stronger in New England communities than elsewhere. On average, the rate of persistence was greater in New England towns than anywhere in the British colonies: in any one decade, only 10 or 15 percent of the residents left. The region was knit together by an intricate network of roads and rivers, and the landscape gradually took on an appearance of stability and permanence, with fields and meadows enclosed by stone walls. Dotting the landscape were simple yet substantial timber-framed wooden farmhouses in the traditional salt-box and Cape Cod styles. Many still stand today.

Owing to a relatively short growing season and poor soil, New England farms produced few commercial crops. Most families grew corn and rye, vegetables and fruit, and bartered them with others in the community. Eight of ten families owned 50 to 100 acres, land enough to support themselves. As a result, New England's distribution of wealth was the most egalitarian on the continent, and perhaps in the entire eighteenth-century Atlantic world. After the Indians of southern New England suffered their final defeat in King Philip's War (1675–76), Puritan farm communities took up most of the available land of Massachusetts, Connecticut, and Rhode Island over the next seventy-five years. Northern Algonquians, allied with the French in Quebec, however, maintained a defensive barrier preventing New Englanders from expanding into Maine, New Hampshire, and the region later called Vermont. By midcentury, then, as the result of growing population and limited area, New England was reaching the limit of its land supply.

The "House of the Seven Gables" in Salem, Massachusetts, was constructed in the seventeenth century. In this style of architecture, function prevailed over form as structures grew to accommodate their residents; rooms were added where and when they were needed. In England, wood for building was scarce, but the abundance of forests in North America created the conditions for a golden age of wood construction.

Young men unable to obtain land in hometowns such as Northampton often moved to the towns and cities of the seaboard, for New England also enjoyed a strong seafaring tradition. Fishing and shipping had first become important during the late seventeenth century, as merchants struggled to find a successful method of earning foreign exchange. The expanding slave market in the South opened new opportunities for them, and led to the growth of thriving coastal ports such as New Haven, Newport, Salem, and Boston. Merchants there participated widely in the markets of the Atlantic. Although the overwhelming majority of the people continued to live in the countryside, by midcentury New England had become the most urban of North America's regions. Boston, the largest city in the British colonies, was the metropolis of a region that included not only New England but the maritime settlements of Nova Scotia and Newfoundland as well, where New England merchants dominated commerce and recruited seamen for their fishing and shipping fleets.

Travelers moving from New York to Boston along the Post Road could hear the patterns of speech change. The Yankee twang, high-pitched and nasal, sounded harsh to outsiders. *Harvard* was pronounced "Haa-v'd," but *follow* became "foller" and *asked* became "arst." In 1750 a traveler could tell by listening that New England was a clearly demarked region.

Immigration

Immigration had little effect on the growth of population in New England, New France, and the Spanish Borderlands. The Spanish monarchy required any subject wishing to emigrate to obtain a license — a difficult process — and filled the demand for labor with thousands of African slaves. Dedicated to keeping its colony Catholic, France turned down the thousands of Protestant Huguenots who desperately sought emigration to Canada. English colonial officials of the late seventeenth century also held a negative view of movement from the mother country. Following the devastation of the Civil War, and particularly after fire and plague ravaged the city of London, many expressed fears about "underpopulation." A total of 150,000 English men and women had relocated to British North America during the seventeenth century, a massive migration that provided the colonies with a substantial population base. But by 1700 English emigration had been reduced to a trickle. In New England, authorities demanded that new arrivals adhere strictly to the Puritan tradition, and in the early eighteenth century the first Presbyterian settlers from the north of Britain were greeted by hostile mobs.

Committed to promoting the growth of their North American colonies, however, British colonial officials began to open the way for non-English immigrants, something the French and Spanish were unwilling to do. As early as the 1680s, William Penn, wishing to populate his proprietary colony of Pennsylvania, received permission to recruit settlers in Holland, France, and the German principalities along the Rhine River. Other colonies began sending recruiting agents to Europe as well. Most British colonies enacted liberal naturalization policies during the early eighteenth century. Aliens who professed Protestantism and swore allegiance to the English crown were allowed to become free "denizens," with all the freedoms and privileges of natural-born subjects. In 1740 Parliament passed a general naturalization law for all the British colonies, which forced even New England to open the door to immigrants. There continued, however, to be severe restrictions throughout the British colonies on the naturalization of Catholics and Jews.

Movements of European men, women, and families in search of land or work was common before this great cross-Atlantic migration began. North America was simply one of many destina-

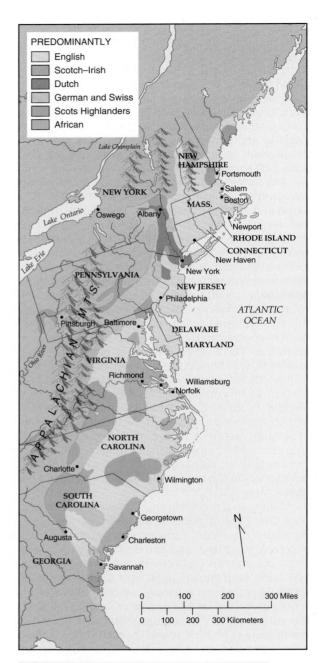

Distribution of Ethnic Groups in British North America

The first federal census of 1790 revealed the remarkable ethnic diversity of the eighteenth-century British colonies. New England was predominantly English, but portions of the South were predominantly African American, and Pennsylvania and the Backcountry were ethnic patchworks.

tions. Mobility was particularly significant in the German communities of the Rhine, especially after they were struck by devastating warfare during the early eighteenth century. Soon thereafter, German emigration to the colonies began to rise, and before the Revolution at least 100,000 Germans settled in North America, where they were known as the Dutch (from *Deutsch,* their self-designation in German). Another area of importance was the northern British Isles. Squeezed by economic hardship, by tariff regulations that hurt their stock-raising economy, and by religious discrimination, large numbers of North Britons from Scotland and northern Ireland emigrated to North America. An estimated 250,000 of them arrived before the end of the colonial period.

The results of the first federal census, taken in 1790, provide a snapshot of the ethnic origins of the eighteenth-century population of British America. Less than half the population was English in origin and nearly a fifth was African; 15 percent were Irish or Scottish, and 7 percent German, with other ethnic backgrounds making up the remainder. There were significant differences by region. Because of its restrictive policies and attitudes, New England remained more than three-quarters English. Pennsylvania, however, was only a quarter English and nearly 40 percent German. The region known as the backcountry — which ran along the Appalachian Mountains from western Pennsylvania to Georgia and over the crest to Tennessee and Kentucky — was populated largely by North Britons. The population of the coastal South was nearly half African. The legacy of eighteenth-century immigration to the British colonies was a population of unprecedented diversity.

The Middle Colonies

New York, with one of the most ethnically diverse populations on the continent, offered a striking contrast to New England, the most homogeneous. The society that developed along the lower Hudson River, including counties in northern New Jersey (long known as West Jersey) as well as New York, was at midcentury a mosaic of ethnic communities: the Dutch of Flatbush, the Flemish of Bergen, the Huguenots of New Rochelle, and the Scots of Perth Amboy, to mention but a few. Africans, both slave and free, made up more than 15 percent of the lower Hudson population. The population of New York and the adjacent New Jersey counties grew from about 25,000 in 1700 to more than 100,000 in 1750, greatly increasing the density of the settlements within easy reach of New York City. Congregations of Puritans,

Baptists, Quakers, and Jews worshiped without legal hindrance. These different communities long retained their ethnic and religious distinctions. There was also a great deal of intermingling, which made New York a cultural melting pot.

Less attractive to immigrants were the rich lands along the upper Hudson, which New York's governors had carved into great manors and be-

---

The Ancestry of the British Colonial Population
The legacy of eighteenth-century immigration to the British colonies was a population of unprecedented ethnic diversity.

Source: Thomas L. Purvis, "The European Ancestry of the United States Population," *William and Mary Quarterly, 61* (1984):85–101.

1700

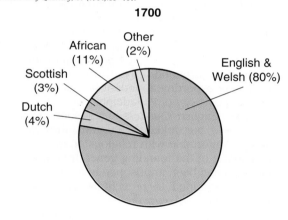

African (11%)
Other (2%)
Scottish (3%)
English & Welsh (80%)
Dutch (4%)

1755

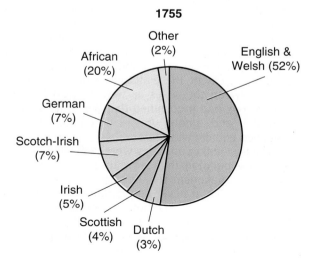

Other (2%)
African (20%)
English & Welsh (52%)
German (7%)
Scotch-Irish (7%)
Irish (5%)
Scottish (4%)
Dutch (3%)

stowed on favored families. Rather than selling these to settlers, the landlords of Fordham, Pelham, Scarsdale, Courtlandt, and Livingston chose to rent this farmland to tenants, mostly descendants of the earliest Dutch immigrants. Class differences here were sharp, and wealthy manor lords ruled imperiously over rural society. New York was "a monstrous monopoly," declared an official from neighboring Pennsylvania.

The Quaker colony, however, was what one German immigrant called "heaven for farmers." Pennsylvania's proprietors were wiling to sell their land to anyone who could pay the relatively modest prices. Thus as the region around New York City filled up, immigrants were attracted by the thousands to Philadelphia, Pennsylvania's port of entry on the Delaware River. During the eighteenth century the population of this region — which included the bordering counties of East Jersey, Delaware, and northern Maryland as well — grew more dramatically than any other in North America. From fewer than 30,000 people in 1700, the population reached nearly 200,000 by 1750. Immigration played the dominant role in achieving this unprecedented annual growth rate of nearly 4 percent. Boasting some of the best farmland in North America, the region was soon exporting abundant produce through the growing port city of Philadelphia.

The English Quakers were soon a minority population, but unlike the Puritans, they were generally comfortable with religious and ethnic pluralism. Many of the founding generation of American Quakers had been imprisoned in England, and they were determined to prevent a repetition of this injustice in their own province. William Penn had been prominent in the struggle for religious toleration. "Force never yet made a good Christian," he argued in 1670. Indeed, the Quakers were opposed to all signs of rank, refusing to doff their hats to superiors but greeting all comers, whatever their station, with the extended hand of brotherhood. To a remarkable extent, these attitudes extended to relations between the sexes as well. English founder George Fox had proclaimed that "in souls there is no sex," and among American Friends women preached equally with men.

These Quaker attitudes were well suited to the diverse population that grew up in Pennsylvania. Although Quakerism remained the religion of the governing elite, it never became an official church. The Germans were Lutherans or Calvinists, the North Britons were Presbyterian, and there were Anglicans and Baptists as well. These churches constituted one of the cornerstones of community life.

The institutions of government were another pillar of local communities. Colonial officials appointed justices of the peace from among the leading men of each community, and these justices provided judicial authority for the countryside. Property-owning farmers chose their own local officials. Country communities were tied by kinship bonds and by bartering and trading among neighbors. The substantial stone houses and great barns of the eastern Pennsylvania countryside testified to the social stability and prosperity. The communities of the middle colonies, however, were more loosely bound than those of New England. Rates of mobility were considerably higher, with about half the population moving on in any given decade. In New England towns like Northampton, land was controlled by the community; but in Pennsylvania, since land was sold in individual lots to families rather than in communal parcels, farmers dispersed themselves at will over the open countryside. Villages gradually developed at crossroads and ferries, but with very little forethought or planning. Emphasizing individual settlement, Pennsylvania, not New England, provided the model for American expansion.

The Backcountry

By midcentury, Pennsylvania's exploding population had pushed beyond the first range of the Appalachian highlands. Settlers occupied the northern reaches of the Great Valley, which extended southwest from Pennsylvania into Virginia. Although these settlers hoped to become commercial farmers, they began more modestly, planting Indian corn and raising hogs, hunting in the woods for meat and furs, and building log cabins. Their strategy had originated with the settlers of the New Sweden colony on the lower Delaware River. Scandinavian immigrants brought their hunting traditions and introduced log cabin construction to North America. From the Delaware Indians they incorporated the methods of New World farming and woodland hunting, just as the Indians took from them the use of firearms and metal tools and began to build log structures of their own.

The movement into the Pennsylvania and Virginia backcountry that began during the 1720s was the first of the great pioneer treks that took Americans into the continental interior. Many, perhaps most, of these pioneers held no legal title to the

This two-story Pennsylvania log house, built in the early eighteenth century, is one of the oldest surviving examples of the method and style of log construction introduced in America by the Scandanavian colonists on the lower Delaware River. Learning New World farming and woodland hunting techniques from the Indians, these settlers forged a tradition of settlement that proved enormously successful for pioneers.

lands they occupied; they simply hacked out and defended their squatters' claims. Coming from the northern borders of England and Ireland, where clan and ethnic violence was endemic, these people adapted well to the violence of the backcountry. The wealthy colonists who themselves planned to acquire and sell those western lands thought of the pioneers as barbarians, "a kind of white people," one sneered, "who live like savages." But from the point of view of the Indians — the Algonquians who had been pushed from the coast into the interior, and the Cherokees who occupied the Appalachian highlands to the south — these pioneers presented a new and deadly threat to their homelands. Rising fears and resentments over this expanding population would be the cause of much eighteenth-century warfare.

In the eighteenth century the people of the backcountry forged another distinctive American region. The settlers cared little for rank. "The rain don't know broadcloth from bluejeans," they said. But the myth of frontier equality was simply that. Most pioneers owned little or no land, while "big men" held great tracts and dominated local communities with their bombastic style of personal leadership. Here the men were warriors, the women workers. The story was told of one pioneer whose wife began to jaw at him. "He pulled off his breeches and threw them down to her, telling her to put them on and wear them." This was also a bawdy culture in which sexuality was open and celebrated. "The young women have a most uncommon practice," wrote an Anglican missionary. "They draw their shift as tight as possible round their breasts and slender waists," and "they expose themselves often quite naked, without ceremony — rubbing themselves and their hair with bears' oil and tying it up behind in a bunch like the Indians." Rates of premarital pregnancy were very high, but the customary response was to laugh and expect the young couple to marry. If they didn't, there would be a "shotgun wedding." Terms such as this were being used as early as the eighteenth century. In backcountry English it was "critter" for *creature,* "sartin" for *certain,* "young-uns" for *young ones,* and "man" for *husband.*

The South

Both the Upper and the Lower South were biracial societies by 1750. From 100,000 people in 1700, the two regions increased to more than 500,000 by midcentury. Much of the growth was due to the forced migration of enslaved Africans, who constituted 40 percent of the population. Not only had the tidewater area of the southern Atlantic coast been filled with colonial settlement, but a good deal of the Piedmont as well. Specializing in rice, tobacco, and other crops, these colonies were overwhelmingly rural. Their farms and plantations were dispersed across the countryside, and villages or towns were rare.

English authorities made the Church of England the state religion in the Chesapeake colonies. Residents paid taxes for its support and had to attend services. No other churches were permitted, and dissenters were excluded or exiled. Before the middle of the eighteenth century, these rules kept other sects out of Virginia and Maryland. But the Anglican establishment was internally weak. There was no colonial bishop, no local institutions for training clergy. Since America was considered a poor assignment, the ministers who arrived from England were not among the best and brightest. In Carolina and Georgia, neither Anglicanism nor any other sect or denomination rested on a firm foundation.

Along the rice coast, the dominant institution of social life was the large plantation. The heavy investment required to transform the tangle of woods and swamps along the rivers into the order of dams, dikes, and flooded fields determined that rice cultivation be undertaken only by men of means. By midcentury, established plantations typically were

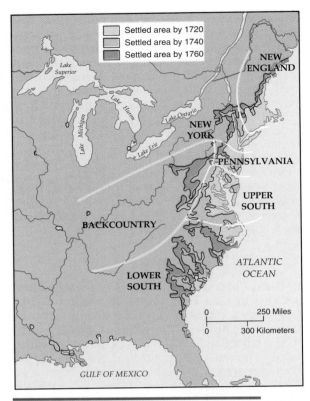

Spread of Settlement in the British Colonies, 1720-1760

The spread of settlement from 1720 to 1760 shows the movement of population into the Backcountry in the midcentury.

miles southeast of Williamsburg. From its location on the summit of a hill, it looked out over spacious acres that included the quarters for the large number of slaves who worked the tobacco fields. Unlike rice, tobacco could be grown profitably in small plots, and therefore the Upper South included a greater variety of farmers and a correspondingly diverse landscape. Tobacco quickly drained the soil of its nutrients, and plantings had to be shifted to fresh ground every few years. Former tobacco land could be planted with corn for several years, but then required rest for twenty years or more to avoid exhaustion. The landscape was thus a patchwork of fields, many in various stages of ragged second growth. The poorest farmers lived in wooden cabins little better than the shacks of the slaves. More prosperous farm families lived with two or three slaves in houses that were considerably smaller than the substantial homes of New England.

Among the elite, extended-family connections were extremely important. Cousin marriage was frequent, and many a southern woman "changed her condition but not her name." The ideal, and the reality in most families, was male supremacy. After the wealthy planter William Byrd II married the equally wealthy Lucy Parke in the early eighteenth century he dominated her, disposing of her estate without consulting her, interfering in her domestic management, even dictating to her the smallest details of her personal grooming. She complained bitterly. During one of their violent arguments, "she lifted up her hands to strike me, but forbore to do it" Byrd wrote in his diary; "she gave me abundance of bad words," but "after acting the mad woman for a long time she was passive again." "Sir," she wrote to him, "your orders must be obeyed whatever reluctance I find thereby."

In the Lower South, where the plantations were little worlds unto themselves, community life was feeble. But by midcentury the Upper South had given rise to well-developed neighborhoods based on kinship networks and economic connections. Encouraging the developing sense of community more than any other institution was the county court, which acted as the executive as well as the judicial power. On court day, white people of all ranks held a great gathering that included public business, horse racing, and perhaps a barbecue. The gentleman justices of the county, appointed by the governor, included the heads of the leading planter families. These men in turn selected the grand jury, composed of substantial freeholders. One of the most significant bonding forces in this free white population was a growing sense of racial solidarity

dominated by a large main house, generally located on a spot of high ground overlooking the fields. Drayton Hall near Charleston, a surviving mansion of the period, was built of pink brick in classically symmetrical style, with hand-carved interior moldings of imported Caribbean mahogany. Nearby, but a world apart, were the slave quarters, rough wooden cabins lining two sides of a muddy pathway near the outbuildings and barns. The contrast between "big house" and "quarters" symbolized the enormous social difference between planters and slaves. The Lower South was the closest thing in North America to the society of the Caribbean sugar islands.

Grand plantation houses could be found in the Upper South as well. One of the more elegant was Carter's Grove, a Georgian-style mansion built a few in response to the increasing proportion of African slaves dispersed throughout the neighborhoods.

The counties of the Upper South repeated the patterns of the communities of rural southern England, with their manors of aristocrats and the cottages of tenants. The distinctive speech of the residents — "I be," "he ain't," "you all" — and their soft, slow, and melodious drawl also originated in the south of England. But this mixed landscape of free and slave, rich and poor, was something uniquely American.

Indian America

By contrast with the eighteenth-century population explosion in the colonies, the Indian peoples of North America continued their long-term population decline. Colonists were relatively immune from dramatic fluctuations in the death rate, but Indian America took a terrific beating from epidemics of European disease. There are no reliable statistics on the numbers of Indians in North America before the nineteenth century, but from an estimated high of 7 to 10 million in 1500, Indian population probably fell to about a million by 1800. Thus it was during the eighteenth century that the colonial population finally overtook the Indian population of the continent. Population loss did not affect all Indian tribes equally, however. Native peoples with a century or more of colonial contact and interaction declined by 50 percent or more, but most Indian societies in the interior had not yet been struck by the pandemics.

Colonization also took a number of unexpected and unintended twists. By the early eighteenth century, Indians on the fringe of the Great Plains were using horses that had escaped or been stolen from the Spanish in the Southwest. The horse enabled hunters to exploit the buffalo herds much more efficiently, and on the base of this more productive subsistence strategy a variety of ethnic groups built a distinctive and elaborate nomadic culture. The mounted Plains Indian, so frequently a symbol of native America, was in fact a product of the colonial era. Vast numbers of Indian peoples moved onto the plains during the eighteenth century, pulled by this new way of life, pushed by colonial invasions and disruptions radiating southwest from Canada and north from the Spanish borderlands. By midcentury, the New Mexicans were regular victims of raids by mounted hunters of the Great Plains.

The early eighteenth century also witnessed a great deal of Indian migration in the eastern portion

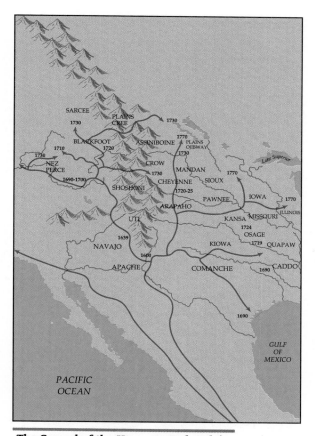

The Spread of the Horse onto the Plains
Spanish settlers introduced horses into their New Mexican colony in the seventeenth century. Through both trading and raiding, horses spread northward in streams both west and east of the Rocky Mountains. The use of the horse allowed the Indian peoples of the Great Plains to create a distinctive hunting and warrior culture.

of the continent, as the Indian peoples of the Atlantic coastal plain lost their lands to colonists through battles or treaties and moved into or beyond the Appalachian Mountains. Their perception of events was evident in the tales they told about how they had lost their land. When the English first arrived, said the Delaware Indians, they asked for land only as big as a bull's hide. But the English then soaked the hide to expand it, cut it into long, thin strips, and used these to enclose a great quantity of ground. "You have cheated us," the angry Indians cried out. "Is this the way you are going to treat us always while you remain in this country?"

This 1728 map of the English colonies is useless as a guide to the geography of the region, but the sketches of Indians and animals to the immediate west emphasize the colonial feeling of living on the periphery of a continent inhabited by natives.

a number of Indian groups. The Fox Indians blocked French passage between the Great Lakes and the upper Mississippi, attempting to become intermediaries in the fur trade. Sporadic fighting continued until the French crushed the tribe in 1716. But Fox warriors rose again in 1726, and the French had to inflict massive punishment before they could force the Fox to sign a treaty in 1738. Farther south, the Natchez and Chickasaw confederacy, a commercial partner of the Carolina traders, opposed the arrival of the French on the lower Mississippi. The two peoples engaged the French in a series of bloody conflicts during the 1720s that concluded with a horrible decimation of the Natchez in 1731. But the biggest concern of the eastern Indians was the tremendous growth of colonial population in the Atlantic coastal colonies, and especially the movement of British settlers westward. Pennsylvania perpetrated a series of fraudulent seizures of land from the Delawares that culminated in 1741. These thefts, which ran counter to that colony's history of fair dealing, offered yet another disturbing sign of things to come. Indian alliances with the French,

A portrait of the Delaware chief Tishcohan by Gustavus Hesselius, painted in 1732. In his purse of chipmunk hide is a clay pipe, a common item of the Indian trade. Tishcohan was one of the Delaware leaders forced by Pennsylvania authorities into signing a fraudulent land deal that overthrew that colony's history of fair dealing with Indians over land. He moved west to the Ohio River as settlers poured into his former homeland.

These Indian migrants, along with the native inhabitants of the Mississippi Valley, became active in the European fur trade and depended upon firearms, metal tools, and other manufactured goods to maintain their way of life. Yet they continued to assert a proud independence. Indians became skilled at playing colonial powers off against each other. The Iroquois had battled the French and their Indian allies in King William's War, but in 1701 they signed a treaty of neutrality with France that kept them out of harm's way during the next round of conflicts. To the south, the Creeks traded with both the French and the English as a means of maintaining their autonomy.

In general the French had better relations with native peoples than the English, but as they pursued their expansionist plans they came into conflict with then, resulted not from great love, but rather from great fears of British expansion.

TRADITION AND CHANGE

There were notable differences among the various colonial societies of eighteenth-century North America, but there were important similarities as well. The family and kinship, the church, and the local community were the most significant factors in everyday life. Colonists came from European societies in which land was scarce and monopolized by property-owning elites, and settled in a continent where for the most part land was abundant and cheap. This was the most important distinction between North America and Europe. With the notable exception of servants and slaves, rural people in the Spanish, French, and British colonies of North America were working lands under their own control by the eighteenth century. American historians once tied the existence of free land directly to the development of American democracy. But although extensive lands were available throughout the colonies of North America, political liberty and democratic values initially developed only in the British areas of the continent.

Charter Principles of Colonial Culture

The history of colonial land policy encouraged a set of assumptions that were anything but democratic. So central to the colonial world view were these beliefs that they may be considered charter principles of North American colonial culture. In the first place, the high rates of population growth and the common expectation of property ownership combined in the demand that more and more land be taken from the Indian inhabitants of North America and given to the colonists. The vast majority of people in all the colonies, therefore, accepted the violence and brutality of the wars of dispossession as a necessary underpinning of colonial life. Thus did the Puritan minister Cotton Mather praise Hannah Dustin, a New England woman who escaped her captors during King William's War by killing and scalping nine sleeping Indians, including two women and six children. The acceptance of massive violence against native peoples was an essential part of the culture of early America.

A second fundamental value was the popular acceptance of forced labor. A good living in the South could be made only by those who "get a few slaves and . . . beat them well to make them work hard," one South Carolina woman wrote. In a land where free men and women could simply work for themselves on their own plot of ground, slavery was thought to be the only way a planter might gain control over an agricultural labor force. In the Spanish borderlands, captured Apache children were made into lifetime household servants. All the colonists came from a European world that believed in social hierarchy and subordination, and involuntary servitude was easily incorporated into their world view. It is important to note that in England and Europe slavery had been outlawed in the late Middle Ages, but in America it sprang back to life.

Bound Labor

At least half of the immigrants to British America, probably more, arrived as bound laborers. This system allowed poor immigrants to arrange passage across the Atlantic in exchange for four or five years of service in America. It also provided colonial employers with a continuing cheap source of workers. Labor in Pennsylvania "is performed chiefly by indentured servants," wrote Benjamin Franklin, "because the high price it bears cannot be performed in any other way." One historian, accounting for the cost of passage and upkeep, estimates that bound laborers earned their masters, on average, about fifty pounds sterling over their terms of service.

Most were indentured servants, their contracts negotiated before they began the journey to America. Usually they were single men, often skilled artisans. Families without the means to pay their passage came as *redemptioners*. They were required to pay upon arrival in North America, where they might have kin to assist them. Failing that, they were sold into service, which sometimes meant the separation of family members. In addition to indentured servants and redemptioners, eighteenth-century England sent over, mostly to the Chesapeake, some 50,000 convicts sentenced to seven or fourteen years at hard labor. All classes of bound laborers remained on board ship after arrival in America, awaiting inspection by potential buyers, who poked muscles, peered into open mouths, and pinched women. Although servants were not slaves, that may have been a distinction without a difference.

There were other similarities with slavery. The ocean crossing was frequently traumatic. One German immigrant described a passage from Rotterdam to Philadelphia in which several hundred people were packed like sardines in the ship's hold. "The ship is filled with pitiful signs of distress," he wrote; "smells, fumes, horrors, vomiting, various kinds of sea sickness, fever, dysentery, headaches, heat, constipation, boils, scurvy, cancer, mouth-rot, and similar afflictions. In such misery all the people on board pray and cry pitifully together." In 1750 Pennsylvania was finally compelled to pass a law to prevent the overcrowding of immigrant ships. Moreover, the period of service was often filled with harsh and grueling labor, especially in the Chesapeake. Running away became a common remedy, although it was usually unsuccessful and resulted in extra time to serve: in Pennsylvania a runaway was liable for five times the lost service, in Maryland ten times!

For those who endured, however, freedom beckoned. "Freedom dues" might include a suit of clothes, tools, money, and sometimes land. But the social mobility of former servants was limited. Of the thousands of men who came to the British colonies as indentured servants during the seventeenth and eighteenth centuries, only about 20 percent achieved positions of moderate comfort. The majority died before their terms were completed, returned to England, or continued in miserable poverty. But opportunities for advancement increased somewhat as the eighteenth century progressed. The majority of German redemptioners, for example, appear to have become small farmers. By midcentury, the chances of moderate success for former servants were probably better than fifty-fifty.

Work in Colonial America

Throughout North America, most colonists continued the traditional European occupation of working the land. Plantation agriculture was designed to be a commercial system, in which crops were commodities for sale. Commercial farming also developed in some particularly fertile areas, notably southeastern Pennsylvania, which became known as the bread-

A carpenter and spinner from *The Book of Trades,* an eighteenth-century British survey of the crafts practiced in colonial America. In colonial cities artisans organized themselves into the traditional European craft system, with apprentices, journeymen, and masters. There were few opportunities for the employment of women outside the household, but women sometimes earned income by establishing sidelines as midwives or spinners.

basket of North America, as well as the country surrounding colonial cities such as New York, Boston, and Quebec. The majority of the farmers of eighteenth-century North America, however, grew crops and raised livestock for their own needs or for local barter, and were largely self-sufficient. Most attempted to produce small surpluses as well, in order to raise enough income to pay their taxes and to buy some manufactured goods. But rather than specializing in the production of one or two crops for sale, they attempted to remain as independent of the market as possible, diversifying their activities. The primary goal was ownership of land, and the assurance that their children and descendants would be able to settle on lands nearby.

Rural households frequently took up the practice of a craft or trade as a sideline. Farmers were also blacksmiths, coopers, weavers, or carpenters. Women too sometimes established careers as independent traders of dairy products or eggs. Others became midwives and medicinal experts serving the community. In one Maine community, for example, the midwife Martha Ballard delivered 797 babies over twenty-seven years of service, and both male and female patients came to her for salves, pills, syrups, ointments, or advice.

In colonial cities, artisans and craftsmen worked at their trades full time. Artisans also followed tradition by organizing themselves according to the European craft system. In the colonial cities of the Atlantic coast, carpenters, iron makers, blacksmiths, shipwrights, and scores of other tradesmen had their own self-governing associations. Young men who wished to pursue a trade served several years as apprentices, working in exchange for learning the skills and secrets of the craft. After completing their apprenticeships they sought employment in a shop. This often required them to migrate to some other area, which accounts for the term *journeyman*. Most craftsmen remained journeymen for the whole of their careers. But by building a good name and carefully saving, journeymen hoped to become master craftsmen, opening a shop and employing journeymen and apprentices of their own. As in farming, the ultimate goal was independence, control over one's work.

With the exception of midwifery, there were few career opportunities for women outside the household. By law, husbands held managerial rights over family property, but widows received support in the form of a one-third interest, known as *dower*, in a deceased husband's real estate. And in certain occupations, such as printing, widows succeeded their husbands in business. As a consequence, a number of colonial women played active roles in eighteenth-century journalism. Ann Smith Franklin, Benjamin Franklin's sister-in-law, took over the operation of her husband's Rhode Island shop after his death. Cornelia Smith Bradford continued to publish her husband's Philadelphia paper and was an important force in publishing throughout the 1750s.

Social Class

Traditional working roles were transferred to North America, but plans for bringing the European class system by creating monopolies on land were far less successful. The Spanish system of encomienda, the seigneurial land grants of New France, and the great manors created by the Dutch and English along the Hudson were all attempts to transplant the essence of European feudalism in North America. But in most areas such monopolies proved difficult or impossible to maintain, because colonial settlers had relatively free access to land. There was, of course, a system of economic ranks, and an unequal distribution of wealth, prestige, and power. North American society was not aristocratic, but neither was it classless.

The colonial societies of Spain and France in North America were more egalitarian than those of the mother countries. The ordinary farmers and ranchers of the borderlands held rights to communally owned land, and the *habitants* of the St. Lawrence suffered few of the miseries of the French peasantry. A rising standard of living in both regions underlay their substantial growth in population. Compared with the social structure of the British colonies, however, the French and Spanish societies of the New World were more in the mold of the Old, with its system of hereditary ranks and titles. A small elite of New Mexican and California families lived on great landed estates amid displays of wealth and prestige, and in New France the seigneurs claimed privileges similar to those enjoyed by their counterparts at home. In both cases, the privileges of the hereditary upper class amounted to far less in practice than in theory.

The upper class of British colonial society — the wealthiest 10 percent of all whites — was made up of large landowners, merchants, and prosperous professionals. In the eighteenth century, property valued at two thousand pounds marked a family as well-to-do, and five thousand pounds was real wealth. Leading merchants enjoyed annual incomes in excess of five hundred pounds, and could live in opulence. Wealthy planters and merchants in the British colonies lived far more extravagantly than the seigneurs of New France or the dons of the borderlands. What separated the culture of class in the British colonies from that of New France or New Mexico, however, was not so much the material conditions of life as the prevailing attitude toward social rank. In the Catholic cultures, the upper class attempted to obscure its origins, claiming descent from European nobility. But in British America, people celebrated social mobility. This was an open class system, and the entrance of newly successful planters, commercial farmers, and merchants into the upper ranks was not only possible, but frequent — although by midcentury most upper-class families had not earned but rather had inherited their wealth.

In the British colonies as a whole, slaves, bound servants, and poor laboring families made up a lower class of workers that constituted at least 40 percent of the population. For these families, the standard of living did not rise above the level of bare subsistence. Most lived from hand to mouth, often suffering through seasons of severe privation. A proportion of poor whites could expect their condition to improve during their lifetimes, but slaves were a permanently servile population. Africans stood apart from gains in the standard of living enjoyed by immigrants from Europe. Their lives had been degraded beyond measure from the conditions prevailing in their native lands.

But the presence of poor people in British North America certainly did not surprise eighteenth-century observers. The feature of the class system most frequently commented upon was not the character or composition of the lower ranks but rather the size and strength of the middle class. As one Pennsylvanian wrote at midcentury, "the people of this province are generally of the middling sort." More than half the population of the British colonies, and nearly 70 percent of all white settlers, might be classified among this "middling sort." Most were families of landowning farmers of small to moderate means, but they also included artisans, craftsmen, and small shopkeepers.

At the low end, the colonial middle class included families whose standard of living was barely above subsistence; at the high end were those whose holdings approached wealth. Households solidly in the center of this broad ranking owned land or other property worth approximately five hundred pounds, and earned the equivalent of about one hundred pounds per year. This allowed them to enjoy a standard of living higher than that of the great majority of people in England and Europe. The low mortality of Americans, probably the result of greater living space and an abundant food supply, was important testimony to generally better living conditions. Touring the British Isles at midcentury, Benjamin Franklin was shocked at the squalid conditions of farmers and workers. He wrote of his renewed appreciation of America, where everyone "lives in a tidy, warm house, has plenty of good food and fuel, with whole cloths from head to foot, the manufacture perhaps of his own family." "Roast beef and apple pie" comfort was possible for the majority of white colonists.

The Progress of Inequality

The total output of the economy of British North America increased dramatically during the eighteenth century. Economic historians estimate that per capita production grew at an annual rate of .5 percent. Granted, this was considerably less than the average annual growth rate of 1.5 percent that prevailed during the era of industrialization that extended from the early nineteenth through the mid-twentieth century. But by steadily increasing the size of the economic pie, economic growth provided for improved living conditions within the lifetimes of most British Americans. Moreover, British colonists enjoyed a standard of living higher than that of any people in Europe. Improving standards of living and relatively open access to land encouraged British colonists to see theirs as a society where hard work and savings could translate into prosperity.

But economic growth also produced increasing social inequality. In the commercial cities, for example, prosperity was accompanied by a concentration of assets in the hands of wealthy families. In Boston and Philadelphia at the beginning of the century, the wealthiest 10 percent owned about half of the taxable property; by about midcentury this figure stood at 65 percent or more. In the commercial farming region of southeastern Pennsylvania, the holdings of the wealthiest tenth increased more modestly, from 24 to 30 percent during the first half of the century. But the share of the poorest third fell from 17 to 6 percent of the taxable property. The general standard of living may have been rising, but the rich were receiving ever larger slices of the pie. The greatest concentrations of wealth occurred in the cities and in those regions dominated by commercial farming, whether slave or free. The greatest economic equality continued to be found in areas of self-sufficient farming, or in the southern backcountry.

Another eighteenth-century trend confounded

the hope of social mobility in the countryside. As population grew, and generations succeeded one another in older settlements like Northampton, all the available land in the towns was taken up. Under the pressure of increased demand, land prices increased almost beyond the reach of families of modest means. As a family's land was divided among the heirs of the second and third generations, parcels became ever smaller and thus were more intensively farmed. Eventually soil exhaustion became a problem. By the eighteenth century, many farm communities did not have sufficient land to provide those of the emerging generation with farms of their own. As the events in Northampton, Massachusetts during the 1730s revealed, this problem was particularly acute among New England communities, where colonists were hemmed in by the French and Indian frontier on the north and the great landed estates of the Hudson Valley on the west. There were notable increases in the number of landless poor in the towns of New England, as well as the disturbing appearance of the "strolling poor" — homeless people who traveled from town to town looking for work or a handout. Poor families crowded into Boston, which by midcentury was expending over five thousand pounds annually in poor relief. Recipients were required to wear a large red *P* on their clothing. In other regions, land shortages in the older settlements almost inevitably prompted people to leave in search of cheap or free land.

The Colonial Mood

Throughout North America, most settlers remained remarkably old-fashioned in their folkways. They tended to live according to the customs prevailing in their European region of origin at the time the colony was first effectively settled. Thus the residents of New England, New France, and New Mex-

ico continued to be attached to the religious passions of the seventeenth century long after their mother countries had abandoned those conflicts in favor of imperial geopolitics. British travelers in the Atlantic colonies consistently remarked on the archaic seventeenth-century speech patterns of Massachusetts and Virginia people. Nostalgia for the mother country helped to fix a conservative colonial attitude toward culture.

The cultures of North America were based on the transmission of information through the spoken word rather than by print or other mass media, on the passage of traditions through storytelling and song, music and crafts. These folk cultures, traditional and suspicious of change, preserved an essentially medieval view of the world. The rhythms of life were regulated by the hours of sunlight and the seasons of the year. People rose with the sun and went to bed soon after the light failed. The demands of the season determined their working routines. They farmed with simple tools, and lived at the whim of nature, for drought, flood, or pestilence might quickly sweep away their efforts. Experience told them that the natural world imposed limitations within which men and women had to learn to live. Even patterns of reproduction conformed to nature's cycle: in nearly every European colonial community of North America the number of births peaked in late winter, then fell to a low point during the summer. Human sexual activity itself seemed to fluctuate with the rural working demands created by the seasons.

For most North American colonists of the mid-eighteenth century, the community was thought to be more important than the individual. In New France, villagers worked together to repair the roads, in New Mexico they collectively determined water rights and maintained the irrigation system, in New England they agreed upon the dates when fields should be plowed, sowed, and harvested. When the Pilgrims and "strangers" of the *Mayflower*

Month of Conception

Jan. Feb. Mar. Apr. May June July Aug. Sept. Oct. Nov. Dec. Jan.

Oct. Nov. Dec. Jan. Feb. Mar. Apr. May June July Sept. Oct.

Month of Birth

— Colonists in Dedham, Massachusetts
---- African Americans in Virginia

Monthly Frequency of Successful Conceptions

Patterns of reproduction corresponded to nature's cycles, but there was a dramatic difference between the practices of European colonists and African American slaves.

Source: James A. Henretta and Gregory H. Nobles, *Evolution and Revolution: American Society, 1600–1820* (Lexington, Mass.: Heath, 1987), 37; Mechal Sobel, *The World They Made Together: Black and White Values in Eighteenth-Century Virginia* (Princeton: Princeton University Press, 1987), 67.

signed their compact, promising "due submission to the general good," they explicitly set down principles with which most North American colonists could agree. Even the artifacts of everyday life reveal this corporate emphasis. Houses offered very little privacy, and the family often slept together in the same room, sat on benches rather than chairs, and took their supper from the common bowl or trencher.

The Enlightenment Challenge

The growth of the economy in the British colonies and the development of a colonial upper class, however, stimulated the emergence of a more cosmopolitan, "Anglican" culture, particularly in the cities of the Atlantic coast. "The culture of minds by the finer arts and sciences," wrote Benjamin Franklin in 1749, "was necessarily postponed to times of more wealth and leisure." And now, he added, "these times are come." A rising demand for drama, poetry, essays, novels, and history was met by urban booksellers who imported British publications. In Boston bookshops at midcentury one could buy the works of Shakespeare and John Milton, the essays of Joseph Addison, Richard Steele, Jonathan Swift, and Samuel Johnson, and editions of the classics. In shops elsewhere around the colonies one might also find editions of eighteenth-century novels such as *Moll Flanders* by Daniel Defoe and *Tom Jones* by Henry Fielding — but not in New England, where such works were considered indecent.

It was through English and European sources that colonists were introduced to the ideas of the Enlightenment. Drawing from the discoveries of Galileo, Copernicus, Decartes, and the seventeenth-century English scientist Sir Isaac Newton, Enlightenment thinkers argued that the universe was governed by natural laws that people could understand and apply for human betterment. The Englishman John Locke developed a philosophy of reason and argued that the state existed to provide for the happiness and security of individuals, who were endowed with inalienable rights to life, liberty, and property. Such writers emphasized rationality, harmony, and order. These themes stood in stark contrast with folk culture's traditional emphasis on the unfathomable mysteries of God and nature and the inevitability of human failure and disorder.

Enlightenment thinking undoubtedly appealed most to those who saw their own lives in terms of progress. It was the sons of the prosperous colonial elite who were most exposed to the new thinking through their college studies. Harvard remained the

Next to the Bible, the narrative of Mary Rowlandson, a pilgrim's progress through the American wilderness, was the best-selling book in British colonial America. Indians captured Rowlandson during King Philip's War in 1676, and it was three months before her husband was able to ransom her. First published in 1682, her book went through fifteen editions and inspired hundreds of other narratives.

only institution of higher education in British America until 1693, when Anglicans established the College of William and Mary at Williamsburg, the new capital of Virginia. Puritans in Connecticut, believing that Harvard was too liberal, founded Yale College in 1701. The curriculum of these colleges, modeled on that of Oxford and Cambridge in England, was designed to train ministers, but gradually each of them introduced courses and professors influenced by the Enlightenment. In the 1730s Harvard endowed a chair of mathematics and natural philosophy and appointed to it John Winthrop, grandson of the Puritan leader and a disciple of Newton. A mixture of traditional and Enlightenment views characterized the colonial colleges, as it did the thought of men such as Cotton Mather. A conservative defender of the old order, Mather wrote a book supporting the reality of witches. But he was also a member of the Royal Society, an early supporter of inoculation against disease, and a defender of the Copernican view of the universe. On hearing a scientific lecture of Mather's that might be construed as raising conflicts with a literal reading of the Bible, one old Boston minister noted in his diary, "I think it inconvenient to assert such problems."

That man's views probably characterized a majority of the public. The tastes of ordinary colonists ran to traditional rather than Enlightenment fare. Rates of literacy among British colonists were relatively high. About half the adult men and a quarter of the women could read, rates comparable to those in England and Scandinavia. In the French and Spanish colonies, in striking contrast, reading was a skill confined to a small upper class of men. In New England, where the Puritans were committed to Bible reading and had developed a system of public education, rates were 85 percent among men and something less than 50 percent among women — the highest in the Atlantic world. But the Puritans' choice of reading material reflected their traditional values. Not surprisingly, the best-selling book of the colonial era was the Bible. In second place was a unique American literary form, the captivity narrative. The first to be published was the *Sovereignty and Goodness of God* (1682), Mary Rowlandson's story of her captivity among the Indians during King Philip's War, a kind of "pilgrim's progress" through the American wilderness. "It is good for me that I have been afflicted," she wrote, for "I have learned to look beyond present and smaller troubles, and to be quieted under them." Appearing in fifteen editions during the colonial period, Rowlandson's account stimulated the publication of at least 500 other such narratives, most with less religion and a great deal more gore.

Another popular literary form was the almanac, a combination calendar, astrological guide, and sourcebook of medical advice and farming tips reflecting the concerns of traditional folk culture. The best remembered is Franklin's *Poor Richard's Almanac* (1732–57), but it was preceded and outlived by a great many others. What was so important about Franklin's almanac was the manner in which he used this traditional form to promote the new Enlightenment emphasis on useful and practical knowledge. Posing as a simple bumpkin, the highly sophisticated Franklin was one of the first to bring Enlightenment thought to ordinary folk.

THE GREAT AWAKENING

In British America, the fire of religious passion burned low in the early eighteenth century; people devoted themselves to more practical matters of making a living. But the religious revivalism that began in Northampton, Massachusetts, and swept across the colonies in the middle decades of the century made evident the tensions produced by economic and cultural change.

"Declension" in Religion

In the middle and southern colonies, population growth and expansion were marked by a decline in the importance of religion. Many families remained "unchurched." The Anglican Church was weak and its ministers uninspiring. South of New England, only one adult in fifteen was a member of a church. Although this figure probably understates the impact of religion on the organization of community life in the middle colonies, it helps keep things in perspective. "Of all opinions there are some, and the most part, of none at all," wrote a visitor to Pennsylvania.

The Puritan churches of New England also suffered declining membership and falling attendance at services, and many ministers began to warn of Puritanism's "declension." By the eighteenth century only one in five New Englanders belonged to an established congregation. When Puritanism had been a sect, membership in the church was voluntary and leaders could demand that congregants testify to their religious conversion. When Puritanism became an established church, however, attendance was expected of all townspeople, and conflicts inevitably arose over the requirement of a conversion experience. An agreement of 1662, the Half-Way Covenant, offered a practical solution: members' children who had not experienced conversion themselves could join as "half-way" members, restricted only from participation in communion. Thus the Puritans chose to manage rather than to resolve the contradiction between attendance and membership. Tensions also developed between congregational autonomy and the central control that traditionally accompanied the establishment of a state church. In 1708 the churches of Connecticut agreed to the Saybrook Platform, which enacted a system of governance by councils of ministers and elders rather than by congregations. These reforms also had the effect of weakening the passion and commitment of church members.

An increasing number of Congregationalists

also began to question the strict Calvinist theology of predestination — the belief that God had predetermined the few men and women who would be saved. Many turned to the more comforting idea that God gave people the freedom to choose salvation by developing their faith and good works, a theological principle known as Arminianism (named for a sixteenth-century Dutch theologian, Jacobus Arminius). This belief was more compatible with the rationalism of the Enlightenment: men and women were not helpless, but could shape their own destinies. Also implicit here was the image of God as a loving rather than a punishing father. In the early eighteenth century, Arminianism became a force at Harvard, and soon a new generation of ministers holding this point of view began to assume leadership in New England's churches. These "liberal" ideas appealed to groups experiencing economic and social improvement, especially commercial farmers, merchants, and the comfortable middle class with its rising expectations. But among ordinary people, especially those in the countryside, there was a good deal of opposition to the new ideas.

The Witchcraft Crisis in Salem

In 1692 a group of girls in Salem, Massachusetts, claimed that they had been bewitched by three old women of the community. In Europe during the previous two centuries, thousands of women had been executed as witches, and there had been a number of episodes of witch hunting in the British colonies. The community was thrown into a panic of accusations. Dragged before the magistrate, one old man considered the charge against him ridiculous. "You tax me for a wizard," he laughed; "you may as well tax me for a buzzard." He was convicted and hanged. Before the colonial governor finally called a halt to the persecutions, twenty persons had been tried, condemned, and executed.

Most of the accused were widows, old women who were suspect because they lived alone, without men. Most came from families whose connections with the Puritan church were weak, families having religious sympathies with Anglicans, Quakers, or Baptists. They were members of prosperous families who lived in the eastern, more commercial part of the community; the majority of their accusers came from the more remote and economically stagnant western side. One of the hallmarks of rationalist Enlightenment thought was the rejection of any belief in witchcraft, and thus the incident also embodied the contest between traditional and cosmopolitan culture. In these ways, the Salem witchcraft episode was an early indication of the tensions in colonial New England.

The Revival of Religion

The increasing rationalism and voluntarism of religion in the eighteenth century were dramatically challenged by the intercolonial revival known as the Great Awakening. During the 1730s there were stirrings of religious enthusiasm, most notably in the movement sparked by Jonathan Edwards of the Northampton community in the Connecticut Valley, but also among German pietists and Scotch-Irish Presbyterians in Pennsylvania, who criticized the spiritual coldness of the Enlightenment. The Great Awakening was the American version of the second phase of the Protestant Reformation, whose leaders condemned the laxity, decadence, and officalism of established Protestantism and reinvigorated it with calls for renewed piety and purity. The American religious radicals were the soulmates of the Methodists in Britain and the pietistic Lutherans and Anabaptists on the European continent.

The first sparks of the Great Awakening were struck by George Whitefield, an evangelical Anglican minister from England who made several tours of the colonies, from Georgia to New England, beginning in 1738. By all accounts, his preaching had a powerful effect. Even Benjamin Franklin, a religious skeptic, wrote of the "extraordinary influence of his oratory" after attending an outdoor service in Philadelphia where 30,000 people crowded the streets to hear him. Whitefield began as Edwards did, chastizing his listeners as "half animals and half devils," but he left them with the hope that God would be responsive to their desire for salvation. "The word was sharper than a two-edged sword," Whitefield wrote after one of his sermons. "The bitter cries and groans were enough to pierce the hardest heart. Some of the people were as pale as death; others were wringing their hands; others lying on the ground; others sinking into the arms of their friends; and most lifting their eyes to heaven and crying to God for mercy. They seemed like persons awakened by the last trumpet, and coming out of their graves to judgement." He avoided sectarian differences. "God help us to forget party names and become Christians in deed and truth," he declared.

In Pennsylvania, two important leaders of the

revival were William Tennent and his son Gilbert. An Irish-born Presbyterian, the elder Tennent was an evangelical preacher who established a school in Pennsylvania to train like-minded men for the ministry. The school was lampooned as the "Log College" by its critics. Tennent accepted the name with pride. He sent a large number of enthusiastic ministers into the field, and the Log College became the model for the College of New Jersey, later called Princeton, a Presbyterian institution founded in 1746. Gilbert Tennent toured with Whitefield in the early 1740s. Disturbed by what he called the "presumptuous security" of the colonial church, he delivered the famous sermon "The Dangers of an Unconverted Ministry," in which he called upon Protestants to examine the religious convictions of their own ministers. Among the Presbyterians, open conflict broke out between New Sides and Old Sides, and in some regions the church hierarchy divided into separate organizations.

In New England the factions were known as New Lights and Old Lights. The New Lights railed against Arminianism, branding it rationalist heresy, and called for a renewal of Calvinism. The Old Lights condemned emotional enthusiasm as part of the heresy of believing in a personal and direct relationship with God outside the order of the church.

Itinerant preachers stirred up trouble in the countryside; ministers found themselves challenged by their newly awakened congregations, and some were removed. Many other congregations split into feuding factions. Never had there been such turmoil in New England churches.

The Awakening came somewhat later to the South. Beginning in the mid-1740s among Scotch-Irish Presbyterians, it did not achieve its full impact until the organization work of the Methodists and particularly the Baptists in the 1760s and early 1770s. The Great Awakening in the South not only affected white Christians, but introduced many slaves to Christianity. The Baptist churches of the South in the era of the American Revolution generally had both white and black members.

The Impact of the Great Awakening

Many other "unchurched" colonists were brought to Protestantism by the Great Awakening. But a careful examination of statistics suggests that the proportion of church members in the general population probably did not increase during the middle decades of the century. While the number of churches more than doubled from 1740 to 1780, the colonial population grew even faster, increasing by a factor of

Baptism by full immersion in the Schuykill River of Pennsylvania, an engraving by Henry Dawkins illustrating events in the history of American Baptists, was published in Philadelphia in 1770. With calls for renewed piety and purity, the Great Awakening reinvigorated American Protestantism. The Baptists preached an egalitarian message, and their congregations in the South often included both white and black Protestants.

SCHUYLKILL

CHRONOLOGY

1636	Harvard College founded
1644	Roger Williams's *The Bloudy Tenent of Persecution*
1662	Half-Way Covenant in New England
1674	Bishopric of Quebec established
1680s	William Penn begins recruiting foreign settlers
1682	Mary Rowlandson's *Sovereignty and Goodness of God*
1689	Toleration Act passed by Parliament
1690s	Beginnings of Franciscan missions in Arizona
1692	Witchcraft crisis in Salem
1693	College of William and Mary founded
1700s	Plains Indians begin adoption of the horse
1701	Yale College founded Iroquois sign treaty of neutrality with France
1708	Saybrook Platform in Connecticut
1716	Spanish begin construction of Texas missions
1730s	French decimate the Natchez and defeat the Fox Indians
1732	Franklin begins publishing *Poor Richard's Almanac*
1734	Religious revival begins in Northampton
1738	George Whitefield first tours the colonies
1740s	Great Awakening in the Northeast
1740	Parliament passes a naturalization law for the colonies
1746	College of New Jersey (Princeton) founded
1760s	Great Awakening achieves full impact in the South
1769	Spanish colonization of California begins
1775	Indian revolt at San Diego
1776	San Francisco founded
1781	Los Angeles founded
1833	Congregational Church disestablished in Massachusetts

three. The greatest impact was on families already associated with the churches. The patterns observed in the Northampton community were repeated throughout the British North American colonies. Before the Awakening, attendance at church had been mostly an adult affair, but throughout the colonies the revival of religion had its deepest effects upon young people, who flocked to church in greater numbers than ever before. Before the Awakening, the number of people experiencing conversion had been steadily falling, but now full membership surged. Church membership previously had been concentrated among women, leading Cotton Mather for one to speculate that perhaps women were indeed more godly. But men were particularly affected by the revival, and their attendance and membership rose. "God has surprisingly seized and subdued the hardest men, and more males have been added here than the tenderer sex," wrote one Massachusetts minister.

The Awakening appealed most to groups who felt bypassed by the development of the British colonies during the first half of the eighteenth century. Religious factions did not divide neatly into haves and have-nots, but New Lights and Baptists tended to draw their greatest strength from small farmers and less prosperous craftsmen. Many members of the upper class and the comfortable "middling sort" were shocked by the excesses of the Great Awakening, saw them as indications of anarchy, and became even more committed to rational religion.

A number of historians have suggested that the Great Awakening had important political implications. In Connecticut, for example, Old Lights politicized the religious dispute by passing a series of laws in the General Assembly designed to suppress the revival. In one town, separatists refused to pay taxes that supported the established church and were jailed. New Light judges were thrown off the bench and others were denied their elected seats in the assembly. The arrogance of these actions was met with popular outrage, and by the 1760s the New Lights had organized the colony and turned the Old Lights out of office. These New Light politicians became the leaders of the Revolution in Connecticut.

CONCLUSION

Such direct connections as those between religion and politics in Connecticut were relatively rare. Yet there is little doubt that for many people the Great Awakening was their first opportunity to actively participate in public debate and public action that affected the direction of their lives. Choices about religious styles, ministers, and doctrine were thrown open for public discourse, and ordinary people began to believe that their opinions actually counted for something. Underlying the debate over these issues were insecurities about warfare, economic growth, and the development of colonial society. These lessons would later be applied in a very different struggle.

Additional Readings

W. J. Eccles, *The Canadian Frontier, 1534–1760* (1983). An introduction to the history of French America by a leading scholar on colonial Canada.

David Hackett Fischer, *Albion's Seed: Four British Folkways in America* (1990). This engaging history supplies fascinating details on the regions of New England, Pennsylvania, Virginia, and the Backcountry.

Jack P. Greene, *Pursuits of Happiness: The Social Development of Early Modern British Colonies and the Formation of American Culture* (1986). A distillation of a tremendous amount of historical material on community and colony life in British North America.

James A. Henretta and Gregory H. Nobles, *Evolution and Revolution: American Society, 1600–1820* (1987). A useful synthesis of the newest social history of the British colonies. Includes an excellent bibliographic essay.

Richard Hofstadter, *America at 1750* (1971). Although more than twenty years old, and left unfinished by the premature death of the author, it remains the single best book on the eighteenth-century British colonies.

Jackson Turner Main, *The Social Structure of Revolutionary America* (1965). Provides a detailed treatment of colonial social structure, with statistics, tables, and enlightening interpretations.

D. W. Meinig, *The Shaping of America: Atlantic America, 1492–1800* (1986). A geographer's overview of the historical development of the North American continent in the era of European colonialism. Provides a survey of the British and French colonies.

David J. Weber, *The Spanish Frontier in North America* (1992). A magnificent treatment of the entire Spanish borderlands, from Florida to California. Includes important chapters on colonial government and social life.

Robert Wells, *The Population of the British Colonies in America before 1776* (1975). The standard source on colonial population growth.

6 FROM EMPIRE TO INDEPENDENCE, 1750–1776

● THE CONTINENTAL CONGRESS IN PHILADELPHIA

The first session of the Continental Congress opened in Carpenter's Hall, Philadelphia, on September 5, 1774. The fifty-six elected delegates from twelve of the colonies of British North America had come together to forge a common response to the closing of the port of Boston, the suspension of Massachusetts government, and other British measures. Labeled the Intolerable Acts by the colonists, they were the empire's latest attempt to force the colonies to accept the power of Parliament to make laws binding them "in all cases whatsoever." This was the first intercolonial meeting since the Stamp Act Congress of 1765. If the colonies now failed to act together, they would be "attacked and destroyed by piecemeal," declared Arthur Lee of Virginia. "Every part will in its turn feel the vengeance which it would not unite to repel." Abigail Adams, the politically astute wife of John Adams of Massachusetts, agreed. "You have before you," she wrote to her husband, "the greatest national concerns that ever came before any people."

A NATIONAL POLITICAL COMMUNITY TAKES SHAPE

But the opening minutes of the first session did not bode well. One delegate moved that they begin with prayer; another responded that they were "so divided in religious sentiments, some Episcopalians, some Quakers, some Aanabaptists, some Presbyterians and some Congregationalists, so that we could not join in the same act of worship." The delegates were confronted immediately with the things that separated rather than united them. It was as if they were "ambassadors from a dozen belligerent powers of Europe," wrote John Adams. The delegates represented different colonies (or provinces, as they now began to style them, in an attempt to see themselves in a new way), whose traditions and histories were as different as those of separate countries. Moreover, these lawyers, merchants, and planters — the upper-class leaders of their respective colonies — were strangers to one another. Their political opinions ranged from loyalty to the British crown and empire to a belief in the necessity of violent revolution. "Every man," Adams wrote, "is a great man, an orator, a critic, a statesman, and therefore every man, upon every question, must show his oratory, his criticism, and his political abilities." As a result, he continued, "business is drawn and spun out to an immeasurable length. I believe that if it was moved and seconded that we should come to a resolution that three and two make five, we

This engraving of the first session of the Continental Congress, published in France in 1782, is the only contemporary illustration of the meeting. Peyton Randolph of Virginia presides from the elevated chair, but otherwise there are no recognizable individuals. The Congress had to find a way to form a community among the leaders from each of the colonies without compromising their local identities.

PREMIÈRE ASSEMBLÉE DU CONGRÈS

should be entertained with logic and rhetorick, law, history, politicks and mathematics concerning the subject for two whole days.''

Would the delegates be blocked here, at the very opening of the first session? Adams's cousin, fellow Massachusetts delegate Samuel Adams, jumped to his feet. He was no bigot, he declared, ''and could hear a prayer from any gentleman of piety and virtue who was at the same time a friend to his country.'' The delegates finally agreed to ask a local clergyman, a supporter of the American cause, to officiate. The minister took for his text the Thirty-fifth Psalm: ''Plead my cause, O Lord, with them that strive with me; fight against them that fight against me.'' John Adams was delighted. He ''prayed with such fervour, such Ardor, such Earnestness and Pathos, and in Language so elegant and sublime,'' he wrote home, that ''it has had an excellent Effect upon every Body here.'' The incident emphasized the most important task before the Continental Congress: finding a way to support the common cause without compromising local and provincial identity.

During seven weeks of deliberations, the men of the Continental Congress forged an agreement on both the principles and the policies they would have to follow in addressing the most serious crisis in the history of Britain's North American colonies. Equally important, the delegates found ways to work together and harmonize their interests. They immediately resolved that each colony would have one vote, thereby committing themselves to preserving provincial autonomy. They sent their most vexing problems to committees, whose members could sound each other out on the issues without speaking for the public record, and they added to their daily routine a round of dinners, parties, and late-night tippling. They had to develop trust in one another, since what they were doing was considered treason by the British authorities. The greatest single accomplishment of the Continental Congress was the creation of a community of leadership for the united colonies. "It has taken us much time to get acquainted," John Adams wrote to Abigail, and although he could be harsh in his judgments of other men, he left Philadelphia thinking of his fellow representatives as "a collection of the greatest men upon this continent."

The First Continental Congress thus took the initial steps toward the creation of a national political community. Communities are not only local, but can be regional or national. When peoples come together as a nation — testing their ability to act together in common purpose, forging a common national identity — they are forming a more general kind of community. The delegates took some of the first steps in this direction. In their final declaration they pledged to "firmly agree and associate, under the sacred ties of virtue, honor and love of our country." They urged their fellow Americans to "encourage frugality, economy, and industry, and promote agriculture, arts and the manufactures of this country," to "discountenance and discourage every species of extravagance and dissipation, especially all horse-racing, and all kinds of gaming, cock fighting, exhibitions of shows, plays, and other expensive diversions and entertainments." In other words, they called upon common Protestant traditions. In asking Americans to remember "the poorer sort" among them during the coming economic troubles, and demanding that they "break off all dealings" and treat with contempt anyone violating the compact, the delegates were deciding who was "in" and who was "out" — an essential first act in the construction of a new community.

Patrick Henry of Virginia, one of the delegates already committed to independence, was exuberant when the Continental Congress adjourned in late October. "Where are your land marks, your boundaries of colonies," he asked rhetorically; "the distinctions between Virginians, Pennsylvanians, New Yorkers, and New Englanders, are no more. I am not a Virginian, but an American." Henry greatly overstated the case, but he struck at an important truth. During the imperial crisis over the Sugar and Stamp Acts, the Intolerable Acts, and the growth of colonial resistance, Great Britain had forced the colonists to recognize that they shared a community of interest distinct from that of the mother country. This unity would be sorely tested as the colonies cautiously moved toward independence and years of bloody warfare. The

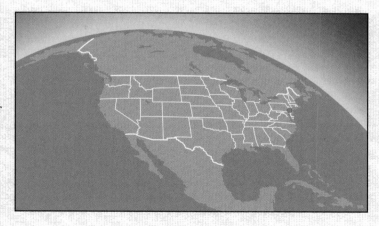

delegates to the Continental Congress would become the core leaders of the national revolutionary generation. Theirs was a first attempt to overcome local diversity and difference in pursuit of a common national goal.

THE GREAT WAR FOR EMPIRE

The first attempt at cooperation among the British colonies had taken place twenty years earlier, in July 1754, when representatives from New England, New York, Pennsylvania, and Maryland met to consider a joint approach to the French and Indian challenge. Even as the delegates met, fighting between Canadians and Virginians began on the Ohio River, the first shots in a great global war for empire pitting Britain (allied with Prussia) against the combined might of France, Austria, and Spain. In North America this would be the final and most destructive of the armed conflicts between the British and the French. It would decide the imperial future of the vast region between the Appalachian Mountains and the Mississippi River, and lay the ground for the conflict between the British and the colonists that would result in the Revolution.

The Albany Conference of 1754

The 1754 meeting, which took place in the New York town of Albany on the Hudson River, had been convened by the British Board of Trade. British officials wanted the colonies to consider a collective response to the continuing conflict with New France and the Indians of the interior. High on the agenda was the negotiation of a settlement with the leaders of the Iroquois Confederacy, who had grown impatient with colonial land grabbing. "Brother, you are not to expect to hear of me any more," the Iroquois chief Hendrick had declared in disgust to New York officials after a swindle that resulted in the loss of a vast tract. "And brother," he added as he departed, "we desire to hear no more of you." But because the powerful Iroquois Confederacy, with its Covenant Chain of alliances with other Indian tribes, occupied such a strategic location between New France and the British colonies, the British could ill afford Iroquois disaffection.

But the Albany Conference underlined the inability of the British colonies to unite in common cause. Behind the scenes, while the negotiations took place, real estate agents bribed some minor Iroquois chiefs for their signatures on a "deed" to an enormous tract of land in Pennsylvania, turning the meeting into a vehicle for the very abuses the British were seeking to correct. Angered by these manipulations, the official Iroquois delegation walked out of the conference, refusing all offers to join a British alliance.

The Albany Conference did, however, adopt the Plan of Union put forward by Benjamin Franklin, representing Pennsylvania. The previous year, British authorities had appointed Franklin postmaster general of the North American colonies, charging him with improving intercolonial communication and commerce, and he had become extremely sensitive to the need for cooperation. His Albany proposal would have placed Indian affairs, western settlement, and other items of mutual interest under the authority of a grand council composed of representatives elected by the colonial assemblies and led by a royally appointed president. "It would be a very strange thing," he declared in reference to the Iroquois Confederacy, if "ignorant savages should be capable of forming a scheme for such a union, and yet a like union should be impracticable for ten or a dozen English colonies." But the colonial assemblies rejected the Albany Plan of Union. As one British official explained, each colony had "a distinct government, wholly independent of the rest, pursuing its own interest and subject to no general command."

Colonial Aims and Indian Interests

An absence of intercolonial cooperation would prove to be one of the greatest weaknesses of the British colonies, for the ensuing war would be fought at a number of widespread locations. There were three principal flash points of conflict in North America. The first was along the northern Atlantic coast. France had ceded to Britain its colony of Acadia in 1713 (which the British renamed Nova Scotia), but continued to occupy the fortress of Louisburg, from which it guarded its fishing grounds and the St. Lawrence approach to New France. New Englanders had captured this prize in 1745 during King George's War (see Chapter 5), but the French had reclaimed it upon the settlement of that conflict in 1748. They subsequently reinforced Louisburg to such an extent that it became known as the Gibraltar of the New World.

A second zone of conflict was the border region between New France and New York, from Niagara Falls to Lake Champlain, where Canadians and New Yorkers competed furiously for the Indian trade. Unable to compete effectively against superior English goods, the French resorted to armed might, constructing fortifications on Lake George, south of Lake Champlain, and reinforcing their base at Niagara. In this zone the strategic advantage was held by the Iroquois Confederacy.

It was the Ohio country — the trans-Appalachian region along the Ohio River — that became the primary focus of British and French attention. This

The War for Empire in North America, 1754–1763

The Seven Years War in America (or the French and Indian War) was fought in three principal areas: the Maritime provinces, the frontier between New France and New York, and the upper Ohio River — gateway to the Great West.

rich land was a prime target of British backcountry settlers and frontier land speculators. The French worried that their isolated settlements at places such as Detroit, Vincennes, and Kaskaskia would be overrun by the expanding British population, and that the loss of the Ohio would threaten their entire Mississippi trading empire. To reinforce their claims, in 1749 the French sent a heavily armed force down the Ohio to warn off the British, and in 1752, supported by their northern Indian allies, they violently expelled a large number of British traders from the region. To prevent the British from returning to the west, they began the next year to construct a series of forts south from Lake Erie to the forks of the Ohio River, the junction of the Allegheny and Monongahela rivers.

The French "have stripped us of more than nine parts in ten of North America," one British official cried, "and left us only a skirt of coast along the Atlantic shore." In preparation for a general war, the British established the port of Halifax in Nova Scotia as a counterpart to Louisburg, and began laying plans to bring new settlers from Scotland and New England to replace the French peasants of Acadia. In northern New York, they strengthened existing forts and constructed new ones. And finally, the king decided to directly challenge the French claim to the upper Ohio Valley: he conferred an enormous grant of land on the Ohio Company, organized by Virginia and London capitalists, and the company made plans to build a fort at the forks of the Ohio River.

The impending conflict did not merely involve competing colonial powers, however, for the Indian peoples of the interior had interests of their own. In addition to its native inhabitants, the Ohio country had become a refuge for Indian peoples who had fled the Northeast — Delawares, Shawnees, Hurons, and Iroquois among them. Most of the Ohio Indians opposed the British, and were anxious to preserve the Appalachians as a barrier to westward expansion. They were also disturbed by the French movement into their country. The French outposts, however, unlike those of the British, did not become centers of expanding agricultural settlements.

The Iroquois Confederacy maintained a position of neutrality between the rival colonial powers. Theirs was not a passive neutrality, however, for Iroquois factions allied themselves with either the British or the French. Rather, the confederacy as a whole sought to play off one power against the other, to its own advantage. In the South, the Cherokees, Creeks, and Choctaws carved out similar roles for themselves between the British colonies on the one hand and those of the French in Louisiana and the Spanish in Florida. It was in the interests of these Indians, in other words, to perpetuate the existing colonial stalemate. Their position would be greatly undermined by an overwhelming victory for either side.

Frontier Warfare

At the Albany Congress the delegates received news that Colonel George Washington, a young militia officer from Virginia, had been forced to surrender his troops to a French force near the headwaters of the Ohio River. The governor of Virginia had sent Washington to expel the French from the region granted to the Ohio Company. Having forced him back, the Canadians now commanded the interior country from their base at Fort Duquesne, which they had built at the forks of the Ohio and named for the governor of Canada.

Taking up the challenge, the British government dispatched two Irish regiments under General Edward Braddock across the Atlantic in 1755. Supplemented with provincial forces, he would march his large army over the mountains to the Ohio River, to attack and destroy Fort Duquesne. Meanwhile, colonial militias commanded by colonial officers would strike at the New York frontier and the north Atlantic coast. An army of New England militiamen succeeded in capturing two important French forts on the border of Nova Scotia, but the other two prongs of the campaign were complete failures. The offensive in New York was repulsed. And in the worst defeat of a British army during the eighteenth century, Braddock's force was destroyed by a smaller number of French and Indians on the upper Ohio, and Braddock himself was killed.

Braddock's defeat resulted in full-scale warfare between Britain and France the next year, a conflict known as the Seven Years' War; in North America it came to be called the French and Indian War. The first few years of fighting were a near catastrophe for Great Britain. Canadians captured the British forts in northern New York. Indians pounded backcountry settlements, killed thousands of settlers, and raided deep into the coastal colonies, throwing British colonists into panic. "There is no surer way to sicken the people of the English colonies," a Canadian commander mused, "and to make them desire the return of peace." The absence of colonial cooperation greatly hampered the British attempt to mount a counterattack. And when British commanders tried to exert direct control over provincial

In this contemporary print, French and Indian forces attack an encampment of British troops on Lake George in September of 1755. The British troops drove off this assault with heavy losses, but two years later the French succeeded in forcing the British to retreat south, exposing New York and New England to punishing raids by Canadian militiamen and their Indian allies.

troops, they succeeded only in angering local authorities. French colonists were delighted at this show of disharmony between British commanders and their provincial troops. "The English on this continent are in dire distress," a Quebec merchant wrote to a friend in 1757. "The poor devils don't know which saint to turn to, for as you know they are not acquainted with many."

In this climate of defeat, the British enacted a draconian policy of retribution against the French-speaking peasants of Acadia (who inhabited what are today the provinces of Nova Scotia and New Brunswick). These people had lived peacefully under British rule for over forty years, but their refusal to swear oaths of allegiance to the crown was now used as an excuse for their expulsion. Over the next several years New England troops forcibly removed approximately 10,000 Acadians, selling their farms at bargain prices to immigrants from New England. Suffering terrible hardship and heartbreak, the Acadians were dispersed throughout the Atlantic world. Approximately 3,000 of them eventually found their way to Louisiana, where, known as the Cajuns, they reassembled their distinctive community, which survives today as a strong culture. The Acadian expulsion is one of the most infamous chapters of the British imperial record in North America.

The Conquest of Canada

In the dark days of 1757, William Pitt, an enthusiastic advocate of British expansion, assumed the prime ministership of Great Britain. "I know that I can save this country," Pitt declared, "and that no one else can." Heavily subsidizing the Prussians to fight the war in Europe, he reserved his own forces and resources for naval and colonial operations, deciding that the global war could be won in North America. Pitt committed the British to the conquest of Canada and the elimination of all French competition in North America. Such a goal could be achieved only with a tremendous outpouring of men and treasure. By promising that the war would be fought "at His Majesty's expense," Pitt was able to buy colonial cooperation. A massive infusion of British specie and credit greatly stimulated the North American economy. Pitt dispatched over 20,000 regular British troops across the Atlantic. Combining them with colonial forces, he massed over 50,000 armed men against Canada.

The British attracted Indian support for their plans by "redressing the grievances complained of by the Indians, with respect to the lands which have been fraudulently taken from them." In 1758 officials promised the Iroquois Confederacy and the Ohio Indians that the crown would "agree upon clear and fixed boundaries between our settlements and their hunting grounds, so that each party may know their own and be a mutual protection to each other of their respective possessions."

Thus did Pitt succeed in reversing the course of the war. Regular and provincial forces captured Louisburg in July 1758, setting the stage for the penetration of the St. Lawrence Valley. A month later a force of New Englanders captured a strategic French fort on Lake Ontario, thereby preventing the Canadians from resupplying their western posts. Encouraged by British promises, many Indian tribes abandoned the French alliance, and the French were forced to give up Fort Duquesne. A large British force soon took control at the forks of the Ohio, renaming the post Fort Pitt (later Pittsburgh) in honor of the prime minister. "Blessed be God," wrote a Boston editor; "the long looked for day is arrived that has now fixed us on the banks of the Ohio." The last of the French forts on the New York frontier fell in 1759. In the South, the Cherokees attempted to maintain the critical balance between the colonial powers by entering the war against the British, but regular and provincial British troops invaded their homeland and crushed them.

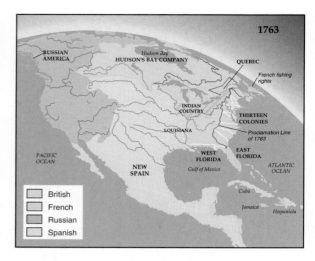

European Claims in North America, 1750 and 1763
As a result of the British victory in the Seven Years War, the map of colonial claims in North America was fundamentally transformed.

British forces now converged on Quebec, the heart of French Canada. In the summer of 1759 British troops, responding to General James Wolfe's order to "burn and lay waste the country," plundered the farms of *habitants* and shelled the city of Quebec. Finally, in an epic battle fought on the Plains of Abraham before the city walls, more than 2,000 British, French, American, and Canadian men lost their lives, including both Wolfe and the French commander, the Marquis de Montcalm. The British army prevailed, and Quebec fell. Although Canadian resistance continued for another year, the conquest of Montreal in 1760 marked the destruction of the French empire in America. "The great day is now come," declared the editor of the *Boston News-Letter*, "the fall of the American Carthage."

In the final two years of the war the British swept French ships from the seas, conquered important French and Spanish colonies in the Caribbean, achieved dominance in India, and even captured the Spanish Philippines. In the Treaty of Paris, signed in 1763, France lost all its American possessions except the sugar islands of Guadeloupe and Martinique. It ceded its claims east of the Mississippi to Great Britain, with the exception of New Orleans. That town, along with the other French trans-Mississippi claims, passed to Spain. In exchange for the return of its Caribbean and Pacific colonies, Spain ceded Florida to Britain. The imperial rivalry in eastern North America that had begun in the sixteenth century now came to an end with complete victory for the British Empire.

Continued Struggles over the West

When the Ohio Indians heard of the French cession of the western country to Britain they were shocked. "The French had no right to give away their country," they told a British trader. "They were never conquered by any nation." A new set of British policies soon shocked them all the more. Both the French and the British had long used gift-giving as a way of gaining favor with Indians. The Spanish officials who replaced the French in Louisiana made an effort to continue the old policy. But the British military governor of the western region, General Jeffery Amherst, in one of his first official actions, banned presents to Indian chiefs and tribes, demanding that they learn to live without "charity." Not only were Indians angered by Amherst's reversal of custom, but they were also frustrated by his refusal to supply them with the ammunition they required for hunting. Many were left starving.

In this climate, hundreds of Ohio Indians became disciples of an Indian visionary named Neolin ("The Enlightened One" in Algonquian), known to the English as the Delaware Prophet. The core of Neolin's teaching was that Indians had been corrupted by European ways and needed to purify themselves by returning to their traditions and preparing for a holy war. "Drive them out," he declared of the settlers. A group of chiefs who had gained influence by adopting Neolin's ideas laid plans for a coordinated attack against the British in the spring of 1763. The principal figure among them was the Ottawa chief Pontiac, renowned as an orator and political leader. This combination of inspirational religious and political leadership was similar to what had taken place among the Algonquians of the Chesapeake in the early seventeenth century (see Chapter 3), and would recur numerous times in the long history of Indian resistance to colonial expansion in North America.

In May of 1763 the Indians simultaneously attacked all the British forts in the west. They overran Fort Michilimackinac, at the narrows between Lakes Michigan and Huron, by scrambling through the gates supposedly in pursuit of a lacrosse ball; they were cheered on by the unsuspecting soldiers. In raids throughout the backcountry, Indians killed over 2,000 settlers. At Fort Pitt, General Amherst proposed that his officers "send the smallpox among the disaffected tribes" by distributing infected blankets from the fort's hospital. This early instance of germ warfare resulted in an epidemic that spread from the Delawares and Shawnees to the southern Creeks, Choctaws, and Chickasaws, killing hundreds of people. The Indians sacked and burned eight British posts, but failed to take the key forts of Niagara, Detroit, and Pitt. Pontiac fought on for another year, but most of the Indians sued for peace, fearing the destruction of their villages. The British came to terms because they knew they could not overwhelm the Indians. The war thus ended in stalemate.

Even before the uprising, the British had been at work on a policy they hoped would help to resolve frontier tensions. In accordance with wartime agreements with the Indian allies, the king assumed jurisdiction from colonial governors over Indian lands. The British government then issued the Proclamation of 1763, which set the terms for British policy toward the Indians. The proclamation set aside the region west of the crest of the Appalachian Mountains as "Indian Country," and required the specific authorization of the crown for any purchase of these protected Indian lands. British authorities promised to maintain commercial posts in the interior for Indian commerce, and to fortify the border to keep out land-hungry settlers. Indians were pleased with the proclamation, but land speculators and backcountry British Americans were outraged.

Colonists had expected that the removal of the French threat would allow them to move unencumbered into the West, regardless of the wishes of the Indian inhabitants. They could not understand why the British would award territory to Indian enemies who had slaughtered more than 4,000 settlers during the previous war. Angered by these regulations, a mob of Pennsylvanians known as the Paxton Boys massacred twenty Indian men, women, and children at the small village of Conestoga on the Susquehanna River in December of 1763. When colonial authorities moved to arrest them, 600 frontiersmen marched into Philadelphia in protest. Negotiations led by Benjamin Franklin helped to prevent a bloody confrontation, but the incident illustrated the aggressive attitude of the backcountry settlers in the aftermath of the Seven Years' War.

In fact, the British proved unable and ultimately unwilling to prevent the westward migration that was a dynamic part of the colonization of British North America. Within a few years of the war, New Englanders by the thousands were moving into the northern Green Mountain district, known by the

A treaty between the Delaware, Shawnee, and Mingo (western Iroquois) Indians and Great Britain, July 13, 1765, at the conclusion of the Indian uprising. The Indian chiefs signed with pictographs symbolizing their clans.

corrupted French name of Vermont. In the middle colonies, New York settlers pushed ever closer to the homeland of the Iroquois, while others located within the protective radius of Fort Pitt in western Pennsylvania. Hunters, stock herders, and farmers crossed over the first range of the Appalachians in Virginia and North Carolina, planting pioneer communities in what are now West Virginia and eastern Tennessee.

Moreover, the press of population growth and economic development turned the attention of investors and land speculators to the area west of the Appalachians. George Washington, member of a wealthy planter family and a prominent investor in western lands, believed that the proclamation declaring an Appalachian boundary to western expansion was merely "a temporary expedient." In 1768 the Ohio Company sent surveyors to mark out their grant in the upper Ohio Valley. In response to demands by settlers and speculators, British authorities were soon pressing the Iroquois and Cherokees for cessions of land in Indian Country. No longer able to play off rival colonial powers, Indians were reduced to a choice between compliance and resistance. Weakened by the recent war, they chose to sign away their land rights. In the Treaty of Hard Labor in 1768, the Cherokees ceded a vast tract on the waters of the upper Tennessee River, where British settlers had already planted communities. In the Treaty of Fort Stanwix of the same year, the Iroquois gave up their claim to the Ohio Valley, hoping thereby to deflect English settlement away from their own homeland.

The individual colonies were even more aggressive. Locked in a dispute with Pennsylvania about jurisdiction in the Ohio country, the Virginia governor, John Murray, Earl of Dunmore, sent a force to occupy Fort Pitt. In 1774, in an attempt to gain legitimacy for his dispute with Pennsylvania, Dunmore provoked a frontier war with the Shawnees. After defeating them he forced them to cede the region to Virginia. The Iroquois and Ohio Indians angrily complained about the outcome of Dunmore's War. The king, they argued, had guaranteed that the boundary between colonial and Indian land "should forever after be looked upon as a barrier between us." But the Americans "entirely disregard, and despise the settlement agreed upon by their superiors and us." They "are come in vast numbers to the Ohio, and [give] our people to understand that they would settle wherever they pleased. If this is the case we must look upon every engagement you made with us as void and of no effect." This

continuing struggle for the West would be an important issue in the coming Revolution.

THE IMPERIAL CRISIS IN BRITISH NORTH AMERICA

No colonial power of the mid-eighteenth century could match Britain in projecting imperial power over the face of the globe. During the years following its victory in the Seven Years' War, Britain turned confidently to the reorganization of its North American empire. This new colonial policy plunged British authorities into a new and ultimately more threatening conflict with the colonists, who had begun to develop a sense of their own nationality.

The Emergence of American Nationalism

Despite the anger of frontiersmen over the Proclamation of 1763, the conclusion of the Seven Years' War had left most colonists proud of their place in the British Empire. But during the war many had begun to note important contrasts between themselves and the mother country. The regular soldiers of the British army, for example, shocked Americans with their profane, lewd, and violent behavior. But the colonists were equally shocked by the swift and terrible punishment that aristocratic officers used to keep these soldiers in line. David Perry of Massachusetts witnessed the punishment of two soldiers sentenced to 800 lashes apiece. "The flesh appeared to be entirely whipped from their shoulders," he wrote, "and they hung as mute and motionless as though they had long since been deprived of life." A military doctor stood nearby with a vial of smelling salts, periodically reviving the men and taunting them: "Damn you, you can bear it yet." It was, Perry concluded, "a specimen of British cruelty." Men who had witnessed such scenes found it easy to believe in the threat of British "slavery."

Colonial forces, by contrast, were composed of volunteer companies. Officers tempered their administration of punishment, knowing they had to maintain the enthusiasm of these troops. Discipline thus fell considerably below the standards to which British officers were accustomed. "Riff-raff," one British general said of the colonials, "the lowest dregs of the people, both officers and men." The British made no secret of their poor opinion of colonial fighting men. "The Americans are in general the dirtiest, most contemptible, cowardly dogs that you can conceive," wrote General Wolfe. For their part, many colonial officers believed that the British ignored the important role the Americans had played in the Seven Years' War. Massachusetts, for example, lost between 1,500 and 2,000 fighting men. This mutual suspicion and hostility was often expressed in name calling: British soldiers called New Englanders "Yankees," while colonists heckled the redcoated British with taunts of "Lobster." During the war many colonists began to see themselves as distinct from the British.

The Seven Years' War also strengthened a sense of intercolonial, American identity. Farm boys who never before had ventured outside the communities of their birth fought in distant regions with men like themselves from other colonies. Such experiences reinforced a developing nationalist perspective. From 1735 to 1775, while trade with Britain doubled, commerce among the colonies increased by a factor of four. People and ideas moved along with these goods. The first stage lines linking seaboard cities began operation in the 1750s. Spurred by Postmaster Franklin, many colonies built or improved post roads for transporting the mails.

One of the most important means of intercolonial communication was the weekly newspaper. Early in the eighteenth century the colonial press functioned as a mouthpiece for the government; editors who criticized public officials could land in jail. In 1735, for example, the New York City editor John Peter Zenger was indicted for seditious libel after printing antigovernment articles. But as it turned out, the Zenger case provided the precedent for greater freedom of the press. "Shall the press be silenced that evil governors may have their way?" Zenger's attorney asked the jury. "The question before the court is not the cause of a poor printer," he declared, but the cause "of every free man that lives under a British government on the main of America." Zenger was acquitted. By 1760, more than twenty highly opinionated weekly newspapers circulated in the British colonies, and according to one estimate, a quarter of all male colonists were regular readers.

The midcentury American press focused increasingly on intercolonial affairs. One study of colonial newspapers indicates that intercolonial coverage increased sixfold over the four decades preceding the Revolution. Editors of local papers increasingly looked at events from a "continental" perspective. This trend accelerated during the Seven Years' War, when families demanded coverage of events in distant colonies where their men might be fighting. During these years the British colonists of

James Franklin began publishing *The New-England Courant* in Boston in 1721. When Franklin criticized the government, he was jailed, and the paper continued under the editorship of brother Benjamin. The *Courant* ceased publication in 1726, and the Franklin brothers went on to other papers — James to *The Rhode Island State Gazette*, Benjamin to *The Pennsylvania Gazette* in Philadelphia. Before the Zenger case in 1735, few editors dared to challenge the government.

North America first began to use the term *American* to denote their common identity. More than any previous event, the Seven Years' War promoted a new spirit of nationalism and a wider notion of community. This was the social base of the political community later forged at the Continental Congress.

Colonial newspapers reflected the views of their editors, few of whom held to contemporary standards of journalistic objectivity; these papers were as much journals of opinion as sources of news. Yet most of America's newspapers shared the same point of view, portraying the struggle with France, for example, as a Protestant crusade against Catholic attempts to block the progress of liberty. This uniformity of opinion in the press was reinforced by the widespread editorial practice of reprinting articles that had appeared in other colonial papers.

Editorials, letters to the editor, and pamphlets published in these years provide a sense of the political assumptions held by influential colonists. Americans were thought to possess all the rights and protections of native Englishmen; the common law of custom and precedent, after all, had been extended explicitly to North America by the provisions of the colonial charters. Prominent among these protections was the "balanced" government of the English constitution. Like the common law, this constitution was unwritten, consisting of a bundle of traditions that included the principle of shared power. The power to raise public revenues belonged exclusively to the representatives of the people. The British Parliament might legitimately regulate international trade, most Americans believed, but only the colonial assemblies enjoyed the power to raise domestic taxes. Royal governors had struggled with the assemblies over this question for decades. (For a discussion of colonial government, see Chapter 5.)

These struggles left Americans receptive to the views of the radical Whigs of eighteenth-century England, whose writings were frequently reprinted in the colonial press. These radicals warned of the growing threat to liberty posed by the unchecked exercise of power. In their more emotional writings they argued that a conspiracy existed among the powerful — kings, aristocrats, and Catholics — to quash liberty and institute tyranny. Their political principles included extension of the ballot to greater numbers of men, apportionment of legislative representation on the basis of population, and responsiveness by representatives to their constituents. The only effective counterweight to the abuse of power was the constant vigilance of the people and their exercise of public virtue — the sacrifice of self-interest for the public good. Although these ideas were put forward as the basic political principles of Englishmen, in fact they were well outside the mainstream of opinion in Britain itself.

The emerging sense of American political identity was soon tested by British measures designed to raise revenues in the colonies. To quell Indian uprisings and stifle discontent among the French and Spanish populations of Quebec and Florida, 10,000 British regular troops remained stationed in North America at the conclusion of the Seven Years' War. The cost of maintaining this force added to the enormous debt Britain had run up during the fighting, and created a desperate need for additional revenues. Increased excise taxes at home, however, resulted in disruptive demonstrations in the south of England, and Parliament was flooded by petitions from landlords and merchants protesting any attempt to raise revenues at their expense. In 1764 the Chancellor of the Exchequer, George Grenville, deciding to obtain the needed revenue from America, pushed through Parliament a measure known as the Sugar Act. "It is just and necessary," Parliament declared, "that a revenue be raised in America for defraying the expenses of defending, protecting, and securing the same."

The old Molasses Act of 1733 had not been designed to raise revenues. Rather, by placing a prohibitive duty on sugar imported into the colonies from outside the British empire, it was supposed to help regulate trade. Moreover, the understaffed and corrupt customs service in North America had not been able to enforce the act effectively, and the law had been widely ignored by American smugglers. The Sugar Act, however, revitalized the customs service, introducing stricter registration procedures for ships and adding more officers. In anticipation of American resistance, the legislation also increased the jurisdiction of the vice-admiralty court at Halifax, where customs cases were heard. In this court, there was no presumption of innocence and the accused had no right to a jury trial.

These new regulations promised not only to squeeze the incomes of American merchants, but to cut off their lucrative smuggling operations. The merchants had already been hurt by an economic depression that accompanied the decline in public spending at the end of the Seven Years' War. Colonial taxes, moreover, which had been raised during the war, remained at an all-time high. In many cities, merchants as well as artisans protested loudly. Boston was especially vocal: in response to the sugar tax, the town meeting proposed a boycott of certain English imports. This movement for non-importation soon spread to other port towns.

Colonial agents in London protested that the

new taxes violated traditional British rights. "A tax laid upon a country without the consent of the legislature of that country," said Jared Ingersoll of Connecticut, was "contrary to the foundation principles of the natural and constitutional rights and liberties." The rhetoric was even stronger at home. James Otis, Jr., a Massachusetts lawyer fond of grand oratory, was one of the first Americans to strike a number of themes that would become familiar over the next fifteen years. A man's "right to his life, his liberty, his property" was "written on the heart, and revealed to him by his maker," he argued in language echoing the rhetoric of the Great Awakening. It was "inherent, inalienable, and indefeasible by any laws, pacts, contracts, covenants, or stipulations which man could devise." "An act against the Constitution is void," he declared; there could be "no taxation without representation."

But it was only fair, Grenville argued, that the colonists help pay the costs of the empire, and what better way to do so than by a tax? "Will these Americans," asked one of his colleagues in Parliament, "grudge to contribute their mite to relieve us from the heavy weight of that burden which we lie under?" In early 1765 Grenville, unswayed by American protests, introduced a second and considerably more sweeping revenue measure, the Stamp Act. This tax required the purchase of specially embossed paper for all newspapers, legal documents, licenses, insurance policies, ship's papers, and even dice and playing cards.

The Stamp Act Crisis

During the summer and autumn of 1765 the American reaction to the Stamp Act created a crisis of unprecedented proportions. Unlike the Sugar Act, which struck only at merchants, the stamp tax affected lawyers, printers, tavern owners, and other influential colonists. It had to be paid in hard money, and it came during a period of economic stagnation. Many colonists complained, as one did, of being "miserably burdened and oppressed with taxes." And indeed, most of the complaints focused on the economic issue.

Of more importance for the longer term, however, were the constitutional implications. The British argued that Americans were subject to the acts of Parliament because of *virtual representation.* That is, members of Parliament were thought to represent not just their districts, but all citizens of the empire. As one British writer put it, the colonists were "represented in Parliament in the same manner as those inhabitants of Britain are who have not voices

During the Stamp Act Crisis of 1765 — provoked by the new British requirement that required the purchase of specially embossed paper for newspapers, legal documents, and even playing cards — one American newspaper cynically proposed that the stamp be in the form of this skull and crossbones.

in elections." But in an influential pamphlet of 1765, *Considerations on the Propriety of Imposing Taxes,* Maryland lawyer Daniel Dulany rejected this theory. Because Americans were members of a separate political community, he insisted, Parliament could impose no tax on them. Instead, he argued for *actual representation,* emphasizing the direct relationship that must exist between the people and their political representatives. "The colonies are dependent upon Great Britain," Dulany admitted, but there was a great difference between dependency and "absolute vassalage and slavery."

It was just such constitutional issues that were emphasized in the Virginia Stamp Act Resolutions, pushed through the Virginia assembly by the passionate young lawyer Patrick Henry in May of 1765. Two years before, Henry had established his reputation as a radical by arguing that George III had degenerated "into a tyrant, and forfeits all rights to his subjects' obedience." Now, speaking in favor of these resolutions in the Virginia House of Burgesses, Henry warned the king to heed the fate of earlier tyrants such as Caesar and Charles I, both of whom had lost their lives. To howls of "Treason!" from his conservative colleagues, Henry cried that he spoke in "the interest of his country's dying liberty." Although the Burgesses rejected the most radical of his resolutions, they were all reprinted throughout the colonies. By the end of 1765 the assemblies of eight other colonies had approved similar measures denouncing the Stamp Act and declaring the principle of "no taxation without representation."

In Massachusetts, the leaders of the opposition to the Stamp Act came from a group of upper- and middle-class men who had long opposed the conservative leaders of the colony. These men had worked years to establish a political alliance with Boston craftsmen and workers who met at taverns, in volunteer fire companies, or at social clubs. One of these clubs, known as the Loyall Nine, included Samuel Adams, an associate and friend of James Otis who had made his career in local politics. Using his contacts with professionals, craftsmen, and laboring men as well, Adams helped put together an anti-British alliance that spanned Boston's social classes. "If our trade may be taxed," he reasoned with working men, "why not our lands? Why not the produce of our lands and everything we possess or make use of?" In August of 1765 Adams and the Loyall Nine were instrumental in organizing a protest of Boston workingmen against the Stamp Act.

The working people of Boston had reasons of their own to be angry. While Boston's elite had prospered during the eighteenth century, the conditions for workers and the poor had worsened. Unemployment, inflation, and high taxes had greatly increased the level of poverty during the depression that followed the Seven Years' War, and many were resentful. Concerted action by crowds, as when people took to the streets to demand fair prices for bread, or when posses formed to capture criminals, were commonplace in the eighteenth-century communities throughout Europe and the colonies. In 1747, a crowd outraged at the British impressment of fifty Boston residents seized control of the city and demanded their release. Annual street demonstrations on Guy Fawkes Day (November 5), celebrating the failure of a seventeenth-century Catholic plot against the English government, frequently turned to fighting among mobs from different neighborhoods. It was in this tradition that a large Boston crowd assembled on August 14, 1765, in the shade of a broad "liberty tree" and strung up effigies of several British officials, including Boston's stamp distributor, Andrew Oliver. The restless crowd then proceeded to vandalize Oliver's office and home. At the order of Oliver's brother-in-law, Lieutenant Governor Thomas Hutchinson, leader of the Massachusetts conservatives, the town sheriff tried to break up the crowd, but he was pelted with paving stones and bricks. Soon thereafter, Oliver resigned his commission. The unified action of Boston's social groups had had its intended effect.

Twelve days later, however, a similar crowd gathered at the aristocratic home of Hutchinson himself. As the family fled through the back door, the crowd smashed through the front with axes. Inside they demolished furniture, chopped down the interior walls, consumed the contents of the wine cellar, and looted everything of value, leaving the house a

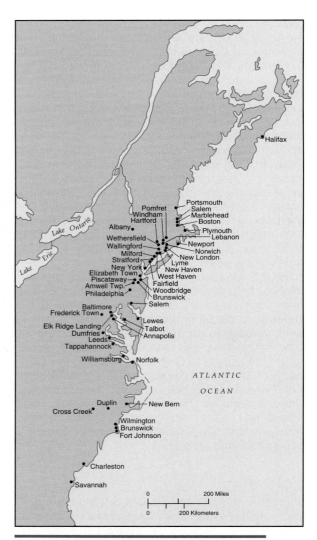

Demonstrations Against the Stamp Act, 1765
From Halifax in the north to Savannah in the south, popular demonstrations against the Stamp Act forced the resignation of British tax officials.

mere shell. Upper- and middle-class radicals were appalled, for the crowd seemed to be acting against wealth itself. Hutchinson, though, had made himself particularly odious by leading a movement to dismantle the traditional town meeting form of government, which was open to all property owners, big and small, and was responsive to the poor as well. The ordinary people of Boston had their own concerns, and popular resistance to authority gave them an opportunity to act on those issues.

As these events demonstrated, it was not always possible to keep popular protests within bounds. During the fall and winter, urban crowds in commercial towns from Halifax in the north to Savannah in the south forced the resignation of British tax officials. Sometimes things got out of hand, as when a Connecticut mob stuffed a stubborn tax official into a coffin, nailed it shut, and began to bury it before releasing the terrified man, who immediately submitted his resignation. Houses were wrecked in Newport, and a stamp distributor's store was destroyed in Baltimore. The divergent goals of different social groups could be seen in these demonstrations. In Charleston, the day after a protest by white citizens, a group of black slaves paraded in favor of liberty, throwing conservatives and radicals alike into a panic.

In many colonial cities and towns, merchants, lawyers, and respectable craftsmen sought to moderate the resistance movement by seizing control of it. The groups they formed took their name from the remarks of Englishman Isaac Barre, who spoke up for the Americans during the parliamentary debates over the Stamp Act. The Americans would not surrender their rights without a fight, said Barre, for they were "sons of liberty." The Sons of Liberty encouraged moderate forms of protest. They circulated petitions, published pamphlets, and encouraged crowd actions only as a last resort; always they emphasized limited political goals. There were few repetitions of mob attacks, but by the end of 1765 almost all the stamp distributors had resigned or fled, making it impossible for Britain to enforce the Stamp Act.

There were even more conservative forms of protest. Merchants formed nonimportation associations, reviving the tactic they had used during the protests over the Sugar Act. In October 1765, acting on a call from the Massachusetts assembly, delegates from nine colonies convened the Stamp Act Congress in New York City, the first official intercolonial meeting since the Albany Congress of 1754. The delegates issued a moderate appeal to the British crown and government in which they pledged their allegiance to George III and offered "all due subordination" to Parliament, but protested that "no taxes be imposed on them but with their own consent." Behind the scenes, however, many of the delegates argued that the British were conspiring to deprive Americans of their liberties and reduce them to slavery, and that the Stamp Act was merely the first step.

Fears of conspiracy and threats to liberties were familiar themes that had been rehearsed for years in the popular press. As evidence, radicals pointed to the standing army that Britain had left in the colonies, to the subversion of the common law right to trial by jury, and to the attack on the right of self-government implicit in the revenue measures.

The Stamp Act, John Adams wrote in his diary, was part of an "enormous engine, fabricated by the British Parliament, for battering down all the rights and liberties of America." The British measures thus helped to focus a new sense of American community, though, as the work of the Stamp Act Congress demonstrated, the colonists were still a long way from the notion of independence.

Repeal of the Stamp Act

In the fall of 1765, a growing number of British merchants, worried about the effects of the growing nonimportation movement among the colonists, began petitioning Parliament to repeal the Stamp Act. The British colonies in North America were the destination for about 40 percent of England's exports. "I rejoice that America has resisted," said William Pitt, who was no longer prime minister but spoke for the merchant interests in Parliament; "it is my opinion that this kingdom has no right to lay a tax upon the colonies." Grenville demanded that the British army be used to enforce the act. "Tell me," he demanded of Pitt, "when the Americans were emancipated." Pitt's response was memorable: "I desire to know when they were made slaves." Parliament heard the testimony of a number of interested parties, including Benjamin Franklin, colonial agent for Pennsylvania, who warned that Grenville's proposal to use troops could bring on a rebellion.

It was not, however, until Grenville was replaced by Lord Rockingham, who opposed the Stamp Act, that in March of 1766 a bill for repeal passed the House of Commons. This news was greeted with celebrations throughout the American colonies, and the nonimportation associations were disbanded. Overlooked in the mood of optimism was Parliament's assertion in this Declaratory Act of its full authority to make laws binding the colonies "in all cases whatsoever." The notion of absolute parliamentary supremacy over colonial matters was basic to the British theory of empire. Even Pitt, friend of America that he was, asserted "the authority of this kingdom over the colonies to be sovereign and supreme, in every circumstance of government and legislation whatsoever." The Declaratory Act signaled that the conflict had not been resolved, but merely postponed.

"SAVE YOUR MONEY AND SAVE YOUR COUNTRY"

Colonial resistance to the Stamp Act was stronger in urban than in rural communities, stronger among merchants, craftsmen, and planters than among farmers and frontiersmen. When the Parliament next moved to impose its will, as it had promised to do in the Declaratory Act, imposing new duties on imported goods, the American opposition again adopted the tactic of nonimportation. But this time resistance spread from the cities and towns into the countryside. As the editor of the *Boston Gazette* phrased the issue, "Save your money and you save your country." It became the slogan of the movement.

The Townshend Acts

King George III had assumed the throne in 1760 when he was only twenty-two years old. Unlike his father, Frederick, and his grandfather, George II, who were native Germans, George III had been born and raised in England, was well educated, and wished to strengthen the administration of the empire. Unfortunately, he was a poor judge of men, and a rigid personality made it difficult for him to cooperate with his own ministers. Consequently, during the 1760s there was a rapid turnover of government leaders that made it difficult for Britain to form a consistent and even-handed policy toward the colonies. In 1767, after several failed governments, George III asked William Pitt to again become prime minister. Pitt enjoyed enormous good will in America, and a government under his leadership stood a good chance of reclaiming colonial credibility. But, suffering from a prolonged illness, he was soon forced to retire, and his place as head of the cabinet was assumed by Charles Townshend, Chancellor of the Exchequer.

One of the first problems facing the new government was the national debt. At home there was massive unemployment, riots over high prices, and tax protests. The large landowners forced a bill through Parliament slashing their taxes by 25 percent. The government feared continued opposition at home far more than opposition in America. So as part of his plan to close the budget gap, Townshend proposed a new revenue measure for the colonies that placed import duties on commodities such as lead, glass, paint, paper, and tea. Townshend hoped that this *external tax,* a duty imposed on goods before they entered colonial markets, would satisfy colonial grievances against *internal taxes* such as those the Stamp Act had levied against goods sold in colonial shops. This was a distinction that Benjamin Franklin, for example, had made in his presentation to the House of Commons. For most colonists, however, it proved to be a distinction without a difference.

John Dickinson, a wealthy Philadelphia lawyer, adopted the pose of a humble husbandman for his 1768 pamphlet, the most influential American response to the Townshend Acts. Dickinson argued against the constitutionality of a revenue tax, but urged resistance rather than revolution. He remained a moderate, and as a delegate from Pennsylvania voted against the Declaration of Independence in 1776. But immediately afterward he volunteered for service in the Patriot army.

The most influential response to these Revenue Acts came in a series of articles by John Dickinson, *Letters from a Farmer in Pennsylvania,* that were reprinted in nearly every colonial newspaper. Dickinson was a wealthy Philadelphia lawyer, but in this work he adopted the pose of a humble husbandman. Parliament had the right to regulate trade through the use of duties, he conceded. It could place prohibitive tariffs, for example, on foreign products. But it had no constitutional authority to tax goods in order to raise revenues in America. As the preface to the Revenue Acts made clear, the income they produced would be used to pay the salaries of royal officials in America. Thus, Dickinson pointed out, colonial administrators would not be subject to the financial oversight of elected representatives.

Other Americans warned again that this was

part of the British conspiracy to suppress American liberties. Their fears were reinforced by Townshend's stringent enforcement of the Revenue Acts. He created a new and strengthened Board of Commissioners of the Customs, and established a series of vice-admiralty courts at Boston, Philadelphia, and Charleston to prosecute violators of the duties — the first time these hated institutions had appeared in the most important American port cities. And to demonstrate his power, he also suspended New York's assembly. That body had refused to vote public funds to support the British troops garrisoned in the colony. Until the citizens of New York relented, Townshend declared, they would no longer be represented. In response to these measures, some men argued for violent resistance. But it was Dickinson's essays that had the greatest effect on the public debate, not only because of their convincing argument, but because of their mild and reasonable tone. "Let us behave like dutiful children," Dickinson urged, "who have received unmerited blows from a beloved parent." As yet, no sentiment for independence existed in America. The colonial response was one of resistance to what were considered unconstitutional measures by the British authorities.

The Revival of Nonimportation

Associations of nonimportation and nonconsumption, revived in October 1767 when the Boston town meeting drew up a long list of British products to boycott, became the main weapon of the resistance movement. Over the next few months other port cities, including Providence, Newport, and New York, set up nonimportation associations of their own. Towns such as Philadelphia, however, were unable to overcome conflicts between merchants and artisans. The economy had begun to improve since the earlier boycott, and many merchants saw little advantage in curtailing imports. Craftsmen, on the other hand, enthusiastically supported nonimportation, because it meant that consumers would buy their products rather than foreign ones. Supported by workers, artisans took to the streets in towns and cities throughout the colonies to force merchants to stop importing British goods. The associations published the names of uncooperative importers and retailers. These people then became the object of protesters, who sometimes resorted to violence. Coercion was very much a part of the movement.

Adopting the language of the Protestant ethic, nonimportation associations pledged to curtail luxuries and stimulate local industry. These values held great appeal in small towns and rural districts, which previously had been relatively uninvolved in the anti-British struggle. In 1768 and 1769, colonial newspapers paid a great deal of attention to women's support for the boycott. Groups of women, some styling themselves Daughters of Liberty, organized spinning bees to produce homespun for local consumption. The actual work performed at these bees was less important than the symbolic message. "The industry and frugality of American ladies," wrote the editor of the *Boston Evening Post*, "are contributing to bring about the political salvation of a whole continent." Other women renounced silks and satins and pledged to stop serving tea to their husbands. Women sang:

> Throw aside your topknots of pride,
> Wear none but your own country linen;
> Of economy boast, let your pride be the most,
> To show clothes of your own make and spinning.

This British cartoon, "A Society of Patriotic Ladies," ridiculed the efforts of American women to support the Patriot cause by boycotting tea. The moderator of the meeting appears coarse and masculine, while an attractive scribe is swayed by the amorous attention of a gentleman. The events under the table suggest that these women are neglecting their true duty.

The poet Milcah Martha Moore urged American women to

Stand firmly resolv'd, and bid Grenville to see,
That rather than freedom we part with our tea,
And well as we love the dear draught when a-dry,
As American patriots our taste we deny.

Nonimportation appealed to the traditional values of rural communities — self-sufficiency and independence — and for the first time brought country people into the growing community of resistance.

Nonimporation was greatly strengthened in May of 1769 when the Virginia House of Burgesses enacted the first provincial association. The association banned the importation of goods enumerated in the Townshend Acts, and slaves and luxury commodities as well. Over the next few months all the colonies but New Hampshire enacted similar associations. Because of these efforts, nonimportation was a great success. The value of colonial imports from Britain fell from £2.2 million in 1768 to £1.3 million in 1769, a decline of 41 percent. In the largest port cities the decrease was even greater — 54 percent in Philadelphia and over 80 percent in New York. The Townshend duties, meanwhile, collected only about £20,000 in revenue. By 1770 English merchants were again protesting their hardship before Parliament.

The Massachusetts Circular Letter

Boston and Massachusetts were at the center of the agitation over the Townshend Acts. In February of 1768 the Massachusetts House of Representatives approved a letter, drawn up by Samuel Adams, addressed to the speakers of the other provincial assemblies. Designed largely as a propaganda device and having little practical significance, the letter denounced the Townshend Acts, attacked the British plan to make royal officials independent of colonial assemblies, and urged the colonies to find a way to "harmonize with each other." Massachusetts governor Francis Bernard condemned the document for stirring up rebellion and dissolved the legislature. In Britain Lord Hillsborough, Secretary of State for the Colonies, ordered each royal governor in America to likewise dissolve his colony's assembly if it should endorse the letter. Before this demand reached America, the assemblies of New Hampshire, New Jersey, and Connecticut had commended Massachusetts. Virginia, moreover, had issued a circular letter encouraging a "hearty union" among the colonies and urging common action against the

British measures that "have an immediate tendency to enslave us."

Hillsborough now ordered Governor Bernard to force the newly elected House of Representatives to rescind Adams's letter and delete all mention of it from its journal. The radicals could have asked for nothing better; resistance to the Townshend duties had been flagging, but there was great support for the prerogative and independence of the assembly. After protracted debate in June of 1768, the representatives voted ninety-two to seventeen to defy Bernard, who immediately shut them down. The "Glorious Ninety-two" became heroes of the hour, and men in taverns throughout the colonies drank "ninety-two toasts" to the brave men of Massachusetts. The "rescinders," meanwhile, were condemned by public and press; in local elections the next year, seven of them lost their seats.

Throughout this crisis there were rumors and threats of mob rule in Boston. "I am no friend to riots, tumult, and unlawful assemblies," Samuel Adams declared, "but when the people are oppressed . . . they are not to be blamed." Because customs agents pressed on smugglers and honest traders alike, they enraged merchants, seamen, and dockworkers. In June of 1768 a crowd assaulted customs officials who had seized John Hancock's sloop *Liberty* for nonpayment of duties. So frightened were the officials that they fled the city. Hancock, reportedly the wealthiest merchant in the colonies, and a vocal opponent of the British measures, had become a principal target of the customs officers. In September, the Boston town meeting called on the people to arm themselves, and in the absence of an elected assembly it invited all the other towns to send delegates to a provincial convention. There were threats of armed resistance, but little support for it in the convention, which broke up in chaos. Nevertheless the British, fearing insurrection, occupied Boston with infantry and artillery regiments on October 1, 1768. With this action, they sacrificed a great deal of good will and respect and added greatly to the growing tensions.

The Boston Massacre

The British troops stationed in the colonies were the object of scorn and hostility over the next two years. There were regular conflicts between soldiers and radicals in New York City, often focusing on the Sons of Liberty. These men would erect "liberty poles" festooned with banners and flags proclaiming their cause, and the British troops would promptly destroy them. When the New York assembly finally bowed to Townshend in December of 1769 and voted an appropriation to support the troops, the New York City Sons of Liberty organized a demonstration and erected a large liberty pole. The soldiers chopped it down, sawed it into pieces, and left the wood on the steps of a tavern frequented by the Sons. This led to a riot in which British troops used their bayonets against several thousand New Yorkers armed with cutlasses and clubs. Several men were wounded.

Confrontations also took place in Boston. In September 1769, James Otis provoked a melee by picking a fight in a tavern catering to British officers. The next month an encounter between a mob and soldiers ended with the troops firing a volley into the air. The demonstrators were "mutinous desperadoes," wrote General Thomas Gage; they were guilty of "sedition." Sam Adams played up reports and rumors of soldiers harassing women, picking fights, or simply taunting residents with versions of "Yankee Doodle." Soldiers were frequently hauled into Boston's courts, and local judges adopted a completely unfriendly attitude toward these members of the occupying army. In February 1770, an eleven-year-old boy was killed when a customs officer opened fire on a rock-throwing crowd. Although no soldiers were involved, this incident inflamed the tensions between citizens and troops.

A persistent source of conflict was the competition between troops and townsmen over jobs.

Soldiers were permitted to work when off duty, and this put them in competition with day laborers. In early March of 1770, an off-duty soldier walked into a ropewalk in search of a job. "You can clean my shithouse," he was told. The soldier left but returned with his friends, and a small riot ensued. Over the next few days the fighting continued in the streets between the wharf and the Common, where the soldiers were encamped. On the evening of March 5, a crowd gathered at the Customs House and began taunting a guard, calling him a "damned rascally scoundrel lobster son of a bitch." A captain and seven soldiers went to his rescue, only to be pelted with snowballs and stones. Suddenly, without orders, the frightened soldiers began to fire. Five of the crowd fell dead and six more were wounded. The soldiers escaped to their barracks, but a mob numbering in the hundreds rampaged through the streets demanding vengeance.

Fearing for the safety of his men and the security of the state, Thomas Hutchinson, now governor of Massachusetts, ordered British troops out of Boston and arrested the soldiers who had fired the shots. The soldiers were tried later that year. Defending them were John Adams and Josiah Quincy, Jr., two leaders of the radicals. Adams and Quincy established a reputation for fairness and statesmanship by convincing a jury of Bostonians that the soldiers had fired in fear of their lives. The "Boston Massacre" became infamous throughout the colonies, in

The Bloody Massacre perpetrated in King Street Boston on March 5th 1770 by a party of the 29th Regt.

In Paul Revere's version of the Boston Massacre, issued three weeks after the incident, the British fire an organized volley into a defenseless crowd. Revere's print — which he plagiarized from another Boston engraver — may have been inaccurate, but was enormously effective propaganda. It hung in so many Patriot homes that the judge hearing the murder trial of these British soldiers warned the jury not to be swayed by "the prints exhibited in our houses."

part because of the circulation of an inflammatory print produced by the Boston engraver Paul Revere, which depicted the British as firing on a crowd of unresisting civilians. But for many colonists, the incident was a disturbing reminder of the extent to which relations with the mother country had deteriorated. During the next two years, many people found themselves pulling back from the brink. "There seems," one Bostonian wrote, "to be a pause in politics."

The growth of American resistance was slowed as well by the news that Parliament had repealed most of the Townshend duties on March 5, 1770 — the same day as the Boston Massacre. In the climate of apprehension and confusion, there were few celebrations of the repeal, and the nonimportation associations almost immediately collapsed. Over the next three years, the value of British imports rose by 80 percent. The parliamentary retreat on the question of duties, like the earlier repeal of the Stamp Act, was accompanied by a face-saving measure — retention of the tax on tea "as a mark of the supremacy of Parliament," in the words of Frederick Lord North, the new prime minister.

From Resistance to Rebellion

No great issues replaced the Townshend duties during the early 1770s, and there was a lull in agitation. But the situation turned violent in 1773, when Parliament again infuriated the Americans. This time it was an ill-advised Tea Act, and it propelled the colonists on a swift track from resistance to outright rebellion. The groundwork for these developments, however, were laid during the quiet years that preceded them.

Committees of Correspondence

The Townshend Acts had declared Britain's intention of using customs revenues to pay the salaries of royal officials in the colonies. In June of 1772, Governor Hutchinson inaugurated another controversy by announcing that henceforth his salary and those of other royally appointed Massachusetts officials would be paid by the crown. In effect, this made the executive and judiciary branches of the colony's government independent of elected representatives. In October, the Boston town meeting appointed a Committee of Correspondence to communicate with other towns regarding this challenge. The next month the meeting issued what became known as the *Boston Pamphlet,* a series of declarations written

by Adams and other radicals, concluding that British encroachments upon colonial rights pointed to a plot to enslave Americans. The Boston committee asked others to consider the evidence: Parliament's continual assertion of total supremacy over the colonies, its imposition of a standing army in America, governors and judges placed at the bidding of royal power, vice-admiralty courts abusing the common law rights of Englishmen, taxation without representation, and ravenous customs collectors. It amounted to a powerful case.

Another incident further inflamed American opinion. The same month as Hutchinson's announcement, the British schooner *Gaspee,* a customs warship, ran aground on the Rhode Island coast, and was sacked and burned by a crowd of merchants and seamen. British officials created a commission of inquiry armed with orders to send suspects to England for trial. Although the commission failed to locate the culprits, its instructions provided further evidence of the British intention to subvert common law rights — in this case, trial by a local jury of peers. In March of 1773 the Virginia House of Burgesses appointed a standing committee for intercolonial correspondence "to obtain the most early and authentic intelligence" of British actions affecting America, "and to keep up and maintain a correspondence and communication with our sister colonies." The Virginia committee, including Patrick Henry, Richard Henry Lee, and young Thomas Jefferson, served as a model, and within a year all the colonies except Pennsylvania, where conservatives controlled the legislature, had created committees of their own. These committees became the principal channel for sharing information, shaping public opinion, and building intercolonial cooperation before the Continental Congress of 1774.

The information most damaging to British influence came from the radicals in Boston. Governor Hutchinson put himself at the center of controversy by declaring early in 1773 that the colonists were mistaken if they thought they enjoyed all the rights of Englishmen. Furthermore, even though they had removed themselves across the Atlantic, he argued, they were still subordinate to Parliament. "I know of no line that can be drawn," he asserted, "between the supreme authority of Parliament and the total independence of the colonies." This bold declaration outraged colonists who during the years of agitation against taxes and duties had convinced themselves of the case against parliamentary supremacy.

In June, the Boston committee circulated a set of

confidential letters from Hutchinson to the ministry in Britain, obtained in London by Benjamin Franklin from friends within the British government. Because Franklin had pledged to keep the letters to himself, he became the center of a scandal in London, and was dismissed from his position as postmaster general. But the British cause in the colonies suffered much more than Franklin's reputation. The letters revealed Hutchinson's call for "an abridgement of what are called English liberties" in the colonies. "I wish to see some further restraint of liberty," he had written, "rather than the connection with the parent state should be broken." This seemed to be the "smoking gun" of the conspiracy theory, and it created a torrent of anger against the British and their officials in the colonies.

The Boston Tea Party

It was in this context that the colonists received the news that Parliament had passed a Tea Act. Colonists were major consumers of tea, but because of the tax on it that remained from the Townshend duties, the market for colonial tea had collapsed, bringing the East India Company to the brink of bankruptcy. This company was the sole agent of British power in India, and Parliament could not allow it to fail. The British therefore devised a scheme in which they offered tea to Americans at prices that would tempt the most patriotic tea drinker. The radicals argued that this was merely a device to make palatable the payment of unconstitutional taxes — further evidence of the British conspiracy to corrupt the colonists. Since shipments of tea had been consigned to a handpicked group of agents, many of them connected to royal appointees, local merchants also believed that the British were attempting to undermine their prosperity and independence. Opposition to the Tea Act, coordinated through the Committees of Correspondence, was widespread.

In October a mass meeting in Philadelphia denounced anyone importing the tea as "an enemy of his country." A group calling itself the Committee for Tarring and Feathering plastered a poster all over the city asking if the pilots of ships carrying the tea might like "ten gallons of liquid tar decanted on your pate — with the feathers of a dozen wild geese laid over that to enliven your appearance?" The Philadelphia consignees resigned in terror. Similar protests in New York City forced resignations there as well. The town meeting in Boston passed resolutions patterned on those of Philadelphia, but the tea agents there, among them two of Governor Hutchin-

E. Tisdale   *del. et sculp.*

The PROCESSION.

A British tax official is paraded in tar and feathers by a crowd of Patriots in a contemporary engraving. Such tactics became common during the commotion over the Tea Act in 1773.

son's sons, resisted the call to refuse the shipments.

The first of the tea ships arrived in Boston Harbor late in November. Mass meetings in Old South Church, which included many country people drawn to the scene of the crisis, resolved to keep the tea from being unloaded. Governor Hutchinson was equally firm in refusing to allow the ship to leave the harbor. On December 16, 1773, 5,000 people crowded into the church to hear the captain of the tea ship report to Samuel Adams that he could not move his ship. ''This meeting can do nothing more to save the country,'' Adams declared. This was the signal for a disciplined group of fifty or sixty men, including farmers, artisans, merchants, professionals, and even apprentices, to march to the wharf disguised as Indians. There they boarded the ship and dumped into the harbor 45 tons of tea, valued at £18,000, all the while cheered on by Boston's citizens. ''Boston Harbor's a tea-pot tonight,'' the crowd chanted.

Boston's was the first tea party, and other incidents of property destruction followed. When the Sons of Liberty learned that a cargo of tea had landed secretly in New York, they too dressed themselves as Indians and dumped the tea chests into the harbor. At Annapolis a ship loaded with tea was destroyed by fire, and arson also consumed a shipment stored at a warehouse in New Jersey. But it was the action in Boston at which the British railed. The government became convinced that something had to be done about the rebellious colony of Massachusetts. Strong measures were required, King George wrote to Lord North, for ''we are now to dispute whether we have, or have not, any authority in that country.''

The Intolerable Acts

During the spring of 1774 an angry Parliament passed a series of acts calculated to punish Massachusetts and strengthen the British hand. The Boston Port Bill prohibited the loading or unloading of ships in any part of Boston Harbor until the town fully compensated the East India Company and the customs service for the destroyed tea. The Massachusetts Government Act annulled the colonial charter: delegates to the upper house would no longer be elected by the assembly, but henceforth were to be appointed by the king. Civil officers throughout the province were placed under the authority of the royal governor, and the selection of juries was given over to governor-appointed sheriffs. Town meetings, an important institution of the resistance movement, were prohibited from convening more than once a year except with the approval of the governor, who was to control their agendas. By these measures the British terminated the long history of self-rule by communities in the colony of Massachusetts. The Administration of Justice Act protected British officials from colonial courts, thereby encouraging them to vigorously

pursue the work of suppression. Those accused of capital crimes committed while putting down riots or collecting revenue, such as the soldiers involved in the Boston Massacre, were now to be sent to England for trial.

Two additional measures affected the other colonies and encouraged them to see themselves in league with suffering Massachusetts. The Quartering Act legalized the housing of troops at public expense not only in taverns and abandoned buildings, as allowed by an earlier act of Parliament, but in occupied dwellings and private homes as well. Finally, the Quebec Act created a permanent government for Canada. Several features of this measure aroused the anger of the colonists. In the first place, to protect the western Indians against incur-

---

The Quebec Act
With the Quebec Act, Britain created a centralized colonial government for Canada, and extended that colony's administrative control southwest to the Ohio River, invalidating the sea-to-sea boundaries of many colonial charters.

---

sions by American settlers, the borders of Quebec were extended southwest to the Ohio River, invalidating the sea-to-sea boundaries of charter colonies such as Connecticut, Pennsylvania, and Virginia. The act also established a highly centralized government in Quebec, which included taxation by Parliament, no provincial legislature, and no jury trials for civil cases. Catholicism was granted religious toleration, and the special privileges of the Roman church were recognized at law. Although most of these provisions simply continued the traditions of French government in Quebec, to British colonists they seemed a frightening preview of what imperial authorities had in store for them. Americans referred to all these measures as the Intolerable Acts. The Committees of Correspondence had publicized the theory of a British conspiracy. The Intolerable Acts provided the evidence that convinced a majority of colonists that the conspiracy was all too real.

In May, General Thomas Gage arrived in Boston to replace Hutchinson as governor. The same day, the Boston town meeting called for a revival of nonimportation measures against Britain. In Virginia, the Burgesses declared that Boston was enduring a "hostile invasion," and made provision for a "day of fasting, humiliation, and prayer, devoutly to implore the divine interposition for averting the heavy calamity, which threatens destruction to our civil rights and the evils of civil war." For this expression of sympathy, Governor Dunmore suspended the legislature. Nevertheless, throughout the colony on the first of June, funeral bells tolled, flags flew at half mast, and people flocked to the churches.

The Continental Congress

It was amid this crisis that town meetings and colonial assemblies alike chose representatives for a Continental Congress to assemble in Philadelphia. The delegates who arrived in September of 1774 included the most important leaders of the American cause. Cousins Samuel and John Adams, the radicals from Massachusetts, were joined by Patrick Henry and George Washington from Virginia and Christopher Gadsden of South Carolina. Many of the delegates were conservatives: John Dickinson and Joseph Galloway of Philadelphia, John Jay and James Duane from New York. With the exception of Gadsden, a hothead who proposed an attack on British forces in Boston, the delegates wished to avoid war and favored a policy of economic coercion.

In one of their first debates, the delegates narrowly defeated a Plan of Union proposed by Galloway. This plan called for a grand council, its members chosen by the provincial assemblies and led by a royally appointed president, that would legislate for all the colonies in cooperation with Parliament. Instead, they passed a Declaration and Resolves, in which they asserted that all the colonists sprang from a common tradition and enjoyed rights guaranteed "by the immutable laws of nature, the principles of the English constitution, and the several charters or compacts" of their provinces. Thirteen acts of Parliament, passed since 1763, were declared in violation of these rights. Until these acts were repealed, the delegates pledged, they would impose a set of sanctions against the British. These would include not only the nonimportation and nonconsumption of British goods, but a prohibition on the export of colonial commodities to Britain or its other colonies.

To enforce these sanctions, the Continental Congress urged that "a committee be chosen in every county, city, and town, by those who are qualified to vote for the legislature, whose business it shall be attentively to observe the conduct of all persons." This call for democratically elected local committees in each community had important political ramifications. The following year, these groups, known as Committees of Observation and Safety, took over the functions of local government throughout the colonies. They organized militia companies, called extralegal courts, and combined to form colony-wide congresses. By dissolving colonial legislatures, royal governors often unwittingly aided the work of these community committees. The committees also scrutinized the activities of fellow citizens, suppressed the expression of Loyalist opinion from pulpit or press, and practiced other forms of coercion.

The rise of committee government affected the countryside as much as the cities. Across Virginia, community committees closed down the county courts. In North Carolina they chose representatives to a provincial convention, forcing Governor Josiah Martin to admit that his government had become "absolutely prostrate, impotent." Western Massachusetts witnessed a popular uprising that closed county courts, put conservative leaders under house arrest, and reorganized town governments. This political revolution failed to penetrate certain areas of strong Loyalist sentiment, but throughout most of the colonies the committees formed a bridge between the old colonial administrations and the revolutionary governments organized over the next few years. Committees began to link localities together in the cause of a wider American community. It was at this point that people began to refer to the colonies as the American "states."

Lexington and Concord

On September 1, 1774, General Gage sent troops from Boston to sieze the stores of cannon and ammunition the Massachusetts militia had stored at armories in Charlestown and Cambridge. In response, the Massachusetts House of Representatives, calling itself the Provincial Congress, created a Committee of Safety empowered to call up the militia. On October 15 the committee authorized the creation of special units, to be known as minutemen, who stood ready to be called at a moment's notice. The armed militia of the towns and communities surrounding Boston faced the British army, quartered in the city. It was no rabble he was up against, Gage wrote to his superiors, but "the freeholders and farmers" of New England who believed they were defending their communities. Worrying that his forces were insufficient to suppress the rebellion, he requested reinforcements. The stalemate continued through the fall and winter. To raise their spirits, the New England militia ridiculed the British army:

And what have you got now with all your designing,
But a town without victuals to sit down and dine in;
And to look on the ground like a parcel of noodles,
And sing, how the Yankees have beaten the Doodles.
I'm sure if you're wise you'll make peace for a dinner,
For fighting and fasting will soon make ye thinner.

But King George was convinced that the time had come for war. "The New England governments are in a state of rebellion," he wrote privately. "Blows must decide whether they are to be subject to this country or independent." In Parliament, Pitt proposed withdrawing troops from Boston, but was overruled by a large margin. Attempting to find a balance between hardliners and advocates of conciliation, Lord North organized majority support in the House of Commons for a plan in which Parliament would "forbear" to levy taxes for purposes of revenue once the colonies had agreed to tax themselves for the common defense. But simultaneously Parliament passed legislation severely restraining colonial commerce. "A great empire and little minds go ill together," Edmund Burke quipped in March 1775 in a brilliant speech opposing this bill. "Let it be once understood that your government may be one

thing and their privileges another, that these two things may exist without any mutual relation." Then he declared in prophetic words, "The cement is gone, the cohesion is loosened, and everything hastens to decay and dissolution."

In Virginia, at almost the same moment, Patrick Henry predicted that hostilities would soon begin in New England. "Gentlemen may cry peace, peace!— but there is no peace," he thundered in prose later memorized by millions of American schoolchildren. "Is life so dear, or peace so sweet, as to be purchased at the price of chains and slavery? Forbid it, Almighty God! I know not what course others may take, but as for me give me liberty or give me death!" Three weeks later, on April 14, General Gage received instructions to strike at once against the Massachusetts militia. "It will surely be better that the conflict should be brought on upon such ground," argued his superior, "than in a riper state of rebellion."

On the evening of April 18, Gage ordered 700 men to capture the store of American ammunition at the town of Concord. Learning of the operation, the Boston committee dispatched two men, Paul Revere and William Dawes, to alert the militia of the countryside. By the time the British forces had reached Lexington at dawn, midway to their destination, some seventy armed minutemen had assembled on the green in the center of town. They were disorganized and confused. "Lay down your arms, you damned rebels, and disperse!" cried one of the British officers. The Americans began to withdraw in the face of overwhelming opposition, but they took their arms with them. "Damn you, why don't you lay down your arms!" someone shouted from the British lines. "Damn them! We will have them!" No order to fire was given, but shots rang out, killing eight Americans and wounding ten others.

The British marched on to Concord, where they burned a small quantity of supplies and cut down a liberty pole. Meanwhile, news of the skirmish at Lexington had spread through the country, and the militia companies of communities from miles around converged on the town. Seeing smoke, they mistakenly concluded that the troops were firing homes. "Will you let them burn the town!" one man cried, and the Americans moved to the Concord bridge. There they attacked a British company, killing three soldiers — the first British casualties of the Revolution. The British immediately turned back for Boston, but were attacked by Americans at many points along the way. Reinforcements met them at Lexington, preventing a complete disaster, but by the time they finally marched into Boston 73 were

Soon after the fighting at Lexington and Concord, the artist Ralph Earl and the engraver Amos Doolittle visited the location and interviewed participants. They produced a series of four engravings of the incident, the first popular prints of the battles of the Revolutionary War. This view shows the British soldiers marching back to Boston through the hail of sniper fire of colonial militiamen.

dead and 202 wounded or missing. The British troops were vastly outnumbered by the approximately 4,000 Massachusetts militiamen, who suffered 95 casualties. The engagement forecast what would be a central problem for the British: they would be forced to fight amidst an armed population, defending their own communities against outsiders.

AMERICAN INDEPENDENCE

"We send you momentous intelligence," read the letter received by the Charleston, South Carolina, committee of correspondence on May 8, reporting the violence in Massachusetts. Community militia companies mobilized throughout the colonies. At Boston, thousands of militiamen from Massachusetts and the surrounding provinces besieged the city, leaving the British no escape but by sea; their siege would last for nearly a year. Meanwhile, delegates from twelve colonies reconverged on Philadelphia; the second session of the Continental Congress was about to begin. What would be the political consequences of the armed struggle now under way?

The Second Continental Congress

The members of the Second Continental Congress, which opened on May 10, 1775, represented twelve of the British colonies on the mainland of North America. From New Hampshire to South Carolina,

committees of observation and safety had elected colony-wide conventions, and these extralegal bodies in turn had chosen delegates. Consequently, few conservatives or Loyalists were among them. Georgia, unrepresented at the first session of the Continental Congress, remained absent at the opening of the second. The newest mainland colony, it depended heavily on British subsidies, and its leaders were cautious, fearing both slave and Indian uprisings. But the political balance in Georgia began to shift in favor of the radicals in 1775, when frontier settlers came to believe that the Continental Congress would be more supportive than the British in the matter of encroachments against the Creek Indians. Leaders from the backcountry then joined Whig merchants from Savannah to form a provincial Committee of Safety, and by the end of the summer the colony had delegates in Philadelphia.

The addition of Georgia made thirteen colonies in the revolutionary camp. But what of the other British possessions? The Continental Congress made overtures to a number of them. In one of their first acts, delegates called on "the oppressed inhabitants of Canada" to join in the struggle for "common liberty." After the Seven Years' War, the British had treated Quebec as a conquered province, and Canadians had little sympathy for the British Empire. On the other hand, the Americans were traditional enemies, much feared because of their aggressive expansionism. Indeed, when the Canadians failed to respond positively and immediately, the delegates reversed themselves and voted to authorize a military expedition against Quebec to eliminate any possibility of a British invasion from that quarter. They thus killed any chance of the Canadians joining the anti-British cause, and set a course toward the development of separate nations.

Many of the other British colonies, however, harbored significant sympathy for the American cause. Nova Scotia's population included a large number of New Englanders who had relocated there after the expulsion of the Acadians. When the British attempted to recruit among them for soldiers to serve in Boston, one community responded that since "[we are] almost all of us born in New England, [we are] divided betwixt natural affection to our nearest relations and good faith and friendship to our king and country." But the British had established a naval stronghold at Halifax, and the province remained secure within the empire. The presence of the British military was decisive in several other locations as well. In Florida, where there was minimal local government, the British army kept the province completely outside the revolutionary struggles. The popular assemblies of Jamaica, Grenada, and Barbados all formally declared themselves in sympathy with the Continental Congress, but the powerful British navy prevented them from sending representatives. Bermuda succeeded in sending a delegation to Philadelphia to plead for support, but so preoccupied were the Americans with more pressing matters that they found themselves unable to assist. Thus it was thirteen colonies against the empire.

Among the delegates at the Continental Congress were many familiar faces and a few new ones, including Thomas Jefferson, a thirty-two-year-old plantation owner and lawyer from Virginia, gifted with one of the most imaginative and analytical minds of his time. All the delegates carried news of the enthusiasm for war that raged in their home provinces. "A frenzy of revenge seems to have seized all ranks of people," said Jefferson. George Washington attended all the sessions in uniform. "Oh that I was a soldier," Adams wrote to his wife, Abigail. The delegates agreed that defense was the first issue on their agenda.

On May 15 the Continental Congress resolved to put the colonies in a state of defense, but the delegates were divided on how best to do it. They lacked the power and the funds to immediately raise and supply an army. After debate and deliberation, John Adams made the practical proposal that the delegates simply designate as a "Continental Army" the militia forces besieging Boston. On June 14 the Congress resolved to supplement the New England militiamen with six companies of expert riflemen

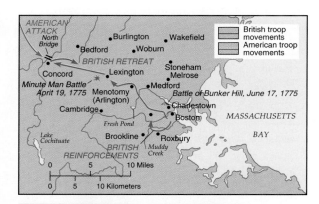

The First Engagements of the Revolution
The first military engagements of the American Revolution took place in the spring of 1775 in the countryside surrounding Boston.

raised in Pennsylvania, Maryland, and Virginia. The delegates agreed that in order to emphasize their national aspirations, they had to select a man from the South to command these New England forces. All eyes turned to George Washington, who was something of a legend because of his exploits during the Seven Years' War. On June 15 Jefferson and Adams nominated Washington to be commander in chief of all Continental forces, and he was elected by a unanimous vote. He served without salary. The Continental Congress soon appointed a staff of major generals to support him. On June 22, in a highly significant move, the Congress voted to finance the army with an issue of $2 million in bills of credit, backed by the good faith of the "Confederated Colonies." Thus began the long and complicated process of financing the Revolution.

During its first session in the spring of 1775, the Continental Congress had begun to move cautiously down the path toward independence. Few would admit, even to themselves, however, that this was their goal. John Adams, who was as close to advocating independence as any delegate, wrote that he was "as fond of reconciliation as any man," but found the hope of peaceful resolution unreasonable. "The cancer is too deeply rooted," he thought, "and too far spread to be cured by anything short of cutting it out entire." Still, on July 5, 1775, the delegates passed the so-called Olive Branch Petition, written by John Dickinson of Pennsylvania, in which they professed their attachment to King George and begged him to prevent further hostilities so that there might be an accommodation. The next day they approved a Declaration of the Causes and

Necessities of Taking Up Arms, written by Jefferson and Dickinson. Here the delegates adopted a harder tone, resolving "to die freemen rather than to live slaves." Before the Second Continental Congress adjourned at the beginning of August, the delegates appointed commissioners to negotiate with the Indian nations in an attempt to keep them out of the conflict. They also made Benjamin Franklin postmaster general to keep the mails moving and protect communication among the colonies.

A State of Rebellion

A number of important military engagements took place before the creation of the Continental army. On the evening of May 10, 1775, a small force of New Englanders under the command of Ethan Allen of Vermont surprised the British garrison at Fort Ticonderoga on Lake Champlain. Allen hailed the British commander, who was still in his nightshirt: "Come out of there, you damned old bastard." By whose authority, the commander demanded. "In the name of Great Jehovah and the Continental Congress," Allen thundered back. The Continental Congress, in fact, knew nothing of this campaign, and when news of it arrived, members of the New York delegation were distressed at this New England violation of their territorial sovereignty. With great effort, the Americans transported the fort's cannon overland to be used in the siege of Boston.

At Boston, the British reinforced Gage's forces and by the middle of June had approximately 6,500 soldiers in the city. By that time the American forces had increased to nearly 10,000. Fearing Gage would occupy the heights south of town, the Americans countered by occupying the Charlestown peninsula to the north. On June 17, British ships in the harbor began to fire on the American positions and Gage

The Connecticut artist John Trumbull painted *The Battle of Bunker Hill* in 1785, the first of a series that earned him the informal title of the "painter of the Revolution." He was careful to research the details of his paintings, but composed them in the grand style of historical romance. In the early nineteenth century he repainted this work, and three other Revolutionary scenes, for the rotunda of the Capitol in Washington, D.C.

decided on a frontal assault to dislodge them. In bloody fighting at Breed's and Bunker hills, the British finally succeeded in routing the Americans, killing 140 men, but not before suffering over a thousand casualties of their own, including 226 dead. The fierce reaction in England to this enormous loss ended all possibility of any last-minute reconciliation. In August of 1775, King George rejected the Olive Branch Petition and issued a royal proclamation declaring the colonists to be in "open and avowed rebellion." "Divers wicked and desperate persons" were the cause of the problem, said the king, and he called on his loyal subjects in America to "bring the traitors to justice."

Early Conflict North and South

Both north and south saw fighting in 1775 and early 1776. In June, the Continental Congress assembled its expeditionary force against Canada. One thousand Americans moved north up the Hudson River corridor, and in November General Richard Montgomery forced the capitulation of Montreal. Meanwhile, Benedict Arnold set out from Massachusetts with another American army, and after a torturous march through the forests and mountains of Maine, he joined Montgomery outside the walls of Quebec. Their assault, however, failed to take the city. Montgomery and 100 Americans were killed, and another 300 were taken prisoner. Although Arnold held his position, the American siege was broken the following spring by British reinforcements who had come down the St. Lawrence. By the summer of 1776 the Americans had been forced back from Canada.

Elsewhere there were successes. The artillery from Ticonderoga reached Boston in January of 1776, and Washington installed it on the heights, placing the city and harbor within cannon range. General William Howe, who had replaced Gage, had little choice but to evacuate the city. In March, the British sailed out of Boston Harbor for the last time, heading north to Halifax with at least 1,000 American Loyalists. In the South, American militia rose against the Loyalist forces of Virginia's Governor Dunmore, who had alienated the planter class by promising freedom to any slave who would fight with the British. After a decisive defeat, Dunmore retreated to British naval vessels, from which he shelled and destroyed much of the city of Norfolk, Virginia, on January 1, 1776. In North Carolina, the rebel militia crushed a Loyalist force at the Battle of Moore's Creek Bridge near Wilmington in February, ending British plans for an invasion of that province.

The British decided to attack Charleston, but at Fort Moultrie in Charleston harbor an American force turned back the assault. It would be more than two years before the British would try to invade the South again.

The Movement toward Independence

Hopes of reconciliation died with the mounting casualties. The Second Continental Congress reconvened in September and received news of the king's proclamation of rebellion. Although the delegates disclaimed any intention of denying the sovereignty of the king, they now moved to organize an American navy. They declared British vessels open to capture and authorized privateering. The Congress took further steps toward de facto independence when it authorized contacts with foreign powers through its agents in Europe. In the spring of 1776, after a period of secret negotiations, France and Spain approved the shipping of supplies to the rebellious provinces. The Continental Congress then declared colonial ports open to the trade of all nations but Britain.

The emotional ties to Britain proved difficult to break. But then in 1776 there appeared a pamphlet written by Thomas Paine, a radical Englishman recently arrived in Philadelphia. In *Common Sense,* Paine proposed to offer "simple fact, plain argument, and common sense" on the crisis. For years Americans had defended their actions by wrapping themselves in the mantle of British traditions. But Paine argued that the British system rested on "the base remains of two ancient tyrannies," aristocracy and monarchy, neither of which was appropriate for America. Paine placed the blame for the oppression of the colonists on the shoulders of King George, whom he labeled the "royal Brute." Appealing to the millennial spirit of American Protestant culture, Paine wrote: "We have it in our power to begin the world over again. A situation, similar to the present, hath not happened since the days of Noah until now." *Common Sense* was the single most important piece of writing during the Revolutionary era, selling more than 100,000 copies within a few months of its publication in January 1776. It reshaped popular thinking, and put independence squarely on the agenda.

In April the North Carolina convention became the first to empower its delegates to vote for a declaration of independence. News that the British were recruiting a force of German mercenaries to use against the Americans provided an additional push toward what now began to seem inevitable. In

May the delegates recommended that the colonies move as quickly as possible toward the adoption of state constitutions. When John Adams wrote, in the preamble to this statement, that "the exercise of every kind of authority under the said crown should be totally suppressed," he sent a strong signal that the delegates were on the verge of approving a momentous declaration.

The Declaration of Independence

On June 7, Richard Henry Lee of Virginia offered a motion to the Continental Congress: "That these united colonies are, and of right ought to be, free and independent states, that they are absolved from all allegiance to the British crown, and that all political connection between them and the state of Great Britain is, and ought to be, totally dissolved." After some debate, a vote was postponed until July, but a committee composed of John Adams, Thomas Jefferson, Roger Sherman of Connecticut, and Robert Livingston of New York was asked to prepare a draft declaration of American independence. The committee assigned the writing to Jefferson.

The intervening month allowed the delegates to sample the public discussion and debate and receive instructions from their state conventions. By the end of the month, all the states but New York had authorized a vote for independence. When the question came up for debate again on July 1, a large majority in the Continental Congress supported independence. The final vote, taken on July 2, was twelve in favor of independence, none against, with New York abstaining. The delegates then turned to the declaration itself and made a number of changes in Jefferson's draft, striking out, for example, a long passage condemning slavery. In this and a number of other ways the final version was somewhat more cautious than the draft, but it was still a stirring document.

Its central section reiterated the "long train of abuses and usurpations" on the part of King George that had led the Americans to their drastic course; there was no mention of Parliament, the principal opponent since 1764. But it was the first section that expressed the highest ideals of the delegates:

> We hold these truths to be self-evident, that all men are created equal, that they are endowed by their creator with certain unalienable rights, that among these are life, liberty, and the pursuit of happiness. That to secure these rights, governments are instituted among men, deriving their just powers from the consent of the governed. That whenever any form of government becomes

The Manner in which the American Colonies Declared themselves INDEPENDENT of the King of ENGLAND, a 1783 English print. Understanding that the coming struggle would require the steady support of ordinary people, in the Declaration of Independence the upper class men of the Continental Congress asserted the right of popular revolution and the great principle of human equality.

> destructive of these ends, it is the right of the people to alter or to abolish it, and to institute a new government, laying its foundation on such principles, and organizing its powers in such form, as to them shall seem most likely to effect their safety and happiness.

There was very little debate in the Continental Congress about these "truths" and principles. But the delegates, mostly men of wealth and position, realized that the coming struggle for independence would require the steady support of ordinary people, and so they asserted this great principle of equality and the right of revolution. The language of the Declaration and the ideal of equality would reverberate throughout American history, inspiring the

CHRONOLOGY

1713	France cedes Acadia to Britain
1745	New Englanders capture Louisburg
1749	French send an expeditionary force down the Ohio River
1753	French begin building forts from Lake Erie to the Ohio
1754	Albany Congress
1755	Braddock's defeat
1756	Seven Years' War begins
1757	William Pitt becomes prime minister
1758	Louisburg captured for the second time
1759	British capture Quebec
1763	Treaty of Paris Pontiac's uprising Paxton Boys massacre
1765	Stamp Act and Stamp Act Congress
1766	Declaratory Act
1767	Townshend Acts
1768	Treaties of Hard Labor and Fort Stanwix
1770	Boston Massacre
1772	Committees of Correspondence organized
1773	Boston Tea Party
1774	Intolerable Acts First Continental Congress Dunmore's War
1775	Fighting begins at Lexington and Concord Second Continental Congress
1776	Americans invade Canada Thomas Paine's *Common Sense* Declaration of Independence

poor as well as the wealthy, women as well as men, blacks as well as whites.

But it was the third and final section that may have contained the most meaning for the delegates: "For the support of this declaration, with a firm reliance on the protection of divine providence, we mutually pledge to each other our lives, our fortunes, and our sacred honor." In voting for independence, the delegates were committing treason against their king and empire; they would be condemned as traitors, hunted as criminals, and might soon stand on the scaffold to pay for their sentiments. These men approved the text of the Declaration on July 4 without dissent.

Conclusion

Great Britain emerged from the Seven Years' War as the dominant power in North America. Yet despite its attempts to strictly regulate and determine the course of events in its colonies, it faced consistent resistance and often complete failure. Perhaps British leaders felt as John Adams had when he attended the first session of the Continental Congress in 1774: How could a motley collection of "ambassadors from a dozen belligerent powers" effectively organize as a single, independent, and defiant body? The British consistently underestimated the ability of the colonists to inform one another, to work together, to build a sentiment of nationalism that cut across the boundaries of ethnicity, region, and economic status. Through newspapers, pamphlets, committees of correspondence, community organizations, and group protest, the colonists discovered the concerns they shared, and in so doing they fostered a new, "American" identity. Without that identity it would have been difficult for them to consent to the treasonous act of declaring independence — especially when the independence they sought was from an international power that dominated much of the globe.

Additional Readings

BERNARD BAILYN, *The Ideological Origins of the American Revolution* (1967). While other accounts stress the economic or social causes, this classic argument concerns the role of ideas in the advent of the Revolution. Includes an analysis of American views of the imperial crisis.

ERIC FONER, *Tom Paine and Revolutionary America* (1976). Not only a biography of Paine, but a community study of the Revolution in Philadelphia and Pennsylvania.

LAWRENCE H. GIPSON, *British Empire before the American Revolution,* 8 vols. (1936–49). Although these volumes are heavy going, they include the most comprehensive and still the best treatment of the Seven Years' War in America.

ROBERT A. GROSS, *The Minute Men and Their World* (1976). This fascinating and readable history examines the coming of the Revolution from the viewpoint of a New England community.

FRANCIS JENNINGS, *Empire of Fortune: Crowns, Colonies, and Tribes in the Seven Years War in America* (1988). The French and Indian War examined from the point of view of the Iroquois Confederacy. This is opinionated but exciting history.

PAULINE MAIER, *From Resistance to Revolution: Colonial Radicals and the Development of American Opposition to Britain, 1765–1776* (1972). Argues that the American leaders were preoccupied with maintaining political and social order. A conservative interpretation of the Revolution.

RICHARD L. MERRITT, *Symbols of American Community, 1735–1775* (1966). A study of colonial newspapers that provides evidence for a rising sense of national community. The French and Indian War emerges as the key period for the growth of nationalist sentiment.

RICHARD WHITE, *The Middle Ground: Indians, Empires, and Republics in the Great Lakes Region, 1650–1815* (1991). This well-researched history provides a fascinating account of the western question from the point of view of imperialists, settlers, and Indians.

7

THE CREATION OF THE UNITED STATES, 1776–1786

AMERICAN COMMUNITIES

● VALLEY FORGE, PENNSYLVANIA

A drum roll ushered in a January morning in 1778, summoning the Continental Army to roll call, and along a two-mile line of log cabins, doors slowly opened and ragged men stepped out onto the frozen ground of Valley Forge. "There comes a soldier," wrote army surgeon Albigense Waldo. "His bare feet are seen through his worn-out shoes, his legs nearly naked from the tattered remains of an only pair of stockings, his breeches not sufficient to cover his nakedness, his shirt hanging in strings, his hair disheveled, his face meagre." The reek of foul straw and unwashed bodies filled the air. "No bread, no soldier!" The chant began as a barely audible murmur, then was picked up by men all along the line. "No bread, no soldier! No bread, no soldier!" At last the chanting

THE CONTINENTAL ARMY BUILDS A NATIONALIST COMMUNITY

grew so loud it could be heard at General Washington's headquarters, a mile away. The ten thousand men of the American army were surviving on little more than "firecake," a mixture of flour and water baked hard before the fire that, according to Waldo, turned "guts to pasteboard." Two thousand men were without shoes, others were without blankets and had to sit up all night about the fires to keep from freezing. "Three or four days of bad weather would prove our destruction," Washington wrote to the Continental Congress. In the folklore of the Revolution, Valley Forge would become the symbol of suffering and endurance.

These soldiers were the seasoned veterans of one of the most arduous campaigns in American military history. They had marched hundreds of weary miles and suffered three terrible defeats at the hands of a British force nearly twice their number. But they had succeeded in retreating intact to winter quarters in this cold Pennsylvania valley between the sheltering hills on the southside of the Schuylkill River, only twenty miles from the British army, comfortably settled in Philadelphia. The problem was not the site, nor was it the relatively mild winter weather. The problem was supply. There was an abundance of food and clothing in Pennsylvania and New Jersey, but mismanagement, greed, and indifference prevented it from reaching the troops. Congress refused to pay the exorbitant rates contractors demanded to haul provisions. Many teamsters who agreed to work lightened their wagons by draining the brine from casks of salt meat or dumping their loads by the roadside. Many local farmers refused to sell their surpluses to the army, preferring to deal with the British in

This popular print of 1779, entitled *A New Touch on the Times,* depicted an American "Daughter of Liberty" ready to defend her country. In the encampment at Valley Forge more than 700 women served as cooks, laundresses, and nurses, as well as wives and lovers. One of them, Mary McCauley, earned the name "Molly Pitcher" for her courage in bringing water to the men during battle. And when her husband was overcome by the heat of battle, she took his place at the cannon.

Philadelphia, who paid in specie, not depreciated Continental currency. The soldiers had not been paid since August.

The 11,000 men of the Continental Army were divided into sixteen brigades composed of regiments from nine states. A Loyalist observer described them as "a vagabond army of ragamuffins," and indeed many of the men were drawn from the ranks of the poor: indentured servants, landless farmers, and recent immigrants. The army also included nearly a thousand African Americans, both slave and free. Most of the men came from thinly settled farm districts or small towns where precautions regarding sanitation had been unnecessary. Every thaw revealed ground covered with "much filth and nastiness," and officers ordered sentinels to fire on any man "easing himself elsewhere than at ye vaults." Typhoid fever and other infectious diseases spread quickly: along with dysentery, malnutrition, and exposure they claimed as many as 2,500 lives that winter. The busy burial detail was composed largely of women. Cooks, laundresses, and prostitutes made up some of the more than 700 camp followers who lived at Valley Forge that winter; among the others were many wives and lovers. General George Washington's wife, Martha, stayed with him. Although Washington generally disapproved of the presence of women in camp, he allowed them to remain in order to minimize desertion.

"What then is to become of this army?" Washington wrote during the depth of the winter. But six months later the force he marched out of Valley Forge was considerably stronger for its experience there. Most important were the strong relationships that formed among the men. Washington referred to his general staff as his "family," and during the coming trials of battle his officers would rely greatly upon the bonds of affection that had developed during the hard winter. Twelve enlisted men bunked together in each of the cabins, which were clustered by state regiments and grouped by brigade. In these units they "shared with each other their hardships, dangers, and sufferings," wrote common soldier Joseph Plumb Martin, "sympathized with each other in trouble and sickness, assisted in bearing each other's burdens, [and] endeavored to conceal each other's faults." In short, he concluded, the men fashioned "a band of brotherhood" among themselves. Psychologists studying men in modern warfare have learned that it is this sense of community that contributes most to success.

Thrown together under the most trying of circumstances, men from hundreds of localities and a variety of ethnic backgrounds found a common identity in their common struggle. In so doing, they were among the first of their countrymen to truly think of themselves as Americans. On May Day 1778 they celebrated the coming of spring by raising a maypole before the cabins of each state regiment. The men paraded through the rough streets of camp, pausing at each maypole to dance and sing together. They were led by thirteen honor guards in Indian costume and a sergeant decked out as King Tammany, the great Delaware chief of American folklore.

> In freedom's bright cause, Tammany plead with applause,
> And reasoned most justly from nature;
> For this, this was his song, all, all the day long:
> Liberty's the right of each creature, brave boys.
>
> No duties, nor stamps, their blest liberty cramps,
> A king, though no tyrant, was he;
> He did oft 'times declare, nay sometimes would swear,
> The least of his subjects were free, my brave boys.

In this ritual celebration of their new sense of national community, the men sang of the liberty once enjoyed by the Indians.

To some American Patriots, the European-style Continental Army betrayed the ideals of the citizen-soldier and the autonomy of local communities — central tenets of the Revolution. Washington argued strongly, however, that the Revolution could not be won without a national army, one insulated from politics and able to withstand the shifting popular mood. Through their developing sense of community, the poor and motley crew of Continentals became living examples of the egalitarian ideals of the Revolution. They constituted a popular democratic force that counterbalanced the conservatism of the new republic's elite leadership. The national spirit they built at Valley Forge would sustain them through four more years of war, and provide momentum for the long process of forging a national political system out of the persistent localism of American politics. "I admire them tremendously!" wrote one European officer serving with Washington. "It is incredible that soldiers composed

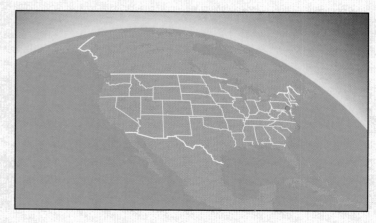

of men of every age, even children of fifteen, of whites and blacks, almost naked, unpaid, and rather poorly fed, can march so well and withstand fire so steadfastly." Asked to explain why his men served, another officer declared: "Nothing but virtue and that great principle, the love of our country."

THE WAR FOR INDEPENDENCE

At the beginning of the Revolution, the British had the world's best-equipped and most disciplined army and a navy that was unopposed in American waters. But they greatly underestimated the American capacity to fight. With a native officer corps and considerable experience in the colonial wars of the eighteenth century, Patriot soldiers proved themselves a formidable force. The British also misperceived the sources of the conflict. They believed that the rebellion was the work of a small group of disgruntled conspirators, and initially defined their objective as defeating the organized Patriot opposition. In the wake of a military victory, they believed, they could easily reassert political control. But the geography of eastern North America offered no single vital center whose conquest would end the war. The Americans had the advantage of fighting on their own ground, among a population thinly spread over a territory stretching along 1,500 miles of coastline and extending 100 miles or more into the interior. When the British succeeded in defeating the Patriots in one area, resistance sprang up in another. The key factor in the outcome of the war, then, was the popular support for the American cause.

The Patriot Forces

Most American men of fighting age had to face the call to arms. From a population of approximately 350,000 eligible men, more than 200,000 saw action, though no more than 25,000 were engaged at any one time. More than half this number served in the Continental Army, under Washington's command and the authority of the Continental Congress; the other soldiers served in Patriot militia companies.

These militias — armed bodies of men drawn from local communities — proved most important in the defense of their own areas, for they had homes as well as local reputations to protect. In the exuberant days of 1776, many Patriots believed that militias alone could win the war against the British. As one observer wrote, "The Rage Militaire, as the French call a passion for arms, has taken possession of the whole Continent." Congress initially refused to invoke a draft, or mandate army enlistments exceeding one year. Because men preferred to serve with their neighbors in local companies rather than subject themselves to the discipline of the regular army, the states failed to meet their quotas for regiments in the Continental Army. But despite legends to the contrary, the Revolution was not won by citizen-soldiers who exchanged plows for guns, or backcountry riflemen who picked off British soldiers from behind trees. Serving short terms of enlistment, often with officers of their own choosing, militiamen resisted discipline. Washington's deputy, General Nathanael Greene, declared that they lacked the fortitude "to stand the shocking scenes of war," having never been "steeled by habit or fortified by military pride." Indeed, in the face of battle militia companies demonstrated appalling rates of desertion. During the fierce fighting on Long Island, for example, three-quarters of Connecticut's 8,000 militiamen simply abandoned the field and headed home.

The final victory, rather, was due primarily to the steady struggle of the Continental Army. The American Revolution had little in common with modern national liberation movements in which armed populations engage in guerrilla warfare. Washington and his officers required a force that could directly engage the British, and from the beginning of the war he argued with a skeptical Congress that victory could be won only with a full

Overview of the Revolutionary War
The fighting during the American Revolution took place in four principal areas (see following maps for details).

commitment to a truly national army. His views conflicted with popular fears of a standing army. Would they not be defeating their own purpose, many Patriots wondered, by adopting the corrupt institutions of their British enemies? "Soldiers are apt to consider themselves as a body distinct from the rest of the citizens," Samuel Adams warned; "they soon become attached to their officers and disposed to yield implicit obedience to their commands. Such a power should be watched with a jealous eye."

The failings of the militias in the early battles of the war, however, sobered Congress and forced it to greatly enlarge state quotas for the army and to extend the term of service to three years or the war's duration. To spur enlistment Congress offered bounties, regular wages, and promises of free land after victory. Although the states consistently failed to meet their quotas, by the spring of 1777 Washington's army had grown to nearly 9,000 men, armed and clothed through supplies and loans from France. To improve discipline, Congress followed Washington's advice and authorized stiffer corporal punishment and expansion of the list of capital crimes.

Discipline was essential in a conflict in which men fired at close range, charged each other with bayonets, and engaged in hand-to-hand combat. One Connecticut man wrote of the effects of cannon on his regiment: "The ball first cut off the head of Smith, a stout heavy man, and dashed it open, then took Taylor across the bowels; it then struck Sergeant Garret of our company on the hip, took off the point of the hip bone." "Oh! What a sight that was," he concluded, "to see within a distance of six rods those men with their legs and arms and guns and packs all in a heap." In New Jersey, a sergeant in the Continental Army witnessed British troops slaughtering Americans lying on the field: "The men that was wounded in the thigh or leg, they dashed out their brains with their muskets and run them through with their bayonets, made them like sieves. This was barbarity to the utmost."

The best estimate is that a total of 25,674 American men died in the Revolution, approximately 6,000 from wounds suffered in battle, 10,000 from the effects of disease, the rest as prisoners of war or missing in action. Regiments of the Continental Army experienced the highest casualty rates, sometimes 30 or 40 percent. Indeed, the casualty ratio overall was higher than in any other American conflict except the Civil War. In most areas the war claimed few civilian lives, for it was confined largely to direct engagements between the armies — though in the backcountry and in regions of the South where Patriot and Loyalist militias waged vicious campaigns, noncombatant casualties were considerable.

Both the Continentals and the militias played important political roles as well. At a time when Americans identified most strongly with their local communities or perhaps their states, the Continental Army became a powerful force for nationalist sentiment. During the dark days of 1780 and early 1781 shortages of food and pay caused a series of mutinies in the army. In the most serious incident, among the Pennsylvania Line in January of 1781, enlisted men killed one officer, wounded two others, and set off from their winter quarters in New Jersey for Philadelphia. They did not want to abandon the American cause; they merely wanted Congress to uphold its commitments to the soldiers who were fighting for the nation. As they marched they were

Jean Baptiste Antoine de Verger, a French officer serving with the Continental Army, made these watercolors of American soldiers during the Revolution. More than 200,000 men saw action, including at least 5,000 African Americans; more than half of these troops served with the Continental Army.

joined by British agents who encouraged them to go over to the king. Enraged at this attempt at subversion, the mutineers hanged the Tories. Angry as they were at Congress, they were Americans first and hated the British. Over a hundred thousand men from every state served in the Continental Army, contributing mightily to the unity of purpose—the formation of a national community—that was essential to the process of nation making.

In most communities Patriots seized control of local government during the period of committee organizing in 1774 and 1775 (see Chapter 6), and with war imminent they pressed the obligation to serve in a Patriot militia upon most eligible men. In Farmington, Connecticut, in 1776, eighteen men were imprisoned "on suspicion of their being inimical to America" upon failing to join the muster of the local militia. After individual grilling by the authorities, they petitioned for pardon. "They appeared to be penitent of their former conduct," it was reported, and understood "that there was no such thing as remaining neuters." Probably the most important role of the Patriot militias was to force even the most apathetic of Americans to think seriously about the Revolution, and to choose sides under the scrutiny of their neighbors.

The Loyalists

But not all Americans were Patriots. Many sat on the fence, confused by the conflict and waiting for a clear turn in the tide of the struggle before declaring their allegiance. About a fifth of the population, perhaps as many as half a million people, remained loyal to the British crown. Loyalism was strongest in the Lower South, weakest in New England. British colonial officials were almost always Loyalists, as were most Anglican clergymen and large numbers of lawyers who had worked with colonial administrators. Loyalists included members of ethnic minorities that had been persecuted by the dominant majority, such as the Highland Scots of the Carolinas and western New York, and southern tenant farmers who had Patriot landlords. Moreover, many slaves and most Indians, the latter fearing aggressive expansion by independent American states, identified with the Loyalists. Other Loyalists were conservatives, fearful of political or social upheaval, or were temperamentally opposed to resistance to established authority.

Patriots passed state treason acts that prohibited speaking or writing against the Revolution. They also issued proclamations of attainder, by

A Patriot mob torments Loyalists in this print published during the Revolution. Loyalists faced mob violence in many areas, most notably in Massachusetts, New York, Pennsylvania, and South Carolina. During and after the Revolution as many as 80,000 Loyalists fled the country.

which Loyalists lost their civil rights and their property. In some areas, notably New York, South Carolina, Massachusetts, and Pennsylvania, Loyalists faced mob violence. One favorite punishment was the "grand Tory ride," in which a crowd hauled the victim through the streets astride a sharp fence rail. Another was tarring and feathering, in which men were stripped to "buff and breeches" and their naked flesh coated liberally with heated tar and then feathers. One broadside recommended that Patriots "then hold a lighted Candle to the feathers, and try to set it all on fire." The torment rarely went that far, but it was brutally painful nonetheless.

The most infamous American supporter of the

British cause was Benedict Arnold, whose name has become synonymous with treason in the United States. Arnold was a hero of the early battles of the Revolution. But in 1779, angry and resentful about what he perceived to be assignments and rank below his station, he became a paid informer of General Clinton, head of the British army in New York City. In 1780 Patriots uncovered Arnold's plot to betray the strategic post of West Point, which he commanded. After fleeing to the British, who paid him a handsome stipend and pension, he became a brigadier general in the British army. The bête noire of the Revolution, Arnold became the most hated man in America. In his hometown of Norwich, Connecticut, a crowd destroyed the gravestones of his family, and in cities and towns throughout America thousands burned his effigy. During the last two years of the war he led British raids against his home state as well as Virginia, and after the Revolution he lived in England until his death in 1801.

The British strategy for suppressing the Revolution depended upon mobilizing the Loyalists, but in most areas this proved impossible. Many Loyalists were sympathetic to Patriot arguments but unwilling to consider disloyalty to the crown. After 1776, when the initiative passed to the advocates of independence, they found themselves outside the debate. Others believed in British invincibility and were apathetic. As many as 50,000, however, fought for the king during the Revolution. Many joined Loyalist militias or engaged in irregular warfare, especially in the Lower South. In 1780, when Washington's Continentals numbered about 9,000, there were 8,000 American Loyalists serving in the British army in America.

As many as 80,000 Loyalists fled the country during and after the Revolution, taking up residence in England, the British West Indies, or Canada, where they are venerated as the founding fathers of the province of Ontario. Their property was confiscated by the states and sold at public auction. Although the British government compensated many for their losses, as a group they were reluctant and unhappy exiles. "I earnestly wish to spend the remainder of my days in America," wrote William Pepperell, formerly of Maine, from London in 1778. "I love the country, I love the people." Former governor Thomas Hutchinson of Massachusetts wrote that he "had rather die in a little country farm-house in New England than in the best nobleman's seat in old England." Their melancholy reflected the realization that they had lost their country.

The Campaign for New York and New Jersey

During the winter of 1775–76 the British developed a strategic plan for the war. From his base at Halifax, Nova Scotia, Sir William Howe was to take his army to New York City, which the British navy would make impregnable. From there he would drive north along the Hudson, while another British army marched south from Canada to Albany. The two armies would converge, cutting New England off from the rest of the colonies, then turn eastward to reduce the rebellious Yankees into submission. Washington, who had arrived at Boston to take command of the militia forces there in the summer of 1775, anticipated this strategy, and in the spring of 1776 he shifted his forces southward toward New York.

In early July, as Congress was taking its final vote on the Declaration of Independence, the British began their operation at New York City, landing 32,000 men, a third of them Hessian mercenaries from Germany, on Staten Island. The Americans, meanwhile, set up fortified positions across the harbor in Brooklyn. Attacking in late August, the British inflicted heavy casualties on the Americans, and the militia forces under Washington's command proved unreliable under fire. The Battle of Long Island ended in disaster for the Patriots, and they were forced to withdraw across the East River to Manhattan.

The Principal Engagement of the Northern Theater of the War, 1775–1777

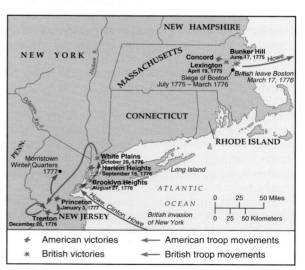

The British now offered Congress an opportunity to negotiate, and on September 6, Benjamin Franklin, John Adams, and Edward Rutledge sat down with General Howe and his brother, Admiral Richard Howe, on Staten Island. But the meeting broke up when the Howes demanded revocation of the Declaration of Independence. The stage was set for another round of violence. Six days later the British invaded Manhattan island, and only an American stand at Harlem Heights prevented the destruction of a large portion of the Patriot army. Enjoying naval control of the harbor, the British quickly outflanked the American positions. In a series of battles over the next few months, they forced Washington back at White Plains and overran the American posts of Fort Washington and Fort Lee, on either side of the Hudson River. By November the Americans were fleeing south across New Jersey in a frantic attempt to avoid the British under General Charles Cornwallis.

With morale desperately low, whole militia companies deserted; others, announcing the end of their terms of enlistment, left for home. American resistance seemed to be collapsing all around Washington. "Our troops will not do their duty," he wrote painfully to Congress as he crossed the Delaware River into Pennsylvania. Upon receiving his message, the delegates in Philadelphia fled for Baltimore. "I think the game is pretty near up," Washington admitted to his brother. But rather than fall back further, which would surely have meant the dissolution of his entire force, he decided to risk a counterattack. On Christmas night Washington led 2,400 troops back across the Delaware, and the next morning defeated the Hessian forces in a surprise attack on their headquarters at Trenton, New Jersey. The Americans inflicted further heavy losses on the British at Princeton, then drove them all the way back to the environs of New York.

Although these small victories had little tactical importance, they salvaged American morale. As Washington settled into winter headquarters at Morristown, he realized he had to pursue a defensive strategy, avoiding direct confrontations with the British while checking their advances and hurting them wherever possible. "We cannot conquer the British force at once," wrote General Greene, "but they cannot conquer us at all." This last sentiment was more of a hope than a conviction, but it defined the essential American strategy of the Revolution. Most important to that strategy was the survival of the Continental Army.

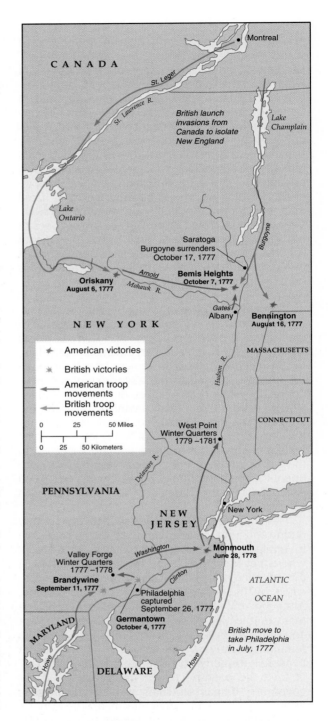

The Principal Engagements of the Middle Theater of the War, 1777–1778

The Campaigns of 1777

The fighting with the American forces had prevented Howe from moving north up the Hudson, and the British advance southward from Canada had been stalled by American resistance at Lake Champlain. In 1777, however, the British decided to replay their strategy. From Canada they dispatched General John Burgoyne with nearly 8,000 British and German troops. Howe was to move his force from New York, first taking the city of Philadelphia, capital of the Continental Congress, then moving north to meet Burgoyne.

Fort Ticonderoga fell to Burgoyne on July 6, but by August the general found himself bogged down and harassed by Patriot militias in the rough country south of Lake George. After several defeats in September at the hands of an American army commanded by General Horatio Gates, Burgoyne retreated to Saratoga. There his army was surrounded by a considerably larger force of Americans, and on October 19, lacking alternatives, he surrendered his nearly 6,000 men. It would be the biggest British defeat until Yorktown, decisive because it forced the nations of Europe to recognize that the Americans had a fighting chance to win their Revolution. Within a few weeks Patriots all over the colonies were dancing a new step known as "Burgoyne's Surrender."

The Americans were less successful against Howe. A force of 15,000 British troops left New York in July, landing a month later at the northern end of Chesapeake Bay. At Brandywine Creek the British outflanked the Americans, inflicting heavy casualties and forcing a retreat. The terrible fighting lasted the whole day, according to one American private, continuing "without much sessation of arms, cannons roaring, muskets cracking, drums beating, bombs flying all round. Men a-dying, wounds, horrid groans which would grieve the hardest of hearts to see such a doleful sight." Ten days later the British routed the Americans a second time with a frightful bayonet charge at Paoli that cost many Patriot dead. When they occupied Philadelphia on September 26, Congress had already fled. Washington attempted a valiant counterattack at Germantown on October 4, but his initial success was followed by miscoordination that eventually doomed the operation.

It was after this campaign that the Continentals headed for Valley Forge, the bitterness of their defeats muted somewhat by news of the surrender at Saratoga. The British had taken the most important city in North America, but it proved to have little strategic value. The Continental Congress moved to the Pennsylvania backcountry. In any event, central government was virtually nonexistent, and so the unified effort suffered little disruption. The British would have done better to move north instead,

The surrender of Gen. John Burgoyne at Saratoga, on October 17, 1777, as depicted in a French illustration of 1784. This was the biggest British defeat before their final surrender at Yorktown in 1781, and it convinced the French to recognize American independence. Within a few weeks Patriots all over the colonies were joyously dancing a new step known as "Burgoyne's Surrender."

where they might have saved Burgoyne. At the end of two years of fighting, the British strategy for winning the war had to be judged a failure.

The French Alliance

During these first two years of fighting, the Americans were sustained by loans from France and Spain. The Continental Congress maintained a diplomatic delegation in Paris headed by Benjamin Franklin. One of the world's most urbane and cosmopolitan citizens, Franklin captured French hearts by dressing in the plain clothing of a Pennsylvania Quaker and wearing a beaver hat. He maintained excellent relations with the French foreign minister, the Comte de Vergennes, with whom he negotiated for recognition of American independence, a Franco-American alliance against the British, and loans to finance the Revolution. Wishing to weaken the British empire any way it could, the French state was inclined to support the Americans. At the same time, it was reluctant to encourage a revolution against monarchy and colonialism. Despite his charms, through 1777 Franklin was unable to convince Vergennes to commit his country to an alliance.

In England, meanwhile, the Whig opposition argued strongly against the war. "The measures toward America are erroneous," declared Lord Rockingham, "the adherence to them is destruction." William Pitt warned his countrymen to beware "the gathering storm" if France decided to actively support the Americans. When, in December 1777, North received the news of Burgoyne's surrender, he dispatched agents to begin peace discussions with Franklin in Paris. Fears of British conciliation with the revolutionaries, in addition to word of the victory at Saratoga, finally persuaded Vergennes to tie France to the United States. In mid-December he informed Franklin that the king's council had decided to recognize American independence.

In February 1778 the American delegation submitted to Congress a treaty of commerce and alliance it had negotiated with the French. In the treaty, to take effect upon a declaration of war between France and Britain, the French pledged to "maintain effectually the liberty, sovereignty, and independence" of the United States. "Neither of the two parties," the document read, "shall conclude either truce or peace with Great Britain, without the formal consent of the other." France guaranteed to the United States all the "northern parts of America" as well as other "conquests" made in the war, while the United States promised to recognize French acquisitions of British islands in the West Indies. Warfare between France and Britain broke out in June.

France was allied with Spain in the "family compact" of monarchs, and a year later Spain also entered the war against Britain. Congressional attempts to establish a formal alliance with the Spanish met with failure, however, for Spain looked with great suspicion on the Revolution, regarding the Americans as a threat to its New World empire. The first French ambassador to the United States arrived with instructions to do everything he could to prevent the Americans from enlarging their territory at the expense of the Spanish empire, which stretched into the Mississippi Valley. Vergennes also feared the potential power of an independent United States. Several years before, he had warned the British that the states "would immediately set about forming a great marine," using it in the Caribbean to "conquer both your islands and ours," then sweeping south, where it would "not leave a foot of that hemisphere in the possession of any European power." American leaders understood that the treaty with the French was an expedient for both sides, and they recognized the dangers that France and Spain posed to the United States. But far more important was the prospect the treaty offered of victory over Britain.

In the spring of 1778 Congress made clear its support for the alliance with the French when it rejected a new British offer of negotiations. Lord North's government had sent a peace commission to America with promises to repeal the parliamentary legislation that had provoked the crisis and never again to impose revenue taxes on the colonies. Three years earlier, such pledges would surely have forestalled the movement toward independence. But the Continental Congress now declared that any person coming to terms with the peace commission was a traitor; the only possible topics of negotiation were the withdrawal of British forces and the recognition of American independence. The peace commission was reduced to attempting to bribe members of Congress, and finally to threatening a war of devastation, but to no avail.

Fighting in the East, the West, and at Sea

The American Loyalists struck a brave pose when they heard the announcement of the French alliance.

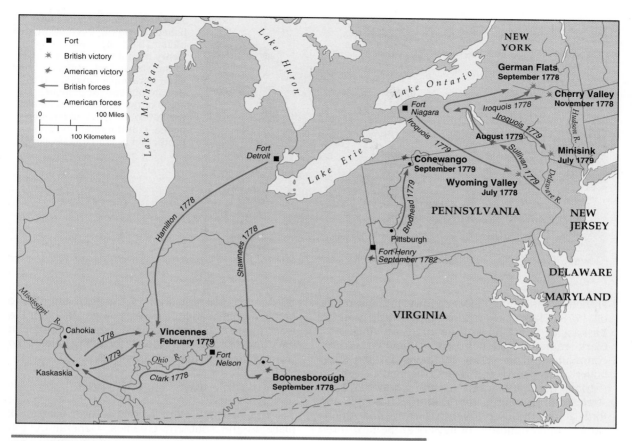

The Principal Engagements of the Western Theater of the War, 1778–1779

The Congress did boast of their mighty ally,
But George does both France and the Congress defy;
And when Britons unite, there's no force can withstand
Their fleets and their armies, by sea and on land.

But the entry of France into the war forced the British to rethink their strategy. The West Indies were now at risk, and the British shipped 5,000 men from New York to the Caribbean, where they beat back a French attack. Fearing the arrival of the French fleet along the North American coast, the new British commander in America, General Henry Clinton, evacuated Philadelphia in June of 1778. In hot pursuit were Washington's Continentals, fresh out of Valley Forge. At the Battle of Monmouth on June 28, the British blunted the American drive and retreated to New York. The Americans, centered at West Point, took up defensive positions surrounding the lower Hudson. Confidence in an impending victory now spread through the Patriot forces. But after a failed campaign with the French against the British forces at Newport, Rhode Island, Washington settled for a defensive strategy. Although the Americans enjoyed a number of small successes in the Northeast over the next two years, the war there went into a stall.

Elsewhere, however, the fighting picked up. Through the summer and fall of 1778, Iroquois and Loyalist forces raided the northern frontiers of Pennsylvania and New York. The following year, an American army attacked the Iroquois, defeating a strong force in the summer and destroying dozens of western Iroquois villages and thousands of acres of crops during the fall. Across the mountains in Kentucky, American settlements barely held out against attacks by the Ohio Indians in 1777 and 1778. Virginian George Rogers Clark countered by organizing an expedition of militia forces against the

This American cartoon, published during the Revolution, depicts "The Scalp Buyer," Col. Henry Hamilton paying bounties to Indians. In fact, Indian fighters were not simply pawns of the British, but sought to insure some of the same values as did the Patriots — political independence, cultural integrity, and protection of land and property.

French towns in the Illinois country. In the summer of 1778 Clark's men took the British post at Kaskaskia. The following February at Vincennes, Clark captured Colonel Henry Hamilton, British commander in the West, infamous as "the scalp buyer" because of the bounty he had placed on Patriots. But Clark lacked the strength to attack the strategic British garrison at Detroit. Raids back and forth across the Ohio River by Indians and Americans claimed hundreds of lives over the next three years.

Once the Spanish entered the war, they advanced on British posts, taking Natchez and Baton Rouge in 1779, Mobile in 1780, and Pensacola in 1781. Alarmed by the quick spread of American settlements west of the Appalachians, they attempted to establish a claim of their own to the British territory north of the Ohio by sending an expedition into the Northwest in 1781. The minor British post of St. Joseph, in present-day Michigan, fell to them.

The war at sea was fought mostly between the British and the French. But Continental, state, and private vessels played a role, raiding British merchant ships and conducting isolated naval patrols. The foremost naval hero of the war was John Paul Jones. In 1777 Jones raided the coast of Scotland. In 1779, while commanding the French ship *Bonhomme Richard* (which Jones had named in honor of Franklin's *Poor Richard*), he engaged in a celebrated battle with the British warship *Serapis*. When the two ships locked together, the British captain hailed Jones, asking if he was ready to surrender. Jones's reply — "I have not yet begun to fight" — became one of the most quoted lines of the Revolution. The battle, though, had little military value, and after the war Congress decommissioned the small American navy and dismissed its officers, including Jones, who went on to serve in the Russian navy.

The War Shifts to the South

The most important fighting of these years took place in the southern colonies. General Clinton regained the initiative for Britain in December 1778 by sending a force from New York against Georgia, the weakest of the colonies. The British crushed the Patriot militia at Savannah and began to organize the Loyalists in an effort to reclaim the colony. Several American counterattacks failed, including one with the French fleet against Savannah in September and October. Encouraged by their success in Georgia, the British decided to apply the lessons learned there throughout the South. This involved a fundamental change from a strategy of military conquest to one of pacification: territory would be retaken step by step, then handed over to Loyalists who would reassert colonial authority loyal to the crown. In early 1780 Clinton evacuated Rhode Island, the last British stronghold in New England, and proceeded with 8,000 troops for a campaign against Charleston.

The siege of Charleston began in February of 1780. Outflanking the American defenders, Clinton forced the surrender of over 5,000 troops in May — the most significant American defeat of the war. Horatio Gates, the hero of Saratoga, led a detachment of Continentals southward, but in August they

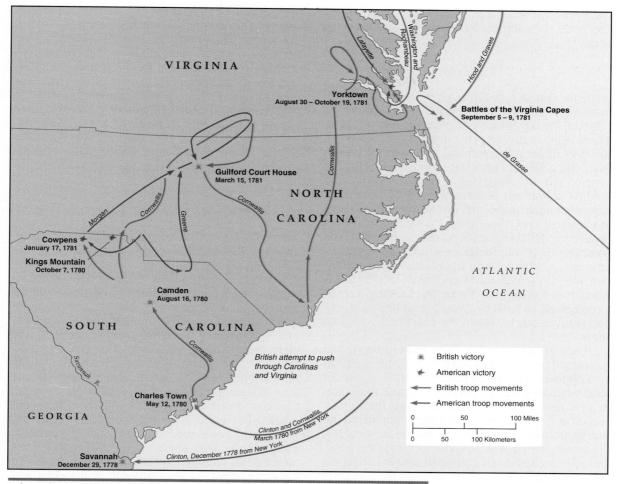

✳	British victory
✷	American victory
←	British troop movements
←	American troop movements

0   50   100 Miles
0   50   100 Kilometers

The Principal Engagements of the Southern Theater of the War, 1778–1781

were defeated by Cornwallis at Camden, South Carolina. Patriot resistance to the British collapsed in the Lower South, and American fortunes were suddenly at their lowest ebb since the beginning of the war.

The southern campaign was marked by vicious violence between partisan militias of Patriots and Loyalists. "The Whigs and Tories persecute each other with little less than savage fury," wrote General Greene, appointed to succeed Gates after the disaster at Camden; "there is nothing but murders and devastations in every quarter." The violence peaked in September of 1780 with Cornwallis's invasion of North Carolina, where the Patriots were stronger and better organized. There the British found their southern strategy untenable: plundering towns and farms in order to feed the army in the interior, where it was detached from lines of supply, had the effect of producing angry support for the Patriots.

Into 1781 the Continentals and militias waged what General Greene called a "fugitive" war of hit and run against the British. "I am quite tired of marching about the country in quest of adventures," Cornwallis wrote; he declared himself "totally in the dark" about what to do next. Finally deciding that he would not be able to hold the Carolinas so long as Virginia remained a base of support and supply for the Americans, Cornwallis led his army northward in the summer of 1781. After marauding throughout the Virginia countryside he reached the Chesapeake, where he expected reinforcements from New York.

The British withdrawal from North Carolina allowed Greene to reestablish Patriot control of the Lower South.

Yorktown

While the British raged through the South the stalemate continued in the Northeast. In the summer of 1780, taking advantage of the British evacuation of Rhode Island, the French landed 5,000 troops at Newport under the command of General Rochambeau. But it was not until the spring of 1781 that the general risked joining his force to Washington's Continentals north of New York. They planned a campaign against the city, but in August Washington learned that the French Caribbean fleet was headed for the Chesapeake. Washington sensed the possibility of a coup de grâce if only he and Rochambeau could move their troops south in coordination with the French naval operation, locking Cornwallis into his camp at Yorktown. Leaving a small force behind as a decoy, Washington and Rochambeau moved quickly down the coast to the Virginia shore.

Over 16,000 American and French troops had converged on the almost 8,000-man British garrison at Yorktown by mid-September. "If you cannot relieve me very soon," Cornwallis wrote to Clinton in New York, "you must expect to hear the worst." French and American heavy artillery hammered the British unmercifully until the middle of October. Cornwallis found it impossible to break the siege, and after the failure of a planned retreat across the York River, he opened negotiations for the surrender of his army. Two days later, on October 19, 1781, between lines of victorious American and French soldiers, the British troops came out from their trenches to surrender, marching to the melancholy tune of "The World Turned Upside Down":

> If buttercups buzzed after the bee,
> If boats were on land, churches on sea,
> If summer were spring and t'other way round,
> Then all the world would be upside down.

It must have seemed that way to Cornwallis, who, pleading illness, sent his second-in-command, General O'Hara, to surrender. O'Hara first approached General Rochambeau, but the Frenchman waved him toward Washington. It was almost incomprehensible to the British that they would be surrendering to former subordinates. Everyone knew this was an event of incalculable importance, but few guessed it was the end of the war, for the British still controlled New York.

In London, at the end of November, Lord North received the news "as he would have taken a ball in the breast," reported the colonial secretary. "Oh God!" he moaned. "It is all over!" British fortunes were at low ebb in India, the West Indies, Florida, and the Mediterranean; the cost of the war was enormous; and there was little support among the public and members of Parliament. King George wished to press on, but North submitted his resignation, and in March 1782 the king was forced to accept the ministry of Lord Rockingham, who favored granting Americans their independence.

OUTSIDERS AND THE REVOLUTION

In March 1776 Abigail Adams wrote to her husband, away at the independence deliberations of the Continental Congress. In her letter were these famous lines: "In the new code of laws which I suppose it will be necessary for you to make I desire you would remember the ladies, and be more generous and favourable to them than your ancestors." Otherwise, if we women are ignored, she playfully concluded, "we are determined to foment a rebellion, and will not hold ourselves bound by any laws in which we have no voice, or representation." John Adams responded in an equally playful tone: "As to your extraordinary code of laws, I cannot but laugh," he wrote. "We have been told that our struggle has loosened the bands of government every where. That children and apprentices were disobedient — that schools and colleges were grown turbulent — that Indians slighted their guardians and Negroes grew insolent to their masters. But your letter was the first intimation that another tribe more numerous and powerful than all the rest were grown discontented." His answer reflected the concern of many Patriots about the dislocations produced by the Revolution.

Revolutionary Women

In many ways the Revolution was a turning point for American women. Although traditional roles remained intact, they were often questioned during this period of turmoil. As men marched off to war, women assumed management of family farms and businesses. Abigail Adams, for example, ran the family farm at Quincy for years. Women volunteered as seamstresses, cooks, nurses, and even spies when the fighting shifted to their locales. A number of women participated more directly in patriotic politics. The Boston home of Mercy Otis Warren, daughter of James Otis, was a center of activity, and this dedicated revolutionary woman published a series of satirical plays in the 1770s supporting the American cause and scorning the Loyalists.

As the months of fighting lengthened into years, many women left their homes to join husbands and lovers, fathers and brothers in army encampments. Some were officially employed, but most took care of their own men, and many fought side by side with them. Some of the better-known camp women included Martha Washington and Catherine Greene, whose husbands were the two most important American generals of the war. But less socially prominent women are remembered as well. Mary Ludwig Hays (later McCauley), who was with her husband at Valley Forge, earned the name "Molly Pitcher" for her courage in bringing water to the men during the Battle of Monmouth; when her husband was overcome by heat, she took his place at the cannon. When Margaret Corbin's husband died while defending Fort Washington, she stepped into his position. Some women, such as Deborah Sampson of Massachusetts, disguised themselves as men and enlisted.

The post-revolutionary years marked a series of advances for American women. There is evidence, for example, of increasing sympathy in the courts for women's property rights and fairer adjudication of women's petitions for divorce. And the 1780s witnessed an increase in opportunities for women seeking an education. From a strictly legal and political point of view, the Revolution may have done little to change women's role in society. It did, however, seem to help change expectations. Abigail Adams's request to her husband was directed less toward the shape of the new republic than toward the structure of family life. "Do not put such unlimited powers into the hands of the husbands," she wrote, "for all men would be tyrants if they could." She had in mind a new, companionate ideal of marriage that contrasted with older notions of patriarchy. Men and women ought to be more like partners, less like master and servant. This new ideal took root among the middle class during the late eighteenth century.

In a number of other, more social ways the Revolutionary era wrought change in the lives of ordinary women. Historians have discovered that premarital conception increased late in the century, and that sisters increasingly tended to marry out of their birth order, selecting husbands whose economic status differed from that of their parents. These patterns suggest that parents had less and less control over their daughters.

African Americans in the Revolution

In late 1775 Lord Dunmore, the last royal governor of Virginia, issued a proclamation calling on slaves to desert their masters and take up arms with the British. Chesapeake planters were terrified when 800 slaves responded to his call. The Patriot who routed Dunmore's force in December saw a large number of African American troops wearing sashes emblazoned with the words "Liberty to Slaves." Many of these black soldiers succumbed to smallpox, but at least 300 sailed with Dunmore when he departed for England in 1777. When the British returned to the South in 1779, thousands of slaves responded to General Clinton's promise of liberty to those who would fight. When the British troops departed at the end of the war, thousands of African American fighters and their families left as well, settling in Great Britain, the West Indies, Canada, and even Africa. Thousands of others eluded their masters and remained in the United States as free men and women. Virginia and South Carolina were said to have lost 30,000 and 25,000 slaves, respectively, as a result of the war. But for many African Americans, the American victory was nothing to celebrate, for it perpetuated the institution of slavery.

Thousands of African Americans, though, did fight for the Patriots. Americans were at first reluctant to arm black men, but were eventually persuaded by the critical need for manpower. The northern states, led by New England, solicited African American recruits early in the war, and Rhode Island went so far as to create an African American regiment. When the war shifted southward, the states of the Upper South grudgingly allowed free persons of color into the armed forces. Some of these men served in the infantry; many more were commissary workers or teamsters. By war's end at least 5,000 African Americans had served in Patriot militias or the Continental army, and in the Upper South some slaves won their freedom through military service. In the Lower South, however, where the numerical superiority of slaves bred white fears of rebellion, there was no similar movement.

To many Americans there was an obvious contradiction in waging a war for liberty while continuing to support the institution of slavery. Slavery was first abolished in the state constitution of Vermont in 1777, and in Massachusetts and New Hampshire in 1780 and 1784, respectively. Pennsylvania, Connecticut, and Rhode Island adopted systems of gradual emancipation during these years, freeing the children of slaves at birth. By 1804 every northern state had provided for abolition or gradual emancipation, although as late as 1810, 30,000 African Americans remained enslaved in the North.

In the Upper South, revolutionary idealism, the Christian egalitarianism of Methodists and Baptists, and a shift from tobacco farming to the cultivation of cereal grains such as wheat and corn combined to weaken the commitment of many planters to the slave system. There was a great increase in manumissions — grants of freedom to slaves by individual masters. George Washington, for example, freed several hundred of his slaves, developing an elaborate plan for apprenticeship and tenancy for the able-bodied, lodging and pensions for the aged. But most masters interested in freeing their slaves saw little reason to go beyond simple manumission. Planters in the Lower South, heavily dependent upon slave labor, resisted the growing calls for an end to slavery. Between 1776 and 1786 all the states but South Carolina and Georgia prohibited or heavily taxed the international slave trade, and this issue became an important point of contention at the Constitutional Convention.

Perhaps the most important result of these developments was the growth of the free African American population from a mere few thousand in 1750 to more than 200,000 by the end of the century. The increase was most notable in the Upper South. The free African American population of Virginia, for example, grew from less than 2,000 in 1780 to approximately 20,000 in 1800. Largely excluded from the institutions of white Americans, the African American community now had sufficient strength to establish schools, churches, and other institutions of its own. Initially this development was opposed. In Williamsburg, Virginia, for instance, the leader of a black congregation was seized and whipped when he attempted to gain recognition from the Baptist Association. But by the 1790s the Williamsburg African Church had grown to over 500 members, and the association reluctantly recognized it. In Philadelphia Absalom Jones established St. Thomas's African Episcoal Church. The incorporation of the term *African* in the names of many churches, schools, and mutual benefit societies reflected the pride African Americans took in their heritage. New York's African Marine Fund, to take one example, described itself as an organization for assisting "our African brethren and the descendants of our mother country."

A small group of African American writers rose to prominence during the revolutionary era. Benjamin Banneker, born free in Maryland, where he received an education, was one of the most accomplished mathematicians and astronomers of late-eighteenth-century America. From 1792 until his death in 1806 he published a popular almanac, consulted by Americans both white and black. Jupiter Hammon, a Long Island slave, took up contemporary issues in his poems and essays, including an important "Address to the Negroes of the State of New York" in 1787.

The most famous African American writer,

This portrait of the African American poet Phillis Wheatley was included in the collection of her work published in London in 1773, when she was only twenty. Kidnapped in Africa when a girl, then purchased off the Boston docks, she was more like a daughter than a slave to the Wheatley family, and later married and lived as a free woman of color before her untimely death in 1784.

however, was Phillis Wheatley, who came to public attention when her *Poems on Various Subjects, Religious and Moral* appeared in London in 1773, while she was still a domestic slave in Boston. Kidnapped as a young girl and converted to Christianity during the Great Awakening, Wheatley wrote poems that combined her piety with a concern for her people. "On Being Brought from Africa to America" is a good example:

'Twas mercy brought me from my pagan land,
Taught my benighted soul to understand
That there's a God, that there's a Saviour too;
Once I redemption neither sought nor knew.
Some view our sable race with scornful eye,
"Their colour is a diabolic dye."
Remember, Christians, Negros, black as Cain,
May be refin'd, and join th'angelic train.

"In every human breast God has implanted a principle, which we call love of freedom; it is impatient of oppression, and pants for deliverance," she wrote in a letter. "The same principle lives in us."

Indian Peoples

Native peoples fought in the Revolution for some of the same values the Patriots did — political independence, cultural integrity, and protection of land and property. Their fears of American expansion, however, led them to oppose those who claimed the cause of natural rights and the equality of all men. Like the Americans, Indian tribes also faced serious problems in overcoming traditions of local autonomy and factionalism. They were far less successful than the Americans, however, in meeting this challenge.

The first significant Indian conflict of the Revolution came in 1776, when a large faction of Cherokees led by the warrior chief Dragging Canoe (Tsiyu-Gunsini) attacked American settlements in the North Carolina backcountry. Over the next two years, militia companies from the southern states managed to drive the Cherokees into the mountains, destroying many of their towns. Americans assumed that Britain sponsored the Indian attacks, but it was not until 1777 that the British adopted a policy of arming Indians. British agents pressed the Iroquois Confederacy, long one of the most significant political forces in colonial North America, to unite against the Americans. "We are unwilling to join on either side of such a contest," an Oneida chief responded, "for we love you both — old England and new." But there were British supporters, principal

Joseph Brant, the brilliant chief of the Mohawks who sided with Great Britain during the Revolution, in a 1786 painting by the American artist Gilbert Stuart. After the Treaty of Paris, Brant led a large faction of Iroquois people north into British Canada where they established a separate Iroquois Confederacy.
(Gilbert Stuart. Joseph Brant. *1786. Oil on canvas. 30" × 25". New York Historical Association, Cooperstown.)*

among them the Mohawk leaders Joseph Brant and his sister Mary, widow of Sir William Johnson, Indian agent for the northern region. The confederacy ultimately split, with the pro-American Oneidas leading one side, the pro-British Mohawks the other. Not only did the Iroquois suffer devastating raids by the Americans, but for the first time since the birth of their confederacy in the fifteenth century, they were torn by civil war.

In the West, the Ohio Indians formed an effective alliance under the British at Detroit, and enjoyed considerable success against western settlers. In 1782, militiamen from western Pennsylvania slaughtered 90 peaceful Christian Delawares north of the Ohio River; soon thereafter Indian fighters killed 146 Kentucky militiamen at the Battle of the Blue Licks. There were atrocities on both sides. The war in the West would not conclude with the end of the Revolution, but would continue for another twenty years.

After Yorktown, the British abandoned their Indian allies. When the Indians learned of the armistice, according to a British officer in the West, they were "thunderstruck." Neither the Iroquois nor the Ohio tribes considered themselves defeated, but the United States nevertheless claimed that the victory over Great Britain was a victory over the Indians as well. A heavily armed American nation now pressed for large grants of territory according to the right of conquest. Even Patriot allies were not exempt. The Oneida suffered territorial demands along with the other Iroquois. The Penobscot and Passamaquoddy of northern New England fought with the Americans in exchange for a promise that Massachusetts would protect their homelands, but after the war that state wrested large amounts of territory from them. For most Indian communities, the American Revolution was an unmitigated disaster.

THE UNITED STATES IN CONGRESS ASSEMBLED

The motion for independence, offered to the Continental Congress by Richard Henry Lee on June 7, 1776, called for a confederation of the states. The Articles of Confederation, the first written constitution of the United States, created a national government of sharply curtailed powers. This arrangement reflected the concerns of people fighting to free themselves from a coercive central government.

The Articles of Confederation

The debate over confederation that took place in the Continental Congress following the Declaration of Independence made it clear that the localists — delegates favoring a loose union of autonomous states — outnumbered those who considered themselves nationalists. Not until the following year did a consensus finally emerge. In November of 1777 the Articles of Confederation were formally adopted by the Continental Congress and sent to the states for ratification. The Articles created a national assembly, called the Congress, in which each state had a single vote. Delegates, selected annually in a manner determined by the individual state legislatures, could serve no more than three years out of six. A presiding president elected annually by Congress was eligible no more than one year out of three. Votes would be decided by a simple majority of the states, except for major questions, which would require the agreement of nine states.

Congress was granted national authority in the conduct of foreign affairs, matters of war and peace,

and maintenance of the armed forces. It could raise loans, issue bills of credit, establish a coinage, and regulate trade with Indian peoples, and it was to be the final authority in jurisdictional disputes between states. It was charged with establishing a national postal system as well as a common standard of weights and measures. Lacking the power to tax citizens directly, however, the national government was to apportion its financial burdens among the states according to the extent of their surveyed land. The Articles explicitly guaranteed the sovereignty of the individual states, reserving to them all powers not expressly delegated to Congress. Ratification or amendment required the agreement of all thirteen states. This constitution thus created a national government of specific, yet sharply circumscribed powers.

The legislatures of twelve states soon voted in favor of the Articles, but final ratification was held up for over three years by the state of Maryland. Representing the interests of states without claims to lands west of the Appalachians, Maryland demanded that states cede to Congress their western claims, the new nation's most valuable resource, for "the good of the whole." Excepted, however, would be the colonial grants made to land companies. The eight states with western claims were reluctant to give them up, and the remaining states included powerful land speculators among their most influential citizens. While the stalemate over western lands continued, Congress remained an extralegal body, but it agreed to work under the terms of the unratified document. It was 1781 before all eight states with western claims voted to cede them. Maryland then agreed to ratification, and in March the Articles of Confederation took effect.

Financing the War

Before 1781, Congress administered the national government by appointing standing committees on finance, the postal system, foreign affairs, and the conduct of the war. During the dark days of 1780, Americans turned to the leadership of nationalists favoring stronger central control, and these men pushed Congress to create governmental departments headed by strong superintendents with ministerial authority. In the most important of these appointments, Robert Morris, one of the wealthiest merchants in the country, became secretary of finance.

Congress had financed the Revolution through grants and loans from friendly foreign powers, and by issuing paper currency. As a measure of nationalistic pride, Congress chose the dollar as its unit of value instead of the British pound. (For the development of this monetary unit, see Chapter 5.) The total foreign subsidy by the end of the war had approached $9 million, but this was insufficient to back the circulating Continental currency, whose face value was nearly $200 million. Congress called on the states to raise taxes, payable in Continental dollars, so that this currency could be retired. But most of the states proved unwilling to do this. In fact, the states resorted to printing currency of their own, which totaled another $200 million by the end of the war. The results of this growth in the money supply were rapid depreciation of Continental currency and runaway inflation. People who received fixed incomes for services — Continental soldiers, for example, as well as merchants, landlords, and other creditors — were devastated. When Morris took office in May of 1781, Continental currency had ceased to circulate; things of no value were said to be "not worth a Continental."

Congress granted Morris great power. His primary goals were to provide the Confederation with a stable currency, redeemable in coin, and to pay the interest on the war debt. He persuaded Congress to charter the Bank of North America in Philadelphia, the first private commercial bank in the United States. There he deposited large quantities of specie and bills of exchange obtained through loans from Holland and France. Morris then issued new paper currency backed by this supply. Once confidence in the bank had developed, he was able to begin supplying the army through private contracts, paid with "Morris Warrants." He was also able to meet the interest payments on the debt, which in 1783 he estimated to be about $30 million. Morris deserved a great deal of credit for setting the financial house of the Confederation in order. He also received a good deal of criticism, however, for he had insisted as a condition of accepting office that he be allowed to retain his private commercial connections, and during his term both he and his associates profited handsomely from his dealings.

Morris was associated with the nationalists who controlled Congress in the early 1780s. With their support, he proposed amending the Articles of Confederation to empower Congress to levy a 5 percent duty on imports. The Confederation would then have a source of revenue independent of state requisitions. By the fall of 1782, twelve states had approved the "impost amendment." Rhode Island refused, objecting that state control of import duties was essential to its own revenues. Localists, who continued to believe in a decentralized Confedera-

tion, also voiced much opposition to the Morris plan. "Let the United States keep the sovereignty divided among themselves, or at least keep the purse in their own power," one argued. Morris and the nationalists continued to press for an independent congressional revenue; failing in this, Morris resigned office in 1784.

Negotiating Independence

Peace talks between the United States and Great Britain opened in July 1782, when Benjamin Franklin sat down with the British emissary in Paris. Congress had first issued instructions to its peace commissioners in 1779. The fundamental demands were recognition of American independence and withdrawal of British forces. Negotiators were to press for as much territory as possible, including Canada, but in no event should settle for less than boundaries along the forty-fifth parallel in the North, the thirty-first parallel in the South, and the Mississippi River in the West. Moreover, the American right to fish the North Atlantic had to be guaranteed. As for its French ally, Congress instructed the commissioners to be guided by friendly advice, but also by "knowledge of our interests, and by your own discretion, in which we repose the fullest confidence." But as the British pushed through the South over the next two years and the Americans grew increasingly dependent upon French loans and military might, the French ambassador in Philadelphia worked to limit potential American power. In June 1781, partly as a result of French pressure, Congress issued a new set of instructions: the commissioners were to settle merely for a grant of independence and withdrawal of troops, and to be subject to the guidance and control of the French in the negotiations.

Franklin, John Jay, and John Adams, the peace commissioners in Paris, were aware of French attempts to manipulate the outcome of negotiations. In violation of instructions and treaty obligations, and without consulting the French, they signed a preliminary treaty with Britain in November. The British were delighted at the thought of separating the wartime allies. In the treaty, Britain acknowledged the United States as "free, sovereign & independent," and agreed to withdraw its troops from all forts within American territory "with all convenient speed." They guaranteed Americans "the right to take fish" in northern waters. The American commissioners had pressed the British for Canada, but settled for territorial boundaries that

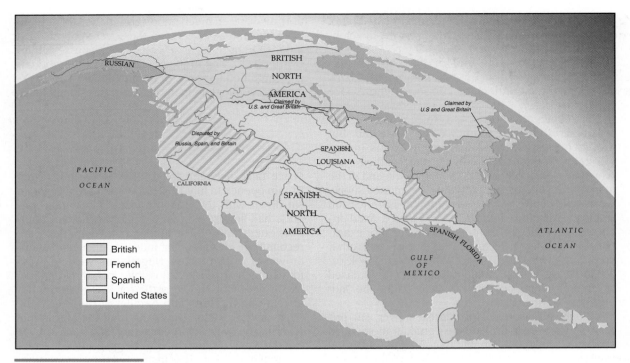

North America in 1783

The map of European and American claims to North America was radically altered by the results of the American Revolution.

extended to the Mississippi. Britain received American promises to erect "no lawful impediments" to the recovery of debts, to cease confiscating Loyalist property, and to try to persuade the states to fairly compensate Loyalist exiles. Finally, the two nations agreed to unencumbered navigation of the Mississippi. The American commissioners had accomplished an astounding coup. The new boundaries, they wrote to Congress, "appear to leave us little to complain of and not much to desire."

France was thus confronted with a *fait accompli.* When Vergennes criticized the commissioners, the Americans responded by hinting that resistance to the treaty provisions could result in a British-American alliance. France thereupon quickly made an agreement of its own with the British.

Spain claimed sovereignty over much of the trans-Appalachian territory granted to the United States. It had not been consulted on Mississippi navigation, which it controlled through its possession of the port of New Orleans. Spain too arranged a separate peace with Great Britain, in which it won

the return of Florida. The final Treaty of Paris was signed at Versailles on September 3, 1783.

The Crisis of Demobilization

During the two years between the surrender at Yorktown and the signing of the Treaty of Paris, the British continued to occupy New York City, Charleston, and a series of western posts. The Continental Army remained on wartime alert, with some 10,000 men and an estimated 1,000 women encamped at Newburgh, New York, north of West Point. The soldiers had long been awaiting their pay, and were very concerned about the postwar bounties and land warrants promised them. The most serious problem, however, lay not among the enlisted men but in the officer corps.

Continental officers had extracted a promise from Congress of life pensions at half pay in exchange for enlistment for the duration of the war. By 1783, however, Congress had still not made specific provisions for the pensions. With peace at hand,

A British cartoon lampooning the Treaty of Paris in 1783 depicts an Englishman, Dutchman, Indian, Spaniard, and Frenchman joining in "A General P--s, or Peace." The caption read in part: "A hundred hard millions in war we have spent, / And American lost by all patriots' consent, / Yet let us be quiet, nor any one hiss, / But rejoice at this hearty and general P--."

officers began to fear that the army would be disbanded before the problem was resolved, and they would lose whatever power they had to pressure Congress. In January 1783 a group of prominent senior officers, including General Henry Knox, petitioned Congress. "We have borne all that men can bear," they wrote. "Our property is expended — our private resources are at an end." They demanded that Congress commute the pensions to a bonus equal to five years of full pay. "Any further experiments on their patience," they warned, "may have fatal effects." This demand was "mercenary," complained some congressmen, and might result in the creation of an aristocracy dangerous to democratic institutions. Despite the barely veiled threat of military intervention, Congress rejected commutation.

These officers were encouraged, however, by a number of nationalist congressmen who saw in the military threat an opportunity to coerce the states into yielding more power to Congress on the critical question of an independent revenue. One of the nationalists, Alexander Hamilton of New York, had served as Washington's aide-de-camp during the war. "The great *desideratum*," he wrote to Washington in February, "is the establishment of general funds, which alone can do justice to the creditors of the United States," and "in this, the influence of the army, properly directed, may cooperate." With the backing of congressional nationalists, a group of army officers associated with General Horatio Gates issued the first of what became known as the Newburgh Addresses, again threatening military force if Congress failed to act, and calling an extraordinary meeting of the officer corps at Newburgh.

But Washington, whom the nationalists counted on for support, condemned the meeting as "disorderly" and called an official meeting of his own, also at Newburgh. There was enormous tension when the officers assembled on March 15, for at stake was nothing less than the possibility of a military coup at the very moment of American victory. Washington strode into the room and mounted the platform. Turning his back in disdain on General Gates, he told the assembly that he wished to read a statement, then pulled a pair of glasses from his pocket. None of his officers had seen their leader wearing glasses before. "Gentlemen, you must pardon me," said Washington when he noticed their surprise; "I have grown gray in your service and now find myself growing blind." He then denounced any resort to force. But the decisive moment had already passed with his offhand remark about growing gray. Who had sacrificed more than their commander in chief? the officers realized in shame. After he left, they adopted resolutions rejecting the "infamous propositions" contained in the Newburgh Addresses. A week later, on Washington's urging, Congress decided to commute the pensions to bonuses after all.

Washington's role in this crisis was one of his greatest contributions to the nation. There is little doubt he could have assumed the role of American dictator. Instead, the principle of military subordination to civil authority was firmly established.

As for the common soldiers, they wanted simply to be discharged. "It is not in the power of Congress or their officers to hold them much, if any, longer," Washington wrote Hamilton in April. The next month, Congress voted the soldiers three months' pay as a bonus and instructed Washington to begin dismissing them. Some troops remained at Newburgh until the British evacuated New York in November, but by the beginning of 1784 the Continental Army had shrunk to no more than a few hundred men.

The Problem of the West

The new nation was also confronted with a mounting crisis in its western territory. Even during the Revolution, thousands migrated west, and after the war, settlers poured over the mountains and down the Ohio River. The population of Kentucky, still a part of Virginia, had grown to more than 30,000 by 1785; in 1790 it numbered 74,000, and the Tennessee area held another 36,000. Thousands of Americans pressed against the Indian country north of the Ohio River, and destructive violence continued along the frontier. British troops continued to occupy posts in the Northwest, and encouraged Indian attacks on vulnerable settlements. To the southwest, Spain, refusing to accept the territorial settlement of the Treaty of Paris, closed the Mississippi River to Americans. Westerners who saw that route as their primary access to markets were outraged.

The British told John Jay, appointed secretary for foreign affairs in 1784, that they would not evacuate the Northwest until all outstanding debts from before the war were settled. Jay negotiated with the Spanish for guarantees of territorial sovereignty and commercial relations, but they insisted that the United States in return would have to relinquish free navigation of the Mississippi. Congress would approve no treaty under those conditions. Under these frustrating circumstances, some westerners considered leaving the Confederation. Kentuckians threatened to rejoin the British. "When once reunited," one Kentuckian declared to Congress, "a long farewell to all your boasted greatness," for then "the inhabitants of these waters, of themselves, in time, will be able to conquer *you*." The Spanish secretly employed a number of prominent westerners, including George Rogers Clark and General James Wilkinson, as informants and spies. The people of the West "stand as it were upon a pivot," wrote Washington in 1784 after a trip down the Ohio. "The touch of a feather would turn them any way." In the West, local community interest continued to override the fragile development of national community sentiment.

In that year, Congress took up the problem of extending national authority over the West. Legislation was drafted, principally by Thomas Jefferson, providing for "Government for the Western Territory." The legislation was a remarkable attempt to create a democratic colonial policy. The public domain was to be divided into states, and Congress guaranteed the settlers in them immediate self-

State Claims to Western Lands, 1782–1802

The ratification of the Articles of Confederation in 1781 awaited settlement of the western claims of eight states.

The Northwest Territory

The greatest achievement of the Confederation government was the Land Ordinance of 1785, which made provision for the survey of newly incorporated lands, and the Northwest Ordinance of 1787, which established a system of government for the western country. Meanwhile, the British continued to occupy several strategic forts in American territory along the northern border with Canada.

government and republican institutions. Once the population of a territory numbered 20,000, the residents could call a convention and establish a constitution and government of their own choosing. And once the population grew to equal that of the smallest of the original thirteen states, the territory could obtain statehood, provided it agreed to remain forever a member of the Confederation. Fortunately, Congress rejected Jefferson's proposal to provide the future states with names such as Assenisippia and Metropotamia. But it also rejected, by a vote of seven to six, his clause prohibiting slavery.

Passed the following year, the Land Ordinance of 1785 provided for the survey and sale of western lands. To avoid the chaos of overlapping surveys and land claims that had characterized Kentucky, the authors of the ordinance created an ordered system of survey, dividing the land into townships composed of thirty-six sections of one square mile (640 acres) each. This measure would have an enormous impact on the North American landscape, as can be seen by anyone who has flown over the United States and looked down at the patchwork pattern. Jefferson argued that land ought to be given away to actual settlers. But Congress, eager to establish a revenue base for the government, provided for the auction of public lands for not less than one dollar per acre. In the treaties of Fort Stanwix in 1784 and Fort McIntosh in 1785, congressional commissioners forced the Iroquois and some of the Ohio Indians to cede a portion of their territory in what is now eastern Ohio, and surveyors were sent there to divide up the land. These treaties were not the result of negotiation; the commissioners dictated the terms by seizing hostages and forcing compliance. The first surveyed lands were not available for sale until the fall of 1788. In the meantime, Congress, desperate for revenue, sold a tract of more than 1.5 million acres to a new land company, the Ohio Company, for a million dollars.

Thousands of westerners chose not to wait for the official opening of the public land north of the Ohio River, but settled illegally. In 1785 Congress raised troops and evicted many of them, but once the troops left the squatters returned. The persistence of this problem convinced many congressmen to revise Jefferson's democratic territorial plan. It was necessary, explained Richard Henry Lee of Virginia, "for the security of property among uninformed and perhaps licentious people, as the greater part of those who go there are, that a strong toned government should exist." In the Northwest Ordinance of 1787, Congress established a system of government for the territory north of the Ohio. Three to five states were to be carved out of the giant Northwest Territory and admitted "on an equal footing with the original states in all respects whatsoever." Slavery was prohibited. But the guarantee of initial self-government in Jefferson's plan was replaced by the rule of a court of judges and a governor appointed by Congress. Once the free white male population of the territory had grown to 5,000, these citizens would be permitted to choose an assembly, but the governor was to have the power of absolute veto on all territorial legislation. National interest would be imposed on the localistic western communities. In an early instance of government in the hands of developers, Congress chose Arthur St. Clair, president of the Ohio Company, as the first governor of the Northwest Territory.

The creation of the land system of the United States was the major achievement of the Confederation government. But there were other important accomplishments. Under the Articles of Confederation, Congress led the country through the Revolution and its commissioners negotiated the terms of a comprehensive peace treaty. The Confederation government organized departments of war, foreign affairs, the post office, and finance — the origins of the national bureaucracy. But the focus of most Americans was not Philadelphia, but the states. The organization of state government was, said Thomas Jefferson, "the whole object of the present controversy."

REVOLUTIONARY POLITICS IN THE STATES

During the revolutionary era and for many years thereafter, most Americans identified politically and socially with their local community and state rather than the American nation. The national community feeling of the Revolution was overwhelmed by persistent localism. The national government was distant and had relatively little effect on people's lives. People spoke of "these United States," emphasizing the plural. The states were the setting for the most important political struggles of the Confederation period and for long after.

The Broadened Base of Politics

The political mobilization that took place in 1774 and 1775 greatly broadened political participation. Mass meetings in which ordinary people expressed their opinions, voted, and gained political experience were common, not only in the cities but in small towns and rural communities as well. During these years, a greater proportion of the population participated in elections. South Carolina, for example, employed a system of universal white manhood suffrage for the selection of delegates to the Continental Congress; many other states relaxed property qualifications. Compared with the colonial assemblies, the new state legislatures included more men from rural and western districts — farmers and artisans as well as lawyers, merchants, and large landowners. Many delegates to the Massachusetts provincial congress of 1774 were men from small farming communities; they lacked formal education and owned little property.

This transformation was accompanied by a dramatic shift in the political debate. During the colonial period, the principal argument had been between Tories and Whigs. The Tory position, argued by royal officials, was that colonial governments were simply convenient instruments of the king's prerogative, serving at his pleasure. Colonial elites, seeking to preserve and increase their power, argued for stronger assemblies. These they justified with traditional Whig arguments about the need for a balanced government of monarchic, aristocratic, and democratic elements, represented by the governor, the upper house, and the assembly, respectively. One of the first important political effects of the American Revolution was the elimination of the Tories as a legitimate political voice. There was a sudden and radical shift to the left, and conservative Patriots found themselves challenged by farmers, artisans, and other ordinary people armed with a new and radical democratic ideology.

With the collapse of colonial government, political debate focused on the appropriate governmental structure for the new states. The thinking of democrats was indicated by the title of a New England pamphlet of 1776, *The People the Best Governors.* Power, the anonymous author argued, should be vested in a single, popularly elected assembly. There should be no property qualifications for either voting or holding office. The governor should simply execute the wishes of the people as voiced by their representatives in the assembly. Judges too should be popularly elected, and their decisions reviewed by the assembly. The people, the pamphlet concluded, "best know their wants and necessities, and therefore are best able to govern themselves." The ideal form of government, according to democrats, was the community or town meeting, in which the people set their own tax rates, created a militia, controlled their own schools and churches, and regulated the local economy. State government was necessary only for coordination among communities.

Conservative voices continued to stress the need for a balanced government. The "unthinking many," wrote another pamphleteer, should be checked by a strong executive and an upper house. Both of these would be insulated from popular control by property qualifications and long terms in office, the latter designed to draw forth the wisdom and talent of the country's wealthiest and most accomplished men. The greatest danger, according to conservatives, was the possibility of majority tyranny, which might lead to the violation of property rights and to dictatorship. "We must take mankind as they are," one conservative wrote, "and not as we could wish them to be."

The First State Constitutions

Fourteen states — the original thirteen plus Vermont — adopted constitutions between 1776 and 1780. Each of these documents was shaped by debate between radicals and conservatives, democrats and Whigs, and reflected a political balance of power. The constitutions of Pennsylvania, Maryland, and New York typified the political range of the times. Pennsylvania instituted a radical democracy, Maryland created a conservative set of institutions designed to keep citizens and rulers as far apart as possible, and New York adopted a system somewhere in the middle.

In Pennsylvania, a majority of the conservatives had become Loyalists, allowing the democrats to seize power in 1776. The election of delegates to the constitutional convention was open to every man in

By giving the vote to "all free inhabitants," the 1776 constitution of New Jersey enfranchised women as well as men who met the property requirements. The number of women voters eventually led to male protests. Wrote one: "What tho' we read, in days of yore, / The woman's occupation / Was to direct the wheel and loom, / Not to direct the nation." In 1807 a new state law explicitly limited the right of franchise to "free white male citizens."

the militia, which further strengthened the advocates of democracy. The document this convention adopted clearly reflected the democratic agenda. It created a unicameral assembly elected annually by all free male taxpayers. So that delegates would be responsive to their constituents, sessions of the assembly were open to the public and included roll-call votes — the latter somewhat rare in colonial assemblies. There was no governor, but rather an elected executive committee. Judges were removable by the assembly.

By contrast, the Maryland constitution, adopted the same year, was written by conservative planters. It created property requirements for officeholding that left only about 10 percent of Maryland men eligible to serve in the assembly, 7 percent in the senate. A powerful governor, elected by large property owners, controlled a highly centralized government. Judges and other high executive officers served for life. These two states, Maryland and Pennsylvania, represented the political extremes. Georgia, Vermont, and North Carolina followed Pennsylvania's example; South Carolina's constitution was much like Maryland's.

In New York, the constitutional convention of 1777 included a large democratic faction. But conservatives such as John Jay, Gouverneur Morris, and Robert R. Livingston, managing the convention with great skill, helped to produce a document that reflected Whiggish principles while appealing to the people. There would be a bicameral legislature, with each house having equal powers. But there were stiff property qualifications for election to the senate, and senators represented districts apportioned by wealth, not population. The governor, also elected by property owners, had the power of veto, which could be overridden only by a two-thirds vote of both houses. Ultraconservatives wanted a constitution more like Maryland's, but Jay argued that "another turn of the winch would have cracked the cord"; conservatives, in other words, had gotten about as much as they could without alienating the mass of voters. Other states whose constitutions blended democratic and conservative elements were New Hampshire, New Jersey, and Massachusetts.

Declarations of Rights

One of the most important innovations of these constitutions was a guarantee of rights patterned on the Virginia Declaration of Rights of June 1776. Written by George Mason — wealthy planter, democrat, and brilliant political philosopher — the Virginia declaration set a distinct tone in its very first article: "That all men are by nature equally free and independent, and have certain inherent rights, . . . namely, the enjoyment of life and liberty, with the means of acquiring and possessing property and pursuing and obtaining happiness and safety." The fifteen articles declared, among other things, that sovereignty resided in the people, that government was the servant of the people, and that the people had the "right to reform, alter, or abolish" that government. There were guarantees of due process and trial by jury in criminal prosecutions, and prohibitions of excessive bail and "cruel and unusual punishments." Freedom of the press was guaranteed as "one of the great bulwarks of liberty," and the people were assured of "the free exercise of religion, according to the dictates of conscience."

Eight state constitutions included a general declaration of rights similar to the first article of the Virginia declaration; others incorporated specific guarantees. A number of states proclaimed the right of the people to engage in free speech and free assembly, to instruct their representatives, and to petition for the redress of grievances — rights either inadvertently or deliberately omitted from Virginia's declaration. These declarations were important precedents for the Bill of Rights, the first ten amendments to the federal constitution. Indeed, George Mason of Virginia was a leader of those democrats who insisted that the Constitution stipulate such rights.

A Spirit of Reform

The political upheaval of the Revolution raised the possibility of other reforms in American society. In 1776, after completing work on the Declaration of Independence, Thomas Jefferson returned to Virginia to take a seat in the House of Delegates, convinced that the most important political work lay within his own state. Over the next several years he led attempts to reform landholding, the penal code, the legal status of African Americans, and education of the young, and to broaden the freedom of religion.

In 1776 Jefferson introduced a bill that abolished the law of entails, which had confined inheritance to particular heirs in order that landed property remain undivided. Jefferson believed that entail and primogeniture (inheritance of all the family property by the firstborn son) — legal customs long in effect in aristocratic England — had no place in a republican society. The legislation had little practical effect, since relatively few estates were entailed, but the repeal was symbolically important, for it repudiated an aristocratic custom. By 1790, every state but one had followed Virginia's lead (Rhode Island acted in 1798).

Jefferson's other notable success was his Bill for Establishing Religious Freedom. Indeed, he considered this document one of his greatest accomplishments. At the beginning of the Revolution, there were established churches in nine of the thirteen colonies — the Congregationalists in Massachusetts, New Hampshire and Connecticut, the Anglicans in New York and the South. (For further discussion of colonial religion, see Chapter 5.) Established religion was increasingly opposed in the eighteenth century, in part because of Enlightenment criticism of the power it had over free and open inquiry, but more importantly because of the growing sectarian diversity produced by the religious revival of the Great Awakening. Many Anglican clergymen harbored Loyalist sympathies, and as part of an anti-Loyalist backlash New York, Maryland, the Carolinas, and Georgia had little difficulty passing acts that disestablished the Anglican church. In Virginia, however, many planters viewed Anglicanism as a bulwark against Baptist and Methodist democrats, resulting in bitter and protracted opposition to Jefferson's bill. Patrick Henry, grown conservative, defended state support for the church, and it was not until 1786 that the bill passed.

New England Congregationalists proved even more resistant to change. Although Massachusetts, New Hampshire, and Connecticut allowed dissenters to receive tax support, they maintained the official relationship between church and state well into the nineteenth century. Other states, despite disestablishment, retained religious tests in their legal codes. Georgia, the Carolinas, and New Jersey limited officeholding to Protestants; New York required legislators to renounce allegiance to the pope; and even Pennsylvania, where religious freedom had a long history, required officials to swear to a belief in the divine inspiration of the Old and New Testaments.

Jefferson proposed several more reforms of Virginia law, all of which failed to pass. He would have created a system of public education, revised the penal code to restrict capital punishment to the crimes of murder and treason, and established the gradual emancipation of slaves by law. Other states witnessed more progress on these issues, but on the whole, the Revolutionary generation, like Jefferson, were more successful in raising these issues than in accomplishing reforms. The problems of penal reform, establishment of free public education, and slavery remained for later generations of Americans to resolve.

During the Revolution, the shortage of goods resulting from the British blockade, the demand for supplies by the army and militias, and the flood of paper currency issued by Congress and the states combined to create the worst inflation that Americans have ever experienced. Continental dollars traded against Spanish dollars at the rate of 3 to 1 in 1777, 40 to 1 in 1779, and 146 to 1 in 1781, by which time Congress had issued over $190 million in Continentals. Most of this paper ended up in the hands of merchants who paid only a fraction of its face value. There was a popular outcry at the incredible increase in prices, and communities and states in the North responded with laws regulating wages and prices. Several states attempted to enact detailed rate schedules, and Congress voted approval of regional cooperation, but little was ever done to provide for enforcement.

The sponsors of wage and price schedules often attributed high prices to hoarding and profiteering. Although it is doubtful that such practices caused the inflation, many merchants did gouge their customers. Numerous communities experienced demonstrations and food riots; men and women demanded fair prices, and when they did not receive them they broke into storehouses and took what they needed. People organized local committees to monitor economic activity and punish wrongdoers. Abigail Adams told of a Boston merchant who refused to sell coffee for the price demanded by the committee. "A number of females, some say a hundred, some say more," she wrote, "seized him by his neck and tossed him into the cart. Upon his finding no quarter he delivered the keys," and the

The shortage of goods resulting from the British blockade, and the flood of Continental currency issued by Congress, combined to create the worst inflation that Americans have ever experienced. Things of no value were said to be "not worth a Continental."

women opened his warehouse and took the coffee. "A large concourse of men stood amazed, silent spectators of the whole transaction."

After the war the primary economic problem was no longer inflation but depression. Political revolution could not alter economic realities: the independent United States continued to be a supplier of raw materials and an importer of manufactured products, and Great Britain remained its most important trading partner. After the Treaty of Paris was signed in 1783, British exporters dumped their unsold goods on the American market, offering easy terms of credit to induce merchants to buy. The production of exportable commodities, however, had been drastically reduced by the fighting. In the South the loss of manpower and the destruction of plantations led to an 18 percent decline in production from prewar levels; rice exports fell by more than half. Britain now declared its West Indian colonies off-limits to Americans. The loss of this commerce was sorely felt in the North. There was still a great deal of smuggling, but it accounted for no more than 50 percent of the lost trade. "The Revolution has robbed us of our trade with the West Indies," James Madison declared in 1785, "without reopening any other channels to compensate for it."

With few exports to offset all the imports, the trade deficit with Britain for the period 1784–86 rose to approximately £5 million. The deficit acted like a magnet, drawing hard currency—gold and silver coin—from American accounts: according to one estimate, merchants exported £1.3 million in gold and silver coin during these two years. In turn, these merchants demanded immediate payment from their customers. Short of hard currency, the three commercial banks in the United States — the Bank of North America (Philadelphia), the Bank of New York, and the Bank of Massachusetts (Boston)—insisted on immediate repayment of old loans and refused to issue new ones. The country was left with very little coin in circulation. "The scarcity of money is beyond . . . conception," James Warren wrote from Boston. It all added up to a serious depression, lasting from 1784 to 1788. At their lowest level, in 1786, prices had fallen 25 percent.

The depression struck while the country was burdened with the huge debt incurred during the Revolution. Some of it was owed to foreign lenders, most to American creditors. Many of the latter had purchased for a considerable discount bills of credit issued to soldiers and farmers, and now expected the government to redeem the notes at full face value. The total debt owed by the national and state governments amounted to more than $50 million in 1785. (To place this figure in perspective, consider that this debt was approximately sixty-four times greater than the value of American exports for the year 1785; by contrast, the national debt in 1990 was only five times greater than the value of exports that year.) Not allowed to raise taxes on its own, the Confederation Congress requisitioned the states for the funds necessary for debt repayment. The states in turn taxed their residents. At a time when there was almost no money in circulation, people rightly feared being crushed by the burden of private debt and public taxes. Thus the economic problem became a political problem.

State Remedies

Where there were manufacturing interests, as in the Northeast, states erected high tariffs to curb imports and protect infant industries. But shippers could avoid these duties simply by unloading their cargo in nearby seaboard states that lacked tariffs; domestic merchants then distributed the products overland. In New England, imports came into duty-free Connecticut, eventually forcing the states of New Hampshire, Massachusetts, and Rhode Island to suspend enforcement of their tariff laws. To be effective, commercial regulation had to be national. Local sentiment had to give way to the unity of a national community. The "means of preserving ourselves," wrote John Adams, "[will] never be secured entirely, until Congress shall be made supreme in foreign commerce, and shall have digested a plan for all the states."

The most controversial economic remedies were those designed to relieve the burden on debtors and ordinary taxpayers. In some areas, farmers called for laws permitting payment of taxes or debts in goods and commodities, a kind of institutionalized barter. More commonly, farmers and debtors pressed their state governments for "legal tender" laws, laws that would require creditors to accept at specified rates of exchange a state's paper currency—regardless of its worth—for all debts public and private. Understandably, creditors opposed such a plan. But farmers were strong enough to enact currency laws in seven states during the depression. For the most part, these were modest programs that worked rather well, resulted in little depreciation, and did not result in the problems feared by creditors. In most instances, the notes were loaned to farmers, who put up the value of their land as collateral.

It was the radical plan of the state of Rhode Island, however, that received most of the attention. A rural political party campaigning under the slogan "To Relieve the Distressed" captured the legislature in 1786 and enacted a currency law. The supply of paper money issued in relation to population was much greater under this program than in any other state. The law declared the currency legal tender for all debts. If creditors refused to accept it, people could satisfy their obligations by depositing the money with a county judge, who would then advertise the debt as paid. "In the state of *Rogue Island,*" wrote a shocked merchant, "fraud and injustice" had been "enjoined by solemn law." Conservatives pointed to Rhode Island as an example of the evils that could accompany unchecked democracy.

Shays' Rebellion

In 1786 a rural uprising of communities in Massachusetts shook the nation. Farmers in the western part of the state had been hit particularly hard during the depression, when country merchants pressed them to pay their debts in hard currency they didn't possess. About a third of all male heads of household were sued for debt during the 1780s, and the county jails filled with debtors who couldn't pay. Dozens of towns petitioned the state government for relief, but the legislature, dominated by urban and merchant interests, rejected legal tender and paper currency laws. During the spring and summer of 1786, farmers throughout the rural parts of the state mustered their community militia companies and closed the courts — precisely what they had done during the Revolution. "Whenever any encroachments are made either upon the liberties or properties of the people," declared one rebel, "if redress cannot be had without, it is virtue in them to disturb government."

This uprising quickly became known as Shays' Rebellion, after Daniel Shays, one of the leaders of the "committee of the people who had also been a leader in the Revolution. Although the rebellion was most widespread in Massachusetts, similar disorders occurred in every other New England state except Rhode Island, where the farmers had already taken power. There were a number of incidents outside New England as well. A "tumultuary assemblage of the people" closed the court of one Maryland county, and in York, Pennsylvania, 200 armed men stopped a farm auction whose proceeds were marked for debt payment. "Following the example of the insurgents in Massachusetts," a conservative wrote, debtor associations in Virginia prevented auctions, and according to James Madison, officials throughout the state watched "prisons and courthouses and clerks' offices willfully burnt."

To James Wilson of Philadelphia, it appeared that "the flames of internal insurrection were ready

A mocking pamphlet of 1787 pictured Daniel Shays and Job Shattuck, two leaders of Shays' Rebellion. The artist gives them uniforms, a flag, and artillery, but the rebels were actually an unorganized group of farmers armed only with clubs and simple muskets. When the rebellion was crushed, Shattuck was wounded and jailed, and Shays along with many others left Massachusetts to settle in a remote region of Vermont.

to burst out in every quarter." His fears were wildly exaggerated, but he was not the only one to express them. Secretary of War Henry Knox, formerly a general in the Continental Army, wrote to George Washington that the insurgents "are determined to annihilate all debts public and private," and Edward Rutledge of South Carolina believed that they would "stop little short of a distribution of property — I speak of a general distribution."

The crisis ended when a militia force raised in communities from eastern Massachusetts marched west and crushed the Shaysites in January 1787 as they marched on the armory in Springfield. Fifteen of the leaders were subsequently sentenced to death; two were hanged before the remainder were pardoned, and several hundred farmers had to swear an oath of allegiance to the state. In fact, these men had wanted little more than temporary relief from their indebtedness, and rural discontent quickly disappeared once the depression began to lift in 1788.

The most important consequence of Shays' Rebellion was its effect on conservative nationalists unhappy with the distribution of power between the states and national government under the Articles of Confederation. The uprising "wrought prodigious changes in the minds of men respecting the powers of government," wrote Henry Knox. "Everybody says they must be strengthened and that unless this shall be effected, there is no security for liberty and property." It was time, he declared, "to clip the wings of a mad democracy."

CHRONOLOGY

1775	Dunmore appeals to slaves to support Britain
1776	August: Battle of Long Island September: British landing on Manhattan Island December: Washington counterattacks at Trenton
1777	Slavery abolished in Vermont September: Howe captures Philadelphia October: Burgoyne surrenders at Saratoga December: France recognizes American independence Continentals settle into winter quarters at Valley Forge
1778	June: France enters the war Battle of Monmouth July: George Rogers Clark captures Kaskaskia December: British capture Savannah
1779	Spain enters the war
1780	February: British land at Charleston July: French land at Newport September: Cornwallis invades North Carolina Articles of Confederation ratified October: Cornwallis surrenders at Yorktown
1781	Robert Morris appointed minister of finance
1782	Peace talks begin
1783	Washington mediates on question of officer pensions Treaty of Paris signed British evacuate New York
1784	Treaty of Fort Stanwix Postwar depression begins
1785	Land Ordinance of 1785
1786	Jefferson's Bill for Establishing Religious Freedom Rhode Island currency law Shays' Rebellion

CONCLUSION

The Revolution was a tulmultuous era, marked by violent conflict between Patriots and Loyalists, masters and slaves, settlers and Indian peoples. But the advocates of independence emerged successful, largely because of their ability to pull together and begin to define their national community. By the mid-1780s, however, many nationalists were paraphrasing Washington's question of 1777: ''What then is to become of this nation?'' Most Americans would seek to answer that question not by retreating to the security of their localities and states, but by attempting to reform the national government and build a strong new national community.

Additional Readings

ROBERT COUNTRYMAN, *The American Revolution* (1985). The best short introduction to the social and political history of the Revolution. Informed by the great outpouring of studies during the twenty years preceding its publication.

MERRILL JENSEN, *The New Nation: A History of the United States during the Confederation, 1781–1789* (1950). Remains the standard work on the 1780s.

ROBERT MIDDLEDAUFF, *The Glorious Cause: The American Revolution, 1763–1789* (1982). Provides a good account of the military and diplomatic side of the conflict.

MARY BETH NORTON, *Liberty's Daughters: The Revolutionary Experience of American Women, 1750–1800* (1980). A provocative and comprehensive history of women in the revolutionary era. Treats not only legal and institutional change, but the more subtle changes in habits and expectations.

CHARLES ROYSTER, *A Revolutionary People at War* (1979). A pathbreaking study of the Continental army and popular attitudes toward it. Emphasizes the important role played by the officer corps and the enlisted men in the formation of the first nationalist constituency.

JOHN SHY, *A People Numerous and Armed* (1976). A series of studies of the local and state militias, demonstrating that their most important contribution was political, not military.

DAVID P. SZATMARY, *Shays' Rebellion: The Making of an Agrarian Insurrection* (1980). An excellent study of the famous farmers' rebellion that stimulated conservatives to write the Constitution. Includes a great deal of general background material on the Confederation period, as well as excellent coverage of the specifics of the revolt.

ALFRED F. YOUNG, ed., *The American Revolution: Explorations in American Radicalism* (1976). Includes provocative essays on African Americans, Indians, and women.

8 THE UNITED STATES OF NORTH AMERICA, 1787–1800

• MINGO CREEK IN THE OHIO COUNTRY

It was a hot July afternoon in 1794 when the federal marshall and the tax collector arrived at the backcountry farm of William Miller in Mingo Creek, a community south of Pittsburgh. Like most of his neighbors, Miller had failed to pay the federal excise tax on his homemade whiskey still, and these men had come to serve him with a notice to appear in federal court in Philadelphia. "I felt myself mad with passion," said the farmer, knowing that the fine and the cost of the trip back east "would ruin me." As the men argued, thirty or forty of Miller's neighbors suddenly appeared, armed with muskets and pitchforks. Members of the Mingo Creek Democratic Society, they had come to fight off this infringement upon liberty. There was an angry confrontation, and someone fired a gun into the air.

A COMMUNITY OF SETTLERS REFUSE TO PAY THE WHISKEY TAX

No one was hit, but the marshall "upbraided" the farmers, and they answered him, as he put it, "in a language peculiar to themselves," that is, in a dialect unfamiliar to a man from the East. After this nasty confrontation, the two officials rode off unmolested. But the farmers were fuming, and decided to make a "citizen's arrest" of the officials the next day.

At Mingo Creek, poverty was the outstanding fact of life. A third of the farm families owned no land, but rented or simply squatted on the acres of others. The tax collector was one of the great local landlords, not only controlling most of the local wealth but monopolizing political office as well. Other landlords lived outside the community, the most powerful being President George Washington himself, who owned thousands of acres in the West, much of it in the vicinity of Mingo Creek. The president had evicted so many squatters from his land that local people considered him a grasping speculator. Washington returned the compliment by describing these frontier settlers as "a parcel of barbarians" who lived little better than "dogs or cats."

Certainly this place had little in common with what Washington thought of as an ideal community. Farm families lived in miserable mud-floored log huts scattered along the creeks of the Monongahela valley. One visitor described the local farms as nothing more than "little clearings detached from each other by intervening forest, through which foot paths, bridle paths, and narrow wagon roads, obstructed with stumps, wound their way." But despite appearances, the

This cartoon appeared during the protests over the Congressional tax (or excise) on whiskey passed in 1791. In western Pennsylvania the opposition to the exciseman turned to popular rebellion in 1794, arousing conservative fears that the United States might be on the brink of the same kind of disorder that characterized the French Revolution.

farmers of Mingo Creek were bound together in networks of family and clan, work and barter, religion and politics. The militiamen acted together in what they perceived to be the interests of their community.

Along with the rest of the West, this was a violent place in a violent time. No-holds-barred fights at local taverns were frequent, and travelers remarked on the presence of one-eyed men, the victims of brutal gougings. Everyone knew of men or women lost in the continuing Indian wars. In 1782 militia companies from the area took their revenge by massacring ninety-six unresisting Christian Indians at Gnadenhutten, north of the Ohio River, hacking their bodies and bringing home their scalps as trophies. The new federal government had committed over 80 percent of its operating budget to defeating the Indians, but the failure of its campaigns left backcountry families resentful.

It was to help pay the costs of these campaigns that Congress had placed the tax on whiskey in 1791. The tax applied to the owners of stills, whether they produced commercially or simply for family and neighbors. Farmers throughout America protested that the excise ran counter to revolutionary principles. "Internal taxes upon consumption," declared the citizens of Mingo Creek, are "most dangerous to the civil rights of freemen, and must in the end destroy the liberties of every country in which they are introduced." Hugh Henry Brackenridge, editor of The Pittsburg Gazette, *argued for a tax on the "unsettled lands which all around us have been purchased by speculating men, who keep them up in large bodies and obstruct the population of the country."*

Protest followed the course familiar from the Revolution. At first citizens gathered peacefully and petitioned their representatives, but when the tax collectors appeared there was vigilante action. Faces blackened or covered with handkerchiefs, farmers tarred and feathered the tax men. Although the immediate issue was taxation, larger matters were at stake. The Mingo Creek Democratic Society was part of Thomas Jefferson's political movement that supported republicanism and the French Revolution, in opposition to the conservative principles of the Washington administration. The tax protesters made this linkage explicit when they raised banners proclaiming the French slogan of "Liberty, Equality, Fraternity" and adding their own phrase, "and No Excise!" In North Carolina the rebels sang:

> Some chaps whom freedom's spirit warms
> Are threatening hard to take up arms,
> And headstrong in rebellion rise
> 'Fore they'll submit to that excise:
> Their liberty they will maintain,
> They fought for't, and they'll fight again.

But only in western Pennsylvania did the protests turn to riot. When the Mingo Creek militia went to arrest the tax man, several of their number were killed in the confrontation. The tax man and his family escaped from their house as it was consumed by a fire set by the farmers. In a community meeting afterward, they resolved to attack and destroy Pittsburgh, where the wealthy and powerful local landlords resided. Terrified residents of the town saved the day by welcoming the rebels with free food and drink. "It cost me four barrels of whiskey that day," declared one man, but "I would rather spare that than a single quart of blood." Destruction was averted, but an angry farmer rode through the street waving a tomahawk and warning: "It is not the excise law only that must go down. A great deal more is to be done. I am but beginning yet."

Declaring the Whiskey Rebellion "the first ripe fruit" of the democratic sentiment sweeping the country, Washington organized a federal army of 13,000 men, larger than the one he had commanded during the Revolution, and ordered the occupation of western Pennsylvania. Soldiers dragged half-naked men from their beds and forced them into open pens, where they remained for days in the freezing rain. Authorities arrested twenty obscure characters, and a judge convicted two of treason. The protest gradually died down. Most of the leaders fled for points west, where they continued their lives of independent poverty. The money spent by the army of occupation helped stimulate the local economy. And federal forces soon defeated the Indian confederation in the Ohio country.

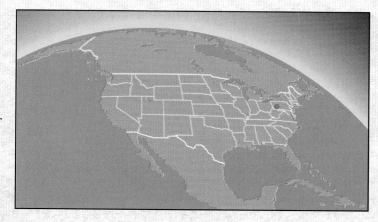

Federal power had prevailed over the local community. In his Farewell Address, Washington warned of an excessive spirit of localism that "agitates the community with ill-founded jealousies and false alarms; kindles the animosity of one part against another; foments occasionally riot and insurrection." But resistance to the excise remained widespread, and no substantial revenue was ever collected from the tax on whiskey. More important, the whiskey rebels had raised some of the most important issues of the day: the power and authority of the new federal government; the relation of the West to the rest of the nation; the nature of political dissent; and the meaning of the revolutionary tradition.

THE CONSTITUTION

The Whiskey Rebellion was the first test of the sovereignty of the newly formed federal government. Federal power had prevailed over a local community. A similar rural uprising eight years before, Shays' Rebellion (see Chapter 7), had helped pull together a nationalist movement that ultimately replaced the Articles of Confederation with a powerful new central government.

Sentiment for a Strong National Government

Nationalists had long argued for a strengthened union of the states. Even before ratification of the Articles of Confederation, Alexander Hamilton, a New York lawyer and close associate of Washington who had served during the Revolution as his aide, was advocating a "solid, coercive union" having "complete sovereignty" over the civil, military, and economic life of the states, along with permanent revenues from taxes and duties. But after victory in the revolutionary war, most Americans turned their attention back to the states.

In general, the nationalists were drawn from the elite circles of American life. "Although there are no nobles in America, there is a class of men denominated 'gentlemen,'" the French ambassador to America wrote home in 1786. "They are creditors, and therefore interested in strengthening the government, and watching over the execution of the law. The majority of them being merchants, it is for their interest to establish the credit of the United States in Europe on a solid foundation by the exact payment of debts, and to grant to Congress powers extensive enough to compel the people to contribute for this purpose." Other nationalists included former officers in the Continental Army whose experience with the Congress had made them firm believers in a stronger central government, as well as conservatives who wanted to check what they considered the excessive democracy of the states.

The economic crisis of the 1780s provided the nationalists with their most important opportunity to organize. In March of 1785 a group of men from Virginia and Maryland, including James Madison, George Mason, and George Washington, met to consider commercial problems relating to the navigation of Chesapeake Bay and the Potomac River. They drafted an agreement recommending to their legislatures uniform commercial regulations, duties, and currency laws. The Maryland legislature endorsed the plan, and requested the inclusion of

Pennsylvania and Delaware. Early the next year, at Madison's urging, the Virginia legislature invited all the states to send representatives to a commercial conference to be held at Annapolis in the fall.

Five states sent strong nationalist delegates to the Annapolis Convention in September of 1786. Lacking representatives from a majority of the states, these men knew it would be useless to attempt to resolve the commercial problems besetting the country. But Hamilton, who played a leading role at the meeting, drew up a report calling on Congress to endorse a new convention to be held in Philadelphia to discuss all matters necessary "to render the constitution of the federal government adequate to the exigencies of the union." By this time most Americans agreed that the Articles needed strengthening, especially in regard to commercial regulation and the generation of revenue. Shays' Rebellion in Massachusetts further helped to mobilize conservative opinion. Early in 1787, the Confederation Congress cautiously endorsed the plan for a convention "for the sole and express purpose of revising the Articles of Confederation."

The Constitutional Convention

Fifty-five men from twelve states assembled at the Pennsylvania State House in Philadelphia in late May of 1787. Rhode Island, where radical democrats held power, refused to send a delegation. A number of prominent men were missing. Thomas Jefferson and John Adams were serving as ambassadors in Europe, and crusty Patrick Henry declared that he "smelt a rat." Henry was a localist, and perhaps what bothered him was the predominantly cosmopolitan cast of the meeting. But most of America's best-known leaders were present: George Washington, Benjamin Franklin, Alexander Hamilton, James Madison, George Mason, Robert Morris. Twenty-nine of them were college educated, thirty-four were lawyers, twenty-four had served in Congress, and twenty-one were veteran officers of the Revolution. At least nineteen owned slaves, and there were also land speculators and merchants. But there were no ordinary farmers or artisans present, and obviously no African Americans, Indians, or women. The Constitution was framed by men who represented America's social elite.

On their first day of work, the delegates agreed to vote by states, in the fashion of Congress. They chose Washington to chair the meeting, and to insure candid debate they decided to keep their sessions secret. James Madison took voluminous

A Northwest View of the State House in Philadelphia, a 1787 engraving by James Trenchard. This had been the regular place of meeting for the Confederation Congress between 1777 and 1783, and now it became the location for the gathering of the Constitutional Convention.

daily minutes, however, allowing historians to know what happened behind the convention's locked doors. Madison, a young, conservative Virginian with a profound knowledge of history and political philosophy, had arrived several days before the Convention opened, and with his fellow Virginians had drafted what became known as the Virginia Plan. Presented by governor Edmund Randolph of Virginia on May 29, it set the convention's agenda.

Convinced by events of the previous few years that the individual states could not be counted on to respect the national interest, or even the rights of private property, the authors of the Virginia Plan proposed scrapping the Articles of Confederation in favor of a "consolidated government" having the power to tax and to enforce its laws directly rather than through the states. "A spirit of locality," Madison declared, was destroying "the aggregate interests of the community," by which he meant the great community of the nation. It was much the same as what Washington would say about the Whiskey rebels. Madison's plan would have reduced the states to little more than administrative districts. Representation in the bicameral national legislature was to be based on population districts, the members of the House of Representatives elected by popular vote, but senators chosen indirectly so that they might be insulated from democratic pressure. The Senate would lead, controlling foreign affairs and the appointment of officials. An appointed chief executive and a national judiciary would together form a Council of Revision having the power to veto both national and state legislation.

The main opposition to these proposals came from the delegates from small states, who feared being swallowed up by the large ones. After two weeks of debate, William Paterson of New Jersey introduced an alternative, a set of "purely federal" principles known since as the New Jersey Plan. He proposed increasing the powers of the central government but retaining a single-house Congress in which the states were equally represented. After much debate, and a series of votes that split the convention down the middle, the delegates finally agreed to what has been called the Great Compromise: proportional representation in the House, representation by states in the Senate. Few were happy with this solution, but it allowed the creation of a strong national government while still providing an important role for the states.

Part of this agreement was a second, fundamental compromise that brought together the delegates from North and South. In the matter of counting population for purposes of representation, southern delegates insisted on including their slaves. Ultimately it was agreed that five slaves would be counted as the equal of three freemen — the "three-fifths rule." Furthermore, the representatives of South Carolina and Georgia demanded protection for the slave trade, and after bitter debate the delegates included a provision preventing any prohibition of the trade for twenty years. Another article legitimized the return of fugitive slaves from free states. The word *slave* was nowhere used in the text of the Constitution, but these provisions amounted to national guarantees for southern slav-

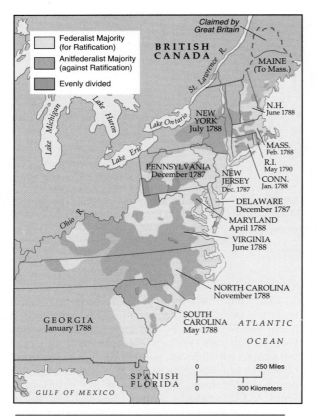

The Ratification of the Constitution, 1787–1790

The distribution of the vote for the ratification of the Constitution demonstrated its wide support in sections of the country linked to the commercial economy, and disapproval in more remote and backcountry sections.

ery. Although many delegates were opposed to slavery, and regretted having to give in on this issue, they agreed with Madison, who wrote that "great as the evil is, a dismemberment of the union would be worse."

There was still much to decide regarding the other branches of government. Madison's Council of Revision was scratched in favor of a strong federal judiciary having the implicit power to declare acts of Congress unconstitutional. Demands for a powerful chief executive raised fears that the office might prove to be, in the words of Edmund Randolph of Virginia, "the fetus of monarchy." But there was considerable support for a president with veto power to check the legislature. In fact, according to James McHenry, a delegate from Maryland, twenty-one delegates favored some form of monarchy, and Alexander Hamilton went on record supporting the

creation of a constitutional monarch. To keep the president independent of Congress, the delegates decided he should be elected, but fearing that the people could never "be sufficiently informed" to select wisely, they created an electoral college to insulate the process from popular choice.

In early September the delegates turned their rough draft of the Constitution over to a Committee of Style that shaped it into an elegant and concise document providing the general principles and basic framework of government. But Madison, known to later generations as the Father of the Constitution, was gloomy, believing that the revisions of his original plan doomed the union to the kind of inaction that had characterized government under the Articles of Confederation. It was left for Franklin to make the final speech to the convention. "Can a perfect production be expected?" he asked. "I consent, Sir, to this Constitution, because I expect no better, and because I am not sure that it is not the best." The delegates voted their approval on September 17, 1787, and transmitted the document to Congress, agreeing it would become operative after ratification by nine states. Despite some congressmen who were outraged that the convention had exceeded its charge of simply modifying the Confederation, Congress called for a special ratifying convention in each of the states.

Ratification

The supporters of the new Constitution immediately adopted the name Federalists to describe themselves. Their outraged opponents objected that it was really the existing Confederation that provided for a "federal" government of balanced power between the states and the union, and that the Constitution would replace it with a "national" government. But in this, as in much of the subsequent process of ratification, the nationalists grabbed the initiative, and their opponents had to content themselves with the label Anti-Federalists. Mercy Otis Warren, a leading critic of the Constitution, commented on the dilemma in which the Anti-Federalists found themselves. "On the one hand," she wrote, "we stand in need of a strong federal government, founded on principles that will support the prosperity and union of the colonies. On the other, we have struggled for liberty and made costly sacrifices at her shrine and there are still many among us who revere her name too much to relinquish, beyond a certain medium, the rights of man for the dignity of government."

The critics of the Constitution were by no means

a unified group. Because most of them were local-ists, they represented a variety of social and regional interests. But most believed the Constitution granted far too much power to the center, weakening the autonomy of communities and states. As local governments "will always possess a better repre-sentation of the feelings and interests of the people at large," one critic wrote, "it is obvious that these powers can be deposited with much greater safety with the state than the general government." An-other Anti-Federalist worried that the Constitution would transform the country from a confederation of small republics into a single great one, "and as our territory is much too large for a democracy, or even an aristocracy, some Caesar or Cromwell, finding absolute authority within his reach, would presently start up in kingly shape to rule over North America."

All the great political thinkers of the eighteenth century had argued that a republican form of gov-ernment could work only for small countries. As the French philosopher Montesquieu had observed, "In an extensive republic, the public good is sacrificed to a thousand private views." But in *The Federalist,* a brilliant series of essays in defense of the Constitu-tion written in 1787 and 1788 by Madison, Hamilton, and John Jay, Madison stood Montesquieu's as-sumption on its head. Rhode Island had demon-strated that the rights of property, and minorities such as creditors, were not protected in even the smallest of states. Asserting that "the most common and durable source of factions has been the various and unequal distribution of property," Madison con-cluded that the best way to control such factions was to "extend the sphere" of government. That way, he continued, "you take in a greater variety of parties and interest; you make it less probable that a majority of the whole will have a common motive to invade the rights of other citizens; or, if such a common motive exists, it will be more difficult for all who feel it to discover their own strength and to act in unison with each other." Rather than a disability, Madison argued, great size is an advantage: inter-ests are so diverse that no single faction is able to gain control of the state, threatening the freedoms of others.

It is doubtful whether Madison's sophisticated argument, or the arguments of the Anti-Federalists for that matter, made much of a difference in the popular voting in the states to select delegates for the state ratification conventions. The alignment of forces generally followed the lines laid down during the fights over economic issues in the years since the Revolution. For example, in Pennsylvania (the first

state to convene, in December of 1787), 48 percent of the Anti-Federalist delegates to the ratification convention were farmers. By contrast, 54 percent of the Federalists were merchants, manufacturers, large landowners, or professionals. What tipped the Pennsylvania convention in favor of the Constitution was the wide support the document enjoyed among artisans and commercial farmers, who saw their interests tied to the growth of a commercial society. As one observer pointed out, "The counties nearest [navigable waters] were in favor of it generally, those more remote, in opposition."

Similar agrarian—localist and commercial—cos-mopolitan alignments characterized most of the other states. The most critical convention took place in Massachusetts in early 1788. Five states — Dela-ware, Pennsylvania, New Jersey, Georgia, and Con-necticut — had already voted to ratify, but the states with the strongest Anti-Federalist movements had yet to convene. If the Constitution lost in Massachu-setts, its fate would be in great danger. At the convention, opponents of ratification enjoyed a small majority. But several important Anti-Federalist leaders, including Samuel Adams, were swayed by the enthusiastic support for the Constitution among Boston's townspeople, and on February 16 the convention voted narrowly in favor of ratification. To no one's surprise, Rhode Island rejected in March, but Maryland and South Carolina approved in April and May. On June 21, New Hampshire became the ninth state to ratify.

New York, Virginia, and North Carolina were left with the decision of whether or not to join the new union. Anti-Federalist support was strong in

A cartoon published in July 1788 when New York be-came the eleventh state to ratify the Constitution. Af-ter initially voting to reject, North Carolina soon re-considered, but radical and still reluctant Rhode Island did not join the union until 1790.

each of these states. North Carolina voted to reject. (It did not join the union until the next year, followed by a still reluctant Rhode Island in 1790.) In New York, the delegates were moved to vote their support by a threat from New York City to secede from the state and join the union separately if the convention failed to ratify. The Virginia convention was almost evenly divided, but promises to amend the Constitution to protect individual rights persuaded enough delegates to produce a victory for the Constitution. The promise of a Bill of Rights, in fact, was important in the ratification vote of five states.

The Bill of Rights

Although the Bill of Rights — the first ten amendments to the Constitution — was adopted during the first session of the new federal Congress, it was first proposed during the debates over ratification. The Constitutional Convention had considered a Bill of Rights, patterned on the declarations of rights in the state constitutions (see Chapter 7), but rejected it as superfluous, agreeing with Madison that the federal government would exercise only those powers expressly delegated to it. George Mason, however, author of the Declaration of Rights in Virginia, refused to sign the Constitution because it failed to contain similar provisions. He played an important role in getting the Virginia ratifying convention to endorse a set of constitutional amendments. Campaigning for a seat in the new Congress, Madison was pressed to affirm his willingness to propose and support a set of amendments guaranteeing "essential rights."

The various state ratification conventions had proposed a grab bag of over two hundred potential amendments. Madison set about transforming these into a series that he introduced into the new Congress on June 8, 1789. Congress passed twelve and sent them to the states, and ten survived the ratification process to become the Bill of Rights in 1791. The First Amendment prohibits Congress from establishing an official religion and provides for the freedoms of assembly, speech, and the press and the right of petition. The other amendments guarantee the right to bear arms, limit the government's power to quarter troops in private homes, and restrain the government from unreasonable searches or seizures; they assure the people their legal rights under the common law, including the prohibition of double jeopardy, the right not to be compelled to testify against oneself, and due process of law before life, liberty, or property can be taken. Finally, the unenumerated rights of the people are protected, and those powers not delegated to the federal government are reserved to the states.

The first ten amendments to the Constitution have been a restraining influence on the growth of government power over American citizens. Their provisions have become an admired aspect of the American political tradition throughout the world. The Bill of Rights was the most important constitutional legacy of the Anti-Federalists.

THE NEW NATION

Ratification of the Constitution was followed by congressional and presidential elections, and in the spring of 1789 the new federal government assumed power in the temporary capital of New York City. The inauguration of George Washington as the first president of the United States took place on April 30, 1789, on the balcony of Federal Hall, at the corner of Wall and Broad streets. The activities of the first federal government were far removed from the everyday lives of most Americans, but as the Whiskey Rebellion demonstrated, there were moments when the two intersected dramatically. Moreover, the first years under the new federal Constitution were especially important for the future, because they shaped the structure of the American state in ways that would be enormously significant for later generations.

The Washington Presidency

During its first month, the Congress debated what to call the president of the United States. Believing that no government could long endure without the awe and veneration of its citizens, Vice-President John Adams, sitting as the president of the Senate, proposed "His Highness the President of the United States." But a majority in the House of Representatives saw this as a dangerous flirtation with "monarchism." When someone proposed that the nation's coinage be stamped with a bust of the president, men of republican persuasion protested that this would be too much like the customs of the Roman or British empire. The president himself finally resolved the controversy by declaring the whole topic had been raised "without any privity of knowledge of it on my part," and by custom he came to be addressed simply as "Mr. President." This issue encapsulated an important conflict of these early years — the desire of some nationalists to add to the power of executive authority, versus the faith of localists in a strong Congress.

Although he dressed in plain American broadcloth at his inauguration and claimed to be content with a plain republican title, Washington was counted among the nationalists. He was anything but a man of the people, by nature reserved and solemn, choosing to ride about town in a grand carriage drawn by six horses and escorted by uniformed liverymen. He delivered his addresses personally to Congress, in the tradition of British royalty, and received from both houses an official reply. These customs were continued by John Adams, Washington's successor, but ended by Thomas Jefferson, who considered them "rags of royalty." On the other hand, Washington worked hard to adhere to the letter of the Constitution, refusing, for example, to use the veto power except where he thought the Congress had acted unconstitutionally, and personally seeking the "advice and consent" of the Senate.

Congress quickly moved to establish departments to run the executive affairs of state, and Washington soon appointed Jefferson his secretary of state, Alexander Hamilton to run the Treasury, Henry Knox the War Department, and Edmund Randolph the Justice Department as attorney general. The president consulted each of these men regularly, and during his first term met with them as a group to discuss matters of policy. By the end of Washington's presidency the secretaries had coalesced into the Cabinet, a group that has survived to the present despite the absence of constitutional authority or enabling legislation. Washington was a powerful and commanding personality, but he understood the importance of national unity, and in his style of leadership, his consultations, and his appointments he sought to achieve a balance of conflicting political perspectives and sectional interests. These intentions would be sorely tested during the eight years of his administration.

The Federal Judiciary

The most important piece of legislation to emerge from the first session of Congress was the Judiciary Act of 1789, which implemented the judicial clause of the Constitution and set up a system of federal courts. Congress provided that the Supreme Court consist of six members, and established three circuit and thirteen district courts. Strong nationalists argued for a powerful federal legal system that would provide a uniform code of civil and criminal justice throughout the country. But the localists in Congress fought successfully to retain the various bodies of law that had developed the states. They wanted to preserve local community autonomy. The act gave federal courts limited original jurisdiction, restricting them mostly to appeals from state courts. But it thereby established the principle of federal judicial review of state legislation, despite the silence of the Constitution on this point. Washington would be the only president in American history with the privilege of naming the entire roster of federal judges.

Under the leadership of Chief Justice John Jay, the Supreme Court heard relatively few cases during its first decade. Still, it managed to raise considerable political controversy. In *Chisholm v. Georgia* (1793) it ruled in favor of two South Carolina residents who had sued the state of Georgia for the

Daniel Huntington's *The Republican Court* emphasized the similarities between American republican government and the royal courts of Europe. When Vice President John Adams proposed that the president be addressed as "His Highness," democrats in the Congress argued this was a dangerous flirtation with "monarchism," and Thomas Jefferson urged that the government give up these "rags of royalty."
(Daniel Huntington. The Republican Court. *1861. The Brooklyn Museum.)*

recovery of confiscated property. Thus did the Court overthrow the common law principle that a sovereignty could not be sued without its consent, and supported the Constitution's grant of federal jurisdiction over disputes "between a state and citizens of another state." Many localists feared that this nationalist ruling threatened the integrity of the states. In response, they proposed the Eleventh Amendment to the Constitution, ratified in 1798, which declared that no state could be sued by citizens from another state. The Supreme Court nevertheless established itself as the final authority on questions of law when it invalidated a Virginia statute in *Ware v. Hylton* (1796) and upheld the constitutionality of an act of Congress in *Hylton v. U.S.* (1796).

Hamilton's Fiscal Program

Fiscal and economic affairs pressed upon the new government. Lacking revenues, and faced with the massive national debt contracted during the Revolution, it took power in a condition of virtual bankruptcy. At the urging of James Madison, whose first official position in the United States was floor leader for the Washington administration in the House of Representatives, Congress passed the Tariff of 1789. This was a compromise between advocates of protective tariffs (duties so high that they made foreign products prohibitively expensive, thus "protecting" American products) and those who wanted moderate tariffs that produced income. Duties on imported goods, rather than direct taxes on property or incomes, would constitute the bulk of federal revenues until the twentieth century. After setting this system of duties in place, Congress turned to the problem of the debt. In January 1790, Hamilton submitted a "Report on the Public Credit." In it he recommended that the federal government assume the obligations accumulated by the states during the previous fifteen years, and redeem the national debt, owed to both domestic and foreign leaders, by agreeing to a new issue of interest-bearing bonds.

By this means, Hamilton sought to inspire the confidence of domestic and foreign investors in the public credit of the new nation. Congress endorsed his plan to pay off the $11 million owed to foreign creditors, but balked at funding the domestic debt of $27 million and assuming the state debts of $25 million. In the first place, necessity had forced many individuals to sell off at deep discounts the notes, warrants, and securities the government had issued them during the Revolution. Yet Hamilton now advocated paying these obligations at face value, providing any speculator who held them with fabulous profits. At the first rumor of Hamilton's pro-gram, speculators fanned out through the countryside trying to buy as cheaply as they could whatever remained of the revolutionary notes. Hamilton's plan for redemption would be "radically immoral," Madison declared, breaking with the administration. He proposed a complicated plan whereby the profits of speculators would be divided with thousands of "hardy veterans." Although this effort helped to establish Madison's reputation as a friend of the common man, Congress rejected his plan by a wide margin, fearing its cost.

An even greater debate took place over the assumption of the state debts, for some states, mostly those in the South, had already arranged to liquidate their debts, while others had left theirs unpaid. Congress remained deadlocked on this issue for six months, until congressmen from Pennsylvania and Virginia arranged a compromise. But final agreement now stalled on a sectional dispute over the location of the new national capital. Southerners supported Washington's desire to plant it on the Potomac River, but northerners argued for Philadelphia. In return for Madison's pledge to obtain enough southern votes to pass Hamilton's assumption plan, northern congressmen agreed to a location for the new federal district on the boundary of Virginia and Maryland. In July of 1790, Congress passed legislation making Philadelphia the temporary capital until the completion of the federal city in the District of Columbia in 1800. Two weeks later they adopted Hamilton's credit program. This was the first of many sectional compromises.

Hamilton now proposed the second component of his fiscal program, the establishment of a Bank of the United States. The bank, a public corporation funded by private capital, would serve as the depository of government funds and the fiscal agent of the Treasury. Congress narrowly approved, but Madison's opposition raised doubts in the president's mind about the constitutionality of the measure, and Washington solicited the opinion of his Cabinet. Here for the first time were articulated the classic interpretations of constitutional authority. Jefferson took a *strict constructionist* position, arguing that the powers of the federal government must be limited to those specifically enumerated in the Constitution. This position came closest to the basic agreement of the men who had drafted the document. Hamilton, on the other hand, reasoned that the Constitution "implied" the power to use whatever means were "necessary and proper" to carry out its enumerated powers — a *loose constructionist* position. Persuaded by Hamilton's opinion, Washington signed the bill, and the bank went into operation in 1791.

Hamilton's "Report on Manufactures," submitted to Congress in December 1791, was the capstone to his comprehensive economic program. It contained an ambitious plan involving the use of government securities as investment capital for infant industries; federal bounties to encourage innovation; and high protective tariffs. This system, Hamilton hoped, would result in the development of an industrial economy. Congressmen from farming areas, whose previous objections to Hamilton's preference for the "monied interests" had not prevailed, were finally able to frustrate him on this proposal. Hamilton's views, they argued, would limit them to roles exactly like those they had played within the British Empire; in effect they would be exchanging British masters for Boston and New York masters. Of equal importance, the plan failed to inspire American capitalists, who continued to be more interested in investments in shipping or in land speculation than in industrial production.

Many of Hamilton's specific proposals for increased tariff protection, however, became part of a revision of duties that took place in 1792. Moreover, his fiscal program as a whole dramatically restored the financial health of the United States. Foreign investment in government securities increased from $5 million in 1790 to more than $33 million in 1801 and, along with domestic capital, provided the Bank of the United States with enormous reserves. The notes of the bank became the most important circulating medium of the North American commercial economy, and their wide acceptance greatly stimulated business enterprise. This was especially important in view of the federal mint's inability to issue much American coin because of a shortage of precious metals in the country. Although Congress established a decimal system of money in 1793, foreign coins remained in circulation, and most ordinary people continued to reckon values in pounds, shillings, and pence until well into the nineteenth century. Most of the paper money in circulation was issued by state and private banks, but the Bank of the United States was able to stabilize this currency through the use of its enormous capital reserves. "Our public credit," Washington declared toward the end of his first term, "stands on that ground which three years ago it would have been considered as a species of madness to have foretold."

The International Situation

The Federalist political coalition, forged during the ratification of the Constitution, was sorely strained by these debates over fiscal policy. By the middle of 1792, Jefferson, representing the southern agrarians, and Hamilton, speaking for northern capitalists, were locked in a full-scale feud within the Washington administration. Hamilton conducted himself more like a prime minister than a cabinet secretary, greatly offending Jefferson, who considered himself the president's heir apparent. But the dispute went deeper than a mere conflict of personalities. Hamilton stated the difference clearly when he wrote that "one side appears to believe that there is a serious plot to overturn the State governments, and substitute a monarchy to the present republican system," while "the other side firmly believes that there is a serious plot to overturn the general government and elevate the separate powers of the States upon its ruins." Although on this occasion he concluded that "both sides may be equally wrong," Hamilton generally pursued the argument, as did Jefferson, with acrimony. Washington urged them both to make "mutual yieldings," and in an attempt to preserve the unity of the Federalist coalition he agreed to serve a second presidential term. But the conflict between Hamilton and Jefferson was to grow even more bitter over the issue of American foreign policy.

The commanding event of the Atlantic world during the 1790s was the French Revolution, which had begun in 1789 after several years of disastrous harvests and the bankruptcy of the French state. Most Americans enthusiastically welcomed the fall of the French monarchy. After the people of Paris stormed the Bastille, Lafayette sent Washington the key to its doors as a symbol of the relationship between the two revolutions. But with the beginning of the Reign of Terror in 1793, which claimed upon the guillotine the lives of hundreds of aristocrats, American conservatives began to voice their opposition. The execution of King Louis XVI, and especially the onset of war between revolutionary France and monarchical Great Britain in 1793, firmly divided American opinion.

Most at issue was whether the Franco-American alliance of 1778 required the United States to support France in its war with Britain. All of Washington's cabinet agreed on the importance of American neutrality. With France and Britain prowling for each other's vessels on the high seas, the vast colonial trade of Europe was delivered up to neutral powers, the United States prominent among them. Neutrality, in other words, meant windfall profits. From 1793 to 1801 there was a fivefold increase in the value of exports and in earnings to the United States from the carrying trade. Jefferson believed it highly unlikely that the French would call upon the Americans to honor the 1778 treaty; the administration should simply wait and see but Hamilton argued that so great was the danger, Washington should immediately declare the treaty "temporarily and provisionally suspended."

These disagreements revealed two contrasting perspectives on the course the United States should chart in international waters. Hamilton believed in the necessity of an accommodation with Great Britain, the most important trading partner of the United States and the world's greatest naval power. Jefferson and Madison, on the other hand, looked for more international independence, pinning their hopes on the future of western expansion. In fact, there was room for compromise between these two points of view, but in the debate over the French Revolution positions tended to become polarized. Throughout the Atlantic world there was a similar bitter division between democrats and conservatives. Not since the Reformation had there been an issue of such international importance, and there would not be another until the Russian Revolution of the early twentieth century.

The debate in the United States grew hotter with the arrival in early 1793 of French ambassador Edmond Genêt. Large crowds of supporters greeted him throughout the nation, and among them he solicited contributions and distributed commissions authorizing American privateering raids against the British. Understandably, a majority of Americans still nursed a hatred of imperial Britain, and these people expressed a great deal of sympathy for republican France. Conservatives such as Hamilton, however, favored a continuation of traditional commercial relations with Britain and feared the anti-aristocratic violence of the French. Washington sympathized with Hamilton's position, but most of all he wished to preserve American independence and neutrality. Knowing he must act before "Citizen" Genêt (as the ambassador was popularly known) compromised American sovereignty and involved the United States in war with Britain, the president issued a proclamation of neutrality on April 22, 1793. In it he assured the world that the United States intended to pursue "a conduct friendly and impartial towards the belligerent powers," and to this end he prohibited Americans from "aiding or abetting hostilities." While remaining neutral, Americans would continue doing business with all sides, for, as any practical-minded person realized, when all the rhetoric is stripped away, neutrality is really a trade policy.

Hamilton's supporters applauded the president, but Jefferson's were outraged. "The cause of France is the cause of man," declared Hugh Henry Brackenridge of Pittsburgh, "and neutrality is desertion."

Throughout the country those sympathetic to France organized Democratic Societies, political clubs modeled after the Sons of Liberty. Society members corresponded with each other, campaigned on behalf of candidates, and lobbied with congressmen. People interpreted the international question in the light of issues of local importance. Thus the members of the Mingo Creek Democratic Society used enthusiasm for the French Revolution as a way of organizing political opposition to the Washington administration. Brackenridge described the Mingo Creek chapter as "an engine of election," a political machine. In a speech to Congress, President Washington denounced what he called these "self-created societies," declaring them "the most diabolical attempt to destroy the best fabric of human government and happiness."

Citizen Genêt miscalculated, however, alienating even his supporters, when he demanded that Washington call Congress into special session to debate neutrality. Jefferson, previously a confidant of the ambassador, now denounced Genêt as "hot-headed" and "indecent towards the President." But these words came too late to save his reputation in the eyes of Washington, and at the end of 1793 Jefferson left the administration. The continuing upheaval in France soon swept Genêt's party from power and he was recalled, but fearing the guillotine he claimed sanctuary and remained in the United States. But during his time in the limelight, he furthered the division of the Federalist coalition into a faction identifying with Washington, Hamilton, and conservative principles and a faction supporting Jefferson, Madison, democracy, and the French Revolution.

Indian Affairs

Among the many problems of the Washington presidency, one of the most pressing concerned the West. The Spanish held the former French territory of Louisiana, as well as Florida, the oldest European colony on the North American mainland, and insisted that its northern boundary ran somewhere in the vicinity of the Ohio River. Moreover, Spanish officials continued to bar Americans from access to the port of New Orleans, effectively closing the Mississippi River to American commercial traffic. In the Northwest Territory, organized by Congress in the Northwest Ordinance of 1787, Great Britain maintained a force of at least a thousand troops at posts such as Detroit. From these positions they managed the fur trade and supplied the Indians with goods, including guns and ammunition.

A medallion given by President Washington to the Seneca chief Red Jacket in 1792. While the federal government frequently applied military pressure to facilitate cessions of land, the procedure of treaty-making preserved a semblance of legality and protected Indian sovereignty over their own affairs.

The American attempt to treat the western tribes as conquered peoples after the Revolution had resulted only in further violence and warfare. The Northwest Ordinance signaled a new approach. "The utmost good faith shall always be observed towards the Indians," read the statute. "Their lands and property shall never be taken from them without their consent; and in their property, rights, and liberty, they shall never be invaded or disturbed, unless in just and lawful wars authorized by Congress." Although the Constitution was silent regarding Indian policy, this statutory recognition of the largely independent character of the Indian tribes was endorsed by Congress in the Intercourse Act of 1790, the basic law by which the United States would "regulate trade and intercourse with the Indian tribes." To eliminate the abuses of unscrupulous traders, the act created a federal licensing system; subsequent amendments authorized the creation of subsidized trading houses, or "facto-

ries," where Indians could obtain goods at reasonable prices. Trade abuses continued unabated for lack of adequate policing power, but these provisions indicated the good intentions of the administration.

To clarify the question of Indian sovereignty, the Intercourse Act declared public treaties between the United States and the independent Indian "nations" to be the only legal means of obtaining Indian land. Treaty making thus became the procedure for establishing and maintaining relations. Typical was a treaty the Washington administration negotiated with the Creek Indians in 1790. In exchange for peace and cessions of land, the United States pledged to protect the boundaries of the "Creek Nation of Indians," and acknowledged the right of the Indians to punish Americans who violated their boundaries or their laws "as they please." The chiefs acknowledged themselves "to be under the protection of the United States of America, and of no other sovereign whosoever." Although the federal government frequently applied military pressure to facilitate the signing of such treaties, the process preserved a semblance of legality. In the twentieth century, a number of Indian tribes have successfully appealed for the return of lands obtained by states or individuals in violation of this provision of the Intercourse Act.

Yet conflict continued to characterize the relationship of Americans and Indians, for the acquisition of Indian land to supply a growing population of farmers remained the highest priority of American policy toward the Indians. The American frontiersmen along the Ohio, wrote one officer, "carry on private expeditions against the Indians and kill them whenever they meet them." There was not a jury in the West, he said, who would punish a man for these crimes. To defend their homelands, villages of Shawnees, Delawares, and other Indian peoples confederated with the Miamis under their war chief Little Turtle. In the fall of 1790, Little Turtle lured an American expeditionary force led by General Josiah Harmar into the confederacy's stronghold in Ohio and badly mauled them. In November 1791 the confederation inflicted an even more disastrous defeat on a large American force under General Arthur St. Clair, governor of the Northwest Territory. More than 900 Americans were killed or wounded, making this the worst defeat of an army by Indians in North American history. Blaming St. Clair's inept leadership for the defeat, Washington cursed his general as "worse than a murderer."

In early 1794 the governor general of Canada told an assembly of Indian leaders from the Ohio country that war between Britain and the United States was almost certain, and that when it broke out, "a line must then be drawn by the warriors." British soldiers began constructing Fort Miami in the Maumee Valley, west of Lake Erie, well within the region supposedly ceded by Britain to the United States at the end of the Revolution. In the Southwest, the Spanish followed a similar course, continuing to occupy forts within territory claimed by the United States, and encouraging Indian resistance to American expansion.

The Crisis of 1794

Washington faced the gravest crisis of his presidency in 1794. In the West, the inability of the federal government to subdue the Indians, or to arrange with the Spanish for unencumbered use of the Mississippi River, turned frontiersmen to loud protests. There were rumblings of rebellion and secession from western communities. This discontent was strengthened by the federal excise tax on whiskey, which hit backcountry farmers hardest. "The people of the western counties," wrote an English commentator, find "themselves grievously taxed for the support of the government without enjoying the blessings of it." London and Madrid believed that American settlers in the Northwest and Southwest might quit the union and join themselves to Canada or Florida, and both English and Spanish secret agents worked to enhance such possibilities with liberal bribes.

In the Atlantic, Great Britain had declared a blockade of France, including the seizure of vessels trading with the French West Indies. From 1793 to the beginning of 1794 the British confiscated the cargoes of more than 250 American ships, threatening hundreds of merchants with ruin. The United States was being "kicked, cuffed, and plundered all over the ocean," declared Madison, and in Congress he introduced legislation imposing retaliatory duties upon British ships and merchandise.

The Whiskey Rebellion, which broke out in the summer of 1794, thus came at a time when President Washington considered the nation to be under siege. The combination of Indian attack, international intrigue, and domestic insurrection, he believed, made for the greatest threat to the nation since the Revolution. In April, the president had dispatched Chief Justice John Jay to London to arrange a settlement with the British. At the same time, war seemed increasingly likely, and Washington feared that any sign of federal weakness in the face of western rebellion would invite British or Spanish intervention. With Hamilton's urging he took a decisive course, raising a large militia even as he pursued halfhearted negotiations with local authorities, and made preparations to occupy the area around Pittsburgh, including Mingo Creek. It is clear that the president overreacted, for although there was riot and violence in western Pennsylvania, there was no organized insurrection. Nevertheless, his mobilization of federal military power dramatically demonstrated the federal commitment to the

In this 1784 painting, President George Washington reviews some of the 13,000 troops he dispatched to suppress the Whiskey Rebellion from Fort Cumberland on the Potomac River. Washington's mobilization of federal military power dramatically demonstrated the federal commitment to the preservation of the Union and the protection of the Western boundary. *(F. Kemmelmeyer.* General George Washington Reviewing the Western Army at Fort Cumberland the 18th of October, 1794. *After Oct. 1794. Oil on paper backed w/linen. 23-1/8" wide × 18-1/8" high. Courtesy, The Henry Francis du Pont Winterthur Museum.)*

preservation of the union, the protection of the western boundary, and the supremacy of the national over the local community.

This action was reinforced by an impressive American victory against the Indian confederacy. Following St. Clair's defeat, Washington appointed General Anthony Wayne to lead a greatly strengthened American force to subdue the Indian confederacy and secure the Northwest. At the Battle of Fallen Timbers, fought in the Maumee on August 20, 1794, "Mad Anthony" Wayne, as he was known to his 3,000 men because of his fierce discipline, crushed the Indians. Retreating, the warriors found the gates of Fort Miami closed and barred, the British inside thinking better of engaging the powerful American force. The victory set the stage for the Treaty of Greenville, in which the representatives of twelve Indian nations ceded a huge territory encompassing most of present-day Ohio, much of Indiana, and other enclaves in the Northwest, including the town of Detroit and the tiny village of Chicago.

Jay's and Pinckney's Treaties

The strengthened American position in the West encouraged the British to settle their dispute with the U.S. in order that they might concentrate on defeating republican France. In November 1794 Jay and the British signed an agreement providing for British withdrawal from American soil by 1796, limited American trade with the British East and West Indies, and the status of most-favored nation for both countries (meaning that each would enjoy benefits equal to those the other accorded any other state). Boundary questions and claims for compensation were to be submitted to joint commissions of arbitration. The treaty represented a solid gain for the young republic. Having only a small army, and no navy to speak of, the United States was in no position to wage war.

As it did on all matters of importance, the Senate debated the treaty in secret session, and Washington refused to release its text until it was ratified. Details thus leaked out in a piecemeal fashion that inflamed public debate. The treaty represented a victory for Hamilton's conception of American neutrality. The Jeffersonians might well have opposed any agreement with Great Britain, but they were enraged over this accommodation at France's expense. The African slaves in the French Caribbean colony of Haiti had staged a successful insurrection, and British support of this revolt reminded southern slave owners of the similar position Britain had taken toward American slaves

during the Revolution. The absence in the treaty of any mention of compensation for the slaves who had fled to the British side further alienated southerners. Throughout the country Democratic Societies and Jeffersonian partisans organized protests and demonstrations. Upon his return to the United States, Jay joked, he could find his way across the country by the light of his burning effigies. He soon resigned his position as Chief Justice to accept the governorship of New York. Despite these protests, the Senate, dominated by supporters of Hamilton, ratified the agreement in June of 1795.

In the House, a coalition of southerners, westerners, agrarians, democrats, and friends of France attempted to stall the treaty by threatening to withhold the appropriations necessary for its implementation. They demanded that they be allowed to examine the diplomatic correspondence regarding the whole affair, but the president refused, establishing the precedent of *executive privilege* in matters of state. The deadlock continued until late in the year, when word arrived in Philadelphia that Thomas Pinckney had negotiated a treaty with Spain recognizing the thirty-first parallel as the southern boundary of the United States and granting Americans free navigation of the Mississippi River with the right to deposit goods at the port of New Orleans. Fearing both the French and the British, and worried about the loss of its American empire, the Spanish suddenly found it expedient to mollify the quarrelsome Americans. This treaty fit the Jeffersonian conception of empire, and congressmen from the West and South were delighted with its terms. But administration supporters demanded their acquiescence in Jay's Treaty before the approval of Pinckney's. With this compromise, the long political controversy finally reached a conclusion.

These two important treaties finally established American sovereignty over the land west of the Appalachians and opened to American commerce a vast market extending from Atlantic ports to the Mississippi Valley. From a political standpoint, however, the battle over Jay's Treaty was costly for Washington, for it provided the Jeffersonians an opportunity to claim that the administration had sold out American neutrality, as well as the republican principles embodied by the French Revolution, in exchange for British gold. His role in the events of 1794 and 1795 brought Washington down from his pedestal and subjected him to the rough-and-tumble of political warfare. In the opposition press, he was vilified as "the source of all the misfortunes of our country," and was even accused of having been a traitor during the Revolution. Sick of politics, and

Spanish Claims to American Territory, 1783–1796
Before 1795 the Spanish claimed the American territory of the Old Southwest, and barred Americans from access to the port of New Orleans, effectively closing the Mississippi River. This dispute was settled by Pickney's Treaty in 1795.

longing to return to private life, Washington rejected the offer of a third term.

The Farewell Address

During the last months of his term, Washington published his "Farewell Address" to the nation. This was a collaborative effort: Washington worked from a draft prepared by Madison, and was assisted in its revision by Hamilton. The address was an appeal for national unity. "With slight shades of difference," Washington said to his countrymen, "you have the same religion, manners, habits, and political principles," and "union ought to be considered as a main prop of your liberty." He warned against sectional loyalty and "the baneful effects of the spirit of party." In the increasingly polarized political debate, however, this appeal fell on deaf ears.

The second part of the address was considerably more influential. "Our detached and distant situation," Washington argued, invited the nation to "defy material injury from external annoyance." He argued not for American isolation, but rather for American disinterest in the affairs of Europe. "The great rule of conduct for us in regard to foreign nations is, in extending our commercial relations to have with them as little *political* connection as possible." Why, he asked "entangle our peace and prosperity in the toils of European ambition, rivalship, interest, humor, or caprice?" In this address, Washington did not actually use a phrase generally attributed to him; it was Thomas Jefferson, in his inaugural address of 1801, who stated the principle of American foreign policy as "peace, commerce, and honest friendship with all nations, *entangling alliances with none.*" That Jefferson chose to paraphrase the "Farewell Address" in his first presidential statement underscored the extent to which Washington articulated principles agreed to by all the major political figures of his day.

FEDERALISTS AND REPUBLICANS

The framers of the Constitution envisioned a one-party state, in which partisan distinctions were absorbed by patriotism and public virtue. "Among the numerous advantages promised by a well constructed Union," Madison had written in *The Federalist,* is "its tendency to break and control the violence of faction." Not only did he fail to anticipate the rise of political parties or factions, but he saw them as potentially harmful to the new nation. Ironically, when Madison broke with the Washington administration on questions of fiscal policy, he was the first to take steps towards organizing a political opposition. At the height of the agitation of the Democratic Societies in 1794, Hamilton cried that "unless soon checked," the "spirit of faction" would "involve the country in all the horrors of anarchy." Yet in acting as Washington's political lieutenant, he did more than anyone else to solidify the Friends of Order, as the Federalists were first known, into a disciplined political party. Despite the framers' intentions, in the twelve years between the ratification of the Constitution and the federal election of 1800, political parties became a fundamental part of the American system of government.

The Rise of Political Parties

Evident in the debates and votes of Congress from 1789 to 1795 were a series of shifting coalitions that pitted commercial against agrarian interests, representatives from the Atlantic seaboard against those from the frontier, Anglophiles against Francophiles. The greatest potential division, that of northerners versus southerners, inspired the greatest fears, and congressmen worked hard to achieve sectional compromise by agreeing to avoid the issue of slavery. Antislavery petitions submitted to the Congress were dismissed by nearly unanimous votes, and a law for the apprehension of fugitive slaves by federal officers anywhere in the union was approved by a large majority in 1793.

These shifting coalitions first began to polarize into political factions during the debate over Jay's Treaty in 1795, when agrarians, westerners, southerners, and supporters of France came together in opposition to the treaty. In the House, Madison acted as a leader of this coalition when it met for the first time and attempted to implement a collective strategy. By the elections of 1796, people had begun to label these factions. The supporters of Hamilton claimed the mantle of Federalism. "I am what the phraseology of politicians has denominated a FEDERALIST," declared one North Carolina candidate for office, "the friend of order, of government, and of the present administration." Forced to find another term, the opposition chose *Republican,* implying that the Federalists were really monarchists at heart. "There are two parties at present in the United States," wrote a Jeffersonian editor in New York, "aristocrats, endeavoring to lay the foundations of monarchical government, and Republicans, the real supports of independence, friends to equal rights, and warm advocates of free elective government." Hamilton insisted on calling his opponents Anti-Federalists, while others scorned them as anarchists, Jacobins, or sans-culottes—all labels from the French Revolution. But gradually the Jeffersonian coalition came to be called the Republicans.

These coalitions played a fitful role in the Presidential election of 1796, which pitted John Adams against Thomas Jefferson. In Pennsylvania, for example, Republicans supplied voters with premarked ballots to carry to the polls, a strategy that paid off handsomely for Jefferson. Partisan organization was strongest in the middle states, where there was a real contest of political forces, weakest in New England and the South, where sectional loyalty prevailed and organized opposition was weaker. The absence of party discipline was demonstrated when the ballots of the presidential electors, cast in their respective state capitals, were counted in the Senate. According to the rules established by the Constitution, each elector cast two votes. The candidate with the highest number became president, the one with next-highest number vice-president. Although Adams was victorious, the electors chose Jefferson rather than a Federalist for

vice-president. Thus the new administration was born divided.

The Adams Presidency

Adams was put in the difficult situation of facing a political opposition led by his own vice-president. He nevertheless attempted to conduct his presidency along the lines laid down by Washington, and retained most of the former president's appointees. This presented Adams with another problem. Although Hamilton had retired the year before, the cabinet remained committed to his advice, actively seeking his opinion and following it. As a result, Adams's authority was further undercut.

On the other hand, Adams benefited from the rising tensions between the United States and France. Angered by Jay's Treaty, the French suspended diplomatic relations at the end of 1796 and inaugurated a tough new policy toward American shipping. During the next two years they seized more than 300 American vessels and confiscated cargoes valued at an estimated $20 million. Hoping to resolve the crisis, Adams sent an American delegation to France. But in dispatches sent back to the United States the American envoys reported that agents of the French foreign ministry had demanded a bribe before any negotiations could be undertaken. Pressed for copies of these dispatches by suspicious Republicans in Congress, Adams released them after substituting the letters X, Y, and Z for the names of the French agents. The documents proved a major liability for the Republicans, producing powerful anti-French sentiment throughout the country. To the demand for a bribe, the American delegates had actually answered "Not a sixpence," but in the inflated rhetoric of the day the response became the infinitely more memorable "Millions for defense, but not one cent for tribute!" The XYZ Affair, as it became known, sent Adams's popularity soaring.

Adams and the Federalists prepared the country for war during the spring of 1798. Congress authorized tripling the size of the army to 10,000 officers and men, and Washington came out of retirement to command the force. Congress also passed legislation reestablishing the Department of the Navy and authorizing the construction or purchase of two dozen ships. Fourteen American men-of-war were at sea within two years, clearing American coastal waters of French vessels and taking the defensive effort to the high seas. Although there was no declaration of war, American ships captured 80 French prizes. Fears of a French invasion declined after word arrived of the British naval victory over the French in August 1798 at Aboukir Bay in Egypt, but the "Quasi-War" between France and the United States continued.

The Alien and Sedition Acts

In the summer of 1798 the Federalist majority in Congress, with the acquiescence of President Adams, passed four acts severely limiting the freedoms of speech and the press and threatening the liberty of foreigners in the United States. Embodying the fear that immigrants, in the words of one Massachusetts Federalist, "contaminate the purity and simplicity of the American character" by introducing dangerous democratic and republican ideas, the Naturalization Act extended the period of residence required for citizenship from five to fourteen years. The Alien Act and the Alien Enemies Act authorized the president to order the imprisonment or deportation of suspected aliens during wartime. Finally, the Sedition Act provided heavy fines and imprisonment for anyone convicted of writing, publishing, or speaking anything of "a false, scandalous and malicious" nature against the government or any of its officers.

The Federalists intended these repressive laws as weapons to defeat the Republicans. Led by Albert Gallatin, a Swiss immigrant and congressman from Pennsylvania (replacing Madison, who had retired from politics to devote his time to his plantation), the Republicans contested all the Federalist war measures and for the first time acted as a genuine opposition party, complete with caucuses, floor leaders, and partisan discipline. For the first time, the two parties contested the election of Speaker of the House of Representatives, which became a partisan office. The more effective the Republicans became, the more treasonous they appeared in the eyes of the Federalists. On at least one occasion acrimonious debate in the House gave way to fisticuffs. Matthew Lyon, Republican of Vermont, spit in the eye of Connecticut Federalist Roger Griswold, Griswold responded by attacking Lyon with a cane, Lyon defended himself with a pair of fire tongs, and the two had to be pulled apart. There was only a weak understanding of the concept of the loyal opposition. Disagreement with the administration was misconstrued by the Federalists as opposition to the state itself.

The Federalists thus pursued the prosecution of dissent, indicting leading Republican newspaper editors and writers, fining and imprisoning at least twenty-five. Thomas Cooper, an English-born scientist who had immigrated to the United States because of his love of democracy, received a six-month sentence and a $400 fine. Supreme Court justice Samuel Chase, a conservative Federalist, declared Cooper's pamphlet to be "the boldest attempt I have known to poison the minds of the people, to mislead the ignorant, and inflame their minds against the President, and to influence their

In this contemporary cartoon, "Congressional Pugilists, Congress Hall in Philadelphia, February 15, 1798," Roger Griswold, a Connecticut Federalist, uses his cane to attack Matthew Lyon, Vermont Republican, who retaliates with fire tongs. During the first years of the American republic there was little understanding of the concept of a "loyal opposition," and disagreement with the policy of the Federalist administration was misconstrued as disloyalty.

votes on the next election." The most infamous victim of the Sedition Act was congressman Lyon, scorned by Federalists as "Ragged Matt the Democrat." Convicted in July 1798 of publishing libelous statements about President Adams, and thrown into a Vermont prison along with horse thieves, counterfeiters, and fugitive slaves, Lyon drew national attention by writing letters and articles reprinted widely in Republican papers. Later that year, after a campaign conducted from his cell, he was reelected to Congress.

From Virginia, Madison wrote that the Sedition Act "ought to produce universal alarm, because it is levelled against the right of freely examining public characters and measures, and of free communication among the people thereon, which has ever been deemed the only effectual guardian of every other right." He and Jefferson authored sets of resolutions, passed by the Virginia and Kentucky legislatures, that declared the Constitution to be nothing more than a compact between the sovereign states and advocated the power of those states to "nullify" unconstitutional laws. When threatened with overbearing central authority, the Republicans argued, the states had the right to go their own way. These declarations had grave implications for the future of the union, for they stamped the notion of secession with the approval of two of the founding fathers. The resolutions would later be used to justify the secession of the southern states at the beginning of the Civil War.

The Revolution of 1800

But the Alien and Sedition Acts did not require state nullification, for they were overthrown by the Republican victory in the national elections of 1800. As the term of President Adams drew to a close, Federalists found themselves seriously divided. In 1799, by releasing seized American ships and requesting negotiations, the French convinced Adams that they were ready to settle their dispute with the United States. The president also sensed the public mood running toward peace. But the Hamiltonian wing of the party, always scornful of public sentiment, continued to beat the drums of war. When Federalists in Congress tried to block the president's attempt to negotiate, Adams threatened to resign and turn the government over to Jefferson. In the Convention of 1800, the United States abandoned its demand of compensation for seized cargoes in exchange for French abrogation of the Alliance of 1778. "The end of war is peace," Adams declared,

"and peace was offered me." Adams considered the settlement of this conflict with France to be one of the greatest accomplishments of his career, but it earned him the scorn of conservative Federalists.

The Federalists also divided over a domestic controversy. Under their leadership Congress had enacted direct tax on houses, similar to the earlier tax on whiskey. In eastern Pennsylvania several dozen farmers, displaying symbols of the French Revolution, routed the tax collectors and freed from jail a tax resister, one John Fries, who had been involved in the Whiskey Rebellion. Adams sent federal troops to restore order, and for leading "Fries Rebellion," a court sentenced to death three men, including Fries. The president's cabinet demanded that Adams enforce "exemplary rigor" by allowing the sentence to be carried out, but in 1800 Adams responded to popular pressure and pardoned the three. To the jeers of Conservative Federalists, Adams now dumped the Hamiltonians from his cabinet. During the war scare with France, Washington had insisted that Hamilton be appointed as second in command of the enlarged army. "You crammed him down my throat!" Adams cried. Now he denounced Hamilton as "a bastard, and as much an alien as Gallatin." Hamilton responded by circulating a private letter in which he condemned Adams for his "disgusting egotism," "distempered jealousy," and "vanity without bounds." This letter fell into the hands of Aaron Burr, leader of the New York Republicans, and he published it, to the consternation of the Federalists.

The Federalists divided at precisely the time when only unity might have prevented the Republicans from consolidating their strengths. The spectacle of the army chasing down Pennsylvania farmers during the Fries Rebellion reinforced popular concern about government oppression under the Sedition Act. The defusing of the crisis with France also helped the Republicans, who could claim opposition to Federalist warmongering. They captured the state governments of Pennsylvania and New York in 1799, the first important inroads of the party in the North. These states had been taken over, cried a shocked Federalist, by "the most God-provoking Democrats on this side of Hell." From Virginia, Jefferson proclaimed his hope that "with Pennsylvania we can defy the universe!"

The presidential campaign of 1800 was the first in which Republicans and Federalists operated as two national political parties. Caucuses of congressmen nominated respective slates: Adams and Charles Cotesworth Pinckney of South Carolina,

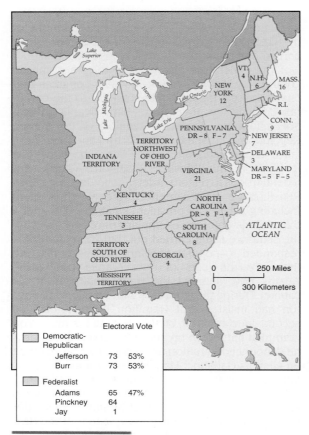

The Election of 1800

In the presidential election of 1800, Republican victories in New York and the divided vote in Pennsylvania threw the election to Jefferson. The combination of the South and these crucial middle states would keep the Republicans in control of the federal government for the next generation.

Electoral Vote

Democratic-Republican
Jefferson 73 53%
Burr 73 53%

Federalist
Adams 65 47%
Pinckney 64
Jay 1

The balloting for presidential electors took place between October and December of 1800. Adams took all the New England states while Jefferson captured the South and West. It was New York and Pennsylvania that threw the election to Jefferson; the combination of the South and these crucial middle states would keep the Republicans in control of the federal government for the next generation. It was, Jefferson said, "the Revolution of 1800." Party discipline was so effective that one of the provisions of the Constitution was shown to be badly outmoded. The candidate receiving a majority of electoral votes became president and the runner-up became vice-president, but by casting all their ballots for Jefferson and Burr, Republican electors unintentionally created a tie and forced the election into the House of Representaives. Since the new Republican-controlled Congress did not convene until March 1801, the Federalist majority was given a last chance to decide the election. They attempted to make a deal with Burr, who refused but also would not withdraw his name from consideration. Finally, on the thirty-fifth ballot the Federalists gave up and arranged with their opponents to elect Jefferson without any of them having to cast a single vote in his favor. Congressman Lyon, "Ragged Matt the Democrat," cast the symbolic final vote in a gesture of sweet revenge. The Twelfth Amendment, creating separate ballots for president and vice-president, was ratified in time for the next presidential election.

With the rise of partisan politics came a transformation in political participation. In 1789, state regulations limited the franchise to a small percentage of the adult population. Women, African Americans, and Indians, of course, could not vote, but taxpaying or property-owing requirements also excluded a third to a half of all free adult males. Moreover, among the eligible, the turnout was generally low. The traditional manner of voting was *viva voce,* by voice. At the polling place in each community individuals announced their selections aloud to the clerk of elections, a system that allowed wealthy men, landlords, and employers of the community to pressure voters.

These practices changed with the increasing competition between Republicans and Federalists. Popular pressure resulted in the introduction of universal white manhood suffrage in four states by 1800 and the reduction of property requirements in others. Thus was inaugurating a movement that would sweep the nation over the next quarter century. Among the states, only Virginia and Kentucky retained viva voce voting in the election of 1800; the others experimented with systems of

Jefferson and Aaron Burr of New York. Both tickets thus represented attempts at sectional balance. The Republicans presented themselves as the party of traditional agrarian purity, of liberty and states' rights, of "government rigorously frugal and simple," in the words of Jefferson. They were optimistic, convinced that they were riding the wave of the future. Divided and embittered, the Federalists waged a defensive struggle for strong central government and public order, and resorted frequently to negative campaigning. They denounced Jefferson as an athiest, a Jacobin, and the father of mulatto children. One campaign placard put the issue succinctly: "GOD — AND A RELIGIOUS PRESIDENT" or "JEFFERSON — AND NO GOD!"

A walnut Pennsylvania ballot box used during the elections of the late eighteenth century. In the British colonies voters had announced their choice aloud to the clerk of elections, a system that provided wealthy and powerful men the opportunity to apply pressure. After the Revolution many states experimented with more democratic systems, including the use of marked ballots inserted into boxes like this one.

secret balloting. Massachusetts for a time employed "corn and bean" balloting, the voter dropping a kernel of corn to indicate one choice, a bean for the other. Elsewhere voters marked paper slips with the name of their choice. Voter turnout increased in all the states. The growth of popular interest in politics was a transformation as important as the peaceful transition from Federalists to Republicans in national government.

"THE RISING GLORY OF AMERICA"

In 1770, graduating senior John Trumbull read a long commencement poem to his Yale classmates in which he predicted great things for American culture: "In mighty pomp America shall rise / Her glories spreading to the boundless skies." The following year Philip Freneau and Henry Hugh Brackenridge read an epic poem of their own, "The Rising Glory of America," to their graduating class at Princeton. These young men admitted that American contributions to learning and the arts had thus far been slim, but they were boundlessly optimistic about the potential of their country. It was perhaps inevitable that the achievements of the next thirty years would fall short of their hopes. But judged against the record of the colonial period, the Revolutionary generation accomplished a great deal in their effort to build a national culture.

The first American to achieve prominence in the artistic world of Europe was Benjamin West, who painted portraits in his native Pennsylvania before leaving for the Continent and England, where he became popular as a painter of historical scenes. His *Death of Wolfe* (1771) was one of the more acclaimed paintings of its day, and the first to elevate an American scene to the high status of monumental historical painting. In 1774 West was joined in London by John Singleton Copley, a Boston portraitist who left America because of his loyalist sentiments. Copley's work is renowned for the truth and straightforwardness of his depictions, as in the famous portrait *Paul Revere* (1769). Both West and Copley remained in England after the Revolution. Their most promising student was Gilbert Stuart, who painted in the fashionable style of the day. Stuart returned to the United States in 1792 to paint what became the most famous portrait of President Washington.

The preeminent painter of the Revolution was Charles Willson Peale, who studied for a time with West in London. He returned to America, however, and during the Revolution turned his talents to producing wartime propaganda. Although the almond eyes and bloated torsos of his figures suggest his technical limitations, Peale's work has a naive charm. His paintings of Washington, for example, seem more revealing of character than Stuart's placid portrait. Inspired by nationalist zeal, Peale planned a public gallery of heroes in Philadelphia that eventually grew into a famous museum of curios, reflecting his interest in natural history, archaeology, and exotic cultures. Federalists joked that its chaotic arrangement of exhibits mirrored Peale's Jeffersonian politics. Part science, part circus, the collection was purchased after Peale's death by the pioneer American entertainer P. T. Barnum.

John Trumbull of Connecticut, who had predicted America's rise to his Yale classmates, served as a soldier during the Revolution, then went to London to study with West. There he painted *The Battle of Bunker's Hill* (1785), the first of a series of Revolutionary scenes, four of which he repainted in the Capitol rotunda in the early nineteenth century. Influenced by the grand style of eighteenth-century historical painting, Trumbull was concerned above all else with documentary detail in his depictions of the great birth scenes of American nationhood.

Nationalism was also evident in architecture. The greatest architectural project of the day was the new federal capital city, named for President Wash-

George Town and Federal City, or City of Washington, a colored aquatint of 1801 by T. Cartwright. When President John Adams first occupied the White House in 1800, Washington was still a small village, its streets merely muddy pathways.

ington. In 1790, after Congress had agreed on the site, Washington retained Pierre Charles L'Enfant, a French engineer who had served as an officer during the Revolution, to lay out the city. The survey was conducted by Andrew Elliott, assisted by the African American mathematician Benjamin Banneker. L'Enfant took full advantage of the lay of the land and the Potomac River, placing the Capitol building on a hill "which stands as a pedestal waiting for a monument." He linked public buildings such as the president's house and the Capitol with radial avenues, allowing for what he called "a reciprocity of sight." And he planned a grand mall from the Capitol to the river, along which there would be public museums, academies, and assembly halls. Development during the nineteenth century obscured L'Enfant's original design, but it was revived in 1901. Jefferson recommended "the models of antiquity"

for the public buildings of the federal city, a suggestion carried out in William Thornton's original design for the Capitol.

"Architecture is worth great attention," declared Jefferson, for "as we double our numbers every twenty years, we must double our houses. It is, then, among the most important arts; and it is desirable to introduce taste into an art which shows so much." In New England, architect Asher Benjamin popularized an American variant of the Georgian style, emphasizing economy of decoration and the use of indigenous materials in his handbooks such as *The Country Builder's Assistant* (1797). A great deal of the urban building undertaken in coastal cities during the shipping boom of the nineties was characterized by this restrained classicism known as the Federal style.

But the majority of Americans lived in small,

bare, even squalid conditions. The nationwide tax on houses in 1798 that spawned the Fries Rebellion also produced the first comprehensive survey of the nation's housing. There was tremendous variation in living conditions. The wealthiest 10 percent lived in dwellings estimated to be worth more than half the total value of all houses. By contrast, the value of housing owned by the wealthiest tenth of Americans today is 30 percent of the total. Forty percent of American houses in 1798 were valued at $100 or less. In the expanding cities, many residents lived along dingy back alleys and in damp basements. In the country, the typical house was a one-story structure of two or three rooms. As the population continued to grow, and Americans continued to move west, many more would be found in log hovels like those in the community along Mingo Creek.

The Liberty of the Press

At the beginning of the Revolution in 1775 there were thirty-seven weekly or semiweekly newspapers in the thirteen colonies, only seven of which were loyalist in sentiment. By 1789 the number of papers in the United States had grown to ninety-two, including eight dailies; three papers were being published west of the Appalachians. Relative to population, there were more newspapers in the United States than in any other country in the world — a reflection of the remarkably high literacy rate of the American people. In New England, readers approached 90 percent of the population, and even on the frontier, where Brackenridge edited the *Pittsburgh Gazette,* about two-thirds of the male population were literate.

During the political controversy of the 1790s, the press became the principal medium of Federalist and Republican opinion, and papers came to be identified by their politics. In 1789 John Fenno, aided by Alexander Hamilton, began publication of the Federalist *Gazette of the United States,* and in 1791 Jefferson encouraged Philip Freneau to establish the competing *National Gazette.* The columns of these papers broadcast the feud between the two cabinet secretaries. The most notorious Jeffersonian paper was the Philadelphia *Aurora,* edited by Benjamin Franklin Bache, named for his grandfather, himself a pioneer editor. The *Aurora* attacked Federalist politicians, and even accused President Washington of personal raids on the Treasury. It first published the leaked text of Jay's Treaty, and in 1798 Bache was arrested under the Sedition Act for libeling President Adams. On the other side, Noah Webster's *American Minerva* in New York took an increasingly acerbic

conservative Federalist position. In 1801 Webster bragged that he had spent "the largest part of eighteen years in opposing democracy."

The prosecutions under the Sedition Act threatened to curb the further development of the media, and in their opposition to these measures Republicans played an important role in establishing the principle of a free press. In *An Essay on Liberty of the Press* (1799), the Virginia lawyer George Hay, later appointed to the federal bench by President Jefferson, wrote that "a man may say everything which his passions suggest." Otherwise, he argued, the First Amendment was "the grossest absurdity that was ever conceived by the human mind." In *A Treatise Concerning Political Enquiry and the Liberty of the Press* (1800), Tunis Wortman, a lawyer active in the Tammany Society, a New York Republican stronghold, declared that only open and free debate enabled society to determine the wisest course of action. Which was better, he asked rhetorically, to defeat erroneous opinion "by the convincing and circumstantial narrative of truth, or by the terrors of imprisonment and the singular logic of the pillory"? "Confidence should be reposed," he concluded, "in the wisdom and virtues of the people." In his first inaugural address Jefferson echoed these early champions of the freedom of expression. "Error of opinion may be tolerated," he declared, "where reason is left free to combat it."

American Books

During the post-revolutionary years there was an enormous outpouring of American publications. In the cities the number of bookstores grew in response to the demand for reading matter. Perhaps even more significant was the appearance in the countryside of numerous book peddlers who supplied farm households with Bibles, gazettes, almanacs, sermons, and political pamphlets. One such peddler was Mason Locke Weems, a man trained as a doctor and ordained an Anglican minister, who gave up these careers in the early 1790s for bookselling. Parson Weems, as he was known, wrote that he found his southern backcountry customers "uninformed, their minds bitter, and their manners savage," but that they cried out for "books, books, books!"

The literature of the Revolution understandably reflected the dominating political concerns of the times. Mercy Otis Warren and Hugh Henry Brackenridge wrote propagandistic dramas, and the poet Joel Barlow composed a nationalist epic, *The Vision of Columbus* (1787). *M'Fingal* (1782), a mock epic satirizing the British, was written by John Trumbull (a cousin of the painter), who associated with a literary group known as the Connecticut Wits. It sold copies enough to be considered the best-selling fictional work of the war. But the majority of "best sellers" during the revolutionary era were political. The most important were Thomas Paine's *Common Sense* (1776) and his series of stirring pamphlets, published under the running title *The American Crisis* (1776–83), the first of which began with the memorable phrase "These are the times that try men's souls."

In the cause of revolution, Paine later returned to England and published *The Rights of Man* (1791), a defense of the French Revolution. Banished from Britain for this expression of radical politics, he went to France, jumped into politics, and, in one of the periodic political turns of the revolution, found himself imprisoned for a time. From his jail cell Paine wrote *The Age of Reason* (1795), a powerful attack on organized religion as an institution created "to terrify and enslave mankind, and monopolize power and profit," and a book that ridiculed the Bible for its inconsistencies and fallibility. It became one of the most popular American books of its day, loved by Jeffersonians and loathed by Federalists. Bookselling Parson Weems, for example, made a steady profit from the sale of Paine, though he offered pious sermons and religious tracts to placate those objecting to Paine's politics.

Some of the most interesting American books of the postwar years examined the developing American character. The French immigrant Michel-Guillaume Jean de Crevecoeur, in *Letters from an American Farmer* (1782), proposed that the American, a product of many cultures, was a "new man" with ideas new to the world. John Filson, the author of the *Discovery, Settlement, and Present State of Kentucke* (1784), presented the narrative of one such new man, the Kentucky pioneer Daniel Boone. In doing so he took an important step in the creation of that most American of literary genres, the Western. In a satirical novel entitled *Modern Chivalry* (1792), featuring incidents from the Whiskey Rebellion, Pittsburgh editor Brackenridge dipped his pen "in the inkstand of human nature" and produced one of the first dialect portraits of "dat son o'd a whore," the American frontiersman. Brackenridge wrote with an appreciation for his crude characters but expressed frustration that the Revolution had failed to elevate the culture of ordinary people. By shunning simple celebration, however, he was one of the first to take a critical look at the American character.

The single best-selling book of the revolutionary era was Noah Webster's *American Spelling Book* (1783), the famous "Blue-Backed Speller," which soon after publication was selling 200,000 copies annually. Over two centuries it became the largest-selling of all American books. With it, Webster launched a lifelong campaign for a distinctive American form of English, which culminated in his *American Dictionary of the English Language* (1828). In a belief that "the King's English" reflected aristocratic standards, Webster argued that "the American language" must be guided by "republican principles," for example, spelling words as they sounded. "Ther iz no alternativ," he wrote. Eventually he abandoned the most radical of his suggestions, although many of his reforms stuck. The speller was the first in a graded series of textbooks that included a grammar and a reader designed to "diffuse the principles of virtue and patriotism." These texts included standard selections not only from British but from American writers. Webster compiled a list of important dates beginning with Columbus's voyage and ending with the British surrender at Yorktown — the first attempt at a distinctively American chronology.

Other writers wrote more formal histories. Republican authors emphasized the tradition of resistance to authority, while Federalists concentrated on the necessity for central direction and unity during the war. In his *History of the American Revolution* (1789), the Jeffersonian David Ramsay upheld "the right of the people to resist their rulers." Mercy Otis Warren delayed publishing her *History of the Rise, Progress, and Termination of the American Revolution* (1805) until after Jefferson's victory in 1800, for fear of persecution by the Federalists. John Marshall's turgid *Life of George Washington* (1805), intended as a "life and times," offered a Federalist view, but people complained that the book had too little *life* and took too much *time* to read.

Parson Weems found it difficult to sell these histories, for they were expensive and his customers found them boring. But he found readers fascinated by the heroes of the Revolution, so he drew up plans for a series of "quarter of dollar books on subjects calculated to strike the popular curiosity, printed in very large numbers and properly distributed." When Washington died in December of 1799, Weems was already at work on a short biography of the first president. "Washington, you know, is gone!" he wrote to his publisher. "Millions are gaping to read something about him. I am very nearly primed and cocked for 'em." His *Life of Washington* (1800, tually promifed to affift each other, if they fhould happen to be affaulted. They had not proceeded far, before they perceived a Bear making towards them with great rage. There were no hopes in flight; but one of them, being very active, fprung up into a tree; upon which the other, throwing himfelf flat on the ground, held his breath, and pretended to be dead; remembering to have heard it afferted, that this creature will not prey upon a dead carcafe. The bear came up, and after fmelling to him fome time, left him, and went on. When he was fairly out of fight and hearing, the hero from the tree calls out—Well, my friend, what faid the bear? He feemed to whifper you very clofely. He did fo, replied the other, and gave me this good piece of advice; never to affociate with a wretch, who in the hour of danger will defert his friend.

TABLE XXXIII.

Words in which *ch* have the found of *k*.

CHRIST	cho-rus	chol-ic	char-ac-ter
chyle	te-trarch	chol-er	cat-e-chifm
fcheme	cha-os	fchol-ar	pen-ta-teuch
ache	cho-ral	mon-arch	fep-ul-cher
chafm	e-poch	or-chal	tech-nic-al
chrifm	o-cher	tro-chee	al-chy-my
tach	tro-chee	fchir-rous	an-cho-ret
	an-chor	ftom-ach	brach-i-al
chord	chrif-ten		lach-ry-mal
loch	chym-ift	pa-tri-arch	mach-i-nate
fchool	ech-o	eu-cha-rift	fac-char-ine
choir	chal-ice		syn-chro-nifm
	fched-ule	an-ar-chy	mich-ael-mas
	paf-chal	chryf-o-lite	chor-if-ter

chron-i-cle	cha-lyb-e-rate	the-om-a-chy
or-chef-tra	a-nach-ro-nifm	
och-i-my	fyn-ec-do-che	ar-chi-tec-ture
chi-me-ra	pyr-rhich-i-us	an-ti-bac-chus
pa-ro-chi-al	am-phib-ra-chus	cat-e-chet-ic-al
cha-mel-ion	mel-an-chol-y	bac-cha-nal-ian
tri-bach-us	chro-nol-o-gy	cat-e-chu-men
arch-an-gel	chi-rog-ra-phy	ich-thy-ol-o-gy
me-chan-ic	cho-rog-ra-phy	
ca-chex-y	chro-nom-e-ter	

FABLE VII.—*The* TWO DOGS.

HASTY and inconfiderate connections are generally attended with great difadvantages; and much of every man's good or ill fortune depends upon the choice he makes of his friends.

A goodnatured Spaniel overtook a furly Maftiff, as he was travelling upon the high road. Tray, although an entire ftranger to Tyger, very civilly accofted him; and if it would be no interruption, he faid, he fhould be glad to bear him company on his way. Tyger

Noah Webster (below), and pages from his famous American Spelling Book (left), the largest seller of all American books during the nineteenth century. Believing that "the King's English" reflected aristocratic standards, Webster argued for spelling reform to create "the American language."
(James Sharples. Noah Webster. *Pastel on laid paper (rubbed to a smooth surface). 7-3/4 in wide × 8-7/8 in. high. The Metropolitan Museum of Art, Bequest of Charles Allen Munn, 1924. [24.109.99])*

enlarged edition 1806), became the most popular history of the Revolution, and introduced a series of popular and completely fabricated anecdotes, including the story of young Washington and the cherry tree. Weems tirelessly promoted his book through twenty-nine printings before his death in 1825. "You have a great deal of money lying in the bones of old George," he wrote his publisher, "if you will but exert yourself to extract it." The book was a pioneering effort in mass culture, and Weems, as one historian put it, was "the father of the Father of his Country."

Condemned by serious writers and scholars, even at the time of its publication, Weems's biography was loved by ordinary Americans of all political persuasions. In the mid-nineteenth century, Abraham Lincoln recalled that he had read Weems "away back in my childhood, the earliest days of my being able to read," and had been profoundly impressed by "the struggles for the liberties of the country." In praise of Washington, Weems wrote, "all parties join with equal alacrity and earnestness." Although Washington had in fact become a partisan leader of the Federalists during his second term, Weems presented him as a unifying figure for the political culture of the new nation, and this was the way he would be remembered. Jefferson echoed these sentiments in his inaugural address in 1801, when as a gesture of conciliation to his opponents he declared, "We have called by different names brethren of the same principle. We are all Republicans, we are all Federalists."

Republican Motherhood

One of the most interesting literary trends of the 1790s was the growing demand for books that appealed to women readers. Susanna Haswell Rowson's *Charlotte Temple* (1791), a tale of seduction and abandonment, ran up tremendous sales and remained in print for more than a century. Other romantic works of fiction included *The Power of Sympathy* (1789) by William Hill Brown, sometimes called the first American novel; the gothic novels of Charles Brockden Brown, such as *Arthur Mervyn* (1797); and *The Coquette* (1797) by Hannah Webster Foster. The young republic thus marked the first dramatic appearance of women readers and women writers. Although women's literacy rates continued to be lower than men's, they rose steadily as girls joined boys in common schools. This increase was one of the most important social legacies of the democratic struggles of the revolutionary era.

Some writers argued that the new republican order ought to provide new roles for women as well as for men. Protests from women about their treatment at the hands of men had long been heard in America. In 1736 an anonymous poet writing in the *Virginia Gazette* had urged:

> Then equal laws let custom find,
> And neither sex oppress;
> More freedom give to womankind,
> Or give to mankind less.

Several years later another unnamed woman wrote in the *South-Carolina Gazette:*

> How wretched is a woman's fate,
> No happy change her fortune knows,
> Subject to man in every state.
> How can she then be free from woes?

That these women had to remain anonymous was a telling fact. The first avowed feminist in American history was Judith Sargent Murray, who publicly stated her belief that women "should be taught to depend on their own efforts, for the procurement of an establishment in life." She was greatly influenced

In this 1792 cartoon from *The Lady's Magazine* the allegorical figure of "Columbia" receives a petition for the "Rights of Woman." In the aftermath of the Revolution Americans debated the issue of an expanded role for women in the new republic. Many Federalists condemned "women of masculine minds," but there was general agreement among both conservatives and democrats that the time had come for better education for American women.

by the English feminist Mary Wollstonecraft, but developed her line of thinking independently, as demonstrated by her essay "On the Equality of the Sexes," written in 1779 and finally published in 1790 in a Massachusetts magazine. "I expect to see our young women forming a new era in female history," Murray predicted. Federalists listened to such opinions with horror. "Women of masculine minds," one Boston minister sneered, "have generally masculine

The Spread of Settlement, 1770–1790

From 1770 to 1790 the Backcountry became the focus of the accelerated pace of settlement.

manners," and Parson Weems admitted that "a masculine air in a woman frightens us."

There seemed to be general agreement among all parties, however, that the time had come for better-educated and -informed women. Republican institutions of self-government were widely thought to depend upon the wisdom and self-discipline of the American people. Civic virtue, so indispensable for the republic, must be taught at home. The share that every male citizen had in the government of the country, Benjamin Rush said in 1787, required that women have "suitable education, to concur in instructing their sons in the principles of liberty and government." By placing her learning at the service of her family, the "republican mother" was spared the criticism of independent-minded women such as Murray. "A woman will have more commendation in being the mother of heroes," said a Federalist, "than in setting up, Amazon-like, for a heroine herself." Thus were women provided the opportunity to be not simply "helpmates," but people "learned and wise." But they were also expected to be content with a narrow role, to not wish for fuller participation in American democracy.

CONCLUSION

In 1800, Canada (then known as British North America) numbered about 500,000 persons. Those of European background in New Mexico and the other Spanish North American colonies constituted approximately 25,000. And the Indian people of the continent made up anywhere from 500,000 to a million. Overwhelming all these groups was the population of the United States, which stood at 5.3 million and was growing at the astounding annual rate of 3 percent. The nation that unified this population had withstood a first decade of stress, but tensions continued to divide the people. As some of the rebel supporters had promised at the beginning of the Whiskey Rebellion, "their liberty they will maintain, / they fought for't, and they'll fight again." At the beginning of the new century it remained uncertain if the new nation would find a way to control and channel the energies of an expanding people.

CHRONOLOGY

1786	Annapolis Convention
1787	Constitutional Convention
1787–88	*The Federalist* published
1788	Constitution ratified; first federal elections
1789	President Washington inaugurated in New York City Judiciary Act French Revolution begins
1790	Agreement on location of capital at Washington, D.C. Intercourse Act Judith Sargent Murray's "On the Equality of the Sexes"
1791	Bill of Rights ratified Bank of the United States chartered Hamilton's "Report on Manufactures" Ohio Indians defeat St. Clair's army
1793	England and France at war; America reaps trade windfall Citizen Genêt affair Washington proclaims American neutrality in Europe British confiscate American vessels *Chisholm v. Georgia*
1794	Whiskey Rebellion Battle of Fallen Timbers Jay concludes treaty with British
1795	Pinckney's Treaty negotiated Thomas Paine's *The Age of Reason* published
1796	Washington's Farewell Address John Adams elected president
1797	French begin seizing American ships
1798	XYZ Affair "Quasi-War" with France Alien and Sedition Acts Kentucky and Virginia Resolutions
1799	Fries Rebellion
1800	Convention of 1800 Thomas Jefferson elected president Mason Locke Weems's *Life of Washington* published

Additional Readings

WILLIAM N. CHAMBERS, *Political Parties in a New Nation: The American Experience, 1776–1809* (1963). An introduction to the formation of the American party system. Though several decades old, it remains essential.

JOSEPH J. ELLIS, *After the Revolution: Profiles of Early American Culture* (1979). A series of portraits of the more important cultural innovators in the young republic.

JAMES T. FLEXNER, *Washington, The Indispensable Man* (1974). The best one-volume biography of the "father of his country."

REGINALD HORSMAN, *The Frontier in the Formative Years, 1783–1815* (1970). A sensitive survey of developments in the West, emphasizing that the "western question" was one of the most important facing the young republic.

JACKSON TURNER MAIN, *The Antifederalists: Critics of the Constitution, 1781–1788* (1961). A detailed examination of the localist tradition in early American politics. Includes a discussion of the ratification of the Constitution from the point of view of its opponents.

JOHN C. MILLER, *The Federalist Era, 1789–1801* (1960). Remains the best overview of the first decade of the American republic.

THOMAS P. SLAUGHTER, *The Whiskey Rebellion: Frontier Epilogue to the American Revolution* (1986). A detailed history of the rebellion in western Pennsylvania during the 1790s. Includes a thorough examination of the politics and culture of both the backcountry and the federal government at a moment of crisis.

JAMES M. SMITH, *Freedom's Fetters: The Alien and Sedition Laws and American Civil Liberties* (1966). Remains the best overview of the Federalist threat to liberty, as well as the Republican counterattack.

GERALD STOURZH, *Alexander Hamilton and the Idea of Republican Government* (1970). A solid biography of both the ultimate Federalist man and his politics.

GORDON WOOD, *The Creation of the American Republic, 1776–1787* (1969). This general survey provides the best overview of the Constitutional Convention.

9 THE AGRARIAN REPUBLIC, 1790–1824

(Pavel Petrovich Svinin. Deck Life on the Paragon, one of Fulton's steamboats. Fort Putnam in the background. Watercolor on paper. 9-7/8 × 14-5/16 in. The Metropolitan Museum of Art, Rogers Fund, 1942.)

It was mid-October 1804 when the news arrived at the Mandan villages on the upper Missouri: an American expedition was coming up the river. Cold winds blowing from the north signaled the beginning of a harsh winter, and the visitors wanted to know if they could hole up for the next few months near the well-supplied towns. The principal chiefs, pleased to hear of this first visit from the Americans, readily agreed. They had visions of expanded trade as well as support against their Sioux enemies, the hunting people who blocked commerce with St. Louis traders. Meriwether Lewis and William Clark guided their three boats and forty-four men toward the villages, prominently situated on the Missouri bluffs. "Great numbers on both sides flocked down to the bank to view us as we passed," wrote Clark, and that evening the Mandans welcomed the Americans with an enthusiastic dance and gifts of food.

AMERICAN EXPANSION TOUCHES A WESTERN INDIAN COMMUNITY

Since the fourteenth century, when they migrated from the East, the Mandans had lived along the Missouri, on the cusp of the Great Plains in what is now North Dakota. They believed their homeland was "the very center of the world," and indeed it is the heart of the North American continent. The women grew corn, beans, squash, sunflowers, and tobacco, and the fertile soil of the river bottom kept their storage pits ever full. The men hunted buffalo and traded crops with the nomadic tribes of the plains. Well before any of them had ever met a European they were receiving kettles, knives, and guns originating among the French and English to the east, and exchanging them for leatherwork, glassware, and horses brought by nomads from the Spanish in the Southwest. The Mandan villages were the central marketplace of the Northern Plains. At trading time in late summer, they were crowded with Crows, Assiniboins, Cheyennes, Kiowas, Arapahoes, British traders from Canada, and French and American traders from St. Louis. Thus the Mandans themselves were key players in a vigorous international trade that stretched from Mexico to the Canadian North and that involved Europeans and many different Indian peoples.

The eighteenth century was a golden age for this communal people, who with their closely related Hidatsa neighbors numbered about 3,000 people in 1804. Each of their five villages controlled its own affairs. At the center of each was a large plaza with earth lodges clustered about it, giving the

The artist George Catlin climbed on top of one of the earth-covered lodges like those in his painting to achieve this panoramic view of a Mandan village in 1832. While scalp-poles waved over his head, Catlin strove to capture the full activity of the busy village. Just five years later, the village was destroyed by a devastating smallpox epidemic.

appearance, one European observer noted, of "so many large hives clustered together." Except for a large ceremonial lodge used for community gatherings, these were family dwellings. A family lodge was home to a senior woman, her husband, her sisters (perhaps married to the same man as she, for the Mandans practiced polygamy), their daughters and their unmarried sons, along with numerous grandchildren. Matrilineal clans, the principal institution of the community, distributed food to the sick, adopted orphans, cared for the dependent elderly, and punished wrongdoers. Male clan leaders made up a village council that selected chiefs. These men led solely on the basis of consensus; they lost power when the people no longer accepted their opinions.

These chiefs met with Lewis and Clark soon after their arrival. Sent by President Jefferson to survey the Louisiana Purchase, the two leaders were also instructed to challenge British economic power in the West by establishing an American fur trading network. The Americans found Frenchmen with Indian wives and children living among the Mandans. This was now American territory, Lewis warned, and a number of the French hired on to the expedition as interpreters. One Frenchman, Touissant Charbonneau, also offered the interpretive skills of one of his wives, a 15-year old Shoshoni captive named Sacajawea. She became the only woman to accompany the expedition on its westward journey. The presence of Sacajawea and her baby son, as Clark noted, "reconciles all the Indians as to our friendly intentions," for everyone knew that women and children did not go on war parties.

In pursuit of their strategic purpose, the Americans offered the Mandans a military and economic alliance. His people would like nothing better, responded Chief Black Cat, for the Mandans had fallen on hard times over the past decade. "The smallpox [had] destroyed the greater part of the nation" some twenty years before, he said. "All the nations before this malady, [were] afraid of them, [but] after they were reduced the Sioux and other Indians waged war, and killed a great many." Black Cat was skeptical of the American promises, however, for the French and the Spanish had said the same thing, but had been unable to break the Sioux barrier. "We were ready to protect them," Clark wrote in his journal, "and kill those who would not listen to our good talk." From the very beginning, American interests were pitted against those of the expansive Sioux.

Before they resumed their westward journey the next spring, the Americans established firm and friendly relations with the Mandans. The Americans became part of the social life that bound the Mandan communities together. There were dances and joint hunting parties. There were frequent visits to the earth lodges, long talks around the fire, and, for many of the men, pleasant nights in the company of Mandan women. The Mandans drew charts and maps from which Lewis and Clark gained critical information on the course and distances of the Missouri, the ranges of the Rocky Mountains, and the crossing of the Continental Divide. The information and support of the Mandans (and of other Indian peoples to the West) was vital to the success of the Lewis and Clark expedition. Their pathfinding voyage of discovery was in actuality a cooperative undertaking by the Americans and the Indian peoples who helped them along their way. When the party left [the Mandan villages] in March, Clark wrote, his men were "generally healthy, except [for] venereal complaints which is very common amongst the natives and the men catch it from them." Two years later, when the Americans returned from their explorations, one of the Mandan chiefs accompanied them back to St. Louis to arrange for a permanent mission to his people.

Before long the Americans had established Fort Clark at the Mandan villages, making the continental heartland a base for penetrating the trans-Mississippi West. But blowing on the American trade wind from the southeast were seeds of destruction for the Mandans and Hidatsas. The permanent American presence brought increased contact, and with it much more disease. In 1837 a terrible smallpox epidemic carried away the vast majority of the Mandans, reducing the population to fewer than 150. Four Bears, a Mandan chief who had been a child at the time of the Lewis and Clark visit, spoke these last words to the remnants of his people. "I have loved the whites," he declared. "I have lived with them ever since I was a boy." But in return for the kindness of all the Mandans, the Americans had brought this plague. "I do not fear death, my friends," he said, "but to die with my face rotten, that even the wolves will shrink with horror at seeing me, and say to themselves, that is Four Bears, the friend of the whites." "They have deceived me," he pronounced with his last breath, "them that I always considered as brothers [have] turned out to be my worst enemies."

President Jefferson had sent Lewis and Clark on their momentous journey to claim the land and the loyalty of the Mandans and other western Indian communities. He was motivated to do so in large part by his vision of an expanding American republic of self-sufficient farmers. During Jefferson's presidency and those of his successors, expansion became a key element of national policy and pride.

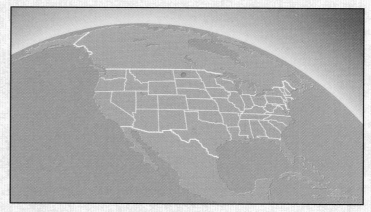

Yet, as the experience of the Mandans showed, expansion was paradoxical. What Jefferson viewed as enlargement of "the empire for liberty" caused the death and destruction of the communities created by America's first peoples. The effects — economic, political, and social — of continental expansion dominate the history of American communities in the first half of the nineteenth century.

European Communities From Coast to Coast

At first glance, the United States of America in 1800 seemed little changed from the scattered colonies of the pre-Revolution era. A long, thin line of settlements still clung to the eastern seacoast and two-thirds of the nation's people still lived within fifty miles of the Atlantic Ocean. From New Hampshire to Georgia, most people lived on farms or in small towns. Because few people had traveled far from home, their horizons were limited and local.

Transportation between the states was slow and difficult. The roads were so bad — snowbound in winter, muddy in spring, rutted in summer — that travel times of only three or four miles an hour were common. At that slow pace, it took two days to travel from New York to Philadelphia by horse and carriage, and at least four days to travel to Boston.

As famed historian Henry Adams observed, at the beginning of the new century "nature was rather man's master than his servant" in the young American republic. Nevertheless, the new nation was already transforming itself, not by ignoring nature but by plunging more deeply into it. Between 1790 and 1800, according to the first and second federal censuses, the American population grew from 3.9 million to 5.3 million. (By comparison, Canada, known then as British North America, had a population of 500,000 in 1800, and the population of European background in New Mexico and the other Spanish colonies in North America was just 25,000.) Growth was most rapid west of the Appalachian Mountains. Settlers poured into this area, confronting the approximately 100,000 Indian people who lived there. Elsewhere on the continent the Indian population totaled 500,000 to 1 million people.

From 1800 to 1850, in an extraordinary territorial expansion, Americans surged westward all the way to the Pacific. As they did so, their lives and attitudes changed in ways unimaginable in 1800. Few people then would have predicted that by 1850 America would be a continental nation. In fact, in 1800 the colonization and settlement efforts of several other European nations seemed equally significant.

America in 1800

In 1800, the new United States of America was surrounded by territories held by the European powers: British Canada, French Louisiana, Spanish Mexico, and Russian Alaska expanding southward along the Pacific coast. Few people could have imagined that by 1850 the United States would span the continent. But the American settlers who had crossed the Appalachians to the Ohio River Valley were already convinced that opportunity lay in the West.

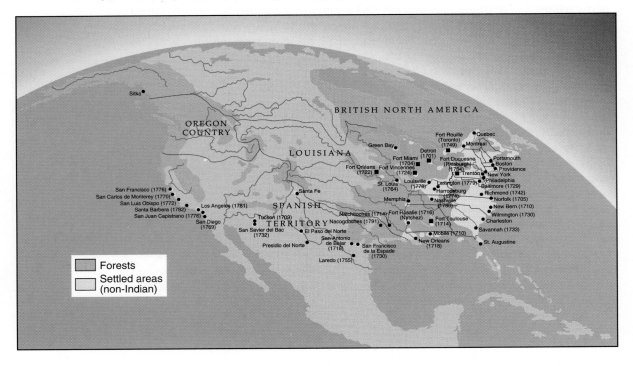

Russian America: Sitka

Russian inroads into the area later known as Alaska were an extension of Russia's conquest of Siberia, which was driven by the fur trade. In 1724 Tsar Peter the Great commissioned the Danish-born naval officer Vitus Bering to lead an expedition across the Pacific to the American continent. In 1741, after several preliminary voyages, Bering sailed east from Kamchatka across the sea that now bears his name, explored the Aleutian Islands, and made landfall on the southern coast of Alaska. Although Bering died in a shipwreck on his return voyage, his associates brought back a cargo of otter furs, news of the discovery of Alaska, and a navigational report on the arctic waters of the northern Pacific. In the aftermath of these voyages, Russian and Siberian fur trappers, known as *Promyshleniki,* became regular visitors to the Aleutian Islands and the Alaskan coast. By the late 1750s they were shipping a steady supply of furs from Russian America.

The Russians sometimes took furs by force, holding whole villages hostage and brutalizing the native Inuit and Aleut peoples. Native resistance was at first sporadic and local, but within a decade it had broadened into a large-scale network. In 1762 the Aleuts destroyed a fleet of Russian ships from Kamchatka, beginning a series of attacks known as the Aleut Revolt. Not until 1766 were the Russians able to crush the Aleuts. The distant state in Moscow subsequently promised to protect the Aleuts from abuse, but little actually changed in Alaska. By the end of the century, the precontact population of 25,000 Aleuts had been greatly reduced. At the same time, extensive sexual relations and intermarriage between fur trappers and Aleut women resulted in a substantial group of Russian creoles who assumed an increasingly prominent position in the Alaskan fur trade as navigators, explorers, clerks, and traders.

In 1784, the merchant trader Gregory Shelikhov established a post on Kodiak Island, and over the next several years he established the first permanent Russian settlements in the Gulf of Alaska. In 1799, after his death, Shelikhov's company combined with smaller groups and received a state charter as a quasi-governmental monopoly with rights to the lucrative trade in sea otter pelts. The Russian-American Company set up American headquarters at Sitka, and by 1805 there were 470 Russians in Alaska. Alexander Baranov, director of company operations for a generation, established a string of nineteen Russian settlements along the Pacific coast. These extended as far south as Fort Ross, founded in 1811 at the mouth of the Russian River,

north of San Francisco Bay. This was well within what Spain considered its own territory.

The North of New Spain: Los Angeles

Spain had long been concerned about threats to its New World empire from other nations. From the port of San Blas, on the western coast of Mexico, the Spanish sent naval squadrons north to establish their claim to the Pacific coast. By the 1770s, Spain had explored and made claim to the mouth of the Columbia River, Nootka Sound (on Vancouver Island), and the coast of southern Alaska. On a voyage in 1789, a Spanish ship in Nootka Sound encountered a British ship exploring the rich resources of sea otter hides on the northern Pacific coast. When the British, under Captain James Colnett, built a

---

Spanish California

Beginning in 1769, the Spanish colonized Alta California by establishing a chain of missions, presidios (forts) and pueblos (towns) linked by the Royal Road, *El Camino Real.* They sought to convert members of California's many Indian groups to Christianity while using them as a labor force to grow crops and raise cattle. European diseases and disruption devastated the California Indians: by the end of the Spanish period, their numbers had been halved.

Source: James Rawls, *Indians at California* (Norman: University of Oklahoma Press), Map 1; and Warren A. Beck and Ynez D. Haase, *Historical Atlas of California* (Norman: University of Oklahoma Press, 1974), Map 19.

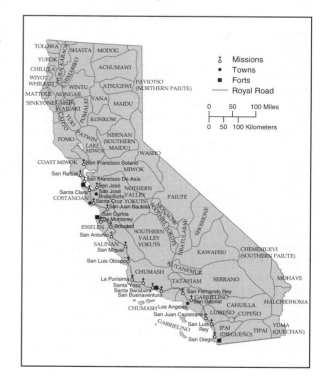

trading post at Nootka Sound, the Spanish arrested him and his crew and sent them to Mexico as prisoners. This chance encounter on the faraway Pacific Northwest coast became an international incident that nearly led Spain and Britain to war.

To protect their rich colony of Mexico against possible Russian or British claims, the Spanish had already pushed north into Alta (Upper) California. There they established a chain of twenty-one missions that stretched from San Diego (1769) to Sonoma (1823) in the north (see Chapter 5). Along with the missions in California, the Spanish founded forts (presidios) and several small farming settlements (pueblos). Of the latter, the largest was Los Angeles, which had a largely mestizo (mixed Spanish and Indian ancestry) population of 300 in 1800. The settlers, some of them retired soldiers enriched by large land grants, employed the Gabrielino Indians to produce more grain, cattle, horses, and sheep than any other community in California. The town functioned chiefly as a center of government authority. It was also the social center for the vast California countryside surrounding it. In 1803 came the first American ship, the *Lelia Bird.* There soon developed a brisk but illegal trade in otter skins, hides, and tallow, in spite of Spain's desire to seal off its territory from American commerce.

Louisiana: New Orleans

New Orleans was hacked out of the swamps near the mouth of the Mississippi River in 1718 by the Frenchman Jean Baptiste le Moyne, Sieur de Bienville. For half a century thereafter New Orleans flourished under French rule, partly as a frontier outpost, partly as a disreputable international port that attracted pirates and smugglers as well as honest merchants. But what made New Orleans really distinctive was that it was also a center of Parisian culture and luxury, supplied by royal governors such as the Marquis de Vaudreuil. Vaudreuil, who ruled lavishly from 1743 to 1753, set an early standard for graft, corruption, and pleasure.

New Orleans came under Spanish rule in 1763 as a result of the Seven Years' War, but it continued to be a polyglot, French-dominated society. Its 1800 population of about 8,000 was half white and half black. Two-thirds of the black population were slaves; the remainder were "free persons of color," who under French law enjoyed legal rights equal to those of whites. The white population was a mixture of French people of European and West Indian origin. Among these were the exiles from Acadia, who became known in New Orleans as Cajuns (see Chapter 5). But there were also Spanish, Germans, English, Irish, Americans, and native-born Creoles, causing one observer to call the community "a veritable tower of Babel." They were all there because New Orleans was a thriving international port, shipping tobacco, sugar, rice, cotton, fruits, and vegetables worth over $3 million to Europe in 1801. Every year, more of the New Orleans trade was supplied by Americans living some distance up the Mississippi River. In 1801 alone, an observer in Natchez counted nearly 600 flatboats on their way to New Orleans from American settlements upriver. Pinckney's 1795 treaty with Spain guaranteed Americans free navigation of the Mississippi River and the right to deposit goods at the port of New Orleans (see Chapter 8). Nevertheless, Americans were uncomfortably aware that the city's crucial location at the mouth of the Mississippi meant that whatever foreign nation possessed New Orleans had the power to choke off all of the flourishing trade in the vast Mississippi Valley river system.

Trans-Appalachia: Cincinnati

Within the United States itself, the region of greatest growth was the area west of the Appalachian Mountains. Far upriver from French New Orleans was the frontier town of Cincinnati, which was destined to become the "Queen City of the West" in the early nineteenth century. Located on the heavily wooded banks of the Ohio River, Cincinnati became a magnet for thousands of settlers who streamed west over the Appalachian Mountains in the closing years of the eighteenth century.

In the Proclamation of 1763, the British had drawn a line at the crest of the Appalachian Mountains and forbidden the American colonists to move west of it. Backcountry pioneers, led by legendary figures such as Daniel Boone, simply ignored the British injunction. Following the Revolutionary War, thousands of settlers funneled through the Cumberland Gap into Kentucky, following Boone's footsteps.

By 1800, 500,000 people (the vast majority from Virginia and North Carolina) had found rich and fertile land along the splendid rivers of the interior — the Tennessee, the Cumberland, and the Ohio, all draining into the Mississippi River, which marked the western boundary of the United States. Soon there was enough population for statehood. Kentucky (1792) and Tennessee (1796) were the first trans-Appalachian states admitted to the Union.

Migration was a principal feature of American life. A reasonable estimate is that 5 to 10 percent of

Founded in 1788 as a military fort for defense against the Shawnee and Miami Indians, Cincinnati's development mirrored the rapid growth of American settlements in the Ohio country. In this view, dated 1807, Cincinnati is well on its way to becoming "The Queen City of the West."

all American households relocated each year during the period from 1790 to 1825. In the rural areas of the Atlantic seaboard, a third of the households enumerated in the 1790 census had left by 1800; in cities the proportion was closer to half. In the West, meanwhile, rates of migration rose to as high as two-thirds of the community every ten years. Most moves were between neighboring communities or towns, but many families underwent the painful process of long-distance relocation. Migration was generally a family affair, with groups of kin moving together to a new area. One observer wrote of a caravan moving across the mountains, "They had prepared baskets made of fine hickory withe or splints, and fastening two of them together with ropes they put a child in each basket and put it across a pack saddle." Once pioneers had managed to struggle by road over the Appalachians, they gladly took to the rivers, and especially the Ohio River, to move farther west.

Cincinnati, strategically situated 450 miles downstream from Pittsburgh, was a particularly dramatic example of the rapid community growth and development that characterized the trans-Appalachian region. Founded in 1788, Cincinnati was located across the Ohio River from the Licking River, which reached south into Kentucky's rich bluegrass country. Cincinnati began life as a military fort defending settlers in the fertile Miami River valleys of Ohio from resistance by Shawnee and Miami Indians. Conflict between these Indian peoples and the new settlers was so fierce that the district was grimly referred to as "the slaughter house."

Cincinnati got its commercial start by serving as the supply point for military actions against Indian tribes throughout Ohio. After Indian resistance was broken in the Battle of Fallen Timbers in 1794 (see Chapter 8), Cincinnati became the point of departure for immigrants arriving by the Ohio River on their way to settle the interior of the Old Northwest: Ohio, Illinois, and Indiana. In the boom years of settlement, the number of people passing through was so great that the entire town seemed to consist of hotels and eating places. Francis Baily, author of *A Tour in the Unsettled Parts of North America,* based on his travels in 1796 and 1797, referred to Cincinnati as "the metropolis of the north-western territory." By 1800, the town had a population of about 750 people.

Cincinnati merchants were quick to forge good relations with farmers in the fertile Miami Valley nearby. Merchants were soon shipping farm goods down the Ohio–Mississippi River system to New Orleans, 1,500 miles away. The trip on barge or keelboat was chancy: snags could rip a boat apart, or the vessel could run aground on a sandbar and cost as much to refloat as the cargo was worth. Otherwise the downriver trip was rapid. Most difficult was the return trip, which could take as long as a hundred days from New Orleans to Cincinnati. Frequently rivermen simply abandoned their flatboats in New Orleans and traveled home overland, on foot or horseback, by the long and dangerous Natchez Trace that linked Natchez with Nashville, Tennessee. Steamboats, introduced on the Ohio River in 1815, dramatically reduced the return trip to as little as twenty-six days. Nevertheless, even before the age of steam, river traffic increased yearly, and the control of New Orleans became a key concern of western farmers and merchants. If New Orleans refused to accept American goods, Cincinnati merchants and many thousands of trans-Appalachian farmers would be ruined.

Atlantic Ports: Charleston to Boston

Although only 3 percent of the nation's population lived in cities, the Atlantic ports continued to exert the economic and political dominance they had exhibited in the colonial era. Seaports benefited from waterborne trade and communication, which were much faster than travel by land. Merchants in the seaboard cities found it much easier to cross the Atlantic than to venture into their own backcountry in search of trade. In 1800 the nation's most important urban centers were all Atlantic seaports: Philadelphia (which had a population of 70,000), Baltimore (26,000), Charleston (20,000), Boston (25,000), and New York (60,000). Each had a distinct regional identity.

Philadelphia, William Penn's "City of Brotherly Love," was distinguished by the commercial and banking skills of Quaker merchants. These merchants had built international trade networks for shipping the farm produce of Pennsylvania's German farmers. Philadelphia served as the nation's capital in the 1790s and was acknowledged as its cultural and intellectual leader as well.

Baltimore was the major port for the tobacco of the Chesapeake Bay region, and thus was connected with the slave-owning aristocracy of the Upper South. But proximity to the wheat-growing regions of the Pennsylvania backcountry increasingly inclined the city's merchants to look westward and to consider ways to tap the trade of the burgeoning Ohio country.

Charleston, South Carolina, was the South's premier port. In colonial days, Charleston had grown rich on its links with the British West Indies and on trade with England in rice, long-staple cotton, and indigo. The social center for the great low-country plantation owners, Charleston was a multicultural city (10,000 whites and 10,000 African Americans, 2,000 of them free). One was as likely to hear French, Spanish, or Gullah (the dialect of low-country African American slaves) as English. This graceful, elegant city was a center for the slave trade until 1808.

Boston, the cockpit of the American Revolution, was the capital of Massachusetts. In 1795, Bostonians built a handsome new State House on Beacon Hill, facing away from the seaport and toward the meadows of Boston Common. But they did not forget the source of their wealth: a carved wooden codfish occupied a place of honor in the new building. Boston's merchant wealth, founded first on West Indian and European markets for fish, had diversified into shipbuilding and shipping, and banking and insurance. Boston's merchant class soon built new homes near the State House. These stylish row houses signaled the dignity and affluence of New England's leading city.

New York, still faintly Dutch in architecture and social customs, was soon to outgrow all the other cities. New York merchants had already distinguished the port through their aggressive pursuit of trade. Unlike their counterparts in Philadelphia and Boston, they accepted the British system of auctioning merchandise, which cut out the middleman and allowed British exporters to sell goods in large lots directly to American customers. As a result, British merchants shipped their goods to America through New York. Middlemen importers suffered, but New York's shipping, banking, insurance, and supporting industries boomed. As early as 1800, a quarter of all American shipping was owned by New York merchants.

Though small in population, these Atlantic cities led the nation—socially, politically, and above all economically. The growth and change that they were yet to experience vividly illustrate the dramatic economic development of the new nation. In the coming half century, the seaports that developed the strongest ties with the trans-Appalachian West were the cities that thrived.

A NATIONAL ECONOMY

In 1800 the new United States was a producer of raw materials. Today countries that export raw materials find themselves at the mercy of fluctuating world commodity prices that they cannot control. They have great difficulty finding ways to strengthen and diversify their economies. Just such a challenge faced the United States in 1800.

The Economy of the Young Republic

In 1800, the nation was predominantly rural and agricultural. According to the census of 1800, 94 in 100 Americans lived in communities of fewer than 2,500 people and four in five families farmed the land, either for themselves or for others. Farming families followed centuries-old traditions of working with hand tools and draft animals, producing most of their own food and fiber. Most Americans dressed in cloth that had been spun, woven, and tailored by women in their own families. It is difficult to say with any precision what proportion of farm produce outside the South ended up on the market. Seaboard farmers of the middle states and those near urban centers engaged in commercial farming, but they were a small minority. For most, production of a "surplus" to sell was a small sideline; crops were generally intended for home use. Commodities such as whiskey and hogs (both easy to transport, one in kegs and the other on the hoof) provided small and irregular cash incomes or items for barter. As late as 1820, only 20 percent of the produce of American farms was consumed outside the local community.

By contrast with the farms of the North, the plantation agriculture of the South was wholly commercial — and international. But slave owners were faced with a growing dilemma: their heavy capital investment in African American slave labor was not matched by a growth in the demand for traditional export crops. The tobacco trade, accounting for about a third of the value of all colonial exports, remained at or below pre-revolutionary levels, and the demand for rice had actually declined. The demand for cotton, on the other hand, grew rapidly, accompanying the boom in the industrial production of textiles in England and Europe. But the variety of cotton that grew best in the southern interior required an enormous investment of labor for extracting the seeds from the fiber. The cotton gin, perfected in 1793, mechanized this process. In so doing it provided the South with an export commodity for which there was an almost infinitely expanding demand.

The century turned, however, before cotton assumed a commanding place in the foreign trade of the United States. In 1790, increasing foreign demand for American goods and services hardly seemed likely. Trade with Great Britain, still the biggest customer for American raw materials, was considerably less than it had been before the Revolution. As an independent nation, the United States no longer received favored treatment from Great Britain, and was subject to the restrictive mercantilist regulations of the European powers. Americans were largely excluded from the lucrative West Indian trade, and their ships were taxed with discriminatory duties.

Shipping and the Economic Boom

In spite of those restrictions, the strong American shipping trade begun during the colonial era and centered in the Atlantic ports became a major asset in the 1790s. Seafaring Americans had both the

experience and the capital to take advantage of opportunities in international trade.

Events in Europe in the 1790s provided American shipping with extraordinary opportunities. The French Revolution, which began in 1789, marked the start of twenty-five years of continual warfare between Britain and France. As the European powers converted their ships from international trade to military purposes, American vessels were ready to replace them. All along the Atlantic seaboard, urban centers thrived as American ships carried European goods that could no longer be transported on British ships without danger of French attack (or vice versa). Because America was neutral, its merchants had the legal right to import European goods and promptly reexport them to other European countries without breaking international neutrality laws. (Even so, as described in Chapter 8, both the British and the French tried to prevent the practice.) Total exports tripled in value from 1793 to 1807, with reexports accounting for half of the total.

In every seaport, this booming trade stimulated the development of financial services, such as insurance companies, banks, and brokers, geared to international rather than local concerns. This financial infrastructure was to benefit both the southern export trade in cotton and the new factories of the North.

The vigorous international shipping trade had dramatic effects within the United States. The coastal cities all grew substantially in the period 1790–1820. In 1790, only twelve cities in the U.S. held more than 5,000 people and only 3 percent of the population was urban; by 1820 city dwellers made up 7 percent of the population and thirty-five cities had a population exceeding 5,000. This rapid urbanization occurred because rural workers were attracted to cities by expanding opportunities, not because (as in some Third World countries today) they were pushed off the farm by poverty. In fact, the rapid growth of cities stimulated farmers to produce the food to feed the new urban dwellers. Thus American urbanization in this period was a sign of vigorous economic growth.

The long series of European wars also allowed enterprising Americans to seize such lucrative international opportunities as the China trade. In 1784 the *Empress of China* set sail from New York for Canton with forty tons of ginseng. When it returned in 1785 with a cargo of teas, silks, and chinaware, the sponsors of the voyage, New York financier Robert Morris and his partners, made a 30 percent profit. Other merchants were quick to follow Morris's example, and to improve on it. In 1787 Robert Gray steered the Boston ship *Columbia* south around

Cape Horn, then north to Nootka Sound in the Pacific Northwest, where he bought sea otter skins cheaply from the coastal Chinook Indians. Then Gray sailed west across the Pacific to China, where he sold the furs at fabulous profits, before returning home, laden with tea, via the Cape of Good Hope. Gray thus became the first American captain to circumnavigate the globe. On his second voyage in 1792, Gray discovered the mouth of a major Northwest river, which he named for his ship. New England so dominated the China trade that the Chinook Indians called all whites "Bostons." Many an elegant mansion in Boston and other New England cities, such as Portland, Maine, Salem, Massachusetts, and Providence, Rhode Island, was built and furnished with the proceeds of that trade.

The active American participation in international trade fostered a strong and diversified shipbuilding industry. All of the major Atlantic ports boasted large shipbuilding enterprises. Each specialized in certain kinds of ships, from small sloops for the coastal trade to full-rigged sailing ships built ever larger as trade concentrated in major ports and the need to carry bulky cargo such as cotton grew. The average size of full-rigged ships built in a shipyard in Portsmouth, New Hampshire, for example, increased from 361 tons in 1825 to 833 tons in 1835 and 2,145 tons in 1855. Demands for speed increased as well, resulting in what many people have regarded as the flower of American shipbuild-

ing, the clipper ship. Built for speed, the narrow-hulled, many-sailed clipper ships of the 1840s and 1850s set records unequaled by any other ships of their size. In 1854, *Flying Cloud,* built in the Boston shipyards of Donald McKay, sailed from Boston to San Francisco — a 16,000-mile trip that usually took 150 to 200 days — in a mere 89 days. The clipper ships' average of 300 miles a day made them competitive with steamships through the 1850s.

The Export of Cotton and Regional Markets

The surge in international shipping that marked America's first success in the world economy largely benefited the North, where shipping had been important since early colonial times. The second success was the worldwide demand for cotton, which transformed the South (see Chapter 11).

The contribution of cotton to the American economy was immense. Cotton was America's single largest export, rising from 40 percent of total exports in 1816 to 63 percent in the late 1830s, then declining slightly but remaining at least half of the export total until the Civil War. Such figures made it inevitable that the southern planter class would demand a dominant voice in the politics of the nation.

The southern cotton boom had effects far beyond the South, for it provided opportunity for other regions to supply southern needs. The financial,

This picture shows the launching of the ship *Fame* from Becket's Shipyard in Essex, Massachusetts in 1802. Shipbuilding was a major New England industry. As this picture shows, a launching was a community event.
(George Ropes. Launching of the Ship FAME. 1802. Oil on canvas. Accession #108,332. Photograph by Mark Sexton. James Duncan Phillips Library. Peabody & Essex Museum.)

brokerage, and transportation aspects of the cotton trade were largely managed in the North. For example, merchants in New York, Baltimore, and Philadelphia owned most of the ships that carried southern cotton to England. The South became a major market for the manufactured goods produced by the new northern factories and workshops that we will examine in Chapter 12. Even imported European goods often traveled to the South by way of northern ports. The West, in turn, provided much of the food for the South, a market that was a powerful spur toward commercial agriculture.

Thus by 1820 each region of the country had developed distinctive characteristics. The North provided the commercial and financial spirit and institutions for the nation. The rural South supported a plantation society on the rich profits of the international demand for cotton. And the West rapidly moved toward commercial agriculture. The regions became increasingly interdependent economically. Bolstered first by the shipping boom and then by the surge in cotton exports, the United States in 1820 was well on its way to building a strong and diversified national economy. At the same time, the building of national unity was the preeminent political concern.

THE JEFFERSONIANS

Thomas Jefferson began his presidency with a symbolic action worthy of a twentieth-century media-wise politician. At noon on March 4, 1801, Jefferson walked from his modest boardinghouse through the swampy streets of the new federal city of Washington to the unfinished Capitol. Washington and Adams had ridden in carriages to their inaugurals. Jefferson, refusing even a military honor guard, demonstrated by his actions that he rejected the elaborate, quasi-monarchical style of the two Federalist presidents, and their (to his mind) autocratic style of government as well.

Tall, ungainly, and diffident in manner, Thomas Jefferson was nonetheless a man of genius. Jefferson designed and supervised every aspect of the building and furnishing of Monticello, his classical home atop a hill in Charlottesville, Virginia. The process took almost 40 years (from 1770 to 1809), for Jefferson constantly changed and refined his design, subjecting both himself and his family to years of uncomfortable living in the partially-completed structure. The result, however, was one of the most civilized — and the most autobiographical — houses ever built.

For all its lack of pretension, Jefferson's inauguration as the third president of the United States was a truly momentous occasion in American history, for it marked the peaceful transition from one political party, the Federalists, to their hated rivals, the Republicans. Some Federalists were convinced that Jefferson's election meant a government of "the worthless, the dishonest, . . . the merciless and the ungodly," as a party newspaper bluntly put it. When the election was thrown into the House of Representatives (see Chapter 8), Federalist congressmen had tried to block Jefferson. In this context of political bitterness, one of the greatest achievements of Jefferson's presidency was to demonstrate that a strongly led party system could shape national policy without leading either to dictatorship or to revolt.

Republican Agrarianism

Jefferson brought to the presidency a clearly defined political philosophy. Behind all the events of his administration (1801–09) and those of his successors in what became known as the Virginia Dynasty — James Madison (1809–17) and James Monroe (1817–25) — was a clear set of beliefs, frequently called Jeffersonianism.

Jefferson's years as ambassador to France in the 1780s were particularly important in shaping his political thinking. Although he was strongly attracted to Parisian culture and advanced philosophical thinking, Jefferson recoiled from the extremes of wealth and poverty he saw in France. He came to believe that it was impossible for Europe to achieve a just society that could guarantee to most of its members the "life, liberty and . . . pursuit of happiness" of which he had written in the Declaration of Independence. Only America, Jefferson believed, provided fertile earth for the true citizenship necessary to a republican form of government. Governments that encouraged concentrations of wealth and inequalities between rich and poor, as Jefferson believed the Federalists did, destroyed the possibility of republicanism.

What America had, and Europe lacked, was room to grow in — enough room for any man so inclined to own his own land. (Although single women could own land, a married woman's property belonged to her husband, and farming was a family enterprise.) Jefferson envisaged a nation of small family farms clustered together in rural communities — an agrarian republic. He believed that only a nation of roughly equal yeoman farmers, each secure in his own possessions and not dependent

This symbol of the Philadelphia Society for Promoting Agriculture illustrates the principles of Republican agrarianism. The yeoman farmer is shown ploughing his field under the approving gaze of the female figure of Columbia. His activity expresses the values of the American republic that she represents.

upon someone else for his livelihood, would exhibit the concern for the community good that was essential in a republic. When Jefferson thought of politics, he thought only of men, for although Republican mothers played a vital role in building the nation by shaping the character of their sons, women did not have the right to vote. More romantically, Jefferson also believed that rural contact with the cycles and rhythms of nature was essential to the republican character. Indeed, Jefferson said that "those who labor in the earth are the chosen people of God," and so he viewed himself, though his "farm" was the large slave-owning plantation of Monticello.

Jefferson's pessimism about the inevitable injustice of European societies seemed to be confirmed by the failure of the French Revolution. By 1799, the electrifying revolutionary cry of "Liberté, égalité, fraternité" had been replaced by the military dictatorship of Napoleon Bonaparte. Another European development, the growth of the factory system in England, seemed almost as horrifying. Jefferson was not alone in deploring the environmental and personal squalor of teeming new factory towns such as Manchester in the north of England. He opposed industrialization in America: in the 1790s, when Alexander Hamilton and the Federalists had proposed fostering manufactures in the United States, Jefferson had responded with outrage (see Chapter 8). He was convinced that the Federalist program would create precisely the same extremes of wealth and the same sort of unjust government that prevailed in Europe.

Yet another European event influenced Jefferson's thinking. In 1798, the Englishman Thomas Malthus published a deeply pessimistic and widely influential *Essay on the Principle of Population.* Warning of an impending population explosion, Malthus predicted that the British population would soon outstrip the country's food supply. Unless this population growth were checked, misery and poverty would soon be widespread. Other European countries would suffer the same fate, and so, Malthus warned, would America. Until then, Americans had taken pride in having one of the fastest rates of population growth in the world. Benjamin Franklin had boasted that the natural health and opportunity of America had caused the population to grow by a third every decade. (His estimate was low. The actual rate was closer to 40 percent per decade: 3,930,000 in 1790, 5,310,000 in 1800, 7,240,000 in 1810.) Now, however, Malthus's forecast worried many Americans — but not Thomas Jefferson, who simply pointed to America's vast land resources. The Malthusian prediction need not trouble the United States, Jefferson said, as long as the country kept expanding.

Jefferson, avid naturalist and geographer, knew better than most of his contemporaries just how great a potential the American West actually held. Space was critical: room for city dwellers to acquire land and become farmers, room for farmers' sons to move to land of their own, room for industrious immigrants to get a fresh start, room for them all to grow the crops that would feed Malthus's predicted hordes, room for people of different political opinions to spread out and not interfere with one another.

Jefferson's vision of an expanding agrarian republic was politically persuasive in his own day. Thanks to the votes primarily of southern and western farmers, Jefferson's Republicans controlled both the presidency and the Congress from 1801 to 1825. His bitter political opponents, the Federalists, opposed expansion and dwindled to a small sectional party, disappearing after 1816. Jefferson's philosophy has remained one of the most compelling statements of American uniqueness and special destiny. But the expansionist spirit contained some negative aspects. The lure of the western lands fostered constant mobility and dissatisfaction rather than the stable, settled communities of yeoman farmers that Jefferson had envisaged. Expansionism caused environmental damage, in particular soil exhaustion — a consequence of abandoning old lands, rather than conserving them, and moving on to new ones. Finally, expansionism bred a ruthlessness toward the Indian peoples, who were pushed out of the way for white settlement or who, like the Mandans, were devastated by the diseases that accompanied European trade and contact. Jeffersonianism thus bred some of the best and some of the worst traits of the developing nation.

Jefferson's Government

Thomas Jefferson took office with a program of "simplicity and frugality," promising to cut all internal taxes, reduce the size of the army (from 4,000 to 2,500 men), navy (from twenty-five ships to seven), and government staff, and to reduce the national debt. He kept all of these promises, even the last, although the Louisiana Purchase of 1803 cost the Treasury $15 million. This diminishment of government was a key matter of republican principle to Jefferson. If his ideal yeoman farmer was to be a truly self-governing citizen, the federal government must not, Jefferson believed, be either large or powerful. His cost-cutting measures simply carried out the pledge he had made in his inaugural address for

> a wise and frugal government, which shall restrain men from injuring one another, which shall leave them otherwise free to regulate their own pursuits.

Perhaps one reason for Jefferson's success was that the federal government he headed was small and unimportant by today's standards. For instance, Jefferson found only 130 federal officials in Washington (a grand total of nine in the State Department, including the secretary of state). The national government's main function for ordinary people was mail delivery, and already in 1800 there were persistent complaints about slowness, unreliability, and expense in the Postal Service! Everything else — law and order, education, welfare, road maintenance, economic control — rested with state or local governments. Power and political loyalty were still local, not national.

This also explains why for years the nation's capital was so small and unimpressive. The French designer Pierre L'Enfant had laid out a magnificent plan of broad streets and sweeping vistas reminiscent of Paris. Congress planned to pay for the grand buildings with money from land sales in the new city, but few people besides politicians and boardinghouse keepers (a largely female occupation) chose to live in Washington. Construction lagged: the President's House lacked a staircase to the second floor until 1808, and although the House and Senate chambers were soon completed, the central portion of the Capitol was missing. Instead of the imposing dome we know so well today, the early Capitol consisted of two white marble boxes connected by a boardwalk. It is a telling indicator of the true location of national power that a people who repeatedly built new local communities across the continent should have had such difficulty establishing their federal city.

An Independent Judiciary

While cutting back on the size and expense of government and (not incidentally) removing Federalist officeholders, Jefferson provoked a landmark decision from the third branch of government, the Supreme Court. In the last days of the Adams administration, the Federalist-dominated Congress passed a Judiciary Act that created sixteen new judgeships and six new circuit courts and provided for officials to staff them. President Adams, in one of his last acts in office, appointed Federalists — quickly dubbed the "midnight appointees" — to the new positions. This last-minute action angered the Republicans, who had won control of Congress as well as the presidency in the 1800 election. They feared that the Federalist party, though it had lost the election, would use the judiciary to continue the political struggle between the two parties. Soon Congress was complaining about biased decisions by Federalist judges, and it repealed the Judiciary Act, thus rendering the new judges unemployed. One of these hapless appointees, William Marbury, sued James Madison, Jefferson's secretary of state, to recover the position he had lost.

At issue in the judiciary controversy was the question of the role of the courts in the federal government. Should judges change when party control of government changed, or was the judiciary independent and thus protected from political attack? In his celebrated 1803 decision, *Marbury v. Madison,* Chief Justice John Marshall, himself a strong Federalist and an Adams appointee, managed to find a way to please both parties. On the one hand, Marshall proclaimed that the courts had a duty "to say what the law is," thus unequivocally defending the independence of the judiciary and the principle of judicial review. On the other hand, Marshall conceded that the Supreme Court could not force the executive branch to appoint Marbury to a position that no longer existed. At first glance, Jefferson's government appeared to have won the battle over Adams's midnight appointees. But in the long run, Marshall established the principle that only the federal judiciary — not the Congress, not state legislatures — could decide what was constitutional. This was a vital step in realizing the three-part balance of power envisaged in the Constitution — president, Congress, judiciary. Equally important, during his long tenure in office (1801–35) Chief Justice Marshall consistently led the Supreme Court in a series of decisions that favored the federal government over state governments. Under Marshall's direction, the Supreme Court became a powerful nationalizing and unifying force.

Opportunity: The Louisiana Purchase

Thomas Jefferson's overriding concern as president was with the domestic politics of the United States, but he could never ignore foreign affairs. In 1800 the United States was a new and fragile democracy in a world of contending great powers: Great Britain and France. During the past half century, the two great European enemies had repeatedly used the North American continent as a battleground and had involved Americans in their struggles. First the British (with American help) had won Canada and the Ohio River drainage from the French and their Indian allies in 1763. In retaliation, the French had given money, military support, and diplomatic assistance to the Americans in their struggle for independence. In the 1790s, the French Revolution had dangerously polarized attitudes within the American government. Now, in 1800, another chapter in the French–British struggle was about to begin, one that would offer both opportunities and problems for the American republic.

In 1799 the young general Napoleon Bonaparte, promising the French people a glorious future, seized control of France and began a career of military conquests. Four years later Great Britain went to war against him, beginning a twelve-year duel that ended only with Napoleon's defeat at the Battle of Waterloo in 1815. As had his predecessors, Napoleon looked at North America as a potential battleground on which to fight the British. In 1800, in a secret treaty, Napoleon acquired the Louisiana Territory, the vast western drainage of the Mississippi and Missouri rivers, from Spain, which had held the region since 1763. From Louisiana, if he chose, Napoleon could launch an attack to regain Canada from the British.

When President Jefferson learned of the secret

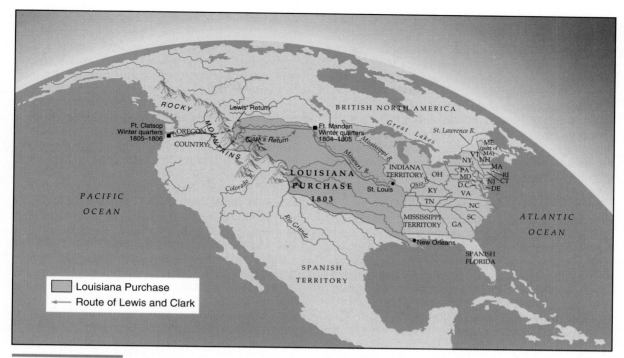

Louisiana Purchase

The Louisiana Purchase of 1803, the largest peaceful acquisition of territory in United States history, more than doubled the size of the nation. The Lewis and Clark Expedition, (1804–06) was the first to survey and document the natural and human richness of the area. The American sense of expansiveness and continental destiny owes more to the extraordinary opportunity of the Louisiana Purchase than to any other single source.

agreement in 1801, he was alarmed. He was not eager to have the belligerent French as neighbors. In particular, Jefferson feared that French control would threaten the growing American trade on the Mississippi River. In fact, in 1802 the Spanish commander at New Orleans (the French had not yet taken formal control) refused Americans the right to deposit their cargoes there before transferring them to ocean-going ships. This action effectively closed the port to American shippers, thus disrupting commerce as far away as Cincinnati.

Responding to these events, Jefferson instructed James Monroe and Robert R. Livingston to buy New Orleans and the surrounding area (then known as West Florida) for $2 million (or up to $10 million, if necessary). Arriving in France in 1803 to join Livingston, who was the American ambassador, Monroe found a golden opportunity. Napoleon had decided that there were better military opportunities closer to hand in Europe. He offered the entire Louisiana Territory, including the crucial port of New Orleans, to the Americans for $15 million. In April 1803 Monroe and Livingston seized the moment and bought the Louisiana Territory of approximately

825,000 square miles, thereby more than doubling the size of the United States overnight. It was the largest peaceful acquisition of territory in United States history.

At home, Jefferson suffered brief qualms. The Constitution did not explicitly authorize the president to purchase territory, and Jefferson had heretofore favored a limited interpretation of executive rights. But he had long held a sense of destiny about the West, and had planned Lewis and Clark's famous exploration long before the Louisiana Purchase was a reality. In any case, the prize was too rich to pass up. Jefferson soon came to believe that the Louisiana Purchase was vital to the nation's republican future. "By enlarging the empire of liberty," Jefferson wrote, "we . . . provide new sources of renovation, should its principles, at any time, degenerate, in those portions of our country which gave them birth." In other words, expansion was essential to liberty.

Both Congress and the general public joined Jefferson in welcoming the wonderful purchase. Of course, the support was not unanimous. Some New Englanders were alarmed at the dramatic expansion of the nation's territory. They feared, said Federalist senator William Plumer of New Hampshire, that New England interests would "shrink into a state of insignificance" as new western states were admitted to the Union. But the vast majority of Americans supported the purchase.

Thus when Lewis and Clark set forth from St. Louis in May of 1804, they were exploring American territory. After their winter with the Mandans, the party made an epic journey to the Pacific Ocean at the mouth of the Columbia River, and returned triumphantly to St. Louis in September of 1806. Their treasure trove of journals, maps, sketches, and scientific samples filled in a vast blank spot in American geographic and scientific knowledge. As well, the Lewis and Clark expedition opened up to trade a heretofore unknown territory and unfamiliar Indian tribes. Unfortunately, as the fate of the hospitable Mandan community shows, the biological effect of white contact was tragic for the natives, who had no immunity to European diseases.

The immediate issue following the Louisiana Purchase was how to treat the French and Spanish inhabitants of Louisiana Territory. Many people thought that the only way to deal with a population so "foreign" was to wipe out its customs and laws and impose American ones as quickly as possible. But this did not happen. The incorporation of Louisiana into the American federal system was a remarkable story of adaptation between two different communities — American and French.

In 1803, when the region that is now the state of Louisiana became American property, it had a racially and ethnically diverse population of 43,000 people, of whom only 6,000 were American. French and French-speaking people were numerically and culturally dominant, especially in the city of New Orleans. The French community of New Orleans effectively challenged the initial American plan of rapidly supplanting French culture and institutions with American ones. The first sign of French resistance came at a public ball held in New Orleans in January of 1804, where American and French military officers almost came to blows over whether an English country dance or a French waltz would be played first. Although officials in Washington dismissed the conflict as mere frivolity, the U.S. representative in New Orleans, William Claiborne, governor of Lower Louisiana Territory, did not. Over the next four years Claiborne came to accept the value of French institutions to the region. As a result, with Claiborne's full support, the Louisiana legal code established in 1808 was based on French civil law rather than English common law. This was not a small concession. French law differed from English

law in many fundamental respects, such as family property (communal versus male ownership), inheritance (forced heirship versus free disposal), and even contracts, which were much more strictly regulated in the French system. Statehood loomed next, and in 1812, with the required 60,000 free inhabitants having been counted in the thriving region, Louisiana was admitted to the Union as a slave state. New Orleans remained for years a distinctively French city, illustrating the flexibility possible under a federal system.

Aaron Burr, Jefferson's vice-president, played a small part in the New Orleans drama. Burr was notorious for his ambition and political intrigue. When Burr's bitter political enemy, Alexander Hamilton, said so publicly, Burr challenged him to a duel and in July of 1804 shot him dead. The vice-president thereupon became a fugitive from justice. Fleeing west, Burr raised a volunteer military force, supposedly to capture Mexico from the Spanish but perhaps to declare an independent state in the Southwest as well. In 1806, Burr was arrested by federal forces just as it seemed that he and his followers were about to attack New Orleans. Tried for treason in October of 1807, Burr was acquitted for lack of evidence, but he was ruined both personally and politically. His frightening escapade served to convince American officials in New Orleans and in Washington that accepting French and Spanish communities into the Union was preferable to secessionist conspiracies.

In November of 1804, Jefferson (and his new vice-president, George Clinton) scored a major victory over the Federalist Charles Cotesworth Pinckney, garnering 162 electoral votes to Pinckney's 14. This was not an accident. Jefferson was a shrewd party leader, and under his direction the Republican party had since 1800 worked through policy and patronage to woo moderate Federalists. The remaining Federalists, unwilling to be flexible like Jefferson, dwindled to a highly principled but sectional group. Although it contested the next several elections, the party found itself unable to attract voters outside of its home base in New England. The difficulties over neutral shipping that beset the country in the next few years bore particularly hard on New England, and served to underscore the Federalists' powerlessness and discontent.

Problems with Neutral Rights

In his first inaugural address in 1801, Jefferson had announced a foreign policy of "peace, commerce, and honest friendship with all nations, entangling alliance with none." This was a difficult policy to pursue after 1803, when the Napoleonic Wars resumed. By 1805 Napoleon had conquered most of Europe, but Britain, the victor at the great naval battle of Trafalger, controlled the seas. The United States, trying to profit from trade with both countries, was caught in the middle. The British did not look kindly on their former colonists trying to evade their blockade of the French by claiming neutrality. Beginning in 1805, the British targeted the American reexport trade between the French West Indies and France by seizing American ships bringing such goods to Europe. Angry Americans viewed such seizures as violations of their neutral rights as shippers.

An even more contentious issue arose from the substantial desertion rate of British sailors. Many deserters promptly signed up on American ships, where they drew better pay and sometimes false naturalization papers as well. The numbers involved were large: as many as a quarter of the 50,000 to 100,000 seamen on American ships were British. Soon the British were stopping American merchant vessels and removing any man they believed to be British, regardless of his papers. The British refusal to recognize genuine naturalization papers (on the principle "once a British subject, always a British

subject") was particularly insulting to the new American sense of nationhood.

At least 6,000 innocent American citizens suffered this impressment from 1803 to 1812, in addition, of course, to much larger numbers of British deserters. In 1807 impressment turned bloody when the British ship *Leopard* stopped the American ship *Chesapeake* in American territorial waters and demanded to search for deserters. When the American captain refused, the *Leopard* opened fire, killing three men, wounding eighteen, and removing four deserters (three with American naturalization papers) from the damaged ship. An indignant public protested British interference and the death of innocent sailors. Had Congress been in session, and had the country been militarily strong, public pressure might very well have forced a declaration of war against Britain then.

The Embargo Act

Jefferson, indignant as anyone, could not find a solution to the controversy over neutral rights. He realized that commerce was essential to the new nation. With the Louisiana Purchase, he had moved decisively to ensure Mississippi River trade through New Orleans, and he was equally determined to insist on America's right as neutrals to ship goods to Europe. But Britain possessed the world's largest and strongest navy. The small American navy could not effectively challenge the British (especially, Federalists pointed out, after the deep cuts Jefferson had inflicted upon it).

To find a peaceful solution, Jefferson tried diplomatic protests, negotiations, then threats, all to no avail. In 1806 Congress passed the Non-Importation Act, hoping that a boycott of British goods, which had worked so well during the Revolutionary War, would be effective once again. Jefferson hoped that British manufacturers, denied their customary American markets, would force a change in their government's policy. They did not. The boycott was suspended late in 1806 while the Jefferson administration tried to negotiate; when that effort failed, the boycott was resumed. Finally, in desperation, Jefferson imposed the Embargo Act in December of 1807. The act forbade American ships from sailing to any foreign port, thereby cutting off all exports as well as imports. In addition to loss of markets, British industry was now deprived of the raw materials they customarily bought from the United States. Again Jefferson hoped for a speedy change of British government policy.

But the results were a disaster, for the United States was deprived as well. The commerce of the

This official certificate of United States citizenship was issued to protect American sailors from British impressment. Frequently, however, British naval officers ignored them, claiming they were forged (as they sometimes were).

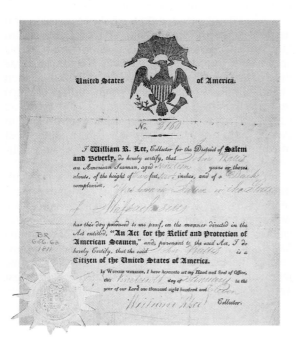

new nation, which Jefferson himself had done so much to promote, came to a standstill. Exports fell from $108 million in 1807 to $22 million in 1808, and the nation was driven into a deep depression. There was widespread evasion of the embargo. A remarkable number of ships in the coastal trade found themselves "blown off course" to the West Indies or Canada. Other ships simply left port illegally. Smuggling flourished. The Federalist party, at the brink of extinction in 1804, sprang to life with a campaign of outspoken opposition to Jefferson's policy. New England, hardest hit by the embargo, was ready to listen even to such radical statements as those of Governor Jonathan Trumbull of Connecticut. Trumbull warned that states had the right to "interpose" their authority between "the rights and liberties of the people and the assumed power of the general government."

The Election of 1808

In this troubled atmosphere, Thomas Jefferson despondently ended his second term, acknowledging the failure of what he called "peaceable coercion." He was followed in office by his friend and colleague, James Madison of Virginia. Madison received 122 electoral votes to only 47 for the Federalist ticket of Charles Pinckney and Rufus King. Nevertheless the Federalists' total marked a threefold increase over their share of the 1804 vote, reflecting the disproportionate hardships imposed upon New England by the Embargo Act.

Ironically, the Embargo Act had almost no effect on its intended victims. The French used the embargo as a pretext for seizing American ships, claiming they must be British ships in disguise. The British, in the absence of American competition, developed new markets for their goods in South America. And at home, as John Randolph sarcastically remarked, the embargo was attempting "to cure corns by cutting off the toes."

In March of 1809 Congress admitted failure, and the Embargo Act was repealed. But the struggle to remain neutral in the confrontation between the European giants continued. The next two years saw passage of several acts prohibiting trade with Britain and France unless they ceased their hostile treatment of U.S. shipping — among them the Non-Intercourse Act of 1809 and Macon's Bill Number 2 in 1810 — all to no avail. Frustration with the ineffectiveness of government policy mounted.

A Contradictory Indian Policy

Arguments with Britain and France over neutral shipping rights were not the only military troubles the United States faced. In the West, the powerful Indian nations of the Ohio Valley were determined to resist the wave of expansion that had carried thousands of white settlers onto their lands.

North of the Ohio River lived the Northwest Confederation of the Shawnee, Delaware, Miami, Potawatomi, and a number of smaller tribes. To the south of the Ohio were five major groups, the Cherokees, Creeks, Choctaws, Chickasaws, and (in Florida) the Seminoles. Pioneer settlement, first in the Kentucky–Tennessee area and later north of the Ohio River, had produced almost twenty years (1775–94) of undeclared warfare as the Indian groups resisted white incursions. The Shawnee, who resided in what is now Ohio but had hunting grounds in Kentucky, were particularly fierce in their resistance.

The constant state of warfare explains why trans-Appalachian settlement was predominantly *community* settlement. Fear of attack led the white settlers in these regions to group together for protection. The basic form of settlement in early Kentucky was the "station," or fort; north of the Ohio River, compact settlements on the New England model were favored. Few settlers sought the solitude of the wilderness: it was too dangerous. Few settlers were Indian sympathizers, either. The bloody nature of frontier warfare confirmed in most whites their fear and hatred of Indians.

According to United States policy toward Indian peoples since the Intercourse Act of 1790, Indian lands must be ceded by treaty rather than simply seized. But the reality of westward expansion was much harsher. Commonly, white settlers pushed ahead of treaty boundaries. When Indian peoples resisted the invasion of their lands, the pioneers called for military protection. Defeat of an Indian people led to further land cessions, and made almost inevitable a cycle of invasion, resistance, and military defeat.

Thomas Jefferson was deeply concerned with the fate of the western Indian peoples. Unlike most of the pioneers, who saw them simply as dangerous obstacles to be removed, Jefferson believed in coexistence and assimilation. Convinced that Indians had to give up hunting in favor of the yeoman-farmer lifestyle he so favored for all Americans, Jefferson directed the governors of the Northwest Territory, Michigan Territory, and Indiana Territory

This double portrait of two Sac Indians by John Wesley Jarvis, painted in 1833, symbolized the hopes of official American Indian policy. The traditional Indian ways of the father (shown in Black Hawk's hair and dress) would be superceded by the "civilized" attire and attitude of the son (as shown in Whirling Thunder's European dress). *(John Wesley Jarvis.* Black Hawk and His Son, Whirling Thunder. *1833. Oil on canvas. 23-3/4 × 30 in. (60.3 × 76 cm). Gilcrease Museum, Tulsa, Oklahoma.)*

to "promote energetically" his vision of civilizing the Indians.

Although he himself was notoriously indifferent to organized religion, Jefferson strongly supported efforts to Christianize Indian peoples and educate them in white ways. A number of denominations, among them the Moravians, Quakers, and Baptists, were eager to undertake missionary efforts among the transAppalachian Indians. Others formed special missionary societies, such as the Society for Propagating the Gospel among Indians (1797) and the American Board of Commissioners for Foreign Missions (1810). The latter was a joint effort of the Congregationalist, Presbyterian, and Dutch Reformed churches. The effect of the missionaries was mixed: although they promoted literacy and a knowledge of white ways, their general disdain for traditional Indian culture caused tribal splits between Christian and traditional groups. Thus, even well-intentioned missionary efforts served to further weaken tribes already disoriented by their enforced cession of lands and lifestyle.

Jefferson's Indian policy was designed to solve the dilemma of expansion — the conflicting needs of white and Indian peoples. The Indians would cede the lands the pioneers craved, and in return whites would teach farming and the white lifestyle on the Indians' new, compressed reservations. But Jefferson's Indian civilization plan was never adequately funded by Congress or supported by territorial governors and settlers.

Furthermore, the plan faced Indian resistance. Each tribe contained groups unwilling to give up traditional ways, especially hunting. After the Louisiana Purchase, Jefferson offered the unreconciled Indians new lands west of the Mississippi River. He meant this proposal sincerely, believing removed Indians would be able to live undisturbed by white settlers for centuries. But he failed to consider the pace of westward expansion. Less than twenty years later, Missouri, the first trans-Mississippi state, was admitted to the Union. The Indians living in Missouri, some of whom had been removed from the Old Northwest in accord with Jefferson's plan, were forced to move again to lands farther west. Western Indians like the Mandans and the Sioux, who had seemed so remote when Lewis and Clark wintered with them in 1804, were now threatened by further westward expansion.

Jefferson's removal plan was unrealistic, but the issue it raised did not disappear. Traditional Indian cultures could not survive the relentless and ever-accelerating white expansion. Deprived of hunting lands, decimated by disease, increasingly dependent on the white economy for trade goods and annuity payments in exchange for land cessions, and at the mercy of missionaries bent on civilizing them, many Indian peoples watched in dismay as their traditional lifestyles eroded. The choices they faced were stark: assimilation, removal, or extinction. Like the Mandans after Lewis and Clark's visit, Indian peoples came to dread the effects of white contact.

Many Indian nations did devise strategies of survival. In the South, the Cherokees and associated tribes adopted agricultural lifestyles and pursued a pattern of peaceful accommodation (see Chapter 11). In the Northwest Territory, however, the Shawnee followed the path of armed resistance.

Shawnee Resistance

The Shawnee, a hunting and farming tribe (the men hunted, the women farmed) of the Ohio Valley, had resisted white settlement in Kentucky and Ohio since the 1750s. Allied with the British in the Revolutionary War, the Shawnee maintained trade relations with them thereafter. Although the Treaty of Paris (1783) compelled the British to withdraw from the Ohio Valley, they did not do so. Not only did they retain their forts at Detroit and Michilimackinac, they built a third fort, Miami, in northwestern Ohio, in 1794. The Shawnee formed part of the fur trade that the British were eager to maintain, and they continued to use arms and supplies from the British forts to resist American settlement. Americans correctly suspected that the British were supporting the Shawnee, but their belief that Shawnee resistance would collapse without this aid was mistaken.

For their part, the Shawnee viewed white trans-Appalachian settlement as an invasion, and the various land treaties (Fort Stanwix, 1784; Fort McIntosh, 1785; Fort Finney, 1786; and Fort Harmar, 1789) as frauds. In some cases, the Indian signatories had no legitimate claim to the lands they had ceded; in other cases, minor chiefs inaccurately claimed to speak for all of their peoples. In Shawnee eyes the treaties were meaningless, and with other tribes of the Northwest Confederation they continued to fight white settlement. Perhaps as many as 1,500 Ohio country settlers were killed in the period 1783–90, and the confederated tribes embarrassed American military forces with victories in 1790 and 1791. The tide finally turned in the Americans' favor with the Battle of Fallen Timbers (1794) and the Treaty of Greenville (1795).

The decisive defeat at Fallen Timbers and the continuing pressure of American settlement split the Shawnee. One group, led by Black Hoof, accepted assimilation. Soon Quaker and Moravian missionaries were converting Black Hoof's band and teaching them farming. Most of the other Shawnee broke into small bands and tried to eke out a living by hunting, but they were demoralized by disease and by alcohol illegally offered by private traders. One group of traditional Shawnee, led by the warrior Tecumseh, escaped demoralization by moving farther west, away from the Americans, and attempting to continue their traditional seminomadic life of hunting and farming.

But there was no escape from white settlement. Between 1801 and 1809, William Henry Harrison, governor of Indiana Territory, concluded fifteen treaties with the Delaware, Potawatomi, Miami, and other tribes. These treaties opened eastern Michigan, southern Indiana, and most of Illinois to white settlement and compressed the Indians into ever-smaller reservations. Many of these treaties were obtained by coercion, bribery, and outright trickery, and most Indians did not accept them.

In 1805 Tecumseh's brother, Tenskwatawa, The Prophet, began preaching a message of Indian revitalization: a return to traditional ways and a rejection of all contact with the Americans. Tenskwatawa urged his listeners to reject American alcohol, clothing, and trade goods and to return to traditional practices of hunting and farming. He preached an end to quarreling, violence, and sexual promiscuity, and to the accumulation of private property. Wealth was only valuable if it was given away, he said. If the Northwest Indians returned to traditional ways, Tenskwatawa promised, "the land will be overturned so that all the white people will be covered and you alone shall inhabit the land."

This was a powerful message, but it was not new. Just six years earlier, Handsome Lake had led the Seneca people of upstate New York in a similar revitalization movement. What made Tenskwatawa's message different was that it enabled Tecumseh to mold his brother's religious following into a powerful pan-Indian resistance movement. With each new treaty that Harrison concluded, Tecumseh gained new followers among the Northwest Confederation tribes who shared his determination to gain back the lost lands.

After 1807 (the year of the incident involving the *Chesapeake* and the *Leopard*), the British, expecting the Americans to declare war, began sending food and guns to Tecumseh from Canada. They also promised an alliance with the Indians if war broke out between Britain and America. Harrison, aware of Tecumseh's contacts with the British, seriously overestimated both the extent of British support and Tecumseh's readiness to go to war. Tecumseh's strategy was at first primarily defensive: he wished to prevent further westward expansion.

But after the Treaty of Fort Wayne in 1809, in which the United States gained 3 million acres of Delaware and Potawatomi land in Indiana, Tecumseh moved from passive to active resistance. Confronting Harrison directly, Tecumseh argued that the

Indian Lands, 1812

American westward expansion put relentless pressure on Indian nations. Some lands were ceded peacefully, but violence was common. The Trans-Appalachian region was marked by constant warfare from the time of the earliest settlements in Kentucky in the 1780s to the War of 1812. Tecumseh's Alliance in the Northwest (1809–11) and the Creek Rebellion in the Southwest (1813–14) were the culminating struggles in the Indian resistance to the American invasion of the Trans-Appalachian region.

Tecumseh (shown here) and his brother Tenskwatawa (The Prophet) led an Indian revitalization and resistance movement that posed a serious threat to American settlement of the Old Northwest. British abandonment of their Shawnee allies at the end of the War of 1812 and Tecumseh's death at the Battle of Thames (1813) marked the end of organized Indian resistance in the Old Northwest.

land belonged to the larger community of all the Indian peoples; no one tribe could give away the common property of all. He then warned that any surveyors or settlers who ventured into the 3 million acres would risk their lives.

Tecumseh took his message of common land ownership and military resistance to all the Indian peoples of the Northwest Confederacy. Even among the Shawnee, though, Tecumseh was not uniformly successful. Black Hoof, for example, refused to join. Nevertheless, by 1811 over 1,000 warriors were gathered at a common village, Tippecanoe (Prophetstown) in northern Indiana.

Tecumseh also recruited among the tribes south of the Ohio River. In councils with Choctaws, Chickasaws, Creeks, and Cherokees, he preached a stark message:

> The white race is a wicked race. Since the days when the white race first came in contact with the red men, there has been a continual series of aggressions. The hunting grounds are fast disappearing, and they are driving the red man farther and farther to the west. Such has been the fate of the Shawnees, and surely will be the fate of all tribes if the power of the whites is not forever crushed. The mere presence of the white man is a source of evil to the red men. His whiskey destroys the bravery of our warriors, and his lust corrupts the virtue of our women. The only hope for the red man is a war of extermination against the paleface.

But the southern tribes, who had chosen assimilation, refused to join with Tecumseh.

In November of 1811, while Tecumseh was still recruiting among the southern tribes, Harrison marched to Tippecanoe with 1,000 soldiers. The 600 to 700 Indian fighters at the town, urged on by Tenskwatawa, attacked Harrison's forces before dawn on November 7, hoping to surprise them. The attack failed, and in the battle that followed the Americans inflicted about 150 Indian casualties, while sustaining about as many themselves. This was a costly victory to the Americans, but it achieved its aim: Tecumseh's military alliance was shattered.

But that was not the end of warfare in the Northwest. Dispersed from Tippecanoe, Tecumseh's angry followers fell upon American settlements in Indiana and southern Michigan, killing many pioneers and forcing the rest to flee to fortified towns. To western settlers, the Indian threat seemed greater than ever. Their fears and anger now joined with those of other Americans to produce war fever.

The War of 1812

Many westerners blamed the British for Tecumseh's attacks on pioneer settlements in the Northwest. Control over western Indians and the long-standing difficulties over neutral shipping rights were the two grievances cited by President Madison when he asked Congress for a declaration of war against Britain on June 1, 1812; Congress obliged him on June 18. But the war had other, more general causes as well.

A rising young generation of political leaders, first elected to Congress in 1810, felt a strong sense of colonial resentment against Britain, the former mother country. These War Hawks, who included such future leaders as Henry Clay of Kentucky and John C. Calhoun of South Carolina, were young Republicans from the South and West. They found all aspects of continuing British dominance, such as impressment and the support of western Indians, intolerable. The War Hawks were eager to strike a blow for national honor by asserting complete independence from England once and for all. These young men saw themselves finishing the job begun by the aging revolutionary generation.

The War Hawks were vehemently expansionist. Southerners wanted to occupy Florida to prevent runaway slaves from seeking refuge with the Seminole Indians. Westerners wanted to invade Canada, hoping thereby to end threats from British-supported Northwest Indians such as Tecumseh. What powered these dreams of expansion, then, was a concern about control over peoples of other races at the edges of the national boundaries. As resentments against England and frustrations over border issues merged, war — always a strong force for national unity — increasingly seemed the solution.

James Madison, Jefferson's long-time collaborator and Virginia neighbor, had succeeded to the presidency in 1809. Madison possessed the finest theoretical mind of the Revolutionary generation, and had contributed his best thought to the framing of the Constitution. But in day-to-day affairs he was indecisive. He yielded to the War Hawks' clamor for action in June of 1812, not realizing that the British,

The War of 1812

On land, the War of 1812 was fought to define the nation's boundaries. In the north, American armies attacked British forts in the Great Lakes region with little success, and the invasion of Canada was a failure. In the south, the Battle of New Orleans made a national hero of Andrew Jackson, but occurred after the peace treaty had been signed. On the sea, with the exception of Perry's victory in the Great Lakes, British dominance was so complete and their blockade so effective that they were able to burn the capital, Washington.

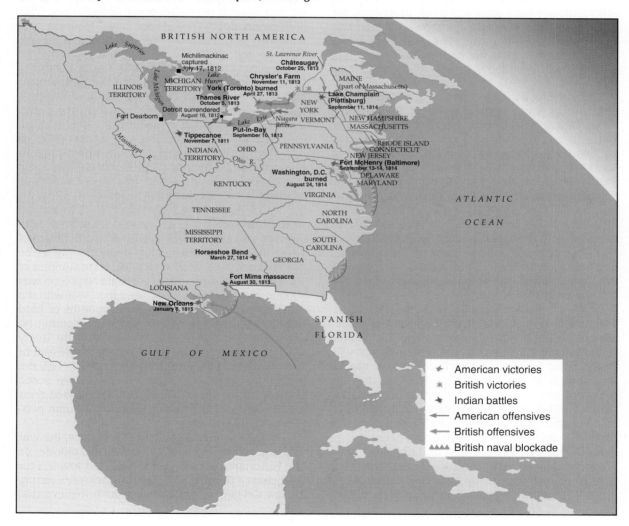

hurt by the American trade embargo, were just then adopting a more conciliatory policy. In the slow world of nineteenth century communications, when it could take 6 weeks for a British ship to reach America, Madison did not yet know of the British willingness to compromise when he declared war.

Madison's declaration of war passed the U.S. Senate by the close vote of 19 to 13 and the House by 79 to 49. All the Federalists voted against the war. (The division along party lines continued in the 1812 presidential election, in which Madison garnered 128 electoral votes to 89 for his Federalist opponent, DeWitt Clinton.) The vote was sectional, with New England and the Middle Atlantic states in opposition and the West and South strongly prowar. Thus the United States entered the War of 1812 more deeply divided along sectional lines than in any other foreign war in American history.

Nor was that the end of the difficulties. As a result of Jefferson's economizing, the American army and navy were small and weak. In contrast, the British, fresh from almost ten years of Napoleonic Wars, were in fighting trim. The Americans had a few glorious moments, but on the whole the War of 1812 was an ignominious struggle that gained them little.

Expansion, a major American goal, fared badly. Southerners were unable to wrest Florida from Spain (Britain's ally). Grand claims about a quick victory over Canada proved mistaken: a quick foray into western Canada by General William Hull of Michigan Territory was repulsed by British and Indian forces, which went on to capture Detroit and Fort Dearborn from the Americans. The American burning of York (now Toronto) in 1813 achieved little. Ironically, the most decisive effect of the abortive American attacks was the formation of a Canadian sense of national identity. The Canadian determination never to be invaded or absorbed by the United States was an unintended by-product of the War of 1812.

Overall, the war went badly for the Americans. The British navy quickly established a strong blockade, harassing coastal shipping along the Atlantic seaboard and attacking coastal settlements at will. In the most humiliating attack, the British burned Washington in the summer of 1814, forcing the president and Congress to flee. (After the war, the damaged President's House was repainted white, thus becoming the White House.) There were a few American military successes. Commodore Oliver Perry's ships defeated a British fleet on Lake Erie in 1813, whereupon Perry sent the famous message "We have met the enemy and they are ours." In early 1815 (after the peace treaty had been signed)

Andrew Jackson improbably won a lopsided victory over veteran British troops in the Battle of New Orleans.

One reason for the failure of the Canadian invasion, aside from overconfidence, was the active opposition of the New England states to the war. Massachusetts, Rhode Island, and Connecticut refused to provide militia or supplies, and other New England governors turned a blind eye to the flourishing illegal trade across the U.S.–Canadian border. Opposition to the war culminated in the Hartford Convention of 1814, where representatives — all Federalists — from the five New England states met to discuss their grievances. At first the air was full of talk of secession from the Union, but soon cooler heads prevailed.

The final document contained a long list of grievances, but it did not mention secession. The convention did, however, insist that a state had the right "to interpose its authority" to protect its citizens against unconstitutional federal laws. This *nullification* doctrine was not new. Madison and Jefferson (anonymously) had proposed it in the Virginia and Kentucky resolutions opposing the Sedition Act in 1798. Nor was the Hartford Convention's proposal for nullification the last in American history. In 1832 South Carolina's threat of nullification would endanger national unity. In any event, the nullification threat from Hartford was ignored, for peace with Britain was announced as delegates from the convention made their way to Washington to deliver their message to Congress. There the convention's grievances were treated not as serious business but as an anticlimactic joke.

By 1814, the long Napoleonic Wars in Europe were slowly drawing to a close. Napoleon was deposed and exiled to the island of Elba in March of 1814. In 1815, he escaped to France, only to be defeated at the Battle of Waterloo. In the summer of 1814 the British (unaware of the fright Napoleon was soon to give them) decided to end their war with the Americans. The peace treaty, after months of hard negotiation, was signed at Ghent, Belgium, on Christmas Eve in 1814. Like the war itself, the treaty was inconclusive. The big issues of impressment and neutral rights were not mentioned, but the British did agree to evacuate their western posts, and late in the negotiations they abandoned their insistence on a buffer state for neutral Indian peoples in the Northwest.

For all its international inconsequence, the war did have an important effect on national morale. As one historian has said, Americans had fought "for their chance to grow up." Andrew Jackson's victory at New Orleans allowed Americans to believe that they had defeated the British. It would be more accurate to say that by not losing the war the Americans had ended their own feelings of colonial dependency. Equally important, they convinced the British government to stop thinking of America as its colony. As it turned out, the War of 1812 was the last war the United States and Britain were to fight with each other.

The War of 1812 was America's most unpopular war, arousing more intense opposition than any other American conflict, including Vietnam. What made the opposition so serious was its sectional nature, which might have led to the secession of New England if the conflict had continued. Today most historians regard the war as both unnecessary and a dangerous risk to new and fragile ideas of national unity. Fortunately for its future, the United States as a whole came out relatively unscathed, and the Battle of New Orleans had provided last-minute balm for its hurt pride.

The only clear losers of the war were the northwestern Indian nations. In October of 1813 William Henry Harrison, assisted by Commodore Perry, defeated a British–Indian force at the Battle of the Thames. Among those slain in the battle was Tecumseh. With him died the last hope of a united Indian resistance to white expansion. Britain's abandonment of its Indian allies in the Treaty of Ghent sealed their fate. By 1815, American settlers were on their way west again.

DEFINING THE BOUNDARIES

With the War of 1812 behind them, Americans turned, more seriously than ever before, to the task of building the identity of the United States of America. In this process, expansion and the definition of national interest were both important.

Another Westward Surge

The end of the war was followed by a westward surge to the Mississippi River and beyond, which populated the Old Northwest (Ohio, Indiana, Illinois) and the Old Southwest (western Georgia, Alabama, Mississippi, Louisiana). The extent of the population redistribution was dramatic: in 1790, 95 percent of the nation's population had lived in states bordering the Atlantic Ocean; by 1820 fully 25 percent of the population lived west of the Appalachians.

What accounted for the westward surge? There were both push and pull factors. Between 1800 and 1820, the nation's population almost doubled, increasing from 5.3 million to 9.6 million. Although a number of easterners were attracted to the rapidly growing seacoast cities, 2.5 million, most of them farmers, chose to go west. Overpopulated farmland in all of the seaboard states pushed farmers off the land, while new land pulled them westward. Removal of the Indian threat by the War of 1812 was another important pull factor.

There were four major migration routes. In upstate New York, the Mohawk and Genesee turnpike led New England migrants to Lake Erie, where they traveled by boat to northern Ohio. In the Middle Atlantic region, the turnpike from Philadelphia to Pittsburgh led to the Ohio River, as did the road that began in Baltimore, linked with the National Road, and led through the Cumberland Gap to Wheeling. In the South, there were passes in the mountains of North and South Carolina that led to Tennessee, but the main route skirted the southern edge of the Appalachians and allowed farmers from South

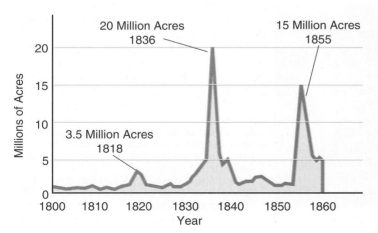

Western Land Sales

Western land sales illustrate the surges of westward expansion. The western land sales surge after the War of 1812 reached 3.5 million acres, dwarfing all earlier expansions. But it was tiny in comparison to the later land sales of the 1830s and the 1850s. Not all land sales reflected actual settlement, however. Speculation in western lands was rampant: Collapse of the postwar speculative boom helped to cause the Panic of 1819, and the abrupt end to the boom of the 1830s led to the Panic of 1837.

Source: Robert Riegel and Robert Athearn, *America Moves West* (New York: Holt, Rinehart, 1964).

Carolina and eastern Georgia to move directly into Alabama and Mississippi. In this way, geography facilitated lateral westward movement (northerners tended to migrate to the Old Northwest, southerners to the Old Southwest). Except in southern Ohio and parts of Kentucky and Tennessee, there was very little contact between regional cultures. New Englanders carried their values and lifestyles directly west and settled largely with their own communities, and southerners did the same, as the following two examples show.

One section of northern Ohio along Lake Erie had been Connecticut's western land claim since the days of its colonial charter. Rather than give up the land when the Northwest Territory was established in 1787, Connecticut held onto the Western Reserve (as it was known) and encouraged its citizens to move there. Group settlement was common. Revolutionary general Moses Cleaveland led one of the first groups of Yankees, fifty-two in all. In 1795 they settled the community that bears his name (though

not his spelling of it). Many other groups followed, naming towns such as Norwalk after those they had left in Connecticut. These New Englanders brought to the Western Reserve their religion (Congregational), their love of learning (tiny Norwalk soon boasted a three-story academy), and their adamant opposition to slavery.

A very different migration occurred to the south. Just as on other frontiers, pioneers hacked wagon roads through the wilderness, encountered resistance from Indian peoples, and cleared the land for settlements and farms. But on this frontier, the hands on the ax handle were likely to be black, clearing land not for themselves but to create plantations for slave owners. More than half of the people who flooded into the Old Southwest after 1812 were enslaved African Americans.

Even before the war, plantation owners in the Natchez district of Mississippi had made fortunes growing cotton, which they shipped to Britain from New Orleans. After the war, as cotton growing

Settlement of the heavily-forested Old Northwest and Old Southwest required much heavy labor to clear the land. One common labor-saving method was to "girdle" the trees (cutting the bark all around), thereby killing them. Dead trees could be more easily chopped and burned.

expanded, hopeful slave owners from older parts of the South (Virginia, North and South Carolina, Georgia) flooded into the region, and so, involuntarily, did their slaves. The movement was like a gold rush, characterized by high hopes, land speculation, and riches — for a few. Most of the settlers in the Old Southwest were small farmers living in forest clearings. Most did not own slaves, but they hoped to, for ownership of slaves was the means to wealth. Quickly, the lifestyle and values of older southern states were replicated on this new frontier.

Thus were distinctive regional cultures transplanted to the West. This explains why, although western states accounted for over a third of the states (eight out of twenty-three) by 1820, the West did not develop as a distinct third region in political terms. In general, communities in the Old Northwest shared New England political attitudes, while those in the Old Southwest shared southern attitudes.

The Election of 1816 and the Era of Good Feelings

In 1816 James Monroe, the last of the "Virginia Dynasty" (following Jefferson and Madison), was easily elected president over his Federalist opponent, Rufus King (183 to 34 electoral votes). This was the last election in which Federalists ran a candidate. Monroe had no opponent in 1820 and was reelected nearly unanimously (231 to 1). The triumph of the Jeffersonian Republicans appeared complete. But new forces, both economic and sectional, were germinating that would dramatically affect the political system in years to come. In the meantime, unwittingly, Monroe presided over a transitional period.

Tall, dignified, dressed in the old-fashioned style of knee breeches and white-topped boots that Washington had worn, Monroe looked like a traditional figure. But his politics reflected changing times. Soon after his inauguration, Monroe made a goodwill tour of the country, the first president since Washington to do so. Monroe's tour illustrated the new shape of the nation, for he visited the frontier post of Detroit, the farthest west any president had ever traveled. He also exemplified a new mood. Monroe visited Boston, as recently as 1815 the heart of a secession-minded Federalist region. Now he was greeted with enthusiastic welcomes, prompting the Federalist *Columbian Centinel* to report that "during the late Presidential Jubilee many persons have met at festive boards, in pleasant converse, whom party politics had long severed." The news-

paper characterized the mood as an "Era of Good Feelings", a phrase that has been applied to Monroe's presidency (1817–25) ever since.

Monroe sought a government of national unity, and he chose men from North and South, Republicans and Federalists, for his Cabinet. He selected John Quincy Adams, a former Federalist, as his secretary of state, virtually assuring that Adams, like his father, would become president. To balance Adams, Monroe picked John C. Calhoun of South Carolina, a prominent War Hawk, as secretary of war. And Monroe supported the American System, a program of national economic development that became identified with westerner Henry Clay, Speaker of the House of Representatives.

In supporting the American System, Monroe was following President Madison, who had proposed the program in his message to Congress of December 1815. Madison and Monroe broke with Jeffersonian Republicanism to embrace much of the Federalist program for economic development, including the chartering of a national bank, a tax on imported goods to protect American manufacturers, and a national system of roads and canals. All three of these had first been proposed by Alexander Hamilton in his second "Report on Public Credit" (1790) and his "Report on Manufactures" (1791). At the time they had met with bitter Republican opposition. The support that Madison and Monroe gave to Hamilton's ideas following the War of 1812 was a crucial sign of the American nation's economic growth and development during the twenty-odd years since.

In 1816 Congress chartered the Second Bank of the United States for twenty years. Located in Philadelphia, the bank had a capital of $35 million, of which the government contributed $7 million. The bank was to provide large-scale financing that the smaller state banks could not handle, and to create a strong national currency. Because they feared concentrated economic power, Republicans had allowed the charter of the original Bank of the United States to expire in 1811. The Republican about-face in 1816 was a sign that the strength of commercial interests had grown to rival that of farmers, whose distrust for central banks persisted.

The Tariff of 1816 was the first substantial protective tariff in American history. In 1815, British manufacturers, who had been excluded for eight years (from the Embargo Act of 1807 to the end of the War of 1812), flooded the United States market with their goods. American manufacturers complained that the British were dumping their goods below cost to prevent the growth of American industries. Congress responded with a tariff on imported woolens and cottons, on iron, leather, hats, paper, and sugar. The measure had southern as well as northern support, although in later years the passage of higher tariffs would become one of the most persistent sources of sectional conflict.

The third item in the American System, funding for roads and canals — internal improvements, as they came to be known — was also destined for long-standing contention. Monroe and Madison both believed it was unconstitutional for the federal government to pay for anything but genuinely national (that is, interstate) projects. Congressmen, however, aware of the urgent need to improve transportation in general and scenting the possibility of funding for their districts, proposed spending federal money on local projects. Both Madison and Monroe vetoed such proposals. Thus it was that some of the most famous projects of the day, such as the Erie Canal (see Chapter 10) and the early railroads, were financed by state or private money.

The support of Madison and Monroe for measures initially identified with their political opposition was an indicator of their realism. The three aspects of the American System — bank, tariff, roads — were all parts of the basic infrastructure that the American economy needed to develop. Briefly, during the Era of Good Feelings, politicians agreed about the need for them. Later, the same three topics would be hot sources of partisan argument.

Building Cultural Institutions

Just as the politics of the Era of Good Feelings was transitional, so was cultural life. The United States was a provincial culture, still looking to Britain for values, standards, and literature, and still mocked by the British. In a famous essay in the *Edinburgh Review* in 1820, Sidney Smith bitingly inquired, "In the four quarters of the globe, who reads an American book? or goes to an American play? or looks at an American picture or statue? What does the world yet owe to American physicians or surgeons? What new substances have their chemists discovered . . . ?" The answer was nothing — yet.

In the early years of the nineteenth century, the eastern seaboard cities were actively building a cultural foundation that would eventually produce the American works Smith found so lacking. Philadelphia had long been recognized as the nation's intellectual and cultural center. The American Philosophical Society, founded by Benjamin Franklin in 1743, drew together leading intellectuals and scien-

tists such as physician Benjamin Rush, astronomer David Rittenhouse, and painters Charles and Rembrandt Peale. When Thomas Jefferson began preparing his private secretary, Meriwether Lewis, to undertake the exploration of the West, he sent him to members of the society to get training in the skills he would need — astronomy, natural history, health, and botany. Jefferson himself was concurrently president of the American Philosophical Society and president of the United States. In 1805, wealthy Philadelphians founded the Pennsylvania Academy of Fine Arts, beginning their art collection with plaster casts of the most famous classical statues from the Louvre in Paris. Because most of the statues were nudes, propriety dictated that they be exhibited separately to ladies, and that the male statues have a fig leaf added.

Culturally, Boston ran a close second to Philadelphia. In the early nineteenth century, Boston leaders founded the Massachusetts General Hospital (1811) and the American Antiquarian Society (1812). They also founded the Boston Athenaeum (1807), a gentlemen's library and reading room (it cost $100 to join) containing "the works of learning and science in all languages; particularly such rare and expensive publications as are not generally to be obtained in this country." It soon became one of the largest libraries in the country. The establishment of the Athenaeum led to the founding of the *North American Review*, which was to become the most important and long-lasting intellectual magazine in the country. It covered natural history, the law, economics, history, philosophy, and literature and aimed to keep its readers in touch with European intellectual developments. In 1826 it had a circulation of 3,000, about the same as better-known British equivalents such as the *Edinburgh Review*.

Southern cities were much less successful in creating civic cultural institutions. Charleston had a Literary and Philosophical Society (founded in 1814), but the widely dispersed residences of the southern elite made it difficult to sustain. Thus, unwittingly, the South ceded cultural leadership to the North.

Of the eastern cities, it was New York that produced the first widely recognized American writers. In 1819, Washington Irving published *The Sketch Book,* thus immortalizing Rip Van Winkle and the Headless Horseman. Within a few years James Fenimore Cooper's frontiersman Natty Bumppo would become an even better-known symbol of a distinctive American literature.

The cultural picture was much spottier in the West. A few cities, such as Lexington, Kentucky, and Cincinnati, had civic cultural institutions, and a

Rip Van Winkle, one of Washington Irving's most famous characters, is shown returning home after his twenty-year "nap." Irving's *Sketch-book* drew on folk tales well known to the descendants of New York's original Dutch settlers.
(John Quidor. The Return of Rip Van Winkle. 1849. Canvas. 39-3/4 in. × 49-3/4 in. Andrew W. Mellon Collection. National Gallery of Art.)

number of transplanted New Englanders maintained cultural connections. A group of pioneers in Ames, Ohio, for example, founded a "coonskin library" composed of books purchased from Boston and paid for in coonskins. But most pioneers were at best uninterested and at worst actively hostile to traditional literary culture. This was not from lack of literacy, nor from failure to read. By 1810, more than 22 million copies of 376 newspapers circulated annually, a greater number than anywhere else in the world. Similarly, religious tracts and journals had a great readership. The Methodist *Christian Advocate,* for example, reached 25,000 people yearly (compared with the *North American Review*'s 3,000).

The frontier emphasis on the practical was hard to distinguish from anti-intellectualism. As writer Hugh Henry Brackenridge lamented from Pittsburgh, it was not "the want of learning I consider as a defect, but the *contempt of it.*"

Thus in the early part of the nineteenth century, the gap between the intellectual and cultural horizons of a wealthy Bostonian and a frontier farmer in Michigan widened. Part of the unfinished task of building a national society would be the creation of a national culture that could fill this gap. This national culture, a literary and artistic flowering that became known as the American Renaissance, began to flourish in the 1830s (see Chapter 10).

The Second Great Awakening

Still another source of growing national unity was religion. Although the individual experience of conversion was profoundly personal, the sweeping set of enthusiastic revivals known as the Second Great Awakening were uniquely communal experiences. Conversion became a public act of faith in which the entire revival community shared, and participants in every revival meeting felt they were part of a national movement toward salvation.

The Second Great Awakening began quietly in the 1790s in the Congregational churches of New England, but by 1800 it had spread through the Protestant churches of the entire country and caught the public's attention. Young men had been the principal converts of the Great Awakening of the early eighteenth century (see Chapter 5), but in the Second Great Awakening female converts outnumbered males by a ratio of three to two. "We look to you, ladies, to raise the standard of character in our own sex," declared the New England minister Joseph Buckminster. "We look to you for the continuance of domestic purity, for the revival of domestic religion, for the increase of our charities, and the support of what remains of religion in our private habits and public institutions." In many churches during the early nineteenth century, women led prayer groups, Sunday schools, and charitable societies, and many people commented on their influence in American Protestantism. One visitor to the United States later declared that she had never seen a country "where religion had so strong a hold upon the women, or a slighter hold upon the men."

The Second Great Awakening was most dramatic on the American frontier, where churches had traditionally been weak. The great institution of western Protestantism became the camp meeting, an outdoor gathering that included many sects and might go on for days. The greatest of the early camp meetings took place at Cane Ridge, Kentucky, in 1801 when an estimated 20,000 people came together for a week of preaching and singing. This was a remarkable assembly if we consider that the largest town in the West at the time had fewer than 2,000 inhabitants. Preachers shouted from the stand, and in the flickering firelight of evening hundreds of people, overcome with religious enthusiasm, fell to speaking in tongues or jerking uncontrollably. "Many things transpired there," one observer wrote, "that had the same effects as miracles on infidels and unbelievers."

Organized religion became one of the most important institutions of the continuing movement of Americans westward. Camp meetings frequently provided the first occasion for the new settlers of an area to come together, and religious meeting houses were often the first public buildings erected in the community. In the absence of resident ministers, preaching was provided by Methodist circuit riders or perhaps a Baptist farmer who heard "the call" and had himself licensed as a lay preacher. On the frontier as well as in the East, women frequently made up the majority of church membership. Churches were fundamental to the planting of the new American communities, and women were among its most important members.

The Second Great Awakening also had a profound impact on the South, for it was in the 1790s that large numbers of African American slaves became Christians. Also then, the African Methodist Episcopal church, founded by black people, and black Baptists began their work among free and enslaved African Americans. In New England, finally, the Second Great Awakening challenged the Calvinist belief in predestination and allowed room for a more open and democratic faith.

Churches throughout the nation remained, as they had long been, the centers around which communities organized. But with the Second Great Awakening, the tone of religion became much more emotional and enthusiastic. Newer, more democratic denominations such as the Methodists and Baptists grew rapidly, eclipsing older, more formal groups such as the Presbyterians, Congregationalists, and Anglicans. This new enthusiasm in religion united people in all parts of the country in a belief in personal and national salvation and thereby made them receptive to change. It was from this widespread religious faith that the reform movements of the 1830s were to spring (see Chapter 13).

Diplomatic Achievements

The diplomatic achievements of the Era of Good Feelings were due almost entirely to the efforts of one man, John Quincy Adams, Monroe's secretary of state. Adams set himself the task of tidying up the borders of the United States. In two accords with Britain, the Rush-Bagot Treaty of 1817 and the Convention of 1818, the border between the United States and Canada was demilitarized and fixed at the forty-ninth parallel; west of the Rocky Mountains, joint occupancy of Oregon was agreed upon for ten (eventually twenty) years. The American claim to Oregon was based on China trader Robert Gray's discovery of the Columbia River in 1792, and on the Lewis and Clark expedition.

The rural and community nature of the Second Great Awakening is captured in this illustration. The preacher exhorts the large audience, which responds with emotion. Many of the most enthusiastic converts were women, who gained a new feeling of moral and social consequence through their religious experience.

In 1819 Adams turned to Spain and negotiated the Adams-Onís Treaty: the United States gained East and West Florida in return for assuming $5 million in U.S. citizens' claims against Spain and relinquishing an American claim to Texas. Adams negotiated the treaty at the same time that General Andrew Jackson, charged with ending raids by Seminole Indians on American settlements, exceeded his orders and invaded Florida (see Chapter 11). Jackson's success made it clear that the United States could easily have snatched Florida from Spain by force; Adams, without using force, gained the same end diplomatically.

Finally, Adams picked his way through the minefield of Spain's disintegrating Latin American empire to the policy that bears his president's name, the Monroe Doctrine. The United States was the first country outside Latin America to recognize the independence of Spain's former colonies (Argentina, Chile, Columbia, and Mexico), all of which had broken free by 1822. Many Americans enthusiastically supported the Latin American revolts, and were proud to think that they were modeled on the American Revolution, as the Latin American liberator Simón Bolívar, had claimed.

But then the European powers (France, Austria, Russia, and Prussia) began talk of a plan to help Spain recover the lost colonies. What was the United States to do? The British, suspicious of the European powers, proposed a British–American declaration against European intervention in the hemisphere.

Others might have been flattered by an approach from the British Empire, but Adams would have none of it. Showing the national pride that was so characteristic of the era, Adams insisted on an independent American policy. He therefore drafted for the president the hemispheric policy that the United States has followed ever since.

On December 2, 1823, the president presented the Monroe Doctrine to Congress and the world. He called for the end of colonization of the Western Hemisphere by European nations (this was aimed as much at Russia and its West Coast settlements as at other European powers). Intervention by European powers in the affairs of the independent New World nations would be considered by the United States a danger to its own peace and safety. Finally, Monroe pledged that the United States would not interfere in the affairs of European countries or in the affairs of their remaining New World colonies.

All of this was a very large bark from a very small dog. In 1823, the United States lacked the military and economic force to back up its grand statement. In fact, what kept the European powers out of Latin America was British opposition to European intervention, enforced by the Royal Navy. But the Monroe Doctrine was to take on quite another aspect at the end of the century, when the United States did have the power to enforce it.

This trio of diplomatic achievements — the treaties with Britain and Spain and the Monroe Doctrine — represented a great personal triumph for the stubborn, principled John Quincy Adams. A committed nationalist and expansionist, he showed that reason and diplomacy were in some circumstances more effective than force. Adams's diplomatic achievements were a fitting end to the period dominated by the Virginia Dynasty, the trio of enlightened revolutionaries who did so much to shape the new nation.

The Panic of 1819

Across this impressive record of political, economic, and cultural nation building fell the shadow of the Panic of 1819. A delayed reaction to the end of the War of 1812 and the Napoleonic Wars, the panic forced Americans to come to terms with their economic place in a peaceful world. The American shipping boom came to an end as British merchant ships resumed their earlier trade routes. American farmers, as well as American shippers, were hurt by diminished international demand for American foodstuffs as European farms resumed production after the long wars.

Domestic economic conditions made matters worse. The western land boom that began in 1815 turned into a speculative frenzy. Land sales, which had totaled 1 million acres in 1815, mushroomed to 3.5 million in 1818. The official price of public lands was $2 an acre, but some lands in Mississippi and Alabama, made valuable by the international demand for cotton, were selling for $100 an acre. Many settlers bought on credit, aided by loans from small and irresponsible "wildcat" state banks. A number of speculators, carried away by the excitement of it all, also bought large tracts of land on credit and promoted them heavily. This was not the first — or the last — speculative boom in western lands. But it ended like all the rest — with a sharp contraction of credit, begun on this occasion by the Second Bank of the United States, which in 1819 forced state banks to foreclose on many bad loans. Many small farmers were ruined, and six years of depression followed.

In response to farmer protests, Congress passed a relief act in 1821 that extended the payment period for western lands and lowered prices, and some state legislatures passed "stay laws" that prevented banks from executing foreclosures. Nonetheless, many small banks failed, taking down their creditors with them. Many western farmers blamed the faraway Bank of the United States for their troubles. In the 1830s Andrew Jackson would build a political movement upon their resentment.

Urban workers suffered both from the decline in international trade and from manufacturing failures caused by competition from British imports. As urban workers lobbied for local relief (there was no federal welfare) they found themselves deeply involved in urban politics, where they could express their resentment against the merchants and owners who had laid them off. Thus developed another component of Andrew Jackson's new political coalition.

Another confrontation arose over the tariff. Southern planters, hurt by a decline in the price of cotton, began to actively protest the protective tariff, which kept the price of imported goods high even when cotton prices were low. Manufacturers, hurt by British competition, lobbied for even higher rates, which they achieved in 1824 over southern protests. Southerners then began to raise doubts about the fairness of a political system in which they were always outvoted.

The panic of 1819 was a symbol of this transitional time. It showed how far the country had moved since 1800 from Jefferson's republic of yeoman farmers toward commercial activity. And the anger and resentment expressed by the groups harmed by the depression — farmers, urban workers, and southern planters — were portents of the politics of the upcoming Jackson era.

The Missouri Compromise

An even more serious portent of future politics was the Missouri crisis of 1819–21. For the first time the nation confronted a momentous question: As America expanded, would slavery expand as well? Until 1819, this question was decided regionally. As residents of the northern states moved west, the territory into which they expanded (the Old Northwest) was free of slavery. As southerners moved into Alabama, Mississippi, and Louisiana, (the Old Southwest) they brought their slaves with them. This regional difference had been mandated by Congress in the Northwest Ordinance of 1787, which explicitly banned slavery in the northern section of trans-Appalachia but made no mention of it elsewhere. Because so much of the expansion into the Old Northwest and Southwest was lateral (northerners stayed in the north, southerners in the south), there was little conflict over sectional differences. In 1819, however, the sections collided — in Missouri.

In 1819, Missouri applied for admission to the Union as a slave state. To the slave-owning Kentuckians and Tennesseans who were the territory's major settlers, this extension of slavery seemed natural and inevitable. But Illinois, the adjacent state, prohibited slavery. The northern states, most of whom had abolished slavery by 1819, looked askance at the extension of slavery northward.

In addition to the moral issue of slavery, the

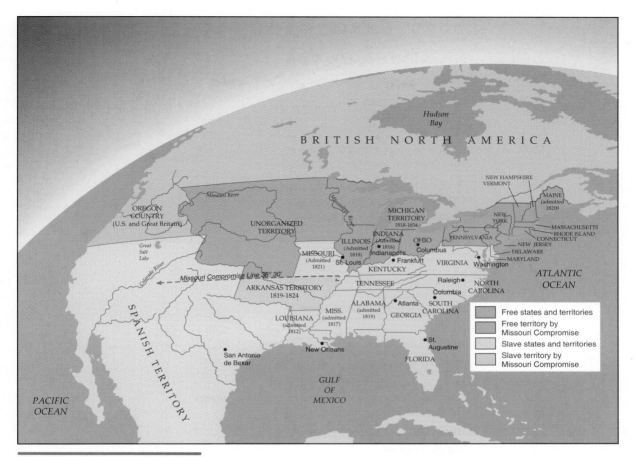

The Missouri Compromise, 1820

Before the Missouri Compromise of 1820, the Ohio River was the dividing line between the free states of the Old Northwest and the slaveholding states of the Old Southwest. The Compromise stipulated that Missouri would enter the Union as a slave state (balanced by Maine, a free state), but slavery would be prohibited in the Louisiana Territory north of 36°30′ (Missouri's southern boundary). This awkward compromise lasted until the Mexican-American War of 1846 reopened the issue of the expansion of slavery.

Missouri question raised the political issue of sectional balance. Northern politicians did not want to admit another slave state. To do so would tip the balance of power in the Senate, where the 1819 count of slave and free states was eleven apiece. For their part, southerners believed they needed an advantage in the Senate; because of faster population growth in the North, they were already outnumbered (105 to 81) in the House of Representatives. But above all, southerners did not believe Congress had the power to limit the expansion of slavery. They were alarmed that northerners were considering national legislation on the matter. Slavery, in southern eyes, was a question of property, and therefore was a matter for state rather than federal legislation. Thus, from the very beginning the expansion of slavery raised constitutional issues.

The urgency of these considerations among politicians in 1819 illustrates how delicate matters of sectional balance had already become. Indeed, the aging politician of Monticello, Thomas Jefferson, immediately grasped the seriousness of the question of the expansion of slavery. As he prophetically wrote to a friend, "This momentous question like a fire bell in the night, awakened and filled me with terror. I considered it at once the [death] knell of the Union."

In 1819 Representative James Tallmadge, Jr., of New York began more than a year of congressional controversy when he demanded that Missouri agree to the gradual end of slavery as the price of entering the Union. At first, the general public paid little attention, but northern religious reformers (Quakers prominent among them) organized a number of

CHRONOLOGY

1790s	Second Great Awakening begins
1800	Thomas Jefferson elected president
1803	Louisiana Purchase
	Marbury v. Madison
	Ohio admitted to the Union
1804	Lewis and Clark expedition begins
	Thomas Jefferson reelected president
1807	*Chesapeake-Leopard* incident
	Embargo Act
1808	James Madison elected president
1809	Tecumseh forms military alliance among Northwest Confederacy peoples
1811	Battle of Tippecanoe
1812	James Madison reelected president
	War of 1812 begins
	Louisiana admitted to the Union
1814	Hartford Convention
	Treaty of Ghent
1815	Battle of New Orleans
1816	James Monroe elected president
	Congress charters Second Bank of the United States
	Indiana admitted to the Union
1817	Mississippi admitted to the Union
1818	Illinois admitted to the Union
	Andrew Jackson invades East Florida
1819	The Panic of 1819
	Adams-Onís Treaty
	Alabama admitted to the Union
1819–20	Missouri controversy
1820	James Monroe reelected president
	Maine admitted to the Union
1821	Missouri admitted to the Union
1823	Monroe Doctrine

antislavery rallies in northern cities that made both northern and southern politicians take notice. Former Federalists in the North, who had seen their party destroyed by the achievements of Jefferson and his successors in the Virginia Dynasty, seized upon the Missouri issue eagerly. This was the first time that the growing northern reform impulse had intersected with sectional politics. It would also be the first time for southern threats of secession to be made openly in Congress.

The Senate debate over the admission of Missouri, held in the early months of 1820, was the nation's first extended debate over slavery. Observers noted the high proportion of free African Americans among the listeners in the Senate gallery. They, like Thomas Jefferson, clearly realized that the fate of the Union and the fate of the black race in America were inseparable. But the full realization that the future of slavery was central to the future of the nation was not apparent to the general public until the 1850s.

In 1820, Congress achieved compromise over the sectional differences. Henry Clay forged the first of the many agreements that were to earn him the title of "The Great Pacificator" (peacemaker). A glance at the map shows the state of Missouri as an awkward intrusion into an otherwise slave-free area, a visual break in the smooth westward continuation of sectionalism. This visual impression is reflected in the Missouri Compromise itself, which was difficult to arrange and had an awkward air about it. The compromise maintained the balance between free and slave states: Maine (which had been part of Massachusetts) was admitted as a free state in 1820 and Missouri as a slave state in the following year. A policy was also enacted with respect to slavery in the rest of the Louisiana Purchase: slavery was prohibited north of 36° 30′ north latitude — the southern boundary of Missouri — and permitted south of that line. This meant that the vast majority of the Louisiana Territory would be free. In reality, then, the Missouri Compromise could be only a temporary solution, because it left open the question of how the balance between slave and free states would be maintained.

The seriousness of the sectional struggle over the Missouri question also directed popular attention to the changing nature of national politics. To that subject we will turn in the next chapter.

CONCLUSION

In complex ways a developing economy, geographical expansion, and even a minor war helped shape American unity. Locally, small, settled face-to-face communities in both the North and the South began to send their more mobile, expectant members west to form new settlements, displacing Indian communities in the process.

The westward movement was the novel element in the American national drama. Europeans believed that large size and a population in motion bred instability and political disintegration. Thomas Jefferson thought otherwise, and the Louisiana Purchase was the gamble that confirmed his guess. The westward population movement dramatically changed the political landscape and Americans' view of themselves. Few of those changes, though, were fully apparent in 1820.

The consequences of expansion are a major theme in the next seven chapters. But we can already say that expansion did not foster the settled communities of yeoman farmers Jefferson had hoped for. Rather, it bred a nation of restless and acquisitive people and a new kind of national democratic politics that reflected their search for broader definitions of community.

Additional Readings

FRANK BERGON, ed., *The Journals of Lewis and Clark* (1989). A handy abridgment of the fascinating history of the expedition. (For more intensive study, Gary Moulton's six-volume unabridged edition of the expedition journals is unsurpassed.)

JOHN BOLES, *The Great Revival, 1787–1805* (1972). The standard source on the Second Great Awakening.

R. DAVID EDMUNDS, *Tecumseh and the Quest for Indian Leadership* (1984). A sympathetic portrait.

JOHN MACK FARAGHER, *Sugar Creek* (1987). The fullest examination of the lives of pioneers in the Old Northwest.

DONALD HICKEY, *The War of 1812: A Forgotten Conflict* (1989), Takes a fresh look at the events and historiography of the war.

DREW McCOY, *The Elusive Republic: Political Economy in Jeffersonian America* (1980). The most useful discussion of the ties between expansion and Jeffersonian republicanism.

JEAN MATTHEWS, *Toward a New Society: American Thought and Culture 1800–1830* (1991). Considers the development of American culture.

GLOVER MOORE, *The Missouri Controversy 1819–1821* (1953). The standard account.

CURTIS P. NETTELS, *The Emergence of a National Economy, 1775–1815* (1962). A useful overview.

MERRILL PETERSON, *Thomas Jefferson and the New Nation* (1970). A good one-volume biography of Jefferson. (The major biography, by Dumas Malone, is a multivolume work.)

JAMES RONDA, *Lewis and Clark Among the Indians* (1984). An innovative look at the famous explorers through the eyes of the Indian peoples they encountered.

10 THE GROWTH OF DEMOCRACY, 1824–1840

● MARTIN VAN BUREN AND THE BUCKTAILS

When Martin Van Buren left Albany for Washington in the fall of 1821 to take up his new position as junior senator from New York, he wrote complacently:

> I left the service of the state [of New York] for that of the federal government with my friends in full and almost unquestioned possession of the state government in all its branches, at peace with each other and overflowing with kindly feelings towards myself. . . .

Thus did Van Buren sum up more than ten years of intense activity in New York State politics in which he and his allies, nicknamed the Bucktails (named for the Indian-inspired insignia, the tail of a buck, that members wore on their hats), created one of the first modern democratic political parties. At first glance, the Little Magician (as Van Buren was known) seemed unimpressive. How could it be, Washington politicians asked, that this short, invariably pleasant but rather nondescript man had triumphed over the renowned DeWitt Clinton?

THE FORGING OF POLITICAL COMMUNITIES

Tall, handsome, and arrogant, DeWitt Clinton, father of the Erie Canal and governor of New York since 1817, represented old-style politics. An aristocrat in wealth, connections, and attitude, Clinton ran the New York (Jeffersonian) Republican party as though it was his personal property. He dispensed patronage to his own relatives and friends (many of whom were Federalists) on the basis of their loyalty to him rather than on the basis of agreed matters of political principle. New York politics, dominated by feuds and counterfeuds among a few great political families (the Clintons, the DeLanceys, and the Livingstons among them) baffled outsiders by its complexity. Swept into office in 1817 on a tide of popularity generated by his promotion of a statewide canal, Clinton soon gained legislative approval for the project. The result was the Erie Canal, the most ambitious and successful canal project of the era (see the discussion of the Erie Canal later in this chapter).

Martin Van Buren, the man who engineered Clinton's downfall, was a new kind of politician. Van Buren was the son of a tavern keeper, not a member of the wealthy elite. Raised in the small Dutch-dominated town of Kinderhook (the model for Washington Irving's Sleepy Hollow), Van Buren never lost his resentment of the aristocratic landowning families such as the

(John Lewis Krimmel. Interior of an American Inn. 1813. Toledo Museum of Art, Ohio. Gift of Florence Scott Libbey.)

This portrait of Martin Van Buren, painted when he was a young man, captures the personal charm that made him such an effective politician, but reveals little of the manipulative ability that earned him the nickname, "The Sly Fox of Kinderhook."

Van Schaacks and the Van Rensselaers (and, by extension, the Clintons) who had disdained him when he was young. Masking his anger with charming manners, Van Buren took advantage of the growing strength of the Jeffersonian Republican party in New York State to make a different kind of career in politics. Van Buren and other rising politicians were infuriated as they watched Clinton dispense patronage to his friends at the expense of young men who were loyal to the party. Two years after Clinton became governor, Van Buren wrote bitterly to a friend:

> A man to be a sound politician and in any degree useful to his country must be guided by higher and steadier considerations than those of personal sympathy and private regard. . . . In the name of all that is holy, where is the evidence of that towering mind and those superior talents which it has been the business of puffers and toad eaters to attribute to [Clinton]?

By 1819, Van Buren had gathered together enough other disgruntled Republicans to form the Bucktails and openly challenge Clinton for control of the Republican party. Two years later, the Albany constitutional convention of 1821 (three-fourths of whose 126 delegates were Bucktails) sealed their victory.

From August to October of 1821, delegates to a special state convention gathered in Albany to revise the out-of-date state constitution of 1777. Carefully managed by Martin Van Buren (himself a delegate), the convention voted to streamline the organization of state government and sharply curtail the patronage powers of the governor. They enacted nearly total manhood suffrage: All adult male citizens who paid state or local taxes, served in the militia, or worked on state roads — more than four-fifths of the adult male population — were now eligible to vote directly for state legislators, governor, and members of Congress. This dramatic democratization of politics reflected the state's changing population. Already the bustling port of New York was the nation's largest city, and commercial opportunity was attracting shrewd Yankee traders from New England, "whose laws, customs and usages," conservative senator Rufus King complained, "differ from those of New York." The old ruling families, swamped by the newcomers, were losing their grip on politics. In the years ahead, the state's economy and population were permanently changed by the remarkable financial success of the Erie Canal, proposed by Clinton himself.

In challenging Clinton, Martin Van Buren and the Bucktails formulated a new and enduring definition of political parties. In contrast with elite groups bound together only by family ties and political favors, the Bucktails asserted that the party should be a democratic organization, expressing the will of all its members. All party members, including the leaders, were expected to abide by majority rule. Party loyalty, rather than personal opinion or friendship, became the bond that kept the party together. Leaders were now the most loyal, not the most aristocratic. Still smarting from the factionalism and favoritism of the Clinton years, Bucktail Silas Wright, Jr., sharply stressed the imperative of loyalty: "The first man we see step to the rear we cut down."

When he departed for Washington in the fall of 1821, Van Buren left behind in Albany a closely knit group of friends and allies who practiced these new political principles. Party decisions, reached by discussion in legislative caucus and publicized by the party newspaper (the Albany Argus), were binding on all members and enforced by patronage decisions. The group, dubbed the Albany Regency, ran New York State politics for twenty years. For all of those years Martin Van Buren was in Washington, where he was a major architect of the new democratic politics of mass participation that has been called the second American party system. This new movement created, for the first time in American history, national communities of political partisans. Van Buren understood this. Organization and discipline were essential not for their own sake, but because they allowed the political leader to reach out to public opinion. "Those who have wrought great changes in the world," Van Buren wrote, "never succeeded by gaining over chiefs; but always by exciting the multitude. The first is the resource of intrigue and produces only secondary results, the second is the resort

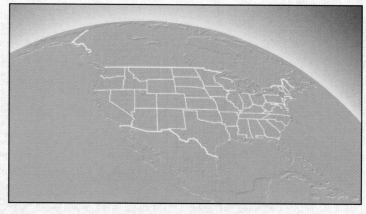

of genius and transforms the face of the universe." In this chapter we will examine the sources and expression of the new transformational politics as well as wider economic and cultural factors encouraging national cohesion.

THE NEW DEMOCRATIC POLITICS

The early years of the nineteenth century were a period of extraordinary growth and change for the new republic. The changes were of two very different kinds: divergent and unifying.

The two major regions, the North and the South, had always had different social systems, and political disagreements invariably resulted. Economic changes in the early nineteenth century increased the divergence between the two regions: The South committed itself to cotton growing and the slave system and the North moved rapidly to a commercial and industrializing economy. Although economically interconnected, the two regions were on different social and cultural paths. Had the new United States of America consisted only of the thirteen original colonies, the North–South compromises might well have broken down by the 1820s and split the nation into two parts.

Westward expansion, however, became a unifying force. Because of developments in transporta-

Population and Westward Expansion, 1830

Westward population movement, relatively small in 1800, had achieved major proportions by 1830. Between 1800 and 1830 the U.S. population more than doubled (from 5,308,881 to 12,866,020) but the transAppalachian population grew tenfold (from 370,000 to 3.7 million). By 1830 over a third of the nation's inhabitants lived west of the original thirteen states.

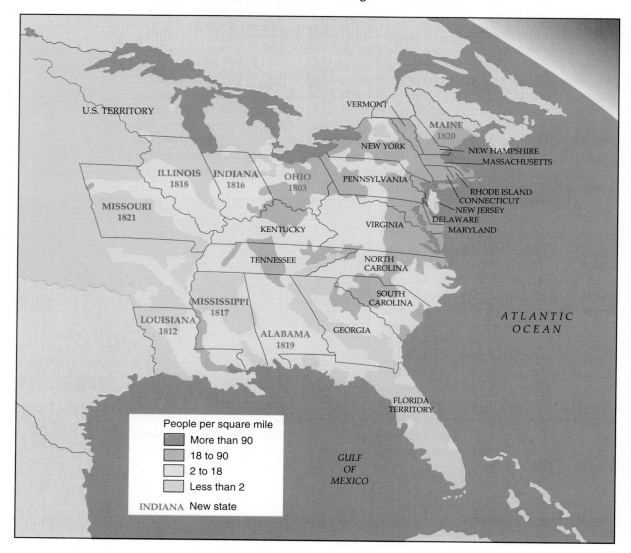

tion, most of the enlarged United States was more closely knit in 1840 than the original thirteen states had been in 1787. And the fifteen new states from west of the Appalachians that entered the Union between 1791 and 1850, making up half of the membership of the U.S. Senate, contributed another regional perspective to national politics. Although the settlement patterns discussed in Chapter 9 tended to align the Old Northwest with New England and the Old Southwest with the South, westerners as a whole also shared common concerns and attitudes. As a result, national politicians from the two older sections found themselves vying for political allegiances in the new region.

While this complicated regional rivalry was taking place, the nation as a whole was coming to grips with the consequences of rapid economic change. It is no wonder that the politics of the period 1820–50 were so dramatic. To understand them, we must look first at changes in politics at the local and state levels.

The Expansion of Suffrage

The partisan competition between Republicans and Federalists in the 1790s had caused some easing of restrictions on voting (See Chapter 8). Even so, before 1800 most of the original thirteen states limited the vote to property owners or taxpayers, thus permitting less than half of the white male population to vote. Turnout among eligible voters was low, in part because voice voting (viva voce) made each man's vote a matter of public knowledge. Furthermore, most state constitutions stipulated that presidential electors and U.S. senators be chosen by state legislators, and not by popular vote.

This system of limited and indirect voting mirrored the social structure of late-eighteenth-century America: Everywhere (except on the frontier) wealthy merchants and slave owners (in the South) dominated officeholding. At the local and state levels, financial and kinship ties were important factors in political advancement, tending to create a small group of active politicians, like DeWitt Clinton in New York, who were connected more by personal loyalties than by ideological beliefs. Because members of this local elite were elected to Congress, state and national politics were closely linked. Southern planters and northern merchants worked together in the early administrations of Washington, Adams, Jefferson, Madison, and Monroe. Although far from unanimous on issues, they shared a background of wealth and privilege, as well an ideology of political responsibility (we might call it paternalism) toward the majority of the American people.

This political structure matched economic reality. The wealthy held the levers of political power, as well as the economic ones. In spite of occasional revolts from below such as the Whiskey Rebellion of 1794 (see Chapter 8) and a strong tradition of republican outspokenness among urban artisans, political control remained in the hands of the traditional elite until the end of the Virginia Dynasty of presidents in 1824.

Westward expansion changed the nature of American politics. The new western states extended the right to vote to all white males over the age of twenty-one. Kentucky entered the Union with universal manhood suffrage in 1792, Tennessee in 1796, Ohio in 1803. Soon older states such as New Jersey (1807) and Maryland (1810) dropped their property qualification for voting. By 1820, most of the older states had followed suit, acting less out of democratic belief than for the practical purpose of attempting to dissuade disgruntled nonvoters from moving west. There were laggards — Rhode Island, Virginia, and Louisiana did not liberalize their voting qualifications until later — but by 1840, more than 90 percent of adult white males in the nation could vote. And they could vote for more officials: Governors and (most important) presidential electors were now elected by direct vote, rather than chosen by small groups of state legislators. As Martin Van Buren proved in New York, these changes transformed politics.

Nowhere in the world, at the time, was the right to vote so widespread as it was in the United States. The extension of suffrage to the common man marked a major step beyond the republicanism advocated by the revolutionary generation. Jefferson, as we have seen, envisaged a republic of independent (that is, property-owning) yeoman farmers. Now, however, propertyless farm workers and members of the laboring poor in the nation's cities could vote as well. European observers were very curious about the democratization of voting: Could "mob rule" possibly succeed?

Nevertheless, even in America voting was not a universal right, and the extent of suffrage tells us something about the limits of American democracy in the early nineteenth century. The right to vote was limited to adult white males: Neither free black men nor women of any race could vote.

When white Americans thought about black people, they thought about slaves, thereby ignoring the rights of the nation's 500,000 free African Americans. Only in five New England states (Maine, New Hampshire, Vermont, Massachusetts, and Rhode Island) could free black men vote before 1865. In most of the other northern states the right of free

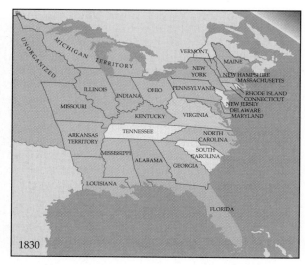

The Growth of Universal White Manhood Suffrage

Kentucky was the first western state to enact white male suffrage without tax or property qualifications. Other western states followed, and by 1820 most of the older states had dropped their suffrage restrictions as well. By 1840, more than 90 percent of the nation's white males could vote. But while voting was democratized for them, restrictions on free black male voters actually increased, and women were excluded completely. Politics was the most engrossing entertainment of the age. In the six elections between 1840 and 1860, voter turnout averaged 77 percent.

African American men to vote was limited, first by custom and later by law. In New York, for example, the Bucktails curtailed the right of African American men to vote in 1821, at the very same session in which they voted to democratize the franchise to include most white men. Although a bill in the New York State legislature to limit the vote only to whites was defeated, African Americans were required to own property of $250 or more, an impossible qualification: Of the nearly 13,000 blacks in New York City in 1825, only 68 were qualified to vote.

Restrictions on the civil rights of free African Americans were even worse in the new western states. The Ohio constitution of 1802 denied African Americans the vote, the right to hold public office, and the right to testify against white men in court cases. Later restrictions barred black men from serving in the state militia and on juries. The constitutions of other western states — Illinois, Indiana, Michigan, Iowa, Wisconsin — and later, Oregon — attempted to solve the "problem" of free black people by simply denying them entry into the state at all!

The denial of suffrage to white women stemmed from patriarchal attitudes that men were always the head of the household and women always subordinate. Even wealthy single women who lived alone were denied the vote (although New Jersey had permitted them to vote until 1807). The extension of

suffrage to all classes of white males had the effect of officially restricting the role of women in public activities (although women were extremely active in social reform movements). Increasingly, as "manhood" rather than property became the qualification for voting, women's participation in politics came to be regarded as inappropriate. Thus, in this period famous for democratization and "the rise of the common man," important groups — black men and women of all races — were excluded by liberalization.

Popular Politics

As important as the spread of universal manhood suffrage was the change in popular attitudes that accompanied it. Popular interest in politics grew dramatically, and the earlier pattern of unquestioned control by a wealthy elite came to an end. The triumph of Van Buren and the Bucktails in New York in 1821 was one example of this sort of change, but there were other politicians in other states who shared Van Buren's vision of tightly organized, mass-based political organizations. John C. Calhoun of South Carolina was first elected to his state legislature in 1808, the year that suffrage was liberalized and the iron political grip of the lowland planters was weakened. Calhoun built his political organization on the newly enfranchised upland

Politics, abetted by the publication of inexpensive party newspapers, was a great topic of male attention and conversation in early 19th century America. As this painting suggests, however, interest in politics did not necessarily lead to agreement on the issues.

voters. In Virginia the Richmond Junto had control of state politics by 1816, and in Tennessee the Nashville Junto, masterminded by John Overton, held sway by 1822. In New Hampshire, Isaac Hill's Concord Regency was firmly in control by 1825. Each of these organizations, to a greater or lesser extent, aspired to the same discipline and control as the Albany Regency, and each had wider aspirations. The Nashville Junto led the way by nominating Andrew Jackson for president in 1824, and in 1828 all five of these new political organizations worked together to elect Jackson president.

The crucial element in the success of the new party system, as Van Buren had realized, was its mass appeal. Just as the religion of the day emphasized emotion over reason, so too the new political parties appealed to popular enthusiasms. The techniques of mass campaigns — huge political rallies, parades (nighttime torchlight parades were particularly effective), and candidates with wide "name recognition," such as military heroes — were quickly adopted by the new political parties. So were less savory techniques such as lavish food and (especially) drink at polling places, which frequently turned elections into rowdy, brawling occasions.

These mass campaigns were something new. In 1834, the French visitor Michel Chevalier witnessed a mile-long nighttime parade in support of Andrew Jackson. Stunned by the orderly stream of banners lit by torchlight, the portraits of Washington, Jefferson, and Jackson, and the enthusiastic cheering of the crowd, Chevalier wrote, "These scenes belong to history. They are the episodes of wondrous epic which will bequeath a lasting memory to posterity, that of the coming of democracy."

The new politics placed great emphasis on party loyalty. Just as professional politicians such as Van Buren were expected to be loyal, so the average voter was encouraged to make a permanent commitment to a political party. The party provided some of the same satisfactions that popular sports offer today: excitement, entertainment, and a sense of belonging. In effect, political parties functioned as giant national men's clubs. They made politics an immediate and engrossing topic of conversation and argument for men of all walks of life, much the way that conversation about sports is today. The new political party was a national example of the grouping together of like-minded people that was so characteristic of early-nineteenth-century America. As the older, local, status-based social order gave way to a more open and mobile one, people sought stability by joining clubs and groups. The political party was simply the political manifestation of a wider social impulse toward community.

The Election of 1824

The expanded electorate and the direct vote had their initial national impact in the presidential election of 1824. Popular election of presidential electors (rather than election by the state legislature) was by then the rule in eighteen states—all but Delaware, Georgia, Louisiana, New York, South Carolina, and Vermont. The 1824 election marked a dramatic end to the political truce that had characterized the Era of Good Feelings since Monroe's election in 1816 (see Chapter 9). Only one party, the Democratic Republicans, ran candidates, but this was misleading, for the party was divided internally. The candidate chosen by the usual method of congressional caucus was William H. Crawford of Georgia. But another candidate, John Quincy Adams of Massachusetts, President Monroe's secretary of state, had a strong claim, as did John C. Calhoun of South Carolina, Monroe's secretary of war. Both were nominated by their state legislature, as were two more candidates, Henry Clay of Kentucky and Andrew Jackson of Tennessee. A latecomer to the race, Jackson was at first not taken seriously because his record as a legislator was lackluster and his political views unknown. Each candidate was clearly identified with a region: New England (Adams), the South (Crawford and Calhoun, who withdrew before the election), and the West (Clay and Jackson). Although Jackson was deeply identified with the Old Southwest, he was able to use his reputation as a military hero to run as a national candidate, one who was opposed to traditional politics. He won the most electoral votes—ninety-nine. John Quincy Adams was the runner-up with eighty-four.

Because no candidate had a majority, however, the election was thrown into the House of Representatives, as the election of 1800 had been. Political deals were made, with the result that Clay (who hated Jackson) supported Adams and became his secretary of state, a strong position from which he could launch a presidential bid in 1828. All of this was customary: The Constitution gave the House the power to decide, and Clay had every right to advise his followers how to vote. But times had changed. Jackson, the man with the most electoral votes (and 43 percent of the popular vote) promptly accused Clay and Adams of a "corrupt bargain," and it was clear that he had popular opinion on his side. John Quincy Adams served four miserable years as president, knowing that Jackson would challenge him, and win, in 1828.

THE JACKSON PRESIDENCY

Andrew Jackson's election symbolized something new in American politics, an era that historians have called the Age of the Common Man. Historians have also determined that Jackson himself was not a common man: He was a military hero, a rich slave owner, and an imperious and decidedly undemocratic personality. Old Hickory, as Jackson was affectionately called, was tough and unbending, just like hickory itself, one of the hardest of woods. Yet he had a mass appeal to ordinary people unmatched — and indeed unsought — by previous presidents. The secret to Jackson's extraordinary appeal

The Election of 1824

The sectional nature of the presidential vote of 1824 is shown in this map. John Quincy Adams carried his native New England and little else, Henry Clay carried only his own state of Kentucky and two adjoining states, Crawford's appeal was limited to Virginia and Georgia. Only Andrew Jackson moved beyond the regional support of the Old Southwest to wider appeal and the greatest number of electoral votes. Because no candidate had a majority, the election was decided by the House of Representatives which chose John Quincy Adams.

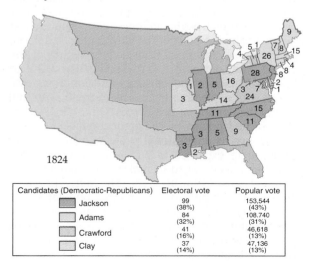

1824

Candidates (Democratic-Republicans)	Electoral vote	Popular vote
Jackson	99 (38%)	153,544 (43%)
Adams	84 (32%)	108,740 (31%)
Crawford	41 (16%)	46,618 (13%)
Clay	37 (14%)	47,136 (13%)

lies in the changing nature of American society. Jackson was the first to respond to the ways in which westward expansion and the extension of the suffrage were changing politics at the national as well as the local and state levels.

Jackson was born in 1767 and raised in North Carolina. During the American Revolution he was captured and mistreated by the British, an insult he never forgot. As a young man without wealth or family support, he moved west to the frontier "station" of Nashville, Tennessee, in 1788. There he made his career as a lawyer and his considerable wealth as a slave-owning planter. His first plantation was in the Natchez district of Mississippi, a 550-mile trip from Nashville along the notoriously rough and dangerous Natchez Trace. It was a journey Jackson made with remarkable frequency. Known throughout his life for his touchy sense of pride and honor (he fought a succession of duels), Jackson expressed a ruthless attitude toward Indians in the military campaigns he waged against the "Five Civilized Tribes" in the Old Southwest during the War of 1812 (see Chapter 11). He first became a national hero with his underdog win against the British in the Battle of New Orleans. In the popular mind, his fierce belligerence came to symbolize pioneer independence.

Sectionalism and the Election of 1828

The election of 1828 was the first to demonstrate the effectiveness of the new party system. With the help of Martin Van Buren, his campaign manager, Jackson rode the wave of the new democratic politics to the presidency. Jackson's party, the Democratic Republicans (they soon dropped *Republicans* and became simply the Democrats), spoke the campaign language of democracy and opposition to the special privilege personified (they claimed) by President John Quincy Adams and his party, who now called themselves National Republicans to distinguish themselves from Jackson's party. Neither Jackson nor Adams campaigned on his own—that was considered undignified. But the supporters of both candidates campaigned vigorously, freely, and negatively. Jackson's supporters portrayed the campaign as a contest between "the *democracy* of the *country,* on the one hand, and a *lordly purse-proud aristocracy* on the other." In their turn, Adams's supporters depicted Jackson as an illiterate backwoodsman, a murderer (he had killed several men in duels), and an adulterer (apparently unwittingly; he had married Rachel Robards before her divorce was final).

Jackson won 56 percent of the popular vote (well over 80 percent in large parts of the South and West) and a decisive electoral majority of 178 votes to Adams's 83. The victory was interpreted as a victory for the common man. But the most important thing about Jackson's victory was the coalition that achieved it. The four new democratically based political organizations mentioned earlier—the Richmond and Nashville Juntos, the Albany and Concord Regencies—with help from Calhoun's organization in South Carolina, worked together to elect him. Popular appeal, which Jackson the military hero certainly possessed, was not enough to ensure victory. To be truly national, a party had to create and maintain a coalition of North, South, and West. The Democrats were the first to do this.

National Political Figures

Suddenly, the new democratic politics, with its mass appeal to ordinary voters superimposed on older sectional issues, had engrossed the nation. In an earlier time, voters were most familiar with their local and state representatives. Now, for the first time, leading senators and representatives became nationally known, their speeches printed and reprinted in newspapers, journals, and textbooks, where generations of schoolchildren memorized them to present at community speaking contests or Fourth of July celebrations. Three sectional leaders stood out: Daniel Webster of the North, John C. Calhoun of the South, and Henry Clay of the West.

Senator Daniel Webster of Massachusetts was the outstanding orator of the age. Large, dark, and stern, Webster delivered his speeches in a deep, booming voice that, listeners said, "shook the world." He was capable of pathos as well, bringing tears to the eyes of those who heard him say, while defending Dartmouth College before the Supreme Court (in the case of the same name), "It is a small college, sir, but there are those who love it." Webster, a lawyer for business interests, became the main spokesman for the new northern commercial interests, supporting a high protective tariff, a national bank, and a strong federal government. Webster's fondness for comfortable living, and especially brandy, made him less effective as he grew older, but then, as a contemporary of his remarked, "no man could be as great as Daniel Webster looked."

Equally formidable was the spokesman for the South, the intense, dogmatic, and uncompromising Senator John C. Calhoun of South Carolina. In his early days as a War Hawk before the War of 1812,

Calhoun was an ardent nationalist and expansionist. Since the debate over the Missouri Compromise in 1820, however, Calhoun had wholeheartedly identified with southern interests, which were first and foremost the expansion and preservation of slavery. As the South's minority position in Congress became clear over the years, Calhoun's defense of southern economic interests and slavery became more and more rigid. Not for nothing did he earn his nickname the "Cast-Iron Man."

In contrast with the other two, Henry Clay of Kentucky, spokesman of the West, was charming, witty, and always eager to forge political compromises. Clay held the powerful position of Speaker of the House of Representatives. A spellbinding storyteller and well known for his ability to make a deal, Clay worked to incorporate western desires for cheap and and good transportation into national politics. He put forward a political agenda that became known as the American System: a national bank, a protective tariff, and a proposal for substantial federal money for roads, canals, and railroads — internal improvements Clay might well have forged a political alliance between the North and the West if not for the policies of President Jackson, his fellow westerner and greatest rival. Jackson's preeminence

thwarted Clay's own ambition to be president. Clay is best known, then, for the skill with which he used his sectional leadership to bring about the two great compromises over expansion, the Missouri Compromise (see Chapter 9) and the Compromise of 1850 (see Chapter 15).

All three sectional representatives — Webster, Calhoun, and Clay — were extraordinary political figures who embodied the hopes, and the fears, of their region. But the man who became president of the United States in 1828, Andrew Jackson, outdid them all. Jackson overrode sectional interests and had national appeal.

On March 4, 1829, Andrew Jackson was inaugurated as president of the United States. Jackson himself was still in mourning for his beloved wife Rachel, who had died, he believed, because of the slanders of the campaign. But everyone else was celebrating. The small community of Washington was crowded with strangers, many of them westerners and common people who had come especially for Jackson's inauguration. Their celebrating dismayed the more respectable members of the community. Jackson's brief inaugural address was almost drowned out by the cheering of the crowd, and after the ceremony the new president was mobbed

Until 1828, presidential inaugurations had been small, polite, and ceremonial occasions. Jackson's popularity brought a horde of well-wishers to Washington. As they all arrived to attend Jackson's frontier-style open house at the White House, conservative critics claimed that "the reign of King Mob" had begun.

by well-wishers. The same unrestrained enthusiasm was evident at a White House reception, where the crowd was large and disorderly. People stood on chairs and sofas to catch glimpses of Jackson, and shoved and pushed to reach the food and drink, which was finally carried out to the lawn. In the rush to follow, some people exited through windows rather than the doors. All in all, a disapproving observer noted, this behavior indicated the end of proper government and the beginning of "the reign of King Mob." Indeed, Jackson's administration was different from those before it.

The Spoils System and the New Politics

Jackson began his term rewarding party loyalists by giving them positions in the national government. While Jackson himself spoke loftily of democratizing the holding of public office, New York Bucktail William Marcy put the matter more bluntly: There was "nothing wrong in the rule, that to the victor belong the spoils of the enemy." Hence the expression *spoils system* to describe the practice of awarding government appointments to loyalists of the winning party. This attitude toward public office, as we have seen in the case of New York State politics, was one of the strongest points of difference between the new politics and the old.

What Jackson did was to transfer a common state practice to the national level, and to set a precedent that was followed in national politics until passage of the Pendleton Act of 1883, which began the reform of the civil service system. Unfortunately for Jackson, he soon found that appointments based primarily on party loyalty were not always successful. His opponents were quick to make accusations of corruption and inefficiency among the new officeholders. It is doubtful, though, if any alternative to the spoils system — such as the elite, independent civil service that the British were developing at the time — would have been consistent with the democratic spirit of American politics in the 1820s.

In fact, although the spoils system upset Jackson's opponents more than most of his other controversial actions, the number of officeholders he replaced was rather small — only about 10 percent (of a total of 10,093 offices). As was true in so many other cases, it was the *manner* in which Jackson made appointments, brooking no argument, not even from supporters, that opponents found so aggravating.

A Strong Executive

The mob scene that accompanied Jackson's inauguration was more than a reflection of the popular enthusiasm for Old Hickory. It also signaled a higher level of controversy in national politics. Jackson's personal style quickly stripped national politics of the polite and gentlemanly aura of cooperation it had acquired during the Era of Good Feelings and that Adams had vainly tried to maintain. Jackson had played rough all his life and he relished controversy. His administration (1829–37) had plenty of it.

Andrew Jackson dominated his own administration. With the exception of Van Buren, who became secretary of state, Jackson ignored most of his Cabinet. Instead he consulted with an informal group, the Kitchen Cabinet, composed of Van Buren and old western friends; it did *not* include Calhoun, the vice-president. Nor was Jackson any friendlier with the two other great sectional representatives of the day. He never forgave Henry Clay for his role in the "corrupt bargain" of 1824, and Daniel Webster represented the privileged elite who were Jackson's favorite target.

One of the ways in which Jackson separated himself from other politicians was by creating social distance. When Jackson's secretary of war, John Henry Eaton, married a beautiful woman of flamboyant reputation, he transgressed the social code of the time. It was rumored that Peggy Eaton had been John's mistress for some time, and that there were a number of other men in her past. She was, in nineteenth-century thinking, a fallen woman and unfit for polite society. The respectable ladies of Washington shunned her. But Jackson, aroused by memories of the slanders against his own wife, defended Peggy Eaton, and urged his Cabinet members to force their wives to call on her. When, to a woman, they refused, Jackson called the husbands henpecked. This episode shattered the social life of Cabinet members and drove a wedge between Jackson and Calhoun, whose wife was a leader in the anti-Eaton group. Jackson claimed to be motivated only by chivalry, but this social disagreement served his political purposes very well. Ironically, it may have occurred only because Jackson was a widower. Had his wife Rachel been alive, she would surely have sided with Mrs. Calhoun in upholding the moral code of the time.

For all of his western origins, Jackson saw himself not as a sectional candidate but as a national one. He was more interested in asserting strong national leadership than promoting sectional compromise. He believed that the president, who symbolized the popular will of the people, ought to dominate the government. As he put it in his first annual message, "the first principle of our system [is that] *the majority is to govern.*" In this, as in other respects, Jackson showed his debt to the new politics. The founders of the Constitution had not envisaged either direct popular elections or party politics. Nor had they foreseen that a president such as Jackson would use his popular mandate to strengthen the executive branch of government at the expense of the legislature and judiciary. By using the veto more frequently than all previous presidents combined (twelve vetoes compared with nine by the first six presidents), Jackson forced Congress to constantly consider his opinions. Even more important, Jackson's "negative activism" *restricted* federal activity, thereby allowing more power to remain in state hands.

In one of his most famous and unexpected actions, the veto of the Maysville Road Bill of 1830, Jackson refused to allow federal funding of a southern spur of the National Road in Kentucky, claiming such funding should be left to the state. Like Presidents Madison and Monroe before him, Jackson believed that federal funding for extensive and expensive internal improvements was unconstitutional, because it infringed on the "reserved powers" specified by the Constitution for the states. What made the veto surprising was that Jackson's western supporters strongly desired better transportation. But by aiming his message to a popular audience, and by couching his objection in terms of states' rights (and by making it clear that he was not opposed to *all* internal improvements), Jackson actually gained political support. He also had the satisfaction of defeating a measure central to the American System proposed by his western rival, Henry Clay.

Indian Removal

In an even more controversial example of presidential authority, Jackson defied his own Supreme Court over the question of Indian removal. Jackson, a famous Indian fighter, undoubtedly expressed the majority will (at least of southerners and westerners) when he supported the state of Georgia in its efforts to remove the "Five Civilized Tribes" (the Choctaws, Cherokees, Creeks, Chickasaws, and Seminoles) to Oklahoma. Jackson himself had played a large role in forcing major land cessions from the tribes following the War of 1812 (see

Chapter 11). By the 1830s, under constant pressure from settlers, each of the five tribes had ceded most of its lands. But sizable self-governing groups remained in Georgia, Alabama, Mississippi, and Florida. All of these (except the Seminoles) had moved far in the direction of coexistence with whites. They had adopted white clothes and housing styles, welcomed white missionaries, established farms and businesses, and even modeled new government structures on those of whites.

The policy of the United States government from the time of Jefferson's administration had been to remove Indian tribes from settled areas to the new Indian Territory west of the Mississippi River. Officially, the reason for this practice was to humanely shelter an inferior race while they learned to adjust to "civilization" (see Chapter 9). But what if, as in the case of the Cherokees, the tribe had changed its "inferior" ways and adopted the customs of the "superior" group? No matter, said the legislatures of Georgia, Alabama, and Mississippi, which passed laws in the 1820s invalidating federal treaties granting special status to Indian lands.

Unluckily for the Cherokees, gold was discovered in 1829 in northern Georgia, within the Cherokee nation. More than 3,000 whites invaded the region, damaging Cherokee crops and property. When the Cherokees appealed to the Georgia courts, their petitions were ignored. As a final indignity, the Georgia legislature passed a law forbidding the Cherokees to mine or prospect for gold on their own lands.

In 1830, the U.S. Congress (at President Jackson's urging) passed the Removal Act, which appropriated funds for relocation. Jackson helped by sending federal officials to negotiate removal treaties with the southern tribes. The Cherokees fought their removal by using the white man's weapon — the law. In *Cherokee Nation v. Georgia* (1831) and *Worcester v. Georgia* (1832) Chief Justice John Marshall ruled that the Cherokees, though not a state or a foreign nation, were a "domestic dependent nation" that could not be forced by the state of Georgia to give up its land against its will. When he heard the Supreme Court's decision, Jackson is reputed to have said, "John Marshall has made his decision. Now let him enforce it." Ignoring the decision, Jackson continued his support for removal.

In the face of all these pressures, what could the Indian tribes do? The Seminoles of Florida chose to fight. Aided by runaway slaves and by their unsurpassed knowledge of their homeland, the Florida Everglades, some Seminole bands fought a guerrilla war that lasted into the 1840s before the U.S.

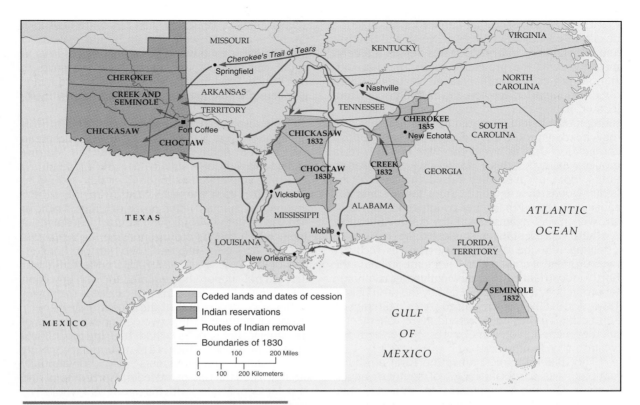

Southern Indian Cessions and Removals, 1830s

Pressure on the five southern Indian peoples — the Creek, Choctaw, Chickasaw, Cherokee, and Seminole — that began during the War of 1812 culminated with their removal in the 1830s. Some groups from every tribe ceded their southern homelands peacefully and moved to the newly established Indian Territory west of Arkansas and Missouri. Some, like the Seminole, resisted by force. Others, like the Cherokee, resisted in the courts but finally lost when President Jackson refused to enforce a Supreme Court decision in their favor. The Cherokee, the last to move, were forcibly removed by the U.S. Army along the "Trail of Tears" in 1838.

military gave up. Other tribes were much less fortunate: the Choctaws moved west in 1830; the Creeks were forcibly moved by the military in 1836, and the Chickasaws a year later. The last and most infamous removal was that of the Cherokees, who were driven west to Oklahoma along the "Trail of Tears" in 1838. A 7,000-man army escorting them watched thousands (perhaps a quarter of the 16,000 Cherokees) die along the way. Although Protestant missionaries had pleaded for a more humane policy, protest in Congress against this brutal removal was unavailing.

In both the Maysville Road veto and the issue of Indian removal, Andrew Jackson took the political position that states had the right to decide their own affairs without interference from the federal government. This was a popular position, garnering him widespread support, especially in the South and

West. But in the next major event of his administration, the nullification crisis, Jackson was forced to define the limits of states' rights.

Sectionalism and Nullification

The men who met to write a new federal constitution in Philadelphia in 1787 were forced to make many compromises in the course of their deliberations. Perhaps the most delicate compromise of all left the federal structure itself ambiguous: The line between the rights of the states and the powers of the central government was blurred. Because there was disagreement about where that line should be drawn, all subsequent sectional disagreements were also constitutional arguments. That was certainly the case with the most serious event of Andrew Jackson's presidency, the nullification crisis.

The political issue that came to symbolize the divergent economic interests of North and South—and the rights of individual states versus a federal majority—was the protective tariff. The first substantial protective tariff, enacted in 1816, placed duties on imported woolen and cotton goods, iron, leather, hats, paper, and sugar. Northern manufacturing interests had clamored for the tariff, because they needed protection from the ruthless British competition that followed the War of 1812. As a group, wealthy southern planters were opposed to tariffs, both because they raised the cost of the luxury goods they imported from Europe and because they feared that other countries might retaliate with tariffs against southern cotton. But most southern representatives supported the 1816 tariff, believing it to be a temporary postwar recovery measure. But of course it was not temporary: As the North industrialized and new industries clamored for protection, it was superseded by the tariff bills of 1824 and 1828, which raised rates still higher. Southerners protested more and more vehemently, but they were outvoted in Congress by northern and western representatives.

The 1828 tariff, nicknamed the Tariff of Abominations, was a special target of southern anger, because Jackson's supporters in Congress had passed it in order to increase northern support for him in the presidential campaign of that year. The taxes on imported textiles and iron were high, ranging from a third to a half of the total value of the item. Lacking the votes to block the tariff, southerners in Congress faced the bleak prospect that their economic interests would always be ignored by the majority. Southern opposition to the protective tariff, they claimed, was based on a constitutional principle: The tariff was not a truly national measure but a sectional one that helped only some groups while harming others.

South Carolina, Calhoun's home state, reacted the most forcefully to the tariff of 1828. Of the older southern states, South Carolina had been the hardest hit by the opening of the new cotton lands to the west, which had drained both population and commerce from the state. Still suffering from the depression that followed the panic of 1819, and from the scare caused by Denmark Vesey's abortive slave revolt of 1822 (see Chapter 11), South Carolinians were in no mood to compromise. One index of South Carolina's changed status was the declining position of Charleston, once the equal of New York and Boston as a port. Much of Charleston's shipping business now went to Mobile and New Orleans instead. Furthermore, South Carolinians, who had always enjoyed especially close ties with the British Caribbean islands, were shaken by the realization that Parliament, bowing to popular pressure at home, was planning to emancipate all the slaves in the British West Indies. What, South Carolinians wondered, would prevent Congress from following suit?

The response to these fears was the doctrine of nullification, and it was the topic of widespread discussion in South Carolina in 1828. The doctrine upheld the right of a state to declare a federal law null and void (unconstitutional) and to refuse to enforce it within the state. This was not a new argument. Thomas Jefferson and James Madison had used it in the Virginia and Kentucky Resolves of 1798, which they wrote in opposing the Alien and Sedition Acts (see Chapter 8). The Hartford Convention of 1814, at which Federalists protested a war they did not support, had adopted the same position (see Chapter 9). At issue in each case was the power of the state versus that of the federal government. However, neither of these two earlier expressions of the nullification doctrine had had much political impact. Moreover, since 1814 national economic and political developments had substantially strengthened the role of the federal government and popular identification with the nation as a whole. For these reasons, South Carolina's nullification doctrine seemed to belong to an earlier age.

Nevertheless, South Carolina had an important supporter of nullification in the person of Calhoun, who wrote a widely circulated defense of the doctrine, the *Exposition and Protest,* in 1828. Because he was soon to be elected as Andrew Jackson's vice-president, he wrote the *Exposition* anonymously. Calhoun hoped to use his influence with Jackson to gain support for nullification, but he was disappointed.

Where Calhoun saw nullification as a safeguard of the rights of the minority, Jackson saw it simply as treason. As the president said at a famous exchange of toasts at the annual Jefferson Day Dinner in 1830, "Our Federal Union, *it must be preserved.*" While Jackson was, as we have seen, a strong supporter of the rights of states over their own affairs, he would not countenance a state veto on matters of national policy, such as the tariff. In response to Jackson, Calhoun offered his own toast: "The Union—next to our liberty most dear. May we always remember that it can only be preserved by distributing equally the benefits and burdens of the Union." The president and the vice-president were thus in open disagreement on a matter of crucial national importance. The outcome was inevitable: Calhoun lost all influ-

A nationalist and expansionist in the War of 1812, Calhoun increasingly identified with southern regional interests. While serving as Jackson's Vice President (1829–32) Calhoun supported South Carolina's nullification doctrine because he believed that the Constitution guaranteed the rights of the states. But his open defiance of the president at the Jefferson Day dinner in 1830, when he gave a toast, "The Union — next to our liberty most dear," earned him Jackson's undying enmity.

Force Bill authorizing the federal government to collect the tariff in South Carolina at gunpoint if necessary. Intimidated, the other southern states refused to follow South Carolina's lead. More quietly, Jackson also asked Congress to revise the tariff. Henry Clay, the Great Pacificator, swung into action and soon, with Calhoun's support, had crafted the Tariff Act of 1833. This measure gradually lowered tariffs over a ten-year period (giving domestic manufacturers time to adjust) but called for an end to all tariffs in 1842 (thus pleasing the South). The South Carolina legislature thereupon repealed its nullification of the Tariff of 1832, but in a continuing spirit of bravado the legislature nullified the Force Bill. Jackson defused the crisis by ignoring this second nullification.

This was the most serious threat to national unity that the United States had ever experienced. South Carolinians, by threatening to secede, had forced concessions on a matter they believed of vital economic importance. They — and a number of other southerners — believed that the resolution of the crisis illustrated the success of their uncompromising tactics. But most of the rest of the nation breathed a sigh of relief, echoing Daniel Webster's sentiment, spoken in the heat of the debate over nullification, "Liberty and Union, now and forever, one and inseparable!" Most Americans firmly believed that while every effort should be made to address sectional concerns, national unity had to come first. Their support of national parties reflected this opinion. Indeed, Van Buren could not have repeated his New York success at the federal level unless voters supported the concept of national unity.

ence with Jackson. Two years later he resigned the vice-presidency, and Martin Van Buren was elected to the office for Jackson's second term. Calhoun became a senator from South Carolina, and in that capacity participated in the last act of the nullification drama.

In 1832 the nullification controversy became a full-blown crisis. In passing the Tariff of 1832, Congress (in spite of Jackson's urging) retained high taxes on woolens, iron, and hemp, although it reduced duties on other items. South Carolina responded with a special convention and an Ordinance of Nullification, in which it rejected the tariff and refused to collect the required taxes. The state further issued a call for a volunteer militia and threatened to secede from the Union if Jackson used force against it. Jackson responded vehemently, denouncing the nullifiers — "Disunion by armed force is *treason*" — and obtaining from Congress a

INTERNAL IMPROVEMENTS

Jackson's presidency was more controversial than any Americans had ever known. Much of the controversy stemmed from Jackson's belligerent personality, but there were deeper reasons as well. In many respects, national politics simply mirrored the dramatic economic events of the time. One such event, the transportation revolution, occurred as the United States attempted to unify itself territorially. As North, South, and West became more closely connected economically, old attitudes of regional isolationism were challenged. The interdependence of North, South, and West, and the points of conflict among these three regions, made the politics of the Jacksonian period lively and memorable.

The Role of Federal and State Government

Beneath the surface of the political debates of the time was basic agreement that the federal and state governments had an important role in promoting economic growth and in fostering the growth of a national market. Not until later in the century did officials come to believe that the government should leave private enterprise alone. Instead, people expected government not only to create an atmosphere conducive to growth, but to actually subsidize risky undertakings, such as canals and railroads. At issue was not whether but how much government assistance there should be. There was also disagreement (as Jackson's Maysville Road veto showed) over whether the state or the federal government should pay.

In his *Report on Manufactures* (1791) Alexander Hamilton had pointed out the financial and commercial requirements for economic development: the banking system and other financial institutions, transportation and communication systems, and support for innovation and technological development — what we now call the *infrastructure* (see Chapter 8). National governments in the 1790s and beyond largely followed the Hamiltonian blueprint, as we saw in Chapter 9. This was particularly evident in 1816, when the Madison administration adopted virtually all of the Federalist program. Madison's successor, James Monroe (1817–25), continued these policies.

Government-sponsored enterprise was most evident in the exploration and development of the trans-Mississippi West (see Chapter 14). It was also prominent in nonwestern federal activities, especially those involving new technologies. Federal arsenals, funded by the government, developed interchangeable parts for army rifles. The United States Post Office gave Samuel F. B. Morse the money to construct the first telegraph line (from Washington to Baltimore, in 1844) and paid him to run it during its first year of operation. Federal patent laws protected him and less famous inventors, giving them a seventeen-year monopoly on their inventions.

Accompanying the federal government's financial encouragement of economic growth was a series of decisions by federal courts asserting broad federal powers over interstate commerce. The effect of these decisions was to prevent states from interfering with such commerce, thus providing the freedom — and the legal predictability — that entre-preneurs needed to operate. Two key decisions were handed down by Chief Justice John Marshall (who had been on the bench since 1801). In *Dartmouth College v. Woodward* (1819) the Supreme Court prevented states from interfering in contracts, and in *Gibbons v. Ogden* (1824) it enjoined the state of New York from giving a monopoly over a steamboat line to Robert Fulton, inventor of the vessel. Although Fulton's invention was protected by patent, its commercial application was not. Patenting thus encouraged technology, but not at the expense of competition. A decision handed down by Marshall's successor, Roger Taney, *Charles River Bridge v. Warren Bridge* (1837), again supported economic opportunity by denying a monopoly. Each of these three decisions, it should be noted, involved federal reversal of decisions made at the state level. They show clearly how the Supreme Court, under Marshall's leadership, strengthened the power of the federal government and thus fostered national unity rather than localism.

But these three Supreme Court decisions did not discourage the states from economic activity. In fact, the states spent much more money than the federal government to build roads, canals, and railroads. By 1860 the state of Pennsylvania alone had invested $100 million in canals, railroads, banks, and industry. States and towns, especially in newly populated areas of the West, competed against each other in giving land, subsidies, and other forms of encouragement to industries (particularly railroads) and institutions (colleges, especially) to settle in their locality.

Another crucial state activity was the passage of laws concerning incorporation of businesses that had grown too large for individual proprietorship, family ownership, or limited partnership. Businesses that needed to raise large amounts of capital by attracting many investors found contractual guarantees of incorporation by the states essential. The state guarantee that investors wanted most was limited liability — the assurance that investors could lose no more than an amount of money proportionate to the amount of stock they held in the company. Thus, if the company went bankrupt or was sued, the amount of money that could be claimed from each investor was limited. State charters of incorporation were strong encouragement to transportation companies and banks. They were less commonly used by merchants and manufacturers until later in the century. Incorporation could be restrictive, in that the business not only gained privileges but was also subject to state regulation. Nevertheless, the net effect of state incorporation laws was to encourage large-scale economic activity.

The Transportation Revolution

The most visible evidence of state and federal encouragement of economic growth was the utterly remarkable transformation of transportation. No single development did as much as transportation improvements to encourage Americans to look beyond their local communities or to stimulate the enterprising, commercial spirit for which Americans became so widely known.

The improvements in transportation in the period 1800–1850 had dramatic effects both on individual mobility and on the economy. By 1850 it was easier for people to move, but an even more remarkable change was the ease with which commercial goods could reach them. Even people who remained in one place found that their horizons were much broader in 1850 than they were fifty years before. The difference lay in improvements in road and water transport, in the invention and speedy development of railroads, and in improved communications, of which the telegraph came to symbolize the new age.

In 1800, travel by road was difficult for much of the year. Mud in the spring, dust in the summer, snow in the winter all made travel by horseback or carriage uncomfortable, slow, and sometimes dangerous. Over the years, localities and states attempted to improve local roads or contracted with private turnpike companies to complete, maintain, and collect tolls on important stretches of road from town to town. In general, the condition of local roads remained poor. The more important development was the commitment of the federal government to the improvement of interregional transportation. The greatest single federal transportation expense, the National Road, built of gravel rather than dirt, spanned the Appalachian Mountains at the Cumberland Gap, thereby opening up the West. Built in stages (to Wheeling by 1818, to Columbus by 1833, to Vandalia, Illinois — almost at the Mississippi River — by 1850), the National Road was one answer to the need, especially urgent among westerners, to link the different regions of the expanding United States. At the same time, the road facilitated the westward movement of population. As a result of this, fifteen states from west of the Appalachians were admitted to the Union between 1790 and 1850. The National Road was an appropriate symbol of the nation's commitment to expansion *and* cohesion,

Travel Times, 1800 and 1857

The effect of the Transportation Revolution is dramatically shown in this comparison of travel times in 1800 to those of 1857. Improved roads, canals, steamboats, and railroads vastly expanded everyone's horizons. Americans now found it easier to move than ever before. Even for those who stayed at home, the new communication links diminished the rural isolation that had been so common in 1800. Easier transportation linked the developing West to the eastern seaboard and fostered a national identity and pride.

for by tying two regions together it helped to foster a national community.

Canals

On the other hand, the National Road and other federally financed interregional roads were unsatisfactory in a commercial sense. Transportation of bulky goods (grain, for example) was too slow and expensive by road. Waterborne transportation was much cheaper, and was still the major commercial link among the Atlantic seaboard states and in the Mississippi–Ohio River system. But prior to the 1820s most water routes were north–south or coastal (Boston to Charleston, for example); east–

west links were urgently needed. Canals, most famously the Erie Canal, turned out to be the answer.

This canal was the brainchild of New York governor DeWitt Clinton, who had the grandiose vision of linking New York City and the Great Lakes by means of the Hudson River and a 364-mile-long canal from Albany to Buffalo. When Clinton proposed the canal in 1817 it was derisively called Clinton's Ditch, for the longest existing American canal was only 27 miles long and had taken nine years to build. Nevertheless, Clinton convinced the New York legislature to approve a bond issue, and investors (New York and British merchants) subscribed to the tune of $7 million, an immense sum for the day.

Building the canal — 40 feet wide, 4 feet deep, 364 miles long, with 83 locks and more than 300 bridges along the way — was a vast engineering and construction challenge. Yankee ingenuity showed at every step of the way, from the creation of stump pullers, to substitutes for cement (previously imported from England), to the widespread use of Dupont blasting powder, the forerunner of dynamite, which wasn't invented for another forty years.

Manpower was another concern. In the early stages nearby farmers worked for eight dollars a month, but when malaria hit the work force in the summer of 1819 many wisely went home. They were replaced by 3,000 Irish contract laborers, who were much more expensive — fifty cents a day plus room and board — but more reliable (if they survived). Local people regarded the Irish workers as strange and rather frightening, but the importation of foreign contract labor was a portent of the future. Much of the heavy construction work on later canals and railroads was performed by immigrant labor. The

This view of the Erie Canal, painted four years after its opening in 1825, shows how rural was most of the countryside through which the canal passed. It also shows the canal's immense commercial success, for three boats can be seen in this small picture alone.
(John William Hill. View on the Erie Canal. *1829. Watercolor. The New York Public Library. Astor, Lenox and Tilden Foundations.)*

best-known example was the first Central Pacific railroad line through the rugged Sierra Nevada in California, built by Chinese contract laborers in the 1860s.

As DeWitt Clinton had promised, to general disbelief, the Erie Canal was completed in less than ten years. It was the wonder of the age. On October 26, 1825, Clinton declared the canal open in Buffalo and sent the first boat, the *Seneca Chief,* on its way to New York, at the incredible speed of four miles an hour. (Ironically, the Seneca Indians, for whom the boat was named, had been removed from the path of the canal and confined to a small reservation.) The boat reached New York on November 4, to be greeted with elaborate ceremonies, including one in which vials of water from the great rivers of the world—the Nile, Ganges, Mississippi, Rhine, and Danube—were emptied into New York harbor to symbolize the opening of commerce between the heart of America and the world.

This grand gesture was appropriate. The Erie Canal provided easy passage to and from the interior, both for people and for goods. It drew settlers like a magnet, both from the East and increasingly from overseas: by 1830, 50,000 people a year were moving west on the canal to the rich farmland of Indiana, Illinois, and territory farther west. Earlier settlers now had a national, indeed an international, market for their produce. Farm families became consumers themselves. One of the most dramatic illustrations of the canal's impact can be found in statistics for home-produced textiles. In 1825, the year the Erie Canal opened, New York homesteads produced 16.5 million yards of textiles. By 1835 the figure was almost half that—8.8 million yards—and by 1855 it was under 1 million.

Towns along the canal—Utica, Rochester, Buffalo—became instant cities, each an important commercial center in its own right. Perhaps the greatest beneficiary was the city of New York, which quickly established a commercial and financial supremacy no other American city could match. The Erie Canal, more than any other development, decisively turned New York's merchants away from Europe and toward America's own heartland. That this shift was soon reflected in American art and literature is not at all surprising.

Everywhere along its route the Erie Canal did much to foster regional feeling. As the famous song put it,

You'll always know your neighbor,
You'll always know your pal,
If you've ever navigated
On the Erie Canal.

The phenomenal success of the Erie Canal ($8.5 million in tolls were collected in the first nine years) prompted a canal mania: $200 million was invested in canals (three-quarters of it by state governments) between 1820 and 1840. Soon nearly every state boasted canals. There was the Cumberland and Oxford Canal in Maine; the Blackstone Canal, linking Worcester, Massachusetts, with Providence, Rhode Island; the Pennsylvania Main Line Canal, reaching all the way from Philadelphia to Pittsburgh; Maryland's Chesapeake and Ohio Canal; and canals in Ohio, Illinois, and Indiana. No other canal achieved the success of the Erie, but most did contribute to the building of east—west links. In 1800 it had often been easier and cheaper to ship goods across the Atlantic than, for example, from western Massachusetts to Boston. Canals helped to change that.

Steamboats

An even more important improvement in water transportation, especially in the American interior, was the steamboat. Robert Fulton first demonstrated the commercial feasibility of steamboats in 1807, and they were soon operating in the East. But the first steamboats were too expensive and cumbersome for western rivers. Redesigned with more efficient engines and shallower, broader hulls, steamboats transformed commerce on the country's great rivers: the Ohio, the Mississippi, the Missouri, and their tributaries. Steamboats were dangerous: frequent boiler explosions prompted one of the first public demands for regulation of private enterprise. The first federal law, passed in 1838, was so weak that the public demanded stronger legislation. The result was the Steamboat Act of 1852. It set standards for the construction, equipment, and operation of steamboat boilers, required measures to prevent fire and collisions, and established an inspection system to make sure the new regulations were carried out.

Dangerous as they were, steamboats greatly stimulated trade on western rivers. Downstream trade had long been possible, but the long return trip overland on the Natchez Trace had been too arduous and dangerous for most. For a time, steamboats actually increased the downriver flatboat trade, because boatmen could now make more round trips in the same amount of time, traveling home by steamboat in speed and comfort.

Cities such as Cincinnati, already notable for its rapid growth, experienced a new economic surge that, like New England shipping of a generation before (see Chapter 9), increased urbanization and commerce of all kinds. Cincinnati, a frontier outpost in 1790, was by the 1830s a center of steamboat manufacture and machine tool production, as well as a central shipping point for food for the southern market. Even in sleepy agricultural villages, such as Mark Twain's hometown of Hannibal, Missouri, the steamboat was a powerful symbol of energy and international commerce. As Twain recounts in *Old Times on the Mississippi:*

> After all these years I can picture that old time to myself now, just as it was then: the white town drowsing in the sunshine of a summer's morning; the streets empty, or pretty nearly so; one or two clerks sitting in front of the Water Street stores, with their splint-bottomed chairs tilted back against the wall, chins on breasts, hats slouched over their faces, asleep . . . ; two or three lonely little freight piles scattered about the "levee"; a pile of "skids" on the slope of the stone-paved wharf, and the fragrant town drunkard asleep in the shadow of them; . . . the great Mississippi, the majestic, magnificent Mississippi, rolling its mile-wide tide along, shining in the sun; the dense forest away on the other side; the "point" above the town, and the "point" below. Presently a film of dark smoke appears above one of those remote "points"; instantly a negro drayman, famous for his quick eye and prodigious voice, lifts up the cry, "S-t-e-a-m-boat a-comin'!" and the scene changes! The town drunkard stirs, the clerks wake up, a furious clatter of drays follows, every house and store pours out a human contribution, and all in a twinkling the dead town is alive and moving. Drays, carts, men, boys, all go hurrying from many quarters to a common center, the wharf. Assembled there, the people fasten their eyes upon the coming boat as upon a wonder they are seeing for the first time . . . . the crew are grouped on the forecastle; the broad stage is run far out over the port bow, and an envied deck-hand stands picturesquely on the end of it with a coil of rope in his hand; . . . the captain lifts his hand, a bell rings, the wheels stop; then they turn back, churning the water to foam, and the steamer is at rest. Then such a scramble as there is to get aboard, and to get ashore, and to take in freight and to discharge freight, all at one and the same time; and such a yelling and cursing as the mates facilitate it all with! Ten minutes later the steamer is under way again. . . . After ten more minutes the town is dead again, and the town drunkard asleep by the skids once more.

Steam also transformed oceangoing transportation, albeit more slowly. In 1817, the Black Ball Line established the first regularly scheduled service from New York to Liverpool on packet sailing ships, so named because they carried packets of mail in addition to cargo and passengers. It was not until 1848 that the Cunard Line began dispatching passenger steamships on the transatlantic route, more than halving the travel time (from as long as fifty days by sail, depending on the wind, to ten or fifteen). For a time the swift and elegant New England-built clipper ships held their own, but they depended on wind to power them, and eventually they were eclipsed by the speed and reliability of the new steamships. New York, which pioneered transatlantic packet service, already enjoyed commercial preeminence, but now its role as the terminus for Atlantic passenger ships earned it a new title, "Gateway to America."

Railroads

Remarkable as all these transportation changes were, the most remarkable was still to come. Railroads, newcomers in 1830 (when the Baltimore and Ohio Railroad opened with 13 miles of track), grew to an astounding 31,000 miles by 1860. By that date, New England and the Old Northwest had laid a dense network of rails, and several lines had reached west beyond the Mississippi. The South, the least industrialized section of the nation, had many fewer railroads (a situation that placed the Confederate army at a considerable disadvantage during the Civil War). "Railroad mania" surpassed even canal mania, as investors — as many as one-quarter of them British — rushed to invest in the new invention.

As with the steamboat, the early years of the railroads were devoted to the solving of technological and supply problems. For example, adequate power required heavy locomotives, which led to the need for iron rather than wooden rails. This in turn forced America's iron industry to modernize (at first, railroad iron was imported from England) and led to the development of a specialized industry, represented by Philadelphia's Baldwin Locomotive Works, for building and servicing locomotives. Heavy engines required a solid gravel roadbed and strong wooden ties. Arranging steady supplies of both and the labor to lay them was a construction challenge on a new scale. Finally, there was the problem of establishing a standard gauge, or width between the rails. Because so many early railroads were short and local, builders had been content to use any gauge that served their purposes. This meant the railroads were built in varying widths, which in turn necessitated frequent train changes for long-haul passengers and freight. At one time, the trip from Philadelphia to Charleston involved eight gauge changes. This was not only an inconve-

The Bank War and the Rise of the Whigs

The last major event of Jackson's presidency, the controversy surrounding his refusal to renew the charter of the Second Bank of the United States, had lasting political consequences. Jackson's opponents, irritated by his earlier actions, were so infuriated by the bank episode that they formed a permanent opposition party, the Whigs. From the heat of the Bank War emerged the two-party system that has characterized American politics ever since.

The Bank War

The first Bank of the United States had been chartered by Congress in 1791, at Alexander Hamilton's urging (see Chapter 8). Federalists supported it, Jeffersonians opposed it, and the latter allowed its charter to expire in 1811. But after the War of 1812 almost all Jeffersonians came to appreciate the stability provided by a central bank. The Second Bank of the United States was granted a twenty-year charter by Congress in 1816. Like its predecessor, the Bank had played a powerful role in the expanding American economy, encouraging the growth of strong and stable financial interests and curbing less stable and irresponsible ones.

Also, like its predecessor, the Bank was not a government agency but a private institution the majority of whose directors were appointed by the government. Its stockholders were some of the nation's richest men (New York's John Jacob Astor and Philadelphia's Stephen Girard among them). The bank was directed by the erudite and aristocratic Nicholas Biddle of Philadelphia. Biddle, a friend of Thomas Jefferson's and an avid amateur scientist, was the editor of the journals of Lewis and Clark.

The Bank, which was the nation's largest (it had thirty branches), performed a variety of functions: It held the government's money (about $10 million), sold government bonds, and made commercial loans. But its most important function was the control it exercised over state banks. At the time, America lacked a national currency. The money in circulation was a mixture of paper money (U.S. notes and the notes of state banks) and gold and silver coins (specie), many of them of foreign origin. Because state banks tended to issue more paper money than they could back with hard currency, the Bank always demanded repayment of its loans to them in coin. This policy forced state banks to maintain adequate reserves, curbed inflationary pressures (overprinting of banknotes), and restricted speculative activities such as risky loans. In times of recession, the Bank eased the pressure on state banks, demanding only partial payment in coin. Thus the Bank acted as a currency stabilizer by helping to control the money supply. It brought a semblance of order to what we today would consider a chaotic money system — coins of various weights and a multitude of state banknotes, many of which were discounted (not accepted at full face value) in other states.

The concept of a strong national bank was supported by the majority of the nation's merchants and businessmen, and was a key element in Henry Clay's American System. Nevertheless, the Bank had many opponents. The objections arose from both sectional and political resentments. A number of state bank directors felt overshadowed by the central bank's size and power. Western land speculators, and many western farmers, chafed at the bank's tight control over the currency reserves of state banks, claiming it was harmful to western development. Both western farmers and urban workers had bitter memories of the Panic of 1819, which the Bank had caused (at least in part) by sharply contracting credit. To some people, the economic power of the Bank was frightening; they feared that monied elites would use it to their own advantage. Although the rapid growth of the national economy made some sort of control necessary, many ordinary people were uneasy not only about the Bank but about banks of all kinds. They believed that a system based on paper currency would be manipulated by bankers in unpredictable and dangerous ways. Among those who held that opinion was Andrew Jackson, who had hated and feared banks ever since the 1790s, when he had lost a great deal of money in a speculative venture.

Early in his administration, Jackson hastened to tell Nicholas Biddle, "I do not dislike your Bank any more than all banks." By 1832, Jackson's opinion had changed and he and Biddle were locked in a personal conflict that harmed not only the national economy but the reputations of both men. Biddle, urged on by Henry Clay and Daniel Webster, precipitated the conflict by making early application for rechartering the Bank. Congress approved the application in July of 1832. Clay and Webster, though well

Cyrus McCormick is shown demonstrating his reaper to skeptical farmers. When they saw that the machine cut four times as much wheat per day as a hand-held scythe, farmers flocked to buy McCormick's invention. Agricultural practices, little changed for centuries, were revolutionized by inventions such as these.

wheat. So they concentrated on products they could sell in nearby towns and cities: vegetables, fruits, and dairy products. In the production of butter and cheese for market, the work of farm women was essential. But many young farm women left their homes in the 1820s and 1830s to work in the early textile mills, such as those in Lowell, Massachusetts (see Chapter 12).

Thus, even farmers who did not directly participate in the new western agriculture found their lives changed by it. This was less true in the South, where cotton remained the staple crop for anyone who could grow it. The lifestyle of the planter class was the aspiration of many white farmers who could afford to own only a few slaves. A number of other southern farmers resisted the pressures of commercialization, raising corn and hogs for home use and

clinging jealously to economic independence and traditional community ties (see Chapter 11). But in the North, and in particular in New England, the dramatic success of western farmers meant major change and adaptation for those who stayed behind. As we shall see in Chapter 12, northern farmers were already being drawn into the market economy by the putting-out system and the lure of work in the many small textile mills. Competition from western farmers thus sped up a transition that was already under way.

The transportation revolution and the commercialization of agriculture were exciting and disturbing experiences for everyone affected by them. For many people, the change was too rapid. It was on these people that Andrew Jackson's war against the Bank of the United States had its greatest impact.

ment of the region, ongoing since the 1790s, accelerated. In the 1830s, after the opening of the Erie Canal, migrants from New England streamed into northern Ohio, Illinois, Indiana, southern Wisconsin, and Michigan and began to reach into Iowa.

New Lands

Government policy strongly encouraged western settlement. The easy terms of federal land sales were an important inducement: from an initial rate of $2.00 per acre for a minimum of 640 acres in 1800, terms by 1820 had eased to $1.25 an acre for 80 acres. Still, this was too much for most settlers to pay all at once. So some people simply squatted, taking their chances that they could make enough money to buy the land before someone else bought it. Less daring settlers relied on credit, which was extended by banks, storekeepers, speculators, promoters, and, somewhat later, railroads, which received large grants of federal lands.

The very need for cash to purchase one's land involved western settlers in commercial agriculture from the beginning. Farmers, and the towns and cities that grew up to supply them, needed access to markets for their crops. Canals, steamboats, and railroads ensured that access, immediately tying the individual farm into national and international commercial networks. The long period of subsistence farming that had characterized colonial New England and the early Ohio Valley frontier (see Chapter 9) was superseded by commercial agriculture stimulated by the transportation revolution.

Commercial agriculture in turn encouraged regional specialization. Ohioans shipped corn and hogs by flatboat (and later by steamboat) to New Orleans. Cincinnati, the center of the Ohio trade, earned the nickname Porkopolis because of the importance of its slaughterhouses. Wheat flowed from the upper Midwest along the Erie Canal (and later, railroads) to eastern cities and increasingly to Europe. The center of wheat production continued to move west, from Ohio in the 1830s to Illinois in the 1850s and then to Wisconsin in the 1860s. In each new area, yields were higher than in the previous one. As the *Prairie Farmer* said in 1850, "the wheat crop is the great crop of the North-west for exchange purposes. It pays debts, buys groceries, clothing and land, and answers more emphatically the purposes of trade among the farmers, than any other crop."

At the same time, farmers who grew wheat or any other cash crop found themselves at the mercy of far-off markets, which established crop prices; faceless canal or railroad companies, which set transportation rates; and the state of the national economy, which determined the availability of local credit. This direct dependence on economic forces outside the control of the local community was something new. So too was the dependence on technology, embodied in expensive new machines that farmers often bought on credit.

The newly settled western lands were more fertile than eastern ones, and new tools made western farmers unusually productive. John Deere's steel plow (invented in 1837) cut in half the labor of plowing, making cultivation of larger acreages possible. Seed drills were another important advance. But the most remarkable innovation was Cyrus McCormick's reaper, invented in 1834. Earlier, harvesting had depended on manpower alone. A man could cut two or three acres of wheat a day with a cradle scythe, but with the horse-drawn reaper he could cut twelve acres. Impressed by these figures, western farmers rushed to buy the new technology, confident that increased production would rapidly pay for the new plow or reaper. In most years, their confidence was justified. Agricultural productivity on the new western lands increased dramatically. In the 1850s, for example, wheat production in the Mississippi Valley increased a stunning 72 percent. Agricultural production on this scale provided yet another stimulus to national economic growth.

Agriculture in New England and the South

By the 1830s it was clear to New England farmers that they could not compete with farmers working the expansive and fertile lands of the West. Wheat production per acre in Ohio, to take but one example, was twice that of New York farms. In response, many New Englanders left their farms, either to move west themselves or to settle in urban centers offering employment in factories and commercial enterprises. There was a Yankee exodus: Between 1820 and 1860 the rural proportion of New England's population fell from 70 to 40 percent. (The population of the South was also flooding westward. In South Carolina, for example, nearly half of those born after 1800 left the state.)

Farmers who stayed on their lands realized they couldn't compete in the national markets for corn or

Leading Domestic Exports of Manufactured Products (millions of dollars)

Rank	1820		1830		1840	
1	Chemicals, etc.	$1.0	Cotton, manuf.	$1.3	Cotton, manuf.	$3.5
2	Soap	0.8	Chemicals, etc.	1.2	Sugar, refined	1.2
3	Spirits, dist'l'd	0.5	Soap	0.6	Iron and steel	1.1
4	Candles	0.3	Leather, manuf.	0.4	Tobacco, manuf.	0.8
5	Leather, manuf.	0.2	Iron and steel	0.3	Chemicals, etc.	0.7
6	Wood[a]	0.2	Spirits dist'l'd	0.3	Wood[a]	0.6
7	Wood[b]	0.2	Candles	0.2	Soap	0.5
8	Tobacco, manuf.	0.1	Tobacco, manuf.	0.2	Spirits, dist'l'd	0.4

Rank	1850		1860	
1	Cotton, manuf.	$4.7	Cotton, manuf.	$10.9
2	Wood[a]	2.0	Iron and steel	5.9
3	Iron and steel	2.0	Tobacco	3.4
4	Chemicals, etc.	0.9	Wood[a]	2.7
5	Soap	0.7	Chemicals, etc.	1.9
6	Tobacco	0.6	Copper and brass	1.7
7	Spirits, dist'l'd	0.3	Leather, manuf.	1.5
8	Sugar, refined	0.3	Spirits, dist'l'd	1.5

[a] Wood, not including household furnishings.
[b] Wood, household furnishings.
Source: Monthly Summary of Commerce and Finance, April, 1903, Bureau of Statistics, Treasury Department, *House Document* No. 15, Pt. 10, 57 Cong., 2 Sess., XLII, 3313–3315.

There were other, less directly economic effects. Every east–west road, canal, and railroad helped to reorient Americans away from the Atlantic and toward the heartland. This was decisive in the creation of a postcolonial sense of national pride and identity. Transportation improvements such as the Erie Canal and the National Road linked Americans together in larger communities of interest beyond the local community in which they lived. Other results were less positive. The technological triumphs of canal building and rail laying fostered a brash spirit of conquest over nature that was to become part of the American myth of the frontier. Furthermore, although every new transportation or communication link broke down local and regional isolation and helped to build a spirit of pride in the nation, it also refocused attention on questions of national, not merely local, politics. In this sense, the new modes of communication and transportation served to heat up the politics of the era.

Commercial Agriculture

The impact of the transportation revolution on rural people (who in spite of the growth of cities still constituted more than two-thirds of the American population) went far beyond the breaking down of rural isolation. Every advance in transportation — better roads, canals, steamboats, railroads — made it easier for farmers to get their produce to market. Improvements in agricultural machinery increased the amount of acreage a farmer could cultivate. These two developments, added to the availability of rich, inexpensive land in the heartland, moved American farmers permanently away from subsistence agriculture and into production for sale. Vastly increased agricultural productivity was also essential to industrialization, for factory workers and urban people could no longer feed themselves.

The effect of the transportation revolution on the Old Northwest was particularly marked. Settle-

Roads ════════

Canals ════════

Navigable rivers ════════

Routes of Commerce: Major Roads, Canals, and Rivers in 1830

By 1830, the United States was tied together by a network of roads, canals, and rivers. The "Transportation Revolution" fostered a tremendous burst of commercial activity and economic growth. The transportation network accelerated commercial agriculture by aiding the movement of the farmer's products to wider, nonlocal markets. It allowed new manufacturers such as those in cotton textiles to engage in large-scale production because they knew their finished goods could reach a large commercial market.

Exciting Trial of Speed between Mr. Peter Cooper's Locomotive, "Tom Thumb" and one of Stockton & Stokes' Horse-Cars.

The locomotive "Tom Thumb" passes the horse-car, leaving it in a cloud of soot and decisively demonstrating the superiority of steampower. From these rather quaint beginnings in 1830, a nationwide network of 31,000 miles of track grew by 1860.

nience for passengers but a major deterrent for commercial shippers, who had to pay to have their goods moved from one railroad to another eight times. The most pleasant — and profitable — way to travel to Charleston was still by ship! Unlike canals, which were usually dug by states, the first railroads were built hurriedly by private companies, usually for only a short distance (to connect two towns, for example). Many were poorly constructed by companies trying to save money. It is no wonder that these early railroads experienced frequent breakdowns and accidents.

Until the 1850s, canalboats and coastal steamers carried more freight than the railroads, and at lower cost. But in the 1850s isolated and local railroads began a process of national consolidation. In the North and the Old Northwest (but to a lesser degree in the South), *trunk* (through) *lines* were superimposed on the old patchwork system of various gauges, railroad rates declined, and for the first time more freight moved by rail than by water. The regional pattern of consolidation gave the North still another commercial advantage compared to the South, and dramatically encouraged westward migration into and beyond the Old Northwest. The new traffic pattern had particularly dramatic effects on cities. Cincinnati, for example, lost its midwestern preeminence as steamboat freight declined, whereas newly settled Chicago, located at the junction of several trunk lines, was already America's eighth largest city by 1860. As we shall see in a later section, much of the freight moving by rail was the agricultural produce — especially wheat — of the Old Northwest.

Effects of the Transportation Revolution

Accompanying all these accelerations in transportation was an invention that outsped them all: the telegraph. By the 1860s, messages in Morse code (named for its inventor, Samuel F. B. Morse) could be transmitted instantaneously across the continent by this device. The impact of this revolutionary invention, the first to separate the message from the speed at which a human messenger could travel, was immediate. The amount of information available to the individual, from important national news to the next train's arrival time, vastly increased. Everyone's horizon was broadened.

The overall effects of the transportation and communication revolutions were many. The new ease of transportation undergirded economic growth by making distant markets accessible. The startling successes of innovations such as canals and railroads attracted large capital investments ($500 million from Europe between 1790 and 1861), which fueled further growth. In turn the new modes of transportation, as we have seen, required technological innovation (in the iron industry, for example) and encouraged technological spinoffs. The transportation revolution fostered an optimistic, risk-taking mentality in the United States that encouraged invention and innovation. More than anything, the transportation revolution allowed people to move with unaccustomed ease. Already a restless people compared with Europeans, Americans took advantage of new transport to move even more often — and farther away — than they had before.

In 1833, Andrew Jackson withdrew $10 million in government deposits from the Bank of the United States. Although this pro-Jackson cartoon shows the Bank crumbling before his thunderbolt, in fact Jackson's highhanded campaign against the Bank mobilized his political opposition and led to the creation of the Whig party.

aware of Jackson's antibank feelings, believed the president would not risk a veto in an election year. They were wrong. Jackson immediately decided on a stinging veto, announcing to Van Buren, "The bank . . . is trying to kill me, *but I will kill it!*"

And kill it he did that same July, with one of the strongest veto messages in American history. Denouncing the bank as unconstitutional, harmful to states' rights, and "dangerous to the liberties of the people," Jackson presented himself as the spokesman for the majority of ordinary people and the enemy of special privilege. Asserting that the bank's "exclusive privileges" were benefiting only the rich, Jackson claimed to speak for the "humble members of society—the farmers, mechanics and laborers" —and to oppose injustice and inequality. Nor did Jackson's veto message speak only of the sharp division between social classes. It also aroused sectional and national feelings by emphasizing the large number of British and eastern stockholders who were, through the bank's loans, making profits from the debts of poor southerners and westerners. In short, the veto spoke directly to many of the fears and resentments that Americans felt at this time of exceptionally rapid economic and social change. Jackson's message was a campaign document, written to appeal to voters. Most of the financial community was appalled, believing both the veto and the accompanying message to be reckless demagoguery.

The Election of 1832

Nevertheless, Jackson's veto message was a great popular success, and it set the terms for the presidential election of 1832. Henry Clay, the nominee of the anti-Jackson forces, lost the battle for popular opinion. Democrats successfully painted Clay as the defender of the Bank and privilege. His defeat was decisive: He drew only 49 electoral votes, to Jackson's 219. A handful of votes went to the first third party in American history, the short-lived Anti-Masonic party. This party played on the resentments of the newly enfranchised "common man" against the traditional elite political leadership, many of whom (including both Jackson and Clay) were members of the Masonic order, a fraternal society with secret rituals and special customs. The Anti-Masonic party did, however, make a lasting contribution to the political process. It was the first to hold a national nominating convention, an innovation quickly adopted by the other political parties.

Although the election was a triumph for Jackson, the Bank War continued. It was to have serious effects on the economy and on political principle. The Bank charter did not expire until 1836, but Jackson, declaring that "the hydra of corruption is only scotched, not dead," decided to kill the bank by transferring its $10 million in government deposits to favored state banks ("pet banks," critics called them). Cabinet members objected, but Jackson ignored them. Two secretaries of the Treasury refused to carry out Jackson's orders and were abruptly removed. Jackson then found a more pliant man, Roger Taney, for the job. (Jackson later rewarded him with the post of chief justice of the Supreme Court.) Henry Clay led a vote of censure in the Senate (loyal Democrats in the House prevented a censure vote there). To all of these protests, Jackson responded that the election had given him a popular mandate to act against the bank. The president was the direct representative of the people, he claimed, and could act upon the popular will, regardless of the opinion of Congress or even the Cabinet. Short of impeachment, there was nothing Congress could do to prevent Jackson's vast — and novel — interpretation of presidential powers.

The Rise of the Whigs and the Election of 1836

But there was someone outside Congress with power to respond: Nicholas Biddle. "This worthy President thinks that because he has scalped Indians . . . he is to have his way with the Bank," Biddle commented. "He is mistaken." As the government withdrew its deposits, Biddle abruptly called in the bank's commercial loans, thereby causing a sharp panic and recession in the winter of 1833–34. Merchants, businessmen, and southern planters were all furious — at Jackson. His opponents, only a loose coalition up to this time, coalesced into a formal opposition party that called itself the Whigs. Evoking the memory of the patriots who had resisted King George III in the American Revolution, the new party called on everyone to resist tyrannical "King Andrew." Just as Jackson's own calls for popular democracy had appealed to voters in all regions, so his opponents overcame their sectional differences to unite in opposition to Jackson's economic policies and his arbitrary methods.

Meanwhile, the consequences of the Bank War continued. The recession was followed by a wild speculative boom, caused largely by foreign investment as well as by the expiration of the Bank. Many new state banks were chartered that were eager to give loans, the price of cotton rose rapidly, and speculation in western lands was feverish (in Alabama and Mississippi, the mid-1830s were known as the "Flush Times"). A government surplus of $37 million distributed to the states in 1836 made the inflationary pressures worse. Jackson became alarmed, especially at the widespread use of paper money, and in July 1836 he issued the Specie Circular, announcing that the government would accept payment for public lands only in hard currency. At the same time, foreign investors, especially British banks, affected by a world recession, called in their American loans. The result was inevitable: The sharp contraction of credit led to the Panic of 1837 and a six-year recession, the worst the American economy had ever known. Ironically, Andrew Jackson, whose bad experience with speculation had led him to destroy the Bank of the United States, set in motion the events that caused the boom and bust he so feared. And he left his successor, Martin Van Buren, an impossible political legacy.

Against Martin Van Buren the Whigs, unable to agree on a common presidential candidate, ran four sectional candidates: William Henry Harrison of Ohio, Hugh Lawson White of Tennessee, W. P. Mangum of North Carolina, and Daniel Webster of Massachusetts. The Whigs hoped the combined votes for these regional candidates would deny Van Buren a majority and force the election into the House of Representatives, where they hoped to win. The strategy failed, but not by much: Although Van Buren captured 170 electoral votes to the Whigs' 124, the popular vote was much closer, 50.9 percent to 49.1 percent. The Whig defeat drove home the weakness of sectional politics, but the closeness of the popular vote showed that the basis for a united national opposition did exist. In 1840, the Whigs would prove that they had learned this lesson.

The Panic of 1837

In 1837, 800 banks suspended business, refusing to pay out any of the $150 million of their deposits. The collapse of the banking system led inevitably to business closures and outright failures. In the winter of 1837–38 in New York City alone, one-third of all manual laborers were unemployed and an estimated 10,000 were living in abject poverty. New York laborers took to the streets. Four or five thousand protesters carrying signs reading "Bread, Meat, Rent, Fuel!" gathered at City Hall on February 10, 1838, then marched to the warehouse of a leading merchant, Eli Hart. Breaking down the door, they took possession of the thousands of barrels of flour Hart had stored there rather than selling at what the mob considered a fair price. Policemen and state militia who tried to prevent the break-in were

This contemporary cartoon bitterly depicts the terrible effects of the Panic of 1837 on ordinary people: bank failures, unemployment, drunkenness, and destitution, while the rich insist on payment in specie (as Jackson had in 1836). Over the scene waves the American flag, accompanied by the ironic message, "61st Anniversary of our independence."

beaten by the angry mob. Nationwide, the unemployment rate was estimated at more than 10 percent.

Nor were the working class and the poor the only victims. Among the many hurt by the panic was Philip Hone, former mayor of New York and once a man of considerable wealth. Hone lost two-thirds of his own fortune and was unable to help his three grown sons when they lost their jobs. The wealthy reformer Arthur Tappan, a leading abolitionist and founder of Oberlin College, went bankrupt. "Business of all kinds [is] completely at a stand," Hone noted in 1840, wondering "how the poor man manages to get a dinner for his family." The Panic of 1837 lasted six long years, causing widespread misery. Not until 1843 did the economy show signs of recovery.

In neither the panic of 1837 nor that of 1819 did the federal government take any action to aid victims. No banks were bailed out, no bank depositors were saved by federal insurance, no laid-off workers got unemployment insurance. Nor did the government undertake any public works projects or pump money into the economy. All of these steps, now seen as essential to prevent economic collapse and to alleviate human suffering, were unheard of in 1819 and 1837. Soup kitchens and private charity were mobilized in major cities, but always by volunteer groups, not by local or state governments. Panics and depressions were believed to be natural stages in the business cycle, and government intervention was considered unwarranted — although, as we have seen, it was perfectly acceptable for government to intervene to *promote* growth. As a result, workers, farmers, and businessmen soon realized that participation in America's booming economy was very dangerous. The rewards were great, but so were the penalties. America's great economic success was attended by substantial risk and anxiety.

Martin Van Buren (quickly nicknamed "Van Ruin") spent a dismal four years in the White House presiding over bank failures, bankruptcies, and massive unemployment. Lacking Jackson's compelling personality, Van Buren could find no remedies to the depression. His misfortune gave the opposition party, the newly formed Whigs, their opportunity.

The Second American Party System

Andrew Jackson's presidency not only symbolized the Age of the Common Man but gave lasting political form to that expression. The political struggles of the Jackson era, coupled with the dramatic social changes caused by expansion and economic growth, created the basic pattern of American politics: two major parties, appealing to voters in all sections of the country and in all social classes. That pattern remains to this day. The paradox was that the national political parties owed their very existence to difference, yet worked as powerful nationalizing forces, subduing sectional antagonisms.

Whigs and Democrats

There were genuine differences between the Whigs and the Democrats, but they were *not* sectional differences. Instead, the two parties reflected just-emerging class and cultural differences. The Democrats, as they themselves were quick to point out, had inherited Thomas Jefferson's belief in the democratic rights of the small, independent yeoman farmer. As most of the country was rural, it is not surprising that the Democrats had nationwide appeal, especially in the South and West, the most rural regions. But some Democrats were workers in northern cities, where the emerging issues of class and ethnicity counted; these people voted *against* the wealthier, native-born Americans, who were mostly Whigs. As a result of Jackson's presidency, Democrats came to be identified with individualism and a distaste for interference, whether from the government or from economic monopolies such as the Bank of the United States. In the politics of the

time, these were *conservative* values. They expressed the opposition of most Democratic voters to the rapid social and economic change that accompanied the replacement of subsistence farming and artisanal labor with commercial agriculture and factory work.

The Whigs were more receptive to these changes, in which they were often participants. Whigs were generally wealthier than Democrats. They supported Henry Clay's American System: a strong central government, the Bank of the United States, a protective tariff, and internal improvements. In fact, Whigs wanted to improve not only roads but people as well. Religion was an important element in political affiliation, and many Whigs were members of evangelical reforming denominations. Northern Whigs were in favor of education and social reforms such as temperance that aimed to improve the ordinary citizen. Southern Whigs, although prevented by the slave system from advocating personal reform too vigorously, were in favor of federal aid for internal improvements and economic development. A number of southern planters, who had close ties to merchant and banking interests, and residents of the South's commercial cities were attracted to the Whig party. In both North and South, Whigs were more forward-looking than Democrats in their social attitudes and were receptive to the personal and social changes that industrialization required. They favored government intervention both in economic and in social affairs. The Whigs' greatest strength was in New England and the northern part of the West (the Old Northwest). Their strength reflected rather accurately those areas most affected by commercial agriculture and factory work.

Each of the parties departed in certain respects from its predecessor. Although the Democrats were clearly the inheritors of Jeffersonian republicanism, Andrew Jackson's dynamic appeals to "the will of the people" during the Bank War fueled the resentment of the "common man" toward the rich one. Jackson's praise of democracy, in other words, encouraged differences along class lines. Yet Jackson himself was a wealthy man, as were many other southern and western Democrats. The Whigs, while just as clearly the heirs of the Federalist belief in the role of a strong federal government in the national economy, were now also the party of moral reform. As we shall see more fully in Chapter 13, reformers believed that everyone, rich and poor, was capable of the self-discipline that would lead to a good life. Many rich men were Whigs, but so were many poorer men who had a democratic faith in the perfectibility of all Americans.

The Campaign of 1840

In 1840, the Whigs set out to beat the Democrats at their own game. Passing over the ever hopeful Henry Clay, the Whigs nominated a man as much like Andrew Jackson as possible, the aging Indian fighter William Henry Harrison, former governor of Indiana Territory. In a clear bid for sectional support they nominated a southerner, John Tyler, for vice-president. The campaign slogan was "Tippecanoe and Tyler too" (Tippecanoe being the site of Harrison's famous victory over Tecumseh's Indian confederation in 1811). As if this were not enough, Whigs made Harrison out to be a humble man who would be happy to live in a log cabin. Thus began another long-lived political legend. (Harrison obligingly posed in front of a log cabin for campaign appearances, but he actually lived in a large and comfortable house.) The Whigs reached out to ordinary people with torchlight parades, barbecues, songs, coonskin caps, bottomless jugs of (hard) cider, and claims that Martin Van Buren, Harrison's hapless opponent, was a man of privilege and aristocratic tastes. As we saw in the introduction to this chapter, nothing could be further from the truth. But Van Buren, a short man who lacked a com-

The Election of 1840

The 1840 Whig electoral triumph was achieved by beating the Democrats at their own game. Whigs could expect to do well in the commercializing areas of New England and the Old Northwest. But the Whig strategy of popular campaigning worked well in the largely rural South and West, contributing to Harrison's victory. Another strategy to appeal to southern voters was the choice of John Tyler as Vice President. This choice robbed the Whigs of their victory when Harrison died and Tyler, who did not share Whig principles, became America's first accidental president.

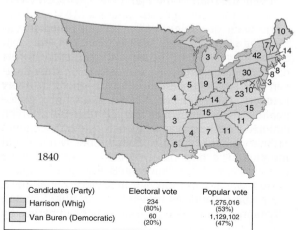

Candidates (Party)	Electoral vote	Popular vote
Harrison (Whig)	234 (80%)	1,275,016 (53%)
Van Buren (Democratic)	60 (20%)	1,129,102 (47%)

1840

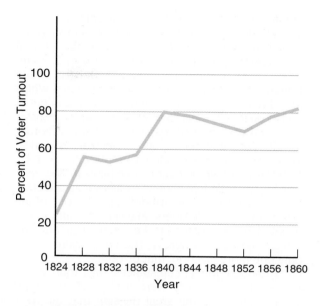

Pre-Civil War Voter Turnout

The turnout of voters in presidential elections more than doubled from 1824 to 1828, the year Andrew Jackson was first elected. Turnout surged to 80 percent in 1840, the year the Whigs triumphed. Democratization of suffrage, coupled with the creation of two mass political parties, made presidential election campaigns events with great popular appeal.

manding presence, had always dressed meticulously, and now even his taste in coats and ties was used against him.

The Whig campaign tactics, combined with popular anger at Van Buren over the continuing depression, gave Harrison a sweeping electoral victory, 234 votes to 60. Even more remarkable, the campaign achieved the greatest voter turnout up to that time (and rarely equaled since), 80 percent.

Tyler Too: The Irony of the 1840 Whig Victory

Although the Whig victory of 1840 was a milestone in American politics, the triumph of Whig principles was short-lived. William Henry Harrison, who was sixty-eight, died of pneumonia a month after his inauguration. For the first time in American history the vice-president was forced to step up to the presidency. Not for the last time, important differences between the dead president and his successor reshaped the direction of American politics.

John Tyler of Virginia was a former Democrat who had left the party because he disagreed with Jackson's autocratic style. The Whigs had sought him primarily for his sectional appeal and had not inquired too closely into his political opinions, which turned out to be anti-Whig as well as anti-Jackson. President Tyler vetoed a series of bills embodying all the elements of Henry Clay's American System: tariffs, internal improvements, a new Bank of the United States. In exasperation, congressional Whigs read Tyler out of the party, and his entire Cabinet of Whigs resigned. (Secretary of State Daniel Webster remained until he had resolved a Canadian border dispute by negotiating the Webster-Ashburton Treaty of 1842 with Britain.) To replace them, Tyler appointed former Democrats like himself. The most startling selection was John C. Calhoun as secretary of state. Thus the Whig triumph of 1840, one of the clearest victories in American electoral politics, was negated by the stalemate between Tyler and the Whig majority in Congress. The Whigs were to win only one more election, that of 1848.

Although the circumstances that robbed the Whigs of their victory were accidental, the Tyler debacle laid bare the great division that the two-party system was intended to hide: the ever growing gap between the North and the South. The Whigs were a short-lived national party because they could not bridge that gap. And by the 1850s not even the Democrats could remain united.

American Arts and Letters

Jackson's presidency was a defining moment in the development of a distinct American identity. Jackson's combination of western belligerency and combative individualism was the strongest statement of American distinctiveness since Thomas Jefferson's agrarianism. Did Jackson speak for all of America? The Whigs did not think so. And the definitions of American identity that were beginning to be formulated by intellectual and cultural figures were more complex than the message coming from the White House. Underlying the work of intellectuals, however, was a widespread interest in information and literature of all kinds.

The Spread of the Written Word

The rapidly growing number of newspapers, magazines, and books played an important role in broadening people's horizons beyond their own community. A print revolution began in 1826 when the American Tract Society (a religious organization) installed the country's first steam-powered press. Three years later, 300,000 Bibles and 6 million tracts had been produced by the new presses. Reform

organizations of all kinds quickly followed the religious organizations into print. Temperance tracts, which frequently told lurid tales of the perils of alcohol, were widely distributed.

At the same time, newspapers made constant improvements in their technology, culminating in the 1845 invention of the rotary press, a machine with a rotating cylinder that could produce 20,000 sheets per hour. Newspaper production and circulation soared: There were 375 newspapers in 1810, 1,200 in 1835, 2,526 in 1850. This rise paralleled the growth of interest in politics. Most newspapers were published by political parties, were openly partisan, and were affordable to all (they were known as "penny papers"). Much of the appeal of these papers was not political but sensational. Typical headlines read "A Secret Tryst," "Double Suicide," "Bloody Murder." These were such standard fare that in 1859 one observer commented, "No narrative of human depravity or crime can shock or horrify an American reader."

For western readers, the popular Crockett almanacs offered a mix of humorous stories and tall tales attributed to Davy Crockett (the famous Tennessee "roarer" who died defending the Alamo in 1836) along with meteorological and climate information. Fifty issues of these almanacs were published between 1835 and 1856.

Amidst all this popular, melodramatic, and amusing material, religious literature was still the most widely read. In addition, a small middle-class audience existed for literary magazines and lectures, and for sentimental magazines and novels read mostly by women.

Emerson and the Transcendentalists

Among intellectuals, Boston's Ralph Waldo Emerson was the man of the age. Originally a Unitarian minister, Emerson quit the pulpit in 1831 and became what one might call a secular minister. Famous as a lecturer — his 1837 lecture "The American Scholar" was one of the most quoted pieces of its day — Emerson preached a message of individualism and self-reliance that struck a chord in many listeners. Emerson popularized a romantic philosophical theory known as transcendentalism, which claimed that there was an ideal reality transcending ordinary life that could be known only by individual intuition. The best place to achieve that intuitive connection with the Universal Being, Emerson suggested, was not in church or in society, but alone in the natural world. As he wrote in "Nature" (1836), "Standing on the bare ground — my head bathed by

Emerson's romantic glorification of nature included the notion of himself as "a transparent Eyeball," (as he wrote in *Nature* in 1836) provoking this cartoon from a literal-minded contemporary.

the blithe air, and uplifted into infinite space — all mean egotism vanishes. I become a transparent Eyeball; I am nothing; I see all; the currents of the Universal Being circulate through me; I am part and parcel of God." This "spiritualization" of nature was new. Emerson's thinking had a strong effect on younger writers, among them Henry David Thoreau, Margaret Fuller, and Nathaniel Hawthorne, who were part of his intellectual circle.

Emerson's public impact was truly remarkable. He was the star of the lyceum circuit, a lecture network that sent speakers on cultural subjects to all parts of the country. Emerson himself gave more than 1,500 lectures in twenty states in the period 1833–60. His emphasis on self-knowledge and intuition encouraged individualism, and his insistence that God was everywhere encouraged his listeners to pay attention to ordinary life. In "The American Scholar," his most popular lecture, Emerson declared that American writers should find their inspiration in the "familiar, the low . . . the milk in the pan; the ballad in the street; the news of the boat; the glance of the eye; the form and gait of the body." His social message was plain: "What is man born for, but to be a Reformer?" Inspirational but down-to-earth, Emerson was just the philosopher to in-

spire young businessmen of the 1830s and 1840s to achieve success in a responsible manner and to encourage writers to find their themes in everyday American life. Emerson's definition of individualism was central to the new middle class notions of family and community that we will explore in Chapters 12 and 13.

The American Renaissance

In this period American writing came of age. Following in the footsteps of Washington Irving and James Fenimore Cooper (both of whom were still writing), a younger generation of writers began to find distinctive American themes. Henry David Thoreau, Emerson's closest associate, followed the transcendental theme of association with nature to Walden Pond, near Concord, Massachusetts, where he lived in solitude in a primitive cabin for two years confronting "the essential facts of life." "On Civil Disobedience" (1849), an essay written in protest of the Mexican War, and *Walden* (1854) are classic individualistic statements of moral indignation at the injustices of society.

Essayist Margaret Fuller, perhaps the most intellectually gifted of the transcendental circle, was handicapped by being female. Patronized by Emerson, Fuller finally achieved some independence by moving to New York City, where she wrote for Horace Greeley's *Herald Tribune*. Fuller expressed her sense of women's wasted potential in her pathbreaking work *Woman in the Nineteenth Century* (1845). Intellectually and emotionally, however, Fuller achieved liberation only when she moved to Europe and participated in the liberal Italian revolution of 1848. She, her Italian husband, and their child died in a shipwreck off the New York coast as they returned to America in 1850.

Other transcendentalists held a darker and more complex view than Emerson of the tension between the individual and the community. In both *The Scarlet Letter* (1850) and *The House of the Seven Gables* (1851), Nathaniel Hawthorne brilliantly contrasted the apparent repressiveness of New England's Puritan heritage with the arrogance of individual pride. The most profound criticism of Emersonian self-reliance, however, was to be found in Herman Melville's great work *Moby Dick* (1851). Dismissed at the time as merely an overly detailed description of a whaling voyage, Melville's novel of Captain Ahab's obsessive search for the white whale has yielded deeper layers of meaning while becoming an American classic.

Neither Hawthorne nor Melville was financially

successful as an author. That honor went instead to the women novelists whom the disgruntled Hawthorne once dismissed as "a damned mob of scribbling women," but whose works sold in the hundreds of thousands. The domestic novels written by "lady novelists" found a ready female audience. Using the marketing techniques of the day, which included advertising, discounts to booksellers, and a small army of sales agents, publishing companies found a lucrative market, one that increased from $2.5 million in 1820 to $12.5 million in 1850. By 1850, *Harper's Magazine* estimated, four-fifths of the reading public were women.

Novels such as Catharine Maria Sedgwick's *Clarence* (1830), Susan Warner's *The Wide Wide World* (1851), and Maria Cummins's *The Lamplighter* (1854) are examples of a particular kind of "women's novel" that found a ready market. *The Wide Wide World*, for example, went through fourteen editions in two years, and Elizabeth Phelps's *The Sunny Side* (1851) sold 100,000 copies. Like their male counterparts, women novelists were preoccupied with the tension between the individual and community. But because they wrote about heroines rather than heroes, the sphere of action was limited to the domestic and family realm. Adventure stories for women were unthinkable — women ventured very little on their own — but stirring stories of female character development found a wide reading audience.

The standard story began with a young orphan girl, or a rich girl suddenly made penniless, who must find within herself the courage, intelligence, and moral fortitude to take control over her life and to overcome hardships. Although the heroine usually marries at the end, these stories were not primarily romances. They focus rather on the heroine's discovery of her own strengths within a close and loving family circle, which she often helps to create. Emerson's famous essay on self-reliance had encouraged the individualism of the era; female novelists spoke of another kind of self-reliance, one that emphasized responsibility and community based upon moral and caring family life.

Religious feeling, antipathy toward the dog-eat-dog world of the commercial economy, and a heavy emphasis on preparedness to cope with unforeseen troubles were common themes in women's novels. They may have originated in the authors' own lives: several of these women, such as Susan Warner, were driven to novel writing when their fathers lost their fortunes in the Panic of 1837. The greatest novelist of the age in terms of book sales was also a woman — Harriet Beecher Stowe, who drew on certain aspects of the domestic novel as well as on

current events to write the famous abolitionist novel *Uncle Tom's Cabin* (1852).

Other writers, neglected in their day, utilized the darker themes and emotions of urban life as it was reflected in the "penny papers" and the lurid temperance tracts. Edgar Allan Poe's stories such as "The Murders in the Rue Morgue" drew directly from newspapers, and for tales like "The Pit and the Pendulum" he followed the model of popular adventure stories. Poet and journalist Walt Whitman drew his sense of life and the rhythms of his poetry from the vibrant streets of New York, which he described in the 1840s as "the most radical city in the world." In *Leaves of Grass* (1855) and other poetry, Whitman tried to capture the lives and feelings of ordinary people.

Romantic Art

Artists as well as novelists found American themes. Thomas Cole, who came to America from England in 1818, found great inspiration in the American landscape. Cole applied the British romantic school of landscape painting to American scenes, founding the Hudson River school of American painting, a style and subject that was frankly nationalistic in tone. Cole's paintings were romantic landscapes of New York State's Catskill and Adirondack Mountains. New Yorker Philip Hone, an admirer of Cole's work, said, "Every American is bound to prove his love of country by admiring Cole." Asher Durand, another member of the Hudson River School, painted his famous *Kindred Spirits* in memory of Cole, who is one of the two figures standing harmoniously in a romantic wilderness.

The western painters — realists such as Karl Bodmer and George Catlin as well as the romantics who followed them, like Alfred Bierstadt and Thomas Moran — drew on the dramatic western landscape and its peoples. Their art was an important contribution to the American sense of the land and to the nation's identity. Catlin, driven by a need to document Indian life before it disappeared, spent eight years among the tribes of the upper Missouri River. Then he assembled his collection — more than 500 paintings in all — and toured the country from 1837 to 1851 in an unsuccessful attempt to arouse public indignation about the plight of the western Indian nations. Another unusual western painter, John James Audubon, who was French, could at first find no publisher in this country for his striking and sometimes grotesque etchings of American birds. George Caleb Bingham, an accomplished genre painter, produced somewhat tidied-up scenes of real-life American workers, such as flatboatmen on

Asher Durand, a member of the Hudson River School of landscape painting, produced this work, *Kindred Spirits,* as a tribute to Thomas Cole, the leader of the school. Cole is one of the figures depicted standing in a romantic wilderness.

the Ohio River. All of these painters found much to record and to celebrate in American life. Ironically, the inspiration for the most prevalent theme, the American wilderness, was profoundly endangered by the rapid western settlement of which the nation was so proud. The Age of the Common Man was the period when American writers and painters found the national themes that first produced distinctively American literature and art.

Building America

The haste and transiency of American life are nowhere so obvious as in the architectural record of this era, which is practically nonexistent. The Greek Revival style that Jefferson had recommended for official buildings in Washington continued to be favored for public buildings elsewhere and by private concerns trying to be imposing, such as banks. A few southern planters built impressive mansions, and there were odd experiments such as the prison built in Philadelphia in the 1820s that was designed to look like a medieval castle. The effect of this building on the imagination, one admiring commentator remarked, was "peculiarly impressive, solemn and instructive."

But in general Americans were in too much of a hurry to build for the future, and in balloon-frame construction they found the perfect technique for the present. The basic frame of wooden studs fastened

CHRONOLOGY

1817	Erie Canal begun
1819	*Dartmouth College v. Woodward*
1821	Martin Van Buren's Bucktails oust DeWitt Clinton
1824	John Quincy Adams elected president by House
	Gibbons v. Ogden
1825	Erie Canal opened
1826	First American use of the steam press
1828	Congress passes Tariff of Abominations
	Andrew Jackson elected president
	John C. Calhoun anonymously publishes *Exposition and Protest*
1830	Jackson vetoes Maysville Road Bill
	Congress passes Indian Removal Act
	Baltimore and Ohio Railroad (thirteen miles) opens
1832	Nullification crisis begins
	Jackson issues bank veto
	Jackson reelected president
1834	Cyrus McCormick patents the McCormick reaper
	Whig party organized
1836	Jackson issues Specie Circular
	Martin Van Buren elected president
1837	*Charles River Bridge v. Warren Bridge*
	John Deere invents steel plow
	Ralph Waldo Emerson publishes "The American Scholar"
	Panic of 1837
1838	Cherokee removal along "Trail of Tears"
1844	Samuel F. B. Morse operates first telegraph
1845	Margaret Fuller, *Woman in the Nineteenth Century*
1850	Nathaniel Hawthorne, *The Scarlet Letter*
1851	Hawthorne, *The House of the Seven Gables*
	Herman Melville, *Moby Dick*
1854	Henry David Thoreau, *Walden*

with crosspieces top and bottom could be put up quickly, cheaply, and without the help of a skilled carpenter. Covering the frame with wooden siding was equally simple, and the resultant dwelling was as strong, although not as well insulated, as a house of solid timber or logs. Balloon-frame construction, first used in Chicago in the 1830s, created an almost instant city. The four-room balloon-frame house became standard in that decade, making houses affordable to many who could not have paid for a traditionally built dwelling. This was indeed housing for the common man and his family.

CONCLUSION

Andrew Jackson's presidency witnessed the building of a strong national party system based on nearly universal white manhood suffrage. At the same time, the roads, canals, and other improvements in transportation and communication began to unify the nation, physically and intellectually. A new national impulse was also apparent in the arts. At first glance, sectionalism and localism seemed to have been swept away. In particular, the party system exemplified by Van Buren and the Bucktails seemed to promise a new kind of national community based on political belief. But the forces of sectionalism still existed. Coupled with new national expansion in the 1840s, they were to destroy political unity. To understand these sectional forces, we turn in the next two chapters to a detailed look at the diverging societies of the South and the North.

Additional Readings

DONALD B. COLE, *Martin Van Buren and the American Political System* (1984). An excellent study of Van Buren's key role in the transformation of politics.

RONALD P. FORMISANO, *The Transformation of Political Culture: Massachusetts Parties, 1790s–1840s* (1983). One of many detailed studies that have contributed to our understanding of the development of the second party system.

WILLIAM W. FREEHLING, *Prelude to Civil War* (1966). An examination of the nullification crisis that stresses the centrality of slavery to the dispute.

PAUL W. GATES, *The Farmer's Age: Agriculture, 1815–1860* (1966). The standard source on the growth of commercial agriculture.

JOHN NIVEN, *Martin Van Buren: The Romantic Age of American Politics* (1983). Valuable in the same way as Cole's book, cited earlier.

EDWARD PESSEN, *Jacksonian America: Society, Personality and Politics,* rev. ed. (1979). A heroic effort to synthesize the vast and changing literature on Jacksonian politics.

MERRILL D. PETERSON, *The Great Triumvirate: Webster, Clay, and Calhoun* (1987). A biography of the famous trio that is also a "life and times."

ROBERT REMINI, *Andrew Jackson and the Source of American Freedom* (1981). An account of Jackson's White House years by his most recent biographer.

DAVID REYNOLDS, *Beneath the American Renaissance* (1988). A fascinating study of the popular literature from which, Reynolds argues, authors such as Whitman, Poe, and Melville drew their themes.

GEORGE ROGERS TAYLOR, *The Transportation Revolution 1815–1860* (1951). The indispensable book on all aspects of the American economy during this period.

JANE TOMPKINS, *Sensational Designs* (1985). An argument for the literary value of the popular women's novels of the period.

HARRY L. WATSON, *Liberty and Power: The Politics of Jacksonian America* (1990). An excellent recent overview of Jacksonian politics.-

11 THE SOUTH AND SLAVERY, 1790s–1850s

The wharfmaster had just opened the public auction of confiscated cargoes in the center of Natchez when a great cry was heard. All present turned to see an angry crowd of flatboatmen, their bowie knives flashing, storming up the bluffs from the Mississippi shouting "threats of violence and death upon all who attempted to sell and buy their property," according to the local newspaper. It was November 1837, and the town council had just enacted a restrictive tax of ten dollars per flatboat, a measure designed to rid the wharf district known as Natchez-under-the-Hill of the most impoverished and disreputable of the riverboatmen. The first confiscation of cargo had taken place after nine captains refused to pay. As the boatmen approached, merchants and onlookers shrank back in fear.

SLAVEOWNERS SHUT DOWN AN OPEN COMMUNITY

But the local authorities had taken the precaution of calling out the militia, and a company of farmers and planters now came marching into the square with their rifles primed and lowered. "The cold and sullen bayonets of the Guards were too hard meat for the Arkansas toothpicks," reported the local press, and "there was no fight." The boatmen sullenly turned back down the bluffs. It was the first confrontation in the "Flatboat Wars," which erupted as Mississippi ports tried to bring their troublesome riverfronts under regulation.

The first European to take notice of this "land abundant in subsistence" was a participant in the de Soto expedition of the early sixteenth century. The area was "thickly peopled" by the Natchez Indians, he wrote. The French established the port there when they built Fort Rosalie in the 1720s. They destroyed the highly organized society of the Natchez in the 1730s, but the port remained as a major Mississippi River trading center. From Fort Rosalie, the French conducted an extensive multiracial frontier trade. A large export market for deerskins — 50,000 were shipped in 1726 alone — connected French traders with hunters among the Choctaws, Chickasaws and Creeks. This trade, like the fur trade in Canada and further west, led to intermarriage and the growth of a mixed race population. During the same time period, some of the Africans imported by the French to work as slaves on plantations found roles in the French-Indian trade as boatmen, hunters, soldiers, and interpreters. The Spanish, who controlled the territory after 1763 and inherited this multiracial trade from the French, laid out a new town high on the bluffs, safe from Mississippi

This rough trading community on the Mississippi River still shows signs of the frontier origins that its companion community, rich slave-owning Natchez at the top of the hill, was eager to leave behind.

flooding. But Under-The-Hill (formerly Fort Rosalie) continued to flourish with the growing commercial traffic of Kentucky and Tennessee farms that moved downriver each year on hundreds of flatboats. The boatmen made their way back to Kentucky and Tennessee along the Natchez Trace, a 600-mile Indian trail that began in Natchez and ended in Nashville. Along the route the returning American boatmen met Choctaw and Chickasaw Indians who had been trading with white men for generations. Americans were only the newest participants in this old multiracial trade.

The Americans took possession in 1798, and the district surrounding the port became the most important center of settlement in the Old Southwest. Once again this abundant land of rich, black soil became thickly peopled, this time with cotton planters and slaves rather than agricultural Indians.

Under-the-Hill became renowned as the last stop for boatmen before New Orleans. Minstrel performers sang of their exploits:

> Den dance de boatmen dance,
> O dance de boatmen dance,
> O dance all night till broad daylight,
> An go home wid de gals in de morning.

"They feel the same inclination to dissipation as sailors who have long been out of port," one traveler wrote, "and generally remain there a day or two to indulge it." There were often as many as 150 boats drawn up at the wharves. The crowds along the riverfront, noted John James Audubon, who visited in the 1820s, "formed a medley which it is beyond my power to describe." Mingling among American rivermen of all descriptions were trappers and hunters in fur caps, Spanish shopkeepers in bright smocks, French gentlemen from New Orleans in velvet coats, Indians wrapped in their trade blankets, African Americans both free and slave—a pageant of nations and races. In clapboard shacks and flatboats dragged on shore and converted into storefronts could be found grog shops, card rooms, dance halls, and hotels, as well as plenty of whorehouses with women of every age and color.

On the bluffs, meanwhile, the town of Natchez had become the winter home to the southwestern planter elite. They built their mansions with commanding views of the river. Stanton Hall, open to the public today, is a masterwork of Natchez plantation architecture, with its double portico supported by huge columns, its marble mantles carved into pomegranates, grapes, and flowers, its imported Italian woodwork, and its huge French mirrors, designed to reflect the light from spectacular bronze chandeliers. A visitor attending a ball at one of these homes was dazzled by the display: "Myriads of wax candles burning in wall sconces, sparkling chandeliers, entrancing music, the scent of jasmine, rose and sweet olive, the sparkle of wine mellowed by age, the flow of wit and brilliant repartee, all were there." Sustaining this American aristocracy was the labor of thousands of enslaved men and women, who lived in the squalid quarters behind the great house and worked the endless fields of cotton. It was they who made possible the greatest accumulations of wealth in early-nineteenth-century America.

The majority of farmers in the Mississippi country owned few if any slaves. But they commonly aspired to become plantation masters themselves, and identified with the interests of the small plantation elite. As the planters grew wealthier and more confident, and as the trade in cotton came to dominate the local economy, Under-the-Hill became an increasing irritant. "A gentleman may game with a gambler by the hour," one resident remembered, "and yet despise him and refuse to recognize him afterward." But the riverfront elite — gamblers, saloon keepers, and pimps — began to appear in Natchez town, staying at the hotels and even building town houses. A greater source of tension was Nat Turner's slave revolt of 1831, after which southerners adopted a more militant defense of slave society. Now the mingling that went on down at the riverfront began to feel threatening to the planters, who had built their fortunes on racial exploitation.

In the late 1830s the district was jolted by rumors of a conspiracy among African Americans and Under-the-Hill desperadoes that was supposed to take place on a Fourth of July. The planter elite was to be murdered by their slaves as they gathered for the celebration, and the Under-the-Hill crowd would loot the mansions. It is unlikely there was any conspiracy, but the rumors illustrated the growing conviction among planters that they could no longer tolerate the polyglot society of the riverfront. The measures to clean up the district soon followed.

In response to the flatboatmen's threats on that November day in 1837, the planters issued an extralegal order giving all the gamblers, pimps, and whores of Under-the-Hill twenty-four hours to evacuate the district. As the Mississippi militia sharpened their bayonets, panic swept the wharves, and that night dozens of flatboats loaded with a motley human cargo headed for the more tolerant community of New Orleans. There were similar orders of expulsion in other river ports. Thus, one resident remembered, "the towns on the river became purified from a moral pestilence which the law could not cure." Three years later a great torna-do hit Under-the-Hill, claiming nearly all the shacks that had served so long as a rendezvous for the rivermen, and gradually the Mississippi reclaimed the bottom.

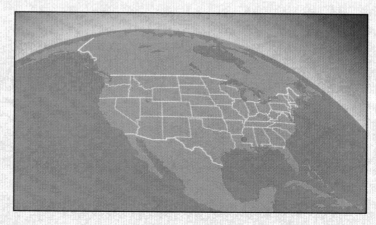

These two communities — Natchez, home to the rich slave-owning elite, and Natchez-under-the-Hill, the bustling polyglot trading community — epitomize the two faces of the American South in the early nineteenth century. Aristo-cratic southerners built a sumptuous lifestyle with the international profits of the region's major crop, cotton. But both cotton growing and the bustling trade that depended on it rested ultimately on enslaved black workers. The contradictions of slavery entangled the South at the very moment of its greatest commercial success.

KING COTTON

The distinctive southern society that by 1850 stretched from Baltimore to Natchez and beyond was based on one crop, cotton, and one form of labor, slavery. Cotton was the dominant crop in a vastly expanded South that included not only the original states of Maryland, Delaware, Virginia, North and South Carolina, and Georgia, but Kentucky, Tennessee, Alabama, Mississippi, Louisiana (the Old Southwest), Arkansas, and Texas as well. In this chapter, we will explore the ways in which the overwhelming economic success of cotton created a distinctive regional culture different from that developing in the North. We will understand how slavery, which had little to do directly with the flatboatmen of Natchez-under-the-Hill, nevertheless shaped their lives and those of every other stratum of southern communities.

The Cotton Gin and the Growth of Cotton Cultivation

In 1790, short-staple cotton had been a minor southern crop. Other crops — tobacco, rice, indigo, sugar, hemp — were what southern planters had sold on the world market since colonial times. But by 1820 short-staple cotton had eclipsed them all. In the thirty years after 1793 the production of cotton increased an astounding 1,000 percent (from 3,135 bales in 1790 to 334,378 in 1820). And the yield kept on soaring, up to 4.8 million bales in 1860. During this time the South experienced a series of expan-

Steamboats at New Orleans await loads of cotton, the nation's major export. Just as the giant bales crowd the wharf, so too the culture created by "King Cotton" dominated southern life.

sionist surges (1816–20, 1832–38, and again in the mid-1850s) that carried cotton cultivation as far west as Texas.

Short-staple cotton had long been recognized as a crop ideally suited to southern soils and growing conditions. But there was one major drawback: The seeds were so difficult to remove from the lint that it took an entire day to hand-clean a single pound of cotton. The invention in 1793 that made cotton growing profitable was the result of collaboration between a young northerner named Eli Whitney, recently graduated from Yale University, and Catherine Greene, a South Carolina plantation owner and widow of Revolutionary War General Nathanael Greene, who hired Whitney to tutor her children. The cotton engine (*gin* for short) was a simple device consisting of a hand-cranked cylinder with teeth that tore the lint away from the seeds. Greene's contribution to the invention was the suggestion that the teeth be made of wire rather than wood. With the cotton gin it was possible to clean more than fifty pounds of cotton a day. Soon large and small planters, especially in the inland regions of Georgia and South Carolina, had begun to grow cotton. By 1811, this area was producing 60 million pounds of cotton a year, and exporting most of it to England.

The rapid growth of cotton production was an international phenomenon, prompted by events occurring far from the American South. The insatiable demand for cotton was a result of the technological and social changes that we know today as the Industrial Revolution. Beginning early in the eighteenth century, a series of small inventions mechanized spinning and weaving. This led in turn to the world's first factories, in the north of England. The ability of these factories to produce cotton cloth revolutionized the world economy. The invention of the cotton gin came at just the right time. British textile manufacturers were eager to buy all the cotton that the South could produce.

Other areas of the South quickly followed South Carolina and Georgia into cotton production. New land was most suitable, for cotton growing rapidly depleted the soil. The profits to be made from cotton growing drew a rush of southern farmers into the "black belt" — those parts of western Georgia, Alabama, and Mississippi blessed with exceptionally fertile soil. As we have seen, several surges of western settlement carried cotton planting over the Mississippi River into Louisiana and deep into Texas. Each surge ignited speculative frenzies, as in the "Flush Times" of the early 1830s. In the minds of the mobile, enterprising southerners who sought their fortunes in the West, cotton profits and expansion went hand in hand.

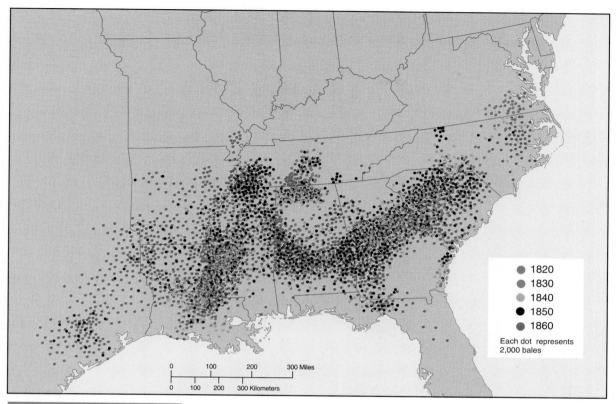

Cotton Production, 1820–1860

In the forty year period from 1820 to 1860, cotton production grew dramatically both in quantity and in extent. Cotton production encouraged expansion. The westward surges of the 1830s and 1850s (shown in the figures for 1840 and 1860) are evident, as is the growing concentration of cotton production in the "black belt" region (so-called for its rich soils) of the Lower South.

Source: Sam Bowers Hilliard, *Atlas of Antebellum Southern Agriculture* (Baton Rouge: Louisiana State University Press,), pp. 67–71.

Increased Demand for Slave Labor

One immediate result of the cotton boom was a vast increase in the demand for slave labor. Cotton growing was well suited to the southern plantation system of agriculture. That system was characterized by large plantings of a single crop tended by gangs of workers who performed the same operation (planting, hoeing, picking) under the supervision of an overseer. Cotton profits depended on slavery, for, as the earlier failure of indentured labor had shown, whites preferred to farm their own land rather than perform plantation work for others. The solution to the South's labor shortage was the creation of a racially distinct, enslaved group of workers, captured and transported from Africa against their will (see Chapter 4). White southerners believed that only African slaves could be forced to work day after day, year after year, at the rapid and brutal pace required in the cotton fields of large plantations in the steamy southern summer. As the

production of cotton climbed higher every year, so did the demand for slaves. The slave system, on the decline in the 1780s, rapidly expanded. Prices for "prime" slaves increased, and human beings became a profitable investment.

After 1808, as agreed upon in the Constitution, the United States chose to end its participation in the international slave trade. Nevertheless, a small number of slaves continued to be smuggled from Africa. On the other hand, the domestic slave trade grew. In the older areas of the South, plantation owners were increasingly tempted to sell their surplus labor "down the river" (the Mississippi) to meet the demand for slave labor in the new and expanding cotton-growing regions to the southwest.

The Economics of Slavery

Was the southern plantation system profitable? Economists have criticized it because the high rate of capital investment in slaves diverted money from

●	1810
●	1820
●	1830
●	1840
●	1850
●	1860

Each dot represents 2,000 slaves

0   100   200   300 Miles

0   100   200   300 Kilometers

Slave Population, 1810–1860

The growth of cotton production caused a redistribution of the enslaved African American population in the South. Although slaves were still used to grow tobacco in Virginia and rice in coastal South Carolina, after 1830 an increasing number were sold "down the river" to work new cotton plantations in the Lower South. Thus although U.S. participation in the international slave trade was outlawed after 1808, the domestic trade in slaves flourished.

Source: Sam Bowers Hilliard, *Atlas of Antebellum, Southern Agriculture* (Baton Rouge: Louisiana State University Press,), pp. 29–34.

the development of more efficient farming methods and from the industrial development occurring in the North. But clearly, in the years before 1860, southern farmers believed that their system was profitable. The figures for cotton production support this conclusion: from 720,000 bales in 1830, to 2.85 million bales in 1850, to nearly 5 million in 1860. By the time of the Civil War, cotton accounted for almost two-thirds of American exports, representing a total value of nearly $200 million a year. Cotton's central place in the national economy and its international importance led Senator James Henry Hammond of South Carolina to make a famous boast in 1858:

> Without firing a gun, without drawing a sword, should they make war on us, we could bring the whole world to our feet . . . . What would happen if no cotton was furnished for three years? . . . England would topple headlong and carry the whole civilized world with her save the

south. No, you dare not to make war on cotton. No power on the earth dares to make war upon it. Cotton *is* King.

However profitable cotton may have been, concentration on plantation agriculture did divert energy and resources from the South's cities. At a time when the North was experiencing the greatest spurt of urban growth in the nation's history, southern cities did not keep pace. Charleston, for example, one of America's five largest cities in 1800, had a population of only 41,000 in 1860, compared with Boston's 177,840 and Baltimore's 212,418. The one exception was New Orleans, the great port at the mouth of the extensive Mississippi River transportation system. In 1860 New Orleans was the nation's fifth largest city, with a population of 169,000. The nine other leading cities were all northern or western. Most of the South remained rural: less than 3 percent of Mississippi's population lived in cities of

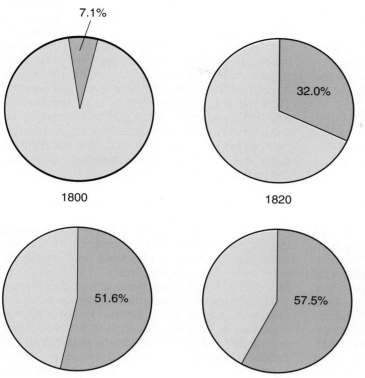

1800 7.1%

1820 32.0%

1840 51.6%

1860 57.5%

Value of Cotton Exports as a Percentage of All U.S. Exports

Another consequence of the growth of cotton production was its importance in international trade. The growing share of the export market, and the great value (nearly $200 million in 1860) led southern slaveowners to believe that "Cotton is King." The importance of cotton to the national economy entitled the South to a commanding voice in national policy, many southerners believed.

more than 2,500 residents, and only 10 percent of Virginia's did.

The South also lagged behind the North in industrialization and in canals and railroads. In 1860, only 15 percent of the nation's factories were located in the South. Noteworthy exceptions were the iron industry near Richmond, Virginia, which in 1860 boasted four rolling mills, fourteen foundries, and various machine shops employing 1,600 mechanics, and William Gregg's cotton textile mills in Charleston. Similarly, the South was being left behind by the transportation revolution (see Chapter 10). In 1850, only 26 percent of the nation's railroads were in the South; in 1860, only 35 percent.

Furthermore, the majority of the mercantile services associated with the cotton trade (insurance, financing, and shipping, for example) were in northern hands. Thus, although cotton dominated American exports, southerners often felt as their predecessors had before the Revolution, when British merchants controlled the sale of southern crops. In spite of American independence, many southern planters still felt like colonists because their economic fate was in the hands of "outside" northern agents. For their part, northerners, who were in the

midst of rapid industrialization and urbanization (see Chapter 12), increasingly regarded the South as a backward region. Northern politician William H. Seward, on his first visit to Virginia, found ample justification for his antislavery convictions:

> It was necessary that I should travel in Virginia to have any idea of a slave state . . . . An exhausted soil, old and decaying towns, wretchedly-neglected roads, and in every respect, an absence of enterprise and improvement, distinguish the region through which we have come, in contrast to that in which we live. Such has been the effect of slavery.

The cotton boom created a distinctive regional culture. Although cotton was far from being the only crop (the South actually devoted more acreage to corn than to cotton in 1860), its vast profitability affected all aspects of society. In the first half of the nineteenth century, King Cotton reigned supreme over an expanding domain as southerners increasingly tied their fortunes to the slave system of cotton production. As a British tourist to Mobile wryly noted in the 1850s, the South was a place where "people live in cotton houses and ride in cotton carriages.

They buy cotton, sell cotton, think cotton, eat cotton, drink cotton, and dream cotton. They marry cotton wives, and unto them are born cotton children . . . ." The South was truly in thrall to King Cotton. This regional identification with cotton created a society that was increasingly at odds with the developing commercial culture of the North.

SOUTHERN EXPANSION

The possibility of profits from cotton served to fuel the South's customary expansionism. Southerners had historically taken the lead in westward expansion. Backcountry residents of Virginia and North Carolina were the first to venture over the Appalachians, and Virginians and Carolinians were the major settlers of the first two trans-Appalachian states, Kentucky (1792) and Tennessee (1796). John C. Calhoun of South Carolina and Henry Clay of Kentucky had been two of the most prominent War Hawks in the War of 1812 (see Chapter 9). Thus there was nothing unusual about southern expansion following the War of 1812. Like the expansion into the Old Northwest, settlement took place rapidly, and at the expense of the region's Indian population. But southern expansion meant the expansion of slavery. This issue, which first emerged in the Missouri controversy of 1819–20, was eventually to strain the American political system to the breaking point.

The Settlement of the Old Southwest

Following the War of 1812, southerners were seized by "Alabama fever." In one of the swiftest migrations in American history, white southerners and their slaves flooded into western Georgia and the areas that would become Alabama and Mississippi. This migration caused the population of Mississippi to double and that of Alabama to grow sixteen times (from 31,306 to 74,448 in Mississippi; from 9,046 to 144,317 in Alabama) in the decade 1810–20. This migration and subsequent western land booms dramatically changed the population of the original southern states as well. Nearly half of all white South Carolinians born after 1800 eventually left the state, usually to move west. By 1850 there more than 50,000 South Carolina natives living in Georgia, almost as many in Alabama, and 26,000 in Mississippi.

The new settlers found it very difficult to clear the land in the Old Southwest. Massive forests, swamps, and dense canebrakes required immense effort to remove, and much of the work was accomplished by slaves. But for a select few the rewards were great: Even before 1812, plantation owners in the Natchez district of Mississippi were among the richest people in the country. Although only a fraction of the settlers became large and wealthy slave owners, the possibility of such success impelled many migrants. And a generation later, in the Flush Times of the 1830s, when the price of cotton rose to twenty cents a pound, the same rapid expansion of the slave and plantation system occurred farther west in Louisiana and Texas.

Expansion and Indian Resistance

As we saw in Chapter 10, the major Indian groups in the Old Southwest were the Cherokees, the Chickasaws, the Creeks, the Choctaws, and the Seminoles — the "Five Civilized Tribes." The twenty-year history of their defeat and removal from their homelands is intertwined with the history of the most famous man of the times, Andrew Jackson. What is important in the following account is not so much Jackson himself as the attitudes he personified. The details of his well-documented life as an Indian fighter illustrate how and why the ruthless anti-Indian attitudes of settlers in the Old Southwest developed.

The first of the Indian peoples to battle the Americans in the Southwest were the Creeks. The war between the Creeks and the whites began, as had the resistance of the Shawnees north of the Ohio River (see Chapter 9), when whites occupied Indian lands — in this case, in northwestern Georgia and central Alabama early in the century. Although some Creeks argued for accommodation, a group known as the Red Sticks were determined to fight. On the other side, Andrew Jackson, then an unknown leader of the Tennessee militia, urged army action against the Creeks as early as 1808, insisting that only an all-out campaign would stop this "ruthless foe." When he had moved west as a young man in 1788, Nashville, Tennessee, was still a "station," fortified but still vulnerable to Indian attack. Jackson, like his neighbors, came to hate the "savages" who made white frontier life so dangerous and terrifying.

Responding to the white invasion, the Creeks *were* ruthless: they killed, scalped, and took captives. Their largest effort, in 1813 (during the War of 1812, when they had British and Spanish encouragement), was an attack on Fort Mims on the Alabama

River, where white families had gathered for safety. They killed over 500 whites, including women and children.

Under Andrew Jackson, Tennessee and Kentucky militias combined with the Creek's traditional foes—the Cherokees, Choctaws, and Chickasaws—to exact revenge. Jackson's troops matched the Creeks in ferocity, shooting the Red Sticks "like dogs," one soldier reported. At the Battle of Horseshoe Bend in March of 1814, the Creeks were trapped between American cannonfire and their Indian enemies: over 800 were killed, more than in any other battle in the history of Indian–white warfare. Jackson then marched on the remaining Red Stick villages, burning and killing as he went. Cornered, one remaining Red Stick leader, Red Eagle, personally confronted Jackson:

> General Jackson, I am not afraid of you. I fear no man, for I am a Creek warrior. I have nothing to request in behalf of myself . . . . But I come to beg you to send for the women and children of the war party, who are now starving in the woods . . . . If I could fight you any longer I would most heartily do so. Send for the women and children. They never did you any harm. But kill me, if the white people want it done.

Impressed by Red Eagle's courage, Jackson allowed him to return home. At the same time, Jackson and most of the region's settlers remained convinced that pitiless warfare against the Red Sticks was fully justified. Of such contradictions—one might call it slaughter with honor—was Jackson's reputation as an Indian fighter made.

At the end of the Creek War in 1814 Jackson demanded land concessions from the Creeks (including land from some Creek bands that had fought on his side) that far exceeded their expectations: 23 million acres, or more than half of their domain. It was the opening of this huge tract of land (three-fifths of Alabama and one-fifth of Georgia) that precipitated the first land rush into the Old Southwest, which led in turn to continuing demands for Indian land. The Treaty of Fort Jackson (1814) also earned Jackson his Indian name, Sharp Knife. Other treaties with other local Indian tribes soon followed. In 1816 the Choctaws ceded millions of acres, as did the Cherokees in 1819. Further cessions from every tribe followed in the 1820s.

Faced with the defeat of the Creeks, and continuing white pressure on their lands, the remaining Creeks and the Cherokees, Choctaws, and Chickasaws decided on a policy of accommodation. The Cherokees took the most dramatic steps to adopt white ways. Their tribal lands in northwestern Georgia boasted prosperous farms, businesses, grain and lumber mills, and even plantations with black slaves. Intermarriage with whites and African Americans had produced an influential group of mixed bloods within the Cherokee nation, some of whom were eager to accept white ways. Schooled by Congregationalist, Presbyterian, and Moravian missionaries, the Cherokees were almost totally literate. They took special pride in their alphabet, developed by the scholar Sequoyah, and in a tribal newspaper, the *Cherokee Phoenix,* established in 1828 and published in both Cherokee and English. In 1827, the tribe abolished its traditional form of government and established a constitutional republic.

Impressive as these changes were, they were not enough to withstand white pressures. During the Jackson and Van Buren presidencies (1829–40) the Cherokees were forced to move west of the Mississippi to Indian Territory (see Chapter 10). One reason for their removal was white land hunger, which was present in all frontier areas throughout the nation. But another reason was rooted in slavery: there was simply no room in the southern social order for anything other than white and black, master and slave. Literate, slave-owning "redskins" confused this simple picture: They were too "civilized" to be like slaves, but the wrong color to be masters. By the 1830s, this ambiguity was too dangerous to be tolerated. In Georgia, as in Natchez, the mood of the South by the 1830s was increasingly hostile to any circumstances that might create a breach in the rigid system that kept slavery intact. Thus southern Indian removal, like southern expansion, was dictated by the needs of the slave system.

Southerners had long been unhappy that Spain held Florida and the southern part of Mississippi, Alabama, and Louisiana, cutting off American access to ports on the Gulf of Mexico (see Chapter 5). In addition, slaves frequently escaped into Florida, and the Seminole Indians, with whom they rapidly intermarried, could attack and then retreat across the border in safety (see Chapter 4). During the War of 1812 the United States annexed West Florida (now Mississippi and Louisiana) over Spain's objections.

But southerners continued to desire all of Florida. Jackson was instrumental in achieving that goal. In 1817 he was sent with troops to the Florida frontier with orders from the War Department to defend American territory against Seminole raids. On his own initiative Jackson invaded Florida,

Sequoyah is shown with the Cherokee alphabet he invented. The bilingual newspaper (right) contains an excerpt from the Cherokee constitution. In spite of these proofs of "civilization," the Cherokee were removed from their Georgia homeland to Indian Territory in 1838.

(Lehman & Duval. Se-Quo-Yah (Inventor of Cherokee Alphabet.) 19th Century. Lithograph. Accession # '37-40-1d. Given by Charles Bird King. Philadelphia Museum of Art.)

seized two Spanish forts, and hanged two British citizens suspected of helping the Indians. These ruthless actions caused a storm in Congress, but southern popular opinion clearly supported Jackson. More important, Spain decided not to try to defend Florida. As we saw in Chapter 9, the Spanish agreed, in the Adams-Onís Treaty of 1819, to cede all of Florida to the United States. Jackson's bold adventuring appeared to be vindicated, but in fact it was John Quincy Adams's careful diplomacy that was decisive in the negotiations.

On every American frontier, white expansion and settlement meant the killing, confining, or removal of Indian peoples and the combating of foreign presences such as the Spanish in Florida. In these respects, the expansion into the Old Southwest fit the national pattern. But there was one aspect of southern westward migration that *was* unique, and that was its inextricable ties to the expansion of slavery.

YEOMEN AND PLANTERS

The pervasive influence of the slave system in the South is demonstrated by one startling statistic: Two-thirds of all southerners did not own slaves, yet slave owners dominated the social and political life of the region. Who were the two-thirds of white southerners who did not own slaves, and how did they live? Throughout the south, slave owners occupied the most productive land: tobacco-producing areas in Virginia and Tennessee, coastal areas of South Carolina and Georgia where rice and sea-island cotton grew, sugar lands in Louisiana, and large sections of the cotton-producing black belt, which stretched westward from South Carolina to Texas. Small farmers, usually without slaves, occupied the rest of the land. This ranged from adequate to poor, from depleted, once-rich lands in Virginia to the Carolina hill country and the pine barrens of Mississippi.

Yeomen

The word *yeoman* is originally a British term for a farmer who works his own land. Southern yeomen were small farmers, most of whom lived self-sufficient lives on family-sized farms. Many grew corn, which they could eat themselves or feed to hogs. They raised enough other vegetables to feed their families and perhaps enough cotton (usually no more than one or two bales) to bring in a little cash. In South Carolina's upcountry Anderson County, for example, Gabriel Cox and his family raised four bales of cotton and 600 bushels of corn as well as nineteen hogs on their seventy-five-acre farm in 1849. They were comfortably self-sufficient. The Coxes and most other yeoman families led what we have come to think of as a frontier lifestyle: subsistence farming, a log cabin (southern style — two rooms with a breezeway, or "dogtrot," between), community social and religious gatherings that fit into the farming cycle, and, underlying everything, a kin-based network of barter and mutual assistance. These were the yeoman farmers of whom Thomas Jefferson dreamed: economically independent yet intimately tied to a larger but still very local group.

Kin-based community links were of major importance. Farm men and women depended on their relatives and neighbors for assistance in large farm tasks such as planting, harvesting, and construction. They repaid this help, and obtained needed goods, through complex systems of barter. In their organization, southern farm communities were no different from northern or western ones, with one major exception: slavery. In the South, one of the key items in the community barter system was the labor of slaves, who were frequently loaned out by small slave owners (who lived side by side with non-slaveholding farmers) to fulfill a master's obligation to another farmer.

Where yeomen and large slave owners lived side by side, as in Edgefield County, South Carolina, slavery provided a link between richer and poorer. Large plantation owners often bought food supplies from small local farmers, ground the latter's corn in the plantation mill, ginned their cotton, and often transported and marketed it as well. Edgefield County slave owner James Henry Hammond (whose "King Cotton" speech was noted earlier) performed all of these services for his poorer neighbors. He also provided medical assistance and allowed the sons of some of the more respectable neighbors to be tutored with his own children. These were the customary obligations of the elite, and Hammond, with 10,000 acres and over 100 slaves, was expected to play this role, although he grumbled that his neighbors were "the most ignorant, vulgar & I may add most narrow-minded set of people in the world." Thus in many areas both the largest farmers (plantation owners) and much smaller yeomen were part of the larger community network of obligation and loyalty.

The goal of yeoman farm families was economic independence. Their mixed farming and grazing enterprises afforded them a self-sufficiency epitomized by this rough but comfortable log cabin. Kinship and community ties were also important.

Of course not all small farmers were on an equal footing. Some 25 percent were tenant farmers or farm laborers, hoping to save enough to buy their own land. Others lived miserable lives on the worst and frequently most isolated land, such as the pine barrens, sand hills, and swamp regions. Prey to debilitating diseases such as malaria and hookworm and suffering from dietary deficiencies, poor farmers were widely scorned as shiftless and ignorant. In reality they were simply unable to coax enough crops out of the poor soil of their small farms. Thomas Beatty, for example, an upcountry neighbor of Gabriel Cox, was unable to feed his family on the unproductive thirty-five acres he rented. He produced one bale of cotton, but was not able to grow enough food to subsist. Many black slaves, better nourished, better dressed, and healthier, dismissed farmers such as Beatty as "poor white trash." Yet even the most degraded "white folks" believed they were better, because of their race, than all African Americans. Indeed, the poorest whites were often the most violent in their assertions of racial superiority. Here we can clearly see how racial ideology diverted attention from class inequities among whites.

Yeoman Politics

In 1828 and 1832, southern yeomen voted overwhelmingly for Andrew Jackson. They were drawn variously to his outspoken policy of ruthless expansionism, his appeals to the common man, and his rags-to-riches ascent from poor boy to rich slave owner. It was a career many hoped to emulate. The dominance of the large planters was due at least in part to the ambition of many yeomen, especially those with two or three slaves, to expand their holdings and become rich. These farmers supported the leaders they hoped to join.

But for a larger group of yeomen, independence and not wealth was most important. Many southern yeomen lived apart from large slaveholders, in the upcountry regions where plantation agriculture was unsuitable. The very high value southern yeomen placed on freedom grew directly from their own experience as self-sufficient property-owning farmers in small, family-based communities. This was a way of life that southern "plain folk" were determined to preserve. It made them resistant to the economic opportunities and challenges that capitalism and industrialization posed for northern farmers (see Chapter 12).

The irony was that the freedom yeomen so prized rested upon slavery. Whites could count on slaves to perform the hardest and worst labor, and the degradation of slave life was a daily reminder of the freedom they enjoyed in comparison. Slavery meant that all whites, rich and poor, were equal in the sense that they were all free. The enslavement of black people made possible relative freedom and equality among white people.

Southern yeomen did not blindly follow the rich slave owners who were their political leaders. Rather, they supported what they believed was a system that brought them a freedom they wouldn't have under any other system. But southern unanimity on this point, which looked so strong, was in actuality very fragile. Anything that appeared to threaten slavery threatened the entire southern social structure, trapping southerners in ever more rigid and defensive positions.

Planters

Remarkably few slave owners fit the popular stereotype of the rich and leisured plantation owner with hundreds of acres of land and hundreds of slaves. Of the 36 percent of southern whites who owned slaves in 1830, half owned five or fewer. At the other extreme, only 2.5 percent of whites owned fifty slaves or more.

White Class Structure in the South, 1830

The great mass of the southern white population were yeoman farmers. In 1830, slaveowners made up only 36 percent of the southern white population; owners of more than 50 slaves comprised a tiny 2.5 percent. Yet they and the others who were middling planters dominated politics, retaining the support of yeoman farmers who prized their freedom as white men above class-based politics.

Source: U.S. Bureau of the Census.

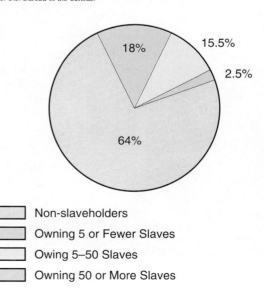

- Non-slaveholders
- Owning 5 or Fewer Slaves
- Owing 5–50 Slaves
- Owning 50 or More Slaves

The largest group of slave owners were small yeomen taking the step from subsistence agriculture to commercial production. To do this in the South's agricultural economy, they had to own slaves. But upward mobility was difficult. Owning one or two slaves increased farm production only slightly, and it was difficult to accumulate the capital to buy more. One common pattern was for a slave owner to leave one or two slaves to farm while he worked another job (usually this meant that his wife had unacknowledged responsibility for their supervision). In other cases, small farmers worked side by side with their slaves in the fields. In still other cases, owners hired out their slaves to larger slave owners.

In every case, the owner was economically vulnerable: A poor crop or a downturn in cotton prices could wipe out his gains and force him to sell his slaves. When times improved, he might buy a new slave or two and try again.

This was the experience of John Flintoff, who moved from North Carolina to Mississippi in 1841, hoping to make his fortune. Working as an overseer on his uncle's land, Flintoff began his career as a slave owner by buying three slave children (one was seven years old), the cheapest slaves available. Over the years he bought nine in all. While an overseer, Flintoff married and began a family. But he was a bad overseer: As he confessed in his diary, "managing negroes and large farms is soul destroying." In 1853 his uncle fired him. Flintoff was forced to sell his slaves and return to North Carolina, where, with the help of his in-laws, he bought 124 acres of land. With the help of several slaves he grew corn, wheat, and tobacco — not the wonderfully profitable cotton of which he had dreamed. By 1860, Flintoff was modestly successful: wealthy enough to send his son to college and to free his wife from routine farm chores. As he boasted, his wife "has lived a *Lady*."

This example shows the difficulty of getting a secure footing on the bottom rung of the slave-owning ladder. Farmers were not helped by the roller-coaster economy of the early nineteenth century; in particular, the Panic of 1837 was a serious setback to many. This struggling group made up by far the largest number of slave owners.

For a smaller group of slave owners, the economic struggle was not so hard. Middle-class professional men — lawyers, doctors, merchants — frequently managed to become large slave owners, because they already had capital (the pay from their professions) to invest in land and slaves. Sometimes they received payment for their services not in money but in slaves. These owners were the most likely to own skilled slaves — carpenters, blacksmiths, other artisans — and to rent them out for profit. By steady accumulation, the most successful members of this middle class were able to buy their way into the slave-owning elite, and to confirm that position by marrying their sons or daughters into the aristocracy. These middle-class men were also the most likely slave owners to be elected to political office.

Here the career of Andrew Jackson of Tennessee is instructive. Jackson, an orphan, had no family money. He began a profitable career as a prosecutor in Nashville in the 1790s, frequently taking small plots of land as payment for his services. In 1794 he owned 10 slaves, and two years later he was elected Tennessee's delegate to the U.S. House of Representatives. In 1798 Jackson owned 15 slaves and was elected a senator. He widened his economic activities, buying land, partnership in a store, a plantation for himself (the Hermitage), and a racetrack. Then came some bad years — the mercantile business failed, and debts on land came due — and Jackson was soon preoccupied with military matters. But he continued to accumulate slaves: 44 by 1820, 95 by 1828 (the year he was elected president), 150 a few years later, and almost 200 by the time of his death in 1845.

The Planter Elite

The slaveowning elite, those 2.5 percent who owned fifty slaves or more, enjoyed the prestige, the political leadership, and the lifestyle to which many white southerners aspired. Great slave owners expected to be political leaders. Men of wealth and property had led southern politics since colonial times. But increasingly after 1820, as the nation moved toward universal manhood suffrage, slave owners had to learn how to appeal to the popular vote. Most of the great slave owners never did acquire the "common touch," and it was the smaller slave owners who formed a clear majority in every southern state legislature before 1860. This political preponderance of planters, elected by the nonslaveholding majority, shows clearly that the defense of slavery was a popular issue.

Who were the members of this privileged minority? In almost every case, elite slave owners inherited their wealth. They were rarely self-made men, although most tried to add to the land and slaves they had inherited. Yet theirs was far from being a closed group, and the aristocratic lifestyle they were so proud of was a relatively recent creation rather than a long-standing tradition.

James Henry Hammond, son of a schoolteacher, became a slave owner by marrying seventeen-year-old Catherine Fitzsimons, a Charleston heiress who was, in the polite words of a friend, "not I should judge from her appearance & manners calculated to make many . . . conquests." The Fitzsimonses, who feared (accurately) that Hammond was marrying for money rather than love, had initially insisted on limiting his power over Catherine's money. Hammond had protested vigorously, claiming that anything less than full ownership of her property would "recognize & establish forever an inequality" between him and his wife. The Fitzsimonses had relented and Hammond had become a member of the rich slave-owning class, but throughout his life he remained touchy about his modest beginnings.

The eastern seaboard had given rise to a class of rich planters nearly a century earlier, as attested by the plantations of Willim Byrd and George Washington of Virginia and the cultured life of the planter elite, centered in Charleston, that had established itself in the South Carolina low country and Sea Islands. One such planter was Thomas Chaplin, owner of Tombee Plantation on St. Helena Island near Beaufort, South Carolina. Chaplin was descended from an indentured servant who arrived in 1672 from the British sugar-producing island of Barbados. In 1839 he married Mary McDowell, granddaughter of a rich Charleston merchant, and in 1840 they moved into the old family house on the 376-acre Tombee Plantation. Master of sixty to seventy slaves, Chaplin grew sea-island cotton (a long-staple variety), potatoes, and corn and raised beef and mutton. Although St. Helena land was rich and fertile, the climate was unhealthy. Malaria was epidemic during the "sickly season" from mid-May until November, causing most planters and their families to flee to Charleston or to the healthier upcountry, and discouraging poorer whites from living there at all. As a consequence, by 1845 black people outnumbered white people eight to one on St. Helena (2,000 African Americans to 250 whites). Like the other Sea Islands of South Carolina, St. Helena was unique in the relative autonomy of the black population and the persistence of African customs and language, as in the use of the Gullah dialect, a mixture of English and African.

Soon after he took possession of Tombee Plantation, Chaplin was forced to sell off more than half his slaves to settle family debts and lawsuits. Land rich but labor poor, Chaplin fretted in 1850: "So many mouths to feed & so few to work that it is *impossible* for me to get along." Completely dependent on his black labor force, Chaplin was indifferent to them as individuals. For example, he would carefully note the birth of each black child but not the identity of the father. Unlike many planters, Chaplin refused to attend slave weddings, dismissing them as "tomfoolery," and only grudgingly did

he permit his slaves to choose husbands and wives from other plantations. He complained unceasingly about the high rate of infant mortality among slaves, going so far as to accuse mothers of killing their own babies. He failed to realize that overwork and poor nutrition (counteracted only in part by the constant pilfering from his storehouses and barns) were to blame. Unlike most planters, Chaplin never hired an overseer for the work in his fields, but after 1852 he increasingly left the details of management to a slave driver. In contrast, James Henry Hammond was deeply involved in agricultural improvement on his upcountry plantation. He also took a personal interest in his slaves, naming slave children, advising about their upbringing, encouraging large families, and punishing marital infidelity.

As southerners and slave owning spread westward, membership in the elite broadened to include the new wealth of Alabama, Mississippi, Louisiana, and Texas. The rich planters of the Natchez community were popularly called *nabobs* (from a Hindi word for Europeans who had amassed fabulous wealth in India). Frederick Stanton, owner of Stanton Hall in Natchez, was a physician who had immigrated from Northern Ireland. The source of his wealth was not medicine but the cotton-commission business. At the time of his death he owned 444 slaves and 15,109 acres of land on six Louisiana and Mississippi plantations that produced over 3,000 bales of cotton a year. Another great Natchez family, the Surgets, of French origin, traced their wealth further back, to a Spanish land grant of 2,500 acres to Pierre Surget. In the 1850s, his grandsons Frank and James Surget, controlled some 93,000 acres in Mississippi, Arkansas, and Louisiana (half of it plantation land and half bought on speculation, for resale). Each brother sold 4,000 bales of cotton a year, and between them they owned upwards of 1,000 slaves. Each also owned palatial mansions in Natchez, Cherry Hill, and Clifton.

The extraordinary concentration of wealth in Natchez — in 1850 it was the richest county in the nation — fostered an elite lifestyle. As the Natchez *Mississippi Free Trader* complained in 1842, "the large planters — the one-thousand-bale planters — do not contribute most to the prosperity of Natchez. They, for the most part, sell their cotton in Liverpool; buy their wines in London or Havre; their negro clothing in Boston; their plantation implements and supplies in Cincinnati; and their groceries and fancy articles in New Orleans." But in spite of their elegant lifestyle, many of the nabobs of Natchez were not so different in their personal habits from the freewheeling boatsmen of Natchez-

Stanton Hall was the elegant mansion built by Frederick Stanton, a Natchez "nabob" who owned almost 500 slaves. Clearly, Stanton's mansion was intended to symbolize the success he had achieved since his arrival in the United States as an Irish immigrant.

under-the-Hill. Fastidious northerners such as Thomas Taylor, a Pennsylvania Quaker who visited Natchez in 1847, noted:

> Many of the *chivalric gentry* whom I have been permitted to see dashing about here on highbred horses, seem to find their greatest enjoyment in recounting their bear hunts, "great fights," and occasional exploits with revolvers and Bowie knives — swearing "terribly" and sucking mint juleps & cherry cobblers with straws . . . ."

The urban life of the Natchez planters was unusual. Many wealthy planters, especially those on new lands in the Old Southwest, lived in isolation on their plantations with their families and slaves. Through family networks, common boarding school experience, political activity, and frequent visiting, the small planter elite consciously worked to create and maintain a distinctive lifestyle.

As Taylor's comments about the Natchez nabobs indicate, the planter lifestyle was self-consciously modeled on the English aristocracy, as southerners understood it. (Some southerners even tried to imitate the chivalric medieval world depicted in the popular novels of Sir Walter Scott). It entailed a large estate, a spacious, elegant mansion, and lavish hospitality. For men, the gentlemanly lifestyle meant immersion in masculine activities such as hunting, soldiering, or politics and a touchy concern with honor that could lead to duels and other acts of bravado. Here again, Andrew Jackson's reputation as a dueling man is representative. Women of the slave-owning elite, in contrast, were expected to be gentle, charming, and always welcoming.

But this gracious image was at odds with the economic reality: Large numbers of black slaves had to be forced to work to produce the wealth of the large plantations. Each plantation, like the yeoman farm but on a larger scale, aimed to be self-sufficient, producing not only the cash crop but most of the food and clothing for both slaves and family. There were stables full of horses for plowing, transportation, and show. There were livestock and vegetable gardens to be tended, and carpentering, blacksmithing, weaving, and sewing to be done. A large plantation was an enterprise that required many hands, many skills, and a lot of management. Large plantation owners might have overseers or black drivers to supervise field work, but frequently they themselves had direct financial control of daily operations. Even if they were absentee landlords (like, for example, Thomas Chaplin on a South Carolina lowland plantation and the richest of the Natchez elite), planters usually required careful accounts from their overseers and often exercised the right to overrule their decisions.

Plantation mistresses spent most of their lives in close supervision of slave operations such as cooking, weaving, and sewing as well as tending to childbirth and illness. The mistress's role as elegant and gracious hostess to crowds of guests, some of whom stayed for weeks, required hours of behind-the-scenes preparations.

Planters reconciled the plantation's gracious image and its reality of toil with the ideology of paternalism. In theory, each plantation was a family composed of both black and white. The master, as head of the plantation, was head of the family, and the mistress was his "helpmate." The master was obligated to provide for all of his family, both black and white, and to treat them with humanity. In return, slaves were to work properly and do as they were told, as children would. Most elite slave owners spoke of their position of privilege as a duty and a burden. (Their wives were more outspoken about the burdensome aspects of supervision of slaves, which they bore more directly than their husbands.) John C. Calhoun spoke for many slave owners when he described the plantation as "a little community with the master at its head," directing operations so that the abilities and needs of every member, black and white, were "perfectly harmonized." Convinced of their own benevolence, slave owners expected not only obedience but gratitude from their slaves. We shall look at paternalism from the slave's point of view in a later section.

The Plantation Mistress

The ideology of paternalism laid special burdens on plantation mistresses that northern women of the same social rank did not share. The difficulties experienced by these privileged women illustrate yet again that the slave system affected every aspect of the personal life of slave owners. As with northern women, southern women were barred from public life and taught that their proper activities should be domestic and family-based. In the North, women came to control the domestic "sphere" and to carry domestic concerns outside the family and into a wide range of reform movements (see Chapter 13). Such autonomy was impossible for plantation mistresses. Paternalism locked them into positions of heavy responsibility but no real authority.

The plantation mistress may have run her own household, but she did not rule it — her husband did. *He* was the source of authority to whom slaves were expected to look for both rewards and punishments. A wife who challenged her husband or sought more independence from him threatened the entire paternalistic system of control over slaves. If she was not dependent and obedient, why should slaves be? Likewise, although many southern women were deeply affected by evangelical religion, their response was personal rather than social. Reform movements, in which many northern women found a voice, were too threatening to the system of slave control to be tolerated in the South.

In addition to their strictly defined family roles, many southern women also suffered deeply from isolation from friends and kin. Sometimes the isolation of life on rural plantations could be overcome by long visits, but mistresses with many small children and extensive responsibilities found it difficult to leave. On the other hand, plantation masters often traveled widely for political and business reasons. John C. Calhoun, for example, who spoke so earnestly about the plantation community, spent much less time than his wife on the family plantation, Fort Hill. He spent years in Washington as a politician while Floride Calhoun, who had accompanied him in his early career, remained at Fort Hill after the first five of their ten children were born. John Calhoun soon came to complain about her "suspicious and fault-finding temper," which he claimed not to understand.

Plantation women in the Old Southwest, many of whom had moved unwillingly and now were far from their families on the eastern seaboard, were particularly lonely. "I seldom see any person aside from our own family, and those employed upon the plantation," Mary Kendall wrote. "For about three weeks I did not have the pleasure of seeing one white female face, there being no white family except our own upon the plantation." The irony is that she was surrounded by women, but the gap between the white mistress and her black slave women was unbridgable.

On every plantation, black women served as nursemaids to young white children and as lifelong maids to white girls and women, usually following them in marriage — an enforced move that often meant leaving their own husbands and children behind. Yet there are few historical examples of genuine sympathy and understanding of black women by white women of the slave-owning class. Although a number of southern women railed against "the curse of slavery," what most were complaining about was not the inhumanity of the system but the extra work entailed by housekeeping with slaves. As one plantation mistress explained, "Slaves are a continual source of more trouble to housekeepers than all other things, vexing them, and causing much sin. We are compelled to keep them in ignorance and much responsibility rests on us." Years later many former slaves remembered their mistresses as being kinder than their masters, but fully a third of their accounts mention cruel whippings and other punishments by white women. As a white mistress named Lucilla McCorkle coolly noted, "I should myself feel a natural repugnance toward slavery if I did not find it existing and myself an owner lawfully . . . ."

Coercion and Violence

There were generous and benevolent masters, but most large slave owners believed that constant discipline and coercion were necessary to make slaves work hard. There were slave owners who used their slaves with great brutality. Owners who killed slaves were occasionally brought to trial (and usually acquitted), but no legal action was taken in the much more frequent cases of excessive punishment, rape, and general abuse.

One of the most common transgressions of the ideology of paternalism (and of southern laws) was sexual abuse of female slaves by their masters. Usually these were casual and forced encounters, but sometimes longer relationships developed. James Henry Hammond kept two slave mistresses, Sally and Louisa Johnson, for twenty years and fathered several children by them. In 1850, Catherine Hammond discovered her husband's relation-

This man bears the permanent scars of the violence that lay at the heart of the slave system. Few slaves were so brutally marked, but all lived with the threat of similar beatings if they failed to obey.

ship with the slave women and demanded they be sold. When Hammond refused, she went to live with relatives and remained apart from her husband for five years. She did not publicly announce the reason for the separation, but rumors flew. When Catherine returned, Sally and Louisa Johnson were still on the plantation, although Hammond had moved them away from the main house.

Hammond gave serious consideration to the future of his mistresses and slave children. His solution tells us much about the boundaries of the slave system. In 1856 Hammond wrote to his (white) son Harry:

> In the last will I made I left to you . . . Sally Johnson the mother of Louisa & all the children of both . . . . I cannot free these people & send them North. It would be cruelty to them . . . Do not let Louisa or any of my children . . . be the slaves of strangers. Slavery *in the family* will be their happiest earthly condition.

It was rare for slave owners to publicly acknowlege fathering slave children or to free the children. Black women and their families were helpless to protest their treatment. Equally silenced was the master's wife, who because of modesty as well as her subordinate position was not supposed to notice this flagrant crossing of the color lines. As Mary Boykin Chesnut, wife of a South Carolina slave owner, vehemently confided to her diary:

> God forgive us, but ours is a monstrous system . . . . Like the patriarchs of old, our men live all in one house with their wives and their concubines, and the mulattoes one sees in every family partly resemble the white children. Any lady is ready to tell you who is the father of all the mulatto children in everybody's household but her own. Those, she seems to think, drop from the clouds.

An owner could do what he chose on his plantation, and his sons grew up expecting to do likewise. Unchecked power is always dangerous, and it is not surprising that on the plantation it was sometimes misused. Perhaps the most suprising thing about the southern slave system is how much humanity survived despite the intolerable conditions. For that, most of the credit goes to the slaves themselves and the life they created under slavery.

TO BE A SLAVE

The slave population, estimated at 7,000 in 1680, had grown to 700,000 by 1790. In the next seven decades it multiplied fivefold, to 4 million. Much of the population increase in the eighteenth century occurred because of the constant importation of slaves from Africa. After 1808 (when official American participation in the international slave trade ceased) the growth occurred because of natural increase — that is, births within the slave population. In spite of the burden of slavery, a distinctive African American community, begun in the eighteenth century (see Chapter 4), flourished in the years before the Civil War.

The Maturing of the American Slave System

Dependence on King Cotton meant dependence on slave labor. In 1850, 55 percent of all slaves were engaged in cotton growing. Another 20 percent labored to produce other crops: tobacco (10 percent), rice, sugar, and hemp. About 15 percent of all slaves were domestic servants, and the remaining

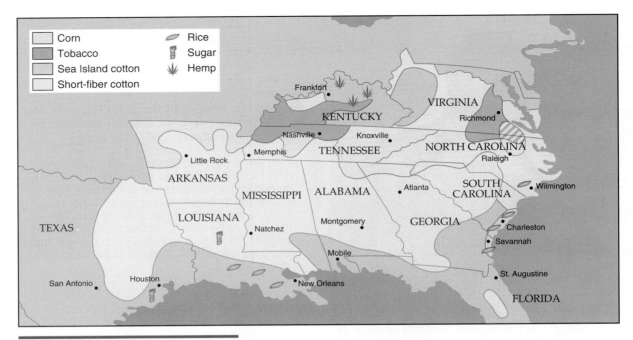

Southern Crop Distribution and Slavery

The distribution of the slave population was determined by agricultural patterns. In 1850, 55 percent of all slaves worked in cotton, 10 percent in tobacco, and another 10 percent in rice, sugar and hemp. Ten percent worked in mining, lumbering, construction and industry, while 15 percent worked as domestic servants. Slaves were not generally used to grow corn, the staple crop of the yeoman farmer.

10 percent worked in mining, lumbering, construction, and industry. In addition, 250,000 free African Americans lived in the South.

Slavery had become distinctively southern: By 1820, most of the northern states had abolished slaveholding. Slaves were increasingly clustered in the Lower South, as Upper South slave owners sold slaves "down the river" or migrated westward with their entire households. Finally, slaves were not distributed equally among southern slaveowners. As we have seen, over half of all slave owners owned five slaves or fewer. But 75 percent of all slaves lived in groups of ten or more. This disproportionate distribution could have a major impact on a slave's life, for it was a very different matter to be the single slave of a small farmer as opposed to a member of a 100-person black community on a large plantation.

Furthermore, slavery was far from static. There were many fewer slaves, and more free black people, in the Upper South, and a correspondingly increasing number of slaves in the new frontier areas of the Southwest. There was a major "slave drain" from north to south: an estimated 2 million slaves migrated involuntarily to the Lower South between 1820 and 1860.

The Challenge to Survive

The first challenge facing African Americans was survival. The first generation had to contend with the notorious Middle Passage from Africa to the Caribbean or the United States, a voyage that commonly claimed the lives of 20 percent of the captives. For later generations of black people born into slavery in the United States, the very young were at risk: Mortality rates for slave children under five were twice those for their white counterparts. The reason was clear: Pregnant black women were inadequately nourished, worked too hard, or were too frequently pregnant (six to eight births). When the British actress Fanny Kemble came to live on her husband's Georgia plantation in 1837, what shocked her more deeply than any other aspect of the slave system was the treatment of pregnant black women. Sensing her sympathy, pregnant slave women came to Kemble to plead for relief from field work, only to be brusquely ordered back to the fields by the overseer and Kemble's husband.

Health remained a lifelong issue for slaves. Malaria, as well as infectious diseases such as yellow fever and cholera, was endemic in the South. White people as well as black died, as the life expectancy

In this 1853 painting, *After the Sale: Slaves Going South from Richmond*, artist Eyre Crowe portrays the poignant farewells among members of slave families at the moment of parting. Separations were especially common in the 1850s, when an estimated one quarter million slaves were sold from the Upper to the Lower South.

figures for 1850 show: 25.5 years for white people but only 21.4 years for African Americans. Slaves were more at risk because of the circumstances of slave life: poor housing, poor diet, and constant, usually heavy work. Sickness was chronic: 20 percent or more of the slave labor force on most plantations were sick at any one time. Many owners believed their slaves weren't sick but only malingering. Because of the poor medical knowledge of the time, they failed to realize that adequate diet, warm housing, and basic sanitation might have prevented the pneumonia and dysentery that killed or debilitated many slaves.

From Cradle to Grave

Slavery was a lifelong labor system, and the constant and inescapable issue between master and slave was how much work the latter would—or could be forced—to do. Southern white slaveowners claimed that by housing, feeding, and clothing their slaves from infancy to death they were acting more humanely than northern industrialists who only employed people during their working years.

But the fact remained that slavery was almost inescapable. In spite of occasional instances of manumission, or freeing of a slave, (more common before 1800 than after), the child born of a slave was destined to remain a slave.

Children lived with their parents (or with their mother if the father was a slave on another farm or plantation) in housing provided by the owner. Slaves owned by small farmers usually had only a bed or mattress to sleep on in the attic or a back room. Larger slave owners housed slaves in one-room cabins with dirt floors and few furnishings (a table, stools, a cooking pot and a few dishes, a bed or corn-shuck mattresses). Fanny Kemble described, with some horror, the one-room slave cabins she found on her husband's plantation:

> These cabins consist of one room, about twelve feet by fifteen, with a couple of closets smaller and closer than the state-rooms of a ship, divided off from the main room and each other by rough wooden partitions, in which the inhabitants sleep. They have almost all of them a rude bedstead, with the gray moss of the forests for mattress, and filthy, pestilential-looking blankets

for covering. Two families (sometimes eight and ten in number) reside in one of these huts, which are mere wooden frames pinned, as it were, to the earth by a brick chimney outside . . . . A wide ditch runs immediately at the back of these dwellings, which is filled and emptied daily by the tide . . . .

A former slave on another plantation remembered that "the log cabin where my mammy lived had so many cracks in it that . . . I could lie in bed and count the stars through the cracks."

Masters supplied food to their slaves. One common ration for a week was three pounds of meat, a quart of corn meal, and some molasses for each person. Often slaves were encouraged to supplement their diet by keeping their own gardens, and by hunting — though not, of course, with guns. Slaves were also provided with clothes, usually of rough homespun cloth: two shirts, two pairs of pants, and a pair of shoes a year for men, and enough cloth for women to make an equal number of smocks for themselves and their children yearly. This clothing was barely adequate, and in severe winters slaves suffered badly.

From birth to about age seven, slave children played with one another and with white children, observing and learning how to survive. They saw the penalties: black adults, perhaps their own parents, whipped for disobedience; black women, perhaps their own sisters, violated by white men. And they might see one or both parents sold away as punishment or out of financial necessity. They would also see signs of white benevolence: special treats for children at holidays, appeals to loyalty from the master or mistress, perhaps friendship with a white child. One former slave recalled:

Yes, ma'am, my white folks was proud of they niggers. Um, yessum, when they used to have company in the big house, Miss Ross would bring them to the door to show them us children. And, my blessed, the yard would be black with us children, all string up there next the doorstep looking up in they eyes. Old Missus would say, "Ain't I got a pretty crop of little niggers coming on?"

The children would learn slave ways of getting along: apparent acquiescence in white demands; pilfering; malingering, sabotage, and other methods of slowing the relentless work pace. Fanny Kemble, an accomplished actress, was quick to note the pretense in the "outrageous flattery" she received from her husband's slaves. But many white southerners genuinely believed that their slaves were both stupider and more loyal than they really were. An escaped slave, Jermain Loguen, recalled with some distaste the charade of "servile bows and counterfeit smiles . . . and other false expressions of gladness" with which he placated his master and mistress. Frederick Douglass, whose fearless leadership of the abolitionist movement made him the most famous African American of his time, wryly noted, "As the master studies to keep the slave ignorant, the slave is cunning enough to make the master think he succeeds."

Most slaves spent their lives as field hands, working in gangs with other slaves under a white overseer, who was usually quick to use his whip to keep up the work pace. But there were other occupations. In the "big house" there were jobs for women as cooks, maids, seamstresses, laundresses, weavers, and nurses. Black men became coachmen, valets, and gardeners, or skilled craftsmen — carpenters, mechanics, and blacksmiths. Some children began learning these occupations at age seven or eight, often in an informal apprentice system. Other children, both boys and girls, were expected to take full care of younger children while the parents were working. Of course black children had no schooling of any kind: In all the southern states, it was against the law to teach a slave to read. At age twelve, slaves were considered full-grown and put to work in the fields or in their designated occupation. Mary Raines, a former South Carolina slave, recalled this time of her life:

I was a strong gal, went to de field when I's twelve years old, hoe my acre of cotton, 'long wid de grown ones, and pick my 150 pounds of cotton. As I wasn't scared of de cows, they set me to milkin' and churnin'. Bless God! Dat took me out of de field. House servants 'bove de field servants, them days. If you didn't get better rations and things to eat in de house, it was your own fault, I tells you!

House Servants

At first glance, working in the big house might seem to have been preferable to working in the fields. Physically it was much less demanding, and house slaves were often better fed and clothed. They also had much more access to information, for whites, accustomed to their servants and generally confident of their loyalty, often forgot their presence and spoke among themselves about matters of interest to the slaves: local gossip, changes in laws or attitudes, policies toward disobedient or rebellious slaves. As Benjamin Russel, a former slave in South Carolina, recalled,

> How did we get the news? Many plantations were strict about this, but the greater the precaution the alerter became the slave, the wider they opened their ears and the more eager they became for outside information. The sources were: girls that waited on the tables, the ladies' maids and the drivers; they would pick up everything they heard and pass it on to the other slaves.

For many whites, one of the worst surprises of the Civil War was the eagerness of their house slaves to flee. Considered by their masters the best treated and the most loyal, these slaves were commonly the first to leave or to organize mass desertions.

From the point of view of the slave, the most unpleasant thing about being a house servant (or the single slave of a small owner) was the constant presence of whites. There was no escape from white supervision. Many slaves who were personal maids and children's nurses were required to live in the big house and rarely saw their own families. Cooks and other house servants were exposed to the tempers and whims of all members of the white family, including the children, who prepared themselves for lives of mastery by practicing giving orders to slaves many times their own age. And house servants, more than any others, were forced to act grateful and ingratiating. The demeaning images of Uncle Tom and the ever smiling mammy derive from the roles slaves learned as the price of survival. At the same time, genuine intimacy was possible, especially between black nurses and white children. But these were bonds that the white children were ultimately forced to reject as the price of joining the master class.

Artisans and Skilled Workers

A small number of slaves were skilled workers: weavers, seamstresses, carpenters, blacksmiths, mechanics. More slave men than women achieved skilled status (partly because demanding work such as cooking, a female task, was not thought of as skilled). Solomon Northup, a northern free African

Population Patterns in the South

In South Carolina and Mississippi the enslaved African American population outnumbered whites; in four other Lower South states the percentage was above forty percent. These ratios frightened many white southerners. Whites also feared the free black population, though it is difficult to see why, for only three states in the Upper South and Louisiana had free black populations over three percent. Six states had free black populations that were so small (less than one percent) as to be statistically insignificant.

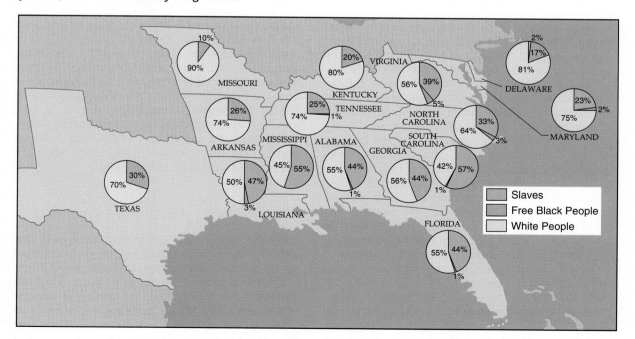

American kidnapped into slavery, explained in his 1853 narrative, *Twelve Years a Slave,* that he had been forced to do a variety of work. He had had three owners and had been hired out repeatedly as a carpenter, as a driver of other slaves in a sugar mill, to clear land for a new Louisiana plantation, and to cut sugar cane. Because of a shortage of white labor throughout the South, black people worked as lumberjacks (of the 16,000 lumber workers, almost all were slaves), as miners, as deckhands and stokers on Mississippi riverboats, as stevedores loading cotton on the docks of Charleston, Savannah, and New Orleans, and in the handful of southern factories. Both the Tregedar Iron Works, near Richmond, and William Gregg's cotton textile mills in Charleston employed slave as well as white workers. The extent to which slaves made up the laboring class was most apparent in cities. A British visitor to Natchez in 1835 noted slave "mechanics, draymen, hosteIers, labourers, hucksters and washwomen and the heterogeneous multitude of every other occupation." In the North, all of this work was performed by whites. In part because the South failed to attract as much immigrant labor as the North, Southern cities offered both enslaved and free black people opportunities in skilled occupations such as blacksmithing and carpentering that free African Americans in the North were denied.

Field Work

A full 75 percent of all slaves were field workers. Field hands, both men and women, worked from "can see to can't see" (sunup to sundown) summer and winter, and frequently longer at harvest, when eighteen hour days were common. On most plantations, the bell sounded an hour before sunup, and slaves were expected to be on their way to the fields as soon as it was light. The usual pattern of working in groups of twenty to twenty-five harked back to African communal systems of agricultural work. Many work gangs had black drivers in addition to white overseers. Work continued till noon, and after an hour or so for lunch and rest the slaves worked nearly until dark. In the evening the women prepared dinner at the cabins and everyone snatched a few hours of socializing before bedtime. Work days were shorter in the winter, perhaps only ten hours.

Work was tedious in the hot and humid southern fields, and the overseer's whip was never far away. Cotton required hard work throughout: plowing and planting, chopping weeds with a heavy hoe, and picking the ripe cotton from the stiff and scratchy bolls at the rate of 150 pounds a day. In the rice fields, slaves spent days knee-deep in water. On sugar plantations, harvesting the cane and getting it ready for boiling was exceptionally heavy work. A strong, hardworking slave — a "prime field hand" — was valuable property, worth as much as $1,800 to the master. Slaves justifiably took pride in their strength, as observed by a white northerner traveling in Mississippi in 1854 who came across a work gang happy to be going home early because of rain:

> First came, led by an old driver carrying a whip, forty of the largest and strongest women I ever saw together . . . they carried themselves loftily, each having a hoe over the shoulder, and walking with a free, powerful stride. Behind them came the . . . plowhands and their mules, thirty strong, mostly men, but a few of them women . . . a lean and vigilant white overseer, on a brisk pony, brought up the rear.

That, of course, is only one side of the story. Compare Solomon Northup's memory of cotton picking:

> It was rarely that a day passed by without one or more whippings. The delinquent [who had not picked enough cotton] was taken out, stripped, made to lie upon the ground, face downwards, when he received a punishment proportioned to his offence. It is the literal, unvarnished truth, that the crack of the lash, and the shrieking of the slaves, can be heard from dark till bed time, on [this] plantation, any day almost during the entire period of the cotton-picking season.

Slaves aged fast in this regime of poor health, poor diet, and heavy labor. When they were too old to work, they took on other tasks within the black community, such as caring for young children. Honored by the slave community, the elderly were tolerated by white owners, who continued to feed and clothe them until their deaths. Few actions show the hypocrisy of southern paternalism more clearly than the speed with which white owners evicted their elderly slaves in the 1860s when the end of the slave system was in sight.

THE AFRICAN AMERICAN COMMUNITY

Few black slaves were unfortunate enough to live their lives alone among white people. Over half of all slaves lived on plantations with twenty or more other slaves. Others, on smaller farms, had links with slaves on nearby properties. Urban slaves were able to make and sustain so many secret contacts with other African Americans in cities or towns that slave owners wondered whether slave discipline could be maintained in urban settings. There can be no question that the bonds among African Americans were what sustained them during the years of slavery. In fact, "the world the slaves made" influenced all of southern society.

Surely no group in American history has faced a harder job of community building than the black people of the antebellum South. Living in intimate, daily contact with their oppressors, African Americans nevertheless created an enduring culture. Their values and attitudes permeated all of southern life. Music, food, speech patterns, even the forms of southern Christianity — all show the influence of the slave community. The slave system created complicated links of knowledge, guilt, anger, and pain between black and white that endure to this day.

In law, slaves were property, to be bought, sold, rented, worked, and otherwise used (but not abused or killed) as the owner saw fit. But slaves were also human beings, with feelings, needs, and hopes. Even though most white southerners believed black people to be members of an inferior, childish race, all but the most brutal masters acknowledged the humanity of their slaves. Furthermore, as a practical matter, white owners had long since learned that unhappy or rebellious slaves were poor workers. White masters learned to live with the two key institutions of African American community life: the family and the African American church.

Five generations of one family on a South Carolina plantation are gathered together for this picture, providing living evidence of the importance of kinship in the building of African American communities.

Slave Families

No southern state recognized slave marriages in law. Most owners, though, not only recognized but encouraged them, sometimes even performing a kind of wedding ceremony for the couple. James Henry Hammond conducted a special ceremony for his slaves, to whom he gave $5.00 for a first marriage and $3.50 for a second marriage. In any case, slaves had their own rituals for celebrating the event: jumping over a broomstick was one common custom. Masters sometimes tried to arrange marriages, but slaves usually found their own mates, sometimes on their own plantation, sometimes elsewhere. Masters encouraged marriage among their slaves, believing it made the men less rebellious, and for economic reasons they were eager for women to have children. Thomas Jefferson, always a clear thinker, put the matter bluntly:

> I consider a [slave] woman who [gives birth to] a child every two years as more profitable than the best man on the farm . . . . What she produces is an addition to the capital.

Whatever marriages meant to the masters, to slaves they were a haven of love and intimacy in a cruel world and the basis of the African American community. Husbands and wives had a chance, in their own cabins, to live their own lives among loved ones. The relationship between slave husband and wife was different from that of the white husband and wife. The patriarchal system dictated that the white marriage be unequal, for the man had to be dominant and the woman dependent and submissive. Slave marriages were more equal, for husband and wife were both powerless within the slave system. Realistically, they each knew they could not protect the other from abuse at the hands of whites.

Husband and wife cooperated in loving and sheltering their children and teaching them survival skills. Above all, family meant continuity. Parents made great efforts to teach their children the family history. (As "Roots," the famous television series of the 1970s illustrated, many African American families today maintain strong oral traditions dating back to their African origins). Parents did their best to surround children with a supportive and protective kinship network.

The strength of these ties is shown by the great numbers of separated husbands and wives and children and parents who searched for each other after the Civil War when slavery came to an end.

Seeking to explain the postwar migrations of blacks, a Freedman's Bureau agent said:

> They had a passion, not so much for wandering, as for getting together, and every mother's son among them seemed to be in search of his mother; every mother in search of her children.

As the ads in black newspapers indicate, some family searches went on into the 1870s and 1880s and many ended in failure. A missionary teacher in South Carolina recalled a poignant conversation with an elderly black woman:

> As soon as she heard I had travelled through Virginia, she came to me to know if I had ever seen her "little gal." . . . And she begged me to look out for her when I went back. She was sure I should know her, she "was such a pretty little gal." It was useless to tell her the girl was now a woman, and doubtless had children of her own. She always had been and always would be her "baby."

Strong as the family was, it was frequently not strong enough to prevent separation, Although masters were often persuaded not to separate hard-working slave husbands and wives, many parents suffered the selling off of children, especially their strong and healthy teenage sons and daughters. As expansion to the Southwest accelerated, so did the demand for slaves in the newly settled regions. *Coffles*— slaves marched together in chains to a new location by a slave trader — were a common sight on the roads to the Southwest in the 1850s, when an estimated 250,000 slaves suffered involuntary migration.

Because of the ever present reality of separation, slave communities often acted like larger families, building kinlike networks to support individuals. Children were taught to respect and learn from all the elders (whom whites tended to regard as useless because they couldn't work any more), to call all adults of a certain age "Aunt" or "Uncle," and to call children of their own age "Brother" or "Sister." Thus, in the absence of their own family, separated children could quickly find a place and a source of comfort in the slave community to which they had been sold.

This emphasis on family and on kinship networks, whether real or *fictive* (as the anthropologists call them), had an even more fundamental purpose. The kinship of the entire community, where old people were respected and young ones cared for, represented a conscious rejection of white paternalism. The slaves' ability, in the most difficult of situations, to structure a community that expressed *their* values, and not their masters', was extraordinary. Equally remarkable was the way in which African Americans reshaped Christianity to serve their needs.

African American Religion

Slaves brought religions from Africa, but were not allowed to practice them, for whites feared religion would create a bond among slaves that might lead to rebellion. African religions survived in the slave community in forms that whites considered "superstition" or "folk belief," such as the medical use of roots by conjurers. Religious ceremonies survived too, in late-night gatherings deep in the woods where the sound of drumming, singing, and dancing could not reach white ears. Impressive as these African survivals were, the reshaping of white Christianity by African Americans was even more significant.

Most masters of the eighteenth century made little effort to Christianize their slaves, apparently believing it was unimportant to do so as long as the slaves worked satisfactorily. The Second Great Awakening (see Chapter 9), which swept the South in the 1790s, changed that. As whites themselves increasingly viewed religion with evangelical fervor, they made sustained efforts to convert their slaves. Doubtless, most whites who preached to African Americans had sincere motives, but the evangelical religion of the early nineteenth century was also a powerful form of social control. Southern slave owners expected Christianity to make their slaves obedient and peaceful. Slaves were quick to realize the owners' purpose. As a former Texas slave recalled,

> We went to church on the place and you ought to heard that preachin'. Obey your massa and missy, don't steal chickens and eggs and meat, but nary a word 'bout havin' a soul to save.

On many plantations, slaves attended religious services with their masters every Sunday, sitting quietly in the back of the church as the minister preached messages justifying slavery and urging obedience. But at night, away from white eyes, they held their own prayer meetings. Another former Texas slave recalled:

> Us niggers used to have a prayin' ground down in the hollow and sometimes we come out of the field, between eleven and twelve at night,

African American religious observances often took place deep in the forest, away from white supervision. In this scene of a slave funeral, painted by John Antrobus around 1860, the community nature of the mourning is evident.

scorchin' and burnin' up with nothin' to eat, and we wants to ask the good Lawd to have mercy. We put grease in a snuff pan or bottle and make a lamp. We takes a pine torch, too, and goes down to the hollow to pray. Some gits so joyous they starts to holler loud and we has to stop up they mouth [so the whites won't hear]. I see niggers git so full of the Lawd and so happy they draps unconscious.

Behind these spontaneous religious expressions lay the concerted action of both free and enslaved African Americans. Beginning in the 1790s (as part of the Second Great Awakening), free black people created their own Baptist and African Methodist Episocal (AME) churches. Free black ministers such as Andrew Marshall of Savannah, Georgia, and many more enslaved black preachers and lay ministers preached, sometimes secretly, to slaves. Their message was very different from that of white ministers. They preached of faith and love, of deliverance, of the coming of the promised land. In this way, the black community made Christianity its own. Fusing Christian texts with African elements of group activity such as the circle dance, the call-and-response pattern, and, above all, group singing, black people created a unique community religion full of emotion, enthusiasm, and protest. Nowhere is this spirit more compelling than in the famous spirituals: "Go Down Moses," with its mournful refrain "Let my people go"; the rousing "Didn't My Lord Deliver Daniel . . . and why not every man"; the haunting "Steal Away." Some of these spirituals became as well known to whites as to blacks, but only African Americans seem to have appreciated the full meaning of their subversive messages.

Nevertheless, this was not a religion of rebellion, for that was unrealistic for most slaves. Black Christianity was an enabling religion: It helped slaves to survive, not as passive victims of white tyranny but as active opponents of an oppressive system that they daily protested in small but meaningful ways. In their faith, African Americans expressed a spiritual freedom that whites could not destroy.

Freedom and Resistance

Whatever their dreams, most slaves knew they would never escape. Freedom was too far away. Almost all successful escapes in the nineteenth century (approximately 1,000 a year) were from the Upper South (Maryland, Virginia, Kentucky, Missouri). A slave in the Deep South or the Southwest simply had too far to go to reach freedom. In addition, white southerners were determined to prevent escapes. "Paterollers" (slave patrols) were a common sight on southern roads after 1830. Any black person without a pass from his or her master was captured (usually roughly) and returned home to certain punishment. But despite almost certain recapture, slaves continued to flee and to help others do so. Harriet Tubman of Maryland, who made nineteen rescue missions freeing 300 slaves in all, is an extraordinary example of determination and skill. She was unusual in another way too: most escapees were young men, for women often had small children whom they were unable to take and unwilling to leave behind.

Much more common was the practice of running away nearby. Hidden in forests or swamps, the runaway was provided with food smuggled by other slaves from the plantation. If the runaway was not caught by bloodhounds and the paterollers, he returned home after a week or so, often to rather mild punishment. As these runaways demonstrated, slaves frequently knew every inch of the land surrounding their plantation. And as we have seen, slaves were practiced at slipping away from plantations for communal activities such as religious gatherings deep in the woods. By running away slaves demonstrated their desire for liberty, however temporary, and put the master on notice that they were discontented. This was a warning sign that a wise master did not ignore.

Free Black People

A little-noticed aspect of the slave system was the existence of free black people. In 1860 nearly 250,000 free African Americans lived in the South. For most, freedom dated from before 1800, when antislavery feeling among slave owners was widespread and cotton cultivation had yet to boom. In Virginia, for example, a manumission law of 1782 made it possible for any slave owner to free a slave under the age of forty-five simply by the stroke of a pen. Consequently, the free black population of towns such as Petersburg tripled in the space of twenty years. In 1805 Virginia's manumission laws were tightened — the freed person was required to leave the state within a year or be sold back into slavery — and after 1830 manumission was virtually impossible. Many free black people were women and their light-skinned children, living proof of the ties of affection and kinship that linked some white masters to slave women.

Most free black people lived in the countryside of the Upper South, where they worked as tenant farmers or farm laborers. Urban African Americans were much more visible. Many urban black families consisted of women and their children. Life was especially difficult for such families because only the most menial work — street peddling and laundry work, for example — was available to free black women. The situation for black males was somewhat better. Although they were discriminated against in employment and in social life, there were

Harriet Tubman escaped in 1849 from slavery in Maryland, and returned nineteen times to free almost 300 other slaves. Here Tubman (at left), the most famous "conductor" on the Underground Railroad, is shown with some of those she led to freedom.

One of the ways Charleston attempted to control its African American population was to require all slaves to wear badges showing their occupation. After 1848, free black people also had to wear badges which were decorated, ironically, with a liberty cap.

opportunities for skilled black craftsmen in trades such as blacksmithing and carpentering.

Cities such as Charleston, Savannah, and Natchez were home to flourishing free black communities that formed their own churches and fraternal orders. In Natchez, a free black barber, William Johnson, owned several barber shops, a small farm, and an estate valued at $25,000 in 1851 that included fifteen slaves. Johnson had a white attorney and friends among the city's leading politicians, and he lived in a white neighborhood. Half a dozen other free blacks in Natchez were similarly prosperous, and they too were slave owners. This tiny elite kept a careful social distance from most of Natchez's approximately 1,000 free black people (one-quarter of all free African Americans in Mississippi in 1840), who were miserably poor. And, as Johnson's diary reveals, they treated whites with great tact and deference.

They had reason to be careful, for their position was precarious. Throughout the South in the 1830s, state legislatures tightened the Black Codes — those laws concerning free black people. Free African Americans could not carry firearms, could not purchase slaves (unless they were members of their own family), and were liable to the criminal penalties meted out to slaves (that is, whippings and summary judgments without a jury trial). They could not testify against whites, hold office, vote, or serve in the militia. In other words, except for the right to own property, free blacks had no civil rights. Following the cleanup of the alarming race mixing in Natchez-under-the-Hill (described in the chapter introduction), the Natchez nabobs focused on free blacks. In 1841, whites mounted a campaign to deport from the state any free black person who adopted ''the practices of the rogue, the incendiary, and the abolitionist.'' Many poor free black people

were deported from Natchez that summer and in the following years. William Johnson, whose own security was not threatened, aided some poor black people by quietly helping them obtain attestations of good character from the nabobs. For all of his (comparative) wealth, as a black man he could do nothing openly to help his own people.

As this episode shows, whites increasingly feared the influence free black people might have on slaves. For free African Americans were a living challenge to the slave system. Their very existence disproved the basic southern equations of white equals free and black equals slave.

Slave Revolts

The ultimate resistance, however, was the slave revolt. Southern history was dotted with stories of former slave conspiracies and rumors of current plots. Every white southerner knew about the last-minute failure of Gabriel Prosser's insurrection in Richmond in 1800 and the chance discovery of Denmark Vesey's plot in Charleston in 1822. In 1831, southern fears were magnified by Nat Turner's rebellion, which was *not* discovered until a number of whites had been killed.

Gabriel Prosser had gathered over a thousand slaves for an assault on Richmond. Although the attempt was aborted at the last minute and Prosser and thirty-five others were caught and hanged, whites were especially frightened to learn that Prosser had organized under a banner proclaiming ''Death or Liberty'' and had hoped for help from the independent black people of Haiti. The notion of an international force of revolutionary slaves demanding their freedom was a serious challenge to slave owners' assumptions about their own liberty and power.

Denmark Vesey's conspiracy raised fears among white people concerning African American religion and free black people. Vesey was a well-traveled former seaman who lived in Charleston and worked as a carpenter. Free, well read, and eloquent, Vesey was a lay preacher at Charleston's African Methodist Episcopal Church, where he drew on quotations from the Bible and from the congressional debates during the Missouri controversy (1819–20) to make a forceful argument against slavery. His co-conspirator, Gullah Jack, was a "conjure-man" who drew on the African religious traditions that flourished among the slaves in the South Carolina low country. Vesey and Gullah Jack drew up a plan to evade the lax city patrol and steal weapons from the Charleston arsenal and horses from livery stables. Then, while mounted and armed slaves beat back white counterattacks in the streets of Charleston, house slaves would capture their owners and murder any who tried to escape. Vesey's aim was to seize Charleston and ultimately to sail to the free black Caribbean nation of Haiti.

Vesey and Gullah Jack recruited at least eighty country and city slaves into the conspiracy, including several trusted house slaves of South Carolina governor Thomas Bennett. Two weeks before the date fixed for the insurrection, the plot was betrayed by a loyal house servant who reported the two slaves who had tried to recruit him into the conspiracy. The accused slaves laughed at the charge, and coolly managed to convince the authorities that

there was no plot. But two days before the revolt, another house servant confessed, and this time the authorities believed him. In the frantic roundup that followed, thirty-five black people were hanged (Vesey among them) and thirty-seven others sold down the river. But some rebels were not caught, because their fellow conspirators died without betraying them. Charlestonians had to live with the knowledge that some of their most trusted servants had conspired to kill them — and might still plan to do so.

In the wake of the Vesey conspiracy, Charlestonians turned their fear and anger outward. Planter Robert J. Turnbull wrote bitterly, "By the Missouri question, our slaves thought, there was a charter of liberties granted them by Congress . . . . [The Vesey Conspiracy] will long be remembered, as amongst the choicest fruits of that question in Congress." Whites attempted to seal off the city from dangerous outside influences. The AME Church (where radical ideas such as the Missouri question had been discussed) was destroyed, and in December of 1822 the South Carolina legislature passed a bill requiring that all black seamen be seized and jailed while their ships were in Charleston harbor. Initially most alarmed about free blacks from Haiti, Charlestonians soon came to believe that northern free black seamen were spreading antislavery ideas among their slaves.

The most famous slave revolt was the one that was not discovered beforehand: Nat Turner's revolt in Southampton County, Virginia. Literate, intelli-

This drawing shows the moment, almost two months after the failure of his famous and bloody slave revolt, when Nat Turner was accidentally discovered in the woods near his home plantation. Turner's cool murder of his owner and methodical organization of his revolt deeply frightened many white southerners.

gent, and religious, Nat Turner was a lay preacher, like Denmark Vesey. Unlike Vesey, Turner was a slave. His intelligence and strong religious sentiments made him a leader in the slave community. These same qualities led his master, Joseph Travis, to treat him with kindness even though Turner had once run away for a month after being mistreated by an overseer. Turner began plotting his revolt after a religious vision in which he saw "white spirits and black spirits engaged in battle"; "the sun was darkened—the thunder rolled in the Heavens, and blood flowed in streams . . . ." Turner and five other slaves struck on the night of August 20, 1831, first killing Travis, about whom Turner said, "[he] was to me a kind master, and placed the greatest confidence in me; in fact, I had no cause to complain of his treatment of me." Moving from plantation to plantation, killing a total of fifty-five whites (including women and children), the rebels numbered sixty by the next morning, when they fled from a group of armed whites. More than forty blacks were executed after the revolt, including Turner, who was captured accidentally after he had hidden for two months in the woods. Thomas R. Gray, a white lawyer to whom Turner dictated a lengthy confession before his death, was impressed by Turner's calmness and composure. "I looked on him," Gray said, "and my blood curdled in my veins." If intelligent, well-treated slaves such as Turner could plot revolts, how could white southerners ever feel safe? After 1831, fear of slave insurrection was never far from southern minds.

The Defense of Slavery

"Slavery informs all our modes of life, all our habits of thought, lies at the basis of our social existence, and of our political faith," announced South Carolina planter William Henry Trescot in 1850, explaining why the South would secede from the Union before giving up slavery. Slavery bound white and black southerners together in tortuous ways that eventually led, as Trescot had warned, to the Civil War.

Population figures tell much of the complex relationship between whites and blacks: of the 12 million people who lived in the South in 1860, 4 million were slaves. Indeed, in the richest agricultural regions, such as the Sea Islands of South Carolina and Georgia and parts of the black belt, black people outnumbered whites. These sheer numbers of African Americans reinforced whites' perpetual fears of black retaliation for the violence exercised by the slavemaster. Every rumor of slave revolts, real or imagined, kept those fears alive. The basic question was this: What might slaves do if they were not controlled? Thomas Jefferson summed up this dilemma:

> We have the wolf by the ears; and we can neither hold him nor safely let him go. Justice is in one scale, and self-preservation in the other.

Developing Proslavery Arguments

At the time of the American Revolution, slavery appeared to be in decline. The paradox that "the loudest yelps for liberty come from the slave drivers" (as Samuel Johnson caustically remarked) could be glossed over if slavery was indeed dying a natural death.

As we have seen, the rise of King Cotton changed the future of slavery in the American South. The international demand for cotton seemed inexhaustible, and slavery appeared to most southerners to be an economic necessity. But at the very moment that the South committed its future to cotton, worldwide opinion about slavery was changing. Britain outlawed the slave trade in 1807 and abolished slavery in its West Indian islands in 1833. Elsewhere in the Americas (with the exception of Cuba and Brazil) slavery had already been abolished or soon would be. It was now much harder to justify slavery in the United States, the most democratic country (for whites) in the world.

Southern apologists had several conventional lines of defense. They found justifications for slavery in the Bible and in the histories of Greece and Rome, both slave-owning societies. The strongest defense was a legal one: The Constitution allowed slavery. Though never specifically mentioned in the final document, slavery had been a major issue between North and South at the Constitutional Convention in 1787. In the end, the delegates agreed that seats in the House of Representatives would be apportioned by counting all of the white population and three-fifths of the black people; they included a clause requiring the return of runaway slaves who had crossed state lines; and they agreed that Congress could not abolish the international slave trade for twenty years. There was absolutely no question: The Constitution did recognize slavery.

The Missouri controversy of 1819–20 alarmed most southerners. They were shocked by the northern hostility toward slavery, by the limitations on its expansion contained in the Missouri Compromise, and by the possibility of becoming a minority voice in national affairs. At the most basic level, most southerners saw the controversy as a matter of property rights. An Alabama agricultural society document put the matter bluntly:

> Our condition is quite different from that of the non-slaveholding section of the United States. With them their only property consists of lands, cattle and planting implements. Their laborers are merely hirelings, while with us our laborers are our property.

As we have seen, South Carolinians viewed Denmark Vesey's conspiracy, happening only two years after the Missouri debate, as an example of the harm that irresponsible northern antislavery talk could cause. After Nat Turner's revolt in 1831, Governor John Floyd of Virginia blamed the uprising on "Yankee peddlers and traders" who would supposedly tell slaves that "all men were born free and equal." Thus northern antislavery opinion and the fear of slave uprisings were firmly linked in southern minds.

After 1830

In 1831 the South began to close ranks in defense of slavery. Several factors contributed to this regional solidarity. Nat Turner's revolt was important, linked as it was in the minds of many southerners with antislavery agitation from the North. As it happened, 1831 was the year that militant abolitionist William Lloyd Garrison began publishing *The Liberator*, the newspaper that was to become the leading antislavery organ (see Chapter 13). The British gave notice that they would soon abolish slavery on the sugar plantations of the West Indies, an action that seemed to many southerners much too close to home. Emancipation for West Indian slaves came in 1833. Finally, 1831 was the year before the nullification crisis was resolved (see Chapter 10). Although the other southern states did not support the hot-headed South Carolinians who called for secession, they did sympathize with the argument that the federal government had no right to interfere with a state's special interest (namely, slavery).

In the 1830s, southern states began to barricade themselves against "outside" antislavery literature. In 1835, a crowd broke into a Charleston post office, made off with bundles of antislavery literature, and set an enormous bonfire, to fervent state and regional acclaim. Southern legislatures tried to blunt the effect of abolitionist literature by passing stringent laws forbidding slaves to learn how to read. These laws were so effective that by 1860, it is estimated, only 5 percent of all slaves were literate. Other laws made the freeing of slaves illegal and placed even more restrictions on the lives of free black people (as we saw in the example of Natchez). In many areas slave patrols were augmented and became more vigilant in restricting African American movement and communication between plantations. Attempts were made to stifle all open debate about slavery; dissenters were encouraged to remain silent or to leave. A few, such as James Birney

This 1841 proslavery cartoon contrasts healthy, well-cared-for African American slaves with unemployed British factory workers living in desperate poverty. The comparison between contented southern slaves and miserable northern "wage slaves" was frequently made by proslavery advocates.

and Sarah and Angelina Grimké of South Carolina, left for the North to act upon their antislavery convictions (see Chapter 13), but most chose silence.

In addition to fueling fears of slave rebellions, the growing abolitionist sentiment of the 1830s raised the worry that southern opportunities for expansion would be cut off. Southern politicians painted melodramatic pictures of a beleaguered white South:

> Hemmed in on the North, West and Southwest by a chain of nonslaveholding States; fanaticism and power, hand in hand, preaching a crusade against her institutions; her post offices flooded with incendiary documents; . . . the value of her property depreciated and her agricultural industry paralyzed, what would become of the people of the Southern States, when they would be forced at last to let loose among them, freed from the wholesome restraints of patriarchal authority . . . an idle, worthless, profligate set of free negroes prowling about our streets at night and haunting the woods during the day armed with whatever weapons they could lay their hands on. . . .

Finally, southern apologists moved beyond defensiveness to develop proslavery arguments. One of the first to do this was James Henry Hammond, elected a South Carolina congressman in 1834. In 1836 Hammond delivered a major address to Congress, in which he said:

> [Slavery] is no evil. On the contrary, I believe it to be the greatest of all the great blessings which a kind Providence had bestowed upon our glorious region. . . . [It has produced] the highest toned, the purest, best organization of society that has ever existed on the face of the earth.

One wonders what Hammond's slaves, especially Sally and Louisa Johnson, would have thought of this argument.

A few years later another southern spokesman, George Fitzhugh, asserted that "the negro slaves of the South are the happiest, and, in some sense, the freest people in the world" because all the responsibility for their care was borne by concerned white masters. Fitzhugh contrasted southern paternalism with the heartless individualism that ruled the lives of northern "wage slaves." Northern employers did not take care of their workers, Fitzhugh claimed, because "selfishness is almost the only motive of human conduct in free society, where every man is taught that it is his first duty to change and better his pecuniary situation." In contrast, Fitzhugh argued, southern masters and their slaves were bound together by a "*community* of interests."

Changes in the South

In spite of these defensive and repressive proslavery measures, which made the South seem monolithic in northern eyes, there were a few indicators of dissent. Most came from upcountry nonslaveholders. One protest occurred in the Virginia state legislature in 1832, when nonslaveholding delegates, alarmed by the Nat Turner rebellion, forced a two-week debate on the merits of gradual abolition. In the final vote, abolition was defeated seventy-three to fifty-eight, and the subject was never raised again.

Moreover, slavery was not a static system. From the 1830s on, it was harder to become a slaveholder. In fact, from 1830 to 1860 the percentage of slaveholders in the South declined from 36 to 25 percent, and in 1860 the average slaveholder was ten times as wealthy as the average nonslaveholder. One reason for the disparity in wealth was the rapidly increasing price of slaves: a "prime field hand" was worth more than $1,500 in 1855. Such prices caused still another change: Slavery decreased markedly in the Upper South (Virginia, Maryland, Delaware, and Tennessee) in the 1850s, as slave owners sold 250,000 slaves to the Lower South (Texas, Louisiana, Mississippi, Alabama, and Georgia) for handsome profits. Such a difference in the extent of slaveholding between Upper and Lower South threatened regional political unity and provoked concern. One remedy suggested in South Carolina was to reopen the slave trade! In North Carolina, disputes between slave owners and nonslaveholders erupted in print in 1857, when North Carolinian Hinton Helper published an antislavery book titled *The Impending Crisis.* His protest was an indicator of the growing tensions between the haves and the have-nots in the South. Equally significant, though, Helper's book was published in New York, and not in the South.

In spite of these signs of tension and dissent, the main lines of the southern argument were drawn in the 1830s and remained fixed thereafter. The defense of slavery stifled debate within the South, prevented a search for alternative labor systems, and narrowed the possibility of cooperation in national politics. In time, it made compromise impossible.

CHRONOLOGY

1790s	Second Great Awakening
	Black Baptist and African Methodist Episcopal churches founded
1792	Kentucky admitted to the Union as a slave state
1793	Cotton gin invented
1796	Tennessee admitted to the Union as a slave state
1800	Gabriel Prosser's revolt discovered in Virginia
1808	Congress prohibits U.S. participation in the international slave trade
1812	Louisiana admitted to the Union as a slave state
1814	Battle of Horseshoe Bend; Treaty of Fort Jackson
1815	Battle of New Orleans makes Andrew Jackson a national hero
1816	Land cessions by Choctaws, Chickasaws, and Creeks
1816–19	"Alabama Fever": Migration to the Old Southwest
1817	Mississippi admitted to the Union as a slave state
	Andrew Jackson raids Florida
1819	Land cessions by the Cherokees
	Adams-Onis Treaty adds Florida to the U.S.
1819–20	Missouri controversy
1820s	Further land cessions by Choctaws, Creeks, and Seminoles
1821	Missouri admitted to the Union as a slave state
1822	Denmark Vesey's conspiracy in Charleston
1830s	Tightening of Black Codes throughout the South
	Final land cessions and removal of the Creeks, Seminoles, Chickasaws, and Cherokees
	Censorship of abolitionist literature
1831	Nat Turner's revolt in Virginia
1832	Nullification crisis
1833	Britain frees West Indian slaves
1836	Arkansas admitted to the Union as a slave state

CONCLUSION

The slave labor system enriched and shaped the American South, but by the mid-nineteenth century slavery was an international anachronism. No matter how many defensive measures were taken—removing "civilized" Indian peoples, shutting down the mixed community of Natchez-under-the-Hill, burning antislavery literature, drafting legal changes—slavery was simply out of place in the modern world. What doomed the slave system in the South was the growth of the United States as a nation. The irony is that the tremendous international demand for cotton contributed substantially to that growth. Throughout the country, people began to think beyond their local and regional communities. In doing so they found things in other regions that they considered intolerable. Northerners disliked slavery; southerners just as genuinely disliked the competitive capitalism of the North. So began the direct conflict of regional cultures that eventually led to civil war. In this chapter we have considered southern regional culture. We turn now to the free labor system that was developing in the North.

Additional Readings

IRA BERLIN, *Slaves without Masters* (1974). A full portrait of the lives of free black people in the South before the Civil War.

B. A. BOTKIN, ed., *Lay My Burden Down: A Folk History of Slavery* (1945). One of the first of many volumes drawing on the words of former slaves concerning their memories of slavery.

ORVILLE VERNON BURTON, *In My Father's House Are Many Mansions: Family and Community in Edgefield, South Carolina* (1985). A detailed community study that considers the farms, families, and everyday relations of white and black people in the period 1850–80.

THOMAS D. CLARK and JOHN D. W. GUICE, *Frontiers in Conflict: The Old Southwest, 1795–1830* (1989). Considers the Indian nations and their removal; white settlement; and the economic development of the region.

CATHERINE CLINTON, *The Plantation Mistress: Woman's World in the Old South* (1982). Illustrates how slavery shaped the lives of elite white women. The exclusive focus on white women, however, neglects the black women with whom they lived on a daily basis.

DREW GILPIN FAUST, *James Henry Hammond and the Old South* (1982). This outstanding biography uses the complex and interesting story of one man's life and ambitions to tell a larger story about southern attitudes and politics.

LACY K. FORD, JR., *Origins of Southern Radicalism: The South Carolina Upcountry, 1800–1860* (1988). One of a growing number of studies of upcountry nonslaveholders and their commitment to liberty and equality.

EUGENE GENOVESE, *Roll, Jordan, Roll: The World the Slaves Made* (1974). The landmark book that redirected the attention of historians from slaves as victims to the slave community as an active participant in the paternalism of the southern slave system.

HERBERT GUTMAN, *The Black Family in Slavery and Freedom, 1750–1925* (1977). A sometimes overly statistical study that proves the centrality and durability of the African American family under slavery and after emancipation.

BRUCE LEVINE, *Half Slave and Half Free: The Roots of Civil War* (1992). A useful survey of the different lines of development of the northern and southern economies and the political conflicts between the regions.

JAMES OAKES, *The Ruling Race: A History of American Slaveholders* (1982). Oakes disagrees with Genovese's characterization of paternalism and sees slave owners instead as entrepreneurial capitalists. Especially useful for distinguishing the various classes of slave owners.

PETER J. PARISH, *Slavery: History and Historians* (1989). A useful survey and synopsis of a large literature.

DANIEL H. USNER, JR. *Indians, Settlers, and Slave in a Frontier Exchange Economy: The Lower Mississippi Valley Before 1783* (1992) This sophisticated book looks at the complex trade and relationships among Europeans, African slaves, and Indian peoples of the lower Mississippi.

12 INDUSTRY AND THE NORTH, 1790s–1840s

AMERICAN COMMUNITIES

• THE WOMEN OF LOWELL, MASSACHUSETTS

In the 1820s and 1830s, young farm women from all over New England flocked to Lowell, the model community in rural Massachusetts. They came to work a twelve-hour day in one of the first cotton textile factories in America, and to live six to eight to a room in boardinghouses nearby. They earned an average of three dollars a week. Some not only earned but learned, attending the nighttime lectures and classes for which Lowell was famous. This unusual factory town and its educated workers drew worldwide attention. As one admirer said, Lowell was less a factory than a "philanthropic manufacturing college."

The Boston businessmen who founded Lowell were philanthropic — but for intensely practical reasons. Eager to be

INDUSTRIALIZATION
CREATES A COMMUNITY
OF WORKERS

as financially successful as Britain's new textile manufacturers, the Bostonians were at the same time anxious to avoid the dirt, poverty, and social disorder of English factory towns. In 1823, at the junction of the Concord and Merrimack Rivers (which provided necessary water power), they opened a model factory town: six neat factory buildings grouped around a central clock tower, the area pleasantly landscaped with flowers, shrubs, and trees. The housing was similarly well ordered: a Georgian mansion for the company agent; neat houses for the overseers; row houses for the mechanics and their families; and boardinghouses, each supervised by a responsible matron, for the model work force that made Lowell famous, young New England farm women.

The choice of young women as factory workers seemed shockingly unconventional. In the 1820s and 1830s, young unmarried women simply did not live alone; they lived and worked with their parents until marriage. Yet, as the Lowell manufacturers shrewdly realized, young farm women were an untapped labor force. In these years of growth and westward expansion, America was chronically short of labor. For young men, the lure of a farm of one's own was much stronger than factory work. But for their sisters, a chance to escape from rural isolation and earn wages was an appealing way to spend a few years before marriage. To attract respectable young women, Lowell offered supervised boardinghouses with strict rules of conduct, compulsory religious services, cultural opportunities such as concerts and lectures, and wages in cash.

These young women, typical of thousands who worked at Lowell, show the respectability, companionship, and pride in their work (evidenced by the weaving shuttles they hold in their hands) that made Lowell a model factory town.

When they first arrived in Lowell, the young women were often bewildered by the large number of people and embarrassed by their own rural clothing and ways of speech. Their adjustment was eased by other women, often their own sisters or neighbors, who had preceded them into the mill. The biggest adjustment was to "the buzzing and hissing and whizzing of pulleys and rollers and spindles and flyers" of the factory. Here too women helped women: as a matter of company policy, senior women carefully trained the newcomers. Most women enjoyed the work. One woman wrote home: "The work is not disagreeable. . . . It tried my patience sadly at first . . . but in general, I like it very much. It is easy to do, and does not require very violent exertion, as much of our farm work does."

Cotton textile mills were the first and best-known American factories. They all had certain things in common. They were laid out according to an elaborate division of labor that established a hierarchy of value and pay. For example, in the mills at Lowell, each floor was devoted to a single operation. Located in the basement was the water wheel that powered the pulleys for the machines. On the first floor were the carding and roving machines, which cleaned the cotton and prepared it for spinning. On the second floor were all the spinning frames: the job of the women who worked here was to change bobbins. On the next floor were the large power looms: the loom tenders had more responsibility, more skill, and more pay than the women on the floor below.

The second common characteristic of textile mills was the rigid work schedules. These were designed to accustom workers to the sustained pace of power-driven machinery. Every mill published elaborate schedules and insisted that the workers adhere to them: there were fines and penalties for latecomers. Every mill also had one or two overseers per floor to make sure the pace was maintained. Men held these positions and the skilled mechanic positions, and they earned more than the women and children who made up most of the work force; this was unquestioned.

To workers unaccustomed to the constant hum of machinery, the cotton mills were noisy. The air was hot, humid, and full of cotton lint. At first most workers found the mills confusing and rather frightening. But once accustomed to the job, most found it not very difficult, even when it involved tending several machines. The women at Lowell said the work was much less physically demanding than farm work. And they were not particularly distressed at the long hours — twelve hours a day — for farm people were accustomed to long days. What they didn't like, and had trouble getting used to, was the need to keep to a precise timetable. This represented the single largest change from preindustrial work habits.

The owners of Lowell made large profits. They also derived substantial acclaim for their carefully managed community with its intelligent and independent work force. But their success was short-lived. In the 1830s, because of competition and poor economic conditions, the owners imposed wage cuts and speedups that provoked a strong reaction from their model work force. Although the Lowell women had been brought together under a system of paternalistic control, they formed their own bonds at work. These led to concerted protests in the form of spontaneous "turnouts" and even sustained strikes. By 1850, all thoughts of a "philanthropic manufacturing college" had ended. The original Lowell work force of New England farm girls had been replaced by impoverished Irish immigrants, who worked much harder and for much less pay than their predecessors. Now Lowell was simply another mill town.

The history of Lowell epitomizes the process by which the North (both New England and the Middle Atlantic states) began to change from a society composed largely of self-sufficient farm families (Jefferson's "yeoman farmers") to one of urban workers in an industrial economy. This process — the Market Revolution — was probably the most fundamental change American communities ever experienced. The Market Revolution encompassed three broad, interrelated economic changes: exceptionally rapid improvements in transportation, which accelerated ongoing westward expansion and urbanization; commercialization; and the industrialization of manufacturing. We looked at the transportation revolution in Chapter 10. In this chapter we will examine the effects of commercialization and industrialization on the lives of ordinary people. Together, they added up to the Market Revolution.

Industrialization did not occur overnight. Large factories were not common until the 1880s, but by that decade most workers had already experienced a fundamental change in their working patterns. Once under way, the Market Revolution changed the very basis of communities: how people worked, how they thought, how they lived. In the early years of the nineteenth century, northern communities led this transformation. In so doing, they fostered attitudes far different from those prevalent in the South.

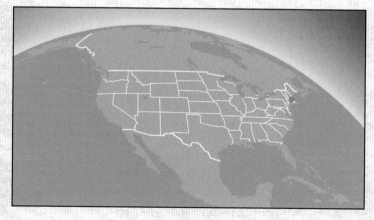

PREINDUSTRIAL WAYS OF WORKING

Because the Market Revolution represented a basic change in long-established patterns of work, we will begin by looking at traditional ways of working, first on farms (where 97 percent of all Americans lived in 1800) and then in cities.

Rural Life: The Springer Family

At first, commercial change came to American farm families gradually. The experience of Thomas and Elizabeth Springer, who began farming in Mill Creek, Delaware (near Wilmington), in the 1790s, illustrates this early change. In 1792, twenty-nine-year-old Thomas Springer, his wife Elizabeth, and their two infant daughters lived on 129 acres of farmland, 104 of which Springer had bought from his well-off father for less than the market price. Springer owned four slaves: Ace, a young man; Sara and Amelia, young girls; and Will, aged sixty. Family wealth had given Thomas Springer, still a young man, a substantial advantage over many of his neighbors in both land and work force.

The presence of slaves on the Springer farm is one of several similarities shared by yeoman farmers in the North and the South in the 1790s. But Springer's slave Ace was in the process of buying his freedom, something he probably could not have done had he lived in the South. Northern dislike of the slave system was already evident. By 1790 five northern states had abolished slavery (Massachusetts, New Hampshire, Pennsylvania, Rhode Island, and Connecticut), and New York and New Jersey followed in 1799 and 1804, respectively. Delaware remained a slave state, but in 1861, when the Civil War broke out, only 2 percent of the state's population were slaves, and there was no question of Delaware's loyalty to the Union.

Even more than attitudes toward slavery, farming decisions contributed to regional divergence. When the invention of the cotton gin made cotton growing profitable after 1793, many southern yeomen devoted at least part of their land to it. Thomas Springer did not. The soil on his farm was not suited to cotton, and Springer already had access, in a small way, to a commercial market that wanted other products from him.

The Springers raised thirty or forty sheep and at least fifteen milking cows. Some of this livestock was fattened for sale to butchers in nearby Wilmington. The Springers also sold the wool from the sheep and the milk and butter from the cows. Spinning the wool and dairying were women's work, and added

Edward Hicks painted this idealized picture of his childhood home in the 1840s. The prosperous preindustrial farm was similar in its mixed yield — sheep, cattle, dairy products, and field crops — to that owned by the Springers. Another similarity is the African-American farm worker, shown plowing. The painting's idealized image of rural harmony, however, owes more to faith in republican agrarianism than to the artist's factual memory.

considerably to Elizabeth Springer's ordinary domestic tasks of food preparation and preservation. She would not have been able to do all that work without the help of the female slaves and perhaps several of her young female relatives as well. In addition to livestock, the Springers raised oats, hay, and Indian corn to feed the livestock, vegetables for the family, and wheat for family use and commercial sale. Probably some of the wheat was bought by Wilmington merchants for transshipment to Philadelphia and then Europe.

The Springers had family ties—parents, a brother, cousins—in the neighborhood. Both Elizabeth and Thomas were part of a community of farms involved in constant labor exchanges (for example, helping with construction, picking apples, threshing wheat, cutting firewood, and pruning trees) and an intricate system of barter. Neighbor women also assisted one another in childbirth. Thus the Springers, with the help of their African American slaves and perhaps some younger relatives as well, produced goods for their own use, for a community network that operated largely by barter, and for a larger, cash market.

The Springers' region of Delaware offers a dramatic example of the transition from community network to a larger commercial market. As early as the 1780s, the milling of flour, which had been a part-time activity for farmers along the Brandywine River near Wilmington, became a full-time commercial occupation. Millers began grinding wheat from as far away as New Jersey, Maryland, Virginia, and New York. By the 1790s, when demand from Europe increased, they were grinding 300,000 to 500,000 bushels of wheat a year. The press of this business prompted millers to begin refusing to grind local wheat and corn for nearby families, a sharp break with the neighborly custom of bartering. Brandywine farmers protested to the state legislature, which agreed to fine millers who did not set aside one day a week to grind local grain. Soon, however, the commercial market won. According to a French traveler late in the 1790s, milling families now believed that "their Mill is not employed for the public but solely for their own private service. It is called a flour manufactory."

The community network of barter and mutual obligation that still worked for the Springers just a few miles away had been replaced on the Brandywine by a new commercial system. In addition, some millowners, especially those who branched out into the shipping and selling of flour, became very rich. This too was something new.

The Traditional Labor System

As the example of the Springers shows, most work occurred in or near the home. One kind of traditional work was the domestic work of women and girls: spinning, weaving, and sewing clothes for every member of the family. Domestic work was a time-consuming, multistage activity that occupied women for much of the year. It could be broken down into tasks of varying difficulty: carding was easier than spinning, which in turn was easier than weaving. Mothers introduced their daughters to the easiest tasks at a young age, and taught them more difficult skills as they grew older. This informal family apprenticeship system was echoed outside the house in the barn and field tasks a young boy would learn from his father. In this way one generation passed along essential skills to the next generation.

On the rocky farms of New England, where cash was often short and a home-produced item was cheaper and easier to obtain than an item from Britain or even Boston, many farmers had another skill besides farming. Or entire families might develop skills such as shoemaking that they could practice over the long New England winters. Much of what was crafted was for local and immediate use, not for a distant or unknown market. Such circumstances bred ingenuity—a better way to do things—and flexibility. As Noah Webster remarked about New England farmers in 1785, "every man is in some measure an artist—he makes a variety of utensils, rough indeed, but such as will answer his purpose—he is a husbandman [farmer] in summer and mechanic in winter."

Two other characteristics of rural home production are notable, because they were soon to disappear. First, lack of cash was the common experience. A home-crafted item or a neighbor's service was usually paid for in foodstuffs, a piece of clothing, or another service. As a result, no item had a fixed price. Rather, goods and services originating in the home were all part of the complicated reciprocal arrangements among townspeople and rural folks in the local community who knew each other well. The second notable characteristic was the slow, unscheduled, task-oriented nature of the work. A job got done when it needed to get done, not on a fixed production schedule. This task orientation, which derived directly from farm work, was just as suitable for making shoes, for example, as for planting a field. A rural artisan worked when he had orders.

Urban Artisans and the Apprenticeship System

In urban areas, preindustrial production was in the hands of skilled craftsmen. Trades were perpetuated through a formal apprenticeship in which a boy went to work in the shop of a master. Over the years he would learn all aspects of the craft and gain increasing responsibility and status until the day he could strike out on his own. In other words, the family model of learning was made formal in the apprenticeship system. Frequently, the apprentice lived with the master craftsman and was treated more like a member of his family than like a servant. Often, master and apprentice were related. Benjamin Franklin, for example, was apprenticed (unhappily) to his older brother James.

Every small rural community had artisans such as blacksmiths and wheelrights who performed essential work such as shoeing horses and mending wagons for local farmers. Artist John Neagle's heroic (and remarkably clean) image of the blacksmith Pat Lyon presents him as the very model of honest industry.
(John Neagle. Pat Lyon at the Forge. 1826-27. Oil on canvas. 93 × 68 in. (236.1 × 172.6 cm). Herman and Zoe Oliver Sherman Fund, 1975. The Museum of Fine Arts, Boston.)

A young man became a skilled worker — an artisan — by becoming an apprentice at the age of twelve or fourteen. There were contracts to be signed between the master and the boy's father. Generally, they bound the apprentice to the master for a period of three to seven years. During that time, the master housed, fed, and clothed the boy while teaching him the trade. Sometimes the master also agreed to make sure the boy went to school. In return, the master had the full use of the boy's labor for no wages. At the end of the term, the boy, now in his late teens or early twenties, became a journeyman craftsman. As the name implies, he could travel anyplace he could find work in his trade. Journeymen worked for wages in the shop of a master craftsman until they had enough capital to set up shop for themselves. At that point they became master craftsmen and took on journeymen and apprentices of their own.

Americans had inherited this system from Europe, where traditions deriving from the orderly medieval guilds ensured that contracts and work standards were rigorously enforced. But as with so many other things inherited from abroad, the guild system was less orderly in the freer air of America. Mobility, the constant labor shortage, and democratic ideas of social equality prevented the apprenticeship system from being enforced as rigorously in America. Runaway apprentices were common, if the frequency of advertisements for runaways in colonial newspapers is any indication. Often the stated reason for running away was unfair treatment by the master. If an apprentice ran to another state or region, he might claim to be a journeyman or enter a new trade, and no one would be the wiser. In just such a fashion, sixteen-year-old Benjamin Franklin ran away from his overbearing brother in Boston and made a fresh start in Philadelphia.

Patriarchy in Family, Work, and Society

Commonly, an entire urban household was organized around a trade. For example, a printer and his family lived at the shop. Though the trade was the husband's, his wife was perfectly capable of carrying out some of the operations in his absence and supervising the work of children or apprentices. She would also be responsible for feeding and clothing apprentices who lived with the family. A blacksmith needed a separate shop, but he probably relied upon his children to fetch and carry and to help him with some of the operations. In a bakery, the husband might bake (which frequently meant getting up in the middle of the night) while the wife sold the goods.

These working families were organized along strictly patriarchal lines. The husband had the unquestioned authority to direct the work of the household — family members and apprentices — and to decide occupations for his sons and marriages for his daughters. His wife had her own responsibilities: feeding, clothing, child rearing, and all the other domestic affairs of the household. But important as those activities were, they too were subject to the direction of the husband. The father was head of the family as well as boss of the work. Because the husband was the person who had been trained in the trade, he was officially the craftsman. Although the entire family was engaged in the enterprise, family assistance was informal and unrecognized.

Urban artisans usually kept long hours: sunup to sundown was common. But the pace of work varied enormously with the time of year and the number of orders. And work was frequently interrupted by family activities and neighborliness. Most cities were densely settled, and one bumped into one's neighbors all the time.

Although women as well as men did task-oriented skilled work, the formal occupational system, as we have just seen, was exclusively for men. It was assumed that all women would marry; therefore, domestic skills were all that were necessary or appropriate for them. Single, widowed, or deserted women were expected to turn to family members for lodging and support. Of course there were nonetheless women who needed or wanted work, and they found a small niche in the occupational structure. In the early nineteenth century, all paid jobs for women involved household skills: domestic service, laundry work, or sewing for wealthy families; cooking in small restaurants or selling food on the streets; running boardinghouses. All were respectable female occupations. Prostitution was not respectable, but as every woman knew, it was also an occupation.

The patriarchal organization of the family was reflected in society as a whole. Legally, the man had all the power: neither women nor children had property or legal rights. For example, a married woman's property belonged to her husband, a woman could not testify on her own behalf in court, and in the rare cases of divorce the husband kept the children, for they were considered his property. Only men could vote, and usually only if they owned a certain amount of property. (This was soon to change: see Chapter 10.) When a man died, his son

The Russian artist Pavel Svinin observed a slice of Philadelphia nightlife in this painting of a woman, assisted by her African American helper, selling oysters to a trio of men enjoying a night on the town. Nighttime street selling was not a respectable female occupation.
(Pavel Petrovich Svinin. Night Life in Philadelphia — An Oyster Barrow in Front of the Chestnut Street Theater. *Watercolor on paper. 6-13/16 in. wide × 9-7/16 in. high. The Metropolitan Museum of Art. Rogers Fund, 1942.)*

inherited. It was customary to allow widows the use of one-third of the property, but unfilial sons could deprive their mothers of support if they chose. There were widows who successfully continued the family business, and single daughters with inheritances from rich fathers, but these were exceptions. The underlying principle, in both legal and voting rights, was that the man, as head of the household, represented the common interests of everyone for whom he was responsible.

The Social Order

On a grander scale, each household, from that of the smallest yeoman farmer to the largest urban merchant, had a fixed place in the social order. The social status of artisans was below that of wealthy merchants but decidedly above that of common laborers. Although men of all social ranks mingled in their daily work, they did not mingle as equals. Great importance was placed on rank and status, which were immediately visible in such things as dress and manner. Although by the 1790s many artisans who owned property were voters and vocal participants in politics, few directly challenged the traditional authority of the rich and powerful to run civic affairs.

Nevertheless, there were a few wealthy artisans in the seacoast cities who, somewhat like the Brandywine millers, were beginning to upset the social order. New York City offered a number of examples. Cabinetmaker Duncan Phyfe, who gave his name to a distinctive style of furniture, opened his first shop in 1792, soon after immigrating from Scotland. Phyfe struggled for several years, but then his furniture was discovered by New York's rich merchant class. By 1815 Phyfe had an elegant salesroom, three workshops employing up to 100 journeymen, and a fortune of $500,000, much of it from real estate investments. Another successful artisan, Stephen Allen, began as an apprentice sailmaker. He made his fortune when he arranged to bypass the traditional middlemen and buy his materials directly from wholesalers. His sailmaking operation made a profit of $100,000 between 1802 and 1825, and when he retired he was elected mayor of New York, customarily a position reserved for gentlemen.

The New York artisans, like the Brandywine millers, owed much of their success to the emerging Market Revolution. New and larger markets provided opportunities that had not existed before.

The Industrial Revolution

The technological innovations that transformed production from the home or farm to the factory, which began in Britain in the late eighteenth century, were to have a dramatic impact on America as well. But before factories were built, certain economic conditions had to exist.

The Accumulation of Capital

In the northern states, the business community (as we would call it today) was composed largely of merchants in the seaboard cities: Boston, Providence, New York, Philadelphia, and Baltimore. Many had made substantial profits in the international shipping boom of the period 1790–1807 (as discussed in Chapter 9). During those years, the pro-portion of American trade carried in American ships jumped from 59 percent to 92 percent, and earnings to American merchants rose from $5.9 million to $42.1 million.

Such extraordinary opportunities attracted enterprising people. Established merchants like New York's Robert Morris opened up markets such as the China trade, but there was room for newcomers as well. John Jacob Astor, who had arrived penniless from Germany in 1784, made his first fortune in the Pacific Northwest fur trade with China. Then, through his American Fur Company, he came to dominate the fur trade in the United States as well. He made his second fortune in New York real estate. When he retired in 1834 with $25 million, he was reputed to be the wealthiest man in America. Both Astor and less fabulous success stories (such as the Brandywine millers who branched out into shipping and selling) demonstrated that risk-takers might reap rich rewards in trade.

The years 1807–15 posed difficulties for international trade. As we saw in Chapter 9, the Napoleonic Wars involved the young United States in controversies over neutral rights, driving Presidents Jefferson and Madison to the disastrous Embargo Act of 1807 and to subsequent efforts to restrict trade. For some American merchants, these difficulties were financial opportunities. The most daring merchants risked blockades and embargoes to reap exceptional profits, but more cautious men turned their eyes toward home. What they saw was the traditional system of hand manufacturing we have just reviewed — localized, slow-paced, and family-centered. They also saw a growing American market deprived of cheap British goods because of the European wars. In short, they saw opportunity. Mobilizing the capital available within the business community, merchants began taking control of and transforming American manufacturing.

Some of the nation's wealthiest men turned to local investments. Philadelphia's Stephen Girard had made his fortune in shipowning and banking enterprises connected to the West Indies trade. Now he invested in the Lehigh Valley coalfields, and later in the canals and railroads that were to link them to factories such as the Baldwin Locomotive Works in Philadelphia. The Brown brothers of Providence, Rhode Island had developed a worldwide trade in iron, candles, rum, and slaves. In the 1780s, Moses Brown and his son-in-law William Almy invested some of the family profits in the new cotton textile trade. Cincinnati merchants banded together to finance the building of the first steamboats to operate on the Ohio River. Much smaller merchants and shopkeepers in rural towns invested in local crafts.

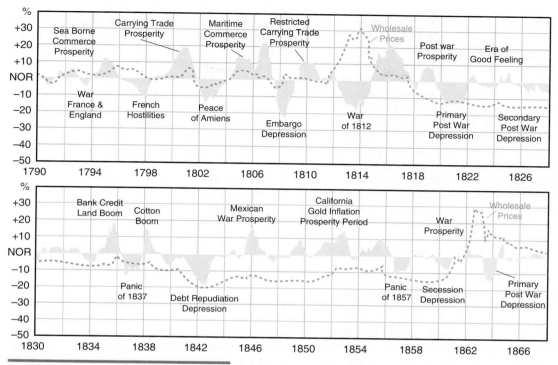

American Business Activity, 1790–1869

Until the 1820s, merchants dominated the national economy. Prosperity or depression was decided primarily by events in the European countries to whom merchants shipped raw materials. This chart, vividly shows how European peace or war affected merchants' profits. Merchants who did well in the prosperous years had capital to invest in domestic manufacturing when the international market was bad. After 1820, investment and speculation in factories, canals and railroads, western land, and cotton made the economy much more diverse and complicated than it had been earlier.

Source: Harold Faulkner, *American Economic History* (Sharon, CA: Quest Editions, 1924).

Much of the capital for the new investments came from banks (such as Stephen Girard's in Philadelphia) that had been established for international trade, and from local banks such as the Lynn Mechanics Bank, founded in 1814 by a group of Quaker merchants. Much of the money for transportation improvements came from the federal and state governments, and from foreign (especially British) investors (see Chapter 10). But an astonishing amount of capital was raised through family connections. Beginning in the late eighteenth century, the business communities in each of the seaboard cities consolidated their position by intermarriage. Marriage between cousins was one way to keep property within the family. In Boston, such a strong community developed that when Francis Cabot Lowell needed $300,000 in 1813 to build the world's first automated cotton mill in Waltham, he had only to turn to his family network to get it.

The Putting-Out System

Most of the merchants who invested in American industry in the early nineteenth century did so in the small putting-out system of home manufactures. The putting-out system marked a significant departure from preindustrial manufacture. The work was still done at home, but now the merchant, not the worker, provided the raw materials and sold the product. The worker only made the item — or part of it. A look at the shoe trade in Lynn, Massachusetts, shows how the change occurred.

Lynn had become one of the centers of the American shoe trade well before 1800. In that year, Lynn produced 400,000 pairs of shoes, enough for every fifth person in the country. Lynn boasted 200 master artisans in 1800, each with a number of journeymen and apprentices, organized in hundreds of small home workshops called *ten-footers* (from their size). The entire family worked on shoes. The artisan and journeymen cut the leather, wives and daughters did the binding of the upper parts of the shoe, the men stitched the shoe together, and children and apprentices helped out. The artisan might barter his shoes with a local shopkeeper, or sell them to larger retailers in Boston or Salem. In the early days, as we have seen, barter was commonplace. In 1773, a Lynn shopkeeper wrote to Nicholas Brown (Moses Brown's brother) offering to trade 100 pairs of shoes for 100 pounds of tea! Sometimes sea captains loaned artisans money for the raw materials, then sold the finished shoes at every port their ship visited. Although the production of shoes in Lynn increased yearly, the shoemaking trade was still organized along traditional apprentice–journeyman–master lines. All that had changed was the scale, not the method, of production.

The investment of merchant capital changed not only the amount of production but its organization. Shoemaking became rationalized, and this standardization directly affected both the work and the workers. In Lynn, a small group of Quaker shopkeepers and merchants, connected by family, religious, and business ties, took the lead in reorganizing the trade. As the demand for shoes grew, Lynn capitalists such as Micajah Pratt built large, two-story central workshops to replace the scattered ten-footers. Pratt employed skilled craftsmen to cut leather for shoes, but he put out the rest of the shoemaking to less skilled workers. The sewing of the uppers was done by farm women and children (no longer just the wives and daughters of artisans), who were paid on a piecework basis. The completed uppers were put out a second time to be soled, this time by rural men and boys (such as the farmers who made shoes in the winter). These workers were paid more than the women and children who did the sewing, but much less than a master craftsman or a journeyman. As a result of these changes, production increased enormously: the largest central shop in 1832 turned out ten times more shoes than the largest shopkeeper had sold in 1789. The new central workshops did not replace artisans' shops overnight, but gradually the economy of the new system won out.

From the point of view of the merchant capitalists, the putting-out system had great advantages. A heretofore individualistic trade was now standardized and controllable. This led not only to a predictable product but to standard wages for workers and lower prices for shoes. Furthermore, the putting-out system was highly flexible. There were no long training periods, because the work was broken into easy stages. Unsatisfactory workers could be easily replaced. Most important from the merchant's point of view was the ability to cut back or expand the labor force as economic conditions or competition warranted. The unaccustomed severity of economic slumps such as the panic of 1819 (see Chapter 9) made this flexibility especially desirable.

The putting-out system first became prevalent in New England around 1805, in the making of shoes. Soon thereafter it was applied to textiles: by 1810 there were an estimated 2,500 outwork weavers in New England. Other crafts that rapidly became organized on an outwork basis were flax and wool spinning, straw braiding, glove making, and stocking knitting.

At first, the response of ordinary New Englanders to the new system was positive, for increased production meant the need for more workers. Significantly, from the beginning most outwork was done by women, who combined it with their domestic work. Many New England farm households were drawn into the cash economy for the first time when the women and children began doing outwork. Wages for piecework replaced the barter system, and many families experienced a sudden new prosperity. Families found it more profitable for women to do outwork than to produce all of the family's food and clothing at home. They used their new wages to buy mass-produced goods — among them shoes, boots, hats, buttons, stockings, suspenders, horsewhips, machine-made textiles and men's work clothes — at the store. In this way, farm families moved away from self-sufficiency and into the market economy. The longer-term consequences of industrial capitalism — the destruction of the artisan tradition and the undermining of the patriarchal family — took some years to work out. For example, apprentices were still taken on in the Lynn shoemaking trade until 1840.

The putting-out system represented a great loss of independence to most artisans. Now the merchant — the owner of the capital — controlled production and the worker only saw part of the process. The merchant was also the employer, paying wages to artisans who had been accustomed to being their own bosses. Finally, the work was unreliable and the merchant could lay off workers or cut back on their work, and therefore their wages, at any time. The only thing the putting-out system shared with the master–apprentice system was that the work still occurred at home.

Household Manufacture of Woolen Cloths in New York State, 1820 and 1845

This map shows the effect of the market revolution on American families. The 1820 map shows the counties with the highest home production of textiles. The second map, in 1845, illustrates the effect of the Erie Canal (opened in 1825). Because they could now buy cheap manufactured textiles, New York women near to the canal no longer made fabric for their families. Many now earned cash as outworkers.

Source: Arthur Harrison Cole, *The American Wool Manufacture* (Cambridge: Harvard University Press, 1926), p. 280.

British Technology and American Industrialization

The Industrial Revolution began in Britain. Industrialization was the result of a series of small inventions in the textile trade — the flying shuttle in 1733, the spinning jenny in 1764, the water frame in 1769, the spinning mule in 1779 — that mechanized the spinning and weaving of cloth. These inventions, when coupled with capital, produced the revolutionary new factory system of manufacturing. Machines, not human hands, made the product. The first factories depended on water power; steam power came later.

Factories represented a sharp break with tradition, and many British people, especially the elite, looked at them with horror. In England, the first factory work force consisted of orphaned children, women, and poor Irish immigrants. These people flooded into ill-prepared rural factory towns. Horrified at the dirt and squalor of these towns, and by the relentless pace of power-driven machinery, British essayist Thomas Carlyle condemned the entire concept of industrialization, writing ominously of "dark, satanic mills." If this was progress, he wanted no part of it.

Predictably, attitudes in America (or at least in the North) were more favorable toward industrialization. America's revolutionary heritage inclined many to welcome change and new ideas, and "inventiveness" was common among New England farmers. As we have seen, the Embargo Act of 1807 encouraged merchant capitalists to redirect their investments from international to domestic commerce. Dramatic improvements in transportation accompanied American industrialization (see Chapter 10), encouraging manufacturers and merchant capitalists like those in Lynn to think in terms of large-scale production rather than small, local markets. New England also had swift rivers that could provide power for factory machinery. And of course the region was closer than Britain to the source of the raw material — southern cotton. In other words, the conditions existed for rapid industrialization.

Slater's Mill

The first and simplest way for America to industrialize was to copy the British. The British, well aware of the value of their machinery, were not eager to be imitated. To prevent copying, they enacted laws forbidding the export of textile machinery — and even skilled textile workers. But laws could be evaded, and over the years a number of British artisans, lured by American offers, emigrated in disguise to the United States.

One of the first and most important of these workers was young Samuel Slater, who had just finished an apprenticeship in the most up-to-date

Slater's Mill, the first cotton textile mill in the United States, depended on the water power of Pawtucket Falls for its energy. New England was rich in swiftly-flowing streams that could provide power to spinning machines and power looms.

cotton spinning factory in England. Disguising himself as a farm laborer, Slater slipped out of England without even telling his mother goodbye, and made his way to Providence. There he met the team of Moses Brown and William Almy, who had been trying without success to duplicate British industrial technology. They hired Slater to manage their cotton mill, where he promptly built copies of the latest British machinery, whose design he had carefully committed to memory before leaving England. The year was 1790, and Slater's Mill, as it was commonly known, was the most advanced cotton mill in America. Slater, a skilled mechanic, later made improvements on the British machines. Nevertheless, it is accurate to say that the beginnings of industrial technology in America date from his successful example of industrial espionage.

For his work force, Slater followed the British example and hired young children (ages seven to twelve) and women, who could be paid much less than skilled male workers. The yarn spun at Slater's Mill, much more than could be produced by home spinning, was then put out to local home weavers, who turned it into cloth on handlooms. Home weaving flourished, for it represented a new opportunity for families to make money at a task with which they were already familiar. Home production of textiles had always been a large part of women's work. Almost every home had a spinning wheel, and girls were expected to learn to card and spin wool, cotton, and flax. Handlooms were less common, for

they were large and cumbersome, but most adult women knew how to weave. In 1790, home weavers had no way of knowing that their profitable occupation would soon be challenged by power looms in factories.

Soon many other merchants and mechanics had followed Slater's lead, and the rivers of New England were dotted with mills wherever water power could be tapped. American factories were sheltered from British competition from 1807 to 1815, but when the War of 1812 ended, the British cut prices ruthlessly to drive the newcomers out of business. It was no wonder that New England manufacturers clamored for a national tariff that would protect their young industry. Congress passed the first tariff (20 percent) against British cotton manufactures in 1816, in spite of protests from many New England merchants in the seaport cities, who were firm believers in international free trade (from which they had profited so richly).

The Lowell Mills

Another tactic for meeting British competition was to beat the British at their own game, by designing better machinery. This was the approach embodied in the most famous example of early American industrialization, the Lowell mills. The story began with another episode of industrial espionage. In this case the spy was not a British apprentice but a proper young Bostonian, Francis Cabot Lowell, who made an apparently casual tour of British textile mills in 1811. His hosts were pleased by his interest and by his intelligent questions. They didn't know that each night, in his hotel room, Lowell made sketches from memory of the machines he had inspected during the day.

Francis C. Lowell was more than a spy, however. When he returned to the United States, he worked closely with a Boston mechanic, Paul Moody, to improve upon the British models. They not only improved the machinery for spinning cotton, but they also invented a power loom. This was a great advance, for it allowed all aspects of textile manufacture (carding, spinning, weaving, and dressing) to be gathered together in the same factory. But it also represented a much larger capital investment than that required by a small spinning mill such as Slater's. Lowell, as we have seen, turned to his family network for the money he needed. The world's first integrated cotton mill began operation in Waltham, near Boston, in 1814. It was a great success: in 1815, the Boston Associates (Lowell's family partners) made profits of 25 percent, and their efficiency allowed them to survive the intense British competition. Many smaller New England mills did not survive, even with the tariff protection voted in 1816. The lesson was clear: size mattered.

The Boston Associates took the lesson to heart, and when they moved their enterprise to a new location in 1823, they thought big. They built an entire town at the junction of the Concord and Merrimack rivers, and named it Lowell (in memory of Francis, who had died, still a young man, in 1817). As described earlier, the new industrial community boasted six mills and company housing for all the workers. In 1826 the town had 2,500 inhabitants; ten years later the population was 17,000.

The Family System

Lowell was unique: no other textile mill was ever such a showplace, relied so completely on the labor of young farm women, or was such a fully integrated operation. Much more common in the early days of industrialization were small rural spinning mills, on the model of Slater's first mill, that put out the yarn they spun to local, home-based weavers. The owners of these mills were much less concerned than the Lowell Associates about whom they recruited as workers. Frequently they hired entire families (hence the name *family mills*). The customary job for children (ages eight to twelve) was doffing (chang-

ing) spindles on the spinning machines. Children made up an estimated 50 percent of the work force, women about 25 percent, and men (who usually had more skilled jobs and were paid more) the rest. This was the pattern Slater had established at his first mill in 1790, and that he and his many imitators followed in subsequent years.

There was nothing unusual in the employment of entire families. After all, both farm and artisanal families were accustomed to working at the family enterprise. And unless a family member was very highly skilled, more than one worker per family was a necessity. To take one example, in the Rockdale mills, located on Chester Creek in Delaware (not far from where the Springers had farmed), wages in the 1840s ranged from $1 a week for unskilled children to $12 a week for skilled spinners. Unskilled adult laborers earned between $2.50 and $3.50 per week, or between $110 and $150 a year, allowing for sickness and temporary layoffs. Wages of $300 a year were necessary to keep a family safely above the poverty line. Single workers, who had to pay $70 to $100 a year for board and room, were at a disadvantage compared with a family, who could rent a house for $25 a year and survive on an estimated $200 a year for food.

Relations between these small rural mill communities and the surrounding farming communities were often difficult, as the history of the towns of Dudley and Oxford, Massachusetts, shows. In the early years of the century, fifteen cotton and woolen factories were founded in the area, three of them by Slater (now a millionaire). Near the two towns (but not in them) Slater built three small mill communities, each consisting of a small factory, a store, and cottages and a boardinghouse for workers. Slater or one of his sons ran the mills personally; they were not absentee owners. Most of Slater's workers came from outside the Dudley-Oxford area. They were a mixed group: single young farm women and men of the kind Lowell attracted, the poor and destitute, and workers from other textile factories looking for better conditions. They rarely stayed long: almost 50 percent of the work force left every year.

Initially, Slater's mills put out work such as cleaning the raw cotton and weaving to local people. But in spite of this economic link, relations between Slater and his workers on one side and the farmers and shopkeepers of the Dudley and Oxford communities on the other were stormy. They disagreed over mill dams (which sometimes flooded local fields), taxes, schools (Slater, hoping to save money and exercise more control, wanted to set up his own school for factory children), and the upkeep of local roads. The debates were so constant, and so heated, that in 1831 Slater petitioned the Massachusetts General Court to create a separate town, Webster, that would encompass his three mill communities. For their part, the residents of Dudley and Oxford became increasingly hostile to Slater, believing he exercised excessive control over his workers. Their dislike carried over to the workers as well. Disdaining them for their poverty and transiency, people in the rural communities began referring to the millworker as an *operatives,* a sort of worker different from themselves. Industrial work thus led to new social distinctions. Even though the people of Dudley and Oxford benefited from the mills, they did not fully accept the social organization on which their new prosperity rested, nor did they feel a sense of community with workers who did.

The American System of Manufacturers

Not all industrialization occurred as a result of copying British inventions. There were many home-grown inventors. Indeed, as one Frenchman observed after seeing the number of New England inventions, Americans were "mechanic[s] by nature." "In Massachusetts and Connecticut," he claimed, "there is not a labourer who had not invented a machine or tool." The Market Revolution gave inventor-manufacturers the opportunity they needed. By the 1840s, for example, the areas around Windsor and St. Johnsbury, Vermont, boasted small local industries based on the inventions of Erastus Fairbanks in scales and plows, Lemuel Hubbard in pumps, and Nicanor Kendall in guns. Still another New Englander, Eli Whitney of cotton gin fame, was among the pioneers of interchangeable parts.

In 1798 Whitney contracted with the government to make 10,000 rifles in twenty-eight months, an incredibly short period had Whitney been planning to produce each rifle in the traditional way, individually and by hand. Instead, Whitney broke down the rifle into standard components and made an exact mold for each. All pieces from the same mold (after being hand-filed by inexpensive unskilled laborers) matched a uniform standard and thus were interchangeable. The concept of interchangeability not only hastened production but also meant that a broken part could be easily replaced by a new one, rather than laboriously handcrafted.

Whitney's ideas far outran his performance. It took him ten years, rather than twenty-eight

months, to fulfill his contract, and even then he had not managed to perfect the production of all the rifle parts. This second crucial step, the invention of milling machines that would grind each part to exact specifications, was achieved not by Whitney but by another New Englander, Simeon North, in 1816. A third New Englander, John Hall, brought the idea to fruition in 1824. Subsidized by the government to make rifles for the national armory at Harpers Ferry, Virginia, Hall wrote triumphantly to the secretary of war, "I have succeeded in an object which has hitherto baffled . . . all the endeavors of those who have heretofore attempted it *—I have succeeded in*

The Growth of Cotton Textile Manufacturing, 1810–1839

Although cotton textile manufacturing spread to other parts of the country after 1810, New England never lost its early lead. By 1839, the extent of industrialization in New England far outstripped that of other regions. Although much of New England was still rural, more and more residents were drawn into the market economy. Nationally, the proportion of wage laborers rose from 12 percent in 1800 to 20 percent in 1860. The majority of them were New England who had made the transition from artisan to worker.

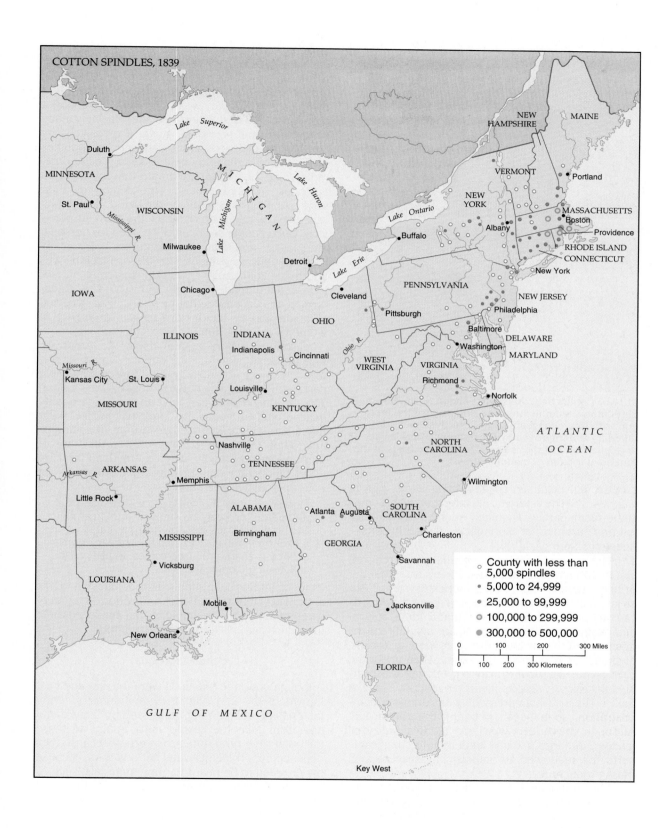

COTTON SPINDLES, 1839

MINNESOTA

Duluth

St. Paul

Lake Superior

WISCONSIN

Milwaukee

MICHIGAN

Lake Michigan

Lake Huron

Detroit

Lake Erie

Lake Ontario

Buffalo

Albany

NEW
HAMPSHIRE

VERMONT

Portland

MAINE

MASSACHUSETTS
Boston
Providence
RHODE ISLAND
CONNECTICUT

NEW YORK

New York

IOWA

Chicago

ILLINOIS

INDIANA

Indianapolis

OHIO

Cleveland

Pittsburgh

Cincinnati

Ohio R.

PENNSYLVANIA

NEW JERSEY

Philadelphia

Baltimore

Washington

DELAWARE

MARYLAND

Missouri R.

Kansas City   St. Louis

MISSOURI

Louisville

KENTUCKY

WEST
VIRGINIA

VIRGINIA

Richmond

Norfolk

ATLANTIC

OCEAN

Arkansas R.

ARKANSAS

Little Rock

Nashville

TENNESSEE

Memphis

NORTH
CAROLINA

Wilmington

ALABAMA

Birmingham

Atlanta Augusta

SOUTH
CAROLINA

Charleston

MISSISSIPPI

Vicksburg

GEORGIA

Savannah

LOUISIANA

Mobile

Jacksonville

New Orleans

○ County with less than
5,000 spindles

• 5,000 to 24,999

● 25,000 to 99,999

○ 100,000 to 299,999

● 300,000 to 500,000

0   100   200   300 Miles

0   100   200   300 Kilometers

FLORIDA

GULF OF MEXICO

Key West

In 1816 Connecticut gunsmith Simeon North did what Eli Whitney had only hoped to do: produce the first gun with interchangeable parts. North's inventions, taken up and improved by the national armories at Springfield and Harper's Ferry, formed the basis of the American system of manufactures.

establishing methods of fabricating arms exactly alike. . . ." The system of interchangeable machine-made parts was quickly adopted by the other national armory, at Springfield, Massachusetts — hence the Springfield rifle.

The concept of interchangeable parts, realized first in gun manufacturing, was so unusual that the British soon dubbed it "the American system." But as late as 1854, British skepticism about the American achievement led to a demand for a special demonstration at the Springfield armory. Rifles manufactured in the previous ten years were disassembled and the parts placed in boxes. Then under the eyes of the skeptical British, a workman reassembled the rifles by selecting parts at random from the boxes. The British, impressed by this dramatic demonstration, soon began imitating the Americans! Although the British were the world's industrial leaders, America's early lead in interchangeable parts foreshadowed its subsequent successes in mass production.

The American system quickly spread throughout American industries, revolutionizing the production of items as varied as steam engines and nails. By 1810 a machine had been developed that could produce 100 nails a minute, cutting the cost of nail-making by two-thirds. Cyrus McCormick's reaper, so ungainly that observers compared it to a monster grasshopper, was built with interchangeable parts. Standardization also affected finely made consumer items previously made (expensively) by hand. Mass-produced clocks and pocket watches now allowed ordinary people to keep precise time, rather than keeping approximate time by the sun. Factories required precise timekeeping of their workers. Railroads, which ran on "clockwork" schedules, would soon reinforce the need for precision. Once people discovered the need for personal timepieces, American manufacturers were ready with inexpensive versions. The sewing machine was another revolutionary invention, fostering an immense ready-made clothing industry. This transformed an occupation that previously had occurred at home and by hand, occupying a large part of women's domestic time.

Like the factory system itself, the American system spread slowly. For example, Singer sewing machines were not made with fully interchangeable parts until 1873, when the company was selling 230,000 machines a year. Nevertheless, high-quality mass-produced goods for ordinary people were manufactured earlier in America than in Britain or any other European country. The availability of these goods profoundly affected American thinking about democracy and equality. As historian David Potter perceptively remarked:

> European radical thought is prone to demand that the man of property be stripped of his carriage and his fine clothes. But American radical thought is likely to insist, instead, that the ordinary man is entitled to mass-produced copies, indistinguishable from the originals.

Other historians have supplied the conclusion to this argument — that the American devotion to equality owes much to the technology that made possible inexpensive goods for mass consumption.

Other Factories

Although cotton textile mills were the first and best known of the early factories, a number of early factories produced other items, among them metal and iron. Like the textile mills, many of these factories were rural rather than urban because they depended upon falling water for power or because they needed to be near their raw materials, such as iron ore. Iron making and forging were dirty and noisy activities that visibly and audibly disrupted the rural landscape. Yet like the early textile mills, these

This panorama of the Cincinnati waterfront in 1848 shows the "Queen City" at the height of its importance as a center of steamboat manufacture and riverborne agricultural trade. Soon railroads surpassed steamboats, and Cincinnati's supremacy dwindled.

first heavy industries initially coexisted with the traditional artisanal system

The rapid development of the steamship industry in Cincinnati illustrates both the role of merchant capital and the coexistence of old and new production methods. The first steamboat appeared on the Ohio River in 1811, and Cincinnati's merchants, who heretofore had invested their profits in land and in real estate speculation, were quick to see its advantages. Cincinnati's first steamboat, financed by local merchant capital, was commissioned in 1816. It proved so successful that by 1819 one-quarter of all western steamboats were being built in Cincinnati. By 1826, Cincinnati's steamship industry had grown to include four iron foundries employing 54 men, five steam engine and finishing factories employing 126 people, and three boatyards with 200 workers. At the same time, much of the detail work on the steamboat was performed by traditional artisans such as cabinetmakers, upholsterers, tinsmiths, and blacksmiths, who did record-breaking amounts of work in their small, independent shops. In this way, new factory methods and industrial techniques were often coupled with old craft techniques.

These techniques of specialization and speedup of work were basic to the system of industrial capitalism. They led to vast increases in wealth and in living standards for many — eventually most — of the inhabitants of industrial nations. But for many workers in early-nineteenth-century America, the transition from the old method of production to the new one did not come without a price.

FROM ARTISAN TO WORKER

The changes in methods of production caused by industrialization had permanent effects on ordinary Americans. But like most historical changes, the transition happened so slowly that most people were unaware of how fundamentally their lives had been changed. The young farm woman who worked at Lowell for a year or two, then returned home; the master craftsman in Lynn who expanded his shop with the aid of merchant capital; the home weaver who prospered on outwork from Slater's Mill — all of these probably regarded the changes in their lives as temporary. As late as 1831, only 67,000 people were employed in New England cotton textile factories, by far the most common new industry. But in fact an irreversible change was under way. As artisans became workers, their lives were completely transformed.

Personal Relationships

The apprenticeship system, as we have seen, was based on a family model of learning: apprentices learned the craft from the master in the same way children learned skills from their parents. Like the family, the hierarchical craft structure ensured that the apprentice would experience a process of maturation (as a journeyman) before becoming a master craftsman. The patriarchal pattern of the apprenticeship system was reflected in the larger society. Men of wealth and learning simply assumed political control as a responsibility that accompanied their status, and regarded the "lesser orders" as they would children or servants.

The putting-out system, with its division of each craft into separate tasks, effectively destroyed the apprenticeship system. For example, in New York by the mid-1820s, although apprenticeship was still the rule, the reality had changed. Tailors and shoemakers taught apprentices only a few simple operations, in effect using them as helpers. Printers undercut the system by hiring partly trained apprentices as journeymen. In almost every trade, apprentices no longer lived in the master's household. Instead, artisans paid a cash amount to the boy's parents, effectively creating a child labor system in place of the older pattern. These artisans who helped to destroy the older system did so because they faced harsh new competition. For example, in the 1850s Philadelphia's 7,000 shoemakers, shut out of the cheap shoe market by the industrialized shoe manufacturers of Lynn, turned to the specialty markets of ladies' shoes and expensive men's shoes and boots. But even in this luxury market, the pressure of cheaper competition forced these artisans to accept the central shop and the putting-out system.

The breakdown of the personal relationship between the master and his workers soon became an issue in the growing political battle between the North and the South over slavery. As we have seen, southern defenders of slavery were fond of comparing their cradle-to-grave responsibility to slaves with northern employers' "heartless" treatment of their "wage slaves." In comparison with traditional ways, the northern employer *did* show less responsibility to individual workers in the new industrial system. Although the earliest textile manufacturers provided housing for their workers, the custom soon ceased, and workers became responsible for their own food and housing. Impersonal wage packets replaced personal contact between employer and wage earner, and employers felt no obligation to old or disabled workers. Southerners were right: this *was* a heartless system. But northerners were also right: industrialization was certainly freer than the slave system, freer even than the hierarchical craft system, though it sometimes really offered only the freedom to starve.

Mechanization and Women's Work

In trade after trade, the subdivision of labor meant that most tasks could be performed by unskilled labor. For example, the textile mills at Lowell and elsewhere hired a mere handful of skilled mechanics; the rest of the workers were unskilled and lower-paid. In fact, the work in the textile mills was so simple that children came to form a large part of the work force. The shoe industry at Lynn, which relied on the putting-out system rather than factory work, used women and children to do the shoe binding; men drew higher wages for the more complex operations. By 1850, a number of skilled trades had been transformed, among them shoemaking, weaving, silversmithing, pottery making, and cabinetmaking. The work was now performed by machines tended by unskilled, low-paid workers. This change had serious effects on the male occupational structure, robbing many men of artisan status and pay and reducing them to laborers.

Mechanization adversely affected women's work as well. The industrialization of textiles—first in spinning, then in weaving—robbed women of their most reliable home occupation. Women now had the choice of following textile work into the factory for low pay or finding other kinds of home work. The palm-leaf hat industry, for example, relied completely on women (and their children), who braided the straw for the hats at home part-time. The inexpensive hats were eventually sold to farm laborers and slaves in the South and the West. In Massachusetts in 1837, 33,000 women were employed in the palm-leaf hat industry (in comparison with only 20,000 cotton textile workers in the state).

In New York in the 1820s, a new work possibility for women was ready-made clothing (at first rough, unfitted clothing for sailors and southern slaves, later overalls and shirts for westerners and finer items such as men's shirts). This booming trade depended on sewing that women did at home. In 1860, Brooks Brothers had 70 "inside" workers in a central workshop, but put out work to 3,000 "outside" workers, all women.

Soon the problems of the garment trade became notorious: seasonal work, deferred wages, wage cutting, and more. These were due in part to ruthless competition, but there were wider causes as well. Women were barred from most occupations, and the funneling of women into the few trades that were considered appropriate for them inevitably led to wage cutting. The prejudice against "respectable" women doing factory work (except for Lowell in its "model" years) condemned women to poorly paid outwork in miserable conditions.

The division of labor, the basic principle of factory work, disadvantaged women outworkers. Manufacturers in the garment trade made their profits not from efficient production, but by obtaining intensive labor for very low wages. The lower the piece rate, the more each woman, sewing at home, had to produce to earn enough to live. Ironically, the invention of the sewing machine, which immensely speeded up work formerly done by hand, only made matters worse. Manufacturers dropped their piecework rates still lower, so that women's output, now aided by sewing machines, would remain as high as or higher than before. Some women found themselves working fifteen to eighteen hours a day.

Work and Leisure

As we have seen, preindustrial work had a flexibility that factory work did not, and it took factory workers a while to get accustomed to the new demands. The hardest thing to get used to was not the task itself but the constant pace. Twelve-hour days and six-day work weeks were not unusual, but the expectation of constant attendance was. In the early days of Samuel Slater's mill in Rhode Island, workers sometimes took a few hours off to go berry picking or to attend to other business. And when Slater first insisted on the twelve-hour day, which required candles for night work, one upset father demanded that his children be sent home at sunset, the traditional end of the workday.

Gradually factory workers adjusted to having their lives regulated by the sound of the factory bell, but not necessarily by becoming the docile "hands" the owners might desire. Absenteeism was common, accounting for about 15 percent of working hours, and there was much pilfering. Workers were beginning to think of themselves as a separate community whose interests differed from those of owners. The tyranny of time over their work was certainly one reason for this. As we shall see in Chapter 13, the length and pace of the working day drew some of the first labor protests.

Time was now divided into two separate activities: work and leisure. No such division existed in the preindustrial lives of farmers and artisans. The place of their work — often their home — and the pace allowed for a blend of work and relaxation: time to stop and have a chat or a friendly drink with a visitor. Now, however, the separation of home and workplace and the pace of industrial work squeezed the leisure out of the workday and into a separate category.

For many workingmen, the favored spot for after-hours and Sunday leisure became the local tavern rather than the workplace. Community-wide celebrations and casual sociability, still common in rural areas, began to be replaced in cities by spec-tator sports — horse racing, boxing, and (beginning in the 1850s) baseball — and by popular entertainments such as plays, operas, minstrel shows, concerts, and circuses. Some of these diversions, such as plays and horse racing, appealed to all social classes. But the working class had its own forms of amusement, from parades to rowdy dance halls to tavern games like quoits and ninepins. Increasingly, the upper classes disapproved of lower-class leisure pursuits, especially Sunday drinking, and tried to regulate or abolish them (see the discussion of the temperance movement in Chapter 13).

The Cash Economy

Another effect of the Market Revolution was the spread of the cash economy. In preindustrial days, as we have seen, much work was bartered in the community. For example, if a farm woman ordered a pair of shoes from the local shoemaker, she might pay him over several months in butter and eggs, not in cash. A few years later, that same woman might be part of the vast New England outwork industry, braiding straw for hats, making gloves, or sewing shirts at home. Now when she needed new footwear, she would pay cash for shoes that were commercially manufactured, perhaps in Lynn. In this way, in hundreds of thousands of small transactions, community economic ties were replaced by distant and national ones. This fundamental economic change affected basic patterns of community interchange throughout the country.

In contrast with the daily contact of the artisanal workshop, the connection between factory worker and (often distant) owner became the pay envelope. For workers, this change was both unsettling and liberating. On the minus side, they were no longer part of a settled, orderly, and familiar community. On the other hand, they were now free to labor wherever they could, at whatever wages their skills or their bargaining power could command. That workers took their freedom seriously is evidenced by the very high turnover in the New England textile mills.

In some family mills, such as Slater's near Dudley and Oxford, Massachusetts, almost half the work force left every year. At Lowell in 1836, half of the work force had been there less than a year. The greatest effect of the cash economy, however, was to make workers totally dependent on wages for their livelihood for the first time. Historians have estimated that the proportion of wage laborers in the nation's labor force rose from 12 percent in 1800 to 40 percent in 1860. Most of these workers were employed in the North. Almost half of all manufacturing workers were women, performing outwork in their homes.

Free Labor

At the heart of the industrializing economy was the notion of free labor. Originally, *free* referred to individual economic choice — that is, to the right of workers to move to another job rather than be held to a position by customary obligation or the formal contract of apprenticeship or journeyman labor. But *free labor* soon came to encompass as well the range of attitudes — hard work, self-discipline, and a striving for economic independence — that were necessary for success in a competitive, industrializing economy. These were profoundly individualistic attitudes, and owners cited them in opposing labor unions and the use of strikes to achieve wage goals. As the Cincinnati *Gazette* put it in 1857: "We are not speaking of *leaving* work — that all men have the right to do; but of combining to interrupt and arrest the machinery. The first is a plain, individual right. The last is a conspiracy against the interest, and even the safety of the public." Owners opposed government action, such as legislation mandating a ten-hour day, on the same grounds: it limited worker freedom.

For their part, many workers were inclined to define freedom more collectively, arguing that their just grievances as free American citizens were not being heard. As a group of New Hampshire female workers rhetorically asked, "Why [is] there . . . so much want, dependence and misery among us, if forsooth, we are *freemen* and *freewomen*?" Or, as the Lowell strikers of 1836 sang as they paraded through the streets:

Oh! Isn't it a pity, such a pretty girl as I,
Should be sent to the factory to pine away and die?
Oh! I cannot be a slave,
I will not be a slave,
For I'm so fond of liberty
That I cannot be a slave.

Early Strikes

Rural women workers led some of the first strikes in American labor history. In that young women formed the majority of the work force in the early textile mills, their participation in spontaneous protests is not surprising. What was surprising, in view of the limited public role of women, was their leadership of these protests. One of the first actions occurred at a Pawtucket, Rhode Island, textile mill in 1824. Women protesting wage cuts and longer hours led their co-workers, female and male, out on strike. They had the support of many townspeople as well.

More famous women-led strikes occurred at Lowell, the model mill. The first serious trouble at Lowell came in 1834, when 800 women participated in a spontaneous "turnout" to protest a wage cut of 25 percent. The owners were shocked and outraged by the strike, considering it both unfeminine and ungrateful. For their part, the workers, bound together by a sense of sisterhood, were protesting not just the attack on their economic independence but also the blow to their position as "daughters of freemen still." Nevertheless the wage cuts were enforced, as were more cuts in 1836, again in the face of a turnout. Many women simply packed their clothes in disgust and returned home to the family farm.

Like the Lowell strikes, most turnouts by factory workers in the 1830s — male or female — were unsuccessful. Owners, claiming that increasing competition made wage cuts inevitable, were always able to find new workers who would work at lower wages. Many discouraged workers moved on to another mill or, like the Lowell women, returned to the farm. The workers who remained found it impossible to form permanent organizations to resist wage cuts. Significantly, female workers received scant help from male unionists, who feared that women's participation in the work force would lower their own wages. Thus, in spite of women's pioneering role in factory protests, there began the myth that it was impossible to organize women into unions.

The Patch Family

The history of an obscure New England family illustrates many of the changes in personal lives that the Market Revolution made possible. Mayo Greenleaf Patch, a newcomer to town, married Abigail McIntire of Reading, Massachusetts, in 1788. Her well-to-do father probably objected to her marriage with an outsider, but Abigail was pregnant, so he had little choice. Abigail's situation was not uncommon: fully a third of the women of her generation were pregnant on their wedding day. Pregnancy was a reason for marriage, not the other way around.

McIntire set up his daughter and her new husband on a portion of his land in Reading, building a small house and a shoemaker's shop for them.

Eight hundred women "operatives," followed by four thousand workmen, participate in a strike for higher wages in Lynn in 1860. The women's banner expresses a demand for rights that was a recurrent theme of women's strikes: "American Ladies Will Not Be Slaves."

Farming was the Patch family's major occupation. Shoemaking was a winter occupation at which the entire family worked (without any formal apprenticeship) to earn a little extra money. Patch sold the completed shoes to merchants in Boston, who also supplied him with leather for new ones. Here was an example of the beginnings of the putting-out system.

Greenleaf and Abigail Patch were recognized as responsible members of their community. In 1793 the town built a schoolhouse near their home, and for the next two years the Patches boarded the schoolteacher, who had several young Patches as students. But in 1799 the Patch family left Reading in disgrace. When Abigail's father died in 1791, Patch became the legal guardian for the inheriting son, Archelaus McIntire, Jr., who was still a minor. Patch, it will be remembered, did not own the land he farmed; it had belonged to his father-in-law, and was now passed on to the son. Apparently, Patch made improper use of the property, and in 1798 the local courts stripped him of his guardianship. Since 1795, Patch had been embroiled in almost constant legal battles with his neighbors as well. His dishonorable behavior finally forced the family to leave town. Abigail Patch, who had no legal rights of her own, was helpless to stop her husband's arguments with her own family.

Seeking other economic opportunities, the Patch family went first to Danvers, a shoemaking community where Abigail had relatives, and then to Marblehead, where Patch had inherited a small legacy. But they were unable to succeed in either place. In 1807 they moved to Pawtucket, Rhode Island, a textile community, where the children went to work in the mills and Abigail did outwork, probably as a weaver. Greenleaf Patch did not work. He drank, abused his family, and finally, in 1812, ran away. Abigail divorced him in 1818. She and the children continued to live in Pawtucket, earning a living by working in the textile mills. Employment in the textile mills thus provided Abigail with the opportunity to support her children without having to depend on her irresponsible and abusive husband.

This family story illustrates only one of the many ways in which artisans became workers. Other families and individuals sought work in thriving cities like Boston, or they moved west. In making this transition, they lost the security of traditional methods of work and community life but gained freedom of movement and the opportunity to realize their aspirations.

A NEW SOCIAL ORDER

The Market Revolution reached into every aspect of life, from the social structure to the most personal family decisions. It also fundamentally changed the social order.

Wealth and Class

There had always been social classes in America. A wealthy elite had existed since the early colonial

This painting by Henry Sargent depicts an elegant gathering of the small and wealthy Boston elite, known as the Brahmins. Intermarriage tended to concentrate wealth in this group and to separate them from the "middling sort."
(Henry Sargent. The Tea Party. Oil on canvas. 64-1/4 × 52-1/4 in. (163.8 × 132.7 cm.) Gift of Mrs. Horatio A. Lamb, in memory of Mr. and Mrs. Winthrop Sargent. Courtesy of The Museum of Fine Arts, Boston.)

period: planters in the South and merchants in the North. So had "mechanics and farmers" — skilled artisans and independent farmers — and the laboring poor, consisting of ordinary laborers and servants and marginal farmers. At the very bottom were the paupers — those dependent on public charity — and the enslaved. Somewhere below the elite but above the mass of people were the "middling sort": a small professional class (lawyers, ministers, schoolteachers, and doctors), public officials, some prosperous farmers, prosperous urban shopkeepers and innkeepers, and a few highly skilled artisans such as the Boston silversmith Paul Revere. American society in the early 1800s was not a democratic system, although it certainly offered more opportunity than European societies dominated by a hereditary aristocracy. The political and social dominance of the small, wealthy elite was largely unquestioned, as was the "natural" social order that fixed most people in the social rank to which they were born. Although many a servant in early America aspired to

become a small farmer or artisan, he did not usually aspire to become a member of the wealthy elite, nor did serving maids often marry rich men.

The Market Revolution ended the old social order, creating the dynamic and unstable one we recognize today: upper, middle, and working classes, whose members all share the hope of climbing as far up the social ladder as they can. This social mobility was new, and it fascinated French observer Alexis de Tocqueville: "The first thing that strikes one in the United States is the innumerable crowd of those striving to escape from their original social condition." In the early nineteenth century the upper class remained about the same in size and composition, for the people who benefited most from industrialization were already rich. In the seacoast cities, as we have seen, the elite was a small, intermarried group, so distinctive in its superior cultural style that in Boston its members were nicknamed Brahmins (a reference to the exclusive caste in the British colony of India).

The major change came in the lives of the "middling sort." Just as the Market Revolution downgraded many independent artisans to the role of worker, others, such as Duncan Phyfe and Stephen Allen of New York, became wealthy businessmen and manufacturers. Others joined the rapidly growing ranks of managers and white-collar workers such as accountants, bank tellers, clerks, bookkeepers, and insurance agents. Occupational opportunities shifted dramatically in just one generation. In Utica, New York, for example, 16 percent of the city's young men held white-collar jobs in 1855, compared with only 6 percent of their fathers. At the same time, the proportion of younger men in artisanal occupations was 15 percent less than that of the older generation.

The new white-collar workers owed not only their jobs but their attitudes to the new economic order, as historical studies of the emerging middle class in Rochester and Utica, New York, have shown. Both cities owed their prosperity to the Erie Canal, which opened in 1825, connecting the agricultural heartland to the bustling international port of New York City (see Chapter 10). Utica's population tripled between 1820 and 1830, then grew by another 50 percent in the following decade. Rochester, which had a population of 300 in 1815, had grown to 10,000 by 1830, making it the fastest-growing city in America. In this pressure-cooker environment, a new middle class with distinctively new attitudes was formed.

The new structure and organization of industry demanded certain habits and attitudes in middle-class individuals: sobriety, responsibility, steadiness, and hard work, coupled with a dislike (amounting almost to fear) of the spontaneity and boisterous sociability of many members of the working class. The change in attitudes could be remarkable. Historian Paul Johnson has sketched this change in lifestyle in his study of Rochester:

> In 1825 a northern businessman dominated his wife and children, worked irregular hours, consumed enormous amounts of alcohol, and seldom voted or went to church. Ten years later the same man went to church twice a week, treated his family with gentleness and love, drank nothing but water, worked steady hours and forced his employees to do the same. . . .

Religion and Personal Life

Religion played a key role in the new attitudes. Dramatic changes had occurred in religion since the 1790s. The Second Great Awakening (see Chapter 9) had supplanted the orderly and intellectual Puritan religion of early New England. The new religious spirit known as *evangelism*, which stressed the achievement of salvation through personal faith, was more democratic and more enthusiastic than before. The old concern with individual sin survived in spellbinding sermons that vividly portrayed hell-fire and damnation. But the way to salvation was much wider than in colonial times. Original sin, the cornerstone of Puritan belief, was replaced by the optimistic belief that a willingness to be saved was enough for salvation. Conversion and repentance were now community experiences, often taking place in huge revival meetings where the eyes and emotions of the entire congregation were focused on the sinners about to be saved. But although continued support from the religious community was important, the converted bore a heavy personal responsibility to demonstrate their faith in their own daily lives through morally respectable behavior. In this way the new religious feeling fostered individualism and self-discipline.

The Second Great Awakening had its greatest initial success on the southern frontier. But by the 1820s evangelical religion was reaching a new audience: the people whose lives had been changed by the Market Revolution and who needed guidance in adapting to the new economic conditions.

Finney and Urban Revivals

Beginning in 1825, Charles G. Finney held a series of dramatic revival meetings in the towns along the Erie Canal. The canal had recently opened, and these towns were experiencing the first shocks of the Market Revolution. Finney's spellbinding message reached people of all classes, rich and poor, converting them to the new evangelistic religion. In 1830 Finney, made famous by the revivals, was invited by businessmen to preach in Rochester. Finney preached every day for six months, and three times on Sundays. His wife, Lydia, played a vital part, constantly making home visits to the unconverted and mobilizing the women of Rochester for the cause. The Finneys dominated Rochester: "You could not go upon the streets," one person recalled, "and hear any conversation, except upon religion." Prayer meetings were held in schools and businesses, impromptu religious services in people's homes. Middle-class women in particular carried the message by prayer and pleading to the men of their families.

The New Middle-Class Family

As the success of Charles and Lydia Finney in Rochester demonstrates, evangelism rapidly became the religion of the new middle class. The "softer," emotional aspects of this religion might first appeal to women, but many women made sure that all of their family joined them in conversion. Men soon found that evangelism's stress on self-discipline and individual achievement helped them adjust to new business conditions.

The Market Revolution and evangelism also affected the family roles of women, which superficially appeared to change the least. As men were forced to concentrate most of their energies on their careers and occupations, women assumed major new responsibilities for rearing the children and inculcating in them the new attitudes necessary for success in the business world.

In the preindustrial artisanal or farming household, work and family matters had been intertwined. Every member of the family, including journeymen and apprentices, was expected to contribute in his or her own way to production. But when the master craftsman became a small manufacturer, or the small subsistence farm became a large-scale commercial operation, the family's relationship to work changed. Production moved out of the family household and into the hands of paid workers, generally in another location such as a factory. The husband's direct connection with the household was broken: he became a manager of workers, and was no longer the undisputed head of a family unit that combined work and personal life.

Now the wife was able to concentrate only on domestic work. She still had plenty to do, for cooking and cleaning were strenuous and time-consuming, but she no longer had the additional responsibility of contributing directly to what now became defined as the husband's work. In fact, although the wife worked all day at domestic tasks, the household now became defined as the realm of "not-work," a place of leisure and relaxation from the pressures of the industrial world. In family life middle-class men sought refuge from the stresses of industrialization. As Utica author John Mather Austin said in his advice manual *A Voice to the Married,* the husband should regard his home as "an elysium to which he can flee and find rest from the stormy strife of a selfish world."

The major task of middle-class women was to manage their households in such a way as to provide that refuge. In this task they were aided by the new women's magazines, such as Sarah Josepha Hale's *Ladies Magazine,* which described for readers "patterns of virtue, of piety, of intelligence and usefulness in private life" (as Hale explained in 1830). In 1837, hurt by the financial panic of that year, Hale merged her magazine with *Godey's Lady's Book,* which soon became famous for its up-to-date

This sentimental view of middle class domesticity glorifies the role of the mother as the moral and spiritual "constant" providing a variety of nurturing activities in the privacy of her own home.

fashion plates and dress patterns. By 1850 the magazine had a subscription list of 70,000. It offered readers a popular mixture of advice, patterns for everything from embroidery to dresses to "model cottages," and recipes as well.

Another new kind of publication was the housekeeping guide, a sure sign that traditional methods were inadequate for new needs. Catherine Beecher's *Treatise on Domestic Economy,* first published in 1841, became the standard housekeeping guide for a generation of middle-class American women. In it, Beecher combined innovative ideas for household design (especially in the kitchen, where she introduced principles of organization) with medical information, child-rearing advice, recipes, and numerous discussions of the mother's moral role in the family. Beecher thus attempted to help women modernize their traditional housekeeping tasks within the context of their newly defined family role. The book clearly filled a need: for many pioneer women, it was the only book besides the Bible that they carried west with them.

Separate Spheres

As the work of middle-class men and women diverged, so did social attitudes about appropriate male and female roles and qualities. Men, as we have seen, were expected to be steady, industrious, responsible, and painstakingly attentive to their business. They had little choice: in the competitive, uncertain, and rapidly changing business conditions of the early nineteenth century, these qualities were essential for men who hoped to hold their existing positions or to get ahead. In contrast, women's nurturing qualities were stressed. Gentleness, kindness, morality, and selfless devotion to family became the primary virtues for females, who were expected to exercise them within the "woman's sphere" — the home. Neither the division of responsibilities — public affairs for men, home and family for women — nor the difference in personal qualities — industrious for him, nurturing for her — were completely new. They were implicit in much earlier thinking about appropriate sex roles. But now sex roles became a matter of social importance. The unsettling demands of the new industrial order forced a dramatic change in family life and in ways of thinking about family activities.

The maintenance or achievement of a middle-class lifestyle required the joint efforts of husband and wife. More cooperation between husband and wife was called for than in the preindustrial patriarchal family. This new relationship, *companionate marriage,* was yet another result of the Market Revolution. The new family cooperation showed most clearly in decisions concerning children.

Family Limitation

Middle-class couples chose to have fewer children than their predecessors. Children who were being raised to succeed in the middle class placed considerable demands on family resources: they required more care, training, and education than children who could be put to work at traditional tasks at an early age. The dramatic fall in the birth rate during the nineteenth century (from an average of seven children per woman in 1800 to four in 1900) is evidence of conscious decisions about family limitation, first by members of the new middle class and later by working-class families. Few couples used mechanical methods of contraception such as the condom, partly because they were difficult to obtain and partly because they were associated with prostitution and the prevention of venereal disease. Instead people used birth control methods that relied on mutual consent: coitus interruptus (withdrawal before climax), the rhythm method (intercourse only during the woman's infertile period), and, most often, abstinence or infrequent intercourse. Medical manuals suggested that couples consider ending their sex life after they had reached the desired number of children.

When mutual efforts at birth control failed, married women often sought a surgical abortion, a new technique that was much more reliable than the folk remedies women had always shared among themselves. Surgical abortions were widely advertised and widely used after 1830, especially by middle-class married women seeking to limit family size. This widespread practice — some studies estimated that one out of every four pregnancies was aborted (about the same rate as in 1990) — prompted the first legal bans. By 1860, twenty states had outlawed abortions. Even in the absence of accurate statistics, it is clear that dangerous illegal abortions continued, especially among unmarried women who felt they lacked alternatives.

Accompanying the interest in family limitation was a redefinition of sexuality. Doctors recommended in all cases that sexual urges be controlled, but they believed this would be much more difficult for men than for women. It was the task of middle-class women to help their husbands and sons restrain their sexuality by appealing to their higher, moral natures. Many medical manuals of the period asserted that women, because of their superior morality, were uninterested in sexual matters. Women who *were* visibly interested ran the risk of being considered immoral or "fallen," and thereupon shunned by the middle class. Although it is always difficult to measure the extent to which the suggestions in advice books were applied in actual experience, it seems that many middle-class women did not object to this new and limited definition of women's sexuality.

The desire to be free of the risks and responsibilities of too frequent childbearing was common among women of the late eighteenth century. But it was a wish they had little chance of achieving until men became equally interested in family limitation. The rapid change in attitudes toward family size that occurred in the early nineteenth century has been repeated around the world as other societies undergo the dramatic experience of industrialization. It is a striking example of the ways economic changes affect our most private and personal decisions.

Motherhood

New responsibilities toward children led to another major redefinition of women's roles. Childrearing had been shared in the preindustrial household, boys learning farming or craft skills from their fathers while girls learned domestic skills from their mothers. The children of the new middle class, however, needed a new kind of upbringing, one that involved a long period of nurturing in the moral beliefs and personal habits necessary for success — responsibility, hard work, and (especially for boys) ambition. Mothers assumed primary responsibility for this training, in part because fathers were too busy, but also because people believed that women's superior qualities of gentleness, morality, and loving watchfulness were essential to the task.

Fathers retained a strong role in major decisions concerning children, but mothers commonly turned to other women for advice on daily matters. Through their churches, women formed maternal associations for help in raising their children to be religious

The invention of photography made possible family portraits that earlier were too expensive for all but the wealthiest. This family group, the Edward Miner Gallaudet family, was photographed by Matthew Brady in the 1860s. It exhibits the gender differences expected in the middle class family: self-reliant males and softer, more clinging females.

and responsible. In Utica, these extremely popular organizations bonded women into strong networks sustained by mutual advice and by publications such as *Mother's Magazine,* issued by the Presbyterian church, and *Mother's Monthly Journal,* put out by the Baptists.

Middle-class status required another sharp break with tradition. In Utica, as late as 1855, artisanal families expected all children over fifteen to work, whereas middle-class families sacrificed to keep their sons in school or in training for their chosen profession. They housed and fed their sons well into their twenties as the young men worked to consolidate their finances before embarking on marriage. Mothers continued to be concerned about their sons' character and morality, as women's activities in the great religious revivals of the 1830s showed.

Women also took the lead in an important informal activity: making sure her family had friends and contacts that would be useful when her children were old enough to consider careers (for sons) and marriage (for all). Matters such as these, rarely considered by earlier generations living in small communities, now became important in the new middle-class communities of America's towns and cities.

Contrary to the growing myth of the self-made man, middle-class success was *not* a matter of individual achievement. Instead it was usually based on a family strategy in which women's efforts were essential. The reorganization of the family described in this section was successful: from its shelter and support emerged generations of ambitious, responsible, and individualistic middle-class men. But while boys were trained for success, this was not an acceptable goal for their sisters. Women were trained to be the nurturing, silent "support system" that undergirded the male success. Naturally, women took great pride in the successes of their fathers, husbands, and sons. But for many women, that was not enough. The great wave of reform that we will examine in Chapter 13 owed much to women's search for an acceptable outlet for the conflicts created by their new middle-class role.

Industrial Morality

These changes in family roles fostered the attitudes necessary for success in the new middle class. But successful businessmen also demanded new attitudes from their workers. As we have seen, the workplace witnessed a change from the informal, side-by-side relationship between master and helper to formal rules concerning punctuality, attendance, and steady work habits.

Master artisans often took the lead in reforming the habits of younger workers. Stephen Allen, the New York sailmaker who became mayor, attributed his success to long work days, avoidance of debt, and "employing the utmost economy in all my concerns." Another New York artisan, master baker Thomas Mercein, took advantage of the opening of the Apprentices' Library, founded by the General Society of Mechanics and Tradesmen in 1820, to preach a similar message. "Cherish, I beseech you, a deep-rooted abhorrence of the alluring but fatal paths of vice and dissipation," Mercein told the apprentices. "Industry, ardour, sobriety, and perseverence in your different pursuits will lead to a successful competition in the world. . . ."

Individualism and Uncertainty

Industrial morality, whether adopted willingly by workers and the new middle class or enforced by new factory work patterns or social pressure, soon permeated much of northern society. And with it came a new, optimistic, and individualistic message. As economist Francis Bowen boasted in 1856, "Neither theoretically nor practically, in this country, is there any obstacle to any individual's becoming rich, if he will, and almost to any amount that he will."

Although Bowen's opinion was widely shared, it was incorrect. Although national wealth increased substantially (it is estimated that real per capita income doubled between 1800 and 1850), the proportions of haves (property owners) and have-nots in the nation remained what they had been in 1790 — 40 percent property owners, 60 percent propertyless. The extremes of wealth and poverty became more glaring. The expanding opportunities of the Market Revolution had the effect of concentrating wealth: by the 1840s, the top 1 percent of the population owned about 40 percent of the nation's wealth. At the other extreme, fully one-third of the population possessed little more than the clothes they wore and some loose change.

Meanwhile, the economic climate had changed fundamentally. Traditional farmers and artisans had occasionally experienced bad economic times, but most farmers had been able to subsist. In contrast, the developing market economy did not offer anyone a smooth ride. In fact, it was much more like a roller coaster, with times of dizzying growth punctuated by terrible drops. The Panic of 1819 (see Chapter 9) was the first taste of the instability that attended the heady economic growth. The Panic of 1837 (see Chapter 10) was even worse.

In what ways did Americans adjust to the economic uncertainty that accompanied the Market Revolution? In addition to the changes in behavior and attitudes we have described, there were two major geographic strategies: moving on or staying in a familiar community.

Moving on was often forced upon workers: when they lost their jobs, they had to find other work. Even for city dwellers, a job change usually meant a change of location and thus a change of residence as well. Census figures show that in the 1840s, one in every three households in Boston moved every year. Frequently these families moved within the city. Mobility was increasingly imposed upon workers by the Market Revolution's reorganization of traditional occupations. These disruptions were not limited just to the poorest and most mobile workers. In New England, for example, even prosperous artisans and farmers faced disruptive competition from factory goods and western commercial agriculture. They could remain where they were only if they changed their work or their farming practices. Often the more conservative choice was to move west and try to reestablish one's occupation on the frontier. The poorest workers did not move west; they couldn't afford to. The wealthiest workers rarely moved either, for they had no incentive. It was the middle range of workers and farmers who moved west, hoping to maintain or to better their circumstances.

The risks of mobility were considerable. At every turn, newcomers were faced with competing claims from land promoters, town boosters, and outright liars and crooks. It was often difficult to sort out true information from false, to know who was trustworthy and who was not. Migrants from the older states to the West adopted the same strategy that immigrants to the United States from Europe were to use: they followed the lead of family, friends, or neighbors who had gone before. Thus just as immigrants from the same European town clustered together in American cities (see Chapter 13), so New England migrants sought familiar company in western towns. In both cases, the basic instinct was to re-create something as close to the original community as possible.

Persistence is the term demographers use for remaining in one place. At the heart of this "staying-put" strategy was the economic and financial support available from the network of family, friends, fellow workers, and institutions (such as churches) that a person developed after long residence in one place. This network is what we mean when we speak of *community*. Few people can live very well without at least some community supports. Thus we

CHRONOLOGY

1790	Samuel Slater's first mill in Rhode Island
1790s	Brandywine millers form "flour manufactories"
1793	Cotton gin invented
1798	Eli Whitney gets government contract for rifles with interchangeable parts
1807	Embargo Act excludes British manufactures
1811	Francis Cabot Lowell tours British textile factories
1812	Micajah Pratt begins his own shoe business in Lynn, Massachusetts
1813	Francis Cabot Lowell raises $300,000 to build his first cotton textile factory at Waltham
1815	War of 1812 ends; British competition in manufactures resumes
1816	First protective tariff
1820	Large-scale outwork networks develop in New England
1823	Lowell mills open
1824	John Hall successfully achieves interchangeable parts at Harpers Ferry armory
	Women lead strike at Pawtucket textile mill
1825	Erie Canal opens
1830	Charles Finney's Rochester revivals
1834	First strike at Lowell mills
1841	Beecher, *Treatise on Domestic Economy*

find during the Market Revolution that Americans counterbalanced the new emphasis on individualism by working diligently to create community. They did so by joining associations of all kinds. In this way they sought to overcome the insecurity caused by the breakup of traditional work patterns and by the explosive urban growth and dramatic westward expansion of the period.

Associations ranged from the local burial society, into which poor immigrants paid tiny weekly sums so that family members could afford a decent funeral, to great national associations such as political parties. People joined them eagerly, and in record numbers. Those who stayed — the persisters — built dense community networks. Those who moved did the best they could to build new networks in their new homes.

The Spirit of Competitive Capitalism

As we have noted, the Market Revolution caused profound changes in personal behavior. For most people the changes were slow and gradual. Until midcentury, small farmers in the North and the South were probably more similar than different. The Market Revolution had as yet made little impact on them. Their lives were still largely determined by community events, although the spread of democratic politics and the availability of newspapers and other printed material increased their connection to a larger world.

But in northern cities and among the business community, the situation was entirely different. There the impact of the Market Revolution could be seen both in the way business was conducted and in the attitudes of successful businessmen. The spirit of competitive capitalism bred among these people a pride in economic growth and a belief that success came to hardworking, forward-looking people. Failure, on the other hand, was the fate of those who did not apply themselves and did not adapt to changing business conditions. As these competitive capitalists looked south, they saw neither a business climate nor a middle class that they recognized. Instead, they saw a leisured aristocracy, a large class of poor and unsuccessful farmers, and a huge class of enslaved workers. Because the South was organized on economic principles so different from their own, many northern capitalists scorned it. When, as we shall examine in the next chapter, abolitionists insisted that slavery was a moral sin, the gulf in understanding between the two regions widened.

CONCLUSION

In spite of recurrent financial panics, the spirit of the age was optimistic. After all, less than fifty years after achieving independence, the United States had experienced extraordinary economic and physical growth: in national and per capita wealth, in population, in physical extent. In spite of the fundamental ways in which the Market Revolution was changing their lives, most Americans were optimistic about their own prospects. Important as the politics of the period were, we should not forget that the task of coping with the Market Revolution fell on ordinary citizens. The nation's cities led the way in coming to terms with the new age. It was there that the "common man" — and the "common woman" — attempted to shape American society in ways that fulfilled its democratic promise.

Additional Readings

CHRISTOPHER CLARK, *The Roots of Rural Capitalism: Western Massachusetts, 1780–1860* (1990). The most thorough examination to date of how the commercial spirit changed rural life.

ALAN DAWLEY, *Class and Community: The Industrial Revolution in Lynn* (1976). A pathbreaking study of the shift from artisanal to wage labor.

THOMAS DUBLIN, *Women at Work: The Transformation of Work and Community in Lowell, Massachusetts 1826–1860* (1979). A careful look at the female workers of Lowell and their changing conditions.

ERIC FONER, *Free Soil, Free Labor, Free Men: The Ideology of the Republican Party before the Civil War* (1970). Still the most useful book for understanding the new spirit of competitive capitalism in the North.

DAVID HOUNDSHELL, *From the American System to Mass Production 1800–1932* (1984). Strips away the mythology surrounding Eli Whitney and interchangeable parts, to reveal a network of New England "mechanics" who contributed to this invention.

PAUL JOHNSON, *A Shopkeeper's Millennium: Society and Revivals in Rochester, New York, 1815–1837* (1978). A study of the changing relationship between masters and workers in Rochester.

———, "The Modernization of Mayo Greenleaf Patch: Land, Family, and Marginality in New England, 1766–1818," *New England Quarterly* 55:

December 1982. One of the few accounts of an ordinary family's transition from rural tradition to urban capitalism.

JONATHAN PRUDE, *The Coming of Industrial Order: Town and Factory Life in Rural Massachusetts, 1810–1860* (1983). A major source of information on family mills.

STEVEN J. ROSS, *Workers on the Edge: Work, Leisure and Politics in Industrializing Cincinnati, 1788–1890* (1985). Studies the growth of wage labor in a major western city.

MARY RYAN, *The Making of the Middle Class* (1981). The first study to clearly discern the role of women in the family strategies of the new middle class.

CHARLES SELLERS, *The Market Revolution: Jacksonian America 1815–1846* (1991). A remarkable synthesis of the politics, religious sentiment, and economic change of the period.

BARBARA CLARK SMITH, *After the Revolution: The Smithsonian History of Everyday Life in the Eighteenth Century* (1985). The story of the Springer family early in this chapter comes from this volume.

CHRISTINE STANSELL, *City of Women: Sex and Class in New York 1789–1860* (1983). Exceptionally useful in exploring the range of women's work and the social dynamics of rapidly growing New York City.

13 COMING TO TERMS WITH THE NEW AGE, 1820s–1850s

AMERICAN COMMUNITIES

• THE WOMEN OF SENECA FALLS

In the summer of 1848, a small advertisement appeared in an upstate New York newspaper:

> WOMAN'S RIGHTS CONVENTION.— A Convention to discuss the social, civil, and religious condition and rights of woman, will be held in the Wesleyan Chapel, at Seneca Falls, N.Y., on Wednesday and Thursday, the 19th and 20th of July, current; commencing at 10 o'clock A.M. During the first day the meeting will be exclusively for women, who are earnestly invited to attend. The public generally are invited to be present on the second day, when Lucretia Mott of Philadelphia, and other ladies and gentlemen, will address the convention.

Charlotte Woodward, a nineteen-year-old glove maker who did outwork in her rural home, saw the advertisement and persuaded six friends to travel to the convention with her. "At first we travelled quite alone,"

A COMMUNITY OF REFORMERS RESPONDS TO THE MARKET REVOLUTION

she recalled. "But before we had gone many miles we came on other waggon-loads of women, bound in the same direction. As we reached different cross-roads we saw waggons coming from every part of the country, and long before we reached Seneca Falls we were a procession." To the surprise of the convention organizers, almost 300 people attended the two-day meeting, where they discussed a document modeled on the Declaration of Independence. It began thus: "We hold these truths to be self-evident: That all men and women are created equal. . . ."

The resolutions accompanying the declaration pointed out that men had deprived women of legal rights, of the right to own their own property, of custody of their children in cases of divorce, of the right to higher education (only Oberlin College and Mount Holyoke College admitted women), of full participation in religion, and of the right to vote. As the delegates to the Seneca Falls convention discussed and voted on each resolution, all were passed unanimously—except the last. "Why Lizzie, thee will make us ridiculous!" Quaker Lucretia Mott had exclaimed when Elizabeth Cady Stanton proposed the voting rights measure. And in fact the newspapers reporting on the convention made great fun of the idea that some women were foolish enough to demand the right to vote. But for the group assembled in the Wesleyan Chapel, this first women's

373

Serious business is clearly being discussed at this meeting of women strikers in Lynn in 1860. Women's meetings like this one and the first women's rights convention in Seneca Falls in 1848 disproved the widespread assumption that women were incapable of organizing on their own behalf.

rights convention was so successful that they promptly planned another one three weeks later in New York's most important upstate city, Rochester.

What impelled Charlotte Woodward and her friends to ride forty miles to attend this meeting? And what attracted the other participants? In the broadest sense, the dislocations caused by the Market Revolution brought them together. The Seneca Falls region, a farming frontier in 1800, had become connected to national commerce when it was linked to the Erie Canal in 1828. It was drawn even further into the modern age when the railroad arrived in 1841. Seneca Falls itself had grown from a village of 200 in 1824 to a town of over 4,000 in 1842. It had become a center for flour milling (in 1845, the nine mills in the town produced a total of 2,000 barrels of flour a day) and manufacturing, and a hub of the outwork network of which Charlotte Woodward was a part. Swamped by newcomers (among them a growing number of poor and foreign-sounding Irish Catholics), the inhabitants of Seneca Falls struggled to maintain a sense of community. A major way they did so was to group together in volunteer organizations of all kinds — religious, civic, social, educational, recreational. The town of Seneca Falls, like many others beset by rapid social change, was home to a number of active reform organizations whose members hoped to improve community life through social change.

Many reformers belonged to liberal religious groups. Both the Wesleyan Methodist Society of Seneca Falls and the Progressive Quakers of the nearby town of Waterloo had broken away from the national organizations of the Methodists and Quakers because they would not take a strong stand against slavery. Both groups were outspoken in their belief in the moral equality of all humankind and in their commitment to social activism. The Wesleyans, for example, resolved in 1847 that "we cannot identify our Christian and moral character with societies where women and colored persons are excluded." Perhaps as many as a third of those attending the Woman's Rights Convention were members of the Wesleyan Chapel, and a quarter or so were Waterloo Quakers.

Others were members of temperance societies. Seneca Falls had been the site of a "Temperance Reformation" in the early 1840s, when the enthusiasm generated in large revival-like meetings had convinced hundreds to sign pledges of abstinence from alcohol. Among the many women active in temperance organizations was Amelia Bloomer, who attended the final evening of the Woman's Rights Convention. Her newspaper, **The Lily,** *which she began to publish in 1849, promoted temperance, women's rights, and the comfortable, loose-fitting dress known as the Bloomer Costume that so shocked her contemporaries.*

Family connections and personal friendships bound the reform community together. Lucretia Mott, the well-known Philadelphia antislavery reformer, was visiting her sister in Waterloo in July of 1848 (after a reform-related tour of the new penitentiary at Auburn and a nearby Indian reservation). Elizabeth Cady Stanton of Seneca Falls, wife of a well-known antislavery orator and niece of a leading reform philanthropist, came to have tea and to renew her acquaintance with Mott. Stanton brought to the meeting a keen awareness of her own recent personal experience. She and her family had recently moved from Boston, where, she remembered, they had "near neighbors, a new home with all the modern conveniences, and well-trained servants." Living in a house on the outskirts of Seneca Falls, she had none of those things and in addition her three children suffered frequent attacks of malaria. She mused,

> I now fully understood the practical difficulties most women had to contend with . . . The general discontent I felt with woman's portion as wife, mother, housekeeper, physician and spiritual guide, the chaotic conditions into which everything fell without her constant supervision, and the wearied anxious look of the majority of women impressed me with a strong feeling that some active measures should be taken to remedy the wrongs of society in general, and of women in particular.

As she and the other reforming women talked about the difficulties of women's lives, the idea of a women's rights convention was born. Initially, women's rights was just one of many reforms, but it was to be exceptionally long-lasting. Stanton, soon to form a working partnership with former temperance worker Susan B. Anthony, devoted the rest of her life to women's rights.

But what of Charlotte Woodward, a local farm girl, unaware of the national reform community? Why was she there? Because in this age of hopefulness and change she wanted a better life for herself. She was motivated, she said, by

> all the hours that I sat and sewed gloves for a miserable pittance, which, after it was earned, could never be mine. [By law and custom her father, as head of the household, was entitled to her wages.] I wanted to work, but I wanted to choose my task and I wanted to collect my wages.

The reforming women of Seneca Falls, grouped together on behalf of social change, had found in the first women's rights convention a way to speak for the needs of working women such as Charlotte Woodward as well as for their own.

All over the North, local communities such as Seneca Falls as well as large ones like New York became places where Americans gathered together in reform organizations to try to solve the novel problems of the Market Revolution. Through their reform oganizations local women and men became partici-

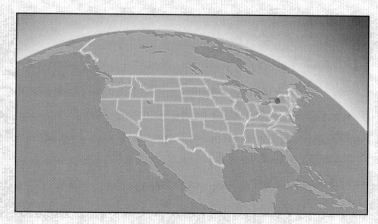

pants in wider communities of concern. From their many local efforts a national reform movement grew.

IMMIGRATION

In previous chapters we examined the personal and political effects of the Market Revolution. In this chapter we look at wider social changes and the response to them. One of the most fundamental changes was in the ethnic composition of the American people.

Patterns of Immigration

Although the United States was, as later generations were accustomed to saying, a nation of immigrants, there were peaks and troughs in the rate of immigration. The years from 1790 to 1820, because of the Napoleonic wars, were not a period of substantial immigration. But then came a surge of immigration that was one of the clearest proofs of the success of the Market Revolution and the belief that America was "the land of opportunity."

Beginning in 1830, immigration to the United States soared, increasing fivefold in the period 1831–40, tripling in the next decade, and then peaking at nearly 450,000 in 1854. The proportion of new immigrants in the population jumped from 1.6 percent in the 1820s to 11.2 percent in 1860. The cumulative effect was much greater: In 1860 one out of three white males in the North was foreign-born (one out of four in the South — an indication of the greater economic diversity and attractiveness of the North).

Irish and German Immigration

Immigration soared in the period 1830–1854. Although the largest percentage of immigrants continued to be English, the Irish Potato Famine of 1845 and economic troubles in Germany caused the numbers of Irish and German immigrants to rise sharply. American cities were ill prepared to cope with this surge of immigrants.

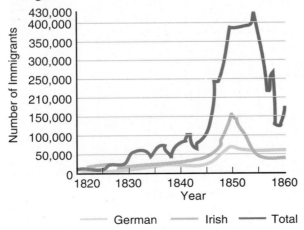

Most of the immigrants to the United States before the Civil War were from Ireland and Germany. They represented the largest influx of non-English immigrants the country had known (most Americans found the Irish dialect as strange as a foreign language). They were also the poorest: Most of the Irish, as we shall see, arrived destitute. In addition, many of them (most of the Irish and half of the Germans) were Catholics, another unwelcome novelty to many Protestant Americans. These characteristics, as well as the rapid increase in immigration, represented a significant new element in the American social structure, one that challenged both the native-born and the newcomers.

It would be a mistake, however, to think that immigration was unwelcome to everyone. Industries needed willing workers, and western states were eager for settlers. In 1852 Wisconsin appointed a commissioner of emigration (from Europe to the U.S.), whose responsibility was to attract settlers. Iowa and Minnesota soon did the same. These states advertised in Europe, as did steamship lines and railroads, particularly later in the century. Some projects simply could not have been accomplished without immigrant labor. The Erie Canal, finished in the 1820s, is a case in point: The labor of Irish contract workers was essential (see Chapter 10). Immigrant labor was also welcomed by manufacturers such as those at Lowell, who faced increased competition and thus sought cheaper and more reliable labor than the farm women who had made up their original labor force. For the rest of the century, industries that demanded heavy physical labor (steelmaking, mining, railroads) drew on the manpower of immigrants. Immigrant women, meanwhile, found jobs as domestic servants and in the needle trades. There was, then, a demand for immigrant labor to fuel the expanding American economy and to turn wilderness into farmland.

Few immigrants found life pleasant or easy. In addition to the psychological difficulties of leaving a home and familiar ways behind, most immigrants endured harsh living and working conditions. America's cities were unprepared for the social problems posed by large numbers of immigrants. Before 1855, immigration was unregulated (anyone could enter) and unprotected (con artists found the newcomers easy pickings). There was no significant federal regulation or responsibility for immigration until the 1880s; the burden fell completely on cities and states. New York City, by far the largest port of entry, did not even establish an official reception center until 1855, when Castle Garden, at the bottom of Manhattan Island (near present-day Battery Park), was so designated.

Irish Immigration

The first major immigrant wave to test American cities was caused by the catastrophic Irish Potato Famine of 1845–49. The Irish, held in unwilling colonial status by the British, subsisted poorly on small plots of farmland on which they grew grain for British landlords and potatoes for their own food. Emigration to the United States, especially by young people who could not hope to own land of their own, occurred at the rate of tens of thousands a year from 1818 to 1845. But in the latter year Ireland's green fields of potatoes turned black with blight. The British government could not cope, leaving the Irish with two choices: starvation or flight. One million people died, and another 1.5 million emigrated, the majority to the United States. Starving, diseased (thousands died of typhus during the voyage), and destitute, hundreds of thousands (250,000 in 1851 alone) disembarked at east coast ports (New York, Philadelphia, Baltimore, and Boston). Lacking the money to go inland and begin farming, they remained in the cities. Crowded together in miserable housing, desperate for work at any wages, foreign in their religion and pastimes (drinking and fighting, their critics said), tenaciously nationalistic and bitterly anti-British, they created ethnic enclaves of a kind new to American cities.

The largest numbers of Irish came to New York, which managed to absorb them. But Boston, a much smaller and more homogeneous city, was overwhelmed by the Irish influx. By 1850, a quarter of Boston's population was Irish, and most of these people were recent immigrants. Boston, the home of Puritanism and the center of American intellectualism, did not welcome illiterate, Catholic Irish peasants. All over the city in places of business and in homes normally eager for domestic servants the signs went up: "No Irish Need Apply." The Irish were able to get only the worst and poorest-paying jobs, and could afford housing only in East Boston. In 1849 a Boston health committee reported that East Boston was "a perfect hive of human beings, without comforts and mostly without common necessaries; in many cases, huddled together like brutes, without regard to sex or age or sense of decency."

The Irish Community

To the Irish, these same slums represented not only family ties and familiar ways, but community support in learning how to survive in new surroundings. Isolated partly by their own beliefs (for Catholics fully reciprocated the hatred and fear Protestants showed them), the Irish created their own community within Boston. They raised the money to erect Catholic churches with Irish priests. They established parochial schools with Irish nuns as teachers, and sent their children there in preference to the openly anti-Catholic public schools. They formed mutual aid societies based on kinship or town of origin in Ireland. Men and women formed religious and social clubs, as well as lodges and brotherhoods and their female auxiliaries. Irishmen manned fire and militia companies as well. This dense network of associations served the same purpose that social welfare organizations do today: providing help in time of need and offering companionship in a hostile environment. And, almost from the moment of their arrival, the Irish sent huge sums of money back to Ireland so that relatives could join them in America. For however bad the conditions in the adopted country, they were better than those in Ireland. As one newcomer wrote, "There is a great many ill conveniences here, but no empty bellies."

For such large amounts of money to be raised from such a poor community, family work strategies were necessary. Families were generally large, and every member contributed to the family income. Young men might work far away on railroad construction or in mines, but most of their wages were sent home. Young women worked in textile mills or, once they had learned the American dialect and some American customs, as live-in domestic servants for Bostonians. In the latter occupation they often had to endure scorn for their "slovenly" ways. For all of their close family ties, Irishwomen eagerly grasped opportunities for independence: In the second, American-born generation, an unusually high percentage of them shunned marriage for careers as schoolteachers.

Their brothers made their way in two occupations: the priesthood and politics. For although the community building and family work strategies just described were common to many immigrant groups throughout American history (even today), the Irish dominated the American Catholic Church and had a special love for politics as well. They quickly took over the local Democratic party. (In contrast, the Boston power structure, as we saw in Chapter 10, consisted mostly of Whigs, the heirs of the Federalists.) Their strength lay at the neighborhood level, where politicians knew everyone personally. Frequently the neighborhood politicians were saloon keepers, for the tavern was the secular center of Irish society—much to the horror of Bostonians, many of whom sternly advocated temperance. Political popularity and loyalty were ensured by the small gestures of aid (a job for a son, a small loan, even a round of free drinks) on which a poor

Emigrants from Europe to the United States endured poor and crowded conditions in the steerage class of Trans-Atlantic passenger ships. The sympathetic artist titled this work *Between Decks in an Emigrant Ship — Feeding Time: A Sketch from Life.*

community depends. By these methods, the Irish elected their first mayor of Boston, Hugh O'Brien, in 1884. With few exceptions, they have held onto City Hall ever since. One such Irish saloon keeper, Patrick Joseph Kennedy, founded one of America's most famous political dynasties. Barely a century after Patrick's birth into a poor immigrant family, his grandson John Fitzgerald Kennedy was elected the first Irish Catholic president of the United States.

German Immigration

Germans had been among America's settlers almost since the beginning. They were concentrated in the Middle Atlantic states, especially Pennsylvania, where in 1790 they made up a third of the population, according to Benjamin Franklin's estimate. William Penn, impressed by the industriousness of Germans, had taken pains to invite them to immigrate to the colony he founded. The nineteenth-century immigration of Germans began somewhat later and more slowly than that of the Irish, but by the 1860s it had surpassed the Irish influx. Some German peasants, like the Irish, were driven from their homeland by potato blight in the mid-1840s. But the typical German immigrant was a small farmer or artisan dislodged by the same market forces at work in America: industrialization of production and consolidation and commercialization of farming. There was also a small group of middle-class liberal intellectuals who left the German states (Germany was not yet a unified nation) after 1848 upon the failure of attempts at revolution. Among them was Carl Schurz, who rose to become secre-tary of the interior in the Hayes administration (1877–81) after many years as a congressman from Missouri. German migrants were thus a more diverse group than the Irish, and their settlement patterns were more diffuse. Nevertheless, like the Irish, they formed their own communities and encountered American hostility for their "foreign" ways.

The first two major ports of embarkation for the Germans were Bremen (in northern Germany) and Le Havre (in northern France), the main ports for American tobacco and cotton. The tobacco boats bore the Bremen passengers to Baltimore, and the cotton ships took them to New Orleans (a major entry point for European immigrants until the Civil War). From these ports, many Germans made their way to the Mississippi and Ohio River valleys — where they settled in Pittsburgh, Cincinnati, and St. Louis — and to farms in Ohio, Indiana, Missouri, and even Texas. In Texas the nucleus of a German community began with a Mexican land grant in the 1830s. Few Germans settled either in northern cities or in the South.

German agricultural communities took a distinctive form that fostered cultural continuity. Although they abandoned the Old World custom of living in villages and going out to their fields every day, immigrants formed predominantly German towns by *clustering,* or taking up adjoining land. A small cluster could support German churches, German schools, and German customs and thereby attract other Germans, some directly from Europe and some from other parts of the United States. Such communities reinforced the traditional values of

German farmers, such as persistence, hard work, and thrift. Non-German neighbors might sell out and move on, but the Germans stayed and improved the land so they could pass it on to the next generation. They used soil conservation practices, for example, that were unusual for the time. Persistence paid: German cluster communities exist to this day in Texas, the Midwest, and the Pacific Northwest, and families of German origin are still the single largest ethnic group in agriculture.

"Little Germanies"

While rural German communities were maintaining their culture as a result of their relative isolation, Germans who settled in urban areas sought with some success to duplicate the rich cultural life of German cities. Initially, as with all immigrant groups, there was residential segregation, most of it voluntary, for new immigrants wanted to live near others who spoke the same language, went to the same church, and shared the same social customs. Soon many cities had a neighborhood known as Little Germany. Like the Irish, the Germans formed church societies, mutual benefit societies, and fire and militia companies for the purpose of mutual support. Partly because their community was more prosperous than the Irish, the Germans also formed a network of leisure organizations: singing societies, debating and political clubs, and turnvereine (gymnastics associations).

Little Germanies had German schools (which were generally better than the public schools), theater groups, and a flourishing German-language press. In the summer, the entire family frequented beer gardens, which were usually in a semirural setting and always had music. This flourishing community culture, with its emphasis on music, intellect, and love of nature, had an impact on American urban life, especially in Baltimore and Cincinnati. At first the Germans were greeted with hostility (temperance societies were especially unhappy about the beer gardens), but by 1860 not only the beer gardens but other German customs such as gymnasiums and candle-lit Christmas trees were shared by Germans and non-Germans alike.

Like the Irish, the Germans enriched American culture. German ideas about education led to the adoption by public schools of kindergartens, music, gymnastics, vocational training, and high schools. But the ethnic neighborhoods and communities, accompanied as they were by the poverty and strangeness of the new immigrants, added to the list of social problems that America's urban centers faced — and were unable to solve — in the early nineteenth century.

URBAN AMERICA

No aspect of American life was unaffected by the Market Revolution. But nowhere was the impact so obvious as in the cities, which experienced a confusing mixture of physical growth, occupational change, and economic competition that was both stimulating and frightening. The cities were also the smelter for the social and political responses to the dramatic changes in American life.

The Growth of Cities

In 1820, only 6 percent of the American population lived in cities. Between 1820 and 1860, the Market Revolution caused cities to grow at a more rapid rate than at any other time in American history. By 1860, almost 20 percent of the population was urban. The great seaports continued to lead the way in population growth.

The nation's five largest cities in 1850 were the same as in 1800, with one exception. New York, Philadelphia, Baltimore, and Boston still topped the list, but Charleston had been replaced by New Orleans (see Chapter 9). The rate of urban growth was extraordinary. Between 1800 and 1860 all four Atlantic seaports grew at least 25 percent each decade, and often much more. New York, for example, grew 64 percent between 1820 and 1830. As we saw in Chapter 10, the opening of the Erie Canal in 1825 gave New York a huge boost, adding much of the new commerce of the American interior to the city's long-standing role in international trade. New York was not only America's largest city (60,500 in 1800, 202,600 in 1830, over 1 million in 1860) but the largest port and financial center. It had far outstripped its rival Atlantic seaports.

Philadelphia, the nation's largest city in 1800, was half the size of New York in 1850. Nevertheless, its growth was substantial — from 70,000 in 1800 to 389,000 in 1850 and to 565,529 in 1860. Philadelphia became as much an industrial as a commercial city. Old artisanal industries such as handloom weaving, tailoring, and shoe manufacture coexisted with new industries such as the huge Baldwin locomotive works, foundries, and chemical companies.

Baltimore was half the size of Philadelphia (212,418 in 1860). Baltimore merchants, attempting to protect trade links with the trans-Appalachian West that were threatened by the Erie Canal, built the first important railroad, the Baltimore and Ohio,

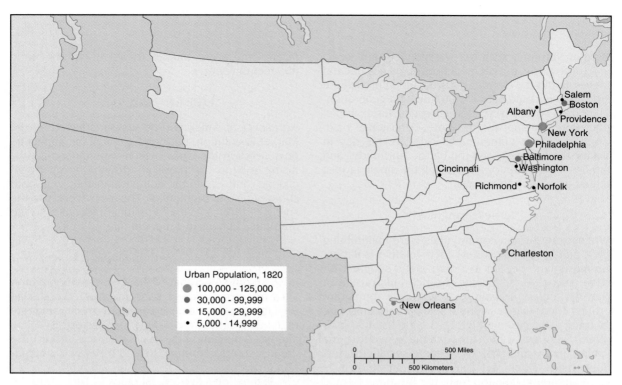

Urban Population, 1820

- ● 100,000 - 125,000
- ● 30,000 - 99,999
- ● 15,000 - 29,999
- · 5,000 - 14,999

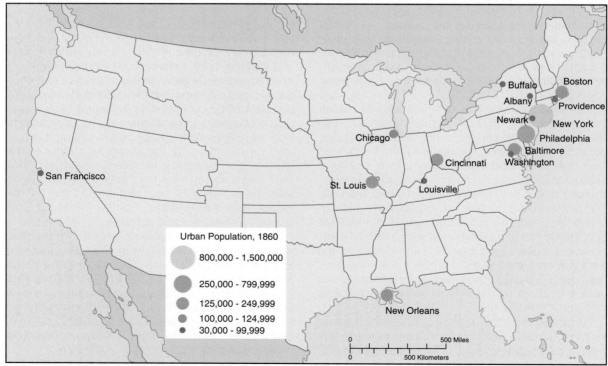

Urban Population, 1860

- ● 800,000 - 1,500,000
- ● 250,000 - 799,999
- ● 125,000 - 249,999
- ● 100,000 - 124,999
- ● 30,000 - 99,999

The Growth of Cities, 1820–1860

American cities grew more rapidly between 1820 and 1860 than at any other time in the nation's history. Eastern seaport cities were still the largest (as they had been in 1800), but New York was now twice the size of the second city, Philadelphia. New York's growth, due in large part to the Erie Canal (opened in 1825), illustrated the importance of trade in the nation's interior. Inland river cities like Cincinnati, St. Louis and the great Mississippi seaport of New Orleans grew rapidly. But the greatest growth was experienced by Chicago, which was both a water and railroad center. It had not even existed as a city in 1820.

in 1830. Although Baltimore remained the east coast center of the tobacco trade with Europe, by 1850 her major foreign trade was with Brazil, to which she shipped flour and from whom she imported coffee.

Boston had 177,840 people in 1860. In colonial times Boston had dominated the triangular trade between Britain and the West Indies. Now Boston merchants had a new triangular trade: Ships carried New England cotton cloth, shoes, and other manufactured goods to the South, delivered southern cotton to British and European ports, and returned to Boston with European manufactured goods. Boston still dominated the China trade as well.

New Orleans, with a population of 168,675 in 1860, fed by the expansion of cotton throughout the South and commercial agriculture in the Mississippi Valley, increased her exports from $5 million in 1815 to $107 million in 1860. In the 1850s, New Orleans handled about half the nation's cotton exports.

By 1860 each of these ports had turned its back to the oceans to reach far into the American interior for trade. Prosperous merchants in these cities now depended on American exports rather than European imports for their profits.

Another result of the Market Revolution was the appearance of "instant" cities, which sprang up at critical points on the new transportation network. Utica, New York, a frontier trading post, was transformed by the opening of the Erie Canal into a commercial and manufacturing center. By 1850 its population was 22,000. A few years later, railroads made the fortune of Chicago, located on the shores of Lake Michigan at a junction of water and rail transport. Grain storage facilities, slaughterhouses, and warehouses of all kinds were built to service the trade that passed through the city. At the same time, farm implement manufacturers such as Cyrus McCormick built manufacturing plants to serve the needs of Midwest farmers. Thus, almost from the start Chicago was a modern, diversified city, well equipped to compete with older eastern urban centers and manufacturers. By 1860 it had a population of 100,000, making it the nation's eighth largest city (after Cincinnati and St. Louis).

The Walking City

For all their diversity, American cities in the early nineteenth century shared certain physical characteristics that have led urban historians to characterize them as *walking cities*. The most common way of getting around in these cities was by foot. (Most laborers—as many as 30,000 in Philadelphia—walked to work daily.) Eighteenth-century cities had been small and compact. Philadelphia, for example, had been laid out by William Penn himself in an orderly grid of streets bordered by neat row houses. This dense, small-scale housing pattern had fostered neighborliness in the preindustrial city. The vastly expanded city of 1850 retained this layout, but now the result was not so much neighborliness as congestion: The large numbers of people packed into small areas created a level of crowding uncommon today. City districts were still a jumble of small dwellings that housed many trades and social classes. There were a few exclusive neighborhoods for the very rich, but most people still lived side by side with commerce and poorer people.

The walking city pattern was ill suited to the rapid urban growth of the early nineteenth century, which overwhelmed the traditional political system. Personal customs and habits could not keep pace with the change either. The most serious problems, sanitation and civic order, were the visible results of the changing class structure.

Class Structure in the Cities

Although economists estimate that per capita income doubled between 1800 and 1850, the growing gap between rich and poor was glaringly apparent in the nation's cities. The benefits of the Market Revolution were unequally distributed. As we have seen, by the 1840s the top 1 percent of the population owned about 40 percent of the nation's wealth; at the other extreme, one-third of the population owned virtually nothing. This dramatic concentration of wealth occurred because the well-to-do (merchants, for example) were best placed to take advantage of new opportunities for wealth. Workers, on the other hand, faced the occupational uncertainties that accompanied industrialization. In the cities, then, there was a very small group of wealthy people worth more than $15,000 (about 3 percent of the population), a very large group of poor people who owned $100 or less (nearly 70 percent), and a middle class with incomes in between (25 to 30 percent).

Differences in income affected every aspect of urban life. Very poor families, including almost all new immigrants, worked at unreliable unskilled labor, lived in cheap rented housing, moved frequently, and depended on more than one income to survive. Artisans and skilled workers with incomes of $500 or more could live adequately, though often in cramped quarters that also served as their shops. Middle-class life was comfortable if a family earned more than $1,000 a year. Then it could afford a larger house of four to six rooms complete with carpeting, wallpaper, and good furniture. The very rich built mansions and large town houses and staffed them with many servants. In the summer they left the cities for country estates or homes at seaside resorts such as Newport, Rhode Island, which attracted wealthy families from all over the country.

Sanitation and Living Patterns

Early-nineteenth-century cities lacked municipal water supplies, sewers, and garbage collection. People drank water from wells, used outdoor privies, and threw garbage and slop out the door, where they were foraged by roaming herds of pigs. Clearly, this was a recipe for disease, and every American city suffered epidemics of sanitation-related diseases such as yellow fever, cholera, and typhus. Philadelphia's yellow fever epidemic of 1793 caused 4,000 deaths and stopped all business with the outside world for over a month.

Yet the cities were slow to take action. In response to the yellow fever epidemic Philadelphia completed a city water system in 1801, but it was not free of charge, and only the richest subscribed in the early days. Neither New York nor Boston had public water systems until the 1840s. Garbage collection remained a private service, and cities charged property owners for the costs of sewers, water mains, and street paving. Poorer areas of the cities could not afford the new sanitation costs.

Provision of municipal services became a powerful force for residential segregation. Richer people clustered in neighborhoods having the new amenities, or escaped to the new suburbs (in New York, one could commute to and from rural Brooklyn by ferry as early as 1814). One of New York's first wealthy areas, Gramercy Park, was developed in 1831 by a speculator who transformed Gramercy Farm into "an ornamental private square or park, with carriageways and footwalks." Only purchasers of the surrounding lots had keys to the park; everyone else was excluded.

Increasingly, the poor gathered in bad neighborhoods — slums. The worst New York slum was Five Points, a stone's throw from City Hall. There, immigrants, free black people, and criminals were crammed into rundown buildings known in the

The New York slum area of Five Points was a dangerous place, frequented by immigrants, the poor, and criminals. Its very existence, only a few blocks from City Hall, was a frightening reminder to New Yorkers of the pressures and inequities that accompanied the city's rapid growth. The style of this illustration stresses the crowded, disreputable nature of the place.

slang of the time as *rookeries.* Notorious gangs of thieves and pickpockets with names such as the Plug Uglies and the Shirt Tails dominated the district. Starvation and murder were commonplace.

Five Points was grim even in comparison with the notorious slums of London. As knowledgeable an Englishman as the author Charles Dickens exclaimed upon viewing the district in 1842, "All that is loathsome, drooping and decayed is here." Speaking specifically of the free black people in Five Points, Dickens went on to say, "Where dogs would howl to lie, women, and men and boys slink off to sleep, forcing the dislodged rats to move away in quest of better lodgings." After 1830, when urban growth was augmented by increasing immigration from Europe, slums were perceived by middle-class Americans as the home of strange and alien peoples who deserved less than native-born Americans. In this way, residential patterns came to embody larger issues of class and citizenship in American life.

Civic Order

Alexis de Tocqueville, the famous French observer who wrote *Democracy in America,* visited the United States in 1831–32 and found much to admire. But, he wrote with foreboding, "I look upon the size of certain American cities, and especially on the nature of their population, as a real danger." Here was an expression of a new fear in American urban life—concern about civic order.

As cities grew, traditions of lower-class amusement that dated back to colonial times began to seem menacing to members of the middle class. New York City's tradition of New Year's Eve "frolics," in which laborers, apprentices, and other members of the lower classes paraded through the streets playing drums, trumpets, whistles, and other noisemakers was just such an example. Like Mardi Gras celebrations, the New Year's Eve parades were dominated by the lower classes—a deliberate and recognized inversion of the usual social order. By the 1820s, however, the revelry had been taken over by gangs of lower-class young workers who called themselves the Callithumpian Band. On New Year's Eve 1828 the band, 4,000 strong and equipped with drums, tin kettles, rattles, horns, and whistles, marched through the city. On their way they overturned carts and broke windows in the commercial district, in some wealthy homes near Battery Park, and in a black church. They then marched to the City Hotel, where middle-class couples were just leaving a ball, and obstructed traffic. The indignant couples watched helplessly as several hundred watchmen called to disperse the mob wisely declined to do so.

The prosperous classes were frightened by the urban poor and by working-class rowdyism. They resented having to avoid many parts of the city that were unsafe for them, and they disliked even more the disturbances in "their" parts of the city. In colonial days, civic disturbances had been handled informally: Members of the city watch asked onlookers for such assistance as was necessary to keep the peace. Clearly that approach was not feasible when the number to be kept peaceful were the 4,000 members of the Callithumpian Band!

New York City's first response in the 1820s and 1830s to concerns about civic order was to hire more city watchmen, and to augment them with constables and marshals. But problems continued, as this irritable notation in the diary of merchant Philip Hone indicates:

> Riot, disorder, and violence increase in our city, every night is marked by some outrage committed by gangs of young ruffians who prowl the streets insulting females, breaking into the houses of unoffending publicans [tavern keepers], making night hideous by yells of disgusting inebriety, and—unchecked by the city authorities—committing every sort of enormity with apparent impunity.

Finally, in 1845 a city police force was created with a clear mandate to keep the poor in order. Here was an indication that earlier notions of a harmonious urban community had broken down.

But the pressures of rapid urbanization, immigration, and the Market Revolution proved to be more than America's cities could contain, even with police forces. Beginning in the 1830s, a series of urban riots broke out against the two poorest urban groups: Catholics and free black people. As if their miserable living conditions were not enough, Irish immigrants were met with virulent anti-Catholicism. In 1834 rioters burned an Ursuline convent in Charlestown, Massachusetts; in 1844 a Philadelphia mob attacked priests and nuns and vandalized Catholic churches; in 1854 a mob destroyed an Irish neighborhood in Lawrence, Massachusetts. But the most common targets of urban violence were free African Americans.

Free Black People

By 1860, there were nearly half a million free people of color in the United States, constituting about 11 percent of the total black population. Some 225,000 lived in the North, mostly in cities, where they competed with immigrants and native-born poor white people for jobs as day laborers and domestic servants. Philadelphia and New York had the largest black communities: 22,000 African Americans in

Philadelphia and 12,500 in New York (another 4,313 lived just across the East River in Brooklyn). The bulk of northern free black people (131,272) lived in the Middle Atlantic states of New York, Pennsylvania, and New Jersey and in the Old Northwest (63,699, more than half of them in Ohio). There were much smaller but still significant black communities in the New England cities of Boston, Providence, and New Haven. The poor position of free black people in the North is suggested by Boston figures from the 1850s: Per capita wealth of blacks was $91 and that of immigrant Irish $131, compared with the Boston-wide figure of $872.

Free black people in northern cities faced residential segregation (except for the domestic servants who lived in with white families), pervasive job discrimination, segregated public schools, and severe limitations on their civil rights. In addition to these legal restrictions there were matters of custom: African Americans of all economic classes endured daily affronts, such as exclusion from public concerts, lectures, and libraries and segregation or exclusion from public transportation. For example, in Massachusetts the famed black abolitionist Frederick Douglass was denied admission to a zoo on Boston Common, a public lecture and revival meeting, a restaurant, and a public omnibus, all within the space of a few days. And Massachusetts had the reputation of being more hospitable to black people than any other northern state!

African Americans found that community support was necessary for survival. They formed associations for aiding the poorest members of the community, for self-improvement, and for socializing. Black communities, tired of being insulted by the white press, supported their own newspapers (*Freedom's Journal,* which began publication in New York City in 1827, was the first). But the major community organization was the black Baptist or African Methodist Episcopal (AME) church, which served, as one historian put it, as "a place of worship, a social and cultural center, a political meeting place, a hiding place for fugitives, a training ground for potential community leaders, and one of the few places where blacks could express their true feelings."

Employment prospects for black men deteriorated from 1820 to 1850. Free black men who had held jobs as skilled artisans were forced from their positions, and their sons denied apprenticeships, by white mechanics and craftsmen who were themselves hurt by industrialization (see Chapter 12).

Free African Americans suffered many forms of discrimination, but as this 1850 daguerreotype of an unknown woman shows, they sought to achieve the same levels of education and economic comfort as other Americans.

Limited to day labor, African Americans found themselves in direct competition with the new immigrants, especially the Irish, for jobs. One of the major areas of competition was the waterfront, where black men lost their jobs as longshoremen and carters to the Irish. One of the few occupations still open was that of seaman. Perhaps half of all American sailors in 1850 were black. Over the years the ranks of black seamen included an increasing number of runaway slaves. The pay was poor and the conditions miserable, but many black men found more equality aboard ship than they did ashore. Mothers, wives, and daughters were left ashore to work as domestic servants (in competition with Irishwomen), washerwomen, and seamstresses.

Free African Americans were a frequent target of urban violence. An 1829 riot in Cincinnati sent a thousand black people fleeing to Canada in fear for their lives; a three-day riot in Providence in 1831 destroyed a black district; and an 1834 New York riot destroyed a church, a school, and a dozen homes.

Philadelphia, the "City of Brotherly Love," had the worst record. Home to the largest free black community in the North, Philadelphia was repeatedly rocked by antiblack riots in the period 1820–49. A riot in 1834 destroyed two churches and thirty-one homes; one African American was killed and many injured. In 1842, a predominatly Irish mob attacked black marchers celebrating Jamaican Emancipation Day. The marchers counterattacked, wounding three Irish boys and provoking widespread arson, which firemen refused to put out for fear of the mob. The Irish rioters then repulsed a sheriff's posse, and the disturbance ended only when the mayor called out seven companies of the militia. Other cities had similar stories. Failure to deal with urban tensions was costly in terms of human life: By 1840 more than 125 people had died, by 1860 more than 1,000.

Changes in Urban Politics

In eighteenth-century cities, rich and poor had lived side by side. Merchants lived next door to their businesses, and they rubbed elbows daily with their employees and with artisans and laborers whom they encountered on the busy city streets and in public places. The wealthy enjoyed unquestioned authority: Merchants sat on the city council, which had broad powers to regulate the public markets, to set prices for basic foodstuffs, to grant licenses to artisans and traders, and to encourage community harmony. The same wealthy men organized charity and relief for the poor in hard times, often walking door to door in their neighborhood to solicit donations. Wealthy men were active in neighborhood volunteer fire departments and in the volunteer watch societies that prevented crime and kept neighborhood order. When larger disturbances such as bread riots broke out, the mayor and other city officials were expected to appear and disperse the mob by force of their own authority. This personal method of governing did not work in the vastly expanded cities of the 1800s.

Universal white manhood suffrage and the development of mass politics (described in Chapter 10), coupled with the rapid growth of cities, changed urban politics. The traditional leadership role of the wealthy elite waned. Members of the wealthiest class gradually withdrew from direct participation in urban politics. In New York City, elite political leaders had disappeared by 1845. In their place were professional politicians from the middle class whose job it was to make party politics work. In New York

and in other large cities, this change in politics was spurred by working-class activism.

The Labor Movement and Urban Politics

As we saw in Chapter 12, the Market Revolution caused profound dislocations in the working life of artisans and apprentices. There was no safety net for workers who lost their jobs — no unemployment insurance or welfare — and no public regulation of wages and conditions of work. The first protests against these harsh conditions came from the women workers at the new cotton textile factories in Lowell and elsewhere. Soon, however, urban workers began a labor movement that helped shape a new kind of urban politics.

The Tradition of Artisanal Politics

The nation's urban centers had long been strongholds of craft associations for artisans and skilled workers. These organizations, and their parades and celebrations, were recognized parts of the urban community. Groups of master craftsmen marching in community parades with signs such as "By Hammer and Hand All Arts Do Stand" were visible symbols of the strength and solidarity of workers' organizations.

Also traditional were riots and demonstrations by workers (usually journeymen or apprentices, not the master artisans themselves) over matters as highly political as the American Revolution or as practical and immediate as the price of bread. In fact, protests by urban workers had been an integral part of the older social order controlled by the wealthy elite. In the eighteenth century, when only men of property could vote, demonstrations usually indicated widespread discontent or economic difficulty among workers. They served as a warning signal that the political elite rarely ignored.

By the 1830s, the status of artisans and independent craftsmen in the nation's cities had changed. Undercut by competition from other cities (the result of the transportation revolution) and by the growth of the putting-out system, the artisanal system was crumbling. Workers' associations changed as well. They came to include defensive and angry workers who were acutely conscious of their declining status in the economic and social order. Tentatively at first, but then with growing conviction, they became active defenders of working-class interests.

This seal of the General Society of Mechanics and Tradesmen illustrates in its motto — "By Hammer and Hand all Arts do Stand" — the personal and community pride artisanal workers took in their work.

What was new was the open antagonism between workers and employers — between, for example, the master craftsman and his journeymen and apprentices. The community of interest between master and workers in preindustrial times broke down. Workers quickly came to see that they must turn to other workers, not to employers, for support. In their turn, employers and members of the middle class began to take alarm at urban disorders that their grandfathers might have viewed as perfectly ordinary.

The Union Movement

Urban worker protest against changing conditions quickly took the form of party politics. The Workingmen's party began in Philadelphia in 1827 and quickly spread to New York and Boston. Using the language of class warfare — "two distinct classes . . . those that live by their own labor and they that live upon the labor of others" — the "Workies" campaigned for the ten-hour day and the preservation of the small artisanal shop. They also called for the end of government-chartered monopolies, of which banks were high on the list, and for a public school system and cheap land in the West. Although the "Workies" themselves did not survive as a party, Jacksonian Democrats were quick to pick up on some of their themes. The Democrats attracted a number of workers' votes in 1832, the year Jackson campaigned against the "monster" Bank of the United States.

Both major parties competed for the votes of urban workers. In New York City in 1835 a radical antimonopoly branch of the Democratic party attracted some worker support. Officially known as the Equal Rights party, the group was popularly called the Locofocos, after the name for the matches they struck at their first evening meeting. For their part, the Whigs wooed workers by assuring them that Henry Clay's American System, and tariff protection in particular, would be good for the economy and for workers' jobs. Nevertheless, neither major political party really spoke to the primary need of workers — well-paid, stable jobs.

Between 1833 and 1837 a wave of strikes in New York City cut the remaining ties between master craftsmen and the journeymen who worked for them. In 1833, journeymen carpenters struck for higher wages. Workers in fifteen other trades came to their support, and within a month the strike was won. The lesson was obvious: If skilled workers banded together across craft lines, they could improve their conditions. The same year, representatives from nine different craft groups formed the General Trades Union of New York. By 1834 similar groups had sprung up in over a dozen cities — Boston, Louisville, and Cincinnati among them. In New York alone, the GTU helped organize almost forty strikes between 1833 and 1837, as well as encouraging the formation of over fifty unions. Also in 1834, representatives of several GTUs met in Baltimore and organized the National Trades Union. In its founding statement the NTU criticized the "unjustifiable distribution of the wealth of society in the hands of a few individuals," which had created for working people "a humiliating, servile dependency, incompatible with . . . natural equality."

Naturally, employers disagreed with the NTU's criticism of the economic system. Convinced that unions were dangerous, New York employers took striking journeymen tailors to court in 1836. Judge Ogden Edwards pronounced the strikers guilty of conspiracy and declared unions un-American. He assured the strikers that "the road of advancement is open to all" and that they would do better to strive to be masters themselves rather than "conspire" with their fellow workers. The GTU responded with a mass rally at which Judge Edwards was burned in effigy. A year later, stunned by the effects of the panic of 1837, the GTU collapsed. These general unions, a visible sign of a class-based community of interest among workers, are generally considered to mark the beginning of the American labor movement. Unfortunately, they included only white men in skilled trades; men in unskilled occupations, all free blacks, and all women were excluded.

The Ten-Hour-Day Movement

The length of the working day, a key issue for the Workingmen's party, reflected the growing gap between workers and the new middle class. Although the workday in the artisanal shop was long, the pace was usually unhurried and there were frequent opportunities for socializing among master, journeymen, and apprentices. In the new mills and industrial workplaces, absentee owners imposed a twelve-hour day, carefully regulated by clock and factory bell, and a rapid and constant work pace. As we saw in Chapter 12, "factory time" was for workers one of the most difficult challenges of the new industrial system.

In 1825 a group of Boston carpenters demanded a ten-hour day. Owners refused, claiming their workers would take up "many temptations and improvident practices" if they were allowed more leisure time! In spite of owner hostility, workers continued to strike and "turn out" for the ten-hour day throughout the 1830s. Finally they won a partial victory: In March of 1840, just as he was leaving office, President Martin Van Buren issued an executive order granting the ten-hour day to all government employees engaged in manual labor. Many skilled workers in private industry (carpenters, mechanics, shipbuilders) soon forced their employers to grant them similar hours. This was the first time that a group of workers had obtained legislation improving their working conditions. Could the tex-

tile mills, which relied mostly on unskilled labor, be forced to follow suit?

In the early 1840s, skilled male factory workers (mechanics and weavers) formed the New England Working Men's Association to force the issue of the ten-hour day in the textile mills. In 1845, female workers did the same, forming the first chapter of the New England Female Labor Reform Association in Lowell. The chapter soon had over 400 members, and other chapters sprang up in mill towns such as Fall River, Massachusetts, and Dover, Nashua, and Manchester, New Hampshire. The Lowell chapter, led by Sarah Bagley, organized a major petition drive on behalf of the ten-hour day and submitted the results to the Massachusetts legislature. When the legislature ignored the petitions on the grounds that many of the signers were female (and thus not voters), Bagley broke with customary notions of female propriety and addressed the legislature herself, the second woman ever to do so (the first was the abolitionist Angelina Grimké). Bagley challenged the legislature directly:

> For the last half century, it has been deemed a violation of woman's sphere to appear before the public as a speaker: but when our rights are trampled upon and we appeal in vain to our legislator, what are we to do? . . . Shall not our voice be heard . . . shall it be [said] to the daughters of New England that they have not political rights?

The answer seemed to be yes, for the legislature ignored the ten-hour-day movement, even in the face of another petition drive in 1846 that yielded more than 10,000 signatures statewide, including over 4,000 from Lowell "girls." But a similar movement in New Hampshire, which included the refusal of Nashua women workers to work after "lighting up" (that is, after dark), was successful. In 1847 New Hampshire passed the nation's first ten-hour-day law. Maine followed in 1848 and Pennsylvania in 1849. In the meantime, however, the militant movement in Lowell collapsed. Its leaders, including the determined Sarah Bagley, are only now beginning to emerge from historical obscurity.

Big-City Machines

Although workers were unable to create strong unions or stable political parties that spoke for their economic interests, the competition for their votes shaped urban politics. As America's cities experienced unprecedented growth, the electorate mushroomed. In New York, for example, the number of voters grew from 20,000 in 1825 to 88,900 in 1855.

This 1837 cartoon, "The Death of Old Tammany and His Wife, Loco Foco," celebrates a local Whig triumph over Tammany, which was affiliated with the national Democratic party. In the cartoon Tammany is represented by an Indian, and the radical workers' Locofoco group is shown as an Irishwoman. Reformers were quick to apply negative ethnic stereotypes to their opponents.

Furthermore, by 1855 half of the voters were foreign-born. The job of serving this electorate and making the new mass political party work at the urban level fell to a new kind of career politician and a new kind of political organization.

In New York, the Tammany Society, begun in the 1780s as a fraternal organization of artisans, slowly evolved into the political center of the new mass politics. (Named after the Delaware chief described in Chapter 3, the society met in a hall called the Wigwam and elected "sachems" as their officers.) To reach the voters Tammany, which was affiliated with the national Democratic party, used many of the techniques of mass appeal made popular by craft organizations — parades, rallies, current songs, and party newspapers.

Along with the new techniques of mass appeal went new methods of organization: a tight system of political control beginning with neighborhood ward committees and topped by a chairman of a citywide general committee. At the citywide level, ward leaders bartered the loyalty and votes of their followers for positions on the city payroll for party members and community services for their neighborhood.

Just as the old system of elite leadership had mirrored the social unity of eighteenth-century cities, so the new system of ward politics reflected the increasing economic and social diversity of the rapidly growing nineteenth-century cities. Feelings of community, which had arisen naturally out of the personal contact that characterized neighborhoods in earlier, smaller cities, now had to be cultivated politically. In America's big cities the result was apparent by midcentury: the political "machine" controlled by the "boss" — the politician who represented the interests of his group and delivered their votes in exchange for patronage and favors. Machine politics served to mediate increasing class divisions and ethnic diversity. The machines themselves offered personal ties and loyalties — community feeling — to recent arrivals in the big cities (increasingly, immigrants from Europe).

Critics claimed that urban career politicians cared more about power than principle, and more about winning the next election than anything else. Furthermore, critics said, big-city machines were corrupt. Antagonism between reformers, who were usually members of the upper and middle classes, and machine politicians, who spoke for the working class, was evident by the 1850s. This antagonism was to become chronic in American urban politics.

SOCIAL REFORM MOVEMENTS

The problems of America's urban centers, though slow to be solved, were not ignored. The passion for "improvement" that was such an important part of the new middle-class thinking was focused on the nation's cities. Indeed it seemed that most middle-class Americans shared a belief in progress and in the perfectibility of individuals as well as society, and that a great number of them were active members of associations devoted to social reform. The widespread movements engendered by these organizations made the period 1825–45 one of the most vibrant in American history.

As illustrated by the Seneca Falls reform community described in the chapter introduction, the first response to the dislocations caused by the Market Revolution was local and voluntary. Associations of people who believed in individual reform tried to deal with the major social changes of the day. The reform message, begun by word of mouth, was vastly amplified by inventions such as the steam printing press, which made mass publication possible. Soon there were national networks of reform groups.

Alexis de Tocqueville remarked upon the vast extent of voluntary associations and their many purposes: "In no country in the world," he noted, "has the principle of association been more successfully used, or more unsparingly applied to a multitude of different objects, than in America." The widespread reform movements of the era depended on the energy and hope of communities of like-minded people.

Evangelism, Reform, and Social Control

Evangelical religion was fundamental to social reform. The Second Great Awakening, which began in the 1790s, spread to the North in the 1820s in a wave of urban revivals (see Chapter 12). Men and women who had been converted to the enthusiastic new faith assumed personal responsibility for making changes in their own lives. It was only a short step from reforming their own behavior to reforming society as a whole. These converts were encouraged in their social activism by such leading revivalists as Charles Finney. (See Chapter 12.) Finney preached a doctrine of "perfectionism," claiming it was possible for all Christians to personally understand and live by God's will and thereby become "as perfect as God." Furthermore, Finney predicted, "the complete reformation of the whole world" could be achieved if only enough converts put their efforts into moral reform. This new religious feeling was intensely hopeful: Members of evangelistic religions really did expect to convert the world and create the perfect moral and religious community on earth.

Much of America was swept by the fervor of moralistic reform, whether through appeals to individual conscience in revivals such as Finney's or by aggressive charity work. The agenda for reform was set by the new middle class, which applied new notions of morality to the movement.

The reforms all shared certain characteristics that were related to the social changes of the time. First of all, they arose from the recognition that the traditional methods of small-scale local relief were no longer adequate. In colonial times, families (sometimes at the request of local government) had housed and cared for the ill or incapacitated. Small local almshouses and prisons had housed the poor and the criminal. Reformers now realized that large cities had to make large-scale provisions for social misfits, and that institutional rather than private efforts were needed. This thinking was especially true of the institutional reform movements that began in the 1830s, such as the push for insane asylums.

A second aspect of reform efforts was a belief in the basic goodness of human nature. All reformers believed that the unfortunate — the poor, the insane, the criminal — would be reformed, or at least improved, in a good environment. Thus insane asylums were built in rural areas, away from the noise and stress of the cities, and orphanages had strict rules that were meant to encourage discipline and self-reliance. Prison reform carried this sentiment to the extreme. On the theory that bad social influences were largely responsible for crime, some "model" prisons completely isolated prisoners from one another, making them eat, sleep, work, and do their required Bible reading in their own cells. The failure of these prisons to achieve dramatic changes in their inmates (a number of isolated prisoners went mad, and some committed suicide) or to reduce the incidence of crime was one of the first indications that perhaps reform was not so simple after all!

A third characteristic of the reform movements was their moralistic dogmatism. Reformers knew what was right, and were determined to see their improvements enacted. As one historian has recently remarked, it is a very short step from individual self-discipline to imposing control on others. These reforms, then, were measures of *social control.* Lazy, sinful, intemperate, or unfit members of society were to be reformed for their own good, whether they wanted to be or not. This attitude was bound to cause controversy; by no means were all Americans members of reform groups, nor did many take kindly to being objects of reform.

Indeed, some aspects of the social reform movements were harmful. The intense religious feeling of the revival movement helped to foster the hostility experienced by Catholic immigrants from Ireland and Germany beginning in the 1830s. The temperance movement targeted immigrants whose drinking habits were freer than those of most older inhabitants. In these and other examples, reformers wished to enforce uniformity of behavior rather than tolerance. Thus social reform helped to foster the virulent nativism of American politics in the period 1840–60 (see Chapter 15).

The extent of reform efforts was unprecedented. Regional and national organizations quickly grew from local efforts to deal with social problems such as drinking, prostitution, mental illness, and crime. As one example, in 1828 Congregationalist minister Lyman Beecher joined other ministers in forming a General Union for Promoting the Observance of the Christian Sabbath; the aim was to prevent business on Sundays. To achieve its goals, the General Union adopted the same methods used by political parties: lobbying, petition drives, fundraising, and special publications. This and other efforts, Beecher said, were all for the purpose of establishing "the moral government of God."

In effect, the sabbath reformers engaged in political action but remained aloof from direct electoral politics, stressing their religious mission. In any case, their goal was controversial. Workingmen (who usually worked six days a week) were angered when the General Union forced the Sunday closure of their favorite taverns, and were quick to vote against the Whigs, the party most sympathetic to reform thinking. Other reforms likewise muddied the distinction between political and social activity. It is not surprising that women, who were barred from electoral politics but not from moral and social activism, were major supporters of reform.

Education and Women Teachers

Through their churches, women were deeply involved in reform efforts. Women did most of the fundraising for the Home Missionary Societies that were beginning to send the evangelical message worldwide — at first by ministers alone, later by married couples. Nearly every church had a Maternal Association, where mothers gathered to discuss ways to raise their children as true Christians. The efforts of these women were evidence of a new and more positive definition of childhood. The Puritans had believed that children were born sinful, and that their wills had to be broken before they could become godly. Early schools reflected these beliefs: teaching was by rote, and punishment was harsh and physical. Educational reformers, however,

Catharine Beecher, a member of one of America's leading families of religious reformers, advocated teaching as a suitable employment for young single women because it called for the nurturing skills and moral values she claimed all women possessed.

tended to believe that children were born innocent and needed gentle nurturing and encouragement if they were to flourish. At home, mothers began to play the central role in child rearing. Outside the home, women helped spread the new public education pioneered by Horace Mann, secretary of the Massachusetts State Board of Education.

Although literacy had long been valued, especially in New England, schooling since colonial times had been a private enterprise and a personal expense. (Town grammar schools, required in Massachusetts since 1647, had been supported primarily by parents' payments, with some help from local property taxes.) In 1827, Massachusetts pioneered compulsory education by legislating that public schools be supported by public taxes. Soon schooling for white children between the ages of five and nineteen was common (although, especially in rural schools, the term might be only a month or so long). Uniformity in curriculum and teacher training, and the grading of classes by ability — measures pioneered by Horace Mann in the 1830s — quickly caught on in other states. In the North and West (the South lagged far behind), more and more children went to school, and more and more teachers, usually young single women, were hired to teach them.

The spread of public education created the first real career opportunity for women. Horace Mann insisted that to learn well children needed schools with a pleasant and friendly atmosphere. One important way to achieve that atmosphere, Mann recommended, was to group children by ages rather than combining everyone in the traditional ungraded classroom, and to pay special attention to the needs of the youngest pupils. Who could better create the friendly atmosphere of the new classroom than women? The great champion of teacher training for women was Catherine Beecher, daughter of Lyman, who clearly saw her efforts as part of the larger work of establishing "the moral government of God." Arguing that women's moral and nurturing nature ideally suited them to be teachers, Beecher campaigned tirelessly on their behalf. Since "the mind is to be guided chiefly by means of the affections," she argued, "is not *woman* best fitted to accomplish these important objects?" By 1850 women dominated primary school teaching, which had come to be regarded as an acceptable occupation for educated young women during the few years between their own schooling and marriage. For some women, teaching was a great adventure: They enthusiastically volunteered to be "schoolmarms" on the distant western frontiers of Wisconsin and Iowa. Still others thought globally: The

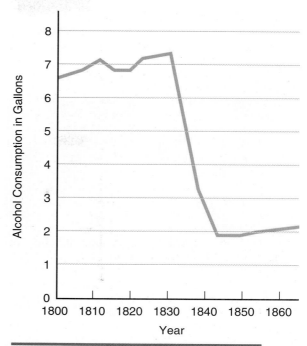

Alcohol Consumption per Capita, 1800–1860
The underlying cause for the dramatic fall in alcohol consumption during the 1830s was the changing nature of work due to the Market Revolution (discussed in Chapter 12). Contributing factors were the shock of the Panic of 1837 and the untiring efforts of temperance reformers.

Source: W. J. Rorabaugh, *The Alcoholic Republic: An American Tradition* (New York: Oxford University Press, 1979).

young women who attended Mary Lyon's Mount Holyoke College in Massachusetts (founded in 1837) hoped to be missionary teachers in distant lands. For other teachers, a few years of teaching was quite enough. Low pay (half of what male schoolteachers earned) and community supervision (the teacher had to board with parents) were probably enough to make almost any marriage proposal look appealing.

Temperance

Reformers believed not only that children could be molded, but that adults could change. The largest reform organization of the period, the American Temperance Society, boasted over 200,000 members in the mid-1830s. Dominated by evangelicals, local chapters used revival methods: massive publication of lurid temperance tracts detailing the evils of alcohol; large prayer meetings; singing; and heavy group pressure to encourage young men to stand up, confess their bad habits, and "take the

The DRUNKARD'S PROGRESS,

OR THE DIRECT ROAD TO POVERTY, WRETCHEDNESS & RUIN.

Designed and Published by J.W.Barber, NewHaven Co. Sept 1826.

The MORNING DRAM.

The GROG SHOP.

The CONFIRMED DRUNKARD.

CONCLUDING SCENE.

Temperance tracts, produced in the hundreds of thousands, painted lurid pictures of the perils of alcohol. Both melodramatic stories of ruin and cartoons like this, "The Drunkard's Progress," spread the temperance message in popular, easily-understood forms.

pledge" (not to drink). Here again, women played an important part.

Excessive drinking was a national problem, and it appears to have been mostly a masculine one, for respectable women did not drink in public. (Many did, however, drink alcohol-based patent medicines. Lydia Pinkham's Vegetable Compound, marketed for "female complaints," was 19 percent alcohol.) Men drank hard liquor — whiskey, rum, and hard cider — in abundance. Drinking was a basic part of American social life. It concluded occasions as formal as the signing of a contract and accompanied such informal activities as card games. And as we have seen, it was a staple offering at political speeches, rallies, and elections. In the old artisanal workshops, drinking had been a customary pastime. Much of the drinking was well within the bounds of sociability, but the widespread use (upwards of five gallons of hard liquor per capita in 1830 — more than twice as much as today's rate) must have encouraged some to partake in excess.

There were a number of reasons to support temperance. Heavy-drinking men hurt their families economically by spending their wages on drink.

Women had no recourse: The laws of the time gave men complete financial control of the household, and divorce was difficult as well as socially unacceptable. Excessive drinking also led to violence and crime, both within and without the family.

But there were other reasons as well. The new middle class, preoccupied with respectability and morality, found the old easygoing drinking ways unacceptable. As work patterns changed, employers banned alcohol at work and increasingly suspected drinking men of unreliability. Temperance became a social and political issue. Whigs, who embraced the new morality, favored it; Democrats (who in northern cities consisted increasingly of immigrant workers) were opposed.

The panic of 1837 affected the temperance movement. Whereas most temperance crusaders in the 1820s had been members of the middle class, the long recession of 1837–44 prompted artisans and skilled workers to reform. Forming associations known as Washington Temperance Societies, these workers spread the word that temperance was the workingman's best chance to survive economically and maintain his independence. Their wives, gathered together in Martha Washington Societies, were often even more committed to temperance than their husbands. While the men's temperance groups were often deeply involved in working-class politics, the women's groups stressed the harm that alcoholism could do to homes and families and provided financial help to distressed women and children.

Campaigns against alcohol were frequent — and successful. By the mid-1840s alcohol consumption had been more than halved, to less than two gallons per capita, about the level of today. Concern over drinking was constant throughout the nineteenth century and on into the twentieth. In the 1870s the Women's Christian Temperance Union, a powerful and increasingly political reform group, joined with other groups to pass *local option* laws. The movement achieved national success in 1919 with the Eighteenth Amendment to the Constitution, which prohibited alcohol, but the amendment was abolished thirteen years later (see Chapters 21 and 23).

Moral Reform, Asylums, and Prisons

Alcohol was not the only "social evil" reform groups attacked. Another was prostitution, which was common in the nation's port cities. The customary approach of evangelical reformers was to "rescue" prostitutes, offering them the salvation of religion, prayer, and temporary shelter. The success rate was not very high. As an alternative to prostitution, reformers usually offered domestic work, a low-paying and restrictive occupation that many women scorned. Nevertheless, campaigns against prostitution, like those against temperance, continued throughout the nineteenth century, and were generally organized by women.

One of the earliest and most effective antiprostitution groups was the Female Moral Reform Society. Founded by evangelical women in New York in 1834 (the first president was Lydia Finney), it boasted 555 affiliates throughout the country by 1840. It was surprising that so many respectable women were willing to acknowledge the existence of something so disreputable as prostitution. Even more surprising was the speed with which the societies realized the economic roots of prostitution. In addition to religious work, the societies rapidly moved to organize charity for poor women and orphans. They also took direct action against the patrons of prostitutes by printing their names in local papers, and they successfully lobbied the New York State legislature for criminal penalties against seducers as well as prostitutes.

Another dramatic example of reform was the asylum movement, spearheaded by an evangelical woman, Dorothea Dix. In 1843, after several years of investigation, Dix horrified the Massachusetts state legislature with a graphic description of the conditions of insane women, who were incarcerated with ordinary prisoners. They were locked up, she said, in "cages, closets, stalls, pens! Chained, naked, beaten with rods, and lashed into obedience!" Dix's efforts led to the establishment of a state asylum for the insane in Massachusetts, and to similar institutions in other states. Between 1843 and 1854 Dix traveled more than 30,000 miles to publicize the movement for humane treatment of the insane. By 1860 twenty-eight states had public institutions for the insane.

Other reformers were active in related causes, such as prison reform and the establishment of orphanages, homes of refuge, and hospitals. Model penitentiaries were built in Auburn and Ossining (Sing Sing), New York, and in Philadelphia and Pittsburgh. Characterized by strict order and discipline, these prisons were supposed to reform rather than simply incarcerate their inmates.

UTOPIANISM

Amidst all the political activism and reform fervor of the 1830s, a small number of people chose another route: escape into utopian communities. On the one hand, these communities were a true measure of social change, in that their experimentation with alternatives reflected their members' liberation from social constraints (never an easy thing). But they were also a sign of disillusion, in that most of the communities considered isolation from the general society essential to their survival. Since it was difficult to maintain that isolation, most utopian communities failed within a few years or modified their original goals.

The Burned-Over District
and Utopian Communities

The upstate New York area along the Erie Canal was a center for religious revivals (such as those led by Charles Finney) in the 1830s. It was also the seedbed for new religions — the Mormons and the Millerites among them — utopian communities such as John Noyes's Oneida Community, and many Shaker settlements. In fact, the area was so notable for its enthusiasms that it has been termed the Burned-Over District (referring to the waves of reform that swept through like forest fires).

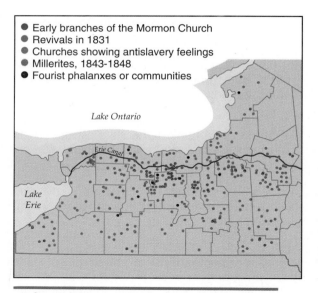

- Early branches of the Mormon Church
- Revivals in 1831
- Churches showing antislavery feelings
- Millerites, 1843-1848
- Fourist phalanxes or communities

Lake Ontario

Erie Canal

Lake Erie

Reform Movements in the Burned-Over District
The Burned-Over District, the region of New York
state most changed by the opening of the Erie Canal,
was a seedbed of religious and reform movements.
Utopian groups such as the Millerites and the Mormons had their origin there, and other sects such as
the Fourierists flourished. Charles Finney held some of
his most successful evangelical revivals in the district.
Antislavery feeling was common in the region, and the
women's rights movement began there at Seneca
Falls. Such widespread reform sentiment was rare
elsewhere; the Burned-Over District certainly deserved its nickname!

Source: Whitney Cross, *The Burned-Over District* (New York: Hippocrene Books, 1981;
orig. published 1950).

Apocalyptic religions tend to spring up at times
of rapid social change. The early nineteenth century
was such a time. A second catalyst is hard times,
and the prolonged depression that began with the
panic of 1837 led some people to embrace a belief in
imminent catastrophe. The Millerites (named for
William Miller, their founder) believed that the Second Coming of Christ would occur on October 22,
1843. In anticipation, members of the church sold
their belongings and bought white robes for their
ascension to heaven. When the Day of Judgment did
not take place as expected, most of Miller's followers drifted away. But a small group persisted. Revising their expectations, they formed the core of the
Seventh-Day Adventist faith, which is still active
today.

The Shakers, founded by "Mother" Ann Lee in
1774, were the oldest utopian group. An offshoot of
the Quakers, the Shakers espoused a radical social-
philosophy involving abolishment of the traditional
family in favor of a family of brothers and sisters
joined in equal fellowship. A basic rule of the sect
was celibacy, which meant that the faith could not
be perpetuated from within. But in the period 1820–
30, beginning from the communal center at New
Lebanon, New York, Shaker colonies multiplied,
eventually reaching twenty settlements in eight
states and a total membership of 6,000. The simple
and highly structured lifestyle, isolation from the
changing world, and the lure of equality drew new
followers, especially among women. Distinctive
Shaker crafts and furniture became well known, and
the sale of these items earned communities a
comfortable living. After 1850 new recruits declined
and the communities withered. Several communities survived into the twentieth century, however,
and a few elderly Shaker women are still alive today.

A much smaller New York settlement, the
Oneida Community, became notorious for its sexual
arrangements. The sect, founded by John Humphrey
Noyes in Vermont in 1836, moved to Oneida in 1848.
Like the Shakers, the Oneida community was one
family. But rather than celibacy they practiced
"complex marriage," a system of highly regulated
group sexual activity. Noyes carried his sexual radicalism even further by insisting that members
practice intercourse without male orgasm, thus
sparing the women frequent pregnancies. Childbearing was regulated: Only "spiritually advanced"
males (usually Noyes himself) could father children.
Children were raised communally, and work was
allocated equally. All this raised outside cries about
"free love" and "socialism," which Noyes ignored.
Eventually he built his sect to 200 members. Today
the sect is long vanished, but the name continues in
the successful Oneida Silverware company, founded
by Noyes.

New Harmony and Fourierist Phalanxes

Still other forthrightly socialist communities flourished briefly. New Harmony, founded by the famous
Scottish industrialist Robert Owen in 1824, was to be
a manufacturing community without poverty and
unemployment. The community survived only three
years; the experiment was not a success.

Faring little better were the phalanxes, huge
communal buildings structured on the socialist theories of the French thinker Charles Fourier. Fourier,
who thought there was a rational way to divide
work, suggested that children would make the best
garbage collectors because they didn't mind dirt!

The Shaker commitment to frugality and simplicity was evident in all aspects of their lives, including the chairs and tables they built for their communal homes. The beauty of Shaker crafts appealed to many outside the sect, and sales of their simple furniture provided a good income to Shaker communities. Examples of Shaker arts can be found today in major museums.

Angelina Grimké and her husband, the abolitionist orator Theodore Weld, lived for a time in a Fourierist phalanx in New Jersey. Louisa May Alcott (who later wrote *Little Women*) and her family lived at Brook Farm in Massachusetts, which had begun as a rural community of transcendentalists.

The rapid failure of these socialist communities was due largely to inadequate planning and organization. Another reason may have been, as Alcott suggested in her satire *Transcendental Wild Oats,* that the women were left to do all the work while the men philosophized. Nevertheless, it is striking that so few cooperative communities succeeded when so many voluntary organizations were flourishing.

The Mormons

The most successful of the nineteenth-century communitarian movements was also a product of the Burned-Over District. In 1830, a young man named Joseph Smith organized a church based on the teachings of The Book of Mormon, which he claimed to have received from an angel in a vision. Smith founded the Church of Jesus Christ of Latter-day Saints, popularly known as the Mormons.

Initially, Mormonism seemed little different from the many other new religious groups and utopian communities of the time. But it rapidly became distinctive because of the extraordinary communitarianism it achieved under the benevolent but absolute authority of the patriarch, Joseph Smith. Close cooperation and hard work made the Mormon community very successful, attracting both new followers and the animosity of neighbors, who resented Mormon exclusiveness and economic success. The Mormons were harassed in New York and driven west to Ohio and then Missouri. Finally they seemed to find an ideal home in Nauvoo, Illinois, where in 1839 they built a model community, achieving almost complete self-government and isolation from non-Mormon neighbors. But in 1844, dissension within the community over Joseph Smith's new doctrine of polygamy (plural wives) gave outsiders a chance to intervene. Smith and his brother were arrested peacefully, but were killed by a mob from which their jailors failed to protect them.

The beleaguered Mormon community decided to move again — this time beyond reach of harm. Led by Brigham Young, the Mormons migrated in 1846 to the Great Salt Lake in present-day Utah.

The arid Great Basin country called forth all of the Mormons' communitarian commitment, for they had to organize irrigation to make the desert bloom sufficiently to feed them all. Young and other church

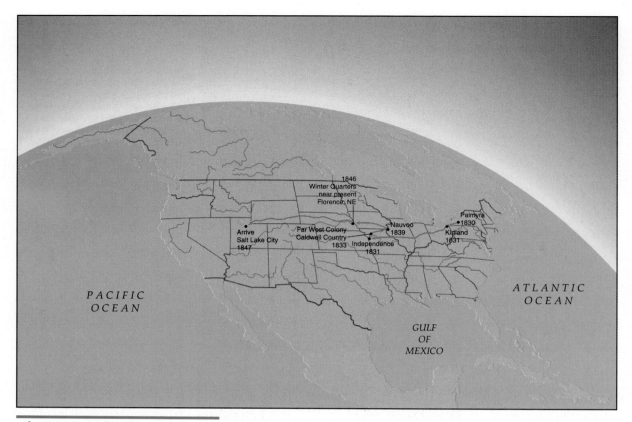

The Mormon Migration, 1830–1847
The Mormon church and community, founded by Joseph Smith in Palmyra New York in 1830, aroused intense opposition. Two early settlements, one in Kirtland, Ohio and another near Independence, Missouri, were driven out in 1838. The Mormons regrouped and prospered in Nauvoo, Illinois until the mob murder of Joseph Smith in 1844. Their escape to the West began in 1846, first to Winter Quarters, Nebraska, and finally to the desolate Great Salt Lake region of Utah, where the Mormons hoped to be free of outside interference.

elders carefully planned Salt Lake City and all subsequent Mormon communities. The land, which belonged to everyone, was allotted to men on the basis of family size (men with many wives got more land than men with only one wife). Families who didn't work the land adequately could have it taken away from them. In contrast with every other frontier, land speculation was prohibited, because the community (through the church) owned it all. Water rights were also shared, as opposed to the first-come-first-served rule observed on other frontiers. After several lean years to begin with (once, a grasshopper plague was stopped by the providential arrival of sea gulls, who ate the bugs), the Mormon method of communal settlement proved successful.

They did indeed make the desert bloom by creating one of the most extensive irrigation systems in the West.

Nevertheless, Mormon troubles were not over. The California gold rush of 1849 transformed Salt Lake City from an isolated settlement into a stopping-off point on the trail west. In doing so it destroyed Mormon hopes of building an autonomous society. Mormon separatism, and especially the doctrine of polygamy, aroused bitter opposition in other Americans. These aspects of Mormonism led to the occupation of Utah Territory by federal troops in 1857 and to the requirement that Utah abolish polygamy in order to be admitted to the Union (it obtained statehood in 1896). A degree of conformity was exacted, but to this day Utah remains a distinctively Mormon society, and the only state in the Union to have remained faithful to its utopian origins in the early nineteenth century.

ANTISLAVERY AND ABOLITIONISM

The antislavery feeling that was to play such an important role in the politics of the 1840s and 1850s also had its roots in the religious reform movement that began in the 1820s and 1830s. Three groups—the Quakers and a few slave owners, free black people, and militant white reformers—worked to bring an end to slavery, but each in different ways. Their efforts eventually turned a minor reform movement into the dominating political issue of the day.

As we have seen in previous chapters, significant antislavery measures had been taken in the early years of the republic. In 1787 antislavery advocates had secured in the Constitution a clause specifying a date after which American participation in the international slave trade could be made illegal, and Congress passed such a law in 1808. By 1800 slavery had been abolished in most northern states. In 1820 the Missouri Compromise prohibited slavery in most of the Louisiana Purchase lands. None of these measures, however, addressed the continuing reality of slavery in the South.

The American Colonization Society

The first attempt to "solve" the problem of slavery was a plan for gradual emancipation of slaves (with compensation to their owners) and their resettlement in Africa. This plan was the work of the American Colonization Society, formed in 1817 by northern religious reformers (Quakers prominent among them) and a number of southern slave owners, most from the Upper South and the border states (Kentuckian Henry Clay was a supporter). Northerners were especially eager to send the North's 250,000 free black people back to Africa, describing them, in the words of the society's 1829 report, as "notoriously ignorant, degraded and miserable, mentally diseased, [and] broken-spirited." Some northern members of the society also supported laws disenfranchising and restricting the rights of free African Americans. Southerners, for their part, favored colonization because they were worried about the potential for race war if freed

slaves remained in the South, where they made up one third of the population. The society was remarkably ineffective: By 1830, it had managed to send only 1,400 black people to a colony in Liberia, West Africa. Critics pointed out that more slaves were born in a week than the society sent back to Africa in a year.

The Black Antislavery Movement

Most free African Americans rejected colonization, insisting instead on a commitment to the immediate end of slavery and the equal treatment of black people in America. "We are *natives* of this country," a black minister in New York pointed out. Then he added bitterly, "We only ask that we be treated as well as *foreigners.*" By 1830 there were at least fifty black abolitionist societies in the North. These organizations held yearly national conventions, where famous black abolitionists such as Frederick Douglass, Harriet Tubman, and Sojourner Truth spoke. The first black newspaper, founded in 1827 by John Russwurm and Samuel Cornish, announced its antislavery position in its title, *Freedom's Journal.* Northern free black people played a major role in helping fugitive slaves and in trying to reach both free African Americans and slaves in the South with their abolitionist message.

In 1829 David Walker, a free African American in Boston, wrote a widely distributed pamphlet, *Appeal . . . to the Colored Citizens,* that encouraged slave rebellion. "We must and shall be free . . . in spite of you," Walker warned whites. "And woe, woe will be it to you if we have to obtain our freedom by fighting." White southerners blamed pamphlets such as these and the militant articles of black journalists for stirring up trouble among southern slaves. They held up the 1831 Nat Turner revolt (see Chapter 11) as a horrifying example of northern interference. The vehemence of their protests is a testament to the courage of a handful of determined free black people in speaking for all of their enslaved brothers and sisters long before most white northerners had even noticed.

Abolitionists

The third and best-known group of antislavery reformers was headed by William Lloyd Garrison. In 1831 Garrison broke with the gradualist persuaders of the American Colonization Society and began publishing his own paper, *The Liberator.* In the first

This poignant engraving of a chained female slave was made by Patrick Reason, a black artist, in 1835. The accompanying message, "Am I Not a Woman and a Sister?" spoke especially to female abolitionists in the North.

issue Garrison declared, "I am in earnest — I will not equivocate — I will not excuse — I will not retreat a single inch — AND I WILL BE HEARD." Garrison, the embodiment of moral indignation, was totally incapable of compromise. His approach was to mount a sweeping crusade condemning slavery as sinful and demanding its immediate abolishment (hence *abolitionism*). Garrison's crusade, like evangelical religion, was personal and moral. In reality, Garrison did not expect that all slaves would be freed immediately, but only that everyone should acknowledge the immorality of slavery. On the other hand, Garrison took the truly radical step of demanding full social equality for black people, referring to them individually as "a man and a brother" and "a woman and a sister." Garrison's determination electrified the antislavery movement, but his inability to compromise made him a difficult leader. After failing to convince the entire country to accept abolition, Garrison came to believe that slavery had corrupted all American institutions. He denounced the recognition of slavery in the Constitution as "a covenant with death, an agreement with Hell," and in 1854 he publicly burned a copy, announcing, "So perish all compromises with tyranny."

Garrison's moral vehemence radicalized northern antislavery religious groups. Theodore Weld, an evangelical minister, joined Garrison in 1833 in forming the American Anti-Slavery Society. The following year, Weld encouraged a group of students at Lane Theological Seminary in Cincinnati to form an antislavery society. When the seminary's president, Lyman Beecher, sought to suppress it, the students withdrew and moved en masse to Oberlin College in northern Ohio. Oberlin soon became known as the most liberal college in the country, not only for its antislavery stance but for its acceptance of black and female students as well.

Moral horror over slavery engaged a number of northerners deeply in the abolitionist movement. They flocked to hear firsthand accounts of slavery by Frederick Douglass and Sojourner Truth, and by the sisters from South Carolina, Angelina and Sarah Grimké. Northerners eagerly read slave narratives and books such as Theodore Weld's 1838 *American Slavery as It Is* (based in part on the recollections of Angelina Grimké, whom Weld had married) that provided graphic details of abuse. Lyman Beecher's daughter, Harriet Beecher Stowe, was to draw on the Grimké–Weld book for her immensely popular antislavery novel, *Uncle Tom's Cabin,* published in 1852.

The style of abolitionist writings and speeches was similar to the oratorical style of the religious revivalists. Northern abolitionists believed that a full description of the evils of slavery would force southern slave owners to confront their wrongdoing and lead to a true act of repentance — freeing their slaves. They were confrontational, denunciatory, and personal in their message, much like the evangelical preachers. Southerners regarded abolitionist attacks as libelous and abusive. Abolitionists also adopted the reform tactic of mass publishing of tracts (much used by revivalists and temperance workers) as a method of persuasion. In 1835 alone, they mailed over a million pieces of antislavery literature to southern states. This tactic also drew a backlash: Southern legislatures banned abolitionist literature, encouraged the harassment and abuse of anyone distributing it, and looked the other way when (as in South Carolina) proslavery mobs seized and burned it. As we have seen, they also prohibited the teaching of reading to slaves, so that they would be unable to read abolitionist literature. The Georgia legislature even offered a $5,000 reward to anyone who would kidnap William Lloyd Garrison and bring him to the South to stand trial for inciting rebellion. Most seriously, they passed laws impeding the emancipation of slaves, and they toughened the laws governing slave behavior. Ironically, then, the immediate impact of abolitionism in the South was to stifle dissent and make the lives of slaves harder (see Chapter 11).

Even in the North, controversy over abolitionism was frequent. Some locales were prone to violence. The Ohio Valley, settled largely by southerners, was one such place, as were northern cities experiencing the tension of urban growth, such as Philadelphia. Immigrant Irish, who found themselves pitted against free black people for jobs, were often violently antiabolitionist. The abolitionist tactic (adopted from the revivalists) of large and emotional meetings opened the door to mob action. Disruption of meetings was common, especially those addressed by Theodore Weld, whose emotional oratory earned him the title of "the most mobbed man in the United States." William Lloyd Garrison was stoned, dragged through the streets, and on one occasion almost hanged by a Boston mob. Property of leading abolitionists was destroyed by arson, and a Connecticut schoolteacher, Prudence Crandall, was forced by community pressure to close her private integrated school. In 1837, antislavery editor Elijah P. Lovejoy of Alton, Illinois, was killed and his press destroyed.

Abolitionism and Politics

Antislavery began as a social movement but soon intersected with sectional interests and became a national political issue. A massive abolitionist petition drive — nearly 700,000 petitions in all — requesting the abolition of slavery and the slave trade in the District of Columbia was rebuffed by Congress. At southern insistence and with President Andrew Jackson's approval, Congress passed a "gag rule" in 1836 that prohibited discussion of antislavery petitions.

The gag rule and censorship of the mails, which southerners saw as necessary defenses against abolitionist frenzy, were greeted differently in the North. Many people became alarmed at these threats to free speech. First among them was former president John Quincy Adams, then a congressman from Massachusetts. Adams so publicly and persistently denounced the gag rule as a violation of the constitutional right to petition, that it was repealed in 1844. Less well-known northerners, such as the thousands of women who canvassed their neighborhoods with petitions, made personal commitments to abolitionism that they did not intend to abandon.

Having raised the nation's emotional temperature, but failing to achieve the moral unity they had hoped to arouse, abolitionist groups began to splinter. One perhaps inevitable but nonetheless distressing split was between white and black abolitionists. Frederick Douglass and William Lloyd Garrison parted ways when Douglass, refusing to be limited to a simple recital of his life as a slave, began to make specific suggestions for improvements in the lives of free black people. When Douglass chose the path of political action, Garrison denounced him as "ungrateful." Douglass and other free African Americans worked under persistent discrimination, even from antislavery whites, some of whom refused to hire black people or meet with them as equals. For example, some Philadelphia Quaker meetings, though devoted to the antislavery cause, maintained segregated seating for black people in their churches. While many white reformers eagerly pressed for *civil* equality for African Americans, they did not accept the idea of *social* equality. On the other hand, black and white "stations" worked closely in the risky enterprise of passing fugitive slaves north over the famous Underground Railroad. Contrary to abolitionist legend, however, it was free black people, rather than whites, who played the major part in helping the fugitives.

Among white abolitionists, William Lloyd Garrison, not surprisingly, remained controversial, especially after 1837, when he espoused a radical program that included women's rights, pacifism, and the abolition of prisons and asylums (which other reformers were working to establish). In 1840 the abolitionist movement formally split. The majority moved toward party politics (which Garrison abhorred), founding the Liberty Party and choosing James G. Birney (whom Theodore Weld had converted to abolitionism) as their presidential candidate. Thus the abolitionist movement, which began

as an individual moral reform, took the first major step toward the eventual formation of the Republican party and the Civil War (see Chapter 15).

For one particular group of antislavery reformers, the abolitionist movement opened up new possibilities for action. Through their participation in antislavery activity, some women came to a vivid realization of the social constraints on their activism.

THE WOMEN'S RIGHTS MOVEMENT

American women, denied a vote in party politics, found a field of activity in social reform movements. There was scarcely a movement in which women were not actively involved, even if, as was fre-

The Philadelphia Anti-Slavery Society was one of the largest and best-known local chapters of the American Anti-Slavery Society, founded in 1833. The national society depended on local chapters such as this one to collect signatures for petitions (nearly 700,000 in all), to organize local abolitionist meetings, and to raise the money to print and distribute more than a million pieces of antislavery literature. The Philadelphia society was distinguished by the high percentage of Quakers among its membership, prominent among them Lucretia Mott, shown in this picture second from the right.

quently the case, men were the official leaders. Rather than accept male leadership, women often formed all-female chapters (for example, in temperance, moral reform, and abolition), which allowed them to define their own reform policies.

The majority of women, of course, did not participate in reform, for they were fully occupied with the time-consuming tasks of housekeeping and child rearing (families with five children were the average). A small number of women, usually members of the new middle class, had the time and energy (because of servants) to look beyond their immediate tasks. Women such as these, touched by the religious revival, enthusiastically joined reform movements. Sometimes, however, their commitment carried them beyond the limits of what was considered acceptable for women and led them to challenge traditional social restrictions.

The Grimké Sisters

The lives of Sarah and Angelina Grimké illustrate the point. The Grimké sisters, members of a prominent South Carolina slaveholding family, rejected slavery out of religious conviction and moved north to join a Quaker community near Philadelphia. In the 1830s, the sisters found themselves drawn into the growing antislavery agitation in the North. Because the Grimké sisters knew about slavery firsthand, they were in great demand as speakers. At first they spoke to "parlor meetings" of women only, as was considered proper. But interested men kept sneaking into the talks, and soon the sisters found themselves speaking to mixed gatherings. The meetings got larger and larger, and soon the sisters realized that they had become the first female public speakers in American history. In 1837 Angelina Grimké became the first woman to address a meeting of the Massachusetts state legislature.

Antislavery was a controversial reform of which many people disapproved, and many famous male antislavery orators were criticized by the press and by conservative ministers. The Grimké sisters were criticized because they were women. A letter from a group of ministers cited the Bible in reprimanding the sisters for stepping out of "woman's proper sphere" of silence and subordination. Sarah Grimké answered the ministers in her 1837 *Letters on the Condition of Women and the Equality of the Sexes.* She claimed that "men and women were CREATED EQUAL. . . . whatever is right for a man to do, is *right* for woman." She followed with this ringing

assertion: "I seek no favors for my sex. I surrender not our claim to equality. All I ask of our brethren is, that they will take their feet from off our necks and permit us to stand upright on that ground which God designed us to occupy."

Although this was the most dramatic incident, women in the antislavery movement found themselves continually struggling with the men to have their voices heard. Sometimes, as in the case of the Philadelphia Female Anti-Slavery Society, women solved the problem by forming their own group. Still, in the antislavery movement and other reform groups as well, men accorded women a secondary role, even when, as was frequently the case, women constituted a majority of the members.

Women's Rights

The Seneca Falls Convention of 1848, the first women's rights convention in American history, was an outgrowth of almost twenty years of female activity in social reform. Every year after 1848 women gathered to hold women's rights conventions and to work for political, legal, and social equality. Over the years, in response to persistent lobbying, states passed property laws more favorable to women and changed divorce laws. Higher education and some occupations opened up to women, and beginning with Wyoming in 1869, women could vote in some states. Nationally, female suffrage was finally enacted in 1920 in the Nineteenth Amendment to the Constitution, seventy-two years after it was first proposed at Seneca Falls.

Historians have only recently realized how much the reform movements of this "Age of the Common Man" were due to the efforts of the "common woman." Women played a vital role in all of the social movements of the day. In doing so they implicitly challenged the popular notion of separate spheres for men and women — the public world for him, home and family for her. The separate-spheres argument was meant to exclude women from political life while heaping them with praise for their allegedly superior moral qualities. The reforms discussed in this chapter show clearly that women reformers believed they had a right and a duty to propose solutions for the moral and social problems of the day. Empowered by their own religious beliefs and activism, the Seneca Falls reformers spoke for all American women when they demanded an end to the unfair restrictions they suffered as women.

CHRONOLOGY

1817	American Colonization Society founded
1820s	Shaker colonies grow
1824	New Harmony founded; fails three years later
1826	American Society for the Promotion of Temperance founded
1827	Workingmen's Party founded in Philadelphia
	Freedom's Journal begins publication
	Public school movement begun in Massachusetts
1829	Daniel Walker, *Appeal . . . to the Colored Citizens*
1830	Joseph Smith founds Church of Jesus Christ of Latter-day Saints (Mormons)
	Finney's revivals in Rochester
	Immigration increases
1831	William Lloyd Garrison begins publishing *The Liberator*
1833	American Anti-Slavery Society founded by Garrison and Weld
1834	First Female Moral Reform Society founded in New York
	National Trades Union formed
1836	Congress passes gag rule
	John Noyes founds Oneida Community
1837	Antislavery editor Elijah O. Lovejoy killed
	Angelina Grimké addresses Massachusetts legislature; Sarah Grimké, *Letters on the Condition of Women and the Equality of the Sexes*
	Panic begins seven-year recession
1840s	New York and Boston complete public water systems
1840	Liberty Party founded
	President Van Buren enacts ten-hour day for government workers
1843	Millerites await the end of the world
	Dorothea Dix spearheads asylum movement
1844	Mormon leader Joseph Smith killed by mob
1845	New England Female Labor Reform Association formed
	New York creates city police force
	Beginning of Irish Potato Famine and heavy Irish immigration
1846	Mormons begin migration to the Great Salt Lake
1848	Woman's Rights Convention at Seneca Falls

CONCLUSION

The various associations (the political party, the religious crusade, the reform movement) that sprung up in the first half of the 1800s replaced the small residential communities of an earlier period. They were new manifestations of the deep human desire for social connection and for continuity — and, especially in the growing cities, for social order. But a striking aspect of these associations was the uncompromising attitudes on which much of the politics (witness Andrew Jackson) and much of the reform efforts (witness temperance) were based. Most associations were bands of like-minded people who desired to impose their will on others. Such intolerance boded ill for the future. If political parties, religious bodies, and reform groups were to splinter along sectional lines (as happened in the 1850s), political compromise would be very difficult. In the meantime, however, the passion for improvement was directed elsewhere. As a perceptive foreign observer, Francis Grund, noted, "Americans love their country not as it is but as it will be." No area of the country seemed so full of such possibilities as the American West.

Additional Readings

ARTHUR BESTOR, *Backwoods Utopias* (1950). The standard work on utopian communities.

STUART BLUMIN, *The Emergence of the Middle Class: Social Experience in the American City, 1760–1900* (1989). A thorough and wide-ranging examination of the changing housing, workplaces, and expectations of the "middling folk" who became the urban middle class.

AMY BRIDGES, *A City in the Republic: Antebellum New York and the Origins of Machine Politics* (1984). An innovative look at the transition from deference to ward politics.

PAUL A. GILJE, *The Road to Mobocracy: Popular Disorder in New York City,* 1763–1834 (1987).

OSCAR HANDLIN, *Boston's Immigrants: A Study in Acculturation* (rev. ed., 1959). A pathbreaking exploration of conflict and adaptation among Boston's Irish community.

DANIEL WALKER HOWE, "The Evangelical Movement and Political Culture in the North during the Second Party System, in *Journal of American History* (March 1991). An award-winning article that explores the connections among religion, politics, and reform.

LEON LITWACK, *North of Slavery: The Negro in the Free States, 1790–1860* (1961). The standard source on free black people in the North.

W. J. RORABAUGH, *The Alcoholic Republic: An American Tradition* (1979). Amusingly informative.

DAVID ROTHMAN, *The Discovery of the Asylum: Social Order and Disorder in the New Republic* (1971). Explores institutional reforms.

KATHRYN SKLAR, *Catherine Beecher: A Study in American Domesticity* (1973). An absorbing "life and times" that explores the possibilities and limits of women's roles in the early nineteenth century.

RONALD G. WALTERS, *American Reformers, 1815–1860* (1978). A survey of antebellum reform, now dated because the role of women in reform is understated.

SEAN WILENTZ, *Chants Democratic: New York City and the Rise of the American Working Class, 1788–1850* (1983). An important book, rooted in social history, that reveals how workers acted upon their understanding of republicanism in confronting the changes wrought by the Market Revolution.

14 THE TERRITORIAL EXPANSION OF THE UNITED STATES, 1830s–1850s

AMERICAN COMMUNITIES

● "REMEMBER THE ALAMO!"

For thirteen days late in the winter of 1836 a force of 187 Texans held the mission fortress known as the Alamo, in San Antonio, against a siege by 5,000 Mexican troops under General Antonio López de Santa Anna, president of Mexico. Santa Anna had come north to subdue this rebellious territory and place it under central authority. On March 6 he ordered a final assault, and in brutal fighting that claimed over 1,500 Mexican lives, his army took the mission. All the defenders were killed, including Commander William Travis and the well-known leaders Jim Bowie and Davy Crockett. It was a crushing defeat, but the cry "Remember the Alamo!" rallied the Texans. Less than two months later they routed the Mexican army and forced Santa Anna to grant them independence from Mexico. The Alamo has indeed been remembered, and today is one of the most cherished historic shrines in the United States. But memory is selective; some things have been forgotten.

TEXANS AND TEJANOS FORM A COMMUNITY TO FIGHT FOR INDEPENDENCE

It has often been forgotten, for example, that the Texas uprising was an alliance between Americans and native Spanish-speaking residents who called themselves Tejanos. The Americans were concentrated in the central and eastern portions of the huge Texas territory, where during the 1820s the Mexican government had authorized several colonies managed by empresarios *(land agents) such as Stephen F. Austin. These settler communities consisted mostly of farmers from the Mississippi Valley, who introduced slavery and cotton growing to the rich lands of coastal and upland Texas. The Tejano community, descended from eighteenth-century Mexican settlers, included wealthy rancheros who raised cattle on the shortgrass prairies of south Texas, as well as the cowboys known as vaqueros and the peons, or poor tenant farmers. Although there was relatively little contact between the Americans and Tejanos, their leaders interacted at places such as San Antonio. The Tejano elite welcomed the American immigrants and were enthusiastic about their plans for the economic development of Texas. For their part, many Americans married into Tejano families. The Tejano elite hoped that by incorporating the Americans and sharing power with them, they could maintain—and indeed strengthen—their community.*

This folk-art painting shows the central plaza of San Antonio, the most important city in Texas under Spanish and Mexican rule. Culturally, it remained Spanish long after the successful American revolt against Mexico in 1836.

(William G.M. Samuel. East Side Main Plaza, San Antonio, Texas. *Oil on canvas, mounted on panel. 22 × 36". San Antonio Museum Association, on loan from Bexar County.)*

The Mexican state, however, was politically and socially unstable during these first years of its independence from Spain. Liberals favored a loose federal union, conservatives a strong central state. As a northern frontier province, Texas had never enjoyed the benefit of statehood, and thus most Tejanos found themselves taking the liberal side in the struggle. When the conservative centralists came to power in Mexico City in1828 and decided the Americans had too much influence in Texas, it was natural for many Tejanos to rise up in opposition. In 1832 the Tejano elite of San Antonio and a number of prominent rancheros went on record in favor of provincial autonomy and a strong role for the Americans.

One of the leaders of the San Antonio community was the wealthy ranchero Juan Nepomuceno Seguin. As Santa Anna's army approached from the south, he recruited a company of Tejano volunteers and joined the American force inside the walls of the Alamo. During the siege, Commander Travis sent Seguin and some of his men for reinforcements. Stopped by Mexican troops on his way across the lines, Seguin called out, "¡Somas paisanos!" ("We are countrymen.") This confused the guards long enough for Seguin and his men to make their escape through a hail of gunfire. He returned from his unsuccessful mission to find the burned bodies of the Alamo defenders, including seven Tejanos from San Antonio, who had died fighting. "Texas sera libre!" Seguin called out as he directed the burial of the Alamo defenders. "Texas shall be free!" He went on to lead a regiment of Tejanos in the Texan victory at the Battle of San Jacinto.

At first, Tejanos were pleased with postwar conditions. For one thing, they played an important political role in the new Texas republic. The liberal Lorenzo de Zavala, for example, was chosen the first vice-president. Seguin became the mayor of San Antonio. But soon things began to change. Many Americans, fired by anti-Mexican passion, suspected all Spanish-speakers of treachery. Unscrupulous men exploited these prejudices to acquire Tejano property. If the rancheros were "sufficiently scared," one wrote, they would "make an advantageous sale of their lands," and if "two or three hundred of our troops should be stationed here, I have no doubt but a man could make some good speculations." Tejanos were attacked and forced from their homes; some of their villages were burned to the ground. "On the pretext that they were Mexicans," Seguin wrote, Americans treated Tejanos "worse than brutes . . . my countrymen ran to me for protection against the assaults or exactions of these adventurers." But even in his capacity as mayor Seguin could do little. In 1842 the Seguins, like hundreds of other Tejano families, were forced to flee south to Mexico in fear for their lives.

The Spanish-speaking community in Texas (and later, those in New Mexico and California), like the communities of Indians throughout the West, became conquered peoples. "White folks and Mexicans were never made to live together," a Texas woman told a traveler a few years after the revolution. "The Mexicans had no business here," she said, and the Americans might "just have to get together and drive them all out of the country." The Tejanos had become foreigners in their native land.

The events in Texas illustrate a recurring pattern in the American occupation of the frontier — the changing relations between two cultures. Most commonly the initial stage of the relationship involved a blending of the newcomers with the native peoples. The first hunters, trappers, and traders on every American frontier — west of the Appalachians, in the Southwest, and in the Far West — married into the local community and tried to learn native ways. Outnumbered European Americans adapted to local societies as a matter of simple survival. The result was a frontier of inclusion, a racially inclusive community. A second, unstable stage occurred when the number of European Americans increased and they began settling or, as in California, "rushing" to mine gold with no intention of permanent settlement. The usual result was warfare and the rapid growth of hostility and racial prejudice — all of which was largely absent in earlier days. A third stage — that of stable settlement — occurred when the native community had been completely removed or subdued. This produced a frontier of exclusion, which was racially exclusive. Generally, when American Indians were removed to reservations, their history went with them. White settlers thus cut themselves off from sources of human history that could

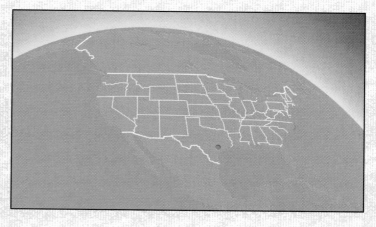

have helped them more fully understand the new country into which they had moved. Or, as in Texas, a conquered people with different cultural values — the Tejanos — survived as a symbol of a romanticized past rather than as full participants in the building of western communities.

EXPLORING THE WEST

Americans were expansionist people. By 1840 they had occupied all of the land east of the Mississippi River and organized all of it (except for Florida and Wisconsin) into states. Ten states were admitted to the Union between 1800 and 1840, three of them from west of the Mississippi (Louisiana, Missouri, and Arkansas). The majority of the U.S. population now lived west of the original thirteen states.

The speed and success of this expansion were a source of deep national pride that whetted appetites for more. Many Americans looked eagerly westward to Texas, to the vast unsettled reaches of the Louisiana Purchase, to Santa Fe and trade with Mexico, and even to the Far West, where New

Exploration of the Continent, 1804–1830

Lewis and Clark's pathbreaking "Voyage of Discovery" of 1804–06 was the first of many government-sponsored western military expeditions. Lt. Zebulon Pike crossed the Great Plains in 1806, but was captured by the Spanish in their territory and taken to Mexico. He returned in 1807 via Texas. Major Stephen Long crossed the Plains in 1820 and found them "arid and forbidding." Meanwhile fur trappers, among them the much travelled Jedidiah Smith, became well acquainted with much of the West as they searched for beaver.

The artist Alfred Jacob Miller, a careful observer of the western fur trade, shows in this sketch a mountain man and his Indian wife. They worked together to trap and prepare beaver pelts for market.

England sea captains had been trading for furs since the 1790s. By 1848 the United States had gained all of these coveted western lands. In this chapter we will look at how the United States became a continental nation, and at the kinds of frontier communities created in the process.

Before European Americans could settle the West, they had to understand its geography. Exploration took several centuries, and was the result of many individual efforts.

The Fur Trade

The fur trade, which flourished from the 1670s to the 1840s, was the greatest spur to exploration on the North American continent. In the 1670s the British Hudson's Bay Company and French Canadians based in Montreal began exploring beyond the Great Lakes in the Canadian west in search of beaver pelts. Both groups were dependent upon the goodwill and cooperation of the native peoples of the region, in particular the Assiniboins, Crees, Gros Ventres, and Blackfeet, all of whom moved freely across what later became the U.S.–Canadian border. From the marriages of European men with native women arose a distinctive mixed-race group, the métis (from the French word for "mixed"). In 1821, the Hudson's Bay Company absorbed its Montreal rival, the North West Company, and ran the fur trade from trading posts in the far Canadian north such as Norway House, Cumberland House, and Fort George. British, French Canadian, and métis employees of the Hudson's Bay Company

also trapped and explored throughout the Canadian west and in the Oregon Territory, which was jointly occupied by the British and Americans (see Chapter 9).

Not until the 1820s were American companies able to challenge British dominance of the trans-Mississippi fur trade. In 1824, William Henry Ashley of the Rocky Mountain Fur Company instituted the rendezvous system. This was a yearly trade fair, deep in the Rocky Mountains (Green River and Jackson Hole were favored locations), to which trappers brought their catch of furs. There they traded them for goods transported by the fur companies from St. Louis: traps, guns, ammunition, tobacco, beads and fabrics for the Indian trade — and alcohol. The yearly fur rendezvous were modeled on Indian trade gatherings such as the huge gathering at Celilo Falls on the Columbia River, which took place at the height of the annual salmon run. Like its Indian model, the fur rendezvous was a boisterous, polyglot, many-day affair at which trappers of many nationalities — European Americans and Indian peoples, French Canadians and métis, as well as Mexicans from Santa Fe and Taos — gathered to trade, drink, and gamble.

For the "mountain men" employed by the American fur companies, the rendezvous was their only contact with "civilization." The rest of the year they spent deep in the mountains trapping beaver and living in some sort of relationship with local Indian peoples. Some lived in a constant state of danger, always alert to the possibility of attack by parties of local people. But most trappers sought accommodation and friendship: more than 40 percent married Indian women, who not only helped in the trapping and curing of furs but also acted as vital diplomatic links between the white and Indian-worlds. Contemporaries often viewed the mountain men — tough, bearded, leather-clad, fluent in Indian tongues — as half savage, but we might better see them as an example of successful adaptation to frontier life. Indeed, legendary trappers such as the African American Jim Beckwourth married a Crow woman and later was accepted as a chief in her tribe.

For all its adventure, the American fur trade was short-lived. By the 1840s, the beaver in western streams were virtually trapped out. The day of the mountain man was over, but a clear sense of western geography had been forged by the daring journeys of indomitable figures such as the much-traveled Jedediah Smith. Soon permanent settlers would follow the trails blazed by the mountain men.

Government-Sponsored Exploration

The federal government played a major role in the exploration and development of the West. Thomas Jefferson decisively influenced American westward expansion with the Louisiana Purchase of 1803. Probably Jefferson dispatched the Lewis and Clark expedition the next year largely to satisfy his own intense scientific and geographic curiosity about the West. But he also instructed them to draw the western Indians into the American rather than the British trading network. (See Chapter 9.)

The exploratory and scientific aspects of the Lewis and Clark expedition set a precedent for many government-financed quasi-military expeditions. In 1806 and 1807, Lt. Zebulon Pike led an expedition to the Rocky Mountains in Colorado. Major Stephen Long's exploration and mapping of the Great Plains in the years 1819–20 was part of a show of force meant to frighten British fur trappers out of the West. In 1843 and 1844 another military explorer, John C. Frémont, mapped the overland trails to Oregon and California. He was on hand in California in 1845 to encourage the Bear Flag Revolt of American settlers against the Mexican governors of the territory. In the 1850s, the Pacific Railroad Surveys explored possible transcontinental railroad routes. The tradition of government-sponsored western exploration continued after the Civil War in the famous Geological Surveys, of which the best known is the 1869 Grand Canyon exploration by Major John Wesley Powell.

Beginning with Long's expedition, the results of these surveys were published by the government complete with maps, illustrations, and, after the Civil War, photographs. These publications fed a deep popular appetite for pictures of the strange and-beautiful scenery of the Far West and information about its inhabitants. Artists such as Karl Bodmer, who accompanied the private expedition of the scientifically inclined German prince Maximilian in the years 1833–34, produced stunning portraits of American Indians. Over the next three decades landscape artists such as Thomas Moran and Albert Bierstadt traveled west with government expeditions and came home to paint grand (and sometimes fanciful) pictures of Yosemite Valley and Yellowstone (later designated the first two national parks). All these images of the American West made a powerful contribution to the emerging American self-image. American pride in the land — the biggest of this, the longest of that, the most spectacular of something else — was founded on the images brought home by government surveyors and explorers.

In the wake of the pathfinders came a horde of government geologists and botanists as well as the surveyors who mapped and platted the West for settlement according to the Northwest Ordinances of 1785 and 1787. Those two measures had established the basic pattern of land survey and sale, and it was followed all the way to the Pacific Ocean. The federal government sold the western public lands at low prices and gave away land in the Old Northwest to veterans of the War of 1812. The government also shouldered the expense of Indian removal, paying the soldiers or the officials who fought or talked Indian peoples into giving up their lands, and making long-term commitments to compensate the Indian people themselves. Where necessary, the government also supported the forts and soldiers who defended settlers (and sometimes protected Indian peoples) in newly opened areas.

Expansion and Indian Policy

While American trappers and traders were learning how to live among the western Indians and artists were painting their way of life, eastern Indian tribes were being removed from the Old Northwest and the Old Southwest. In 1815, President James Monroe proposed a plan to relocate all eastern tribes to western territory. Accordingly, an "Indian Territory" was established west of Missouri and Arkansas on the eastern edge of the Great Plains (a region widely regarded as unfarmable and popularly known as the Great American Desert). It was to these marginal lands that eastern tribes were relocated, at first voluntarily but later by force, following the passage of Andrew Jackson's Indian Removal Act in 1830. The most notorious case of removal was that of theso-called Five Civilized Tribes, the Cherokees, Chocktaws, Chickasaws, Creeks, and Seminoles, culminating in the Cherokee Trail of Tears (see Chapter 10). Most other migrations occurred peacefully, as dispirited eastern tribes accepted their inevitable displacement.

The justification for western removal, as Thomas Jefferson had explained early in the century, was the creation of a space where Indian people could live undisturbed by whites while they slowly learned "civilized" ways. But Jefferson and other government officials failed to realize the tremendous speed at which whites were settling the West. The pace of westward expansion was so swift that there was no permanent way to separate whites and Indians. For example, the Kickapoos, moved west in 1819 to western Missouri Territory, were forced to move again two years later when Missouri became a state.

Encroachment on the new Indian Territory was not long in coming. The territory was crossed by the Santa Fe Trail, established in 1821; in the 1840s the northern part was crossed by the heavily traveled Overland Trail to California, Oregon, and the Mormon community in Utah. In 1854, under pressure from transportation interests who wanted to build a transcontinental railroad, the government abolished the northern half of Indian Territory. In its place it established the Kansas and Nebraska territories, which were immediately opened to white settlement. (See Chapter 15.) The tribes of the area — the Potawatomis, Wyandots, Kickapoos, Sauks and Foxes, Delawares, Shawnees, Kaskaskias, Peorias, Piankashaws, Weas, Miamis, Omahas, Otos, and Missouris — signed treaties accepting either vastly reduced reservations or allotments (private land, which they sold, often under pressure, to whites). Thus many lost both their autonomy and their tribal identity.

The southern part of Indian Territory, in what is now Oklahoma, fared somewhat better. Those members of the southern tribes — the Cherokees, Choctaws, Seminoles, Creeks, and Chickasaws — who had survived the trauma of forcible removal quickly created impressive new communities. The five tribes divided up the territory and established self-governing nations with their own schools and churches. The societies they created were not so different from the European American societies from which they had been expelled. The five tribes even carried slavery west with them: An elite economic group established plantations and shipped their cotton to New Orleans like other southerners.

These southern tribes were able to withstand outside pressures and remain self-governing — as they had been promised by treaties — until after the Civil War.

The removal of the eastern tribes did not solve the Indian "problem." West of Indian Territory were the nomadic and warlike Indians of the Great Plains: the Sioux, Cheyennes, Arapahos, Comanches, and Kiowas. Beyond them were the seminomadic tribes of the Rocky Mountains — the Blackfeet, Crows, Utes, Arikaras, Shoshonis, Nez Perces, and Salish peoples — and, in the Southwest, the sedentary groups of Pueblos, Hopis, Acomas, Zunis, Pimas, and Papagos and the migratory Apaches and Navahos. Even farther west were hundreds of small tribes in California and the Pacific Northwest. Clearly, all of these people could not be removed, and besides, where could they be removed to? The answer came after the Civil War: a series of Indian wars that penned up the remaining Indians on small reservations (see Chapter 18). For the moment, the first western pioneers ignored the issue. Beginning in the 1840s, they simply passed through the far western tribal lands on their way to establish new frontiers of settlement in California and Oregon.

MANIFEST DESTINY

America's rapid expansion had many consequences, but perhaps the greatest was its reinforcement of Americans' sense of themselves as pioneering people. In the 1890s Frederick Jackson Turner, America's most famous historian, stated the case thus: The repeated experience of settling new frontiers across the continent had shaped America into a uniquely adventurous, optimistic, and democratic nation. Other historians have disagreed with Turner, but there is no question that his view of the frontier long ago won the battle for popular opinion. Ever since the time of Daniel Boone, venturing into the wilderness has held a special place in the American imagination. This adventurous expansion quickly began to seem like an American *right*.

The Ideology of Expansion

How did Americans justify their restless expansionism? After all, the United States was already a very large country with much undeveloped land. To push beyond the national boundaries was to risk war with Mexico, which held what is now Texas, New Mexico, Arizona, Utah, Nevada, and California, and with Great Britain, which claimed the Pacific Northwest. Even if successful, such wars would reduce 75,000

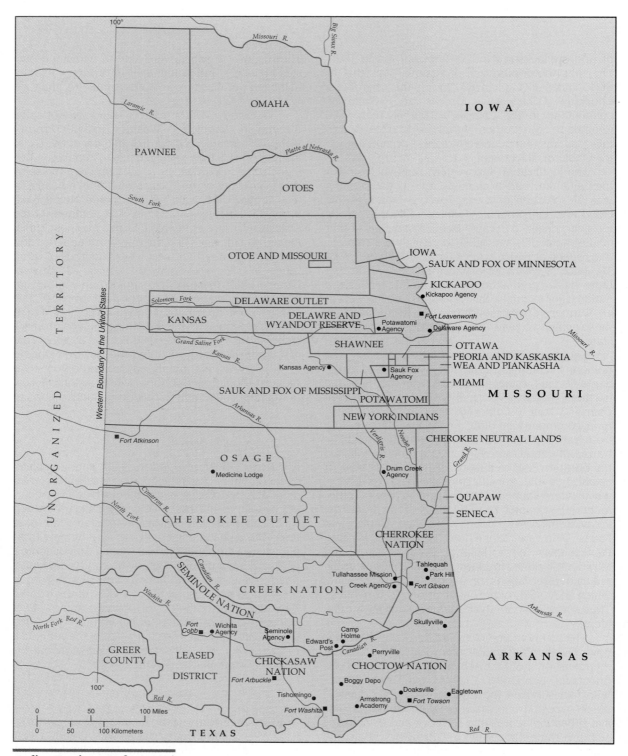

Indian Territory Before 1854

Indian Territory was the land west of Arkansas, Missouri, and Iowa and east of the border with Spanish Territory. In the 1830s and the 1840s most of the Indian peoples who lived there had been removed from east of the Mississippi River. In the southern part (in what is now Oklahoma) lived the groups removed from the Old Southwest: the Creeks, Cherokees, Chickasaw, Choctaw, and Seminole. To the north (in what is now Kansas) were the groups that had been removed from the Old Northwest. All of the removed groups had trouble adjusting to a new climate and to the close proximity of other Indian tribes, some of whom were traditional enemies.

Spanish-speakers and 150,000 Indian people (who could not be removed farther west) to the status of conquered peoples. The United States needed a rationale for conquest.

In 1845 newspaperman John O'Sullivan provided it. In the process he coined the phrase by which expansionism became famous. It was, O'Sullivan said, "our *manifest destiny* to overspread the continent allotted by Providence for the free development of our yearly multiplying millions." Sullivan argued that Americans had a God-given right to bring the benefits of American democracy to other, more backward peoples — meaning Mexicans and Indian nations — by force, if necessary. The notion of manifest destiny summed up the thinking of many expansionists. Pride in American democracy together with racist attitudes toward other peoples made for a powerful combination.

One source of expansionist sentiment was national pride. Americans were proud of their rapid development: the surge in population, the remarkable canals and railroads, the grand scale of the American enterprise. Why shouldn't it be even bigger? Almost swaggering, Americans dared other countries — Great Britain in particular — to stop them.

Behind the bravado was concern about the economic future of the United States. After the devastating Panic of 1837 (see Chapter 10), a number of politicians convinced themselves that the nation's prosperity depended on vastly expanded trade with Asia. One of them, Missouri senator Thomas Hart Benton, a leading expansionist, had been advocating trade with India by way of the Missouri and Columbia rivers since the 1820s. (This was not the easiest of routes, as Lewis and Clark had shown!) Soon he and others were pointing out how greatly Pacific trade would increase if the United States held the magnificent harbors of the West Coast, among them Puget Sound in the jointly held Oregon Territory and San Francisco Bay and San Diego Bay in Mexican-held California. Benton, unlike some other expansionists (including the explorer Frémont, his son-in-law), always believed the United States could acquire the western ports peacefully.

In another sense, manifest destiny was simply evangelical religion on a larger scale. The same revivalist fervor that Charles Finney had sparked in Rochester in 1830 had a continental echo: Missionaries were among the first to travel to the Far West to Christianize Indian people. Just as many of Finney's eastern converts mounted reform movements aimed at changing the lives of workers, so did the western missionaries attempt to "civilize" the In-

dian peoples. They believed that the only way to do so was to destroy their cultures and to surround them with good American examples.

Expansionism was tied to national politics. "Manifest destiny" was not a term coined by a neutral observer: John O'Sullivan was the editor of the *Democratic Review*, a party newspaper. Most Democrats were wholehearted supporters of expansion; many Whigs (especially in the North) were opposed. As we saw in Chapter 10, the two parties held different attitudes toward American society. Whigs welcomed most of the changes wrought by industrialization, and advocated strong government policies (Henry Clay's American System) that would guide growth and development within the existing boundaries of the United States. They also feared (correctly, as we shall see) that expansion would raise the contentious issue of the extension of slavery to new territories.

On the other hand, most Democrats favored expansion as a way to preserve customary social patterns. Many Democrats feared the industrialization that the Whigs welcomed. Where the Whigs saw economic progress, Democrats saw economic depression (the Panic of 1837 was the worst the nation had experienced), uncontrolled urban growth, and growing social unrest — all of which, as we saw in Chapters 12 and 13, did indeed accompany the country's economic growth. For many Democrats, the answer to the nation's social ills was to continue to follow Thomas Jefferson's vision of establishing agriculture in the new territories in order to counterbalance industrialization (see Chapter 9). Another factor in the political struggle over expansion in the 1840s was that many Democrats were southerners, for whom the continual expansion of cotton-growing lands was a matter of social faith as well as economic necessity.

These were politicians' reasons. For the average farmer, the move west was made for many other reasons: land hunger, national pride, plain and simple curiosity, and a sense of adventure.

The Overland Trail

No account of the settling of Oregon — or, somewhat later, California — would be complete without a description of the journey there on the Overland Trail. The 2,000-mile trip from the "jumping-off places" on the banks of the Missouri River — Independence, St. Joseph, Kansas City, Council Bluffs — usually took seven months, sometimes more. Travel was slow, dangerous, tedious, and exhausting. Pioneers often arrived in Oregon with little food and belongings, having been forced to lighten their loads

The Overland Trails, 1840

All of the great trails west started at the Missouri River. The Oregon, California, and Mormon Trails followed the Platte River into Wyoming, crossed South Pass, and divided in western Wyoming. The Santa Fe Trail, a much harsher trip, stretched 900 miles southwest across the Great Plains. The trails west of Santa Fe were less travelled because of the great heat and aridity. All of the trails crossed Indian Territory and, to greater or lesser extent, Mexican Territory as well.

as animals died and winter weather threatened. Uprooted from family and familiar surroundings, pioneers faced the prospect of being, in the poignant nineteenth-century phrase, "strangers in a strange land." Yet with all of the risks, settlers streamed west: 5,000 to Oregon by 1845 and about 3,000 to California by 1848 (before the discovery of gold). Some residents arrived by ship, but this was expensive. Nor was the overland journey cheap. A wagon, a team of oxen, food, clothing, and essential tools cost between $500 and $1000.

A number of motives impelled the pioneers to make the trip. Glowing reports from Oregon's Willamette Valley seemed to promise economic opportunity and healthy surroundings, an alluring combination to farmers in the malaria-prone Midwest who had been hard hit by the panic of 1837. But rational motives do not tell the whole story. Many men—and some women—were motivated by a sense of adventure, by a desire to experience the unknown, or, as they put it, to "see the elephant."

Women were more likely to explain the trip as "a pioneer's search for an ideal home," as Phoebe Judson titled an account of her 1852 trip.

Many pioneers, aware of the epic nature of their journey, kept diaries or wrote accounts to pass on to their grandchildren. These diaries give us a vivid overall picture of the westward movement, and some striking details. Arriving at one of the jumping-off places in April, pioneers bought supplies if they didn't already have them. "Leave Missouri in April with a good light wagon, 150 lbs. of flour to the person, 60 lbs. of bacon, 40 lbs. of sugar, 25 lbs. dried fruit, 10 lbs of rice and plenty of pickles and vinegar, tea, coffee, etc," advised Caleb and Alice Richie, Oregon pioneers of 1852, to the relatives who were to follow them.

Few pioneers traveled alone, partly because of fear of Indian attack (which was rare) but largely because cooperative effort was needed for fording rivers or crossing mountains with heavy wagons. Most Oregon pioneers were family parties, but usually they joined a larger group, forming a "train." In the earliest years, when the route was still uncertain, trains hired a "pilot," generally a former fur trapper. Often the men of the wagon train drew up semimilitary constitutions, electing a leader. Democratic as this process appeared, not everyone was willing to obey the leader, and many trains experienced dissension and breakups along the trail. But in essence all pioneers — men, women, and children — were part of a westward-moving community, and experienced the various supports and tensions that community membership entailed.

Trains started westward as soon as the prairies were green (thus ensuring feed for the livestock). But too early a start meant a muddy trail, in which case the early days of the trip were spent digging out stuck wagons.

The daily routine was soon established. Men took care of the moving equipment and the animals. In the morning they hitched the teams to the wagons and drove them, usually on foot, leading the oxen. At night, after a suitable resting place had been chosen, they circled the wagons and pastured the stock. Then they took turns guarding the stock, to prevent wandering and Indian theft. (Plains Indian men, trained since boyhood to steal the horses of other tribes, saw no reason why the horses of whites should be off-limits.) Men were also responsible for fixing things. And as the months wore on, more and more equipment needed repair. They also did the dangerous work of heaving wagons out of ruts and up steep terrain and swimming wagons and stock across rivers.

Women had a different routine. Up first in the morning to make breakfast (usually around four), during the day they rode in the wagons or walked, trying to keep a careful eye on their children. Lunch was usually only a brief stop for a cold meal. The real work for women came at night. While the men were resting after a day of driving, women were cooking, usually the evening meal and lunch the next day, arranging the nighttime bedding, and watching the children. As pioneer Amelia Buss irritably wrote in her diary: "I fail to see any thing *desirable* in such traveling; it is hurry up in the morning and get a hasty breakfast and have a cold lunch for dinner and at night get supper and bake bread and not get through till 9." A surprising number of women began the trip pregnant and gave birth along the trail. Usually the wagon train rested for a day after the birth; the recovering mother then rode in the rolling wagon. Women were generally among those most insistent on Sunday as a day of rest. It is difficult to avoid the suspicion that they were thinking as much about an opportunity to do the laundry as they were about the need for faithful religious observance!

ACROSS THE CONTINENT.
"WESTWARD THE COURSE OF EMPIRE TAKES ITS WAY"

Crossing rivers was one of the most difficult parts of the overland journey, and called for the greatest cooperation. Floating the wagons, which often had to be unloaded before the crossing, and swimming the stock across rivers was dangerous and often led to accidental deaths by drowning.

Slowly, at a rate of about fifteen miles a day, the wagon trains followed the Platte River west across the Great Plains. Famous landmarks were Chimney Rock and Scotts Bluff in present-day Nebraska and the last military outpost, Fort Laramie, which trains hoped to reach by late June. Next, around the Fourth of July, the emigrants came to Independence Rock, and then to the mercifully gentle transit of the Continental Divide at South Pass in Wyoming. Usually, parties stopped near South Pass to celebrate their progress.

But in fact the second and much rougher part of the trip lay ahead. West of the Rockies the climate was much drier. There was less grass for the tiring stock, and people were tired too. The long, dusty stretch along the Snake River in present-day southern Idaho seemed endless. But awaiting them were the steep and difficult crossing of Oregon's Blue Mountains and finally the dangerous rafting down the Columbia River, in which many drowned and all were drenched by the cold winter rains of the Pacific Northwest. California-bound emigrants faced even worse hazards: the complete lack of water in the Humbolt Sink region of northern Nevada and the looming Sierra Nevada, which had to be crossed before the winter snows came. (Members of the ill-fated Donner party, snowbound on the Nevada side of that range, resorted to cannibalism before they were rescued.) Exhausted travelers, many of them ill from scurvy because of lack of vegetables, watched their animals slacken and often die just when speed was essential. Amicable members of

wagon trains argued and split. Some, in desperation, chose foolhardy "shortcuts"; others fell farther behind. Almost every wagon was forced to lighten its load, leaving cherished family treasures behind. Families buckled and sometimes broke under the strain.

In addition to tedium and exhaustion, there were other, more dramatic trail hazards. As we have noted, danger from Indian attack, which all the pioneers feared, was actually very small. Before 1849 — that is, before the California gold rush — thirty-four whites were killed (twenty-four in one wagon train) and twenty-five Indians. In subsequent years, as thousands of gold rushers flocked west, the deaths increased. Significantly, more Indians than whites died. It appears that unprovoked white attacks on Indians were more common than the reverse.

Another major killer was cholera, which in 1849 and the early 1850s stalked sections of the trail along the Platte River. Cholera, spread by contaminated water, caused vomiting and diarrhea, which in turn led to extreme dehydration and death, often overnight. In the afflicted regions, trailside graves were a frequent and grim sight. The other major killer was accidents: drownings, accidental ax wounds or shootings, children falling out of wagons and getting run over. The members of the wagon train community did what they could to arrange decent burials, and they provided support for survivors: Men helped widows drive their wagons onward, nursing babies were fed and tended by other

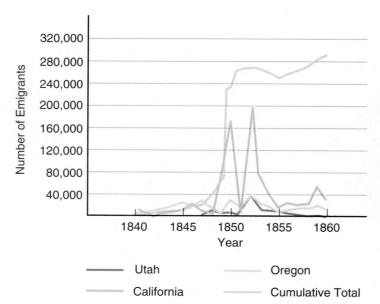

Overland Emigration to Oregon, California, and Utah, 1840–1860

Prior to 1849 most of the westward migration was composed of family groups going to Oregon or Utah. The discovery of gold in California dramatically changed the migration: through 1854 most of the migration was single men "rushing" to California, and up until 1860 it remained the favored destination. Over the twenty year period covered by these figures, the Overland Trails were transformed from difficult and dangerous routes to well-marked and well-served thoroughfares.

Source: John Unruh, Jr., *The Plains Across* (Champaign/Urbana: University of Illinois Press, 1979), pp. 119–120.

mothers, and one whole parentless family, the seven Sager children, were brought to Oregon in safety.

By 1860 almost 300,000 people had traveled the Oregon and California Trails. Ruts from the wagon wheels can be seen in a number of places along the route even today. In 1869, the completion of the transcontinental railroad marked the end of the wagon train era (although many people made shorter trips to other western locations by wagon). In retrospect, the Oregon pioneers remembered their journey as more dangerous and less tedious than it actually was. The stories that came down to their grandchildren told of a heroic adventure. These "pioneers' tales" were not the truth as it had really happened, but an effort to acknowledge the true heroism of an important episode in one's life in the best way one could—by making a good story out of it.

Oregon

The American settlement of Oregon provides a capsule example of some of the frontier impulses we have considered thus far. The first contacts between the region's Indian peoples and Europeans were commercial. Spanish, British, Russian, and American ships traded for sea otter skins from the 1780s to about 1810. Subsequently land-based groups scoured the region for beaver. The effect of the fur trade on the native tribes was catastrophic: Long before many Indian peoples had ever seen a white person, European diseases had decimated their populations. For example, the Nez Perces suffered a major smallpox epidemic in 1781 and 1782, almost twenty-five years before Lewis and Clark established the first direct white contact with them.

Both Great Britain and the United States claimed the Oregon Country by right of discovery. In the Convention of 1818, the two nations agreed to joint occupation, thus postponing a final decision. In reality, the British clearly dominated the region. In 1824 the Hudson's Bay Company consolidated Britain's position by establishing a major fur trading post, Fort Vancouver, on the banks of the Columbia River. Like all fur-trading ventures, it attracted a polyglot population of eastern Indians (Delawares and Iroquois), local Chinook Indians, French and métis from Canada, Hawaiians, and British.

The first permanent European settlers in Oregon were retired fur trappers and their Indian wives and families. They favored a spot in the lush and temperate Willamette Valley that became known as French Prairie, although the inhabitants were a mixed group of Americans, British, French Canadi-ans, Indian peoples, and métis. The next to arrive were Protestant and Catholic missionaries. Methodist Jason Lee established a mission in the Willamette Valley in 1834. Marcus and Narcissa Whitman and other members of their group (mostly Congregationalists) arrived in the years 1837–39 and opened missions farther inland to convert the Cayuses, Spokans, and Nez Perces. Two Franciscan priests, Frances Blanchet and Modeste Demers, arrived in 1838, followed in 1840 by Jesuit Pierre DeSmet, who established a mission among the Flathead Indians in what is now western Montana. None of these missions was very successful. Epidemics had devastated all the region's peoples, and those who were left were disinclined to give up their nomadic life and settle down as the missionaries wanted them to do.

The tragic career of Narcissa Whitman in Oregon exemplified the best and the worst of the missionary impulse. Raised in an evangelical household in upstate New York, she ventured to the Pacific Northwest with her husband, Marcus, in 1837 to Christianize the Cayuse Indians. Ironically, the Whitmans were guided west by fur trappers, whose accommodating attitude toward Indian peoples was the opposite of their own reform impulse. Disappointed and angry when the Cayuses refused their religious instruction, the Whitmans turned to encouraging the migration of white settlers to Oregon. For their part, the Cayuses were equally disappointed and angered. They had expected the missionaries to bring them a new sort of power, not demands for fundamental changes in their way of life. The Whitmans wanted the Cayuses to give up their nomadic fishing-and-gathering lifestyle and to settle down as docile farm laborers under white direction. Then too, the Whitmans' encouragement of migration to Oregon brought white settlers who encroached on Indian fishing grounds and brought devastating diseases. In 1847, during a measles epidemic that decimated the native people but left most whites alive, the Whitmans were killed by the Cayuses they had tried to Christianize. In retaliation, Oregon settlers waged a war of extermination against the Cayuses. Not all missionary efforts in Oregon and elsewhere ended this badly, but it was true that the missionaries had more success encouraging white settlement than they did converting Indian peoples.

It was not difficult to find people eager to make the overland journey to the Oregon Country. Settlers were lured not only by the glowing reports of the healthy climate and fertile soil, but also by the chance to "tweak the lion's tail" (irritate the British) and to gain free land. Oregon's Donation Land Claim

This watercolor of tiny Oregon City in 1846 shows the small American numbers during Oregon's first years as a U.S. territory. By 1850, boasting 953 inhabitants, it was the largest city in Oregon.

Act of 1850 codified the practice of giving 320 acres to each white male age 18 or over and 640 acres to each married couple (African Americans and Hawaiians were excluded from the largesse). Guidebooks to the overland journey were soon available, although a number of them, such as Lansford Hasting's *Emigrant's Guide to Oregon and California* (1845) seriously understated the dangers and difficulties of the trip. Finally, noted expansionists such as Thomas Hart Benton urged the peaceful settlement of Oregon as the best way to settle the dispute with Great Britain. The result was "Oregon fever," a wave of enthusiasm that struck farmers (especially in the Midwest) in the mid-1840s and sent them west.

So the pioneers came to Oregon, some by sea but most overland. Because most were farmers and intended to settle permanently, they traveled in family groups. Three-generation family parties (older parents, their adult children, and young grandchildren) were not unusual. By 1845, as we have seen, there were 5,000 American settlers in Oregon. Most had settled in the Willamette Valley.

For these early settlers, life was at first very difficult. Most arrived in late autumn, exhausted from the strenuous overland journey. They could not begin to farm until the spring, and so they were dependent upon the earlier settlers for their survival over the winter. Ironically, in the earliest years American settlers got vital help from the Hudson's Bay Company, even though the HBC factor (director), John McLoughlin, had been ordered by the British government not to encourage American settlement. McLoughlin disregarded his orders, motivated by sympathy for the plight of the newcomers and a keen sense of the dangers his enterprise would face if he were outnumbered by angry Americans.

Joint occupancy of Oregon by the Americans and the British continued until 1846. American occupation of Oregon was an issue in the 1844 presidential race, as we shall see later in this chapter. Democratic candidate James K. Polk campaigned on the belligerent slogan "Fifty-four Forty [the Russian–Alaskan border] or Fight," but in fact he was willing to compromise. In the spring of 1846, the British offered to accept the forty-ninth parallel as the U.S.–Canada border if the island of Vancouver remained in their hands, and a treaty was signed peacefully on June 15 of that year. The British then quietly wound up their declining fur trade in the region. In 1849 the Hudson's Bay Company closed Fort Vancouver and moved its operations to Victoria, thus ending the Pacific Northwest's largely successful experience with joint occupancy.

The Frontier Community

The handful of American settlers in Oregon found themselves in possession of a remote frontier. One of the first things they did (even before the American claim was finally settled) was to draw up their own constitution. When the first Oregon settlers (including a number of former mountain men) met in the summer of 1843 to arrange for self-government, they voted (among other things) to prohibit African Americans from settling in the territory. By this ostrichlike measure, they vainly hoped to avoid the divisive issue of slavery.

The white settlers realized that they had to forge

strong community bonds if they hoped to survive on their distant frontier. Cooperation and mutual aid were the rule. Until well into the 1850s, residents organized yearly parties to travel back along the last stretches of the Overland Trail to help straggling parties making their way to Oregon. Kinship networks were strong and vital: Many pioneers came to join family who had migrated before them. Although most settlers lived on their own land claims rather than in towns, neighborly cooperation was crucial. Food sharing and mutual labor were essential in the early years, when crop and livestock loss to weather or natural predators was common. Help, even to total strangers, was customary in times of illness or death.

Community feeling did not, however, extend to the Indian peoples. Relationships with the small and unthreatening groups of disease-thinned local Indian people were generally peaceful until 1847, when the killing of the Whitmans initiated a series of "wars" against those remaining. Until the California gold rush of 1849 gave a boost to grain production and cattle raising, Oregon remained an outpost of subsistence farms far from the United States.

American expansion into Oregon was a success, and the area became part of the United States peaceably. But expansion into the Spanish provinces of New Mexico and Texas was more troubled.

New Spain's Texas Frontier

In 1716, a mixed band of pioneers from New Spain (Mexico)—soldiers, missionary priests, and settlers—built a frontier border post in the far northeast of the state of Coahuila. The settlement was Nacogdoches, in what is now Texas. Catholic priests were sent to this northern border, as were others to New Mexico and California at other times, to convert the native Indians to Christianity and to "civilize" them by turning them into farmers. But the success of the Spanish settlements ultimately rested with the mestizo (mixed-race) pioneers who possessed basic farming and artisanal skills. Soldiers accompanied the priests and settlers for defense, for although some of the coastal tribes were friendly, the Comanche Indians who inhabited the interior highlands most decidedly were not.

The Comanches were the finest example of the revolution that occurred in the lives of Plains Indians once they had horses (originally brought to the American continent by the Spanish in 1519). "A Comanche on his feet is out of his element . . . but the moment he lays his hands upon his horse," said artist George Catlin, "I doubt very much whether any people in the world can surpass [him]." Legendary warriors, the Comanches raided the small Texas settlements at will, and even struck deep into Mexico itself. Once they raided so far south that they saw brightly plumed birds (parrots) and "tiny men with tails" (monkeys); apparently they had reached the tropical Yucatan. The nomadic Comanches followed the immense buffalo herds (on whom they depended for food and clothing) in the north and west of Texas. Their relentless raids on the Texas settlements rose from a determination to hold onto this rich buffalo-hunting territory.

The beleagured Spanish settlements had a distinctive character. As was customary throughout New Spain, communities were organized around three centers: the mission, the presidio (the army fort), and large ranchos, which specialized in cattle raising and on which rural living depended. The

This George Catlin painting, done around 1834, shows the ways in which the everyday life of a Comanche village was tied to buffalo. The women in the foreground are scraping buffalo hide, and buffalo meat can be seen drying on racks. The men and boys are no doubt planning their next buffalo hunt.

mixed-blood vaqueros were renowned for their horsemanship; later generations taught American cowboys their skills, becoming "buckaroos" in the process. As was true everywhere in New Spain, society was divided into two classes: the *ricos* (the rich) who claimed Spanish descent, and the mixed-blood *pobres* (the poor). Some of the *ricos* lived grandly on large ranchos, but most settlers led hardscrabble frontier lives as small farmers or common laborers. In 1821 there were only 2,240 residents of New Spain's Texas frontier.

The Santa Fe Trade

Santa Fe, first settled by colonists from Mexico in 1609 and the center of the Spanish frontier province of New Mexico, had long attracted western frontiersmen and traders. But Spain had forcefully resisted American penetration. For example, Lieutenant Zebulon Pike's Great Plains and Rocky Mountain exploration of 1806 and 1807 ended ignominiously with his capture by Spanish soldiers. This exclusionary policy changed after Mexico gained its independence.

In 1821 Mexico seized its independence from Spain in a military coup. But the sprawling Mexican empire, which included California, Texas and the Southwest, and all of Central America except Panama, was wracked by political instability. The small governing class was bitterly divided between liberals who favored provincial autonomy and centralizers who wished to keep power in the hands of the church and the army. As a result, between 1833 and 1855 the Mexican presidency changed hands thirty-six times, often by force. One man, General Antonio López de Santa Anna, held the presidency eleven times.

Independence opened up the northern Mexican provinces to American trade and residence, which the Spanish had forbidden. American traders were now welcome in Santa Fe, but the trip over the legendary Santa Fe Trail from Independence, Missouri, was a forbidding 900 miles of arid plains, deserts, and mountains. There was serious danger of Indian attack, for neither the Comanches nor the Apaches of the southern high plains tolerated trespassers. Nevertheless, in 1825, at the urging of Senator Benton and others, Congress voted federal protection for the Santa Fe Trail, even though much of it lay in Mexican territory. The number of people venturing west in the trading caravans increased yearly because the profits were so great (the first trader, William Becknell, realized a thousand percent profit). By the 1840s a few hundred American trappers and traders (*extranjeros,* or foreigners) lived permanently in New Mexico. In Santa Fe, a number of American merchants married daughters of important local families. This pattern of assimilation into the local elite had been followed by early American traders in Texas as well.

Settlements and trading posts soon grew up along the long Santa Fe Trail. One of the most famous was Bent's Fort, on the Arkansas River in what is now eastern Colorado, which did a brisk trade in beaver skins and buffalo robes. Like most trading posts, it had a multiethnic population. In the 1840s the occupants included housekeeper Josefa Tafoya of Taos, whose husband was a carpenter from Pennsylvania; an African American cook named Andrew Green; a French tailor from New Orleans; Mexican muleteers; and a number of Indian women, including the two Cheyenne women who were the (successive) wives of William Bent, co-founder of the fort. The three small communities of Pueblo, Hardscrabble, and Greenhorn were spinoffs of Bent's Fort. They were populated by former trappers of all nationalities and younger men eager for frontier experience, along with their Mexican and Indian wives. They lived by trapping, hunting, and a little farming. This racially and economically mixed existence was characteristic of all early trading frontiers, but it was very different from the American agricultural settlements in Texas.

Americans in Texas

The Texas frontier that was so remote and hostile when viewed from Mexico City was inviting to southern Americans who had seen its areas of rich land suitable for growing cotton. Invited to settle by the Mexican government (which wanted a better-populated buffer between its heartland and the Comanches), Americans were willing to do so on Mexican terms. In 1821, Stephen F. Austin, the first American *empresario* (land agent) was granted an area of 18,000 square miles. In exchange he agreed that he and his colonists would take on the Catholic religion and Mexican citizenship. In startling contrast with the usual frontier free-for-all, Austin handpicked his settlers, for all the world like the owner of a proprietary colony in long-ago colonial America. Neither Austin nor later *empresarios* had any trouble finding Americans to apply, for the simple reason that Mexican land grants were magnificent: a square league (4,605 acres) per family. Soon Americans (including black slaves, whose presence the Mexican government winked at) vastly outnumbered the Mexican inhabitants. By 1830 there were at least 20,000 Americans in Texas.

From the beginning the American settlement of

This painting by Alfred Jacob Miller shows the busy life of Fort Laramie. Bent's Fort, a trading post with a multiracial population, must have looked like this.

Texas differed markedly from the customary frontier pattern. Elsewhere, Americans had frequently settled on land to which Indian peoples still held title. Or, as in the case of Oregon, they had occupied lands of uncertain nationality. In contrast, the Texas settlement was legal: *empresarios* entered into formal contracts with the Mexican government in which they agreed that they and their settlers would observe Mexican laws. The Austin settlement of 1821 was followed by others, twenty-six in all, concentrating in the fertile river bottoms of east Texas (along the Sabine River) and south central Texas (the Brazos and the Colorado). The principal crop was cotton, planted and grown by black slave labor. Austin's colonists and those who settled later were predominantly southerners who viewed Texas as a natural extension of settlement in Mississippi and Louisiana.

Although a growing number of independent hunters, trappers, and subsistence farmers lived in the woods of eastern Texas, most of the settlers of the large land grants were of another type. Stephen Austin, for example, had some rigorous requirements for his handpicked group: "No frontiersman who has no other occupation than that of hunter will be received — no drunkard, no gambler, no profane swearer, no idler." These large Texas settlements were highly organized farming enterprises that produced cotton for the international market. By the early 1830s, Americans in Texas were exporting an estimated $500,000 worth of goods yearly to New

Orleans, two-thirds of it cotton. Finally, the American settlers created self-contained communities that had little contact with Tejanos or Indian peoples. In fact, although they lived in Mexican territory, most Americans never bothered to learn Spanish. Yet unlike the Oregon settlers, who wrote their own constitution within three years of settlement, the Americans in Texas were not self-governing.

There were only 4,000 Mexicans in Texas in the mid-1830s, clustered mainly in three towns — Nacogdoches, Goliad, and San Antonio — and in large ranchos in the surrounding countryside. Life in towns was traditionally hierarchical, dominated by a rich elite that was connected by blood or marriage with the great ranching families. At the elite level — and this was true in Santa Fe and California as well — the isolation of the Americans disappeared. As we saw in the chapter introduction, wealthy Americans married into the Tejano elite with ease. One such marriage in San Antonio linked wealthy Louisianan James Bowie, the legendary fighter for whom the Bowie knife is named, and Ursula Veramendi, daughter of the vice-governor of Texas. With the marriage, Bowie became a wealthy, honored, and well-connected Mexican citizen. Only after the death of his wife and children in a cholera epidemic in 1833 did Bowie support the cause of Anglo-Texan independence, going on to fight — and die — at the Alamo.

The great ranchos excited the admiration of many Americans, who later made cattle raising a major western industry. In these early days in Texas, Americans watched and learned as Tejanos rounded up range cattle, branded them, and drove more than 20,000 yearly to Nacogdoches for the United States market. Praise for Tejano horsemanship was unstinting: They are "not surpassed perhaps by any other people in the Globe," enthused one American immigrant. Tejano customs, especially multi-day celebrations that mixed religious ceremonies, feasting, horse racing, and elaborate fandangos (dances), offered striking evidence of the richly textured community life created by Tejanos of all social classes.

Unlike the Mexicans, the Americans devoted little effort to towns. San Felipe, the capital of the Austin land grant, amounted to little more than a scattering of log cabins. Even where the Americans adopted the formal Spanish town plan of a central plaza bordered by the church and official buildings, Mexican observers were shocked to see that citizens built their houses wherever they chose. From the Mexican point of view, Americans lacked civic order. The Americans thought Mexicans lacked enterprise. Both agreed, however, that they had a common enemy in the Comanche raiders, who prevented westward expansion.

For a brief period Texas was big enough to hold all three communities: Comanche, Mexican, and American. As we have seen, the nomadic Comanches rode the high plains of northern and western Texas, raiding settlements primarily for horses. The Mexicans maintained their ranches and missions mostly in the south, while American farmers swept into the eastern and south central sections. Each group viewed the land differently: The Comanches would fight to hold their rich hunting grounds, the Mexicans to maintain their frontier; and the newcomers, the Americans, to keep the land granted them.

The three-way balance was broken in 1830, when centrists gained control of the government of Mexico and, in a dramatic shift of policy, decided to exercise firm control over the northern province. What ensued was reminiscent of the American Revolution (which Anglo-Texans never tired of invoking). As the Mexican government restricted American immigration, outlawed slavery, levied customs duties and taxes, and planned other measures, Americans seethed with rebellious talk — which was backed up by the presence of as many as 10,000 Americans, many of them openly expansionist, who emigrated to Texas after 1830. They did not intend to become Mexican citizens. Instead, they planned to take over Texas. For all the invocations of the American Revolution, the real issue in Texas was a conflict of cultures.

Whereas many of the older Anglo-Texan set-

The Settlement of Texas, ca. 1835

Three major groups lived in Texas: the Spanish Mexicans, the Comanches, and the Americans. The Spanish Mexicans, largely ranchers and small farmers, clustered in and around Nacogdoches and San Antonio. The Americans settled the fertile river bottoms of southcentral Texas and established cotton plantations. The Comanches rode the high plains to the north, following the buffalo.

Source: T. R. Fehrenbach, *Lone Star* (New York: Macmillan, 1968).

tlers found much that was admirable, or at least understandable, in Spanish Mexican culture, many of the post-1830 immigrants were vehemently anti-Mexican. Many had grievances: failure to obtain a land grant, restrictions on trade because of Mexican customs regulations, difficulties in understanding Hispanic law, which differed markedly from the Anglo-American legal tradition. Above all, in the eyes of many Americans, there was the matter of race. Statements of racial superiority were commonplace, and even so evenhanded a figure as Stephen Austin wrote in 1836 that he saw the Texas conflict as one of barbarism on the part of "a mongrel Spanish-Indian and negro race, against civilization and the Anglo-American race."

War in Texas

Between 1830 and 1836, in spite of the mediation efforts of Austin (who was imprisoned for eighteen months by the Mexican government for his pains), the "war parties" in both Mexico and Anglo Texas gained ground. In the fall of 1835 war finally broke out, and a volunteer Anglo-Texan army seized Goliad and San Antonio, in the heart of Mexican Texas, from the small Mexican army that was sent to quell them. Believing they had won, the Americans were caught off guard by a major counterattack led by the Mexican general and president Antonio López de Santa Anna. On March 6, 1836, Santa Anna and his forces overwhelmed the 187 men who refused to surrender—or to escape from—the Alamo in San Antonio. In addition to James Bowie, other legendary figures to meet their fate at the Alamo were Davy Crockett and William Travis (see the chapter introduction). At Santa Anna's orders, the women at the Alamo—the wife of a Texas lieutenant, and several Mexicans—and a black slave named Joe were spared so that Anglo-Texans could hear their eyewitness accounts. From those accounts the legend of the Alamo was born.

From San Antonio, Santa Anna divided his army and led part of it in pursuit of the undisciplined volunteer Texas army that General Sam Houston was trying to train while on the run. On April 21, 1836, at the San Jacinto River in eastern Texas, Santa Anna thought he had Houston trapped at last. Confident of victory against the exhausted Anglo-Texans, Santa Anna's army rested in the afternoon, failing even to post sentries. Houston's men democratically voted (against Houston's advice) to attack immediately rather than the next morning. Shouting for the first time "Remember the Alamo!" the Texans completely surprised their opponents and won an overwhelming victory. Santa Anna fled from the field clad only in his silk shirt and drawers; he was captured later wearing a private's uniform. On May 14, 1836, he signed a treaty fixing the southern boundary of the newly independent Republic of Texas at the Rio Grande. The Mexican Congress, however, repudiated the treaty and refused to recognize Texan independence. They also rejected an offer from President Andrew Jackson to purchase Texas.

The Republic of Texas

Despite the military triumph of the Americans who had proclaimed the Republic of Texas, the land between the Rio Grande and the Nueces River remained disputed territory. An effort by the Texans in 1841 to capture Santa Fe was easily repulsed.

The Texas Republic was unexpectedly rebuffed in another quarter as well: the United States Congress. Immediately after independence in 1836 Texas applied for admission to the Union. But petitions opposing the admission of a fourteenth slave state (versus thirteen free states) poured into Congress. Former president John Quincy Adams, now serving formally as a congressman from Massachusetts and informally as the conscience of New England, led the opposition to the admission of Texas. Congress debated and ultimately dropped the application.

During his administration Adams, like Andrew Jackson after him, had tried to buy Texas from Mexico, but he was not now willing to add another slave state to the Union. Although Jackson was sympathetic to the Texan cause, he knew that he did not have the power to quell the controversy that the admission of Texas would arouse. But he did manage to extend diplomatic recognition to the Texas Republic, on March 3, 1837, less than twenty-four hours before he left office. Breaking the good news to Texas agents at the White House, Jackson offered toasts to the Republic of Texas and to its president, his old friend Sam Houston.

Houston must have frequently wondered whether the presidency of the Texas Republic was an honor worth having. The unresolved situation with Mexico put heavy stress on Anglo–Tejano relations. Immediately after the revolt, many Tejano residents fled to Mexico, and Anglo squatters moved in to claim their lands. In some regions, vigilantes forced Tejanos to leave. San Antonio, however, the most important city of Mexican Texas, saw an accommodation between the old Tejano elite and the new Anglo authorities (see the chapter introduction). Although they slowly lost political power, members of the elite were not immediately dispossessed of their property. As before, ambitious Anglos could marry into the group, while fostering the changes in law and commerce by which it would eventually be displaced.

This arrangement was upset in 1842, when two expeditions from Mexico briefly captured San Antonio. Upon regaining control, Anglos became much harsher, and many of the Tejano elite fled to Mexico. Fearful and angry, Anglos briefly discussed banishing or imprisoning all Tejanos until the border issue was settled. This was, of course, impossible. Culturally, San Antonio remained a Mexican city long after the Americans had declared independence. The Americans in the Republic of Texas faced the problem of reconciling American ideals of democracy with the reality of subordinating those with a prior claim, the Tejanos, to the status of a conquered people.

Nationally, ethnocentric attitudes toward Mexicans quickly triumphed. Tejanos and other Mexicans were soon being blamed for their subordination. Senator Edward Hannagan of Indiana was one of the most outspoken. "Mexico and the United

States are peopled by two distinct and utterly un-homogeneous races," he announced (incorrectly) in 1847. "In no reasonable period could we amalgamate." In the same year, the *Democratic Review* offered the following smooth rationalization of conquest:

> Had Mexico been settled by a vigorous race of Europeans . . . that would have turned its advantages to account, developed its wealth, increased its commerce and multiplied its settlements, she would not now be in danger of losing her lands by emigration from the North.

American control over the other Texas residents, the Indians, was also slow in coming. Although the coastal peoples were soon killed or removed, the Comanches still rode the high plains of northern and western Texas. West of the Rio Grande, equally fierce Apache bands were in control. Both groups soon learned to distrust American promises to stay out of their territory, and they did not hesitate to raid and kill trespassers. Not until after the Civil War, and major campaigns by the U.S. Army, would these fierce Indian tribes be conquered.

Texas Annexation and the Election of 1844

Martin Van Buren, who succeeded Andrew Jackson as president in 1837, was too cautious to raise the Texas issue during his term of office. But Texans themselves continued to press for annexation, and at the same time they sought recognition and support from Great Britain. The idea of an independent and expansionist republic on their southern border, and one supported by America's traditional enemy no less, alarmed many Americans. Annexation thus became an urgent matter of national politics, adding to the troubles of the governing Whig party. The Whigs, as we saw in Chapter 10, were already deeply divided by the policies of John Tyler, the accidental president. Tyler raised the issue of annexation in 1844, hoping thereby to ensure his reelection. But the strategy backfired. Secretary of State John Calhoun awakened sectional fears by presenting the annexation treaty to Congress in language stressing the urgent need of southern slave owners for the extension of slavery.

In a storm of protest, Whigs rejected the treaty proposed by their own president, and ejected Tyler himself from the party. In his place they chose Henry Clay, the party's long-time standard-bearer, as their presidential candidate. Clay took a noncommittal stance on Texas, favoring annexation, but only if Mexico approved. Since Mexico's emphatic disapproval was well known, Clay's statement was widely interpreted as a politician's effort not to alienate voters on either side of the fence.

In contrast, wholehearted and outspoken expansionists seized control of the Democratic party. Sweeping aside their own senior politician, Van Buren, who like Clay tried to remain noncommittal, the Democrats nominated their first dark horse candidate, James K. Polk of Tennessee. Southerners and westerners among the Democrats — including such notables as Robert Walker of Mississippi, Stephen Douglas of Illinois, and Lewis Cass of Michigan — beat the drum of manifest destiny (the phrase was coined during this election), promising that expansion meant a glorious extension of democracy. They enthusiastically endorsed Polk's platform, which called for "the re-occupation of Oregon and the re-annexation of Texas at the earliest practicable period."

Polk won the 1844 election by the narrow margin of 40,000 votes (although he gained 170 electoral votes to Clay's 105). An ominous portent for the Whigs was the showing of James G. Birney of the Liberty party. He polled 62,000 votes, largely from northern antislavery Whigs who found even Henry Clay's lukewarm expansionism unacceptable. Birney's third-party campaign was the first political sign of the growing strength of antislavery opinion. In 1845 John Tyler, ignoring this signal of sectional division, pushed through Congress a joint resolution (which did not require the two-thirds approval by the Senate necessary for treaties) for the annexation of Texas. Thus nine years after its founding the Republic of Texas disappeared and Texas entered the Union as the twenty-eighth state and the fourteenth slave state.

THE MEXICAN—AMERICAN WAR

James K. Polk entered the presidency an avowed expansionist, and he certainly lived up to his convictions. In 1846 Polk peacefully added Oregon south of the forty-ninth parallel to the United States; in 1848, following the Mexican-American War, he acquired Mexico's northern provinces of California and New Mexico as well. With the annexation of Texas, the United States had added 1.5 million

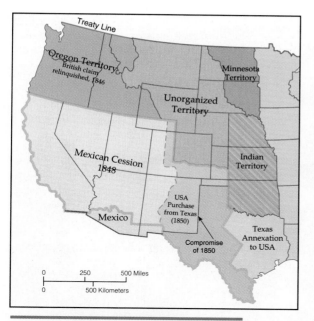

Territory Added During Polk's Presidency

James K. Polk was elected president in 1844 on an expansionist platform. He lived up to most of his campaign rhetoric by gaining the Oregon Territory peacefully from the British, Texas by the presidential action of his predecessor John Tyler, and present-day California, Arizona, Nevada, Utah, and New Mexico by war with Mexico. In the short space of three years, the size of the United States was doubled.

square miles of territory, doubling its size in the short space of three years. Polk was indeed "the manifest destiny" president.

War Begins

In the spring of 1846, just as the Oregon controversy was drawing to a peaceful conclusion, tensions with Mexico grew more serious. As soon as Texas was granted statehood in 1845, the Mexican government broke diplomatic relations with the United States. In addition, because the United States accepted the Texas claim of all land north of the Rio Grande, it found itself embroiled in a border dispute with Mexico. In the summer of 1845, Polk sent General Zachary Taylor and a force of 3,500 to the Nueces River with orders to defend Texas in the event of a Mexican invasion.

Polk had larger goals in mind than settling a mere border dispute. He coveted the area that is now Texas, New Mexico, Arizona, Nevada, Utah, and especially California. At the same time that he sent Taylor to Texas, Polk secretly instructed the Pacific naval squadron to seize the California ports if Mexico declared war. He also wrote the American consul in Monterey, Thomas Larkin, that a peaceful takeover by Californians (Spanish Mexicans and Americans alike) would not be unwelcome. When, in addition the federally commissioned explorer John C. Frémont and a band of armed men appeared in California in the winter of 1845–46, Mexican authorities became alarmed and ordered him to leave. After withdrawing briefly to Oregon, Frémont returned to California and was on hand in June to assist in the Bear Flag Revolt (to be discussed later in the chapter).

Meanwhile, Polk followed up his warlike gestures by sending a secret envoy, John Slidell, to Mexico with an offer of $30 million (or more) for the Rio Grande border, New Mexico, and California. When the Mexican government refused in January of 1846 to even receive Slidell, an angry Polk ordered General Taylor and his forces south into the disputed territory between the Nueces and the Rio Grande. In April of 1846 a brief skirmish broke out between American and Mexican soldiers. Polk seized upon the event, sending a war message to Congress: "Mexico has passed the boundary of the United States . . . and shed American blood upon American soil. . . . War exists by the act of Mexico herself, notwithstanding all our efforts to avoid it." This last claim of President Polk's was, of course, contrary to fact. On May 13, 1846, Congress declared war upon Mexico.

Mr. Polk's War

From the beginning, the Mexican-American War was politically divisive. Whig critics in Congress, among them a gawky young congressman from Illinois named Abraham Lincoln, questioned Polk's account of the border incident. They accused the president of misleading Congress and maneuvering the country into an unnecessary war. Congressional concern over the president's use of his war powers — a recurrent issue in the Vietnam War and again in the Reagan years — begins here in the suspicious opening of the Mexican-American War. As the war dragged on and casualties and costs mounted — 13,000 American and 50,000 Mexican lives, $97 million in American military costs — opposition in-

This vivid sketch of a California engagement (San Pasqual) during the Mexican-American War captures the excitement of battle. It also reveals the very small number of soldiers whose victories decided the fates of two large nations.

creased, especially among northern antislavery Whigs. More and more people came to the opinion that the war was nothing more than a plot by southerners to expand slavery. Many northerners asked why Polk had been willing to settle for only a part of Oregon but was so eager to pursue a war for slave territory. Thus expansionist dreams served to fuel sectional antagonisms.

The northern states witnessed both mass and individual protests against the war. In Massachusetts, the legislature passed a resolution condemning Polk's declaration of war as unconstitutional, and Concord's Henry David Thoreau went to jail rather than pay the taxes he believed would support the war effort. (His dramatic gesture was undercut by his aunt, who paid his fine after he had spent only one night in jail.) After his release Thoreau went back to his cabin on Walden Pond, where he wrote his essay "Civil Disobedience," justifying his moral right to oppose an immoral government. Years later, the Indian nationalist Mohandas Gandhi used Thoreau's essay to justify his campaign of civil disobedience against the British Empire. Still later, Martin

Luther King and others used Gandhi's model of civil disobedience, derived from Thoreau's protest against a war of expansion, as a basis for their actions in the civil rights movement of the 1960s.

The claim that the conflict was "Mr. Polk's War" was not just a Whig jibe. Although he lacked a military background, Polk assumed the overall planning of strategy (a practice that the critical Mr. Lincoln was to follow in the Civil War). It was Polk who defined the role of the president as commander in chief during wartime, coordinating civilian political goals and military requirements. In 1846 Polk sent General Taylor south into northeastern Mexico and Colonel Stephen Kearny to New Mexico and California. Taylor captured the northern Mexico city of Monterrey in September. Meanwhile, Kearney marched his men the 900 miles to Santa Fe, which surrendered peacefully. Another march of roughly the same distance brought him by fall to southern California, which he took with the help of naval forces and Frémont's irregular troops.

The northern provinces that Polk had coveted were now secured, but contrary to his expectations,

Mexico refused to negotiate. In response, General Winfield Scott launched an amphibious attack on the coastal city of Veracruz. General Santa Anna, victor at the Alamo eleven years earlier, attacked American troops at Buena Vista in February of 1847, but failed to defeat Taylor's small force. Scott, with a force of 12,000 men, thereupon succeeded in capturing Veracruz, and in September of that year he took Mexico City. It was a brilliant feat for an all-volunteer, poorly supplied army fighting on foreign soil.

With the American army went a special envoy, Nicholas Trist, who delivered Polk's terms for peace. In the Treaty of Guadalupe Hidalgo, signed February 2, 1848, Mexico ceded their northern provinces of California and New Mexico (which included present-day Arizona, Utah, and Nevada) and accepted the Rio Grande as the boundary of Texas. The United States agreed to pay Mexico $15 million and assume about $2 million in individual claims against that nation. When Trist returned to Washington with the treaty, Polk was furious. Polk's appetite had grown after General Scott's sweeping victory, and he had recalled Trist, intending to replace him with an envoy who would make greater demands. Trist had ignored the recall order and completed the treaty. "All Mexico!" was the phrase widely used by expansionists. But a vocal group opposed further expansion. Among them were such notables as Ralph Waldo Emerson, who grimly warned, "The United

The Mexican-American War, 1846–1848

The Mexican-American War began with an advance by U.S. forces into the disputed area between the Nueces River and the Rio Grande in Texas. The war's major battles were fought by General Zachary Taylor in northern Mexico and General Winfield Scott in Veracruz and Mexico City. Meanwhile Colonel Stephen Kearney secured New Mexico and, with the help of the U.S. Navy and Fremont's troops, California.

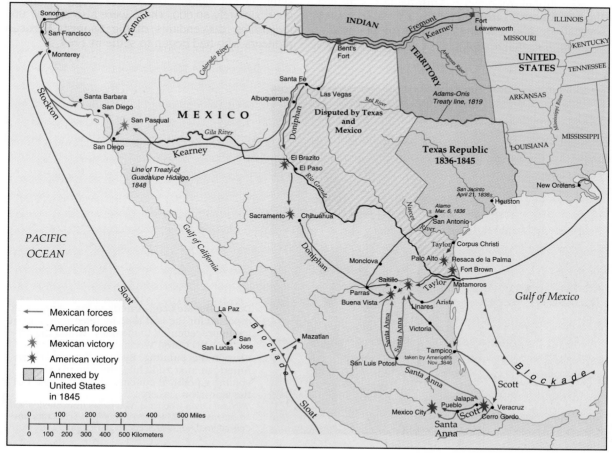

States will conquer Mexico, but it will be as the man swallows arsenic, which brings him down in turn. Mexico will poison us." Bowing to the political reality posed by the antislavery forces, Polk reluctantly accepted the treaty, but not without firing Trist, whom he denounced as an "impudent and unqualified scoundrel." Later, in 1853, the $10 million Gadsden Purchase added another 285,000 square miles (in present-day New Mexico and Arizona) to the United States.

A Popular War

The Mexican-American War was America's first popular war. For the first time, ordinary citizens could follow the events of the war almost daily. Thanks to the recently invented telegraph, newspapers could get up-to-date reports from their reporters, who were among the world's first war correspondents. Publishers of the *penny press,* as inexpensive, mass-circulation newspapers were known, soon discovered that the public's appetite for sensational war news was insatiable. For the first time in American history, on-the-spot accounts by journalists, and not the opinions of politicians, became the major shapers of popular attitudes toward a war. From beginning to end, news of the war stirred unprecedented popular excitement. The reports from the battlefield united Americans in a new way: They became part of a temporary but highly emotional community linked by newsprint and buttressed by public gatherings. In the spring of 1846, news of Zachary Taylor's first victory (at Palo Alto) prompted the largest meeting ever held in the cotton textile town of Lowell, Massachusetts. In May of 1847, New York City celebrated the twin victories at Vera Cruz and Buena Vista with fireworks, illuminations, and a "grand procession" estimated at 400,000 people. Generals Taylor and Scott became overnight heroes; in time, both became presidential candidates. Exciting, sobering, and terrible, war news had a deep hold on the popular imagination. It was a lesson newspaper publishers never forgot.

THE CALIFORNIA GOLD RUSH

In the early 1840s California was inhabited by many seminomadic Indian tribes, whose people numbered approximately 50,000. There were also some 7,000 *Californios,* descendants of the Spanish Mexican pioneers who had begun to settle in 1769.

During the Mexican-American War, news was reported for the first time by telegraph, imparting unprecedented immediacy, which the artist, Richard Caton Woodville, perfectly captures in this painting. By including an African American man and child, the artist is also voicing a political concern about the effect of the war upon slavery.
(Richard Caton Woodville. War News from Mexico. *Oil on canvas. 27 × 25 inches. Gift of John D.B. Crimmins. Collection of National Academy of Design.)*

Russian–Californio Trade

Under Spanish rule California had been neglected and isolated. The elaborate system of twenty-one missions had been difficult to maintain so far from the home country (see Chapter 5). Evading Spanish regulations, the *Californios* conducted a small illegal trade in cattle hides (for the shoe factories of Massachusetts) with American ships, and a much larger trade with the Russian American Fur Company in Sitka, Alaska. A mutually beneficial barter of California food for iron tools and woven cloth from Russia was established in 1806. This arrangement became even brisker after the Russians settled Fort Ross (near present-day Mendocino) in 1812, and led in time to regular trade with Mission San Rafael and Mission Sonoma. That the Russians in Alaska, so far from their own capital, were better supplied with manufactured goods than the *Californios* is an index of the latter's isolation.

Until 1822 the Russian–*Californio* trade was officially illegal, but with Mexican independence the California trade was thrown open to ships of all nations. Nevertheless, *Californios* continued their cordial relations with the Russians, exempting them from the taxes and inspections that they required of the Americans. For its part, the Russian American Fur Company encouraged company agent Kyrill Khlebnikov to become fluent in spoken and written Spanish and to develop close relations with California officials. In 1832 Khlebnikov was recalled to Russia for a promotion. The same year, the Mexican government ordered the secularization of the California missions. This meant that the Indians who lived there were released from their virtual bondage, and much of the mission land was claimed by *Californios*. Agricultural productivity declined, and the Russians turned more and more to the rich farms of the Hudson's Bay Company in the Pacific Northwest for their food supply. In 1841, they sold Fort Ross to John Sutter and the Russian–Californio connection came to an end.

Early American Settlement

John Sutter, a Swiss who had migrated to California in 1839 and become a Mexican citizen, held a magnificent land grant in the Sacramento Valley. At the center of his holdings was Sutter's Fort, a walled compound that was part living quarters and part supply shop for his vast cattle ranch, which was largely run on enforced Indian labor. In the 1840s, Sutter offered valuable support to the handful of Americans who chose to travel the Overland Trail to California rather than to Oregon, the preferred destination. Most of these Americans, keenly aware that they were interlopers in Mexican territory, settled near Sutter in California's Central Valley, away from the *Californios* clustered along the coast.

The 1840s immigrants made no effort to intermarry with the *Californios* or to conform to Spanish ways. They were bent on taking over the territory. In June of 1846 these Americans banded together at Sonoma in the Bear Flag Revolt (so called because of the emblem on their flag), declaring independence from Mexico. The American takeover of California was not confirmed until the Treaty of Guadalupe Hidalgo in 1848. In the meantime, California was regarded merely as a remote, sparsely populated frontier.

Gold!

In January 1848 carpenter James Marshall noticed small flakes of gold in the millrace at Sutter's Mill (present-day Coloma). Soon he and all the rest of Sutter's employees were panning for gold in California's streams. The news, which they had hoped to keep secret, spread, and before long it seemed that all the men in California were at the mines. When explorer John Frémont reached San Francisco in June of 1848, he found it almost deserted because of "gold fever."

In the autumn of 1848, rumors reached the east coast that gold had been discovered in California. The reports were confirmed in mid-November when an army courier arrived in Washington carrying a tea caddy full of gold dust and nuggets. The spirit of excitement and adventure so recently aroused by the Mexican-American War was now directed toward California, the new El Dorado. Thousands left farms and jobs and headed west, by ship and overland trail, to make their fortune. These "forty-niners" from all parts of the United States — and indeed, from all over the world — transformed a quiet ranching paradise into a tumultuous search for wealth in California's rivers and streams.

Eighty percent of the forty-niners were American. They came from every state — an eye-opening realization for the many people who had known only their hometown folks before. The second largest group of migrants were from nearby Mexico and the west coast of Latin America (13 percent). The remainder came from Europe and Asia.

In 1849, as the gold rush began in earnest, San Francisco, the major entry port and supply point,

California in the Gold Rush Period

This map shows the major gold camps along the Mother Lode in the western foothills of the Sierra Nevada mountains. Goldseekers reached the camps by crossing the Sierra Nevada near Placerville on the Overland Trail or by sea via San Francisco. San Francisco, formerly a sleepy village, became a major city overnight. The main area of Spanish-Mexican settlement, the coastal region between Monterey and Los Angeles, was remote from the gold fields.

Source: Warren A. Beck and Ynez D. Haase, *Historical Atlas of California* (Norman: University of Oklahoma Press, 1974), map 50.

money than now presents itself in this place. . . . We are satisfied to dig our gold in San Francisco." From these "instant" beginnings (including several years of vigilante justice in the early 1850s), San Francisco stabilized to become a major American city. Meanwhile, the white population of California had jumped from an estimated pre–gold rush figure of 11,000 to over 100,000.

Mining Camps

Most mining camps, though they shared San Francisco's instant beginnings, were empty within a few years. In spite of the aura of glamour that surrounds the names of the famous camps — Poker Flat, Angels Camp, Whiskey Bar, Placerville, Mariposa — they were generally dirty and dreary places. Most miners lived in tents or hovels, unwilling to take time from mining to build themselves decent quarters. They cooked monotonous meals of beans, bread, and bacon or, if they had money, bought meals at expensive restaurants and boardinghouses. Many migrants traveled to the mines with relatives or fellow townspeople. But often they split up in California — each man with his own idea of where he could find gold the easiest — and ended up on their own. They led a cheerless, uncomfortable, and unhealthy existence, especially during the long, rainy winter months, with few distractions apart from the saloon, the gambling hall, and the prostitute's crib.

Most miners were young, unmarried, and unsuccessful. Only a small percentage ever struck it rich in California, because the most accessible gold deposits played out early and the deeper deposits required capital and machinery, not a single pick and shovel. (Some of the workings at the Comstock Lode in Virginia City, Nevada, a later mining center, were half a mile deep.) But many men were ashamed to come home until they had made their pile. Increasingly, those who stayed on in California were no longer independent miners but wage earners for large mining concerns.

As in San Francisco, a more reliable way to earn money was to supply the miners. Every mining community had its saloon keepers, gamblers, prostitutes, merchants, and restauranters (even if the table was only a plank on top of two flour barrels). Like the miners themselves, these people were transients, always ready to pick up and move at the word of a new strike. The majority of women in the early mining camps were prostitutes. Some grew rich or married respectably, but most died young of drugs, venereal disease, or violence. Most of the

sprang to life. From a settlement of 1,000 in 1848 it grew to a city of 35,000 in 1850. Amazing as it might appear, this surge of growth should not surprise us. For the real money to be made in California was not in panning for gold but in supplying the miners, who needed to be fed, clothed, housed, supplied with tools, and entertained. Among the first to learn that lesson was the German Jew Levi Strauss, who sold so many tough work pants to miners that his name became synonymous with his product. And Jerusha Marshall, who opened a twenty-room boardinghouse in the city, candidly wrote to her eastern relatives: "Never was there a better field for making

These abandoned ships in San Francisco Bay attest to the strength of "gold fever." Many ships that docked in San Francisco in 1849 and 1850 lost all of their crew, who rushed to the gold fields in the hopes of getting rich.

other women were hardworking wives of miners, and in this predominantly male society they made good money doing domestic work: keeping boardinghouses, cooking, doing laundry. Even the wives of professional men, who in the East might have been restrained by propriety, succumbed to the monetary opportunities and kept boardinghouses.

Although the gold rush lured hundreds of thousands to California, the mining camps could hardly be called "civilized." Few people put any effort into building communities: They were too busy seeking gold. Violence was endemic, and much of it was racial. Discrimination, especially against Chinese, Mexicans, and African Americans, was common. Frequently their claims were "jumped." They were robbed and sometimes killed, and many were forced to move to another area altogether. When violence failed, legal means were used, among them a mining tax on foreigners that was prohibitively high. Finally, most mining camps were at best temporary communities. The gold "played out," people moved on, leaving ghost towns behind.

By the mid-1850s, the immediate effects of the gold rush had passed. California had a booming population, a thriving agriculture, and a corporate mining industry. The gold rush also left California with a population that was larger, more affluent, and (in urban San Francisco) more culturally sophisticated than that in other newly settled territories. But the gold rush left some permanent scars, and not

just on the foothills landscape: the virtual extermination of the California Indians, the dispossession of many *Californios* (forced out of the mines and then legally deprived of their land grants), and the growth of racial animosity toward a new ethnic group, the Chinese. The major characteristics of the mining frontier, evident first in the California gold rush and repeated many times thereafter in "rushes" in Colorado, Montana, Idaho, South Dakota, and Arizona, were a lack of stable communities and a worsening of racial tensions.

THE POLITICS OF MANIFEST DESTINY

As we have seen, in three short years, from 1845 to 1848, the United States grew an incredible 50 percent and became a continental nation. This expansion quickly became the dominant issue in national politics.

Young America

Early in the chapter we saw that one source of manifest destiny sentiment was national pride — the feeling that the superiority of American democracy would lead inevitably to the expansion of the nation. The swift victory in the Mexican-American War and the "prize" of California gold seemed to confirm that

Chinese first came to California in 1848 attracted by the Gold Rush. Frequently, however, they were forced off their claims by intolerant whites and limited to servant occupations rather than allowed equal chance for enterprise in the gold fields.

belief. European events in 1848 also served to foster American pride. In that year a series of democratic revolutions — in Italy, France, Germany, Hungary, and parts of the Austrian Empire — swept the Continent. Expansionists quickly assumed that American democracy and manifest destiny formed the model for these liberal revolutions. When Lajos Kossuth, the famed Hungarian revolutionary, visited the United States in 1851, he was given a hero's welcome, and Daniel Webster complacently assured him that "we shall rejoice to see our American model upon the lower Danube."

In an even more confident gesture, Commodore Matthew Perry was dispatched across the Pacific to Japan. The mission resulted in 1854 in a commercial treaty that opened Japan to American trade. Perry's feat caused a newspaper in tiny Olympia, Washington, to boast, "We shall have the boundless Pacific for a market in manifest destiny. We were born to command it."

But efforts closer to home by the Young America movement, as expansionist Democrats styled themselves, were more controversial. Victory in the Mexican-American War, and the evident weakness of the Mexican government, had whetted the appetite of southern expansionists for more territory. But the majority of American politicians were very cautious about further gains. When in the spring of 1848 Polk recommended American intervention in the civil war in the Mexican province of Yucatán,

Congress rebuffed him. No less a figure than John Calhoun, harking back to Polk's manipulation of Congress in 1846, cautioned, "I did hope that the experience of the Mexican War — that precipitate and rash measure which has cost the country so dearly in blood and treasure — would have taught the administration moderation and caution." In the winter of 1848, rumors swept Washington that Polk had offered Spain up to $100 million for Cuba (compared with the $15 million that had purchased California and New Mexico). The nation was spared a raging political battle when Spain spurned all offers.

Thus the Mexican-American War was divisive even after it was won. A small group of expansionists, most from the South, wanted more, in spite of clear evidence that most Americans had had enough. Throughout the 1850s, these expansionists continued to covet Mexico, Central America, and Cuba. Adventures in these directions, all organized by southerners intent on acquiring new lands for cotton, further inflamed the festering sectional differences of the 1850s (see Chapter 15).

The Wilmot Proviso

In 1846, almost all the northern members of the Whig party opposed Democratic president James Polk's belligerent expansionism on antislavery grounds. Northern Whigs correctly feared that expansion would reopen the issue of slavery in the territories. "We appear . . . to be rushing upon perils headlong, and with our eyes all open," Daniel Webster warned in 1847. His remedy? "We want no extension of territory; we want no accession of new states. The country is already large enough." But the outpouring of enthusiasm for the Mexican-American War drowned out Webster's words and convinced most Whig congressmen that they needed to vote military appropriations for the war in spite of their misgivings.

Ironically it was not the Whigs but a freshman Democratic congressman from Pennsylvania, David Wilmot, who opened the door to sectional controversy over expansion. In August of 1846, only a few short months after the beginning of the Mexican-American War, Wilmot proposed in an amendment to a military appropriations bill that slavery be banned in all the territories acquired from Mexico. He was ready, Wilmot said, to "sustain the institutions of the South as they exist. But sir, the issue now presented is not whether slavery shall exist unmolested where it is now, but whether it shall be carried to new and distant regions, now free, where the footprint of a slave cannot be found." In the debate and voting that followed, something new and ominous occurred: Southern Whigs joined southern Democrats to vote against the measure, while northerners of both parties supported it. Sectional

interest had triumphed over party loyalty. Wilmot's Proviso marked the first breakdown of the national party system and reopened the debate about the place of slavery in the future of the nation.

Final congressional action on the Wilmot Proviso was delayed until the end of the Mexican-American War. But in 1848, following the Treaty of Guadalupe Hidalgo, the question of the expansion of slavery could no longer be avoided or postponed. Antislavery advocates from the North argued with proslavery southerners in a debate that was much more prolonged and more bitter than the Missouri Compromise debate of 1819. Civility quickly wore thin: Threats were uttered and fistfights broke out on the floor of the House of Representatives. The Wilmot Proviso posed a fundamental challenge to both parties. Neither the Democrats nor the Whigs could take a strong stand on the amendment because neither party could get its northern and southern wings to agree. Decisive action, for or against, was a serious threat to party unity. Webster's fear that expansion would lead to sectional conflict had become a reality.

The Free-Soil Movement

Why did David Wilmot propose this controversial measure? In part, for reasons of practical politics: Wilmot was a northern antislavery Democrat who

This Japanese painting shows Commodore Matthew Perry landing in Japan in 1854. The subsequent commercial treaty, which opened a formerly closed Japan to American trade, was viewed in the United States as another fruit of Manifest Destiny.

had, as he said, "battled, time and again, against the abolitionists of the North." Northern politicians — both Democrats and Whigs — needed to stop the loss of votes to the Liberty party. Founded in 1840 by abolitionists, the party won 62,000 votes in the 1844 presidential election, all in the North. This was more than enough to deny victory to the Whig candidate, Henry Clay. Neither party could afford to ignore the strength of this third party.

The Liberty party took an uncompromising stance against slavery. As articulated by Ohio's Salmon P. Chase, the party platform called for the "divorce of the federal government from slavery." The party proposed to prohibit the admission of slave states to the Union, end slavery in the District of Columbia, and abolish the interstate slave trade, which was vital to the expansion of cotton growing into the Old Southwest (see Chapter 11). Liberty party members also favored denying office to all slaveholders (a proposal that would have robbed all the southern states of their senators) and forbidding the use of slave labor on federal construction projects. In short, the party proposed to quickly strangle slavery. The popularity of this radical program among northern voters in 1844 was an indication of the moral fervor of abolitionism (see Chapter 13).

But Liberty party doctrine was too uncompromising for the mass of northern voters, who immediately realized that the southern states would leave the Union before accepting it. Still, as the 1844 vote indicated, many northerners opposed slavery. From this sentiment the Free-Soil party was born. The free-soil argument was a calculated adjustment of abolitionist principles to practical politics. It shifted the focus from the question of the morality of slavery to the ways in which slavery posed a threat to northern expansion. The free-soil doctrine thus established a direct link between expansion, which most Americans supported, and sectional politics.

Free-soilers were willing to allow slavery to continue in the existing slave states — because they supported the Union, not because they approved of slavery — but they were unwilling to allow the extension of slavery to new and unorganized territory. If the South were successful in extending slavery, they argued, northern farmers who moved west would find themselves competing at an economic disadvantage with large planters using slave labor. Free-Soilers also insisted that the northern values of freedom and individualism would be destroyed if the slave-based southern labor system were allowed to spread. To Free-Soilers, the South was composed of little more than corrupt aristocrats, degraded slaves, and a large class of poor whites who were deprived of opportunity because they did not understand the value of honest labor.

Finally, many free-soilers really meant "anti-black" when they said "antislavery." They proposed to ban *all* black people from the new territories (a step that four states — Indiana, Illinois, Iowa, and Oregon — took but did not always enforce). William Lloyd Garrison promptly denounced the free-soil doctrine as "whitemanism," a racist effort to make the territories white. There was much truth to his charge, but there was no denying that the free-soil doctrine was popular. Although abolitionists were making headway in their claim for moral equality regardless of skin color, most northerners were unwilling to consider social equality for African Americans, free or slave. Banning all black people from the western territories seemed a simple solution.

Finally, the free-soil movement was a repudiation of the sectional compromise of 1820. If the Missouri Compromise line were carried westward to the Pacific Ocean (as Secretary of State James Buchanan proposed in 1848), much of present-day New Mexico and Arizona and the southern half of California would have been admitted as slave states, and everything to the north would have been free. Free-Soilers opposed this arrangement. Their opposition in 1848 to the Missouri Compromise line indicated how influential antislavery feeling was becoming in the North.

The Election of 1848

A swirl of emotions — pride, expansionism, sectionalism, abolitionism, free-soil sentiment — surrounded the election of 1848. The Treaty of Guadalupe Hidalgo had been signed, and the vast northern Mexican provinces of New Mexico and California (as well as Texas) incorporated into the United States. But the issues raised by the Wilmot Proviso were unresolved (not to be settled until the Compromise of 1850). Every candidate had to have an answer to the question of whether slavery should be admitted in the new territories.

Lewis Cass of Michigan, the Democratic nominee for president (Polk, in poor health, declined to serve a second term) proposed the notion of popular sovereignty — that is, leaving the decision to the citizens of each territory. This democratic-sounding measure was based on the Jeffersonian faith in the common man's ability to vote both his own self-interest and the common good. But in fact, it shifted decision making on this crucial issue from national politicians to the members of territorial legislatures — and, as it turned out in Kansas (see Chapter 15), to warring bands of ordinary people. In reality, then, popular sovereignty was an admission of the nation's failure to resolve sectional differences.

Moreover, the doctrine was deliberately vague about *when* a territory would choose its status. Would it do so during the territorial stage? At the point of applying for statehood? Clearly, this question was crucial, for no slave owner would invest in new land if the territory could later be declared free, and no abolitionist would move to a territory that was destined to become a slave state. Cass hoped his ambiguity on this point would win him votes in both North and South. Even so, sectional differences ran so deep that the Democrats found it necessary to print two campaign biographies of Cass. The biography circulated in the North touted Cass's doctrine of popular sovereignty as the best way to keep slavery out of the territories; the biography in the South implied the opposite.

For their part, the Whigs passed over perennial candidate Henry Clay and turned once again to a war hero, General Zachary Taylor. Taylor, a Louisiana slaveholder, refused to take a position on the Wilmot Proviso, thus allowing both northern and southern voters to hope that he agreed with them. Privately, Taylor opposed the expansion of slavery. In public, he evaded the issue by running as a war hero and a national leader who was above sectional politics.

The deliberate vagueness of the two major

In 1848, the Whigs once again adopted the campaign strategy that had worked so successfully for them in the presidential election of 1840. They nominated a hero of the Mexican-American War, General Zachary Taylor, and ran on his military exploits. In this poster, every letter of Taylor's name is decorated with scenes from the recent war, which had seized the popular imagination in a way no previous conflict had done. Emphasizing Taylor's reputation as a national hero (and therefore above petty politics), the Whigs were able to evade the question of whether or not he favored the extension of slavery.

CHRONOLOGY

1608	First Spanish settlement in New Mexico
1670s	British and French Canadians begin fur trade in western Canada
1716	First Spanish settlement in Texas
1769	First Spanish settlement in California
1790s	New England ships begin sea otter trade in Pacific Northwest
1803	Louisiana Purchase
1804	Lewis and Clark expedition
1806	Russian-Californio trade begins
1806—07	Zebulon Pike's expedition to Great Plains and Rocky Mountains
1819—20	Stephen Long's expedition to Great Plains
1821	Hudson's Bay Company gains dominance of western fur trade
	Mexico seizes independence from Spain
	Santa Fe Trail opens; soon protected by U.S. military
	Stephen Austin becomes first American *empresario* in Texas
1824	First fur rendezvous sponsored by Rocky Mountain Fur Company
	Hudson's Bay Company establishes Fort Vancouver in Oregon Territory
1830	Indian Removal Act creates Indian Territory
1833—34	Prince Maximilian and Karl Bodmer visit Plains Indians
1834	Jason Lee establishes first mission in Oregon Territory
1836	Texas revolts against Mexico; Republic of Texas formed
1843—44	John C. Frémont maps trails to Oregon and California
1844	Democrat James Polk elected president on an expansionist platform
1845	Texas annexed to U.S. as a slave state
	John O'Sullivan coins the phrase "manifest destiny"
1846	Oregon question settled peacefully with Britain
	Mexican-American War begins
	Bear Flag Revolt in California
	Wilmot Proviso
1847	Missionaries Narcissa and Marcus Whitman killed in Oregon; Cayuse War begins
1848	Treaty of Guadalupe Hidalgo
	General Zachary Taylor, a Whig, elected president
1849	California gold rush

candidates displeased a number of northern voters. An uneasy mixture of disaffected Democrats (among them David Wilmot) and Whigs joined former Liberty party voters to support the candidate of the Free-Soil party, former president Martin Van Buren. Van Buren, angry at the Democratic party for passing him over in 1844 and displeased with the growing southern dominance of the Democratic party, frankly ran as a spoiler. He knew he could not win the election, but he could divide the Democrats. In the end, Van Buren garnered 10 percent of the vote (all in the North). The Free-Soil vote cost Cass the electoral votes of New York and Pennsylvania, and General Taylor won the election with 47 percent of the popular vote. This was the second election (after 1840 and William Henry Harrison) that the Whigs had won by running a war hero who could duck hard questions by claiming to be above politics. Uncannily, history was to repeat itself: Taylor, like Harrison, died before his term was completed, and the chance for national unity—if ever it existed—was lost.

CONCLUSION

If we think of the election of 1848 as a referendum on manifest destiny, the results are deeply ironic. James Polk, who presided over the unprecedented expansion, did not serve a second term and thus gained no electoral victory to match his military one. The electorate that had been so thrilled by the war news voted for a war hero — who led the antiexpansionist party. The election was decided by Martin Van Buren, the Free-Soil candidate who voiced the sentiments of the abolitionists, an insignificant reform group just a few years before. The amazing expansion achieved by the Mexican-American War — America's manifest destiny — made the United States a continental nation but awakened the issue that was to tear the country apart. Sectional rivalries and fears dominated every aspect of the politics of the 1850s. Expansion, once a force for unity, now divided the nation's major sectional communities, the North and the South, who could not agree on the future of their shared community, the federal Union.

Additional Readings

ARNOLDO DE LEON, *The Tejano Community, 1836–1900* (1982). Traces the changing status of Tejanos after Texas came under Anglo control.

JOHN MACK FARAGHER, *Women and Men on the Overland Trail* (1979). One of the first books to consider the experience of women on the journey west.

T. R. FEHRENBACH, *Lone Star: A History of Texas and Texans* (1968) A large and leisurely study with a primary focus on the history of Anglos in Texas.

WILLIAM GOETZMAN, *Exploration and Empire: The Explorer and the Scientist in the Winning of the American West* (1966). Considers the many government-sponsored explorations of the West.

THOMAS R. HIETALA, *Manifest Design: Anxious Aggrandizement in Late Jacksonian America* (1985). An interesting reassessment of manifest destiny from the perspective of party politics.

JULIE ROY JEFFREY, *Converting the West: A Biography of Narcissa Whitman* (1991). Makes a clear connection between Whitman's evangelical upbringing and her failure to understand the culture of the Cayuse Indians.

ROBERT W. JOHANNSEN, *To the Halls of the Montezumas: The Mexican War in the American Imagination* (1985). A lively book that explores the impact of the Mexican War on public opinion.

JANET LECOMPTE, *Pueblo, Hardscrabble, Greenhorn: The Upper Arkansas, 1832–1856* (1978). A social history that portrays the multicultural composition of the trading frontier.

CARLOS SCHWANTES, *The Pacific Northwest: An Interpretive History* (1989). A good regional history.

DAVID J. WEBER, *The Mexican Frontier, 1821–1846: The American Southwest under Mexico* (1982). A fine study of the history of the Southwest before American conquest. The author is a leading borderlands historian.

RICHARD WHITE, *"It's Your Misfortune and None of My Own": A History of the American West* (1991). A major reinterpretation that focuses on the history of the region itself rather than on the westward expansion of Americans. Pays much more attention to Spanish Mexicans and Indian peoples than earlier texts. Devotes substantial space to the twentieth century.

15

THE COMING CRISIS, THE 1850s

Bleeding Kansas, as it came to be called, was a lesson in the harm that two antithetical communities can do to each other. When Kansas was opened to white settlement in 1854, politicians in Washington could not agree on whether it should be a free or a slave state. They left the question to the white settlers of the territory, who tried to solve it by killing each other.

The first to claim land in Kansas were residents of nearby Missouri, itself a slave state. Egged on by Democratic senator David Atchinson of Missouri (who took a leave of absence from Congress to lead them), Missourians took up land claims, established proslavery strongholds such as the towns of Leavenworth, Kickapoo, and Atchinson, and repeatedly and blatantly swamped Kansas elections with Missouri votes. In 1855,

> **TWO LOCAL COMMUNITIES MIRROR THE SECTIONAL DIVISION OF THE NATION**

in the second of a number of notoriously fraudulent elections, 6,307 ballots were cast in a territory that had less than 3,000 eligible voters. The rest of the votes—all proslavery—were cast by "border ruffians," as they proudly called themselves, from Missouri. These were frontiersmen, fond of boasting that they could "scream louder, jump higher, shoot closer, get drunker at night and wake up soberer in the morning than any man this side of the Rocky Mountains."

Northerners quickly responded, with the encouragement of sympathetic politicians. At the beginning of the Kansas struggle, antislavery senator William H. Seward of New York had cried: "Come on then, gentlemen of the slave states! . . . We will engage in competition for the virgin soil of Kansas and God give victory to the side that is stronger in numbers, as it is in right." A number of free-soil (antislavery) New Englanders were recruited to Kansas by the New England Emigrant Aid Society, begun by abolitionist Eli Thayer of Massachusetts. The first party of New Englanders arrived in the summer of 1854 and founded the free-soil town of Lawrence. More than a thousand others had joined them by the following summer. Lawrence quickly blossomed from a town of tent homes to one of solid log cabins, a church, a sawmill, stores, and a stone foundation for a permanent New England Emigrant Aid Society's Free State Hotel. These migrants were all free-soilers, and many were religious reformers as well. The contrast of values between them and the border ruffians was almost total. When nondrinking William Phillips stiffly refused a friendly

The Free State Hotel, built by the New England Emigrant Aid Society to house antislavery migrants to Kansas, was the most notable casualty of the burning and looting of the Lawrence community by proslavery opponents in 1856.

offer of a drink from a Missourian, the border ruffian burst out, "That's just it! This thing of temperance and abolitionism and the Emigrant Aid Society are all the same kind of thing."

Because of the earlier pattern of lateral settlement (northerners to the Old Northwest, southerners to the Old Southwest), New Englanders and southern frontiersmen such as the Missouri border ruffians were meeting each other for the first time in the new western territories like Kansas. Neither side liked what they saw. This clash of regional values might have been amusing if not for the failure of national politicians to solve the problem of slavery. Their failure made the Kansas confrontation lethal. When national politicians could not break the impasse between rival territorial legislatures — one proslave, one antislave — the people of Kansas turned to arms.

Heavy crates arrived in Lawrence. Though marked BOOKS, they were actually Sharp's repeating rifles, sent by eastern supporters. For their part, the already fully armed border ruffians (a typical "walking arsenal" carried a Bowie knife in his boots, revolvers at the waist, a rifle slung from his shoulder, and a sword at his side) called for reinforcements. David Atchinson exhorted Alabamans: "Let your young men come forth to Missouri and Kansas! Let them come well armed!"

The lethal preparations exploded into open warfare in the summer of 1856. The town of Lawrence was burned by proslave forces. In retaliation a grim old man named John Brown led his sons to kill five unarmed proslavery neighbors at Pottawatomie Creek. Described by a New York Tribune reporter as "a strange, resolute, repulsive, iron-willed, inexorable old man," John Brown was undoubtedly a fanatic. Earlier in his career, before he came to Kansas, he had been at work on what he called his "Subterranean Pass Way" scheme to establish a guerilla base in the southern mountains from whence slaves could be snatched from plantations and passed to freedom in the North. Three years after the Pottawatomie massacres, Brown was executed for his dramatic but foolhardy raid on Harper's Ferry, Virginia. But in the Kansas of 1856 what was most remarkable about John Brown was how unexceptional he was. In the wave of burnings and killings that followed Lawrence and Pottawatomie, John Brown and his followers became merely one of a number of bands of marauding murderers who were never arrested, never brought to trial, and never stopped from committing further violence. Armed bands roamed the countryside and killings became commonplace. In Leavenworth, city recorder James Lyle handed a proslave election ballot to a German voter, who scornfully tore it up. Threatened by proslavery bystanders, the German was rescued by abolitionist William Haller. Annoyed at Haller's intervention, Lyle drew his knife and turned to him saying, "What is it to you?" Haller responded by drawing his knife and plunging it into Lyle, deep enough to kill him. The somewhat more peaceable mayor of Leavenworth contented himself by hiring a crier to ride through town warning free-soil families to get out of town if they didn't want to be burned out. Peaceful residents of large sections of rural Kansas were repeatedly forced to flee to the safety of military forts when rumors of one or another armed band of "regulators" reached them. In such an atmosphere, even John Brown's pronouncement that "it is infinitely better that this generation should be swept away from the face of the earth, than that slavery shall continue to exist," raised hardly on eyebrow.

One of the worst aspects of Bleeding Kansas was the unwillingness of the combatants and their national supporters to accept responsibility for the violence. Even as notable a figure as Yale University's Henry Ward Beecher sent young men off to Kansas with Sharp's rifles, Bibles, and a message: "There are times when self-defense is a religious duty. If that duty was ever imperative it is now, and in Kansas." Proslavery Kansans responded by dubbing the rifles "Beecher's Bibles" and calling for "Blood for Blood! Let us purge ourselves of all abolition emissaries . . . and give distinct notice that all who do not leave immediately for the East, will leave for eternity!" In this atmosphere, law and order lost all meaning, even to ordinarily law-abiding citizens. Antislavery supporters even found a way to ignore an event as horrible and inexcusable as John Brown's slaughter of innocent people at Pottawatomie Creek.

"Let the voters decide" is a wonderfully democratic idea — when there is agreement on basic principles. Bleeding Kansas showed the nation what could happen when two irreconcilable communities disagreed. As the rest of the nation watched in horror, the residents of Kansas slaughtered each other in the pursuit of sectional goals. Americans' pride in the nation's great achievements

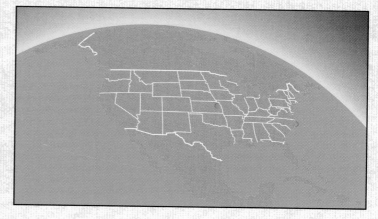

was threatened by the endless violence in one small part — but a part that increasingly seemed to represent the divisions of the whole.

AMERICA IN 1850

In 1850, after half a century of economic growth, America was a very different nation from that of 1800. Its population had grown enormously: from 5.3 million in 1800 to over 23 million, of whom 4 million were black slaves and 2 million new immigrants. America was also a much larger place: in 1850 there were thirty-one states rather than the sixteen of 1800, and more than half of the population lived west of the Appalachians. The nation, through war and diplomacy, had expanded to continental dimensions, as we saw in Chapter 14. Its cities had undergone the most rapid half century of growth they were ever to experience. And America was also a much richer nation: it is estimated that real per capita income doubled between 1800 and 1850. In this half century, America moved decisively out of the "developing nation" category. Increasing prosperity seemed assured and the economic future looked very bright.

The political future, however, was clouded. The year 1850 opened to the most serious political crisis the United States had ever known. The struggle over the issue of slavery in the territories had begun in 1846 with Wilmot's Proviso and was still unresolved (see Chapter 14). Increasingly, both politicians and ordinary people began to consider the almost unthinkable possibility of disunion. As the new year dawned, politician James Buchanan expressed a common fear when he wrote to a friend, "The blessed Union of these states is now in greater danger than it has ever been since the adoption of the federal Constitution."

Politicians had long been concerned about the dangers of sectionalism in American life. But most ordinary people had taken for granted the federal union of states — and the ability of slave and nonslave states to coexist. Although much of this chapter will focus on political actions in Washington, we should remember that politicians were only the tip of the iceberg. In the 1850s, the entire mass of the

U.S. Population and Settlement, 1850

By 1850, the United States was a continental nation and the population, which Thomas Jefferson had once thought would take 40 generations to reach the Mississippi River, had not only passed it but leapfrogged to the west coast. In comparison to the America of 1800 (see map p. 238) the growth was incredible. Population grew from 5.3 million to over 23 million, and the number of states increased from 16 to 31.

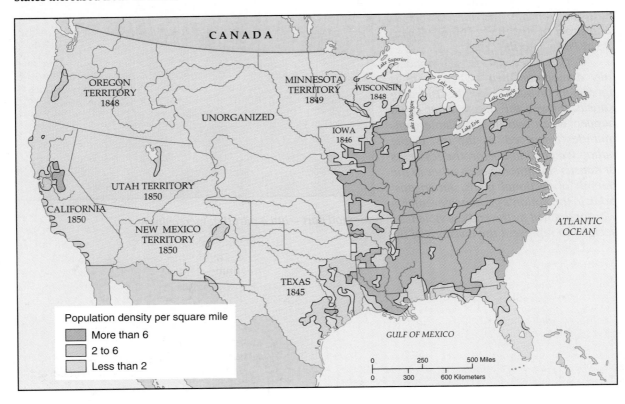

Population density per square mile
- More than 6
- 2 to 6
- Less than 2

iceberg was moving. Over the course of the decade, many Americans came to believe that the place of slavery in the nation's life had to be permanently settled. These Americans lived in two sectional communities — one slave, one free — that had come to seem dramatically different. Ordinary people began to wonder if these two different communities could continue to be part of a unitary national one.

SLAVERY: THE UNASKED QUESTION

Slavery had long been a divisive issue in national politics. Until the 1840s, compromises had always been found, most notably in the Constitution itself (see Chapter 8) and in the Missouri Compromise of 1820 (see Chapter 9). But the struggle over the place of slavery in the vast new territories gained in the Mexican-American War gave rise to new sectional arguments. One of the places where this sectionalism appeared was the national party system.

The National Party System

The national party system had been forged in the great controversies of Andrew Jackson's presidency (see Chapter 10). First Jackson's Democrats and then the Whig party put together stable coalitions of voters from all parts of the country. In their need to mobilize great masses of recently enfranchised voters to elect a president every four years, politicians created an organized party structure that overrode deeply rooted sectional differences. Politicians from all sections of the country cooperated because they knew their party could not succeed without national appeal. At a time when the ordinary person still had very strong sectional loyalties, the mass political party created a national community of like-minded voters.

The national party system was remarkably effective in organizing a mass democratic electorate. Less noticed has been the system's very short duration. The election of 1836 is usually taken as the beginning of the national two-party system, yet by the election of 1848 sectional interests were already eroding the political "glue" in both parties. Indeed, southern Whigs had already deserted their northern colleagues to vote against the Wilmot Proviso in Congress (see Chapter 14). Although Zachary Taylor, the Whig candidate, won the election of 1848, Whigs lost a sizable proportion of their customary vote in New England and in states settled by New Englanders, because Taylor was a southern slave-owner. Similarly, the Democratic party was splin-

tering. While its southern wing vehemently advocated the extension of slavery, a northern group bolted to the Free-Soil party, costing the Democrats a drop of 150,000 votes (three times that of the Whig decline) in the North. Thus although each party still appeared united, sectional fissures already ran deep.

Social splits predated political ones. The country's great religious organizations had already split into two sectional groups, the Presbyterians doing so in 1837 and the Methodists and the Baptists in 1844 and 1845. (Some of these splits turned out to be permanent. The Southern Baptist Convention, for example, is still a separate body.) Theodore Weld, the abolitionist leader, saw these splits as inevitable: "*Events* . . . have for years been silently but without a moment's pause, settling the basis of two great parties, the nucleus of one slavery, of the other, freedom."

Since the 1830s, abolitionists had been posing the choice in just such simple and uncompromising terms: *either* slave *or* free. Since 1840 the Liberty party (and in 1848 the Free-Soil party) had insisted, in the words of abolitionist Salmon P. Chase, that "freedom is national; slavery only is local and sectional."

States' Rights

Was freedom national and slavery sectional, or the other way around? Southern politicians had another answer to this question, which rang through the 1850s. Foremost among them was South Carolina's "cast-iron man," John C. Calhoun.

In 1828 Calhoun had provoked the nullification crisis by asserting the constitutional right of states to "nullify" national laws that were harmful to their interests (see Chapter 10). Calhoun argued, as have others since, that the states' rights doctrine protected the legitimate rights of a minority in a democratic system governed by majority rule.

In 1847, Calhoun responded to the Wilmot Proviso with an elaboration of the states' rights argument. In spite of the apparent precedents of the Northwest Ordinance of 1787 and the Missouri Compromise, Calhoun argued that Congress did not have a constitutional right to prohibit slavery in the territories. The territories, he said, were the common property of *all* the states, North and South, and Congress could not discriminate against slave owners as they moved west. On the contrary, Calhoun argued, slave owners had a constitutional right to the protection of their property wherever they moved. Of course, Calhoun's legally correct description of black slaves as property enraged abolitionists. But on behalf of the South, Calhoun was expressing the belief — and the fear — that his interpretation of the Constitution was the only protection for slave owners whose right to own slaves (a fundamental right in southern eyes) was being attacked. Calhoun's position on the territories quickly became southern dogma: anything less than full access to the territories was unconstitutional. Slavery, Calhoun and other southerners insisted, had to be national.

The Proslavery Argument

Since the Missouri Compromise of 1820, southern politicians had become increasingly defensive about slavery. Abolitionist agitation in the 1830s had the effect of further hardening southern opinion (see Chapter 11). Southern thinking on slavery changed from Jefferson's expectation that slavery would gradually disappear to the kind of defense made memorable by Calhoun in 1837: "a good — a positive good." What had happened in the meantime was the enormous growth of the plantation system of cotton growing, which quickly became the South's economic mainstay. But Calhoun went far beyond a simple defense of a profitable labor system to directly challenge the social organization of the commercial North:

> There never has yet existed a wealthy and civilized society in which one portion of the community did not, in point of fact, live on the labor of the other. . . . I fearlessly assert that the existing relation between the two races in the South . . . forms the most solid and durable foundation upon which to rear free and stable political institutions.

In Calhoun's mind, the most fundamental southern claim was to personal and political equality with any other American. Acutely aware of his own personal honor, Calhoun said in response to abolitionist attacks, "I am a southern man and a slaveholder; a kind and merciful one, I trust — and none the worse for being a slaveholder." Calhoun was no less unyielding in his conception of political equality: "I would rather meet any extremity upon earth than give up one inch of our equality. . . . What, acknowledge inferiority! The surrender of life is nothing to sinking down into acknowledged inferiority."

That personal and political equality were closely linked in the minds of southerners directly affected the issue of slavery extension. As Senator Robert Toombs of Georgia put the case in 1850, there was very little room for compromise:

> I stand upon the great principle that the South has the right to an equal participation in the territories of the United States. . . . She will divide with you if you wish it, but the right to enter all or divide I shall never surrender. . . . Deprive us of this right and appropriate the common property to yourselves, it is then your government, not mine. Then I am its enemy. . . . Give us our just rights, and we are ready . . . to stand by the Union. . . . Refuse [them], and for one, I will strike for *independence.*"

Northern Fears of the "Slave Power"

Southern speeches such as this seemed to many northern listeners to confirm the warning by antislavery leaders of the "slave power." Liberty party leader James Birney was the first to add this menacing image to the nation's political vocabulary. In 1844 Birney declared that southern slave owners posed a danger to free speech and free institutions throughout the nation. The "slave power," Birney explained, was a group of aristocratic slave owners who not only dominated the political and social life of the South but who conspired to control the federal government as well.

Birney's "slave power" was a caricature of the influence slave owners wielded over southern politics, and of the increasingly defensive and monolithic response of southern representatives in national politics after 1830 (see Chapter 11). The proslavery strategy of maintaining supremacy in the Senate by having at least as many slave as free states admitted to the Union (a plan that required slavery expansion) and of maintaining control, or at least veto power, over presidential nominees seemed, in southern eyes, to be nothing less than ordinary self-defense. But to antislavery advocates, these actions looked like a conspiracy by sectional interests to control national politics. Birney's warnings about the "slave power" seemed in 1844 merely the overheated rhetoric of an extremist group of abolitionists. But the defensive southern political strategies of the 1850s, in particular the Fugitive Slave Law and the Kansas-Nebraska Act, convinced an increasing number of northern voters that the "slave power" did in fact exist. Thus in northern eyes the South became demonized as a monolith that threatened the national government.

PEOPLE'S MEETING!!

CITIZENS OF CHESTER COUNTY:—The time has arrived when it is necessary to make preparations for the next general election. In view of existing circumstances, it is proper that the citizens of this County

WITHOUT RESPECT TO PARTY,

Should meet for the purpose of Conferring together, and forming such an organization as will give effect to their views on important public questions. A fixed and resolute determination has recently been manifested on the part of the

SLAVE POWER,

To extend its dominion—to carry its blighting influence to territory now free—to control the government of the nation, and make it subservient to its wicked designs. Compacts entered into, under circumstances the most solemn, have been violated; an extended territory, dedicated by the MISSOURI COMPROMISE to Freedom, in violation of faith and honor, has been thrown open to the traffickers in human flesh, who by disregard of law and order, have seized upon its fertile plains with a view of adding

OTHER SLAVE STATES TO THE UNION

And giving to the Slave Power an ascendancy over freedom in the Nation. Experience has satisfied the people that while the emigration to this country of the peaceable industrious foreigner, should be regarded with favor, the facility with which persons reared abroad, under systems of government radically different from our own, approach the ballot box, and indiscriminate our elections, is an evil dangerous alike to the adopted and native citizens. A change in the

NATURALIZATION LAWS

Extending the probative period of the alien—the separation of Church and State in practice as well as in theory—the freedom of the government from all improper foreign influence—and the protection of the

AMERICAN LABORER

Are believed to be essential to the welfare of all classes of the people. All persons who are willing to co-operate upon the principles here indicated and which we believe to be those of a true democracy, are earnestly invited to meet at the

COURT HOUSE IN THE BOROUGH OF WEST CHESTER

On Saturday the 18th Instant at ten o'clock A. M.   August 1855

This strident poster warns that the Slave Power aims "to control the government of the nation, and make it subservient to its wicked designs." For good measure, the poster also appeals to nativist fears and to workers.

Common Ground, Different Paths

Ironically, it was a basic agreement between northerners and southerners that made their arguments so irreconcilable: both sections of the country believed fervently in expansion. Southerners had been the strongest supporters of the Mexican-American War, and they still hoped to expand into Cuba, believing that the slave system must grow or wither (see Chapter 11). Although many northern Whigs had opposed the Mexican-American War, most did so for antislavery reasons, not because they opposed expansion. The strong showing of the Free-Soil party in the election of 1848 (10 percent of the popular vote) was proof of that. Basically, as we saw in Chapter 14, both North and South believed in manifest destiny, but each on its own terms.

Similarly, both North and South used the language of basic rights and liberties in the debate over

expansion. But free-soilers were speaking of personal liberty, whereas southerners meant their right to own a particular kind of property (slaves) and to maintain a way of life based on that property. In defending its own rights, each side had taken measures that infringed on the rights of the other. Southerners pointed out that abolitionists had libeled slave owners as a class, bombarded the South with unwanted literature, abused the right of petition to Congress, incited slaves to rebellion, and actively helped them to escape. Northerners accused slave owners of censorship of the mails; imposition of the "gag rule," which prohibited any petition against slavery from being read to or discussed by Congress (it was repealed in 1844); suppression of free speech in the South—and, of course, the moral wrong of slavery in the first place.

Two Communities, Two Perspectives

From common principles—liberty, equality, and the superiority of American democracy—North and South had by 1850 created different, and increasingly irreconcilable communities. To antislavery northerners, the South was an economic backwater dominated by a small slave-owning aristocracy that lived off the profits of forced labor and deprived poor whites of their democratic rights and the fruits of honest work. The slave system was not only immoral but a drag on the entire nation, for, in the words of William Seward, it subverted the "intelligence, vigor and energy" that were essential for national growth. In contrast, the dynamic and enterprising commercial North boasted a free-labor ideology that offered economic opportunity to the common man and ensured his democratic rights (see Chapter 12).

The same two communities looked very different through southern eyes. Far from being economically backward, the South, through its export of cotton, was the great engine of national economic growth from which the North benefited. Slavery was not only a blessing to an inferior race, but the cornerstone of democracy, because it ensured the freedom and independence of all white men without entailing the bitter class divisions that marked the North. As we have seen, slave owners accused northern manufacturers of hypocrisy for practicing "wage slavery" rather than treating their work force with the paternalistic care given by slave owners. The North, James Henry Hammond charged, had eliminated the "*name* [of slavery], but not the *thing*," for "your whole hireling class of manual laborers and 'operatives,' . . . are essentially slaves."

These two differing visions did not appear overnight. They were, rather, the result of many years of political controversy. Once the visions were fixed, however, as they were by the early 1850s, the chances of national reconciliation were very slim.

THE COMPROMISE OF 1850

By 1850 the issue raised by the Wilmot Proviso—should slavery be extended to the new territories?—could no longer be ignored. Overnight, the California gold rush had turned a sparse and remote frontier into a territory with a booming population. In 1849 Californians had applied for statehood. The same year, a similar request had come from the Mormons of Utah (or Deseret, as they called it). Should these be admitted as slave or free states? A simmering border war between Texas (a slave state) and New Mexico, which seemed likely to be a free state, had to be settled, as did the issue of the debts Texas had incurred as an independent republic. Closer to home, antislavery forces demanded the end of slavery in the District of Columbia, while slave owners complained that northerners were refusing to return escaped slaves, as federal law mandated.

Debate and Compromise

Once again Henry Clay, author of the Missouri Compromise of 1820, came forward with a solution. This time, though, compromise was much more complicated and difficult to arrange, and the three great political figures associated with the measure were old men. For Henry Clay, now seventy-three, John C. Calhoun, who had entered the final year of his life, and Daniel Webster, the Compromise of 1850 was to be the final act of their political careers. The three men had been active in national politics since the War of 1812, and in the public mind they had come to embody the sections: West, South, and North. It was sadly appropriate to the bitter sectional argument of 1850 that the three men contributed great words to the debate, but that the compromise itself was enacted by younger men. Calhoun brought an aura of death with him to the Senate as he sat, shrouded in flannels, listening to the speech that he was too ill to read for himself. He died less than a month later, still insisting on the right of the South to secede if necessary to preserve its way of life. Daniel Webster claimed to speak "not as a Massachusetts man, nor as a Northern man, but as an American. . . . I speak today for the preservation of the Union." He rejected southern claims that peaceable secession was possible or desirable, but pleaded with abolitionists to compromise enough to keep the

This painting shows the three old men who attempted to resolve the 1850 crisis: Henry Clay (speaking), John C. Calhoun (standing third from right), and Daniel Webster (seated at left with his head in his hand). Both Clay and Webster were ill, and Calhoun died before the issue was settled by a younger group of politicians led by Stephen A. Douglas.

South in the Union. Clay, claiming he had "never before risen to address any assemblage so oppressed, so appalled, and so anxious," argued eloquently for compromise, but left the Senate in ill health before his plea was answered.

In June of 1850, amid the debate, delegates from most of the southern states convened in Nashville, Tennessee, to consider united action. Although Calhoun had died in March, the convention owed its existence to him. Early in 1849, Calhoun had urged all southern congressmen of both parties to join him in creating an all-South party, saying bluntly, "If you become united the North will be brought to a pause." Basically, he was asking southern politicians to form a sectional party in defense of slavery. The Nashville Convention treated Calhoun's proposal gingerly, knowing full well that it was tantamount to secession. Although five states — Virginia, South Carolina, Georgia, Mississippi, and Texas — sent officially elected delegations and four other states were unofficially represented, six states — Delaware, Maryland, Kentucky, Missouri, North Carolina, and Louisiana — were absent. While all assembled were agreed on the need to defend southern rights, they could not agree on how to do so. A small group, the "fire-eaters," advocated immediate secession, arguing that the South would never be safe united with the increasingly antislavery North. The majority of those present were much more moderate, regarding secession as treasonable. But it was the fire-eaters — Robert Barnwell Rhett of South Carolina, William Yancey of Alabama, Edmund Ruffin of Virginia — who attracted national attention. From this time on, although the majority of southerners remained committed to the Union, the threat of secession hung in the air.

A more serious interruption of the debate over the Compromise of 1850 occurred when President Zachary Taylor died on July 9, 1850, of acute gastroenteritis following a hasty meal of fresh fruit and cold milk on a very hot Fourth of July. Taylor, a bluff military man, had been prepared to follow Andrew Jackson's precedent during the nullification crisis of 1832 and simply demand that southern dissidents compromise. A moderate northern Whig, Millard Fillmore, became president. More prosouthern than the southern-born Taylor had been, Fillmore was instrumental in arranging the Compromise of 1850 to southern liking. For although Clay had assembled all the necessary parts of the bargain, it was not he, but members of a younger political generation, and in particular the rising young Democrat from Illinois, Stephen Douglas, who drove the Compromise of 1850 through Congress. The final product consisted of five bills (it had been impossible to obtain a majority for a comprehensive measure), embodying three compromises:

1. California was admitted as a free state. But the rest of the former Mexican possessions would have no "restriction or condition on the subject of slavery." In practice, their status would be decided by popular sovereignty (a vote of the territory's inhabitants). (Utah's application for statehood was not accepted until 1896, not because of slavery, but because of controversy over the Mormon practice of polygamy.)
2. Texas (a slave state) was required to cede land to New Mexico Territory (status undecided). In return the United States assumed $10 million of Texan debts incurred before statehood.
3. The slave trade, but not slavery itself, was ended in the District of Columbia, but a stronger fugitive slave law was enacted.

Jubilation and relief greeted the news that compromise had been achieved. In Washington, where the anxiety and concern had been greatest, drunken crowds serenaded Congress shouting, "The Union is saved!" That was certainly true for the moment, but analysis of the votes on the five bills that made up the compromise revealed no consistent majority. The sectional splits within each party that had existed before the compromise remained. Antislavery northern Whigs and proslavery southern Democrats, each the larger wing of their party, were the least willing to compromise. Southern Whigs and northern Democrats were the forces for moderation, but each group was dwindling in popular appeal as sectional feelings grew. If the question of the territorial extension of slavery came up again, the center might not hold.

In the country as a whole, the feeling was that the problem of slavery in the territories had been solved. The Philadelphia *Pennsylvanian* was confident that "peace and tranquility" had been ensured, and the *Louisville Journal* said that a weight seemed to have been lifted from the heart of America. But as Senator Salmon P. Chase of Ohio soberly noted, "The question of slavery in the territories has been avoided. It has not been settled." And he was correct. However, the most immediately inflamma

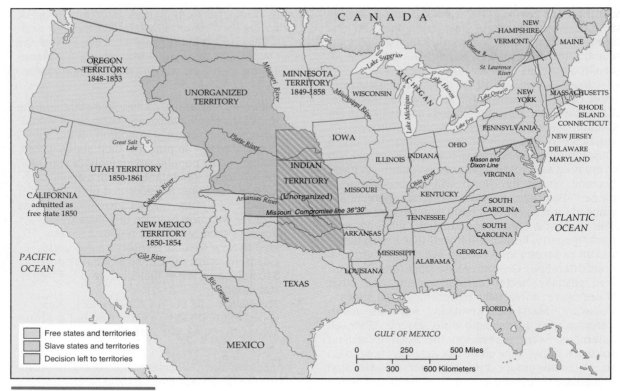

The Compromise of 1850

The Compromise of 1850 reflected heightened sectional tensions by being even messier and more awkward than the Missouri Compromise of 1820. California was admitted as a free state, the borders of Texas were settled, and the status of the rest of the former Mexican territory was to be decided later by popular sovereignty. No consistent majority voted for the five separate bills that made up the compromise.

tory measure of the compromise was the Fugitive Slave Act.

The Fugitive Slave Act

From the early days of their movement, northern abolitionists had urged slaves to escape, promising assistance and support when they reached the North. Some free black people had offered far more than verbal support. Most famously, Harriet Tubman, herself an escaped slave from Maryland, made nineteen return trips and brought almost 300 slaves to freedom, among them all the other members of her family. Northerners had long been appalled by professional slave catchers, who zealously seized African Americans in the North and took them south into slavery again. Most abhorrent in northern eyes was that captured black people were at the mercy of slave catchers because they had no legal right to defend themselves. In more than one case, a north-

ern free African American was captured in his own community and helplessly shipped into slavery.

Solomon Northup was one such person. In his popular account *Twelve Years a Slave*, published in 1853, he told a harrowing tale of being kidnapped in Washington, the nation's capital, and shipped south. Northup spent twelve years as a slave before he was able to send a message to northern friends to bring the legal proof to free him. As a result of such stories, and the very effective publicity generated by abolitionists, nine northern states passed personal liberty laws between 1842 and 1850, serving notice that they would not cooperate with federal recapture efforts. These northern laws enraged southerners, who had long been convinced that all northerners, not just abolitionists, were actively hindering efforts to reclaim their escaped slaves. What was at issue was two different definitions of rights: northerners were upset at the denial of legal and personal rights to escaped slaves; southerners saw illegal infringement of their property rights. The latter insisted that a strong federal law be part of the Compromise of 1850.

The Fugitive Slave Law, enacted in 1850, dramatically increased the power of slave owners to capture escaped slaves. The full force of the federal government now supported slave owners, and while fugitives were guaranteed a hearing before a federal commissioner, they were not allowed to testify on their own behalf. In Boston, the center of the abolitionist movement, reaction to the new law was fierce. When an escaped slave named Shadrach was seized in February of 1851, a group of black men broke into the courtroom, overwhelmed the federal marshals, seized Shadrach, and sent him safely to Canada by the underground railroad. A number of people, including Daniel Webster and President Fillmore, condemned this episode of "mob rule," but the action had community support: a Massachusetts jury defiantly refused to convict the alleged perpetrators.

The federal government responded with overwhelming force. In April of 1851, 300 armed soldiers were mobilized to prevent the rescue of Thomas Sims, who was being shipped back into slavery. In the most famous Boston case, a biracial group of armed abolitionists stormed the federal courthouse in 1854 in an attempt to save escaped slave Anthony Burns. This was no lower-class mob: the leader of the group was Unitarian clergyman Thomas Wentworth Higginson. The rescue effort failed, and a federal deputy marshal was killed. President Pierce sent marines, cavalry, and artillery to Boston to reinforce the guard over Burns, and ordered a revenue cutter to be ready to deliver the fugitive back into slavery. Defense lawyers tried to argue for Burns's freedom. When that failed, Bostonians raised money in the community to buy his freedom. But the U.S. attorney, ordered by the president to enforce the Fugitive Slave Law in all circumstances, blocked the purchase. The case was lost, and Burns was marched to the docks through streets lined with sorrowing abolitionists. Buildings were shrouded in black and draped with American flags hanging upside down, while bells tolled as if for a funeral.

The Burns case radicalized many northerners. Conservative Whig George Hilliard wrote to a friend, "When it was all over, and I was left alone in my office, I put my face in my hands and wept. I could do nothing less." Over the 1850s, 322 black fugitives were sent back into slavery; only 11 were declared free. Northern popular sentiment and the Fugitive Slave Law, rigorously enforced by the federal government, were increasingly at odds. The northern abolitionists who used force to rescue captured slaves were breaking the law, but they were winning the battle for public opinion.

In this volatile atmosphere, escaped African Americans wrote and lectured bravely on behalf of freedom. Frederick Douglass, the most famous and eloquent of the fugitive slaves, spoke out fearlessly in support of armed resistance. "The only way to make the Fugitive Slave Law a dead letter," he said in 1853, "is to make a half dozen or more dead kidnappers." Openly active in the underground network that helped slaves reach safety in Canada, Douglass himself was constantly in danger of capture until his friends bought his freedom. Harriet Jacobs, who escaped to the North after seven years in hiding in the South, wrote bitterly in her *Incidents in the Life of a Slave Girl*, "I was, in fact, a slave in New York, as subject to slave laws as I had been in a slave state. . . . I had been chased during half my life, and it seemed as if the chase was never to end." Threatened by owners who came north for her, Jacobs went into hiding again, until informed that friends had arranged her purchase: "A gentleman near me said, 'It's true; I have seen the bill of sale.' 'The bill of sale!' Those words struck me like a blow. So I was *sold* at last! A human being *sold* in the free city of New York!"

But the most popular piece of abolitionist propaganda came from the pen of a white woman. Harriet Beecher Stowe combined the literary style of women's domestic novels with vivid details of slavery culled from the Grimké–Weld volume *American Slavery as It Is* and from her own experience helping runaway slaves in Cincinnati in the 1830s. The daughter and wife of Congregational clergymen, and herself a member of the evangelical movement, Stowe had long been active in antislavery work. But the Fugitive Slave Law impelled her to write a novel that would persuade everyone of the evils of slavery. While writing nightly at her kitchen table after putting her eight children to bed, she said later, the events of the novel came to her "with a vividness that could not be denied," making her feel like "an instrument of God."

Stowe's famous novel, *Uncle Tom's Cabin,* told a poignant story of a Christ-like black man, Uncle Tom, who patiently endured the cruel treatment of an evil white overseer, Simon Legree. Published in 1852, it was a runaway best seller. More than 300,000 copies were sold in the first year, and within ten years it had sold more than 2 million copies, becoming the all-time American best seller in proportion to population. Turned into a play that re-

This free African American family, the Webbs, toured northern cities performing dramatic readings from *Uncle Tom's Cabin*. Immensely popular in the 1850s, the novel outlasted the Civil War to become one of the most popular plays of the second half of the nineteenth century.

mained popular throughout the nineteenth century, *Uncle Tom's Cabin* reached an even wider audience. Scenes from the novel such as Eliza carrying her son across the ice-choked Ohio River to freedom, Tom weeping for his children as he was sold south, and the death of little Eva are among the best-known passages in all of American literature. *Uncle Tom's Cabin* was more than a heart-tugging story: it was a call to action. Harriet Beecher Stowe succeeded so well at arousing popular opinion that when she met Abraham Lincoln during the Civil War in 1863, he greeted her by saying, "So you're the little woman who wrote the book that made this great war!"

Popular literature and civic outrage worked strongly on public opinion, but it was the Fugitive Slave Law itself that brought home the reality of slavery to residents of the free states. In effect, the Fugitive Slave Law made slavery national and forced northern communities to confront what that meant. Although most people were still unwilling to grant social equality to the free African Americans who

lived in the northern states (see Chapter 13), more and more of them had come to believe that the institution of slavery was wrong. The strong northern reaction against the Fugitive Slave Law also had consequences in the South. As Democrat Cave Johnson of Tennessee warned, "If the fugitive slave bill is not enforced in the North, the moderate men of the South . . . will be overwhelmed by the *'fire-eaters.'*" Northern protests against the Fugitive Slave Law bred suspicion in the South and encouraged secessionist thinking. These new currents of public opinion were reflected in the election of 1852.

The Election of 1852

The first sign of trouble in 1852 was the difficulty both parties experienced at their nominating conventions. The Whigs nominated General Winfield Scott (their third military hero in four elections) rather than Millard Fillmore. Long-time party leaders Henry Clay and Daniel Webster having died, William Seward of New York became the unofficial party head, much to the displeasure of southern Whigs. Seward preferred Scott to the prosouthern Fillmore, but it took him fifty-two ballots to achieve his desire. Many southern Whigs were angered and alienated by the choice and, like Georgia's Alexander Stephens and Robert Toombs, either abstained from voting or cast a protest vote for the Democratic candidate. Although southern Whigs were still elected to Congress, their loyalty to the national party was strained to the breaking point. The Whigs never again fielded a presidential candidate.

The Democrats had a wider variety of candidates: Lewis Cass of popular sovereignty fame; Stephen Douglas, savior of the Compromise of 1850; and James Buchanan, described as a "Northern man with Southern principles." Cass, Douglas, and Buchanan competed for forty-nine ballots, each strong enough to block the others but not strong enough to win. Finally the party turned to a handsome, affable nonentity, Franklin Pierce of New Hampshire, who was thought to have southern sympathies. Uniting on a platform pledging "faithful execution" of all parts of the Compromise of 1850, including the Fugitive Slave Law, Democrats polled well in the South and in the North. Most Democrats who had voted for the Free-Soil party in 1848 voted for Pierce. So, in record numbers, did immigrant Irish and German voters, who were eligible for citizenship after three years' residence. The strong immigrant vote for Pierce was a sign of the strength of the Democratic machines in northern cities (see Chapter 13). Reformers complained, not for the last time, about widespread corruption and "vote buying" by urban ward bosses. Overall, however, "Genl. Apathy is the strongest candidate out here," as one Ohioan reported. Pierce easily won the 1852 election, 254 electoral votes to 42. Voter turnout was below 70 percent, lower than it had been since 1836.

Pierce and "Young America"

Observing the Whig collapse, Democrats prided themselves on their unity. Pierce entered the White House in early 1853 on a wave of good feeling. Massachusetts Whig Amos Lawrence reported, "Never since Washington has an administration commenced with the hearty [good]will of so large a portion of the country." This goodwill was soon strained by the expansionist adventures of the "Young America" movement.

Southern Young America expansionists had glanced covetously toward the Caribbean region since the end of the Mexican War. President Polk himself had wanted to buy Cuba and to intervene in Mexican politics, but was rebuffed by Congress (see Chapter 14). During the Pierce administration, a number of private "filibusters" (from the Spanish *filibustero,* meaning a freebooter or pirate) invaded Caribbean and Central American countries, usually with the declared intention of extending slave territory. All these adventurers drew on southern volunteers and money, and several had supporters within the Pierce administration as well. The best known of the filibusters was also the most improbable: short, slight, soft-spoken William Walker invaded Nicaragua not once, but four times. After his first invasion in 1856, Walker became ruler of the country and encouraged settlement by southern slave owners. In 1857, however, Walker was unseated by a regional revolt. Rescued by the U.S. Navy, he returned to New Orleans and then undertook a wildly popular fundraising tour of the South. The U.S. Navy prevented his second invasion attempt in 1857 by intercepting his ship. His third attempt, in 1858, ended in farce when his ship hit a reef and sank. Unfortunately for Walker, his fourth attempt in 1860 at first succeeded, but soon he was captured and met his death by firing squad in Honduras.

In addition to Walker's adventures, there were several expeditions to Cuba. Because they all depended on uprisings by sympathetic Cubans that never materialized, they all failed. In one such attempt, 50 Americans were executed by a Spanish

Cartoons such as this sought to couple concerns about temperance (shown by the barrels of Irish whiskey and German lager beer) with nativist claims that immigrant voters were voting illegally.

firing squad. This led to southern demands for full-scale war, which the Pierce administration ignored (although it did negotiate the return of more than 300 American prisoners). The Pierce administration was, however, deeply involved in another effort to obtain Cuba. In 1854, Pierce authorized his minister to Spain, Pierre Soulé, to try to force the unwilling Spanish to sell Cuba for $130 million. Soulé met in Ostend, Belgium, with the American ministers to France and England, John Mason and James Buchanan, to compose the offer, which was a mixture of cajolements and threats. At first appealing to Spain to recognize the deep affinities between the Cubans and American southerners that made them "one people with one destiny," the document went on to threaten to "wrest" Cuba from Spain if necessary. This amazing document, which became known as the Ostend Manifesto, was supposed to be secret. But soon it was leaked to the press, causing deep embarrassment to the Pierce administration, which was forced to repudiate it.

The complicity between the Pierce administration and proslavery expansionists was foolhardy. The sectional crisis that preceded the Compromise of 1850 had made obvious the danger of reopening the territorial issue. Ironically, it was not the Young America expansionists but the prime mover of the Compromise of 1850 himself, Stephen A. Douglas, who reignited the sectional struggle over slavery expansion.

THE CRISIS OF THE NATIONAL PARTY SYSTEM

In 1854, Douglas introduced the Kansas-Nebraska Act and thereby reopened the question of slavery in the territories. Douglas knew he was taking a political risk, but he believed he could satisfy both his expansionist aims and his presidential ambitions. He was wrong. Instead, he pushed the national party system into crisis, destroying the Democratic party after killing the Whigs first.

The Kansas-Nebraska Act

Until 1854, white Americans thought of Kansas only as a way to other places farther west. Kansas was part of Indian Territory and home to a great number of tribes. Some of these had been moved, often more than once, from their original homes in the East (see Chapters 9 and 10). In the great Indian removals of the 1830s, these tribes had been promised the Kansas lands "as long as grass grows and water-

flows." The promise was broken in 1854. Treaties were ignored and the northern part of Indian Territory was thrown open to white settlement.

Douglas wanted to open the territory to white settlement because it offered the route he favored for a transcontinental railroad having a terminus in Chicago (in Douglas's state of Illinois) and extending through land in which he had a financial interest. But to open the territory, he needed the votes of southern Democrats, who were unwilling to support him unless the new territory was open to slavery.

Douglas's master stroke (as he thought) was to open up the lands under the principle of popular sovereignty. Ever since 1848, this democratic-sounding slogan had been favored by Democratic politicians, for it was vague enough to appeal to both pro- and anti-slavery voters. By espousing popular sovereignty for Kansas and Nebraska, Douglas expected to gain favor with the southern branch of the Democratic party, which he would need to be nominated for president in 1856, while obtaining northern support because of the railroad route. Privately, Douglas believed that the topography of

---

The Kansas-Nebraska Act, 1854

The Kansas-Nebraska Act, proposed by Steven A. Douglas in 1854, opened the central and northern Great Plains to settlement. The act had two major faults: It robbed Indian peoples of half of the territory guaranteed to them by treaty, and, because it repealed the Missouri Compromise Line, it opened up the lands to warring pro- and anti-slavery factions.

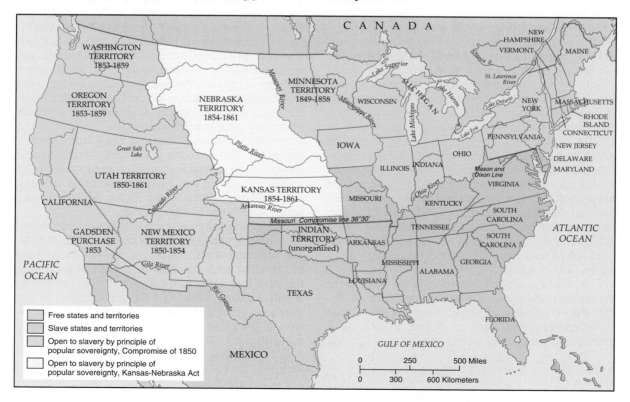

the Kansas-Nebraska region was unsuitable for slave agriculture, and that the region's inhabitants would decide to enter the Union as free states. Douglas chose also to downplay the price he had to pay for southern support — explicit repeal of the Missouri Compromise line of 1820 (36°30′) in his bill.

Douglas's Kansas-Nebraska bill passed, but at a great price. It destroyed the Whig party, for southern Whigs voted with southern Democrats in favor of the measure, while northern Whigs rejected it absolutely. The split was irreconcilable, and the Whigs were unable to field a presidential candidate in 1856. The damage to the Democratic party was almost as great. In the congressional elections of 1854, northern Democrats lost two-thirds of their seats (a drop from ninety-one to twenty-five), giving the southern Democrats (who were solidly in favor of slavery extension) the dominant voice both in Congress and within the party.

Douglas had committed one of the greatest miscalculations in American political history. A storm of protest arose throughout the North. More than 300 large anti-Nebraska rallies occurred during congressional consideration of the bill, and the anger did not subside. Douglas, who confidently believed that "the people of the north will sustain the measure when they come to understand it," found himself shouted down more than once at public rallies in his efforts to explain. "I could travel from Boston to Chicago," he ruefully commented, "by the light of my own [burning] effigy."

The Kansas-Nebraska bill shifted a crucial sector of northern opinion: the wealthy merchants, bankers, and manufacturers — the "Cotton Whigs" — who had economic ties with southern slave owners and who had always disapproved of abolitionist activity. Convinced that the bill would encourage antislavery feeling in the North, Cotton Whigs urged southern politicians to vote against it, only to be ignored. Passage of the Kansas-Nebraska Act convinced a number of northern Whigs that compromise with the South was impossible. Even as sober a newspaper as the *New York Times* regarded the act as "part of this great scheme for extending and perpetuating the supremacy of the Slave Power." Some Cotton Whigs, such as manufacturer Amos Lawrence of Massachusetts, who had so warmly welcomed the prospect of sectional peace at the beginning of the Pierce administration, now joined the antislavery cause. Lawrence provided the financial backing for the first group of antislavery New Englanders who traveled to Kansas in 1854. In gratitude, they named their town for him.

In Kansas itself in 1854, hasty treaties were conducted with the Indian tribes who owned the land. Some, such as the Kickapoos, Shawnees, and

Sauks and Foxes, agreed to relocate to small reservations. Others, like the Delawares, Weas, and Iowas, agreed to sell out to whites. Still others, such as the Cheyennes and Sioux, kept the western part of Kansas Territory (now Colorado) — until gold was discovered there in 1859. Following the treaties, the battle of white settlement began. Although the vast majority of Kansas settlers were peaceful farmers interested primarily in finding good land, pro- and antislavery minorities turned the territory into a bloody battleground of sectional politics, as we saw in the introduction to this chapter.

Nativism and the Know-Nothings

Meanwhile, sectional pressures continued to re-shape national politics. The breakup of the Whig party coincided with one of the strongest bursts of anti-immigrant feeling in American history. The rapid rise in the number of foreign-born Democratic voters drew an equally rapid nativist backlash. The wave of German and Irish newcomers had sent the immigration rate soaring (it tripled in the years 1845–55). As we saw in Chapter 13, most of these immigrants were poor Catholics who clustered in urban centers, where they provided votes for Democratic party bosses. Legally, immigrants could become U.S. citizens after three years' residence, but in practice the time span was often much shorter in Democrat-controlled big cities. Irish immigrants in particular voted Democratic, both in reaction to Whig hostility (as in Boston) and because of their own antiblack prejudices. Frequently pitted against free black people for low-paying jobs, Irish immigrants were more inclined to share the attitudes of southerners than those of abolitionists. Violent urban riots in which free African Americans were the scapegoats periodically erupted in northern cities. Among the largest disturbances were those in Cincinnati in 1829, Providence in 1831, New York in 1834, and Philadelphia in 1834 and 1842.

The reformist and individualistic attitudes of many Whigs inclined them toward nativism. They disapproved of the new immigrants because they were poor, intemperate, and Catholic. Many Whigs were strong supporters of temperance (see Chapter 13) and disapproved of immigrant-supported saloons. The Catholic Church's opposition to the liberal European revolutions of 1848 fueled anti-Catholic fears. If America's new Catholic immigrants opposed the revolutions in which Americans had taken such pride (believing them to be modeled on the American example), how could the future of America's own democracy be ensured? Finally, the failure of urban governments to deal with the sudden growth in urban population was another

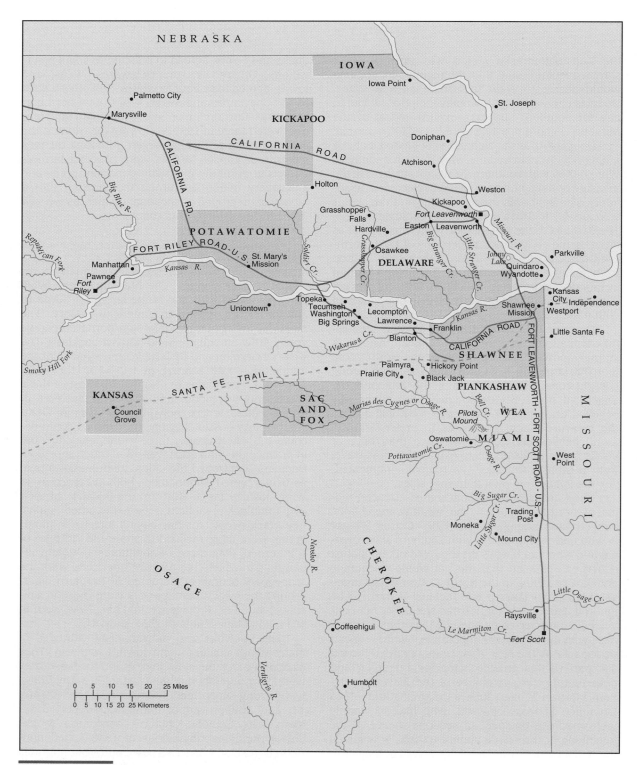

Bleeding Kansas

Kansas, formerly a part of Indian Territory, was opened for white settlement in 1854. Some Indian groups ceded their lands and moved to what is now Oklahoma, but some stayed, on small reservations. Although most white settlers were peaceful farmers, small bands of pro- and anti-slavery supporters warred with each other and made life dangerous for everyone. "Bleeding Kansas" was riven by sectional antagonisms until after the Civil War.

Source: Alice Nichols, *Bleeding Kansas* (New York: Oxford University Press, 1954).

cause of nativism: Whigs resented the increases in crime and in poor relief that they (incorrectly) blamed solely on immigration.

Reform movements in which women played a major role were also concerned about immigrants. As early as 1838, the influential Lydia Sigourney wrote in alarm in her *Letters to Mothers* about the "influx of untutored foreigners" that had made the United States "a repository for the waste and refuse of other nations." Sigourney urged women to organize an internal missionary movement that would carry the principles of middle-class American domesticity to the unenlightened foreigners.

For all of these reasons, former Whigs, especially young men in white-collar and skilled blue-collar occupations, were strongly drawn to the new American party. At the core of the party were several secret fraternal societies open only to native-born Protestants who pledged never to vote for a Catholic (on the grounds that all Catholics took their orders straight from the pope in Rome — a fear voiced again by Southern Baptists when John F. Kennedy ran for president in 1960). When questioned about their beliefs, party members maintained secrecy by answering, "I know nothing." Hence their popular name, the Know-Nothing party. Few Know-Nothings were wealthy: most were workers or small farmers whose jobs or ways of life were threatened by the cheap labor and unfamiliar culture of the new immigrants.

Know-Nothings scored startling victories in northern state elections in 1854, winning control of the legislature in Massachusetts and polling 40 percent of the vote in Pennsylvania. No wonder one Pennsylvania Democrat reported, "Nearly everybody seems to have gone altogether deranged on Nativism." Although most of the new immigrants lived in the North, resentment and anger against them was national and the American party initially polled well in the South, attracting the votes of many former southern Whigs. But the exclusive emphasis on nativism and the attempt to ignore the question of slavery were impossible to sustain, and in 1855 the American party split into northern (antislavery) and southern (proslavery) wings. Soon the Know-Nothings were superseded by another political combination of many of the same Whig attitudes and a westward-looking, expansionist, free-soil policy. This was the Republican party, founded in 1854.

The Organization of the Republican Party

In 1854 a Massachusetts voter described the elections in his state in terms of "freedom, temperance, and Protestantism against slavery, rum, and Romanism." In so doing, he linked nativism with sectional politics. The last three qualities were supposed to describe the national Democratic party, which included large numbers of southern slave owners and northern immigrant Catholics. The first three qualities were the ones that united the Republican party. Many constituencies found room in the new party. There were many former northern Whigs who opposed slavery completely, many free-soilers who opposed the expansion of slavery but were willing to tolerate it in the South, and many northern reformers concerned about temperance and Catholicism. The Republicans also attracted the economic core of the old Whig party — the merchants and industrialists who wanted a strong national government to promote economic growth by supporting a protective tariff, transportation improvements, and cheap land for western farmers. In quieter times it would have taken this party a while to sort out all its differences, and become a true political community. But because of the sectional crisis, the fledgling party nearly won its very first presidential election.

The Election of 1856

The immediate question facing the nation in 1856 was which new party, the Know-Nothings or the

"If I Don't Kill Something Else Soon, *I'll Spile!*" This hostile comment on Know-Nothing violence in Baltimore illustrates the class origins of many members, who were native-born workers venting their frustration about job competition from immigrants through violence.

Republicans, would emerge the stronger. But the more important question was whether the Democratic party could hold together. The two strongest contenders for the Democratic nomination were President Pierce and Stephen A. Douglas. Douglas, as we have seen, had proposed the Kansas-Nebraska Act and Pierce had actively supported it. Both men therefore had the support of the southern wing of the party. But for precisely the same reason, northerners opposed both of them. The Kansas-Nebraska Act's divisive effect on the Democratic Party now became clear: no one who had voted on the bill, either for or against, could satisfy both wings of the party. A compromise candidate was found, James Buchanan of Pennsylvania, long known as a northerner with southern sympathies. Luckily for him, he had been ambassador to Great Britain at the time of the Kansas-Nebraska Act, and thus had not had to commit himself.

The election of 1856 appeared to be a three-way contest that pitted Buchanan against explorer John C. Frémont of the Republican party and former president Millard Fillmore of the American party. In fact, the election was two separate contests, one in the North and one in the South.

The southern race was between Buchanan and Fillmore. Frémont's name appeared on the ballot only in the four Upper South states, and even there he polled almost no votes. Fillmore received strong support from many former southern Whigs. Although he carried only the state of Maryland, he attracted more than 40 percent of the vote in ten other slave states. Buchanan, though, won the electoral votes of all the southern states.

Frémont decisively defeated Buchanan in the North, winning eleven of sixteen free states. Nationwide he garnered 1.3 million votes to Buchanan's 1.8 million. Buchanan won the election with only 45 percent of the popular vote because he was the only national candidate. His southern support, plus the electoral votes of Pennsylvania, New Jersey, Illinois, Indiana, and California gave him the victory. But the Republicans, after studying the election returns, claimed "victorious defeat," for they realized that the addition of two more northern states to their total in 1860 would mean victory for them. Furthermore, the Republican party had clearly defeated the American party in the battle to win designation as a major party. These were grounds for great optimism — and for great concern, for the Republican party was a sectional rather than a national party. Southerners viewed the very existence of the Republican party as an attack upon its vital interests. Thus the rapid rise of the Republicans posed a growing threat to national unity.

The election of 1856 attracted one of the highest voter turnouts in American history — 79 percent. Ordinary people had come to share the politicians' concern about the growing sectional rift. The combined popular vote for Buchanan and Fillmore (67 percent) showed that most voters, North and South, favored politicians who claimed to speak for national rather than sectional interests. But the northern returns showed something else: northerners had decided that the threat posed by the expansion of slavery was greater than that posed by the new immigrants. Nativism subsided, although it never disappeared.

Events in "Bleeding Kansas" and the inability of the Buchanan administration to stop them shaped the next chapter in the slow slide into civil war.

THE DIFFERENCES DEEPEN

In one horrible week in 1856, the people of the United States heard of the looting and burning of Lawrence, Kansas, by proslavery forces, John Brown's retaliatory massacre of five unarmed proslavery men at Pottawatomie, and of violence on the Senate floor. In the last of these incidents, Senator Charles Sumner of Massachusetts suffered permanent injury in a vicious attack by Congressman Preston Brooks of South Carolina. Trapped at his desk, Sumner was helpless as Brooks beat him so hard with his cane that it broke. Blood streaming from his head, Sumner escaped only by wrenching loose his desk from the screws that held it to the floor. A few days earlier, Sumner had given an insulting antislavery speech entitled "The Crime against Kansas." Using the abusive, accusatory style favored by abolitionists, he had singled out for ridicule Senator Andrew Butler of South Carolina, charging him with choosing "the harlot, slavery" as his mistress. Senator Butler was Preston Brooks's uncle; in Brooks's mind, he was simply avenging an intolerable affront to his uncle's honor. So far had the behavioral codes of North and South diverged that each man found his own action perfectly justifiable and the action of the other outrageous. Their attitudes were mirrored in their respective sections.

The Buchanan Presidency

Guerrilla warfare in Kansas, physical attacks in Congress — this was the situation that faced James Buchanan when he entered the White House in March of 1857. Although Buchanan firmly believed that he alone could hold the nation together, his

The beating of Senator Charles Sumner by Congressman Preston Brooks on the Senate floor attracted horrified national attention. This illustration from a leading northern magazine was accompanied by a story, a detailed diagram, and a portrait of Sumner.

self-confidence outran his abilities. At the time, Buchanan was the oldest president (sixty-five) ever elected, but despite his experience, he was indecisive at moments that called for firm leadership. Most of all, he was so deeply indebted to the strong southern wing of the Democratic party that he could not take the impartial actions necessary to heal "Bleeding Kansas." Equally unfortunate, his support of the prosouthern Dred Scott decision encouraged further sectional differences.

The Lecompton Constitution

In Kansas, the application of popular sovereignty led to civil strife and the political travesty of two territorial governments. The election for a territorial government in 1855 produced such lopsided proslavery results that "border ruffian" voting was unmistakable (see the chapter introduction). Free-soilers then formed their own government. As a result, Kansas had both a proslavery territorial legislature in Lecompton and a free-soil government in Topeka. Fearing another fraudulent outcome, free-soil voters boycotted a June 1857 election for a constitutional convention. As a result, the convention had a proslavery majority, which wrote a proslavery constitution and applied to Congress for admission to the Union. In the meantime, free-soil voters had participated in relatively honest elections for the territorial legislature in October 1857. These elections returned a clear free-soil majority. Neverthe-

less, Buchanan, in the single most disastrous mistake of his administration, endorsed the proslave Lecompton constitution because he was anxious not to lose the support of southern Democrats. It seemed that Kansas would enter the Union as a slave state.

Unexpected congressional opposition came from none other than Stephen Douglas, author of the legislation that had begun the Kansas troubles in 1854. Now, in 1857, in what was surely the bravest step of his political career, Douglas opposed the Lecompton constitution on the grounds that it violated the principle of popular sovereignty. He insisted that the Lecompton constitution must be voted upon by Kansas voters in honest elections (as indeed Buchanan had initially promised). Douglas's decision was one of principle, but it was also motivated by the realization that a proslavery vote would never be accepted by the northern wing of the Democratic party. Defying James Buchanan, his own president, Douglas carried the congressional vote of April 1, 1858, that defeated the Lecompton constitution. The people of Kansas also rejected the Lecompton constitution, 11,300 to 1,788. In 1859 Kansas held another constitutional convention, this one dominated by delegates from the new Republican party. Kansas was finally admitted as a free state in January 1861.

The defeat of the Lecompton constitution did not come easily. There was more bloodshed in Kansas: sporadic ambushes and killings, including a mass shooting of nine free-soilers. And there was more violence in Congress: a free-for-all involving almost thirty congressmen broke out in the House late one night after an exchange of insults between Republicans and southern Democrats. And there was conflict on still another level: the Democratic party broke apart. Douglas had intended to preserve the Democrats as a national party, but instead he lost the support of the southern wing. Southerners reviled him, one claiming that Douglas was "stained with the dishonor of treachery without a parallel." Summing up these events, Congressman Alexander Stephens of Georgia wrote glumly to his brother: "All things here are tending my mind to the conclusion that the Union cannot and will not last long." Honest Quitman of Mississippi was even more outspoken:

> National Democracy is worthless. We must . . . see in [the rejection of the Lecompton constitution] a fixed and inexorable determination on the part of the majority never to admit another slave state, to stop forever the extension of slavery, and thus to bind the South to a triumphant car of an antagonistic majority.

The Dred Scott Case

On March 6, 1857, three days after James Buchanan was sworn in, the Supreme Court announced one of its most momentous opinions. In the Dred Scott case, a southern-dominated Court attempted — and failed — to solve the political controversy over slavery. Chief Justice Roger B. Taney, seventy-nine years old, hard of hearing and his sight failing, insisted on reading his majority opinion in its entirety, a process that took four excruciating hours. Declaring the Missouri Compromise unconstitutional, Taney asserted that the federal government had no right to interfere with the free movement of property throughout the territories. This was John C. Calhoun's states' rights position, which had always been considered an extremist southern argument. Now Taney asserted it was the law of the land. Furthermore, Taney dismissed the Dred Scott case, which had been in the courts for eleven years, on the grounds that only citizens could bring suits before federal courts and that black people were not citizens. With this bold judicial intervention into the most heated issue of the day, Taney intended to settle the controversy over the expansion of slavery once and for all. Instead, he enflamed the conflict.

Dred Scott had been a slave all his life. His owner, army surgeon John Emerson, had taken Scott on his military assignments during the 1830s to Illinois (a free state) and Minnesota Territory (a free part of the Louisiana Purchase). Scott married another slave, Harriet, in Minnesota, and their daughter, Eliza, was born in free territory. They all returned to Missouri (a slave state) and there, in 1846, Dred Scott sued for his freedom and that of his wife and daughter (who as women had no legal standing of their own), on the grounds that residence in free lands had made them free. It took eleven years for the case to reach the Supreme Court, and by then its importance was obvious to everyone.

The five southern members of the Supreme Court concurred in Taney's decision, as did one northerner, Robert C. Grier. Historians subsequently found that President-elect Buchanan had pressured Grier, a fellow Pennsylvanian, to support the majority. Two of the three other northerners vigorously dissented, and the last voiced other objections. This was a sectional decision, and the response to it was sectional. Southerners expressed great satisfaction in the decision and strong support for the Court. The *Louisville Democrat* said, "The decision is right . . . but whether or not, what this tribunal decides the Constitution to be, that it is; and all patriotic men will acquiesce." More bluntly, the Georgia *Constitutionalist* announced, "Southern opinion upon the subject of southern slavery . . . is now the supreme law of the land . . . and opposition to southern opinion upon this subject is now opposition to the Constitution, and morally treason against the Government." President Buchanan, knowing the decision in advance, announced somewhat disingenuously in his inaugural address that he would "cheerfully submit . . . in common with all good citizens" to the Supreme Court's decision.

Northerners felt differently. Few were quite so contemptuous as the *New York Tribune,* which declared that the decision was "entitled to just as much moral weight as would be the judgment of a majority of those congregated in any Washington bar-room." Still, many northerners disagreed so strongly with the Dred Scott decision that for the first time they found themselves seriously questioning the power of the Supreme Court to establish the "law of the land." In effect, they were questioning a crucial part of the federal system because it was dominated by their sectional opponents. Many northern legislatures denounced the decision. New York passed a resolution declaring that the Supreme Court had lost the confidence and respect of the people of that state, and another refusing to allow slavery within its borders "in any form or under any

These sympathetic portraits of Harriet and Dred Scott and their daughters were part of the northern reaction to the Supreme Court decision that denied the Scotts' claim for freedom. The famous Dred Scott decision, which was intended to resolve the issue of slavery expansion, instead heightened feelings in both North and South.

pretence, or for any time, however short." New York Republicans also proposed an equal-suffrage amendment for free African Americans (who were largely disenfranchised by a stringent property qualification). But this was too liberal for the state's voters, who defeated it. This racist attitude was a bitter blow to free black people in the North.

For the Republican party, the Dred Scott decision represented a formidable challenge. By invalidating the Missouri Compromise, it swept away the free-soil foundation of the party. But to directly challenge a Supreme Court decision was a weighty matter. The most sensational Republican counterattack was the accusation that President Buchanan had conspired with the southern Supreme Court justices to subvert the American political system by withholding the decision until after the presidential election. Both William H. Seward and Abraham Lincoln made this claim. Lincoln also raised the frightening possibility that "the next Dred Scott decision" would legalize slavery even in free states that abhorred it.

The most considered Republican response to the Dred Scott decision was also the most realistic one. Lincoln pledged not to defy the Supreme Court's decision but to have it reversed. The way to do that was to elect a Republican president who would appoint free-soil judges to the Court. But in the atmosphere of the 1850s, even this democratic answer frightened the South. Now southerners had another reason to dread the election of a Republican president. Politicians — and the general public — began to look anxiously to the next presidential election.

The Panic of 1857

Adding to the growing political tensions was the short but sharp depression of 1857 and 1858. Technology played a part: word of the failure of an Ohio investment house in August of 1857 — the kind of event that had formerly taken weeks to be widely known — flashed immediately over telegraph wires to Wall Street and other financial markets. There ensued a wave of panic selling, which led to business failures and slowdowns that threw thousands out of work. The major cause of the panic was a sharp downturn in agricultural exports caused by the end of the Crimean War in Europe. Recovery was well under way by early 1859 (in contrast with the seven-year depression that had followed the Panic of 1837). In the meantime, Republicans and some northern Democrats in Congress proposed to raise tariffs to help industries hurt by the depression, only to be outvoted by almost all southern representatives and about half of the northern Democrats. The South had resisted protective tariffs since the 1820s (see Chapter 10), but now the opposition was regarded, in the bitter words of one Republican, as yet another example of a Congress "shamelessly prostituted, in a base subserviency to the Slave Power."

Because cotton exports were affected less than northern exports, the Panic of 1857 was less harmful to the South than to the North. Southerners took this as proof of the superiority of their economic system to the free-labor system of the North, and some could not resist the chance to gloat. Senator James Hammond of South Carolina drove home the point

This worried crowd engaged in panic selling on Wall Street demonstrates one new aspect of the Panic of 1857. There had been previous panics, but this was the first in which the telegraph played a part by carrying bad financial news in the West to New York much more rapidly than in the past.

in his celebrated "King Cotton" speech (see Chapter 11) of March 1858:

> When the abuse of credit had destroyed credit and annihilated confidence; when thousands of the strongest commercial houses in the world were coming down . . . when you came to a dead lock, and revolutions were threatened, what brought you up? . . . We have poured in upon you one million six hundred thousand bales of cotton just at the moment to save you from destruction. . . . We have sold it for $65,000,000, and saved you.

It seemed that all matters of political discussion were being drawn into the sectional dispute.

The Lincoln-Douglas Debates

Stephen Douglas of Illinois was already a leading contender for the presidency in 1860, but first he had to win reelection to his Illinois Senate seat in the fall of 1858. The race was of much more than local importance. Douglas's standing in his party had been drastically changed by his vote on the Lecompton constitution. Previously excoriated by northerners, Douglas now found himself praised and courted by northern Republicans as well as Democrats. On the other hand, the southern wing of the Democratic party, which he had done so much to conciliate, now reviled him. Buchanan, furious over the Lecompton defeat, openly opposed Douglas's reelection and encouraged local Democrats in Illinois to work against him.

Douglas's stand on Kansas affected not only his own prospects but those of the Republican party. Until Douglas's disavowal of the Lecompton constitution, Republicans had been able to claim that southerners completely dominated the Democratic party. Douglas had effectively undercut that argument. Because the crisis of the Union was so severe, and Douglas's role so pivotal, his reelection campaign was nothing less than a preview of the 1860 presidential election. The Republican party, for the sake of its future, *had* to field a strong candidate to oppose him. Fortunately, such a man stepped forward: Abraham Lincoln.

Lincoln had been a congressman in the 1840s, had opposed the Mexican-American War, and had lost his bid for reelection to the House as a consequence. He had then developed a prosperous Springfield law practice, and had been an influential member of the Illinois Republican party since its founding in 1856. Beginning as a Whig in the Henry Clay tradition of favoring federal policies that fostered national development, Lincoln, like many other Whigs, was radicalized by the issue of slavery extension. Now, although his wife's family were Kentucky slave owners, Lincoln's commitment to freedom and his resistance to the spread of slavery were absolute. For Lincoln, freedom and Union were inseperable.

Lincoln was the underdog in the 1858 Senate race, being much less well known than Douglas. Consequently, Lincoln challenged Douglas to debate, and Douglas accepted. In August and September of 1858 the two men squared off seven times at different communities in Illinois. Their confrontations have become the most famous political debates in American history. They discussed one issue only: slavery and the future of the Union. This alone indicates how serious sectional differences had become. For most of the decade, politicians trying to find compromises acceptable to everyone had done their best *not* to talk about slavery.

Thousands of farmers and their families drove the dusty roads of rural Illinois to join the residents of small country communities in listening to the debates. These were festive, outdoor occasions, with picnicking, band music, and much socializing. But the central attraction was the debate itself. Politics was of consuming interest to the people of Illinois in the 1850s, part serious business, part entertainment. The voters of Illinois expected, and got, an engrossing show from the two senatorial candidates.

Douglas and Lincoln must have been a funny sight as they took the stump together. Douglas was short (five feet four inches) and very square; his nickname was the Little Giant. Lincoln, on the other hand, was very tall, very thin, and remarkably homely. Both were eloquent and powerful speakers — and they had need to be. The three-hour debates were held without amplification of any kind. Audiences listened with rapt attention to long, carefully reasoned arguments and to the opponent's rebuttals, and they participated actively by shouting questions and comments and punctuating the exchanges with cheers, boos, and groans. The Lincoln-Douglas debates, one noted historian has claimed, were "almost a perfect [example] of nineteenth-century American democratic practice at its best."

Douglas had many strengths going into these debates. He spoke for the Union, he claimed, pointing out that the Democratic Party was national, the Republican Party only sectional. He defended the principle of popular sovereignty, and he was shrewd enough to appeal to the racism of much of his audience with declarations such as, "I would not blot out the great inalienable rights of the white men for all the negroes that ever existed!" He repeatedly

Tall, thin Abraham Lincoln and short, square Stephen A. Douglas are contrasted in this cartoon, which also cleverly illustrates, in the black man trapped in the rail fence, the way in which Lincoln forced Douglas to equivocate over the issue of the extension of slavery.

called his opponent a "Black Republican," a favorite Democratic slur, implying that Lincoln and his party favored the social equality of whites and blacks, and even race mixing.

Lincoln did not, in fact, believe in the social equality of the races. (As we have seen, few whites did, even abolitionists.) But he *did* believe whole-heartedly that slavery was a moral wrong. In one of his most famous speeches, which predated the debates, he announced his position in memorable language: "A House divided against itself cannot stand. I believe this government cannot endure, permanently half *slave* and half *free*. . . . I do not expect the Union to be dissolved—I do not expect the House to fall—but I do expect it to cease to be divided. It will become all one thing or all the other." Pledging the Republican party to the "ultimate extinction" of slavery, Lincoln continually warned that Douglas's position would lead to the opposite result: the spread of slavery everywhere. In this argument, Lincoln was tapping into the popular northern fear of the expansionist "slave power." At the same time, Lincoln strove to present himself as a moderate: he did not favor the breakup of the Union. But he never wavered from his assertion that slavery was a moral wrong, and in so doing he established in the public mind the image of the Republican party as the only force capable of stopping southern domination of the country.

Lincoln cleverly used the Dred Scott decision to corner Douglas. Was there any way, Lincoln asked Douglas in their debate at Freeport, that a territory could exclude slavery if it wished to? Douglas wiggled: if he answered no, he supported the Dred Scott decision and lost northern support; if he answered yes and affirmed his belief in popular sovereignty, the South would be angered. He found a compromise, claiming (in the statement since known as the Freeport Doctrine) that the people of a territory could in effect choose to support or not support slavery, depending on the legislation they passed: "Slavery cannot exist a day in the midst of an unfriendly people with unfriendly laws," Douglas pronounced.

Most historians have agreed that Lincoln "won" the debates. But he did not win the 1858 senatorial election in Illinois. The result of that election mirrored the national divisions: the Democrats won almost all of southern Illinois, the Republicans almost all the northern part of the state. Each candidate polled roughly the same number of votes——but the Democratic-controlled legislature awarded the seat to Douglas. Assured of the support of the northern wing of the party, Douglas emerged the front-runner for his party's presidential nomination in 1860. Lincoln, though, by his skill in debating contentious issues, had vastly enhanced his own credibility within the Republican party. The next step on the path to the presidency, however, was taken not by these two principals but by the grim abolitionist from Kansas, John Brown.

John Brown's Raid

In the heated political mood of the late 1850s, some improbable people became heroes. None was more improbable than John Brown, who had made his name by slaughtering unarmed proslavery men in Kansas in 1856 (see the chapter introduction). Brown's wild scheme in 1859 to raid the South and start a general slave uprising would have been unthinkable in normal political times. Brown believed, as did most northern abolitionists, that discontent among southern slaves was so great that a general uprising needed only a spark to get going. Significantly, free black people, among them Frederick Douglass, did not support Brown, thinking his scheme to raid the federal arsenal at Harpers Ferry, Virginia, was doomed to failure. It did fail. On October 16, 1859, Brown led a group of twenty-two white and African American men against the arsenal. But he had made no provision for escape. Even more incredible, he had not notified the Virginia slaves whose uprising it was supposed to be. In less than a day the raid was over. Eight of Brown's men (including two of his sons) were dead, no slaves had risen, and Brown himself was captured. Moving quickly to prevent a lynching by local mobs, the state of Virginia tried and convicted Brown of treason, murder, and fomenting insurrection while he was still weak from the wounds of battle.

Ludicrous in life, possibly insane, Brown was a noble martyr. In his closing speech prior to sentencing, Brown was magnificently eloquent:

> Now, if it is deemed necessary that I should forfeit my life for the furtherance of the end of justice, and mingle my blood further with the blood of my children and with the blood of millions in this slave country whose rights are disregarded by wicked, cruel, and unjust enactments, I say, let it be done.

Brown's death by hanging on December 2, 1859, was marked throughout northern communi-

This photograph of John Brown, taken in 1859, clearly shows the intense moral fervor that drove him to undertake an unrealistic raid on Harper's Ferry in October of that year. Brown, an eloquent martyr, was executed on December 2, 1859. His death provoked almost unprecedented mourning in the North, a reaction that horrified the South.

ties with public rites of mourning not seen since the death of George Washington. Church bells tolled, buildings were draped in black, ministers preached sermons, prayer meetings were held, abolitionists eulogized the deceased. Ralph Waldo Emerson said that Brown would "make the gallows as glorious as the cross," and Henry David Thoreau called him "an angel of light." In a more militant frame of mind, Wendell Phillips announced, "The lesson of the hour is insurrection." Naturally, not all northerners supported Brown's action. Northern Democrats and conservative opinion generally repudiated him. In New York, for example, 20,000 merchants signed a call for a public meeting designed to reassure the South of northern good intentions. But many people,

while rejecting Brown's raid, did support the antislavery cause that he represented.

Brown's raid shocked the South because it struck at their greatest fear, that of slave rebellion. Southerners believed that northern abolitionists were provoking slave revolts, a suspicion apparently confirmed when documents captured at Harpers Ferry revealed that Brown had the financial support of half a dozen members of the northern elite. These "Secret Six" — Gerrit Smith, George Stearns, Franklin Sanborn, Thomas Wentworth Higginson, Theodore Parker, and Samuel Gridley Howe — had been willing to finance armed attacks on the slave system.

Even more shocking to southerners than the raid itself was the general northern reaction to Brown's death. Although the Republican party disavowed Brown's actions, southerners simply did not believe them. They wondered how they could stay in the Union in the face of what one southerner termed "Northern insolence." The Richmond *Enquirer* reported, "The Harper's Ferry invasion has advanced the cause of disunion more than any other event that has happened since the formation of [the] government." The alarm in upcountry South Carolina was so great that vigilance committees were formed in every district. Throughout the next year, these committees remained armed and ready to deal with strangers (they might be abolitionists) and any hint of slave revolt. This extreme paranoia was not a good portent for the election year of 1860. Looking to the presidential race, Senator Robert Toombs of Georgia warned that the South would "never permit this Federal government to pass into the traitorous hands of the Black Republican party."

Talk of secession as the only possible response to the northern "insults" of the 1850s — the armed protests against the Fugitive Slave Law, the rejection of the Lecompton constitution, and now the support for John Brown's raid — was common throughout the South. Although the majority of southerners probably rejected secession, the political passions of the election year fostered secessionist thinking.

The South Secedes

By 1860, sectional differences had caused one national party, the Whigs, to collapse. The second national party, the Democrats, stood on the brink of dissolution. Not only the politicians but ordinary people in both the North and the South were coming to believe there was no way to avoid what William

Seward (once a Whig, now a Republican) in 1858 had called an "irrepressible conflict."

The Election of 1860

James Buchanan had entered the presidency in 1857 convinced that only he could hold the Democratic party and the nation together. But key events of his administration — the Dred Scott decision, the rejection of the Lecompton constitution, Douglas's re-election in 1858 — irreparably split the Democratic party into northern and southern wings. The split became official at the Democratic nominating conventions in 1860.

The Democrats convened first in Charleston, South Carolina, the center of secessionist agitation. It was the worst possible location in which to attempt to reach unity. Although Stephen Douglas had the support of the majority of delegates, he did not have the plurality necessary for nomination. As the price of their support, southerners insisted that Douglas support a federal slave code — a guarantee that slavery would be protected in the territories. Douglas could not agree without violating his own belief in popular sovereignty and losing his northern support. After ten days, fifty-nine ballots, and two southern walkouts the convention ended where it had begun: deadlocked. Northern supporters of Douglas were angry and bitter: "I never heard Abolitionists talk more uncharitably and rancorously of the people of the South than the Douglas men," one reporter wrote. "They say they do not care a d — — n where the South goes. . . ."

In June, the Democrats met again in Baltimore. The Douglasites, recognizing the need for a united party, were eager to compromise wherever they could; most southern Democrats were not. More than a third of the delegates bolted. Later, holding a

This Republican Party poster for the election of 1860 combines the party's major themes: free land, free soil, opposition to the Slave Power (the slogan "Free Speech"), and higher tariffs. But above all was the message "The Union Shall be Preserved."

convention of their own, they nominated Vice-President John C. Breckinridge of Kentucky. Douglas was duly nominated by the remaining two-thirds of the Democrats, but they all knew a Republican victory was inevitable. To make matters worse, some southern Whigs joined with some border state nativists to form the Constitutional Union party, which nominated John Bell of Tennessee.

Republican strategy was built on the lessons of the 1856 "victorious defeat." The Republicans planned to carry all the states Frémont had won, plus Pennsylvania, Illinois, and Indiana. The two leading contenders were Senator William H. Seward of New York and Abraham Lincoln of Illinois. Seward, the party's best-known figure, had enemies among party moderates, who thought he was too radical, and among nativists with whom he had clashed in the New York Whig party. Lincoln, on the other hand, appeared new, impressive, more moderate than Seward, and certain to carry Illinois. Lincoln won the nomination on the third ballot.

The election of 1860 presented voters with one of the clearest choices in American history. On the key issue of slavery, Breckinridge supported its extension to the territories; Lincoln stood firmly for its exclusion. Douglas attempted to hold the middle ground with his principle of popular sovereignty; Bell vaguely favored compromise as well. The Republicans offered other platform planks designed to appeal to northern voters: a homestead act (free western lands), support for a transcontinental railroad, other internal improvements, and a higher tariff. While speaking clearly against the extension of slavery, Republicans devoted most of their other efforts to dispelling their radical abolitionist image. The Republican platform condemned John Brown's raid as "the gravest of crimes," repeatedly denied that Republicans favored the social equality of blacks, and strenuously denied that they sought the breakup of the Union. In reality, Republicans simply did not believe the South would secede if Lincoln won. In this the Republicans were not alone: few northerners believed southern threats — southerners had threatened too many times before.

Breckinridge insisted that he and his supporters were loyal to the Union — as long as their needs concerning slavery were met. The only candidate who spoke urgently and openly about the impending threat of secession was Douglas. Breaking with convention, Douglas personally campaigned in both the North and the South, warning of the danger of dissolution and presenting himself as the only truly national candidate. Realizing his own chances for election were slight, Douglas bravely campaigned in

a hostile South for national unity. As he told his private secretary, "Mr. Lincoln is the next President. We must try to save the Union. I will go South."

In accordance with tradition, Lincoln did not campaign for himself, but many other Republicans spoke for him. In an estimated 50,000 campaign speeches they built the image of "Honest Abe," the candidate who really *had* been born in a log cabin. The Republicans made a special effort, headed by Missouri congressman Carl Schurz, to attract the German immigrant vote. They were successful with German Protestants but less so with Catholics, who were put off by the Republicans' lingering reputation for nativism. The general mood among the northern electorate was one of excitement and optimism. For the Republicans were almost certain to win and to bring, because of their uncompromising opposition to the expansion of slavery, an end to the long sectional crisis. "I will vote the Republican ticket next Tuesday," wrote New York businessman and former Whig George Templeton Strong. "The only alternative is everlasting submission to the South." The Republicans did not campaign in the South; Breckinridge did not campaign in the North. Each side was therefore free to believe the worst about the other. All parties, North and South, campaigned with oratory, parades and rallies, free food and drink. In spite of the looming crisis, this presidential campaign was the best entertainment there was.

In spite of Breckinridge's disclaimers, the mood in the Deep South was close to mass hysteria. Rumors of slave revolts — in Texas, Alabama, and South Carolina — swept the region, and vigilance committees sprang up to counter the supposed threat. Responding to the rumors, Alabaman Sarah R. Espy wrote in her diary, "The country is getting in a deplorable state owing to the depredations committed by the Abolitionist[s] especially in Texas; and the safety of the country depend[s] on who is elected to the presidency." Apparently, southern voters talked of little else, as Alabaman Benjamin F. Riley recalled:

> Little else was done this year, than discuss politics. Vast crowds would daily assemble at the places of popular resort, to canvass the questions at issue. Stump speaking was a daily occurrence. Men were swayed more by passion than by calm judgment.

In the South Carolina upcountry, the question of secession dominated races for the state legislature. Candidates such as A. S. Wallace of York, who advocated "patriotic forbearance" if Lincoln won, were soundly defeated. Although northerners did

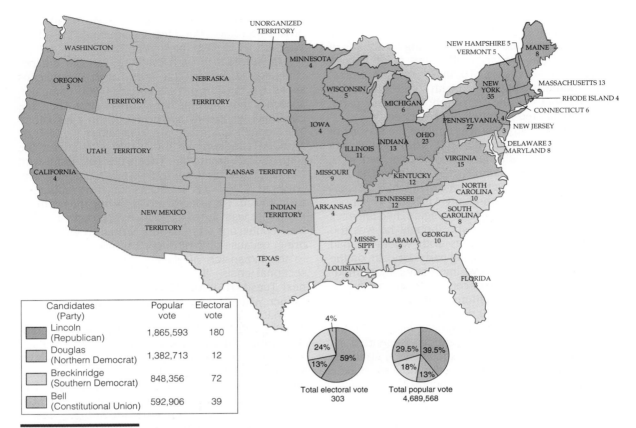

Candidates (Party)	Popular vote	Electoral vote
Lincoln (Republican)	1,865,593	180
Douglas (Northern Democrat)	1,382,713	12
Breckinridge (Southern Democrat)	848,356	72
Bell (Constitutional Union)	592,906	39

Total electoral vote 303

Total popular vote 4,689,568

The Election of 1860

The Election of 1860 was a sectional election. Lincoln gained no votes in the South, Breckinridge none in the North. The contest in the North was between Lincoln and Douglas, and although Lincoln swept the electoral vote, Douglas' popular vote was uncomfortably close. The huge number of northern Democratic voters opposed to Lincoln was a source of much political trouble for him during the Civil War.

not believe the South would secede, the very passion and excitement of the election campaign moved southerners toward extremism. Even the weather — the worst drought and heat wave the South had known for years — contributed to the tension.

The election of 1860 produced the second highest voter turnout in U.S. history (81.2 percent, topped only by 81.8 percent in 1876). The election turned out to be two regional contests: Breckinridge versus Bell in the South, Lincoln versus Douglas in the North. Breckinridge carried ten southern states with 18 percent of the total vote; Bell carried Virginia, Tennessee, and Kentucky. Lincoln won all eighteen of the free states (he split New Jersey with Douglas) and 38 percent of the popular vote. Douglas carried only Missouri, but gained 30 percent of the popular vote. Lincoln's electoral vote total was

overwhelming: 180 to a combined 123 for the other three candidates. But although Lincoln had won 54 percent of the vote in the northern states, his name had not even appeared on the ballot in ten southern states. The true winner of the 1860 election was sectionalism.

Southern Action

Charles Francis Adams, son and grandson of presidents, wrote in his diary on the day Lincoln was elected, "The great revolution has actually taken place. . . . The country has once and for all thrown off the domination of the Slaveholders." That was precisely what the South feared.

The results of the election shocked southerners. They were humiliated and frightened by the prospect of becoming a permanent minority in a political system dominated by a party pledged to the elimination of slavery. Lincoln always presented himself as a moderate, talking about the eventual rather than immediate "extinction" of slavery, but in southern eyes the result was the same. The Republican triumph meant they would become unequal partners in the federal enterprise, their way of life (the slave system) existing on borrowed time. As a Georgia newspaper said, ten days after Lincoln's election, "African slavery, though panoplied by the Federal Constitution, is doomed to a war of extermination. All the powers of a Government which has so long sheltered it will be turned to its destruction. The only hope for its preservation, therefore, is out of the Union." And Mary Boykin Chesnut, member of a well-connected South Carolina family, confided to her diary, "The die is cast — no more vain regrets — sad forebodings are useless. The stake is life or death —"

The governors of South Carolina, Alabama, and Mississippi, each personally committed to secession if Lincoln were elected, immediately issued calls for special state conventions. At the same time, calls went out to southern communities to form vigilance committees and volunteer militia companies. A visiting northerner, Sereno Watson, wrote to his brother in amazement:

> This people is apparently gone crazy. I do not know how to account for it & have no idea what might be the end of it. Union men, Douglas men, Breckinridge men are alike in their loud denunciation of submission to Lincoln's administration. There are of course those who think differently but they scarcely dare or are suffered to open their mouths.

In the face of this frenzy, cooperationists (the term used for those opposed to immediate secession) were either intimidated into silence or simply left behind by the speed of events.

On December 20, 1860, South Carolina, with all the hoopla and excitement of bands, fireworks displays, and huge rallies, seceded from the Union. James Buchanan, the lame-duck president (Lincoln would not be inaugurated until March), did nothing. In the weeks that followed, six other southern states (Mississippi, Florida, Alabama, Georgia, Louisiana, and Texas) followed suit. In none of these states was the vote for secession unanimous, as it had been in South Carolina, but the average vote in favor was 80 percent. Although there was genuine division of opinion in the South (especially in Georgia and Alabama, along customary upcountry/low-country lines) none of the Deep South states held anywhere

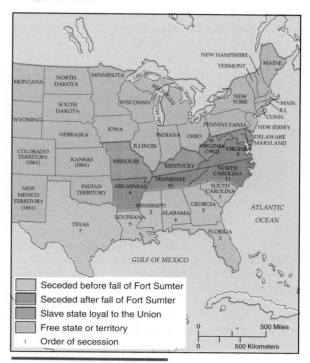

The Southern States Secede

The southern states that would compose the Confederacy seceded in two major groups. The states of the Lower South seceded before Lincoln took office and war began at Fort Sumter. Three states of the Upper South — Virginia, North Carolina and Tennessee — and Arkansas waited until after Fort Sumter. And four border slave states: Delaware, Maryland, Kentucky and Missouri, chose not to secede. Every southern state (except South Carolina) was divided on the issue of secession, generally along upcountry/low country lines. In Virginia, this division was so extreme that West Virginia split off to become a separate nonslave state and was admitted to the Union in 1863.

near the number of Unionists that Republicans had hoped. Throughout the South, secession occurred because southerners no longer believed they had a choice. "Secession is a desperate remedy," acknowledged South Carolina's David Harris, "but of the two evils I do think it is the lesser."

In every state that seceded, the joyous scenes of South Carolina were repeated as the decisiveness of action replaced the long years of anxiety and tension. People danced in the streets, most believing the North had no choice but to accept secession peacefully. They ignored the fact that eight other slave states (Delaware, Maryland, Kentucky, Missouri, Virginia, North Carolina, Tennessee, and Arkansas) had not acted — though the latter four states did join them before war broke out. Just as Republicans had miscalculated in thinking southern threats of secession were just another bluff, so secessionists now miscalculated in believing they would be able to leave the Union in peace.

Northern Response

What should the North do? James Buchanan, true to form, did nothing. The decision rested with Abraham Lincoln, even before he officially became president. One possibility was compromise, and many were suggested, ranging from full adoption of the Breckinridge campaign platform to reinstatement of the Missouri Compromise line. Lincoln cautiously refused them all, making it clear that he would not compromise on the extension of slavery, which was the South's key demand. He hoped, by appearing firm but moderate, to discourage additional southern states from seceding while giving pro-Union southerners time to organize. He succeeded in his first aim, but not in the second. Lincoln and most of the Republican party had seriously overestimated the strength of pro-Union sentiment in the South.

A second possibility, suggested by Horace Greeley of the *New York Tribune*, was to let the seven seceding states "go in peace." This is what many secessionists expected, but too many northerners — including Lincoln himself — believed in the Union for this to happen. As Lincoln said, what was at stake was "the necessity of proving that popular government is not an absurdity. We must settle this question now, whether in a free government the minority have the right to break up the government whenever they choose." At stake was all the accumulated American pride in the federal government as a model for democracies the world over.

The third possibility was force, and this was the crux of the dilemma. Although he believed their action was wrong, Lincoln was loath to go to war to force the seceding states back into the Union. On the other hand, he refused to give up federal powers in the South over military forts and customs posts. These were precisely the powers the seceding states had to command if they were to function as an independent nation. A confrontation was bound to come. Abraham Lincoln, not for the last time, was prepared to wait for the other side to strike the first blow.

Establishment of the Confederacy

In February, delegates from the seven seceding states met in Montgomery, Alabama, and created the Confederate States of America. They wrote a constitution that was identical to the Constitution of the United States, with a few crucial exceptions: it strongly supported states' rights and made the abolition of slavery practically impossible. These two clauses did much to define the Confederate enterprise. It was difficult to avoid the conclusion that the structure of the new Confederate state had been decided by the southern organization of slave labor. L. W. Spratt of South Carolina confessed as much in 1859: "We stand committed to the South, but we stand more vitally committed to the cause of slavery. It is, indeed, to be doubted whether the South [has] any cause apart from the institution which affects her." The South's entire defense of slavery was built on a commitment to individualism and decentralization — the rights of the slave owner over his slaves, and the right of freedom claimed by all white men — and on the rights of the states versus the federal government. But the military defense of the South would require a strong central government. This was to be the South's basic dilemma throughout the Civil War.

The Montgomery convention passed over the fire-eaters — the men who had been the first to urge secession — and chose Jefferson Davis of Mississippi as president and Alexander Stephens of Georgia as vice-president of the new nation. Both men were known as moderates. Davis, a slave owner, a general in the Mexican-American War, secretary of war in the Pierce administration, and senator from Mississippi, had expressed his own uncertainties by retaining his Senate seat for two weeks after Mississippi seceded. Stephens, a former leader in the Whig party, had been a cooperationist delegate to Georgia's convention, where he urged that secession not be undertaken hastily.

The choice of moderates was deliberate, for the strategy of the new Confederate state was to argue that secession was a normal, responsible, and expectable course of action, and nothing for the North to get upset about. This was the theme that President Jefferson Davis of the Confederate States of America struck in his inaugural address, delivered to a crowd of 10,000 from the steps of the state capitol at Montgomery on February 18, 1861. "We have changed the constituent parts," Davis said, "but not the system of our Government." Secession was a legal and peaceful step that, Davis said, quoting from the Declaration of Independence, "illustrates the American idea that governments rest on the consent of the governed . . . and that it is the right of the people to alter or abolish them at will whenever they become destructive of the ends for which they were established." After insisting that "a just perception of mutual interest[should] permit us peaceably to pursue our separate political [course]," Davis concluded, "Obstacles may retard, but they cannot long prevent, the progress of a movement sanctified by its justice and sustained by a virtuous people." This impressive inaugural prompted a deeply moved correspondent for the *New York Herald* to report, "God does not permit evil to be done with such earnest solemnity, such all-pervading trust in His Providence, as was exhibited by the whole people on that day."

Lincoln's Inauguration

The country as a whole waited to see what Abraham Lincoln would do. It appeared he was doing nothing. In Springfield, Lincoln refused to issue public statements before his inaugural (although he sent many private messages to Congress and to key military officers), for fear of making a delicate situation worse. Similarly, during a twelve-day whistle-stopping railroad trip from Springfield to Washington, he was careful to say nothing controversial. Eastern intellectuals, already suspicious of a mere "prairie lawyer," were not impressed. Finally, hard evidence of an assassination plot forced Lincoln to creep into Washington "like a thief in the night," as he complained. These evidences of moderation and caution did not appeal to an American public with a penchant for electing military heroes. Americans wanted leadership and action.

Lincoln continued, however, to offer nonbelligerent firmness and moderation. And at the end of his inaugural speech on March 4, 1861, as he stood ringed by federal troops called out in case of a Confederate attack, the new president offered unexpected eloquence:

Abraham Lincoln's inauguration on March 4, 1861, shown here in *Leslie's Illustrated Newspaper*, symbolized the state of the nation. As he took the oath to become president of a divided country, Lincoln stood before a Capitol building with a half-finished dome and was guarded by soldiers who feared a Confederate attack.

> I am loath to close. We are not enemies, but friends. We must not be enemies. Though passion may have strained, it must not break our bonds of affection. The mystic chords of memory, stretching from every battlefield, and patriot grave, to every living heart and hearthstone, all over this broad land, will yet swell the chorus of the Union, when again touched, as surely they will be, by the better angels of our nature.

CONCLUSION

Two communities with similar origins and many common bonds were now enemies. What had happened in Kansas now happened throughout the nation. Over a period of forty years, the issue of slavery had slowly severed the connections between North and South. The frantic efforts at political compromise that characterized the 1850s could no longer bridge the gap between the ordinary people of the two regions, who demanded a better answer than "half slave and half free." But although Americans were divided, they were still one people. That made the war, when it came, all the more terrible, for it was a civil war.

CHRONOLOGY

1820	Missouri Compromise
1832	Nullification crisis
1846	Wilmot Proviso
1848	Treaty of Guadalupe Hidalgo ends Mexican-American War Zachary Taylor (Whig) elected president Free-Soil party formed
1849	California and Utah (Deseret) seek admission to the Union as free states
1850	Nashville Convention Compromise of 1850; California admitted as a free state Zachary Taylor dies, Millard Fillmore becomes president
1851	North reacts to Fugitive Slave Law
1852	Harriet Beecher Stowe, *Uncle Tom's Cabin* Franklin Pierce (Democrat) elected president
1854	Ostend Manifesto Kansas-Nebraska Act Treaties with Indians in northern part of Indian Territory renegotiated Know-Nothing and Republican parties formed as Whig Party dissolves
1855	William Walker leads first filibustering expedition to Nicaragua
1856	"Sack of Lawrence" John Brown leads Pottawatomie massacre James Buchanan (Democrat) elected president
1857	Dred Scott decision President Buchanan accepts proslavery Lecompton constitution in Kansas Panic of 1857
1858	Congress rejects Lecompton constitution Lincoln-Douglas debates
1859	John Brown's raid on Harpers Ferry
1860	Four parties run presidential candidates Abraham Lincoln (Republican) elected president South Carolina secedes from Union
1861	Six other Deep South states secede Confederate States of America formed Lincoln takes office

Additional Readings

WILLIAM L. BARNEY, *The Secessionist Impulse: Alabama and Mississippi in 1860* (1974). Covers the election of 1860 and the subsequent conventions that led to secession.

DON E. FEHRENBACHER, *The Dred Scott Case: Its Significance in American Law and Politics* (1978). A major study by the leading historian on this controversial decision.

ERIC FONER, *Free Soil, Free Labor, Free Men: The Ideology of the Republican Party before the Civil War* (1970). A landmark effort that was among the first studies to focus on the conflicting ideologies of North and South and their dominant concern with slavery.

LACY K. FORD, JR., *Origins of Southern Radicalism: The South Carolina Upcountry, 1800–1860* (1988). One of a number of recent studies of the attitudes of upcountry farmers, who in South Carolina supported secession wholeheartedly.

HOMAN HAMILTON, *Prologue to Conflict: The Crisis and Compromise of 1850* (1964). The standard source on the Compromise of 1850.

BRUCE LEVINE, *Half Slave and Half Free: The Roots of the Civil War* (1992). Good survey of the contrasting attitudes of North and South.

ALICE NICHOLS, *Bleeding Kansas* (1954). The standard source on the battles over Kansas.

DAVID M. POTTER, *The Impending Crisis, 1848–1861* (1976). A comprehensive account of the politics leading up to the Civil War.

KENNETH M. STAMPP, *America in 1857: A Nation on the Brink* (1990). A study of the "crucial" year by a leading southern historian.

16 *THE CIVIL WAR,*
1861–1865

AMERICAN COMMUNITIES

● WASHINGTON GOES TO WAR

To visitors accustomed to the splendor of European capitals, Washington was a shock. Busy and crowded when Congress was in session, somnolent at other times, Washington was little more than a rural southern town. Partly paved Pennsylvania Avenue connected six unfinished federal buildings, among them the Washington Monument, only one-third built, and the Capitol with its half-finished dome. Pigs rooted in the side streets, and President's Park, south of the White House, was a malarial swamp. Slaves and slave dwellings were everywhere, and most of the permanent white residents were of southern origin, having kin in the bordering slave states of Maryland and Virginia.

The Civil War transformed Washington. Never again would

THE CIVIL WAR
TRANSFORMS THE
WASHINGTON
COMMUNITY AND THE
NATION

it seem like a southern country town. Nor would the nation ever revert to its prewar condition. The dramatic changes, so visible in this small community, mirrored those taking place in the nation as a whole. Throughout the country, com-
munities experienced political division, fear, military mobilization, urgent needs for medical and social care, and examples of wartime prosperity that seemed shocking in the midst of widespread suffering. Washington itself experienced a dramatic growth and centralization of federal power that was never reversed.

The election of Abraham Lincoln to the presidency in November of 1860 divided the Washington community. As southern congressmen and senators withdrew from the city following the secession of seven southern states, Republican office seekers flooded in from the North. This sudden change in politics threw the loyalty of the permanent Washington inhabitants into doubt. Known to be southern in sympathy, would Washington residents give active aid and comfort to Lincoln's enemies? Lincoln's inaugural betrayed the fears and rumors of insurrection, for as he spoke words of peace, he was closely guarded by soldiers standing on the roof and at every window of the Capitol with rifles at the ready.

At the outbreak of war, Washington's vulnerability increased. With the secession of Virginia, Washington became a front-line city and a valuable prize. Proslavery riots in Maryland cut off rail and telegraph communication between Washington and the rest of the North for six long and anxious days.

Winslow Homer. Prisoners from the Front. 1866. Oil on canvas. 24 in. × 38 in. Signed and dated (lower right) "Homer 1866." The Metropolitan Museum of Art, Gift of Mrs. Frank B. Porter, 1922.

Washington, sleepy slaveowning community and unfinished national capital, was transformed by the Civil War into a frontline city, an army base, a hospital, a refuge, and a center of national power.

After the first disastrous Union defeat, at Bull Run (July 1861), panic-stricken soldiers in full retreat streamed down Pennsylvania Avenue, reminding all the inhabitants of just how close the front line was. The feeling of vulnerability never went away: Confederate drives into northern territory (Antietam in 1862 and Gettysburg in 1863) threatened the city of Washington itself and disturbed Maryland's loyalty to the Union.

Soon Washington came to resemble an armed camp. State militias flooded into the capital to be mustered in at the War Department and then sent into battle. At first, the troops were camped everywhere, even in the Capitol building itself. Their drilling and drumming disrupted the quiet streets of Washington, forcing some leading members of the Lincoln administration to move to less noisy neighborhoods. Even after the first rush subsided and troops were moved to orderly encampments outside the city, the military presence was everywhere. It was joked that a boy once threw a stone at a dog on Pennsylvania Avenue and hit three brigadier generals! Moreover, the troops soon attracted a crowd of army contractors and saloon keepers and more prostitutes than the staid people of Washington had ever dreamed existed.

Soon Washington added the role of refuge to its other functions. Clusters of white buildings and tents marked the presence of the base hospital of the Army of the Potomac. Thousands of men suffered and died there, many of diseases (measles, smallpox, typhoid) and minor wounds that we consider easily treatable today. Some of these men were helped in their suffering by female nurses trained by a vast and essential volunteer organization, the United States Sanitary Commission. The "San," as it was nicknamed, organized everything from medical supplies to homeward transportation for wounded soldiers to major fundraising. Almost entirely dependent upon the work of female volunteers, the Sanitary Commission was a major example of the way northern civilian communities actively participated in all aspects of the war effort. Less positively, the Commission's essential services exposed the fact that the U.S. Army was incapable of meeting the needs of the first mass army in the nation's history.

Washington soon became a refuge for another population — escaped slaves, popularly known as contrabands, who crowded into the capital to join the free black people who lived there (at 9,000, they composed one of the largest urban black populations outside the South). Many destitute contrabands received help from the Contraband Relief Association. Modeled on the Sanitary Commission, the association was founded by former slave Elizabeth Keckley, seamstress to Mary Todd Lincoln, the president's wife. The emancipation of Washington's slaves, enacted in April of 1862, distressed many white residents, not just those of southern origin. One complained that abolitionists were determined to make life in Washington "a hell on earth for the white man." In fact, emancipation seemed to make little difference. Most former slaves continued to work for their masters while waiting patiently for the public education that Congress had approved but neglected to vote money for.

As the Civil War went on (far longer than anyone had predicted at the start), Washington prospered as never before. Government contracts, political patronage, and the continued presence of the military made many people rich. Prices, especially for housing, rose substantially. But wages did not keep pace. There were strikes by construction workers, workers in the Printing Office, and drivers of street railways, among others. Although strikes were widely condemned, there was general sympathy for the plight of government workers, whose wages were not keeping up with inflation. After Lincoln's reelection in November of 1864, this prosperous, bustling city clearly symbolized the strength and confidence of the Republican party.

Then, in the spring of 1865, Washington suffered a double shock. The first was joyous: the news, on April 2, that the Confederate capital had yielded. Telegraph operators leaned from their windows, shouting "Richmond has fallen!" Crowds stormed newspaper offices to get copies of the extras. "Glory!!! Hail Columbia!!! Hallelujah!!!" headlined one Washington paper. Lee's surrender at Appomattox on April 9 was almost anticlimactic. The second shock came on April 14, when President Lincoln was assassinated at Ford's Theater. From the ecstasy of victory, Washington was plunged into mourning. After a week of observances in Washington, Lincoln's coffin was loaded on a funeral train that slowly carried him back to Springfield. All along the railroad route, day and night, in small towns and large, people gathered to see the train pass and to pay their last respects. At that moment, the Washington community and the larger Union community were one and the same.

One final event brought the Civil War to a close in Washington. For two days in May, the Union Army passed in grand review before the president, General Grant, and the largest crowd the city had ever seen. On May 23rd, the Army of the Potomac (Washington's own home army) paraded to the tune of war songs like "When This Cruel War Is Over" and "When Johnny Comes Marching Home." It took them all day to pass in review. On May 24th, General Sherman led the Army of the West as they paraded to a new tune, "Marching Through Georgia." Among them, riding sidesaddle, dressed in calico dress and sunbonnet, was the legendary "Mother" Bickerdyke, the tough, hardworking woman who had nursed Sherman's "boys" in the teeth of his initial objections. In all, 150,000 soldiers paraded during the

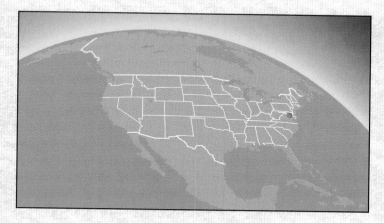

two days of the Grand Review. The Washington crowd met them with a mixture of cheers and tears, for no one could forget the nearly half million soldiers who had not survived. This moment of victory, then, contained a poignant reminder of the nation's loss and a powerful lesson that the unity gained by force of arms now had to be realized peacefully. War had preserved the Union, but the bonds that held the national community together needed to be reknit.

COMMUNITIES MOBILIZE FOR WAR

The country in March of 1861 presented to the observer an ominous series of similarities. Two nations — the United States of America (shorn of seven Deep South states) and the Confederate States of America — each blamed the other for the breakup of the Union. Two new presidents — Abraham Lincoln and Jefferson Davis — were each faced with the challenging task of building and maintaining national unity. Two regions — North and South — scorned each other and boasted of their own superiority. But the most basic similarity was not yet apparent: both sides and all participants were unprepared for the ordeal that lay ahead.

Fort Sumter: The War Begins

In their inaugural addresses, both Lincoln and Davis prayed for peace but positioned themselves for war. Careful listeners to both addresses realized that the two men were on a collision course. Jefferson Davis claimed that the Confederacy would be forced to "appeal to arms . . . if . . . the integrity of our territory and jurisdiction [is] assailed." Lincoln in his turn said, "The power confided to me will be used to hold, occupy, and possess the property and places belonging to the government." One of those places, Fort Sumter, South Carolina, was claimed by both sides.

Fort Sumter, a major federal military installation, sat on a granite island at the entrance to Charleston harbor. So long as it remained in Union hands, Charleston, the center of secessionist sentiment, would be immobilized. Realizing its military and its symbolic importance, South Carolinians had begun clamoring that the fort be turned over to them even before they seceded. Thus it was hardly surprising that Fort Sumter should be the first crisis facing President Lincoln.

Fort Sumter was dangerously low on supplies. Lincoln had to decide whether to withdraw or to risk the fight that was likely if he took action. Using a decision-making process he would follow on many other occasions, Lincoln first hesitated, canvassed opinions of all kinds, and then took cautious and careful action (even as some of his Cabinet urged more decisive steps). On April 6, Lincoln notified the governor of South Carolina that he was sending a relief force carrying only food and no military supplies to the fort. Now the decision rested with Jefferson Davis. Like Lincoln, Davis faced a divided Cabinet; unlike Lincoln, he opted for decisive action. On April 10 President Davis ordered General P. G. T. Beauregard to demand the surrender of Fort Sumter, and to use force if the garrison did not comply. On

April 12, as Lincoln's relief force neared Charleston harbor, Beauregard opened fire on Fort Sumter. Two days later, the defenders surrendered and the Confederate stars and bars rose over the fort. Residents of the Charleston community celebrated wildly. One of them, Mary Boykin Chesnut, wrote in her diary, "I did not know that one could live such days of excitement."

The Call to Arms

Even before Sumter, the Confederate Congress had authorized a volunteer army of 100,000 men to serve for twelve months. There was no difficulty finding volunteers. Men flocked to enlist, and their communities sent them off with bands playing "Dixie" and other martial music. Bonfires and belligerent oratory also accompanied the recruits. Most of the latter, like Jefferson Davis's inaugural address (see Chapter 15) evoked the Revolutionary War and the right of free people to resist tyranny. In many places, the response to the hostilities at Sumter was even more visceral. The first war circular printed in Hickman County, Tennessee, trumpeted, "To Arms! Our Southern soil must be defended. We must not stop to ask who brought about war, who is at fault, but let us go and do battle . . . and then settle the question of who is to blame." Exhilarated by their own rapid mobilization, most southerners believed that Unionists were cowards who would not be able to face up to southern bravery. "Just throw three or four shells among those blue-bellied Yankees," one North Carolinian boasted, "and they'll scatter like sheep." The cry of "On to Washington!" was raised throughout the South, and orators confidently predicted that the city would be captured and the war concluded within sixty days. For the early recruits, war was a patriotic adventure.

The "thunderclap of Sumter" startled the North into an angry response. The apathy and uncertainty that had prevailed since Lincoln's election disappeared, to be replaced by strong feelings of patriotism. On April 15, Lincoln issued a proclamation calling for 75,000 state militiamen to serve in the federal army for 90 days. Enlistment offices were swamped with so many enthusiastic volunteers that many men were sent home. Free African Americans, among the most eager to serve, were turned away: this was not yet a war for or by black people.

Public outpourings of patriotism were common. New Yorker George Templeton Strong recorded one example on April 18:

> Went to the [City] Hall. The [Sixth] Massachusetts Regiment, which arrived here last night, was marching down on its way to Washington. Im-

Community members gather for a formal send-off to men of the First Michigan Infantry, shown here drawn up to hear patriotic speeches by local officials before leaving for Washington, where they and other state regiments were mustered into the Union Army.

mense crowd; immense cheering. My eyes filled with tears, and I was half choked in sympathy with the contagious excitement. God be praised for the unity of feeling here! It is beyond, very far beyond, anything I hoped for.

The mobilization in Chester, Pennsylvania, was typical of the northern response to the outbreak of war. A patriotic rally was held at which a company of volunteers (the first of many from the region) calling themselves the "Union Blues" were mustered into the Ninth Regiment of Pennsylvania Volunteers, amid cheers and band music. As they marched off to Washington (the gathering place for the Union army, as we saw in the chapter introduction), companies of home guards were organized by the men who remained behind. Within a month, the women of the Chester community had organized a countywide system of war relief that sent a stream of clothing, blankets, bandages, and other supplies to the local troops, as well as providing assistance to their families at home. Relief organizations such as this, some formally organized, some informal, existed in every community, North and South, that sent soldiers off to the Civil War. These organizations not only played a vital role in supplying the troops, but they maintained the human, local link upon which so many soldiers depended. In this sense, every American community accompanied its young men to war. And every American community stood to suffer terrible losses when their young men went into battle together.

The Border States

The first secession, between December 20, 1860, and February 1, 1861, had taken seven Deep South states out of the Union. Now, in April, the firing on Fort Sumter and Lincoln's call for state militias forced the other southern states to take sides. Courted — and pressured — by both North and South, four states of the Upper South (Virginia, Arkansas, Tennessee, and North Carolina) joined the original seven in April and May of 1861. Virginia's secession, which was the first, tipped the other three toward the Confederacy. The capital of the Confederacy was now moved to Richmond. This meant that the two capitals — Richmond and Washington — were less than 100 miles apart.

Still undecided was the loyalty of the northern-most tier of slave-owning states: Missouri, Kentucky, Maryland, and Delaware. Each controlled vital strategic assets. Missouri not only bordered the Mississippi River, but controlled the routes to the west. Kentucky controlled the Ohio River. The main railroad link with the West ran through Maryland and the hill region of western Virginia (which split from Virginia to become the free state of West Virginia in 1863). Delaware controlled access to Philadelphia. Finally, the nation's capital, already facing a Confederate enemy nearby in Virginia to the southwest, was bordered on all other sides by Maryland.

Delaware was loyal to the Union (less than 2 percent of its population were slaves), but Maryland's loyalty was divided. The planters and tobacco growers of the southern and eastern parts of the state favored secession, while northwestern Maryland, mainly a region of small farms, was Unionist. Baltimore was divided, as an ugly incident on April 19 showed. The Sixth Massachusetts Regiment (the same one Strong had cheered in New York) met a hostile crowd as it marched through Baltimore. To this crowd, the soldiers represented not the Union but abolitionist feeling, which was stronger in Massachusetts than in any other state. A mob of nearly 10,000 proslavery supporters, flying Confederate flags, pelted the troops with bricks, paving stones, and bullets. Finally, in desperation the troops fired on the crowd, killing twelve of them and wounding others. In retaliation, southern sympathizers burned the railroad bridges to the North and destroyed the telegraph line to Washington, cutting off communication between the capital and the rest of the Union.

Lincoln took swift and stern measures, stationing Union troops along Maryland's crucial railroads, declaring martial law in Baltimore, and arresting the suspected ringleaders of the pro-Confederate mob and holding them without trial. In July Lincoln ordered the detention of thirty-two secessionist legislators and a number of sympathizers. Thus was Maryland's Union loyalty ensured.

Although Chief Justice Roger B. Taney ruled that the president had no right to suspend the writ of habeas corpus, as he had done in detaining the Baltimore agitators, Lincoln at first ignored him. Later Lincoln argued that the suspension of certain civil rights might be necessary to suppress rebellion. This was the first of a number of violations of basic civil rights that occurred during the war, all of which the president justified on the basis of national security.

An even bloodier division occurred in Missouri, where two old foes from "Bleeding Kansas" faced off — abolitionist Nathaniel Lyon, commander of the federal troops at the U.S. arsenal in St. Louis, and Claiborne Fox Jackson, the proslavery governor. Although a special state convention had voted against secession in March, the governor did not accept the result. Warfare broke out between the two factions. The governor and most of the legislature fled to Arkansas, where they declared a Confederate state government in exile. Unionists remained in St. Louis and declared a provisional government that lasted until 1865. Although Missouri had been saved for the Union, the federal military was unable to stop the guerrilla warfare (so reminiscent of Kansas) that raged there. The hostilities were dominated on one side by notorious "bushwhackers" like William Quantrill and on the other side by pro-Union "jayhawkers" from Kansas such as James H. Lane, a former U.S. senator.

Finally, Lincoln kept Kentucky in the Union by accepting its declaration of neutrality at face value — and looking the other way as it became the center of a huge illegal trade with the Confederacy through neighboring Tennessee. By the summer of 1861, Unionists controlled most of the state. A breakaway group led by Governor Beriah Magoffin set up a provisional Confederate government in the southwest corner of the state, but officially Kentucky stayed in the Union.

The conflicting loyalties of the border states were often mirrored within families. Kentucky senator John J. Crittenden had two sons who were major generals, one in the Union army and the other in the Confederate army. "I do not know of a single family," one Kentuckian said, "where all the men were arrayed on one side." The conflicts reached all the way to the White House: Kentucky-born Mary

Todd Lincoln, the president's wife, lost three brothers who fought for the Confederacy.

That these four border states chose to stay in the Union was a severe blow to the Confederacy. Among them, the four states could have added 45 percent to the white population and military manpower of the Confederacy and 80 percent to its manufacturing capacity. Almost as damaging, the decision of four slave states to stay in the Union punched a huge hole in the Confederate argument that the Southern states were forced to secede to protect the right to own slaves.

The Battle of Bull Run

Once sides had been chosen and the initial flush of enthusiasm had passed, the nature of the war, and the mistaken notions about it, soon became clear. The event that shattered the illusions was the first Battle of Bull Run, at Manassas Creek in Virginia in July of 1861. Confident of a quick victory, a Union army of 35,000 men marched south crying "On to Richmond!" So lighthearted and unprepared was the Washington community that the troops were accompanied not only by journalists but by a crowd of politicians and sightseers. At first the Union troops held their ground against the 25,000 Confederate troops commanded by General P. G. T. Beauregard (of Fort Sumter fame). But when 2,300 fresh Confederate troops arrived as reinforcement, the untrained northern troops broke ranks in an uncontrolled retreat that swept up the frightened sightseers as well. Soldiers and civilians alike ran all the way to Washington. Mary Boykin Chesnut recorded in her diary, "A friend in the federal capital writes me that we might have walked into Washington any day for a week after Manassas, such was the consternation and confusion there." But the Confederates lacked the organization and the strength to follow them and capture the capital as well.

Bull Run was sobering—and prophetic. The Civil War was the most lethal military conflict in American history. More than 600,000 died, more than the nation's combined casualties in the First and Second World Wars. One out of every four soldiers did not return home. Devastation on the battlefield and desolation at home—these were two of the major legacies of the Civil War.

Relative Strengths of North and South

Overall, in both population and productive capacity, the Union seemed to have a commanding edge. The North had two and a half times the South's population (22 million to 9 million, 4 million of the latter being slaves) and enjoyed an even greater advantage in industrial capacity (nine times that of the South). The North produced almost all of the nation's firearms (97 percent), had 70 percent of its railroad mileage, and produced 94 percent of its cloth and 90 percent of its footwear. The North seemed able to feed, clothe, arm, and transport all the soldiers it chose. And by the end of the war in 1865, these advantages had proved decisive: the Union had managed to field over 2 million soldiers to the Confederacy's 800,000. But in the short term, the South had some important assets.

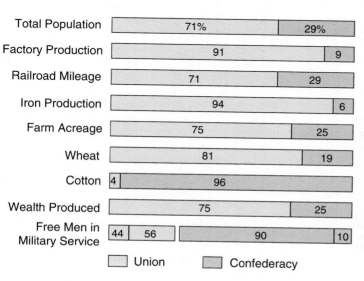

	Union	Confederacy
Total Population	71%	29%
Factory Production	91	9
Railroad Mileage	71	29
Iron Production	94	6
Farm Acreage	75	25
Wheat	81	19
Cotton	4	96
Wealth Produced	75	25
Free Men in Military Service	44 / 56	90 / 10

Comparative Resources, North and South, 1861

By 1865, the North's overwhelming advantage in population, industrial strength, railroad mileage, agriculture and wealth was decisive in the final victory. But initially these strengths made little difference in a struggle that began as a traditional war of maneuver in which the South held the defensive advantage. Only slowly did the Civil War become a modern war in which all of the resources of society, including the lives of civilians, were mobilized for battle.

Source: *The Times Atlas of World History* (New Jersey: Hammond, 1978).

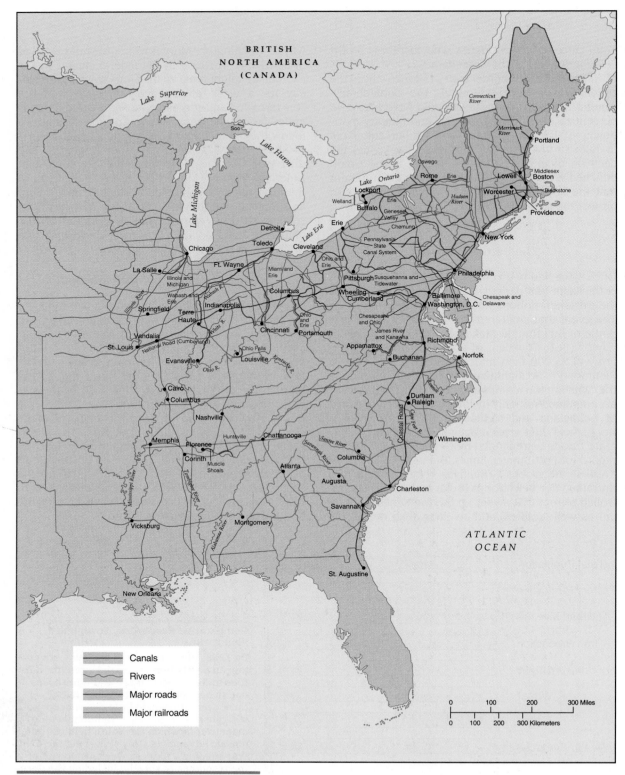

Comparative Transportation Systems, 1860

Transportation systems were an important index of comparative strength: the North had almost three times the railroad mileage of the South. The relative lack of transportation hurt the Confederacy by hindering its ability to move troops and to provide military and medical supplies.

The first was the nature of the struggle. For the South, this was a defensive war, in which, as the early volunteers showed, the most basic principle of the defense of home and community united almost all white southerners, regardless of their views toward slavery. The North would have to invade the South and control guerrilla warfare to win. The parallels with the Revolutionary War were unmistakable. Most white southerners were confident that the North would turn out to be a lumbering giant and that independence would be achieved.

Second, the military disparity was less than it appeared. Although the North had manpower, the troops were mostly untrained. The professional federal army numbered only 16,000, and most of its experience had been gained in small Indian wars. Moreover the South, because of its tradition of honor and belligerence (see Chapter 11), appeared to have an advantage in military leadership. More than a quarter of all the regular army officers chose to side with the South. The most notable was Robert E. Lee. Offered command of the Union army by President Lincoln, Lee hesitated but finally decided to follow his native state, Virginia, into secession, saying, "I cannot raise my hand against my birthplace, my home, my children."

Finally, the economic discrepancy, which was eventually to be decisive, initially seemed unimportant. The South could feed itself, and many soldiers brought their own weapons, uniforms, horses, and sometimes slaves when they enlisted. It was widely believed that the slave system would work to the South's advantage, for slaves could continue to do the vital plantation work while their masters went off to war. But above all, the South had the weapon of cotton. "Cotton is king," James Hammond had announced in 1858, at the height of the cotton boom that made the 1850s the most profitable decade in southern history. Because of the crucial role of southern cotton in industrialization, Hammond had declared, "the slaveholding South is now the controlling power of the world." Southerners were confident that the British and French need for southern cotton would soon bring those states to recognize the Confederacy as a separate nation.

THE LINCOLN PRESIDENCY

The Civil War forced the federal government to assume powers unimaginable just a few years before. Abraham Lincoln took as his primary task his responsibility as commander in chief to lead and unify the nation. He found the challenge almost insurmountable. Fortunately, the nation had found in Lincoln a man with the moral courage and the political skill to chart a course through the many conflicting currents of northern public opinion.

The Cabinet Struggle

Lincoln's first task as president was to assert control over his own Cabinet. Because he had few national contacts outside the Republican party, Lincoln chose to staff his Cabinet with other Republicans, including several who had been his rivals for the presidential nomination. Treasury Secretary Salmon P. Chase, a staunch abolitionist, adamantly opposed concessions to the South and considered Lincoln too conciliatory. Secretary of State William Seward, widely regarded as the leader of the Republican party, at first intended to "manage" Lincoln as he had Zachary Taylor in 1848. But he soon became a willing partner. Chase, a key member of a group known as the Radical Republicans, remained a vocal and dangerous critic. That the Republican Party was a not quite jelled mix of former Whigs, abolitionists, moderate free-soilers, and even some prowar Democrats made Lincoln's task as party leader much more difficult.

Military Necessity: Lincoln as a War President

Following the fall of Fort Sumter, Lincoln took a number of executive actions that were driven by military necessity: calling up the state militias, ordering a naval blockade of the South, and vastly expanding the military budget. He broke with precedent by acting without congressional sanction. But Congress was not in session and Lincoln did not wait. Likewise, other early actions, such as the suspension of habeas corpus for the Maryland pro-slavery agitators and the president's willingness to accept Kentucky's ambiguous neutrality, were driven by the military need to hold the border states. This necessity also led Lincoln to repudiate an unauthorized declaration issued by General John C. Frémont, military commander in Missouri, in August 1861 that would have freed Missouri's slaves. Lincoln's action brought a howl of protest from abolitionists, but it was solidly grounded: the president believed that emancipation in Missouri might cause the defection of divided Kentucky and Maryland, both of which the Union desperately needed.

Although James K. Polk's direction of the Mexican-American War created somewhat of a precedent (see Chapter 14), Lincoln was the first president to act as commander in chief in both a practical and a symbolic way. Lincoln actively directed military

Although as a young Congressman Abraham Lincoln had objected to James K. Polk's active participation in Mexican-American War strategy, he found himself taking a major role as Commander in Chief during the Civil War. His relationship with General George McClellan was especially difficult, for he could never convince the general to overcome his habitual caution.

policy, although he sometimes wondered whether he would ever find generals capable of carrying out his orders. Lincoln's involvement in military strategy sprang from his realization that a civil war presented different problems than a foreign war of conquest. Lincoln wanted above all to *persuade* the South to rejoin the Union, and his every military move was dictated by the hope of eventual reconciliation. Thus his cautiousness, and his acute sense of the role of public opinion. Today we recognize Lincoln's exceptional abilities and eloquent language, but in his own time some of his most moving statements of his war aims fell on deaf ears.

The War Department

The greatest expansion in government power came in the War Department, which by early 1862 was faced with the task of feeding, clothing, and arming 700,000 Union soldiers. This was an organizational challenge of unprecedented size. At first the War Department was unequal to the task, and individual states agreed to equip and supply their vastly expanded militias until the Union army could absorb the costs. States often contracted directly with textile mills and shoe factories to clothe their troops. In many northern cities volunteer groups sprang up to recruit regiments, buy them weapons, and send them to Washington. Other such groups, like the one in Chester, Pennsylvania, focused on clothing and providing medical care to soldiers. After January 1862 the War Department, under the able direction of Edwin M. Stanton, a former Democrat from Ohio, was able to perform many basic functions of procurement and supply without too much delay or corruption. But the size of the Union army and the

complexity of fully supplying it demanded constant efforts at all levels — government, state, and community — throughout the war. Thus, in the matter of procurement and supply, as in mobilization, the battlefront was related to the home front on a scale that Americans had not previously experienced.

The Greenback Dollar

Although Lincoln was an active commander in chief, he did not believe it was the job of the president to direct economic policy. This, he believed, was the task of Congress. In this important respect, the Civil War was fundamentally different from American wars of the twentieth century, where executive control over economic policy was deemed essential. Yet the need for money for the vast war effort was pressing. Secretary of the Treasury Chase worked closely with Congress to develop ways to finance the war. They naturally turned to the nation's economic experts — private bankers, merchants, and managers of large businesses. With the help of Philadelphia financier Jay Cooke, the Treasury used patriotic appeals to sell war bonds to ordinary people in amounts as small as $50. By this means, Cooke sold $400 million in bonds, taking for himself what he considered a "fair commission." This was the first example in American history of the mass financing of war. By war's end, the United States had borrowed $2.6 billion for the war effort. Additional sources of revenue were sales taxes and the first federal income tax (of 3 percent), initiated in August of 1861. The income tax affected only the affluent: anyone with an annual income under $800 was exempt.

Most radical of all, after a bitter congressional

fight Chase received authorization to print Treasury notes (paper money) and have them accepted nationally. Until then, the money in circulation had been a mixture of coins and state banknotes issued by 1,500 different state banks. The Legal Tender Act of February 1862 created a national currency, which, because of the color, was popularly known as the greenback. In 1863 Congress passed the National Bank Act, which prohibited state banks from issuing their own notes and forced them to apply for federal charters. Thus was the first uniform national currency created, at the expense of the independence that many state banks had prized. "These are extraordinary times, and extraordinary measures must be resorted to in order to save our Government and preserve our nationality," pleaded Congressman Elbridge G. Spaulding, sponsor of the legislation. Only through this appeal to wartime necessity were Spaulding and his allies able to overcome the opposition, for the national currency was widely recognized as a major centralization of economic power in the hands of the federal government. Such a measure would have been unthinkable if southern Democrats, the heirs to Jackson's animosity to national banks, had still been part of the national government. The absence of southern Democrats also made possible passage of a number of Republican economic measures not directly related to the war.

The Comprehensive Republican Platform

Although the debate over slavery had overshadowed everything else, the Republican party had campaigned in 1860 on a comprehensive program of economic development. Once in office, Republicans quickly passed the Morrill Tariff Act (1861), and by 1864 subsequent measures had raised tariffs to more than double their prewar rate. In 1862 and 1864, Congress created two federally chartered corporations, the Union Pacific Railroad Company, to build westward from Omaha, and the Central Pacific, to build eastward from California. These plans to create a transcontinental railroad fulfilled the dreams of the many expansionists (among them Stephen A. Douglas, who died before this legislation was enacted) who believed that America's economic future lay in trade with Asia across the Pacific Ocean. Two other measures, both passed in 1862, had long been sought by westerners. The Homestead Act gave 160 acres of public land to any citizen who agreed to live on it for five years, improve it by building a house and cultivating some of the land, and pay a small fee. The Morrill Land Grant Act gave states public land that would allow them to finance land-grant colleges offering education to ordinary citizens in practical skills such as agriculture, engineering, and military science. Coupled with this act, the establishment of a federal Department of Agriculture in 1862 gave American farmers a big push toward modern commercial agriculture.

This package revealed the Whig origins of many Republicans, for the measures were in essence Henry Clay's American System of national economic development brought up to date (see Chapter 9). These were all powerful nationalizing forces, connecting ordinary people to the federal government in new ways. As much as the extraordinary war measures, the enactment of the Republican program served to increase the role of the federal government in national life. Although many of the executive war powers lapsed when the battles ended, the accrual of strength to the federal government was never reversed.

Diplomatic Objectives

To Secretary of State William Seward fell the job of making sure that Britain and France did not extend diplomatic recognition to the Confederacy. Although the South had been certain that King Cotton would gain them European support, they were wrong. British public opinion, which had strongly supported the abolition of slavery within the British Empire in the 1830s, would not now countenance the recognition of a nation based on slavery. British cotton manufacturers found economic alternatives, first using up their backlog of southern cotton and then turning to two British colonies, Egypt and India, for their supply. In spite of Union protests, however, both Britain and France did allow Confederate vessels to use their ports, and British shipyards sold six ships to the Confederacy. But in 1863, when the Confederacy commissioned Britain's Laird shipyard to build two ironclad ships with pointed prows for ramming, the Union threatened war and the British government made sure the Laird rams were never delivered. Seward had wanted to threaten Britain with war earlier, in 1861, when the prospect of diplomatic recognition for the Confederacy seemed most likely. But Lincoln had overruled him, cautioning, "One war at a time."

This was also the reluctant Union response in 1863 when France took advantage of the Civil War to invade Mexico and install the Austrian archduke Maximilian as emperor. This was a serious violation of the Monroe Doctrine, but for fear that France might recognize the Confederacy or invade Texas, Seward had to content himself with refusing to recognize the new Mexican government. In the meantime he directed Union troops to gain a strong-hold in Texas as soon as possible. In November, eight months after Maximilian's accession, Union troops seized Brownsville, on the Texas-Mexico border, sending a clear signal to the French to go no further. In 1866, after the Civil War was won, strong diplomatic pressure from Seward convinced the French to withdraw from Mexico. The following year, the hapless Maximilian was captured and shot during a revolt led by a future Mexican president, Benito Juarez.

Although the goal of Seward's diplomacy—preventing recognition of the Confederacy by the European powers—was always clear, its achievement was uncertain for more than two years. Northern fears and southern hopes seesawed with the fortunes of battle. Not until the victories at Vicksburg and Gettysburg in July of 1863 could Seward be reasonably confident of success.

THE CONFEDERACY

Lincoln faced a major challenge in keeping the North unified enough to win the war, but Jefferson Davis's challenge was even greater. He had to *create* a Confederate nation. The Confederate States of America was a loose grouping of eleven states that each believed strongly in states' rights. Yet the necessities of war, as we have seen in the case of the Union, required central direction.

Jefferson Davis as President

Although Jefferson Davis had held national Cabinet rank, enjoyed experience as an administrator, and was a former military man (none of which Abraham Lincoln was), he was unable to hold the Confederacy together. Perhaps no one could have. Born in Kentucky (Lincoln's birth state), Davis and his family moved south to Mississippi, where they became rich planters. Davis was thus a "cotton nabob" (one of the newly rich class of slave owners), and as such was as scorned by some members of the old southern aristocracy as was Abraham Lincoln by some members of the North's elite. Davis's problems, however, were as much structural as they were personal.

Davis's first Cabinet of six men, appointed in February of 1861, included a representative from each of the states of the first secession except Mississippi, which was represented by Davis himself This careful attention to the equality of the states pointed to the fundamental Confederate problem that Davis was unable to overcome. For all of its drama, secession was a *conservative* strategy for preserving the slavery-based social and political structure that existed in every southern state. Davis, who would have preferred to be a Confederate general rather than president, lacked Lincoln's persuasive skills and political astuteness. Although he saw the need for unity, he was unable to impose it. Soon his autonomous style of leadership—he

Jefferson Davis, a military hero from the Mexican American War, would rather have been a Confederate general than its president. Verena Davis, whose independent manner was greeted with scorn by the ladies of the old southern aristocracy, also appears to wish she were elsewhere.

wanted to decide every detail himself—angered his generals, alienated Cabinet members, and gave southern governors reason to resist his orders. By the second year of the war, when rich slave owners were refusing to give up their privileges for the war effort, Davis no longer had the public confidence and support he needed to coerce them. After the first flush of patriotism had passed, the Confederacy never lived up to its hope of becoming a unified nation.

Diplomatic Hopes

The failure of "cotton diplomacy" was a crushing blow. White southerners were stunned that Britain and France would not recognize their claim to independence. Well into 1863, the South hoped that a decisive battlefield victory would change the minds of cautious Europeans. In the meantime, plantations continued to grow cotton, but not to ship it, hoping that lack of raw material for their textile mills would lead the British and French to recognize the Confederacy. The British reacted indignantly, claiming that to give in to economic blackmail "would be ignominious beyond measure," as Lord Russell put it in 1861. British textile manufacturers found new sources of cotton in India and Egypt. Thus in 1862, when the Confederacy ended the embargo and began to ship its great cotton surplus, the result was to depress the world price of cotton. Then too, the Union naval blockade, weak at first, began to take effect. Cotton turned out to be not so powerful a diplomatic weapon after all.

Financing the Confederacy

Perhaps the greatest southern failure was in the area of finances. The Confederate government at first tried to raise money from the states, but governors refused to impose new taxes on their residents. By the time uniform taxes were levied (1863), it was too late. In the meantime, large amounts of borrowing and the issuance of even greater supplies of paper money had produced runaway inflation (a rate of 9,000 percent, compared with 80 percent in the North). This in turn caused incalculable damage to morale and prospects for unity.

Manpower

After the initial surge of volunteers, enlistment in the military fell off (as it did in the North). In April of 1862, the Confederate Congress passed the first draft law in American history (the Union Congress approved a draft in March of 1863). The southern law

SUBSTITUTE NOTICES.

WANTED—A SUBSTITUTE for a conscript, to serve during the war. Any good man over the age of 35 years, not a resident of Virginia, or a foreigner, may hear of a good situation by calling at Mr. GEORGE BAGBY'S office, Shockoe Slip, to-day, between the hours of 9 and 11 A. M.   [jy 9—1t*]   A COUNTRYMAN.

WANTED—Two SUBSTITUTES—one for artillery, the other for infantry or cavalry service. Also, to sell, a trained, thoroughbred cavalry HORSE.   Apply to   DR. BROOCKS, Corner Main and 12th streets, or to
                    T. T. BROOCKS,
jy 9—3t*   Petersburg, Va.

WANTED—Immediately, a SUBSTITUTE. A man over 35 years old, or under 18, can get a good price by making immediate application to Room No. 50, Monument Hotel, or by addressing "J. W.," through Richmond P. O.   jy 9—1t*

WANTED—A SUBSTITUTE, to go into the 24th North Carolina State troops, for which a liberal price will be paid. Apply to me at Dispatch office this evening at 4 o'clock P. M.
jy 9—1t*   R. R. MOORE.

WANTED—A SUBSTITUTE, to go in a first-rate Georgia company of infantry, under the heroic Jackson. A gentleman whose health is impaired, will give a fair price for a substitute. Apply immediately at ROOM, No. 13, Post-Office Department, third story, between the hours of 10 and 3 o'clock.   jy 9—6t*

WANTED—Two SUBSTITUTES for the war. A good bonus will be given. None need apply except those exempt from Conscript. Apply to-day at   GEORGE I. HERRING'S,
jy 9—1t*   Grocery store, No. 56 Main st.

The contrast between the hope and valor of these young southern volunteer soldiers, photographed shortly before the first Battle of Bull Run, and the later advertisements for substitutes is marked. Southern exemptions for slaveowners and lavish payment for substitutes increasingly bred resentment among the ordinary people of the South.

declared that all able-bodied men between eighteen and thirty-five were eligible for three years of military service. Purchase of substitutes was allowed, as in the North, but in the South the price was uncontrolled, rising eventually to $10,000 in Confederate money. The most disliked part of the draft law was a provision exempting one white man on each plantation that had twenty or more slaves. This not only seemed to disprove the earlier claim that slavery freed up more white men to fight, but it aroused class resentments. In the bitter phrase of the time, "It's a rich man's war but a poor man's fight."

Contradictions of Southern Nationalism

In the early days of the war, Jefferson Davis successfully mobilized feelings of regional identity and patriotism. Many southerners felt part of a beleaguered region that had been forced to resist northern tyranny. But most people felt loyalty to their own state, not to a Confederate *nation*. Jefferson Davis's challenge was to create that feeling of national community, but as we have seen, he could not do it. Although he himself had no qualms about using the powers of the Confederate government to win the war, Davis could not overcome his region's strong beliefs in states' rights and aristocratic privilege. It was such beliefs that undermined the Confederate cause. The very steps necessary for unity, such as moving militias outside their home states, were resisted by some southern governors. Broader measures, such as general taxation, were widely evaded by rich and poor alike. The inequitable draft was only one of a number of steps that convinced the ordinary people of the South that this was a war for privileged slave owners, not for them. The South could not unify because too many people feared (perhaps correctly) that centralization would destroy what was distinctively southern. As a result, the Confederacy was unable to mobilize the resources — financial, human, and otherwise — that might have prevented its destruction by northern armies.

THE FIGHTING THROUGH 1862

Just as political decisions were often driven by military necessity, the basic northern and southern military strategies were affected by political considerations as much as by military ones. The initial policy of limited war, thought to be the best route to ultimate reconciliation, faced public impatience for victories. But victories, as the mounting slaughter made clear, were not easy to achieve.

The Northern Strategy

The initial northern strategy, dubbed by critics the Anaconda Plan (after the constricting snake), envisaged slowly squeezing the South with a blockade at sea and on the Mississippi River. Proposed by Commanding General Winfield Scott, a native of Virginia, it avoided invasion and conquest, in the hope that a straitened South would recognize the inevitability of defeat and surrender. Lincoln accepted the basics of the plan, but public clamor for a fight pushed him to agree to the disastrous Battle of Bull Run and then to a major buildup of Union troops in northern Virginia under General George B. McClellan. Dashing in appearance, McClellan was extremely cautious in battle. In March of 1862, after almost a year of drilling the raw Union recruits, and after repeated exhortations by an impatient Lincoln, McClellan committed 120,000 troops to what became known as the Peninsula campaign. The objective was to capture Richmond, the Confederate capital. All of these troops and their supplies and support were ferried from Washington to Fortress Monroe, near the mouth of the James River, in 400 ships, an effort that took three weeks. Inching up the James Peninsula toward Richmond, McClellan tried to limit Confederate casualties, hoping his overwhelming numbers would convince the South to surrender and thus avoid a brutal war of destruction and conquest. He was also extremely reluctant to commit his own troops to battle. By June, McClellan's troops were close enough to Richmond to hear the church bells ringing — but not close enough for victory. In a series of battles known as the Seven Days, Robert E. Lee boldly counterattacked, repeatedly catching McClellan by surprise. Taking heavy losses as well as inflicting them, Lee drove McClellan back. In August, a disappointed Lincoln ordered McClellan to abandon the campaign and return to Washington.

The Southern Strategy

Jefferson Davis, like Abraham Lincoln, was an active commander in chief. And like Lincoln, he responded to a public that clamored for more action than a strictly defensive war entailed. Following the Seven Days victories, Davis ordered a Confederate attack on Maryland. At the same time, he issued a proclamation urging the people of Maryland to make a separate peace. But the all-out attack failed: in September McClellan turned back Lee at Antietam, at the cost of more than 5,000 dead and 19,000 wounded. Lee retreated to Virginia, where he held

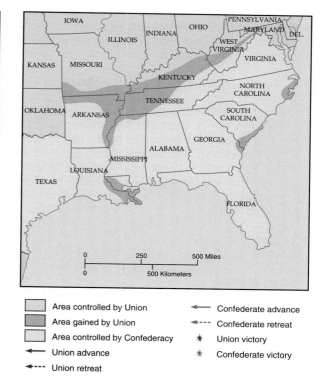

Area controlled by Union
Area gained by Union
Area controlled by Confederacy
Union advance
Union retreat
Confederate advance
Confederate retreat
Union victory
Confederate victory

Major Battles, 1861–62

Northern Virginia was the most crucial and the most constant theater of battle. The prizes were the two opposing capitals, Washington and Richmond, only 70 miles apart. By the summer of 1862, George C. Mc-Clellan, famously cautious, had achieved only stalemate in the Peninsula campaign. He did, however, turn back Lee at Antietam in September. Further west, Ulysses S. Grant waged a more mobile war by winning at Fort Donalson in Tennessee in February 1862 and at Shiloh in April, capturing Memphis in June and moving on to beseige Vickburg. Along the Mississippi, the Union's "Anaconda" strategy of slow strangulation was working, and the capture of the Sea Islands presaged the success of the naval blockade.

off a northern attack at Fredericksburg in December. The war in northern Virginia was stalemated: neither side was strong enough to win, but each was too strong to be defeated.

Shiloh and the War for the Mississippi

Although most public attention was focused on the fighting in Virginia, battles in Tennessee and along the Mississippi River proved to be the key to eventual Union victory. The rising military figure in the West was Ulysses S. Grant, who had once resigned from the service because of a drinking problem. Reenlisting as a colonel after Fort Sumter, Grant was promoted to brigadier general within two months. In February of 1862 Grant captured Fort Henry and Fort Donelson, on the Tennessee and Cumberland Rivers, gaining Union control of much of Tennessee and forcing Confederate troops to retreat into northern Mississippi.

Moving south with 63,000 men, Grant met a 40,000-man Confederate force commanded by General Albert Sidney Johnston at Shiloh Church in April. After two days of bitter and bloody fighting in the rain, the Confederates withdrew. The losses on both sides were enormous: the North lost 13,000 men, the South 11,000, including General Johnston, who bled to death. McClellan's peninsular campaign was already under way when Grant won at Shiloh, and Jefferson Davis, concerned about the defense of Richmond, refused to reinforce the generals who were trying to stop Grant. Consequently, Grant kept moving, capturing Memphis in June and beginning a siege of Vicksburg, Mississippi, in November. Earlier that year, naval forces under Admiral David Farragut had captured New Orleans in April and then continued up the Mississippi River. By the end of 1862 it was clear that only a matter of time was left before the entire river would be in Union hands. Arkansas, Louisiana, Texas, and much of Tennessee would then be cut off from the rest of the Confederacy.

The War in the West

Far removed from the major theaters of battle, the Far West was nevertheless a rich prize in the Civil War. Battles in remote places like Glorieta Pass, New Mexico, were decisive in holding the Far West for the Union. The battles in Kansas and Indian Territory, however, arose primarily from prewar antagonisms and settled little.

Source: Warren Beck and Ynez Haase, *Historical Atlas of the American West* (Norman: University of Oklahoma Press, 1989).

The War in the West

Although only one western state, Texas, seceded from the Union, the Civil War was fought in small ways in many parts of the West. Southern dreams of the extension of slavery into the Southwest were reignited by the war. Texans mounted an attack on New Mexico, which they had long coveted (see Chapter 14), and kept their eyes on the larger prizes of Arizona Territory and California beyond. A Confederate force led by General Henry H. Sibley occupied Santa Fe and Albuquerque early in 1862 without resistance, thus posing a serious Confederate threat to the entire Southwest. Confederate hopes were dashed, however, by a ragtag group of 950 miners and adventurers organized into the first Colorado Volunteer Infantry Regiment. After an epic march of 400 miles from Denver to Fort Union in thirteen days through snow and high winds, the Colorado militia stopped the unsuspecting Confederate troops in the Battle of Glorieta Pass, March 26–28, 1862. This dashing action, coupled with the efforts of California militias to safeguard Arizona and Utah from seizure by Confederate sympathizers, secured the Far West for the Union.

Other military action in the West was less

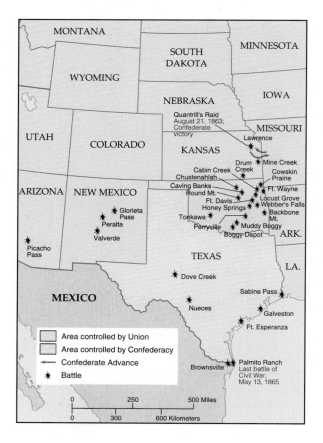

decisive. The chronic fighting along the Kansas-Missouri border set a record for brutality when Quantrill's Raiders made a pre-dawn attack on Lawrence, Kansas, in August of 1863, massacring 150 inhabitants and burning the town. Another civil war took place in Indian Territory, south of Kansas. The southern Indian tribes, who had been removed there from the Old Southwest in the 1820s and 1830s (see Chapters 10 and 11), held a number of Confederate sympathizers. Among them were wealthy slave owners and many who remembered the horrors of removal by federal troops with great bitterness. Others, however, had equally bitter memories of the role of the southern states in forcing the removals. Union victories at Pea Ridge (in northwestern Arkansas) in March of 1862 and near Fort Gibson (in Indian Territory) in 1863 secured the area for the Union but did little to stop the dissension among the Indian groups themselves. This internal conflict was costly, for after the Civil War the victorious federal government used the excuse of Confederate sympathies to insist on further land cessions from the tribes.

The hostilities in the West showed that no part of the country and none of its inhabitants could remain untouched by the Civil War.

The Naval War

Initially, the Union blockade of southern ships was unsuccessful. The U.S. Navy had only thirty-three ships, with which it tried to blockade 189 ports along 3,500 miles of coastline. Southern blockade runners evaded Union ships with ease: only an estimated one-eighth of all Confederate shipping was stopped in 1862. Moreover, the Confederacy licensed British-made privateers to strike at northern shipping. In a two-year period one such Confederate raider, the *Alabama,* destroyed sixty-nine Union ships with cargoes valued at $6 million. Beginning in 1863, however, as the Union navy increased in size, the naval blockade began to take effect. In 1864 a third of the blockade runners were captured, and in 1865 half of them. As a result, fewer and fewer supplies reached the South.

North and South also engaged in a brief technological duel featuring the revolutionary new ironclad ships. In March of 1862, as McClellan began his peninsular campaign, the southern ironclad *Merrimac*—a wooden ship clad in metal plates—steamed out of Norfolk harbor right into the Union blockade. The squadron of Union ships could not harm the *Merrimac* and were defenseless against her ram and powerful guns. More than the entire navy was endangered. "Who," asked Gustavus Fox, assistant secretary of the U.S. Navy, "is to prevent her

dropping her anchor in the Potomac . . . and throwing her hundred-pound shells into [the White House] or battering down the halls of the Capitol?" The answer, fortunately for the North, was an experimental ironclad of its own, the *Monitor,* which was waiting for the *Merrimac* when it next emerged from port. The *Monitor,* which looked like "an immense shingle floating on the water, with a gigantic cheese box rising from its center," was the ship of the future, for the "cheese box" was a revolving turret, a basic component of battleships to come. The historic duel between these first two ironclads, fought on March 9, 1862, was inconclusive, and primitive technology together with limited resources made ironclads of little consequence in the naval war. But this brief duel, as much as the massing of huge armies on the battlefield, prefigured the naval and land battles of World Wars One and Two.

For the Union, the most successful naval operation in the first two years of the war was not the blockade but the seizing of exposed coastal areas. The Sea Islands of South Carolina were taken, as were some of the North Carolina islands and Fort Pulaski, which commanded the harbor of Savannah, Georgia. Most damaging to the South was the capture of New Orleans.

The Black Response

The capture of Port Royal in the South Carolina Sea Islands in 1861 was important for another reason. Whites fled at the Union advance, but 10,000 slaves greeted the troops with jubilation and shouts of gratitude. Union troops had unwittingly freed these slaves, in advance of any official Union policy.

Early in the war, an irate southerner who saw three of his slaves disappear behind Union lines at Fortress Monroe, Virginia, demanded the return of his property, citing the Fugitive Slave Law. The Union commander, Benjamin Butler, replied that the Fugitive Slave Law no longer applied, and that the escaped slaves were "contraband of war." News of Butler's decision spread rapidly among the slaves in the region of Fortress Monroe. Two days later, eight runaway slaves appeared; the next day fifty-nine black men and women arrived at the fort. Union commanders had found an effective way to rob the South of its basic work force. The contrabands, as they were known, were put to work building fortifications and doing other useful work in northern camps.

As Union troops drove deeper into the South, the black response grew. The most dramatic single example happened in 1864 during Sherman's march through Georgia, where 18,000 slaves—entire families, people of all ages—flocked to the Union lines.

By war's end, nearly a million black people, fully a quarter of all the slaves in the South, had "voted with their feet" for the Union.

THE DEATH OF SLAVERY

The overwhelming response of black slaves to Union troops changed the nature of the war. As increasing numbers of slaves flocked to Union lines, the conclusion was unmistakable: the southern war to defend the slave system did not have the support of slaves themselves. Any northern policy that ignored the issue of slavery and the wishes of the slaves was unrealistic.

The Emancipation Proclamation

Abraham Lincoln had always said that this was a war for the Union, not a war about slavery. In his inaugural address, he had promised to leave slavery untouched in the South. Although Lincoln personally abhorred slavery, his official policy was based on a realistic assessment of several factors. At first, he hoped to give pro-Union forces in the South a chance to consolidate and to prevent the outbreak of war. After the war began, as we have seen, Lincoln was impelled by the military necessity of holding the border states (Delaware, Maryland, Kentucky, and Missouri), where slavery was legal.

Finally, Lincoln was worried about unity in the North. Even within the Republican party, only a small group of abolitionists had favored freeing the slaves before the war. Most Republicans were more concerned about the expansion of slavery than they were about the lives of slaves themselves. They did not favor the social equality of black people, whom they believed inferior. The free-soil movement, for example, was as often antiblack as it was antislave (see Chapter 14). For their part, most northern Democrats were openly antiblack. As we saw in Chapter 13, Irish workers in northern cities had rioted against free African Americans, with whom they often competed for jobs. There was also the question of what would become of slaves who were freed. Even the most fervent abolitionists had refused to face up to this issue. Finally, Northern Democrats effectively played on racial fears in the 1862 congressional elections, warning that freed slaves would pour into northern cities and take laborers' jobs.

Nevertheless, the necessities of war edged Lincoln toward a new position. In March 1862 he proposed that every state undertake gradual, compensated emancipation, after which former slaves would be resettled in Haiti and Panama (neither of which was under U.S. control). The unrealistic colonization scheme, as well as the reluctance of border state politicians to consider emancipation, doomed the proposal.

Radical Republicans chafed at Lincoln's conservative stance. In August of 1862, in an open letter to the president, Horace Greeley, editor of the *New York Tribune,* pressed the point: "On the face of this wide earth, Mr. President, there is not one disinterested, determined, intelligent champion of the Union cause who does not feel that all attempts to put down the Rebellion and at the same time uphold its inciting cause are preposterous and futile." Greeley's statement was incorrect for, as we have seen, many northerners did not care what happened to the slaves, but did care what happened to the Union. Lincoln's famous answer implicitly acknowledged the many shades of public opinion and cast his decision in terms of military necessity:

> If I could save the Union without freeing any slave, I would do it; and if I could save it by freeing all the slaves, I would do it; and if I could do it by freeing some and leaving others alone, I would also do that. What I do about Slavery and the colored race, I do because I believe it helps to save this Union.

In fact, Lincoln had already made up his mind to issue an Emancipation Proclamation, and was simply waiting for the right moment. Following the Union victory at Antietam in September of 1862, Lincoln issued a preliminary decree: unless the rebellious states returned to the Union by January 1, 1863, he would declare their slaves "forever free." Although Lincoln did not expect the Confederate states to surrender because of his proclamation, the decree increased the pressure on the South by directly linking the slave system to the war effort. Thus the freedom of black people became part of the struggle. Frederick Douglass, the voice of black America, wrote, "We shout for joy that we live to record this righteous decree."

On January 1, 1863, Lincoln duly issued the final Emancipation Proclamation, which turned out to be just as tortuous as his response to Greeley in August. Lincoln freed the slaves in the areas of rebellion — the areas the Union did not control — but specifically exempted slaves in the border states and in former Confederate areas won by the Union in battle. Lincoln's purpose was to meet the abolitionist demand for a war against slavery while not losing the support of conservatives, especially in the border states. But the proclamation was so equivocal that Lincoln's own secretary of state, William Seward, remarked sarcastically, "We show our sympathy with slavery by emancipating slaves where we cannot reach them and holding them in bondage where we can set them free." And in Britain, where Lincoln had hoped to make a favorable impression on the public, government official Lord Russell commented on the "very strange nature" of the proclamation.

One group greeted the Emancipation Proclamation with open celebration. On New Year's Day, hundreds of African Americans gathered outside the White House and cheered the president. They called to him, as pastor Henry M. Turner recalled, that "if he would come out of that palace, they would hug him to death." Realizing the symbolic importance of the proclamation, free black people predicted that the news would encourage southern slaves either to flee to Union lines or to refuse to work for their masters. Both of these things were already happening as black people seized upon wartime changes to reshape white-black relations in the South. In one sense, then, the Emancipation Proclamation simply gave a name to a process already in motion.

The Thirteenth Amendment

Abolitionists set about to move Lincoln beyond his careful stance in the Emancipation Proclamation. Reformers such as Elizabeth Cady Stanton and Susan B. Anthony lobbied and petitioned for a constitutional amendment outlawing slavery. Lincoln agreed with them, and encouraged the Republican party to support such action in its 1864 election platform. Congress, at Lincoln's urging, passed and sent to the states a statement banning slavery throughout the United States. Quickly ratified by the Union states in 1865, the statement became the Thirteenth Amendment to the Constitution. (The southern states, being in a state of rebellion, could not vote.) Lincoln's firm support for this amendment is a good indicator of his true feelings about slavery when he was free of the kinds of military and political considerations taken into account in the Emancipation Proclamation.

Black Fighting Men

As part of the Emancipation Proclamation, Lincoln gave his support for the first time to the recruitment of black soldiers. Early in the war, eager black volunteers had been bitterly disappointed at being turned away. Many, like Robert Fitzgerald, a free African American from Pennsylvania, found other ways to serve the Union cause. Fitzgerald first drove a wagon and mule for the Quartermaster Corps, and

This unidentified young African American corporal is shown holding his rifle with a fixed bayonet. As Frederick Douglass commented, once black men such as this had served in the Union army, "there is no power on earth that can deny he has earned the right to citizenship."

later, in spite of persistent seasickness, he served in the Union navy. After the Emancipation Proclamation, however, Fitzgerald was able to do what he had wanted to do all along: be a soldier. He enlisted in the Fifth Massachusetts Cavalry, a regiment that, like all the units in which black soldiers served, was 100 percent African American.

In Fitzgerald's company of eighty-three men, half came from slave states and had run away to enlist; the other half came mostly from the North but also from Canada, the West Indies, and France. Other regiments had volunteers from Africa. The proportion of volunteers from the loyal border states (where slavery was still legal) was upwards of 25 percent — a lethal blow to the slave system in those states.

As was customary in black regiments, the commanding officers were white. The most famous black regiment, the fifty-fourth Massachusetts Volunteers, had been commanded by abolitionist Robert Gould Shaw of Boston, who was killed in action along with half of his troops in a fruitless attack on Fort Wagner, South Carolina, in 1863. (A story retold in the film *Glory*.) Thomas Wentworth Higginson, the Unitarian minister who had supported John Brown, led another of the first black regiments, the First South Carolina Volunteers.

After a scant two months of training (two years had been customary for prewar cavalry units) Fitzgerald's company was sent on to Washington and thence to battle in northern Virginia. Uncertain of the reception they would receive in northern cities with their history of antiblack riots, Fitzgerald and his comrades were pleasantly surprised. "We are cheered in every town we pass through," he wrote in his diary. "I was surprised to see a great many white people weeping as the train moved South." White people had reason to cheer: black volunteers, eager and willing to fight, made up 10 percent of the Union army. Nearly 200,000 African Americans (one out of five black males in the nation) served in the Union army or navy. A fifth of them — 37,000 — died defending their own freedom and the Union.

Military service was something no black man could take lightly. He faced prejudice of several kinds. In the North, most whites believed that black people were inferior both in intelligence and in courage. Most army officers shared these opinions — but usually not those who had volunteered to lead black troops. Thus black soldiers had to prove themselves in battle. The performance of black soldiers at Fort Wagner and in battles near Vicksburg, Mississippi, in 1863 helped to change the minds of the Union army command. In the Battle of Milliken's Bend, untrained and poorly armed former slaves fought desperately — and successfully. "The bravery of the blacks . . . completely revolutionized the sentiment of the army with regard to the employment of negro troops," wrote Charles Dana, assistant secretary of war. "I heard prominent officers who formerly in private had sneered at the idea of negroes fighting express themselves after that as heartily in favor of it."

However, Dana went on to say, among the Confederates "the feeling was very different." They hated and feared black troops, and threatened to treat any captured black soldier as an escaped slave subject to execution. On at least one occasion, at Fort Pillow, Tennessee, in 1864, the threats were carried out. Confederate soldiers massacred 262 black soldiers after they had surrendered. Although large-scale episodes such as this were rare (especially after President Lincoln threatened retaliation), smaller ones were not. On duty near Petersburg, Virginia, Robert Fitzgerald's company lost a picket to Confederate hatred: wounded in the leg, he was unable to escape when Confederate soldiers smashed his skull with their musket butts. Fitzgerald wrote in his diary, "Can such men eventually triumph? God forbid!"

Another extraordinary part of the story of the black soldiers was their reception by black people in the South. The sight of armed black men, many of them former slaves themselves, wearing the uniform of the Union army was overwhelming. As his regiment entered Wilmington, North Carolina, one black soldier wrote, "men and women, old and young, were running throughout the streets, shouting and praising God. We could then truly see what we have been fighting for. . . ."

Robert Fitzgerald's own army career was brief. Just five months after he enlisted, he caught typhoid fever. Hearing of his illness, Fitzgerald's mother traveled from Pennsylvania and nursed him, probably saving his life. Eventually, 117 members of his regiment died of disease — and only 7 in battle. Eight months after he had enlisted, Fitzgerald was discharged for poor eyesight. His short military career nevertheless gave him, in the words of a granddaughter, the distinguished lawyer Pauli Murray, "a pride which would be felt throughout his family for the next century."

Black soldiers were not treated equally by the Union army. They were segregated in camp, and given the worst jobs. Many white officers and soldiers treated them as inferiors. In addition, they were paid less than whites (ten dollars a month rather than thirteen). While they might not be able to do much about the other kinds of discrimination, they could protest the pay inequity. The Fifty-fourth Massachusetts regiment found an unusual way to protest: they refused to accept their pay, preferring to serve the army for free until it decided to treat them as free men. The protest was effective: in June 1864 the War Department equalized wages between black and white soldiers.

In other ways the army service of black men made a dent in northern white racism. Massachusetts, the state where abolitionist feeling was the strongest, went the furthest by enacting the first law forbidding discrimination against blacks in public facilities. Some major cities, among them San Francisco, Cincinnati, Cleveland, and New York, desegregated their streetcars. Several states — Ohio, California, Illinois — repealed statutes that had barred black people from testifying in court or serving on juries. But above all, as Frederick Douglass acutely saw, military service permanently changed the status of African Americans. "Once let the black man get upon his person the brass letters, U.S., let him get an eagle on his button and a musket on his shoulder and bullets in his pocket," Douglass said, and "there is no power on earth that can deny that he has earned the right to citizenship."

THE FRONT LINES AND THE HOME FRONT

Civil War soldiers wrote millions of letters home, more proportionately than in any American war. Their letters and the ones they received in return were the links between the front lines and the home front, between the soldiers and their home communities. They are a testament to the patriotism of both Union and Confederate troops, for the story they told was frequently one of slaughter and horror.

The Toll of War

In spite of early hopes for what one might call a "brotherly" war, one that avoided excessive conquest and devastation, Civil War deaths, in battle after battle, were appalling. One reason was technology: improved weapons, in particular modern rifles, had much greater range and accuracy than the muskets they replaced. The Mexican-American War had been fought with smooth-bore muskets, which were slow to reload and accurate only at short distances. As Ulysses Grant said, "At a distance of a few hundred yards, a man could fire at you all day [with a musket] without your finding out." The new Springfield and Enfield rifles were accurate for a quarter of a mile or more. Civil War generals, both North and South, were slow to adjust to this new reality.

It is often said that generals are always prepared to fight the last war rather than the current one. Almost all Union and Confederate generals were committed to the conventional military doctrine of massed infantry offensives—the Jomini doctrine—that they had learned in their military classes at West Point. At an earlier time, artillery "softened up" the defensive line before the infantry assault, but now the range of the new rifles made artillery itself vulnerable to attack. As a result, generals relied less on softening up than on immense numbers of infantrymen, hoping that enough of them would survive the withering rifle fire to overwhelm the enemy line. The enormous casualties, then, were a consequence of basic strategy.

Medical ignorance was another factor in the huge casualty rate, as we saw in the chapter introduction. Because the use of antiseptic procedures was in its infancy, men often died because minor wounds became infected. Gangrene was a common cause of death. Disease was an even more frequent killer, taking twice as many men as were lost in battle. The overcrowded and unsanitary conditions of many camps were breeding grounds for disease: smallpox, dysentery, typhoid, pneumonia, and, in the summer, malaria. The devastating effect of disease was apparent, for example, in McClellan's Peninsula campaign. Among his 130,000 men, nearly a quarter of the unwounded were ill in July of 1862. The knowledge that this situation could only deteriorate during August and September — the most disease-ridden months — was one of the reasons Lincoln decided to recall McClellan and his army.

Yet another factor was both North and South were completely unprepared to handle the supply and health needs of their large armies. Twenty-four hours after the Battle of Shiloh, most of the wounded still lay on the field in the rain. Many died of exposure; some, unable to help themselves, drowned. An equally shocking example was the Confederate prison camp of Andersonville in northern Georgia. An open stockade established early in 1864 to hold 10,000 northern prisoners, it held 33,000 by midsummer, and offered no shade or shelter. During the worst weeks of that summer, 100 prisoners a day died of disease, exposure, or malnutrition.

The United States Sanitary Commission

In the earliest stages of the war, women north and south came together in their communities to make clothing for the local men who had gone off to war. In the North, these efforts rapidly expanded. A number of women, most of them experienced in earlier reform efforts such as abolitionism, temperance, and education, banded together to form the Women's Central Association for Relief. By 1863, 7,000 association chapters throughout the North were doing volunteer work—fundraising; making and sending bandages, food, clothing, medicine, and more than 250,000 quilts and comforters to army camps and hospitals; and providing meals, housing, and transportation to soldiers on furlough. These women's groups supplied an estimated $15 million worth of goods to the Union troops. They provided vital volunteer assistance to an army that was unable to meet its medical and supply needs.

But the work of these groups went even further-

Convincing President Lincoln that it needed official status, the association gained a new name — the United States Sanitary Commission — in June of 1861, along with the power to investigate and advise the Medical Bureau. Henry Bellows, a Unitarian clergyman, became president of the organization and Frederick Law Olmsted its executive secretary. Over 500 "sanitary inspectors" (usually men, and all volunteers) instructed soldiers in matters such as placement of latrines, water supply, and safe cooking. Some soldiers listened, but, as the disease figures showed, not enough. Overall, it is estimated that the U.S. Sanitary Commission and all its branches contributed $50 million to the Union war effort.

Even more radical, at the insistence of the Sanitary, as the commission was known, women became army nurses, in spite of the objections of most army doctors. Hospital nursing, which had been both minimal and disreputable, now became a suitable vocation for middle-class women. Most women had done considerable nursing for their own families; care of the sick was considered one of women's key domestic qualities. But taking care of the bodily needs of strange men in hospitals was another thing. There were strong objections that such work was "unseemly" for respectable women. Many senior army doctors objected because they realized they would now be under the critical eye of women who were no different from their own daughters and wives. Nevertheless, reforming women persisted. Under the leadership of veteran reformer Dorothea Dix (the leader of the asylum movement — see Chapter 13), and in cooperation with the Sanitary Commission, by war's end more than 3,000 northern women had worked as paid army nurses and many more as volunteers.

One of the volunteers was Ellen Ruggles Strong of New York, who, over her husband's objections, insisted on nursing in the Peninsula campaign of 1862. "The little woman has come out amazingly strong during these two months," George Templeton Strong wrote in his diary with a mixture of pride and condescension. "Have never given her credit for a tithe of the enterprise, pluck, discretion, and force of character that she has shown. God bless her." Other women organized other volunteer efforts outside the Sanitary Commission umbrella. Perhaps the best known was Clara Barton, a government clerk before the war who consequently knew a number of influential congressmen. Barton organized nursing and medical supplies; she also used her congressional contacts to force reforms in army medical practice, of which she was very critical. Another strong-minded woman who was a special champion of enlisted men was Mary Ann "Mother" Bickerdyke, an Illinois widow who began working in army camps in 1861, first with Grant and later with William Tecumseh Sherman as he marched through Georgia. Sherman disliked most women, but he liked Mother Bickerdyke's fighting spirit.

Southern women were also active in nursing and otherwise aiding soldiers, though the South never boasted a single large-scale organization like

Nurse Ann Bell is shown preparing medicine for a wounded soldier. Prompted by the medical crisis of the war, the U.S. Sanitary Commission and other reformers helped women such as Bell and Ellen Ruggles Strong make nursing an acceptable activity for respectable women.

the Sanitary Commission. The women of Richmond, Virginia, volunteered when they found the war on their doorstep in the summer of 1862. During the Seven Days' Battles, thousands of wounded poured into Richmond; many died in the streets because there was no room for them in hospitals. Richmond women first established informal "roadside hospitals" to meet the need, and their activities expanded from there. As in the North, middle-class women at first faced strong resistance from army doctors and even their own families, who believed that a field hospital was "no place for a refined lady." Kate Cumming of Mobile, who nursed in Corinth, Mississippi after the Shiloh battle, faced down such reproofs, though she confided to her diary that nursing wounded men was very difficult: "Nothing that I had ever heard or read had given me the faintest idea of the horrors witnessed here." She and her companion nurses persisted and became an important part of the Confederate medical services. For southern women, who had been much less active in the public life of their communities than their northern reforming sisters, this Civil War activity marked an important break with prewar tradition.

Although women had made important advances, most army nurses and medical support staff continued to be men. One volunteer nurse was the poet Walt Whitman, who visited wounded soldiers in the hospital in Washington, D.C. Horrified at the suffering he saw, Whitman also formed a deep admiration for the "incredible dauntlessness" of the common soldier in the face of slaughter and privation. While never denying the senselessness of the slaughter, Whitman nevertheless found hope in the determined spirit of the common man and woman.

The Life of the Common Soldier

The conditions experienced by the eager young volunteers of the Union and Confederate armies included massive, terrifying, and bloody battles, apparently unending, with no sign of victory in sight. Soldiers suffered from the uncertainty of supply, which left troops, especially in the South, without uniforms, tents, and sometimes even food. They endured long marches over muddy, rutted roads while carrying packs of fifty or sixty pounds. Disease was rampant in their dirty, verminous, and unsanitary camps, and hospitals were so dreadful that more men left dead than alive. Many soldiers had entered military service with unrealistic, even romantic ideas about warfare. The Mexican-American War had been short and glorious (or at least far enough away to seem so) and the Revolutionary War was even more shrouded in myth. Reality was

thus a rude shock, and not all soldiers reacted as nobly as those glorified by Walt Whitman. Desertion was common: an estimated one of every nine Confederate soldiers and one of every seven Union soldiers deserted. Absence without leave (AWOL) was another problem. At Antietam Robert E. Lee estimated that a third to a half of his troops were AWOL.

Another widespread phenomenon was fraternization between the two sides. One example among many was provided by a southern private writing about how he celebrated the Fourth of July after the Seven Days' Battles in 1862:

> There are blackberries in the fields so our boys and the Yanks made a bargain not to fire at each other, and went out in the field, leaving one man on each post with the arms, and gathered berries together and talked over the fight, and traded tobacco and coffee and newspapers as peacefully and kindly as if they had not been engaged for . . . seven days in butchering one another.

In October 1861 a Louisiana man wrote to his brother-in-law: "You spoke as if you had some notion of volunteering. I advise you to stay at home." Once the initial patriotic fervor had waned, attitudes such as his, on the battlefield and at home, were increasingly common.

Wartime Politics

In the very earliest days of the war, northerners had joined together in support of the war effort. Democrat Stephen A. Douglas, Lincoln's defeated rival, paid a visit to the White House to offer Lincoln his support, then traveled home to Illinois, where he addressed a huge rally of Democrats in Chicago: "There can be no neutrals in this war, *only patriots — or traitors!*" Within a month, Douglas was dead at age forty-eight. The Democrats had lost the leadership of a large-minded man who might have done much on behalf of northern unity. By 1862 Democrats had split into two factions: the War Democrats (some of whom, like Edwin M. Stanton, accepted positions in the Lincoln administration) and the Peace Democrats, or Copperheads (from the poisonous snake), as their opponents called them.

The Democratic party was a powerful force in northern politics. It had received 44 percent of the popular vote in the 1860 election. The united opposition of the Democratic party to the emancipation of slaves explains much of Lincoln's equivocal action on this issue. But the Peace Democrats went far beyond this: they denounced the draft, martial law, and the high-handed actions of "King Abraham." Echoing old complaints against the Whigs, Peace Democrats appealed to the sympathies of western farmers by warning that agriculture was being hurt by the tariff and industrial policies of the Republican party. At the same time, they used racist arguments to appeal to urban workers and immigrants, warning that Republican policies would bring a flood of black workers into northern cities.

The leader of the Copperheads, Clement Vallandigham, a former Ohio congressman, advocated an armistice and a negotiated peace that would "look only to the welfare, peace and safety of the white race, without reference to the effect that settlement may have on the African." Western Democrats, he threatened, might form their own union with the South, excluding New England with its radical abolitionists and high-tariff industrialists.

At the time, long before Grant captured Vicksburg and gained control of the Mississippi River, Lincoln could not afford to take Vallandigham's threats lightly. Besides, he was convinced that some Peace Democrats were members of secret societies — the Knights of the Golden Circle and the Sons of Liberty — that had been conspiring with the Confederacy. In 1862, Lincoln proclaimed that all people who discouraged enlistments in the army or otherwise engaged in disloyal practices would be subject to martial law. In all, 13,000 people were arrested and imprisoned, including Vallandigham, who was exiled to the Confederacy. Lincoln rejected all protests, claiming his arbitrary actions were necessary for national security.

Lincoln also faced divisions in his own party between Radicals and conservatives. As the war continued, the Radicals gained strength: it was they who pushed for emancipation in the early days of the war and for harsh treatment of the defeated South at the end. The most troublesome Radical was Salmon P. Chase, who caused a Cabinet crisis in December of 1862 when he encouraged Senate Republicans to complain that Secretary of State William Seward was "lukewarm" in his support for emancipation. This Radical-conservative split was a portent of the party's difficulties after the war, which Lincoln did not live to see — or prevent.

Economic and Social Strains in the North

Wartime needs caused a surge in northern economic growth, but the gains were unequally spread. Early in the war, some industries suffered: cotton textile manufacturers could not get cotton, and shoe factories that had made cheap shoes for slaves were without a market. But other industries boomed —

boots, ships, and woolen goods such as blankets and uniforms, to name just three examples. Coal mining expanded, as did iron making, and especially the manufacture of iron rails for railroads. Agricultural goods were in great demand, and this furthered the mechanization of farming. The McCormick brothers grew rich from sales of their reapers. Once scorned as a "metal grasshopper," the ungainly-looking McCormick reaper made the hand-operated harvest of grain a thing of the past and led to great savings in manpower. Women, left to tend the family farm while the men went to war, found they could manage the demanding task of harvesting with mechanized equipment.

Wartime needs enriched some people honestly, but speculators and profiteers also flourished (as they have in every war). By the end of the war, government contracts had exceeded $1 billion. Not all of this business was free from corruption. New wealth was evident in every northern city. *Harper's Monthly* reported that "the suddenly enriched contractors, speculators, and stock-jobbers . . . are spending money with a profusion never before witnessed in our country. . . ." Some people were appalled at the spectacle of wealth in the midst of wartime suffering. Still, some of the new wealth went to good causes. Of the more than $3 million raised by the female volunteers of the United States Sanitary Commission, some came from gala Sanitary Fairs designed to attract those with money to spend.

For most people, however, the war brought the day-to-day hardship of inflation. During the four years of the war, the North suffered an inflation rate of 80 percent, or nearly 15 percent a year. This annual rate, three times what is generally considered tolerable, did much to inflame social tensions in the North. For one thing, wages rose only half as much as prices. Workers responded by joining unions and striking for higher wages (see the chapter introduction). Thirteen occupational groups, among them tailors, coal miners, and railroad engineers, formed unions during the Civil War. Manufacturers, bitterly opposed to unions, freely hired strikebreakers (many of whom were African Americans, women, or immigrants) and formed organizations of their own to prevent further unionization and to blacklist union organizers. Thus both capital and labor moved far beyond the small and local confrontations of the early industrial period. The formation of large-scale organizations, fostered by the wartime demand, laid the groundwork for the national battle between workers and manufacturers that dominated the last part of the nineteenth century.

Another major source of social tension was

conscription, implemented for the first time in U.S. history. The Union introduced a draft in July of 1863. (The Confederacy, as we have seen, had done so the previous year.) Although its major purpose was to stimulate reenlistments (many men had signed up for one-year terms) and to encourage volunteers, it was soon obvious that forcible conscription, backed by federal marshals, was necessary. Especially unpopular in the 1863 draft law was a provision that allowed the hiring of substitutes or the payment of a commutation fee of $300. The most likely source of substitutes was recent immigrants who had not yet filed for citizenship. It is estimated that immigrants (some of whom *were* citizens) made up 20 percent of the Union army. Substitution had been accepted in all previous European and American wars. It was so common that President Lincoln, though overage, tried to set an example by paying for a substitute himself. Even so, substitution became inflammatory in the hands of the Democratic party (88 percent of whose congressmen had voted against the draft). Pointing out that $300 was almost a year's wages for an unskilled laborer, Democrats denounced the draft law. They appealed to popular resentment by calling it "aristocratic legislation" and to fear by running headlines such as "Three Hundred Dollars or Your Life."

Carried out in the local community, conscription was in fact often marred by favoritism and prejudice. Many more poor than rich men were called, and many more immigrants were selected than their proportion of the population would logically dictate. But in reality, only 7 percent of all men called to serve actually did so. About 25 percent of the draftees hired a substitute, another 45 percent were exempted for cause (usually health reasons), and another 20 to 25 percent simply failed to report to the community draft office. Nevertheless, by 1863 many northern urban workers believed that the slogan "a rich man's war but a poor man's fight," though coined in the South, applied to them as well.

The New York City Draft Riots

There were protests against the draft throughout the North in the spring of 1863. Riots and disturbances broke out in a number of northern cities, and several federal enrollment officers were killed. But the worst trouble occurred in New York City, July 13–17, 1863, in a wave of working-class rioting, looting, fighting, and lynching that claimed the lives of 105 people, many of them black. The rioting was quelled only when five units of the U.S. Army were rushed from the battlefield at Gettysburg, where they had been fighting Confederates the week before. It was the most extensive rioting in American history.

The riots had several causes. Anger at the draft and racial prejudice were what most contemporaries saw. George Templeton Strong, a staunch Republican, believed that the "brutal, cowardly ruffianism and plunder" was instigated by Confederate agents stirring up "the rabble" of "the lowest Irish day laborers." A longer historical view reveals that the riots had less to do with the war than with the urban growth and tensions we explored in Chapter 13.

A black man is lynched during the New York City Draft Riots in July of 1863. Free black people and their institutions were major victims of the most extensive rioting in American history. The riots were less a protest against the draft than an outburst of frustration over urban problems that had been festering for decades.

The Civil War made urban problems worse and heightened the visible contrast between the lives of the rich and those of the poor. These tensions exploded, but were not solved, on a hot summer's week in New York in 1863.

Ironically, black men, so favored a target of the rioters' anger, were a major force in easing the national crisis over the draft. As we have seen, black volunteers ultimately composed one-tenth of the Union army, though they had been barred from service until 1863. Nearly 200,000 black soldiers filled the manpower gap that the controversial draft was meant to address.

The Failure of Southern Nationalism

The war brought even greater changes to the South. As in the North, war needs led to expansion and centralization of government control over the economy. In many cases, Jefferson Davis himself initiated government control (over railroads, shipping, and war production, for example), often in the face of protest or inaction by states' rights governors. The expansion of government brought sudden urbanization, a new experience for the predominantly rural South. Richmond, the Confederate capital, almost tripled in population, in large part because the Confederate bureaucracy grew to 70,000 people. Because of the need for military manpower, a good part of the Confederate bureaucracy was female — "government girls," the women were called. All of this — government control, urban growth, women in the paid work force — was new to southerners, but not all of it was welcomed.

Even more than in the North, the voracious need for soldiers fostered class antagonisms. When small yeoman farmers went off to war, their wives and families struggled to farm on their own, without the help of mechanization (a northern innovation) and without the help of slaves, which they had never owned. But wealthy men, as we have seen, could be exempted from the draft if they had more than twenty slaves. Furthermore, many upper-class southerners — at least 50,000 — avoided military service by paying liberally ($5,000 and more) for substitutes. In the face of these inequities, desertions from the Confederate army soared. One Mississippi soldier spoke for many when he said that "he did not propose to fight for the rich men while they were at home having a good time." But the rich men, the South's traditional ruling class, paid little attention.

Worst of all was the starvation, caused by the northern blockade and the breakdown of the southern transportation system and vastly magnified by runaway inflation. As we have seen, the price rise in the South was an unbelievable 9,000 percent. Speculation and hoarding by the rich made matters even worse. Women and children were left destitute, and a government-sponsored civilian relief program was soon diverted to meet the pressing needs of the military. Ordinary people suffered. "It is folly for a poor mother to call on the rich people about here," one woman wrote bitterly. "Their hearts are of steel; they would sooner throw what they have to spare to the dogs than give it to a starving child."

In the spring of 1863 food riots broke out in four Georgia cities (Atlanta among them) and in North Carolina. In Richmond, the capital, more than a thousand people, mostly women, broke into bakeries and snatched loaves of bread, crying "Bread! Bread! Our children are starving while the rich roll in wealth!" When the bread riot threatened to turn into general looting, Jefferson Davis himself appealed to the crowd to disperse — but found he had to threaten the rioters with gunfire before they would leave. A year later, Richmond stores sold eggs for six dollars a dozen and butter for twenty-five dollars a pound. A Richmond woman exclaimed, "My God! How can I pay such prices? I have seven children; what shall I do?"

Increasingly, the ordinary people of the South, preoccupied with staying alive, refused to pay taxes, to provide food, or to serve in the army. Soldiers were drawn home by the desperation of their families as well as the discouraging course of the war. By 1864 the desertion rate had climbed to 40 percent.

At the same time, the life of the southern ruling class was irrevocably changed by the changing nature of slavery. One-quarter of all slaves had fled to the Union lines by war's end, and those who remained often stood in a different relationship to their owners. As white masters and overseers left to join the army, white women were left behind on the plantation to cope with shortages, grow crops, and manage the labor of slaves. Lacking the patriarchal authority of their husbands, white women found that white-black relationships shifted, sometimes drastically (as when slaves fled) and sometimes more subtly. Slaves increasingly made their own decisions about when and how they would work, and they refused to accept the punishments that would have accompanied this insubordination in prewar years. One black woman, implored by her mistress not to reveal the location of a trunk of money and silver plate when the invading Yankees arrived, looked her in the eye and said, "Mistress, I can't lie over that; you bought that silver plate when you sold my three children."

Peace movements in the South were motivated by a confused mixture of realism, war weariness, and states' rights animosity toward Jefferson Davis's efforts to hold the Confederacy together. The anti-Davis faction was led by his own vice-president, Alexander Stephens, who early in 1864 suggested a negotiated peace. Peace sentiment was especially strong in North Carolina, where over a hundred public meetings in support of negotiations were held in the summer of 1863. Davis would have none of it, and he commanded enough votes in the Confederate Congress to enforce his will and to suggest that peace sentiment was traitorous. The Confederacy, which lacked a two-party system, had no official way to consider alternatives. Thus the peace sentiment, which grew throughout 1864, flourished outside the political system in secret societies such as the Heroes of America and the Red Strings. As hopes of Confederate victory slipped away, the military battlefield expanded to include the political battles that southern civilians were fighting among themselves.

THE TIDE TURNS

As Lincoln's timing of the Emancipation Proclamation showed, by 1863 the nature of the war was changing. The proclamation freeing the slaves struck directly at the southern home front and the civilian work force. That same year, the nature of the battlefield war changed as well. McClellan's notion of a limited war with modest battlefield casualties was gone forever. The Civil War became the first total war.

The Turning Point of 1863

In the summer of 1863 the moment finally arrived when the North could begin to hope for victory. But for the Union army the year opened with stalemate in the East and slow and costly progress in the West. For the South, 1863 represented its highest hopes for military success and for diplomatic recognition by Britain or France.

Attempting to break the stalemate in northern Virginia, General Joseph "Fighting Joe" Hooker and a Union army of 130,000 men attacked a Confederate army half that size at Chancellorsville in May. In response, Robert E. Lee took the daring risk of dividing his forces. He sent General Stonewall Jackson and 30,000 men on a day-long flanking movement that caught the Union troops by surprise. Although Jackson was killed (shot by his own men by mistake), Chancellorsville was a great Confeder-

ate victory. However, their losses were also great: 13,000 men, representing more than 20 percent of Lee's army (versus 17,000 Union men). Though weakened, Lee moved to the attack in the war's most dangerous single thrust into Union territory.

In June, Lee moved north into Maryland and Pennsylvania. His purpose was as much political as military: he hoped that a great Confederate victory would lead Britain and France to intervene in the war and demand a negotiated peace. The ensuing Battle of Gettysburg, July 1–3, 1863, was another horrible slaughter. On the last day, Lee sent 15,000 men, commanded by George Pickett, to attack the heavily defended Union center. The charge was suicidal. When the Union forces opened fire at 700 yards, one southern officer reported, "Pickett's division just seemed to melt away. . . . Nothing but stragglers came back." The next day a Union officer reported, "I tried to ride over the field but could not, for dead and wounded lay too thick to guide a horse through them."

Pickett's Charge, one historian has written, was a perfect symbol of the entire Confederate war effort: "matchless valor, apparent initial success, and ultimate disaster." Lee retreated from the field, leaving more than one-third of his army behind— 28,000 men killed, wounded, or missing. Union general George Meade elected not to pursue with his battered Union army (23,000 casualties). "We had them in our grasp," Lincoln said in bitter frustration. "We had only to stretch forth our arms and they were ours. And nothing I could say or do could make the Army move." Lee's great gamble had failed; he never again mounted a major offensive.

The next day, July 4, 1863, Ulysses S. Grant took Vicksburg, Mississippi, after a costly seven-month siege. The combined news of Gettysburg and Vicksburg dissuaded Britain and France from recognizing the Confederacy and checked the northern peace movement. It also tightened the grip of the "anaconda" on the South, for the Union now controlled all of the Mississippi River. In November Generals Grant and Sherman captured Chattanooga, Tennessee, thus opening the way for the capture of Atlanta and the march through Georgia that Sherman would undertake in 1864.

Grant and Sherman

In March of 1864, President Lincoln called Grant east and appointed him general in chief of all the Union forces. Lincoln's critics were appalled. Grant was an uncouth westerner (like the president) and (unlike the president) was rumored to have a drinking

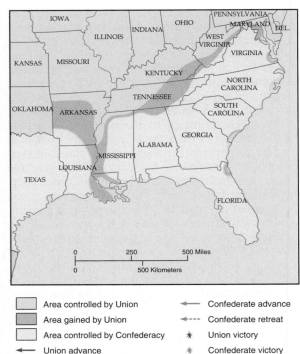

▢ Area controlled by Union	← Confederate advance
▨ Area gained by Union	←--- Confederate retreat
▢ Area controlled by Confederacy	✳ Union victory
← Union advance	✳ Confederate victory

The Turning Point: 1863

Following his victory at Chancellorsville in May, Lee boldly struck north into Maryland and Pennsylvania, hoping for a victory that would cause Britian and France to demand a negotiated peace on Confederate terms. Instead, he lost the hard-fought battle of Gettysburg, July 1–3. The very next day, Grant's seven-month siege of Vicksburg finally succeeded. These two great Fourth of July victories turned the tide in favor of the Union. The Confederates never again mounted a major offensive. Total Union control of the Mississippi exposed the Lower South. After the Union's capture of Chattanooga in November, the threat to Georgia was unmistakable.

This beautifully composed photograph shows a scene of horror: a line of dead Confederate soldiers after the battle of Fredericksburg. The mounting total of dead and wounded on both sides reached into the heart of every American community.

problem. Lincoln replied that if he knew the general's brand he would send a barrel of whiskey to every other commander in the Union army.

Grant devised a plan of strangulation and annihilation. He sent General William Tecumseh Sherman to defeat Confederate general Joe Johnston's Army of Tennessee, while he himself took on Lee in northern Virginia. Both Grant and Sherman exemplified the new kind of warfare. They aimed to inflict maximum damage on the fabric of southern life, hoping the South would choose to surrender rather than face total destruction. This decision to broaden the war so that it directly affected civilians was new in American military history, and prefigured the total wars of the twentieth century.

In northern Virginia, Grant pursued a policy of destroying civilian supplies. He said he "regarded it as humane to both sides to protect the persons of those found at their homes, but to consume everything that could be used to support or supply armies." One of those supports was slaves. Grant welcomed fleeing slaves to Union lines and encouraged army efforts to put them to work or enlist them as soldiers. He also cooperated with the efforts of the Freedmen's Bureau, which sent northern volunteers (many of them women) into Union-occupied parts of the South to educate former slaves. (The Freedman's Bureau continued its work into Reconstruction. One of the northern teachers who went south in 1866 to work for the bureau was Robert

Fitzgerald, the former soldier.) But the most famous example of the new total war strategy was General Sherman's 1864 march through Georgia.

On September 1, 1864, Sherman captured Atlanta, the "Gate City of the South." The rest of Georgia now lay open to him. The battle had been fierce, and the city lay in ruins around the victors. The fall of Atlanta was decisive. Gloom enveloped the South. "Since Atlanta I have felt as if all were dead within me, forever," Mary Boykin Chesnut wrote in her diary. "We are going to be wiped off the earth."

In November Sherman set out to march the 285 miles to the coastal city of Savannah, living off the land and destroying everything else in his path. His military purpose was to tighten the noose around Robert E. Lee's army in northern Virginia by cutting off Mississippi, Alabama, and Georgia from the rest of the Confederacy. But his second purpose, openly stated, was to "make war so terrible" to the people of the South, to "make them so sick of war that generations would pass away before they would again appeal to it." Accordingly, he told his men to seize, burn, or destroy everything in their path (but not, significantly, to harm civilians).

One Union soldier wrote to his father, "You can form no idea of the amount of property destroyed by us on this raid. . . . A tornado 60 miles in width from Chattanooga to this place 290 miles away could not have done half the damage we did." A southern woman supplied the details: "The fields

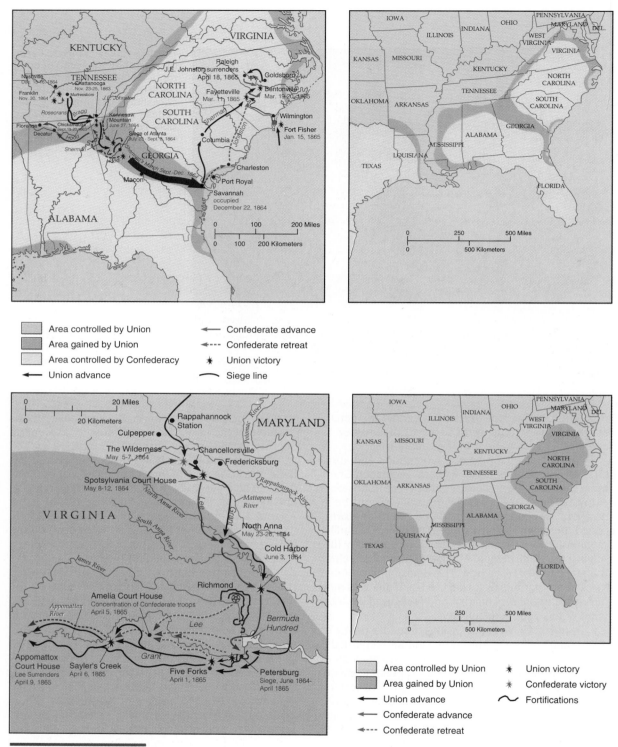

The Battles of 1864—65

Ulysses S. Grant and William Tecumseh Sherman, two like-minded generals, commanded the Union's armies in the final push to victory. While Grant hammered away at Lee in northern Virginia, Sherman captured Atlanta in September (a victory that may have been vital to Lincoln's re-election) and began his March to the Sea in November, 1864. In the war's final phase early in 1865, Sherman closed one arm of the pincers by marching north from Savannah while Grant closed in on Lee's last defensive positions in Petersburg and Richmond. Lee retreated from them on April 2 and surrendered at Appomattox on April 9, 1865, succumbing at last to the overwhelming pressures of shortage and starvation.

were trampled down and the road was lined with carcasses of horses, hogs and cattle that the invaders, unable either to consume or to carry with them, had wantonly shot down to starve our people and prevent them from making their crops. The stench in some places was unbearable." Estimates were that Sherman's army had done $100 million worth of damage. "They say no living thing is found in Sherman's track," Mary Boykin Chesnut wrote, "only chimneys, like telegraph poles, to carry the news of [his] attack backwards."

Terrifying to white southern civilians, Sherman was initially hostile to black southerners as well. In the interests of speed and efficiency, his army turned away many of the 18,000 slaves who flocked to it in Georgia, causing a number to be recaptured and reenslaved. This callous action caused such a scandal in Washington that Secretary of War Edwin Stanton arranged a special meeting in Georgia with Sherman and twenty black ministers who spoke for the freed slaves. This in itself was extraordinary: no one before had asked slaves what they wanted. Equally extraordinary was Sherman's response in Field Order 15, issued in January of 1865: he set aside more than 400,000 acres of Confederate land, to be given to the freed slaves in 40-acre parcels. This was war of a kind that white southerners had never imagined.

The Election of 1864

The war complicated the presidential election of 1864. The usual factionalism of politics was made much worse by the stresses of war. Public opinion rode a roller coaster, soaring to great heights with news of Union victories, plunging low during long periods of stalemate. Just as in the Mexican-American War, the "instant news" provided by the telegraph and special correspondents pulled people out of their daily lives and fixed their attention on the war. But the Civil War was much larger and much nearer. Almost everyone had a son or a father or a brother at the front, or knew someone in their community who did. The war news was *personal*.

Lincoln was renominated during a low period. Opposed by the Radicals, who thought he was too conciliatory toward the South, and by Republican conservatives, who disapproved of the Emancipation Proclamation, Lincoln had little support within his own party. Secretary of the Treasury Salmon P. Chase, a man of immense ego, went so far as to encourage his supporters to propose him, rather than Lincoln, as the party's nominee.

The Democrats had an appealing candidate: General George McClellan, a war hero (always a favorite with American voters) who was known to be sympathetic to the South. McClellan proclaimed the war a failure and proposed an armistice to end it. Other Democrats played shamelessly on the racist fears of the urban working class, accusing Republicans of being "negro-lovers" and warning that race mixing lay ahead.

A deeply depressed Lincoln fully expected to lose the election. "I am going to be beaten," he told an army officer in August of 1864, "and unless some great change takes place *badly* beaten." A great change *did* take place: Sherman captured Atlanta on September 1. Jubilation swept the North: some cities celebrated with 100-gun salutes. Lincoln won the election with 55 percent of the popular vote (78 percent of the soldiers voted for him rather than their former commander). The vote probably saved the Republican party from extinction. Furthermore, the election was important evidence of northern support for Lincoln's policy of unconditional surrender for the South. There would be no negotiated peace; the war would continue.

In many ways, Lincoln's reelection was extraordinary. Both the war-weary soldiers themselves and ordinary people as well had voted to continue a difficult and divisive conflict. This was the first time in American history that the people had been able to *vote* on whether they were willing to continue wartime hardships. That 45 percent of the electorate voted against Lincoln indicates the seriousness of the hardships that the war brought to the Union.

Nearing the End

As Sherman devastated the lower South, Grant was locked in struggle with Lee in northern Virginia. Grant did not favor subtle strategies of warfare. He bluntly said, "The art of war is simple enough. Find out where your enemy is. Get at him as soon as you can. Strike at him as hard as you can, and keep moving on." Following this plan Grant hammered Lee into submission in a year. But victory was expensive. Lee had learned the art of defensive warfare (his troops called him the "King of Spades" because he made them dig trenches so often), and he inflicted heavy losses on the Union army in the spring and summer of 1864: almost 18,000 at the Battle of the Wilderness, more than 8,000 at Spotsylvania, and 12,000 at Cold Harbor. At Cold Harbor, Union troops wrote their names and addresses on scraps of paper and pinned them to their backs, so certain were they of being killed or wounded in battle. Grim and terrible as Grant's strategy was, it eventually proved effective. The North's great advantage in population finally began to show. There were more Union soldiers to replace those lost in battle, but there were no more white Confederates.

In desperation, the South turned to the hitherto unthinkable: arming slaves to serve as soldiers in the Confederate army. As Jefferson Davis said in February of 1865, "We are reduced to choosing whether the negroes shall fight for or against us." But — and this was the bitter irony — the black soldiers and their families would have to be promised freedom or they would desert to the Union the first chance they had. Even though Davis's proposal had the support of Robert E. Lee, the Confederate Congress balked at first. As one Confederate congressman said, the idea was "revolting to Southern sentiment, Southern pride, and Southern honor." Another candidly admitted, "If slaves make good soldiers our whole theory of slavery is wrong." Finally, on March 13, the Confederate Congress authorized a draft of black soldiers — without mentioning freedom. Although two regiments of black soldiers were immediately organized in Richmond, it was too late. The South never had to publicly acknowledge the paradox of having to offer slaves freedom so that they would fight to defend slavery.

By the spring of 1865, public support for the war simply disintegrated in the South. Starvation, inflation, dissension, and the prospect of military defeat were too much. In February, Jefferson Davis sent his vice-president, Alexander Stephens, to negotiate terms at a peace conference at Hampton Roads. Lincoln would not countenance anything less than full surrender, although he did offer gradual emancipation with compensation for slave owners. Davis, however, insisted on southern independence at all costs, and was even willing to offer slaves their freedom if they would fight for it. Consequently, the Hampton Roads conference failed and southern resistance faded away. In March of 1865, Mary Boykin Chesnut recorded in her diary: "I am sure our army is silently dispersing. Men are going the wrong way all the time. They slip by now with no songs nor shouts. They have given the thing up."

Appomattox

Grant's hammering tactics worked — slowly. In the spring of 1865 Lee and his remaining troops, outnumbered two to one, still held Petersburg and Richmond, the Confederate capital. Starving, short of ammunition, and losing men in battle or to desertion every day, Lee retreated from Petersburg on April 2. The Confederate government fled Rich-

Abraham Lincoln toured the ruins of Richmond, the Confederate capital, just hours after Jefferson Davis had fled. In these ruins and in others throughout the South, Lincoln saw firsthand the immense task of rebuilding and reconciliation that he did not live to accomplish.

Lincoln's assassination, just days after Lee's surrender at Appomattox, was a stunning blow. From the most elderly person to the youngest child, from the most distinguished to the obscure, the Union mourned. *(Hermann Faber. Death of Abraham Lincoln. 1865. Pencil on paper. 13-7/8 × 9-7/8". Armed Forces Institute of Pathology, Washington, D.C. Otis Historical Archives, National Museum of Health and Medicine.)*

mond, stripping and burning the city. Seven days later, Lee and his 25,000 troops surrendered to Grant at Appomattox Courthouse. Grant treated Lee with great respect and set a historic precedent by giving the Confederate troops parole. This meant they could not subsequently be prosecuted for treason. Grant then sent the starving army on its way with three days' rations for every man. Jefferson Davis, who had hoped to set up a new government in Texas, was captured in Georgia on May 10. The war was finally over.

Death of a President

Sensing the war was near its end, Abraham Lincoln visited Grant's troops when Lee withdrew from Petersburg on April 2. Thus it was that Lincoln came to visit Richmond, and to sit briefly in Jefferson Davis's presidential office, soon after Davis had left it. As Lincoln walked the streets of the burned and pillaged city, black people poured out to see him and surround him, shouting "Glory to God! Glory! Glory! Glory!" Lincoln in turn said to Admiral David Porter: "Thank God I have lived to see this. It seems to me that I have been dreaming a horrid dream for four years, and now the nightmare is gone." Lincoln had only the briefest time to savor the victory. On the night of April 14, President and Mrs. Lincoln went to Ford's Theater in Washington. There Lincoln was shot at point-blank range by John Wilkes Booth, a Confederate sympathizer. He died the next day. For the people of the Union, the joy of victory was muted by mourning for their great war leader. The nation as a whole was left with Lincoln's vision of peace-

making, expressed in the unforgettable words of his second inaugural address:

> With malice toward none; with charity for all, with firmness in the right, as God give us to see the right, let us strive on to finish the work we are in; to bind up the nation's wounds; to care for him who shall have borne the battle, and for his widow, his orphan — to do all which may achieve and cherish a just and lasting peace among ourselves, and with all nations.

CONCLUSION

In 1865, a divided people had been forcibly reunited by battle. Their nation, the United States of America, had been permanently changed by civil war. Devastating losses among the young men of the country — the greatest such losses the nation was ever to suffer — would affect not only their families but all of postwar society. Politically, the deepest irony of the Civil War was that only by fighting it had America become completely a nation. For it was the war that broke down local isolation. Ordinary citizens in local communities, North and South, developed a national perspective as they sent their sons and brothers to be soldiers, their daughters to be nurses and teachers. Then too, the federal government, vastly strengthened by wartime necessity, now reached the lives of ordinary citizens more than ever before. The question now was whether this strengthened but divided national community, forged in battle (to use Lincoln's words from the Gettysburg Address), could create a just peace.

CHRONOLOGY

1861   Fort Sumter falls; war begins (April)
Virginia, North Carolina, Arkansas, Tennessee secede (April–May)
Mobilization begins
United States Sanitary Commission established (June)
First Battle of Bull Run (July)
Morrill Tariff Act

1862   Legal Tender Act (February)
McClellan's Peninsula campaign (March–August)
Battle of Glorieta Pass (March)
Battle of Pea Ridge (March)
Battle of Shiloh (April)
Confederate Conscription Act (April)
David Farragut captures New Orleans (April)
Homestead Act (May)
Seven Days' Battles (June–July)
Pacific Railroad Act (July)
Morrill Land Grant Act (July)
Battle of Antietam (September)
Battle of Fredericksburg (December)

1863   Emancipation Proclamation (January)
National Bank Act (February)
French install Archduke Maximilian in Mexico (March)
Battle of Chancellorsville (May)
Draft introduced in the North (July)
Battle of Gettysburg (July)
Surrender of Vicksburg (July)
New York City Draft Riots (July)
Battle of Chattanooga (November)
Union troops capture Brownsville, Texas (November)

1864   Grant becomes commanding general of Union forces (March)
Battle of the Wilderness (May)
Battle of Spotsylvania (May)
Battle of Cold Harbor (June)
Atlanta falls (September)
Lincoln reelected president (November)
Sherman's March to the Sea (November–December)

1865   Richmond falls (April)
Grant surrenders at Appomattox (April)
Lincoln assassinated (April)
Thirteenth Amendment to the Constitution becomes law
(December)

Additional Readings

IVER BERNSTEIN, *The New York City Draft Riots* (1990). A social history that places the famous riots in the context of the nineteenth century's extraordinary urbanization.

PAUL ESCOTT, *After Secession: Jefferson Davis and the Failure of Confederate Nationalism* (1978). A thoughtful study of Davis's record as president of the Confederacy.

ALVIN JOSEPHY, *The Civil War in the West* (1992). A long-needed study, by a noted western historian, of the course of the war in the West.

MARGARET LEECH, *Reveille in Washington: 1860–65* (1941). An engaging study of wartime changes, filled with anecdotes.

JAMES M. MCPHERSON, *Battle Cry of Freedom: The Civil War Era* (1988). An acclaimed, highly readable synthesis of much scholarship on the war.

JAMES M. MCPHERSON, *The Negro's Civil War: How American Negroes Felt and Acted during the War for the Union* (1965). One of the earliest documentary collections on African American activity in wartime.

WILLIAM QUENTIN MAXWELL, *Lincoln's Fifth Wheel: The Political History of the United States Sanitary Commission* (1956). A useful study of the major northern volunteer organization.

PAULI MURRAY, *Proud Shoes: The Story of an American Family* (1956). Murray tells the proud story of her African American family and her grandfather Robert Fitzgerald.

PHILIP SHAW PALUDAN, *''A People's Contest'': The Union at War, 1861–1865* (1988). A largely successful social history of the North during the war.

17 RECONSTRUCTION, 1863–1877

American Communities

● Hale County, Alabama

Theodor Kaufmann. On to Liberty. 1867. Oil on canvas. 91.4 × 142.2 cm. The Metropolitan Museum of Art, Gift of Erving and Joyce Wolf, 1982.

On a bright Saturday morning in May 1867, 4,000 former slaves eagerly streamed into the town of Greensboro, bustling seat of Hale County in west central Alabama. They came to hear speeches from two delegates to a recent freedmen's convention in Mobile, and to find out about the political status of black people under the Reconstruction Act just passed by Congress. In the days following this unprecedented gathering of African Americans, tension mounted throughout the surrounding countryside. Military authorities had begun supervising voter registration for elections to the upcoming constitutional convention that would rewrite the laws of Alabama. On June 13 John Orrick, a local white, confronted Alex Webb, a politically active freedman, on the streets of Greensboro. Webb had recently been appointed a voter registrar for the district. Orrick swore he would never be registered by a black man, and shot Webb dead. Hundreds of armed and angry freedmen formed a posse to search for Orrick, but they failed to find him. Webb's murder galvanized 500 local freedmen to form a [local] Union League chapter, which functioned as both a militia company and a forum to agitate for political rights.

FROM SLAVERY TO FREEDOM IN A BLACK BELT COMMUNITY

Such violent political encounters between black and white were common in southern communities. The Civil War had destroyed slavery and the Confederacy, but the political and economic status of newly emancipated African Americans remained to be worked out. The contests over the meaning of freedom reflected the great diversity of circumstances among southern communities. The 4 million freed people composed roughly one-third of the total southern population, but the black-white ratio in individual communities varied enormously. In some places the Union army had been a strong presence during the war, hastening collapse of the slave system and encouraging experiments in free labor. Other areas remained relatively untouched by the fighting. As a region, the South included a wide range of agriculture, with large plantations dominating certain areas and small farms others.

Large plantations dominated the economy and political life of west central Alabama's communities. The region had emerged as a fertile center of cotton production only in the two decades before the Civil War. Typical of the South's "black belt," it was an area in which African Americans constituted over three-quarters of the population. Hale County was virtu-

A group of slaves on a plantation in Edisto Island, South Carolina, in 1862. They were left to fend for themselves after their owner fled approaching Union forces. During the war thousands of former slaves on Edisto and neighboring Sea Islands, encouraged by military authorities and the Freedmen's Bureau, farmed small plots carved out of abandoned plantations. When President Johnson ordered the restoration of these lands to their pre-war white owners, freedpeople bitterly resisted; in some cases federal troops were required to force eviction.

ally untouched by fighting until the very end of the Civil War. The arrival of Union troops there in the spring of 1865 emboldened African Americans to challenge the traditional gang system by which masters had organized plantation labor. With the help of agents from the Freedmen's Bureau, former slaves began signing yearly contracts with plantation owners. These contracts set the conditions of work and payment, usually in the form of share wages *(a share of the cotton crop). Former slaves were paid either collectively, in which case they divided shares among themselves, or else individually, according to working capacity.*

One owner, Henry Watson, found that his entire work force had deserted him at the end of 1865. They did so after discovering that the one-eighth share of the crop they had contracted for came to only $6.06 per hand for the entire year's wage. "I am in the midst of a large and fertile cotton growing country," Watson wrote to a partner. "Many plantations are entirely without labor, many plantations have insufficient labor, and upon none are the laborers doing their former accustomed work." Watson and other local planters complained about what seemed to them to be strange behavior on the part of newly freed slaves. Black women refused to work in the fields, preferring to stay home with their children and tend garden plots. Nor would male field hands do any work, such as caring for hogs, that did not directly increase their share of the cotton crop.

Above all, freed people desired greater autonomy from their old masters, and they began forcing planters to accept changes in the labor system. In 1867 Wilson O'Berry, long-time overseer of the large Cameron plantation, reorganized production along new lines. He decided to withdraw from active control of crop production and work the land "in families," letting the freed people choose their own supervisors and find their own provisions. O'Berry divided his work force into three "squads" supervised by three former slaves, brothers Paul and Jim Hargress and Sandy Cameron. O'Berry soon reported improved productivity and better work habits among the hands. Over the next few years, the Cameron place was leased and eventually sold in small plots to families of former slaves. For men such as the Hargress brothers and Cameron, owning and farming their own land was the best way to secure their freedom, keep their family together, and get ahead. An independent black community still exists on the old Cameron plantation today.

Most African Americans were not so fortunate as to be able to buy land. The majority settled for some version of sharecropping, while others managed to rent land from owners, becoming tenant farmers. Still, planters throughout Hale County had been forced to change the old routines of plantation labor. Local African Americans also organized politically. In 1866 Congress had passed the Civil Rights Act and the Fourteenth Amendment to the Constitution, both of which promised full citizenship rights to former slaves. Hale County freedmen joined Union League chapters and the Republican party, using their new political power to press for better labor contracts and agitate for the more radical goal of land confiscation and redistribution. "The colored people are very anxious to get land of their own to live upon independently; and they want money to buy stock to make crops," reported one black Union League organizer. "The only way to get these necessaries is to give our votes to the [Republican] party . . . making every effort possible to bring these blessings about by reconstructing the State." Two Hale County former slaves, Brister Reese and James K. Green, won election to the Alabama state legislature in 1869.

These new labor arrangements and aggressive black political activism prompted a white counterattack. In the spring of 1868 the Ku Klux Klan came to Hale County. A secret organization of white people devoted to terrorizing and intimidating African Americans and their white Republican allies, the Klan quickly made its presence felt. Disguised in white sheets, armed with guns and whips, and making nighttime raids on horseback, Klansmen flogged, beat, and murdered freed people. The spread of sharecropping and tenant farming dispersed African American families throughout the countryside, making them more vulnerable to violent attack. Planters used Klan terror to dissuade former slaves from leaving plantations or organizing for higher wages. The Klan was also a potent weapon for punishing African American voters and political activists.

A congressional investigation in 1871 found that the Klan was "more widespread and virulent" in the west Alabama black belt than in any other part of the South. But the federal government made no serious effort to stop Klan terror in the region. For by then it had retreated from its immediate postwar policy of active intervention in southern politics. Planters thus reestablished much of their social and political control. Not until the "Second Reconstruction" of the twentieth-century civil rights movement would the descendants of Hale County's African Americans enjoy the full fruits of freedom.

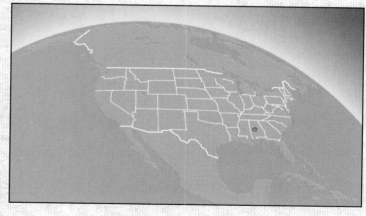

Events in Hale County typified a struggle that took place in hundreds of southern communities in the aftermath of the Civil War. The destruction of slavery and the Confederacy forced African Americans and white people to renegotiate their old economic and political roles. During the Reconstruction era, these community battles both shaped and were shaped by the victorious and newly expansive federal government in Washington.

NATIONAL RECONSTRUCTION

When General Robert E. Lee's men stacked their guns at Appomattox, the bloodiest war in American history ended. Approximately 620,000 soldiers had died during the four years of fighting, 360,000 Union and 260,000 Confederate. Another 275,000 Union and 190,000 Confederate troops were wounded. Decades of vitriolic debate had fed sectional tensions over slavery's extension into the federal territories. Although President Abraham Lincoln insisted early on that the conflict was over the maintenance of the Union, by 1863 the contest had evolved into a war of African American liberation as well as a constitutional struggle. Indeed slavery — as a political, economic, and moral issue — was the root cause of the war. The Civil War ultimately destroyed slavery, though not racism, once and for all.

The Civil War also settled which interpretation of the Constitution — states' rights or federalism — would prevail. Never again would federal authority be tested on the battlefield. The name *United States* would from now on be understood as a singular rather than a plural noun, signaling an important change in the meaning of American nationality. The old notion of the United States as a voluntary union of sovereign states gave way to the new reality of a single nation in which the federal government took precedence over the individual states. The key historical developments of the Reconstruction era revolved around precisely how the newly strengthened national government would define its relationship with the defeated Confederate states and the 4 million newly freed slaves.

The Defeated South

The white South paid an extremely high price for secession, war, and defeat. In addition to the battlefield casualties, the Confederate states sustained deep material and psychological wounds. War had decimated the South's economic infrastructure. Much of the best agricultural land was desolated, including the rich fields of northern Virginia, the Shenandoah Valley, and large sections of Tennessee, Mississippi, Georgia, and South Carolina. Many towns and cities — including Richmond, Atlanta, and Columbia, South Carolina — lay in ruins. By 1865, the South's most precious commodities, cotton and African American slaves, no longer were measures of wealth and prestige. Retreating Confederates destroyed most of the South's cotton to prevent its capture by federal troops. What remained was confiscated by Union agents as contraband of war. The former slaves, many of whom had fled to Union lines during the latter stages of the war, were determined to chart their own course in the reconstructed South as free men and women.

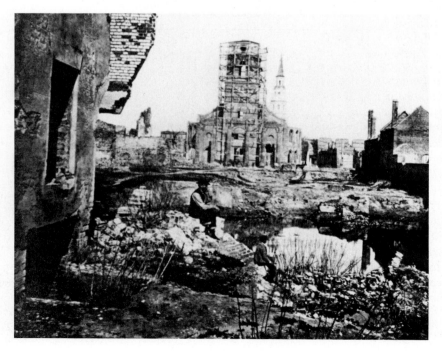

Charleston, South Carolina, in 1865, after Union troops had burned the city. In the aftermath of the Civil War, scenes like this were common throughout the South. The destruction of large portions of so many southern cities and towns contributed to the postwar economic hardships faced by the region.

It would take the South's economy a generation to overcome the severe blows dealt by the war. Farm values diminished 41 percent, the worth of farm machinery and equipment fell by 37 percent, and the value of livestock declined by 28 percent. About $1.5 billion of the South's capital (including slaves) had been destroyed, and the financial assets of individuals and state and local governments were wiped out. In 1860 the South held 30 percent of the nation's wealth; a decade later it controlled only 12 percent. After 1865, each of the former Confederate states (except Florida and Texas) experienced serious reductions in the amount of acreage under cultivation.

The presence of 200,000 Union troops, including U.S. Colored Troops, reminded former Confederates that they were a defeated people. Many white southerners resented their conquered status, and white notions of race, class, and "honor" died hard. A white North Carolinian, for example, who had lost almost everything dear to him in the war — his sons, home, and slaves — recalled in 1865 that in spite of all his tragedy he still retained one thing. "They've left me one inestimable privilege — to hate 'em. I git up at half-past four in the morning, and sit up till twelve at night, to hate 'em." As late as 1870 the Reverend Robert Lewis Dabney of Virginia wrote: "I do not forgive. I try not to forgive. What! forgive those people, who have invaded our country, burned our cities, destroyed our homes, slain our young men, and spread desolation and ruin over our land! No, I do not forgive them."

Emancipation proved the bitterest pill for white Southerners to swallow, especially the planter elite. Conquered and degraded, and in their view robbed of their slave property, white people more than ever perceived African Americans as vastly inferior to themselves. In the antebellum South white skin had defined a social bond that united white people of all economic classes. The lowliest poor white person at least possessed his or her white skin — a badge of superiority over even the most skilled slave or prosperous free African American. Emancipation, however, forced white people to redefine their world. Many believed that without white direction, the freed people would languish, become wards of the state, or die off. Most white people believed that African Americans were too lazy to take care of themselves and survive. At the very least, whites reasoned, the South's agricultural economy would suffer at the hands of allegedly undisciplined and inefficient African Americans. The specter of political power and social equality for African Americans made racial order the consuming passion of most white southerners during the Reconstruction years.

Lincoln's Plan

By late 1863 Union military victories had convinced President Lincoln of the need to fashion a plan for the reconstruction of the South (see Chapter 16). He had already appointed provisional military governors for Louisiana, North Carolina, and Tennessee as sections of these states fell to Union troops. Lincoln based his reconstruction program on bringing the seceded states back into the Union as quickly as possible. He was determined to respect private property (except in the case of slave property) and he opposed imposing harsh punishments for rebellion. His Proclamation of Amnesty and Reconstruction of December 1863 offered "full pardon" and the restoration of property, not including slaves, to white southerners willing to swear an oath of allegiance to the United States and its laws, including the Emancipation Proclamation. Prominent Confederate military and civil leaders were excluded from Lincoln's offer, though he indicated that he would freely pardon these officers.

The president also proposed that when the number of any Confederate state's voters who took the oath of allegiance reached 10 percent of the number who had voted in the election of 1860, this group could establish a state government that Lincoln would recognize as legitimate. Fundamental to this Ten Percent Plan was acceptance by the reconstructed governments of the abolition of slavery. Lincoln added that the states could adopt other policies "which may yet be consistent, as a temporary arrangement, with [slaves'] present condition as a laboring, landless, and homeless class." Lincoln's plan was designed less as a blueprint for Reconstruction than as a way to shorten the war and gain white people's support for emancipation. Lincoln's reconstruction process, then, could begin as soon as 10 percent of the voters took an oath of future loyalty. But in late 1864, when Arkansas and Louisiana met the steps outlined by the president, Congress refused to seat their representatives.

There was a reason for this. Lincoln's amnesty proclamation had angered those Republicans — known as Radical Republicans — who advocated not only equal rights for the freedmen but a tougher stance toward the white South. In July 1864, Senator Benjamin F. Wade of Ohio and Congressman Henry W. Davis of Maryland sought to substitute a harsher alternative to the Ten Percent Plan. The Wade-Davis bill required that 50 percent of the white male citizens had to take a loyalty oath before elections for new state constitutional conventions could be held in the seceded states. The bill also contained

FREEDOM TO SLAVES!

Whereas, the President of the United States did, on the first day of the present month, issue his *Proclamation* declaring "that *all persons held as Slaves in certain designated States, and parts of States, are, and hencefor-ward shall be free,*" and that the Executive Government of the United States, including the Military and Naval authorities thereof, would recognize and maintain the freedom of said persons. *And Whereas,* the county of *Frede-rick* is included in the territory designated by the Proclamation of the Presi-dent, in which the *Slaves should become free,* I therefore hereby notify the citizens of the city of Winchester, and of said County, of said Proclamation, and of my intention to maintain and enforce the same.

I expect all citizens to yield a ready compliance with the Proclamation of the Chief Executive, and I admonish all persons disposed to resist its peaceful enforcement, that upon manifesting such disposition by acts, they will be regarded as rebels in arms against the lawful authority of the Federal Government and dealt with accordingly.

All persons liberated by said Proclamation are admonished to abstain from all violence, and immediately betake themselves to useful occupations.

The officers of this command are admonished and ordered to act in accord-ance with said proclamation and to yield their ready co-operation in its enforcement.

R. H. Milroy,
Brig. Gen'l Commanding.

Winchester Va.
Jan. 5th, 1863.

A Union commander notifies the citizens of Winchester, Virginia of President Lincoln's Emancipation Proclamation. Union officers throughout the South had to improvise arrangements for dealing with African Americans who streamed into Union army camps. For many newly-freed slaves, the call for taking up "useful occupations" meant serving the Union forces in their neighborhood as laborers, cooks, spies, and soldiers.

guarantees of equality before the law (although not suffrage) for former slaves. Unlike the president, the Radicals saw Reconstruction as a chance to effect a fundamental transformation of southern society. They thus wanted to delay the process until war's end and to limit participation to a smaller number of southern Unionists. Lincoln viewed Reconstruction as part of the larger effort to win the war and abolish slavery. He wanted to weaken the Confederacy by creating new state governments that could win broad support from southern white people. The Wade-Davis bill threatened his efforts to build political consensus within the southern states, and Lincoln therefore pocket-vetoed it.

Redistribution of southern land among former slaves posed another thorny issue for Lincoln, Congress, and federal military officers. As Union armies occupied parts of the South, commanders had improvised a variety of arrangements involving the confiscation of plantations and the leasing of land to freedmen. For example, in 1862 General Benjamin F. Butler had initiated a policy of transforming slaves on Louisiana sugar plantations into wage laborers under the close supervision of occupying federal troops. Butler's policy required slaves to remain on the estates of loyal planters, where they would receive wages according to a fixed schedule, as well as food and medical care for the aged and sick. Abandoned plantations would be leased to northern investors. Butler's successor, General Nathaniel P. Banks, extended this system throughout occupied Louisiana. By 1864 some 50,000 African American laborers on nearly 1,500 Louisiana estates worked either directly for the government or for individual planters under contracts supervised by the army.

In January 1865, General William T. Sherman issued Special Field Order No. 15, setting aside the Sea Islands off the Georgia coast and a portion of the South Carolina low-country rice fields for the exclusive settlement of freed people. Each family would receive forty acres of land and the loan of mules from the army — the origin, perhaps, of the famous "forty acres and a mule" idea that would soon capture the imagination of African Americans throughout the South. Sherman's intent was not to revolutionize southern society but to relieve the demands placed on his army by the thousands of impoverished African Americans who followed his march to the sea. By the summer of 1865 some 40,000 freed people, eager to take advantage of the general's order, had been settled on 400,000 acres of "Sherman land."

But conflicts within the Republican party, and Lincoln's opposition based on constitutional grounds, prevented the development of a systematic land distribution program. Still, Lincoln and the Republican Congress supported other measures to aid the emancipated slaves. In March 1865 Congress established the Freedmen's Bureau. Along with offering provisions, clothing, and fuel to destitute former slaves, the bureau was charged with supervising and managing "all the abandoned lands in the South and the control of all subjects relating to refugees and freedmen." The act that established the bureau also stated that forty acres of abandoned or confiscated land could be leased to freed slaves or white Unionists, who would have an option to purchase after three years and "such title thereto as the United States can convey." To guarantee the end of slavery once the war ended, Republicans drafted the Thirteenth Amendment, declaring that "neither slavery nor involuntary servitude, except as punishment for crime. . . , shall exist within the United States." This amendment passed both houses of Congress in January 1865 and was ratified by the necessary three-fourths of the states on December 18, 1865 — eight months after Lee's surrender.

On April 14, 1865, while attending the theater in Washington, President Lincoln was shot by John Wilkes Booth, an actor and Confederate sympathizer. Lincoln died the next day, mourned by African Americans as their emancipator and by northern white people as the savior of the Union. Booth was part of a group that conspired unsuccessfully to kill other prominent Union officials. Booth himself was quickly hunted down and killed; months later several of his fellow conspirators were tried and hanged. At the time of his death, Lincoln's Reconstruction policy remained unsettled and incomplete. In its broad outlines the president's plans had seemed to favor a speedy restoration of the southern states to the Union, and a minimum of federal intervention in their affairs. But now the specifics of postwar Reconstruction would have to be hammered out by a new president, Andrew Johnson of Tennessee, and a Republican-controlled Congress determined to win the peace as well as the war.

Andrew Johnson and Presidential Reconstruction

Andrew Johnson, a Democrat and former slaveholder, was a most unlikely successor to the martyred Lincoln. By trade a tailor, educated by his wife, Johnson overcame his impoverished background and served as state legislator, governor, and U.S. senator. Throughout his career Johnson had championed yeoman farmers and viewed the South's plantation aristocrats with contempt. He was the only southern member of the U.S. Senate to remain loyal to the Union, and he held the planter elite responsible for secession and defeat. In 1862 Lincoln appointed Johnson to the difficult post of military governor of Tennessee. There he successfully began wartime Reconstruction and cultivated Unionist support in the mountainous eastern districts of that state.

In 1864 the Republicans, determined to broaden their appeal to include northern and border state "War Democrats," nominated Johnson for vice-president. But despite Johnson's success in Tennessee and in the 1864 campaign, many Radical Republicans distrusted him, and the hardscrabble Tennessean remained a political outsider in Republican circles. In the immediate aftermath of Lincoln's murder, however, Johnson appeared to side with those Radical Republicans who sought to treat the South as a conquered province. "Treason is a crime and must be made odious," Johnson declared. "Traitors must be impoverished. . . . They must not only be punished, but their social power must be destroyed." The new president also hinted at indicting prominent Confederate officials for treason, disfranchising them, and confiscating their property.

Such tough talk appealed to Republicans. Early in Johnson's presidency one described him approvingly as "a southern loyalist in the midst of traitors, a southern democrat in the midst of aristocrats, . . . lifted at last to the presidency . . . that he might be charged with the duty of dealing punishment to these self-same assassins of the Union." But such support for Johnson quickly faded as the new president's policies unfolded. Johnson defined Reconstruction as the province of the executive, not the legislative branch, and he planned to restore the Union as quickly as possible. He blamed individual southerners — the planter elite — rather than entire states for leading the South down the disastrous road to secession. In line with this philosophy, Johnson outlined mild terms for reentry to the Union.

In the spring of 1865 Johnson granted amnesty and pardon, including restoration of property rights except slaves, to all Confederates who pledged loyalty to the Union and support for emancipation. Fourteen classes of southerners, mostly major Confederate officials and wealthy landowners, were excluded. But these men could apply individually for presidential pardons. The power to pardon his former enemies — the Old South's planter elite — gratified Johnson and reinforced his class bias. It also helped win southern support for his lenient policies, for Johnson pardoned former Confederates liberally. In September 1865 Johnson granted an average of a hundred pardons a day, and during his tenure he pardoned roughly 90 percent of those who applied. Significantly, Johnson instituted this plan while Congress was not in session.

Johnson also appointed provisional governors for seven of the former Confederate states, requiring them to hold elections for state constitutional conventions. Participation in this political process was limited to white people who had been pardoned or who had taken a loyalty oath. Johnson also called upon state conventions to repudiate secession, acknowledge the abolition of slavery, and void state debts incurred during the war. By the fall of 1865 ten of the eleven Confederate states claimed to have met Johnson's requirements to reenter the Union. On December 6, 1865, in his first annual message to Congress, the president declared the "restoration" of the Union virtually complete. But a serious division within the federal government was taking shape, for the Congress was not about to allow the president free rein in determining the conditions of southern readmission.

Andrew Johnson's goal had been simply to create functioning governments in the southern states and avoid pushing for major political or social change. He used the term *restoration* rather than *reconstruction*. A lifelong Democrat with ambitions to be elected president on his own in 1868, Johnson hoped to build a new political coalition composed of northern Democrats, conservative Republicans, and southern Unionists. Firmly committed to white supremacy, he opposed political rights for the freedmen. In 1866, after Frederick Douglass and other black leaders had met with him to discuss black suffrage, Johnson told an aide: "Those damned sons of bitches thought they had me in a trap! I know that damned Douglass; he's just like any nigger, and he would sooner cut a white man's throat than not." Johnson's open sympathy for his fellow white southerners, his antiblack bias, and his determination to control the course of Reconstruction placed him on a collision course with the powerful Radical wing of the Republican party.

Radical Republicans and National Citizenship

The Radicals believed they now had a chance to reshape southern communities in the North's image. Most Radicals were men whose careers had been shaped by the slavery controversy. At the core of their thinking lay a deep belief in equal political rights and equal economic opportunity, both guaranteed by a powerful national government. They argued that once free labor, universal education, and equal rights were implanted in the South, that region would be able to share in the North's material wealth, progress, and fluid social mobility. Representative George W. Julian of Indiana typified the Radical vision for the South. He called for elimination of the region's "large estates, widely scattered settlements, wasteful agriculture, popular ignorance, social degradation, the decline of manufactures, contempt for honest labor, and a pampered oligarchy." This process would allow Republicans to develop "small farms, thrifty tillage, free schools, social independence, flourishing manufactures and the arts, respect for honest labor, and equality of political rights."

In the Radicals' view, the power of the federal government would be central to the remaking of southern society, especially in guaranteeing civil rights and suffrage for freedmen. In the most far-reaching proposal, Representative Thaddeus Stevens of Pennsylvania called for the confiscation of 400 million acres belonging to the wealthiest 10 percent of southerners, to be redistributed to black and white yeomen and northern land buyers. "The whole fabric of southern society *must* be changed," Stevens told Pennsylvania Republicans in September 1865, "and never can it be done if this opportunity is lost. How can republican institutions, free schools, free churches, free social intercourse exist in a mingled community of nabobs and serfs? If the South is ever to be made a safe republic let her lands be cultivated by the toil of the owners."

Northern Republicans were especially outraged by the stringent "Black Codes" passed by South Carolina, Mississippi, Louisiana, and other states. These were designed to restrict the freedom of the black labor force and keep freed people as close to slave status as possible. Laborers who left their jobs before contracts expired would forfeit wages already earned and be subject to arrest by any white citizen. Vagrancy, very broadly defined, was punishable by fines and involuntary plantation labor. Apprenticeship clauses obliged black children to work without pay for employers. Some states attempted to bar African Americans from land ownership. Other laws specifically denied African Americans equality with white people in civil rights, excluding them from juries and prohibiting interracial marriages. In some cities and states African Americans were forced to accept segregated public facilities such as schools,

"Slavery Is Dead" —*Harper's Weekly,* January 12, 1867. This political cartoon typifies the widespread anger among northern Republicans over continued Southern resistance to the Fourteenth Amendment and citizenship rights for the recently freed slaves. Two months later, the Republican Congress passed the First Reconstruction Act over President Johnson's veto, dividing the South into five military districts subject to martial law.

restaurants, theaters, and railroad cars; in others they were simply excluded altogether.

The Black Codes underscored the unwillingness of white southerners to accept the full meaning of freedom for African Americans. Mississippi's version contained a catchall section levying fines and possible imprisonment for any former slaves

> committing riots, routs, affrays, trespasses, malicious mischief, cruel treatment to animals, seditious speeches, insulting gestures, language, or acts, or assaults on any person, disturbance of the peace, exercising the function of a minister of the Gospel without a license . . . vending spiritous or intoxicating liquors, or committing any other misdemeanor, the punishment of which is not specifically provided for by law.

The Radicals, although not a majority of Republicans, gained support as growing numbers of north-

erners grew suspicious of white southern intransigence and the denial of political rights to freedmen. When the Thirty-ninth Congress convened in December 1865, the large Republican majority prevented the seating of the white southerners elected to Congress under President Johnson's provisional state governments. Republicans established the Joint Committee on Reconstruction, including among its members nine representatives and six senators. The committee heard extensive testimony from a broad range of witnesses, including army officers, Freedmen's Bureau agents, southern Unionists, and African Americans. It concluded that not only were old Confederates back in power in the South, but that Black Codes and racial violence directed at African Americans necessitated increased protection for them.

As a result, in the spring of 1866 Congress passed two important bills designed to aid African

Americans. The landmark Civil Rights bill, which bestowed full citizenship upon African Americans, overturned the 1857 Dred Scott decision and the Black Codes. The bill was the first attempt to give meaning to the recently passed Thirteenth Amendment — in effect, to define the essence of freedom. It defined all persons born in the United States (except Indian peoples) as national citizens, and it enumerated various rights, including the rights to make and enforce contracts, to sue, to give evidence, and to buy and sell property. Under this bill, African Americans acquired "full and equal benefit of all laws and proceedings for the security of person and property as is enjoyed by white citizens."

Congress also voted to enlarge the scope of the Freedmen's Bureau, empowering it to build schools and pay teachers, and also to establish courts to prosecute those charged with depriving African Americans of their civil rights. The bureau achieved important, if limited, success in aiding African Americans. Bureau-run schools helped lay the foundation for southern public education. The bureau's network of courts allowed freed people to bring suits against white people in disputes involving violence, nonpayment of wages, or unfair division of crops. Such cases could never have been won in local civil courts controlled by white people. The very existence of courts hearing public testimony by African Americans provided an important psychological challenge to traditional notions of white racial domination.

An angry President Johnson vetoed both of these bills. In opposing the Civil Rights bill, Johnson denounced the assertion of national power to protect African American civil rights, claiming it was a "stride toward centralization, and the concentration of all legislative powers in the national Government." In the case of the Freedmen's Bureau, Johnson argued that Congress lacked jurisdiction over the eleven unrepresented southern states. But Johnson's intemperate attacks on the Radicals — he damned them as traitors unwilling to reunite the Union — rallied the Republicans and they succeeded in overriding the vetoes. Congressional Republicans, led by the Radical faction, were now united in challenging the president's power to direct Reconstruction and in using national authority to define and protect the rights of citizens.

In June 1866, fearful that the Civil Rights Act might be declared unconstitutional and eager to settle the basis for the seating of southern representatives, Congress passed the Fourteenth Amendment. The amendment defined national citizenship to include former slaves ("all persons born or naturalized in the United States") and prohibited the states from violating the privileges of citizens without due process of law. It also empowered Congress to reduce the representation of any state that denied the suffrage to males over twenty-one. Republicans adopted the Fourteenth Amendment as their platform for the 1866 congressional elections and suggested that southern states would have to ratify it as a condition of readmission. President Johnson, meanwhile, took to the stump in August to support conservative Democratic and Republican candidates. Throughout the North, he underscored the South's loyalty and condemned the Radicals' unwillingness to seat southern congressmen. Johnson's unrestrained speeches often degenerated into harangues, alienating many voters and aiding the Republican cause.

For their part, the Republicans skillfully portrayed Johnson and northern Democrats as disloyal and white southerners as unregenerate. Republicans began an effective campaign tradition known as "waving the bloody shirt" — reminding northern voters of the hundreds of thousands of Yankee soldiers left dead or maimed by the war. They praised themselves as saviors of the Union and held Johnson and the South responsible for the failure of Reconstruction. In November 1866 the Republicans captured a two-thirds majority in both the House and the Senate and gained control of all the northern states.

Congressional Reconstruction and the Impeachment Crisis

Flush with electoral victory, Radical Republicans and their moderate allies took control of Reconstruction early in 1867. In March Congress passed the First Reconstruction Act over Johnson's veto. This act divided the South into five military districts subject to martial law. To achieve restoration, southern states were first required to call new constitutional conventions, elected by universal manhood suffrage. Once these states had drafted new constitutions, guaranteed African American voting rights, and ratified the Fourteenth Amendment, they were eligible for readmission to the Union. Supplementary legislation, also passed over the president's veto, invalidated the provisional governments established by Johnson, empowered the military to administer voter registration, and required an oath of loyalty to the United States.

Suspicious that President Johnson would try to

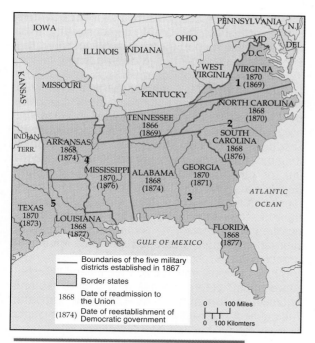

Reconstruction of the South, 1865–1877
Dates for the readmission of southern states to the Union and the return of Democrats to power varied according to the specific political situation in those states.

position and barricaded himself in his office when Johnson attempted to remove him once again.

Outraged by Johnson's relentless obstructionism, and seizing upon his violation of the Tenure of Office Act as a pretext, Republicans in the House of Representatives impeached the president by a vote of 126 to 47 on February 24, 1868. Though some Republicans had sought to impeach Johnson for more than a year, not until February did enough moderates agree to charge Johnson with eleven counts of high crimes and misdemeanors. The articles of impeachment focused on violations of the Tenure of Office Act, leaving unstated the Republicans' real reasons for wanting the president removed: Johnson's political views, his opposition to the Reconstruction Acts, and his incompetence.

Behind the scenes during his Senate trial, Johnson agreed to abide by the Reconstruction Acts. An influential group of moderate Senate Republicans feared the damage a conviction might do to the constitutional separation of powers. They also worried about the political and economic policies that might be pursued by the man who would succeed Johnson — Benjamin Wade, the Radical president pro tem of the Senate. In May, the Senate voted thirty-five for conviction, nineteen for acquittal — one vote shy of the two-thirds necessary for removal from office. Seven moderate Republicans had deserted their party and voted to acquit. Johnson's narrow acquittal established the precedent that only criminal actions by a president — not political disagreements — warranted removal from office.

The Election of 1868

Sobered by the close impeachment vote, Johnson cooperated with Congress for the remainder of his term. One by one the remaining ten unreconstructed southern states (Tennessee had been readmitted to the Union in 1866) revised their constitutions and submitted them to voters. In 1868 seven states (Arkansas, Alabama, Florida, Georgia, Louisiana, North Carolina, and South Carolina) ratified the revised constitutions, elected Republican governments, and ratified the Fourteenth Amendment. Having done so they rejoined the Union. Though Mississippi, Texas, and Virginia still awaited readmission to the Union, the presidential election of 1868 offered some hope that the Civil War's legacy of sectional hate and racial tension might finally ease.

Republicans nominated Ulysses S. Grant, the North's foremost military hero. An Ohio native,

sabotage its harsher plans for the South, Congress passed several laws aimed at limiting his power. One of these, the Tenure of Office Act, stipulated that any officeholder appointed by the president with the Senate's advice and consent could not be removed until the Senate had approved a successor. In this way, congressional leaders could protect Republicans, such as Secretary of War Edwin M. Stanton, entrusted with implementing Congressional Reconstruction. In August 1867, with Congress adjourned, Johnson suspended Stanton and appointed General Ulysses S. Grant interim secretary of war. This enabled the president to remove generals in the field that he judged to be too radical and replace them with men who were sympathetic to his own views. It also served as a challenge to the Tenure of Office Act. In January 1868, when the Senate overruled Stanton's suspension, Grant broke openly with Johnson in a bitter dispute. Stanton resumed his

Grant had graduated from West Point in 1843, served in the Mexican War, and resigned from the army in 1854. Unhappy in civilian life, Grant received a second chance during the Civil War. He rose quickly to become commander in the western theater and he later destroyed Lee's army in Virginia. Although his armies suffered terrible losses, Grant enjoyed tremendous popularity after the war, especially when he broke with Johnson. Totally lacking in political experience, Grant admitted after receiving the nomination that he had been forced into it in spite of himself. "I could not back down without leaving the contest for power for the next four years between mere trading politicians, the elevation of whom, no matter which party won, would lose to us, largely, the results of the costly war which we have gone through."

During the 1868 campaign Republicans vigorously waved the bloody shirt and praised themselves for the fruits of Congressional Reconstruction. Significantly, at the very moment that the South was being forced to enfranchise former slaves as a prerequisite for readmission to the Union, the Republicans rejected a campaign plank endorsing black suffrage in the North. Their platform left "the question of suffrage in all the loyal States . . . to the people of those States." State referendums calling for black suffrage failed in eleven northern states between 1865 and 1868, succeeding only in Iowa and Minnesota. The Democrats, determined to reverse Congressional Reconstruction, nominated Horatio Seymour, former governor of New York and a long-time foe of emancipation and supporter of states' rights. Democrats North and South exploited the race question to garner votes. Their platform blasted the Republicans for subjecting the nation "in time of profound peace, to military despotism and negro supremacy." The party sought "the abolition of the Freedmen's Bureau; and all political instrumentalities designed to secure negro supremacy."

Throughout the South, violence marked the electoral process. The Ku Klux Klan, founded as a Tennessee social club in 1866, emerged as a potent instrument of terror (see the chapter introduction). In Louisiana, Arkansas, Georgia, and South Carolina the Klan threatened, whipped, and murdered black and white Republicans to prevent them from voting. This terrorism enabled the Democrats to carry Georgia and Louisiana, but such tactics ultimately cost the Democrats votes in the North. In the final tally, Grant carried twenty-six of the thirty-four states for an electoral college victory of 214 to 80. But he received a popular majority of less than 53 percent, beating Seymour by only 306,000 votes. Significantly, more than 500,000 African American voters cast their ballots for Grant, demonstrating their overwhelming support for the Republican party. The Republicans also maintained overwhelming majorities in both houses of Congress.

In February 1869, Congress passed the Fifteenth Amendment, providing that "the right of citizens of the United States to vote shall not be abridged . . . on account of race, color, or previous condition of servitude." Noticeably absent was language prohibiting the states from imposing educational, residential, or other qualifications for voting. Moderate Republicans feared that filling these discriminatory loopholes might make it difficult to obtain ratification for the amendment by the required three-quarters of the states. To enhance the chances of ratification, Congress required the three remaining unreconstructed states — Mississippi, Texas, and Virginia — to ratify both the Fourteenth and Fifteenth Amendments before readmission. They did so and rejoined the Union in early 1870. The Fifteenth Amendment was ratified in February 1870. On paper at least, Reconstruction was complete.

Woman Suffrage and Reconstruction

The battles over the political status of African Americans proved an important turning point for women as well. Many women's rights advocates had long been active in the abolitionist movement. During the war, many feminists had actively supported the Union cause through their work in the National Women's Loyal League and the U.S. Sanitary Commission. The Fourteenth and Fifteenth Amendments, which granted citizenship and the vote to freedmen, both inspired and frustrated women's rights activists. For example, Elizabeth Cady Stanton and Susan B. Anthony, two leaders with long involvement in both the antislavery and feminist movements, objected to the inclusion of the word *male* in the Fourteenth Amendment. "If that word 'male' be inserted," Stanton predicted in 1866, "it will take us a century at least to get it out."

Insisting that the causes of the African American vote and women's vote were linked, Stanton, Anthony, and Lucy Stone founded the Equal Rights Association in 1866. The group launched a series of lobbying and petition campaigns to remove racial and sexual restrictions on voting from state constitutions. In Kansas, for example, an old antislavery battlefield, the association vigorously supported two 1867 referendums that would have removed the words *male* and *white* from the state's constitution. But Kansas voters rejected both woman suffrage

Susan B. Anthony (1820–1906) and Elizabeth Cady Stanton (1815–1902), the two most influential leaders of the woman suffrage movement, c. 1870. Anthony and Stanton broke with their longtime abolitionist allies after the Civil War when they opposed the Fifteenth Amendment. They argued that the doctrine of universal manhood suffrage it embodied would give constitutional authority to the claim that men were the social and political superiors of women. As founders of the militant National Woman Suffrage Association, Stanton and Anthony established an independent woman suffrage movement and drew millions of women into public life during the late nineteenth century.

and black suffrage. Throughout the nation, the old abolitionist organizations and the Republican party emphasized passage of the Fourteenth and Fifteenth Amendments and withdrew funds and support from the cause of woman suffrage. Disagreements over these amendments divided woman suffragists into factions that lasted for decades.

The radical wing, led by Stanton and Anthony, opposed the Fifteenth Amendment, arguing that ratification would establish an "aristocracy of sex," enfranchising all men while leaving women without political privileges. They argued for a Sixteenth Amendment that would secure the vote for women. They included racist and elitist arguments in their appeal. They urged "American women of wealth, education, virtue, and refinement" to support the vote for women and oppose the Fifteenth Amendment "if you do not wish the lower orders of Chinese, Africans, Germans, and Irish, with their low ideas of womanhood to make laws for you and your daughters." Other women's rights activists, including Lucy Stone and Frederick Douglass, asserted that "this hour belongs to the Negro." They feared a debate over woman suffrage at the national level would jeopardize passage of the two amendments.

By 1869 woman suffragists had split into two competing organizations. The moderate American Woman Suffrage Association (AWSA), led by Lucy Stone, Julia Ward Howe, and Henry Blackwell, focused on achieving woman suffrage at the state level. It maintained close ties with the Republican party and the old abolitionist networks, worked for the Fifteenth Amendment, and actively sought the support of men. The more radical wing founded the all-female National Woman Suffrage Association (NWSA). For the NWSA, the vote represented only one part of a broad spectrum of goals inherited from the Declaration of Sentiments manifesto adopted at the first women's convention held in 1848 at Seneca Falls (see Chapter 13).

Although women did not win the vote in this period, they did establish an independent suffrage movement that eventually drew millions of women into political life. The NWSA in particular demonstrated that self-government and democratic participation in the public sphere were crucial for women's emancipation. Stanton and Anthony toured the country, speaking to women's audiences and inspiring the formation of suffrage societies. The NWSA's weekly magazine, *Revolution,* became a forum for feminist ideas on divorce laws, unequal pay, women's property rights, and marriage. "The only revolution that we would inaugurate," Elizabeth Cady Stanton told the NWSA in 1870, "is to make woman a self-supporting, dignified, independent, equal partner with man in the state, the church, the home." The failure of woman suffrage after the Civil War was less a result of factional fighting than of the larger defeat of Radical Reconstruction and the ideal of expanded citizenship.

THE MEANING OF FREEDOM

For 4 million slaves, freedom arrived in various ways in different parts of the South. In many areas, slavery had collapsed long before Lee's surrender at Appomattox. In regions far removed from the presence of federal troops, African Americans did not learn of slavery's end until the spring of 1865. But regardless of specific regional circumstances, the meaning of "freedom" would be contested for years to come. The deep desire for independence from white control formed the underlying aspiration of newly freed slaves. For their part, most southern white people sought to restrict the boundaries of that independence. As individuals and as members of communities transformed by emancipation, former slaves struggled to establish economic, political, and cultural autonomy. They built upon the twin pillars of slave culture — the family and the church — to consolidate and expand African American institutions and thereby laid the foundation for the modern African American community.

Emancipation greatly expanded the choices available to African Americans. It helped build confidence in their ability to effect change without deferring to white people. Freedom also meant greater uncertainty and risk. But the vast majority of African Americans were more than willing to take their chances. Many years later, one former Texas slave pondered the question "What I likes bes, to be slave or free?" She answered: "Well, it's dis way. In slavery I owns nothin' and never owns' nothin'. In freedom I's own de home and raise de family. All dat cause me worryment and in slavery I has no worryment, but I takes de freedom."

Moving About

In areas occupied by federal forces, many thousands of slaves had already left home and tasted freedom behind Union lines. But in more remote areas, untouched by fighting, large numbers of slaves waited for their master to confirm their freedom. The Emancipation Proclamation and the military defeat of the Confederacy did not totally wipe out the fear and obedience that masters commanded over their slaves. There were thousands of sharply contrasting stories, many of which revealed the need for freed slaves to confront their owners. One Virginia slave, hired out to another family during the war, had been working in the fields when a friend told her she was now free. "Is dat so?" she exclaimed. Dropping her hoe, she ran the seven miles to her old place, confronted her former mistress, and shouted, "I'se free! Yes, I'se free! Ain't got to work fo' you no mo'. You can't put me in yo' pocket now!" Her mistress burst into tears and ran into the house. That was all the former slave needed to see.

The first impulse of many emancipated slaves was to test their freedom. The simplest, most obvious way to do this involved leaving home. By walking off a plantation, coming and going without restraint or fear of punishment, African Americans could savor the taste of freedom. Throughout the

"Leaving for Kansas," *Harper's Weekly,* May 17, 1879. This drawing depicts a group of southern freedpeople on their way to Kansas. Black disillusionment following the end of Reconstruction led thousands of African Americans to migrate to Kansas, where they hoped to find the political rights, economic opportunities, and freedom from violence denied them in the South. Most of these "Exodusters" (after the biblical story of the Israelite Exodus from Egypt) lacked the capital or experience to establish themselves as independent farmers on the Great Plains. Yet few chose to return to the South where their former masters had returned to political and economic power.

summer and fall of 1865, observers in the South noted the enormous numbers of freed people on the move. One former slave squatting in an abandoned tent outside Selma, Alabama, explained his feeling to a northern journalist: "I's want to be free man, cum when I please, and nobody say nuffin to me, nor order me roun'." When urged to stay on with the South Carolina family she had served for years as a cook, a slave woman replied firmly: "No, Miss, I must go. If I stay here I'll never know I am free." In northern Florida, Richard Edwards, a black preacher, expressed the widely held belief in testing freedom by moving. He told a large crowd of former slaves:

> You ain't, none o' you, gwinter feel rale free till you shakes de dus' ob de Ole Plantashun offen yore feet an' goes ter a new place whey you kin live out o' sight o' de gret house. So long ez de shadder ob de gret house falls acrost you, you ain't gwine ter feel lak no free man, an' you ain't gwine ter feel lak no free 'oman. You mus' all move—you mus' move clar away from de ole places what you knows, ter de new places what you don't know, whey you kin raise up yore head douten no fear o' Marse Dis ur Marse Tudder. Go whey you please—do what you please—furgit erbout de white folks.

Yet many who left their old neighborhoods returned soon afterwards to seek work in the general vicinity, or even on the plantation they had left. Many wanted to separate themselves from former owners, but not from familial ties and friendships. Others moved away altogether, seeking jobs in nearby towns and cities. A large number of former slaves left predominantly white counties, where they felt more vulnerable and isolated, for new lives in the relative comfort of predominantly black communities. In most southern states, there was a significant population shift toward black belt plantation counties and towns after the war. Many African Americans, attracted by schools, churches, and fraternal societies as well as the army, preferred the city. Between 1865 and 1870, the African American population of the South's largest ten cities doubled while the white population increased by only 10 percent.

Disgruntled planters had difficulty accepting African American independence. During slavery, they had expected obedience, submission, and loyalty from African Americans. Now, many could not understand why so many former slaves wanted to leave despite urgent pleas to continue working at the old place. The deference and humility white people expected from African Americans could no longer be taken for granted. Indeed, many freed people went out of their way to reject the old subservience. Moving about freely was one way of doing this, as was refusing to tip one's hat to white people, ignoring former masters or mistresses in the streets, and refusing to step aside on sidewalks. After encountering an African American who would not step aside, Eliza Andrews, a Georgia plantation mistress, complained, "It is the first time in my life that I have ever had to give up the sidewalk to a man, much less to negroes!" When freed people staged parades, dances, and picnics, as they did, for example, when commemorating the Emancipation Proclamation, white people invariably expressed anger. Yet what the white South termed "insolence," "outrageous spectacles," or "putting on airs" were more often than not simply celebrations by former slaves of their new freedom.

The African American Family

Emancipation allowed freed people the chance to strengthen family ties that had existed under slavery. For many former slaves, freedom meant the opportunity to reunite with long-lost family members. To track down relatives, freed people trekked to faraway places, put ads in newspapers, sought the help of Freedmen's Bureau agents, and questioned anyone who might have information about loved ones. Many thousands of family reunions, each with its own story, took place after the war. To William Curtis of Georgia, whose father had been sold to a Virginia planter, "that was the best thing about the war setting us free, he could come back to us." One North Carolina slave, who had seen his parents separated by sale, recalled many years later what for him had been the most significant aspect of freedom. "I has got thirteen great-gran' chilluns an' I know whar dey ever'one am. In slavery times dey'd have been on de block long time ago."

Slave families once separated because they belonged to different owners could now live together. Thousands of African American couples who had lived together under slavery streamed to military and civilian authorities and demanded to be legally married. By 1870, the two-parent household was the norm for a large majority of African Americans. "In their eyes," a Freedmen's Bureau agent reported, "the work of emancipation was incomplete until the families which had been dispersed by slavery were reunited." For many freed people the attempt to find lost relatives dragged on for years. Searches often proved frustrating, exhausting, and ultimately disappointing. Some "reunions" ended painfully with the discovery that spouses had found new partners and started new families.

Emancipation brought changes to gender roles within the African American family as well. By serving in the Union army, African American men played a more direct role than women in the fight for freedom. In the political sphere, black men could now serve on juries, vote, and hold office; black women, like their white counterparts, could not. Freedmen's Bureau agents designated the husband as household head and established lower wage scales for women laborers. African American editors, preachers, and politicians regularly quoted the biblical injunction that wives submit to their husbands. African American men asserted their male authority, denied under slavery, by insisting their wives work at home instead of in the fields.

For years after 1865, southern planters complained about the scarcity of women and children available for field work. African American women generally wanted to devote more time than they had under slavery to caring for their children and to performing such domestic chores as cooking, sewing, gardening, and laundering. Yet African American women continued to work outside the home, engaging in seasonal field labor for wages or working a family's rented plot. Most rural black families barely eked out a living, and thus the labor of every family member was essential to survival. The key difference from slave times was that African American families themselves, not white masters and overseers, decided when and where women and children worked. Freedom did not bring an end to backbreaking labor, but it did offer the chance for African American families to labor on behalf of their own families and kin.

Labor and Land after Slavery

Most newly emancipated African Americans aspired to quit the plantations and to make new lives for themselves. Some freed people did find jobs in railroad building, mining, ranching, or construction work. Others raised subsistence crops and tended vegetable gardens on squatters' land. In the immediate aftermath of the Civil War, however, white planters tried to retain African Americans as perma-

nent agricultural laborers. Restricting the employment of former slaves was an important goal of the Black Codes. For example, South Carolina legislation in 1865 provided that "no person of color shall pursue or practice the art, trade, or business of an artisan, mechanic, or shopkeeper, or any other trade employment, or business, besides that of husbandry, or that of a servant under contract for service or labor" without a special and costly permit.

The majority of African Americans hoped to become self-sufficient farmers. As *DeBow's Review* observed in 1869, the freedman showed "great anxiety to have his little home, with his horse, cow, and hogs, separate and apart from others." Many former slaves believed they were entitled to the land they had worked throughout their lives. General Oliver O. Howard, chief of the Freedmen's Bureau, observed that many "supposed that the Government [would] divide among them the lands of the conquered owners, and furnish them with all that might be necessary to begin life as an independent farmer." This perception was not merely a wishful fantasy. The Freedmen's Bureau Act of 1865 specifically required that abandoned land be leased for three years in forty-acre lots, with an option to buy. Frequent reference in the Congress and the press to the question of land distribution made the idea of "forty acres and a mule" not just a pipe dream but a matter of serious public debate.

Above all, African Americans sought economic autonomy, and ownership of land promised the most independence. "Give us our own land and we take care of ourselves," was how one former slave saw it. "But widout land, de ole massas can hire us or starve us, as dey please." At a Colored Convention in Montgomery, Alabama, in May 1867, delegates argued that the property now owned by planters had been "nearly all earned by the sweat of our brows, not theirs. It has been forfeited to the government by the treason of its owners, and is liable to be confiscated whenever the Republican Party demands it." But by 1866 the federal government had already pulled back from the various wartime experiments involving the breaking up of large plantations and the leasing of small plots to individual families. President Johnson directed General Howard of the Freedmen's Bureau to evict tens of thousands of freed people settled on confiscated and abandoned land in southeastern Virginia, southern Louisiana, and the Georgia and South Carolina low country. These evictions created a deep sense of betrayal among African Americans. A former Mississippi slave, Merrimon Howard, bitterly noted that African Americans had been left with "no

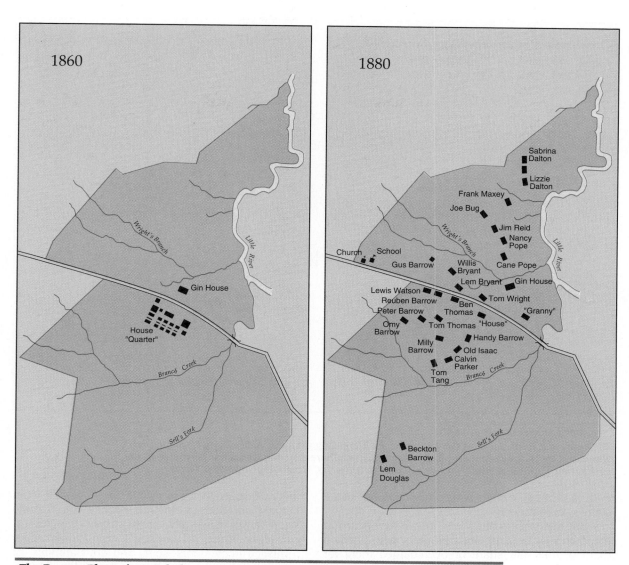

The Barrow Plantation, Oglethorpe County, Georgia, 1860 and 1881 (Appx. 2,000 acres)
These two maps, based on drawings from *Scribner's Monthly,* April 1881, show some of the changes brought by emancipation. In 1860 the plantation's entire black population lived in the communal slave quarters, right next to the white master's house. In 1881 black sharecropper and tenant families lived on individual plots, spread out across the land. The former slaves had also built their own school and church.

land, no house, not so much as a place to lay our head. . . . We were friends on the march, brothers on the battlefield, but in the peaceful pursuits of life it seems that we are strangers.''

A small number of African Americans were able to purchase farmland. But the vast majority lacked the capital to buy or rent land and thus had to hire out as laborers. A system of labor, neither slave nor free, gradually emerged. At first, planters planned to

contract former slaves to work in gangs. In several states, planters secured "enticement" acts to ensure a common wage scale and prevent the development of a free market in labor. The Freedmen's Bureau provided some relief from these and other harsh restrictions on the black work force. Bureau agents helped negotiate labor contracts, usually between planters and large groups of freed slaves. Payment might be made either in standing wages (withheld

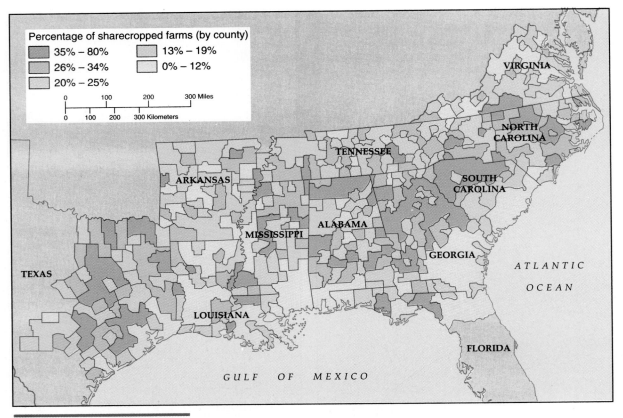

Southern Sharecropping, 1880.
The economic depression of the 1870s forced increasing numbers of southern farmers, both white and black, into sharecropping arrangements. Sharecropping was most pervasive in the cotton belt regions of South Carolina, Georgia, Alabama, Mississippi, and east Texas.

Percentage of sharecropped farms (by county)
- 35% – 80%
- 26% – 34%
- 20% – 25%
- 13% – 19%
- 0% – 12%

until year's end) or share wages, as mentioned in the chapter introduction.

But this system often left African Americans at the mercy of unscrupulous planters who cheated them of their fair share or overcharged them for rations. The African Americans' desire for economic improvement and greater independence led many to revolt against the gang labor system, so reminiscent of slavery. Some black workers preferred to organize themselves into "squads" of a dozen or less. These often included whole families, as well as unrelated men, working under the direction of one of the squad members. The squad system represented an intermediary phase in the decentralization of southern agriculture. By the late 1860s, sharecropping had emerged as the dominant form of working the land.

Sharecropping represented a compromise between planters and former slaves. Under this arrangement, individual families contracted with landowners to be responsible for a specific plot. Large plantations were thus broken into family-sized farms. Generally, sharecropper families received one-third of the year's crop if the owner furnished implements, seed, and draft animals, or one-half if they provided their own supplies. African Americans preferred sharecropping to gang labor, as it allowed families to set their own hours and tasks and offered freedom from white supervision and control. For planters, the system stabilized the work force by requiring sharecroppers to remain until the harvest and to employ all family members. It also offered a way around the chronic shortage of cash and credit that plagued the postwar South. Still, many planters resisted sharecropping as inefficient and considered it a threat to their traditional authority over black labor.

Sharecropping came to dominate the southern agricultural economy and African American life in particular. By 1880 about 80 percent of the land in the black belt states — Mississippi, Alabama, and Georgia — had been divided into family-sized farms. Nearly three-quarters of black southerners were sharecroppers. Through much of the black belt, family and community were one. Often several families worked adjoining parcels of land in common, pooling their labor in order to get by. Men usually oversaw crop production. Women went to the fields seasonally during planting or harvesting, but they mainly tended to household chores and childcare. In addition, women frequently held jobs that might bring in cash, such as raising chickens or taking in laundry. The cotton harvest engaged all members of the community, from the oldest to the youngest. Cotton picking remained a difficult, labor-intensive task that took priority over all other work.

African American Churches and Schools

In the post-Emancipation years African Americans began building institutions that provided the foundations for newly independent communities. The creation of separate African American churches proved the most lasting and important element of this energetic institution building. Before the Civil War southern Protestant churches had relegated slaves and free African Americans to second-class membership. Black worshipers were required to sit in the back during services, they were denied any role in church governance, and they were excluded from Sunday schools. Even in larger cities, where all-black congregations sometimes built their own churches, the law required white pastors. In rural areas, slaves preferred their own preachers to the sermons of local white ministers who quoted Scripture to justify slavery and white supremacy. "That old white preachin' wasn't nothin'," former slave Nancy Williams recalled. "Old white preachers used to talk with their tongues without sayin' nothin', but Jesus told us slaves to talk with our hearts."

In communities around the South, African Americans now pooled their resources to buy land and build their own churches. Before these structures were completed, they might hold services in a railroad boxcar, where Atlanta's First Baptist Church began, or in an outdoor arbor, the original site of the First Baptist Church of Memphis. The first new building erected from the rubble of Charleston was an African American church on Calhoun Street. By late 1866 Charleston's African American community could boast of eleven churches in the city — five Methodist, two Presbyterian, two Episcopalian, one

Baptist, and one Congregational. In rural areas, different denominations frequently shared the same church building. Churches became the center not only for religious life but for many other activities that defined the African American community: schools, picnics, festivals, and political meetings. They also helped spawn a host of organizations devoted to benevolence and mutual aid, such as burial societies, Masonic lodges, temperance clubs, and trade associations.

The church became the first social institution fully controlled by African Americans. In nearly every community ministers, respected for their speaking and organizational skills, were among the most influential leaders. By 1877 the great majority of black southerners had withdrawn from white-dominated churches. In South Carolina, for example, only a few hundred black Methodists attended biracial churches, down from over 40,000 in 1865. The various Protestant denominations competed for the allegiance of African American worshipers. Among Methodists, the African Methodist Episcopal Church gained ascendancy over white-dominated rivals. Black Baptist churches, with their decentralized and democratic structure and more emotional services, attracted the greatest number of freed people. By the end of Reconstruction the vast majority of African American Christians belonged to black Baptist or Methodist churches.

The rapid spread of schools reflected African Americans' thirst for self-improvement. Southern states had prohibited education for slaves. But many free black people managed to attend school and a few slaves had been able to educate themselves. Still, over 90 percent of the South's adult African American population was illiterate in 1860. Access to education thus became a central part of the meaning of freedom. Freedmen's Bureau agents repeatedly expressed amazement at the number of makeshift classrooms organized by African Americans in rural areas. A bureau officer described these "wayside schools": "A negro riding on a loaded wagon, or sitting on a hack waiting for a train, or by the cabin door, is often seen, book in hand delving after the rudiments of knowledge. A group on the platform of a depot, after carefully conning an old spelling book, resolves itself into a class."

African American communities received important educational aid from outside organizations. By 1869 the Freedmen's Bureau was supervising nearly 3,000 schools serving over 150,000 students throughout the South. Over half the roughly 3,300 teachers in these schools were African Americans, many of whom had been free before the Civil War. Other teachers included dedicated northern white women, volunteers sponsored by the American Missionary Association (AMA). The bureau and the AMA also assisted in the founding of several black colleges, including Tougaloo, Hampton, and Fisk, designed to train black teachers. Black self-help proved crucial to the education effort. Throughout the South in 1865 and 1866, African Americans raised money to build schoolhouses, buy supplies, and pay teachers. Black artisans donated labor for construction, and black families offered room and board to teachers. By 1870 black southerners, most of them impoverished, had managed to raise over $1 million for education, a feat that long remained a source of collective pride.

The Origins of African American Politics

Although the desire for autonomy had led African Americans to pursue their economic and religious goals largely apart from white people, inclusion rather than separation formed the keynote of early African American political activity. The most extensive political activity by African Americans occurred in areas occupied by Union forces during the war. In 1865 and 1866, African Americans throughout the South organized scores of mass meetings, parades, and petitions that demanded civil equality and the right to vote. In the cities, the growing web of churches and fraternal societies helped bolster early efforts at political organization. Wilmington, North Carolina, freedmen formed an Equal Rights League in 1865. Worried local white officials noted that the league insisted upon "all the social and political rights of white citizens."

Hundreds of African American delegates, selected by local meetings or churches, attended statewide conventions held throughout the South in 1865 and 1866. Free African Americans and black ministers, artisans, and veterans of the Union Army tended to dominate these proceedings, setting a pattern that would hold throughout Reconstruction. Convention debates sometimes reflected the tensions within African American communities, such as friction between poorer former slaves and better-off free black people, or between lighter- and darker-skinned African Americans. But most of these state gatherings concentrated on passing resolutions on issues that united all African Americans. The central concerns were suffrage and equality

before the law. Black southerners firmly proclaimed their identification with the nation's history and republican traditions. The 1865 North Carolina freedmen's convention was typical in describing universal manhood suffrage as "an essential and inseparable element of self-government." It also praised the Declaration of Independence as "the broadest, the deepest, the most comprehensive and truthful definition of human freedom that was ever given to the world."

The passage of the First Reconstruction Act in 1867 encouraged even more political activity among African Americans. The military started registering the South's electorate, ultimately enrolling approximately 735,000 black and 635,000 white voters in the ten unreconstructed states. Five states — Alabama, Florida, Louisiana, Mississippi, and South Carolina — had black electoral majorities. Fewer than half the registered white voters participated in the elections for state constitutional conventions in 1867 and 1868. In contrast, four-fifths of the registered black voters cast ballots in these elections. Much of this new African American political activism was channeled through local Union League chapters throughout the South.

Begun during the war as a northern, largely middle-class patriotic club, the Union League now became the political voice of the former slaves. Union League chapters brought together local African Americans, soldiers, and Freedmen's Bureau agents to demand the vote and an end to legal discrimination against African Americans. It brought out African American voters, instructed freedmen in the rights and duties of citizenship, and promoted Republican candidates. Not surprisingly, newly enfranchised freedmen voted Republican and formed the core of the Republican party in the South.

In 1867 and 1868, the promise of Radical Reconstruction enlarged the scope of African American political participation and brought new leaders to the fore. In the black belt, local leaders tended to be former slaves of modest means. Many were teachers, preachers, or others possessing useful skills, such as literacy. For most ordinary African Americans, politics was inseparable from economic issues, especially the land question. Grass-roots political organizations frequently intervened in local disputes with planters over the terms of labor contracts. African American political groups closely followed the congressional debates over Reconstruction policy and agitated for land confiscation and distribution. Perhaps most important, politics

"Electioneering at the South," *Harper's Weekly,* July 25, 1868. Throughout the Reconstruction era South, newly freed slaves took a keen interest in both local and national political affairs. The presence of women and children at these campaign gatherings illustrates the importance of contemporary political issues to the entire African American community.

was the only arena where black and white southerners might engage each other on an equal basis. As the delegates to an Alabama convention asserted in 1867:

> We claim exactly the same rights, privileges and immunities as are enjoyed by white men — we ask nothing more and will be content with nothing less. . . . The law no longer knows white nor black, but simply men, and consequently we are entitled to ride in public conveyances, hold office, sit on juries and do everything else which we have in the past been prevented from doing solely on the ground of color.

SOUTHERN POLITICS AND SOCIETY

Most Republican congressmen had conceived of Reconstruction in limited terms. They rejected radical calls for confiscation and redistribution of land, as well as permanent military rule of the South. The Reconstruction Acts of 1867 and 1868 laid out the requirements for the readmission of southern states, along with the procedures for forming and electing new governments. By the summer of 1868, when the South had returned to the Union, the majority of Republicans believed the task of Reconstruction to be finished. Ultimately, they put their faith in a political solution to the problems facing the vanquished South. That meant nurturing a viable two-party system in the southern states, where no Republican party had ever existed. If that could be accomplished, Republicans and Democrats would compete for votes, offices, and influence, just as they did in northern states.

Yet over the next decade the political structure created in the southern states proved too restricted and fragile to sustain itself. Republicans had to employ radical means to protect their essentially conservative goals. To most southern whites the active participation of African Americans in politics seemed extremely dangerous. Federal troops were needed to protect Republican governments and their supporters from violent opposition. Congressional action to monitor southern elections and protect black voting rights became routine. Despite initial successes, southern Republicanism proved an unstable coalition of often conflicting elements, unable to sustain effective power for very long. By 1877, Democrats had regained political control of all the former Confederate states.

Southern Republicans

Three major groups composed the fledgling Republican coalition in the postwar South. African American voters made up a large majority of southern Republicans throughout the Reconstruction era. Yet African Americans outnumbered whites in only three southern states — South Carolina, Mississippi, and Louisiana. They made up roughly one-quarter of the population in Texas, Tennessee, and Arkansas, and between 40 and 50 percent in Virginia, North Carolina, Alabama, Florida, and Georgia. Thus, Republicans would have to attract white support to win elections and sustain power.

A second group consisted of white northerners, derisively called *carpetbaggers* by native white southerners. One Democratic congressman in 1871 said the term "applied to the office seeker from the North who came here seeking office by the negroes, by arraying their political passions and prejudices against the white people of the community." In fact, most carpetbaggers combined a desire for personal gain with a commitment to reform the "unprogressive" South by developing its material resources and introducing Yankee institutions such as free labor and free public schools. Some entered politics only after unsuccessful business ventures. Most were veterans of the Union army who stayed in the South after the war. Others included Freedmen's Bureau agents and businessmen who had invested capital in cotton plantations and other economic enterprises.

Carpetbaggers tended to be well educated and from the middle class. Albert Morgan, for example, was an Army veteran from Ohio who settled in Mississippi after the war. After he and his brother failed at running a cotton plantation and sawmill, Morgan became active in Republican politics as a way to earn a living. He won election to the state constitutional convention, became a power in the state legislature, and risked his life to keep the Republican organization alive in the Mississippi Delta region. Adelbert Ames, a young New Englander who had won the Medal of Honor and risen to brigadier general during the war, headed the Freedmen's Bureau in Mississippi. He became a key force in the state's Republican politics, eventually serving as U.S. senator and governor. Although they made up a tiny percentage of the population, carpetbaggers played a disproportionately large role in southern politics. They won a large share of Reconstruction offices, particularly in Florida, South Carolina, and Louisiana and in areas with large African American constituencies.

The third major group of southern Republicans were the native whites perjoratively termed *scalawags*. They had even more diverse backgrounds and motives than the northern-born Republicans. Some were prominent prewar Whigs who saw the Republican party as their best chance to regain political influence. Others viewed the party as an agent of modernization and economic expansion. "Yankees and Yankee notions are just what we want in this country," argued Thomas Settle of North Carolina. "We want their capital to build factories and workshops. We want their intelligence, their energy and enterprise." Their greatest influence lay in the up-country strongholds of southern Unionism, such as eastern Tennessee, western North Carolina, and northern Alabama. Loyalists during the war, traditional enemies of the planter elite (most were small farmers), these white southerners looked to the Republican party for help in settling old scores and relief from debt and wartime devastation.

Deep contradictions strained the alliance of these three groups. Southern Republicans touted themselves as the "party of progress and civilization," and promised a new era of material progress for the region. Republican state conventions in 1867 and 1868 voiced support for internal improvements, public schools, debt relief, and railroad building. Yet few white southerners identified with the political and economic aspirations of African Americans. Nearly every party convention split between "confiscation radicals" (generally African Americans) and moderate elements committed to white control of the party and to economic development that offered more to outside investors than to impoverished African Americans and poor whites. As in the North, where Democrats gained dramatically in the 1868 elections, the heritage of racism proved difficult to overcome.

Reconstructing the States: A Mixed Record

The First Reconstruction Act required the southern states to write new constitutions before they could be readmitted to Congress. With the old Confederate leaders barred from political participation, and with carpetbaggers and newly enfranchised African Americans representing many of the plantation districts, Republicans managed to dominate the ten southern constitutional conventions of 1867–69. Well-educated carpetbaggers usually chaired the important committees and drafted key provisions of the new constitutions. Southern white Republicans formed the largest number of delegates. African Americans formed a majority of the conventions in Louisiana and South Carolina, but they were generally underrepresented. In all, there were 258 African Americans among the 1,027 convention delegates at the ten conventions.

Most of the conventions produced constitutions that expanded democracy and the public role of the state. The new documents guaranteed the political and civil rights of African Americans, and they abolished property qualifications for officeholding

An 1868 lithograph depicting African Americans elected to the Louisiana constitutional convention and the state assembly, as well as the black lieutenant governor. The majority of the men pictured here were freeborn, rather than former slaves. Prints such as these expressed the pride taken by African American communities in their political leaders and in newly won citizenship rights. Note the special attention given to the equal rights and public education clauses of the new Louisiana constitution.

and jury service, as well as imprisonment for debt. They created the first state-funded systems of education in the South, to be administered by state commissioners. The new constitutions also mandated establishment of orphanages, penitentiaries, and homes for the insane. The changes wrought in the South's political landscape seemed quite radical to many. In 1868, only three years after the end of the war, Republicans came to power in most of the southern states. By 1869 new constitutions had been ratified in all the old Confederate states. "These constitutions and governments," one South Carolina Democratic newspaper vowed bitterly, "will last just as long as the bayonets which ushered them into being, shall keep them in existence, and not one day longer."

Republican governments in the South faced a continual crisis of legitimacy that limited their ability to legislate change. They had to balance reform urges against ongoing efforts to gain acceptance, especially by white southerners. Their achievements were thus mixed. In the realm of race relations there was a clear thrust toward equal rights and against discrimination. Republican legislatures followed up the federal Civil Rights Act of 1866 with various antidiscrimination clauses in new constitutions and laws prescribing harsh penalties for civil rights violations. South Carolina, for example, imposed a fine of $1,000 or a year's imprisonment for owners of businesses that discriminated. While most African Americans supported autonomous African American churches, fraternal societies, and schools, they insisted that the state be color-blind. African Americans could now be employed in police forces and fire departments, serve on juries, school boards, and city councils, and hold public office at all levels of government. Political life and government were the most integrated realms of in southern life.

Segregation, though, became the norm in public school systems. African American leaders often accepted segregation because they feared that insistence upon integrated education might jeopardize funding for the new school systems. They generally agreed with Frederick Douglass's assertion that separate schools were "infinitely superior" to no schools at all. African Americans opposed constitutional language requiring racial segregation in schools. But most were less interested in the abstract ideal of integrated education than in ensuring educational opportunities for their children and employment for African American teachers. Many, in fact, believed all-black schools offered a better chance of securing these goals.

Patterns of discrimination persisted. Demands by African Americans to prohibit segregation in railroad cars, steamboats, theaters, and other public spaces revealed and heightened the divisions within the Republican party. Moderate white Republicans feared such laws would only further alienate potential white supporters. But by the early 1870s, as black influence and assertiveness grew, laws guaranteeing equal access to transportation and public accommodation were passed in many states. By and large, though, civil rights laws were difficult to enforce in local communities.

In economic matters, Republican governments failed to fulfill African Americans' hopes of obtaining land. Few former slaves possessed the cash to buy land in the open market, and they looked to the state for help. As black Republican leader Emanuel Fortune of Florida put it, "We have to purchase land from the Government . . . otherwise we cannot get it." Republicans tried to weaken the plantation and promote black ownership by raising taxes on land. Yet even when state governments seized land for nonpayment of taxes, the property was never used to help create black homesteads. In Mississippi, for example, 6 million acres, or about 20 percent of the land, had been forfeited by 1875. Yet virtually all of it found its way back to the original owners after they paid minimal penalties.

In labor relations, Republican governments did reverse the old pattern of planters using public authority to control the African American labor force. They swept away the remnants of the Black Codes and thus helped protect the rights of farm laborers to move about more freely and bargain for wages.

Republican leaders emphasized the "gospel of prosperity" as the key to improving the economic fortunes of all southerners, black and white. Essentially, they envisioned promoting northern-style capitalist development — factories, large towns, and diversified agriculture — in the South through state aid. Much Republican state lawmaking was devoted to encouraging railroad construction. Between 1868 and 1873 state legislatures passed hundreds of bills promoting railroads. Most of the government aid consisted not of direct cash subsidies but of official endorsements of a company's bonds. This government backing gave railroad companies credibility and helped them raise capital. In exchange, states received liens on railroads as security against defaults on payments to bondholders.

Between 1868 and 1872 the southern railroad

system was rebuilt and over 3,000 new miles of track added, an increase of almost 40 percent. But in spite of all the new laws, it proved impossible to attract significant amounts of northern and European investment capital. The obsession with railroads drew resources from education and other programs. As in the North, it also opened the doors to widespread corruption and bribery of public officials. Finally, the frenzy of railroad promotion soon led to an overextension of credit and to many bankruptcies, saddling Republican governments with enormous debts. Railroad failures eroded public confidence in the Republicans' ability to govern. The "gospel of prosperity" ultimately failed to modernize the economy or solidify the Republican party in the South.

White Resistance and "Redemption"

The emergence of a Republican party in the reconstructed South brought two parties but not a two-party system to the region. The opponents of Reconstruction, the Democrats, refused to acknowledge Republicans' right to participate in southern political life. In their view, the Republican party represented the partisan instrument of the northern Congress, and its support was based primarily upon the votes of former slaves. Since Republicans controlled state governments, this denial of legitimacy meant, in effect, a rejection of state authority itself. The Democrats' position further exacerbated Republican factionalism. In each state, Republicans were split between those who urged conciliation and white acceptance and those who emphasized consolidating the party and military protection.

From 1870 to 1872 a resurgent Ku Klux Klan fought an ongoing terrorist campaign against Reconstruction governments and local leaders. Although not centrally organized, the Klan was a powerful presence in nearly every southern state. It acted as a kind of guerrilla military force in the service of the Democratic party, the planter class, and all those who sought the restoration of white supremacy. Klansmen employed violence to intimidate African Americans and white Republicans, murdering innocent people, driving them from their homes, and destroying their property. Planters sometimes employed Klansmen to enforce labor discipline by driving African Americans off plantations to deprive them of their harvest share.

In October 1870, after Republicans carried Laurens County in South Carolina, bands of white people drove 150 African Americans from their homes and committed 13 murders. The victims included both black and white Republican activists. In March 1871, three African Americans were arrested in Meridian, Mississippi, for giving "incendiary" speeches. At their court hearing, Klansmen killed two of the defendants and the Republican judge, and 30 more African Americans were murdered in a day of rioting. In Jackson County, Florida, Klansmen killed over 150 people in a reign of terror lasting three years. One former Confederate officer observed that the Klan's goal was "to defy the reconstructed State Governments, to treat them with contempt, and show that they have no real existence." The single bloodiest episode of Reconstruction era violence took place in Colfax, Louisiana, on Easter Sunday 1873. Nearly 100 African Americans were murdered, most in cold blood, after they failed to hold a beseiged courthouse during a contested election.

Southern Republicans looked to Washington for help. In 1870 and 1871 Congress passed three Enforcement Acts designed to counter racial terrorism. These declared interference with voting a federal offense, provided for federal supervision of voting, and authorized the president to send the army and suspend the writ of habeas corpus in districts declared to be in a state of insurrection. The most sweeping measure was the Ku Klux Klan Act of April 1871, which made the violent infringement of civil and political rights a federal crime punishable by the national government. Attorney General Amos T. Akerman prosecuted hundreds of Klansmen in North Carolina and Mississippi. In October 1871 President Grant sent federal troops to occupy nine South Carolina counties and round up thousands of Klan members. By the election of 1872 the federal government's intervention had helped break the Klan's hold and restored relative law and order. The Civil Rights Act of 1875 outlawed racial discrimination in theaters, hotels, railroads, and other public places. But the law proved more an assertion of principle than a direct federal intervention in Southern affairs. Enforcement required African Americans to take their cases to the federal courts, a costly and time-consuming procedure.

As wartime idealism faded, northern Republicans became less inclined toward direct intervention in southern affairs. They had enough trouble retaining political control in the North. In 1874 the Democrats gained a majority in the House of Representatives for the first time since 1856. Key northern states also began to fall to the Democrats. Northern Republicans slowly abandoned the freedmen and their white allies in the South. These developments

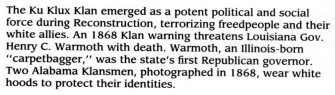

The Ku Klux Klan emerged as a potent political and social force during Reconstruction, terrorizing freedpeople and their white allies. An 1868 Klan warning threatens Louisiana Gov. Henry C. Warmoth with death. Warmoth, an Illinois-born "carpetbagger," was the state's first Republican governor. Two Alabama Klansmen, photographed in 1868, wear white hoods to protect their identities.

pointed to a clear retreat from the ideals of Congressional Reconstruction. In the southern states, Democrats were also able to exploit a deepening fiscal crisis by blaming Republicans for excessive extension of public credit and the sharp increase in tax rates. Before the war, planters had not paid very much in the way of property taxes. And Republican governments had indeed spent more public money for new state school systems, orphanages, roads, and other internal improvements.

Gradually, conservative Democrats "redeemed" one state after another (see map on p. 519). Virginia led the way in 1869, followed by Alabama and North Carolina in 1870, Georgia in 1871, Texas in 1873, and Arkansas in 1874. In Mississippi white conservatives employed violence

and intimidation to wrest control in 1875 and "redeemed" the state the following year. Republican infighting in Louisiana in 1873 and 1874 led to a series of contested election results, including bloody clashes between black militia and armed whites, and finally to "redemption" by the Democrats in 1877. Once under Democratic control, African Americans in these states faced obstacles to voting, more stringent controls on plantation labor, and deep cuts in social services. "Redemption" signaled the demise of Congressional Reconstruction.

Several Supreme Court rulings involving the Fourteenth and Fifteenth Amendments effectively constrained federal protection of African American civil rights. In the so-called Slaughterhouse cases of 1873, the Court issued its first ruling on the Fourteenth Amendment. The cases involved a Louisiana charter that gave a New Orleans meat-packing company a monopoly over the city's butchering business, on the grounds of protecting public health. A rival group of butchers had sued, claiming the law violated the Fourteenth Amendment, which prohibited states from depriving any person of life, liberty, or property without due process of law. The Court held that the Fourteenth Amendment protected only the former slaves, not butchers, and that it protected only *national* citizenship rights, not the regulatory powers of states. The ruling in effect denied the original intent of the Fourteenth Amendment — to protect against state infringement of national citizenship rights as spelled out in the Bill of Rights.

Three other decisions curtailed federal protection of black civil rights. In *U.S. v. Reese* (1876) and *U.S. v. Cruikshank* (1876) the Court restricted congressional power to enforce the Ku Klux Klan Act. Future prosecution would depend on the states rather than on federal authorities. In these rulings the Court held that the Fourteenth Amendment extended the federal power to protect civil rights only in cases involving discrimination by states; discrimination by individuals or groups was not covered. The Court also ruled that the Fifteenth Amendment did not guarantee a citizen's right to vote; it only barred certain specific grounds for denying suffrage — "race, color, or previous condition of servitude." This opened the door for southern states to disfranchise African Americans for allegedly nonracial reasons. States back under Democratic control began to limit African American voting by passing laws restricting voter eligibility through poll taxes and property requirements. "Grandfather clauses," which restricted voting to those descended from a grandfather who had voted, became an effective tool for limiting black suffrage, since most African Americans had been slaves before Reconstruction. Finally, in the 1883 *Civil Rights Cases* decision, the Court declared the Civil Rights Act of 1875 unconstitutional, holding that the federal government had no power to protect social, as opposed to political, rights. Together, these Supreme Court decisions marked the end of federal attempts to protect African American rights until well into the next century.

"King Cotton"

The Republicans' vision of a "New South" remade along the lines of the northern economy failed to materialize. Instead, the South declined into the country's poorest agricultural region. The Civil War had set the stage for a new order based on free labor, but the racial caste system specific to the South, as well as the economic plight of the region as a whole, succeeded rather in shoring up the old plantation system. If the South had previously been *undeveloped,* a rural society with few public services or even adequate transportation, it was now *underdeveloped,* hopelessly in debt to northern merchants and unable to end its reliance upon a single cash crop, cotton.

The spread of the crop lien system as the South's main form of agricultural credit forced more and more farmers, both white and black, into cotton growing. A chronic shortage of capital and banking institutions made local merchants and planters the sole source of credit. They advanced loans to sharecroppers and tenant farmers only in exchange for a lien, or claim, on the year's cotton crop. Merchants and planters frequently charged usurious interest rates on advances, as well as marking up the prices of the goods they sold in their stores. Taking advantage of the high illiteracy rates among poor southerners, landlords and merchants easily altered their books to inflate the figures. At the end of the year, sharecroppers and tenants found themselves deep in debt to stores (many owned by northerners) for seed, supplies, and clothing. Despite hard work and even bountiful harvests, few small farmers could escape from heavy debt.

The near total dominance of "King Cotton" inhibited economic growth across the region. Unlike midwestern and western farm towns burgeoning from trade in wheat, corn, and livestock, southern communities found themselves almost entirely dependent upon the price of one commodity. A Mississippi farmer complained in 1874 that in his community, "the culture of everything but cotton has either been abandoned or greatly curtailed." An economist analyzing southern agriculture compared cotton's power to that of a tyrant. "The majority of cotton growers, including the greater part of the tenant farmers and small land owners, as well as some of the large planters, are bound to cotton by a law as inexorable as any ever promulgated by the most despotic earthly governments."

As more and more farmers turned to cotton growing as the only way to obtain credit, expanding production depressed prices. Competition from new cotton centers in the world market, such as Egypt and India, furthered the downward spiral. As cotton prices declined alarmingly, from roughly eleven cents per pound in 1875 to five cents in 1894, per capita wealth in the South fell steadily, equaling only one-third that of the East, Midwest, or West by the 1890s. Cotton dependency had other repercussions. The planters lacked capital to purchase the farm equipment needed to profitably cultivate wheat or corn, and their reliance on cheap labor kept them wedded to cotton. Planters persisted in employing hand labor and mule power. As soil depletion took its toll, crop outputs, or yields per acre, either remained steady or fell.

By 1880, about one-third of the white farmers and nearly three-quarters of the African American farmers in the cotton states were sharecroppers or tenants. Of the roughly 1.1 million farms in the nine large cotton-planting states that year, sharecroppers worked 301,000 of them. Many former slaves and poor white people had tried subsistence farming in the undeveloped backcountry. Yet to obtain precious credit, most found themselves forced to produce cotton for market and thus became enmeshed in the debt-ridden crop lien system. A cotton-dominated commercial agriculture, with landless tenants and sharecroppers as the main work force, had replaced the more diversified subsistence economy of the antebellum era.

RECONSTRUCTING THE NORTH

Abraham Lincoln liked to cite his own rise as proof of the superiority of the northern system of "free labor" over slavery. "There is no permanent class of hired laborers amongst us," Lincoln asserted. "Twenty-five years ago, I was a hired laborer. The hired laborer of yesterday, labors on his own account today; and will hire others to labor for him tomorrow. Advancement — improvement in condition — is the order of things in a society of equals." But the triumph of the North brought with it fundamental changes in the economy, labor relations, and politics that brought Lincoln's ideal vision into question. The spread of the factory system, the growth of large and powerful corporations, and the rapid expansion of capitalist enterprise all hastened the development of a large unskilled and routinized work force. Rather than becoming independent producers, more and more workers found themselves consigned to a permanent position of wage labor.

The old Republican ideal of a society bound by a harmony of interests had become overshadowed by a grimmer reality of class conflict. A violent national railroad strike in 1877 was broken only with the direct intervention of federal troops. That conflict struck many Americans as a turning point. Northern society, like the society of the South, appeared more hierarchical than equal. That same year, the last federal troops withdrew from their southern posts, marking the end of the Reconstruction era. By then, the North had undergone its own "reconstruction" as well.

The Age of Capital

In the decade following Appomattox, the North's economy continued the industrial boom begun during the Civil War. By 1873, America's industrial production had grown 75 percent over the 1865 level. By that time too, the number of nonagricultural workers in the North had surpassed the number of farmers. Between 1860 and 1880 the number of wage earners in manufacturing and construction more than doubled, from 2 million to over 4 million. Only Great Britain boasted a larger manufacturing economy than the U.S. During the same period, nearly 3 million immigrants arrived in America, almost all of whom settled in the North and West.

The railroad business both symbolized and advanced the new industrial order. Between 1865 and 1873, railroad companies laid 35,000 miles of track, as much as the entire system had boasted in 1860. In a lavish 1869 ceremony, officials of the Union Pacific and Central Pacific railroads hammered a golden spike at Promontory Point, Utah, marking the finish of the first transcontinental line. The transportation revolution that had begun with the road and canal building of the early nineteenth century was now complete. Railroads paved the way for the rapid settlement of the West, and both rural and urban areas grew dramatically over the next several decades. The combined population of Minnesota, the Dakotas, Nebraska, and Kansas jumped from 300,000 in 1860 to over 2 million in 1880.

Railroad corporations became America's first big businesses. Railroads required huge outlays of investment capital, and their growth increased the economic power of banks and investment houses centered in Wall Street. Bankers often gained seats on boards of directors, and their access to capital sometimes gave them the real control of lines. By the early 1870s the Pennsylvania Railroad stood as the nation's largest single company, with over 20,000 employees. A new breed of aggressive entrepreneur sought to ease cutthroat competition by

Completion of the transcontinental railroad, May 10, 1869, as building crews for the Union Pacific and Central Pacific meet at Promontory, Utah. The two locomotive engineers exchange champagne toasts, while the chief engineers for the two railroads shake hands. Construction had begun simultaneously from Omaha and Sacramento in 1863, with the help of generous subsidies from the Congress. Work crews, consisting of thousands of ex-soldiers, Irish immigrants, and imported Chinese laborers, laid nearly 1800 miles of new track.

absorbing smaller companies and forming "pools" that set rates and divided the market. A small group of railroad executives, including Cornelius Vanderbilt, Jay Gould, Collis P. Huntington, and James J. Hill amassed unheard-of fortunes. When he died in 1877, Vanderbilt left his son $100 million. By comparison, a decent annual wage for working a six-day week was around $350.

A growing number of Republican politicians maintained close connections with railroad interests. Railroad promoters, lawyers, and lobbyists became ubiquitous figures in Washington and state capitals, wielding enormous influence among lawmakers. "The galleries and lobbies of every legislature," one Republican leader noted, "are thronged with men seeking . . . an advantage." Railroads benefited enormously from government subsidies. Between 1862 and 1872 Congress alone awarded over 100 million acres of public lands to railroad companies and provided over $64 million in loans and tax incentives.

Some of the nation's most prominent politicians routinely accepted railroad largesse. Republican senator William M. Stewart of Nevada, a member of the Committee on the Pacific Railroad, received a gift of 50,000 acres of land from the Central Pacific for his services. Republican senator Lyman Trumbull of Illinois took an annual retainer from the Illinois Central. The worst scandal of the Grant administration grew out of corruption involving railroad promotion. As a way of diverting funds for the building of the Union Pacific Railroad, an inner circle of Union Pacific stockholders created the dummy Crédit Mobilier construction company. In return for political favors, a group of prominent Republicans received stock in the company. When the scandal broke in

1872, it ruined Vice-President Schuyler Colfax politically and led to the censure of two congressmen.

Other industries also boomed in this period, especially those engaged in extracting minerals and processing natural resources. Railroad growth stimulated expansion in the production of coal, iron, stone, and lumber, and these also received significant government aid. For example, under the National Mineral Act of 1866, mining companies received millions of acres of free public land. Oil refining enjoyed a huge expansion in the 1860s and 1870s. As with railroads, an early period of fierce competition soon gave way to concentration. By the late 1870s John D. Rockefeller's Standard Oil Company controlled almost 90 percent of the nation's oil-refining capacity. The production of pig iron tripled from 1 million tons in 1865 to 3 million tons in 1873. Between 1869 and 1879 both the capital investment and the number of workers in iron nearly doubled. Coal production shot up from 17 million tons in 1861 to 72 million tons in 1880. The size of individual iron works and coal mines — measured by the number of employees and capital invested — also grew in these years, reflecting the expanding scale of industrial enterprise as a whole.

Liberal Republicans and the Election of 1872

Like its southern counterpart, the Republican party in the North also found itself deeply divided by factionalism. With the rapid growth of large-scale, capital-intensive enterprises, Republicans increasingly identified with the interests of business rather than the rights of freedmen or the antebellum ideology of "free labor." The old Civil War era Radicals had declined in influence. Thaddeus Stevens died in 1868, and many other prominent Radicals had lost their congressional seats by 1871. State Republican parties now organized themselves around the spoils of federal patronage rather than grand causes such as preserving the Union or ending slavery. Despite the Crédit Mobilier affair, Republicans had no monopoly on political scandal. In 1871 New York City newspapers reported the shocking story of how Democratic party boss William M. Tweed and his friends had systematically stolen tens of millions from the city treasury. The Tweed Ring had received enormous bribes and kickbacks from city contractors and businessmen. But to many, the scandal represented only the most extreme case of the routine corruption that now plagued American political life.

By the end of President Grant's first term, a large number of disaffected Republicans sought an alternative. They were led by a small but influential number of intellectuals, professionals, businessmen, and reformers who articulated an ideology that helped reshape late-nineteenth-century politics. The Liberal Republicans, as they called themselves, shared several core values. First, they emphasized the doctrines of classical economics, stressing the law of supply and demand, free trade, defense of property rights, and individualism. They called for a return to limited government, arguing that bribery, scandal, and high taxes all flowed from excessive state interference in the economy. "The Government," wrote E. L. Godkin, editor of *The Nation,* "must get out of the 'protective' business and the 'subsidy' business and the 'improvement' and 'development' business. . . . It cannot touch them without breeding corruption."

Liberal Republicans were also suspicious of expanding democracy. "Universal suffrage," Charles Francis Adams, Jr., wrote in 1869, "can only mean in plain English the government of ignorance and vice — it means a European, and especially Celtic, proletariat on the Atlantic coast, an African proletariat on the shores of the Gulf, and a Chinese proletariat on the Pacific." Liberal Republicans believed that politics ought to be the province of "the best men" — educated and well-to-do men like themselves, devoted to the "science of government." They proposed civil service reform as the best way to break the hold of party machines on patronage. Competitive examinations, they argued, were the best way to choose employees for government posts. At a time when only a very small fraction of Americans attended college, this would severely restrict the pool of government workers.

Although most Liberal Republicans had enthusiastically supported abolition, the Union cause, and equal rights for freedmen, they now opposed continued federal intervention in the South. The national government had done all it could for the former slaves; they must now take care of themselves. "Root, Hog, or Die" was the harsh advice offered by Horace Greeley, editor of the *New York Tribune.* In the spring of 1872 a diverse collection of Liberal Republicans nominated Greeley to run for president. A longtime foe of the Democratic party, Greeley nonetheless won that party's presidential nomination as well. He made a new policy for the South the center of his campaign against Grant. The "best men" of both sections, he argued, should support a more generous Reconstruction policy based on "universal amnesty and impartial suffrage." All Americans, Greeley urged, must put the Civil War behind them and "clasp hands across the bloody chasm."

Grant easily defeated Greeley, carrying every state in the North and winning 56 percent of the popular vote. Most Republicans were not willing to abandon the regular party organization, and waving the bloody shirt was still a potent vote getter. But the 1872 election accelerated the trend toward federal abandonment of African American citizenship rights. The Liberal Republicans quickly faded as an organized political force. But their ideas helped define a growing conservative consciousness among the northern public. For the rest of the century, their political and economic views attracted a growing number of middle-class professionals and businessmen. This agenda included retreat from the ideal of racial justice, fear of trade unions, suspicion of working-class and immigrant political power, celebration of competitive individualism, and opposition to government intervention in economic affairs.

The Depression of 1873

In the fall of 1873 the postwar boom came to an abrupt halt as a severe financial panic triggered a deep economic depression. The collapse resulted from commercial overexpansion, especially speculative investing in the nation's railroad system. The investment banking house of Jay Cooke and Company failed in September 1873 when it found itself unable to market millions of dollars in Northern Pacific Railroad bonds. Soon other banks and brokerage houses, especially those dealing in railroad securities, caved in as well, and the New York Stock Exchange suspended operations. By 1876 half the nation's railroads had defaulted on their bonds. Over the next two years over 100 banks folded and 18,000 businesses shut their doors. The depression that began in 1873 lasted 65 months — the longest economic contraction in the nation's history.

The human toll of the depression was enormous. As factories began to close across the nation, the unemployment rate soared to about 15 percent. In many cities the jobless rate was much higher; roughly one-quarter of New York City workers were unemployed in 1874. "The sufferings of the working classes are daily increasing," wrote one Philadelphia worker in the summer of 1875. "Famine has broken into the home of many of us, and is at the door of all." Many thousands of men took to the road in search of work, and the "tramp" emerged as a new and menacing figure on the social landscape. The Pennsylvania Bureau of Labor Statistics noted that never before had "so many of the working classes, skilled and unskilled . . . been moving from place to place seeking employment that was not to be had." Farmers were also hard hit by the depression. Agricultural output continued to grow, but prices and land values fell sharply. The commodity

"The Tramp," *Harper's Weekly*, September 2, 1876. The Depression of 1873 forced many thousands of unemployed workers to go "on the tramp" in search of jobs. Men wandered from town to town, walking or riding railroad cars, desperate for a chance to work for wages, or simply room and board. The "tramp" became a powerful symbol of the misery caused by industrial depression, and, as in this drawing, an image that evoked fear and nervousness among the nation's middle class.

price index plummeted from 81 in 1874 to 59 in 1877. As prices for their crops fell, farmers had a more difficult time repaying their fixed loan obligations; many sank deeper into debt.

During the winter of 1873, New York labor leaders demanded to know what measures would be taken "to relieve the necessities of the 10,000 homeless and hungry men and women of our city whose urgent appeals have apparently been disregarded by our public servants." Mass meetings of workers in New York and other cities issued calls to government officials to create jobs through public works. But these appeals were rejected. Indeed, many business leaders and political figures denounced even meager efforts at charity. E. L. Godkin wrote in the Christmas 1875 issue of *The Nation* that "free soup must be prohibited, and all classes must learn that soup of any kind, beef or turtle, can be had only by being paid for." Men such as Godkin saw the depression as a natural, if painful, part of the business cycle, one that would allow only the strongest enterprises (and workers) to survive. They dismissed any attempts at government interference, in the form of either job creation or poor relief. The American Social Science Association, in a special report on "pauperism," went so far as to blame "indiscriminate" and "over-generous" private relief for encouraging laziness and labor unrest.

Increased tensions, sometimes violent, between labor and capital reinforced the feeling of many Americans that the nation was no longer immune from European-style class conflict. The depression of the 1870s prompted workers and farmers to question the old free-labor ideology that celebrated a harmony of interests in northern society. More people voiced anger at and distrust of large corporations that exercised great economic power from outside their communities. Businessmen and merchants, meanwhile, especially in large cities, became more conscious of their own class interests. New political organizations such as Chicago's Citizens' Association united businessmen in campaigns for fiscal conservatism and defense of property rights. In national politics, the persistent depression made the Republican party, North and South, more vulnerable than ever.

The Electoral Crisis of 1876

With the economy mired in depression, Democrats looked forward to capturing the White House in 1876. New scandals plaguing the Grant administration also weakened the Republican party. In 1875 there surfaced a conspiracy between distillers and U.S. revenue agents to cheat the government out of millions in tax revenues. The government secured indictments against over 200 members of this "Whiskey Ring," including Orville E. Babcock, Grant's private secretary. Though acquitted thanks to Grant's deposition, Babcock resigned in disgrace. In 1876, Secretary of War William W. Belknap was impeached for receiving bribes for the sale of trading posts in Indian Territory.

Though Grant himself was never implicated in any wrongdoing, Democrats hammered away at his administration's low standard of honesty in government. For president they nominated Governor Samuel J. Tilden of New York, who brought impeccable reform credentials to his candidacy. In 1871 he had helped expose and prosecute the Tweed Ring in New York City. As governor he had toppled the Canal Ring, a graft-ridden scheme involving inflated contracts for repairs on the Erie Canal. In their platform, the Democrats linked the issue of corruption to an attack on Reconstruction policies. They blamed the Republicans for instituting "a corrupt centralism" that subjected southern states to "the rapacity of carpetbag tyrannies," riddled the national government "with incapacity, waste, and fraud," and "locked fast the prosperity of an industrious people in the paralysis of hard times."

Republican nominee Rutherford B. Hayes, governor of Ohio, also sought the high ground. As a lawyer in Cincinnati he had defended runaway slaves. Later he had distinguished himself as a general in the Union army. Republicans charged Tilden with disloyalty during the war, income tax evasion, and close relations with powerful railroad interests. Their platform branded the Democrat party "unworthy, recreant, and incapable," the "same in character and spirit as when it sympathized with treason." Hayes promised, if elected, to support an efficient civil service system, to vigorously prosecute officials who betrayed the public trust, and to introduce a system of free universal education.

On an Election Day marred by widespread vote fraud and violent intimidation, Tilden received 250,000 more popular votes than Hayes. But Republicans refused to concede victory, challenging the vote totals in the electoral college. Tilden garnered 184 uncontested electoral votes, one shy of the majority required to win, while Hayes received 165. The problem centered in 20 disputed votes from Florida, Louisiana, South Carolina, and Oregon. In each of the three southern states two sets of electoral votes were returned. In Oregon, which Hayes

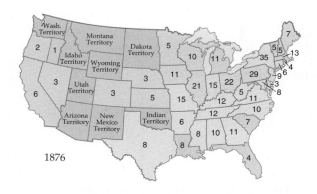

1876

Candidates (Party)	Uncontested electoral vote	Electoral vote	Popular vote
Rutherford B. Hayes (Republican)	165	185	4,034,311 (48%)
Samuel J. Tilden (Democratic)	184	184	4,288,546 (51%)
Peter Cooper (Greenback)	–	–	75,973 (1%)
Disputed			

The Election of 1876
The Presidential election of 1876 left the nation without a clear-cut winner.

had unquestionably carried, the Democratic governor illegally replaced a Republican elector with a Democrat.

The crisis was unprecedented. In January 1877 Congress moved to settle the deadlock, establishing an Electoral Commission composed of five senators, five representatives, and five Supreme Court justices; eight were Republicans and seven were Democrats. The commission voted along strict partisan lines to award all the contested electoral votes to Hayes. Outraged by this decision, Democratic congressmen threatened a filibuster to block Hayes's inauguration. Some Democrats warned ominously of another civil war if Tilden was cheated out of his victory. Violence and stalemate were avoided when Democrats and Republicans struck a compromise in February. In return for Hayes's ascendance to the presidency, the Republicans promised to appropriate more money for southern internal improvements, to appoint a southerner to Hayes's cabinet, and to pursue a policy of noninterference ("home rule") in southern affairs.

Shortly after assuming office, Hayes ordered removal of the remaining federal troops in Louisiana and South Carolina. Without this military presence to sustain them, the Republican governors of those two states quickly lost power to Democrats. "Home rule" meant Republican abandonment of freedpeople, Radicals, carpetbaggers, and scalawags. It also effectively nullified the Fourteenth and Fifteenth Amendments and the Civil Rights Act of 1866. The "Compromise of 1877" completed repudiation of the idea, born during the Civil War and pursued during Congressional Reconstruction, of a powerful federal government protecting the rights of all American citizens. As one black Louisianan lamented, "The whole South—every state in the South—had got into the hands of the very men that held us slaves." Other voices hailed this turning point in policy. "The negro," declared *The Nation,* "will disappear from the field of national politics. Henceforth, the nation, as a nation, will have nothing more to do with him."

CONCLUSION

Reconstruction succeeded in the limited political sense of reuniting a nation torn apart by civil war. But the end of Reconstruction left the way open for the return of white domination in the South. The freedpeople's political and civil equality proved only temporary. It would take a "Second Reconstruction," the civil rights movement of the next century, to establish full black citizenship rights once and for all. The federal government's failure to pursue land reform left former slaves without the economic independence needed for full emancipation. Yet the newly autonomous black family, along with black-controlled churches, schools, and other social institutions, provided the foundations for the modern African American community. If the federal government was not yet fully committed to protecting equal rights in local communities, the Reconstruction era at least pointed to how that goal might be achieved.

Even as the federal government retreated from the defense of equal rights for black people, it took a more aggressive stance as the protector of business interests. The Hayes administration responded decisively to one of the worst outbreaks of class violence in American history by dispatching federal troops to several northern cities to break the Great Railroad Strike of 1877. In the aftermath of Reconstruction, the struggle between capital and labor had clearly replaced "the southern question" as the number one political issue of the day. "The overwhelming labor question has dwarfed all other questions into nothing," wrote an Ohio Republican. "We have *home* questions enough to occupy attention now."

CHRONOLOGY

1865	Abraham Lincoln assassinated
	Andrew Johnson begins Presidential Reconstruction
	Thirteenth Amendment ratified
	Freedmen's Bureau established
	Black Codes enacted in southern states
1866	Congress approves Fourteenth Amendment
	Civil Rights Act passed
	Ku Klux Klan founded
1867	Reconstruction Acts, passed over President Johnson's veto, begin Congressional Reconstruction
	Tenure of Office Act
	Southern states call constitutional conventions
1868	President Johnson impeached by the House, but acquitted in Senate trial
	Fourteenth Amendment ratified
	Most southern states readmitted to Union
	Ulysses S. Grant elected president
1869	Congress approves Fifteenth Amendment
	National Woman Suffrage Association founded
1870	Ratification of Fifteenth Amendment
1871	Ku Klux Klan Act passed
	Tweed Ring in New York City exposed
1872	Liberal Republicans break with Grant and Radicals, nominate Horace Greeley for president
	Crédit Mobilier scandal
	Grant reelected president
1873	Financial panic and beginning of economic depression
	Slaughterhouse cases
1874	Democrats gain control of House for first time since 1856
1875	Civil Rights Act
1876	Disputed election between Samuel Tilden and Rutherford Hayes
1877	Electoral Commission elects Hayes president
	Hayes dispatches federal troops to break Great Railroad Strike

Additional Readings

MICHAEL LES BENEDICT, *The Impeachment and Trial of Andrew Johnson* (1973). The best history of the impeachment crisis.

ELLEN CAROL DuBois, *Feminism and Suffrage* (1978). Analyzes the emergence of an independent woman suffrage movement in the context of Reconstruction politics.

MICHAEL W. FITZGERALD, *The Union League Movement in the Deep South* (1989). Uses the Union League as a lens through which to examine race relations and the close connections between politics and economic change in the post–Civil War South.

ERIC FONER, *Reconstruction: America's Unfinished Revolution, 1863–1877* (1988). The most comprehensive and thoroughly researched overview of the Reconstruction era.

STEVEN HAHN, *The Roots of Southern Populism* (1983). Examines the deteriorating plight of poor white southern farmers after the Civil War and their efforts at political protest.

JACQUELINE JONES, *Labor of Love, Labor of Sorrow* (1985). Includes excellent material on the work and family lives of African American women in slavery and freedom.

LEON F. LITWACK, *Been in the Storm So Long: The Aftermath of Slavery* (1979). A richly detailed analysis of the transition from slavery to freedom; excellent use of African American sources.

WILLIAM S. McFEELY, *Grant: A Biography* (1981). The standard biography of this key Civil War general and Reconstruction era president.

MICHAEL PERMAN, *Emancipation and Reconstruction* (1987). A short but very useful overview of Reconstruction politics emphasizing racial issues and the end of slavery.

HOWARD N. RABINOWITZ, *Race Relations in the Urban South, 1865–1890* (1978). A detailed account of black-white social and political relations in southern cities.

WILLIE LEE ROSE, *Rehearsal for Reconstruction: The Port Royal Experiment* (1964). A pioneering account of the transition from slavery to freedom on the Sea Island plantations during the Civil War.

MARK W. SUMMERS, *Railroads, Reconstruction, and the Gospel of Prosperity* (1984). The best study of the economic and political importance of railroad building in this era.

ALLEN W. TRELEASE, *White Terror: The Ku Klux Klan Conspiracy and Southern Reconstruction* (1971). The most complete account of Klan activity and the efforts to suppress it.

18 CONQUEST AND SURVIVAL: COMMUNITIES IN THE TRANS-MISSISSIPPI WEST, 1860–1900

(William Fuller. Crow Creek Agency, Dakota Territory. *1884. Oil on canvas, 24⅝ × 51¾ in. Amon Carter Museum, Fort Worth, Texas; in memory of René d'Harnoncourt, trustee, 1961–68.)*

Decades later cowboy Evan G. Barnard vividly recalled the preparations made by settlers when Oklahoma territorial officials announced the opening of the Cherokee Strip to the biggest "land rush" in American history. "Thousands of people gathered along the border. . . . As the day for the race drew near the settlers practiced running their horses and driving carts. . . ." Finally, the morning of April 22, 1889, came. "At ten o'clock people lined up . . . ready for the great race of their lives." Like many others, Barnard displayed his guns to dissuade competitors from claiming the 160 acres of prime land that he intended to grab for himself.

Barnard's story was part of a longer regional tale involving the continual breakdown and creation of communities. What was to become Oklahoma in 1907 had been reserved by the federal government since the 1830s for the Five Civilized Tribes (the Seminoles, Cherokees, Choctaws, Chickasaws, and Creeks), who had been forcibly removed from the East.

HOMESTEADERS AND INDIAN PEOPLES CONTEST FOR LAND IN OKLAHOMA

Claiming that these tribes had sided with the Confederacy during the Civil War (some had, some had not), authorities reneged on their promise. During the 1870s and 1880s, the government moved thousands of people from other tribes there, reduced the size of their reservations, and simultaneously opened up much of the region to white settlers. In 1889 Congress enacted yet another treaty, redefining as public domain almost 2 million more acres of the Oklahoma territory. The Cherokee Strip, once explicitly established for the displaced tribes, now became the target of new settlers' land hunger.

"Sooners" (those whites who had arrived "sooner" than others to claim land) moved in illegally by the thousands to seize land and turn fields into farms. Southerners were well represented. Their own region dispossessed by warfare and economic ruin, they hoped to reconstitute their rural communities on the former Indian land.

By the end of the day, "tent cities" had been set up along railroad lines as market-minded settlers claimed land nearest to transportation routes. In a little over two months, 6,000 homestead claims were filed.

Despite this rush for land, the majority of settlers failed to establish themselves as independent farmers. By 1900 more than 60 percent of the farmers in the seven newly settled East

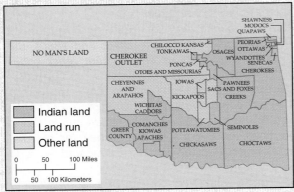

This photograph captures the activity in Guthrie, Oklahoma just five days after the town had been founded in 1889. Rushing to claim newly-opened land, settlers erected their tents as temporary dwellings. Street merchants sold everything from legal advice on filing land claims to buckets of river water.

Oklahoma Territory, 1889

Land earlier ceded to Indian tribes was opened to white settlers.

Oklahoma counties had been reduced to sharecroppers. Some were the Indian peoples who had been deprived of agriculturally rich tribal land. The only ones to prosper were a group of land speculators who included railroad promoters, oil prospectors, and coal operators.

Even if farmers had been able to overcome landlord domination, they lacked the climatic conditions for success. Most of Oklahoma did not have the steady rainfall required for long-term agricultural productivity. Intensive farming rapidly damaged the water-conserving grasslands, and poor land management along with sporadic droughts hastened soil erosion. Those Sooners who could afford to do so usually moved on. The families who stayed in Oklahoma saw their overworked land turn into great clouds of blowing silt in the 1930s — the worst "dust bowl" in American history. During the Great Depression tens of thousands of these "Okies" joined neighboring "Arkies" (from Arkansas) in a long trek to California. The multi-generational quest for a family homestead ended in squalid "jungle camps," where whole families of migrant crop pickers lived in grinding poverty.

Since the 1830s, when the federal government had forced the Five Civilized Tribes onto overlapping tribal territories, the promise of Oklahoma land had set one community against another. In two or three generations, white Oklahomans had pushed most Indian peoples aside (and African Americans downward) in their quest for the prosperity that only a minority would ever enjoy.

During the last half of the nineteenth century, white settlers, and a relatively small number of Mexican Americans and African Americans, built new communities across the Trans-Mississippi West. They helped to shape the emerging national economy by developing cattle ranching, mining, and agriculture into major industries. They succeeded, however, by displacing preexisting peoples as well as by drastically transforming the land itself.

Settlement of the West had many other consequences. It rapidly changed the regional distribution of the population, for instance, along with the relative importance of the regions themselves. Migrations in the 1870s depleted the population of southern states bordering the Mississippi River, except for Arkansas. Tennessee alone lost over 90,000 people, while the Dakotas gained almost an equal number. Texas added more than 300,000 as did Kansas. Even before the century closed, the West had overpowered the South as a zone of great economic promise. By that time over a quarter of the population of the United States lived west of the Mississippi.

Westward movement also changed the way many Americans looked at themselves. Always a frontier society, the United States reached its continental limit without losing its desire for a feeling of frontier excitement, romance, and adventure. Even as settlers entered the most environmentally forbidding territories, armed with new technologies and links to far-flung economic markets, they proceeded to create great legends about the "Wild West." Easterners and Europeans could read lurid tales about gold- and silver-mining exploits and harrowing gunfights, attend a Wild West show of cowboys and Indians, or appreciate the splendor of the landscape as captured in painting and photography. As different as these products of the artistic imagination might be, they all represented parts of a picture that Americans liked to believe made their society new and different from any other.

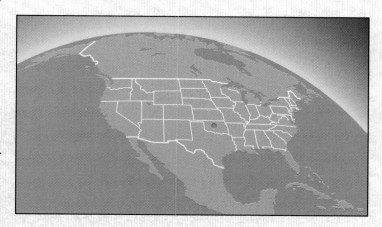

THE GREAT MIGRATION WEST

The vision of a huge garden stretching west of the Appalachians all the way to the Pacific Ocean had inspired Americans since the days of Thomas Jefferson. The United States was to realize its destiny, achieve wealth, and sustain its virtue, they believed, as a nation of family farms. Before the Civil War, when northern cities spread hand in hand with industry and the South grew more adamant in defending slavery, the idea of "free soil, free labor" gained popularity as an alternative. Following the Homestead Act of 1862 and the completion of the transcontinental railroad in 1869, the vast expanse of land west of the Mississippi River, primarily occupied by Indian peoples, opened to new settlers and new communities.

The Homestead Act

Hoping to win votes with the slogan "Vote Yourself a Farm," the Republican party made the demand for free homesteads a major plank in its 1860 platform. According to its promoters, the Homestead Act was to develop the Trans-Mississippi West into a utopia of family farms and simultaneously act as a safety valve for increasingly discontented workers in crowded northeastern cities. The election of Republican Abraham Lincoln in 1860 and the secession of the South ensured the passage of the Homestead Act, because the southern congressional delegation, which foresaw that western settlement would ultimately add free states, would no longer be present to vote against it.

The provisions of the Homestead Act of 1862 were simple. Any family head or adult male who was a citizen or who had filed a declaration to become one could claim 160 acres of surveyed land in the public domain for a small registration fee and a promise to live there for five years. Eighty-three million acres lay open for immediate settlement, and 15 million acres of California, Colorado, Washington, and Wisconsin were added later.

The Homestead Act achieved its greatest success in the central and upper Midwest, where the soil was rich and the climate relatively moderate. Between 1863, when the Homestead Act took effect, and 1880, a little over half of the 242,000 new farms in Minnesota, Dakota Territory, Nebraska, and Kansas were homesteading ventures. Homesteading accounted for approximately two-thirds of Minnesota's new farms.

But the Homestead Act failed to meet the needs of those family farmers who attempted to settle the Great Plains and beyond. Lured by descriptions of land "carpeted with soft grass — a sylvan paradise," settlers discovered a region less than bucolic. West of the ninety-eighth meridian (a north-south line extending through western Oklahoma, central Kansas and Nebraska, and eastern Dakota), the climate was harsh and the water supply minimal. Here, an average homestead of 160 acres of arid land could not, even with hard work, furnish a family livelihood.

Later changes to homesteading legislation did little to improve this situation. In 1877 Congress passed the Desert Land Act, which allowed homesteaders to buy 640 acres of land at $1.25 per acre if

These homesteaders in Nebraska, 1886, confronted the typically harsh conditions of treeless plains by erecting sod huts. They often brought with them an assortment of seeds and seedlings for spring plantings and a small number of livestock. A good fall harvest would provide the cash for building more substantial wood-frame or brick houses and out-buildings and encourage other homesteaders to settle near them. Communities eventually grew from these crude beginnings.

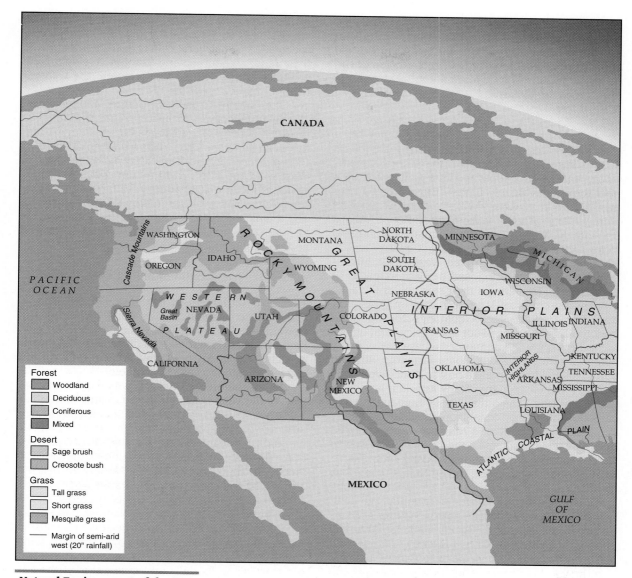

Natural Environment of the West

Rather than being a vast, potentially lush farmland, the West offered settlers relatively small fringes of arable land around huge expanses of mountain and desert, areas unsuited to cultivation but often rich in minerals and other natural resources.

they promised to irrigate it. Few settlers could afford the expense of irrigation, however, and speculators moved in, sometimes fulfilling the promise to irrigate by throwing out a bucket of water. The Enlarged Homestead Act of 1909 encouraged dry farming of the Great Plains, a technique for retaining moisture by plowing the land after each rainfall. By this time, the best land had already been claimed, and few farmers could succeed in the difficult

technique of stimulating germination of seeds buried deep in the soil.

The dream of a homestead nevertheless died hard. Five years after passage of the Homestead Act, *New York Tribune* editor Horace Greeley still advised workers to strike off "into the broad, free West" and "make yourself a farm from Uncle Sam's generous domain, you will crowd nobody, starve nobody, and . . . neither you nor your children need evermore beg for something to do." He was wrong. The most hard-pressed families could not afford to resettle at such a distance. Although the Homestead Act did indeed spark the largest migration in American history, it did not lay the foundation for a nation of prosperous family farms.

Land Acquisition

Most settlers acquired their land outright rather than filing a homestead claim with the federal government. State governments and land companies often held the most valuable lands — those located near transportation and markets — and many farmers were willing to forgo the Homestead Act provisions and buy such land. Railroad companies alone sold more land than the Homestead Act ever provided. Although farm acreage tripled west of the Mississippi before the century closed, perhaps as few as 10 percent of all farmers got their start under the act.

The purchase of land and start-up costs sent most farmers into debt. A quarter section of good land (costing perhaps $500) and agricultural equipment (perhaps $700) demanded a cash outlay many potential farmers lacked. Some farmers cultivated portions too small to yield a profit. Others eventually mortgaged their property. Many lost their land altogether. By 1880, when the Census Bureau began to compile statistics on tenant-operated farms, nearly 18 percent of the farms in Nebraska were operated by tenants; a decade later the portion had risen to nearly a quarter. As the century closed, more than a third of all farmers in the United States worked as tenants.

Land speculation was as common as debt. Large speculators plucked choice locations at $1.25 per acre; smaller speculators claimed more than the allotted one parcel. Both had their eye on eventual resale. In some territories, the bulk of public land fell into the hands of speculators, local politicians, and lumber companies. Paying bargain prices, these buyers ended up with large chunks of the 100 million acres Congress had opened to unlimited purchase. Californian William Chapman held more than 600,000 acres, timber king Thomas B. Walker more than 700,000. After 1898 speculators filed the largest number of claims.

Several other congressional acts inadvertently encouraged speculation in place of homesteading. The Timber Culture Act of 1873 allotted settlers an additional 160 acres of land in return for planting and cultivating 40 acres of trees. The new forests, Congress hoped, would improve the weather and provide a source of fencing and fuel. Because residence was not required, and because tree planting could not be assessed for at least thirteen years, speculators filed several claims at once, then resold their land without having planted a single tree. Although some forests were restored, the weather did not improve.

The director of the U.S. Census announced in 1890 that the country's "unsettled area has been so broken into by isolated bodies of settlement that there can hardly be said to be a frontier line." In fact, though, very large areas of the trans-Mississippi West were too arid or too mountainous for large-scale settlement. So scattered did farming communities remain over the vast region that western cities and towns had come to dominate the total population by 1880, making the West the most urbanized section of the nation.

Transcontinental Railroads

The rapid settlement of the West could not have taken place without the railroad. Whereas the Homestead Act offered prospective farmers free land, it was the railroad that promoted settlement, brought people to their new homes, and carried crops and cattle to eastern markets.

Shortly before the Civil War, when track mileage west of the Mississippi amounted to little more than 3,000 out of 30,000 in the United States, enthusiasm mounted for a transcontinental line. Private companies took on the huge and expensive job of construction. The federal government funded the project, providing the largest subsidy in American history. The Pacific Railway Act of 1862 granted to the Union Pacific and the Central Pacific rights to a broad swath of land extending from Omaha, Nebraska, to Sacramento, California. An 1864 act bestowed a subsidy of $15,000 per mile of track laid over smooth plains country and varying larger amounts up to $48,000 per mile in the foothills and mountains of the Far West. The Union Pacific employed groups of Irish American and African American workers to lay track heading west from Omaha, while the Central Pacific brought in over 10,000 men from China to handle the laborious stints in the Sierra Nevada.

On May 10, 1869, the governor of California, Leland Stanford, traveled to Promontory Point in Utah Territory to plant the ceremonial golden spike marking the completion of the transcontinental line. "Hats off!" a telegraph operator signaled to a nation of celebrants.

Other lines went up with less fanfare. The Southern Pacific, chartered by the state of California, reached from San Francisco to Los Angeles and on

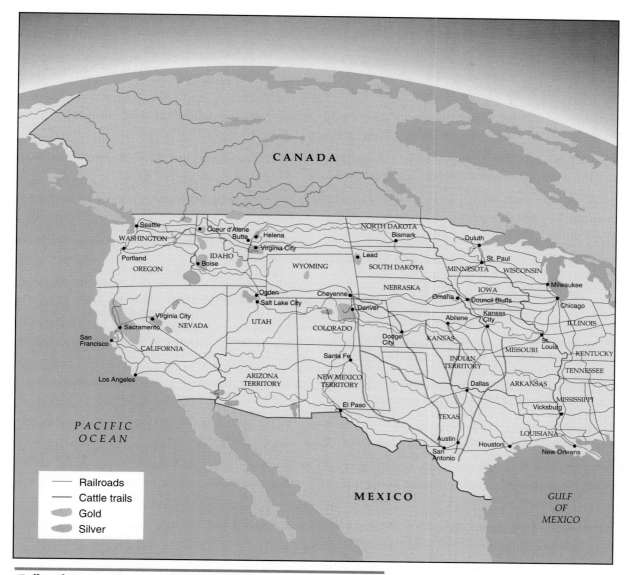

Railroad Routes, Cattle Trails, Gold and Silver Rushes, 1860–1900
By the end of the nineteenth century, the vast region of the West was crosscut by hundreds of lines of transportation and communication. The trade in precious metals and in cattle helped build a population almost constantly on the move, following the rushes for gold or the herds of cattle.

through Arizona and New Mexico to connections with New Orleans. The Atchison, Topeka and Santa Fe reached the Pacific in 1887 by way of a southerly route across the Rocky Mountains. The Great Northern, one of the few lines financed by private capital, extended west from St. Paul, Minnesota, to Washington's Puget Sound.

In the fifty years after 1870, track grew to more than a quarter million miles — more than all the rest of the world's railroad track combined. With the adoption of a standard gauge (size of track), trunk lines (major long-distance routes) were finally able to connect the many smaller systems in the Northeast and South. The large companies absorbed nearly 540 smaller ones in the 1880s alone, leaving in their wake nine major national routes. Various improvements, from more powerful engines, air brakes, and refrigerator cars to accounting procedures, enhanced operations. The railroads even changed the time: in 1883 they established four time zones to bring order to a chaotic national scheduling system involving nearly eighty different zones. By the 1880s, only a small proportion of Americans lived more than a few hundred miles from a railroad depot—only a few days' drive by horse and wagon.

The railroads wielded tremendous economic and political power in western communities. Their agents, known to one and all—and reputed to know every cow in the district—made major decisions affecting the community's welfare. Frequently they bribed public officials and granted discriminatory rates to favored customers. In designing routes and locating depots, railroad companies put whole communities on the map or left them behind.

Traveling West by Train

Along with providing transportation links between the East and West and potential markets as distant as China, the western railroads directly encouraged settlement. Unlike the railroads built before the Civil War, which followed the path of villages and towns, the western lines preceded settlement. Bringing people west became their top priority, and the railroad companies conducted huge promotional and marketing campaigns. Agents enticed easterners and Europeans alike with long-term loans and free transportation by rail to distant points in the West. The railroads also commissioned land companies to sell parcels of their own huge allotments. One of these, the National Land Company, founded in Chicago in 1869, organized sixteen colonies of mainly European immigrants in parts of Kansas and Colorado. Santa Fe Railroad agent C. B. Schmidt in Germany enticed nearly 60,000 Germans to settle along the rail line.

Although the train surpassed the "prairie schooner" (wagon train) in comfort, travel could be slow and even dangerous. Wood-burning trains had to stop often for fueling, and passenger trains were frequently recoupled en route to freight trains traveling in the same direction. In the summer, the stifling heat of the plains was intensified by the closed windows of the coaches; even a gentle breeze brought with it a blinding cloud of dust. Meanwhile, despite the cow catcher at the front of the locomotive, trains often hit wandering cattle, causing a tremendous jolt to passengers. In addition to these annoyances, genuine risks abounded. En-

gineers drove the trains too fast for the roadbeds, which suffered from shoddy construction, and the breaking and signaling system sometimes gave way, causing trains to jump the track or even crash into each other.

For all their problems, the railroads speeded western development. Whereas the wagon trip to Oregon along the Overland Trail had taken six to eight weeks, the rail journey took merely a week. In the process of laying track, the rail companies enticed, organized, and paid wages to tens of thousands of laborers; they opened virgin land for development into farms or mines; and they reaped their profits as trains sped metallic ore and produce eastward and finished goods westward. The railroads were commercial arteries for a flow of badly needed or much-desired manufactured goods, from hats to canned foods.

Railroads helped to concentrate economic and political authority over western lands in the hands of new settlers, who urged yet more rapid development. This concentration and development endangered the ancestral homes of the survivors of an older, sparsely populated West. Various Indian tribes could no longer count on a buffer between themselves and other tribes, Mexicans, or the expanding communities of white settlers. Ultimately, the creation of new communities meant the extinction of others.

THE INTERNAL EMPIRE

The way for expansion had been paved legally by the federal government's acquisition of western land. Through the 1848 Treaty of Guadalupe Hidalgo, which concluded the war with Mexico, and the Gadsden Purchase of 1853, the United States gained huge territories, including all of present-day California and Arizona and part of New Mexico. Congress created the Dakota, Colorado, and Nevada territories in 1861 and the Arizona and Idaho territories in 1863. By 1870 the territories of Montana and Wyoming had been carved out, mainly from the former Oregon Country and the Louisiana Purchase. Twice the size of Texas, Alaska was purchased from Russia for $7.2 million in 1867. Beginning in 1873, the Department of the Interior supervised these territories and directed their appointed governors to keep them orderly, peaceful, and inviting to new settlers.

In creating thirteen territories between 1861 and 1888, the federal government extended its direct rule over large portions of the trans-Mississippi West. Only four states were admitted to the Union from the West during this time—Kansas (1861),

Nevada (1864), Nebraska (1867), and Colorado (1876)—and in the remaining territories popular sovereignty remained limited. The federal government built roads, brought mail service, maintained military posts, subsidized territorial economies, and played a greater role in local governance than in any other region of the country.

Mining Communities

Prospectors were the first white people after the fur traders to sweep over much of this territory. Although ranchers and missionaries established the first white settlements in California, the gold rush of 1849 overran the region with prospecting parties (see Chapter 14). It also set a pattern for intermittent rushes for gold, silver, or copper that extended from the Colorado mountains to the Arizona deserts, from Oregon, Washington, and Alaska to the Black Hills of South Dakota. By 1875 prospectors had located a fortune in precious metals and formed distinctive though often short-lived communities throughout the West.

The mines yielded almost unimaginable wealth. Even before the widespread settlement of the West, their bounty had helped finance the Civil War and had added capital to the industries spreading across the Northeast. The eastern-based corporations that financed the mining projects earned the majority of profits as well as admiration worldwide. Engineers regarded western mining as a showplace of extractive technology. New explosives, compressed-air or diamond-headed rotary drills, wire cable, and other innovations made possible a subterranean world that resembled a vast series of urban tenements filled with hundreds of sweating men.

Along the way, disappointment was far more common than success. The Comstock Lode of gold and silver, discovered by Henry Comstock along the Carson River in Nevada in 1858, prompted a major stampede. But relatively few individuals struck it rich. Of 17,000 claims in Nevada, four-fifths of the dividends came from just two adjacent mines. Comstock himself sold his claims for a mere $11,000 and two mules. At least half of the 50,000 prospectors who headed to Colorado in 1859 with the slogan "Pikes Peak or Bust" left the site "busted." Only in 1897, with news of gold on the Klondike in the Yukon, did miners again hit upon a vein worth millions of dollars.

Miners not only laid the basis for a new economy and interim government but established many of the West's first white communities. Before the spread of railroads, ore had to be brought out and supplies brought in to mining areas by boat, wagon, and mule over hundreds of miles of rough territory. The shipping trade grew up into an important industry of its own, employing thousands of merchants, peddlers, and sailors. The railroad made transportation of supplies easier, but soon the growing population had other demands, which were met by dance halls, saloons, theaters, hospitals, and newspapers.

The mining camps of Nevada, Colorado, Montana, Idaho, and Arizona rapidly grew into sizable communities of a unique type. As throughout the western territories, single men outnumbered women, and in this region at the ratio of two to one. Miners tried to keep favorite aspects of "civilization" close to them. They lived unusually well, eating foods such as oysters trucked in at great expense and drinking oceans of beer and whiskey. Miners also attended public lectures and read large numbers of magazines and books.

When prices and ore production fell sharply, townspeople abandoned the area. Often miners left

Catskill, New Mexico, at the close of the century claimed the "largest tract of timber under one management in the United States." The company transformed trees into railroad ties, mining props, telegraph poles, and firewood. Populated mainly by male timber workers, Catskill attracted small numbers of women. This group organized a community marching band.

behind an environmental disaster. Hydraulic mining, a method of using water cannons to blast hillsides and expose gold deposits, drove tons of rock and earth into the rivers and canyons. By the late 1860s southern California's rivers were clogged, producing floods that wiped out towns and agriculture. In 1893 Congress finally passed the Caminetti Act, giving the state the power to regulate mines, and the hydraulic mines closed. (The act also created the Sacramento River Commission, which began to replace free-flowing California rivers with canals and dams.) Underground mining continued unregulated, using up whole forests for timbers and polluting the air with sulfurous smoke.

Occasionally, ore veins lasted long enough — as in Butte, Montana, a copper mining center — to create a permanent city similar to urban areas elsewhere in the United States or Europe. Back in Ireland, balladeers sang of Butte as the town "where the streets were paved with Irish bones," and departing emigrants promised their mothers that they would never go underground in Montana. Yet jobs drew Irish to Butte for generations. The Catholic Church and the Ancient Order of Hibernians helped Irish families in Butte survive the unremitting dangers of the job and the usual drifting of miners from site to site.

By the end of the century, miners had created the strongest labor unions of the West. Demanding and receiving good pay for their dangerous, life-shortening work, they succeeded in establishing a standard wage for white men. They resisted efforts to reduce wages or safeguards, even if their employers' profits declined. When mineowners' private armies "arrested" miners or fought their unions with rifle fire, miners burned down the camp sites, seized trains loaded with ore, and engaged in various acts of "sabotage" against company property. Yet if violence on both sides characterized western labor relations, so did legislation mandating a maximum eight-hour day for certain jobs and workmen's compensation for injuries. Such bills, enacted in Idaho, Arizona, and New Mexico by the 1910s, long preceded similar laws in most eastern states.

Offering unique if elusive opportunities to native-born white men and European immigrants, western mining underscored the racial dynamics of the region. The unions fought hard, but they did so exclusively for the benefit of white workers. The native-born and the Irish and Cornish immigrants (the latter, natives of Cornwall, England, were commonly known as Cousin Jacks) far outnumbered other groups until century's end, when Italians, Slavs, and Greeks began to replace them. Labor unions eventually admitted these new immigrants, but refused Chinese, Mexican, and Indian workers. White miners at the Comstock Lode rioted in 1869 to protest the employment of Chinese miners. In Arizona, Mexican Americans worked the copper and silver mines from the time of their opening, often outnumbering white miners but almost always receiving less pay and enduring worse conditions.

Mormon Settlements

While the consolidation of the internal empire fostered the growth of new commercial centers, such as the numerous if unstable mining towns, it also placed severe restrictions upon preexisting communities. The Mormons (formally the Church of Jesus Christ of Latter-day Saints) had fled western New York and Illinois in the 1840s and 1850s to escape persecution for their practice of polygamy (plural marriage). Settling around the Great Basin in present-day Utah, the Mormons became the largest communitarian society in the West. By 1860 more than 40,000 Mormons resided in Utah, and by 1900 more than 200,000.

No other single group, secular or religious, played a more important role in the agricultural settling of the West. Contrary to federal law, church officials forbade the selling of land. Instead they apportioned property so as to form a sizable urban settlement complemented by satellite villages joined to communal farmlands and a common pasture. Relying on agricultural techniques learned from local Indian tribes, the Mormons built dams for irrigation and harvested a variety of crops from desert soil. Eventually they founded dozens of communities from Oregon to Idaho to Arizona.

Under tightening territorial rule, which had begun in 1850, the Mormons saw their unique way of life once again threatened by the increasing attention of Congress and the nation. The newspapers and the courts repeatedly assailed the Mormons for their practice of polygamy. Preceded by two prohibitory federal laws of 1862 and 1874, the Supreme Court ruled against polygamy in *United States* v. *George Reynolds* (1878), granting the freedom of belief but not the freedom of practice. In 1887 Congress passed the Edmunds-Tucker Act, which effectively disfranchised those who believed in or practiced polygamy and threatened them with fines and imprisonment. By the early 1890s Mormon leaders had officially renounced plural marriage.

Although polygamy involved no more than 15 to 20 percent of families, Mormons had bolstered their sense of mission by defending this religious tenet. Forced to abandon plural marriage, they eventually gave up most other aspects of their distinctive communal life, including common ownership of land. The Mormon Church became more conservative, and the communities came to resemble the individualist society that the original settlers had sought to escape.

Still, the Mormons managed to create a fabric of close-knit communities, including nearly 500 new settlements by century's end. Close supervision by church leaders promoted the towns' initial prosperity and remained important, especially in Utah, which became a state in 1896.

The Southwest

In the Southwest, the United States absorbed, expanded, and transformed an empire built by Spain. By 1824 a Spanish-speaking population of 20,000 with close ties to Mexico lived in Nuevo Mexico (present-day New Mexico and Arizona). The prospect of further northern expansion by Mexico ended abruptly in 1845, however, when Texas, an independent republic since 1836, became a state.

After annexing Texas, the United States mounted a campaign for regional control. Anglos (as the Mexicans called white Americans) violated treaties established to protect persons of Mexican descent and seized their land. In the border town of Brownsville, the "Cortina War" broke out in 1859. Hostilities spread rapidly across the lower Rio Grande Valley, bringing the Texas Rangers and a militia of Mexicanos (as the Mexican residents called themselves) into armed conflict. Although Mexicans continued to move north to work on the growing number of Anglo-owned cotton farms, sheep ranches, and cattle trails, they found themselves locked into the racial hierarchy of a new empire.

For a time, territorial Arizona and New Mexico seemed to hold out hopes for mutually beneficial interaction between Mexicanos and Anglos. A prosperous class of Mexican landowners had long-standing ties, especially through marriage, to Anglo merchants and craftsmen. Estevan Ochoa, merchant, philanthropist, and the only Mexican to serve as mayor of Tucson following the Gadsden Purchase of 1853, built one of the largest business empires in Arizona. Ochoa and other leading Tucsonenses promoted a system of public schools, the first in the Southwest, and private institutions such as Saint Joseph's Academy for Young Ladies. Mexicano elites continued to wield political power as ranchers, landlords, and real estate developers until the end of the century.

In the mountains and deserts of the Southwest, where the majority of people had lived off the land for well over two centuries, the expansion of Anglo society had far-reaching consequences. The Mexicano residents lived outside the commercial economy, in communities where they farmed and herded sheep primarily for their own subsistence. With the Anglos came land closures as well as commercial expansion, prompted by the development of railroads and the mining and timber industries. Some Mexicanos adapted by taking wage work on the railroad or in the mines, while their wives and daughters managed small family gardens or sought employment as seamstresses or laundresses in the new Anglo-dominated towns. For women, these changes brought a major change in status. Formerly at the center of a communal, subsistence economy, Mexicanas found themselves with fewer resources. What wages they could earn in the new commercial economy fell below even the meager sums paid to their husbands. Their authority within both family and community diminished accordingly.

By century's end, a new social arrangement prevailed in the Southwest. Intermarriage declined rapidly in Tucson, for instance, as incentives for economic cooperation diminished. With federal and state agencies frequently refusing to license Mexicano merchants, Anglos soon took over the choice businesses, jobs, and neighborhoods. The Anglo-led Sante Fe Ring, a group of lawyers, politicians, and land speculators, stole millions of acres from the public domain. At the same time, individual swindlers cut into Mexicano landholdings. Many Mexicano families found themselves crowded onto plots too small for subsistence farming. Large numbers turned to seasonal labor on the new Anglo-owned farms, becoming the first of many generations of poorly paid migratory workers.

The Anglo system of commercial agricultural took a large toll on the land. The new settlers dug agricultural arroyos (canyons), removed trees, and grazed cattle across the flood plains of southwestern rivers. Water levels soon dropped, streams went dry, and many long-tended Mexicano fields had to be abandoned. Anglo techniques also stimulated heavy flooding in the rainy season and severe soil erosion.

The rising Anglo authority and the broadening market economy created new opportunities for a minority of Mexicanos. An exceptional family such as the wealthy Amadors of Las Cruces, New Mexico, could shop by mail from Bloomingdales, travel to the world's fair in Chicago, and send their children to

A Mexican household in Tucson, Arizona, in 1899. This photograph shows community members posed for the camera in their best clothes, including straw hats and suits with ties for the men, long gowns with corsets for the women.

alistes (mutual aid societies) offered political advice while providing sickness and death benefits to Mexican families.

But in the long run, local populations, customs, and even language all grew less important than the connections to national markets and the federal government. Anglos exerted their authority in national politics through congressional and presidential elections, responding to the population rush with demands upon Congress for territorial status and eventually, petitions for statehood. New Mexico and Arizona became states early in the twentieth century.

For Anglos, large regions of the West had been "won," from the previous populations and from nature. Ironically, though, even after statehood the white settlers would still be distant representatives of an empire whose financial, political, and industrial centers remained in the Northeast. In return for produce and ore they received washtubs, clothes, and whiskey; model legal statutes; and doctors, lawyers, and teachers. Although westerners continued to boast of their "local color," and a significant minority made a killing on their investments and hard work, many pioneers were frustrated by their isolation and enraged at the investors and lawyers who seemed poised on all sides to rob them of the fruits of their resettlement. They, along with southerners, formed the core of a nationwide discontent that by century's end would threaten to transform American politics.

Indian Peoples under Siege

Although newspaper editor and reformer Horace Greeley (who advised, "Go west, young man") and other enthusiasts of expansion described the western territories as unoccupied, perhaps 360,000 Indian people lived in the trans-Mississippi West. Most tribes had coexisted with non-Indian people for centuries, though rarely in peace or harmony. Two hundred years earlier, the Plains tribes had learned to ride the horses and shoot the guns introduced by Spanish and British traders. Masters of these new resources, the Pawnees had migrated west to escape harassment by white settlers, while Apaches had moved south for better hunting grounds. Conquered by the Spanish, the southwestern Hopis and Zunis continued to trade regularly with the Mexicans who lived near them. In a few cases, tribal assimilation to European ways had become almost complete. The Cherokees, forcibly removed from Georgia to Oklahoma under orders from President Andrew Jackson, had survived so long among whites that they had adopted aspects of representa-

English-language Catholic schools. By the turn of the century, the small and struggling Mexicano middle class could buy kitchen stoves and sewing machines. The mass of impoverished Mexicanos, on the other hand, persisted in older ways because they had fewer choices and because their family and religion reinforced tradition. As a Protestant missionary to Texas wrote, they "were kindly in home life, particularly to the aged, and clannish to a degree, whole families of several generations occupying one hut." Mexican Catholicism blended European and Indian religious traditions into something unique. Folk beliefs—special saints such as the Virgin of Guadalupe and distinctive holy days like the Day of the Dead—survived along with fiestas celebrating the change of seasons.

In sporadic rebellions and political counteroffensives Mexicanos aimed to reverse these trends or at least to limit the damage done to their way of life. Las Gorras Blancas, agrarian rebels in New Mexico in the late 1880s, so called because of the white caps of their costume, cut the barbed-wire fences (known as "the devil's hatband") that had been strung along the borders of the new Anglo farms and ranches. They also destroyed railroad ties and publicly posted their demands for justice. Less confrontational Mexicano organizations developed sophisticated political skills. Mexicanos formed Los Alianza Hispano-Americana (the Hispanic-American Alliance) "to protect and fight for the rights of Spanish Americans" through political action. The Penitentes, a lay religious brotherhood, sought to influence elections through bloc voting, and mututive government and the Christian religion. By mid-century many Cherokees lived in settled communities of family farmers.

The Great Plains region was home to nearly two-thirds of all Indian people at the end of the Civil War. The Cheyennes occupied large parts of Montana and the Dakotas and extended down to New Mexico, Oklahoma, and Texas. Blackfeet, Crows, and Arapahos along with the Sioux lived in the north, while Osages, Kiowas, Omahas, Pawnees, and Comanches occupied the South. Many of these tribes were known for their fighting ability, and they responded militantly to the threats posed by the massive invasion of white settlers into their ancestral lands. Widespread violence marked Indian-white relations from the 1850s through century's end.

The Plains Indians

Although some tribes planted crops and herded sheep, the grassy, semiarid terrain promoted a

Major Indian Battles and Indian Reservations, 1860–1900

As commercial routes and white populations passed through and occupied Indian lands, warfare inevitably erupted. The displacement of Indians to reservations opened access by farmers, ranchers, and investors to natural resources and to markets.

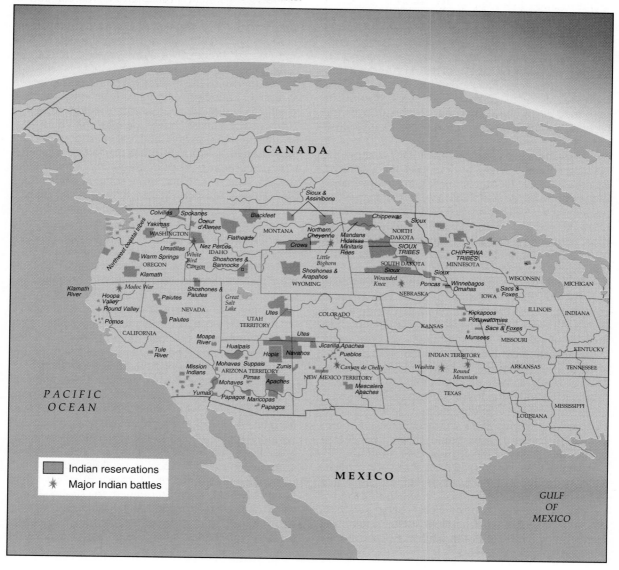

nomadic culture based primarily on hunting and gathering. The Comanches, Kiowas, Kiowa Apaches, and southern Arapahos ranged over wide expanses, often crossing land claimed by other tribes. In the Southwest, the Navahos and Apaches, who raided each other's camps for horses, cattle, and sheep, engaged in fierce wars beginning in the 1850s and flaring up intermittently into the 1880s. The Comanches had conquered large areas of the southern plains, while to the north the prosperous Lakota Sioux with their Arapaho and Cheyenne allies were at the height of their power, unaware that whites would soon eradicate their gains.

The Cheyenne nation had undergone several transformations. Never more than a few thousand people, they had found themselves caught geographically between aggressive tribes in the Great Lakes region during the late eighteenth century and had migrated to the Missouri area, where they split into small, village-sized communities. By the mid-nineteenth century the Cheyennes had become expert horse traders on the Great Plains. Although they practiced the "casual" agriculture of planting and then leaving fields of corn, pumpkins, and beans untended until they returned, their survival and prosperity depended foremost on good grass to feed their horses.

The Cheyennes had prepared well to meet the massive influx of white settlers after the Civil War. By relocating frequently and living in small villages, they minimized their contact with the diseases white people carried. They also survived large-scale intermarriage with the Sioux in the 1860s and 1870s. Like the Cherokees, many Cheyennes took up elements of the Christian religion and became farmers, without losing their tribal identity.

The Sioux, one of the largest, most widespread, and highly adaptive Indian nations, was a loose confederation of bands scattered across the Great Plains. All Sioux tribes relied economically upon the buffalo, which men expertly hunted on horseback. Women tanned the hides, performed menial labors, tended to children, and produced elaborate quilts and embroidered blankets and clothing. Sioux were also known widely as vision seekers. Their religious beliefs led young men and women to seek dreams that would provide them with guidance for a lifetime, and elders to seek grand visions that would shape the destiny of the entire tribe or nation.

The Sioux took pride in their status as warriors. Among the most famous Sioux fighters were Red Cloud and Crazy Horse, both from the Teton, or Lakota, people. The Sioux had long considered tribal war a men's sport or avocation in which relatively few actually died — until the whites approached. By the early 1850s white settlers had encroached on Sioux hunting lands, driving off the buffalo herds and bringing deadly cholera. In response, the Sioux grew markedly more violent and deadly not only toward whites but also toward the Pawnees and Crows and even toward the buffalo, which they hunted with increasing efficiency. By midcentury Lakota bands controlled much of the northern plains.

Reservations and Resistance

The region of present-day Oklahoma once constituted "one big reservation," an "Indian Country" held in public trust. Having driven the Five Civilized Tribes there from the Southeast in the 1830s, the federal government prohibited any white person from entering without a license. But well before the Civil War, the onslaught of wagon trains and various stampedes for gold had pressured various Ojibwa and Dakota Sioux tribes alone to cede millions of acres to the federal government.

By the 1860s the federal government had begun to assign boundaries to each tribe, and in 1866 Washington directed the Bureau of Indian Affairs to "protect and subsist" Indian peoples until they gave up their nomadic ways and resettled as self-sufficient farmers. Although most officials justified the policy as a means to ensure the safety of non-Indian settlers, miners, and investors, some acknowledged that the new reservation system merely disguised a campaign to clear the land for white ownership.

Many small tribes peacefully accommodated to settled farming, but those tribes that had traditionally hunted over vast spaces could not adapt to the reservation system. Moreover, the federal government repeatedly reduced the size of land allotments, forcing tribes to compete with each other for increasingly scarce resources. In many cases, subsistence on the reservation became impossible. Corrupt government officials made a bad situation worse by reducing food supplies, a policy promoting malnutrition, demoralization, and desperation.

A crisis erupted with the mass slaughter of buffalo. In earlier eras, vast herds of bison, perhaps as many as 70 million, had darkened the western horizon. Buffalo grazed over distances of several hundred miles, eating grass, searching for water, and wallowing in mud to fend off insects. When gunpowder came to the range, their number fell. Although only 40 million "Indian cattle" (as white hunters called them) remained in 1840, several tribes continued to depend on buffalo as a source of meat, skins, and even dung for fuel. For white traders, buffalo meant mainly fur coats, leather, and trophy heads. New rifles, such as the .50 caliber Sharps, could kill at 600 feet, and one sharpshooter bragged of killing 3,000 himself. Army commanders encouraged the practice, believing starvation an effective means to break tribal resistance to the reservation system.

By the mid-1880s little remained of the herds but great heaps of bones, which scavengers sold for $7.50 per ton. A mere 5,000 buffalo survived in the United States. A small step toward recovery of the species was taken when several states enacted protective measures in the 1880s.

The influx of white settlers and a commercial economy had already begun to transform Indian life on the plains in various ways. Trading posts introduced metal cookware and traps, coffee and sugar, encouraging tribes to abandon traditional skills and diet without affording them the means to pay for newly acquired habits. Fur traders smoothed their deals with alcohol, swindling Indian people and promoting a narcotic method of relieving mental depression. Nevertheless, tribal identities remained especially vital among the Plains peoples.

"Indian Wars"

Various tribes repeatedly sought peace, resorting to violence only after white settlers had persistently violated treaties. In 1851 the Sioux had willingly relinquished large tracts of land in a demonstration of good faith. But within a decade, a mass invasion of miners and the construction of military forts along the Bozeman Trail in Montana — the Sioux's princi-pal buffalo range — threw the tribe's future into doubt and precipitated the "Great Sioux War" of 1865 – 67. The Battle of One Hundred Slain in December 1866 was a major defeat for U.S. Army troops and forced the government to abandon its forts, which the Sioux later burned to the ground. In 1869 a treaty signed by Red Cloud restored a temporary peace to the region.

In 1864, Governor John Evans of Colorado Territory inaugurated a campaign to terminate all land treaties with tribes in eastern Colorado and encouraged a group of white civilians, the Colorado Volunteers, to stage repeated raids through Cheyenne camping grounds. Seeking protection, Chief Black Kettle brought a band of 800 Cheyennes to a U.S. fort and received orders to set up camp at Sand Creek. Secure in this arrangement, Black Kettle sent out most of his men to hunt. The next morning, on November 29, 1864, 700 Colorado Volunteers attacked. While Black Kettle held up a U.S. flag and white truce banner, the disorderly group of whites, many of them drunk, slaughtered 105 Cheyenne women and children and 28 men. After mutilating the corpses they took scalps back to Denver to exhibit as trophies. One Cheyenne woman, Iron Teeth, lived with the memory of a woman "crawling along on the ground, shot, scalped, crazy, but not yet dead." Months after the Sand Creek Massacre, bands of Cheyenne, Sioux, and Arapaho struck back, burning civilian outposts and killing whole families.

In 1867 a major peace treaty brought together more than 100,000 Arapahos, Cheyennes, Kiowas, Sioux, Shoshones, Bannocks, Navahos, and

Young Kiowa Brave, in crayon and pencil, c.1887. This sketch on paper was made by an Indian artist, Silver Horns, who had himself taken part in the final revolt of the Kiowas in 1874. He later became a medicine man, and then served as a private in the U.S. Cavalry at Fort Sill, Oklahoma Territory. *(Silver Horns.* Young Kiowa Brave. *1887. Crayon and pencil, 9¼ × 13¾ in. Marion Koogler McNay Art Institute, San Antonio, Texas.)*

Apaches to accept reservation status. Over the next decade, Quaker appointees of President Grant attempted to mediate among the tribes, friend and foe alike, and to supply starving peoples with food and the seed needed to rebuild their lives. But despite federal government guarantees of the integrity of Indian land, white settlers, mainly miners, continued to flood Dakota Territory. "They crowded in," Iron Teeth recalled bitterly, "so we had to move out." But numerous tribes, enraged at the U.S. policies or eager for military glory, continued to resist reservation status.

U.S. military policy hardened. Civil War general William Tecumseh Sherman, commander of the western troops, insisted in 1869, "The more we can kill this year, the less will have to be killed the next war, for the more I see of these Indians the more I am convinced that all have to be killed or maintained as a species of pauper."

Civil War hero George Armstrong Custer developed a plan to finish off the rebellious tribes. The most flamboyant (and in the eyes of many of his own troops the most irresponsible) of army commanders, Custer invited newspaper reporters along as he set off to invade the sacred grounds of the Sioux. After several skirmishes, he decided to rush ahead of other army regiments to the site known to white soldiers as the Little Bighorn and to Lakotas as Greasy Grass. This foolhardy move offered the allied Pawnee and Sioux warriors a perfect opportunity to cut off Custer's logistical and military support. On June 25, 1876, Custer and his troops fell before one of the largest Indian contingents ever assembled, an estimated 2,000 to 4,000 warriors led by the Teton Sioux Crazy Horse and Gall, a chief of the Hunkpapa Sioux.

Custer's Last Stand provided Indian haters the emotional ammunition to whip up public excitement. Sioux chief Sitting Bull was said to have uttered on hearing the news of Custer's defeat, "Now they will never let us rest." The U.S. Army eventually claimed victory. Its troops tracked down the disbanded Indian contingents one by one, forced Crazy Horse to surrender in May 1877, and drove the Sioux back to Dakota.

Among the last to hold out against the reservation system were the Apaches. Most bands had abided by the peace treaty of 1867, and Cochise, one of the ablest Apache chiefs, agreed in 1872 to live with his people on a reservation incorporating a portion of the tribe's ancestral land. Cochise died two years later, and some of the bands, unable to tolerate the harsh conditions on the reservation, returned to their old ways. For the next ten years,

Cochise's successor, the famous warrior Geronimo, led intermittent raids against white outposts in the rough Arizona terrain.

Pursued by the U.S. Army, the Apaches earned reputations as intrepid warriors. Lightning-swift raids followed by quick escapes made legends of their brilliant strategists and horse-riding braves. Kiowas and Comanches joined the Apaches in one of the most bloody conflicts, the "Red River War" of 1874–75. At last the U.S. Army scored a decisive victory, less by military might than by denying Indians access to food. Yet small-scale warfare sputtered on. His band reduced to only thirty people, Geronimo surrendered in September 1886. The "Indian Wars" were over.

THE TRANSFORMATION OF INDIAN SOCIETIES

Changes in tribal status after the Civil War alarmed sympathetic white observers. From its inception, the federal government had regarded Indian tribes as autonomous nations within American boundaries and had negotiated numerous treaties with them over land rights and commerce. During President Jackson's administration the government violated numerous treaty agreements, and in 1831 the Supreme Court ruled in *Cherokee Nation* v. *Georgia* that Indians constituted "domestic dependent nations." While continuing to acknowledge the sovereignty of Indian nations, the government reduced the Indians themselves to wards of the American state and established the Bureau of Indian Affairs to oversee their activities. The creation of Indian Territory in the vicinity of present-day Oklahoma and the establishment of reservations further weakened the tribes' political integrity. Whether they resisted or accommodated to these changes ultimately made little difference, for in 1871, when the government formally ended the treaty system, all tribes lost sovereignty. In response, reformers advocated policies designed to promote assimilation into white society.

Reform Policy and the Dawes Severalty Act

In 1869, during President Grant's administration, Congress created the Board of Indian Commissioners. Over the next fifteen years the commissioners, who were nominated by major Protestant denominations, sought to mediate local conflicts while instilling in Indians both Christian virtues and European-originated models of family life and community organization.

Students at Toledo Indian School, Iowa, August, 1899. Young women of various tribes boarded at this school, which offered them lessons in several subjects and training for adult life among white Americans. Their teachers hoped to prepare them for a future Christian marriage and motherhood.

Unlike most Americans, who saw the conquest of the West as a means to national glory, some reformers were genuinely outraged by the government's disregard of treaty obligations and the military enforcement of the reservation policy. One of the most influential of these reformers was Helen Hunt Jackson, a noted poet. In 1879 Jackson had attended a lecture in Hartford, Connecticut, by a Ponca chief, whose destitute people had been forced from their Dakota homeland. Afterward, she lobbied former abolitionists such as Wendell Phillips to work for Indians rights and she herself began to write against government policy. Her exposé *A Century of Dishonor*, published in 1881, detailed the mistreatment of Indian peoples.

Meanwhile, the Women's National Indian Association (WNIA), formed in 1874, attempted to rally public support for a program of assimilation. The Indian Rights Association, an offshoot of the WNIA supported by Jackson, sent missionaries west to eradicate distinct tribal customs such as the relegation of hunting to men and farming to women. According to reformers' plans, families would abandon all communal practices in favor of individually owned homesteads. Men would both farm and hunt while women would take care of home and children. The children, hair trimmed short, would be placed in boarding schools, where, removed from their parents' influence, they would shed traditional values

and cultural practices. To prepare for full citizenship, Indian families were encouraged to commemorate such American holidays as Independence Day and to convert to Christianity. By 1882 the WNIA had gathered 100,000 signatures on petitions urging Congress to phase out the reservation system, establish universal education for Indian children, and award title to 160 acres to any individual willing to accept the land.

The Dawes Severalty Act, passed by Congress in 1887, incorporated many of these measures and established federal Indian policy for decades to come. The act allowed the president to distribute land not to tribes but to individuals legally "severed" from their tribes. The commissioner of Indian affairs rendered the popular interpretation that "tribal relations should be broken up, socialism destroyed and the family and autonomy of the individual substituted. The allotment of land in severalty, the establishment of local courts and police, the development of a personal sense of independence and the universal adoption of the English language are means to this end."

Those individuals who accepted the allotment of 160 acres and agreed to allow the government to sell unallotted tribal lands (with some of the proceeds set aside for education) could petition to become citizens. A little over a decade after its enactment, many reformers believed that the Dawes Act had resolved the basis of the "Indian problem."

The Dawes Act did little to integrate Indians into white society, and nothing to restore tribal sovereignty, lost in 1871 with the end of the treaty system. Indian children fled most white schools, and only a minority dropped their religion for Christianity or their communal ways for the accumulation of private property. Nor did the adults receive much encouragement to become property holders. Government agencies allotted them inferior farmland, inadequate tools, and little training for agricultural self-sufficiency. In the next forty years, Indian peoples would lose 60 percent of the reservation land remaining in 1887, and 66 percent of the land allotted to them. The tenets of the Dawes Act were not reversed until 1934. In that year Congress passed the Tribal Reorganization Act, which affirmed the integrity of Indian cultural institutions and returned land to tribal ownership (see Chapter 24).

The Ghost Dance

After the tribal rebellions had been crushed, there remained one last cycle of attempted self-redemption followed by tragic violence. The Paiute prophet

Sioux encampment, near Pine Ridge, South Dakota, in 1890. Inaccurately captioned by the original publishers as a "great hostile Indian Camp," this photograph shows Sioux gathered to discuss the end of the world, to participate in the Ghost Dance Ceremony which would bring the end closer, and to await the arrival of Sitting Bull.

Wovoka, ill with scarlet fever, had a vision during a total eclipse of the sun in 1889. In it the Creator told him that if Indians learned to love one another, they would be granted a special place in the afterlife. The Creator also gave Wovoka the Ghost Dance, which the prophet performed for others and spread among the nearly devastated Sioux. Tribal members came to believe that on Judgment Day all the Indian peoples who had ever lived would return to their lost world and white peoples would vanish from the earth. The Sioux chant sounded:

> The whole world is coming.
> A nation is coming, a nation is coming.
> The Eagle has brought the message to the tribe.
> The father says so, the father says so.
> Over the whole earth they are coming.
> The buffalo are coming, the buffalo are coming.
> The Crow has brought the message to the tribe,
> The Father says so, the Father says so.

Belief in a sudden divine judgment was familiar to many Christians and Jews. During the 1830s and 1840s, Protestant groups such as the Millerites had renounced personal property and prepared themselves for the millennium (see Chapter 13). But after decades of Indian warfare, white Americans took the Ghost Dance as a warning of tribal retribution rather than a religious ceremony. As thousands of Sioux danced to exhaustion, settlers and federal officials demanded an end to the practice. Two Indian policemen, backed up by U.S. troops, arrested and then shot Sitting Bull, who had been called by his people to direct the dance on the Pine Ridge, South Dakota, reservation.

The Miniconjou people of the Lakota Sioux, led by Big Foot, feared a massacre and moved north to hide. The U.S. Seventh Cavalry, pursued them. On December 29, 1890, surrounded at Wounded Knee Creek, his band of 300 malnourished Sioux freezing, without horses, and almost weaponless, Big Foot flew a white surrender flag. But a gunshot from a young brave provoked a methodical response from the machine gun crews all around. Within minutes 200 were dead. Those straggling away, mostly women and children, were slaughtered outright or buried alive in the snow. Custer had been revenged. Black Elk later recalled, "I can see that something else died there in the bloody mud, and was buried in the blizzard. A people's dream died there. It was a beautiful dream. . . . the nation's hoop is broken and scattered. There is no center any longer, and the sacred tree is dead."

Endurance and Rejuvenation

The fortunate among the tribes occupied land unwanted by white settlers and distant from new communities. Still, not even an insular, peaceful agricultural existence on semiarid, treeless terrain necessarily provided protection. Nor did a total willingness to accept white offers peacefully.

The Pimas of Arizona, for instance, had a well-developed agricultural system adapted to a scarce supply of water, and they rarely warred with other tribes. Following the arrival of white settlers, they integrated Christian symbolism into their religion, learned English, and even fought with U.S. cavalry against the Apaches. Still, the Pimas saw their lands stolen, their precious waterways diverted, and their families reduced to impoverishment.

The similarly peaceful Yana tribes of California, hunters and gatherers rather than farmers, were less fortunate. Enslaved and prostituted by white settlers, ravaged by new diseases, they faced near extinction within a generation. One Yana tribe, the Yahi, chose simply to disappear. They lived in caves and avoided all contact with white settlers for more than a decade.

Many tribes found it difficult to survive in the proximity of white settlers. Indian commissioners in the Bitterroot region of Montana predicted quick assimilation of the Flatheads, on the basis of their resistance to the Ghost Dance and their willingness to sell rich tribal land and move to a reservation. Unable to resettle until all their land had been sold, however, the displaced Flatheads nearly starved. Finally, in October 1891, 250 Flatheads wearing their finest war paint galloped onto their new reservation, whooping and firing their guns to celebrate. But they fared poorly. The federal government drastically reduced the size of the reservation, making a large part of it into a national reserve for buffalo. Handfuls of Flatheads, mostly aged tribal members, continued to live together in pockets of rural poverty.

A majority of tribes, especially smaller ones, sooner or later dwindled to the brink of extinction. Although unions with whites were widely condemned by the white community, intermarriage nevertheless occurred, especially where racial lines were less sharp. Some tribal leaders deliberately chose assimilation. The Quapaw, for example, disbanded in the aftermath of the Dawes Act. The minority who managed to prosper in white society as businessmen or farmers abandoned their native language, religious customs, and traditional ways of life. Later attempts to revive tribes among descendant Quapaws proved futile. Even knowledge of the old customs had vanished by then.

A small minority of peoples, skillful in adapting to changing circumstances, managed to survive and even grow. The Navahos experienced an extraordinary renewal, largely because they built a life in territory considered worthless by whites. Themselves migrants from the North to the Southwest perhaps 700 years earlier, the Dine ("the people," as they called themselves) had already survived invasions by the Spanish. In 1863 they had been conquered again with the cooperation of hostile tribes led by the famous Colonel Kit Carson. Their crops burned, their fruit trees destroyed, 8,000 of them were forced to move to southern New Mexico in what they called the "Long Walk." Four years later, the Bureau of Indian Affairs allowed the badly reduced tribe to return to a fraction of its former lands.

By 1880 Navaho numbers had nearly returned to where they were before the conquest by white Americans. But the hemmed-in population quickly depleted the deer and antelope, so that sheep alone remained a food reserve for years of bad crops. Increasingly Navahos turned to crafting wool rugs and blankets, much in demand in the East, and eventually silver jewelry as well. The Navahos lived on the economic margin, but they persevered.

The nearby Hopis, like the Navahos, survived by stubbornly clinging to lands unwanted by white settlers and by adapting to drastically changing conditions. Famous as a desert people, the Hopis had lived for centuries in their cliff cities. Their highly developed theological beliefs, peaceful social system, sand paintings, and kachina dolls interested many educated and influential whites. The resulting publicity helped them gather the public support and the financial resources to fend off further threats to their reservations.

Northwestern tribes remained relatively isolated from white settlers until the early twentieth century, when anthropologists moved in to study their culture and assert the importance of its survival. These peoples relied largely upon salmon and other resources of the rivers and bays around them, but they had traded skillfully with white visitors for centuries. Northwest tribes measured their prosperity and status through the *potlatch,* a demonstration of tribal superiority in which leaders gave elaborate gifts to competing tribes. They also constructed totem poles (and other intricate wood carvings), which recorded their history and marked their regional status. Northwesterners persisted in part through their connections with kin in Canada, as did southern tribes through ties with members in Mexico. Outside American borders, new Indian populations presented less pressure and governments permitted more tribal authority than in the United States.

By and large, however, a way of life and a distinctive world view vanished with the free lands of the plains, the buffalo, and large populations of western wildlife. Many white settlers came to appreciate their fellow westerners too late. As a woman who migrated to Oklahoma in 1901 testified, she had learned that friendship depended upon the person, and she found in a Chickasaw woman her truest "neighbor and best friend." But the vast majority of the descendants of European immigrants lost, before they knew or even cared to know, their last opportunity to engage with the preexisting cultures of North America. By 1890 the Indian population had declined to its lowest number — 228,000.

THE CATTLE INDUSTRY

The enormous number of new settlers, whether producing wheat in Montana, oranges in California, or copper in Arizona, differed from the pioneers of half a century before, who had cleared woods to live simply off the land. As a group they carried out the largest commercial expansion in American history.

The cattle industry furnished huge profits. Texas longhorns, introduced by the Spanish, numbered over 5 million at the close of the Civil War and represented a potentially plentiful supply of beef for eastern consumers. In the spring of 1866, entrepreneurs such as Joseph G. McCoy began to build a spectacular cattle market in the western part of Kansas, where the Union Pacific Railroad provided crucial transportation links to slaughtering and packing houses and commercial distributors in Kansas City, St. Louis, and Chicago.

In 1867 only 35,000 head reached McCoy's new stockyards in Abilene, but 1868 proved the first of many banner years. Drovers pushed herd after herd of Texas cattle north through Oklahoma on the trail marked out by part-Cherokee trader Jesse Chisholm and maintained for nearly two decades a bonanza industry. Great profits were made on Texas steers bought for $7 to $9 a head and sold in Kansas for upwards of $30. In 1880 nearly 2 million cattle were slaughtered in Chicago alone.

Cowboys

The cattle industry depended on the cowboy, a seasonal, migrant agricultural worker. After the Civil War, cowboys — one for every 300 to 500 head on the trail — rounded up herds of Texas cattle and

Curly Wolves Howled on Saturday Night, a commercial woodcut from the 1870s. The artist, recording this scene at a tavern near Billings, Montana, captured what he called a "Dude and a Waitress" dancing the "Bull Calves' Medley on the Grand Piano." Illustrations depicting a wild and lively West appeared prominently in magazines like *Harper's Weekly,* which circulated mainly among readers east of the Mississippi.

drove them as far as 1,500 miles north to grazing ranches or to the stockyards where they were readied for shipping by rail to eastern markets. The boss supplied the horses, the cowboy his own bedroll, saddle and spurs, and his labor. The work-day lasted from sunup to sundown, with short night shifts for guarding the cattle. Scurvy, a widespread ailment, could be traced to the basic chuckwagon menu of sowbelly, beans, and coffee, a diet bereft of fruits and vegetables. The cowboy worked without protection from rain or hail, and severe dust storms could cause temporary blindness. As late as 1920, veterans of the range complained that no company would sell life insurance to a cowboy.

In return for his labor, the cowboy received at the best of times about $30 a month. Wages were usually paid in one lump sum at the end of a drive, a policy that encouraged cowboys to spend their money quickly and recklessly in the wide-open cattle towns of Dodge City, Kansas, or Cheyenne, Wyoming. In the 1880s, as wages fell along with beef prices, cowboys fought back by stealing cattle or by forming unions. Many Texas cowboys struck for higher wages in 1883 and nearly all Wyoming cowboys struck in 1886. Aided by the legendary camaraderie fostered in the otherwise desolate conditions of the long drive, cowboys were among the first western workers to organize against employers.

Like other parts of the West, the cattle range was ethnically diverse. Between one-fifth and one-third of all workers were Indian, Mexican, or African American. Indian cowboys worked mainly on the northern plains and in Indian Territory; the vaqueros, who had worked on the Mexican cattle haciendas, predominated in southern Texas. After the Civil War, nearly 9,000 African American cowboys took the trail north from south Texas. Some were former slaves or sons of slaves who had been captured from the African territory of Gambia, where cattle raising was an age-old art.

Like the vaqueros, black cowboys were highly skilled managers of cattle. During the early years of the industry, African American cowboys, unlike Mexicans, earned wages comparable to those paid to Anglos and sometimes worked in integrated drover parties. By the 1880s, as the center of the cattle industry shifted to the more settled regions around the northern ranches, African Americans met exclusionary policies, and most sought other kinds of work. The majority of Anglo cowboys also came from the South. Although they shared with former slaves the hope of escaping the postwar economic devastation of their region, many white cowboys had served with the Confederacy during the Civil War and remained fiercely loyal to its racial standards.

Cowgirls and Prostitutes

Few women worked on the open range. Several cowgirls became legendary as fancy shooters, but only a very small number followed the trail. Sally Redus, wife of an early Texas cattleman, accompanied her husband once on the long drive from Texas to Kansas. Carrying her baby boy on her lap, she most likely rode the enormous distance sidesaddle, with both legs on one side of the horse. Only those few women who boldly dressed in pants or who ran their own ranches participated directly in any part of the cattle industry. Although the Homestead Act allowed women who headed families to file a claim, the majority of those women who managed ranches had taken over for absent or deceased husbands. By the end of the century, daughters reared on ranches were riding astride (or "clothespin style"), roping calves, and on occasion branding cattle, castrating bulls, and cutting their ears to mark them. But as late as 1897 the Sears Roebuck catalog offered twenty-one models of sidesaddles, and not until 1901 did a woman enter an official rodeo contest.

Prostitution employed many women. During the first cattle drive to Abilene in 1867, a few women moved there to work as prostitutes. By the following spring, McCoy's assistant recalled, "they came in swarms, & as the weather was warm 4 or 5 girls could huddle together in a tent very comfortably." Although some women worked in trailside "hog-houses," the best-paid prostitutes congregated in dance halls. Most cattle towns boasted at least one dance hall. Dodge City had two: one with white prostitutes for white patrons, another with black prostitutes for both white and black men.

Perhaps 50,000 women engaged in prostitution west of the Mississippi during the second half of the nineteenth century. Many had come from underpaid work such as dressmaking or domestic service, and few other occupations awaited women in the cattle towns, where the cost of food and lodging was notoriously high. Still, earnings in prostitution were slim. At best a fully employed Wichita prostitute might earn thirty dollars a week, but nearly two-thirds of her income had to be paid out in room and board. Nearly all prostitutes, like most cowboys, were young, in their teens or twenties.

Race shaped the character of prostitution, as it did that of cattle herding. Near United States Army forts, Indian women figured prominently in the trade, providing a source of income for an increasingly desperate people. Across the Southwest, Mexicanas occupied the next lowest level of status, pay, and conditions. Black prostitutes were only slightly better off, but like the others they had little protection from violent clients. Even Anglo women, the best-paid workers, led dangerous lives, according to personal testimony and police records. Frequently married to men who lived off their earnings, prostitutes drank heavily, sometimes used drugs such as cocaine or morphine, and often raised their daughters to become prostitutes like themselves. Suicides and deaths from drug overdoses were not uncommon.

Community and Conflict on the Range

The combination of prostitution, gambling, and drinking worked against stable communities. According to a Kansas proverb, "there's no Sunday west of Junction City and no god west of Salina." Personal violence was notoriously commonplace on the streets and in the barrooms of cattle towns and mining camps. Although most western towns had outlawed the carrying and drawing of guns by 1890, enforcement lagged. Local specialty shops and mail-order catalogs continued to sell weapons with little regulation. Contrary to popular belief, however, gunfights were relatively rare, and murders no more common in the West than in most other parts of the country.

Assault, robbery, and other violent crimes took a sharp upturn throughout the United States after the Civil War. Veterans, disoriented and sometimes embittered, furnished a large part of the growing prison population. In the West, the most popular crime was horse theft, which rose sharply during the peak years of the cattle trade but then dwindled by the 1890s. Capital punishment by legal hanging — or illegal "necktie parties," the victims "jerked to Jesus" — was considered a standard sentence. In Lincoln County, New Mexico, in 1878, business rivalry and cattle stealing caused a feud so violent that one faction hired gunman Billy the Kid, and President Rutherford Hayes sent in troops to halt the bloodshed.

The "range wars" of the 1870s also produced violent conflicts that tore communities apart. By this time farmers and sheep ranchers were encroaching on the grassy fields where cows had once freely grazed and fencing in thousands of acres of formerly open land. Farmers also lobbied the state legislatures to win stricter regulation of the cattle industry. The great cattle barons fought back by ordering their cowboys to cut the barbed-wire fences, a practice that often precipitated a hail of gunfire.

The cattle barons helped to bring about their own demise. During the mid-1880s ranchers eager for greater profits and backed by foreign capital overstocked their herds, and within a short time the cows depleted the increasingly limited supply of grass. Meanwhile, the ferocious heat of the summer of 1885, followed by a winter of freezing blizzards, killed off 90 percent of the cattle. Many ranchers went bankrupt; others turned to smaller ranches and scientific methods to improve breeding and feeding.

The Legendary Wild West

While the actual work of cowboys was becoming more routine, the legend of the Wild West grew into a staple of American popular culture. The first "Westerns" appeared in the form of the dime novel, which by the 1860s was selling in editions of 50,000 or more. Competing against stories about pirates, wars, crime, and sea adventures, the Western genre outsold the others. Edward Zane Carroll Judson's *Buffalo Bill, the King of the Border Men,* first published in 1869, spawned hundreds of other novels, thousands of stories, and one entire magazine devoted to Buffalo Bill. Even before farmers had halted the free-grazing of cattle, writers made tough cowboys and high-spirited women into legends of the Wild West. Real-life African American cowboy Nat Love lived on in the imaginations of many generations as Edward L. Wheeler's dime novel hero Deadwood Dick, who rode the range as a white cowboy in black clothes in over thirty stories. His girlfriend Calamity Jane — "the most reckless buchario in ther Hills" — also took on mythic qualities.

Railroad promoters and herd owners actively encouraged these romantic and heroic images. Cowman Joseph McCoy himself staged Wild West shows in St. Louis and Chicago in which Texas cowboys entertained prospective buyers by roping calves and breaking horses. Many cowboys dressed and talked to fit the stories told about them. "The drovers of the seventies were a wild and reckless bunch," recalled cowboy Teddy Blue. Typically, they had worn a "wide brimmed beaver hat, black or brown with a low crown, fancy shirts, high heeled boots, and sometimes a vest." In the 1880s cowboys adopted the high-crowned (preferably white) Stetson hat ornately detailed shirts with pockets, and striped or checked pants. The first professional photographers often made their living touring the West, setting up studios where cowboys and prostitutes posed in elaborate costumes.

The Wild West shows, which toured the United States and Europe for thirty years, further popularized the mythic West. William Cody, a former pony express rider and chief army scout, had lived as a

Buffalo Bill "Wild West Show" poster from 1899. William Cody's theatrical company toured the United States and Europe for decades, re-enacting various battles and occasionally switching to football (cowboys versus Indians). Cody's style set the pace for both rodeos and western silent films.

boy at the frontier and had actually met the famous Kit Carson. Imitating the mannerisms and living out the last adventures of the fading cowboy culture, Cody hit upon the idea of an extravaganza that would bring the legendary West to those who could never experience it. He hired former cowboys to perform mock stagecoach robberies and battles with Indians, and after the massacre at Wounded Knee he even employed former Ghost Dancers. Revamped as the rodeo, the Wild West show long outlasted Buffalo Bill. At the end of the century, veteran cowboys were enlisting themselves on dude ranches and performing in theaters as rope twirlers or yodeling singers. In 1902 Owen Wister's novel *The Virginian* fixed in the popular imagination the scene of the cowboy facing down the villain and saying, "When you call me that, *smile.*"

THE WORLD'S BREADBASKET

During the last half of the nineteenth century the farmland of middle America became the site of the most intensive and extensive methods of grain production in the world. These twin elements of success went hand in hand. The application of new technology allowed farmers to reach an unprecedented level of efficiency in the planting and harvesting of crops. The land itself, unexcelled in its vastness and richness, prompted the largest migration in American history. As settlers arrived from across Europe and the eastern United States, the number of farms grew from 2 million to 6 million.

New Technologies of Production

The land west of the Mississippi did not yield readily to cultivation. Only after the trees had been cleared and grasslands cut free of roots could the soil be prepared for cultivation. On the best locations, the loamy, fertile ground had built up over centuries into eight or more inches of decayed vegetation. But it now required preliminary breaking or "busting," a process where five or six oxen pulled a plow through the soil, one man guiding the team while another regulated the depth of the cut, or furrow. As a North Dakota settler wrote to his wife back in Michigan, after the first crop the soil became as "soft as can be, any team [of men and animals] can work it."

The great productivity of these new farms depended as much on new technology as on the settlers' hard labor. The reaper, which replaced the cutting of grain by hand with scythes, was invented in eighteenth-century England, redesigned by Cyrus McCormick in the 1830s, and produced in his factory in mass quantities in the 1850s. It featured ridges of triangular knives, like sharks' teeth, that sliced through the stalks as the reaper moved forward under horse power or, later, machine power. The harvester, invented in the 1870s, drew the cut stalks upward to a platform where two men could bind them into sheaves (by the 1880s, an automatic

This "Thirty three horse team harvester" was photographed at the turn of the century in Walla Walla, Washington. Binding the grain into sheaves before it could hit the ground, the "harvester" cut, threshed, and sacked wheat in one single motion.

Hand vs. Machine Labor on the Farm

| Crop | Time Worked | | Labor Cost | |
	Hand	Machine	Hand	Machine
Wheat	61 hours	3 hours	$3.55	$0.66
Corn	39 hours	15 hours	3.62	1.51
Oats	66 hours	7 hours	3.73	1.07
Loose Hay	21 hours	4 hours	1.75	0.42
Baled Hay	35 hours	12 hours	3.06	1.29

knotter would tie them together). Drastically reducing the number of people traditionally required for this work, the harvester speeded the pace manyfold.

Improvements were not confined to the reaper and harvester: from the 1840s on, the U.S. Patent Office recorded an astonishing number of agricultural inventions. By 1880 the general techniques of "modern" farming were almost complete. The reaper and harvester themselves continually under-

went redesign, and were enhanced later by steam and eventually gas power. Mechanized corn planters and machines for mowing or raking hay all but completed the technological arsenal.

In the 1890s, the U.S. commissioner of labor measured the impact of technology on farm productivity. Before the introduction of the wire binder in 1875, he reported, a farmer could plant less than 8 acres of wheat if he were to harvest it successfully without help; by 1890 the same farmer could rely on his new machine to handle with relative ease 135 acres without risk of spoilage. The improvements in the last half of the century allowed an average farmer to produce up to ten times more than was possible with the old implements.

Scientific study of soil, grain, and climatic conditions was another factor in the record output. Heretofore, farmers had to rely on tradition or else experiment with what grain merchants had to offer. In the mid-nineteenth century, federal and state governments began to add inducements to the growing body of expertise, scientific information, and hands-on advice. Through the Morrill Act of 1862, "land-grant" colleges acquired space for campuses in return for promising to institute agricultural programs. The Department of Agriculture, which achieved Cabinet status in 1889, and the Weather Bureau (transferred from the War Department in 1891) also made considerable contributions to farmers' knowledge. The federal Hatch Act of 1887,

Agricultural Acreage in Late-Nineteenth Century

The expansion of farming and cattle-raising rapidly produced regional specialties, with much of the Southwest as well as Colorado, Montana, and Wyoming given over to cattle, while wheat and corn production swept through the Plains states. The South remained dominant in sugar cane production along with cotton. Specialty production, like fruit and sheep, favored the distant West with its unique climates and open spaces.

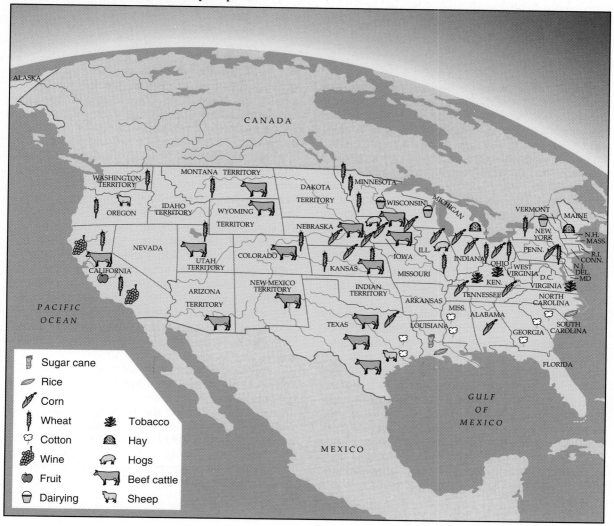

creating a series of experimental agricultural stations, passed along new information especially in the areas of soil minerals and plant growth. Many states added their own agricultural stations, usually connected with state colleges and universities.

Nature nevertheless often reigned over technological innovation and in places seemed to take revenge against these early successes. West of the 98th meridian, perennial dryness from an annual rainfall of less than 28 inches threatened constantly to turn soil into dust and to break plows on the hardened limestone. Summer heat burned out crops and ignited grassfires. Mountains of winter snows turned rivers into spring torrents, flooding fields; heavy fall rains washed crops away. Even good weather invited worms and flying insects to infest the crops. During the 1870s grasshoppers in clouds a mile long ate everything organic, including tree bark and clothes. Mormons erected a statue to the gulls who made a surprise appearance in Utah to eat the 'hoppers. Most farmers were not as lucky as the Mormons.

Producing for Market

From the prairie states of the Midwest to the far reaches of the Great Plains, farming underwent important changes during the last third of the nineteenth century. By 1900 relatively few families still raised all their own provisions. Although farmers tended vegetable gardens and often kept fowl or livestock for household consumption, they raised crops mainly for the market and measured their own success or failure in terms of cash profit. Most farmers specialized in one or two crops, such as wheat and corn or rye and barley, and sent their goods by railroad to eastern distributors and thence national and international markets. In return, they received cash to pay off their mortgages, to buy foodstuffs and factory-made clothing for their families, and to reinvest in the business.

With the aid of their new machinery, farmers had to adapt their crops not only to variable climate but to fluctuating markets. New England farms, decreasing drastically from 1860 to 1900, turned to such specialties as dairy products or fruits and vegetables for nearby urban markets. In the upper Midwest farmers switched from wheat to the production of milk and its by-products. "Cheesedom" moved from its earlier center in western New York and Ohio to the Great Lakes states, and above all to the "dairy state" of Wisconsin.

Farmers experienced all these changes directly. The new machines and expanding market did not guarantee success. Land, draft animals, and equipment remained very expensive, and start-up costs could keep a family in debt for decades. One year of good returns often preceded a year of financial disaster. Weather conditions, international markets, and rail and steam shipping prices all proved equally unpredictable and heartless.

Farmers settling on good lands in the 1860s and 1870s were more fortunate than those to follow. These pioneers who began with only a little capital and worked twenty or thirty years to build up livestock and crops frequently reached old age knowing they could leave productive farmland to their sons or daughters. Latecomers found most of the good land already locked up in production or too expensive to acquire. The new technology and scientific expertise favored the large, well-capitalized farmer over the small one. Between 1880 and 1900 average farm size in the seven leading grain-growing states increased from 64.4 acres to more than 100 acres.

California

The trend toward big farms peaked in California, where farming as a business quickly superseded farming as a way of life. Land reformer and social commentator Henry George pronounced California "not a country of farms but a country of plantations and estates." Well before the Homestead Act, large landowners had acquired the best land and had proceeded to build dams, canals, and other expensive earthworks demanded by the arid soil. Farms of nearly 500 acres dominated the California landscape in 1870; those of 1,000 acres occupied two-thirds of the state's arable land by the turn of the century.

On the "bonanza farms" of the 1870s and 1880s, hundreds of field hands applied the latest technologies, such as great steam-engine tractors. By 1890 California was producing more wheat, mostly for export, than any state save Minnesota. Intense battles in the state legislature over diversion of rivers for irrigation rights underscored the arrival of powerful forces in California to promote large-scale agricultural production.

This scale of production succeeded dramatically with fruit and vegetables. Large- and medium-sized growers, shrewdly combined in cooperative marketing associations during the 1870s and 1880s, used the new refrigerator cars to ship their produce in large quantities to the East and even to Europe. By 1890, cherries, apricots, and oranges, loaded down with mountains of ice, made their way into homes across the United States.

California growers learned quickly that they could satisfy consumer appetites and even create new ones. Orange producers packed their products individually in tissue paper to convince eastern consumers that they were about to eat a luxury fruit. By the turn of the century advertisers were describing oranges as a necessity for good health and had invented the "Sunkist" trademark to be stamped on each orange. California grape growing grew into a big business, promoted by winemaker Paul Masson. Long considered inferior to French wines, California wines found a ready market at lower prices. Other grape growers made their fortunes in raisins. By the early twentieth century these were being packaged for schoolchildren in the famous nickel box wearing the "Sun Maid" trademark.

By 1900, California had become the model for American agribusiness and the dream of the United States as a land of family homesteads had been deeply shaken. If the farm had already become a secondary factor in the northeast economy, it was in the Middle West of Minnesota to Illinois, the plains states, and the South where the future of rural life would be decided.

FARMING COMMUNITIES ON THE PLAINS

Before the Civil War, most Americans regarded the Great Plains as one of the most uninviting areas of the continent. The region stretching west from Kansas and Nebraska, north to Montana and the Dakotas, and south again to Oklahoma and Texas loomed in the popular imagination as the Great Desert, a formidable barrier to expansion and development. There were scarcely any trees to fend off the blazing sun of summer or to provide lumber for homes and fences. In the occasional river or stream flowed a substance described as "muddy gruel." The entire region appeared infinitely vast and hopelessly barren, and only the most adventuresome pioneers were willing to endure its harsh climate in return for little more than desolation.

It took massive improvements in both transportation and farm technology — as well as unrelenting advertising and promotional campaigns — to open this lonely land to settlement. By the 1870s the conditions were met, and within a few years the Great Plains became a vast farming region. In place of the first one-room shanties, sod houses, and log cabins stood substantial frame or brick farmhouses, along with barns, smokehouses, and stables. But the built environment took nothing away from the predominating vista, the expansive fields of grain.

"You have no idea, Beulah," wrote a Dakota farmer to his wife, "of what [the wheat farms] are like until you see them. For mile after mile there is not a sign of a tree or stone and just as level as the floor of your house. . . . Wheat never looked better and it is nothing but wheat, wheat, wheat."

Populating the Plains

Over 2 million Europeans, lured by agents combing the villages for prospects or encouraged by reports from relatives and fellow villagers, settled the Great Plains between 1870 and 1900. Some districts in Minnesota seemed virtual colonies of Sweden; others housed the largest settlements of Finns in the New World. In thinly settled North Dakota Scandinavians constituted 30 percent of the population, with Norwegians the largest group. Nebraska, whose population as early as 1870 was 25 percent foreign-born, concentrated Germans, Swedes, Danes, and Czechs. A smaller proportion of European immigrants settled in Kansas, still fewer in the southwestern territories.

The quality of life on the Great Plains, although difficult, often surpassed the settlers' previous circumstances. Germans and Russians found the soil similar to that of their homeland but the weather more severe. German Mennonites, who had fled religious persecution after the Protestant Reformation, had settled first in the Volga River district of Russia, and moved again in the 1870s to the American Great Plains. Their example of heavy Russian coats and houses of sun-dried bricks helped other settlers survive the arctic winters in areas where lumber was scarce.

Many groups of immigrants formed their own tight-knit communities. The Poles who settled central Nebraska in the 1880s hoped to establish an exclusive colony. The German Hutterites, who disavowed private property, established the Bon Homme colony in South Dakota in 1874 and lived as much as possible in seclusion.

Native-born settlers rarely established long-lasting communities. The largest number had migrated from states bordering the Mississippi River, all of which lost population in the decade after passage of the Homestead Act. Settling as individual families rather than as whole communities, they found life on the Great Plains exceptionally solitary. The usual rectangular homestead of 160 acres placed farm families at least half a mile and often much farther from each other. To stave off isolation, families sometimes purposely settled on adjoining corners of their plots. Still, mobility was so high on

Drawing by Mary Anna Hallock Foote (1847–1938), the first woman to become an important magazine illustrator of the American West. Contributing to *Scribner's* and *Harper's Weekly*, she offered a vision of the West that incorporated the domestic setting of home and family. A resident of Leadville, Colorado, later Idaho and California, Foote also became a famous regional novelist.

the Great Plains that between a third and a half of all households pulled up stakes within a decade.

Communities flourished in towns such as Grand Island, Nebraska, Coffeyville, Kansas, and Fargo, North Dakota, which served the larger agricultural region. Built alongside the railroad, they grew as commercial centers, home to banking, medical, legal, and retail services. Town life fostered a special intimacy; even in the county graveyard, it was said, a town resident remained among neighbors. On the other hand, closeness did not necessarily promote social equality or even deep friendship. On the basis

of education (for the handful of doctors and lawyers) and, more important, investment property (held mainly by railroad officers and bankers), individuals and families in farm districts arranged themselves in a social hierarchy. Reinforced by family ties and religious and ethnic differences, this hierarchy often persisted across generations. Residents also formed exclusive clubs, such as fraternal or secret societies, at a much faster rate than their contemporaries in the East. The Independent Order of Oddfellows, the Benevolent and Protective Order of Elks, and the Good Templers gathered the town's men, while auxiliaries such as the Order of the Eastern Star, Phythia Sisterhood, and Companions of the Forest joined women in secret rituals.

Work, Dawn to Dusk

Most farm families survived, and prospered if they could, through hard work, often from dawn to dusk. Men's activities in the fields tended to be seasonal, with heavy work during planting and harvest. At other times, their labor centered in construction or repair of buildings and care of livestock. Women's activities were usually far more routine, week in and week out: cooking and canning of seasonal fruits and vegetables, washing, ironing, churning cream for butter, and keeping chickens for their eggs. Women might occasionally take in boarders, usually young men working temporarily in railroad construction, and they tended to the young children. Many women complained about the ceaseless drudgery, especially when they watched their husbands invest in farm equipment rather than domestic appliances. Others, however, relished the challenge. An Iowa woman, for example, liked "to have whole control of my house; can say I am monarch of all I survey and none to dispute my right."

While many women found themselves taking on unfamiliar chores, their children also joined in the family's labors. Milking the cows, hauling water, and running errands to neighboring farms could be done once a child had reached the age of nine or so. The one-room school, where all grades learned together, taught the basics of literacy and arithmetic that a future farmer or commercial employee would require. Sons might be expected to work for ten to twenty years on the family farm, generally for their subsistence alone. Older sons and daughters alike might move to the nearest town to find wage work and contribute their earnings to the family coffer.

The harsh climate and unyielding soil nevertheless forced all but the most reclusive families to seek out friends and neighbors. Clearing the land for cultivation or for roadbeds, raising houses and barns, or completing a harvest before a threatening storm demanded many hands. A group of neighbors might agree to work with each other haying, harvesting grain, and threshing it. They also traded their labor, calculated by the hour, with families who needed help with machinery or with small children in the household. The well-to-do farmer might "rent" his reaper in exchange for a small cash fee and, for instance, three days' labor. Housewives routinely traded among themselves, exchanging garden produce for bread and milk or for assistance

during childbirth or disability. For relaxation, neighbors gathered for barn dances and whole communities turned out for picnics on Decoration Day and the Fourth of July. Long-lasting friendships grew from these occasions, including the many quilting bees, husking bees, and apple bees that joined families from across the countryside.

Much of this informal barter and exchange nevertheless resulted from lack of cash rather than a lasting desire to cooperate. But during the last decades of the century, cash transactions took over, and even the practice of bartering goods with other farm wives and local merchants — butter and eggs in return for clothes or seed — diminished sharply. In particular, as farmers began to specialize in single market crops, their wives stopped producing for local markets and devoted more of their time to childcare and housework. Better roads and rural free mail delivery eased the sense of isolation. Nevertheless, many farmers wondering if they had chosen the best life for themselves and their families stood only a step away from financial disaster.

The Garden of Eden was not to be found in the Great Plains, no matter how hard the average farm family worked. Again and again foreclosures wiped out the small landowner, who was vulnerable to dips in commodity prices, bad decisions, natural disasters, or illness. By the century's close, the swift growth of rural population had ended. Although writers of fiction and celebratory orators alike continued to portray farming as the source of virtue and economic well-being, the hard reality of big money and political power told a far different story.

THE WESTERN LANDSCAPE

Throughout the nineteenth century many Americans viewed western expansion as the nation's manifest destiny. Even more marveled at the region's natural and cultural wonders. Their fascination grew with the proliferation of literature, entertainments, and even museums and traveling exhibits featuring western themes. The public east of the Mississippi craved stories about the region and visual images of its sweeping vistas. Many Europeans felt the same way and welcomed Sitting Bull and the other Indian people who toured Europe with Buffalo Bill's Wild West shows. Artists and photographers carved out their reputations in what they saw and imagined. Scholars, from geologists and botanists to historians and anthropologists, toured the trans-Mississippi West in pursuit of new data. The region and its peoples came to represent

Merced River, Yosemite Valley,(1866) by Alfred Bierstadt. Bierstadt became one of the first artists to capture on enormous canvasses the vastness and rugged terrain of mountains and western wilderness. Many other artists joined Bierstadt to form the "Rocky Mountain School." In time, the camera largely replaced the paintbrush, and most Americans formed an image of these majestic peaks from postcards and magazine illustrations.
(Albert Bierstadt. Merced River, Yosemite Valley. 1866. Oil on canvas, 36 × 50 in. The Metropolitan Museum of Art. Gift of the sons of William Paton, 1909.)

what was both unique and magnificent about the American landscape.

Nature's Majesty

Alexis de Tocqueville, the famed commentator on American society, found little beauty in the land west of the Mississippi. Writing in the 1830s, he described the landscape as "more and more uneven and sterile," the soil "punctured in a thousand places by primitive rocks sticking out here and there like the bones of a skeleton when sinews of flesh have perished." By the end of the century, scores of writers had provided an entirely different visual image of the American West, describing such spec-

tacular natural sites as the Tetons and High Sierra, the vast meadows of waving grasses and beautiful flowers, the expansive canyons and rushing white water, and even the exquisite deserts covered with sagebrush or dotted with flowering cactus and enticing precisely for their impression of vacancy. A traveler through the Yellowstone country recalled "the varied scenery" of the West and its "stupendous & remarkable manifestations of nature's forces," an impression destined to stay with him "as long as memory lasts." Moved by such descriptions, President Lincoln set aside Yosemite as a nature preserve in 1864 and appointed the landscape architect Frederick Law Olmstead its first commissioner.

The section of the Rocky Mountains destined to

become Yellowstone National Park inspired numerous reveries. Early visitors created legends of huge sky-high lakes, boiling mud, and spectacular waterfalls. In 1871 the federal government allotted $40,000 for explorations by a team of scientists from the Geological and Geographical Survey of the Territories, which included the early landscape photographer William H. Jackson and the engraver Thomas Moran. They brought back to the U.S. Congress visual proof of the monumental scenery of the West, including the Grand Canyon. Congress named Yellowstone the first national park in 1872. Yosemite and Sequoia in California, Mount Rainier in Washington, Crater Lake in Oregon, and Glacier in Montana were named national parks between 1890 and 1910.

Landscape painters, particularly the group that became known as the Rocky Mountain School, also

The Establishment of National Parks and Forests

The setting aside of land for national parks saved large districts of the West from early commercial development and industrial degradation, establishing a precedent for the later establishment of additional parks in economically marginal but scenic territory. The West, home to the vast majority of park space, became a principal site of tourism by the end of the nineteenth century.

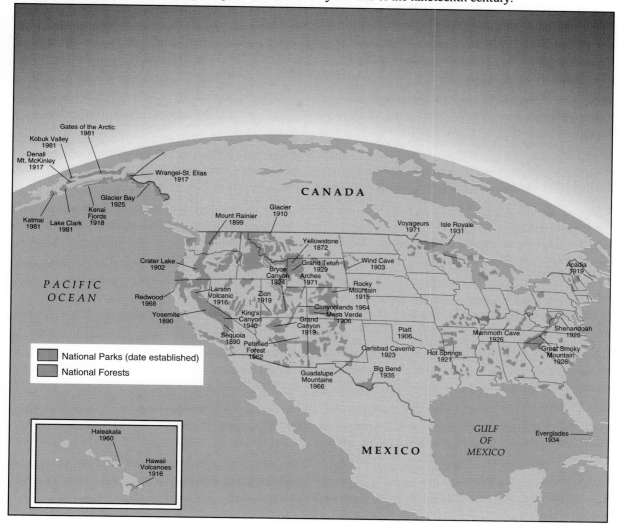

piqued the public's interest in western scenery. Exhibited in galleries and museums and reproduced in popular magazines, their sketches and paintings circulated western imagery throughout the country and through much of Europe. Alfred Bierstadt, the most popular of the Rocky Mountain School, was born in Germany but raised in Massachusetts. Before he set out on the Oregon Trail in the 1860s his brothers, professional photographers, supplied him with a camera. Thus equipped, Bierstadt captured details that he would later elaborate in his paintings. Bierstadt painted mountains so wondrous that they became nearly surreal, projecting a divine aura behind the majesty of nature. His "earthscapes" — huge canvases with exacting details of animals and plants — thrilled viewers and were sold for tens of thousands of dollars each.

Toll on the Land

Although the federal government set aside huge expanses of land for preserves and parks, the early administrators did little to keep them environmentally intact. Railroads lobbied for rights of way through Yellowstone, and hunters went after protected wildlife. Under human pressure, delicate ecologies perished more quickly in the West than anywhere else on the continent. Viewing the land as a resource to command, the new inhabitants often looked past the existing flora and fauna toward a landscape remade strictly for commercial purposes. In some areas they produced changes nearly as cataclysmic as those of the Ice Age.

Rooting out many existing species, farmers "improved" the land by introducing exotic plants and animals — that is, biological colonies indigenous to other regions and continents. Some of the new plants and animals flourished in alien surroundings, many did not. Farmers also unintentionally introduced new varieties of weeds and rats. Surviving portions of older grasslands and meadows eventually could be found only along railroad tracks, in graveyards, or inside national parks. Overall, the biological diversity of the region was drastically reduced.

Inland bodies of water were also depleted. Before white settlement, rainfall had drained into lakes and springs, and throughout the plains watering spots were no more than fifteen miles apart. To irrigate their crops, farmers retained water, thereby causing a significant drop in the water table. Lake Tulare in California's Central Valley, for example,

had occupied up to 760 square miles. After farmers began to irrigate their land by tapping the rivers that fed the Tulare, the lake shrunk to a mere 36 square miles by the early twentieth century. At last Lake Tulare, which for thousands of years had supported rich aquatic and avian life, disappeared entirely. The land left behind, now wholly dependent upon irrigation, grew so alkaline in spots that it could no longer be used for agriculture.

The determination of western farmers to protect their water supply indirectly led to the creation of national forests and the Forest Service. The General Land Revision Act of 1891 indicated the need for forest reserves as watersheds offsetting the threats posed by lumbering, overgrazing, and forest fires. President Benjamin Harrison ordered the protection of fifteen reserves with some 16 million acres, and President Grover Cleveland added more than 21 million acres later in the 1890s. By 1897 the secretary of the interior had gained the authority to regulate the reserves under the Forest Management Act, and the federal government began its widescale regulatory activities.

The "American Primitive"

Since at least the early nineteenth century and the novels of John Fenimore Cooper, many Americans had relished tales about Indian peoples, settlers, and U.S. Army soldiers. The new techniques of graphic reproduction in the popular press of the century's last three decades widened the audience for such stories and encouraged painters and photographers to provide new images, authentic as well as fabricated. The public craved elaborately detailed portrayals of western life, but most fans sought stereotyped depictions of bold cowboys and exotic savages.

As the Wild West vanished, imaginative artists worked fast to create their own version. A young German American artist, Charles Schreyvogel, saw Buffalo Bill's tent show in Buffalo and decided to make the West his life's work. By 1900 Schreyvogel's canvases were valued for their details. His depiction of Indian peoples and soldiers show them fighting furiously but without inflicting visible bloody wounds. Charles Russell, son of a brick manufacturer and himself owner of a sheep ranch, created an imaginary West, producing paintings of buffalo hunts and first encounters between Indian peoples and white homesteaders, events he had never observed.

Frederic Remington, the most famous of all western artists, left Yale Art School to visit Montana in 1881, became a Kansas sheepherder and tavern owner, and then returned to painting. Inspired by newspaper stories of the army campaign against the Apaches, he made himself into a war correspondent and captured in his sketches vivid scenes of battle. Painstakingly accurate in physical details, especially of horses, his paintings nevertheless contributed to the romantic myth of the Old West. By the turn of the century he was the chief magazine illustrator of western history.

Remington joined hundreds of other painters and engravers in reproducing the most popular historic scene: Custer's Last Stand. Totally fictionalized by white artists to show a heroic General Custer personally holding off advancing Indians, these renditions perfectly suited the tastes of their audiences. Indian artists recorded a strikingly different version of the episode in designs sketched onto their robes.

Photographers often rendered more complex views of the West, including its human inhabitants. Dozens of early photographers from the Bureau of American Ethnology captured the gaze of proud Indian peoples in portraits and their actions at work, digging clams or grinding corn. President Theodore Roosevelt praised the photos of Edward Sheriff Curtis as conveying tribal spirituality, and many Americans agreed. Generations later, in the 1960s and 1970s, Curtis's photographs captured the imagination of western enthusiasts who were unaware or unconcerned that this sympathetic artist had often posed his subjects or retouched his photos to blur out any artifacts of white society.

Painters and photographers led the way for scholarly observers of human society. The early ethnographer and pioneer of field work in anthropology, Lewis Henry Morgan, devoted his life to the study of Indian family or kinship patterns, mostly of eastern tribes such as the Iroquois, who adopted him into their Hawk Clan. In 1851 he published *League of the Ho-de-no-sau-nee, or Iroquois,* considered the first scientific account of an Indian tribe. In 1860 Morgan ventured into Cheyenne country to examine the patterns and names given to Cheyenne relatives. His major work, *Ancient Society,* published in 1877, proposed a universal scheme of social evolution, from savagery to barbarism to civilization.

Alice Cunningham Fletcher, a reformer who supported the Dawes Severalty Act, became a prolific writer on the Omaha tribe, especially its music, and transcribed hundreds of songs. She became well known to government officials and was commissioned to prepare the Indian Bureau exhibit for the New Orleans Exposition of 1884. The following year she produced for the U.S. Senate a report entitled *Indian Education and Civilization,* one of the first surveys of the needs and status of Indians. A founder of the American Anthropological Society and president of the American Folk-Lore Society, she encouraged both professional societies to pursue the study of Indians. Many amateur scholars and writers of fiction with less sophistication and no training also collected numerous tribal stories simply by listening and writing down what they heard.

Interest in Indian societies expanded into a hobby for millions of Americans, and not only in western states. As white settlers and the federal government continued to banish the tribes from reservations and drive them further into poverty, scholars and amateurs alike pursued a study of Indian cultures. Adults and children shared delight at turning up arrowheads. Fraternal organizations such as the Elks and Eagles borrowed tribal terminology. The Boy Scouts and Girl Scouts, the nation's premier youth organizations, instilled patriotism but also strength of character through self-reliance in nature outings that incorporated a large dose of tribal lore. Images of tribal chiefs and of buffalo were chosen for the most frequently used American coins.

CONCLUSION

The transformation of the Western landscape pointed up the larger meaning of expansion. Almost overnight, mines opened, cities grew, and vast farms or cattle ranches spread out across the countryside. With the assistance of the railroad and new technologies of development, from mechanical harvesters to Gatling guns, new communities formed and displaced old ones. The new communities soon produced their own conflicts, sometimes bitter and violent, over land and resources. Cowboys battled farmers, cattle and sheep ranchers exchanged legal threats, and mine owners used private militias against miners.

At great human and environmental cost, the development of the West met the nation's demand for mineral resources for its expanding industries and agricultural products for the people of the growing cities. By opening up such huge territory and bringing it into the nation, the West had prepared the way for the industrial age.

CHRONOLOGY

1848	Treaty of Guadalupe Hidalgo
1849–1860s	California gold rush
1853	Gadsden Purchase
1858	Comstock Lode discovered
1859	"Cortina War"
1862	Homestead Act Morrill Act
1865–67	"Great Sioux War"
1866	Southern Homestead Act Texas cattle drive begins
1869	Golden spike struck for transcontinental railroad Board of Indian Commissioners created Edward Zane Carroll Judson's *Buffalo Bill, the King of the Border Men*, sets off "Wild West" publishing craze
1870s	Grasshopper attacks on the plains
1872	Yellowstone National Park created
1873	Timber Culture Act
1875	Sioux war in Black Hills of Dakotas
1876	Colorado statehood Custer's Last Stand
1877	Desert Land Act *Munn v. Illinois*
1881	Helen Hunt Jackson, *A Century of Dishonor*
1882–83	Sante Fe, Southern Pacific, and Northern Pacific railroad link
1886	Bad winter in West ends cattle boom
1887	Dawes Severalty Act
1890	Sioux Ghost Dance movement Massacre of Lakota Sioux at Wounded Knee Wyoming and Idaho statehood Census Bureau officially closes frontier
1896	Utah statehood

Additional Readings

SUSAN ARMITAGE and ELIZABETH JAMESON, eds., *The Women's West* (1987). A collection of essays on women in western settlement. Stresses the varieties of experience among women of differing backgrounds, ethnic groups, and races.

ALLAN G. BOGUE, *From Prairie to Corn Belt: Farming on the Illinois and Iowa Prairies in the Nineteenth Century* (1963). A close economic interpretation of the midwestern agricultural frontier. Examines the growth of farming from the pioneering homesteads to intensive, large-scale businesses and discusses the advantages enjoyed by the early settlers and their descendants over latecomers.

ANNE M. BUTLER, *Daughters of Joy, Sisters of Misery: Prostitutes in the American West, 1865–1890* (1985). A study of ordinary prostitutes rather than the notorious and financially successful madams that fill western lore. Pays special attention to the women's background, age, health, and family status.

WILLIAM CRONON, GEORGE MILES, and JAY GITLIN, eds., *Under an Open Sky: Rethinking America's Western Past* (1992). A useful collection of essays that reinterpret older evidence and add new data. The essays stress the bitter conflicts over territory, the racial and gender barriers to democratic community, and the tragic elements of western history.

PATRICIA NELSON LIMERICK, *The Legacy of Conquest: The Unbroken Past of the American West* (1987). A controversial and popular "revisionist" history of the West. Focused on conflict, Limerick's study shows the frontier most of all as a site of racial antagonism.

FREDERICK C. LUEBKE, ed., *Ethnicity on the Great Plains* (1980). Essays on Germans, Czechs, Russians, and other Europeans resettling in agricultural districts. The essays show that the immigrants, rather than assimilating, often sought to re-create their homeland communities within the United States.

JOHN G. NEIHARDT, *Black Elk Speaks; Being the Life Story of a Holy Man of the Oglala Sioux* (1961). A classic as-told-to autobiographical account published originally in 1932. Black Elk recalls the tragedy of his tribe's destruction following the events involving General Custer and the Battle of the Little Bighorn.

THOMAS E. SHERIDAN, *Los Tucsonenses: The Mexican Community in Tucson, 1854–1941* (1986). A highly readable account of Mexican American communities in the Southwest. Sheridan shows how a midcentury accommodation of Anglos and Mexicanos faded with the absorption of the region into the national economy, and with the steady displacement of the Mexicano community from its agricultural landholdings.

KEVIN STARR, *Americans and the California Dream, 1850–1915* (1973). A study of California as the mythmaking "Golden State." Describes Americans' images of California's potential riches and natural beauty, and the ways the myths themselves became powerful conditions of immigration and development.

JACK WESTON, *The Real American Cowboy* (1985). A lively account of the cowboy. Emphasizes the cowboy's identity as a low-paid, badly treated western agricultural laborer and the cowboys' efforts to better their conditions.

RICHARD WHITE, *"It's Your Misfortune and None of My Own": A History of the American West* (1991). A wide-ranging history that emphasizes cultural contact and the environment. Shows that conflicting cultures with little understanding of each other clashed tragically, with great losses to the environment and the ideal of a democratic American community.

19 THE INCORPORATION OF AMERICA, 1865–1900

AMERICAN COMMUNITIES

● CHICAGO, ILLINOIS

Chicago, a moiling metropolis of energy, was one of the fastest-growing cities in the world in the second half of the nineteenth century. Its population doubled every decade after the Civil War, topping one million by 1890. The nation's second major industrial center, Chicago housed the heartland's basic industries in food, metal, and transportation. The trainlines slicing through its downtown and the stockyards bordering its residential neighborhoods lent distinctive character to what poet Carl Sandburg would later describe as the "city of big shoulders . . . hog butcher of the world."

Sears and Roebuck, Armour, Pullman, and McCormick were all headquartered in Chicago. Marshall Field, the department store magnate known as the richest man west of New York, lived there. So, too, did masses of working people. The city's foreign-born population, 40 percent of its total, transformed Chicago into a mosaic of immigrant communities.

GERMANS AND OTHER IMMIGRANTS FORM NEW COMMUNITIES IN THE INDUSTRIAL HEARTLAND

Germans, who constituted one-quarter of the city's wage-earning population, secured many of the most-skilled and highest-paying blue-collar jobs, especially in woodworking and the machine tool industry. The Irish, prominent in a scattering of highly paid crafts, mostly worked as factory operatives, servants, or common laborers in the construction trades. Firmly entrenched in the local Democratic party, Irish Americans predominated in municipal services such as police, fire, and sanitation. Newly arrived Poles, Czechs, Italians, and other immigrants from eastern and southern Europe lacked either marketable skills or political influence and worked mainly as unskilled laborers in such booming industries as meat-packing and garment manufacturing.

Residential patterns echoed and reinforced the industrial hierarchy. Chicago's business and political leaders concentrated in the "Gold Coast" district, which stretched north along the Lake Michigan shoreline and into woody suburbs, while immigrants clustered in less glamorous neighborhoods. The Irish resided in large numbers along the unhealthy Chicago River until displaced by Poles and Italians. Downtown, African Americans were crowded into run-down districts with fewer city services. Residing on the Northwest Side, with its densely populated blocks of two-story frame houses, Germans generally held the most valuable residential property in Chicago's working-class neighborhoods.

"In a Strange Land — Asking the Way," c.1874. Arriving in the United States during the second largest wave of German immigration, these newcomers of various ages and skills entered a society plunged into economic distress. Nevertheless, they successfully located other immigrants like themselves, found ways to help each other, and built thriving communities.

Like most other groups, German immigrants established their own community. They published daily and weekly newspapers in their mother tongue, and large numbers continued to speak their own language. They rarely intermarried, even with non-German neighbors. Like many immigrant groups, Germans maintained their own school system and parishes. To protect their families from unanticipated hardship, they formed sickness-and-death societies, which paid benefits to stricken members. Such orders as Harugari and Hermannssohne (the Sons of Herman) even demanded that all business be conducted in the German language. Of scarcely less importance was the neighborhood tavern, meeting place for many political and labor organizations.

The children of German immigrants, relatively well educated and prepared for social mobility, usually left behind their parents' language and much of their culture. Although Germans continued to reign as the city's largest ethnic group until after

World War I, large numbers had moved beyond the city limits and scattered themselves among the new suburbs. Their old neighborhood hallmarks, the Old World–style beer gardens or groves that had entertained whole families, had all but vanished.

By the turn of the century the "Stage Dutchman" of the vaudeville circuit was telling jokes and singing sentimental songs in a comical, broken English about the efforts of the first immigrants to make themselves into Americans. Meanwhile, second-generation German Americans were inventing Tin Pan Alley — the sheet music industry — and cleverly devising some of the nation's most popular nostalgic tunes, such as "By the Banks of the Wabash Far Away," later adopted as the state song of Indiana. One of the founders of Tin Pan Alley, Gus Edwards (born Augustus Edward Simon in Germany), had his start entertaining fellow tobacco workers in the 1880s with his renditions of German folk music. Rising into show business through vaudeville and music halls, he composed many popular tunes, including "By the Light of the Silvery Moon." In 1939 Bing Crosby starred in a song-filled movie based on Edwards's life. Through popular culture such German Americans created a lasting rendition of the American past. They also helped to shape the emerging national identity.

Chicago's German immigrants were well situated geographically to play this role. Their city served as gateway to the West for both people and commerce. It furnished the railroad link between East and West that allowed goods and services to soar in both directions. Chicago provided a home to several of the nation's largest law firms, banks, and corporate headquarters in the country. By the end of the century, the Chicago Board of Trade rivaled the New York Stock Exchange as an economic institution of both regional and national significance, and, moreover, the leading merchants of the two cities nurtured a special relationship, allowing capital to flow readily between both commercial centers.

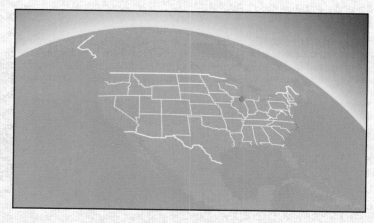

Chicago and its immigrant population thus stood at the center of what the historian Alan Trachtenberg has called "the incorporation of America." During the last third of the nineteenth century, the expansion and consolidation of capital and commerce produced a national economy governed by gigantic corporations — as well as a prestigious new middle class of clerks and managers and a population that found a new kind of livelihood in the factories and shops. Swift material changes, transforming both the cities and the pace of daily life, offered the growing numbers of urban residents a bright commercial world of style and excitement. But these same developments also prompted resentments among those who failed to benefit from this transformation and produced conflict over what Americans might do with their new potential.

RISE OF INDUSTRY, TRIUMPH OF BUSINESS

After the Civil War, the emergence and consolidation of large-scale corporations drastically reshaped the nation's economy. Businesses grew to unforeseen size, their ownership concentrated in a few hands. By century's end, a handful of large corporations ran the nation's key industries. At the helm were unimaginably wealthy capitalists such as Andrew Carnegie, Jay Gould, and John D. Rockefeller, all powerful leaders of a new national business community.

The Great Boom

In the decades after the Civil War American industry made itself a new wonder of the world. The Centennial Exposition of 1876 celebrated not so much the American Revolution one hundred years earlier as the industrial and technological promise of the century to come. Its central theme was *power*. In the main building — at the time the largest on earth — the visiting emperor of Brazil marked the opening day by throwing a switch on a giant steam engine. Examining the telephone, which he had never before seen in operation, he gasped, "My God, it talks!" Patented the same year by Alexander Graham Bell, the telephone signaled the rise of the United States to world leadership in industrial technology.

The year 1876 also marked the opening of Thomas Alva Edison's laboratory in Menlo Park, New Jersey, one of the first devoted to industrial research. Not yet thirty years old, Edison could already claim credit for the mimeograph, the multiplex telegraph, and the stock ticker. In October 1879 his research team hit upon its most marketable invention, a vacuum bulb that burned for over thirteen hours. On December 31 Edison brought 3,000 people by a special train to witness the sight of hundreds of electric lights illuminating his shop and neighborhood streets. By 1892 the Edison Electric Illuminating Company had launched its service in New York City in the financial district. A wondrous source of light and power, electricity revolutionized both industry and urban life.

By this time American inventors, who had filed nearly half a million patents since the close of the

A whimsical rendition of Thomas Edison's laboratories in Menlo Park, New Jersey, c.1880. The commercial artist imagined a great electrical light illuminating the entire region. When Edison announced in 1879 the invention of the electrical light, within six weeks the stock market turned jittery and gas company shares fell sharply: investors feared his "magic."-

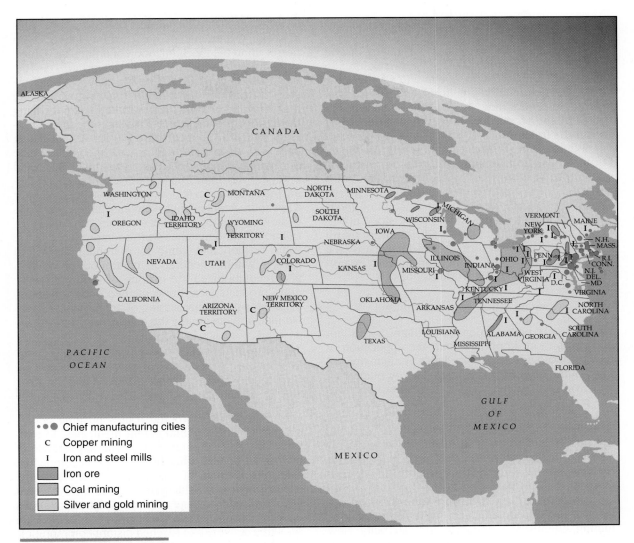

Patterns of Industry, 1900

Industrial manufacturing concentrated in the Northeast and Middle West, while the raw materials for production came mostly from other parts of the nation.

Civil War, were previewing the marvels of the next century. Henry Ford, working as an electrical engineer for the Detroit Edison Company, was already experimenting with the gasoline-burning internal combustion engine and designing his own automobile. By 1900 American companies had produced over 4,000 automobiles. The Wright brothers staged the first airplane flight at Kitty Hawk, North Carolina, in 1903, putting in sight the prospect of commercial aviation.

In the decades after the Civil War, though, the principal agent of industrial growth was the vast transcontinental railroad, completed in 1869. By the early 1880s there were three more major lines (the Southern Pacific, the Northern Pacific, and the Atchison, Topeka and Santa Fe), and the addition of the Great Northern a decade later completed the most extensive transportation network in the world. Railroads linked cities in every state and serviced a nationwide market for goods. Freight trains carried bountiful natural resources such as iron, coal, and minerals, which supplied the raw materials for industry, as well as food for the growing urban labor force.

The monumental advances in transportation and communication facilitated the progressively westward relocation of industry. The geographic center of manufacturing, computed by the gross value of products, was near the middle of Pennsylvania in 1850, in western Pennsylvania by 1880, and near Mansfield, Ohio, in 1900. Flour milling moved from the east coast to Rochester, New York, then to Ohio, and finally to Minneapolis and Kansas City. The manufacture of agricultural equipment relocated from central New York to Illinois and Wisconsin, while the production of wire moved from Massachusetts to Illinois.

Industry grew at a pace not only unprecedented but previously unimaginable. The output of capital goods rose at more than 7 percent per year (compared with less than 5 percent annually before the Civil War). In 1865 the annual production of goods was estimated at $2 billion; by 1900 it stood at $13 billion, and the United States had risen from fourth to first in the world in terms of productivity. By the early twentieth century, American industry manufactured one-third of the world's goods.

Mechanization Takes Command

This industrial boom depended on many factors, but none was more important than the application of new technologies to increase labor productivity and the volume of goods. Machines, factory managers, and workers together created a system of continuous production by which more could be made, and faster, than anywhere else on earth. Higher productivity depended not only on machinery and technology but on economies of scale and speed, reorganization of factory labor and business management, and the unparalleled growth of a market for goods of all kinds.

Mechanized production both fostered and developed from interrelated innovations in metallurgy, mining, chemistry, hydraulics, and electricity. New materials, such as "soft" steel, lubricants for high-powered machines and abrasives for grinding facilitated wide-scale retooling. By the late 1890s many factories had replaced steam power with electricity. This reliable and increasingly inexpensive energy source made possible dramatic changes in the industrial uses of light, heat, and motion.

The meat-packers of Cincinnati set up the earliest production line during the 1860s. The process of converting a domesticated animal into meat began with a live pig. A chain around the hind leg whirled the body to an overhead rail which carried it to the slaughter — all in barely half a minute's time. Then hair and bristles were removed by a scraping machine, the carcass shifted to a conveyor belt where the chest was split and the organs removed, and the body placed in a cooler. These mechanical innovations displaced patterns of hand labor centuries old. Opponents of meat eating looked with horror upon the mechanization of animal slaughter, comparing the process to modern warfare.

Sometimes a single new machine could instantly transform production, mechanizing every stage from processing the raw material to packaging the product. The cigarette-making machine, patented in 1881, shaped the tobacco, encased it in paper into an endless tube, and snipped off the tube at cigarette-length intervals. This machine could produce more than 7,000 cigarettes per hour, replacing the worker who at best made 3,000 per day. After a few more years of improvements, fifteen machines could meet the total market for American cigarettes. Diamond brand matches were soon produced in the same fashion and came to dominate the world market. Within a generation, continuous production also revolutionized the making of furniture, cloth, grain products, soap, and canned goods; refining, distilling, and the processing of animal and vegetable fats; and eventually the automobile.

Mass Retailing

To distribute the growing volume of goods, businesses demanded new techniques of marketing and merchandising. For generations, legions of sellers ("drummers") had worked routes pushing goods, especially hardware and patent medicines, to individual buyers and retail stores. The appearance of mail-order houses after the Civil War accompanied the consolidation of the railroad lines and the expansion of the postal system. Rates were lowered for freight and postage alike, and railroad stations opened post offices and sold money orders. By 1896 rural free delivery had reached distant communities. The successful Chicago-based mail-order houses grew directly out of this service. Sears and Roebuck (which began by selling watches by mail) and Montgomery Ward (which started out with a mail-order catalog of department store items) offered an enormous variety of goods, from shoes to buggies to cream separators for farmers.

High profits depended on making more goods accessible to more customers. This in turn required marketing to keep up with the speed of mass production. At Sears, each department was scheduled to send out an order within fifteen minutes of its placement, or else pay a fine. Each department had its own manager, who controlled specifications, volume, wholesale prices, wage scales, employee discipline, and advertising copy.

The chain store performed a similar consumer

service. By 1900, half a dozen grocery chains had sprung up. A&P (originally named the Great Atlantic and Pacific Tea Company to celebrate the completion of the transcontinental railroad) was the largest. Frank and Charles Woolworth offered inexpensive variety goods in over 1,000 five-and-ten-cent stores established in the United States and Great Britain by 1919. Other chains selling drugs, costume jewelry, shoes, cigars, and furniture soon appeared, offering a greater selection of goods and lower prices than the small, independent stores. Community-based retailers pushed for antichain legislation in several states.

The department stores reigned over the urban market. These palaces of merchandise, with their attractive display and convenient arrangement of goods, enticed buyers and browsers alike. Beginning shortly after the Civil War, department stores began to take up much of the business formerly enjoyed by specialty shops. Soon they had surpassed the shops, offering a spectrum of services that included rest rooms, restaurants, ticket agencies, nurseries, reading rooms, and post offices. Elegantly appointed with imported carpets, sweeping marble staircases, and crystal chandeliers, the department store raised retailing to new heights. By the close of the century, Marshall Field of Chicago, Filene's of Boston, The Emporium of San Francisco, Wanamaker's of Philadelphia, and Macy's of New York had come to represent the splendors of those great cities as well as the apex of mass retailing.

Advertising lured customers to the department stores, the chains, and the independent neighborhood shops. The advertising revolution began in 1869, when Francis Wayland Ayer founded the earliest agency, but the firm hired its first full-time copy writers only in 1891. Ayer's handled the accounts of such companies as Montgomery Ward, Proctor & Gamble, and the National Biscuit Company, and its success encouraged the organization of a powerful advertising industry. With the help of this new sales tool, department stores' gross commercial revenues raced upward from $8 million in 1860 to $102 million in 1900.

Integration, Combination, and Merger

Business leaders moved purposefully to exercise greater control of the American economy and to enlarge their own commercial empires. In every aspect of their business, from sources of raw materials to the organization of production, from the conditions of labor to public opinion, they acted shrewdly. The federal war contracts and high pro-

Montgomery Ward Company, Chicago, c.1870s. This "sectional view" imaginatively strips away exterior walls to show the activity of each department of the great mail-order firm. The artist suggests that all who work at the Ward Company must be overwhelmingly busy simply to meet customer demand.

tective tariffs of the Civil War era had given American businesses an enormous boost. The business cycle, alternating between rapid growth and sharp decline, also promoted the rise of big business. Major economic setbacks in 1873 and 1893 wiped out weaker competitors, allowing the strongest firms to rebound swiftly and to expand their sales and scale of operation during the recovery period. Purchasing more efficient machines and speeding up production, American corporations in the last half of the century commanded the heights of the national and even world markets.

Businesses grew in two distinct if overlapping ways. Through *vertical integration* a firm aspired to control production at every step of the way — from raw materials through processing to transport and merchandising of the finished items. Agricultural processors such as Swift Brothers in meat and James Buchanan Duke's American Tobacco Company often integrated "forward" in this fashion. In 1899 the United Fruit Company began to build a network of wholesale houses, and within two years it had opened distribution centers in twenty-one major cities. Eventually United Fruit controlled an elaborate system of Central American plantations and temperature controlled shipping and storage facilities for their highly perishable bananas. The firm became one of the nation's largest corporations, its "empire in bananas" extending over the economic and political life of whole nations in Central America.

The second means of growth, *horizontal combination,* entailed gaining control of the market for a single product. The most famous case was the Standard Oil Company, founded by John D. Rockefeller in 1870. Operating out of Cleveland in a highly competitive but lucrative field, Rockefeller recognized the urgency of bringing "some order out of what was rapidly become a state of chaos." He first secured preferential rates from railroads eager to ensure a steady supply of oil. He then convinced or coerced other local oil operators to sell their stock to him, and by 1880 Rockefeller controlled over 90 percent of the nation's oil-refining industry.

The Standard Oil Trust, established in 1882, "was the first in the field," wrote journalist Ida Tarbell, "and it has furnished the methods, the charter, and the traditions for its followers." Rockefeller himself recognized the larger implications. "This movement," he wrote proudly, "was the origin of the whole system of modern economic administration. It has revolutionized the way of doing business all over the world. . . . The day of combination is here to stay."

Horizontal combinations, which secured unprecedented control over output and prices, produced a highly concentrated business economy over which a few very large firms prevailed. The Sherman Anti-Trust Act, passed by Congress in 1890, claimed to outlaw "every . . . combination . . . in restraint of trade" and to restore competition by encouraging small business. Ironically, the courts interpreted the law in ways that inhibited the organization of trade unions (on the grounds that they restricted the free flow of labor) while prompting the consolidation of business. Between 1898 and 1902, over 2,600 firms vanished, 1,200 in 1899 alone. By 1910 the industrial giants that would dominate the American economy until the last half of the twentieth century — U.S. Rubber, Goodyear, American Smelting and Refining, Anaconda Copper, General Electric, Westinghouse, Nabisco, Swift and Company, Armour, International Harvester, Eastman-Kodak, and American Can — had already formed.

The Gospel of Wealth

The preeminent financiers and corporation magnates not only took pride in the collective triumph of the business community but felt spiritually fulfilled by the accumulation of wealth. Ninety percent of the nation's business leaders were Protestant, and the majority attended church services regularly. They attributed their personal achievement to hard work and perseverance, and made this a principal tenet of a new faith that imbued the pursuit of wealth with old-time religious zeal. "God gave me my money," declared multimillionaire John D. Rockefeller, and Baptist minister Russell Conwell's pamphlet *Acres of Diamonds,* which sold over one million copies, argued that to build a fortune was a profound Christian duty. "Let us remember," he preached, "there is not a poor person in the United States who was not made poor by his own shortcomings. . . ."

One version of this "gospel of wealth" justified the ruthless behavior of entrepreneurs who accrued unprecedented wealth and power through shady deals and conspiracies. Speculator Jay Gould, known in the popular press as the "Worst Man in the World," wrung his fortune, it was widely believed, from the labor of others. Through a series of financial maneuvers (which allegedly drove a partner to suicide in one case) and such high-handed measures as sending armed employees to seize a factory, he rose quickly from his modest origins in western New York State. After abandoning his tanning business for stock trading, Gould gained notoriety on Wall Street for bribing, threatening, and conspiring against his competitors.

Speculation in railroads proved Gould's forte. He took over the Erie Railroad and paid off New York legislators to get the state to finance its expansion. Now a major player, Gould acquired the U.S. Express Company by pressuring and tricking its stockholders. Threatened with arrest, Gould sold off his shares for $9 million and moved on to the Union Pacific, where he cut wages, precipitated strikes, and manipulated elections in western and plains states. When caricatured in the press as a great swindler, Gould bought the leading newspapers and kept reporters in line by giving them valuable tips on stocks. At his death, the *New York World* called Jay Gould "an incarnation of cupidity and sordidness" whose life symbolized "idolatrous homage [to] the golden calf."

Andrew Carnegie — "the richest man in the

world" — offered a strikingly different model of success. He represented the "captain of industry" who had risen from the ranks through diligence and who refused to worship wealth for its own sake. A poor immigrant boy from Scotland, Carnegie had studied bookkeeping at night while working days in a textile mill. At thirteen he had become a messenger for Western Union, and by age seventeen he was the fastest telegraph key operator in Pittsburgh. In 1852 the superintendent of the Pennsylvania Railroad's western division hired the young man as his secretary and personal telegrapher. Well placed to learn the principles of the railroad business, Carnegie stepped into the superintendent's job seven years later. He improved passenger train service while investing brilliantly to build up funds for his next venture, steel. By exploiting his talents for management and self-promotion, Carnegie was soon able to place the new industry on the same powerful financial footing as the railroads.

A genius at vertical integration, Carnegie built an empire in steel. He consistently undercut his strongest competitors by utilizing the latest technology and following his own system of cost analysis. By 1900 Carnegie managed the most efficient steel mills in the world and accounted for one-third of American output. When he sold out to J. P. Morgan's new United States Steel Corporation in 1901 for $480 million, his personal share of the proceeds came to $225 million.

By 1890 Carnegie, who measured only five feet three inches, was an industrial giant with a personality to match. From one point of view, he was still a factory despot who underpaid his employees and ruthlessly managed their work lives. But to the patrons of the public libraries, art museums, concert halls, colleges, and universities that he funded, Carnegie appeared the greatest single philanthropist of the age. At the time of his death, he had given away his massive personal fortune. "There is no genuine, praiseworthy success in life," he insisted in *The Gospel of Wealth,* published in 1900, "if you are not honest, truthful, and fair-dealing."

Whether following the rough road of Gould or the smooth path of Carnegie, the business community effected sweeping changes in the larger society.

This photograph of steel workers at the turn of the century focuses on the giant ladle used to pour molten steel, making it an overpowering symbol of the industrial age. Averaging a 72-hour work week, pouring crews endured unremittingly hot and dangerous conditions. After 1880, immigrants from eastern or southern Europe filled the majority of unskilled positions in the industry.

One such change took place in the way most Americans perceived greatness. The captains of industry appeared to fulfill the lesson of social Darwinism, or survival of the fittest — the timely doctrine devised from famed naturalist Charles Darwin's scientific theories of evolution. Some Americans feared, however, that the cost of progress achieved by such principles might be more than the nation could afford.

LABOR IN THE AGE OF BIG BUSINESS

It was an item of faith among most working people that, as labor reformer George E. McNeill put it in 1877, "labor produces all the wealth of the world. . . . [the laborer] makes civilization possible." Like the gospel of wealth, the "gospel of work" affirmed the dignity of hard work, thrift, and the importance of individual initiative. Both doctrines elaborated the simple phrase adorning many needlework samplers, "Work Is Prayer." But unlike business leaders, the philosophers of American working people did not believe in riches as the proof of work well done, or in the lust for power as the driving force of progress. On the contrary, they contended that honesty and competence should become the foundation stones of a society "so improved that labor shall become a blessing instead of a curse," a blessing recognized by all as the badge of the morally responsible citizen.

This faith inspired a slender minority, less than 3 percent of the work force, to organize unions in various trades and industries. Despite its small size, the labor movement that formed in the last half of the century represented the most significant and lasting response of workers to the rise of industry and the consolidation of corporate power.

The Changing Status of Labor

The rise of big business dramatically reduced self-employment, creating a nation of wageworkers or employees. The 1870 census revealed that wage earners already totaled almost 5 million (3.5 million in industry) of the nearly 13 million gainfully employed persons. Farmers still counted for 3 million or so, agricultural laborers for nearly 4 million. By century's end, two-thirds of all Americans worked for wages.

The new system required a vast number of people. Many young men and women fled the family farm for the promise of a paying job in industry. A smaller number escaped the peonage system of agricultural labor in the South. By far the largest proportion came from Europe or Asia. Between 1860 and 1890, 10 million people immigrated to the United States. Although the lure of jobs brought many to American shores, political or economic crisis in the homeland also proved a major incentive. The Irish were forced off the land in their native country, while in Germany and Great Britain factory workers fled industrial depressions. In a 1910 report on twenty-one industries it was estimated that nearly 53 percent of all wageworkers were foreign-born, with two-thirds coming from southern and eastern Europe. In many occupations — meat processing, clothing and textile manufacturing, cigar

Immigration to the United States, 1860–1929

This chart shows peak years of immigration in the nineteenth century years of 1873, 1882, and 1892, each also marking the beginning of an economic recession. Immigration slowed when jobs were scarce, especially so following the financial panics of 1873 and 1893, and picked up again during periods of recovery.

Source: *Statistical Abstract of the United States,* 1921 and 1930.

Between the 1849 Gold Rush and the Chinese Exclusion Act of 1882, approximately 250,000 Chinese immigrated to the United States. Many helped to build the Central Pacific Railroad and, after fulfilling their labor contracts, moved on to work as cooks or laundry workers in mining and timber camps. Nearly 90 percent of all American Chinese settled in the West. This family, celebrating a wedding, posed for a photographer in Idaho City, Idaho, their new hometown.

making, and mining, for example — immigrants predominated.

The accelerating growth of industry, especially the steady mechanization of production, shaped this expanding pool of wageworkers in two major ways. It dramatically changed employer-employee relations, and it created wholly new categories of workers. Both in turn fostered competition among workers and created conditions often hazardous to health.

For most skilled workers, the new system destroyed long-standing practices and chipped away at their traditional authority. Craftworkers faced the relentless discipline of scientific management, pioneered by Frederick Winslow Taylor, who succinctly explained that managers should "take all the important decisions . . . out of the hands of workmen." Although only a few corporations adopted Taylor's specific policies before the turn of the century, workers in major industries lost control over production processes. Skilled ironworkers, for example, who had previously set the "legislation" (rules of production) while employers supplied equipment and raw materials, now had to contend with constant supervision, higher production quotas, and new, faster machinery. Highly skilled cabinetmakers, who had for generations brought their own tools to the factory, were largely replaced by "green hands" — immigrants, including many women, who

with minimal training and close supervision could operate new woodworking machines.

Not all trades conformed to this pattern. The garment industry, for example, grew at a very fast pace in New York, Boston, Chicago, Philadelphia, Cleveland, and St. Louis but retained older systems of labor along with the new. On the one hand, the highly mechanized factories employed hundreds of thousands of young immigrant women. At the same time, the outwork system, established well before the Civil War, employed ever larger numbers of families who worked at home on sewing machines or by hand. In exploiting this growing human resource, employers fostered extreme competition between workers, continually speeding up the pace by increasing daily production quotas. Paid by the piece — a seam stitched, a collar turned, a button attached — workers labored faster and longer at home or in the factory to forestall a dip in wages. Meanwhile, in older trades such as machine tooling and textiles, the surviving craft jobs continued to pass from fathers to sons, nephews, or family friends.

Wholly new trades or expanding occupational fields brought an unprecedented number of women into the wage system. In the trades least affected by technological advances, such as domestic service, African American and immigrant women in particular found expanding opportunities for employment in cities such as Atlanta, Boston, New York, and Chicago. Meanwhile English-speaking white women moved into clerical positions in the rapidly expanding business sector. Once the typewriter and telephone came into widespread use in the 1890s, the number of women in office work rose even faster. By 1890 there was a merchandising legion of nearly 60,000 saleswomen ruled over by male superintendents, floorwalkers, and buyers. Overall, at the turn of the century 8.6 million women worked outside their homes — nearly triple the number in 1870.

By contrast, African American men found themselves excluded from many fields. In Cleveland, for example, the number of black carpenters declined after 1870, just as the volume of construction increased rapidly. African American men were also systematically driven from restaurant service and barred from newer trades such as boilermaking, plumbing, electrical work, and paperhanging, which European immigrants secured for themselves.

Discriminatory or exclusionary practices fell hardest on workers recruited earlier from China. Driven by severe famine and political turmoil in their homeland and drawn by news of jobs available in the California gold rush, 30,000 Chinese — mostly young men between sixteen and twenty-four — had immigrated to the Pacific coast between 1850 and 1882. Many signed up as contract laborers, agreeing to work four or five years in railroad construction without wages in return for ocean transport. Once their contracts expired and they sought other jobs, they were viewed as potential competitors by white workers and proprietors of small businesses. In 1877 rioters calling for deportation measures destroyed Chinese neighborhoods. In 1882 Congress passed the Chinese Exclusion Act, which suspended Chinese immigration, limited the civil rights of resident Chinese, and forbade their naturalization.

For even the best-placed wage earners, the new workplace could be unhealthy, even dangerous. Factory owners often failed to mark high-voltage wires, locked fire doors from the outside, and took little or no action to limit the emission of toxic fumes. Extractive workers, such as coal and copper miners, endured the worst conditions of all. Mine shaft air could suddenly turn poisonous, making escape from cave-ins all but impossible. Moreover, machines in American factories ran faster than anywhere else in the world. Those workers who couldn't keep up or who suffered serious injury found themselves without a job.

U.S. Economy, 1873–1900

This chart illustrates the sharp ups and downs of the economy in the late nineteenth century. Each "boom" was swiftly followed by a "bust," often of greater duration. Although wholesale prices fell, most consumers lacked sufficient income to enjoy fully the bounty of cheaper goods.

Even under less hazardous conditions, workers complained about the tedium of performing repetitive tasks for hours each day. Although federal employees had been granted the eight-hour day in 1868, most workers still toiled upwards of ten or twelve hours. "Life in a factory," one textile operative grumbled, is perhaps, with the exception of prison life, the most monotonous life a human being can live. . . ." Nor could glamour be found in the work of saleswomen in the elegant new department stores. Clerks could not sit down despite workdays reaching sixteen hours in the busy season, or hold "unnecessary conversations" with customers or other clerks. Despite these disadvantages, most women preferred sales and manufacturing jobs to domestic service. Household workers, especially live-in servants, were on call seven days a week, enjoying at best an occasional afternoon off. Most workers tolerated unsafe conditions or tedious jobs as the price of steady employment.

The boom-and-bust business cycle made periods of unemployment routine in the lives of most workers. Between 1866 and 1897, fourteen years of prosperity stood against seventeen of hard times. The two major depressions of 1873–79 and 1893–97 were the worst in the nation's history up to that time. Three "minor" recessions (1866–67, 1883–85, and 1890–91) did not seem insignificant to the millions who lost their jobs then. "At one time they drive us like slaves," a labor official complained in 1883, "and at other times we have to beg for work." During that year, 40 percent of all industrial workers lived below the poverty line ($500 per year). Whereas a highly skilled worker might earn $800 to $1,000 a year, a common laborer received only $1.50 for a day's work.

Mobilization against the Wage System

The many workers who abhorred the wage system tried to envision alternatives. Others dismissed such an approach as impractical and concentrated instead on improving conditions and above all shortening hours. In the second half of the nineteenth century, a national labor movement embracing both views took shape.

The National Labor Union (NLU) was formed in 1866. William Sylvis, its founder and president wished to halt the spread of the wage system. He insisted that through "cooperation we will become a nation of employers — the employers of our own labor. The wealth of the land will pass into the hands of those who produce it." Annual NLU conventions passed resolutions advocating drastic banking reforms that would enable workers to establish and manage their own factories. The NLU achieved a maximum enrollment of approximately 300,000, but disintegrated soon after Sylvis's death, its goal unrealized.

The Noble and Holy Order of the Knights of Labor took up the task of redeeming the toilers of the nation. Founded by a group of Philadelphia garment cutters in 1869, the order sought to initiate members into a program of moral regeneration. Those regarded as swindlers and debauchees — bankers, lawyers, stockbrokers, professional gamblers, and liquor dealers — were rigorously excluded from this community of worker-citizens. Organizing slowly during the next decade, the Knights of Labor was the largest labor assembly in the nation by the 1880s.

Grand Master Workman Terence V. Powderly, who headed the order, advocated a variety of measures — cooperatively run workshops, more land set aside for homesteading, the abolition of contract labor, and monetary reform — to offset the power of the manufacturers. He also encouraged a program of self-improvement, including education and the disavowal of intoxicating spirits. He believed that the "producing classes," once freed from the grip of corporate monopoly and the curses of ignorance and alcohol, could surely transform the United States into a genuinely democratic, cooperative order. Powderly's principal suggestion, derived from his own experience as a worker, was to abolish the wage system.

The Knights urged workplace cooperation as the alternative to the wage system. Local assemblies launched thousands of small producer co-ops, such as the Our Girls garment shop, established by Chicago seamstresses who had been fired for joining a parade for shorter hours. These worker-run factories generated great enthusiasm among participants, who shared all profits and made collective decisions on prices and wages. The majority of the cooperatives, small grocery stores often housed in the Knights' own assembly buildings, operated under the auspices of the labor movement itself. Others, such as cooperative cigar shops, intended to sell primarily to working-class customers. Local banks and other businesses, however, viewed them as competitors, and many refused credit or wholesale prices on goods. Ultimately, the cooperatives could not compete against these heavily capitalized enterprises.

Meanwhile, a campaign for a shorter workday gained momentum. The Eight-Hours League, led by Ira Steward, advocated a "natural" rhythm of eight hours for work, eight for sleep, and eight for leisure.

After staging petition campaigns, marches, and a massive strike in New York City, the movement collapsed during the mid-1870s. But it was revived early the next decade, and this time the campaign aroused widespread public support. Consumers boycotted those brands of beer, bread, and other products made in longer-hour shops. Newspaper advertisements announced "eight-hour" shoes, "eight-hour" romance novels, and "eight-hour" picnics and concerts sponsored by groups eager for the reform. During the first weeks of May, 1886, more than a third of a million workers walked off their jobs; approximately 200,000 won shorter hours.

The eight-hour campaign swelled the ranks of the Knights of Labor. The organization grew from a few thousand in 1880 to nearly three-quarters of a million six years later. Workers ordinarily excluded from craft unions joined the Knights. Nearly 3,000 women formed their own "ladies assemblies" or joined mixed locals. Leonora Barry, appointed to organize women, helped to increase their share of membership to 10 percent, or nearly 50,000 workers from the textile, garment, shoe, and carpet industries. African Americans also joined the Knights — 20,000 to 30,000 of them nationally — forming separate assemblies within the organization. Like the NLU, the Knights excluded Chinese laborers and supported total restriction of immigration.

The shorter-hours campaign ended in tragedy when the spotlight turned from the demand for the eight-hour day to urban violence and supposed threats to the public order. On May 4, 1886, at a mass demonstration for the eight-hour day at Chicago's Haymarket Square, an unknown person threw a bomb that killed one policeman and left

Knights of Labor Membership by District Concentration, c.1885

This map indicates that the Knights of Labor frequently organized most successfully outside the major metropolitan areas. In many industrial towns — or even in farm districts where Grangers and Populists had influence — the Knights established strong local assemblies. In 1885 national membership stood at 110,000.

Source: Carville Earle, *Geographical Inquiry and American Historical Problems* (Stanford University Press, 1992).

seven others fatally wounded. Police responded by firing wildly into the crowd, killing an equal number. During the next few weeks, newspaper editorials predicted violent revolution on the nation's streets. Club-wielding police in several cities broke up rallies, raided the offices of labor newspapers, or threatened immigrant union members with deportation. Chicago authorities arrested anarchist leaders and in a sensational trial sentenced them to hang, although no evidence linked them to the actual bombing. Four of the anarchists were hung, another committed suicide, and three others remained jailed until Illinois governor John Peter Altgeld pardoned them in 1893. While many Americans considered the condemnation of the "Haymarket Martyrs" a travesty of justice, conservatives approved the harsh sentence.

The labor movement suffered irreparable setbacks during the rest of 1886 and 1887. Employers' associations pooled funds to rid their factories of troublesome union organizers, and the disoriented Knights of Labor lost the capacity and the will to fight back. Most of its members, discouraged or disillusioned, dropped out, and few of the remaining assemblies survived the sharp economic decline of the 1890s. The wage system had won.

The American Federation of Labor

The events of 1886 spawned a different kind of organization, the American Federation of Labor. Unlike the NLU or the Knights, the AFL accepted the finality of the wage system and set its sights upon advancing a select minority of workers.

The AFL originated in craft unions revived from earlier times or founded in the decade after the Civil War. National organizations for individual major crafts, such as machinists and typographers, set their own agendas. At the same time, combined assemblies of skilled workers appeared in each major city. During the business upswing of the early 1880s, delegates from eight national unions formed the Federation of Organized Trades and Labor Unions of the United States and Canada. In 1886 this organization became the American Federation of Labor.

The new federation, with twelve national unions and 140,000 affiliated members, declared war on the Knights of Labor. In the wake of the Haymarket tragedy and collapse of the eight-hour movement, the AFL pushed ahead of its rival because it enjoyed more resources to support strikes and its skilled members could not easily be replaced by strikebreakers. AFL president Samuel Gompers believed that unskilled workers, racial minorities, women, and immigrants—that "heterogeneous stew of divergent and discordant customs, languages and institutions," as he put it—was "impossible to organize" and even unworthy of equal status. Under Gompers, the AFL sought to control the labor market by excluding competitors. Under his leadership, the AFL member became the "aristocrat" of the factory, the best-paid manual laborer in the world.

By century's end, the AFL had attained a membership of 250,000 and consolidated its hold on the American labor movement. The craft unionists enjoyed a respectability that the Knights of Labor commanded only briefly. Using their full rights of citizenship, AFL members won the favor of politicians, who courted their votes. They made Labor Day, first celebrated in New Haven, Connecticut, in 1883, a national tradition. "Business unionism," pragmatic rather than visionary, emphasized immediate gains such as higher wages, shorter hours, and collective bargaining with employers.

THE INDUSTRIAL CITY

Before the Civil War, manufacturing had centered in the nation's countryside, in burgeoning factory towns such as Lowell, Massachusetts, and Troy, New York. The expanding rail system promoted new growth in the older commercial cities of Boston, Philadelphia, and New York and created urban outposts like Minneapolis, Kansas City, and Denver. By century's end, 90 percent of all manufacturing took place in cities. The metropolis stood at the center of the growing industrial economy, a magnet drawing raw material, capital, and labor. It became the key distribution point for manufactured goods.

The industrial city inspired both great hope and great trepidation. Civic leaders often bragged about its size and rate of growth; immigrants wrote their countryfolk of its pace, both exciting and exhausting. Philosopher Josiah Strong described the city as the nation's "storm center." "Here luxuries are gathered—everything that dazzles the eye, or tempts the appetite," as well as, he pointedly added, "the desperation of starvation." Whatever the assessment, the city dominated the nation's economic, social, and cultural life.

Populating the City

The United States was on its way to becoming an urban nation. The population of cities grew at double the rate of the nation's population as a whole. In 1860 only 16 cities had more than 50,000 residents. By 1890 one-third of all Americans were city dwellers. Eleven cities claimed more than 250,000 people. Both Chicago and Philadelphia had 1 million inhabitants. The New York metropolitan area was by 1900 home to more than 3 million people.

The major cities — New York, Chicago, Philadelphia, St. Louis, Boston, and Baltimore — achieved international fame for the size and diversity of their populations. Many of their new residents had mi-

grated from rural communities in the United States. Between 1870 and 1910, an average of nearly 7,000 African Americans from the South moved north each year, hoping to escape poverty and oppression and find better-paying jobs. By the end of the century, nearly 80 percent of African Americans in the North lived in urban areas. Among those sixteen to thirty-five in all native-born groups, urban women outnumbered men. Whereas young white men in particular aspired to inherit the family farm or seek a fortune in the West, their sisters sought jobs in

Population of Foreign Birth by Region, 1880

As this map indicates, European immigrants after the Civil War settled primarily in the industrial districts of the northern Midwest and parts of the Northeast. French-Canadians continued to settle in Maine, Cubans in Florida, and Mexicans in the Southwest, where earlier immigrants had established thriving communities.

Source: Clifford L. Lord and Elizabeth H. Lord, *Lord & Lord Historical Atlas of the United States* (New York: Holt, 1953).

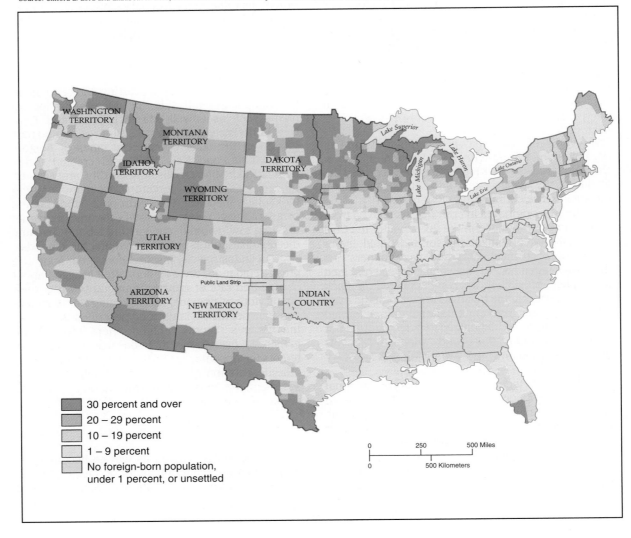

- 30 percent and over
- 20 – 29 percent
- 10 – 19 percent
- 1 – 9 percent
- No foreign-born population, under 1 percent, or unsettled

urban manufacturing, commercial trades, and housekeeping.

Immigrants and their children proved the major source of urban population growth in the late nineteenth century. Whereas the countryside attracted the majority of the first wave of immigration before the Civil War, the industrial city drew the "new immigrants" from Europe, Japan, Latin America, and Canada from the 1880s onward. At the turn of the century Chicago had more Germans than all but a few German cities, more Poles than most Polish cities; New York more Italians than all but a handful of the largest Italian cities, and Boston nearly as many Irish as Dublin. By 1885 immigrants constituted a majority in all major cities outside the South, and in almost every group except the Irish, men outnumbered women.

Like rural in-migrants, immigrants came to the United States to take advantage of the expanding opportunities for employment. While many hoped to build a new home in the land of plenty, a large number intended to work hard, save money, and return to their families in the Old Country. In the 1880s, nearly half of all Italian, Greek, and Serbian men, for example, returned to their native lands. Others could not, or did not wish to, ever return to their homelands. Jews, for instance, had emigrated mainly for economic reasons but also had fled persecution. A Yiddish critic later called this generation "Jews without Jewish memories. . . . They shook them off in the boat when they came across the seas. They emptied out their memories."

The particular city the European immigrants chose, and how well they fared in their new community, depended upon many factors. Of all groups, Jews had the most experience with urban life. Forbidden to own land in most parts of Europe and boxed into *shtetls* (villages), Jews had helped form the thriving urban communities of Vilna, Berlin, London, and Vienna. A large number had worked in garment manufacturing in, for example, London's East End, and followed a path to American cities like New York, Rochester, Philadelphia, and Chicago, where the needle trades flourished.

Other groups, the majority coming from rural parts of Europe, similarly pursued economic opportunities as interpreted for them by predecessors among their kinfolk or by the advertisements of American business recruiters. Thus Bohemians settled largely in Chicago, Pittsburgh, and Cleveland. They worked and lived near German immigrants but occupied less skilled positions as lumberyard laborers, cigar rollers, and garment workers. French Canadians, a relatively small group of a few hundred thousand, emigrated from Quebec and settled almost exclusively in New England and upper New York State. Finding work mainly in textile mills, they transformed smaller industrial cities like Woonsocket, Rhode Island, into French-speaking communities. Cubans, themselves often first- or second-generation immigrants from Spain, moved to Ybor City, a section of Tampa, Florida, to work in cigar factories. Still other groups tended toward cities dominated by fishing, shoemaking, or even glass-blowing, a craft brought directly from the Old Country.

Resettlement in an American city did not necessarily mark the end of the journey. Newcomers, both native-born and immigrant, moved frequently from neighborhood to neighborhood and between cities. As manufacturing advanced outward from the city center, working populations followed. American cities experienced a total population turnover three or four times during each decade of the last half of the century.

The American city was transformed under the pressure of these various groups. In 1882, when 1.2 million people immigrated to the United States, the expatriate novelist Henry James returned to his homeland after a twenty-five-year absence and described a "sharp sense of dispossession." To the immigrants, the scene was also disquieting. Before he left his village, Allesandro DeLuca remembered hearing that New York was not only bigger but better than any city in Italy. After he arrived, he wondered if he would indeed "find here my idea."

The Urban Landscape

Faced with a population explosion and an unprecedented building boom, the cities encouraged the creation of many beautiful and useful structures, including commercial offices, sumptuous homes, and efficient public services. At the same time, cities did little to improve the conditions of the majority of the population, who worked in dingy factories and lived in crowded tenements. Civic and business leaders and politicians disregarded architectural conventions that for centuries had made many European cities both livable and appealing to all social classes. Open space rapidly decreased as American cities grew while adding few amenities, such as European-style pedestrian arches, public fountains, and outdoor cafes.

American streets customarily followed a simple gridiron pattern. Builders leveled hills, filled ponds, and pulled down any farms or houses in the way. City officials usually lacked any master plan save the idea of endless expansion. Factories occupied many of the potentially best housing sites, typically near waterways, where goods could be easily transported and chemical wastes dumped. Space not already occupied by the factory or railroad was given over to residential development.

Built by the thousands in working-class neighborhoods, "dumbbell" tenements were designed to maximize the use of space while narrowly meeting construction codes. The rooms in these narrow six- to eight-story buildings lacked windows or, worse, opened to air shafts where residents threw rotting trash and where rodents gathered. By 1890 New York's Lower East Side packed more than 700 people per acre in back-to-back buildings, producing one of the highest population densities in the world.

At the other end of the urban social scale, New York's Fifth Avenue, St. Paul's Summit Avenue, Chicago's Michigan Avenue, and San Francisco's Nob Hill fairly gleamed with new mansions and townhouses. Commonwealth Avenue marked Boston's fashionable Back Bay district, built on a filled-in 450-acre tidal flat. State engineers planned this community, with its magnificent boulevard, uniform five-story brownstones, and back alleys designed for deliveries. Like wealthy neighborhoods in other cities, Back Bay also provided space for the city's major cultural institutions—its stately public library, fine arts and science museums, and orchestra hall. Back Bay opened to Fenway Park, designed by the nation's premier landscape architect, Frederick Law Olmstead.

Cities such as Boston, Chicago, Baltimore, and San Francisco managed to rebuild after major fires, employing the latest technological and architectural innovations. The Chicago Fire broke out in October 1871—though not, as legend had it, because "Mrs. O'Leary's cow" had kicked over a lantern—and swept through the ramshackle wooden houses which had been thrown up for immigrants. By the time it was doused, the fire had destroyed over 60,000 buildings across four square miles, including much of the commercial district, and left nearly 100,000 people homeless. Architect Louis Sullivan, recently schooled in Europe, surveyed the newly cleared sites in the aftermath of the conflagration. Although Sullivan did little to improve residential living, he came up with a plan for a new type of office building, a "proud and soaring thing, rising in [such] sheer exultation that from bottom to top it is a unit without a single dissenting line." In advance of most other architects, Sullivan emphasized the skyscraper's vertical grandeur.

The commercial and civic architecture of the industrial city established a style not only for contemporary European designers but for American builders throughout the twentieth century. Using fireproof materials, expanded foundations, and internal metal construction, the era's talented young architects focused on the factory and office building. Concentrating as many offices as possible in the downtown, they fashioned hundreds of buildings from steel, sometimes decorating them with elaborate wrought-iron facades. The office building could rise seven, ten, even twenty stories high.

The city inspired other architectural marvels. The Brooklyn Bridge won wide acclaim from engineers, journalists, and poets as the most original American construction of all. Designed by John Roebling, who died on the job, and by his son Washington, who became an invalid while completing it, the bridge opened in 1884. It was immediately considered an aesthetic and practical wonder. The images of strength and elasticity given off by the steel piers, arches, and cables inspired artists and writers to believe in the potential of technology to unite function and beauty.

By the 1890s newer designs had appeared alongside the architectural innovations of the Roe-

Los Angeles trolley, c.1900. Trolleys and street cars allowed populations not only to move swiftly through town, but to live or conduct business in outlying areas. Developing from its suburbs inward, Los Angeles eventually became the West Coast's premier metropolis.

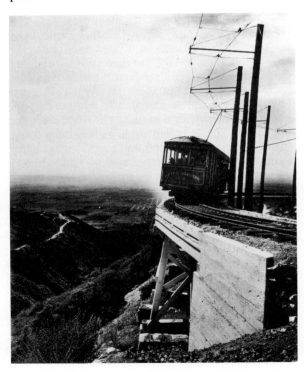

blings and Sullivan. Influenced by American wealth and its enhanced role in the global economy, city planners turned to the monumental or imperial style, laying grand concrete boulevards at enormous public cost. New sports amphitheaters dazzled the public and spread pride in the city's accomplishments. The huge new art galleries, museums, and concert halls promoted a feeling of urban excitement as well as cultural uplift. The imperial style also increased congestion and noise, making the city a more desirable place to visit than to live.

New transportations systems altered the spatial design of cities. Like the railroad but on a smaller scale, the streetcar changed business dramatically, carrying traffic of many different kinds — information, people, and goods — swifter and farther. Although San Francisco introduced the first mechanically driven cable car in 1873, Chicago could claim the most extensive cable car system in the world by the 1880s. By 1895 over 800 cities and towns operated electrically powered cars or trolleys on 10,000 miles of track. Two years later Boston rerouted a mile and a half of track underground, establishing the nation's first subway trolley. In 1902 New York opened its subway system, which would grow to become the largest in the nation.

City and Environment

By making it possible for a great number of workers to live in communities distant from their place of employment, streetcars and subways also allowed cities to increase their size dramatically. In 1880 New York City's surface transit system alone accommodated more than 150 million riders annually, a large proportion traveling into Manhattan from the boroughs of Queens and Brooklyn. Suburbs like Dorchester and Brookline sprang up outside Boston, offering many professional and business workers quiet residential retreats from the city's busy downtown. New retail and service businesses followed as the dynamism of the great city expanded outward — while the mass of population and the bulk of industry and pollution remained behind.

Modern sewer systems, meanwhile, became part of a hidden city of pipes and wires mirroring the growth of the visible city above ground. The home bath with shower and flush toilet had already entered institutions such as hospitals and the middle-class home in the 1880s. Electric lights began to replace gas in streetlights and in house illumination, improving the environment for evening education and leisure — and more intensive factory labor.

These new technologies, however, did not in themselves eradicate serious environmental problems. Most cities continued to dump sewage in nearby bodies of water. Rather than outlawing factory dumping and cleaning rivers at their sources, municipal governments usually established separate clean-water systems through the use of reservoirs. Meanwhile the filthy rivers, such as the Providence and Woonsaquaket in Providence, Rhode Island, were paved over as they passed through downtown. Some, like the Chicago River, were even reversed so as to transport sewage out of town.

Nor did the quality of life in cities necessarily improve. The unrestricted burning of coal to fuel the railroads and to heat factories and homes after 1880 greatly intensified urban air pollution. Noise levels continued to rise in the most compacted living and industrial areas. Overcrowding and inadequate sanitation continued to breed tuberculosis, smallpox, and scarlet fever, among other communicable diseases. Children's diseases like whooping cough and measles swept many a poor neighborhood. Only after the turn of the century, amid an intensive campaign against municipal corruption, did laws and administrative practices begin to address these problems (see Chapter 21).

Meanwhile the distance between city and countryside closed. Naturalists had hoped for large open spaces — a buffer zone — to preserve farmland and wild areas, protect future water supplies, and diminish regional air pollution. Nearby rural lands not destined for private housing or commercial development had, however, already begun to house water treatment and sewage plants, garbage dumps, and graveyards, services essential to the city's growing population.

THE "NEW SOUTH"

"Fifteen years have gone over" since the war, journalist Whitelaw Reid complained, yet the South "still sits crushed, wretched, busy displaying and bemoaning her wounds." Physically and financially devastated by the Civil War, the South held little investment capital and relatively few banks to manage it. It was economically stagnant, its per capita wealth only 27 percent of that of northeastern states. The South's remote countryside receded into deeper insularity while its few urban regions moved very slowly into the era of modern industry and technology. As late as 1880 mining and manufacturing employed only 5 percent of Alabama's work force. At the turn of the century southern industries lagged far behind enterprises in other regions of the

Harper's Weekly published this imaginative sketch of Atlanta in 1887. Only twenty years earlier, the Civil War had left the once-proud city in ruins. Growing up from its ashes, Atlanta appears in this artist's rendition as a "Southern Chicago," heart of the "New South." With eight railroads steaming out of Union Station and factories growing up on every side, Atlanta symbolized the process of re-establishing national unity through industrialization.

country. Their progress was held back by northern business and finance capital, continued dependence on cotton, and the legacy of slavery.

An Internal Colony

In the 1870s a vocal and powerful new group of Southerners headed by Henry Woodfin Grady, editor of the *Atlanta Constitution,* insisted that the region enjoyed great potential in its abundant natural resources of coal, iron, turpentine, tobacco, and lumber. Grady and his peers envisioned a "New South" where modern textile mills operated efficiently and profitably. The mills would be sited close to the sources of raw goods, the expansive fields of cotton, and a plentiful and cheap supply of labor unrestricted by unions or by legal limitations on the employment of children. Arguing against those planters who aspired to rejuvenate the agricultural economy by cultivating a few staple crops, the group forcefully promoted industrial development and welcomed northern investors.

Northern investors secured huge concessions from state legislatures, including land, forest, and mineral rights and large tax exemptions. Exploiting the incentives, railroad companies laid over 22,000 miles of new track, connecting the region with national markets and creating new cities. By 1890 a score of large companies, centered mainly in New York, held more than half of southern track. Northern-owned lumber companies, meanwhile, stripped southern forests.

Northerners also employed various means to protect their investments from southern competi-tion. By the late 1870s southern merchants, with the help of mainly foreign investors, had begun to run iron factories around Birmingham, Alabama. Southern iron production was soon encroaching on the northeastern market. Andrew Carnegie toured the city's iron mills and then declared, "The South is Pennsylvania's most formidable industrial enemy." To stave off competition, he ordered railroads to charge higher freight fees to Birmingham's iron producers. Unable to block Birmingham at first, New York bankers later succeeded in expatriating profits through stock ownership in southern firms. After the turn of the century, U.S. Steel took over much of Birmingham's production.

The production of cotton textiles followed a similar course. The few mills appearing before the Civil War had enjoyed a lucrative business. Powerful merchants and large landowners, realizing they could make high profits by controlling the cotton crop from field to factory, promoted the vertical integration of the cotton industry. With the upturn of business in 1879, local boosters announced a "cotton mill campaign." In 1880 the Mississippi Valley Cotton Planters' Association advised planters to "set up spindles in the cotton fields." The number of mills grew from 161 in 1880 to 400 in 1900. Southern investors supplied large amounts of the capital for industrial expansion and technological improvements. The latest machines ran the new mills, and the South boasted the first factory fully equipped with electricity. Production in the four leading cotton-manufacturing states — Georgia, North Carolina, South Carolina, and Alabama — skyrocketed, far outpacing the New England mills.

Yet this achievement did not necessarily represent an absolute gain for the South. Northern manufacturers, including many New England millowners, responded creatively to the report of the 1900 census of manufacturing that "the return upon investment in southern cotton mills has greatly exceeded that upon factories in the North." Recognizing the potential for great profit in new factories and cheap labor, they shifted their investments to the South. By the 1920s, northern investors held much of the South's wealth, including the major textile mills, but returned only a small share of the profits to the region's people.

Beyond iron or steel and textiles, southern industry remained largely extractive and, like the South itself, rural. Turpentine and lumbering businesses pushed ever farther into diminishing pine forests, the sawmills and distilleries moving with them. Toward the end of the century, fruit canning and sugar refining flourished. For the most part, southern enterprises mainly produced raw materials for consumption or use in the North, perpetuating the economic imbalance between the sections.

The governing role of capital investments from outside the region reinforced long-standing relationships. Even rapid industrialization — in iron, railroads, and textiles — did not carry the same consequences achieved in the North. The rise of the "New South" reinforced, rather than diminished, the region's status as the nation's internal colony.

Southern Labor

Reconstruction and its demise (see Chapter 17) profoundly affected the region's labor market and working conditions. For instance, Captain Ellison Alger Smyth launched the Pelzer Mill of Greenville, South Carolina, in 1881, only a few years after he had organized the Red Shirts, a group of "rifle clubs" dedicated to driving African Americans and northerners from political office and economic influence in the state. Textile barons such as Smyth, later

African American women working as sweepers, Belton, South Carolina, in 1899. Despite the rise of industry in the New South, African Americans found few new avenues for employment. The majority continued to work in agricultural labor or domestic service.

renowned as the "Dean of Southern Cotton Manufacturers," helped to pass new laws and to devise informal rules that established racial segregation throughout southern society. They also strictly enforced a whites-only employment policy in their mills.

The advance of southern industry brought little improvement to the working lives of most African Americans. At best they held onto the occupational positions they had gained during Reconstruction; often they lost ground in skilled trades. African Americans continued to dominate the low-paid "trowel trades" of plastering and bricklaying but found themselves newly excluded from the better-paying building trades as well as from printing and cabinetmaking. In the new industries, African Americans rarely worked alongside white workers and never occupied supervisory positions. Cigarette factories, for example, employed both black and white workers but rigidly segregated them. Black men and women monopolized the highly mechanized menial jobs, while white workers filled the skilled, better-paying positions.

In general, white workers fiercely protected their relatively privileged positions. Locals of the all-white carpenters' union maintained a segregation policy so absolute that if too few members were available for a job, the union would send for out-of-town white workers rather than employ local members of the black carpenters' union. In Atlanta in 1897, 1,400 white women mill operatives went out on strike when the company proposed to hire two black spinners.

Only at rare moments did southern workers unite across racial lines. In the 1880s, the Knights of Labor briefly organized both black and white workers. At its high point, District Assembly 92 enrolled two-thirds of Richmond's 5,000 tobacco operatives and made significant inroads among quarry workers, coopers, typographers, iron molders, and builders. But when white politicians and local newspapers began to raise the specter of black domination, the Knights were forced to retreat. Across the region their assemblies collapsed. Other unions remained the exclusive claim of white skilled workers.

Wages throughout the South were low for both black and white workers. In Richmond, white skilled carpenters and iron-trades workers, including plumbers and gas fitters, made 10 to 30 percent less in 1890 than comparable workers elsewhere in the United States. Southern textile workers' wages were barely half those of New Englanders. In the 1880s, when investors enjoyed profits ranging from 30 to 75 percent, southern millworkers earned as little as twelve cents per hour. Black men earned at or below the poverty line of $300; black women rarely earned more than $120 and white women about $220 annually. The poorest paid were children, a mainstay of southern mill labor.

As industry expanded throughout the nation, so too did the number of children earning wages. This was especially so in the South. In 1896, whereas only one in twenty Massachusetts millworkers was younger than sixteen, one in four cotton mill operatives in North Carolina was. Traditions rooted in the agricultural economy reinforced the practice of utilizing the labor of all family members, even the very young. The same principle operated among the Polish immigrant families in the South: even five-year-olds joined their parents in the oyster-canning factories. Seasonal labor, like picking crops or grinding sugarcane, put families on the move, making community life and formal education all but impossible. Not until well into the twentieth century did compulsory school laws effectively restrict child labor in the South.

A system of convict labor also thrived in the South. Public work projects of all kinds, especially in remote areas, employed disciplinary methods and created living and working conditions reminiscent of slavery. With African Americans constituting up to 90 percent of the convict work force, public officials felt little need to justify the occasional practice of capturing unsuspecting strangers and placing them alongside criminals in labor gangs. Transported and housed like animals — chained together by day and confined in portable cages at night — these workers suffered high mortality rates. Southern leaders took pride in what they called the "good roads movement" — the chief use of convict labor — as proof of regional progress.

Transformation of Piedmont Communities

The impact of the "New South" was nowhere greater than in the Piedmont, the region extending from southern Virginia and the central Carolinas into northern Alabama and Georgia. After 1870 long-established farms and plantations gave way to railroad tracks, textile factories, numerous mill villages, and a few sizable cities. By the turn of the century, five Piedmont communities topped 10,000 in population. Even more dramatic was the swell in the number of small towns with populations between 1,000 and 5,000 — from fourteen in 1870 to fifty-two in 1900. Once the South's backcountry, the

Piedmont now surpassed New England in the production of yarn and cloth to stand first in the world.

Rural poverty, even more than the persuasive arguments of labor recruiters hired by factory owners, encouraged many farm families to strike out for a new life in the mill town. As prices for cotton or tobacco fell and farmers' debts to merchants rose, many other families turned to tenant farming and its life of hopeless indebtedness. Those with the least access to land and credit — mainly widows and their children and single women — went into the mills first. Then families sent their children, initially to help pay off debts. Other families entered the mills on a seasonal basis, between planting and harvesting. As the agricultural crisis deepened, more and more abandoned the countryside entirely for what they called "public work." One former farmer explained, "I worked and toiled from year to year and all the fruits of labor went to the man that never struck a lick." In the mill, they hoped, they could do better.

The majority of these families found themselves residents of a company town, owned "lock, stock, and barrel" by the manufacturers who employed them. A mill community typically comprised rows of single-family houses, a small school, several churches, a company-owned store, and the home of the superintendent, who governed the affairs of the community. The manager of the King Cotton Mill in Burlington, North Carolina, not only kept the company's accounts in order, purchased raw material, and sold the finished yarn, but even bought Christmas presents for the workers' children. It was not unknown for a superintendent to parole the neighborhood at night to see if any families were burning their lamps past the nine o'clock curfew and, finding a violation, knock on the door and tell the offenders to go to bed. Millworkers frequently complained that they had no private life at all. A federal report published shortly after the turn of the century concluded that "all the affairs of the village and the conditions of living of all the people are regulated entirely by the mill company. Practically speaking, the company owns everything and controls everything, and to a large extent controls everybody in the mill village."

Mill superintendents also relied on schoolteachers and clergy to set the tone of community life. They hired Baptist and Methodist ministers to preach a faith encouraging workers to be thrifty, orderly, temperate, and hardworking. Ministers conducted evening prayer services, brought men and women into the choir, and sponsored Bible classes and missionary societies. The schools, similarly subsidized by the company, reinforced the theme of the moral and social discipline required of industrial life and encouraged students to follow their parents into the mill. But it was mainly young children between six and eight years old who attended school. When more hands were needed in the mill, superintendents plucked out these youngsters and sent them to join their older brothers and sisters who were already at work.

Piedmont mill villages like Greenville, South Carolina, and Burlington, Charlotte, and Franklinville, North Carolina, nevertheless developed a cohesive character more typical of rural than urban communities. The new residents maintained many aspects of their agricultural pasts, tilling small gardens and keeping chickens, pigs, and cows in their yards. Factory owners rarely paved roads or sidewalks or provided adequate sanitation. Mud, flies, and diseases such as typhoid fever flourished. Millworkers endured poverty and health hazards by strengthening community ties through intermarriage. Within a few generations most of the village residents had, according to one study, "some connection to each other, however distant, by marriage," blood, or both. Even the men and women without families boarded in households where privacy was scarce and collective meals created a family-like atmosphere. Historians have called this complex of intimate economic, family, and community ties the *customs of incorporation*.

SOCIETY AND CULTURE IN THE GILDED AGE

The growth of industry and spread of cities had a profound impact on all regions of the United States. During the final third of the century the standard of living climbed, although unevenly and erratically. Real wages (pay in relation to the cost of living) rose, fostering improvements in nutrition, clothing, and housing. More and cheaper products came within the reach of all but the very poor. Food from the farms became more abundant and varied — grains for bread or beer; poultry, pork, and beef; fresh fruits and vegetables from California. Although many Americans continued to acknowledge the moral value of hard work, thrift, and self-sacrifice, the explosion of consumer goods and services promoted sweeping changes in behavior and beliefs. Nearly everyone felt the impact of the nation's wealth, although in vastly different ways.

"Conspicuous Consumption"

The era favored the growth of a new class united in its pursuit of money and leisure. The well-to-do enjoyed great status throughout the nineteenth century, but only after the Civil War did upper-class Americans form national networks to consolidate their power. Business leaders built diverse stock portfolios and often served simultaneously on the boards of several corporations. Similarly, they intertwined their interests by joining the same religious, charitable, athletic, and professional societies. They sent their sons to private boarding schools such as St. Paul's, then on to Harvard, Yale, or Princeton. Their wives and children vacationed together in the sumptuous new seashore and mountain resorts, while they themselves made deals at their leisure at the new downtown social clubs and on the golf links of suburban country clubs. Just as *Dun and Brad-street* ranked the nation's leading corporations, the *Social Register* identified the 500 families that controlled most of its wealth.

According to iconoclastic sociologist Thorstein Veblen, the rich had created a new style of "conspicuous consumption." The Chicago mansion of real estate tycoon Potter Palmer was constructed in 1885 without exterior doorknobs. Not only could no one enter from the outside, a visitor's calling card supposedly passed through the hands of twenty-seven servants before admittance was allowed. At the nearby McCormick mansion, a menu printed in French preceded each dinner. A vice-president of the Chicago & Northwestern Railroad, Perry H. Smith, built his marble palace in the style of the Greek Renaissance. Its ebony staircase was trimmed in gold, its butler's pantry equipped with faucets not only for hot and cold water but for iced champagne. The women who oversaw these elaborate households themselves served as measures of their husband's status, according to Veblen, by adorning themselves in jewels, furs, and dresses of the latest Paris design.

Conspicuous consumption reached new heights of extravagance. In New York, wealthy families hosted dinner parties for their dogs or pet monkeys, dressing the animals in fancy outfits for the occasion. Railroad magnate "Diamond Jim" Brady commonly enjoyed after-theater snacks at the city's "lobster palaces," where he consumed vast quantities of food — oysters for an appetizer, two soups, fish, a main dinner of beef and vegetables, punches and sherbet on the side, dessert, and coffee, all washed down with quarts of orange juice.

Perhaps no display of wealth matched the ostentation of the "cottages" of Newport, Rhode Island, where the rich created a summer community of consumption. Architect H. H. Richardson and his proteges built exquisite manor houses more magnificent than the English originals. Here, wealthy young men and women engaged in new amateur sports such as polo, rowing, and lawn tennis. Young and old alike joined in yachting and golf tournaments.

Toward the century's end, the wealthy added a dramatic public dimension to the "high life." New York's Waldorf-Astoria hotel, which opened in 1897, incorporated the grandeur of European royalty, but with an important difference. Because rich Americans wanted to be watched, the elegantly appointed corridors and restaurants were visible to the public through huge windows, and floor-to-ceiling mirrors allowed diners to observe one another. The New York rich also established a unique custom to welcome the New Year: they opened all the curtains

This photograph, taken in 1912, shows the entrance hallway to Pullman Mansion, one of the most sumptuous private dwellings in Chicago. Constructed in 1873 to resemble Paris's Grand Opera theatre, the grand hallway demonstrated its wealthy owner's devotion to "conspicuous consumption." The extremely fine woodwork also displayed the skilled labor of Chicago's immigrant German and Czechoslovakian cabinetmakers.

of their Fifth Avenue mansions so that passersby could marvel at the elegant decor.

The nation's wealthy also became the leading patrons of the arts as well as the chief importers of treasures from Europe and Asia. They provided the bulk of funds for the new symphonies, operas, and ballet companies, which soon rivaled those of continental Europe. Nearly all the major museums and art galleries, including the Boston Museum of Fine Arts, the Philadelphia Museum of Art, the Art Institute of Chicago, and the Metropolitan Museum of Art in New York, were founded during the last decades of the nineteenth century. Many were the gifts of individual donors, such as all the libraries, museums, and galleries in Pittsburgh that bore the name *Carnegie.*

Gentility among the Middle Classes

A new middle class, very different from its predecessor, formed during the last half of the century. The older middle class comprised the owners or superintendents of small businesses, as well as doctors, lawyers, teachers, and ministers and their families.

The new middle class included these professionals but also the growing number of salaried employees—the managers, technicians, clerks, and engineers who worked in the complex web of corporations and government. Long hours of labor earned their families a modest status and sufficient income to live securely in style and comfort.

Most middle-class American families valued their home not simply as a sign of their social station but as a haven from the tumultuous society outside. For as little as ten dollars a month, a family could finance the construction of a suburban faux manor house in which to retreat from the noise, filth, and dangers of the city. This peaceful domestic setting, with its manicured lawns and well-placed shrubs, afforded family members both privacy and rejuvenation. But to accomplish this goal, middle-class families had to separate business activities from leisure, as well as the breadwinner from his family for most of the day. Assisted by modern transportation systems, men often traveled an hour or two a day, five or six days a week, to their city offices and back again. Women and children stayed behind.

The interior design of suburban or metropolitan

The parlor and the piano were the highlights of the middle-class family home. This photograph (c. 1890) shows family and friends gathered to enjoy both privacy and refinement. The parlor displayed reproductions of paintings and sculptures from American and European museums, offering cultural uplift as well as ornamentation.

middle-class homes reflected a desire for refinement. A rush of new magazines and volumes on homemaking, like Harriet Spofford's *Art Decoration* (1879), set the standards, including elaborate front entryways, walls stenciled by housewives themselves, stained-glass windows, and solid furniture. Reserved for visitors, the parlor featured amply upholstered gentlemen's chairs, armless ladies' chairs, inexpensive prints of famous paintings, and framed photographs of family members. Outside, the fenced-in yard served as a safe playground for small children and their pets.

Middle-class women found themselves devoting a large part of their day to home care. They frequently employed one or two servants but relied increasingly on the many new household appliances to get their work done. Improvements in the kitchen stove, such as the conversion from wood fuel to gas, saved a lot of time. Yet, with the widespread circulation of cookbooks and recipes in newspapers and magazines, as well as the availability of new foods, meal preparation became more complex and time-consuming. New devices such as the eggbeater speeded up some familiar tasks, but the era's fancy culinary practices offset any such time savings. Similarly, the new carpet sweepers surpassed the broom in efficiency, but the fashionable high-napped carpeting demanded more care. The foot-powered treadle sewing machine, a staple of the middle-class home, likewise encouraged the fashion-conscious seamstress to spend more time producing fancier clothing for herself and her family. Rather than diminishing with technological innovation, household work expanded to fill the time available.

Almost exclusively white, Anglo-Saxon, and Protestant, the new middle class embraced "culture" not for purposes of conspicuous consumption but as a means of self-improvement and moral uplift. Whole families visited the new museums and art galleries, constituting the majority who utilized these cultural institutions. One of the most cherished institutions, the annual week of lectures at the Chautauqua campgrounds in upstate New York, brought thousands of families together in pursuit of knowledge of literature and the fine arts. The middle class also provided the bulk of patrons for the new public libraries.

Middle-class families applied the same standards of personal improvement to their leisure activities. What one sporting-goods entrepreneur rightly called the "gospel of EXERCISE" involved men and women in calisthenics and outdoor activities, not so much for pleasure as for physical and mental discipline. Hiking was a favorite among men and women and required entirely new outfits: for women, loose upper garments and skirts short enough to prevent dragging; for men, rugged outerwear and jaunty hats. Soon they began camping out, with almost enough amenities to re-create a middle-class home within the woods. Roller skating, which became a craze shortly after the Civil War, was available in specially designed rinks in almost every major town. By the 1890s the "safety" bicycle had been marketed. It replaced the large-wheel variety, which was difficult to stay up on. A good "bike" cost $100, and, as in the case of the piano, ownership signaled middle-class status.

Leisure became the special province of middle-class children. Removed from factories and shops and freed of many domestic chores, children enjoyed a new age of creative play and physical activity. The toy market boomed. Lower printing prices helped children's literature flourish. The *Brownie Book* (1898), about imaginary elflike beings, was tremendously popular. Children's magazines such as *St. Nicholas* were filled with stories, poems, and pictures. Slightly older readers found Westerns galore, Horatio Alger novels (usually describing a boy's ascent from "rags to riches"), sports novels of many kinds, and such perennial and uplifting classics as *Little Women* and *Black Beauty*.

Life in the Streets

Immigrants often weighed the material abundance they found in the United States against their memories of the Old Country. One could "live better" here, but only by working much harder. In letters back home, they described the riches of the new country but warned friends and relatives not to send weaklings, who would surely die of stress and strain. But even if their bodies thrived, their spirits would sink amid the alien and intense commercialism of American society. In many immigrant communities, alcoholism and suicide rates soared above contemporary European standards. Germans in Chicago, it was said half jokingly, drank more beer and whiskey than all the Germans in Germany. Each group had its own phrase to express the feelings of disenchantment. Embittered German immigrants called their new land *Malhuerica,* misfortune; Jews called it *Ama Reka,* Hebrew for "without soul"; and Slavs referred to it as *Dollerica.*

To allay the stress of adjustment to life in an unfamiliar city, newcomers often established close-knit ethnic communities. European immigrants usually preferred to live with people of their own country of origin, and if possible people from their home district. The poorest of new immigrants, like the Italians of Providence, Rhode Island, and the Slavs of Homestead, Pennsylvania, made special sacrifices to resettle with people familiar to them. Aunts and uncles became almost as dear as parents, cousins as close as brothers and sisters. Young adults married within their communities, often setting up households within a few blocks of their parents and not infrequently within the same triple-decker or tenement.

Many newcomers, having little choice about their place of residence, were concentrated in districts marked off by racial or ethnic lines. In San Francisco, city ordinances prevented Chinese from operating laundries in most of the city's neighborhoods, effectively confining the population to Chinatown. In Los Angeles and San Antonio, Mexicans lived in distinctive *barrios*. In most cities, African American families were similarly compelled to inherit and remain in the dingiest, most vicious crime-ridden, and dangerous sections of town.

Young people who had left their families behind, in Europe or the American countryside, usually took rooms in small residential hotels or boarding-houses. Established in several northern cities shortly after the Civil War, the Young Men's Christian Association and the Young Women's Christian Association provided temporary residence mainly to native-born white self-supporting men and women. The most successful "women adrift," such as clerical workers and retail clerks, lived in the new furnished-room districts bordering the city's business center. The least prosperous men and women landed on skid row, where homeless people spent time in the rough taverns, eating free lunches, waiting for casual labor, and sometimes trading sexual favors for money.

The working-class home did not necessarily offer protection from the dangers of the outside world or ensure privacy. In the tenements, families often shared their rooms with other families or, when finances demanded, paying boarders. During the summer heat, adults, children, and boarders alike competed for a sleeping place on the fire escape or roof, and all year round, noises raced through paper-thin walls. But no single pattern emerged, so complex and varied were income levels and social customs. Skilled ironrollers who worked at the Carnegie Steel Company in Homestead, Pennsylvania, often owned their own homes with parlors and even imported Belgian carpets on their floors. At the other extreme, those Italian immigrants who considered themselves fortunate to get work with a

shovel usually lived in overcrowded rented apartments, one paycheck from eviction.

Whether a small cottage or a tenement flat, the working-class home involved women and children in routines of household labor devoid of the new mechanical innovations. In addition to cooking and cleaning, women used the cramped domestic space for homework. They gathered their children — and their husbands after a hard day's work — to sew garments, string beads, or paint vases for a contractor who paid them small wages by the piece. And they cooked and cleaned for the boarder whose rent supplemented the family income. In short, the home remained a second workplace, usually for the entire family.

Despite working people's slim resources, their combined buying power created new and important markets for consumer goods. Often they bought shoddy replicas of products sold to the middle class: cheaper canned goods, inferior cuts of meat, and partially spoiled fruit. Several leading clothing manufacturers specialized in cheap, ready-to-wear items, usually copied from patterns designed for wealthier consumers but constructed hastily from flimsy materials. Patent medicines advertised for ailments caused by working long periods in cramped conditions sold well in working-class neighborhoods where money for doctors was scarce. These nostrums failed to restore health, except perhaps by the power of suggestion. On the other hand, their high alcohol content lifted spirits, if only temporarily.

The close quarters of the urban neighborhood allowed immigrants to preserve many Old World customs. In immigrant communities such as Pittsburgh's Poletown, New York's Lower East Side, or San Francisco's Chinatown, people usually spoke their native language while visiting friends and relatives. The men might play cards while women and children gathered in the stairwell or front stoop to trade stories and gossip. In good weather they walked and talked, an inexpensive pastime common in the great European walking cities. Immigrants also re-created Old World religious institutions such as the church or synagogue, or secular institutions such as German family-style taverns or Russian Jewish tearooms. They replicated their native cuisine (as much as available foods allowed), sang their own songs accompanied by polka, mazurka, or tamburiza music according to tradition, and married, baptized children, and buried the dead by Old World customs.

In the cosmopolitan city, European carryovers also mixed freely with the burgeoning new commer-

New York City's Lower East Side, photographed by Jacob Riis (1849–1914), c.1900. Unlike the middle class who worked and played hidden away in offices and private homes, lower-class immigrants lived the greater parts of their lives in public, on the streets of the city. Here, children and adults mingle, partaking in both business and conversation.

cial entertainments. Ultimately, working-class people helped to shape the emerging popular culture by being innovative entrepreneurs as well as the best customers. Ragtime, for example, quickly found its way north from the Storyville red-light district of New Orleans, where the African American and Creole bands of Buddy Bolden and other early giants first popularized the music. Those who rushed to the dance halls to hear the new tunes were mainly the teenage offspring of immigrants. Disdaining their parents' sentimental favorites, such as "Beautiful Dreamer," they seemed to associate the syncopated sounds with the pulse of urban life. They also gave ragtime musicians paying work and budding musical entrepreneurs the idea that music with African American roots could become the biggest commercial entertainment of all.

In the same years, the first great amusement parks took shape. The most spectacular, Coney Island, at the southern edge of Brooklyn, grew from a series of fancy hotels and gambling (and prostitution) parlors. When developers realized that "wholesome fun" for the masses could pay better than upper-class leisure or lower-class vice, they decided to transform Coney Island into a magnificent working-class resort filled with ingenious amusements such as water slides, mechanized horse races, roller coasters, and fun houses. On the rides or at the nearby beach, young men and women could easily meet apart from their parents, cast off their inhibitions, and enjoy a hug or kiss. Or they could simply stroll through the grounds, looking at

exotic performers and enjoying make-believe trips to the Far East or even the moon, entranced by the fantastic towers, columns, minarets, and lagoons lit up at night to resemble dreams rather than reality. Here, millions of working-class people enjoyed cheap thrills that offset their hard working lives.

CULTURES IN CONFLICT, CULTURE IN COMMON

The new commercial entertainments gave Americans from various backgrounds more in common than they might have otherwise imagined. On New York's Lower East Side, for instance, theater blossomed with dramas that Broadway would adopt years later, while children dreamed of going "uptown" where the popular songs they heard on the streets were transcribed onto sheet music and then sold in stores throughout the city. Even so, nothing could smooth the tensions caused by conflicting claims over the same resources and public institutions, especially their control.

Education

As industries grew and cities expanded, so did the nation's public school system. Business and civic leaders realized that the welfare of society now depended on an educated population, one possessing the requisite skills and knowledge to keep both industry and government running. In the last three decades of the nineteenth century, the idea of universal, free schooling at the primary level, at least for white children, took hold. Kindergartens in particular flourished. The St. Louis public school system opened the first kindergarten in 1873, and by the turn of the century more than 4,000 similar programs were taking in children between the ages of three and seven.

The number of public high schools also increased, from 160 in 1870 to 6,000 by century's end. In Chicago alone, average daily attendance increased sixfold. Despite this spectacular growth, which was concentrated in urban industrial areas, as late as 1890 only 4 percent of children between the ages of fourteen and seventeen were enrolled in school, the majority of them girls preparing for work in schools or offices. The benefits of a high school education did not outweigh the immediate needs of families who depended on the wages of their sons. Most high schools better served the middle class. In 1893 the National Education Association defined the major purpose of the nation's high schools as college preparation, and endorsed a curriculum of rigorous academic training in the classics.

Higher education also took various forms. Agricultural colleges formed earlier in the century developed into institutes of technology and took their places alongside the prestigious liberal arts colleges. To extend learning to the "industrial classes," Representative Justin Morrill of Vermont sponsored the Morrill Act in 1862, which funded a system of state colleges and universities for teaching agriculture and the mechanics "without excluding other scientific and classic studies." One of the most important developments occurred in the area of research and graduate studies, pioneered in this country in 1876 by Johns Hopkins University. By the end of the century several American universities, including Stanford and Chicago, had adopted this model and expanded beyond the undergraduate curriculum to offer advanced degrees in the arts and sciences. Corporate leaders such as Rockefeller and Carnegie provided large endowments to established private institutions like Harvard, Yale, Princeton, and Columbia. Still, as the number of colleges and universities grew from 563 in 1870 to nearly 1,000 by 1910, only 3 percent of the college-age population took advantage of these new opportunities.

Women benefited from this expansion and gained specialized training in the new women's colleges. Vassar College, founded in 1861, established high academic standards for its students and marked a new era in women's higher education.

Smith and Wellesley followed in 1875, Bryn Mawr in 1885. By the end of the century 125 women's colleges offered a first-rate education comparable to that given men at Harvard, Yale, and Princeton. Meanwhile, many of the new colleges welcomed women. Growing from a virtual handful of students before the Civil War, women constituted 21 percent of undergraduate enrollments by 1870, 32 percent by 1880, and 40 percent by 1910.

Outside the women's colleges were institutions that served an entirely different clientele. A greater number of self-supporting women enrolled in vocational courses conducted mainly by philanthropic agencies directed by middle-class women. Boston's first training school for nurses opened in 1873, followed in 1879 by a diet kitchen that trained women as cooks for the city's hospitals. Founded in 1877 by middle-class women, the Women's Educational and Industrial Union offered a multitude of classes to Boston's wage-earning women. These ranged from elementary French and German, to hand drawing and water, oil, and china painting, to dressmaking, millinery, stenography, and typing, and even included crafts less familiar to women, such as upholstering, cabinetmaking, and carpentry. In the early 1890s, when the entering class at a large women's college like Vassar still averaged under 100, the union reported that its staff of 83 served an estimated 1,500 clients per day. By that time, one of its most well-funded programs was a training school for domestic servants.

The leaders of the business community had also begun to agitate for manual training for working-class and immigrant boys. One leading San Francisco merchant described the philosophy behind this movement as a desire to train boys "to earn a living with little study and plenty of work." Craft unionists in several cities actively opposed this development, preferring their own methods of apprenticeship to training programs they could not control. But local associations of merchants and manufacturers lobbied hard for "industrial education" and raised funds themselves to supplement the public school budget. In 1884 the Chicago Manual Training School opened to teach "shop work" along with a few academic subjects, and by 1895 all elementary and high schools in the city offered courses training working-class boys for jobs in industry and business.

The expansion of education did not benefit all Americans or benefit all recipients in the same way. Howard University, funded and planned by former abolitionists, began as an integrated coeducational university in Washington, D.C., shortly after the Civil

War. As one of the first American institutions to admit women to medical school, Howard attracted a sizable population of women students, both black and white. Between 1869 and 1900, twenty-three black women and twenty-five white women received medical degrees, an impressive number for the time. By the end of the century, when other universities like Cornell enrolled women medical students, the number of white women choosing to attend Howard had begun to drop precipitously. Within a few decades, Howard University had become in principle an all-black school. Racial segregation governed the educational system well into the twentieth century.

The educator Booker T. Washington encouraged African Americans to resist "the craze for Greek and Latin learning" and to strive for practical instruction. In 1881 he founded the Tuskegee Institute in Alabama to provide industrial and moral education and to train public schoolteachers. By the turn of the century Tuskegee enrolled 1,400 men and women in over thirty industrial courses, including cooking classes for homemakers and domestic servants.

By the end of the century, the nation's educational system had become more inclusive and yet more differentiated. Public and private elementary schools enrolled the majority of all children and a minority of young adults. The various educational programs tracked students to fill particular roles in the consolidating industrial society.

Leisure and Public Space

Public space, like the public school, became an important arena of conflict. Most large cities set aside land for common leisure-time use by residents. Golden Gate Park in San Francisco, Central Park in Manhattan, and Lincoln Park in Chicago were rolling expanses traversed by streams and pathways and footbridges and set off by groves of trees, numerous shrubs, and neat flower gardens. According to the designers' vision, middle-class urban dwellers could renew themselves and find relief from the stress of modern life by strolling through the picturesque, semirural grounds.

The working classes had their own ideas about the use of parks and open land. Trapped in overcrowded apartments, they wanted space for sports, picnics, and lovers' trysts. Young people openly defied ordinances that prohibited playing on the grassy knolls of parks, while their elders routinely voted against municipal bonds that did not include funds for more recreational space in their communities. Immigrant ward representatives on the Pittsburgh city council, for instance, argued that band shells for classical music meant little to their constituents, but spaces suitable for athletic contests meant much.

Eventually, most park administrators set aside sections for playgrounds and sports and others for public gardens and concerts. Yet, intermittent conflicts erupted. The Worcester, Massachusetts, park system, for example, allowed sports leagues to schedule events but prohibited pickup games. This policy gave city officials more control over the use of the park for outdoor recreation but forced many ball-playing boys into the streets. When working-class parents protested, city officials responded by instituting programs of supervised play, to the further dismay of the children.

Public drinking of alcoholic beverages, especially on Sunday, provoked similar disputes. Pittsburgh blue laws forbidding businesses to open on Sunday were rigidly enforced when it came to neighborhood taverns, while large firms like the railroad corporations enjoyed exemptions. To discourage Sunday drinking, the Carnegie Institute offered as an alternative public organ recitals and other concerts. Many working people, especially beer-loving German immigrants, continued to treat Sunday as their one day of relaxation and casual drinking.

Civic leaders pointed out that money spent on alcohol should go instead to feeding families, and that physical abuse of women and children went hand in hand with excess consumption. Besides, the tavern supposedly led to the underworld of gambling, drugs, and prostitution, and the bartender often bailed out petty criminals. These critics rarely conceded that if the tavern could be a lice-ridden den where men drank themselves into stupors, it also put a roof over the homeless during a wintry day and supplied them a free lunch. Taverns commonly served the entire working-class neighborhood by providing its only telephone.

National Pastimes

Toward the end of the century, the younger members of the urban middle class had begun to find common ground in lower-class pastimes, for example, in rag-time music. Introduced to many northerners by African American composer Scott Joplin at the Chicago World's Fair of 1893, "rag" quickly became the staple of the new cabaret-style musical clubs. After the turn of the century, middle-class urbanites sought out ragtime bands and congregated on the rooftops of posh hotels and uptown restaurants to listen and dance and even to drink.

Vaudeville, the most popular form of commercial entertainment since the 1880s, also bridged middle- and working-class tastes. Drawing on a variety show tradition of singers, dancers, comedians, jugglers, and acrobats that had entertained Americans since colonial days, "vaude" became a big business that made ethnic and racial stereotypes and the daily frustrations of city life into major topics of amusement. Vaudeville palaces — ten in New York, six in Philadelphia, five in Chicago, and at least one in every city of size — attracted huge, "respectable" crowds of men and women who sampled between twenty and thirty acts averaging twelve to fifteen minutes each. One study estimated that before vaudeville gave way to movie theaters in the 1920s, between 14 and 16 percent of all city dwellers attended shows at least once a week.

Sports, however, outdistanced all other commercial entertainments in appealing to all kinds of fans and in creating a sense of national identity. No doubt the most popular parks in the United States were the expanses of green surrounded by grandstands and marked by the unique diamond shape — the baseball fields. During the last quarter of the nineteenth century the amateur sport of gentlemen and Civil War soldiers suddenly became the "national pastime." Both American and English children had for years been playing a form of baseball, known mainly as rounders, when a group of young men in Manhattan formed the Knickerbocker Base

Ball Club in 1845 and proceeded to codify the game's rules in writing. Baseball clubs soon formed in many cities, and shortly after the Civil War traveling teams with regular schedules made baseball a professional sport. The formation of the National League in 1876 encouraged other spectator sports, but for generations baseball remained the most popular.

Rowdy behavior flavored the game with a working-class ambiance. Many well-loved players known for their saloon brawls occasionally disappeared for a few days on "benders." Team owners, themselves often owners of local breweries, counted heavily on liquor sales in the parks. Having to contend with hundreds of drunken fans, officials maintained order with great difficulty. Outfielders occasionally charged into the grandstand to punch spectators who had heckled them. To attract more subdued middle-class fans, the National League raised admission prices, banned the sale of alcohol, and observed Sunday blue laws. Catering to a more working-class audience, the American Association kept the price of admission low, sold liquor, and played ball on Sunday.

Baseball entrepreneur Albert G. Spalding brought order to often chaotic league organization and playing arrangements, but at a price. Manager and then president of the Chicago White Stockings, Spalding quickly came to see baseball as a source of multiple profits. He procured exclusive rights to manufacture the official ball and rule book, while producing a large variety of other sporting equipment. Meanwhile, he built impressive baseball parks

Baseball Players, **watercolor by Thomas Eakins, 1875. One of the finest American painters of the period, known for realistic depictions of physical exertion in amateur athletics, Eakins here turned his attention to the commercial baseball park. The batter and catcher appear as well-poised athletes, dignified in their dress and manner — everything that the baseball player of the late nineteenth century was not very likely to be.**
(Thomas Eakins. Baseball Players. 1875. Watercolor. The Rhode Island School of Design, Museum of Art.)

CHRONOLOGY

1843–84	"Old Immigration"
1866	National Labor Union founded
1869	Knights of Labor founded
1870	Standard Oil Company formed
1871	Chicago Fire
1873	Financial panic brings severe depression Carnegie Steel founded
1876	National League (baseball) formed
1879	Thomas Edison invents incandescent bulb Depression ends
1881	Tuskegee Institute founded
1882	Peak of German immigration to U.S. (1.2 million) Standard Oil Trust founded
1885–1914	"New Immigration"
1886	Campaigns for eight-hour day Haymarket episode AFL founded
1890	Sherman Anti-Trust Act
1893	Stock market panic precipitates severe depression
1895	Coney Island opens
1900	Carnegie, *The Gospel of Wealth*
1901	U.S. Steel Corporation formed

in Chicago with seating for 10,000 and private boxes for the wealthy above the grandstands. He easily became the foremost figure in the National League.

Spalding also tightened the rules of employment. In 1879 he dictated the reserve clause, which prevented players from negotiating a better deal and leaving the team that had originally signed them. Spalding encouraged his player-manager "Cap" Anson to refuse to allow the White Stockings to play any team with an African American, effectively setting the standard for professional baseball. The firing of Moses "Fleet" Walker from Cincinnati in 1884 marked the first time the color line had been drawn in a major professional sport. African Americans organized their own traveling teams, and in the 1920s formed the Negro Leagues, which produced some of the nation's finest ballplayers.

Players occasionally organized to regain control over their sport. They frequently complained about low wages and arbitrary rules. Like factory workers in the 1880s, they formed their own cooperatively run league, the Brotherhood of Professional Baseball Players. Profits were divided between participants and investors. This effort failed, partly because fans would not desert the established leagues, but mostly because successful baseball franchises demanded large quantities of capital. American sports had become big business.

As attendance continued to grow, the enthusiasm for baseball straddled important cultural divisions, bringing Americans of many kinds together, if only on a limited basis. By century's end, no section of the daily newspaper drew more readers than the sports pages. Although interesting relatively few women, sports news riveted the attention of men from all social classes. Loyalty to the home team helped to create an urban identity, while individual players became national heroes.

CONCLUSION

By the end of the nineteenth century, industry and the city had opened a new world for Americans. Fresh from Europe or from the American countryside, ordinary urban dwellers struggled to form communities of fellow newcomers through work and leisure—at the factory and the ballpark, in the neighborhood and the public school. Meanwhile, their "betters," the wealthy members of the business community and the new middle class, made and carried out the decisions of industry and marketing, established the era's grand civic institutions, and set the tone for high fashion and art.

Rich and poor alike bore witness to many developments that inspired fascination and confidence in the emerging order. Yet inequalities increased. Indeed they were as much a part of the new order as the construction of the Brooklyn Bridge or the appearance of advertising. During the mostly prosperous 1880s, optimists believed that unfair treatment based on region, class, and even perhaps race and gender might ease in time. By the depressed 1890s, these hopes had worn thin. The lure of an overseas empire, symbol of manifest destiny, was one of the few goals that seemed to unite a suffering and otherwise divided nation.

Additional Readings

ALFRED D. CHANDLER, JR., *The Visible Hand: The Managerial Revolution in American Business* (1977). A highly acclaimed study of corporate management. Shows how the rapid growth in the scale of business, as well as the influence of business in public life, brought about a new type of executive armed with skills for national decision making and enjoying close links with others of his kind.

HERBERT G. GUTMAN, *Work, Culture and Society in Industrializing America: Essays in American Working-Class and Social History* (1977). Influential essays on the formation of working-class communities in the nineteenth century. Focuses on the role of immigrants in transforming the values and belief systems of working-class Americans undergoing the throes of industrialization.

JOHN F. KASSON, *Amusing the Million: Coney Island at the Turn of the Century* (1978). A heavily illustrated account of America's favorite amusement park. Sees Coney Island as the meeting point for shrewd entrepreneurs and pleasure-seeking immigrants, its amusements and architectural styles emblematic of a special era in American history.

ALICE KESSLER-HARRIS, *Out to Work: A History of Wage-Earning Women in the United States* (1982). A comprehensive survey of women's increasing participation in the labor force. Documents women's role in trade unions but also its impact on family patterns and on ideas about women's role in American society in general.

KENNETH L. KUSMER, *A Ghetto Takes Shape: Black Cleveland, 1870–1930* (1976). A keen analysis of a long-standing African American community. Shows how black workers suffered downward mobility and increased segregation as their skilled jobs and small-business opportunities were given to European immigrants.

LAWRENCE H. LARSEN, *The Rise of the Urban South* (1985). In Larson's view, the true "New South" was the city, for relatively few had lived there before the late nineteenth century. But rural values remained vital, especially in religious life and voting patterns.

DAVID MONTGOMERY, *Workers' Control in America: Studies in the History of Work, Technology, and Labor Struggles* (1979). A detailed analysis of industrial change from the mid-nineteenth century to the early twentieth century, and a study of workers' responses to increased pace and loss of control.

DAVID F. NOBLE, *America by Design: Science, Technology and the Rise of Corporate Capitalism* (1977). A view of scientific advancement and its connections with the expanding economy. Shows how scientific breakthroughs were often created for, and especially adapted to, corporate purposes.

DAVE ROEDIGER and FRANKLIN ROSEMONT, eds., *Haymarket Scrapbook* (1986). A large, beautifully illustrated book about the events and consequences of the Haymarket tragedy.

ROY ROSENZWEIG, *Eight Hours for What We Will: Workers and Leisure in an Industrial City, 1870–1920* (1983). Treats the city park as the arena for conflict over whether public community life should be uplifting (devoted to nature walks and concerts) or entertaining (allowing drinking, courting, and amusement).

ALAN TRACHTENBERG, *The Incorporation of America: Culture and Society in the Gilded Age* (1982). One of the best and most readable overviews of the post–Civil War era. Carefully describes how the corporation rose to become the defining institution of national life, and how culture was reoriented to reflect the tastes of the new middle classes employed by the corporation.

20 COMMONWEALTH AND EMPIRE, 1870s–1900s

● THE COOPERATIVE COMMONWEALTH

(*Childe Hassam. The Electricity Building, World's Columbian Exposition, Chicago. 1893. Watercolor. 17-3/4 × 30 in. Chicago Historical Society.*)

Edward Bellamy's Looking Backward *(1888), the best-selling novel of the nineteenth century after Harriet Beecher Stowe's* Uncle Tom's Cabin, *told the story of Bostonian Julian West, who fell asleep in 1887 and awoke in the year 2000. To his surprise, Americans had solved their major problems peacefully and democratically. Poverty, crime, war, taxes, air pollution, housework, and even politicians, capitalists, and bankers had ceased to exist. Most amazing, the great social division between the powerful rich and what Bellamy referred to as the suffering "dependent classes" was gone. In the year 2000 all citizens lived in material comfort, happily and harmoniously.*

Community and cooperation were the key concepts in Bellamy's utopian tale. Economic activity had been wrested from private corporations and given over to the collective ownership of the people. Formerly subject to the whims of corrupt politicians in league with big business, the government now restricted its functions to organizing the production and distribution of goods for the common good. It ran the factories, operated huge department stores and warehouses full of marvelous manufactured goods, and oversaw majestic apartment complexes with modern facilities for cooking, dining, and laundering.

AMERICANS ENVISION
NEW COMMUNITIES,
REMOVED FROM THE
COMPETITION AND
STRIFE OF THE
INDUSTRIAL AGE

An "industrial army" enlisting all adult men and women performed the necessary labors. After enjoying short workdays, long vacations, and clean and pleasant workplaces, everyone retired at age forty-five to pursue hobbies, sports, and culture. Bellamy's future society promoted the "highest possible physical, as well as mental, development for everyone." There was nothing fantastic in this idea, he insisted. Organized properly, the United States could be voluntarily transformed into a "cooperative commonwealth" as "the logical outcome of the operation of human nature under rational conditions."

Edward Bellamy, a journalist and writer of historical fiction from Chicopee Falls, Massachusetts, moved thousands of his readers into action. Named after Bellamy's program for a "new nation," the Nationalist movement organized quickly, reaching an apex of 165 clubs. Bellamy began to publish his own weekly newspaper and wrote a sequel novel that proved

"Icaria Speranza" in Cloverdale, California, c.1885; and the "Theosophical Temple and Homestead" at Point Loma, California, c.1900. Inspired by the utopian socialist Etienne Cabet, a group of French "Icarians" purchased agricultural land about fifty miles north of San Francisco in 1881, calling their colony "Speranza." This experiment failed after a few years due to inadequate resources and depressed business conditions. The Point Loma colony, based on the more popular philosophical-spiritual idea of Theosophy, was also much better funded.

especially popular among women. *Equality*, published in 1897, showed how women might become "absolutely free agents in the disposition of themselves" by ending their financial dependence on men.

During the 1890s, devotees of **Looking Backward** actually attempted to create new communities along lines outlined by Bellamy. The best known and most long-lasting was established in Point Loma, California, in 1897. Situated on 330 acres, with avenues winding through gardens and orchards in newly planted groves of eucalyptus trees, Point Loma possessed enormous physical beauty. Some residents, especially young couples, lived in bungalows scattered throughout the colony grounds; others opted for private rooms in a large communal building. Either way, they all met twice daily to share meals and usually spent their leisure hours together. On the ocean's edge the residents constructed an outdoor amphitheater and staged their own plays and concerts.

None of Point Loma's 500 residents earned wages for his or her daily labors, but everyone lived comfortably. They dressed simply in clothes manufactured by the community. They conducted agricultural experiments that yielded new types of avocados and fruits, and eventually produced over half of their own food supply. Children, who slept in a special dormitory from school age on, enjoyed an education so outstanding that pupils often displayed their wide-ranging knowledge to news reporters and audiences in nearby San Diego.

The Point Loma community never met all its expenses, but for decades it managed to remain solvent. Admirers across the company sent donations, and baseball entrepreneur Albert Spalding, who lived there during his retirement, helped to make up the financial deficit. Only in 1940 did the community liquidate its landholdings.

The establishment of successful cooperative communities such as Point Loma could not in itself bring the changes that Bellamy hoped to see, and he knew it. Only a mobilization of citizens nationwide could overturn the current hierarchies and establish the egalitarian order depicted in **Looking Backward**. Without such a rigorous challenge, the economic and political leadership emerging since the Civil War would consolidate its power ever further from popular control.

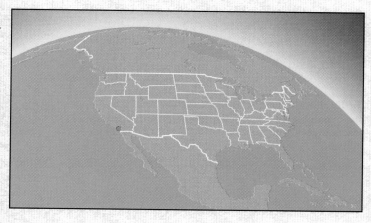

The last quarter of the nineteenth century saw just such a challenge, producing what one historian calls "a moment of democratic promise." Ordinary citizens sought to renew the older values of community through farm and labor organizations, philanthropic and charitable societies. They could not clearly see, however, that the fate of the nation depended increasingly upon events beyond national shores. Business leaders and politicians, most importantly the President himself, worked to create an American empire that would claim distant territories as possessions and expand economic borders to the ends of the earth.

Toward a National Governing Class

The historian and future president Woodrow Wilson observed that the "size of modern democracy necessitates the exercise of persuasive power by dominant minds." The rapid expansion of government, mirroring the growth of the economy during the last quarter of the century, set the stage for the consolidation of the modern two-party political system. The administration of power rapidly became a key concern for the far-sighted elites who sought to balance party influence with the need for competence and honesty in government.

The Growth of the State

State and local governments had been expanding rapidly since midcentury. Well before the Civil War most cities had created professional police and fire-fighting forces, and some municipalities had begun to finance the creation of school systems, parks, and libraries. These services, especially waterworks and sewer systems, demanded huge increases in local taxation. The city government of Boston, for example, spent five times more per resident in 1875 than it had just thirty years earlier, and its municipal debt rose from $784,000 to over $27 million. In New York, one of every eight voters appeared on a government payroll in 1880.

At the national level, meanwhile, mobilization for the Civil War and Reconstruction also demanded an unprecedented degree of coordination. Expanding rapidly under the weight of new tasks and responsibilities, the federal government continued its speedy growth. Federal revenues skyrocketed,

---

Federal Employment by Decade, 1871–1901

The expansion of government created a bureaucracy of employees and great opportunities for political patronage.

Source: David Nachmias and David H. Rosenbloom, *Bureaucratic Government USA* (New York: St. Martin's Press, 1980), p. 39.

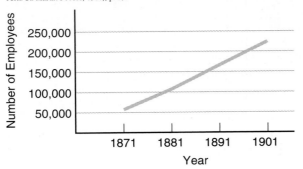

from $257 million in 1878 to $567 million in 1900. The federal bureaucracy grew in tandem, from 50,000 employees in 1871 to 100,000 only a decade later.

The modern apparatus of government commissions, bureaus, and cabinet seats took shape amid this upswing. One of the most important legislative measures of the period, the Interstate Commerce Act of 1887, created the first federal agency delegated to regulate an industry. The five-person Interstate Commerce Commission had the task of requiring reasonable freight and passenger charges by the railroads. By statute, it could take public testimony on possible violations, examine company records, and generally oversee enforcement of the law. In fact, a series of Supreme Court decisions undercut the ICC's decision-making powers, rendering it little more than a public information bureau. But the 1887 act had established a precedent for regulation and expanded the power of the federal government over the states.

A complex of other federal bodies, including the Department of Labor and the Agricultural Bureau, were also founded at this time. The Department of the Interior, the largest and most important bureau after the Post Office, itself comprised more than twenty agencies, including Indian Affairs, the Census, and the Geographical Survey. The next most important department, the Treasury, grew from 4,000 employees in 1873 to nearly 25,000 in 1900. Within a decade after the Pension Act of 1890 made virtually every northern Civil War veteran and his dependents eligible for benefits, the Veterans Bureau, known as "the largest executive bureau in the world," employed nearly 60,000 men and women. The federal government complex in Washington, D.C., assumed permanent status as a major source of employment, a major spender of public revenues, and the butt of complaints from taxpaying citizens.

The Two–Party System

During the 1870s and 1880s, the two-party system solidified as an electoral counterpart to the expanding state. The Republican party continued to derive strength from its control of the federal government, while Democrats gathered support from southern white voters and new groups of naturalized citizens in the North. Each party put up candidates for as many offices as possible, from local and state to national levels. During this era, the two parties established a mode of operation that would persist for at least a century.

Although Republicans and Democrats met in

national conventions every four years, they operated essentially as state or regional organizations that depended on the loyalty of local supporters. Their platforms encompassed broad national issues, such as tariffs, but candidates themselves had to pay close attention to the particular concerns of their constituents. German American voters, for example, regularly opposed any candidate who favored legislation restricting the consumption of alcoholic beverages; farmers mistrusted politicians backed by the railroads. Democrats and Republicans repeatedly crosscut each other on these and other principles, forgoing any claim to consistency.

The election of Ulysses S. Grant in 1872 ushered out the great era of dramatic political reform that had marked early Reconstruction. None of the presidents of the next twenty-four years — Rutherford B. Hayes (1877–81), James A. Garfield (1881), Chester A. Arthur (1881–85), Grover Cleveland (1885–89 and 1893–97), and Benjamin Harrison (1889–93) — held to any clear principles of government. Weak in office, they yielded their power to Congress and the state legislatures. Only 1 percent of the popular vote separated the candidates in three of five presidential elections between 1876 and 1892. The voting pattern for Congress was similarly stable. Democrats tended to represent the majority in the House, while Republicans controlled the Senate.

Political campaigns nevertheless generated enormous enthusiasm. Candidates of both parties urged their "regulars" to turn out and pursued the swing voters furiously. "We work through one campaign," quipped one candidate, "take a bath and start in on the next." Campaign paraphernalia — leaflets or pamphlets, banners, hats, flags, buttons, inscribed playing cards, and clay pipes featuring a likeness of the candidate's face or the party symbol — became a major expense for both parties. Partisans embraced the Democratic donkey or the Republican elephant as symbols of party fidelity. Voters did indeed turn out. During the last quarter of the century, participation in presidential elections peaked at nearly 80 percent of those eligible to vote. Thousands, in fact, voted several times on any given election day; voters who had died, or who had never existed, also miraculously cast ballots.

Politicians covered the rising costs of maintaining local organizations and orchestrating mammoth campaigns through a system of kickbacks and bribes. Lobbying became a high-priced trade with lucrative payoffs. Legislators who supported government subsidies for railroad companies commonly received stock in return. At the local level, powerful bosses and political machines dominated

This wooden noisemaker was designed for Grover Cleveland's presidential campaign in 1892. Pursuing the voters, political campaigners devised ingenious signs, buttons, and other miscellaneous novelties for supporters to display, especially at public demonstrations. When shaken vigorously, noisemakers literally demanded the attention of bystanders.

both parties. Democrats William Marcy Tweed of New York's Tammany Hall and Michael "Hinky Dink" Kenna of Chicago specialized in giving municipal jobs to loyal voters and holiday food baskets to their families. Tweed's machine pushed through city services for working-class neighborhoods and even staged major sporting events or entertainments to woo Irish Americans and German Americans, who made up over half of New York City's population. Hundreds of smaller political machines ruled cities and rural courthouses through a combination of "boodle" (corruption) and personal favors.

Noted critic John Jay Chapman, looking back at the history of American electoral politics, suggested that "the change of motive power behind the party organizations — from principles to money — was silently effected during the thirty years which followed the [Civil] war." No wonder politicians and political parties had ceased to exist in Bellamy's utopian community.

The Spoils System and Civil Service Reform

Each time a new party took national office, a vast army of jobs changed hands. More than 50 percent of all federal jobs — nearly 56,000 in 1881 — were patronage positions. Post offices were centers of a spoils system that sustained a huge excess of administrators; a typical rural area could boast a fourth-class postmaster for every hundred voters. After taking office, President Cleveland alone replaced nearly 40,000 postmasters. Decisions about congressional patronage, observers estimated, filled one-third of all legislators' time.

Critics in both parties called for an end to this abuse of political power but made little headway. As early as 1865, Republican representative Thomas A. Jenckes of Rhode Island had proposed a bill for civil service reform. But Congress feared such legislation would hamper candidates in their relentless pursuit of votes. President Hayes took up the cause, introducing a few reforms in the New York Custom House and federal post offices, but Congress again refused to join in a major sweep.

Although the mass of voters in both parties remained indifferent, a group comprising mainly professors, newspaper editors, lawyers, and ministers organized a Civil Service Reform Association and enlisted Democratic senator George H. Pendleton of Ohio to push legislation in Congress. Following the election of 1882, both parties agreed to support the bill.

In January 1883, a bipartisan congressional majority passed the Pendleton Civil Service Reform Act. This measure allowed the president to create, with Senate approval, a three-person commission that would draw up a set of guidelines for executive and legislative appointments. The commission established a system of standards for various federal jobs and instituted "open, competitive examinations for testing the fitness of applicants for public service." The Pendleton Act also barred political candidates from soliciting campaign contributions from government workers.

Patronage did not disappear altogether. But at the federal level, the reforms imparted a decidedly professional character to civil service, similar to that imposed by doctors, lawyers, and scholars on their respective fields through the formation of professional societies such as the American Medical Association and the American Historical Association. At the same time, the federal judiciary began to act more aggressively to establish the parameters of government. Through the Circuit Courts of Appeals Act of 1891, the U.S. Supreme Court gained the right to review all cases at will.

The move to reconstitute government as a professional enterprise involved people from many walks of life, but no group more than lawyers. With the rise of the corporation, the legal specialist's influence had grown rapidly. In forming the American Bar Association (ABA) in 1878, lawyers sought to establish a merit system and thereby to adjust the legal system to modern society. The ABA hardly needed to improve lawyers' strategic position in American politics: by the turn of the century lawyers occupied more than 40 percent of Congress and had become a permanently dominant force in the Senate. Many judicial and cabinet appointments also went to lawyers.

One Politician's Story

Lawyer James Garfield, the nation's twentieth president, was a typical politician of the age. Born in a frontier Ohio cabin in 1831, he briefly worked as a canal boat driver, an experience later exploited as proof of his rise from humble origins. Honored as a Civil War hero (a major general at war's end, he had fought at Shiloh and was honored for gallantry at Chickamauga), the Ohio legislator carefully prepared his move into the national political arena.

While serving in Congress, Garfield seemed at first committed to social reform. He introduced a bill to create a Department of Education, arguing that public education would prove the best stepping stone to equality. He denounced his own Republican party for allowing corruption to flourish under Grant's administration. The nation's "next great fight," he insisted, would pit the people against the corporations.

But like many Civil War–era leaders, Garfield shifted his stance as the failure of Reconstruction became evident. By the early 1870s he had begun to espouse conservative views. Nearly defeated in the 1874 Democratic congressional landslide, he concluded that "the intelligence of the average American citizen" fell short of the demands of a thoroughgoing democratic system. As a result, he came out against universal suffrage. Garfield now looked upon the increasingly business-oriented Republican party as a vehicle for realizing his personal ambition. After six years of shrewd maneuvering, trading votes and favors to build his reputation, Garfield won the Republican nomination for the 1880 presidential campaign. In a mediocre race with no outstanding issues, he won by 40,000 votes out of 9 million cast.

Garfield the idealist had grown into Garfield the machine politician and lackluster president. He had already shown himself indecisive and even indifferent to governing when a bullet struck him down just 200 days after his inauguration. Other presidents of this period similarly assumed that the chief executive served as the party's titular leader and played mainly a ceremonial role in office. A strong Congress, along with government officials at all levels, presumably guarded the nation's welfare.

To Edward Bellamy, this system looked suspiciously like a reign of "insiders," people pulling the levers of the party machinery or spending money to influence important decisions. He concluded that the vast new army of politicians and civil servants failed to address the needs of ordinary citizens. Envisioning a future society where all shared equally in an abundance of goods and services, Bellamy also advised Americans to organize their communities in order to wrest control from the hands of the entrenched politicians.

FARMERS AND WORKERS ORGANIZE THEIR COMMUNITIES

During the last quarter of the century, farmers and workers laid the foundation for a different kind of mass political movement. The two groups began to organize their respective communities shortly after the close of the Civil War. Within two decades they had built powerful national organizations opposing, as a Nebraska newspaper put it, "the wealthy and powerful classes who want the control of government to plunder the people." Though short on financial resources, farmers and workers waged the most significant challenge to the two-party system since the Civil War — the Populist movement.

The Grange

Farmers on the Great Plains initially sought to organize their communities for "social, intellectual, and moral improvement," as a Declaration of Principles of the Grange announced. Officially known as the Patrons of Husbandry, the Grange was founded by Oliver H. Kelley, an employee of the Department of Agriculture, in 1867. This fraternal society resembled the secretive Masonic lodges: whole families staffing a complex array of offices engaged in elaborate rituals of passwords, flags, songs, and costumes. In many farming communities, the Grange hall became the center of social activity, serving as the site of summer dinners and winter dances.

The Grange organized rapidly in the 1870s, especially among farmers on the Great Plains and in the South, the two areas where agrarian discontent ran deepest. The post–Civil War boom in prices and production had raised expectations, but following the Panic of 1873 families saw their hopes for prosperity wither on the vine. Great Plains farmers barely survived the blizzards, grasshopper infestations, and droughts of the early 1870s. Meanwhile, farmers throughout the trans-Mississippi West and the South watched grain and cotton prices fall year by year against growing competition from producers in Canada, Australia, Argentina, Russia, and India. Most farmers found themselves operating at a loss; large numbers slid to the verge of bankruptcy. The Grange soon swelled to more than 1.5 million members.

Grangers blamed their hard times on a band of "thieves in the night" — railroads, grain elevator operators, banks — who charged exorbitant fees for their services. They fumed at American manufacturers such as Cyrus McCormick who sold farm equipment cheaper in Europe than in the United States. For machinery purchases alone, farmers accrued an average debt twice that of other Americans. Banks, Grangers charged, not only imposed high interest rates but offered mortgages on terms too short for farmers to turn around their fortunes.

Grangers mounted their steadiest assault on the railroad corporations. By bribing state legislators, railroads maintained a highly discriminatory rate policy, commonly charging farmers far more to ship their crops short distances than over long hauls. Responding to Grange pressure, several plains states passed laws in 1874 establishing maximum shipping rates. Chicago grain wholesalers challenged the constitutionality of such rulings, but in *Munn v. Illinois* (1877) the Supreme Court upheld the legislatures, ruling that states had the power to regulate private property when it was devoted to public use.

Determined to "buy less and produce more," Grangers established a vast array of cooperative enterprises for purchasing supplies and marketing crops. They created their own local grain elevators, set up retail stores, and even manufactured some of their own farm machinery. As early as 1872, the Iowa Grange claimed to control one-third of the

The symbols chosen by Grange artists represented their faith that all social value could be traced to honest labor and most of all to the work of the entire farm family. The hardworking American required only the enlightenment offered by the Grange to build a better community.

Source: From the *Kingfisher Reformer*, May 3, 1894.

grain elevators and warehouses in the state. The Ohio Grange boasted that each county Grange in that state operated its own retail store. In other areas, Grangers ran banks as well as fraternal life and fire insurance companies.

The deepening depression of the late 1870s came at the worst possible moment for the Patrons of Husbandry, wiping out most of their cooperative programs. By 1880 Grange membership had fallen to 100,000. Meanwhile, the Supreme Court overturned most of the key legislation regulating railroads. Only in New England and the Middle Atlantic states, far from its old geographical center, did the Grange remain a center of rural and small-town community life. Despite these setbacks, the Patrons of Husbandry had promoted a model of cooperation that would remain the heart of the rural protest movement until the end of the century.

The Farmers' Alliance

Agrarian unrest did not end with the downward turn of the Grange but instead moved south. In the 1880s farmers organized in communities where both pov-

erty and the crop lien system prevailed (see Chapter 17). Conservative newspaper writers and politicians advised farmers to trim expenditures and grow a greater variety of crops, but those farmers whose household budgets had already fallen from fifty dollars to as low as ten dollars per year had nothing to cut back. Nor could they afford to diversify their crops, for the cost of shipping perishable foods far outstripped the price they could get for cotton. In response to diminishing returns, Texas farmers began to organize under the masthead "Equal Rights to All, Special Privileges to None."

Under Charles W. Macune, a self-taught physician and lawyer, several regional organizations joined forces in 1889 as the National Farmers' Alliance and Industrial Union. By the next year the combined movement claimed 3 million white members. Separately, the National Colored Farmers' Alliance and Cooperative Union grew from its beginnings in Arkansas and quickly spread across the South to claim more than a million members of its own. In a region where racial segregation increasingly ruled, the development of parallel organizations was a practical necessity. The racism of white alliance members also shaped this strategy, however.

Farmers black and white recognized that a new governing class held power, and that farmers had to deal with the consequences of "the impoverishment and bondage of so many." The "overthrow and certain destruction of the growing and menacing dangers to the institutions of the country and the liberties of the people," read the Farmers' Alliance's Declaration of Purposes, depended "on agitation, on education, and cooperation, carried on by the means of thorough organization of the masses."

The National Farmers' Alliance was born of several regional alliances. The Southern Farmers' Alliance had successfully organized many local farming communities into producer cooperatives. The falling price of cotton underlined the need for action, and farmers readily translated their anger into intense loyalty to the one organization pledged to their redemption. With more than 500 chapters in Texas alone, and cooperative stores selling a wide range of goods complemented by cooperative merchandizing of crops, the Southern Alliance had become a viable alternative to the capitalist marketplace.

The Northern Farmers' Alliance took shape in the plains states, drawing upon large organizations in Minnesota, Nebraska, Iowa, Kansas, and the Dakotas. During 1886 and 1887, summer drought followed winter blizzards and ice storms, reducing wheat crops by one-third. Locusts and cinch bugs ate much of the rest. As if this were not enough, prices on the world market fell sharply for what little crop remained. Fifty percent of the population left western Kansas in the late 1880s and early 1890s. Skilled agitators played upon these hardships, emphasizing the overpowering influence of railroads over the farmers' lives. By 1890, the Kansas Alliance alone boasted 130,000 members.

Grangers had pushed legislation that would limit the salaries of public officials, provide public school students with books at little or no cost, establish a program of teacher certification, and widen the admissions policy of the new state colleges. But only rarely did they put up candidates for office. In comparison, the Farmers' Alliance had few reservations about taking political stands or entering electoral races. At the end of the 1880s, regional alliances crafted platforms demanding state ownership of the railroads, a graduated income tax, lower tariffs, prohibition of alien land ownership, and "the free and unlimited coinage of silver." In several states, alliance candidates won local and state offices. By 1890 the alliances had gained control of the Nebraska legislature and held the balance of power in Minnesota and South Dakota.

Workers Search For Power

Like farmers, urban workers organized their communities in protest movements during the mid-1870s. The depression following the Panic of 1873, producing 25 percent unemployment in many cities, proved a strong catalyst for organization. In New York City, a group attempted to march to city hall to present a petition on behalf of 10,000 workers who were without jobs or homes. Turned back repeatedly by police, the organizers decided to stage a rally to advertise their demand for a steady job at a living wage. City officials refused to grant a permit. When 7,000 working-class men and women turned out anyway on January 13, 1874, a battalion of 1,600 police — nearly two-thirds of the city's force — rushed into the crowd and began striking out indiscriminately with their clubs. The Tompkins Square Riot inaugurated an era of unprecedented labor conflict and violence.

As among farmers, the railroad corporations provoked a steady stream of protest among workers, culminating in "the Great Uprising of 1877." The first nationwide strike started in July in Martinsburg, West Virginia, where workers responded to a 10 percent wage cut by uncoupling all engines. No more trains would run, they promised, until wages were restored. Within a few days, the strike had spread along the route of the transcontinental railroad lines to New York, Buffalo, Pittsburgh, Chicago, Kansas City, and San Francisco. Workers in other industries and masses of unemployed formed angry crowds across the country, defying armed militias ordered to quell the strike by any means. Dodging hails of bullets, strikers stopped train traffic and seized carloads of food for hungry families. In St. Louis, workers even took over the city administration.

The rioting persisted for nearly a week, spurring business leaders to call for the deportation, arrest, or execution of strike leaders, while Law and Order Leagues swept through working-class neighborhoods and broke up union meetings. President Hayes, fearing a "national insurrection," called in the U.S. Army, setting a precedent for the use of federal troops to suppress a strike. In Pittsburgh, federal troops equipped with Gatling guns fired into a crowd, killing over 20 people. By the time the strike finally ended, over 100 had died.

Memories of the uprising of 1877 haunted leaders in government and business for decades, prompting the creation of the National Guard and the construction of armories near potentially dangerous industrial neighborhoods. Workers also drew lessons from the events. Before the century ended, over 6 million workers would strike in industries

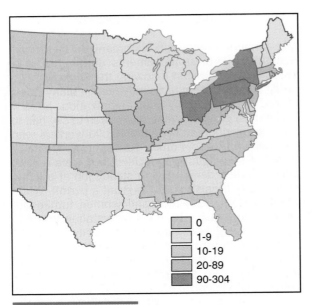

Strikes by State, 1880

Most strikes after the uprising of 1877 could be traced to organized trades, concentrated in the manufacturing districts of the Northeast and Midwest.

☐	0
☐	1–9
☐	10–19
☐	20–89
☐	90–304

Source: Carville Earle, *Geographical Inquiry and American Historical Problems* (Stanford University Press, 1992).

ranging from New England textile to southern tobacco factories to western mines. By the mid-1880s workers also organized to expand their sphere of influence to the halls of city government. While the Farmers' Alliance put up candidates in local and state elections in the South and Plains states, workers launched labor parties in dozens of industrial towns and cities.

In New York City, popular economist and reformer Henry George, with the ardent support of the city's Central Labor Council, put himself forward as candidate for mayor of New York on the Union Labor party ticket. A former prospector, George had observed firsthand the rapid concentration of choice California landholdings in the hands of a few powerful individuals and corporations. In his best-selling *Progress and Poverty* (1879), he explained that a sweeping tax on land would generate enough revenue to allow all Americans to live in comfort. Especially popular among Irish Americans, who had seen their homeland swallowed up by British landlords, George also adopted a program of reforms appealing to German Americans, who along with the Irish constituted the backbone of the New York labor movement.

Tammany Hall delivered many thousands of votes for George straight into the Hudson River, but he managed nevertheless to finish a respectable second: 67,000 to Democrat Abraham S. Hewitt's 90,000 and Republican Theodore Roosevelt's 60,000. Despite its promising beginning, the United Labor party dissolved when the New York State legislature adopted several of George's milder reform planks.

Labor parties elected one or two city council members in many cities, but most groups collapsed with the decline of the Knights of Labor. In smaller industrial towns where workers outnumbered the middle classes, labor parties achieved more success. In Rochester, New Hampshire, with a population of only 7,000, the Knights encouraged workers in the local shoe factories to put up their own candidates for office. From 1889 through 1891 Rochester's workers elected a majority slate, from city council to mayor.

Despite their defeat and disappearance, the local labor parties made a permanent mark on urban politics. The Democratic party in particular responded by running working-class Irish Americans for city offices, usually with a modest set of labor planks in their platforms. Once elected, they often abandoned their ideals for the material rewards of machine politics. But some continued to champion organized labor and the poor by sponsoring appropriations for public relief, refusing to authorize city funds to break strikes, and sometimes urging municipal ownership of public utilities. Many supporters of local labor parties meanwhile moved on to other reform movements, including Bellamy Nationalist Clubs and woman suffrage societies.

Women Build Alliances

Women actively shaped both the labor and agrarian protest movements while campaigning for their own rights as citizens. Like woman suffrage leader Elizabeth Cady Stanton, they believed "government based on caste and class privileges cannot stand." In its place, as Bellamy's novel *Equality* had predicted, would arise a new order where women were "absolutely free agents in the disposition of themselves."

Women in the Knights of Labor endorsed the order's political planks while putting forth their own set of demands. In 1886, sixteen women attending the national convention of the Knights lobbied for the creation of a special department "to investigate the abuses of which our sex is subjected by unscrupulous employers, to agitate the principles which our Order teaches of equal pay for equal work and the abolition of child labor.'' The delegates accepted the plan with little dissent and appointed knit-goods worker Leonora M. Barry general investigator. With perhaps 65,000 women members at its peak, the Knights ran day-care centers for the children of wage-earning mothers and occasionally even bakery cooperatives to reduce the drudgery of cooking.

Women made a similar mark on farmers' organizations. The Patrons of Husbandry issued a charter to a local chapter only when women were well represented on its rolls, and delegates to its conventions in the 1870s routinely gave speeches endorsing woman suffrage and even dress reform. The Farmers' Alliance continued this policy, enjoining women to join their fathers, husbands, or sons in local agitation. Whole families shared in social programs, such as songfests on Sunday afternoons, lecture series, and contests featuring antimonopoly games. In both the Northern and Southern alliances, women constituted perhaps one-quarter of the membership, and several advanced through the ranks to become leading speakers and organizers. Mary E. Lease, who achieved lasting fame for advising farmers to raise less corn and more hell, vividly expressed their sense of purpose. ''Ours is a grand, a holy mission . . . ,'' she proclaimed, ''to drive from our land and forever abolish the triune monopoly of land, money, and transportation.''

Women in both the Knights of Labor and the Farmers' Alliance found their greatest leader in Frances E. Willard, the most famous American woman of the century. Willard assumed that the women who guarded their family's physical and spiritual welfare would, if granted the right to vote, extend their influence throughout the society. From 1878 until her death in 1897, Willard presided over the Woman's Christian Temperance Union (WCTU), the largest organization of women in the world, and encouraged her numerous followers to ''do everything.'' She mobilized nearly one million women in order to, in her words, ''make the whole world HOMELIKE.'' WCTU members worked to reform the prison system, eradicate prostitution, and eliminate the wage system as well as to reduce the consumption of alcoholic beverages. Willard went so far as to draw up plans for a new system of government whereby all offices, right up to the presidency, would be shared equally by a man and a woman. In the late 1880s, Willard took out membership in the Knights of Labor and endorsed the platform of the Farmers' Alliance.

The WCTU grew under Willard's leadership into the major force behind the late-nineteenth-century campaign for woman suffrage, far surpassing the two major woman suffrage associations, the American Woman Suffrage Association and the National Woman Suffrage Association. By 1890, when the rival associations merged to form the National American Woman Suffrage Association, the WCTU

Sixteen women were among the 660 delegates attending the 1886 convention of the Knights of Labor in Richmond, Virginia. Elizabeth Rodgers, who holds her two-week old daughter, joined the organization as a housewife. The mother of twelve children, she was also the first woman elected to head a district assembly. The majority of women delegates worked in shoe factories or textile mills.

had already pushed the heart of the suffrage campaign into the plains states and the West. In Iowa, Nebraska, Colorado, and especially Kansas, the agitation for the right to vote provided a political bridge among women organized in the WCTU, the Farmers' Alliance, the Knights of Labor, and various local suffrage societies.

In 1891, at the invitation of Populist women, members of these various organizations formed the National Women's Alliance. The founding convention called for "full equality of the sexes," "harmony and unity of action among the Sisterhood" of the nation, "prevention of war," and the rejection of alcohol, tobacco, and narcotics as injurious to health. Their newspaper, the *Farmer's Wife,* spelled out basic principles in epigrams such as "Give our women encouragement and victory is yours" and "Put 1000 women lecturers in the field and the revolution is here."

Although women lecturers such as Kansas's Annie Diggs were outstanding crowd pleasers, women failed to gain equality within the Knights of Labor and the Farmers' Alliance. Many women in the Southern Alliance actually opposed the enfranchisement of women. It was, however, the turn to partisan politics that placed voteless women on the sidelines of populism. The People's party refused to put a woman suffrage plank in its platform. Only in Colorado did local Populist men join the successful 1893 campaign that secured for women the right to vote in that state.

The People's Party

Meeting at Ocala, Florida, in December 1890, the Farmers' Alliance began to press for a national third-party movement. This was, however, a risky proposition, because the Farmers' Alliance, like the Grange, had allied locally with Democrats or Republicans. The Southern Alliance hoped to capture control of the Democratic party, while many plains states farmers voted Republican. In some areas, though, the Farmers' Alliance established its own parties, put up full slates of candidates for state elections, won majorities in state legislatures, and even sent a representative to Congress. Reviewing these successes, the delegates at Ocala decided to push ahead and form a national party, and they appealed to other farm, labor, and reform organizations to join them.

The time had come, the alliance announced, "to establish the moral solidarity of the farmer and toiler societies." In February 1892, representatives from the Farmers' Alliance, the Knights of Labor, and the National Colored Alliance, among others, met in St. Louis under a broad banner that read: "We do not ask for sympathy or pity. We ask for justice." After much deliberation, the 1,300 delegates adopted a platform for the new People's party calling for government ownership of the railroads, banks, and telegraph lines, the prohibition of large landholding companies, a graduated income tax, an eight-hour workday, and immigration restriction. Its preamble, written by Minnesota's Ignatius Donnelly, declared: "we seek to restore the government of the Republic to the hands of 'the plain people' with which class it originated." The People's party convened again in Omaha in July 1892 and nominated James B. Weaver of Iowa for president and, to please the South, Confederate veteran James Field of Virginia for vice-president.

The Populists, as supporters of the People's party styled themselves, quickly became a major factor in American politics. In some southern states, Populists cooperated with local Republicans in sponsoring "pepper and salt" state and local tickets that put black and white candidates on one slate. To hold their voters, some Democrats adopted the Populist platform wholesale; others resorted to massive voter fraud and intimidation. In the West, Democrats threw their weight behind the Populist ticket mainly to defeat the ruling Republican party.

Although Democrat Grover Cleveland regained the presidency in 1892 (he had previously served from 1885 to 1888), Populists scored significant local victories. They ran strongest in Idaho, Nevada, Colorado, Kansas, and North Dakota, winning 50 percent or more of the vote. Nationwide they elected three governors, ten representatives, and five senators. The national ticket received over a million votes (8.5 percent of the total) and twenty-two electoral college votes — the only time since the Civil War that a third party had received *any* electoral votes. Despite poor showings among urban workers and throughout New England and the Upper South, Populists looked forward to the next round of state elections in 1894. But the great test would come with the next presidential election in 1896.

THE CRISIS OF THE 1890S

Populist Ignatius Donnelly wrote in the preface to his pessimistic novel *Caesar's Column* that industrial society appeared a "wretched failure" to "the great mass of mankind." On route to disaster rather than to the egalitarian community that Bellamy had envisioned, "the rich, as a rule, hate the poor; and the poor are coming to hate the rich . . . society divides itself into two hostile camps. . . . They wait only for the drum beat and the trumpet to summon them to armed conflict."

A series of events in the 1890s shook the confidence of many citizens in the reigning political system. By 1894 the nation had entered its greatest depression to date. More than 500,000 workers had struck against their own employers or in solidarity with workers in other industries. Neither Republicans nor Democrats responded sufficiently to the crisis, and many feared — while others hoped — that the entire political system would topple.

Financial Collapse and the Depression

At the center of economic growth lay the railroads, which by the early 1890s represented a combined capital of $2.5 billion. While helping to create a national market for goods and labor, the railroad corporations had sparked rage among many workers and farmers. In 1893, when the nation's major lines collapsed, the business boom of nearly two decades ended and the entire economy ground to a halt. The depression that followed made the hard times of the 1870s appear a mere rehearsal for worse misery to come.

The collapse of the Philadelphia and Reading Railroad in March 1893 followed by the downfall of the National Cordage Company precipitated a crisis in the stock market and sent waves of panic splashing over Wall Street–connected banks. In a few months, more than 150 banks went into receivership and hundreds more closed; nearly 200 railroads and more than 15,000 businesses also slipped into bankruptcy. The steel industry alone, which produced the rails, saw thirty companies collapse within six months of the panic. Agricultural prices, meanwhile, plummeted to new lows. Subsequent bank failures and stock market declines held back recovery until 1897, when the economy slowly began to pick up again. The new century arrived before prosperity returned.

The depression brought untold hardships. In many cities, unemployment rates reached 20 to 25 percent. Seasonal layoffs became far more common and long-lasting. Few people starved but many suffered from malnutrition. From farm to city slum communicable diseases related to inadequate diets, such as tuberculosis and pellagra, plagued wide populations. Unable to buy food, clothes, or household items, families learned to survive with the barest minimum.

The "tramp problem," a direct result of unemployment, returned to levels reached during the hungry 1870s. Tens of thousands rode the rails or went "on the tramp" to look for work, hoping a new community might bring employment. Some panhandled for the nickel that could buy a mug of beer and a free lunch at a saloon. By night they slept in

Jacob Coxey's "Commonwealth of Christ Army," 1894. Attracting sympathetic attention of working people and the hostility of most of the wealthier classes, "Industrial Armies" moved through U.S. cities on route to the nation's capitol.

parks or, in the colder months, flocked to the "bum tanks" of the city jail or to fleabag hotels. Vagrancy laws (enacted during the 1870s) forced many into prison. In New York City alone, with over 20,000 homeless people, thousands ended up in jail. Once again newspapers warned against this "menace" and blamed the growing crime rates on these "dangerous classes."

Populist Jacob Sechler Coxey of Massillon, Ohio, attempted to rally masses of unemployed workers into a huge "industrial army" that would carry a demand for a public works program directly to the U.S. Congress. His ally Carl Browne, a California reformer, had ingeniously come up with the idea of a "petition in boots." On Easter Sunday 1894, Coxey left Massillon with several hundred followers, hoping to attract 100,000 more and arrive in Washington, D.C., on May Day. From Boston, Los Angeles, San Francisco, Tacoma, Denver, Salt Lake City, Reno, Butte, and Omaha other small brigades set out. Although many communities welcomed the marchers with food and shelter, U.S. attorney general Richard C. Olney, a former lawyer for the railroad companies, conspired with state and local police to halt the march. Only 600 men and women actually reached the nation's capital, where club-wielding police arrested the leaders and dispersed the crowd. Coxey's army quickly disbanded, but not before the movement generated great sympathy for the masses of unemployed.

Strikes and the Solidarity of Labor

Labor unleashed its own protests, different from both the marches of the unemployed and the riotous strikes of 1877. The majority of strikes during the 1890s were neither spontaneous outbreaks of discontent nor nationwide actions but, rather, carefully organized local events sanctioned by unions. In 1891, three quarters of all walkouts took place with the "official" approval of labor organizations.

Employers provoked some of the most violent strikes by discarding the work rules that regulated the pace of production, standards that unions had negotiated and enforced. More and more workers turned out in "sympathy" with fellow workers striking in other locations in defense of similar prerogatives. These "solidarity" strikes often succeeded temporarily in strengthening local chapters of existing national and international unions. But they could not overcome the economic tide against the craft worker and the power of the legal system to overrule labor's solidarity.

At Homestead, Pennsylvania, members of the Amalgamated Iron, Steel and Tin Workers, the largest and most powerful union of the American Federation of Labor (AFL), had carved out an admirable position for themselves in the Carnegie Steel Company. Well paid, proud of their skills, the unionists owned their own homes and directed their unskilled "helpers" without undue influence from

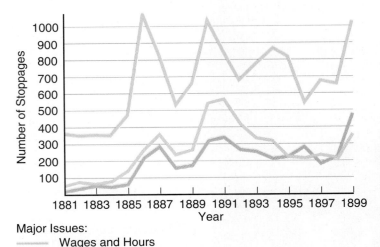

Major Issues:

- - - - - Wages and Hours
········· Union Organization
———— Other and Not Reported

Work Stoppages, 1881–1899

The number of strikes over wages and hours peaked in the years of 1886, 1890, and 1899, as workers in various trades and industries acted to protect or better their situations. By contrast, strikes for union recognition by employers — waged mostly by skilled workers — rose slowly but steadily until the economic depression of the 1890s. As the depression eased, strikes again increased.

Source: *Historical Statistics of the United States (D–970),* p. 179.

company supervisors. Company owner Carnegie and Chairman Henry C. Frick, having determined to gain complete control over production, including the cost and pace of labor, threatened the union's existence.

The Amalgamated and management had fought to a standstill in 1889, but when the union's contract expired in 1892 Frick announced a drastic wage cut. He simultaneously prepared for a strike, ordering the construction around the factory of a wooden stockade with holes for rifles and barbed wire on top. When the city government refused to assign police to disperse strikers, Frick sent a barge with 300 security guards to do the work. Gunfire broke out and continued throughout the day, wounding at least sixty. Eventually the governor sent in the Pennsylvania National Guard to restore order. Carnegie's factory reopened with nonunion scabs doing the work.

After four months the union was forced to concede a crushing defeat, not only for itself but in effect for all steelworkers. The Carnegie company reduced its workforce by a quarter, lengthened the workday, and cut wages 25 percent for those who remained on the job. Within a decade, every major steel company was operating without interference from the Amalgamated.

Many observers of this strike and others at the time pointed out that labor had defeated itself even before the deployment of private armies or government troops. By encouraging the exclusion of unskilled workers (including women and African Americans) from unions, the American Federation of Labor had placed all its faith in the very crafts that were rapidly being displaced by the new machinery. Management's counteroffensive seemed to promise the loss of everything unions had gained — unless skilled workers put aside their claims of privilege in the name of class solidarity. Just two years after Homestead, the most earthshaking railway strike since 1877 built on this lesson.

Like Lowell, Massachusetts, sixty years earlier (see Chapter 12), the town of Pullman, Illinois, just south of Chicago, had been regarded as a model industrial community. Its creator and proprietor, George Pullman, had manufactured luxurious sleeping cars for railroads since 1881. He built his company as a self-contained community. The factory was at the center, surrounded by modern cottages, a library, churches, an independent water supply, and even a company cemetery. The Pullman Palace Car Company deducted rent, water bills, library fees, and grocery tabs from workers' weekly wages. In good times, workers enjoyed a decent livelihood, although many resented Pullman's autocratic control of their daily affairs.

When times grew hard, Pullman cut wages by one-third and in some instances as much as half, down to less than a dollar a day. Food prices and rents remained unchanged. Furthermore, factory supervisors sought to make up for declining profits by driving workers relentlessly to produce greater volume. When Pullman fired members of a committee that had drawn up a list of grievances, workers voted in May 1894 to strike.

The workers at Pullman found their champion in Eugene V. Debs, a former official in the Brotherhood of Locomotive Firemen who had recently formed the American Railway Union in order to embrace all railroad workers in one organization. Architect of the ARU's victory over James J. Hill's Great Northern rail line just one month earlier, Debs advised caution. But delegates to an ARU convention voted to support a nationwide boycott of all Pullman cars. This action soon inspired a sympathy strike by railroad workers across the country. Support for the strike was especially strong in the western states.

Compared with the Uprising of 1877, the orderly Pullman strike produced remarkably little violence. The ARU urged strikers to resist all police provocations and hold their ground peacefully. But Attorney General Olney, claiming that the ARU was interfering with the mails (actually Debs had banned just such interference), issued a blanket injunction against the strike. President Cleveland sent federal troops to Chicago on July 4, over Illinois governor John Peter Altgeld's objections. After a bitter confrontation leaving thirteen dead and over fifty wounded, the army dispersed the strikers. Over the next week, railroad workers in twenty-six other states resisted federal troops and a dozen more people were killed. On July 17, federal marshalls arrested Debs and other leaders, bringing the strike to an end.

The imprisoned labor leader became a national hero overnight. "The Debs of fable," wrote the editor of a Unitarian weekly, "lighted a fire in the car yards of Chicago. The Debs of fact lighted an idea in the dangerous shadows of the Republic." Assailing the arrogance of class privilege that encouraged the government to use brute force against its citizens, Debs concluded that the labor movement could not regain its dignity under the existing political system.

An avid reader of Bellamy's *Looking Backward,* Debs announced his conversion to the ideals of socialism. For a few years after the Pullman strike, he tried to create a utopian colony that would prove the viability of cooperation in both working and living arrangements. This attempt failed to get off the ground, and Debs moved on to help form a political party dedicated to the principles of socialism.

Across the industrial belt, and in the West and Southwest, in railroad towns, factory villages, and farms, tens of thousands followed Debs in taking up the new gospel. Declining the efforts of railroad mechanics to nominate him for vice-president for the Populist ticket in 1896, Debs ran for president as a Socialist in 1900 and four times later. The odds against him grew with the scale of the booming economy, but Debs made his point on moral grounds. His friend James Whitcomb Riley, the nation's most admired sentimental poet, wrote in rural dialect that Debs had "the kindest heart that ever beat/betwixt here and the jedgment [judgment] seat."

The Social Gospel

The unwholesome consequences of an inequitable political economy emerged as a major topic of Protestant sermons and Catholic tracts and inspired many churchgoers to rally in sympathy with the working classes and the poor. Like Edward Bellamy, a growing number of clergy and lay theologians noted a discrepancy between the ideals of Christianity and the assumptions of the social order. Moved by the human suffering accompanying the major depressions of the 1870s and the 1890s, they concluded that environmental factors such as hunger and homelessness made the task of spiritual uplift difficult, if not impossible. Like Bellamy, they could no longer sanction a political system that allowed larger numbers of its citizens to toil long hours under unhealthy conditions and for subsistence wages. They demanded the church lead the way in a massive *social* redemption, envisioning a new cooperative order based on the principles of Christ's gospels. "The spirit of the Master and of His gospels," the Reverend Franklin Monroe Sprague wrote, was "uncompromisingly against the possession of riches amid want and suffering."

Coinciding with an upswing in religious revivals in the nation's cities, some liberal congregations broke away from established churches to side with the working class and the immigrant poor. Ministers called for civil service reform and factory inspection legislation. Supporting labor's right to organize and, if necessary, to strike, they petitioned government officials to regulate corporations and limit profits. Washington Gladden, a Congregationalist minister, warned that if churches continued to ignore the pressing social issues of the day they would devolve into institutions whose sole purpose was to maintain obscure rituals and superstitions. In the wake of the great railroad strikes of 1877, he had called upon his congregation in Columbus, Ohio, to take an active part in the fight against social injustice. In *Applied Christianity* (1886), Gladden appealed to the nation's employers to return to Christ's law.

Less famous but more numerous, local Protestant ministers and community leaders likewise sought to restore what they considered the true spirit of Christianity. As labor reformer and Christian socialist George McNeill wrote in 1890, some ministers might be the servants of wealth, but "the influence of the teachings of the Carpenter's Son" would in the long run "counteract the influence of Mammon," the biblical god of greed. McNeill looked forward to the day when "every man shall have according to his needs." Although the social gospel spread most rapidly among the residents of northern industrial cities, southern African Americans espoused their own version. They reinterpreted the Gospel as Jesus' promise to emancipate their race from satanic white power brokers. The biblical republic of Beulahland became their model of redemption.

A host of writers elaborated these themes during the depression of the 1890s. The very popular *If Christ Came to Chicago* (1894), by British journalist W. T. Stead, forced readers to confront the "ugly sight" of a city filled with 200 millionaires and 200,000 unemployed men. It inspired Edward Everett Hale's *If Jesus Came to Boston* (1894), which similarly questioned contemporary social arrangements. The most famous tract, *In His Steps* (1896), by Methodist minister Charles M. Sheldon of Topeka, Kansas, urged readers to rethink their actions in the light of the simple question "What would Jesus do?" By 1933 Sheldon's book had sold more than 23 million copies.

Catholics, doctrinally more inclined than Protestants to accept poverty as a natural condition, joined the social gospel movement in smaller numbers. In the early 1880s Polish Americans broke off from the Roman Catholic Church to form the Polish National Church, a body more attuned to the interests of working people. Irish Americans, especially prominent in the Knights of Labor, encouraged priests to ally with the labor movement. Leo XIII's papal encyclical *Rerum Novarum* (1891) endorsed the right of workers to form trade unions.

Women guided the social gospel movement in the community. Groups of evangelical women of various Protestant sects in nearly every city of size raised money to establish small, inexpensive residential hotels for working women, whose meager wages rarely covered the price of safe, comfortable shelter. Federated as the Young Women's Christian Association, the YWCA incorporated over 600 local chapters by the turn of the century. The "Y" sponsored a range of services for needy Christian women, ranging from homes for the elderly and for unmarried mothers to elaborate programs of vocational instruction and physical fitness. The Girls Friendly Societies, an organization of young women affiliated with Episcopal churches in several cities, sponsored similar programs. Meanwhile, Catholic lay women and nuns served the poor women of their faith. The Grey Nuns of Boston, for example, strove to bring "good cheer to the multitude of young workers treading the thorny way of privation in the daily struggle for livelihood" and operated several residential homes.

Although centered in the cities, the social gospel rallied women in many small-town and rural communities, especially those ardent admirers of the century's most renowned woman evangelist, Frances Willard. "The time will come," Willard insisted, "when the human heart will be so much alive that no one could sleep in any given community if any of that group of human beings were cold, hungry, or miserable."

THE POLITICS OF REFORM, THE POLITICS OF ORDER

The severe hardships of the 1890s, following decades of popular unrest and economic uncertainty, led to a crisis in the two-party system and pointed to the presidential election of 1896 as the likely turning point in American politics. Republicans and Democrats continued to enjoy long-standing voter loyalties within specific groups or regions, and both parties could depend on masses of white voters to unite against any movement threatening to compromise the "color line." But Populists showed surprising ingenuity and courage in breaking down the barriers against political insurgents.

The Free-Silver Issue

Grover Cleveland owed his victory in 1892 over Republican incumbent Benjamin Harrison to the predictable votes of the Democratic "solid" South

Populists published this cartoon in 1894 to illustrate their argument that life in the United States had degenerated from its egalitarian past.

Source: Worth Robert Miller, *Oklahoma Populism: A History of the People's Party in the Oklahoma Territory* (Norman: University of Oklahoma Press, 1987).

and to the unanticipated support of such northern states as Illinois and Wisconsin, which had not voted Democratic since before the Civil War. But when the economy collapsed the following year, President Cleveland and the Democrats who controlled the Senate faced a public eager for action. Convinced that the crisis could be easily resolved through a familiar combination of lower tariffs, laissez-faire economics, and retention of the gold standard, Cleveland scorned any major federal program that would have provided relief for the homeless and hungry.

With both major parties short on ideas for economic recovery, the currency issue rapidly moved to the center of national debate. Since the early decades of the century, reformers had often urged the adoption of "soft" (inflated) currency, which would help farmers pay their loans to banks at a discount, and would accelerate economic growth by increasing the volume of money in circulation. The issuance of Greenbacks, the devalued currency that had become necessary during the Civil War to meet national debts, had encouraged soft-money enthusiasts to advocate a continuation of inflated currency after the war. Soft-money advocates, including the representatives of western states rich in silver, persuaded President Grant to sign the 1873 Coinage Act, which added silver to gold as the precious-metal basis for currency. This move had little real impact on the economy but opened the door to yet more tinkering.

In hard times especially, the currency question continued to simmer. Philanthropist Peter Cooper ran an independent presidential campaign in 1876 on a platform of soft money and won 50,000 votes. Four years later, Civil War general James B. Weaver ran on similar planks for the Greenback Labor party and gathered an impressive 300,000 votes. Meanwhile, the gold-standard advocates, concentrated mostly in the business community, argued that the introduction of silver had already damaged the economy severely. The compromise Sherman Silver Purchase Act of 1890 directed the Treasury to purchase 4.5 million ounces of silver each month, almost precisely the amount being produced by western silver mines, and to issue Treasury notes equal in value to the cost of these purchases, redeemable to buyers in either gold or silver. Republican members of Congress supported this measure in return for the Democrats' agreement to support the McKinley tariff, which established the highest duties yet on manufactured goods. Known as the "Million Dollar Congress," these legislators angered reformers as well as poor farmers and workers, who gained nothing from these measures.

With the economy in ruins, a desperate President Cleveland called a secret session of Congress and urged repeal of the Sherman Act, insisting that only the gold standard could pull the nation out of depression. By exerting intense pressure on congressional Democrats, Cleveland succeeded in October 1893, but not without ruining his chances for renomination in 1896. The "Silver Democrats" of his own party vowed revenge and began to look more kindly on Populists, who remained firmly wedded to "free silver." Republicans, solidly behind the gold standard, linked their future to a "hard-money," business-oriented candidate, Ohio's William McKinley.

Populism's Last Campaigns

Populists had been buoyed by the 1894 election, which delivered to their candidates nearly 1.5 million votes, a gain of 40 percent over their 1892 totals. They made impressive inroads even into the southern states of Georgia, Alabama, and North Carolina. Only Democrat-instigated fraud and voter harassment, especially pronounced in Louisiana, prevented Populists from winning entire states. In the West, political excitement steadily increased. David

Waite, Populist governor of Colorado, talked of a coming revolution and declared, "It is better, infinitely better, that blood should flow [up] to the horses' bridles rather than our national liberties should be destroyed." Known afterward as "Bloody Bridles" Waite, he was regarded by conservatives as dangerous, even subversive, to established order. In Kansas, rival forces barely averted violence in their contest for the statehouse. An army of reform veterans who had previously supported the Knights of Labor, Henry George, or Edward Bellamy also threw their weight behind the Populist movement.

As Populists prepared for the 1896 election, they found themselves at a crossroads: What were they to do about the growing popularity of Democrat William Jennings Bryan? Son of a southern Illinois judge who had run for Congress unsuccessfully on the Greenback ticket, Bryan had settled in Nebraska to practice law. A spellbinding public speaker, he succeeded where his father failed and won a congressional seat in 1890. Although he courted local business leaders and envisioned only a modest redistribution of power, Bryan adopted the Populist slogan "Equal Rights to All and Special Privileges to None" and soon enlarged his following.

Bryan stumbled into his most important crusade. "I don't know anything about free silver," he had admitted in an 1892 campaign speech, but "the people of Nebraska are for free silver and I am for free silver. I will look up the arguments later." He swiftly took up the currency issue as the one dearest to the voting majority and suddenly became a champion of free silver — as well as the darling of the mining companies, which distributed nearly one million copies of his speech. Bryan's popularity gave new life to a divided Democratic party.

At the 1896 party convention, Democrats thrilled over the thirty-six-year-old Bryan's "Cross of Gold" speech, one of the most famous orations in the history of American politics. "Burn down your cities and leave our farms," he said, "and your cities will spring up again as if by magic; but destroy our farms and the grass will grow in the streets of every city in the country." Bryan closed on a yet more dramatic note, intoning the solidarity of the common folk against the rich and privileged classes. Spreading his arms to suggest the figure of the crucified Jesus Christ, Bryan pledged to answer all demands for a gold standard by saying, "You shall not press down upon the brow of labor this crown of thorns, you shall not crucify mankind upon a cross of gold." With this speech, Bryan swept the gathering.

Populists feared that the Democrats, in nomi-

These political buttons and badges were part of the 1896 presidential race. Republican William McKinley brings luck with the rabbit's foot, and an imitation gold elephant symbolizes his party, the "GOP." The cross and Biblical phrase recall the most memorable passage of William Jennings Bryan's famous speech. The Democrats and Prohibitionists strike a dignified pose for their photographic portrait.

cans, and allow the victors to make important changes in government. Yet as their own convention approached, Populists remained divided on strategy. Western Populists generally favored a merger with Democrats, while southern Populists continued to hold out for third-party campaign.

In the end, Populists put forward a "fusion" Democratic-Populist ticket. Nominating Bryan for president, the convention chose one of their own for vice-president, the popular Georgian Tom Watson. Most state electoral boards, however, refused to put the Populist ticket on the ballot. Worse, Bryan and his running mate on the Democratic ticket, Arthur Sewell, simply ignored the Populist campaign.

The Republican Triumph

Republican leaders, meanwhile, set about to build a national coalition that could claim credit for the development of a powerful, modern industrial nation. They turned to the Protestant business classes, believing them the best suited to rule and the most likely to contribute generously to Republican coffers. After its election defeat in 1892, the party determinedly reorganized to offer a conservative yet appealing answer to the Democratic and Populist challenges.

The Republican party found in William McKinley a handsome, knowledgeable, courteous, and ruthless political candidate. Equally important, McKinley enjoyed the backing of the most formidable machine in American history. Financier Mark Hanna guided a campaign that raised up to $7 million and outspent Bryan more than ten to one. The sheer expense and skill of coordination outdid all previous campaigns and established a precedent for twentieth-century elections. Using innumerable placards, hats, and parades, Republicans advertised their promised "good times to come." Meanwhile, they cast adversary Bryan as a dangerous nay-sayer willing to risk the nation's well-being and cost voters their jobs or worse.

Bryan won 46 percent of the popular vote but could not carry the Midwest, the Far West, or the Upper South. Although many individual Populists were elected as Democrats in the West, or against Democrats in the South, the "fusion" approach fatally damaged the party machinery. Moreover, the single-issue appeal for currency reform failed to convince urban dwellers, who feared that soft money would bring higher prices. Catholics, uncomfortable with Bryan's Protestant evangelicalism, went especially heavily for McKinley and helped elect a Republican Congress. Neither the reform-minded

nating Bryan, had stolen their thunder. For several years, the silver issue had been building within their own ranks. A national conference of the prosilver American Bimetallic League, held in Chicago in 1893, had involved both Bryan and Populist leader Ignatius Donnelly, who prepared its set of resolutions. Although many Populists feared that the growing emphasis on currency would overshadow the more important plan to nationalize the nation's railroads and communication systems, they felt helpless to express their reservations amid so much enthusiasm. They hoped, therefore, that a political victory would unite the silver-mining West and the indebted South, crush the gold-standard Republi-

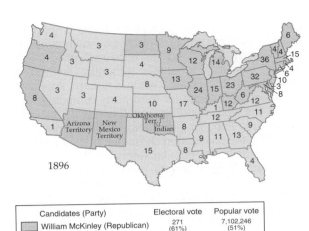

Candidates (Party)	Electoral vote	Popular vote
William McKinley (Republican)	271 (61%)	7,102,246 (51%)
William J. Bryan (Democratic)	176 (39%)	6,492,559 (47%)
Minor parties	–	315,398 (2%)

Election of 1896, by States

Democratic candidate William Jennings Bryan carried most of rural America but could not overcome Republican William McKinley's stronghold in the populous industrial states.

urban middle classes nor impoverished blue-collar workers were convinced, finally, that Bryan's grand reform vision really included them. The Populist following, disappointed and disillusioned, dwindled away.

For sixteen years after the 1896 election, Democrats dominated no region but the South. With Republican victories seemingly inevitable, apathy set in and voter participation spiraled downward.

Once in office, McKinley promoted a mixture of probusiness and expansionist measures. He supported the Dingley Tariff of 1897, raising duties to an all-time high, and committed the United States to the gold standard through the Currency Act of 1900. McKinley also moved toward moderate business regulation. He encouraged Congress to create in 1897 the United States Industrial Commission, which would plan business regulation; promoted an 1898 bankruptcy act that eased the financial situation of small businesses; and proposed the Erdman Act of the same year, which established a system of arbitration designed to prevent rail strikes. The Supreme Court ruled in concert with the president, finding eighteen railways in violation of antitrust laws and granting states the right to regulate hours of labor under certain circumstances.

McKinley's triumph over the ruins of populism ended the popular challenge to the governing sys-

tem. With prosperity returning after 1898 and nationalism rising swiftly, McKinley encouraged Americans to go for "a full dinner pail," the winning Republican slogan of the 1900 election.

The Limits of Democracy

Campaign rhetoric aside, McKinley and Bryan differed only slightly on the major problems facing the nation in 1896. Neither Bryan the reformer nor McKinley the prophet of prosperity addressed the escalation of racism and nativism throughout the nation. After the election, McKinley made white supremacy a major tenet of his foreign policy; Bryan, twice more a presidential contender, championed white rule in the South.

Toward the end of the nineteenth century, many political observers noted, the nation's patriotic fervor had a strongly nationalistic and xenophobic tone. Striking workers and their employers alike tended to blame "foreigners" for the hard times. Fourth of July orators, rather than celebrating freedom and liberty, now boasted about the might and power of their nation, while the sons and daughters of immigrants attacked the new generation of newcomers as unfit for democracy and dangerous to the national way of life. Semisecret organizations such as the American Protective Association sprang up to defend American institutions from an imagined Catholic conspiracy directed by the pope. White violence against African Americans, especially lynchings, reached a level unknown since Reconstruction.

Beginning in the late 1880s, state and local "Jim Crow" laws codified the worsening condition of African Americans in the South. Wealthy planters, merchants, and farmers organized to disfranchise black voters and to extend segregation to facilities such as restaurants, public transportation, and even drinking fountains and phone booths. The U.S. Supreme Court upheld the new discriminatory legislation. Its *Civil Rights* decisions of 1883 overturned the Civil Rights Act of 1875, and in *Plessy v. Ferguson* (1896) the Court upheld a Louisiana state law formally segregating railroad cars on the basis of "separate but equal" facilities for African Americans. In *Cumming v. County Board of Education* (1899), the Court allowed separate schools for blacks and whites on a similar basis, even where facilities for African American children did not exist.

The new restrictions struck especially hard at the already eroded voting rights of African Americans. Southern states enacted new literacy tests and property qualifications for voting, demanding proof of $300 to $500 in property and the ability to read and write. Loopholes permitted poor whites to vote even under these conditions, except where they threatened the Democratic party's rule. "Grandfather clauses," invented in Louisiana, exempted from all restrictions those who were entitled to vote on January 1, 1867, together with their sons and grandsons, a measure that effectively enfranchised whites while barring African Americans. In 1898 the Supreme Court ruled that poll taxes and literacy requirements enacted purposefully to prevent blacks (and some poor whites) from voting were a proper means of restricting the ballot to "qualified" voters. Supreme Court justice John Marshall Harlan, the lone dissenter, lamented that the Court's majority rulings gave power to the states "to place in a condition of legal inferiority a large body of American citizens."

These restrictive measures, enacted against a background of physical violence, deprived African Americans of equal rights and protection under the law and encouraged state legislatures outside the South to pass similar measures. By 1900 only 5 percent of the southern black electorate voted. In the growing southern cities, black people lived almost entirely apart from whites, compelled to put up with inferior schools, neighborhoods, and jobs. Conditions continued to deteriorate in many border states, such as Ohio, and elsewhere throughout the North. Discriminatory legislation based on race expanded steadily until the Supreme Court's *Brown v. Board of Education of Topeka* ruling in 1954 (see Chapter 28).

Although calling for the expansion of democracy, the era's major protest movements failed to overcome their own racial and ethnic prejudices. Trade unions produced a mixed but generally poor record. During the 1877 railroad strike St. Louis leaders formally declared that labor "recognizes neither color, creed, nor nationality." But fearing a loss of support among the city's white majority, they excluded African Americans from participating in their public events. Meanwhile, San Francisco strikers turned into mobs avenging themselves upon Chinese merchants. A California Workingmen's party, which grew out of the racial unrest, operated mainly as an anti-Chinese organization. Even the Knights of Labor, which organized many African American workers, barred Chinese from membership. The American Federation of Labor adopted more comprehensive exclusionary policies. Its leaders imposed no standards upon affiliates but also

WHITE SUPREMACY!

Attention, White Men!

Grand Torch-Light Procession

At JACKSON,

On the Night of the

Fourth of January, 1890.

The Final Settlement of Democratic Rule and White Supremacy in Mississippi.

GRAND PYROTECHNIC DISPLAY!
Transparencies and Torches Free for all.

All in Sympathy with the Grand Cause are Cordially and Earnestly Invited to be on hand, to aid in the Final Overthrow of Radical Rule in our State.

Come on foot or on horse-back; come any way, but be sure to get there.
Brass Bands, Cannon, Flambeau Torches, Transparencies, Sky-rockets, Etc.

A GRAND DISPLAY FOR A GRAND CAUSE.

Billboard produced for the Mississippi constitution convention of 1890. Rallying under the banner of "white supremacy," the delegates successfully disfranchised African Americans.

made no move to discourage the outright ban on nonwhite members in effect in many trades. AFL leader Samuel Gompers, himself a Jewish immigrant from Holland, lobbied Congress to protect the labor market for "real" Americans by restricting immigration from eastern and southern Europe.

Reformers, too, had a mixed record. Many former abolitionists who had routinely called for both the enfranchisement of women and the emancipation of slaves later concluded that African Americans had wrongfully been granted voting rights ahead of white women under the terms of the Fourteenth and Fifteenth amendments. Newer generations explicitly condoned segregation and refused to condemn racial violence. Wishing to appease new southern members, the 1899 convention of the National American Woman Suffrage Association voted down a delegate's appeal for an official resolution condemning racial segregation in public facilities. Frances Willard, prestigious president of the WCTU, similarly refused to condemn the lynchings of African Americans.

Tom Watson

A racist turn in the Populist movement represented a far greater tragedy, because at times its leading figures had challenged white supremacy. The story of Tom Watson, briefly a champion of interracial unity, illustrates the rise and fall of Populist hopes for an egalitarian South.

Son of a prosperous farmer driven into bankruptcy by the depressed cotton prices of the 1870s, young Tom quickly became an orator for agrarian causes. He ridiculed the two major parties for failing to respond to the depression, and attacked "Yankee rule" of the South as demoralizing for both blacks and whites. In the 1880s he found a home in the Southern Farmers' Alliance.

As a Populist leader, Watson courageously defended the voting rights of African Americans, making him the most controversial political leader in the South. "Why is not the colored tenant [farmer] open to the conviction that he is in the same boat as the white tenant; the colored laborer with the white laborer?" he asked. Watson planned to overturn the Democratic domination of the region by capturing and drastically increasing the black vote.

Southerners following Watson were jailed, shot at, denied protection of the courts, and driven from their churches. Yet tens of thousands regarded him as a savior. Flowers decorated the bridges along his rural speaking routes, crowds standing in pouring rain begged him to continue speaking, and wagons of loyalists carried Winchester rifles to defend him from armed attack. Preaching government ownership of railroads and banks and political equality for both races, Watson stirred the only truly grass-roots, interracial movement the South had yet seen.

By early 1896, however, Watson had perceived that the increasing ardor for currency reform and the move toward "fusion" with Democrats would doom the Populist movement. Following McKinley's triumph he withdrew from politics, retiring to his Georgia farm to write popular histories of the United States and to plot his future.

Watson returned to public life after the turn of the century but with a totally different racial approach to politics. Railing against the poverty and demoralization of the South, Watson once again created a devoted following for himself, although not large enough to lift him to the national spotlight. He still bitterly attacked the wealthy classes but now blamed black citizens for conspiring against poor whites. He had concluded that political success now hinged on accommodation to white supremacy. Watson expressed a southern version of a new national creed that prepared Americans to view the luckless inhabitants of distant lands as ripe for colonization by the United States.

THE "IMPERIALISM OF RIGHTEOUSNESS"

Many Americans attributed the Panic of 1893 not simply to the collapse of the railroads and the uncertainty of the stock market but to basic structural problems: an overbuilt economy and an insufficient market for goods. Profits from total sales of manufactured and agricultural products had increased substantially over those of the 1880s, but output increased even more rapidly. While the number of millionaires shot up from 500 in 1860 to more than 4,000 in 1892, the majority of working people lacked the requisite income to buy back a significant portion of what they produced. As Republican senator Albert J. Beveridge of Indiana put it, "We are raising more than we can consume . . . making more than we can use. Therefore, we must find new markets for our produce, new occupation for our capital, new work for our labor."

At an international gathering of historians in 1893, the distinguished scholar Frederick Jackson Turner reminded Americans that the continent had now been settled. The first period in the nation's history was over. "American social development has been continually beginning over again on the frontier," he explained. "This perennial rebirth, this fluidity of American life, this expansion westward with its new opportunities, its continuous touch with the simplicity of primitive society, furnish the forces dominating American character." The nation, "having passed from the task of filling up the vacant spaces of the continent," Turner concluded, "is now thrown back upon itself." The United States needed to redefine its purpose.

The White Man's Burden

Since the nation's founding, many Americans had regarded their republic as a "city upon a hill," a beacon of light for other peoples. But as Turner suggested in his landmark essay "The Significance of the Frontier in American History," if Americans were to preserve their democratic character, they required a new "frontier" beyond the North American continent. Many clergy and politicians agreed, insisting that Americans spread democracy and Christianity together to distant lands.

This optimistic philosophy of nationalism found dramatic expression at the World's Columbian Exposition. Less than two months after the nation's major railroad companies had collapsed, crowds gathered on May Day 1893 in Chicago's "White City," a complex of over 400 new buildings constructed in classical design to display the splendors of American industry and technology.

Agriculture Hall showcased the production of corn, wheat, and other crops and majestically displayed a gigantic globe surrounded by American-manufactured farm machinery. The symbolism escaped no one: all eyes were on worldwide markets for American products. Another building housed a model of a canal cut across Nicaragua, suggesting the ease with which American traders might reach Asian markets if freighters could steam directly from the Caribbean to the Pacific. One of the fair's most popular exhibits, attracting 20,000 people a day, featured a mock ocean liner, built to scale by the International Navigation Company, where fair-goers could imagine themselves as "tourists" sailing in luxury to distant parts of the world.

The World's Fair also "displayed" representatives of the people who populated foreign lands. The Midway Plaisance, an enormous sideshow, re-created Turkish bazaars and South Sea island huts. There were Javanese carpenters, Dahoman drummers, Egyptian swordsmen, and Hungarian Gypsies as well as Eskimos, Syrians, Samoans, and Chinese. According to the guidebook, these peoples had come "from the nightsome North and the splendid South, from the wasty West and the effete East, bringing their manners, customs, dress, religions, legends, amusements, that we might know them better." Very popular was the World Congress of Beauty, displaying "40 Ladies from 40 Nations" dressed in native costume. Another favorite attraction was "Little Egypt," who performed with other dancers at the Persian Palace of Eros; her *danse du ventre* became better known as the hootchy-kootchy.

By celebrating the brilliance of American industry while rendering the rest of the world's people

"Little Egypt," as seen on Midway Plaisance, World's Columbian Exhibition, Chicago, 1893. Advertised as an "exotic" dancer from the Middle East, this performer wears mainly the clothing of contemporary American women, such as stockings and high-heeled shoes, in a greatly abbreviated fashion. Over her head she holds the veil used in the "danse du ventre," more popularly known as the hootchy-kootchy.

into exotic entertainment, the planners of the fair delivered a powerful if unintended message. Former abolitionist Frederick Douglass, who attended the fair on "Colored People's Day," recognized it immediately. He noted that the physical layout of the fair, the careful grouping of exhibits, sharply divided the United States and Europe from the rest of the world, namely from the nations of Africa, Asia, and the Middle East. Douglass objected to the stark contrast between Anglo-Saxons and people of color, an opposition, in the parlance of contemporary ethnographers, between "civilization" and "savagery." Douglass referred to the famed White City as "a whited sepulcher."

The Columbian Exposition gave material shape to prevalent ideas about the superiority of American civilization and its racial order, as Douglass recognized. At the same time, it illustrated the imperative for commercial enterprises abroad. Social gospeler Josiah Strong, a Congregational minister who had begun his career trying to convert Indians to Christianity, provided a timely synthesis. He argued that the United States, as the most economically advanced and most Christian nation in the world, commanded a providential role. Linking economic to spiritual expansion, Strong advocated an "imperialism of righteousness." The rest of the world "is to be Christianized and civilized," Strong insisted, by the white Americans, who were best suited to this greatest task of all time. "Pure spiritual Christianity" and its "genius for colonizing" compelled Americans to move beyond their own national interests to consider the needs of the people of Africa and the Pacific and beyond. It was the white American, Strong argued, who had been "divinely commissioned to be, in a peculiar sense, his brother's keeper."

Senator Beveridge carried this message to Congress, insisting that God "has made us [white, English-speaking people] adept in government that we may administer governments among savages and senile peoples. . . . He has marked the American people as His chosen nation to finally lead in the regeneration of the world." According to many newspaper writers and editorialists, it would be morally wrong for Americans to shirk what the British poet Rudyard Kipling called the "White Man's Burden."

Foreign Missions

The push for overseas expansion coincided with a major wave of religious evangelism and the formation of foreign missions. Early in the nineteenth century, most Protestant missionaries, hoping to fulfill what they believed to be a divine command to carry God's message to all peoples and to win converts for their church, had focused on North America. Like Strong himself, many disciples headed west and stationed themselves on Indian reservations. Others worked among the unchurched people of the nation's growing cities. As early as the 1820s, however, a few missionaries had traveled to the Sandwich Islands (Hawai'i) in an effort to supplant the indigenous religion with Christianity. After the Civil War, following the formation of the Women's Union Missionary Society of Americans for Heathen Lands, the major evangelical Protestant denominations began to sponsor new missions directed at foreign lands.

Funded by wealthy men and the vigorous campaigns waged by female church members, these societies soon attracted a very large membership. By the 1890s college campuses blazed with missionary excitement, and the intercollegiate Student Volunteers for Foreign Missions spread rapidly under the slogan "The Evangelicization of the World in this Generation." Magazines bristled with essays such as "The Anglo-Saxon and the World's Redemption." Young Protestant women rushed to join foreign missionary societies. In 1863 there had been only 94 Methodist women missionaries in China; by 1902 the number had increased to 783. In all, some twenty-three American Protestant churches had established missions in China by the turn of the century, the majority staffed by women. By 1915 more than 3 million women had enrolled in forty denominational missionary societies, easily surpassing in size any other women's organization. Their missions ranged from India and Africa to Syria, the Pacific Islands, and nearby Latin America.

With so many agents in the field, missionaries scored many successes. They managed to recruit numerous "natives," including "rice Christians," those who feigned conversion in order to be fed by the missions. By 1898 Protestants claimed to have converted over 80,000 Chinese, a tiny portion of the population but a significant stronghold for American interests in their nation. The missionaries did more than spread the gospel. They taught school, provided rudimentary medical care, offered vocational training, and sometimes encouraged young men and women to pursue college educations in the U.S. in preparation for careers in their native lands. Such work depended on, and in turn inspired, enthusiastic church members in the United States.

Outside the churches proper, the YMCA and YWCA, which had set up nondenominational missions for the working poor in many American cities, also embarked upon a worldwide crusade to reach non-Christians. By the turn of the century, the YWCA had foreign branches in Ceylon (present-day Sri Lanka) and China. After a decade of proliferation of foreign branches, a close observer ironically suggested that the United States had three great occupying forces: the army, the navy, and the "Y." He was not far wrong.

Missionaries played an important role both in generating public interest in "foreign lands" and in preparing the way for American economic expansion. For this reason, China attracted the most attention among missionaries and American business leaders alike. As Josiah Strong aptly put it, "Commerce follows the missionary."

Architects of Empire

Secretary of State William Henry Seward had established the terms of this crusade in the late 1860s. He outlined "a political law — and when I say political law, I mean higher law, a law of Providence — that empire has [had], for the last three thousand years. . . ." On his advice, the United States acquired Alaska (known at the time as Seward's Icebox), and in 1868 Congress signed a treaty with China allowing western employers to bring in unlimited numbers of cheap Chinese laborers. These were only steps in Seward's plan to build way stations across the Pacific to reach the Asian markets, "the prize" in the battle among imperialist nations and "chief theatre of events in the world's great hereafter."

Seward launched the nation's Pacific empire in several ways. He established a stronghold in the Midway islands while expanding American economic interests in Hawai'i and preparing for wider influence there. By 1875 U.S. sugar businesses had secured commercial dominance, and Hawai'ian sugar arrived duty-free in the United States. In 1887, a new treaty allowed the United States to build a naval base at Pearl Harbor on the island of Oahu. To further American interests in China, Seward ordered military maneuvers against Japan, forcing strict terms of trade on the rival nation. Although Seward stirred congressional opposition at home, he paved the way for further economic expansion outside North America.

The fulfillment of Seward's plans depended on U.S. armed forces capable of defending treaties and protecting overseas investments. In 1884 Congress established the Naval War College in Newport, Rhode Island, to create an officer corps to command the seas. The year before, Congress had appropriated the funds to rebuild the fleet. Beginning with ninety small ships, many of them wooden, the navy became by century's end the Great White Fleet of armor-plated steel battleships.

Captain Alfred Thayer Mahan, early president of the Naval War College, prescribed the imperial strategy of the "large navy." His major work, *The Influence of Sea Power upon History, 1660–1783* (1890), helped to define American foreign policy at the time. By way of example from the British Empire, Mahan perceived that international strength rested upon open markets, the ownership of colonies, and the ability to wage or to threaten naval warfare. The popularity of Mahan's ideas, which were embraced by President McKinley, marked the determination of the United States to move outward from the continent, through naval expansion, into imperial glory.

OVERSEAS EMPIRE

During his 1896 campaign, William McKinley firmly committed himself to the principle of economic expansion. It was for him the proper alternative to the program of Edward Bellamy and the popular novelist's vision of a cooperative commonwealth. Business leaders likewise insisted that sufficient world power and the wealth it guaranteed would bring about prosperity, at least for industrious white Americans.

The "end in view" of foreign policy, McKinley explained, was "always to be the opening up of new markets." As president, McKinley not only reached out for markets but acquired new territories for the United States. Long in the making, this move nevertheless marked a new stage in American foreign policy. The United States, as a global power, joined Japan, Germany, France, and England in the great rush to create overseas empires. Senator Henry Cabot Lodge of Massachusetts spoke for many avowed imperialists in insisting that the United States "must not fall out of the line of march."

Markets and Colonies

Foreign trade, despite periods of boom and bust, became increasingly central to the American economy in the decades after the Civil War. Exports more than tripled, from about $400 million in 1870 to over $1.5 billion in 1900. But as the European market for American goods contracted during the depression of the 1890s, U.S. business leaders by necessity expanded their horizons. They began to look at countries closer by, intent on achieving economic dominance of the entire hemisphere.

Since the American Revolution, many politicians and diplomats had regarded such nearby nations as Canada, Cuba, and Mexico as falling naturally within the American territorial realm, destined to be conquered when opportunity allowed. As early as the 1840s, advocates of expansion de-

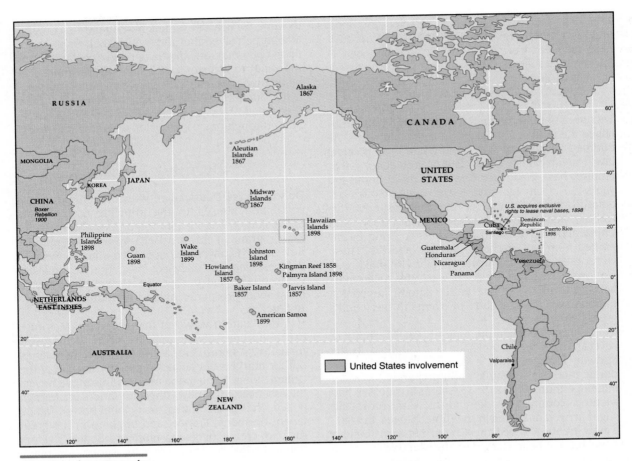

The American Domain

The United States claimed numerous islands in the South Pacific and intervened repeatedly in Latin America to secure its economic interests.

scribed Cuba as a "ripe pear" ready for picking. After the Civil War, while European nations reached farther into Asia and Africa, the United States increasingly viewed the Caribbean as an "American lake" and Asia as a vast potential market for U.S. goods. The economic crisis of the 1890s transformed this long-standing desire into a widely recognized political imperative. But unlike their counterparts in Europe, American expansionists concluded that possession of an empire did not demand permanent military occupation and costly colonial administration. The United States could achieve its commercial goals more easily by other means.

In 1870 Secretary of State Hamilton Fish testified to Congress that the United States would inevitably predominate over European interests in Latin America. His successor, Frederick Frelinghuysen, arranged bilateral economic treaties during the early

1880s with Mexico, Colombia, the British West Indies, El Salvador, the Dominican Republic, Spanish-dominated Puerto Rico, and Cuba. In return for importing more raw materials from these countries, the United States would create a sizable market there for its own manufactured goods. These treaties allowed American business to dominate local economies, whose own potential for development had been undercut by U.S. exports. Often, American investors simply took over the main industries of small nations, as they did in the Cuban sugar fields.

U.S. diplomats and private investors guided Latin American governments in controlling restless populations, calling upon the U.S. Navy when popular uprisings proved too much for local military forces. The State Department warned European powers not to meddle when revolt shook Venezuela in 1875 — only the U.S. government was permitted to do so. In 1881, the same year that Secretary of State James G. Blaine called for a hemispheric conference to promote peace and trade, he ordered three separate military interventions to settle border disputes between Latin American neighbors.

A decade later, President Harrison all but declared war on Chile after drunken American soldiers on shore leave had assaulted civilians and been attacked in return. Only after the Chilean government paid an indemnity of $75,000 did Americans forgive Chile. In 1895, when the British contested the right of the United States to invoke the Monroe Doctrine in cases of international law (referring to a dispute over the border of British Guiana), President Cleveland appointed a congressional commission to settle the Chilean incident unilaterally, without Chil-

ean input. The British, previously dominant in large parts of the region, saw their position now hopelessly eroded by American power, and acquiesced in the new rule.

The annexation of Hawai'i on July 7, 1898, followed nearly a half century of economic penetration and diplomatic maneuvering. American investors in the sugar industry had increasingly gained political control over the island, and in 1887 they went a step further, arranging the overthrow of local rulers in order to secure a government allied to their economic interests. In 1892 the new queen, Liliuokalani, fought back by instituting a new constitution granting her more discretionary power. Prompted by the pineapple magnate Sanford B. Dole, the U.S. minister to Hawai'i called in the U.S. Marines from a nearby cruiser in early 1893, deposed the queen, recognized a new provisional government, and proclaimed Hawai'i an American protectorate (a territory protected and partly controlled by the United States). American diplomat John L. Stevens, stationed in Hawai'i, eagerly wired Washington that the "Hawaiian pear is now fully ripe, and this is the golden hour for the United States to pluck it." President Cleveland refused to consider annexation, but five years later McKinley affirmed a joint congressional resolution that made Hawai'i an American territory in 1900. The residents of Hawai'i were not consulted in this momentous change of national identity.

The Spanish–American War

In the Caribbean, Cuba offered another inviting commercial prize. By 1895, when Americans held an estimated $50 million in Cuban property, rebels seeking independence from Spanish rule made a highly emotional appeal to Americans to aid their popular uprising. Although grisly horror stories of Spain's treatment of insurrectionaries circulated in the U.S. press and aroused popular sympathy, President Cleveland refused to back the Cubans. Even when Congress passed a resolution in 1896 recognizing the independence of Cuba, Cleveland and his advisers demurred, hoping to avoid an almost certain war with Spain.

McKinley saw that the insurrection harmed U.S. investments and might destroy the island's economy. But while many in Congress and the press urged U.S. intervention, he held back, fearing public opposition. The tide of opinion turned in 1897, however, when American newspapers published a private letter by a Spanish diplomat characterizing the president as weak and opportunistic. Public

Brought to power with the assistance of American businessmen, Queen Liliuokalani nevertheless sought to limit the outsiders' influence. American marines, Christian missionaries, and sugar planters joined in 1893 to drive her from her throne. A century later, the U.S. government apologized to Hawai'ians for this illegal act.

The Spanish—American War

In two theatres of action, the United States used its naval power adeptly against a weak foe.

indignation, whipped up by tabloid press headlines and sensational stories, turned into frenzy in 1898 when an explosion hit the U.S. battleship *Maine,* stationed in Havana harbor ostensibly to rescue American citizens living in Cuba.

McKinley, suspecting war was close, had begun to prepare for intervention. Public clamor to avenge the deaths of 266 American sailors speeded up his deliberations, and two weeks later the president asked Congress for a declaration of war against Spain. Yet the Senate barely passed the war resolution, forty-two to thirty-five, and only with the inclusion of an amendment by Senator Henry Teller of Colorado that disclaimed "any disposition or intention to exercise sovereignty, jurisdiction or control over said islands, except for the pacification thereof." The president and his advisers, however, ignored all congressional restraints.

A popular outpouring of patriotic joy for a short and successful military conflict inspired massive parades, topical songs, and an overpowering enthu-siasm. "Populists, Democrats, and Republicans are we," ran one timely jingle, "but we are all Americans to make Cuba free."

War against Spain was declared on April 21, 1898; by August 12 it was over, a smashing success for the U.S. Navy, which demolished the Spanish fleet near Cuba's Santiago harbor. The four-month war resembled less a standard military conflict than a naval assault and a very limited land war against an enemy with few soldiers and badly outdated ships. U.S. troops, led in part by Theodore Roosevelt — who boasted of killing Spaniards "like jackrabbits" — lost less than 400 men in battle, although disease and inept treatment of the wounded claimed more than 5,000 lives. Nevertheless Roosevelt, invigorated by the conflict, agreed with John Hay, former secretary of state, that it had been "a splendid little war."

At the victory ceremony marking Spain's surrender, the United States denied Cuba an official role. While American businesses consolidated their

Rebel Cubans, 1898, painted by Herbert Orth. Badly supplied Cuban *insurrectos* had practiced guerilla warfare against the Spanish colonizers since the mid–1890s, but after the bombing of the *U.S.S. Maine*, American forces took over the war and abandoned the cause of Cuban self-determination. This picture, by a young U.S. volunteer, was one of a series of sketches later transformed into watercolor and oil paintings.

hold on local sugar plantations, the military oversaw the formation of a constitutional convention that made Cuba a protectorate of the United States. In the Platt Amendment, sponsored by Republican senator Orville H. Platt of Connecticut in 1901, Cuba promised to provide land for American bases; to abide by a debt structure that would allow it to repay Americans through revenues; to sign no treaty detrimental to American interests; and to acknowledge the right of the United States to intervene at any time to protect its own interests in Cuba. After American troops withdrew from Cuba, the amendment was incorporated into the Cuban-American Treaty of 1903, which remained in place until 1934.

Rule over Cuba advanced U.S. territorial claims in the Caribbean to include Puerto Rico, ceded by Spain, and the Virgin Islands of St. Thomas and St. John, purchased from Denmark. The acquisition of Pacific territories, including Guam (also ceded by Spain) and the Philippines, marked the emergence of the United States as a global colonial power.

War in the Philippines

The Philippines was an especially attractive prospect, its 7,000 Pacific islands a natural way station to the markets of mainland Asia. In 1897 Assistant Secretary of the Navy Theodore Roosevelt and President McKinley had discussed the merit of taking the Philippines in case of war with Spain. Once war had been declared, Roosevelt himself appointed Commodore George Dewey, a Civil War veteran, to command the American Asiatic Squadron. Ordered to "start offensive action," Dewey destroyed Spanish naval power during seven hours of unimpeded target practice in Manila Bay.

McKinley dispatched 12,000 troops to the region and refused all offers of armistice until the Spaniards agreed to give up all claims to their Pacific islands. Once Spain conceded, McKinley quickly proceeded to draw up plans for colonial administration. He pledged "to educate the Filipinos, and to uplift and civilize and Christianize them. . . ." But after centuries of Spanish rule, the majority of islanders — already Christians — were eager to create their own nation.

At first, Filipino rebels, like the Cubans, welcomed American troops and fought with them against Spain. But when they learned that the Treaty of Paris of 1899, marking the end of the Spanish-American war, allowed the United States to annex their country, rebels led by Emilio Aguinaldo turned against their former allies and attacked the American base of operations in Manila in February 1899.

Predicting a brief skirmish, American commanders seriously underestimated the population's capacity to endure great suffering for the sake of independence.

American military officers had in various ways provoked this conflict. U.S. troops, many of them veterans of the Indian wars, described the natives as "gu-gus" and reported themselves, as one said, "just itching to get at the niggers." While awaiting action, American soldiers frequently insulted or physically abused civilians, raped Filipino women, and otherwise whipped up resentments.

The resulting conflict took the form of a modern guerrilla war. Instructed to regard every male Filipino over ten years of age as a potential enemy who could be shot without provocation, U.S. troops attacked civilians and destroyed their food, housing, and water supplies. Many American soldiers appeared indifferent to the sight of bloodshed. A. A. Barnes of the Third Regiment, describing the slaughter of 1,000 men, women, and children, wrote home, "I am probably growing hard-hearted, for I am in my glory when I can sight my gun on some dark-skin and pull the trigger." Ordered to take no prisoners, American soldiers forced Filipino civilians to dig their own graves and bragged about killing the wounded. By the time the fighting stopped in 1902, over 4,000 American lives had been lost, 20,000 Filipinos had been killed in combat, and an estimated 250,000 civilians lay dead from collateral injury, starvation, or disease.

The conquest of the Philippines, which remained a U.S. territory until 1946, evoked for its defenders the vision of the American commonwealth as empire. Senator Platt likened Dewey's warship in Manila to "a new Mayflower . . . the harbinger and agent of a new civilization." The first Philippine Commission came to the same conclusion, reporting that "only through American occupation . . . is the idea of a free, self-governing and united Philippine commonwealth at all conceivable."

Once again, Josiah Strong proclaimed judgment over an era. His famous treatise *Expansion* (1900) roundly defended American overseas involvements by carefully distinguishing between freedom and independence. People could achieve freedom, he argued, only under the rule of law. And because white Americans had proven themselves superior in the realm of government, they could best bring "freedom" to nonwhite peoples by setting aside the ideals of national independence for a period of enforced guidance. Many wondered, however, whether the United States could become an empire without losing its democratic spirit, and whether the subjugated people were really so fortunate to have U.S. military forces ruling them.

Critics of Empire

No mass movement formed to forestall U.S. expansion, but such distinguished figures as Mark Twain, Andrew Carnegie, William Jennings Bryan, and Harvard philosopher William James voiced their opposition strongly. Dissent followed two broad lines of thought. In 1870, when President Grant urged the annexation of Santo Domingo, the nation-state occupying half of the island of Hispaniola (Haiti occupying the other half), opponents countered by insisting that the United States stood unequivocally for the right of national self-determination and the consent of the governed. Others opposed the move on the ground that dark-skinned and "ignorant" Santo Domingans were unworthy of American citizenship. These two contrary arguments, democratic and racist, sounded throughout the last third of the nineteenth century, especially as the United States joined other nations in the armed struggle for empire.

Organized protest to military action, especially against the widely reported atrocities in the Philippines, owed much to the Anti-Imperialist League, initiated by a small group of prominent Bostonians. In historic Fanueil Hall, which had witnessed the birth of both the American Revolution and the antislavery movement, a mass meeting convened in June 1898 to protest the "insane and wicked ambition which is driving the nation to ruin." Within a few months, the league reported 25,000 members. It drew followers from every walk of life, including such famous writers as Charles Francis Adam, *Nation* editor E. L. Godkin, African-American scholar W. E. B. Du Bois, and Civil War general Thomas Wentworth Higginson.

The Anti-Imperialist League brought together like-minded societies from across the country, encouraged mass meetings, and published pamphlets, poems, and broadsides. The *National Labor Standard,* organ of the New Jersey State Federation of Labor, expressed the common hope that all those "who believe in the *Republic* against *Empire* should join." By 1899, the league claimed half a million members. A few outspoken anti-imperialists, such as former Illinois governor John Peter Altgeld, openly toasted Filipino rebels as heroes. Morrison Swift, leader of the Coxey's Army contingent from Massachusetts, formed a Filipino Liberation Society and sent antiwar materials to American troops.

"Uncle Sam Teaches the Art of Self-Government," editorial cartoon, 1898. Expressing a popular sentiment of the time, a newspaper cartoonist shows the rebels as raucous children who constantly fight among themselves and need to be brought into line by Uncle Sam. The Filipino leader, Aguinaldo, appears as a dunce for failing to learn properly from the teacher. The two major islands where no uprising took place, Puerto Rico and Hawai'i, appear as passive but exotically dressed women, ready to learn their lessons.

Others, such as Samuel Gompers, a league vice-president, felt no sympathy for conquered peoples, describing Filipinos as "perhaps nearer the condition of savages and barbarians than any island possessed by any other civilized nation on earth." Gompers simply wanted to prevent colonized non-whites from immigrating to the United States and "inundating" American labor.

Military leaders and staunch imperialists did not distinguish between racist and nonracist anti-imperialists. They called all dissenters "unhung traitors" and demanded their arrest. Newspaper editors accused universities of harboring antiwar professors, although college students as a group were enthusiastic supporters of the war.

Within the press, which overwhelmingly supported the Spanish-American war, the voice of opposition appeared primarily in African American and labor papers. The *Indianapolis Recorder* asked rhetorically in 1899, "Are the tender-hearted expan-

CHRONOLOGY

1867	Patrons of Husbandry (Grange) founded
1875	Species Resumption Act
1877	Rutherford B. Hayes elected president
1879	Henry George, *Progress and Poverty*
1881	President James Garfield assassinated; Chester Arthur becomes president
1883	Pendleton Civil Service Reform Act
1884	Grover Cleveland elected president
1887	Interstate Commerce Act
1888	Edward Bellamy, *Looking Backward* National Colored Farmers' Alliance and Cooperative Union formed Benjamin Harrison elected president
1889	National Farmers' Alliance and Industrial Union formed
1890	Populist (People's) party formed Sherman Anti-Trust Act Sherman Silver Purchase Act McKinley Tariff National American Woman Suffrage Association formed
1892	Grover Cleveland elected to second term as president Homestead, Pennsylvania, strike
1893	World's Columbian Exhibition, Chicago Financial panic and business recession begin
1894	"Coxey's Army" marches on Washington, D.C. Pullman strike
1896	*Plessy v. Ferguson* opens the way for segregated public schools William McKinley defeats William Jennings Bryan for president
1897	Dingley Tariff
1898	Hawai'i becomes a U.S. possession War declared against Spain; Cuba and Philippines seized
1899	*Cummins v. County Board of Education*
1900	Currency Act commits U.S. to gold standard McKinley reelected

sionists in the United States Congress really actuated by the desire to save the Filipinos from self-destruction or is it the worldly greed for gain?'' The *Railroad Telegrapher* similarly commented, ''The wonder of it all is that the working people are willing to lose blood and treasure in fighting another man's battle.''

Most Americans put aside their doubts and welcomed the new era of aggressive nationalism. Untouched by the private tragedies of dead or wounded American soldiers and the mass destruction of civilian society in the Philippines, the vast majority of Americans could approve Theodore Roosevelt's defense of armed conflict: ''No triumph of peace is quite so great as the supreme triumphs of war.''

CONCLUSION

The conflicts marking the last quarter of the nineteenth century that pitted farmers, workers, and the proprietors of small businesses against powerful outside interests had offered Americans an important moment of democratic promise. By century's end, however, the rural and working-class campaigns to revive community self-government had been defeated, their organizations destroyed, their autonomy eroded. The rise of a national governing class and its counterpart, the large bureaucratic state, established new rules of behavior, new sources of prestige, and new rewards for the most successful citizens as well as greater restrictions for others. As the new century opened, progressive reformers moved to correct flaws in government while accepting the framework of a corporate society and its overseas empire.

Additional Readings

RUTH BORDIN, *Woman and Temperance: The Quest for Power and Liberty, 1873–1900* (1981). Relates the history of the WCTU to other campaigns for women's emancipation in the late nineteenth century and highlights the leadership of Frances E. Willard. Demonstrates the central position of temperance in the political struggles of the era.

JOHN G. CAWELTI, *Apostles of the Self-Made Man* (1965). Examines the popular cultural obsession with the idea of success. Analyzes the myths behind the notion of equal opportunity for all, and the methods of popularizing success in the various media of the time.

LAWRENCE GOODWYN, *Democratic Promise: The Populist Moment in America* (1976). The most detailed study of populism. Focuses on the economic cooperation and visionary schemes that preceded the Populist campaigns of the 1890s. Shows that populism was above all a movement aimed at turning back the monopolistic trend in the market economy and returning power to the nation's citizens.

LEWIS L. GOULD, *The Presidency of William McKinley* (1980). A biography and political study of the president who in several key ways represented a new kind of national leader. Gould presents McKinley as a model Republican, a product of "machine" politics, but also, in his own eyes, an enlightened and modern administrator.

WALTER LAFEBER, *The New Empire: An Interpretation of American Expansion, 1860–1898* (1963). The best overview of U.S. imperial involvement in the late nineteenth century. Shows how overseas commitments grew out of American leaders' faith in economic expansion and grew continuously, if often chaotically, with the opportunities presented by the crises experienced by the older imperial powers.

NELL IRVIN PAINTER, *Standing at Armageddon: The United States, 1877–1919* (1987). Presents a broad overview of racial and industrial conflicts and the political movements that formed in their wake. Attempts to show that this period proved decisive to the future of the United States.

THOMAS C. REEVES, *Gentleman Boss: The Life of Chester Alan Arthur* (1975). A detailed treatment of President Arthur as a product of a particular stage in the American political system. Analyzes the conflicts within the Republican party and the chaos of the Democratic party, which made Arthur's rise possible, and his brief presidency but lasting importance.

EMILY S. ROSENBERG, *Spreading the American Dream: American Economic and Cultural Expansion, 1890–1945* (1982). Insightfully examines the significance of expansionist ideology. Shows the cultural and social roots of American foreign policy.

WILLIAM APPLEMAN WILLIAMS, *Empire as a Way of Life: An Essay on the Causes and Character of America's Present Predicament* (1982). A lucid general exploration of American views of empire. Shows that Americans allowed the idea of empire and, more generally, economic expansion to dominate their concept of democracy, especially in the last half of the nineteenth century.

C. VANN WOODWARD, *The Strange Career of Jim Crow*, 3d rev. ed. (1974). The classic study of southern segregation. Shows how racist laws and customs tightened in the South and in many parts of the North in the last decades of the nineteenth century, and how the ideologies of the society encouraged the rise of Jim Crow legislation.

21 URBAN AMERICA AND THE PROGRESSIVE ERA, 1900–1920

AMERICAN COMMUNITIES

• THE HENRY STREET SETTLEMENT HOUSE

A shy and frightened young girl appeared in the doorway of a weekly home nursing class for women on Manhattan's Lower East Side. The teacher beckoned her to come forward. Tugging on the teacher's skirt, the girl pleaded in broken English for the teacher to come home with her. "Mother," "baby," "blood," she kept repeating. The teacher gathered up the sheets that were part of the interrupted lesson in bedmaking. The two hurried through narrow, garbage-strewn, foul-smelling streets, then groped their way up a pitch-dark, rickety staircase. They reached a cramped, two-room apartment occupied by an immigrant family of seven and several boarders. There, in a vermin-infested bed, encrusted with dried blood, lay a mother and her newborn baby. The mother had been abandoned by a doctor because she could not afford his fee. The teacher quickly brought order to the chaotic scene by caring for the mother and baby, making the bed with fresh linen, and cleaning up the apartment.

WOMEN SETTLEMENT
HOUSE WORKERS
CREATE A COMMUNITY
OF REFORM

Years later, Lillian Wald recalled this scene as her baptism of fire and the turning point in her life. Born in 1867, Wald enjoyed a comfortable upbringing in a middle class, German Jewish family in Rochester. Against her parents' objections, she moved to New York City to become a professional nurse. Wald resented the disdainful treatment nurses received from doctors, and she was horrified by the inhumane conditions she witnessed in her job at a juvenile asylum. She was determined to find a way of caring for the sick more directly, in their neighborhoods and in their homes. Along with her nursing school classmate Mary Brewster, Wald rented a fifth-floor walk-up apartment on the Lower East Side and established a visiting nurse service. The two women offered professional care in the home to hundreds of families for a nominal fee of ten to twenty-five cents. They also offered each family they visited information on basic health care, sanitation, and disease prevention. In 1895, philanthropist Jacob Schiff generously donated a red brick Georgian house on Henry Street as a new base of operation.

The Henry Street Settlement became a model for a new kind of reform community. It was essentially a community of college-educated women who encouraged and supported one another in a wide variety of humanitarian, civic, political, and cultural activities. As a living arrangement, settlement houses

(George Bellows. New York, 1911. Oil on canvas, 42 × 60 in. National Gallery of Art, Washington, D.C. Collection of Mr. and Mrs. Paul Mellon.)

An Infant Welfare Society Nurse makes a home visit to an immigrant family living in a Chicago tenement around 1907. Home visits by nurses, made for a nominal fee, represented one of the most useful and appreciated activities undertaken by settlement houses and other Progressive era social service agencies. This carefully posed photograph conveyed an atmosphere of harmony between the professional and the slum dweller.

closely resembled the dormitory atmosphere found at such new women's colleges as Smith, Wellesley, and Vassar. Like these colleges, the settlement house was an "experiment," but one designed, in Jane Addams's words, "to aid in the solution of the social and industrial problems which are engendered by the modern conditions of urban life." Unlike earlier "moral reformers" who tried to impose their ideas from outside the neighborhood, settlement house residents were committed to living in the midst of poor neighborhoods and working for immediate improvements in the health and welfare of the community. Yet as Addams and others repeatedly stressed, the college-educated women were beneficiaries as well. The settlement house allowed them to preserve a collegial spirit, satisfy the desire for service, and apply their academic training.

A self-sufficient institution serving as a moral and social center for both its occupants and the surrounding neighborhood, the settlement house became the focus of a movement attracting large numbers of educated young women. In 1891 there were 6 settlements in the United States, in 1897 there were 74, by 1900 over 200, and by 1910 over 400. Few made settlement work a career; the average stay was less than five years. Roughly half eventually married. But those who did make a career of this work typically chose not to marry, and most lived together with female companions. As the settlements flourished, the residents described their neighbors in countless articles and lectures, which helped build sympathy for the plight of the poor and fostered respect for different cultural heritages. Settlement houses also transformed their leading residents, such as Jane Addams, Lillian Wald, and Florence Kelley, into influential political figures during the Progressive era.

The Henry Street Settlement stood in the center of the most overcrowded and cosmopolitan neighborhood in America, New York's Lower East Side. Roughly 500,000 people were packed into an area only as large as a midsized Kansas farm. Population density was about 500 per acre; a single city block might have as many as 3,000 residents. Home for most Lower East Siders was a small tenement apartment that might include paying boarders squeezed in alongside the immediate family. The vast majority of residents were recent immigrants from southern and eastern Europe: Jews, Italians, Germans, Greeks, Hungarians, Slavs. Men, women, and children toiled in the garment shops, small factories, retail stores, breweries, and warehouses to be found on nearly every street. A highly organized, Irish-dominated political machine controlled local political affairs.

Wald attracted a dedicated group of nurses, educators, and reformers to live at the Henry Street Settlement. By 1909 Henry Street had over forty residents, supported by the donations of well-to-do New Yorkers. In addition to the nursing service, Wald and her allies convinced the New York Board of Health to assign a nurse to every public school in the city. They lobbied the Board of Education to create the first school lunch programs. They persuaded the city to set up municipal milk stations to insure the purity of milk. Henry Street also pioneered tuberculosis treatment and prevention. Its leaders became powerful advocates for playground construction, improved street cleaning, and tougher housing inspection. The settlement's Neighborhood Playhouse became an internationally acclaimed center for innovative theater, music, and dance.

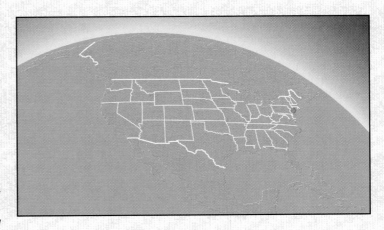

As settlement house workers expanded their influence from local neighborhoods to larger political and social circles, they became, in the phrase of one historian, spearheads for reform. Lillian Wald became a national figure — an outspoken advocate of child labor legislation and woman suffrage and a vigorous opponent of American involvement in World War I. She offered Henry Street as a meeting place to the National Negro Conference in 1909, out of which emerged the National Association for the Advancement of Colored People. It was no cliché for Wald to say, as she did on many occasions, "The whole world is my neighborhood."

COMMUNITIES OF REFORM

During the first two decades of the twentieth century, millions of Americans identified themselves in some way as progressives. Progressivism is perhaps best understood as a varied collection of reform communities, often temporary, that took shape with the aim of curing the ills of an increasingly industrialized and urbanized society. These communities consisted of concerned citizens who united in a host of political, professional, and religious organizations, some of which were national in scope. Reform communities sometimes overlapped, but not to the point that there was a unified progressive movement or a single set of principles. Different regions of the country defined progressivism according to local needs and political realities. Self-styled progressives often found themselves facing each other from opposite sides of contemporary issues. But at the local, state, and finally national levels, progressive energy and ideals defined most of the political, social, and cultural causes of the day.

The Progressive Impulse

As a political movement progressivism drew from deep roots in hundreds of local American communities. At the state level it flowered in the soil of several key issues: ending political corruption, bringing more businesslike methods to governing, and offering a more compassionate legislative response to the excesses of industrialism. As a national movement, progressivism reached its peak in 1912, when the four major presidential candidates all ran on some version of a progressive platform. This last development was an important measure of the extent to which local reform movements and new intellectual currents had captured the political imagination of the nation.

Three basic attitudes underlay the various crusades and movements that emerged in response to the fears gnawing at large segments of the population. The first was anger over the excesses of industrial capitalism and urban growth. At the same time, progressives shared an essential optimism about the ability of citizens to improve social and economic conditions. They were reformers, not revolutionaries. Second, progressives emphasized social cohesion and common bonds as a way of understanding how modern society and economics actually worked. They largely rejected the ideal of individualism that had informed nineteenth-century economic and political theory. For progressives, poverty and success hinged on more than simply individual character; the economy was more than

Lewis Hine took this photo of a young girl working on a thread spinning frame in a North Carolina cotton mill. Between 1908 and 1918 Hine worked for the National Child Labor Committee, documenting the widespread abuse of child labor in the nation's mills, factories, mines, and canneries. "These pictures," Hine wrote, "speak for themselves and prove that the law is being violated."

merely a sum of individual calculations. Along these lines, progressives sought alternatives to social Darwinism. Social Darwinists had long claimed that society operated like a jungle, in which only the "fittest" survived. Efforts to improve social conditions were therefore misguided and futile attempts at interfering with the "natural" order. Third, progressives believed in the need for citizens to actively intervene, both politically and morally, in order to improve social conditions. They pushed for a stronger government role in regulating the economy and solving the nation's social problems.

Progressive rhetoric and methods drew on two distinct sources of inspiration. One was evangelical Protestantism, particularly the late-nineteenth-century social gospel movement. Social gospelers rejected the idea of original sin as the cause of human suffering. They emphasized both the capacity and the duty of Christians to purge the world of poverty, inequality, and economic greed. A second strain of progressive thought looked to natural and social scientists to develop rational measures for improving the human condition, believing that experts trained in statistical analysis and engineering could make government and industry more efficient. Progressivism thus offered an uneasy combination of social justice and social control. Between the 1890s and World War I, a large and diverse number of Americans claimed the label of *progressive.* But there were many contradictions and disagreements surrounding this ambiguous word. The best way to understand progressivism is to examine what key reform groups, thinkers, and political figures actually did and said.

Social Progressives

In the 1890s the settlement house movement had begun to provide an alternative to traditional concepts of private charity and humanitarian reform. Settlement workers found they could not transform their own neighborhoods without confronting a host of broad social questions: chronic poverty, overcrowded tenement houses, child labor, industrial accidents, public health. College-educated, middle-class women constituted a key vanguard in the crusade for social justice. As reform communities, settlement houses soon discovered the need to engage the political and cultural life of the larger communities that surrounded them.

In 1889, Jane Addams had founded Chicago's Hull House after years of struggling to find work and a social identity equal to her talents. She had graduated from Rockford College, one of the first generation of American college women. Settlement work provided an attractive alternative for the growing number of educated women dissatisfied with the life choices presented them: early marriage or the traditional female professions of teaching, nursing, and library work. Located in a run-down slum area of Chicago, Hull House had a day nursery, a dispensary for medicines and medical advice, a boardinghouse, an art gallery, and a music school. Addams often spoke of the "subjective necessity" of settlement houses. By this she meant that they gave young educated women a way to satisfy their powerful desire to connect with the real world. "There is nothing after disease, indigence and guilt," she wrote, "so fatal to life itself as the want of a proper outlet for active faculties."

Social reformer Florence Kelley helped to reshape the settlement house movement in support of groundbreaking state and federal labor legislation. Kelley published numerous reports detailing the dismal conditions in sweatshops and the ill effects of long hours on their women and child workers. She was a driving force behind *Hull House Maps and Papers* (1895), the first scientific study of urban poverty in America. In 1898 she moved to the Henry Street Settlement, where she served as general secretary of the new National Consumers League. She was the single most important lobbyist for the passage of state minimum wage laws for women. With Lillian Wald she established the New York Child Labor Committee and pushed for the creation of the U.S. Children's Bureau, established in 1912. After her death in 1932, Supreme Court justice Felix Frankfurter wrote that Kelley "had probably the largest single share in shaping the social history of the United States during the first thirty years of this century."

The Urban Machine

By the turn of the century Democratic party machines, usually dominated by first- and second-generation Irish, controlled the political life of most large American cities. The keys to machine strength were disciplined organization and the delivery of essential services to both immigrant communities and business elites. The successful machine politician viewed his work as a business, and he accumulated his capital by serving people who needed assistance. For most urban dwellers, the city was a place of economic and social insecurity. Recent immigrants in particular faced frequent unemployment, sickness, and discrimination. In exchange for votes, machine politicians offered their constituents a variety of services. These included municipal jobs in the police and fire departments, work at city construction sites, intervention with legal problems, and food and coal during hard times. The ward heeler, the local cog in the city's machine, provided citizens with their most important — and often only — connection with government.

For those who did business with the city — construction companies, road builders, realtors — staying on the machine's good side was simply another business expense. In exchange for valuable franchises and city contracts, businessmen routinely bribed machine politicians and contributed liberally to their campaign funds. George Washington Plunkitt, a stalwart of New York's Tammany Hall machine, good-naturedly defended what he called "honest graft": making money from inside information on public improvements. "It's just like lookin' ahead in Wall Street or in the coffee or cotton market. . . . I seen my opportunities and I took 'em." As urban America expanded physically, political machines brokered the building of water and sewer systems, municipal parks, government offices, and trolleys and subways.

The machines usually had close ties to a city's vice economy and commercial entertainments. Organized prostitution and gambling, patronized largely by visitors to the city, could flourish only when "protected" by politicians who shared in the profits. Many machine figures began as saloon keepers, and liquor dealers and beer brewers provided important financial support for "the organization." Vaudeville and burlesque theaters, boxing and horse racing, and professional baseball were other urban enterprises with economic and political links to machines. Entertainment and spectacle made up a central element in the machine political style as well. Constituents looked forward to the colorful torchlight parades, free summer picnics, and riverboat excursions regularly sponsored by the machines.

The turn-of-the-century "boss" of New York

City's Lower East Side, Timothy D. "Big Tim" Sullivan, embodied the popular machine style. Critics charged that Sullivan controlled the city's gambling and made money from prostitution. But Big Tim, who had risen from desperate poverty, remained enormously popular with his constituents until his death in 1913. "I believe in liberality," he declared. "I am a thorough New Yorker and have no narrow prejudices. I never ask a hungry man about his past; I feed him, not because he is good, but because he needs food. Help your neighbor but keep your nose out of his affairs." Sullivan, whose district included the largest number of immigrants and transients in the city, provided shoe giveaways and free Christmas dinners to thousands every winter. To pay for these and other charitable activities, he informally taxed the saloons, theaters, and restaurants in the district. Sullivan also made a fortune through his investments in vaudeville and the early movie business.

This publicity photograph of neighborhood children taking an art class at the Henry Street Settlement, New York City, around 1910, suggested that cultural pursuits and learning could flourish in slum neighborhoods with the help of a settlement house.

Progressive critics of machine politics often exaggerated its power and influence. State legislatures, controlled by Republican rural and small-town elements, proved a formidable check on what city-based machines could accomplish. Reform campaigns that publicized excessive graft and corruption sometimes led voters to throw machine-backed mayors and aldermen out of office. And there were never enough patronage jobs for all the people clamoring for appointments. In the early twentieth century, political machines in the Northeast began concentrating more on passing welfare legislation beneficial to working-class and immigrant constituencies. In this way machine politicians often allied themselves with progressive reformers in state legislatures. In New York, for example, Tammany Hall figures such as Timothy Sullivan, Robert Wagner, and Al Smith worked with middle-class progressive groups such as the National Consumers League to pass child labor laws, factory safety regulations, worker compensation plans, and other efforts to make government more responsive to social needs. As Jewish and Catholic immigrants expanded their proportions in the city population, urban machines also began to champion cultural pluralism, opposing prohibition and immigration restrictions and defending the contributions made by new ethnic groups in the cities.

Political Progressives and Urban Reform

Political progressivism originated in the cities. The rapid pace of urbanization between 1890 and 1910 had made city life barely tolerable and downright dangerous for millions of Americans. The rate of urban growth was around double the growth of the nation as a whole. City governments, especially in the Northeast and industrial Midwest, hardly seemed capable of providing the basic services needed to sustain large populations. For example, an impure water supply left Pittsburgh with one of the world's highest rates of death from typhoid, dysentery, and cholera. Most New York City neighborhoods rarely enjoyed street cleaning, and playgrounds were nonexistent. "The challenge of the city," Cleveland progressive Frederic C. Howe said in 1906, "has become one of decent human existence."

Reformers placed much of the blame for urban ills on the machines and looked for ways to restructure city government. The "good government" movement, led by the National Municipal League, fought to make city management a nonpartisan, even nonpolitical, process by bringing the administrative techniques of large corporations to cities. Reformers revised city charters in favor of stronger mayoral power and expanded use of appointed administrators and career civil servants. The New York Bureau of Municipal Research, founded in 1906, became a prototype for similar bureaus around the country. It drew up blueprints for model charters, ordinances, and zoning plans designed by trained experts in public administration.

Business and professional elites became the biggest boosters of structural reforms in urban government. In the summer of 1900 a hurricane in the Gulf of Mexico unleashed a disastrous tidal wave on Galveston, Texas. The flood killed one out of every six people in the city. Leading businessmen convinced the state legislature to replace the mayor-council government with a small board of commissioners. Each commissioner was elected at large and each was responsible for a different city department. Under this plan voters could more easily identify and hold accountable those responsible for city services. Backed-up sewers, for example, might doom reelection hopes for the commissioner of public works. The city commission, enjoying both policy-making and administrative powers, proved very effective in rebuilding Galveston. By 1917 nearly 500 cities, including Houston, Oakland, Kansas City, Denver, and Buffalo had adopted the commission form of government. Another approach, the city manager plan, gained popularity in small and midsized cities. In this system, a city council appointed a professional, nonpartisan city manager to handle the day-to-day operations of the community.

Progressive politicians who focused on the human problems of the industrial city championed a different kind of reform, one based on changing policies rather than the political structure. In Toledo, Samuel "Golden Rule" Jones served as mayor from 1897 to 1904. A capitalist who had made a fortune manufacturing oil well machinery, Jones created a strong base of working-class and ethnic voters around his reform program. He advocated municipal ownership of utilities, built new parks and schools, and established an eight-hour day and a minimum wage for city employees. In Cleveland another wealthy businessman, Thomas L. Johnson, as mayor served from 1901 to 1909. He emphasized both efficiency and social welfare. His popular program included lower streetcar fares, public baths, milk and meat inspection, and an expanded park and playground system.

Progressivism in the Statehouse

Some reformers looked to state politics as a more promising field for change. Their motives and achievements were mixed, but progressive politicians became a powerful force in many state capitols. In Wisconsin, Republican dissident Robert M. La Follette forged a coalition of angry farmers, ethnics, and workers with his fiery attacks on railroads and other large corporations. Leader of the Progressive faction of the state Republicans, "Fighting Bob" won three terms as governor (1900–1906), then served as a U.S. senator until his death in 1925. As governor he pushed through tougher corporate tax rates, a direct primary, an improved civil service code, and a model railroad commission. La Follette used faculty experts at the University of Wisconsin to help research and write his bills. Other states began copying the "Wisconsin Idea" — the application of academic scholarship and theory to the needs of the people.

La Follette railed against "the interests" and invoked the power of the ordinary citizen. In practice, the railroad commission accomplished far less than progressive rhetoric claimed. It essentially represented commercial farmers and businessmen seeking reduced shipping rates. What the politics of regulation boiled down to was conflict between two interest groups, shippers and carriers; ordinary consumers did not see lower passenger fares or reduced food prices. Commissioners also began to see that state regulation was ineffective as long as the larger railroads had a national reach. Although La Follette championed a more open political system, he also enrolled state employees in a tight political machine of his own. The La Follette family would dominate Wisconsin politics for forty years.

Western progressives displayed the greatest enthusiasm for institutional political reform. The "Oregon System" was in many ways the essence of western progressivism. In the early 1900s, Oregon voters approved a series of constitutional amendments designed to strengthen direct democracy. The two most important were the initiative, which allowed a direct vote on specific measures put on the state ballot by petition, and the referendum, which allowed voters to decide upon bills referred to them by the legislature. Other reforms included the direct primary, which allowed voters to cross party lines, and the recall, which gave voters the right to remove elected officials by popular vote. Widely copied throughout the West, all these measures intentionally weakened political parties. Western progressives in both the Democratic and Republican parties typically tended to ignore party discipline more readily than in other parts of the nation.

Western progressives also targeted railroads, mining and timber companies, and public utilities for reform. Large corporations such as Pacific Gas and Electric and the Southern Pacific Railroad had amassed enormous wealth and political influence. They were able to corrupt state legislatures and charge consumers exorbitant rates. An alliance between middle-class progressives and working-class voters reflected growing disillusionment with the ideology of individualism that had helped pave the way for the rise of the big corporation. The old conservative notion of freedom of contract made less sense if individuals could not bargain on equal terms with powerful corporations and overwhelming bureaucracies. In California, attorney Hiram Johnson won a progressive campaign for governor on the slogan "Kick the Southern Pacific Railroad Out of Politics." He served from 1910 to 1916, then went on to five terms in the U.S. Senate. In addition to winning political reforms, Johnson also put through laws regulating utilities and child labor, an eight-hour day for working women, and a state worker compensation plan.

In the South, progressivism drew upon the agrarian program and flamboyant oratory of populism. In the new century's first decade, former Populists such as Tom Watson of Georgia, Benjamin Tillman of South Carolina, Hoke Smith of Georgia, and James Vardaman of Mississippi all gained the governorship of their states. Southern progressives made genuine improvements in educational facilities, regulation of corporations, and reform of city governments.

But southern progressivism was for whites only. A strident racism accompanied reform campaigns against entrenched conservative Democratic machines, reinforcing racial discrimination and segregation. The legal disfranchisement of black voters between 1890 and 1908 virtually eliminated African Americans from southern politics. In the same period, "Jim Crow" laws relegated African Americans to separate and inferior public schools and other services and allowed their exclusion from private theaters, restaurants, and hotels. To some degree these "reforms" were a response to the growth of new black communities in southern cities. Expanding urban communities such as Atlanta, Memphis, and Birmingham presented more of a danger of social mixing and economic competition between the races than did rural areas. Southern progressives thus created more rigid legal and institutional guarantees of white supremacy.

New Journalism: Muckraking

New developments in the mass media drew the attention of millions to urban poverty, political corruption, the plight of industrial workers, and immoral business practices. As early as 1890, journalist Jacob Riis had shocked the nation with his landmark book *How the Other Half Lives,* a portrait of New York City's poor. A Danish immigrant who arrived in New York City in 1871, Riis had himself experienced hard times and loneliness in the big city. He became a newspaper reporter, covering the police beat and learning about the city's desperate underside. For his book, Riis made a remarkable series of photographs in tenements, lodging houses, sweatshops, and saloons. The combination of striking photos and Riis's analysis of slum housing patterns made a powerful impact upon a whole generation of urban reformers.

Within a few years, magazine journalists as well had turned to uncovering the seamier side of American life. The key innovator was S. S. McClure, a young midwestern editor who in 1893 started America's first large-circulation magazine, *McClure's.* Charging only a dime for his monthly, McClure effectively combined popular fiction with articles on science, technology, travel, and recent history. He attracted a new readership among the urban middle class through aggressive subscription and promotional campaigns, as well as newsstand sales. By the turn of the century *McClure's* and several imitators— *Munsey's, Cosmopolitan, Collier's, Everybody's* the *Saturday Evening Post*— had circulations in the hundreds of thousands.

In 1902 McClure began hiring talented reporters to write detailed accounts of the nation's social problems. Lincoln Steffens's series *The Shame of the Cities* revealed the widespread graft at the center of American urban politics. He showed how big-city bosses routinely worked hand in glove with businessmen seeking lucrative municipal contracts for gas, water, electricity, and mass transit. Ida Tarbell, in her *History of the Standard Oil Company,* thoroughly documented how John D. Rockefeller ruthlessly squeezed out competitors with unfair business practices. Ray Stannard Baker wrote detailed portraits of life and labor in Pennsylvania coal towns.

McClure's and other magazines discovered that "exposure journalism" paid off handsomely in terms of increased circulation. The middle-class public responded to this new combination of factual reporting and moral exhortation. A series such as Steffens's fueled reform campaigns that swept individual communities. Between 1902 and 1908, magazines were full of articles exposing insurance scandals, patent medicine frauds, and stock market swindles. Upton Sinclair's 1906 novel *The Jungle,* a socialist tract set among Chicago packinghouse workers, exposed the filthy sanitation and abysmal working conditions in the stockyards and the meatpacking industry. In an effort to boost sales, Sinclair's publisher devoted an entire issue of a monthly magazine it owned, *The World's Work,* to articles

In his landmark book, *How the Other Half Lives* (1890), Jacob Riis made innovative use of photographs and statistics to argue for housing reform. This photograph depicts an Italian immigrant family of seven living in a one-room apartment. Overcrowded and dilapidated tenements threatened the entire city "because they are the hot-beds of the epidemics that carry death to the rich and poor alike; the nurseries of pauperism and crime that fill our jails and police courts."

and photographs that substantiated Sinclair's devastating portrait. The resulting publicity not only helped make *The Jungle* a best seller, it also significantly increased the circulation of *The World's Work,* which had previously avoided "exposure journalism."

Progressives working to reform the nation's food and drug industries exploited the national revelations about the meat-packing industry to push through new legislation. In late 1906, with the support of President Theodore Roosevelt, Congress passed the Meat Inspection Act and the Pure Food and Drug Act. The new laws empowered the Department of Agriculture to enforce sanitary regulations in meat-packing plants and administer a federal inspection of all companies selling meats in interstate commerce. These acts also established a new federal agency, the Food and Drug Administration (FDA), charged with testing and approving drugs before they went on the market. The federal government would now play a new and aggressive role in protecting consumers from impure food and drugs.

That same year, David Graham Phillips's *Cosmopolitan* series *The Treason of the Senate* argued that many conservative U.S. senators were no more than mouthpieces for big business. President Roosevelt, upset by Phillips's attack on several of his friends and supporters, angrily denounced the "muckrakers," saying they "raked the mud of society and never looked up." The muckraking vogue began to wane, partly due to Roosevelt's outburst. By 1907 S. S. McClure's original team of reporters had broken up. Certain subjects failed to draw much interest, such as Baker's series on race relations, *Following the Color Line.* But muckraking had demonstrated the powerful potential for mobilizing public opinion on a national scale. Reform campaigns need not be limited to the local community. Ultimately, they could engage a national community of informed citizens.

Intellectual Currents

On a deeper level than muckraking, a host of early-twentieth-century thinkers challenged several of the core ideas in American intellectual life. Based largely in universities, they did not necessarily identify themselves as progressives. But their new theories of education, law, economics, and society provided effective tools for reformers eager to repair American life. The emergent fields of the social sciences — sociology, anthropology, and econom- ics — offered alternative interpretations of Darwin's evolutionary theory and what it implied for human society. The revolt against nineteenth-century dogmas rejected the harsh language of social Darwinism and the all-consuming faith in individualism (see Chapter 20). The intellectuals who led this revolt emphasized empirical observation of how people actually lived and behaved in their communities. Above all, progressive reformers looked to use systematic intelligence and reason to actively improve the material conditions of their society.

Sociologist Lester Frank Ward, in his pioneering work *Dynamic Sociology* (1883), offered an important critique of reigning orthodoxy. Ward argued that conservative social theorists such as Herbert Spencer and William Graham Sumner had wrongly applied evolutionary theory to human affairs. They had confused organic evolution with social evolution. Nature's method was *genetic:* unplanned, involuntary, automatic, and mechanical. An octopus had to lay 50,000 eggs to maintain itself; a codfish hatched a million young fish a year in order that two might survive. By contrast, civilization had been built on successful human intervention in the natural processes of organic evolution. The human method was *telic:* planned, voluntary, rational, dynamic. "Every implement or utensil," Ward argued, "every mechanical device, every object of design, skill, and labor, every artificial thing that serves a human purpose, is a triumph of mind over the physical forces of nature in ceaseless and aimless competition." In 1905 Ward became the first president of the American Sociological Society.

The new field of American sociology concentrated on the rapidly changing nature of community. German social theorist Ferdinand Tönnies developed an extremely influential model for describing the recent evolution of Western society from *Gemeinschaft* to *Gesellschaft:* from a static, close-knit, morally unified community to a dynamic, impersonal, morally fragmented society. If the new urban-industrial order had weakened traditional sources of morality and values — the family, the church, the small community — then where would the mass of people now learn these values? This question provided the focus for Edward A. Ross's landmark work *Social Control* (1901), a book whose title became a key phrase in progressive thought. Ross argued that society needed an "ethical elite" of citizens "who have at heart the general welfare and know what kinds of conduct will promote this welfare." The "surplus moral energy" of this elite — ministers, educators, professionals — would have to guide the new mechanisms of social control needed in America's *Gesellschaft* communities.

Philosopher John Dewey criticized the excessively rigid and formal approach to education found in most American schools. In books such as *The School and Society* (1902) and *Democracy and Education* (1916), Dewey advocated developing what he called "creative intelligence" in students, which could then be put to use in improving society. Schools ought to be "embryonic communities," miniatures of society, where children were encouraged to participate actively in different types of experience. By cultivating imagination and openness to new experiences, schools could develop creativity and the habits required for systematic inquiry. Dewey placed excessive faith in the power of schools to promote community spirit and democratic values. But his belief that education was the "fundamental method of social progress and reform" inspired generations of progressive educators.

Some progressive social scientists had a direct influence on governing. At the University of Wisconsin, John R. Commons founded the new field of industrial relations and organized a state industrial commission that became a model for other states. Working closely with Robert M. La Follette, Commons and his students helped draft pioneering laws in worker compensation and public utility regulation. Another Wisconsin faculty member, economist Richard Ely, argued that the state was "an educational and ethical agency whose positive aim is an indispensable condition of human progress." Ely believed the state must directly intervene to help solve public problems. He rejected the doctrine of laissez faire as merely "a tool in the hands of the greedy." Like Commons, Ely worked with Wisconsin lawmakers, applying his expertise in economics to reforming the state's labor laws.

Progressive legal theorists began challenging the conservative view of constitutional law that had dominated American courts. Since the 1870s the Supreme Court had interpreted the Fourteenth Amendment (1868) as a guarantee of broad rights for corporations. That amendment, which prevented states from depriving "any person of life, liberty, or property without due process of law," had been designed to protect the civil rights of African Americans against violations by the states. But the Court, led by Justice Stephen J. Field, used the due process clause to consistently strike down state laws regulating business and labor conditions. The Supreme Court and state courts had thus made the Fourteenth Amendment a bulwark for big business and a foe of social welfare measures.

The most important dissenter from this view was Oliver Wendell Holmes, Jr. A scholar and Massachusetts judge, Holmes took a more tolerant view of legislative regulation. Holmes believed the law had to take into account changing social conditions. And courts should take care not to invalidate social legislation enacted democratically. After his appointment to the Supreme Court in 1902, Holmes authored a number of notable dissents to conservative court decisions overturning progressive legislation. Criticizing the majority opinion in *Lochner v. New York* (1905), in which the Court struck down a state law setting a ten-hour day for bakers, Holmes insisted that the Constitution "is not intended to embody a particular theory."

Holmes's pragmatic views of the law seldom convinced a majority of the Supreme Court before the late 1930s. But his views influenced a generation of lawyers who began practicing what came to be called *sociological jurisprudence*. In *Muller v. Oregon* (1908), the Court upheld an Oregon law limiting the maximum hours for working women. Noting that "woman's physical structure and the performance of maternal functions place her at a disadvantage," the Court found that "the physical well-being of woman becomes an object of public interest and care." Louis Brandeis, the state's attorney, amassed statistical, sociological, and economic data, rather than traditional legal arguments, to support his arguments. The "Brandeis Brief" became a common strategy for lawyers defending the constitutionality of progressive legislation.

SOCIAL CONTROL AND ITS LIMITS

Many middle- and upper-class Protestant progressives expressed deep anxiety over the increasing numbers of immigrants, industrial workers, and black people, especially in American cities. They feared that these groups threatened the stability of American democracy, and they worried that alien cultural practices were disrupting what they viewed as traditional American morality. How could all these new people be assimilated into American society? Many progressives saw themselves as part of Edward Ross's "ethical elite." They believed they had a mission to frame laws and regulations for the social control of immigrants, industrial workers, and

African Americans. This was the moralistic and frequently xenophobic side of progressivism, and it provided a powerful source of support for the regulation of drinking, prostitution, leisure activities, and schooling. Organizations devoted to social control constituted other versions of reform communities. But these attempts at moral reform met with mixed success amidst the extraordinary cultural and ethnic diversity of America's cities.

The Prohibition Movement

Agitation against alcohol consumption had a long history in America. During the last two decades of the nineteenth century, the Women's Christian Temperance Union had grown into a powerful mass organization. The WCTU appealed especially to women angered by men who used alcohol and then abused their wives and children. It directed most of its work toward ending the production, sale, and consumption of alcohol. But local WCTU chapters put their energy into nontemperance activities as well, including homeless shelters, Sunday schools, prison reform, child nurseries, and woman suffrage. The WCTU thus created a political space where women could fuse public concerns with their traditional moral posture as guardians of the home. By 1911 the WCTU, with a quarter-million members, was the largest women's organization in American history.

Other temperance groups had a narrower focus. The most influential of these was the Anti-Saloon League, founded in 1893. The league began by organizing local-option campaigns in which rural counties and small towns banned liquor within their geographical limits. It drew much of its financial support from local businessmen who saw a link between closing a community's saloons and increasing the productivity of workers. The league was a one-issue pressure group that played effectively on anti-urban and anti-immigrant prejudice. League lobbyists targeted state legislatures, where big cities were usually underrepresented. They hammered away at the close connections among saloon culture, liquor dealers, brewers, and big-city political machines.

The Prohibition movement found its core strength among Protestant, native-born, small-town and rural Americans. But Prohibition found support in the cities as well—the issue was not simply a rural versus urban conflict. The battle to ban alcohol also revealed the deep ethnic and cultural divides within America's urban communities. Opponents of alcohol were generally "pietists" who viewed the world from a position of moral absolutism. These included native-born, middle-class Protestants associated with evangelical churches, along with some old-stock Protestant immigrant denominations. Opponents of prohibition were generally "ritualists" with less arbitrary notions of personal morality. These were largely new-stock, working-class Catholic and Jewish immigrants, along with some Protestants, such as German Lutherans.

The caption for this cartoon reads, "I cannot tell a lie—I did it with my little hatchet." Carrie Nation had gained wide publicity for her one-woman crusade against drinking. She challenged authorities to arrest her after she used an axe to smash liquor bottles, plate glass, and fixtures in several illegal Kansas saloons.

The Social Evil

Many of the same reformers who battled the saloon and drinking also engaged in efforts to eradicate prostitution. Crusades against "the social evil" had appeared at intervals throughout the nineteenth century. But they reached a new level of intensity between 1895 and 1920. In part, this new sense of urgency stemmed from the sheer growth of cities and the greater visibility of prostitution in red-light districts and neighborhoods. Anti-prostitution campaigns epitomized the diverse makeup and mixed motives of so much progressive reform. Male business and civic leaders joined forces with feminists, social workers, and clergy to eradicate "commercialized vice." Although they could not end prostitution in American communities, they did radically change the organization of the sex trade.

Between 1908 and 1914 exposés of the "white slave" traffic became a national sensation. Dozens of books, articles, and motion pictures alleged an international conspiracy to seduce and sell girls into prostitution. Most of these materials exaggerated the practices they attacked. They also made foreigners, especially Jews and southern Europeans, scapegoats for the sexual anxieties of native-born whites. "The vilest practices are brought here from continental Europe," one report to a Senate committee warned in 1909, including "the most bestial elements of depravity." In 1910 Congress passed legislation that permitted the deportation of foreign-born prostitutes or any foreigner convicted of procuring or employing them. That same year, the Mann Act made it a federal offense to transport women across state lines for "immoral purposes."

But most anti-prostitution activity took place at the local level. Between 1910 and 1915, thirty-five cities and states conducted thorough investigations of prostitution. The progressive bent for defining social problems through statistics was nowhere more evident than in these reports. Vice commission investigators combed red-light districts, tenement houses, hotels, and dance halls, drawing up detailed lists of places where prostitution took place. They interviewed prostitutes, pimps, and customers. These reports agreed that commercialized sex was a business run by and for the profit and pleasure of men. They also documented the dangers of venereal disease to the larger community. The highly publicized vice reports were effective in forcing police crackdowns in urban red-light districts.

Reformers disagreed on why so many women in big cities sold their bodies for money. Most had trouble believing that any woman would freely choose to be a prostitute; this was antithetical to conventional notions of female purity and sexuality. But for wage-earning women, prostitution was a rational choice in a world of limited opportunities. Maimie Pinzer, a prostitute, summed up her feelings in a letter to a wealthy female reformer: "I don't propose to get up at 6:30 to be at work at 8 and work in a close, stuffy room with people I despise, until dark, for $6 or $7 a week! When I could, just by phoning, spend an afternoon with some congenial person and in the end have more than a week's work could pay me." Ultimately, the antivice crusades transformed the structure of prostitution rather than eradicating it. They succeeded in closing down many urban red-light districts and larger brothels, but these were replaced by the streetwalker and call girl, who were more vulnerable to harassment and control by policemen and pimps.

The Redemption of Leisure

In the cities, progressive-minded philanthropists and reformers were in the forefront of efforts to improve recreational opportunities, especially for children. Physical education in the schools and supervised municipal playgrounds were two important legacies of this concern. The Playground Association of America, founded in 1906, helped convince municipal governments to spend millions of dollars on city playgrounds and the staff to supervise them. Settlement workers and educators stressed the value of organized team sports, such as baseball and basketball, in teaching youngsters cooperation and respect for rules. Children's play, in this view, was too important to be left to children.

But progressives faced a thornier issue in the growing popularity of commercial entertainment. For large numbers of working-class adults and children, leisure meant time and money spent at vaudeville and burlesque theaters, amusement parks, dance halls, and motion picture houses. These competed with municipal parks, libraries and museums, YMCAs, and school recreation centers. For many cultural traditionalists who spoke of "the moral significance of play," the flood of new urban commercial amusements posed a grave threat. As with prostitution, urban progressives sponsored a host of recreation and amusement surveys detailing the situation in their individual cities. "Commercialized leisure," warned Frederick C. Howe in 1914, "is molding our civilization — not as it should be molded but as commerce dictates. And leisure must be controlled by the community, if it is to become an agency of civilization rather than the reverse."

By 1908 the enormous and unprecedented popularity of *nickelodeon* theaters made movies the most popular form of cheap entertainment in America. By 1911, an estimated 11,500 movie theaters attracted 5 million patrons each day. For five or ten cents one could see a program that might include a slapstick comedy, a Western, a travelogue, and a melodrama. Early movies were most popular in the tenement and immigrant districts of big cities, and with children. As the films themselves became more sophisticated and as "movie palaces" began to replace cheap storefront theaters, the new medium attracted a large middle-class clientele as well.

Progressive reformers seized the chance to help regulate the new medium as a way of improving the commercial recreation of the urban poor. Movies held out the promise of an alternative to the older entertainment traditions, such as concert saloons and burlesque theater, that had been closely allied with machine politics and the vice economy. In 1909, New York City movie producers and exhibitors joined with the reform-minded People's Institute to establish the voluntary National Board of Censorship (NBC). Movie entrepreneurs, most of whom were themselves immigrants, sought to shed the stigma of the slums, attract more middle-class patronage, and increase profits. A revolving group of civic activists reviewed the movies, passing them, suggesting changes, or condemning them. Local censoring committees all over the nation subscribed

Movies, by John Sloan, 1913, the most talented artist among the so-called "ashcan realist" school of painting. Active in socialist and bohemian circles, Sloan served as art editor for *The Masses* magazine for several years. His work celebrated the vitality and diversity of urban working class life and leisure, including the new commercial culture represented by the motion picture.

to the board's weekly bulletin. They aimed at achieving what John Collier of the NBC called "the redemption of leisure." By 1914 the NBC was reviewing 95 percent of the nation's film output. Filmmakers generally took greater care in avoiding more sensational subjects. The progressive influence could also be found in a growing number of movies that depicted efforts to reform labor conditions, prostitution, and slum housing.

Standardizing Education

Public schools had always provided American children with a combination of cognitive skills and cultural values. Along with reading, writing, and mathematics, schools inculcated patriotism, piety, and respect for authority. In the late nineteenth century, reformers began looking to the public school system as a key agency for socializing young people, especially in the city. Progressive educators looked to the public school primarily as an agent of "Americanization." Elwood Cubberley, a leading educational reformer, expressed the view that schools could be the vehicle by which immigrant children could break free of the parochial ethnic neighborhood. "Our task," he argued in *Changing Conceptions of Education* (1909), "is to break up these groups or settlements, to assimilate and amalgamate these people as a part of our American race, and to implant in their children, so far as can be done, the Anglo-Saxon conception of righteousness, law and order, and popular government."

The most important educational trends in these years were the expansion and bureaucratization of the nation's public school systems. In most cities centralization served to consolidate the power of older urban elites who felt threatened by the large influx of immigrants. Children began school earlier and stayed there longer. Kindergartens spread rapidly in large cities. They presented, as one writer put it in 1903, "the earliest opportunity to catch the little Russian, the little Italian, the little German, Pole, Syrian, and the rest and begin to make good American citizens of them." High schools also multiplied, extending the school's influence beyond the traditional grammar school curriculum. In 1890 only 4 percent of the nation's youth between fourteen and seventeen were enrolled in school; by 1930 the figure was 47 percent. By 1918 every state had some form of compulsory school attendance.

In the nineteenth century, most educators viewed the essential purpose of schooling to be character building. High schools reflected a growing belief that schools be comprehensive, multifunctional institutions. In 1918 the National Education Association offered a report defining *Cardinal Principles of Secondary Education.* These included instruction in health, family life, citizenship, and ethical character. Academic programs prepared a small number of students for college. Vocational programs trained boys and girls for a niche in the new industrial order. Boys took shop courses in metal trades, carpentry, and machine tools. Girls learned typing, bookkeeping, sewing, cooking, and home economics. The Smith-Hughes Act of 1917 provided federal grants to support these programs and set up a Federal Board for Vocational Education.

Progressive educators pushed for greater centralization of boards of education. These boards would oversee school construction, teacher hiring, and curriculum. Educational reformers also established national testing organizations such as the College Entrance Examination Board (founded in 1900) and helped standardize agencies for curriculum development and teacher training. In 1914 E. L. Thorndike published *Educational Psychology,* which laid the groundwork for education research based on experimental and statistical investigations. Progressives led in the development of specialized fields such as educational psychology, guidance counseling, and educational administration. The progressive faith in a "science of education" thus shaped key institutions in modern American schooling.

WORKING-CLASS COMMUNITIES AND PROTEST

The Industrial Revolution, which had begun transforming American life and labor in the nineteenth century, reached maturity in the early twentieth. In 1900, out of a total labor force of 28.5 million, 16 million people worked at industrial occupations and 11 million on farms. By 1920, in a labor force of nearly 42 million, almost 29 million were in industry, but farm labor had declined to 10.4 million. There were enormous variations within the world of the industrial worker. That world included large manufacturing towns in New England; barren mining settlements in the Far West; primitive lumber and turpentine camps in the Deep South; steel and coal-mining cities in Pennsylvania and Ohio; and densely packed immigrant ghettos from New York to San Francisco, where workers toiled in garment trade sweatshops.

All of these industrial workers shared the need to sell their labor for wages in order to survive. This made their world fundamentally different from that of the business and professional classes. At the same time, differences in skill, ethnicity, and race proved powerful barriers to efforts at organizing trade unions that could bargain for improved wages and working conditions. So too did the economic and political power of the large corporations that dominated much of American industry. Yet there were also small, closely knit groups of skilled workers, such as printers and brewers, who exercised real control over their lives and labors. And these years saw many labor struggles that created effective trade unions, or laid the groundwork for others. Industrial workers also became a force in local and national politics, adding a chorus of insistent voices to the calls for social justice.

The New Immigrants

On the eve of World War I, close to 60 percent of the industrial labor force was foreign-born. Most of these workers were among the roughly 9 million new immigrants from southern and eastern Europe who arrived in the United States between 1900 and 1914. In the nineteenth century, much of the overseas migration had come from the industrial districts of northern and western Europe. English, Welsh, and German artisans had brought with them skills critical for emerging industries such as steelmaking and coal mining. Unlike their predecessors, the new Italian, Polish, Hungarian, Jewish, and Greek immigrants nearly all lacked industrial skills. They thus entered the bottom ranks of factories, mines, mills, and sweatshops.

They had been driven from their European farms and towns by several forces. These included the undermining of subsistence farming by commercial agriculture; a falling death rate that brought a shortage of land; and religious and political persecution. American corporations also sent agents to recruit cheap labor. Except for Jewish immigrants, a majority of whom fled virulent anti-Semitism in Russia and Poland, most newcomers planned on earning a stake and then returning home. Hard times in America forced many back to Europe. In the depression year of 1908, for example, more Austro-Hungarians and Italians left than entered the United States.

Family members and friends often supplied practical information to those planning to migrate. One Polish immigrant in Pittsburgh wrote detailed instructions to his brother, who planned to join him.

Now prepare yourself for the trip in the following way. Take rubles for spending. Take a suit with you because you will need it in Prussia. Buy sugar and vinegar and a bottle of vodka. The day when you will be leaving for the ocean don't eat anything cooked or boiled on the ship because they are adding powder to make you throw up. Eat only dry bread and vodka and then maybe you will be well. And when you arrive in New York . . . send me a telegram, and I will wait for you in Pittsburgh.

This San Francisco elementary school photo taken in 1919 illustrates the impact of new immigration on the West Coast.

Sources of Immigrants, 1900–1920

By the early twentieth century immigrants to the United States came mainly from southern and eastern Europe. This trend reversed the older pattern of immigration primarily from northern and western Europe.

The low-paid, backbreaking work in basic industry became nearly the exclusive preserve of the new immigrants. The steelmaking center of Pittsburgh provides a good overview. In 1907, of the 14,359 common laborers employed at the Carnegie steel mills, 11,694 were eastern Europeans. For twelve-hour days and seven-day weeks, two-thirds of these workers made less than $12.50 a week, one-third less than $10.00. This was far less than the minimum of $15.00 that the Pittsburgh Associated Charities had set as the minimum for providing necessities for a family of five. Small wonder that the new immigration was disproportionately male: one-third of the immigrant steelworkers were single, and among married men who had been in the country less than five years, about two-thirds reported that their wives were still in Europe. Workers with families generally supplemented their incomes by taking in single men as boarders.

Not all of the new immigrants came from Europe. Between 1898 and 1907 more than 80,000 Japanese entered the U.S. The vast majority were young men working as contract laborers in the West. By 1906 some 14,000 Japanese worked as section hands on western railroads and nearly 40,000 worked as agricultural laborers in the harvest season, mainly in California. American law prevented Japanese immigrants (the Issei) from obtaining American citizenship, because they were not white. This legal discrimination, along with informal exclusion from many occupations, forced the Japanese to create niches for themselves within local economies. Most Japanese settled around Los Angeles, where they established small communities centered around fishing, truck farming, and the flower and nursery business. In 1920 Japanese farmers produced 10 percent of the dollar volume of California agriculture on 1 percent of the farm acreage. By 1930 over 35,000 Issei and their children (the Nisei) lived in Los Angeles.

Mexican immigration also grew in these years, providing a critical source of labor for the West's farms, railroads, and mines. Economic and political crises spurred tens of thousands of Mexico's rural and urban poor to emigrate to the north. Large numbers of seasonal agricultural workers regularly came up from Mexico to work in the expanding sugar beet industry and then returned. But a number of substantial resident Mexican communities also emerged in the early twentieth century. Between

These Japanese immigrants are shown arriving at the quarantine station at Angel Island, San Francisco Bay, around 1911. Over half the Japanese population was concentrated in California, with an economic focus on agriculture. The so-called Gentlemen's Agreement of 1907–08 ended the immigration of Japanese laborers until 1924. But it did provide for family unification by allowing passports for "laborers who have already been in America and to the parents, wives, and children of laborers resident there."

much higher rates of disease and infant mortality than surrounding Anglo communities.

Company Towns

Immigrant industrial workers and their families often established their communities in a company town, where a single large corporation was dominant. Cities such as Lawrence, Massachusetts, Gary, Indiana, and Butte, Montana, revolved around the industrial enterprises of Pacific Woolen, U.S. Steel, and Anaconda Copper. Workers had little or no influence over the economic and political institutions of these cities. But they did maintain some community control in other ways. Family and kin networks, ethnic lodges, saloons, benefit societies, churches and synagogues, and musical groups affirmed traditional forms of community in a setting governed by individualism and private capital. All these institutions helped mediate the immigrant experience with industrial capitalism.

On the job, modern machinery and industrial discipline meant high rates of injury and death. In Gary, immigrant steelworkers suffered twice the accident rate of English-speaking employees, who could better understand safety instructions and warnings. A 1910 study of work accidents revealed that nearly a fourth of all new steelworkers were killed or injured each year. Steel mills in Allegheny County, Pennsylvania, took the lives of 157 Slavs in just one year. As one Polish worker described the immigrant's lot to his wife: "If he comes home sick then it is trouble, because everybody is looking only for money to get some of it, and during the sickness most will be spent." Mutual aid associations, organized around ethnic groups, offered some protection through cheap insurance and death benefits.

In steel and coal towns, women not only maintained the household and raised the children, they also boosted the family income by taking in boarders, sewing, and laundry. Many women also tended gardens and raised chickens, rabbits, and goats. This helped reduce dependence on the company store. In many communities the company store, owned and operated by the dominant corporation, was the only place where workers could buy groceries and supplies, usually at very high prices. Working-class women felt the burdens of housework more heavily than their middle-class sisters. Running water, indoor plumbing, and sewage disposal were often available only on a pay-as-you-go basis. The daily drudgery endured by working-class women far outlasted the "man-killing" shift worked

1900 and 1914, the number of people of Mexican descent living and working in the United States tripled, from roughly 100,000 to 300,000.

Throughout Texas, California, New Mexico, Arizona, and Colorado, western cities developed *barrios,* distinct communities of Mexicans. Mexican immigrants attracted by jobs in the smelting industry made El Paso the most thoroughly Mexican city in the U.S. In San Antonio Mexicans worked at shelling pecans, becoming perhaps the most underpaid and exploited group of workers in the country. By 1910, San Antonio contained the largest number of Mexican immigrants of any city in the West. In southern California, labor agents for railroads recruited Mexicans to work on building new interurban lines around Los Angeles. Labor camps built to house these workers evolved into several Mexican enclaves. Overcrowding, poor sanitation, and deficient public services made many of these enclaves unhealthy places to live. Mexican barrios suffered

This photograph of Ludlow, Colorado, April 21, 1914, shows the aftermath of the state militia attack that totally destroyed a tent colony of striking miners. The "Ludlow Massacre," which killed fourteen people (including eleven children), demonstrated the intensity of state-supported violence in western company towns.

by the husband. Many women struggled with the effects of their husbands' excessive drinking and faced early widowhood.

The adjustment for immigrant workers was not so much a process of assimilation as one of adaptation and resistance. Efficiency experts, such as Frederick Taylor, tried to increase industrial output by bringing the principles of "scientific management" to factory labor. Taylor and others carefully observed and analyzed the time and energy needed for each job, then set standard methods for each worker. In theory, this would increase efficiency and give managers more control over their workers. But work habits and Old World cultural traditions did not always mesh with factory discipline. A Polish wedding celebration might last three or four days. A drinking bout following a Sunday funeral might cause workers to celebrate "St. Monday" and not show up for work. Employers made much of the few Slavs allowed to work their way up into the ranks of skilled workers and foremen. But most immigrants were far more concerned with job security than with upward mobility. The newcomers learned from more skilled and experienced British and American workers that "slowing down" or "soldiering" spread out the work. As new immigrants became less transient and more permanently settled in company towns, they increased their involvement in local politics and union activity.

The power of large corporations in the life of company towns was most evident among the min-

ing communities of the West, as was violent labor conflict. The Colorado Fuel and Iron Company (CFI) employed roughly half of the 8,000 coal miners who labored in that state's mines. In mining towns such as Ludlow and Trinidad, the CFI thoroughly dominated the lives of miners and their families. "The miner," one contemporary union official observed, "is in this land owned by the corporation that owns the homes, that owns the boarding houses, that owns every single thing there is there . . . not only the mines, but all the grounds, all the buildings, all the places of recreation, as well as the school and church buildings." By the early twentieth century, new immigrants, such as Italians, Greeks, Slavs, and Mexicans, composed a majority of these Western mining communities. About one-fifth of CFI miners spoke no English. Frequent mine explosions and poor housing made for extremely harsh living conditions.

In September of 1913, the United Mine Workers led a strike in the Colorado coal fields, calling for improved safety, higher wages, and recognition of the union. Thousands of miners' families moved out of company housing and into makeshift tent colonies provided by the union. In October, Governor Elias Ammons ordered the Colorado National Guard into the tense strike region to keep order. The troops, supposedly neutral, proceeded to ally themselves with the mine operators. By spring the strike had bankrupted the state, forcing the governor to remove most of the troops. The coal companies then brought in large numbers of private mine guards who were extremely hostile toward the strikers. On April 20, 1914, a combination of guardsmen and private guards surrounded the largest of the tent colonies at Ludlow, where over a thousand mine families lived. A shot rang out (each side accused the other of firing), and there ensued a pitched battle that lasted until the poorly armed miners ran out of ammunition. At dusk, the troops burned the tent village to the ground, routing the families and killing fourteen, including eleven children. Enraged strikers attacked mines throughout southern Colorado in an armed rebellion that lasted ten days, until President Wilson ordered the U.S. Army into the region. News of the "Ludlow Massacre" shocked millions and aroused widespread protests and demonstrations against the policies of Colorado Fuel and Iron and its owner, John D. Rockefeller, Jr. Ludlow remained a potent symbol of the corporate power and violent labor disputes characteristic of many company towns.

Urban Ghettos

In large cities new immigrant communities took the form of densely packed ghettos. By 1920, immigrants and their children constituted almost 60 percent of the population of cities over 100,000. They were an even larger percentage in major industrial centers such as Chicago, Pittsburgh, Philadelphia, and New York. Although ethnic groups clustered together in tight communities based on a common language and nationality, the sheer size and dynamism of these cities made the immigrant experience more complex there than in the company town. Immigrant workers in the urban garment trades toiled for low wages and suffered layoffs, unemployment, and poor health. But conditions in the small, labor-intensive shops of the clothing industry differed significantly from those in the large-scale capital-intensive industries like steel.

New York City had become the center of both Jewish immigration and America's huge industry in ready-to-wear clothing. Almost two-thirds of all the Jews entering the United States between 1890 and 1915 settled in New York. The city's Jewish population was 1.4 million in 1915, almost 30 percent of its inhabitants. New York produced 70 percent of all women's clothing and 40 percent of all men's clothing made in the country. In small factories, lofts, and tenement apartments some 200,000 people, most of them Jews, some of them Italians, worked in the clothing trades. Most of the industry operated on the grueling piece-rate, or task, system, in which manufacturers and subcontractors paid individuals or teams of workers to complete a certain quota of labor within a specific time.

The garment industry was highly seasonal. A typical work week was sixty hours, with seventy common during busy season. But there were long stretches of unemployment in slack times. Even skilled cutters, all men, earned an average of only sixteen dollars per week. Unskilled workers, nearly all of them young single women, made only six or seven dollars a week. Perhaps a quarter of the work force, classified as "learners," earned only three to six dollars a week. Often forced to work in cramped, dirty, and badly lit rooms, garment workers strained under a system in which time equaled money. Morris Rosenfeld, a presser of men's clothing who wrote Yiddish poetry, captured the feeling: "The tick of the clock is the boss in his anger / The face of the clock has the eye of a foe / The clock — I shudder — Dost hear how it draws me? / It calls me 'Machine' and it cries to me 'Sew!'"

In November of 1909 two New York garment manufacturers responded to strikes by unskilled women workers by hiring thugs and prostitutes to beat up pickets. The strikers won the support of the Women's Trade Union League, a group of sympathetic female reformers that included Lillian Wald, Mary Drier, and prominent society figures. At a dramatic mass meeting in Cooper Union Hall, Clara Lemlich, a teenage working girl speaking in Yiddish, made an emotional plea for a general strike. She called for everyone in the crowd to take an old Jewish oath: "If I turn traitor to the cause I now pledge, may this hand wither from the arm I now raise." The "uprising of the 20,000" swept through the city's garment district.

The strikers demanded union recognition, better wages, and safer and more sanitary conditions. They drew support from thousands of suffragists, trade unionists, and sympathetic middle-class women as well. Hundreds of strikers were arrested and many were beaten by police. After three cold months on the picket line the strikers returned to work without union recognition. But the International Ladies Garment Workers Union (ILGWU), founded in 1900, did gain strength and negotiated contracts with some of the city's shirtwaist makers. The strike was an important breakthrough in the drive to organize unskilled workers into industrial unions. It opened the doors to women's involvement in the labor movement and created new leaders, such as Lemlich, Pauline Newman, and Rose Schneiderman. And it showed the power that could be achieved through an alliance between working-class and middle-class women.

On March 25, 1911, the issues raised by the strike took on new urgency when a fire raced through three floors of the Triangle Shirtwaist Company. As the flames spread, workers found themselves trapped by exit doors locked from the outside. Fire escapes were nonexistent. Within half an hour, 146 people, mostly young Jewish women, had been killed by smoke or had leaped to their death. In the bitter aftermath, women progressives led by Florence Kelley and Frances Perkins of the National Consumers League joined with Tammany Hall leaders Al Smith, Robert Wagner, and Timothy Sullivan to create a New York State Factory Investigation Commission. Under Perkins's vigorous leadership, the FIC conducted an unprecedented round of public hearings and on-site inspections, leading to a series of state laws that dramatically improved safety conditions and limited the hours for working women and children.

The AFL: "Unions, Pure and Simple"

Following the depression of the 1890s, the American Federation of Labor emerged as the strongest and most stable organization of workers. Samuel Gompers's strategy of recruiting skilled labor into unions organized by craft had paid off. Union membership climbed from under 500,000 in 1897 to over 2 million by 1904. Most of this growth took place in AFL affiliates in coal mining, the building trades, transportation, and machine shops. The national unions — the United Mine Workers of America, the Brotherhood of Carpenters and Joiners, the International Association of Machinists — represented workers of specific occupations in collective bargaining. Trade autonomy and exclusive jurisdiction were the ruling principles within the AFL.

But the strength of craft organization also gave rise to weakness. In 1905 Gompers told a union gathering in Minneapolis that "caucasians" would not "let their standard of living be destroyed by negroes, Chinamen, Japs, or any others." Those "others" included the new immigrants from eastern and southern Europe, men and women, who labored in the steel mills and garment trades. Each trade looked mainly to the welfare of its own. Many explicitly barred women and African Americans from membership. The national affiliates generally perceived unorganized workers as threats to the economic position of unions. There were some important exceptions. The United Mine Workers of America followed a more inclusive policy, recruiting both skilled underground pitmen and the unskilled above-ground workers. The UMWA even tried to recruit strikebreakers brought in by coal operators. With 260,000 members in 1904, the UMWA became the largest AFL affiliate.

AFL unions had a difficult time holding on to their gains. Economic slumps, technological changes, and aggressive counterattacks by employer organizations could be devastating. Trade associations using management-controlled efficiency drives fought union efforts to regulate output and shop practices. The National Association of Manufacturers, a group of smaller industrialists founded in 1903, launched an "open shop" campaign to eradicate unions altogether. *Open shop* was simply a new name for a workplace where unions were not allowed. The NAM supplied strikebreakers, private guards, and labor spies to employers. It also formed antiboycott associations to prevent unions in one trade from supporting walkouts in another.

Unfriendly judicial decisions also hurt organizing efforts. In 1906 a federal judge issued a permanent injunction against an iron molders strike at the Allis Chalmers Company of Milwaukee. The ruling forbid "any interference with the plaintiff's business, peaceful persuasion to induce its employees to stop work, and all picketing." In the so-called Danbury Hatters Case (*Loewe v. Lawler*, 1908), a federal court ruled that the Sherman Anti-Trust Act could be applied to trade unions engaged in boycotting manufacturers. Such *secondary boycotts*, long an effective labor tactic, were now declared a conspiracy in restraint of trade. Not until the 1930s would unions be able to count on legal support for collective bargaining and the right to strike.

The IWW: "One Big Union"

Some workers developed more radical visions of labor organizing. The Western Federation of Miners (WFM) had gained strength in the metal mining regions of the West by leading several violent strikes. In the harsh and isolated company towns of Idaho, Montana, and Colorado, miners suffered from low wages, poor food, and primitive sanitation, as well as injuries and death from frequent cave-ins and explosions. In 1899, during a strike in the silver mining district of Coeur d'Alene, Idaho, the Bunker Hill and Sullivan Mining Company had enraged the miners by hiring armed detectives and firing all union members. Desperate miners retaliated by destroying a company mill with dynamite. Idaho's governor declared martial law and obtained federal troops to enforce it. In a pattern that would become familiar in western labor relations, the soldiers served as strikebreakers, rounding up hundreds of miners and imprisoning them for months in makeshift bullpens.

In response to the brutal realities of labor organizing in the West, most WFM leaders embraced socialism and industrial unionism. In 1905, leaders of the WFM, the Socialist party, and various radical groups gathered in Chicago to found the

Industrial Workers of the World (IWW). The IWW charter proclaimed bluntly, "The working class and the employing class have nothing in common. . . . Between these two classes a struggle must go on until the workers of the world unite as a class, take possession of the earth and the machinery of production, and abolish the wage system."

William D. "Big Bill" Haywood, an imposing, one-eyed, hard-rock miner, emerged as the most influential and flamboyant spokesman for the IWW, or Wobblies, as they were called. Haywood, a charismatic speaker and effective organizer, regularly denounced the conservative, craft consciousness of the AFL. He insisted that "society can be no better than its most miserable," and boasted that the IWW would exclude no one from its ranks. The Wobblies concentrated their efforts on miners, lumberjacks, sailors, "harvest stiffs," and other casual laborers. They glorified transient and unskilled workers in speeches and songs, aiming to counter their hopelessness and degradation. Openly contemptuous of bourgeois respectability, the IWW stressed the power of collective direct action on the job — strikes and, occasionally, sabotage.

The IWW briefly became a force among eastern industrial workers, tapping the rage and growing militance of the immigrants and unskilled. In 1909, an IWW-led steel strike at McKees Rocks, Pennsylvania, challenged the power of U.S. Steel. In the 1912 "Bread and Roses" strike in Lawrence, Massachusetts, IWW organizers turned a spontaneous walkout of textile workers into a successful struggle for union recognition. Wobbly leaders such as Haywood, Elizabeth Gurley Flynn, and Joseph Ettor showed that class-conscious rhetoric and multilingual appeals could forge unity among the ethnically diverse Lawrence work force of 25,000.

These battles gained the IWW a great deal of sympathy from radical intellectuals, along with public scorn from the AFL and employers' groups. The IWW failed to establish permanent organizations in the eastern cities, but it remained a force in the lumber camps, mines, and wheat fields of the west. In spite of its militant rhetoric, the IWW concerned itself with practical gains. "The final aim is revolution," said one Wobbly organizer, "but for the present let's see if we can get a bed to sleep in, water enough to take a bath in and decent food to eat." When the United States entered World War I, the Justice Department used the IWW's anticapitalist rhetoric and antiwar stance to crush it.

The occasional use of violence by union organizers sometimes backfired against the labor movement. On October 1, 1910, two explosions destroyed the printing plant of the *Los Angeles Times,* killing twenty-one workmen. When John and James McNamara, two brothers active in the ironworkers union, were charged with the bombing and indicted for murder, unionists of all political persuasions rallied to their defense. Leaders of the AFL, IWW, and Socialist party joined in a massive defense campaign that stressed the labor-versus-capital aspects of the case. They emphasized the strong antiunion stance of the *Times* and its influential owner, Harrison Gray Otis, noting that the paper had helped keep Los Angeles a largely nonunion city. On Labor Day 1911, as the trial approached, huge crowds in America's largest cities gathered to proclaim the McNamara brothers innocent. But they were guilty. In the middle of the trial, the McNamaras confessed to the dynamiting, shocking their many supporters. A Socialist candidate for mayor of Los Angeles, favored to win the election, was decisively defeated. And the city remained a nonunion stronghold.

Rebels in Bohemia

During the 1910s, a small but influential community of cultural radicals coalesced in the New York City neighborhood of Greenwich Village. These several hundred men and women, nearly all of middle-class background and hailing from provincial American towns, included painters, journalists, poets, social workers, lawyers, and political activists. They shared a deep sympathy toward the struggles of labor, a passion for modern art, and an openness to socialism and anarchism. "Village bohemians," especially the women among them, challenged the double standard of Victorian sexual morality, rejected traditional marriage and sex roles, advocated birth control, and experimented with homosexual relations. They became a powerful national symbol for rebellion and the merger of political and cultural radicalism.

Other American cities, notably Chicago at the turn of the century, had supported bohemian communities. The term *bohemian* came to mean anyone who had artistic or intellectual aspirations, and who lived with disregard for conventional rules of behavior. But the Village scene was unique, if fleeting. The Village offered cheap rents, studio space, and good ethnic restaurants, and it was close to the exciting political and labor activism of Manhattan's Lower East Side. *The Masses,* a monthly magazine begun in 1911 and edited by its founder, socialist critic Max Eastman, summed up the bohemian world view of the Village. "The broad purpose of *The Masses,*" wrote John Reed, one of its leading writers, "is a social one — to everlastingly attack old systems, old morals, old prejudices — the whole weight of out-

Joseph Stella, *Battle of Lights, Coney Island* (1913). Stella's painting of Coney Island met with harsh criticism when first exhibited, but it is now considered a classic example of American Futurist painting. Stella used the illusion of motion, abstracted form and color, and diagonal lines of force to capture the mood and energy at the nation's best known amusement park.

worn thought that dead men have saddled upon us.'' Regular contributors included radical labor journalist Mary Heaton Vorse, artists John Sloan and George Bellows, and writers Floyd Dell and Sherwood Anderson.

At private parties and public events, the Village brought together a wide variety of men and women looking to combine politics, art, and support for the labor movement. Birth control activist Margaret Sanger found a sympathetic audience, as did IWW leader Big Bill Haywood. Journalist Walter Lippmann lectured on the new psychological theory of Sigmund Freud. Anarchist and feminist Emma Goldman wooed financial supporters for her magazine *Mother Earth*. Photographer Alfred Stieglitz welcomed artists to his gallery-studio ''291.''

Greenwich Village took on different meanings for the various people who sought refuge there. For some it offered a chance to experiment with sexual relationships or work arrangements. For others it was an escape from small-town conformity or a haven for like-minded artists and activists. Yet the Village bohemians were united in their search for a new sense of community. Mary Heaton Vorse expressed their deeply pessimistic conviction that

modern American society could no longer satisfy the elemental needs of community. ''This is our weakness,'' she wrote. ''Our strength does not multiply in our daily lives. There is a creative force in people doing things together.'' Intellectuals and artists, as well as workers, were victims of alienation and sought shelter in the collective life and close-knit social relations offered by the Village community. ''The horror of capitalism,'' Walter Lippmann argued, ''is not alone in the poverty and suffering it entails, but in its ruthless denial of life to millions of men. The most cruel of all denials is to deprive a human being of joyous activity.''

The Paterson, New Jersey, silk workers' strike of 1913 provided the most memorable fusion of bohemian sensibility and radical activism. After hearing Haywood speak about the strike at Mabel Dodge's apartment, John Reed offered to organize a pageant on the strikers' behalf at Madison Square Garden. The idea was to publicize the strike to the world and also raise money. The Villagers helped write a script, designed sets and scenery, and took care of publicity. A huge crowd watched over a thousand workers reenact the strike, complete with picket line songs, a funeral, and speeches by IWW organizers Haywood and Elizabeth Gurley Flynn.

The spectacular production was an artistic triumph. One critic described the pageant as ''a new art form, a form in which the workers would present their own story without artifice or theatricality, and therefore with a new kind of dramatic power.'' But the pageant was also a financial disaster. Still, it suggested a powerful new way of combining artistic talent and vision with the labor struggles of the day. The Village bohemia lasted only a few years, a flame snuffed out by the chill political winds accompanying America's entry into World War I. But for decades Greenwich Village remained a mecca for young men and women searching for alternatives to conventional ways of living.

WOMEN'S MOVEMENTS AND BLACK AWAKENING

Progressive era women were at the forefront of several reform campaigns, such as the settlement house movement, prohibition, suffrage, and birth control. Millions of others took an active role in new women's associations that combined self-help and social mission. These organizations created a separate space for women in public life, gave women greater influence in civic affairs, and nurtured a new generation of female leaders.

In fighting racial discrimination, African Americans had a more difficult task. As racism gained ground in the political and cultural spheres, black progressives fought mostly defensive battles for equal rights. Still, they managed to produce leaders, ideas, and organizations that would have a long-range impact on American race relations.

The New Woman

The settlement house movement was just one of the new avenues of opportunity for Progressive era women. A steady proliferation of women's organizations attracted growing numbers of educated, middle-class women in the early twentieth century. Single-sex associations had existed throughout the nineteenth century, but their rapid expansion by the 1890s reflected the changing conditions of middle-class women. The middle-class home had lost many of its traditional productive functions, and was now more properly defined as a unit of consumption. With more men working in offices, with more children attending school, and with family size declining, it was also emptier. At the same time, more middle-class women were graduating from high school and college. In 1900, only 7 percent of Americans went to high school, but 60 percent of those who graduated were women. In 1870, 1 percent of college-age Americans had attended college; about 20 percent of these were women. By 1910 about 5 percent of college-age Americans attended college, but the proportion of women had doubled to 40 percent.

Single-sex clubs brought middle-class women into the public sphere by celebrating the distinctive strengths associated with women's culture: cooperation, uplift, service. The formation of the General Federation of Women's Clubs in 1890 brought together 200 local clubs representing 20,000 women. By 1900 the GFWC boasted 150,000 members, and by World War I it claimed to represent over a million women. The women's club movement combined an earlier focus on self-improvement and intellectual pursuits with newer benevolent efforts on behalf of working women and children. The Buffalo Union, for example, sponsored art lectures for housewives and classes in typing, stenography, and bookkeeping for young working women. It also maintained a library, set up a "noon rest" downtown where women could eat lunch, and ran a school for training domestics. In Chicago the Women's Club became a powerful ally for the reformers of Hull House. Club member Louise Bowen, a Hull House trustee, gave the settlement three-quarters of a million dollars. The Chicago Women's Club helped

settlement workers found the Legal Aid Society, the Public Art Association, and the Protective Agency for Women and Children.

For many middle-class women the club movement provided a new kind of female-centered community. As one member put it: "What college life is to the young woman, club life is to the woman of riper years, who amidst the responsibilities and cares of home life still wishes to keep abreast of the time, still longs for the companionship of those who, like herself, do not wish to cease to be students because they have left school." Club activity often led members to participate in other civic ventures, particularly "child-saving" reforms, such as child labor laws and mothers' pensions. Some took up the cause of working-class women, fighting for protective legislation and offering aid to trade unions. As wives and daughters of influential and well-off men in their communities, clubwomen had access to funds and could generate support for projects they undertook.

Other women's associations made even more explicit efforts to bridge class lines between middle-class homemakers and working-class women. The National Consumers League (NCL), started in 1898 by Maud Nathan and Josephine Lowell, sponsored a "white label" campaign in which manufacturers who met safety and sanitary standards could put NCL labels on their food and clothing. "It is the duty of consumers," Nathan argued, "to find out under what conditions the articles they purchase are produced and to insist that these conditions be at least decent." Under the dynamic leadership of Florence Kelley, the NCL took an even more aggressive stance by publicizing labor abuses in department stores and lobbying for maximum hour and minimum wage laws in state legislatures. In its efforts to protect home and housewife, worker and consumer, the NCL embodied the ideal of "social housekeeping." "The home does not stop at the street door," said Marion Talbot, dean of women at the University of Chicago in 1911. "It is as wide as the world into which the individual steps forth."

Birth Control

Another mass movement with crucial implications for the lives of women grew out of the Greenwich Village community of radicals. The phrase *birth control,* coined by Margaret Sanger around 1913, described her campaign to provide contraceptive information and devices for women. In 1910, Sanger was a thirty-year-old nurse and housewife living with her husband and three children in a New York City suburb. Excited by a socialist lecture she had

Margaret Sanger (second from left) is shown outside the first birth control clinic, which she founded in Brooklyn, New York, in 1916. Sanger campaigned tirelessly to educate working class women about contraception: she wrote and distributed pamphlets, lectured around the country, and invited arrest by publicly breaking obscenity laws. "Women cannot be on an equal footing with men," she wrote, "until they have full and complete control over their reproductive function."

attended, Sanger convinced her husband to move to the city, where she threw herself into the bohemian milieu. She became an organizer for the IWW, and in 1912 she wrote a series of articles on female sexuality for a socialist newspaper.

When postal officials confiscated the paper for violating obscenity laws, Sanger left for Europe to learn more about contraception. She returned to New York determined to challenge the obscenity statutes with her own magazine, *The Woman Rebel.* Sanger's journal celebrated female autonomy, including the right to sexual expression and control over one's body. When she distributed her pamphlet *Family Limitation,* postal inspectors confiscated copies and she found herself facing forty-five years in prison. In October 1914 she fled to Europe again. In her absence, anarchist agitator Emma Goldman and many women in the Socialist party took up the cause.

An older generation of feminists had advocated "voluntary motherhood," or the right to say no to a husband's sexual demands. The new birth control advocates embraced contraception as a way of advancing sexual freedom for middle-class women as well as responding to the misery of those working-class women who bore numerous children while living in poverty. Sanger returned to the U.S. in October 1915. After the government dropped the obscenity charges she embarked on a national speaking tour. In 1916 she again defied the law by opening a birth control clinic in a working-class neighborhood in Brooklyn and offering birth control information without a physician present. Arrested and jailed, she gained more publicity for her cru-

sade. Within a few years, birth control leagues and clinics could be found in every major city and most large towns in the country. Many thousands of women eagerly sought birth control information and services and defended the clinics from political attack.

Racism and Accommodation

At the turn of the century, African Americans remained clustered primarily in rural southern communities. Four-fifths of the nation's 10 million African Americans still lived in the South, most working in agriculture and at menial jobs in cities. The systematic disfranchisement of African American voters began in the 1890s and continued through the 1900s. Southern progressivism also institutionalized racial segregation in every public sphere. Schools, restaurants, streetcars, beaches, and theaters all became legally segregated in the southern states. Violence against African Americans, often on the flimsiest excuse, was on the rise. From 1882 to 1901 the annual number of lynchings usually exceeded 100, with a record 230 reported in 1892.

African Americans also endured a deeply racist popular culture that made hateful stereotypes of black people a normal feature of political debate and everyday life. White southern politicians and writers claimed that African Americans had undergone a natural "reversion to savagery" upon the end of slavery. Benjamin Tillman, a U.S. senator from South Carolina, denounced the African American as "a fiend, a wild beast, seeking whom he may devour." Thomas Dixon's popular novel *The Clans-*

man (1905) described the typical African American as "half child, half animal, the sport of impulse, whim, and conceit . . . a being who, left to his will, roams at night and sleeps in the day, whose speech knows no word of love, whose passions, once aroused, are as the fury of a tiger." In northern cities "coon songs," based on gross caricatures of black life, were extremely popular in theaters and as sheet music. As in the antebellum minstrel shows, these songs reduced African Americans to creatures of pure appetite — for food, sex, alcohol, and violence.

Amidst this political and cultural climate, Booker T. Washington won recognition as the most influential black leader of the day. Born a slave in 1856, Washington was educated at Hampton Institute in Virginia, one of the first freedmen's schools devoted to industrial education. In 1881 he founded Tuskegee Institute, a black school in Alabama devoted to industrial and moral education. He became the leading spokesman for racial accommodation, urging blacks to focus on economic improvement and self-reliance, as opposed to political and civil rights. In an 1895 speech delivered at the Cotton States Exposition in Atlanta, Washington outlined the key themes of accommodationist philosophy. "Cast down your buckets where you are," Washington told black people, meaning they should focus on improving their vocational skills as industrial workers and farmers. "In all things that are purely social," he told attentive whites, "we can be as separate as the fingers, yet one as the hand in all things essential to mutual progress."

Washington's message won him the financial backing of leading white philanthropists. His widely read autobiography, *Up From Slavery* (1901), stands as a classic narrative of an American self-made man. Written with a shrewd eye toward cementing his support among white Americans, it stressed the importance of learning values such as frugality, cleanliness, and personal morality. But Washington also gained a large following among African Americans, especially those who aspired to business success. With the help of Andrew Carnegie he founded the National Negro Business League to preach the virtue of black business development in black communities. Publicly he insisted that "agitation of questions of social equality is the extremest folly." But privately Washington also spent money and worked behind the scenes trying to halt disfranchisement and segregation.

Racial Justice and the NAACP

Washington's focus on economic self-help remained deeply influential in African American communities long after his death in 1915. But alternative black voices challenged his racial philosophy while he lived. One issue that galvanized protest was lynching. Lynching was not used exclusively against black people. In south Texas, for example, white mobs used lynching as a way of terrorizing Latino farm workers. But African Americans bore the great brunt of the steady increase in lynchings. After three black businessmen were lynched in Memphis in 1892, Ida B. Wells, young editor of a local black newspaper, vigorously denounced the outrage, blaming white business competitors of the victims. Her stand aroused the anger of local whites, who destroyed her office and forced the outspoken editor to leave the city.

Wells set out to investigate lynching in a systematic fashion. She paid special attention to the common defense of lynching — that it was a necessary response to attempts by black men to rape white women. Her 1895 pamphlet *A Red Record* showed that the vast majority of black lynching victims had not even been accused of rape. In fact, Wells showed, lynching was primarily a brutal device for eliminating African Americans who had become too prosperous or competed with white businesses. Wells created a one-woman crusade against lynching, lecturing across the country and in Europe, urging black people to break the silence about this awful crime. Wells's work also inspired the growth of a black women's club movement. The National Association of Colored Women, founded in 1896, provided a home for activist black women who had been excluded from the General Federation of Women's Clubs. United by a growing sense of racial pride, black women's clubs took up the antilynching cause and fought to protect black women from exploitation by white men and charges of moral looseness. Like white women's clubs, they also sponsored classes, recreation, welfare institutions, and public health campaigns in their local communities.

In the early 1900s, scholar and activist W. E. B. Du Bois created a significant alternative to Washington's leadership. A product of the black middle class, Du Bois had been educated at Fisk University and Harvard, where in 1895 he became the first African American to receive a Ph.D. His first book, *The Philadelphia Negro* (1899), was a pioneering work of social science that refuted racist stereotypes. In *The Souls of Black Folk* (1903), Du Bois declared prophetically that "the problem of the twentieth century is the problem of the color line." Through essays on black history, culture, education, and politics, Du Bois explored the concept of "double consciousness." Black people, he argued, would always feel the tension between an African heritage and their desire to assimilate as Americans.

Du Bois criticized Booker T. Washington's philosophy for its acceptance of "the alleged inferiority of the Negro." The black community, he argued, must fight for the right to vote, for civic equality, and for higher education for the "talented tenth" of their youth. In 1905 Du Bois and editor William Monroe Trotter brought together a group of educated black men to oppose Washington's conciliatory views. Discrimination they encountered in Buffalo, New York, prompted the men to move their meeting to Niagara Falls, Ontario. "Any discrimination based simply on race or color is barbarous," they declared. "Persistent manly agitation is the way to liberty." The Niagara movement protested legal segregation, the exclusion of blacks from labor unions, and the curtailment of voting and other civil rights.

The Niagara movement failed to generate much

change. But in 1909 many of its members, led by Du Bois, attended a National Negro Conference held at the Henry Street Settlement in New York. The group included a number of white progressives sympathetic to the idea of challenging Washington's philosophy. A new, interracial organization emerged from this conference, the National Association for the Advancement of Colored People. Du Bois, the only black officer of the original NAACP, founded and edited *The Crisis,* the influential NAACP monthly journal. For the next several decades the NAACP would lead struggles to overturn legal and economic barriers to equal opportunity.

NATIONAL PROGRESSIVISM

The progressive impulse had begun at local levels and percolated up. Progressive forces in both major political parties pushed older, entrenched elements to take a more aggressive stance on reform issues of the day. Both Republican Theodore Roosevelt and Democrat Woodrow Wilson laid claim to the progressive mantle during their presidencies. In their pursuit of reform agendas, both significantly reshaped the office of the president. As progressivism moved to Washington, American politics moved firmly into the twentieth century. Nationally organized interest groups and public opinion would begin to rival the influence of the old political parties in shaping the political landscape.

Theodore Roosevelt and Presidential Activism

The assassination of William McKinley in 1901 made forty-two-year-old Theodore Roosevelt the youngest man to hold the office of president before or since. Born to a moderately wealthy New York family in 1858, Roosevelt overcame a sickly childhood through strenuous physical exercise and rugged outdoor living. After graduating from Harvard he immediately threw himself into a career in the rough and tumble of New York politics. He won election to the state assembly, ran an unsuccessful campaign for mayor of New York, served as president of the New York City Board of Police Commissioners, and went to Washington as assistant secretary of the navy. During the Spanish-American War, he won national fame as leader of the Rough Rider regiment in Cuba. Upon his return, he was elected governor of New York and then in 1900 vice-president. Roosevelt viewed the presidency as a "bully pulpit" and aimed to make the most of it.

Although he had served a twenty-year apprenticeship in Republican politics, Roosevelt had always

In July 1905, a group of African American leaders met in Niagara Falls, Ontario, to protest legal segregation and the denial of civil rights to the nation's black population. This portrait was taken against a studio backdrop of the Falls. In 1909, the leader of the "Niagara Movement," W.E.B. DuBois (second from right, middle row) founded and edited *The Crisis,* the influential monthly journal of the National Association for the Advancement of Colored People (NAACP).

made party leaders nervous. He was a uniquely colorful figure, a shrewd publicist, and a creative politician. His three-year stint as a rancher in the Dakota Territory; his fondness for hunting and nature study; his passion for scholarship, which resulted in ten books before he became president — all these set "T.R." apart from most of his upper-class peers. Roosevelt preached the virtues of "the strenuous life," and he believed that educated and wealthy Americans had a special responsibility to serve, guide, and inspire those less fortunate.

In style, Roosevelt made key contributions to national progressivism. He knew how to inspire and guide public opinion. He stimulated discussion and aroused curiosity like no one before him. The young journalist Walter Lippmann spoke for many when he described Roosevelt as "the image of the great leader and the prototype of Presidents." In 1902 Roosevelt demonstrated his unique style of activism when he personally intervened in a bitter strike by anthracite coal miners. Using public calls for concili-ation, a series of White House bargaining sessions, and private pressure on the mineowners, Roosevelt secured a settlement that won better pay and work-ing conditions for the miners, but without recogni-tion of their union. Roosevelt also pushed for effi-cient government as the solution to social problems. Unlike most nineteenth-century Republicans, who had largely denied economic and social differences, Roosevelt frankly acknowledged them. Administra-tive agencies run by experts, he believed, could find rational solutions that could satisfy everyone.

Trust-Busting and Regulation

One of the first issues Roosevelt faced was growing public concern with the rapid business consolida-tions taking place in the American economy. In 1902 he directed the Justice Department to begin a series of prosecutions under the Sherman Anti-Trust Act. The first target was the Northern Securities Com-pany, a huge merger of transcontinental railroads brought about by financier J. P. Morgan. The deal would have created a giant holding company con-trolling nearly all the long-distance rail lines from Chicago to California. The Justice Department won the case all the way through a challenge before the Supreme Court. In *Northern Securities v. U.S.* (1904), the Court held that the stock transactions consti-tuted an illegal combination in restraint of interstate commerce.

This case established Roosevelt's reputation as a "trustbuster." During his two terms, the Justice

"The President's Dream," *Washington Post,* 1903. The cartoonist Clifford Berryman had previously depicted Theodore Roosevelt's refusal to shoot a small, de-fenseless bear while on a hunt, thereby creating the popular image of the "Teddy bear." Here, Berryman used the symbol to illustrate Roosevelt's own distinc-tion between "good trusts" (those open to govern-ment regulation) and "bad trusts" (those opposed to any government interference in business affairs).

Department filed forty-three cases under the Sher-man Anti-Trust Act to restrain or dissolve business monopolies. These included actions against the so-called tobacco and beef trusts and the Standard Oil Company. Roosevelt viewed these suits as nec-essary to publicize the issue and assert the federal government's ultimate authority over big business. But he did not really believe in the need to break up large corporations. Unlike many progressives, who were nostalgic for smaller companies and freer competition, Roosevelt accepted centralization as a fact of modern economic life. "This is an age of combination," he said in 1905, "and any effort to prevent all combination will not only be useless, but in the end vicious, because of the contempt for law which the failure to enforce law inevitably pro-duces."

Roosevelt considered government regulation the best way to deal with big business. After easily defeating Democrat Alton B. Parker in the 1904 election, Roosevelt felt more secure in pushing for regulatory legislation. In 1906 Roosevelt responded to public pressure for greater government intervention and, overcoming objections from a conservative Congress, three important measures. The Hepburn Act strengthened the Interstate Commerce Commission (ICC), established in 1887 as the first independent regulatory agency, by authorizing it to set maximum railroad rates and inspect financial records. The Pure Food and Drug Act established the Food and Drug Administration (FDA), which tested and approved drugs before they went on the market. The Meat Inspection Act (passed with help from the shocking publicity surrounding Upton Sinclair's muckraking novel *The Jungle*) empowered the Department of Agriculture to inspect and label meat products.

As a naturalist and outdoorsman, Roosevelt also believed in the need for government regulation of the natural environment. He worried about the destruction of forests, prairies, streams, and the wilderness. The conservation of forest and water resources, he argued, was a national problem of vital import. In 1905 he created the U.S. Forest Service and named conservationist Gifford Pinchot to head it. Pinchot recruited a force of forest rangers to manage the reserves. By 1909 total timber and forest reserves had increased from 45 to 195 million acres, and more than 80 million acres of mineral lands had been withdrawn from public sale. Roosevelt also sponsored a National Conservation Commission, which produced the first comprehensive study of the nation's mineral, water, forest, and soil resources.

Conservation, Preservation, and the Environment

On the broad issue of managing America's natural resources, the Roosevelt administration took the middle ground between preservation and unrestricted commercial development. Gifford Pinchot established the basic pattern of federal regulation based on a philosophy of "wise use" of forest reserves. "Wilderness is waste," Pinchot was fond of saying, reflecting an essentially utilitarian vision that balanced the demands of business with wilderness conservation. But other voices championed a more radical vision of conservation, emphasizing the preservation of wilderness lands against the encroachment of commercial exploitation. The most influential and committed of these was John Muir, an essayist and founder of the modern environmentalist movement. Muir made a passionate and spiritual defense of the inherent value of the American

wilderness. Wild country, he argued, had a mystical power to inspire and refresh. "Climb the mountains and get their good tidings," he advised. "Nature's peace will flow into you as the sunshine into the trees. The winds will blow their freshness into you, and the storms their energy, while cares will drop off like autumn leaves."

Muir had been a driving force behind the Yosemite Act of 1890. Yosemite Park, located in a valley amidst California's majestic Sierra Nevada range, became the nation's first preserve consciously designed to protect wilderness. Muir served as first president of the Sierra Club, founded in 1892 to preserve and protect the mountain regions of the West Coast, as well as Yellowstone National Park in Wyoming. Muir was a tireless publicist, and his writings won wide popularity among Americans, who were increasingly drawn to explore and enjoy the outdoors. By the turn of the century, misgivings about the effects of "overcivilization" and the association of untamed lands with the nation's frontier and pioneer past had attracted many to his thinking. As Muir put it, "Thousands of tired, nerve-shaken, over-civilized people are beginning to find out that going to the mountains is going home; that wildness is a necessity; and that mountain parks and reservations are useful not only as fountains of timber and irrigating rivers, but as fountains of life."

A bitter, drawn-out struggle over new water sources for San Francisco revealed the deep conflicts between conservationists, represented by Pinchot, and preservationists, represented by Muir. After the 1906 earthquake, San Francisco sought federal approval to dam and flood the spectacular Hetch Hetchy Valley, located 150 miles from the city in Yosemite National Park. The project promised to ease the city's chronic freshwater shortage and to generate hydroelectric power. To San Francisco's public officials and their sympathizers, the scenic beauty of the valley was, as Gifford Pinchot put it, "altogether unimportant compared with the benefits to be derived from its use as a reservoir." Conservationists and their urban progressive allies argued that developing Hetch Hetchy would be a victory for the public good over greedy private developers, since the plan called for municipal control of the water supply. To John Muir and the Sierra Club, Hetch Hetchy was a "temple" threatened with destruction by the "devotees of ravaging commercialism."

Both sides lobbied furiously in Congress and wrote scores of articles in newspapers and magazines. Congress finally approved the reservoir plan

Thomas Moran, *The Grand Canyon of the Yellowstone* (1872). While on an 1871 government expedition exploring the Rocky Mountains, Thomas Moran painted a series of striking watercolors depicting the Yellowstone country. Congress established Yellowstone as the first national park in 1872. Moran's paintings, along with the photographs of William H. Jackson, helped convince Congress of the uniqueness of Yellowstone's natural beauty.

in 1913; utility and public development triumphed over the preservation of nature. Although they lost the battle for Hetch Hetchy, the preservationists gained much ground in the larger campaign of alerting the nation to the dangers of a vanishing wilderness. A disappointed John Muir took some consolation from the fact that "the conscience of the whole country has been aroused from sleep." Defenders of national parks now realized that they could not make their case simply on scenic merit alone. They began to use their own utilitarian rationales, arguing that national parks would encourage economic growth through tourism and provide Americans with a healthy escape from urban and industrial areas. In 1916 the preservationists obtained their own bureaucracy in Washington with the creation of the National Park Service.

Republican Split

When he won reelection in 1904 Roosevelt proclaimed his support for a "Square Deal" for all people. He was still essentially a conservative who supported progressive reform as the best way to head off the potential of class war. "The friends of property, of order, of law," he warned "must realize that the surest way to provoke an explosion of wrong and injustice is to be shortsighted, narrow-minded, greedy, and arrogant." By the end of his second term, Roosevelt had moved beyond the idea of regulation to push for the most far-reaching federal economic and social programs ever proposed. He saw the central problem as "how to exercise . . . responsible control over the business use of vast wealth." To that end, he proposed restrictions on the use of court injunctions against labor strikes, an eight-hour day for federal employees, a worker compensation law, and federal income and inheritance taxes.

In 1908, Roosevelt kept his promise to retire after a second term. He chose Secretary of War William Howard Taft as his successor. Taft easily defeated Democrat William Jennings Bryan in the 1908 election. During Taft's presidency, the gulf between "insurgent" progressives and the "stand pat" wing split the Republican Party wide open. To some degree, the battles were as much over style as substance. Compared with Roosevelt, the reflective and judicious Taft brought a much more restrained concept of the presidency to the White House. He supported some progressive measures, including the amendment legalizing a graduated income tax (ratified in 1913), safety codes for mines and railroads, and the creation of a federal Children's Bureau. But in a series of bitter political fights involving tariff, antitrust, and conservation policies, Taft alienated Roosevelt and many other progressives.

After returning from an African safari and a triumphant European tour in 1910, Roosevelt threw himself back into national politics. He directly challenged Taft for the Republican party leadership. In a dozen bitter state presidential primaries (the first ever held) Taft and Roosevelt fought for the nomination. Although Roosevelt won most of these contests, the old guard still controlled the national convention and narrowly renominated Taft in June 1912. Roosevelt's supporters stormed out, and in August the new Progressive party nominated Roosevelt and Hiram Johnson of California as its presidential ticket. Roosevelt's "New Nationalism" presented a vision of a strong federal government, led by an activist president, regulating and protecting the various interests in American society. The platform called for woman suffrage, the eight-hour day, prohibition of child labor, minimum wage standards for working women, and stricter regulation of large corporations.

The Election of 1912

With the Republicans so badly divided, the Democrats sensed a chance for their first presidential victory in twenty years. They chose Governor Woodrow Wilson of New Jersey as their candidate. Although not nearly as well known nationally as Taft and Roosevelt, Wilson had built a strong reputation as a reformer. He had only recently entered professional politics. The son of a Virginia Presbyterian minister, Wilson spent most of his early career in academia. He earned a law degree at the University of Virginia and then a Ph.D. from John Hopkins. After teaching history and political science at several schools, he became president of Princeton University in 1902. In 1910, he won election as New Jersey's governor, running against the state Democratic machine. He won the Democratic nomination for president with the support of many of the party's progressives, including William Jennings Bryan.

Wilson declared himself and the Democratic party to be the true progressives. Viewing Roosevelt rather than Taft as his main rival, Wilson contrasted his "New Freedom" campaign with Roosevelt's New

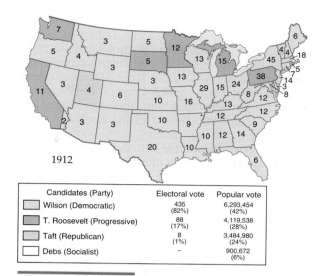

Candidates (Party)	Electoral vote	Popular vote
Wilson (Democratic)	435 (82%)	6,293,454 (42%)
T. Roosevelt (Progressive)	88 (17%)	4,119,538 (28%)
Taft (Republican)	8 (1%)	3,484,980 (24%)
Debs (Socialist)	–	900,672 (6%)

The Election of 1912

The split within the Republican Party allowed Woodrow Wilson to become only the second Democrat since the Civil War to be elected President. Eugene Debs's vote was the highest ever polled by a Socialist candidate.

Nationalism. Crafted largely by progressive lawyer Louis Brandeis, Wilson's platform was far more ambiguous than Roosevelt's. The New Freedom emphasized restoring conditions of free competition and equality of economic opportunity. "Ours is a program of liberty," Wilson said, "and theirs is a program of regulation." Wilson did favor a variety of progressive reforms for workers, farmers, and consumers. But in sounding older, nineteenth-century Democratic themes of states' rights and small government, Wilson argued against allowing the federal government to become as large and paternalistic as Roosevelt advocated. "What this country needs above everything else," Wilson argued, "is a body of laws which will look after the men who are on the make rather than the men who are already made."

Socialist party nominee Eugene Debs offered the fourth and most radical choice to voters. The Socialists had more than doubled their membership since 1908, to over 100,000. On election days Socialist strength was far greater than that, as the party's candidates attracted increasing numbers of voters. By 1912 more than a thousand Socialists held elective office in thirty-three states and 160 cities. Geographically, Socialist strength had shifted to the trans-Mississippi South and West. In Oklahoma, Texas, California, Oregon, and Washington, where industrial conflicts often provoked more violent repression, the Socialist vote doubled and tripled between 1904 and 1912. Debs had been a national figure in American politics since the 1890s and he had already run for president three times. An inspiring orator who drew large and sympathetic crowds wherever he spoke, Debs proved especially popular in areas with strong labor movements and populist traditions. Debs and the Socialists could also take credit for pushing both Roosevelt and Wilson further toward the Left. Both the Democratic and Progressive party platforms contained proposals considered extremely radical only ten years earlier.

In the end, the divisions in the Republican party gave the election to Wilson. He won easily, polling 6.3 million votes to Roosevelt's 4.1 million. Taft came in third with 3.5 million. Eugene Debs won 900,000 votes, 6 percent of the total, for the strongest Socialist showing in American history. Even though he won with only 42 percent of the popular vote, Wilson swept the electoral college with 435 votes to Roosevelt's 88 and Taft's 8, giving him the largest electoral majority ever to that time. In several respects, the election of 1912 was the first "modern" presidential race. It featured the first direct primaries, challenges to traditional party loyalties, an issue-oriented campaign, and a high degree of interest group activity. It thus resembled the election of 1980 more than that of 1896.

Woodrow Wilson's First Term

As president, Wilson followed Roosevelt's lead in expanding the activist dimensions of the office. He became more responsive to pressure for a greater federal role in regulating business and the economy. This pressure came from hundreds of local and national reform groups, Washington-based lobbys, and the new Progressive party. With the help of a Democratic-controlled Congress, Wilson pushed through a significant battery of reform proposals. By 1916 his reform program looked more like the New Nationalism than the New Freedom. Four legislative achievements in Wilson's first term stand out.

The Underwood-Simmons Act of 1913 substantially reduced tariff duties on a variety of raw materials and manufactured goods, including wool, sugar, agricultural machinery, shoes, iron, and steel. Taking advantage of the newly ratified Sixteenth Amendment, it also imposed the first graduated tax (up to 6 percent) on personal incomes. The Federal Reserve Act that same year restructured the nation's banking and currency system. It created twelve Federal Reserve Banks regulated by a central board in Washington. By giving central direction to banking and monetary policy, the Federal Reserve Board diminished the power of large private banks.

Wilson also supported the Clayton Anti-Trust Act of 1914, which replaced the old Sherman Act of 1890 as the nation's basic antitrust law. Clayton reflected the growing political clout of the American Federation of Labor. It exempted unions from being construed as illegal combinations in restraint of trade and it forbade federal courts to issue injunctions against strikers. But Wilson adopted the view that permanent federal regulation was necessary for checking the abuses of big business. The Federal Trade Commission (FTC), established in 1914, sought to give the federal government the same sort of regulatory control over corporations that the ICC had over railroads. The FTC would provide a method for doing this superior to trust-busting. Wilson's hope that the FTC would usher in an era of harmony between government and business recalled the aims of Roosevelt and his big business backers in 1912.

On social issues, Wilson proved more cautious in his first two years. His initial failure to support federal child labor legislation and rural credits to farm banks angered many progressives. A southerner, Wilson also sanctioned the spread of racial segregation in federal offices. "I would say," he explained in 1913, "that I do approve of the segregation that is being attempted in several of the departments." As the reelection campaign of 1916 approached, Wilson worried about defections from the labor and social justice wings of his party. He proceeded to support a rural credits act providing government capital to federal farm banks, as well as federal aid to agricultural extension programs in schools. He also came out in favor of child labor reform and a worker compensation bill for federal employees. But by 1916 the dark cloud of the European War had already begun to cast its long shadow over progressive reform.

Conclusion

The American political and social landscape was significantly different in 1916 than 1900. These changes reflected the tensions and ambiguities of progressivism itself. Nearly every new election law had the effect of excluding some people from voting

CHRONOLOGY

1889	Jane Addams founds Hull House in Chicago
1890	Jacob Riis, *How the Other Half Lives*
1895	Booker T. Washington addresses Cotton States Exposition in Atlanta Lillian Wald establishes Henry Street Settlement in New York
1898	Florence Kelley becomes general secretary of National Consumers League
1900	Robert M. La Follette elected governor of Wisconsin
1901	Theodore Roosevelt succeeds the assassinated William McKinley as president
1902	Lincoln Steffens, *The Shame of the Cities*
1905	President Roosevelt creates U.S. Forest Service and names Gifford Pinchot head
1906	Upton Sinclair, *The Jungle* Congress passes Pure Food and Drug Act and Meat Inspection Act and establishes Food and Drug Administration (FDA)
1908	In *Muller v. Oregon* Supreme Court upholds a state law limiting maximum hours for working women
1909	Founding of the National Association for the Advancement of Colored People (NAACP)
1911	Triangle Shirtwaist Company fire kills 146 garment workers in New York City *The Masses* magazine begun by socialist Max Eastman
1912	Democrat Woodrow Wilson wins presidency, defeating Republican William H. Taft, Progressive Theodore Roosevelt, and Socialist Eugene V. Debs "Bread and Roses" strike involves 25,000 textile workers in Lawrence, Massachusetts
1913	Sixteenth Amendment, legalizing a graduated income tax, is ratified Margaret Sanger begins writing and speaking in support of birth control for women
1914	Passage of Clayton Anti-Trust Act Establishment of the Federal Trade Commission (FTC) Ludlow Massacre
1917	Congress passes Eighteenth Amendment, prohibiting the manufacture and sale of alcoholic beverages; ratified in 1919

while including others. For African Americans, progressivism largely meant disfranchisement from voting altogether. Direct primary laws eliminated some of the most blatant abuses of big-city machines, but they also left party leaders in substantial control of candidate selection. In cities and states dominated by one party, the majority party's primary effectively decided the general election. Stricter election laws made it more difficult for third parties to get on the ballot. Voting itself steadily declined in these years.

Overall, party voting became a less important form of political participation. Interest group activity, congressional and statehouse lobbying, and direct appeals to public opinion gained currently as ways of influencing government. Business groups such as the National Association of Manufacturers and individual trade associations were among the most active groups pressing their demands on government. Political action often shifted from legislatures to the new administrative agencies and commissions created to deal with social and economic problems. Politicians such as Theodore Roosevelt cultivated public opinion outside the old party circles, as did numerous reform organizations and interest groups. Popular magazines and journals grew significantly in both number and circulation, becoming more influential in shaping and appealing to national public opinion.

Social progressives and their allies could point to significant improvements in the everyday lives of ordinary Americans. On the state level, real advances had been made through a range of social legislation covering working conditions, child labor, minimum wages, and worker compensation. Social progressives, too, had discovered the power of organizing into extraparty lobbying groups such as the National Consumers League and the National Woman Suffrage Association. Yet the tensions between fighting for social justice and the urge toward social control remained unresolved. The emphasis on efficiency, uplift, and rational administration often collided with humane impulses to aid the poor, the immigrant, the slum dweller. The large majority of African Americans, blue-collar workers, and urban poor remained untouched by federal assistance programs.

In communities all over the nation progressives had succeeded in setting new agendas for reform. Using varied means and sometimes working for conflicting ends, progressives had tried to confront the new realities of urban and industrial society. What had begun as a discrete collection of local and state struggles had by 1912 come to redefine state and national politics. Politics itself had been transformed by the calls for social justice. Federal and state power would now play a more decisive role than ever in shaping work, play, and social life in local communities. That there was so much contention over the "true meaning" of progressivism is but one measure of its defining role in shaping early-twentieth-century America.

Additional Readings

PAUL M. BOYER, *Urban Masses and Moral Order in America, 1820–1920* (1978). Contains useful material on the social control side of progressivism.

JOHN D. BUENKER, *Urban Liberalism and Progressive Reform* (1973). Explores the contributions of urban ethnic voters and machine-based politicians to the progressive movement.

JOHN D. BUENKER, JOHN C. BURNHAM, and ROBERT M. CRUNDEN, *Progressivism* (1977). Reviews the large scholarly output on the subject and emphasizes the diversity within progressivism.

ELLEN CHESLER, *Woman of Valor: The Life of Margaret Sanger* (1992). The definitive biography of the birth control pioneer.

JOHN M. COOPER, JR., *The Pivotal Decades: The United States, 1900–1920* (1990). A good overview focusing on American political history of the era, with special attention to the national scene.

ROBERT M. CRUNDEN, *Ministers of Reform: The Progressives' Achievement in American Civilization, 1889–1920* (1982). Emphasizes the moral and religious traditions of middle-class Protestants as the core of the progressive ethos.

ALLEN F. DAVIS, *Spearheads of Reform: The Social Settlements and the Progressive Movement, 1890–1914.* Focuses on the influence of the settlement house movement on progressive reform.

ALLEN F. DAVIS, *American Heroine: The Life and Legend of Jane Addams* (1973). The standard biography of this central figure of the Progressive era.

MELVYN DUBOFSKY, *We Shall Be All: A History of the Industrial Workers of the World* (1969). The best overview of this radical labor group.

LOUIS FILLER, *The Muckrakers* (rev. ed., 1980). Offers a useful synthesis of these influential journalists.

LESLIE FISHBEIN, *Rebels in Bohemia* (1982). Surveys the people and causes clustered around *The Masses* magazine and Greenwich Village.

SUSAN A. GLENN, *Daughters of the Shtetl: Life and Labor in the Immigrant Generation* (1990). A sensitive analysis of the experiences of immigrant Jewish women in the garment trades.

DEWEY GRANTHAM, *Southern Progressivism: The Reconciliation of Progress and Tradition* (1983). Examines the contradictions within the southern progressive tradition.

JAMES R. GREEN, *The World of the Worker: Labor in Twentieth-Century America* (1980). Includes a fine overview of life and work in company towns and urban ghettos in the early twentieth century.

LOUIS HARLAN, *Booker T. Washington: The Wizard of Tuskegee, 1901–1915* (1983). The most comprehensive analysis of Washington's thought, leadership, and influence.

Arthur Link and Richard L. McCormick, *Progressivism* (1983). The best recent overview of progressivism and electoral politics.

Roderick Nash, *Wilderness and the American Mind* (1967). Contains good material on John Muir, the Hetch Hetchy controversy, and the intellectual origins of environmentalism.

David W. Noble, ed., *The Progressive Mind* (rev. ed., 1981). A compendium of important strains in progressive thought.

Kathy Peiss, *Cheap Amusements: Working Women and Leisure in Turn-of-the-Century New York* (1986). Explores how working-class women both shaped and were shaped by new forms of commercial leisure.

Ruth Rosen, *The Lost Sisterhood: Prostitutes in America, 1900–1918* (1982). Examines prostitution from the perspectives of both prostitutes and reformers.

Nick Salvatore, *Eugene V. Debs: Citizen and Socialist* (1982). The best biography of America's most important socialist leader.

David P. Thelen, *Robert M. La Follette and the Insurgent Spirit* (1976). The best analysis of this pivotal midwestern progressive leader.

James Weinstein, *The Corporate Ideal in the Liberal State, 1900–1918* (1969). Emphasizes the important role of business leaders in various reform movements.

Richard White, *"It's Your Misfortune and None of My Own": A History of the American West* (1991). Contains excellent material on progressive politics in the West.

Robert Wiebe, *The Search for Order, 1877–1920* (1967). A pathbreaking study of how the professional middle classes responded to the upheavals of industrialism and urbanization.

Nancy Woloch, *Women and the American Experience* (1984). Includes excellent material on women's crucial contributions to progressive reform, as well as an analysis of the larger changes in women's public and private lives during this period.

22 WORLD WAR I, 1914–1920

• MILWAUKEE GOES TO WAR; VICTOR BERGER GOES TO CONGRESS

As the Sixty-sixth Congress — the first since the end of "the Great War" — prepared to convene in May 1919, one issue took precedence over all others. Should the House allow the feisty Victor Berger to take his seat? As a prominent voice of the Socialist party and editor of the **Milwaukee Leader,** Berger had vigorously opposed American involvement in the European War. In 1917 the Postmaster General had shut down the Leader as a "disloyal publication," and Berger was sentenced to twenty years in prison for violating the recently passed Espionage Act. While appealing his conviction, Berger won election to Congress from Milwaukee's Fifth District. Although the war had ended, the deep passions it had aroused about

WORLD WAR I DIVIDES AND UNITES AN AMERICAN CITY

loyalty and "Americanism" burned hotter than ever. In the House, member after member rose to denounce Berger, and cities around the nation held anti-Berger rallies. One congressman called his defense "the untrue, unjust, unpatriotic, un-American ravings of one who would destroy our system of government."

After weeks of hearings the House voted that Victor Berger was ineligible to serve in the Congress because he had given "comfort to the enemy" during the war. Only one congressman opposed the otherwise unanimous vote. Berger steadfastly refused to retract anything, insisting he was being punished for his membership in the Socialist party rather than for any disloyal acts. As a self-proclaimed "spokesman of evolutionary Socialism," Berger warned that throwing out legal elections could only give comfort to more radical Socialists, such as the Bolsheviks who had recently seized power in Russia. "It is fundamentally a question whether representative government and political action are to be thrown to the scrapheap as inadequate," he said.

Berger's struggle to be seated in Congress and Milwaukee's World War I experience were microcosms of how the conflict divided American communities and the nation as a whole. A manufacturing and port city on Lake Michigan, Milwaukee had won a reputation as a well-run, efficient, progressive, and "Europeanized" city. Half of its nearly 500,000 people were of German descent, and the city boasted a vibrant German-language culture that included German newspapers, theaters, clubs, and music societies. There were

George Luks. Armistice Night. 1918. Oil on canvas, 37 × 68-3/4 in. (94 × 174.6 cm). Gift of an anonymous donor. Whitney Museum of American Art, New York.

Milwaukee Socialists Victor Berger (far left), with Mr. and Mrs. Emil Seidel. In the first two decades of the century, hundreds of socialists won election to state and local offices, especially in the Midwest. Berger was elected to Congress on the Socialist party ticket and Seidel became Milwaukee's first Socialist mayor.

smaller pockets of Poles, Russian Jews, Czechs, and Italians as well. The city had voted for Democrat Woodrow Wilson for president in 1912 and 1916, but Socialists controlled local politics.

The coming of war to Europe brought enormous concerns about the loyalties of "hyphenated" Americans. Thousands of Milwaukee residents belonged to the National German-American Alliance, founded in 1901 to promote the interests of German communities around the nation. In the first week of March 1916, 175,000 Milwaukeeans attended an Alliance sponsored relief bazaar that raised $150,000 for German, Austrian, and Hungarian victims of the war. When German sympathizers criticized President Wilson for favoring Great Britain, the Milwaukee Journal, the city's largest newspaper, began a relentless campaign attacking pro-German sentiment. The Journal vigorously supported preparedness for war, and it printed testimonials from loyal German-Americans to prove that Milwaukee was a "real American community."

Socialists, too, immediately came under suspicion for their longtime opposition to the war. They had been in the forefront of peace groups working to stave off the growing war fever. Berger criticized the Europan war in the pages of the Leader *as a capitalist war*, "of no concern to the good people of Milwaukee and to the country at large." In February, 1917 Berger presided over an anti-interventionist demonstration of 4,000 socialists and non-socialists in Milwaukee. "There are many Americans," he told the crowd, "who will protest against the war because America has nothing to gain and a great deal to lose. We are bound to lose lives, civil liberties and money."

Precisely for these reasons, the wartime pressures for conformity were especially strong in Milwaukee. The head of the Wisconsin Defense League adamantly declared in 1917 that Milwaukee "must not, and shall not, subscribe, or be accused of subscribing, to any doctrine that does not venerate the constitution, love the flag, and keep step to the music of the Union." Milwaukee's chapter of the American Protective League, loosely affiliated with the Justice Department, claimed it investigated 10,000 enemy aliens during the war and made 2,400 reports of sedition. Milwaukee's Loyalty Legion pressured the school board to ban the teaching of German, and it shut down German theaters and music halls.

At the same time, Milwaukee was the first large city to complete its draft registration under the Selective Service law. Its Liberty Loan drives raised more than $122 million in bonds to help finance the war. The Socialist mayor, Daniel Hoan, threw himself into organizing the activities of the Milwaukee Council of Defense: staging going-away parties for soldiers; organizing Liberty Loan rallies; handling food shortages and emergency relief; setting up a labor board to mediate industrial disputes. Hoan, who remained in office for twenty-four years, saw the war as an opportunity to further his goal of making municipal government more directly responsive to the needs of its citizens. The Federated Trades Council now embraced patriotism and war bond drives and drifted away from its Socialist ties from before the war. Wartime Americanization programs put German Americans on the defensive: many changed their names, and the once flourishing German cultural institutions declined.

As in many other cities, the war proved a boon to the local economy. Milwaukee manufacturers filled over $50 million in defense contracts. The war brought great demands for the city's steel, heavy machinery, packed meat, and leather products. Milwaukee's famous breweries and malt houses gained access to new markets formerly supplied by Germany. Wartime orders increased the value of manufactured products by over 150 percent in just four years.

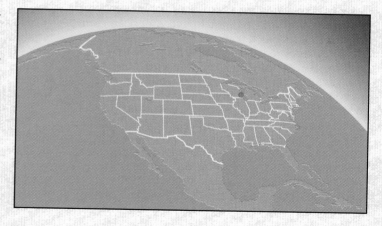

In a special 1919 election to fill the vacant congressional seat, Milwaukee voters again elected Berger. He drew support from Socialists, German Americans, and thousands of other voters who admired his spirit. Milwaukee's largest newspaper, the Journal, thought the district "declared itself against the United States." In January 1920, Congress refused to seat Berger a second time. But the Supreme Court threw out his Espionage Act conviction on a technicality, and in 1923 Berger at last took his seat in the House. He was by then only a fading reminder of the powerful political emotions aroused by the United States entry into World War I.

A NEW WORLD POWER

In the first years of the new century the United States pursued a more vigorous and aggressive foreign policy than it had in the past. Presidents Theodore Roosevelt, William Howard Taft, and Woodrow Wilson all contributed to "progressive diplomacy," in which commercial expansion was backed by a growing military presence in the Caribbean, Asia, and Mexico. At root, this was a view of world affairs that stressed moralism, order, and a special, even God-given, role for the United States. By 1917, when the U.S. entered the Great War, this policy had already secured the country's place as a new world power.

Roosevelt: The Big Stick

Theodore Roosevelt left a strong imprint on the nation's foreign policy. Like many of his class and background, T.R. took for granted the superiority of Protestant Anglo-American culture and the goal of spreading its values and influence. To avoid falling into "a life of slothful ease," he preached, Americans needed to pursue "the strenuous life." Similarly, to maintain and increase its economic and political stature, America must be militarily strong. In 1900 Roosevelt summarized his activist views, declaring, "I have always been fond of the West African proverb, 'Speak softly and carry a big stick, you will go far.'"

Roosevelt brought the "big stick" approach to several disputes in the Caribbean region. Since the 1880s, several British, French, and American companies had pursued various plans for building a canal across the Isthmus of Panama, thereby connecting the Atlantic and Pacific oceans. The canal was a top priority for Roosevelt, and he tried to negotiate a leasing agreement with Colombia, of which Panama was a province. But when the Colombian Senate rejected a final American offer in the fall of 1903, Roosevelt invented a new strategy. A combination of native forces and foreign promoters associated with the canal project plotted a revolt against Colombia. Roosevelt kept in touch with at least one leader of the revolt, Philippe Bunau-Varilla, an engineer and agent for the New Panama Canal Company, and the president let him know that U.S. warships were steaming toward Panama.

On November 3, 1903, just as the USS Nashville arrived in Colón harbor, the province of Panama declared itself independent of Colombia. America immediately recognized the new Republic of Panama. Less than two weeks later, Bunau-Varilla, serving as a minister from Panama, signed a treaty

President Theodore Roosevelt poses at the controls of a steam shovel during his 1906 inspection tour of the Panama Canal. This widely circulated photograph reinforced Roosevelt's image as an empire builder, and it demonstrated his flair for publicity. The trip to Panama made TR the first president to leave the United States while in office.

granting the U.S. full sovereignty in perpetuity over a ten-mile-wide canal zone. America guaranteed Panama's independence and agreed to a down payment of $10 million and a regular installment of $250,000 per year. Years after the canal was completed, the U.S. Senate voted another $25 million to Colombia as compensation.

The Panama Canal was a triumph of modern engineering and gave the U.S. a tremendous strategic and commercial advantage in the Western Hemisphere. The actual building of the canal took eight years and hundreds of lives of badly paid manual workers. The U.S. avoided the failure of earlier attempts at canal building by using better equipment and mounting a vigorous campaign against disease. Army colonel William Gorgas guided a drainage project that protected many more of the largely imported Caribbean laborers from the ill effects of fever-bearing mosquitoes. Finally, in 1914, after $720 million in construction costs, the first merchant ships sailed through the canal.

"The inevitable effect of our building the Canal," wrote Secretary of State Elihu Root in 1905, "must be to require us to police the surrounding premises." As a former police commissioner of New York City, Roosevelt agreed with the necessity for "proper policing of the world." He was especially concerned that European powers might step in if America did not. In 1903 Great Britain, Germany, and Italy had imposed a blockade on Venezuela in a dispute over debt payments owed to private investors. To prevent armed intervention by the Europeans, Roosevelt proclaimed what became known as the Roosevelt Corollary to the Monroe Doctrine. "Chronic wrongdoing, or an impotence which results in a general loosening of the ties of civilized society," the statement read, justified "the exercise of an international police power" anywhere in the hemisphere. Roosevelt invoked the corollary to justify U.S. intervention in the region, beginning with the Dominican Republic in 1905. To counter the protests of European creditors (and the implied threat of armed intervention), Washington assumed management of the Dominican debt and customs services. Roosevelt and later presidents cited the corollary to justify armed intervention in the internal affairs of Cuba, Haiti, Nicaragua, and Mexico.

With the outbreak of the Russo-Japanese War in 1904, Roosevelt worried about the future of the Open Door policy in Asia. That policy had been formulated by Secretary of State John Hay in 1899. Japan and the western European powers had carved much of China into spheres of influence, in which individual nations enjoyed economic dominance. Since the U.S. was a latecomer to the potentially lucrative China market, Hay sought guarantees of equal investment opportunities for American commercial interests in China. In a series of diplomatic notes Hay won approval for the so-called Open Door approach, giving all nations equal access to trading and development rights in China. A total victory by Russia or Japan could upset the balance of power in the Far East and threaten American business enterprises. Roosevelt became especially concerned after the Japanese scored a series of military victories over Russia and began to loom as a dominant power in the Pacific.

Roosevelt mediated a settlement of the Russo-Japanese War at Portsmouth, New Hampshire, in 1905 (for which he was awarded the 1906 Nobel Peace Prize). In this settlement, Japan won recognition of its dominant position in Korea and consolidated its economic and territorial control over Manchuria. Yet American-Japanese relations remained strained over repeated outbursts of anti-Japanese racism in California — a nativist response to the "yellow peril" — which angered Japan. Roosevelt

built up American naval strength in the Pacific, and in 1908 he sent battleships to visit Japan in a muscle-flexing display of sea power. But in that same year, the two burgeoning Pacific powers reached a reconciliation. The Root-Takahira Agreement affirmed the territorial status quo in Asia and the Open Door trade policy in China.

Taft: Dollar Diplomacy

Roosevelt's successor, William Howard Taft, believed he could replace the military Big Stick with the more subtle and effective weapon of business investment. Taft and his secretary of state, corporate lawyer Philander C. Knox, followed a strategy (called "dollar diplomacy" by critics) in which they assumed that political influence would follow increased U.S. trade. As Taft explained in 1910, he advocated "active intervention to secure for our merchandise and our capitalists opportunity for profitable investment." Although he had hoped to substitute "dollars for bullets," Taft discovered the limits of this approach in both the Caribbean and Asia.

Overall American investment in Central America grew rapidly, from $41 million in 1908 to $93 million by 1914. Most of this money went into railroad construction, mining, and plantations. The United Fruit Company alone owned about 160,000 acres of land in the Caribbean by 1913. But dollar diplomacy ended up requiring military support, and the Taft administration sent the navy and the marines to intervene in political disputes in Honduras and Nicaragua. In both cases, U.S. military power propped up political factions pledged to protect American business interests. A contingent of U.S. Marines remained in Nicaragua until 1923. The economic and political structures of Honduras and Nicaragua were controlled by both the dollar and the bullet.

In China, Taft and Knox pressed for a greater share of the pie for U.S. investors. They gained a place for U.S. bankers in the European consortium building the massive new Hu-kuang Railways in southern and central China. But Knox blundered by attempting to "neutralize" the existing railroads in China. He tried to secure a huge international loan for the Chinese government that would allow it to buy up all the foreign railways and develop new ones. Knox ignored the fact that railway development had been the historical key to foreign intervention in China. Both Russia and Japan, which had fought wars over their railroad interests in Manchuria, resisted this plan as a threat to the arrangements hammered out at Portsmouth with the help of

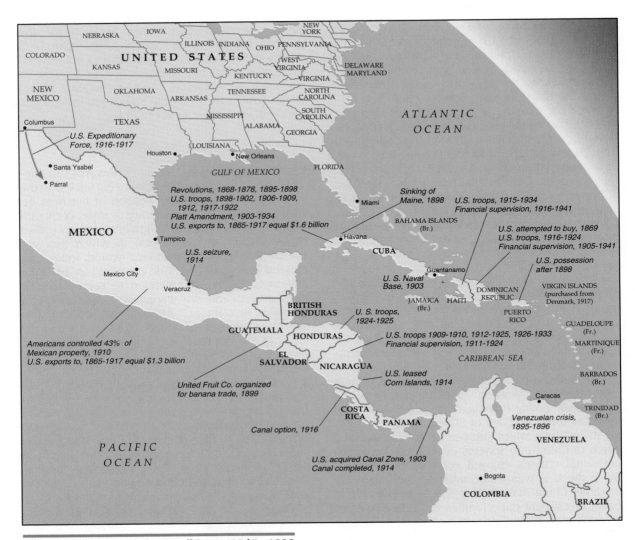

The United States in the Carribbean, 1865—1933

An overview of U.S. economic and military involvement in the Carribbean during the late nineteenth and early twentieth centuries. Victory in the Spanish American War, the Panama Canal project, and rapid economic investment in Mexico and Cuba all contributed to a permanent and growing U.S. military presence in the region.

Theodore Roosevelt. The "neutralization" scheme pushed by Knox, and the U.S. support for the Chinese Nationalists in their 1911 revolt against the ruling Manchu dynasty, prompted Japan to sign a new friendship treaty with Russia. The Open Door to China was now effectively closed, and American relations with Japan began a slow deterioration that ended in war thirty years later.

Wilson: Moralism and Realism

Right after he took office in 1913, President Woodrow Wilson observed that "it would be the irony of fate if my administration had to deal chiefly with foreign affairs." As it turned out, Wilson had to face international crises from his first day in office. These were of a scope and complexity unprecedented in U.S. history. Wilson had no experience in diplomacy, but he brought to foreign affairs a set of fundamental principles that combined a moralist's faith in American democracy with a realist's understanding of the power of international commerce. He believed that American economic expansion, accompanied by democratic principles and Christianity, was a civilizing force in the world. "Our industries," he told the Democratic National Convention in 1912, "have expanded to such a point that they will burst their jackets if they cannot find a free outlet to the markets of the world. . . . Our domestic markets no longer suffice. We need foreign markets.''

Wilson, like most corporate and political leaders of the day, emphasized foreign investments and industrial exports as the keys to the nation's prosperity. ''There is nothing in which I am more interested,'' he told a National Foreign Trade Convention in 1914, ''than the fullest development of the trade of this country and its righteous conquest of foreign markets.'' Wilson believed that the U.S., with its superior industrial efficiency, could achieve supremacy in world commerce if artificial barriers to free trade were removed. He championed and extended the Open Door Policy of John Hay, advocating strong diplomatic and military measures ''for making ourselves supreme in the world from an economic point of view.'' Wilson often couched his vision of a dynamic, expansive American capitalism in terms of a moral crusade. As he put it in a speech to a congress of salesmen, ''[Since] you are Americans and are meant to carry liberty and justice and the principles of humanity wherever you go, go out and sell goods that will make the world more comfortable and more happy, and convert them to the principles of America.'' Yet he quickly found that the complex realities of power politics could interfere with moral vision.

Wilson's policies toward Mexico, which foreshadowed the problems he would encounter in World War I, best illustrate his difficulties. The 1911 Mexican Revolution had overthrown the brutally corrupt dictatorship of Porfirio Diaz, and popular leader Francisco Madero had won wide support by promising democracy and economic reform for millions of landless peasants. U.S. businessmen, however, were nervous about the future of their investments, which totaled over $1 billion. This was greater than Mexico's own investment and more than all other foreign investment in that country combined. Wilson at first gave his blessing to the revolutionary movement, expressed regret over the Mexican War of 1846–48, and disavowed any interest in another war. ''I have constantly to remind myself,'' he told a friend, ''that I am not the servant of those who wish to enhance the value of their Mexican investments.''

But right before he took office, Wilson was stunned by the ousting and murder of Madero by his chief lieutenant, General Victoriano Huerta. Other nations, including Great Britain and Japan, recognized the Huerta regime, but Wilson refused. He announced that the U.S. would support only such governments as rested upon the rule of law. An armed opposition to Huerta, known as the Constitutionalists and led by Venustiano Carranza, emerged in northern Mexico. Wilson tried to broker a compromise between the two factions, but both sides refused. Carranza, an ardent nationalist, pressed for the right to buy U.S. arms, which he won in 1914. Wilson also isolated Huerta diplomatically by persuading the British to withdraw their support in exchange for American guarantees of English property interests in Mexico.

But Huerta stubbornly remained in power. In

Mexican revolutionary leaders and sometime allies Francisco ''Pancho'' Villa (center) and Emiliano Zapata (right) are shown at the National Palace in Mexico City, c.1916. Zapata's army operated out of a base in the southern agricultural state of Morelos, while Villa's army controlled large portions of Mexico's north. In 1914 Villa captured the imagination of American reformers, journalists, and movie makers with his military exploits against the oppressive Huerta regime. But in 1916, after several border clashes with U.S. military units, President Wilson dispatched a punitive expedition in pursuit of Villa.

April 1914 Wilson used a minor insult to U.S. sailors in Tampico as an excuse to invade. American naval forces bombarded and then occupied the port of Veracruz, the main entry for arms shipments to Huerta. The battle, which killed 19 Americans and 126 Mexicans, brought the two countries close to war and set off anti-American demonstrations in Mexico and throughout Latin America. Wilson accepted the offer of the ABC Powers — Argentina, Brazil, and Chile — to mediate the dispute. Mexico rejected a plan to replace Huerta with a provisional government, but Carranza managed to overthrow Huerta in August. Far from expressing gratitude, Carranza himself denounced Wilson's intervention and played to nationalist sentiment. He refused Wilson's advice on setting up a new government and threatened to confiscate U.S. business properties.

As war loomed in Europe, Wilson found himself frustrated by his inability to control Mexico's complex revolutionary politics. For a brief period Wilson threw his support behind Pancho Villa, Carranza's former ally who now led a rebel army of his own in the north. But Carranza defeated Villa's army, and in October 1915, with more attention being given to the war in Europe, the Wilson administration finally recognized Carranza as Mexico's de facto president. Meanwhile Pancho Villa, feeling betrayed, turned on the U.S. and tried to provoke a crisis that might draw Washington into war with Mexico. Villa led several raids in Mexico and across the border in early 1916 that killed a few dozen Americans. The man once viewed by Wilson as a fighter for democracy was now dismissed as a dangerous bandit.

In March 1916, enraged by Villa's defiance, Wilson dispatched General John J. Pershing and an army that eventually numbered 15,000. For a year, Pershing's troops chased Villa in vain, penetrating 300 miles into Mexico. The invasion made Villa a symbol of national resistance in Mexico, and his army grew from 500 men to 10,000 by the end of 1916. Villa's effective hit-and-run guerrilla tactics kept the U.S. forces at bay. A frustrated General Pershing complained that he felt "just a little bit like a man looking for a needle in a haystack." He urged the U.S. government to occupy the northern Mexican state of Chihuahua, and later called for the occupation of the entire country. One of Pershing's lieutenants, George S. Patton, expressed the basis for this proposed solution to the Mexican crisis. "One must be a fool indeed," Patton wrote, "to think that people half savaged and wholly ignorant will ever form a republic. It is a joke. A despot is all they know or want."

The presence of the U.S. forces strained relations with the Carranza government and the Mexican public. Skirmishes between Pershing and Carranza's army brought the two nations to the brink of war in June 1916. Wilson prepared a message to Congress in which he requested permission for American troops to occupy all of northern Mexico. But he never delivered it. The possibility of a Mexican-American war aroused fierce opposition around the United States. Perhaps more important, Wilson feared such a war because of mounting tensions with Germany. He told an aide that "Germany is anxious to have us at war with Mexico, so that our minds and our energies will be taken off the great war across the sea." Wilson thus accepted negotiations by a face-saving international commission. In early 1917, with America moving toward direct involvement in the European War, Wilson began withdrawing American troops. Just a month before the U.S. entered World War I, Wilson officially recognized the Carranza regime.

Wilson's attempt to guide the course of Mexico's revolution and protect U.S. interests left a bitter legacy of suspicion and distrust. It also suggested the limits of a foreign policy tied to a moral vision rooted in the idea of American exceptionalism. Militarism and imperialism, Wilson had believed, were hallmarks of the old European way. American liberal values — rooted in capitalist development, democracy, and free trade — were the wave of the future. Wilson believed the U.S. could lead the world in establishing a new international system based on peaceful commerce and political stability. In both the 1914 invasion and the 1916 punitive expedition, Wilson declared that he had no desire to interfere with Mexican sovereignty. But in both cases that is exactly what he did. The U.S., he argued, must actively use its enormous moral and material power to create the new order. That principle would soon engage America in Europe's bloodiest war and its most momentous revolution. As in Mexico, the contradictions of using armed might in the name of protecting democratic ideals and liberal values would become more tangled than ever.

THE GREAT WAR

World War I, or the Great War, as it was originally called, took an enormous human toll on an entire generation of Europeans. The unprecedented slaughter on the battlefields of Verdun, Ypres, Gallipoli, and scores of other places appalled the combatant nations. At the war's start in August

1914, both sides had confidently predicted a quick victory. Instead, the killing dragged on for over four years, and in the end transformed the old power relations and political map of Europe. The United States entered the war reluctantly, and American forces played a supportive rather than a central role in the military outcome. Yet the wartime experience left a sharp imprint on the nation's economy, politics, and cultural life, one that would last into the next decades.

The Guns of August

In August 1914 a relatively minor incident plunged the European continent into the most destructive war in history. The last decades of the nineteenth century had seen the major European nations, especially Germany, enjoy a great rush of industrial development at the same time that they acquired extensive colonial empires in Africa, Asia, and the Middle East. Only a complex and fragile system of alliances had kept the European powers at peace with each other since 1870. Two great competing camps had evolved by 1907: the Triple Alliance united Germany, Austria-Hungary, and Italy (also known as the Central Powers), and the Triple Entente linked Great Britain, France, and Russia (also known as the Allies). At the heart of this rivalry was the competition between Great Britain, long the world's dominant colonial and commercial power, and Germany, which had powerful aspirations for an empire of its own.

The alliance system managed to keep small conflicts from escalating into larger ones for most of the late nineteenth and early twentieth centuries. But its inclusiveness was also its weakness: it had the potential for drawing many nations into any war that erupted. On June 28, 1914, Archduke Franz Ferdinand, heir to the throne of the unstable Austro-Hungarian Empire, was assassinated in Sarajevo, Bosnia. The archduke's killer was a Slavic nationalist who believed the Austro-Hungarian province of Bosnia ought to be annexed to neighboring Serbia. Germany pushed Austria-Hungary to retaliate against Serbia, and the Serbians in turn asked Russia for help in defense.

By early August both sides had exchanged declarations of war and begun mobilizing their forces. Germany invaded Belgium and prepared to move across the French border. But after the German armies were stopped at the River Marne in September, the war settled into a long, bloody stalemate. New and grimly efficient weapons, such as the machine gun and the tank, and the horrors of trench warfare meant unprecedented casualties for all involved. Centered in northern France, the fighting killed 5 million people over the next two and a half years.

American Neutrality

The outbreak of war in Europe shocked Americans. President Wilson issued a formal proclamation of neutrality and urged citizens to be "impartial in thought as well as in action." Most of the country shared the editorial view expressed that August in the *New York Sun:* "There is nothing reasonable in such a war, and it would be folly for the country to sacrifice itself to the frenzy of dynastic policies and the clash of ancient hatreds which is urging the Old World to destruction." Americans could at least take comfort in the long-established tradition of staying out of faraway European wars.

In practice, powerful cultural, political, and economic factors made the impartiality advocated by Wilson impossible. The U.S. population included many ethnic groups with close emotional ties to the Old World. Out of a total population of 92 million in 1914, about one-third were "hyphenated" Americans, either foreign-born or having one or both parents who were immigrants. Strong support for the Central Powers could be found among the 8 million German Americans, as well as the 4 million Irish Americans, who shared their ancestral homeland's historical hatred for English rule. On the other side, many Americans were at least mildly pro-Allies due to cultural and language bonds with Great Britain and the tradition of Franco-American friendship. President Wilson and most of his advisers had long admired English culture, and they saw its political system as the source of America's own.

Both sides bombarded the U.S. with vigorous propaganda campaigns. The British effectively exploited their natural advantage of common language and heritage. Reports of looting, raping, and the killing of innocent civilians circulated widely in the press. Many of these atrocity stories were exaggerated, but they were given some credibility by German actions — the invasion of neutral Belgium, submarine attacks on merchant ships, and the razing of towns. German propagandists blamed the war on Russian expansionism and France's desire to avenge its defeat by Germany in 1870. It is difficult to accurately measure the impact of war propaganda on American public opinion. As a whole, though, it highlighted the terrible human costs of the war and thus strengthened the conviction that America should stay out of it.

Economic ties between the U.S. and the Allies were perhaps the greatest barrier to true neutrality. A key tactic for the British was a naval blockade on all shipping to Germany. Theoretically, Wilson's neutrality would mean the right of nonbelligerents such as the U.S. to trade with both sides. In practice, although he protested the blockade, the president had to accept the situation and allow trade with the Allies to continue while commerce with Germany all but ended. As war orders poured in from Britain and France, the value of American trade with the Allies shot up from $824 million in 1914 to $3.2 billion in 1916. By 1917 loans to the Allies had exceeded $2.5 billion; loans to the Central Powers were only $27 million. Increased trade with the Allies helped produce a great economic boom at home, and the U.S. became neutral in name only.

Preparedness and Peace

Germany's use of submarine warfare to break the British blockade proved the greatest challenge to President Wilson's ideal of neutrality. In February 1915, Germany declared the waters around the British Isles to be a war zone. Previously, the procedure had been for submarines to surface, stop a ship, check its cargo, and unload all passengers before attacking. Now, all enemy shipping would be subject to surprise submarine attack. Neutral powers were warned that the problems of identification at sea put their ships at risk. The U.S. issued a sharp protest to this policy, calling it "an indefensible violation of neutral rights," and threatened to hold Germany accountable.

On May 7, 1915, a German U-boat sank the Cunard liner *Lusitania* off the coast of Ireland. Among the 1,198 people who died were 128 American citizens. The *Lusitania* was in fact secretly carrying war materials, and passengers had been warned about a possible attack. Wilson nevertheless denounced the sinking as illegal and inhuman, and the American press loudly condemned the act as barbaric. An angry exchange of diplomatic notes led Secretary of State William Jennings Bryan to resign in protest against a policy he thought too warlike.

Tensions heated up again in March 1916 when a German U-boat torpedoed the *Sussex,* an unarmed French passenger ship, injuring four Americans. President Wilson threatened to break off diplomatic relations with Germany unless it abandoned its methods of submarine warfare. He won a temporary diplomatic victory when Germany promised that all vessels would be visited prior to attack. But the crisis also prompted Wilson to begin preparing for war. He was aided by private lobbying groups that stressed the danger of America's military weakness. The most influential and best-organized of these was the National Security League, active in large eastern cities and bankrolled by conservative banking and commercial interests. It pushed for a bigger army and navy, and, most important, a system of universal military training. In June 1916 Congress passed the National Defense Act, which more than doubled the size of the regular army to 220,000 and integrated the state National Guards under federal control. In August, Congress passed a bill that dramatically increased spending for new battleships, cruisers, and destroyers.

Not all Americans supported these preparations for battle and opposition to military build-up found expression in scores of American communities. As early as August 29, 1914, 1,500 women clad in black had marched down New York's Fifth Avenue in the Woman's Peace Parade. Out of this gathering evolved the American Union against Militarism, which lobbied against the preparedness campaign and against intervention in Mexico. Antiwar feeling was especially strong in the South and Middle West. The South generally had weaker economic ties to the Allies, as well as a historical suspicion of military power concentrated in Washington. The Midwest included communities with large German and Socialist influences, both of which opposed U.S. aid to the Allies. A group of thirty to fifty House Democrats, led by majority leader Claude Kitchin of North Carolina, stubbornly opposed Wilson's build-up. Jane Addams, Lillian D. Wald, and many other prominent progressive reformers spoke out for peace. One of these, Oswald Garrison Villard, warned Wilson that he was "sowing the seeds of militarism, raising up a military and naval caste."

A large reservoir of popular antiwar sentiment flowed through the culture in various ways. Movie director Thomas Ince won a huge audience for his 1916 film *Civilization,* which depicted Christ returning to reveal the horrors of war to world leaders. Two of the most popular songs of 1915 were "Don't Take My Darling Boy Away" and "I Didn't Raise My Boy to Be a Soldier." The chorus of the latter went:

I didn't raise my boy to be a soldier
I brought him up to be my pride and joy
Who dares place a musket on his shoulder
To shoot some other mother's darling boy?
Let nations arbitrate their future troubles,
It's time to lay the sword and gun away.
There'd be no war today,
If mothers all would say,
"I didn't raise my boy to be a soldier."

Members of the Women's Peace Party demonstrating in New York City, 1917. Formed in 1915, the new party quickly attracted over 25,000 members, including many women from the suffrage and social settlement movements. Its pacifist platform represented the views of "the mother half of humanity," but the American entry into World War I led to the party's rapid demise.

Wilson had to acknowledge the strong opposition to involvement in the war. In the 1916 presidential campaign Democrats adopted the winning slogan "He Kept Us Out of War." Wilson made a strong showing in the West, where antiwar sentiment was strong, and managed to draw hundreds of thousands of votes away from the antiwar Socialist party as well. Wilson made a point of appealing to progressives of all kinds, stressing his support for the eight-hour day and his administration's efforts on behalf of farmers. The war-induced prosperity no doubt helped him to defeat conservative Republican Charles Evans Hughes in a very close election. But Wilson knew that the peace was as fragile as his victory. "I can't keep the country out of war," he privately worried during the campaign. "Any little German lieutenant can put us into war at any time by some calculated outrage."

Safe for Democracy

By the end of January 1917 Germany's leaders had decided against the possibility of a negotiated peace settlement. Their only hope lay in a final decisive offensive against the Allies. On February 1, 1917, Germany announced a new policy of unrestricted submarine warfare, with no warnings, against all neutral and belligerent shipping. This decision was made with full knowledge that it might bring America into the conflict. In effect, German leaders were gambling that they could destroy the ability of the Allies to fight before the U.S. would be able to effectively mobilize manpower and resources.

Wilson was indignant and disappointed. He still hoped for peace, but Germany had made it impossible for him to preserve his twin goals of U.S. neutrality and freedom of the seas. Reluctantly, Wilson broke off diplomatic relations with Germany and called upon Congress to approve the arming of U.S. merchant ships. On March 1, the White House shocked the country when it made public a recently intercepted coded message from German foreign secretary Arthur Zimmerman to the German ambassador in Mexico. The Zimmerman note proposed that an alliance be made between Germany and Mexico if the U.S. entered the war. Zimmerman suggested that Mexico take up arms against the U.S. and receive in return the "lost territory in New Mexico, Texas, and Arizona." The note caused a sensation and became a very effective propaganda tool for those who favored U.S. entry in the war. "As soon as I saw it," wrote Republican senator Henry Cabot Lodge of Massachusetts, an interventionist, "I knew it would arouse the country more than any other event." The specter of a German-Mexican alliance helped turn the tide of public opinion in the Southwest, where opposition to U.S. involvement in the war had been strong.

Revelation of the Zimmerman note stiffened Wilson's resolve. Ignoring his defeat in the Senate, he issued an executive order in mid-March authorizing the arming of all merchant ships and allowing them to shoot at submarines. In that month, German U-boats sank seven U.S. merchant ships, leaving a heavy death toll. Anti-German feeling increased, and thousands took part in prowar demonstrations in New York, Boston, Philadelphia, and other cities. Wilson finally called a special session of Congress to ask for a declaration of war.

On April 2, on a rainy night before a packed and very quiet assembly, Wilson made his case. He reviewed the escalation of submarine warfare, which he called "warfare against mankind," and said that neutrality was no longer feasible or desirable. But the conflict was not merely about U.S. shipping rights, Wilson argued. With idealistic zeal, he laid out what the U.S. would fight for:

> The world must be made safe for democracy. Its peace must be planted upon the tested foundations of political liberty. We have no selfish ends to serve. We shall fight for the things which we have always carried nearest our hearts,— for democracy, for the right of those who submit to authority to have a voice in their own Governments, for the rights and liberties of small nations.

This was a bold bid to give the United States a new role in international affairs. It asserted not just the right to protect U.S. interests, but called also for change in basic international structures. Wilson's eloquent speech won over the Congress, most of the press, and even his bitterest political critics, such as Theodore Roosevelt. The Senate adopted the war resolution 82 to 6, the House 373 to 50. On April 6 President Wilson signed the declaration of war. All that remained was to win over the American public.

AMERICAN MOBILIZATION

The overall public response to Wilson's war message was enthusiastic. Most newspapers, ministers, state legislatures, and prominent public figures endorsed the call to arms. But the Wilson administration was less certain about the feelings of ordinary Americans. It therefore took immediate steps to win over public support for the war effort, place a legal muzzle on antiwar dissenters, and establish a universal military draft. War mobilization was above all a campaign to unify the country.

Selling the War

Just a week after signing the war declaration, Wilson created the Committee on Public Information (CPI) to organize public opinion. It was dominated by its civilian chairman, the journalist and reformer George Creel. Creel had edited newspapers in Kansas City and Denver, where he also served as a reform police commissioner. He became a personal

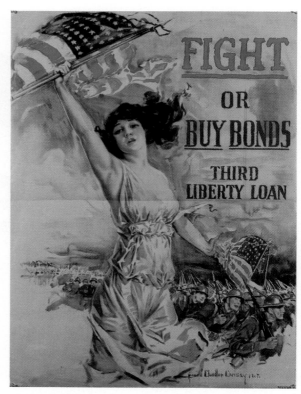

"Fight or Buy Bonds", 1917, by Howard Chandler Christy; Liberty Bond posters such as these appeared in public places as part of the government's effort to sell the war. Such posters often combined traditional gender imagery (Liberty as a woman) with appeals to patriotism.

friend of Wilson's while handling publicity for the 1916 Democratic campaign. Creel quickly transformed the CPI from its original function as coordinator of government news to a much more aggressive role in promoting the war. In his drive to create what he called "a national ideology," Creel raised the art of public relations to new heights.

Creel enlisted over 150,000 people to work on a score of CPI committees. They produced over 100 million pieces of literature — pamphlets, articles, books — that explained the causes and meaning of the war. The CPI also created posters, slides, newspaper advertising, and films to promote the war. It called upon movie stars such as Charlie Chaplin, Mary Pickford, and Douglas Fairbanks to help sell war bonds at huge rallies. Famous journalists like the muckraker Ida Tarbell and well-known artists like Charles Dana Gibson were recruited. Across the nation, a volunteer army of 75,000 "Four Minute Men" gave brief patriotic speeches before stage and movie shows.

The CPI also led an aggressively negative campaign against all things German. Its posters and advertisements depicted the Germans as Huns, bestial monsters outside the civilized world. It supported films such as *The Kaiser: The Beast of Berlin* and *The Prussian Cur*. German music and literature, indeed the German language itself, were suspect, and were banished from the concert halls, schools, and libraries of many communities. The CPI also urged ethnic Americans to abandon their Old World ties, to become "unhyphenated Americans." The CPI's push for conformity would soon encourage thousands of local, sometimes violent, campaigns of harassment against German Americans, radicals, and peace activists.

Opposing the War

What happened to the war's opponents? By defining the call to war as a great moral crusade, President Wilson was able to win over many Americans who had been reluctant to go to war. In particular, many liberals and progressives were attracted to the possibilities of war as a positive force for social change. *The New Republic,* a leading liberal magazine, spoke for many reform-minded Americans when it endorsed the idealism of Wilson's war message: "For the first time in history a wholly independent nation has entered a great and costly war under the influence of ideas rather than immediate interests and without any expectation of gains."

Many progressives identified with President Wilson's definition of the war as an idealistic crusade to defend democracy, spread liberal principles, and redeem European decadence and militarism. John Dewey, the influential philosopher, believed the war offered great "social possibilities" for developing the public good through science and greater efficiency. Dewey believed that wartime mobilization would forge the United States into a more cohesive community by "enforcing the public interest in all the agencies of production and exchange." Social welfare advocates, suffragists, tax reformers, even many Socialists, now viewed war as a unique opportunity. War would require greater direct and coordinated involvement by the government in nearly every phase of American life. A group of prominent progressives quickly issued a statement of support for Wilson's war policy. They argued that "out of the sacrifice of war we may achieve broader democracy in Government, more equitable distribution of wealth, and greater national efficiency in raising the level of the general welfare."

The writer and cultural critic Randolph Bourne was an important, if lonely, voice of dissent among intellectuals. A former student of Dewey's at Columbia University, Bourne wrote a series of antiwar essays warning of the disastrous consequences for reform movements of all kinds. He was particularly critical of "war intellectuals" such as Dewey who were so eager to shift their energies to serving the war effort. "War is essentially the health of the State," Bourne wrote, and he accurately predicted sharp infringements on political and intellectual freedoms.

The Women's Peace party, founded in 1915 by feminists opposed to the preparedness campaign, dissolved. Most of its leading lights — Florence Kelley, Lillian D. Wald, and Carrie Chapman Catt — threw themselves into volunteer war work. Catt, leader of the huge National American Woman Suffrage Association (NAWSA), believed that supporting the war might help women win the right to vote. She joined the Women's Committee of the Council of National Defense, and encouraged suffragists to mobilize women for war service of various kinds. A few lonely feminist voices, such as Jane Addams, continued steadfastly to oppose the war effort. But war work proved very popular among activist middle-class women. They played a leading role in their communities by selling bonds, coordinating food conservation drives, and working for hospitals and the Red Cross. The NAWSA's membership doubled during the war, reaching 2 million by 1919.

"You're in the Army Now"

The central military issue facing the administration was how to raise and deploy U.S. armed forces. When war was declared, there were only about 200,000 men in the army. Traditionally, the U.S. had relied upon volunteer forces organized at the state level. But volunteer rates after April 6 were less than they had been for the Civil War or the Spanish-American War, reflecting the softness of prowar sentiment. The administration thus introduced the Selective Service Act, which provided for the registration and classification for military service of all men between ages twenty-one and thirty-five. Secretary of War Newton D. Baker was anxious to prevent the widespread, even violent, opposition to the draft that had occurred during the Civil War. Much of the anger over the Civil War draft stemmed from the unpopular provision that allowed draftees to buy their way out by paying $300 for a substitute. The new draft made no such allowances. Baker stressed the democratic procedures for registration and the active role of local draft boards in administering the process.

U.S. soldiers leaving training camp, on their way to the European front, 1918. In just over a year national mobilization expanded the armed forces twenty fold, to nearly five million men and women. By November, 1918, when the fighting ended, over two million American troops were in Europe.

On June 5, 1917, nearly 10 million men registered for the draft. There was scattered organized resistance, notably in Oklahoma, Montana, Minnesota, and Texas. But overall, registration records offered impressive evidence of national support. A supplemental registration in August 1918 extended the age limits to eighteen and forty-five. By the end of the war some 24 million men had registered. Resistance was most likely to occur individually, at the time of induction. Of the 2.8 million men eventually called up for service, about 340,000, or 12 percent, failed to show up. Another 2 million Americans volunteered for the various armed services.

The vast, polyglot army posed unprecedented challenges of organization and control. But progressive elements within the administration also saw opportunities for pressing reform measures involving education, alcohol, and sex. Army psychologists gave the new Stanford-Binet intelligence test to all recruits and were shocked to find illiteracy rates as high as 25 percent. Low test scores among many recent immigrants and rural African Americans no doubt resulted from difficulty with language and from the cultural biases embedded in the tests. How could everyone be expected to know the author of "The Raven" or the importance of painter Rosa Bonheur? But for many psychologists low scores reinforced racial theories of innate differences in intelligence. After the war, intelligence testing became a standard feature of America's educational system.

Concerned with the moral health of recruits, the army banned drinking by soldiers in uniform and prohibited liquor on military bases and in surrounding towns. This imposed temperance gave strength to the movement for national prohibition, which became the law after the war ended. Even more ambitious was the army's educational campaign against venereal disease. Under the direction of Raymond Fosdick and the Commission on Training Camp Activities, the military aggressively educated troops on the dangers of contracting syphilis and gonorrhea. "A Soldier who gets a dose," warned a typical poster, "is a Traitor." Over a hundred redlight districts near army bases were closed down. The army distributed condoms to soldiers, and the scientific discussions of sex in lectures, pamphlets, and films were surely a first for the vast majority of the men. Venereal disease rates for soldiers declined by over 300 percent during the war, and the army's fight for "social purity" inspired a postwar movement against sexually transmitted diseases.

Ideally, the army provided a field for social reform and education, especially for the one-fifth of U.S. soldiers born in another country. "The military tent where they all sleep side by side," Theodore Roosevelt predicted, "will rank next to the public schools among the great agents of democratization." The recruits themselves took a more lighthearted view, while singing the army's praises:

Oh, the army, the army, the democratic army,
They clothe you and feed you because the army needs you

Hash for breakfast, beans for dinner, stew for suppertime,
Thirty dollars every month, deducting twenty-nine.
Oh, the army, the army, the democratic army,
The Jews, the Wops, and the Dutch and Irish Cops,
They're all in the army now!

But African Americans who served found severe limitations in the U.S. military. They were organized into totally segregated units, barred entirely from the marines and the Coast Guard, and largely relegated to working as cooks, laundrymen, stevedores, and the like in the army and navy. Thousands of black soldiers endured humiliating, sometimes violent treatment, particularly from white southern officers. African American servicemen faced hostility from white civilians as well, North and South, often being denied service in restaurants and admission to theaters near training camps. The ugliest incident occurred in Houston, Texas, in August 1917 when black infantrymen, insulted and harassed by local segregation laws, killed seventeen civilians. The army court-martialed over a hundred black soldiers and executed thirteen of them without appeal.

Over 200,000 African Americans eventually served in France, but only about one in five saw combat, as opposed to two out of three white soldiers. Black combat units served with distinction in various divisions of the French army. The all-black 369th U.S. Infantry, for example, saw the first and longest service of any American regiment deployed in a foreign army, serving in the trenches for 191 days. The French government awarded the Croix de Guerre to the entire regiment, and 171 officers and enlisted men were cited individually for exceptional bravery in action. African American soldiers by and large enjoyed a friendly reception from French civilians as well, which caused resentment among white American soldiers. The contrast with their treatment at home would remain a sore point with these troops upon their return to the U.S.

Americans in Battle

Naively, many Americans had assumed that the nation's participation in the war could be limited to supplying economic aid and military hardware. At first, the main contribution came on the sea. German U-boats were sinking Allied ships at a rate of 900,000 tons each month; one of four British ships never returned to port. The U.S. began sending warships and destroyers to protect large convoys of merchant ships and to aid the British navy in assaulting U-boats. Within a year, shipping tonnage lost each month to submarine warfare had been

The military reinforced old patterns of racism in American life by segregating African American troops and assigning most of them to menial and support tasks. Yet African Americans generally supported the war effort. The leading black newspaper of the day, the *Chicago Defender*, predicted optimistically: "The colored soldier who fights side by side with the white American will hardly be begrudged a fair chance when the victorious armies return."

reduced to 200,000; the flow of weapons, supplies, and troops continued. No American soldiers were lost on the way to Europe.

President Wilson appointed General John J. Pershing, recently returned from pursuing Pancho Villa in Mexico, as commander of the American Expeditionary Force (AEF). Pershing insisted that the AEF maintain its own identity, distinct from that of the French and British armies. He was also reluctant to send American troops into battle before they had received at least six months' training. The AEF's combat role would be brief but intense: not until early 1918 did AEF units reach the front in large numbers; eight months later the war was over.

Pershing's view of the war had been shaped by his military education at West Point and the strategic legacies of the Civil War. Like Ulysses S. Grant, Pershing believed the object of war to be total destruction of the enemy's military power. He expressed contempt for the essentially defensive tactics of trench warfare pursued by both sides. But the brutal power of modern military technology had made trench warfare a necessity from 1914 to 1917. The awesome firepower of the machine gun and long-range artillery made the massed frontal confrontations of the Civil War era obsolete. The grim reality of life in the trenches — cold, wet, lice-ridden,

The Western Front, 1918

American units saw their first substantial action in late May, helping to stop the German offensive at the battle of Cantigny. By September, over one million American troops were fighting in a counteroffensive campaign at St. Mihiel, the largest single American engagement of the war.

with long periods of boredom and sleeplessness — also made a mockery of older notions about the glory of combat.

In the early spring of 1918 the Germans launched a major offensive that brought them to within fifty miles of Paris. Allied leaders called for an infusion of fresh American troops. In early June about 70,000 AEF soldiers helped the French stop the Germans in the battles of Château-Thierry and Belleau Wood. In July Allied forces led by Marshal Foch of France, began a counteroffensive designed to defeat Germany once and for all. American reinforcements began flooding the ports of Liverpool in England and Brest and Saint-Nazaire in France. The "doughboys" streamed in at a rate of over 250,000 a month. By September, General Pershing had over a million Americans in his army.

In late September 1918, the AEF took over the southern part of a 200-mile front in the Meuse-Argonne offensive. In seven weeks of fighting, most through terrible mud and rain, the U.S. army used more ammunition than the entire Union army had in four years of the Civil War. The Germans, exhausted and badly outnumbered, began to fall back and look for a ceasefire. On November 11, 1918, the war ended with the signing of an armistice.

The massive influx of American troops and supplies no doubt hastened the end of the war. About two-thirds of the U.S. soldiers saw at least some fighting, but even they managed to avoid the horrors of the sustained trench warfare that had marked the earlier years of the war. In all, over 52,000 Americans died in battle. Another 60,000 died from influenza and pneumonia, half of these while still in training camp. Over 200,000 Americans were wounded in the war. These figures, awful as they were, paled against the estimated casualties (killed and wounded) suffered by the European nations: 9 million for Russia, more than 6 million for Germany, nearly 5 million for France, and over 2 million each for Great Britain and Italy. For most Americans at the front, the war experience was a mixture of fear, exhaustion, and fatigue. Many of the rest experienced the war more as tourists than as soldiers.

Historian William Langer, a young doughboy in 1917, would later recall that many in the army "were simply fascinated by the prospect of adventure and heroism. Here was our one great chance for excitement and risk. We could not afford to pass it up." Novelist John Dos Passos, who served in the volunteer ambulance corps, had similar memories. "We had spent our boyhood in the afterglow of the peaceful nineteenth century. What was war like? We wanted to see with our own eyes." For most of the 2 million Americans who passed through the AEF, the time in France would remain a decisive moment in their lives.

OVER HERE

In one sense World War I can be understood as the ultimate progressive crusade, a reform movement of its own. Nearly all the reform energy of the previous two decades was turned toward the central goal of winning the war. The federal government would play a larger role than ever in managing and regulating the wartime economy. Planning, efficiency, scientific analysis, and cooperation were key principles for government agencies and large volunteer organizations. Although much of the regulatory spirit was temporary, the war experience introduced some important and lasting organizational trends in American life.

Organizing the Economy

In the summer of 1917 President Wilson established the War Industries Board (WIB) as a clearing house for industrial mobilization. Led by the successful Wall Street speculator Bernard M. Baruch, the WIB proved a major innovation in expanding the regulatory power of the federal government. It was given broad authority over the conversion of industrial plants to wartime needs, the manufacture of war materials, and the purchase of supplies for the U.S. and the Allies. The WIB had to balance price controls against war profits. Only by ensuring a fair rate of return on investment could it encourage stepped-up production.

The WIB eventually handled 3,000 contracts worth $14.5 billion with various businesses. Working with the U.S. Chamber of Commerce, it oversaw a huge network of War Service Committees, each made up largely of representatives from leading industries. Standardization of goods effected large savings and streamlined production. Baruch continually negotiated with business leaders, describing the system as "voluntary cooperation with the big stick in the cupboard." Baruch threatened to bring the big stick out in two key cases — when Elbert Gary of U.S. Steel refused to accept the government's price for steel, and when Henry Ford balked at limiting private car production. When Baruch warned that he would instruct the military to take over their plants, both industrialists backed down.

In August 1917, Congress passed the Food and Fuel Act, authorizing the president to regulate the production and distribution of the food and fuel necessary for the war effort. To lead the Food Administration (FA), Wilson appointed Herbert Hoover, a millionaire engineer who had already won fame for directing the Belgian relief effort. He became one of the best-known figures of the war administration. Hoover enacted price controls on certain agricultural commodities, such as sugar, pork, and wheat. These were purchased by the government and then sold to the public through licensed dealers. But he stopped short of imposing mandatory food rationing, preferring to rely upon persuasion and voluntary controls.

Hoover's success, like George Creel's at the CPI, depended upon mobilizing hundreds of thousands of volunteers in thousands of American communities. The FA coordinated the work of local committees that distributed posters and leaflets urging people to save food, recycle scraps, and substitute for scarce produce. The FA directed patriotic appeals for "Wheatless Mondays, Meatless Tuesdays, and Porkless Thursdays." Hoover exhorted Americans to "go back to simple food, simple clothes, simple pleasures." He urged them to grow their own vegetables. These efforts resulted in a sharp cutback in the consumption of sugar and wheat, as well as a boost in the supply of livestock. An increase in food exports helped sustain the Allied war effort. Hoover's reputation for efficient administration would make him a key political figure in the postwar decade.

The enormous cost of fighting the war, about $33 billion, meant unprecedentedly large expenditures for the federal government. Roughly one-third of the money came from new taxes. The entire structure of American taxation shifted during the war as taxes on incomes and profits replaced excise and customs levies as the major source of revenue. A graduated federal income tax had been in effect only since 1913, with ratification of the Sixteenth Amendment. Lowering the minimum level of taxable income to $1,000 brought many more households into the federal tax system. Thus, in 1916 only 437,000 Americans paid income tax; by 1918 the figure was 4,425,000. Tax rates were as steep as 70 percent in the highest brackets.

The bulk of war financing came from government borrowing, especially in the form of the popular Liberty Bonds sold to the American public. Treasury Secretary McAdoo orchestrated a sophisticated sales campaign that employed the latest techniques in advertising and public relations: slogans, huge public rallies, celebrity endorsements. Bond drives became highly organized patriotic campaigns that ultimately raised a total of $23 billion for the war effort. The administration also used the new Federal Reserve Banks to expand the money supply, making borrowing easier. The federal debt jumped from $1 billion in 1915 to $20 billion in 1920.

The Business of War

Overall, the war meant expansion and high profits for American business. The boom had begun in 1915 as American industry and agriculture responded to Allied war orders. Now, the American army needed millions of uniforms, blankets, and shoes, as well as hundreds of thousands of trucks, cars, and tanks. Between 1916 and 1918, Ford Motor Company increased its work force from 32,000 to 48,000, General Motors from 10,000 to 50,000. Total capital expenditure in U.S. manufacturing jumped from $600 million in 1915 to $2.5 billion in 1918.

Corporate profits as a whole nearly tripled between 1914 and 1919, and many large businesses did much better than that. Annual prewar profits for U.S. Steel had averaged $76 million; in 1917 they were $478 million. The Bethlehem Shipbuilding Company increased its annual profits from $6 million in peacetime to $49 million in wartime. Du Pont quadrupled its assets. The demand for foodstuffs led to a boom in agriculture as well. The total value of farm produce rose from $9.8 billion in 1914 to $21.3 billion by 1918. Expanded farm acreage and increased investment in farm machinery led to a jump of 20 to 30 percent in overall farm production. As agricultural prices dropped in the 1920s and during the Great Depression, American farmers would remember the prosperity of the war years as their golden age.

The most important and long-lasting economic legacy of the war was the organizational shift toward corporatism in American business. The wartime need for efficient management, manufacturing, and distribution could be met only by a greater reliance on the productive and marketing power of large corporations. Never before had business and the federal government cooperated so closely. Under war administrators such as Baruch and Hoover, entire industries (such as radio manufacturing) and economic sectors (such as agriculture and energy) were organized, regulated, and subsidized as never before. War agencies coordinated industrial committees, volunteer organizations, congressional committees, and Cabinet departments, all in the name of winning the war. They used both public and private power — legal authority and voluntarism — to hammer out and enforce agreements. Here was the genesis of the modern bureaucratic state.

Some Americans worried about the wartime trend toward a greater federal presence in their lives. As the *Saturday Evening Post* noted, "all this government activity will be called to account and re-examined in due time." Although many aspects of the government-business partnership proved temporary, some institutions and practices grew stronger in the postwar years. Among these were the Federal Reserve Board, the income tax system, the Chamber of Commerce and the Farm Bureau, and the growing horde of lobbying groups that pressed Washington for special interest legislation.

One key example of the long-range impact of the government-business partnership was the infant radio industry. Wireless communication technology found many uses among naval and ground forces in wartime. As in most industries, the Justice Department guaranteed radio manufacturers protection against patent infringement and antitrust suits. These guarantees helped stimulate research and the mass production of radios for airplanes, ships, and infantry. In 1919 the government helped create the Radio Corporation of America (RCA), which bought out a British company that had dominated America's wireless system. As part of the deal, the U.S. military was allowed a permanent representative on the RCA board of directors. The creation of RCA, jointly owned by General Electric, American Telephone and Telegraph, and Westinghouse, assured the U.S. a powerful position in the new age of global communications. It also set the stage for the new radio broadcasting industry of the 1920s.

Labor and the War

The expansion of the economy, combined with army mobilization and a decline in immigration from Europe, caused a growing wartime labor shortage. As the demand for workers intensified, the federal government was forced to recognize that labor, like any other resource or commodity, would have to be more carefully tended to than in peacetime. For the war's duration, working people generally enjoyed higher wages and a better standard of living. Trade unions, especially those affiliated with the American Federation of Labor (AFL), enjoyed a sharp rise in membership. In effect, the government took in labor as a junior partner in the mobilization of the economy.

Samuel Gompers, president of the AFL, emerged as the leading spokesman for the nation's trade union movement. An English immigrant and cigar maker by trade, Gompers had rejected the socialism of his youth for a philosophy of ''business unionism.'' By stressing the concrete gains that workers could win through collective bargaining with employers, the AFL had reached a total membership of about 2 million in 1914. Virtually all its members were skilled white males, organized in highly selective crafts in the building trades, railroads, and coal mines.

When the U.S. entered the war, Gompers pledged the AFL's patriotic support, and in April 1918 President Wilson appointed him to the National War Labor Board (NWLB). During 1917 the nation had seen thousands of strikes involving more than a million workers. Wages were usually at issue, reflecting workers' concerns with spiraling inflation and higher prices. The NWLB, cochaired by labor attorney Frank Walsh and former president William H. Taft, acted as a kind of supreme court for labor, arbitrating disputes and working to prevent disruptions in production. The Department of Labor estimated that between 1917 and 1919 NWLB decisions affected nearly 5 million men and women on the job, mostly through mediation and arbitration of wage and hour disputes. The great majority of these interventions resulted in improved wages and reduced hours of work.

Most important, the NWLB supported the right of workers to organize unions and furthered the acceptance of the eight-hour day for war workers — central aims of the labor movement. It also backed time-and-a-half pay for overtime, as well as the principle of equal pay for women workers. AFL unions gained over a million new members during the war, and overall union membership rose from 2.7 million in 1914 to over 5 million by 1920. The NWLB established important precedents for government intervention on behalf of labor. Organized labor's power and prestige, though by no means equal to business or government's, clearly grew during the war.

Wartime conditions often meant severe disruptions and discomfort for America's workers. Overcrowding, rapid work-force turnover, and high inflation rates were typical in war-boom communities. In Bridgeport, Connecticut, a center for small-arms manufacturing, the population grew by 50,000 in less than a year. In 1917 the number of families grew by 12,000 but available housing stock increased by only 6,000 units. Chronic congestion became common in many cities. In the steel center of Gary, Indiana, thirty-one men were found in one attic sharing thirteen beds. Philadelphia reported the worst housing shortage in its history.

If the war boosted the fortunes of the AFL, it also spelled the end for more radical elements of the U.S. labor movement. The Industrial Workers of the World (IWW) had followed a different path from the ''pure and simple'' trade unionism of Gompers. Unlike the AFL, the IWW concentrated on organizing unskilled workers into all-inclusive industrial unions. The Wobblies denounced capitalism as an unreformable system based on exploitation and they opposed United States entry into the war. IWW leaders advised their members to refuse induction for ''the capitalists' war.''

With vigorous organizing, especially in the West, the IWW had grown in 1916 and 1917. It gained strength among workers in several areas crucial to the war effort: copper mining, lumbering, and wheat harvesting. In September 1917, the Wilson administration responded to appeals from western business leaders for a crackdown on the Wobblies. Justice Department agents, acting under the broad authority of the recently passed Espionage Act, swooped down upon IWW offices in over sixty towns and cities, arresting over 300 people and confiscating files. The mass trials and convictions that followed broke the back of America's radical labor movement and marked the beginning of a powerful wave of political repression.

Women at Work

For American women, the war provided new opportunities for wage labor. About a million women workers joined the labor force for the first time. For many of the 8 million women already in the labor force, the war meant a chance to switch from low-paying jobs, such as domestic service, to higher-paying industrial fields. Of the estimated 9.4 million workers directly engaged in war work, some 2.25 million were women, 1.25 million of them in manufacturing. Female munitions plant workers, train engineers, drill press operators, streetcar conductors, and mail carriers became a common sight around the country.

In response to the widened range of female employment, the Labor Department created the Women in Industry Service (WIS). Directed by Mary Van Kleeck, the service advised employers on using

"For Every Fighter A Woman Worker," 1917, by Ernest Hamlin Baker. This poster, part of the United War Work Campaign of the Young Women's Christian Association, depicted America's women as a civilian army, ready and able to take the place of male workers gone off to fight.

female labor and formulated general standards. Although these goals had no legal force, it marked the first time the federal government had taken a practical stand on improving working conditions for women. Gains included the eight-hour day, equal pay for equal work, a minimum wage, the prohibition of night work, and the provision of rest periods, meal breaks, and restroom facilities. Nonetheless, WIS inspectors found that in spite of their recommendations women were often employed for long hours in difficult and dangerous occupations. Although WIS standards were unevenly adopted, they were accepted as goals by nearly every group concerned with improving the conditions of working women.

Yet many women resented restrictions. Myrtle Altenburg, a Wisconsin widow, complained of being prevented from working on a local railroad. "It is my belief," she wrote the state railway commission, "that a woman can do everything that a man can do that is within her strength. Hundreds and hundreds

of women might work and release men for war or war work, could they, the women, be employed on the railroads." Even when hired, women suffered discrimination over pay. And the established trade unions of the AFL were adamantly opposed to women workers. Government surveys found that women's average earnings were roughly half of men's in the same industries.

At war's end, women lost nearly all their defense-related jobs. But the war accelerated female employment in fields already dominated by women. By 1920, more women who worked outside the home did so in white-collar occupations — such as telephone operators, secretaries, and clerks — than in manufacturing or domestic service. They found a large niche in the expanding fields of communications, advertising, public relations, and finance. The new awareness of women's work led Congress to create the Women's Bureau in the Labor Department, which continued the WIS wartime program of education and investigation through the postwar years.

Woman Suffrage

If the wartime gains by working-class women were fleeting, the war substantially advanced women's status in other ways. Along with the presence of so many new women wageworkers, the highly visible volunteer efforts of millions of middle-class women helped to finally secure the vote for women. Volunteer war work — selling bonds, saving food, organizing benefits — was very popular among housewives and clubwomen. These women played a key role in the success of the Food Administration, and the Women's Committee of the Council of National Defense included a variety of women's organizations.

Until World War I, the fight for woman suffrage had been waged largely within individual states. Western states had led the way. Various forms of woman suffrage had become law in Wyoming in 1869, followed by Utah (1870), Colorado (1893), Idaho (1896), Washington (1910), California (1911), Arizona and Oregon (1912), and Montana and Nevada (1914). The reasons for this regional pattern had less to do with dramatically different notions of gender roles in the West than with the distinctiveness of western politics and society. Rocky Mountain and Pacific Coast states did not have the sharp ethnocultural divisions between Catholics and Protestants that hindered suffrage efforts in the East. The close identification in the East between suffrage and Prohibition led many Catholic immigrants to oppose the vote for women because they feared it would lead to Prohibition. Mormons in Utah supported woman suffrage as a way to preserve polygamy and defend their distinctive social order from attack.

The U.S. entry into the war provided a unique opportunity for suffrage groups to shift their strategy to a national campaign for a constitutional amendment granting the vote to women. The most important of these groups was the National American Woman Suffrage Association. Before 1917, most American suffragists had opposed the war. Under the leadership of Carrie Chapman Catt, NAWSA threw its support behind the war effort and doubled its membership to 2 million. Catt gambled that a strong show of patriotism would help clinch the century-old fight to win the vote for women. The NAWSA pursued a moderate policy of lobbying Congress for a constitutional amendment and calling for state referendums on woman suffrage.

At the same time, more militant suffragists led by a young Quaker activist, Alice Paul, injected new energy and more radical tactics into the movement. Paul had spent several years in England working with militant suffragists there, and in 1913 she returned to the U.S. to form the Congressional Union within the NAWSA to lobby for a federal amendment. Dissatisfied with the NAWSA's conservative strategy of quiet lobbying and orderly demonstrations, Paul left the organization in 1916. She joined forces with western women voters to form the

National Woman's Party. Borrowing from English suffragists, the NWP pursued a more aggressive and dramatic strategy of agitation. Paul and her supporters picketed the White House, publicly burned President Wilson's speeches, and condemned the president and the Democrats for failing to produce an amendment. In one demonstration they chained themselves to the White House fence and after their arrest went on a hunger strike in jail. The militants generated a great deal of publicity and sympathy.

Although some in the NAWSA objected to these tactics, Paul's radical approach helped make the NAWSA position more acceptable to Wilson. Carrie Chapman Catt used the president's war rhetoric as an argument for granting the vote to women. The fight for democracy, she argued, must begin at home, and she urged passage of the woman suffrage amendment as a "war measure." She won Wilson's support, and in 1917 the president urged Congress to pass a woman suffrage amendment as "vital to the winning of the war." The House did so in January 1918 and a more reluctant Senate approved it in June 1919. Another year of hard work was spent convincing the state legislatures. In August 1920 Tennessee gave the final vote needed to ratify the Nineteenth Amendment to the Constitution, finally making woman's vote legal nationwide. The war, Carrie Chapman Catt wrote, had "a tremendous effect on woman suffrage by revolutionizing the whole sphere of women."

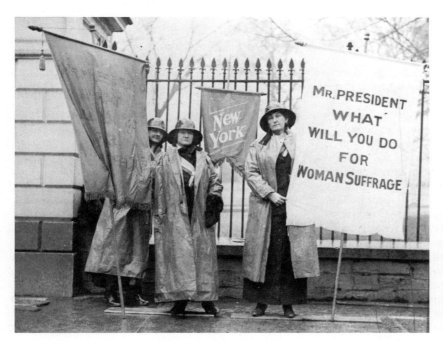

Members of the National Woman's Party picketed President Wilson at the White House in 1917. Their militant action in the midst of the war crisis aroused both anger and sympathy. The NWP campaign helped push the President and the Congress to accept woman suffrage as "a war measure."

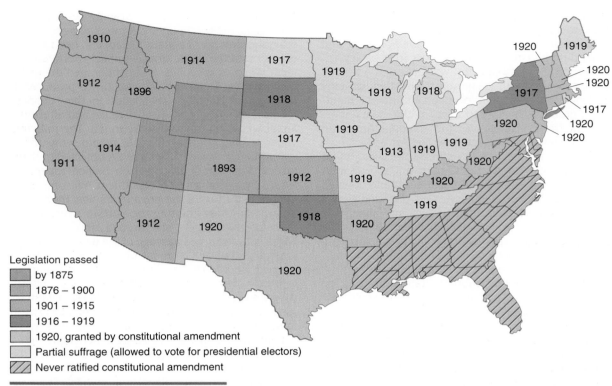

Woman Suffrage By State, 1869–1919

Dates for the enactment of woman suffrage in the individual states. Years before ratification of the Nineteenth Amendment in 1920, a number of western states had legislated full or partial voting rights for women. In 1917 Montana suffragist Jeannette Rankin became the first woman elected to Congress.

Legislation passed
- by 1875
- 1876 – 1900
- 1901 – 1915
- 1916 – 1919
- 1920, granted by constitutional amendment
- Partial suffrage (allowed to vote for presidential electors)
- Never ratified constitutional amendment

Source: Barbara G. Shortridge, *Atlas of American Women* (New York: Macmillan, 1987).

Prohibition

Significantly, another reform effort closely associated with women's groups triumphed at the same time. The movement to eliminate alcohol from American life had attracted large numbers of Americans, especially women, since before the Civil War. Temperance advocates saw drinking as the source of many of the worst problems faced by the working class, including family violence, unemployment, and poverty. By the early twentieth century the Women's Christian Temperance Union, with a quarter million members, had become the single largest women's organization in American history.

Many progressives joined the fight, believing the saloon culture was intimately tied to the corruption of city bosses and their largely immigrant constituents. In 1913 the Anti-Saloon League had announced support for a constitutional amendment enacting a national prohibition. The moral fervor that accompanied America's entry into the war provided a crucial boost to the cause. With so many breweries bearing German names, the movement benefited as well from the strong anti-German feeling of the war years. Outlawing beer and whiskey would also help to conserve precious grain, prohibitionists argued.

In 1917, a coalition of progressives and rural fundamentalists in Congress pushed through a constitutional amendment making the ban national. The Eighteenth Amendment was ratified by the states in January 1919 and became the law of the land one year later. The postwar years would show that Prohibition created a host of new problems, especially its encouragement of organized crime. At the time, however, many Americans, particularly native Protestants, considered Prohibition a worthy moral reform.

REPRESSION AND REACTION

World War I exposed and intensified many of the deepest social tensions in American life. The push for national unity led the federal government to crack down on a wide spectrum of dissenters from its war policies. On the local level, vigilantes increasingly took the law into their own hands to punish those suspected of disloyalty. The war inflamed racial hatred, and the worst race riots in the nation's history exploded in several cities. At war's end, a newly militant labor movement briefly asserted itself in mass strikes around the nation. Over all these developments hung the specter of the 1917 Bolshevik Revolution in Russia. Radicals around the world had drawn inspiration from what looked like the first successful revolution against a capitalist state. Many conservatives worried that similar revolutions were imminent. From 1918 through 1920 the federal government directed a repressive antiradical campaign that had crucial implications for the nation's future.

Muzzling Dissent: The Espionage and Sedition Acts

The case brought against Victor Berger and his socialist newspaper, the *Milwaukee Leader,* was only one of many examples of federally sponsored repression during the war. The Espionage Act of June 1917 became the government's key tool for the suppression of antiwar sentiment. It set severe penalties (up to twenty years' imprisonment and a $10,000 fine) for anyone found guilty of aiding the enemy, obstructing recruitment, or causing insubordination in the armed forces. The act also empowered the postmaster general, Albert Burleson, to exclude from the mails any newspapers or magazines he thought treasonous. Burleson interpreted the act quite broadly and within a year had revoked the mailing rights of forty-five newspapers. These included several anti-British and pro-Irish publications, as well as such leading journals of American socialism as *The Masses* and *The Appeal to Reason,* which had enjoyed a prewar circulation of half a million.

To enforce the Espionage Act, the government had to increase its overall police and surveillance machinery. Military intelligence grew from a staff of 2 officers in 1917 to 300 in 1918 assisted by 1,000 civilians. Civilian intelligence was coordinated by the newly created Bureau of Investigation in the Justice Department. This agency was reorganized after the war as the Federal Bureau of Investigation (FBI). In May 1918 the Sedition Act, an amendment to the Espionage Act, significantly widened the government's power to crush opposition to the war. The new act outlawed "any disloyal, profane, scurrilous, or abusive language intended to cause contempt, scorn, contumely, or disrepute" to the government, constitution, or flag.

In all, over 2,100 cases were brought to trial under these acts. They became a convenient vehicle for striking out at Socialists, pacifists, radical labor activists, and others who resisted the patriotic tide. The most celebrated prosecution came in June 1918 when federal agents arrested Eugene Debs in Canton, Ohio, after he gave a speech defending antiwar protesters. Sentenced to ten years in prison, Debs defiantly told the court: "I have been accused of having obstructed the war. I admit it. Gentlemen, I abhor war. I would oppose the war if I stood alone." Debs served thirty-two months in federal prison before being pardoned by President Harding on Christmas Day 1921.

The Supreme Court upheld the constitutionality of the acts in several 1919 decisions. In *Schenck v. United States* the Court unanimously agreed with Justice Oliver Wendell Holmes's claim that Congress could restrict speech if the words "are used in such circumstances and are of such a nature as to create a clear and present danger." It upheld the conviction of Charles Schenck for having mailed pamphlets urging potential army inductees to resist conscription. In *Debs v. United States,* the Court affirmed the guilt of Eugene Debs for his antiwar speech in Canton, even though he had not explicitly urged violation of the draft laws. Finally, in *Abrams v. United States,* the Court upheld Sedition Act convictions of four Russian immigrants who had printed pamphlets denouncing American military intervention in the Russian Revolution. The nation's highest court thus endorsed the extreme wartime restrictions on free speech.

Vigilantism

Outbreaks of vigilantism provided the starkest examples of how the war divided American communities. By the fall of 1917 news stories from all over the country told of people being beaten, or worse, by mobs of superpatriots. The reasons varied: for not displaying a flag, for failing to buy bonds, for objecting to the draft law, for criticizing war aims and policies, for alleged spying. In Emerson, Nebraska, Rudolph Schopke was tarred and feathered for declining to contribute to the Red Cross. At Rutgers University, Samuel Chovenson, an antiwar Socialist, refused a demand by fellow students that he address a Liberty Loan rally. He was stripped, blindfolded, covered with molasses and feathers, then paraded through the streets of town. In Tulsa, Oklahoma, S. L. Miller shot and killed Joe Spring, a waiter in a restaurant, for allegedly making pro-

German remarks. Local vigilantes rallied around Miller, who was found not guilty of murder.

Government repression and local vigilantes reinforced each other. The American Protective League, founded with the blessing of the Justice Department, mobilized 250,000 self-appointed "operatives" in over 600 towns and cities. APL members, mostly businessmen, bankers, and former policemen, spied on their neighbors and staged a series of well-publicized "slacker" raids on antiwar protesters and draft evaders. Many communities, inspired by Committee on Public Information campaigns, sought to ban the teaching of the German language in their schools or the performance of German music in concert halls.

Vigilantes, especially in the West, used the super patriotic mood to settle scores with labor organizers and radicals. In Butte, Montana, a strike of 15,000 copper miners in the summer of 1917 attracted IWW organizer Frank Little. After making a series of speeches denouncing the war and the capitalist class, Little was seized by local vigilantes, dragged through the streets by a car, then hanged from a railroad bridge. In Bisbee, Arizona, vigilantes from the Citizens Protective League joined the local sheriff in rounding up 1,200 workers suspected of belonging to the IWW. They placed them in twenty-three boxcars and transported them to New Mexico, where they were abandoned in the desert without food or water. They were finally rescued by the military.

Local businessmen, politicians, and newspapers had the IWW identified in the public mind with pro-Germanism, sabotage, and disloyalty. Indeed, the Sedition Act was passed largely in response to local appeals from vigilantes active against Wobblies and other radicals. While a few voices, such as the new American Civil Liberties Union, spoke out against the intolerance, the vast majority of the nation's press, government leaders, and citizens seemed to agree with the *Atlanta Constitution.* Supporting the new Sedition Act, the paper argued that "for the red-blooded, 100 percent American members of society," no measure "can be 'too drastic' in its applications to traitors and disloyalists."

The Great Migration and Racial Tensions

Economic opportunity brought on by war prosperity triggered a massive migration of rural black southerners to northern cities. From 1914 to 1920, somewhere between 300,000 and 500,000 African Americans left the rural South for the North. Chicago's black population increased by 65,000, or 150 per-

This southern African American family is shown arriving in Chicago around 1915. Black migrants to northern cities often faced overcrowding, inferior housing, and a high death rate from disease. But the chance to earn daily wages of six to eight dollars (the equivalent of a week's wages in much of the South), as well as the desire to escape persistent racial violence, kept the migrants coming.

Black Population of Selected Northern Cities, 1910–1920

	1910		1920		
	No.	Percent	No.	Percent	Percent Increase
New York	91,709	1.9	152,467	2.7	66.3
Chicago	44,103	2.0	109,458	4.1	148.2
Philadelphia	84,459	5.5	134,229	7.4	58.9
Detroit	5,741	1.2	40,838	4.1	611.3
St. Louis	43,960	6.4	69,854	9.0	58.9
Cleveland	8,448	1.5	34,451	4.3	307.8
Pittsburgh	25,623	4.8	37,725	6.4	47.2
Cincinnati	19,739	5.4	30,079	7.5	53.2
Indianapolis	21,816	9.3	34,678	11.0	59.0
Newark	9,475	2.7	16,977	4.1	79.2
Kansas City	23,566	9.5	30,719	9.5	30.4
Columbus	12,739	7.0	22,181	9.4	74.1
Gary	383	2.3	5,299	9.6	1,283.6
Youngstown	1,936	2.4	6,662	5.0	244.1
Buffalo	1,773	.4	4,511	.9	154.4
Toledo	1,877	1.1	5,691	2.3	203.2
Akron	657	1.0	5,580	2.7	749.3

Source: U.S. Department of Commerce.

cent; Detroit's by 35,000, or 600 percent. Acute labor shortages led northern factory managers to recruit black migrants to the booming industrial centers. The Pennsylvania Railroad alone drew 10,000 black workers from Florida and south Georgia. Black workers eagerly left low-paying jobs as field hands and domestic servants for the chance at relatively high-paying work in meat-packing plants, shipyards, and steel mills.

Kinship and community networks were crucial in shaping what came to be called the Great Migration. African American families and individuals usually had specific destinations, based on information gathered from family members and friends who had gone first. They shared news about job openings, urban residential districts, and boardinghouses in northern cities. Black clubs, churches, and fraternal lodges in southern communities frequently sponsored the migration of their members, as well as return trips to the South. Single African American women often made the trip first because they could more easily obtain steady work as maids, cooks, and laundresses. One recalled that "if [white employers] liked the way the women would work in their homes or did ironing, they might throw some work to your husband or son." Relatively few African American

men actually secured high-paying skilled jobs in industry or manufacturing. Most had to settle for work as construction laborers, teamsters, janitors, porters, or other lower-paid jobs.

The lure of the North was not based entirely on economic factors. The persistence of lynching and other racial violence in the South no doubt contributed to the Great Migration. But racial violence was not limited to the South. Two of the worst race riots in American history occurred as a result of tensions brought on by wartime migration. On July 2, 1917, in East St. Louis, Illinois, a ferocious mob of whites attacked African Americans, killing at least 200. Before this riot, some of the city's manufacturers had been steadily recruiting black labor as a way to keep local union demands down. Unions had refused to allow black workers as members, and politicians had cynically exploited white racism. In Chicago, on July 27, 1919, antiblack rioting broke out on a Lake Michigan beach. For two weeks white gangs hunted African Americans in the streets and burned hundreds out of their homes. Twenty-three African Americans and 15 whites died, and over 500 were injured.

In both East St. Louis and Chicago, local authorities held African Americans responsible for the violence, even though the latter were largely victims, not aggressors. President Wilson refused requests for federal intervention or investigation. A few weeks after the East St. Louis riot, some 8,000 black residents of New York City staged a silent protest march down Fifth Avenue. A young black veteran who had been chased by a mob in the Chicago riot asked: "Had the ten months I spent in France been all in vain? Were all those white crosses over dead bodies of those dark skinned boys lying in Flanders field for naught? Was democracy a hollow sentiment?"

In terms of service in the armed forces, compliance with the draft, and involvement in volunteer work, African Americans had supported the war effort as faithfully as any group. In 1917, despite a segregated army and discrimination in the defense industry, most African Americans thought the war might improve their lot. "If we again demonstrate our loyalty and devotion to our country," advised the *Chicago Defender*, "those injustices will disappear and the grounds for complaint will no longer exist." By the fall of 1919, writing in the NAACP journal *Crisis*, black author James Weldon Johnson gloomily concluded that "an increased hatred of race was an integral part of wartime intolerance."

The sense of black disillusionment about the war grew quickly. So did a newly militant spirit. In 1919 W. E. B. Du Bois urged African Americans to "marshal every ounce of our brain and brawn. We return, we return from fighting, we return fighting." A heightened sense of race consciousness and activism was evident among black veterans and the growing black communities of northern cities. Taking the lead in the fight against bigotry and injustice, the NAACP held a national conference in 1919 on lynching. It pledged to defend persecuted African Americans, publicize the horrors of lynch law, and seek federal legislation against "Judge Lynch." By 1919 membership in the NAACP had reached 60,000 and the circulation of its journal, *Crisis*, exceeded half a million.

The General Strike Committee of Seattle distributed groceries to union families in February, 1919. The Seattle General Strike had been triggered when shipyard workers walked off the job after failing to gain wage hikes to offset spiralling postwar inflation. The conservative *Los Angeles Times* saw the strike as evidence that Bolshevism was a "right-here now American menace."

Labor Strife

The relative labor peace of 1917 and 1918 dissolved after the armistice. Over 4 million American workers were involved in some 3,600 strikes in 1919 alone. This unprecedented strike wave had several causes. Most of the modest wartime wage gains were wiped out by spiraling inflation and high prices for food, fuel, and housing. With the end of government controls on industry, many employers withdrew their recognition of unions. Difficult working conditions were still routine in some industries, such as the twelve-hour day in steel mills. The quick return of demobilized servicemen to the labor force meant layoffs and new concerns about job security.

Several of the postwar strikes received widespread national attention. They seemed to be more than simply economic conflicts, and they provoked deep fears about the larger social order. Seattle, Washington, a shipbuilding and lumber center, had grown rapidly during the war. In February 1919 a strike in the shipyards over wages escalated into a general citywide strike involving 60,000 workers. A strike committee coordinated the city's essential services for a week in a disciplined, nonviolent fashion. But the local press and Mayor Ole Hanson denounced the strikers as revolutionaries. Hanson effectively ended the strike by requesting federal troops to occupy the city.

In September, Boston policemen shocked the city by going out on strike. The walkout was triggered when the police commissioner rejected a citizens' commission study that recommended a pay raise. Local veterans, college students, and other volunteers struggled to keep order amidst looting and violence. Massachusetts governor Calvin Coolidge called in the National Guard to restore order and won a national reputation by crushing the strike. The entire police force was fired. Coolidge declared, "There is no right to strike against the public safety by anybody, anywhere, any time."

The biggest strike took place in the steel industry, involving some 350,000 steelworkers. Centered in several midwestern cities, this epic struggle lasted from September 1919 to January 1920. The AFL had hoped to build on wartime gains in an industry that had successfully resisted unionization before the war. The major demands were union recognition, the eight-hour day, and wage increases. The steel companies used black strikebreakers and armed guards to keep the mills running. Elbert Gary, president of U.S. Steel, directed a sophisticated propaganda campaign that tied the strikers to revolutionaries. Public opinion turned against the strike and condoned the widespread use of state and federal troops. A violent riot in Gary, Indiana, left eighteen strikers dead. The failed steel strike proved to be the era's most bitter and devastating defeat for organized labor.

The Red Scare

The revolutionary changes taking place in Russia became an important backdrop for domestic politics. In the United States, strikes, antiwar agitation, even racial disturbances were increasingly blamed on foreign radicals and alien ideologies. It became easy to lump together pro-German sentiment with socialism, the IWW, and trade unionism in general. The accusation of bolshevism became a powerful weapon for turning public opinion against strikers and political dissenters of all kinds. In the 1919 Seattle general strike, for example, Mayor Hanson claimed against all evidence that the strikers "want to take possession of our American Government and try to duplicate the anarchy of Russia." Months later the *Seattle Post-Intelligencer*, referring to the IWW, said: "We must smash every un-American and anti-American organization in the land. We must put to death the leaders of this gigantic conspiracy of murder, pillage, and revolution."

In truth, by 1919 the American radical Left was already weakened and badly split by factions. The Socialist party had around 40,000 members. Two small Communist parties, made up largely of immigrants, had a total of perhaps 70,000. In the spring of 1919, a few extremists mailed bombs to a number of prominent business and political leaders. In June, simultaneous bombings in eight cities killed two people and damaged the residence of Attorney General A. Mitchell Palmer. With public alarm growing, state and federal officials began a coordinated campaign to root out communists and their alleged Russian connections.

Palmer used the broad authority of the 1918 Alien Act, which enabled the government to deport any immigrant found to be a member of a revolutionary organization prior to or after coming to the U.S. In a series of raids in late 1919 Justice Department agents in eleven cities arrested and roughed up several hundred members of the IWW and the Union of Russian Workers. Little evidence of revolutionary intent was found, but 249 people were deported, including prominent anarchists Emma

Goldman and Alexander Berkman. In early 1920 some 6,000 people in thirty-three cities, including many U.S. citizens and noncommunists, were arrested and herded into prisons and bullpens. Again, no evidence of a grand plot was found, but another 600 aliens were deported.

Motivated in part by presidential ambitions, Palmer kept up a high public profile in his fight against "alien agitators." He defended the rough treatment of the apprehended, saying his agents were angry at radicals "seeking to destroy their homes, their religion, and their country." The Palmer raids had a ripple effect around the nation by encouraging extralegal mob action and other repressive measures against radicals. In New York, the state assembly refused to seat five duly elected Socialists.

A report prepared by a group of distinguished lawyers, including Felix Frankfurter and Zechariah Chafee, questioned the legality of the attorney general's tactics. Palmer's popularity had waned by the spring of 1920, when it became clear that his predictions of revolutionary uprisings were wildly exaggerated. But the Red Scare left an ugly legacy: wholesale violations of constitutional rights, deportations of hundreds of innocent people, fuel for the fires of nativism and intolerance. Business groups, such as the National Association of Manufacturers, found "redbaiting" to be an effective tool in postwar efforts to keep unions out of their factories. Indeed, the government-sanctioned Red Scare was to return as a key element in the century's politics.

The Red Scare took its toll on the women's movement as well. Before the war, many suffragists and feminists had maintained ties and shared platforms with Socialist and labor groups. The suffrage movement in particular had brought together women from very different class backgrounds and political perspectives. But the calls for "100 percent Americanism" during and after the war destroyed the fragile alliances that had made a group such as the National American Woman Suffrage Association so powerful. After the war, a large number of women's organizations that had been divided over American involvement in the war reunited under the umbrella of the National Council for Prevention of War. But when military spokesmen in the early 1920s attacked the group for advocating communism, two of its largest affiliates — the General Federation of Women's Clubs and the Parent-Teacher Association — withdrew in fear. Hostility to radicalism marked the political climate of the 1920s, and

this helped to narrow the political spectrum for women activists. As Elizabeth Kent, a National Woman's party officer from California put it, "Many of our women long to drop everything controversial."

An Uneasy Peace

The armistice of November 1918 ended the fighting on battlefields, but the war continued at the peace conference. In the old royal palace of Versailles near Paris, delegates from twenty-seven countries spent five months hammering out a settlement. Yet neither Germany nor Russia was represented. The proceedings were dominated by leaders of the "Big Four": David Lloyd George (Great Britain), Georges Clemenceau (France), Vittorio Orlando (Italy), and Woodrow Wilson (U.S.). President Wilson saw the peace conference as a historic opportunity to project his domestic liberalism onto the world stage. But the stubborn realities of power politics would frustrate Wilson at Versailles and lead to his most crushing defeat at home.

The Fourteen Points

Wilson arrived in Paris with the United States delegation in January 1919. He brought with him a plan for peace that he had outlined a year earlier in a speech to Congress on U.S. war aims. The Fourteen Points, as they were called, contained three main elements. First, Wilson offered a series of specific proposals for setting postwar boundaries in Europe and creating new countries out of the collapsed Austro-Hungarian and Ottoman empires. The key idea here was the right of all peoples to "national self-determination." Second, Wilson listed general principles for governing international conduct, including freedom of the seas, free trade, open covenants instead of secret treaties, reduced armaments, and mediation for competing colonial claims. Third, and most important, Wilson called for a League of Nations to help implement these principles and resolve future disputes.

In essence, the Fourteen Points offered a plan for world order deeply rooted in the liberal progressivism long associated with Wilson. The plan reflected a faith in efficient government and the rule of law as means for solving international problems. It looked to free trade and commercial development as the key to spreading prosperity. It advocated a dynamic democratic capitalism as a middle ground between Old World autocracy and revolutionary socialism. Wilson's vision was a profoundly moral one, and he was certain it was the only road to a lasting and humane peace.

The most controversial element, both at home and abroad, would prove to be the league. The heart of the league covenant, Article X, called for collective security as the ultimate method of keeping the peace: "The members of the League undertake to respect and preserve as against external aggression the territorial integrity and existing political independence of all Members." In the United States, Wilson's critics would focus on this provision as an unacceptable surrender of the nation's sovereignty and independence in foreign affairs.

Wilson in Paris

The president was pleased when the conference at first accepted his plan as the basis for discussions. He also enjoyed wildly enthusiastic receptions from the public in Paris and several other European capitals he visited. France's Clemenceau was less enamored. He sarcastically observed, "God gave us the Ten Commandments, and we broke them. Wilson gave us the Fourteen Points. We shall see." Wilson's plan could not survive the hostile atmosphere at Versailles. He was unable to win support for most of his broad principles, such as freedom of the seas, free trade, and open covenants.

Much of the negotiating at Versailles was in fact done in secret among the Big Four. The ideal of self-determination found limited expression. The independent states of Austria, Hungary, Poland, Yugoslavia, and Czechoslovakia were carved out of the homelands of the beaten Central Powers. But the Allies, looking to maintain the prewar imperial system, resisted Wilson's call for independence for the colonies of the defeated nations. A compromise mandate system of protectorates gave the French and British control of parts of the old German and Turkish empires in Africa and the Middle East. In Asia, Japan won control of former German colonies in China. Among those trying, but failing, to influence the treaty negotiations were the sixty-odd delegates to the first Pan African Congress, held in Paris at the same time as the peace talks. The group included Americans W. E. B. Du Bois and William Monroe Trotter, as well as representatives from Africa and the West Indies. All were disappointed

Sir William Orpen's portrait of President Woodrow Wilson. The painting captured Wilson's penetrating gaze and intensity of purpose. In October, 1919, exhausted from the political battles over the Versailles peace treaty, Wilson suffered a massive stroke, from which he never fully recovered.

with the failure of the peace conference to grant self-determination to thousands of Africans living in former German colonies.

Another disappointment for Wilson came with the issue of war guilt. He had strongly opposed the extraction of harsh economic reparations from the Central Powers. But the French and British, with their awful war losses fresh in mind, insisted on making Germany pay. The final treaty contained a clause attributing the war to "the aggression of Germany," and a commission later set German war reparations at $33 billion. Bitter resentment in Germany over the punitive treaty helped sow the seeds for the Nazi rise to power in the 1930s. Wilson also alienated the Italians, who walked out of the conference when he refused to support their claims to the city of Fiume, an Adriatic port surrounded by Yugoslav land.

Hovering over the proceedings was the specter of the Russian Revolution. The repressive and corrupt regime of Czar Nicholas II had been overthrown in March 1917 by a coalition of forces demanding change. The new provisional government, headed by Alexander Kerensky, vowed to keep Russia in the fight against Germany. But the war had taken a terrible toll on Russian soldiers and civilians, and had become very unpopular. The radical Bolsheviks, led by V. I. Lenin, gained a large following by promising "peace, land, and bread," and they began plotting to seize power. The Bolsheviks followed the teachings of German revolutionary Karl Marx, emphasizing the inevitability of class struggle and the replacement of capitalism by communism.

In November 1917 the Bolsheviks took control of the Russian government. In February 1918, to the dismay of the Allies, Russia signed a separate peace with Germany. A civil war raged within Russia for three more years before the Bolsheviks consolidated their power. Allied troops from Britain, France, and the U.S. intervened in Russia, ostensibly to reclaim military supplies sent for use against the kaiser. But British and French leaders wanted to help counter-revolutionary forces overthrow the new Bolshevik regime, and many Allied troops wound up fighting on the side of the anti-Bolshevik forces. Wilson dispatched 15,000 American troops to northern and eastern Russia, where some remained until 1920. This armed intervention widened the gulf between Russia and the West. In March 1919, Russian Communists established the Third International, or Comintern. Their call for a worldwide revolution deepened Allied mistrust, and the Paris Peace Conference essentially ignored the new political reality posed by the Russian Revolution.

The final treaty was signed on June 28, 1919, in the Hall of Mirrors at the Versailles palace. The Germans had no choice but to accept its harsh terms. President Wilson had been disappointed by the secret deals and the endless compromising of his ideals, no doubt underestimating the stubborn reality of power politics in the wake of Europe's most devastating war. He had nonetheless won a commitment to the League of Nations, the centerpiece of his plan, and he was confident that the American people would accept the treaty. The tougher fight would be with the Senate, where a two-thirds vote was needed for ratification.

The Treaty Fight

When Woodrow Wilson returned to Washington in July he had spent only ten days in the U.S. over the past six months. Preoccupied with peace conference politics in Paris, he had neglected politics at home.

His troubles had actually started earlier. He had alienated many voters in the November 1918 elections by calling for loyal Democratic majorities in Congress. Instead, Republicans had captured both the House and the Senate. Wilson had then made a tactical error by including no prominent Republicans in the U.S. peace delegation. He therefore faced a variety of tough opponents to the treaty he brought home.

His most extreme enemies in the Senate were a group of about eighteen "irreconcilables," opposed to a treaty in any form. Some were isolationist progressives, such as Republicans Robert M. La Follette of Wisconsin and William Borah of Idaho, who opposed the league as steadfastly as they opposed American entry into the war. Others were racist xenophobes like Democrat James Reed of Missouri. He objected, he said, to submitting questions to a tribunal "on which a nigger from Liberia, a nigger from Honduras, a nigger from India, and an unlettered gentleman from Siam, each have votes equal to the great United States of America."

The less dogmatic but more influential opponents were led by Republican Henry Cabot Lodge of Massachusetts, powerful majority leader of the Senate. They had strong reservations about the League of Nations, especially the provisions for collective security in the event of a member being attacked. Lodge argued that this provision impinged on congressional authority to declare war and placed unacceptable restraints on the nation's ability to pursue an independent foreign policy. Lodge proposed a series of amendments that would have weakened the league. But Wilson refused to compromise, motivated in part by the long-standing hatred he and Lodge felt toward each other. The president decided instead to take his case directly to the American people.

In September, Wilson set out on a speaking tour across the country to drum up support for the league and the treaty. His train traveled 8,000 miles — through the Midwest, to the Pacific, and then back East. The crowds were large and responsive, but they did not change any votes in the Senate. The strain took its toll. On September 25, after speaking in Pueblo, Colorado, the sixty-three-year-old Wilson collapsed from exhaustion. His doctor canceled the rest of the trip. A week later, back in Washington, the president suffered a stroke that left him partially paralyzed. In November, Lodge brought the treaty out of committee for a vote, having appended to it fourteen reservations — that is, recommended changes. A bedridden Wilson stubbornly refused to compromise and instructed Democrats to vote against the Lodge version of the treaty. On November 19 Democrats joined with the "irreconcilables" to defeat the amended treaty, fifty-nine to thirty-five.

Wilson refused to budge. In January, he urged Democrats to either stand by the original treaty or vote it down. The 1920 election, he warned, would be "a great and solemn referendum" on the whole issue. In the final vote, on March 19, 1920, twenty-one Democrats broke with the president and voted for the Lodge version, giving it a majority of forty-nine to thirty-five. But this was seven votes short of the two-thirds needed for ratification. As a result, the United States never signed the Versailles treaty, nor did it join the League of Nations. The absence of the U.S. weakened the League and made it more difficult for the organization to realize Wilson's dream of a peaceful community of nations. When Wilson died in 1924, British prime minister David Lloyd George observed, "He was as much a victim of the war as any soldier who died in the trenches."

THE ELECTION OF 1920

The presidential contest of 1920 suggested that Americans wanted to retreat from the internationalism, reform fervor, and social tensions associated with the war. Woodrow Wilson had wanted the 1920 election to be a referendum on the League of Nations and his conduct of the war. Ill and exhausted, Wilson did not run for reelection. A badly divided Democratic party compromised on Governor James M. Cox of Ohio as their candidate. A proven vote getter, Cox distanced himself from Wilson's policies, which had come under withering attack from many quarters.

The Republicans nominated Senator Warren G. Harding of Ohio. A political hack, the handsome and genial Harding had virtually no qualifications to be president, except that he looked like one. Harding's campaign was vague and ambiguous about the Versailles treaty and almost everything else. He struck a chord with the electorate in calling for a retreat from Wilsonian idealism. "America's present need," he said, "is not heroics but healing; not nostrums but normalcy; not revolution but restoration."

The notion of a "return to normalcy" proved very attractive to voters exhausted by the war, inflation, big government, and social dislocation. Harding won the greatest landslide in history to that date, carrying every state outside the South and taking the popular vote by 16 million to 9 million. Republicans retained their majorities in the House and Senate as well. Socialist Eugene Debs, still a powerful symbol of the dream of radical social change, managed to poll 900,000 votes from jail. But the overall vote repudiated Wilson and the progressive movement. Americans seemed eager to pull back from moralism in public and international controversies. But many of the underlying economic, social, and cultural changes wrought by the war would accelerate during the 1920s. In truth, there would never be a "return to normalcy."

CONCLUSION

Compared to the casualties and social upheavals endured by the European powers, the Great War's impact upon American life might appear slight. Yet the war brought underlying economic, social, and political dislocations that helped reshape American life long after the Armistice Day. Republican administrations invoked the wartime partnership between government and industry to justify an aggressive peacetime policy fostering cooperation between the state and business. Wartime production needs contributed to what economists later called "the second industrial revolution." Patriotic fervor and the exaggerated specter of "Bolshevism" could be used to repress radicalism, organized labor, feminism, and the entire legacy of progressive reform. The wartime measure of national prohibition evolved into perhaps the most contentious social issue of peacetime. Sophisticated use of sales techniques, psychology, and propaganda during the war helped define the newly powerful advertising and public relations industries of the 1920s. The growing visibility of immigrants and African Americans, especially in the nation's cities, provoked a xenophobic and racist backlash in the politics of the 1920s. More than anything else, the desire for "normalcy" reflected the deep anxieties evoked by America's wartime experience.

CHRONOLOGY

1903	U.S. obtains canal rights in Panama
1904	Roosevelt Corollary to Monroe Doctrine
1905	Theodore Roosevelt mediates peace treaty between Japan and Russia at Portsmouth Conference
1907	Root–Takahira Agreement
1911	Mexican Revolution begins
1912	U.S. troops intervene in Cuba and Nicaragua
1914	U.S. forces invade Mexico Panama Canal opens First World War begins
1915	Germany declares war zone around Great Britain; German U-boat sinks *Lusitania*
1916	Wilson reelected on pledge to keep U.S. out of war National Defense Act establishes preparedness program
1917	Germany declares new policy of unrestricted submarine warfare Zimmerman note U.S. declares war Selective Service Act Espionage Act Race riot in East St. Louis, Illinois Bolshevik Revolution begins in Russia
1918	Creation of War Industries Board, National War Labor Board, Food Administration, Fuel Administration, Committee on Public Information Sedition Act Eugene Debs imprisoned U.S. troops in action in France Armistice ends war Wilson unveils Fourteen Points
1919	Eighteenth Amendment (Prohibition) ratified Wilson travels to Paris Peace Conference Wilson suffers stroke while touring country in support of Versailles treaty Race riot in Chicago Steel strike begins Versailles treaty rejected by Senate Red Scare and Palmer raids begin
1920	Nineteenth Amendment (woman suffrage) ratified Warren Harding elected president

Additional Readings

EDWARD M. COFFMAN, *The War to End All Wars* (1968). A solid overview of the U.S. military during the war.

ROBERT H. FERRELL, *Woodrow Wilson and World War I* (1985). A close analysis of Wilson's handling of wartime diplomacy and domestic politics.

MAURINE GREENWALD, *Women, War, and Work* (1980). The best account of the impact of the war upon working women.

ELLIS W. HAWLEY, *The Great War and the Search for Modern Order* (1979). An important study arguing that World War I was a turning point in the evolution of the managerial institutions and values of modern capitalism.

FRIEDRICH KATZ, *The Secret War in Mexico* (1981). A detailed study of the complex relations among the U.S., the European powers, and the Mexican Revolution.

DAVID M. KENNEDY, *Over Here: The First World War and American Society* (1980). The best, most comprehensive one-volume analysis of the political and economic impact of the war on the domestic front.

WALTER LAFEBER, *The American Age* (1989). A fine survey of the history of U.S. foreign policy that includes a good analysis of the pre–World War I era.

N. GORDON LEVIN, JR., *Woodrow Wilson and World Politics* (1968). A pathbreaking study of Wilson's response to the Russian Revolution and his role at Versailles.

C. ROLAND MARCHAND, *The American Peace Movement and Social Reform, 1898–1918* (1973). A very useful overview of antiwar activists and their connection with prewar reform movements.

SALLY M. MILLER, *Victor Berger and the Promises of Constructive Socialism* (1973). Includes a detailed account of Berger's fight against the Espionage Act.

PAUL L. MURPHY, *World War I and the Origin of Civil Liberties* (1979). A good overview of the various civil liberties issues raised by the war and government efforts to suppress dissent.

ROBERT K. MURRAY, *The Red Scare: A Study in National Hysteria, 1919–1920* (1955). A pioneering analysis of the impact of the Bolshevik Revolution on domestic postwar politics.

JOE WILLIAM TROTTER, JR., ed., *The Great Migration in Historical Perspective* (1991). An excellent collection of essays analyzing the Great Migration, with special attention to issues of class and gender within the African American community.

NEIL A. WYNN, *From Progressivism to Prosperity: World War I and American Society* (1986). An illuminating account of the social impact of the war on American life. Effectively connects the war experience both with Progressive era trends and with postwar developments in the 1920s.

23 THE TWENTIES, 1920–1929

● THE MOVIE AUDIENCE AND HOLLYWOOD

Thomas Hart Benton. "Instruments of Power" from America Today. 1930. Distemper and egg tempera with oil glaze on gessoed linen. 92 × 160". Collection, The Equitable.

Inside midtown Manhattan's magnificent new Roxy Theater, a sellout crowd eagerly settled in for opening night. Outside, thousands of fans cheered wildly at the arrival of movie stars such as Charlie Chaplin, Gloria Swanson, and Harold Lloyd. A squadron of smartly uniformed ushers guided patrons under a five-story-tall rotunda to some 6,200 velvet-covered seats. The audience marveled at the huge gold-and-rose-colored murals, classical statuary, plush carpeting, and Gothic-style windows. It was easy to believe newspaper reports that the theater had cost $10 million to build. Suddenly, a flood of illumination lit up a pit orchestra of 110 musicians playing "The Star Spangled Banner." An array of 100 dancers then took the stage, performing ballet numbers and singing old southern melodies such as "My Old Kentucky Home" and "Swanee River." Congratulatory telegrams from President Calvin Coolidge and other dignitaries were projected onto a screen. Finally,

MASS CULTURE CREATES A NEW NATIONAL COMMUNITY

the evening's feature presentation, The Love of Sunya, *starring Gloria Swanson, began. The grand dream of Samuel L. "Roxy" Rothapfel, the theater's designer, to build what he called "the cathedral of the motion picture" was now a reality.*

At the time of the Roxy's opening in March of 1927, nearly 60 million Americans worshiped each week at movie theaters across the nation. The "movie palaces" of the 1920s were designed to transport patrons to exotic places and different times. As film pioneer Marcus Loew put it, "We sell tickets to theaters, not movies." Every large community boasted at least one opulent movie theater. Houston's Majestic was built to represent an ancient Italian garden; it had a ceiling made to look like an open sky, complete with stars and cloud formations. The Tivoli in Chicago featured opulent French Renaissance decor; Grauman's Egyptian in Los Angeles re-created the look of a pharaoh's tomb; and Albuquerque's Kimo drew inspiration from Navaho art and religion.

The remarkable popularity of motion pictures, and later radio, forged a new kind of community. A huge national audience regularly went to the movies, and the same entertainment could be enjoyed virtually anywhere in the country by just about everyone. Movies emerged as the most popular form in the new mass culture, and the appeal extended far beyond the films themselves, or even the theaters. Americans em-

An enthusiastic and youthful crowd of movie fans gathered outside Warners' Theatre in New York City, August, 1926. The main attraction, *Don Juan*, starring John Barrymore, featured the new "Vitaphone" sound process, which provided musical accompaniment to the film from a phonograph disc rather than a live orchestra. The next year Warner Brothers used "Vitaphone" for dialogue as well as music in *The Jazz Singer*, ushering in the "talkie" revolution in Hollywood films.

braced the cult of celebrity, voraciously consuming fan magazines, gossip columns, and news of the stars. By the 1920s, the production center for this dream world was Hollywood, California, a suburb of Los Angeles that had barely existed in 1890.

Motion picture companies found Hollywood an alluring alternative to the East Coast cities where they had been born. The reliably sunny and dry climate was ideal for the year-round shooting of film. The unique physical environment offered a perfect variety of scenic locations — mountains, desert, ocean — and downtown Los Angeles was only an hour away. Land was cheap and plentiful. Producers found the political environment attractive as well. Los Angeles was the leading non-union, open shop city in the country, and lower labor costs provided a powerful incentive to relocate. By the early 1920s Hollywood produced over 80 percent of the nation's motion pictures, and the myth of this new community was already emerging. The physical isolation of the town, its great distance from the Eastern cities, the absence of traditional sources of culture and learning, all contributed to movie folk looking at life in a self-consciously "Hollywood" way.

Hollywood, with its feel of a modern frontier boom town, was a new kind of American community. It attracted a young, cosmopolitan group of people lured by an ideal of urban mobility and a new way of life. In the 1920s, its untypically Americanwork force redefined the nation's cultural values around the consumption ideal associated with the movies and Southern California. Most of the top studio executives were Jewish immigrants from eastern and central Europe. Over half of the writers, directors, editors, and actors in Hollywood were born in large cities of over 100,000, at a time when most Americans hailed from rural areas or small towns. Two thirds of the performers were under thirty-five, and three-fourths of the actresses were under twenty-five. Over 90 percent of the writers had either higher education or journalism experience. Women made up one-third to one-half of this key group.

But it was the movie stars that dominated the Hollywood community. In the 1920s, Hollywood achieved a mythic power in American life as its movies came to symbolize the pleasures of leisure, consumption, and personal freedom. Film stars such as Charlie Chaplin, Mary Pickford, Rudolph Valentino, Gloria Swanson, and Douglas Fairbanks became popular idols as much for their highly publicized private lives as for their work lives. They were the nation's experts on how to live well. Movie folk built luxurious mansions in a variety of architectural styles and outfitted them with swimming pools, tennis courts, golf courses, and lavish gardens. The lines between movie roles and private lives blurred in the public eye.

Visitors often noted that Hollywood had no museums, art galleries, theaters, or other traditional institutions of high culture. How would the town's wealthy movie elite spend their time and money? By 1916 Charlie Chaplin, a working-class immigrant from the London slums, was earning $10,000 a week for the comedies that made him the most famous face in the world. He recalled trying to figure out what to do with his new wealth. "The money I earned was legendary, a symbol in figures, for I had never actually seen it. I therefore had to do something to prove I had it. So I procured a secretary, a valet, a car, a chauffeur."

When Mary Pickford announced one summer that she might take a vacation from moviemaking, she noted she would stay right at her estate, Pickfair. "I can't see why anyone would leave Los Angeles for a vacation," she told reporters. Ordinary Americans found it easy to identify with movie stars, many of whom had achieved enormous wealth and status. Unlike traditionally powerful individuals, such as industrialists or politicians, movie stars had no social authority over large groups of employees or voters. They too had to answer to a boss, and most had risen from humble beginnings. But above all, Hollywood, like the movies it churned out, represented for millions of Americans new possibilities: freedom, material success, upward mobility, and the chance to remake one's very identity. Only a relatively few Americans actually realized these during the 1920s. But by the end of the decade the Hollywood "dream factory" had helped forge a national community whose collective aspirations and desires were increasingly defined by those possibilities.

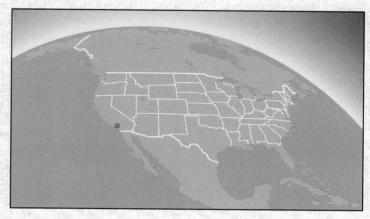

The State and Business

Throughout the 1920s, a confident Republican party maintained that it had ushered in a "new era" in American life. There was no doubt that Republicans controlled the national politics of the 1920s. There were important continuities between the administrations of Warren Harding, Calvin Coolidge, and Herbert Hoover. A new and closer relationship between the federal government and American business became the hallmark of Republican policy in both domestic and foreign affairs. And Republicans never tired of claiming that the business-government partnership their policies promoted was responsible for the nation's economic prosperity.

Harding and Coolidge

Handsome, genial, and well-spoken, Warren Harding may have looked the part of a president — but acting like one was another matter. Harding was a product of small-town Marion, Ohio, and the machine politics in his native state. Republican party officials had made a point of keeping Senator Harding, a compromise choice, as removed from the public eye as possible in the 1920 election. They correctly saw that active campaigning could only hurt their candidate by exposing his shallowness and intellectual weakness. Harding understood his own limitations. He sadly told one visitor to the White House shortly after taking office, "I knew that this job would be too much for me."

Harding surrounded himself with a close circle of friends, "the Ohio gang," delegating to them a great deal of administrative power. The president often conducted business as if he were in the relaxed, convivial, and masculine confines of a small-town saloon. Alice Roosevelt Longworth described the scene she encountered in Harding's crony-filled study when she tagged along with her husband, Congressman Nicholas Longworth, to a card game: "the air heavy with tobacco smoke, trays with bottles containing every imaginable brand of whiskey [standing] about, cards and poker chips ready at hand — a general atmosphere of waistcoat unbuttoned, feet on the desk, and spitoons alongside."

Shortly before his death from a coronary embolism in August 1923, Harding began to get wind of the scandals for which his administration is best remembered. He wearily told his friend Kansas journalist William Allen White: "My God, this is a hell of a job! I have no trouble with my ene-mies. . . . But my damned friends, my God-damn friends, White, they're the ones that keep me walking the floor nights."

A series of congressional investigations soon revealed a deep pattern of corruption. Attorney General Harry M. Daugherty had received bribes from violators of the Prohibition statutes. He had also failed to investigate graft in the Veterans Bureau, where Charles R. Forbes had pocketed a large chunk of the $250 million spent on hospitals and supplies. The worst affair was the Teapot Dome scandal involving Interior Secretary Albert Fall. Fall received hundreds of thousands of dollars in payoffs when he secretly leased navy oil reserves in Teapot Dome, Wyoming, and Elk Hills, California, to two private oil developers. He eventually became the first Cabinet officer ever to go to jail.

But the Harding administration's legacy was not all scandal. Andrew Mellon, an influential Pittsburgh banker, served as secretary of the Treasury under all three Republican presidents of the 1920s. One of the richest men in America, and a leading investor in the Aluminum Corporation of America and Gulf Oil, Mellon believed government ought to run on the same conservative principles as a corporation. He was a leading voice for trimming the federal budget and cutting taxes on incomes, corporate profits, and inheritances. These cuts, he argued, would free up capital for new investment and thus promote general economic growth. Mellon's tax program sharply cut taxes for both higher-income brackets and businesses. By 1926 a person earning a million a year paid less than a third of the income tax paid in 1921. Overall, Mellon's policies succeeded in rolling back much of the progressive taxation associated with Woodrow Wilson.

When Calvin Coolidge succeeded to the presidency in 1923, he seemed to most people the temperamental opposite of Harding. Born and raised in rural Vermont, elected governor of Massachusetts, and coming to national prominence only through the 1919 Boston police strike, "Silent Cal" was the quintessential New England Yankee. Taciturn, genteel, and completely honest, Coolidge believed in the least amount of government possible. He spent only four hours a day at the office. The core philosophy of the Republican "new era" was best expressed by Coolidge's famous aphorism "The business of America is business." He was in awe of wealthy men such as Andrew Mellon, and he thought them best suited to make society's key decisions.

Coolidge easily won election on his own in 1924. He benefited from the general prosperity and

Calvin Coolidge combined a spare, laconic political style with a flair for publicity. He frequently posed in the dress of a cowboy, farmer, or Indian chief.

the contrast he provided with the disgraced Harding. Coolidge defeated little-known Democrat John W. Davis, the compromise choice of a party badly divided between its rural and urban wings. Also running was Progressive party candidate Robert M. La Follette of Wisconsin, who mounted a reform campaign that attacked economic monopolies and called for government ownership of utilities.

In his full term, Coolidge showed most interest in reducing federal spending, lowering taxes, and blocking congressional initiatives. His saw his primary function as clearing the way for American businessmen. They, after all, were the agents of the era's unprecedented prosperity.

Herbert Hoover and the "Associative State"

The most influential figure of the "new era" was Herbert Hoover, who as secretary of commerce dominated the cabinets of Harding and Coolidge before becoming president himself in 1928. As an administrator, intellectual, and politician, Hoover effectively embodied the belief that enlightened business, encouraged and informed by the government, would act in the public interest. In the modern industrial age, Hoover believed, the government needed only to advise private groups about what national or international polices to pursue. "Reactionaries and radicals," he wrote in *American Individualism* (1922), "would assume that all reform and human advance must come through government. They have forgotten that progress must come from the steady lift of the individual and that the measure of national idealism and progress is the quality of idealism in the individual."

Hoover thus fused a faith in old-fashioned individualism with a strong commitment to the progressive possibilities offered by efficiency and rationality. Unlike an earlier generation of Republicans, Hoover wanted not just to create a favorable climate for business but to actively assist the business community. He spoke of creating an "associative state," in which the government would encourage voluntary cooperation among businesses and social groups. This became the central occupation of the Department of Commerce under Hoover's leadership. Under Hoover, the Bureau of Standards became one of the nation's leading research centers. It was especially involved with setting engineering standards for key American industries such as machine tools and automobiles. The bureau also helped standardize the styles, sizes, and designs of many consumer products, such as canned goods and refrigerators. The Commerce Department oversaw operational and safety standards in the emerging industries of commercial aviation and radio broadcasting.

Hoover actively encouraged the creation and expansion of national trade associations. By 1929 there were about 2,000 of them. At industrial conferences called by the Commerce Department, government officials explained the advantages of mutual cooperation in figuring prices and costs and then publishing the information. The idea was to improve efficiency by reducing competition. To some this practice violated the spirit of antitrust laws, but in the 1920s the Justice Department's Anti-Trust Division took a very lax view of its responsibility. In addition, the Supreme Court consistently upheld the legality of trade associations. Hoover also had a strong influence on presidential appointments to regulatory commissions; most of these went to men who had worked for the very firms the commissions had been designed to supervise. Regulatory commissions thus benefited from the technical expertise brought by industry leaders, but they in turn tended to remain uncritical of the industries they oversaw.

The government thus provided an ideal climate for the concentration of corporate wealth and power. The trend toward large corporate trusts and holding companies had been well under way since the late nineteenth century, but it accelerated in the 1920s. By 1929, the 200 largest American corporations owned almost half the total corporate wealth and about a fifth of the total national wealth. Concentration was particularly strong in manufacturing, retailing, mining, banking, and utilities. Vertical combinations also increased, through which large, integrated firms controlled raw materials, finished products, and distribution networks. These became common not only in older fields but in newer ones as well, such as the automobile, electrical, radio, and motion picture industries.

War Debts, Reparations, Keeping the Peace

America emerged from World War I the strongest economic power in the world. The war transformed the U.S. from the world's leading debtor nation to its most important creditor. European governments owed the U.S. government about $10 billion in 1919. In the private sector, the war ushered in an era of expanding American investment abroad. As late as 1914 foreign investments in the U.S. were about $3 billion more than the total of American capital invested abroad. By 1919 that situation was reversed: America had $3 billion more invested abroad than foreigners had invested in the U.S. By 1929 the surplus was $8 billion. New York replaced London as the center of international finance and capital markets.

During the 1920s, war debts and reparations were the single most divisive issue in international economics. In France and Great Britain, which both owed the U.S. large amounts in war loans, many concluded that the Uncle Sam who had offered assistance during wartime was really "Uncle Shylock" in disguise. In turn, many Americans viewed Europeans as ungrateful debtors. As President Coolidge acidly remarked, "They hired the money, didn't they?" In 1922 the U.S. Foreign Debt Commission negotiated an agreement with the debtor nations that called for them to repay $11.5 billion over a sixty-two-year period. But by the late 1920s, the European financial situation had become so desperate that the U.S. agreed to cancel a large part of these debts. Continued insistence by the U.S. that the Europeans pay at least a portion of the debt fed anti-American feeling in Europe and isolationism at home.

The Germans believed that war reparations, set at $33 billion by the Treaty of Versailles, not only unfairly punished the losers of the conflict but, by

This cartoon expressed the disgust many Americans felt over the failure of European nations to pay their war debts. Isolationist sentiment was a potent political force during the 1920s, yet the United States was more deeply tied to the world economy than ever before.

saddling their civilian economies with such massive debt, also deprived them of the very means to repay. In 1924 Herbert Hoover and Chicago banker Charles Dawes worked out a plan to aid the recovery of the German economy. The Dawes Plan reduced Germany's debt, stretched out the repayment period, and had American bankers lend funds to Germany. These measures helped stabilize Germany's currency and allowed it to make reparations payments to France and Great Britain. The Allies, in turn, were better able to pay their war debts to the U.S.

The horrors of the Great War led millions of citizens, as well as government officials, to advocate curbs on the world's armed forces. In 1921 Secretary of State Charles Evans Hughes took the initiative on arms limitations by inviting representatives from Great Britain, Japan, Italy, France, and China to meet in Washington to discuss reductions in military budgets. Hughes offered to scrap thirty American battleships and asked for comparable actions by the British and Japanese. He asked for a ten-year moratorium on the construction of new battleships and cruisers, and proposed a fixed ratio limiting naval tonnage. The following year the Five Power Treaty agreed to this scaling down of navies, and also pledged to respect the territorial integrity of China.

But the Italians and Japanese soon complained about the treaty's restraints, and ultimately the limits placed on navy construction were abandoned.

The U.S. never joined the League of Nations but it maintained an active, if selective, involvement in world affairs. In addition to the Dawes Plan and the American role in naval disarmament, the U.S. joined the league-sponsored World Court in 1926 and was represented at numerous league conferences. In 1928, with great fanfare, the U.S. joined sixty-two other nations in signing the Pact of Paris, better known as the Kellogg-Briand Pact, which grandly and naively renounced war in principle. Peace groups, such as the Women's Peace party and the Quaker-based Fellowship of Reconciliation, hailed the pact for formally outlawing war. But critics charged the Kellogg-Briand Pact was essentially meaningless since it lacked powers of enforcement and relied solely on the moral force of world opinion. Within weeks of its ratification, the U.S. Congress had appropriated $250 million for new battleships.

Commerce and Foreign Policy

Throughout the 1920s, Republican leaders pursued policies designed to expand American economic activity abroad. They understood that capitalist economies must be dynamic; they must expand their markets if they are to thrive. The goal was to increase the sales of American products and the investment of American capital abroad. But this also required stability in the international economic realm, especially with regard to currencies and capital flow. A key case was Germany. The Dawes Plan brought together private investors and government officials to ensure that the flow of American capital provided a solid foundation for the entire structure of international finance. American businesses began investing in Germany more extensively than in any other European nation.

During the 1920s, American oil, autos, farm machinery, and electrical equipment supplied a growing world market. Much of this expansion took place through the establishment of branch plants overseas by American companies. America's direct investment abroad increased from $3.8 billion in 1919 to $7.5 billion by 1929. Leading the American domination of the world market were General Electric, Ford, and Monsanto Chemical. American oil companies, with the support of the State Department, also challenged Great Britain's dominance in the oil fields of the Middle East and Latin America, forming powerful cartels with English firms. Ameri-can rubber companies, encouraged by Hoover, invested in new plantations in the Dutch East Indies and Brazil. For Hoover and other policy makers, American business abroad was simply rugged individualism at work around the globe.

The strategy of maximum freedom for private enterprise, backed by limited government advice and assistance, significantly boosted the power and profit levels of American overseas investors. But in Central and Latin America, in particular, aggressive U.S. investment also fostered chronically underdeveloped economies, dependent upon a few staple crops (sugar, coffee, cocoa, bananas) grown for export. The growing wealth and power of such U.S. companies as United Fruit made it more difficult for these nations to grow their own food or diversify their economies. U.S. economic dominance in the hemisphere also hampered the growth of democratic politics by favoring autocratic, military regimes that could be counted upon to protect U.S. investments.

During the 1920s, the U.S. peacefully resolved long-simmering disputes with Mexico over oil and mineral concessions held by American companies. In Central America, the U.S. withdrew its marines from the Dominican Republic in 1924, after many years of direct military intervention. But in Nicaragua, American troops continued to prop up the conservative government of Adolfo Diaz, who had worked closely with the State Department since 1911 and the first U.S. intervention. When a popular revolt led by General Augustino Sandino broke out in 1927, American marines landed and wound up supervising Nicaraguan elections over the next five years. They were not finally withdrawn until 1933, leaving a bitter legacy that would lead to crisis once again in the 1980s.

THE PRICE OF PROSPERITY

Warren G. Harding won the presidency in 1920 largely on his nostalgic call for a "return to normalcy." But in the decade following the end of World War I, the American economy underwent profound structural changes that guaranteed life would never be "normal" again. The 1920s saw an enormous increase in the efficiency of production, a steady climb in real wages, a decline in the average employee's work week, and a boom in consumer goods industries. Americans shared unevenly in the postwar prosperity, and by the end of the decade certain basic weaknesses in the economy helped to bring on the worst depression in American history.

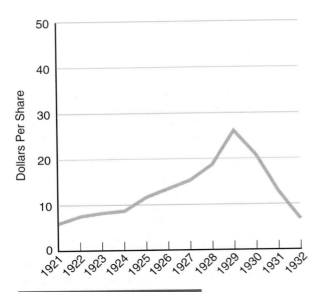

Stock Market Prices, 1921–1932

This graph charts the steep rise in common stock prices during the 1920s. Although only about 4 million Americans owned stocks during the period, "stock watching" became something of a national sport.

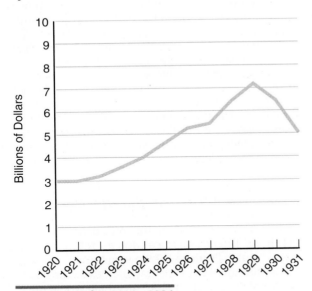

Consumer Debt, 1920–1931

The expansion of consumer borrowing was a key component of the era's prosperity. These figures do not include mortgages or money borrowed to purchase stocks. They reveal the great increase in "installment buying" for such consumer durable goods as automobiles and household appliances.

Yet overall, the nation experienced crucial transformations in how it organized its business, earned its living, and enjoyed its leisure time.

The Second Industrial Revolution

At the base of 1920s prosperity lay what historians have called the "second industrial revolution" in American manufacturing, in which technological innovations led the way to increasing industrial output without expansion of the labor force. Electricity replaced steam as the main power source for industry in these years. In 1914 only 30 percent of the nation's factories were electrified; by 1929, 70 percent relied on the electric motor rather than the steam engine. The spread of electricity enabled companies to use machinery that was far more efficient and flexible than steam- or water-powered equipment.

Much of the newer, automatic machinery could be used by unskilled and semiskilled workers, and it boosted the overall efficiency of American industry. Thus, in 1929 the average worker in manufacturing produced roughly three-quarters more per hour than he or she had in 1919. The machine industry itself, particularly electrical machinery, led in productivity gains, enjoying one of the fastest rates of expansion. It employed more workers than any other manufacturing sector—some 1.1 million in 1929—and not only satisfied a growing home market but provided 35 percent of the world's export of machinery.

During the late nineteenth century heavy industries such as machine tools, railroads, iron, and steel had pioneered mass production techniques. These were what economists call *producer-durable goods*. In the 1920s, newer *consumer-durable goods*, such as automobiles, radios, washing machines, and telephones, increasingly were produced by modern mass production techniques that allowed firms to make large profits while keeping prices affordable for consumers. Other consumer-based industries, such as canning, chemicals, synthetics, and plastics, began to change the everyday lives of millions of Americans. With more efficient management, greater mechanization, intensive product research, and ingenious sales and advertising methods, the consumer-based industries helped to nearly double industrial production in the 1920s.

America experienced a building boom during the 1920s, and its construction industry played a large role in the new prosperity. Expenditures for residential housing, nonresidential building, and public construction projects all showed steady growth after 1921. The demand for new housing was unprecedented, particularly with the backlog created during World War I, when little new construction took place. One and a half million people were being added to the population each year through immigration and a high birth rate. Extensive migration from rural areas to the cities and from the cities to suburbia stimulated the need for houses and apartments. The growth in automobile ownership, as well as improvements in public mass transit, made suburban living more attractive to families and more profitable for developers. Greatly expanded credit for home buying was available from commercial banks, savings and loan associations, and insurance companies. America's residential mortgage debt jumped from about $8 billion in 1919 to $27 billion in 1929.

The Modern Corporation

The postwar decade brought crucial underlying changes in the organization and techniques of American business, extending trends begun in the late nineteenth century. Large, bureaucratically complex corporations dominated the economy as never before. In the late nineteenth century, individual entrepreneurs such as John D. Rockefeller in oil and Andrew Carnegie in steel had provided a model for success. They maintained both corporate control (ownership) and business leadership (management) in their enterprises. In the 1920s, a managerial revolution increasingly divorced ownership of corporate stock from the everyday control of businesses. The new corporate ideal was to be found in men such as Alfred P. Sloan of General Motors and Owen D. Young of the Radio Corporation of America. These executives made their reputations as bureaucratic managers who coordinated production and sales, concentrated on long-range planning, and emphasized scientific research and development.

During the 1920s, the most successful corporations were those that led the way in three key areas: the thorough integration of production and distribution; diversification of products as an explicit strategy for growth; and the expansion of industrial research. The chemical and electrical machine industries led the way in these developments. For example, through World War I the Du Pont Company was a chemical manufacturer that had long specialized in explosives, such as gunpowder. After the war Du Pont aggressively diversified its production,

branching out to manufacture a variety of consumer goods. The company created separate but integrated divisions that produced and distributed new fabrics (such as rayon), paints, dyes, and celluloid products. Similarly, the great electrical manufacturers — General Electric and Westinghouse — transformed themselves after the war. Previously concentrating on manufacturing lighting and power equipment, they now diversified into household appliances, such as radios, washing machines, and refrigerators. The chemical and electrical industries also led the way in industrial research, where personnel developed and tested the commercial viability of new products. By 1929 roughly half of the people employed in industrial research worked in those two industries.

Merger and consolidation were making the economy more centralized than ever. By 1929 the 200 largest corporations owned nearly half the nation's corporate wealth — that is, physical plant, stock, and property. Half the total industrial income — revenue from sales of goods — was concentrated in 100 corporations. Oligopolies, where a few large producers controlled the market for a product, became the norm. Four companies packed almost three-quarters of all American meat. Another four rolled nine out of every ten cigarettes. National chain grocery, clothing, and drugstores began squeezing out local neighborhood businesses. One grocery chain alone, the Great Atlantic and Pacific Tea Company (A&P), accounted for 10 percent of all retail food sales in America. Its 15,000 stores sold a greater volume of goods than Ford Motor Company at its peak. These changes meant that Americans were increasingly members of national consumer communities, buying the same brands all over the country, as opposed to locally produced goods.

Modern corporate techniques were exploited most successfully by the leaders of newer industries: General Motors in automobiles, General Electric and Westinghouse in electrical goods, Du Pont in chemicals, American Telephone and Telegraph in communications. For example, AT&T's formal incorporation of Bell Laboratories in 1925 reflected the importance of ongoing research aimed at winning new patents, developing products, and cutting production costs. A growing class of salaried executives, plant managers, and engineers formed a new elite who made corporate policy without owning the business. They stressed scientific management and adapted the latest theories of behavioral psychology in their effort to make their workplaces more productive, stable, and profitable. "Industry's most

The red-fronted A & P grocery store became a familiar sight in communities across America, as the chain expanded from 400 stores in 1912 to over 15,000 by the end of the 1920s. A & P advertisements emphasized the availability of name brand goods at discount prices.

important task in this day of large-scale production," declared Bethlehem Steel chief Charles M. Schwab, "is management of men on a human basis."

Welfare Capitalism

The war experience had shown that the orderly and peaceful resolution of labor disputes through government mediation could significantly improve overall output and efficiency. Yet the wartime gains made by organized labor and the active sympathy shown to trade unions by the government war boards troubled most corporate leaders. Large employers aggressively promoted a variety of new programs designed to improve worker well-being and morale and thereby challenge the power and appeal of trade unions and collective bargaining. These schemes, collectively known as *welfare capitalism*, became a key part of corporate strategy in the 1920s.

One approach encouraged workers to acquire property through stock-purchasing plans or, less frequently, home ownership plans. By 1927, 800,000 employees had over $1 billion invested in over 300 companies. Other programs offered workers insurance policies covering accidents, illness, old age, and death. By 1928 some 6 million workers had group insurance coverage valued at $7.5 billion. Many plant managers and personnel departments consciously worked to improve safety conditions, provide more medical services, and establish sports and recreation programs. A 1926 survey of the 1,500

largest companies found that nearly half had comprehensive worker welfare programs; 80 percent had at least some such provisions. Employers hoped such measures would encourage workers to identify personally with the company and would discourage complaints on the job. To some extent they succeeded. But welfare capitalism could not solve the most chronic problems faced by industrial workers: seasonal unemployment, low wages, long hours, and unhealthy factory conditions.

Large corporations also mounted an effective antiunion campaign in the early 1920s. This drive was also called "the American plan," a tactic to associate unionism with foreign and un-American ideas. Backed by powerful business lobbies such as the National Association of Manufacturers and the Chamber of Commerce, campaign leaders called for the *open shop,* in which no employee would be compelled to join a union. If a union existed, nonmembers would still get whatever wages and rights the union had won — a policy that put organizers at a disadvantage in signing up new members.

The open shop undercut the gains won in a *union shop,* where new employees had to join an existing union, or a *closed shop,* where employers agreed to hire only union members. As alternatives, large employers such as U.S. Steel and International Harvester began setting up *company unions.* Here largely symbolic employee representation in management conferences was meant to substitute for the more confrontational process of collective bargaining. Company unions were often established simultaneously with antiunion campaigns in specific industries or communities.

These management strategies contributed to a sharp decline in the ranks of organized labor. Total union membership dropped from about 5 million in 1920 to 3.5 million in 1926. A large proportion of the remaining union members were concentrated in the skilled crafts of the building and printing trades. A conservative and timid union leadership was also responsible for the trend. After the death of Samuel Gompers in 1924, new American Federation of Labor president William Green showed no real interest in getting the unorganized into unions. Workers in the growing mass production industries such as automobiles, steel, and electrical goods were largely ignored. The federal government, which had provided limited wartime support for unions, now reverted to a more probusiness posture. The Supreme Court in particular was very unsympathetic toward unions, consistently upholding the use of injunctions to prevent strikes, picketing, and other union activities.

The Auto Age

In their classic community study *Middletown* (1929), sociologists Robert and Helen Lynd noted the dramatic impact of the car on the social life of Muncie, Indiana. "Why on earth do you need to study what's changing this country?" asked one lifelong Muncie resident in 1924. "I can tell you what's happening in just four letters: A–U–T–O!" This remark hardly seems much of an exaggeration today. No single development could match the automobile explosion of the postwar years for changing how Americans worked, lived, and played. The auto industry offered the clearest example of the rise to prominence of consumer durables. During the 1920s, America made approximately 85 percent of all the world's passenger cars. By 1929 motor vehicle producers were the most productive industry in the U.S. in terms of value, producing some 4.8 million cars in 1929. Over 26 million cars were on American roads by then, roughly one car for every five people.

This extraordinary new industry had mushroomed in less than a generation. Its great pioneer, Henry Ford, had shown how the use of a continuous assembly line could drastically reduce the number of worker-hours required to produce a single vehicle. Ford revolutionized the factory shop floor with new, custom-built machinery, such as the engine-boring drill press and the pneumatic wrench, and a more efficient layout. "Every piece of work in the shop moves," Ford boasted. "It may move on hooks or overhead chains, going to assembly in the exact order in which the parts are required; it may travel on a moving platform, or it may go by gravity, but the point is that there is no lifting or trucking of anything other than materials." In 1913 it took thirteen hours to produce one automobile. In 1914, at his sprawling new Highland Park assembly plant just outside Detroit, Ford's system finished one car every ninety minutes. By 1925, cars were rolling off his assembly line at the rate of one every ten seconds.

In 1914 Ford startled American industry by inaugurating a new wage scale: five dollars for an eight-hour day. This was roughly double the going pay rate for industrial labor, and a shorter work day as well. But in defying the conventional economic

Finished automobiles roll off the moving assembly line at the Ford Motor Company, Highland Park, Michigan, c.1920. During the 1920s Henry Ford achieved the status of folk hero, as his name became synonymous with the techniques of mass production. Ford cultivated a public image of himself as the heroic genius of the auto industry, greatly exaggerating his individual achievements.

wisdom of the day, Ford acted less out of benevolence than out of shrewdness. He understood that workers were consumers as well as producers, and the new wage scale helped boost sales of Ford cars. It also reduced the high turnover rate in his labor force and increased worker efficiency, thus cutting production costs. In hiring new workers, Ford emphasized not skill level but rather stamina, speed, and the ability to concentrate on repetitive tasks. Roughly two-thirds of the labor force at Ford consisted of immigrants from southern and eastern Europe. By the early 1920s Ford also employed about 5,000 African Americans, more than any other large American corporation. Ford's mass production system and economies of scale meant he could progressively reduce the price of the automobile, bringing it within the reach of millions of Americans. The famous Model T, thoroughly standardized and available only in black, cost just under $300 in 1924 — about three months' wages for the best-paid factory workers.

By 1927 Ford had produced 15 million Model Ts. But by then Ford's major competitor, General Motors, had pioneered an effective new strategy based on changing models every year and offering consumers more choice in their cars. GM, under the guidance of Alfred P. Sloan, was organized around separate divisions that appealed to particular segments of the market. Cadillac, for example, produced the most expensive GM cars, Chevrolet the cheapest. Sloan established the General Motors Acceptance Corporation, the first consumer credit organization to finance car sales through time payments. The GM business structure, along with its attempts to match production with demand through sophisticated market research and sales forecasting, became a widely copied model for other large American corporations.

The auto industry had a powerful ripple effect on the entire economy. It provided a large market for makers of steel, rubber, glass, and petroleum products. It stimulated public spending for good roads and extended the housing boom to new suburbs. Showrooms, repair shops, and gas stations appeared in thousands of communities. New small enterprises, from motels to billboard advertising to roadside diners, sprang up as motorists took to the highway. The rapid development of Florida and California, in particular, was partly a response to the growing influence of the automobile. All over the country the holiday business became more lucrative; the modern tourist industry owed much to the spread of auto ownership in the 1920s.

As a mechanical extension of the self, automobiles widened the experiences of millions of Ameri-

Until 1924 Henry Ford had disdained national advertising for his cars. But as General Motors gained a competitive edge by making yearly changes in style and technology, Ford was forced to pay more attention to advertising. This ad was directed at "Mrs. Consumer," combining appeals to both female independence and motherly duties.

cans. They made the exploration of the world outside one's local community much easier and more attractive than ever. Cars allowed people to go when and where they wished, to travel at high speeds, alone or with others. If for some car ownership merely reinforced old social patterns — for example, driving to church on Sunday or visiting with neighbors — others used their cars to explore new places, shop in the nearest city, or take vacations. Leisure, in the sense of getting away from the routines of work and school, became a more regular part of everyday life. The courtship practices of America's youth were undoubtedly altered by the auto. "What on earth do you want me to do?" complained one Middletown high school girl to her anxious father. "Just sit around home all evening?" Young people took advantage of the car to gain privacy and distance from their parents, and for many the car became the site of their first sexual experiences.

Cities and Suburbs

One critical trend in living patterns had become apparent by 1920. The federal census for that year showed that for the first time in American history, the proportion of the population classified as urban — 51 percent — was greater than that classified as rural. The census definition of an urban place — one with more than 2,500 people — was not a very useful indicator of urban growth. More revealing was the steady increase in the number of big cities. In 1910 there were sixty cities with more than 100,000 inhabitants, in 1920 there were sixty-eight, and by 1930 there were ninety-two. New York grew by 25 percent, to over 7 million. Detroit, home of the auto industry, doubled its population, to nearly 2 million.

Houston offers a good example of how the automobile shaped an urban community. A sleepy railroad town that served the Texas Gulf Coast and interior, Houston contained about 75,000 people in 1910. The enormous demand for gasoline and other petroleum products helped transform the city into a busy center for oil refining. Population soared to 300,000 by the end of the 1920s. Abundant cheap land and the absence of government zoning ordinances, combined with the availability of the automobile, pushed Houston to expand horizontally rather than vertically. It became the archetypal decentralized, low-density city, sprawling miles in each direction from downtown, and thoroughly dependent upon automobiles and roads for its sense of community. Other Sunbelt cities, such as Los Angeles, Miami, and San Diego, experienced similar land use patterns and sharp population growth during the decade.

In the 1920s it was these large metropolitan districts that came to play a central role in defining American culture and politics. Cities attracted millions of Americans, white and black, from small towns and farms, as well as immigrants from abroad. They were centers for business opportunity, for better jobs, for cultural enjoyment, and for greater personal freedom. The presence of large ethnic communities attracted immigrants with family ties or simply looking for familiar cultures. The Great Migration of African Americans begun in the World War I years continued apace during the 1920s, as black southerners left rural areas in search of better economic opportunity. Roughly 1.5 million African Americans migrated to cities during the decade, doubling the black populations of New York, Chicago, Detroit, and Houston.

Cities grew both vertically and horizontally in these years. Skylines around the country were re-made as architects took advantage of steel-skeleton construction technology to build skyscrapers. By 1930, American cities boasted nearly 400 buildings over 20 stories tall. New York's Empire State Building, completed in 1931, was the tallest building in the world, rising 1,250 feet into the sky. It had room for 25,000 commercial and residential tenants in its 102 stories. As in the case of Houston, cities expanded on the ground too, sprawling into the surrounding countryside. Los Angeles provided a model for future cities heavily dependent on the automobile. A spreading network of roads connected new subdivisions over a large area, boosting the Los Angeles population from around 100,000 in 1900 to over 1 million by 1930.

The 1920s saw an acceleration of suburban communities as well, made possible in large part by the automobile boom. Undeveloped land on the fringes of cities became valuable real estate, and the rate of growth of these suburbs was twice that of their core communities. Grosse Pointe, near Detroit, and Elmwood Park, near Chicago, grew by over 700 percent in ten years. Long Island's Nassau County, just east of New York City, tripled in population. All of the new "automobile suburbs" differed in important ways from earlier suburbs built along mass transit lines. The car allowed for a larger average lot size, and in turn lower residential density. It also became essential for commuting to work and encouraged deconcentration of employment. The suburbs would increasingly become not only places to live, but centers for working and shopping as well.

Exceptions: Agriculture, Sick Industries

Amidst prosperity and progress, there were large pockets of the country that lagged behind. Advances in real income and improvements in the standard of living for workers and farmers were uneven at best. During the 1920s one-quarter of all American workers were employed in agriculture; yet the farm sector failed to share in the general prosperity. The years 1914–19 had been a kind of golden age for the nation's farmers. Increased wartime demands, along with the devastation of much of European agriculture, had led to record-high prices for many crops. In addition, the wartime Food Administration had encouraged a great increase in agricultural production. But with the war's end American farmers began to suffer from a chronic worldwide surplus of agricultural commodities.

Prices began to drop sharply in 1920. A bushel of wheat that brought $2.58 in June of that year fetched only $1.43 in December. By the end of 1921 the price had dropped below $1.00 a bushel. Cotton, which sold at $.37 a pound in mid-1920, fell to $.14 by year's end. Hog and cattle prices declined nearly 50 percent. By 1921 net farm income was down more than half from the year before. Land values also dropped, wiping out billions in capital investment. Behind these aggregate statistics were hundreds of thousands of individual human tragedies on the nation's 6 million farms. A 1928 song, "Eleven Cent Cotton," expressed the farmer's lament:

" 'Leven cent cotton, forty cent meat,
How in the world can a poor man eat?
Pray for the sunshine, 'cause it will rain,
Things gettin' worse, drivin' us insane.

Many farmers were squeezed between low prices and high operating expenses. Farm debts, incurred by purchase of real estate and equipment, were fixed expenses and proved to be crushing burdens as prices spiraled downward. During the war many had gone heavily into debt to buy land and expand operations with new machinery. Farm mortgages had doubled between 1910 and 1920, from $3.3 billion to $6.7 billion, and another $2.7 billion was added to the total by 1925. American farm products, moreover, faced stiffer competition abroad from reviving European agriculture and the expanding output from countries such as Canada, Argentina, and Australia. Efforts to ease the farmer's plight through governmental reform were largely unsuccessful. Individual farmers, traditionally independent, could not influence the price of commodities they sold or bought. It was extremely difficult for farmers to act collectively.

To be sure, some farmers thrived, especially those engaged in citrus, dairy, and truck farming, as well as large corporate enterprises that farmed the new wheat lands of the high plains. These farmers profited from the growing importance of national markets. Improved transportation and chain supermarkets allowed for a wider and more regular distribution of such foods as oranges, lemons, and fresh green vegetables. But per capita farm income remained well below what it had been in 1919, and the gap between farm and nonfarm income widened. By 1929 the average income per person on farms was $223, compared with $870 for nonfarm workers. By the end of the decade, hundreds of thousands had quit farming altogether for jobs in mills and factories. And fewer farmers owned their land. In 1930, 42 percent of all farmers were tenants, compared with 37 percent in 1919.

The American Farm Bureau Federation, founded in 1921, became an influential yet conservative lobby for agricultural interests in Washington.

The most important initiatives for federal farm relief were the McNary-Haugen bills, a series of complicated measures designed to prop up and stabilize farm prices. The basic idea, borrowed from the old Populist proposals of the 1890s, called for the government to purchase farm surpluses and either store them until prices rose or sell them on the world market. The result was supposed to be higher domestic prices for farm products. After the McNary-Haugen bill of 1927 finally passed Congress, President Coolidge vetoed it as unwarranted federal interference in the economy. Government relief for hard-pressed farmers would not arrive until the New Deal programs implemented in response to the Great Depression.

There were also large sectors of American industry that failed to share in the decade's prosperity. As oil and natural gas gained in importance, America's coal mines became a less important source of energy. A combination of shrinking demand, new mining technology, and a series of losing strikes reduced the coal labor force by one-quarter. The United Mine Workers, perhaps the strongest AFL union in 1920 with 500,000 members, had shrunk to 75,000 by 1928. Economic hardship was widespread in many mining communities dependent upon coal, particularly in Appalachia and the southern Midwest. And those miners who did work earned lower hourly wages.

Other big industries in serious decline included railroads and textiles. The number of miles of railroad track actually began to decrease after 1920 as automobiles and trucks began to displace trains. In textiles, shrinking demand and overcapacity (too many factories) were chronic problems. The women's fashions of the 1920s generally required less material for dresses, and competition from synthetic fibers such as rayon depressed demand for cotton textiles. To improve profit margins, textile manufacturers in New England and other parts of the Northeast began a long-range shift of operations to the South, where nonunion shops and substandard wages became the rule. Between 1923 and 1933, 40 percent of New England's textile factories closed and nearly 100,000 of the 190,000 workers employed there lost their jobs. Many older New England manufacturing centers, such as Lawrence, Lowell, Nashua, Manchester, and Fall River, were hard hit by this shift.

The center of the American textile industry shifted permanently to the Piedmont region of North and South Carolina. Southern mills increased their work force from 220,000 to 257,000 between 1923 and 1933. By the latter year they employed nearly 70 percent of the workers in the industry. One of the biggest new textile communities was Gastonia, North Carolina, which proudly called itself "the South's City of Spindles." As the dominant employers and overall economic powers in southern textile communities, manufacturers aggressively tried to improve productivity and cut costs. Southern mills generally operated night and day, used the newest labor-saving machinery, and cut back on the wage gains of the World War I years. Southern millhands paid the price for what they called *stretch-out* — a catchall term describing the changes that had them tending more and more machines, receiving lower wages, working nights, and losing nearly all control over the pace and method of production.

THE NEW MASS CULTURE

New media of communication reshaped American culture in the 1920s. The phrase "Roaring Twenties" makes best sense as a shorthand description for the explosion of image- and sound-making machinery that came to dominate so much of American life. Radio, movies, new kinds of journalism, and the recording industry were deeply connected with the new culture of consumption. They also encouraged the parallel emergence of celebrity as a defining element in modern life. As technologies of mass impression, the media established national standards and norms for much of our culture — habit, dress, language, sounds, social behavior. For millions of Americans, the new media radically altered the rhythms of everyday life and redefined what it meant to be "normal." To be sure, most working-class families had only limited access to the world of mass consumption — and many had only limited interest in it. But the new mass culture helped redefine the ideal of "the good life" and made the images, if not the substance, of it available to a national community.

Advertising Modernity

A thriving advertising industry both reflected and encouraged the growing importance of consumer goods in American life. Earlier efforts at advertising products had been confined mostly to staid newspaper and magazine spreads that offered basic information about products. The most creative advertising was usually for dubious products, such as patent medicines. The successful efforts of the government's Committee on Public Information, set up to "sell" World War I to Americans, suggested that

Cigarette smoking increased enormously in the 1920s among both men and women, and tobacco companies were among the largest national advertisers. This 1927 ad linked smoking Camels to male sexual prowess, and it also made an appeal to the new market of female smokers.

new techniques using modern communication media could convince people to buy a wide range of goods and services. As a profession, advertising reached a higher level of respectability, sophistication, and economic power in American life during the 1920s.

The larger ad agencies moved toward a more scientific approach by sponsoring market research and welcoming the language of psychology to their profession. John B. Watson, influential founder of behavioral psychology, left Johns Hopkins University in 1927 to join the prominent J. Walter Thompson ad agency in New York. "As a psychologist," Watson said, "I decry the fact that we are all trained so much alike — that there is so little individuality in the world. But, as an advertising man, I rejoice; my bread and butter depends on it."

Advertisers began focusing on the needs, desires, and anxieties of the consumer rather than the qualities of the product. "There are certain things that most people believe," noted one ad agency executive in 1927. "The moment your copy is linked to one of those beliefs, more than half your battle is won." Ad agencies and their clients invested extraordinary amounts of time, energy, and money trying to discover and, to some extent, shape those beliefs. Leading agencies such as Lord and Thomas in Chicago and J. Walter Thompson in New York combined knowledge gained from market research and consumer surveys with carefully prepared graphics and text to sell their clients' wares. High-powered ad campaigns made new products like Fleischmann's Yeast and Kotex household words across the country. One of the more spectacular examples of advertising effectiveness involved an old product, Listerine, which had been marketed as a general antiseptic for years by Lambert Pharmaceuticals. A new ad campaign touting Listerine as a cure for halitosis — a scientific-sounding term for bad breath — boosted Lambert's profits from $100,000 in 1922 to over $4 million in 1927.

Above all, advertising celebrated consumption itself as a positive good. In this sense the new advertising ethic was a therapeutic one, promising that products would contribute to the buyer's physical, psychic, or emotional well-being. Certain strategies, such as appeals to nature, medical authority, and personal freedom, were utilized with great success. Many of these themes and techniques are still familiar today. Well-financed ad campaigns were especially crucial for marketing newer consumer goods such as cars, electrical appliances, and personal hygiene products. Total advertising volume in all media — newspapers, magazines, radio, billboards — jumped from $1.4 billion in 1919 to $3 billion in 1929.

Radio Broadcasting

In the fall of 1920, Westinghouse executive Harry P. Davis noticed that amateur broadcasts from the garage of an employee had attracted attention in the local Pittsburgh press. A department store advertised radio sets capable of picking up these "wireless concerts." Davis converted this amateur station to a stronger one at the Westinghouse main plant. Beginning with the presidential election returns that November, station KDKA offered regular nightly broadcasts that were probably heard by only a few hundred people. Radio broadcasting, begun as a service for selling cheap radio sets left over from World War I, would soon sweep the nation.

Before KDKA, wireless technology had been of interest only to the military, the telephone industry, and a few thousand "ham" (amateur) operators who enjoyed communicating with each other. The "radio mania" of the early 1920s was a response to the new possibilities offered by broadcasting. By 1923 nearly 600 stations had been licensed by the Department of Commerce and about 600,000 Americans had bought radios. Most of the early stations were owned by radio equipment manufacturers, newspapers, department stores, and universities. Early programs included live popular music, phonograph records, talks by college professors, church services, and news and weather reports. For millions of Americans, especially in rural areas and small towns, radio provided a new and exciting link to the larger national community of consumption.

Who would pay for radio programs? This was the essential question for the new industry. A variety of plans were put forward. In the early 1920s, owners and operators of radio stations included state universities, cities, ethnic societies, labor unions, and churches. But by the end of the decade commercial (or "toll") broadcasting emerged as the answer. The dominant corporations in the industry — General Electric, Westinghouse, RCA, and AT&T — settled on the idea that advertisers would foot the bill for radio. Millions of listeners might be the consumers of radio shows, but sponsors were to be the customers. Only the sponsors and their advertising agencies enjoyed a direct relationship with broadcasters. Sponsors advertised directly or indirectly to the mass audience through such shows as the "Eveready Hour," the "Ipana Troubadors," and the "Taystee Loafers." AT&T leased its nationwide system of telephone wires to allow the linking of many stations into powerful radio networks, such as the National Broadcasting System (1926) and the Columbia Broadcasting System (1928).

Radio broadcasting created a national community of listeners, just as motion pictures created one of viewers. NBC and CBS led the way in creating popular radio programs that relied heavily upon older cultural forms. Variety shows, hosted by vaudeville comedians, became the first important style of network radio. Radio's first truly national hit, "The Amos 'n' Andy Show" (1928), was a direct descendant of nineteenth-century "blackface" minstrel entertainment. Radio did more than any previous medium to publicize and commercialize previously isolated forms of American music, such as country-and-western, blues, and jazz. Broadcasts of baseball and college football games proved especially popular; millions of fans closely followed the exploits of new heroes such as Babe Ruth and Red Grange. In 1930, some 600 stations were broadcasting to over 12 million radio homes, or roughly 40 percent of American families. By that time all the elements that characterize the present American system of broadcasting could be found in radio.

Movie-Made America

The other great national medium of communication, motion pictures, also matured in the decade after World War I. The early movie industry, centered in New York and a few other big cities, had made moviegoing a regular habit for millions of Americans, especially immigrants and the working class. They flocked to cheap, storefront theaters, called *nickelodeons,* to watch short Westerns, slapstick comedies, melodramas, and travelogues. By 1914 there were about 18,000 places showing motion pictures, over 7 million daily admissions, and $300 million in annual receipts. With the shift of the industry westward to Hollywood, movies entered a new phase of business expansion.

By the 1920s, the "Big Eight" Hollywood studios produced 90 percent of the 800 movies made each year. Large studios such as Paramount, Fox, M-G-M, Universal, and Warner Brothers dominated the business with longer and more expensively produced movies—feature films. These companies were founded and controlled by Jewish immigrants from Europe, all of whom had a talent for discovering and exploiting changes in popular tastes. Adolph Zukor, the Hungarian-born head of Paramount, had been a furrier in New York City. Samuel Goldwyn, a founder of M-G-M, had been a glove salesman. William Fox, of Fox Pictures, began as a garment cutter in Brooklyn. Most of the immigrant moguls had started in the business by buying or managing small movie theaters and then entering the production phase.

The studio system, which came to dominate moviemaking, was based on industrial principles. Each studio combined the three functions of production, distribution, and exhibition, and each controlled hundreds of movie theaters around the country. When Warner Brothers scored a huge hit with *The Jazz Singer* in 1927, starring Al Jolson, Hollywood added the dimension of sound to its movies. New genres—musicals, gangster films, and screwball comedies—soon became popular. The higher costs associated with "talkies" also increased the studios' reliance upon Wall Street investors and banks for working capital.

At the heart of Hollywood's success was the star system and the accompanying cult of celebrity. Stars

Mary Pickford, one of the most popular movie stars of the 1910s and 1920s, shown here reading a feminist newspaper in a publicity photo c.1917. Pickford frequently portrayed young women struggling for economic freedom from men. She wrote weekly columns for women in which she backed suffrage and urged her female readers to be more self sufficient. Pickford embodied the new, mass media based "celebrity" of the 1920s.

like Charlie Chaplin, Mary Pickford, Douglas Fairbanks, Rudolph Valentino, and Greta Garbo became vital to the fantasy lives of millions. Films that emphasized sexual themes, by such directors as Cecil B. DeMille and Erich von Stroheim, tended to celebrate youth, play, athleticism, and the liberating power of consumer goods, as much as anything. For many fans, there was only a vague line separating the on-screen and off-screen adventures of the stars. Studio publicity, fan magazines, and gossip columns reinforced this ambiguity. Film idols, with their mansions, cars, parties, and private escapades, became the national experts on leisure and consumption. Young Americans in particular looked to movies to learn how to dress, wear their hair, talk, or kiss.

In the 1920s Hollywood tried to broaden its appeal to women and middle-class Americans. Moviemakers attracted new fans by producing more spectacular movies and by building elegant "movie palaces" in which to watch them. But many Americans, particularly in rural areas and small towns, worried about Hollywood's impact on traditional sexual morality. They attacked the permissiveness associated with Hollywood life, and many states created censorship boards to pass upon movies before allowing them to be screened in theaters. In 1921, a highly publicized sex scandal involving popular comedian Roscoe "Fatty" Arbuckle brought a wave of negative publicity to Hollywood. Frightened studio heads resolved to improve their public image.

To counter the growing calls for government censorship, Hollywood's studios came up with a plan to censor themselves. They hired Will Hays to head the Motion Picture Producers and Distributors Association. Hays was just what the immigrant moguls needed. An Indiana Republican, elder in the Presbyterian Church, and former postmaster general under President Harding, he personified midwestern Protestant respectability. As the movie industry's czar, Hays lobbyied against censorship laws, wrote pamphlets defending the movie business, and began setting guidelines for what could and could not be depicted on the screen. Above all, he insisted that movies be treated like any other industrial enterprise. Hays understood, too, the relationship between Hollywood's success and the growth of the nation's consumer culture. "More and more," Hays argued in 1926, "is the motion picture being recognized as a stimulant to trade. No longer does the girl in Sullivan, Indiana, guess what the styles are going to be in three months. She knows because she sees them on the screen."

New Forms of Journalism

Sensationalism in American journalism was not invented in the 1920s. But a new kind of newspaper, the tabloid, became quite popular in the postwar years. The *New York Daily News,* founded in 1919 by Joseph M. Patterson, was the first to develop the tabloid style. Its folded-in-half page size made it convenient to read on buses or subways. The *News* devoted much of its space to photographs and other illustrations. It offered readers a terse, lively reporting style that emphasized news about crime, sex, scandal, and sports. The gossip column, focusing on the lives of entertainers and celebrities, was another very popular tabloid feature.

Daily News circulation reached 400,000 in 1922 and 1.3 million by 1929. Its success spawned a host of imitators in New York and elsewhere. New papers like the *Chicago Times* and the *Los Angeles Daily News* brought the tabloid style to cities across America, while some older papers, such as the *Denver Rocky Mountain News,* adopted the new format. The circulation of existing dailies was little affected. Tabloids had instead discovered an audience of millions who had never read newspapers before. Most of these new readers were poorly educated working-class city dwellers, many of whom were immigrants or their children. Many critics dismissed the tabloids for being, as one put it, "synonomous with bad taste, vulgarity, and a degenerate sensationalism." But the popularity of the tabloids forced advertising agencies to expand their definition of the consumer market to include working-class and immigrant readers. And advertisers borrowed freely from tabloid techniques—"true confession" stories, racy headlines, shocking photos—to reach that market.

Journalism followed the larger economic trend toward consolidation and merger. Newspaper chains like Hearst, Gannett, and Scripps-Howard flourished during the 1920s. There was a sizable increase in the number of these chains and in the percentage of total daily circulation that was chain-owned. By the early 1930s, the Hearst organization alone controlled twenty-six dailies in eighteen cities, accounting for 14 percent of the nation's newspaper circulation. One of every four Sunday papers sold in America was owned by the Hearst group. One journalist lamented this standardization in 1930: "When one travels through the country on a Sunday on a fast train and buys Sunday papers, one finds the same 'comics,' the same Sunday magazines, the same special 'features' in almost all of them and, of course, in most of them precisely the same Associated Press news." New forms of journalism, like radio and the movies, contributed to the growth of a national consumer community.

The Phonograph and the Recording Industry

Like radio and movies, the phonograph came into its own in the 1920s as a popular means of entertainment. Originally marketed in the 1890s, early phonographs used wax cylinders that could both record and replay. But the sound quality was quite poor and the cylinders were difficult to handle. The convenient permanently grooved disc recordings introduced around World War I were eagerly snapped up by the public, even though discs could not be used to make recordings at home. The popularity of records transformed the popular music business, displacing both cylinders and sheet music as the major source of music in the home.

The phonograph business boomed. Dance crazes such as the fox trot, tango, and grizzly bear, done to complex ragtime and Latin rhythms, boosted the record business tremendously. Dixieland jazz, which recorded well, also captured the public's fancy in the early 1920s, and records provided the music for newer popular dances like the

Charleston and the black bottom. In 1921 annual record sales exceeded 100 million, and over 200 companies produced some 2 million phonographs. That year Americans spent $106 million on records, more than any other leisure-time expenditure.

Record sales declined toward the end of the decade due to competition from radio. But in a broader cultural sense, records continued to transform American popular culture. Most important, record companies discovered lucrative regional and ethnic markets for country music, which appealed primarily to white southerners, and blues and jazz, which appealed primarily to African Americans. Country musicians like the Carter Family and Jimmie Rodgers and blues singers like Blind Lemon Jefferson and Ma Rainey had their performances put on record for the first time. Their records sold mainly in specialized "hillbilly" and "race" markets. Yet they were also played over the radio, and millions of Americans began to hear musical styles and performers who had previously been isolated. Blues great Bessie Smith sold hundreds of thousands of records and single-handedly kept the fledgling Columbia Record Company profitable. The combination of records and radio started an extraordinary cross-fertilization of American musics that continues to this day.

A New Morality?

The new mass media intensified the place of consumption in American life during the 1920s. Happiness, success, personal fulfillment — "the good life" — were increasingly defined by what one owned. Movie stars, radio personalities, sports heroes, and popular musicians became the elite figures in a new culture of celebrity defined by the mass media. They were the ultimate consumers and the model for achievement in the new age. Great events and abstract issues were made real through movie close-ups, radio interviews, and tabloid photos. The new media relentlessly created and disseminated images that are still familiar today. Think of Babe Ruth, Al Capone, Mary Pickford, Charles Lindbergh, or Amelia Earhart, to name just a few.

But images do not tell the whole story. Consider one of the most enduring images of the "Roaring Twenties," the flapper. She was usually portrayed on screen, in novels, and in the press as a young, sexually aggressive woman with bobbed hair, rouged cheeks, and short skirt. She loved to dance to jazz music, enjoyed smoking cigarettes, and drank bootleg liquor in cabarets and dance halls. She could also be competitive, assertive, and a good pal. As writer Zelda Fitzgerald put it in 1924: "I think a woman gets more happiness out of being gay, light hearted, unconventional, mistress of her own fate. . . . I want [my daughter] to be a flapper, because flappers are brave and gay and beautiful."

Was the flapper a genuine representative of the 1920s? Did she embody the "new morality" that was so widely discussed and chronicled in the media of the day? Historians have discovered that the flapper certainly did exist, but she was neither as new nor as widespread a phenomenon as the image would suggest. The delight in sensuality, individual pleasure, and rhythmically complex dance and music had long been key elements of subcultures on the fringes of middle-class society: bohemian enclaves, communities of political radicals, African American ghettoes, working-class dance halls. In the 1920s, these activities became normative for a growing number of white middle-class Americans, including women. Jazz, sexual experimentation, heavy use of makeup, and cigarette smoking spread to college campuses and were heavily documented by the new media as well.

Several sources, most of them rooted in earlier years, can be found for the more open and widespread treatment of sexuality in the 1920s. The social purity movement had reached a high point during World War I, with the government supporting sex education for the troops. The writings of Havelock Ellis, Ellen Key, and Sigmund Freud stressed the central role of sexuality in human experience, arguing that sex was a positive, healthy impulse and repression could be damaging to mental and emotional health. The pioneering efforts of Margaret Sanger in educating women about birth control had begun before World War I (see Chapter 21). She had started by taking direct action, through pamphlets and free clinics, to liberate working-class women from "enforced motherhood." In the 1920s, Sanger campaigned vigorously — through her journal *Birth Control Review,* in books, on speaking tours — to make contraception freely available to all women.

Sexuality was also a key component in the new mass media. Advertisers routinely used sex appeal to sell products. Tabloid newspapers exploited sex with cheesecake photos, but they also provided features giving advice on sex hygiene and venereal disease. And movies, of course, featured powerful sex symbols, such as Rudolph Valentino, Gloria Swanson, John Gilbert, and Clara Bow, whose popularity depended upon their attraction to the opposite sex. Movies also taught young people the etiquette of sex. This was clear in many motion picture diaries kept by young people, part of the movie research conducted by social scientists. One typical eighteen-year-old college student wrote:

"These passionate pictures stir such longings, desires, and urges as I never expected any person to possess. Just the way the passionate lover held his sweetheart suggests so many beautiful and intimate relations, which even my reenacting a scene does not satisfy any more."

Sociological surveys also suggested that genuine changes in sexual behavior occurred, beginning in the prewar years, for both married and single women. Katherine Bement Davis's pioneering study of 2200 middle-class women, carried out in 1918 and published in 1929, revealed that most used contraceptives and described sexual relations in positive terms. A 1938 survey of 777 middle-class females found that among those born between 1890 and 1900, 74 percent were virgins before marriage; for those born after 1910 the figure dropped to 32 percent. A later survey by sex researcher Alfred Kinsey, based on a much larger sample, corroborated this finding. Women born after the turn of the century were twice as likely to have experienced premarital sex as those born before 1900. The critical change took place in the generation that came of age in the late teens and early 1920s. By the 1920s, male and female "morals" were becoming more alike.

RESISTANCE TO MODERNITY

One measure of the profound cultural changes of the 1920s was the hostility and opposition expressed toward them by large sectors of the American public. Deep and persistent tensions, with ethnic, racial, and geographical overtones, characterized much of the decade's politics. The postwar Red Scare had given strength to the forces of antiradicalism in politics and traditionalism in culture. Resentments over the growing power of urban culture were very strong in rural and small-town America. The big city, in this view, stood for all that was alien, corrupt, and immoral in the country's life. Several trends and mass movements reflected this anger and the longing for a less complicated past.

Prohibition

The Eighteenth Amendment, banning the manufacture and sale of alcoholic beverages, took effect in January 1920. Prohibition was the culmination of a long campaign that associated drinking with the degradation of working-class family life and the worst evils of urban politics. Supporters, a coalition of women's temperance groups, middle-class pro-

gressives, and rural Protestants, hailed the new law as "a noble experiment." But it became clear rather quickly that enforcing the new law would be extremely difficult. The Volstead Act of 1919 established a federal Prohibition Bureau to enforce the Eighteenth Amendment. Yet the bureau was severely understaffed, with only about 1,500 agents to police the entire country. The bureau depended upon federal and state appropriations, and these proved difficult to obtain.

The public demand for alcohol, especially in the big cities, led to widespread lawbreaking. Drinking was such a routine part of life for so many Americans that bootlegging quickly became a big business. Illegal stills and breweries, as well as liquor imported from Canada, supplied the needs of those Americans who continued to drink. Nearly every town and city had at least one speakeasy, where people could drink and be entertained. Local law enforcement personnel, especially in the cities, were easily bribed. By the early 1920s many eastern states no longer made even a token effort at enforcing the law.

Prohibition gave an enormous boost to violent organized crime. The profits to be made in the illegal liquor trade dwarfed the traditional sources of income for criminals — gambling, prostitution, and robbery. The pattern of organized crime in the 1920s closely resembled the larger trends in American business: smaller operations gave way to more complex and carefully organized combinations. Successful organized crime figures, like Chicago's Al "Scarface" Capone, became celebrities in their own right and received heavy coverage in the mass media. Capone himself shrewdly used the rhetoric of the "new era" to defend himself: "Everybody calls me a racketeer. I call myself a businessman. When I sell liquor it's bootlegging. When my patrons serve it on a silver tray on Lake Shore Drive, it's hospitality."

Organized crime, based on its huge profits from liquor, also made significant inroads into legitimate businesses, labor unions, and city government. By the time Congress and the states ratified the Twenty-first Amendment in 1933, repealing Prohibition, organized crime was a permanent feature of American life. Politically, Prohibition continued to be a controversial issue in national politics, as "wets" and "drys" debated the merits of the law. The struggle was transformed into a contest of political power between cities and rural and small-town districts.

Studies have shown that Prohibition did, in fact, significantly reduce per capita consumption of alcohol. In 1910, annual per capita consumption stood at

2.6 gallons; in 1934 the figure was less than a gallon. Many drinkers — especially wage earners — probably consumed less because of the higher price of bootleg beer and spirits. Yet among young people, especially college students, the excitement associated with speakeasies and lawbreaking contributed to increased drinking during Prohibition.

Immigration Restriction

The movement to limit immigration into the U.S. embodied some of the most intolerant currents of the 1920s. Sentiment for restricting immigration, growing since the late nineteenth century, reached its peak immediately after World War I. Anti-immigrant feeling reflected major shifts in both the size and makeup of the immigrant stream. Before 1890, the majority of immigrants to America had come mainly from countries in northern and western Europe: Great Britain, Germany, and Scandinavia. Most were Protestant, and many of those who were Catholic, such as the Irish, spoke the English language. But between 1891 and 1920 roughly 10.5 million immigrants arrived from southern and eastern Europe: Poland, Russia, Austria-Hungary, Italy, and Greece. This was nearly twice as many as arrived in the same years from northern and western Europe.

The "new immigrants" were mostly Catholic and Jewish, and were darker-skinned than the "old immigrants." To many Americans they seemed more exotic, more foreign, and less willing and able to assimilate the nation's political and cultural values. They were also relatively poorer, more physically isolated, and less politically strong than earlier immigrants. In the 1890s, the anti-Catholic American Protective Association called for a curb on immigration, and by exploiting the economic depression of that decade it reached a membership of 2.5 million. In 1894 a group of prominent Harvard graduates, including Henry Cabot Lodge and John Fiske, founded the Immigration Restriction League, providing an influential forum for the fears of the nation's elite. The league used newer scientific arguments, based on Darwinism and genetics, to support its call for literacy tests for all would-be immigrants.

Theories of scientific racism had become more popular in the early 1900s, and they reinforced anti-immigrant bias. The most influential statement of racial hierarchy was Madison Grant's *The Passing of the Great Race* (1916). It used a distorted version of genetic theory to argue that America was committing "race suicide." According to Grant, inferior Alpine, Mediterranean, and Jewish stock threatened to extinguish the superior Nordic race that had made America great. Eugenicists, who also enjoyed a large vogue in these years, held that heredity determined almost all of a person's capacities, and that genetic inferiority predisposed people to crime and poverty. Such pseudoscientific thinking sought to explain historical and social development solely as a function of racial differences.

Against this background, the war and its aftermath provided the final push for immigration restriction. The "100 percent American" fervor of the war years fueled nativist passions. So did the Red Scare of 1919–20, in which foreigners became closely associated in the popular mind with bolshevism and radicalism of all kinds. The postwar depression coincided with the resumption of massive immigration, bringing much hostile comment on the relationship between rising unemployment and the new influx of foreigners. The American Federation of

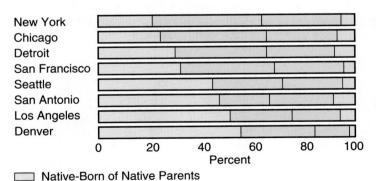

New York
Chicago
Detroit
San Francisco
Seattle
San Antonio
Los Angeles
Denver

0   20   40   60   80   100
Percent

☐ Native-Born of Native Parents
☐ Native-Born of Foreign Parents
☐ Foreign-Born
☐ Non-White (including Asian)

Population Composition of Selected Cities, 1920

By 1920 the demographic impact of several decades of heavy immigration was especially evident in the nation's cities. The combined population of the foreign born and those born of foreign parents frequently surpassed that of the native born of native parents.

Labor proposed stopping all immigration for two years. Sensational press coverage of organized crime figures, many of them Italian and Jewish, also played a part. In 1920 Henry Ford, one of the nation's most popular and well-known figures, launched a viciously anti-Semitic campaign against what he claimed was a vast international network of Jewish bankers who dominated the American economy.

In 1921 Congress passed the Immigration Act, setting a maximum of 357,000 new immigrants each year. Quotas limited annual immigration from any European country to 3 percent of the number of its natives counted in the 1910 American census. But restrictionists complained that the new law still allowed too many southern and eastern Europeans in, especially since the northern and western Europeans did not fill their quotas. The Johnson-Reed Immigration Act of 1924 revised the quotas to 2 percent of the number of foreign-born counted for each nationality in the census for 1890, when far fewer southern or eastern Europeans were present in the U.S. The maximum total allowed each year was also halved, to 164,000. The quota laws did not apply to Canada, Mexico, or any other New World nation.

The immigration restriction laws reversed ear-lier practices and became a permanent feature of national policy. Republican congressman Albert Johnson of Washington, coauthor of the 1924 act, defended it by claiming that "our capacity to main-tain our cherished institutions stands diluted by a stream of alien blood, with all its inherited miscon-ceptions respecting the relationships of the govern-ing power to the governed. . . . The day of unal-loyed welcome to all peoples, the day of indiscriminate acceptance of all races, has definitely ended." In effect, Congress had accepted the racial assumptions of nativists such as Madison Grant, basing immigration restriction upon a discrimina-tory hierarchy of superior and inferior "races."

The Ku Klux Klan

If immigration restriction was resurgent nativism's most significant legislative expression, a revived Ku Klux Klan was its most effective mass movement. The original Klan had been formed in the Recon-struction South as an instrument of white racial terror against newly freed slaves. It had died out in the 1870s. The new Klan, born in Stone Mountain, Georgia, in 1915, was inspired by D. W. Griffith's racist spectacle *The Birth of a Nation*, a film that

Women members of the Ku Klux Klan in New Castle, Indiana, August 1, 1923. The revived Klan was a powerful presence in scores of American communities during the early 1920s, especially among native born white Protestants who feared cultural and political change. In addition to preaching "100 percent Americanism," local Klan chapters also served a social function for its members and their families.

depicted the original KKK as a heroic organization. The new Klan patterned itself on the secret rituals and antiblack hostility of its predecessor, and until 1920 it was limited to a few local chapters in Georgia and Alabama.

But the new Klan soon grew into something quite different. When Hiram W. Evans, a racist dentist from Dallas, became imperial wizard in 1922 he transformed the organization. Evans hired professional fundraisers and publicists and directed an effective recruiting scheme that paid a commission to sponsors of new members. The Klan preached hatred not only of African Americans but of Catholics, Jews, and immigrants as well. In the name of "100 per cent Americanism," it also staunchly supported Prohibition and patriotism and attacked birth control and Darwinism. In sum, the Klan presented itself as the righteous defender of the embattled values of small-town Protestant America.

By 1924 the new Klan counted over 3 million members across the country. Its slogan, "Native, White, Protestant Supremacy," proved especially attractive in the Midwest and South, including many cities. Klan members frequently terrorized African Americans, Jews, and Catholics in local communities. Klansmen boycotted businesses, threatened families, and sometimes resorted to violence against its chosen enemies: public whippings, arson, and lynching. Its targets sometimes included white Protestants thought to be guilty of sexual promiscuity, blasphemy, or drunkenness.

At its height, the Klan also became a powerful force in Democratic party politics in Texas, Oklahoma, Indiana, Colorado, Oregon, and other states. It had a strong presence among delegates to the 1924 Democratic National Convention. It began to fade in 1925 when its Midwest leader, Grand Dragon David C. Stephenson, became involved in a sordid personal affair. Stephenson had picked up a young secretary at a party, got her drunk on bootleg liquor, and then assaulted her on a train. After the woman took poison and died, Stephenson was convicted of manslaughter. With one of its most famous leaders disgraced and in jail, the new Klan began to lose members and influence. The success of immigration restriction, the receding concern with "bolshevism," wrangling among Klan leaders, and the general economic prosperity also contributed to the movement's rapid decline by the late 1920s.

Religious Fundamentalism

Paralleling political nativism in the 1920s was the growth of religious fundamentalism. Many middle-class and urban Protestants had reconciled their religious faith with the teachings of modern science. In large numbers of Protestant churches, congregations focused less on religious practice and worship than on social and reform activities in the larger community. By the early 1920s, a fundamentalist revival had developed in reaction to these tendencies. The fundamentalists emphasized a literal reading of the Bible, and they rejected the tenets of modern science as inconsistent with the revealed word of God. Fundamentalist publications and Bible colleges flourished, particularly among Southern Baptists.

One special target of the fundamentalists was the theory of evolution, first put forth by Charles Darwin in his landmark work *The Origin of Species* (1859). Evolutionary theory directly contradicted the account of creation given in the Book of Genesis. Although most Protestant clergymen had long since found ways of blending the scientific theory with their theology, fundamentalists launched an attack on the teaching of Darwinism in schools and universities. By 1925 five southern state legislatures had passed laws restricting the teaching of evolution. In Tennessee it was illegal for public schoolteachers to "teach any theory that denies the story of the divine creation of man as taught in the Bible."

A young biology teacher, John T. Scopes, deliberately broke the Tennessee law in 1925 in order to challenge it in court. The resulting trial that summer in Dayton, a small town near Chattanooga, drew international attention to the controversy. Scopes's defense team included attorneys from the American Civil Liberties Union and Clarence Darrow, the most famous trial lawyer in America. The prosecution was led by William Jennings Bryan, the old Populist standard-bearer who had thrown himself into the fundamentalist and antievolutionist cause. Bryan had recently defined his creed: "I fear the plutocracy of wealth; I respect the aristocracy of learning; but I thank God for the democracy of the heart." Held in a circus atmosphere in sweltering heat, the trial attracted thousands of reporters and partisans to Dayton, and was broadcast nationally over the radio.

The Scopes "monkey trial" — so called because fundamentalists trivialized Darwin's theory into a claim that humans were descended from monkeys — became one of the most publicized and definitive moments of the decade. The real drama was the confrontation between Darrow and Bryan. Darrow, denied the right to call scientists to testify for the defense, put the "Great Commoner" himself on the stand as an expert witness on the Bible. Bryan delighted his supporters with a staunch defense of biblical literalism. But he also drew scorn from many of the assembled journalists, including cosmopolitan types such as H. L. Mencken of the *Baltimore Sun,* who ridiculed Bryan's simplistic faith. Scopes's guilt was never in question. The jury convicted him quickly, although the verdict was later thrown out on a technicality. Bryan died a week after the trial; his epitaph read simply, "He kept the Faith." The struggle over the teaching of evolution continued in an uneasy stalemate; state statutes were not repealed, but prosecutions ceased. Fundamentalism, a religious creed and a bulwark against the uncertainties of modern life, continued to have a strong appeal for millions of Americans.

PROMISES POSTPONED

The overall prosperity of the decade, it is clear, was unevenly distributed and enjoyed across America. Older reform movements that had pointed out inequities came upon hard times amidst the conservative political climate. But the "new era" did inspire a range of critics deeply troubled by unfulfilled promises in American life. Feminists sought to redefine their movement in the wake of the suffrage victory. Mexican immigration to the U.S. shot up, and in the burgeoning Mexican American communities of the Southwest and Midwest, economic and social conditions were very difficult. African Americans, bitterly disappointed by their treatment during and after the war, turned to new political and cultural strategies. Many American intellectuals found themselves deeply alienated from the temper and direction of modern American society.

Feminism in Transition

The dream of women remaking American politics with their votes faded quickly. Few women in the 1920s sought elective office, and the percentage of women voting would not equal that of men for thirty years. The achievement of the suffrage removed the central issue that had given cohesion to the disparate forces of female reform activism. In addition, female activists of all persuasions found themselves swimming against a national tide of hostility to political idealism. During the 1920s, the women's movement split into two main wings over a fundamental disagreement about female identity. Should activists stress women's differences from men — their vulnerability and the double burden of work and family — and continue to press for protective

legislation? Or should they emphasize the ways that women were like men — sharing similar aspirations — and push for full legal and civil equality? These two perspectives dominated a bitter fight over goals and strategies for American women.

In 1920, the National American Woman Suffrage Association reorganized itself as the League of Women Voters. The League represented the historical mainstream of the suffrage movement, those who believed that the vote for women would bring a nurturing sensibility and a reform vision to American politics. This view was rooted in *politicized domesticity,* the notion that women had a special role to play in bettering society: improving conditions for working women, abolishing child labor, humanizing prisons and mental hospitals, and serving the urban poor. Most League members continued working in a variety of reform organizations, and the League itself concentrated on educating the new female electorate, encouraging women to run for office, and supporting laws for the protection of women and children.

A newer, smaller, and more militant group was the National Woman's Party, founded in 1916 by militant suffragist Alice Paul. The NWP downplayed the significance of suffrage and argued that women were still subordinate to men in every facet of life. The NWP opposed protective legislation for women, claiming that such laws reinforced sex stereotyping and prevented women from competing with men in many fields. Largely representing the interests of professional and business women, the NWP offered a narrowed version of feminism by severing ties with other reform issues. It focused on passage of a brief Equal Rights Amendment to the Constitution, introduced to Congress in 1923: "Men and women shall have equal rights throughout the United States and every place subject to its jurisdiction."

Since the ERA would wipe out sex as a legal category, its opponents worried about the loss of hard-won protective legislation that benefited poor and working-class women. Many of the older generation of women reformers opposed the ERA as an elitist idea, arguing that far more women benefited from protective laws than were injured by them. "So long as men cannot be mothers," Florence Kelley declared, "so long legislation adequate for them can never be adequate for wage-earning women; and the cry Equality, Equality, where nature has created inequality, is as stupid and as deadly as the cry of Peace, Peace, where there is no Peace." Mary Anderson, director of the Women's Bureau in the Department of Labor, argued that "women who are wage earners, with one job in the factory and another in the home, have little time and energy left to carry on the fight to better their economic status. They need the help of other women and they need labor laws."

ERA supporters countered that maximum hours laws or laws prohibiting women from night work prevented women from getting many lucrative jobs. According to Harriot Stanton Blatch, "In many highly paid trades women have been pushed into the lower grades of work, limited in earning capacity, if not shut out of the trade entirely by these so-called protective laws." M. Carey Thomas, president of Bryn Mawr College, defended the ERA with language reminiscent of laissez faire: "How much better by one blow to do away with discriminating against women in work, salaries, promotion and opportunities to compete with men in a fair field with no favour on either side!"

But most women's groups did not think there was a "fair field," and they opposed the ERA. These included the League of Women Voters, the National Consumers League, and the Women's Trade Union League. ERA supporters generally stressed individualism, competition, and the abstract language of "equality" and "rights." ERA opponents emphasized the grim reality of industrial exploitation and the concentration of women workers in low-paying jobs in which they did not compete directly with men. ERA advocates dreamed of a labor market that might be — one where women might have the widest opportunity. Anti-ERA forces looked at the labor market as it was, insisting it was more important to protect women from existing exploitation. The NWP campaign failed to get the ERA passed by Congress, but the debates it sparked would be echoed during the feminist movement of the 1970s.

The changing nature of women's work during the 1920s provided a crucial context for the ERA debate. A small number of professional women made real gains in the fields of real estate, banking, and journalism. The press regularly announced new "firsts" for women, such as Amelia Earhart's 1928 airplane flight across the Atlantic. As business expanded, a greater percentage of working women were employed in white-collar positions, as opposed to manufacturing and domestic service. In 1900 less than 18 percent of employed women worked in clerical, managerial, sales, and professional areas. By 1930 the number was 44 percent. But studies showed that most of these women were clustered in the low-paying areas of typing, stenography, bookkeeping, cashiering, and salesclerking.

Men still dominated in the higher-paid and managerial white-collar occupations.

The most significant, if limited, victory for feminist reformers was the 1921 Sheppard-Towner Act, a landmark measure designed to reduce infant and maternal mortality. This act, which established the first federally funded health care program, provided matching funds for states to set up prenatal and child health care centers. These centers also provided public health nurses for house calls. Although hailed as a genuine reform breakthrough, especially for women in rural and isolated communities, the act aroused much opposition. The NWP disliked it for its assumption that all women were mothers. Birth control advocates such as Margaret Sanger complained that contraception was not part of the health program at the centers. Most important, Sheppard Towner drew fire from the American Medical Association, which objected to government-sponsored health care and to nurses who functioned outside the supervision of physicians. By 1929, largely as a result of intense AMA lobbying, Congress cut off funds for the program.

Mexican Immigration

While immigration restriction sharply cut the flow of new arrivals from Europe, the 1920s also brought a dramatic and unprecedented influx of Mexicans to the United States. (Mexico was not included in the immigration laws of 1921 and 1924.) Mexican migration had picked up substantially after the outbreak of the Mexican Revolution in 1911, as political instability and economic hardships provided incentives to cross the border to *El Norte.* According to the U.S. Immigration Service, an estimated 219,000 Mexicans entered the U.S. between 1911 and 1920. The figure for 1921 to 1930 was 459,000. Yet in all probability these numbers underrepresent the true size of Mexican immigration. Many Mexicans shunned the main border crossing at El Paso, Texas; Nogales, Arizona; and Calexico, California, and thus avoided paying the eight-dollar head tax and ten-dollar visa fee.

The primary pull factor in this new movement was the tremendous agricultural expansion occurring in the American Southwest. Irrigation and large-scale agribusiness investment had begun transforming California's Imperial and San Joaquin valleys from arid desert into lucrative fruit and vegetable fields. Cotton pickers were needed in the vast plantations of Lower Rio Grande valley in Texas and the Salt River valley in Arizona. The sugar beet fields of Michigan, Minnesota, and Colorado also attracted large numbers of Mexican farm workers. American industry, moreover, had begun recruiting Mexican workers, first to fill wartime needs and later to stop the gap left by the decline in European immigration. Among the most aggressive industrial recruiters were Ford Motor Company, Bethlehem Steel, and the Southern Pacific Railroad.

The new Mexican immigration appeared more permanent than previous waves — that is, more and more newcomers stayed. And as in the rest of the U.S. during the 1920s, Mexicans settled in urban centers in growing numbers. By 1930 San Antonio's Mexican community accounted for roughly 70,000 people out of a total population of a quarter million. Around 100,000 Mexicans lived in Los Angeles, including 55,000 who attended city schools. Substantial Mexican communities also flourished in midwestern cities such as Chicago, Detroit, Kansas City, and Gary. Many of the immigrants alternated between agricultural and factory jobs, depending upon seasonal availability of work. Mexican women often worked in the fields alongside their husbands. They also toiled as domestics and seamstresses, or took in laundry and boarders.

Mexican Immigration to the U.S. in the 1920s
Many Mexican migrants avoided official border crossing stations so they would not have to pay visa fees. Thus, these official figures probably underestimated the true size of the decade's Mexican migration. As the economy contracted with the onset of the Great Depression, immigration from Mexico dropped off sharply.

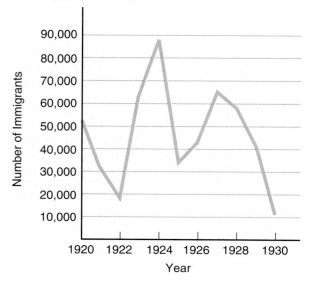

Racism and local patterns of residential segregation confined most Mexicans to barrios in American cities. Housing conditions were generally poor, particularly for recent arrivals, who were forced to live in rude shacks without running water or electricity. Disease and infant mortality rates were much higher than average, and most Mexicans worked at low-paying, unskilled jobs and received inadequate health care. Legal restrictions passed by states and cities made it difficult for Mexicans to enter teaching, legal, and other professions. Mexicans were routinely banned from local public works projects as well. Many felt a deep ambivalence about applying for American citizenship. Loyalty to the old country was strong, and many cherished dreams of returning to live out their days in Mexico. Many Mexicans living in a *colonia* felt social pressure not to apply for citizenship. And most Anglos would look down upon them whether they were citizens or not.

Ugly racist campaigns against Mexicans were common in the 1920s, especially when "cheap Mexican labor" was blamed for local unemployment or hard times. Stereotypes of Mexicans as "greasers" or "wetbacks" were prevalent in newspapers and movies of the day. Nativist efforts to limit Mexican immigration were thwarted by the lobbying of powerful agribusiness interests. The Los Angeles Chamber of Commerce typically employed racist stereotyping in arguing to keep the borders open. Mexicans, it claimed, were naturally suited for agriculture, "due to their crouching and bending habits . . . , while the white is physically unable to adapt himself to them."

A key social and political institution in the Mexican communities of the Southwest and Midwest were the *mutualistas*. These were mutual aid societies that provided death benefits and widow's pensions for members. They also served as centers of resistance to civil rights violations and discrimination. In 1928, the Federation of Mexican Workers Unions formed in response to a large farm labor strike in the Imperial Valley. Meanwhile, a group of middle-class Mexican professionals in Texas organized the League of United Latin American Citizens. This organization focused on civil rights issues, improvements in schools, and voter registration drives. These marked only the beginnings of a long struggle to bring economic, social, and racial equality to Mexican Americans.

The "New Negro"

The Great Migration spurred by World War I showed no signs of letting up during the 1920s, and African

Mexican American farm workers are shown pitting apricots near Canoga Park, Los Angeles County, 1924. Most of the over half million Mexicans who migrated to the United States during the 1920s worked as farm laborers. Migrant families usually travelled and worked together, as in this photo, following the crop harvests.

American communities in northern cities grew rapidly. By far the largest and most influential of these communities was New York City's Harlem, the demographic and cultural capital of black America. Previously a residential suburb, Harlem began attracting middle-class African Americans in the prewar years. After the war, heavy black migration from the South and the Carribbean encouraged real estate speculators and landlords to remake Harlem as an exclusively black neighborhood. Between 1920 and 1930 nearly 90,000 new arrivals settled in Harlem, giving it a black population of nearly 200,000.

The demand for housing in this restricted geographical area led to skyrocketing rents. Most Harlemites held low-wage jobs. This combination helped lead to extremely overcrowded apartments, unsanitary conditions, and the rapid deterioration of

housing stock. Disease and death rates were abnormally high. Harlem was well on its way to becoming a slum. Yet Harlem also boasted a large middle-class population and supported a wide array of churches, theaters, newspapers and journals, and black-owned businesses. It became a magnet for African American intellectuals, artists, musicians, and writers from all over the world. Poet Langston Hughes expressed the excitement of arriving in the community in 1921: "I can never put on paper the thrill of the underground ride to Harlem. I went up the steps and out into the bright September sunlight. Harlem! I stood there, dropped my bags, took a deep breath and felt happy again."

Harlem became the political and intellectual-center for what writer Alain Locke called the "New Negro." Locke was referring to a new spirit in the

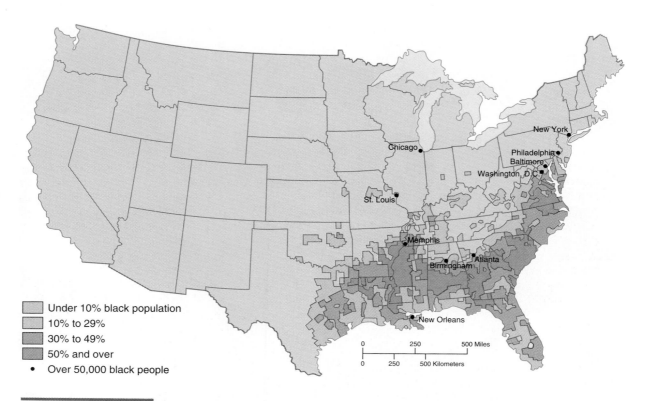

Black Population, 1920

Although the "Great Migration" had drawn hundreds of thousands of African Americans to the urban north, the southern states of the Confederacy still remained the center of the African American population in 1920.

Legend:
- Under 10% black population
- 10% to 29%
- 30% to 49%
- 50% and over
- • Over 50,000 black people

work of black writers and intellectuals, an optimistic faith that African Americans should develop and celebrate their distinctive culture. These achievements would be firmly rooted in the history, folk culture, and experiences of African American people. This was the common denominator uniting the disparate figures associated with the Harlem Renaissance. The assertion of cultural independence resonated in the poetry of Langston Hughes and Claude McKay, the novels of Zora Neale Hurston and Jessie Fauset, the essays of Countee Cullen and James Weldon Johnson, the acting of Paul Robeson, and the blues singing of Bessie Smith. Most would agree with Johnson when he wrote in 1927 that "nothing can go farther to destroy race prejudice than the recognition of the Negro as a creator and contributor to American civilization."

There was a political side to the "New Negro" as well. The newly militant spirit that black veterans had brought home from World War I matured and found a variety of expression in the Harlem of the 1920s. New leaders and movements began to ap-

pear alongside established organizations like the NAACP. A. Philip Randolph began a long career as a labor leader, socialist, and civil rights activist in these years, editing *The Messenger* and organizing the Brotherhood of Sleeping Car Porters. Harlem was also headquarters to Marcus Garvey's Universal Negro Improvement Association. An ambitious Jamaican immigrant who had moved to Harlem in 1916, Garvey created a mass movement that stressed black economic self-determination and unity among the black communities of the United States, the Caribbean, and Africa. His newspaper, the *Negro World*, spoke to black communities around the world, urging black businesses to trade among themselves. With colorful parades and rallies, and a central message affirming pride in black identity, Garvey attracted as many as a million members worldwide.

Garvey's best-publicized project was the Black Star Line, a black-owned and -operated fleet of ships that would link people of African descent around the world. But insufficient capital and serious financial mismanagement resulted in the spectacular failure of the enterprise. In 1923, Garvey was found guilty of mail fraud in his fundraising efforts; he later went to jail and was subsequently deported to England. Despite the disgrace, Harlem's largest newspaper, the *Amsterdam News,* explained Garvey's continuing appeal to African Americans: "In a world where black is despised, he taught them that black is beautiful. He taught them to admire and praise black things and black people."

Harlem in the 1920s also became a popular tourist attraction for "slumming" whites. Nightclubs like the Cotton Club and Small's Paradise were controlled by white organized crime figures. They featured bootleg liquor, floor shows, and the best jazz bands of the day, led by Duke Ellington, Fletcher Henderson, Cab Calloway, and Louis Armstrong. Yet these clubs were rigidly segregated. Black dancers, singers, and musicians provided the entertainment, but no African Americans were allowed in the audience. Chronicled in novels and newspapers, Harlem became a potent symbol to white America of the ultimate good time. Yet the average Harlemite never saw the inside of a nightclub. For the vast majority of Harlem residents, working a menial job for a low wage and forced to pay high rent, the day-to-day reality was depressingly different.

Marcus Garvey, head of the Universal Negro Improvement Association, c.1920. Garvey used twin appeals to black nationalism and economic self determination to forge the first real mass movement of African Americans. His movement gained strength especially among the burgeoning African American communities of northern cities.

Intellectuals and Alienation

In the early 1920s Gertrude Stein, an American expatriate writer living in Paris, told the young novelist Ernest Hemingway: "All of you young people who served in the war, you are a lost generation." Stein's widely quoted phrase "a lost generation" became perhaps the best-known image of American writers, artists, and intellectuals of the postwar era. Yet it is difficult to generalize about a community so diverse, especially for the 1920s. For one thing, the experience of living abroad attracted only a handful of American writers. Alienation and disillusion with American life were prominent subjects in the literature and thought of the 1920s, but artists and thinkers developed these themes in very different ways.

The war experience itself had led not just to revulsion against the mass slaughter of people, but to a deep cynicism about describing war in the heroic and moralistic style so popular in the nineteenth century. Novelists Hemingway and John Dos Passos, who both served at the front as ambulance drivers, depicted the war and its aftermath in more world-weary and unsentimental tones. Hemingway's *The Sun Also Rises* (1926) and *A Farewell To Arms* (1929) used taut, spare language to express his distrust of idealism, abstractions, and large meanings. As Jake Barnes, the wounded war hero of *The Sun Also Rises* explained, "I did not care what it was all about. All I wanted to know was how to live it." The search for personal moral codes that would allow one to endure life with dignity and authenticity was at the center of Hemingway's fiction.

F. Scott Fitzgerald, along with Hemingway the most influential novelist of the era, had not served overseas. Fitzgerald's work celebrated the youthful vitality of the "Jazz Age" (a phrase he coined), but was also deeply distrustful of the promises of American prosperity and politics. His first novel, *This Side of Paradise* (1920), won a wide readership around the country with its exuberant portrait of "a new generation." They were "dedicated more than the last to the fear of poverty and the worship of success; grown up to find all Gods dead, all wars fought, all faiths in man shaken." Fitzgerald's greatest work, *The Great Gatsby* (1925), was written in the south of France. It highlighted the glamorous world of the wealthy and their parties while evoking the tragic limits of material success.

At home, many American writers engaged in sharp attacks on small-town America and what they viewed as its provincial values. Essayist H. L. Mencken, caustic editor of the *American Mercury,* heaped scorn on fundamentalists, Prohibition, and nativists, while ridiculing what he called the "American booboisie." Mencken understood the power of the small town and despaired of reforming politics. "Our laws," he wrote, "are invented, in the main, by frauds and fanatics, and put upon the statute books by poltroons and scoundrels." Fiction writers also skewered small-town America with commercial and critical success. Sherwood Anderson's *Winesburg, Ohio* (1919), offered a spare, laconic, pessimistic yet compassionate view of middle America. He had a lasting influence on younger novelists of the 1920s.

The most popular and acclaimed (at the time) writer of the era was novelist Sinclair Lewis. He wrote a series of novels that satirized small-town life in affectionate terms. In *Main Street* (1920) and especially *Babbitt* (1922), Lewis mocked his characters as absurd. Yet there was a strong element of self-mockery in Lewis's treatment of his most famous character, the real estate man George Babbitt of Zenith. For Lewis could offer no alternative set of values to Babbit's crass self-promotion, hunger for success, and craving for social acceptance. In 1930 Lewis became the first American author to win the Nobel Prize for literature.

In the world of theater, Eugene O'Neill revolutionized the American stage with his naturalistic and brooding dramas. He depicted the darker side of family life, explored race relations, and generally helped to lift American playwriting out of the melodramatic conventions of late-nineteenth-century theater. Among his influential early plays were *Beyond the Horizon* (1920), *The Emperor Jones* (1921), and *The Great God Brown* (1926). Two expatriate poets, T. S. Eliot and Ezra Pound, were breaking Victorian conventions by pushing American verse in revolutionary new directions. Eliot's *The Waste Land* (1922) used the metaphor of impotence to comment on the postwar world and became perhaps the most influential poem of the century.

Another side of intellectual alienation was expressed by writers critical of industrial progress and the new mass culture. The most important of these were a group of poets and scholars centered in Vanderbilt University in Nashville, Tennessee, collectively known as the Fugitives. They included Allen Tate, John Crowe Ransom, and Donald Davidson, all of whom invoked traditional authority, respect for the past, and older agrarian ways as ideals to live by. The Fugitives attacked industrialism and materialism as modern-day ills. Self-conscious Southerners, they looked to the antebellum plantation-based society as a model for community based on benevolence toward dependents (such as black people and women) and respect for the land. Their

book of essays, *I'll Take My Stand* (1930), was a collective manifesto of their ideas.

Not all intellectuals, of course, were critics of modern trends. Some, like the philosopher John Dewey, retained much of the prewar optimism and belief in progress. But many others, such as Walter Lippmann and Joseph Wood Krutch, articulated a profound uneasiness with the limits of material growth. In his 1928 book *A Preface to Morals*, the urbane and sophisticated Lippmann expressed doubts about the moral health of the nation. Modern science and technological advances could not address more cosmic questions of belief. The erosion of old religious faiths and moral standards, along with the triumph of the new mass culture, had left many people with nothing to believe in. Lippmann called for a new "religion of the spirit" to offer a guide for living an ethical life. He was unclear as to just what the "religion of the spirit" might be. But he was certain that the moralist would have to persuade rather than command people to live the good life. His job would be "not to exhort men to be good but to elucidate what the good is."

THE ELECTION OF 1928

The 1928 campaign featured two politicians who represented profoundly different sides of American life. Al Smith, the Democratic nominee for president,

---

Election of 1928

Although Al Smith managed to carry the nation's twelve largest cities, Herbert Hoover's victory in 1928 was one of the largest popular and electoral landslides in the nation's history.

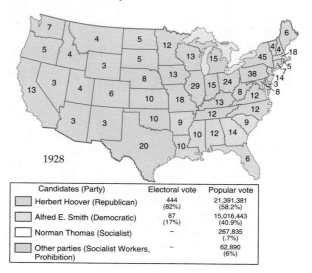

1928

Candidates (Party)	Electoral vote	Popular vote
Herbert Hoover (Republican)	444 (82%)	21,391,381 (58.2%)
Alfred E. Smith (Democratic)	87 (17%)	15,016,443 (40.9%)
Norman Thomas (Socialist)	–	267,835 (.7%)
Other parties (Socialist Workers, Prohibition)	–	62,890 (6%)

JUST STICK YOUR HEAD IN THERE RUBE, AND ALL YOUR TROUBLES WILL BE OVER!

Al Smith, Democratic nominee for president in 1920, faced a great deal of anti-urban and anti-Catholic prejudice, especially in the West and the South. This cartoon portrayed Smith as the city slicker candidate looking to trick the virtuous farmer. The image of the Tammany Hall "tiger" had long been used to symbolize the corrupt urban political machine.

was a pure product of New York City's Lower East Side. Smith came from a mixed immigrant background that included Irish, German, and Italian ancestry, and he was raised as a Roman Catholic. After attending parochial school and working in the Fulton Fish Market, he rose through the political ranks of New York's Tammany Hall machine. A personable man with a deep sympathy for poor and working-class people, Smith won a reputation as an effective state legislator in Albany. He served four terms as governor of New York, pushing through an array of laws reforming factory conditions, housing, and welfare programs. Two of his closest advisers were the progressives Frances Perkins and Belle Moskowitz. Smith thus fused older-style machine politics with the newer reform emphasis on state intervention to solve social problems.

Herbert Hoover easily won the Republican nomination after Calvin Coolidge announced he would not run for reelection. Hoover epitomized the successful and forward-looking American. An engineer and self-made millionaire, he offered a unique combination of experience in humanitarian war relief, administrative efficiency, and pro-business policies. Above all, Hoover stood for a commitment to voluntarism, or what he sometimes called "spiritual individualism," as the best method for advancing the public welfare. He was one of the best-known men in America and promised to continue the Republican control of national politics.

Smith himself quickly became the central issue of the campaign. His sharp New York accent, jarring to many Americans who heard it over the radio, marked him clearly as a man of the city. So did his brown derby and fashionable suits, as well as his promise to work for the repeal of Prohibition. As the first Roman Catholic nominee of a major party, Smith also drew a torrent of anti-Catholic bigotry, especially in the South and Midwest. Nativists and Ku Klux Klanners shamelessly exploited old anti-Catholic prejudices and intimidated participants in Democratic election rallies. But Smith was also attacked from more respectable quarters. Bishop James Cannon, head of the Southern Methodist Episcopal Church, insisted that "no subject of the Pope" should be permitted to occupy the White House. William Allen White, the old and influential progressive editor from Kansas, denounced Smith as the candidate of gambling, prostitution, and liquor interests.

For his part, Smith ran a largely conservative race. He appointed John Raskob, a Republican vice-president of General Motors, to manage his campaign, and tried to outdo Hoover in his praise for business. He avoided economic issues such as the unevenness of the prosperity, the plight of farmers, or the growing unemployment. Democrats remained regionally divided over Prohibition, Smith's religion, and the widening split between rural and urban values. Hoover did not have to do much, other than take credit for the continued prosperity. In a speech on Smith's home turf, in Madison Square Garden, Hoover reiterated his objections to government interference in business. "It would cramp and cripple the mental and spiritual energies of our people. It would extinguish equality and opportunity. It would dry up the spirit of liberty and progress."

In retrospect, probably no Democrat could have won in 1928. Hoover polled 21 million votes to Smith's 15 million, and swept the electoral college 444 to 87, including New York State. Even the Solid South, reliably Democratic since the Civil War, gave five states to Hoover—a clear reflection of the ethnocultural split in the party. Yet the election offered important clues to the future of the Democrats. Smith ran better in the big cities of the North and East than any Democrat in modern times: he carried the nation's twelve largest cities and thus

CHRONOLOGY

1920	Prohibition takes effect
	Warren Harding elected president
	Station KDKA in Pittsburgh goes on the air
	Census reports that urban population is greater than rural population for first time
1921	First immigration quotas established by Congress
	Sheppard-Towner Act
1923	Equal Rights Amendment introduced to Congress
	Harding dies in office; Calvin Coolidge becomes president
1924	Dawes Plan for war reparations
	Johnson-Reed Immigration Act tightens quotas established in 1921
1925	Ku Klux Klan at height of its influence
	Scopes trial
	F. Scott Fitzgerald, *The Great Gatsby*
1926	National Broadcasting Company establishes first national radio network
1927	Warner Brothers produces *The Jazz Singer*, first feature-length motion picture with sound
	Charles Lindbergh makes first solo flight across Atlantic
1928	Kellogg-Briand Pact signed
	Herbert Hoover defeats Al Smith for the presidency

pointed the way to the Democrats' return to national power in 1932.

CONCLUSION

The presidential election of 1928 served as a kind of national referendum on the Republican "new age." It also revealed just how important ethnic and cultural differences had become in defining American politics. The contest reflected many of the deepest tensions and conflicts that marked American society in the 1920s: native-born versus immigrant; Protestant versus Catholic; Prohibition versus legal drinking; small-town life versus the cosmopolitan city; fundamentalism versus modernism; traditional sources of culture versus the new mass media. Al Smith, quintessential voice of the city, had failed to win the presidency. But even in defeat, he embodied the growing political and cultural strength of urban America.

Additional Readings

RODOLFO ACUNA, *Occupied America: A History of Chicanos* (3rd. ed., 1980). This survey of Mexican American history contains good material on the large-scale immigration of the 1920s.

ERIK BARNOUW, *A Tower of Babel: A History of Broadcasting in the U.S. to 1933* (1966). Pathbreaking history of early development of radio.

JOHN BRAEMER et al., eds., *Change and Continuity in Twentieth Century America: The 1920s* (1968). A wide-ranging collection of essays on the period, with especially good studies of the resistance to modernity.

DAVID BRODY, *Workers in Industrial America* (1980). A fine collection of essays that includes good material on the decline of the labor movement during the 1920s.

DAVID BURNER, *Herbert Hoover* (1978). One of the best biographies of this key political figure.

ALFRED D. CHANDLER, JR., *The Visible Hand: The Managerial Revolution in American Business* (1977). Includes an excellent analysis of the crucial changes in American business practices after World War I.

NANCY F. COTT, *The Grounding of Modern Feminism* (1987). Includes a sophisticated analysis of the debates among and between feminists during the 1920s. Connects the varied positions of the principal figures with earlier and later feminist movements.

SARA M. EVANS, *Born for Liberty: A History of Women in America* (1989). Includes an excellent discussion of the debate over the changing morality of the 1920s.

JAMES J. FLINK, *The Car Culture* (1975). The best single volume on the history of the automobile and how it changed American life.

NATHAN I. HUGGINS, *Harlem Renaissance* (1971). The most insightful history of the Harlem Renaissance.

KENNETH JACKSON, *Crabgrass Frontier* (1985). The best history of the suburbs. Includes a good survey of suburbanization in the 1920s.

ROBERT LYND AND HELEN LYND, *Middletown* (1929). A pioneering and still useful sociological analysis, documenting the changes in Muncie, Indiana, between the 1890s and 1920s.

ROBERT S. McELVAINE, *The Great Depression: America, 1929–1941* (1984). Includes an excellent analysis of the weaknesses in the American economy in the pre-Depression decade.

RONALD MARCHAND, *Advertising the American Dream* (1985). A brilliant, beautifully illustrated account of the rise of the advertising industry.

GILBERT OSOFSKY, *Harlem: The Making of a Ghetto* (1965). A solid and succinct social history of this key African American community.

EMILY S. ROSENBERG, *Spreading the American Dream* (1982). An important study of American economic and cultural expansion around the world from 1890 to 1945.

ROBERT SKLAR, *Movie-Made America* (1976). A fine cultural history of the motion picture. Especially strong on the early years of Hollywood.

24 THE GREAT DEPRESSION AND THE NEW DEAL, 1929–1940

Isaac Soyer. *Employment Agency. 1937. Oil on canvas, 34-1/4 × 45 in. (87 × 114.3). Whitney Museum of American Art, New York.*

AMERICAN COMMUNITIES

• SIT-DOWN STRIKE AT FLINT

In the gloomy evening of February 11, 1937, 400 tired, unshaven, but very happy strikers marched out of the sprawling automobile factory known as Fisher Body Number 1. Most carried American flags and small bundles of clothing. A makeshift banner on top of the plant announced "Victory Is Ours." A wildly cheering parade line of a thousand supporters greeted them at the gates. Shouting with joy, honking horns, and singing songs, the celebrants marched to two other factories to greet other emerging strikers. After forty-four days, the great Flint sit-down strike was over.

Flint, Michigan, was the heart of production for General Motors, the largest corporation in the world. In 1936 GM's net profits had reached $285 million, and its total assets were

AUTOMOBILE WORKERS ORGANIZE A NEW UNION

$1.5 billion. Originally a center for lumbering and then carriage making, Flint had boomed with the auto industry during the 1920s. Thousands of migrants streamed into the city, attracted by assembly line jobs averaging about thirty dollars a week. By 1930 Flint had grown to about 150,000 people, 80 percent of whom depended upon work at General Motors. A severe housing shortage made living conditions difficult. Tarpaper shacks, tents, even railroad cars were the only shelter available for many. Parts of the city resembled a mining camp.

The Great Depression hit Flint very hard. Employment at GM fell from a 1929 high of 56,000 to under 17,000 in 1932. As late as 1938 close to half the city's families were receiving some kind of emergency relief. By that time, as in thousands of other American communities, Flint's private and county relief agencies had been overwhelmed by the needs of the unemployed and their families. Two new national agencies based in Washington, D.C., the Federal Emergency Relief Administration and the Works Progress Administration, had replaced local sources of aid during the economic crisis.

The United Automobile Workers came to Flint in 1936 seeking to organize GM workers into one industrial union. The previous year, Congress had passed the National Labor Relations Act (also known as the Wagner Act), which facilitated union organizing by guaranteeing the right of workers to join unions and bargain collectively. The act established the National Labor Relations Board to oversee union elections and prohibit illegal antiunion activities by employers. But the obstacles to labor organizing were still enormous. Unemploy-

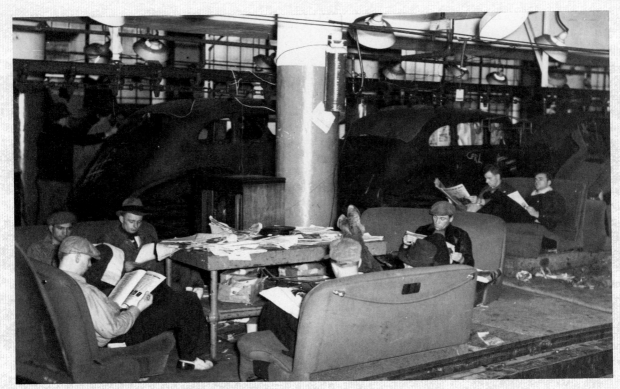

"Sit-down" strikers at a Flint, Michigan General Motors plant poured over newspaper accounts during their landmark 44 day strike in 1937. This makeshift reading room was part of the carefully organized community created by automobile workers striking for union recognition against the largest corporation in the world.

ment was high and the company had maintained a vigorous antiunion policy for years. By the fall of 1936, the UAW had signed up only a thousand members. The key moment came with the seizure of two Flint GM plants by a few hundred auto workers on December 30, 1936. The idea was to stay in the factories until strikers could achieve a collective bargaining agreement with General Motors. "We don't aim to keep the plants or try to run them," explained one sit-downer to a reporter, "but we want to see that nobody takes our jobs. We don't think we're breaking the law, or at least we don't think we're doing anything really bad."

The sit-down strike was a new and daring tactic that gained popularity among American industrial workers during the 1930s. In 1936 there were 48 sit-downs involving nearly 90,000 workers, and in 1937 some 400,000 workers participated in 477 sit-down strikes. Sit-downs expressed the militant exuberance of the rank and file. As one union song of the day put it:

> "When they tie the can to a union man,
>   Sit down! Sit down!
> When they give him the sack they'll take him back,
>   Sit down! Sit down!
> When the speed up comes, just twiddle your thumbs,
>   Sit down! Sit down!
> When the boss won't talk don't take a walk,
>   Sit down! Sit down!"

The strikers carefully organized themselves into what one historian called "the sit down community." Each plant elected a strike committee and appointed its own police chief and sanitary engineer. Strikers were divided into "families" of fifteen, each with a captain. No alcohol was allowed and strikers were careful not to destroy company property. Committees were organized for every conceivable purpose: food, recreation, sanitation, education, and contact with the outside. Sit-downers formed glee clubs and small orchestras to entertain themselves. Using loudspeakers, they broadcast concerts and speeches to their supporters outside the gates. A Women's Emergency Brigade — the strikers' wives, mothers, and daughters — provided crucial support preparing food and maintaining militant picket lines.

As the sit-down strike continued through January, support in Flint and around the nation grew. Overall production in the GM empire dropped from 53,000 vehicles per week to 1,500. Reporters and union supporters flocked to the plants. On January 11, in the "Battle of Running Bulls," strikers and their supporters clashed violently with Flint police and private GM guards. Michigan governor Frank Murphy, sympathetic to the strikers, brought in the National Guard to protect them. He refused to enforce an injunction obtained by GM to evict the strikers.

In the face of determined unity by the sit-downers, GM gave in and recognized the UAW as the exclusive bargaining agent in all sixty of its factories. The strike was perhaps the most important in American labor history, sparking a huge growth in union membership in the automobile and other mass production industries. Rose Pesotta, a textile union organizer, described the wild victory celebration in Flint's overflowing Pengelly Building: "People sang and joked and laughed and cried, deliriously joyful. Victory meant a freedom they had never known before. No longer would they be afraid to join unions."

Out of the tight-knit, temporary community of the sit-down strike emerged a looser yet more permanent kind of community: a powerful, nationwide trade union of automobile workers. The UAW struggled successfully to win recognition and collective bargaining rights from other carmakers, such as Chrysler and Ford. The national UAW, like other new unions in the mass production industries, was composed of chapters around the country. The permanent community of unionized auto workers won significant improvements in wages, working conditions, and benefits. Local chapters also became quite influential in the political and social lives of their larger com-

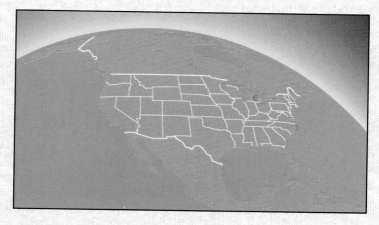

munities — industrial cities such as Flint, Detroit, and Toledo. Nationally, organized labor became a crucial component of the New Deal political coalition and a key power broker in the Democratic party. The new reality of a national community of organized labor would alter the national political and economic landscape for decades to come.

Hard Times

No event of the twentieth century had a more profound impact on American life than the Great Depression of the 1930s. Statistics can document a slumping economy, mass unemployment, and swelling relief rolls—but these numbers tell only part of the story. The emotional and psychological toll of these years, what one writer called "the invisible scar," must also be considered in understanding the worst economic crisis in American history. Even today, depression-era experiences retain a central, even mythical, place in the lives and memories of millions of American families. Nearly every aspect of the nation's life would be transformed by the painful encounter with "hard times."

The Bull Market

Stock trading in the late 1920s captured the imagination of the broad American public. The stock market resembled a sporting arena, millions following stock prices as they did the exploits of a Babe Ruth or a Jack Dempsey. Many business leaders and economists as much as told Americans that it was their duty to buy stocks. John J. Raskob, chairman of the board of General Motors, wrote an article for the *Ladies Home Journal* titled "Everybody Ought to Be Rich." A person who saved $15 each month and invested it in good common stocks would have $80,000 within twenty years. The *Saturday Evening Post* printed a poem that captured the fever:

> "Oh, hush thee, my babe, granny's bought some more shares
> Daddy's gone out to play with the bulls and the bears,
> Mother's buying on tips and she simply can't lose,
> And baby shall have some expensive new shoes!"

During the bull market of the 1920s stock prices increased at roughly twice the rate of industrial production. Paper value far outran real value. By the end of the decade stocks that had been bought mainly on the basis of their earning power, which was passed on to stockholders in the form of dividends, now came to be purchased only for the resale value after their prices rose. Anyone reading the financial pages of a newspaper would be amazed at the upward climb. In 1928 alone, for example, the price of Radio Corporation of America stock shot up from 85 to 420; Chrysler stock more than doubled, from 63 to 132; General Electric rose from 136 to 221. Overall, trading volume that year expanded from 577 million to 920 million shares.

Yet only about 4 million Americans owned any stocks at all, out of a total population of 120 million. Many of these stock buyers had been lured into the market through easy-credit, margin accounts. These allowed investors to purchase stocks by making a small down payment (as low as 10 percent), borrowing the rest from a broker, and using the shares as collateral, or security, on the loan. Just as installment plans had stimulated the automobile and other industries, "buying on the margin" brought new customers to the stock market. Investment trusts, existing for the sole purpose of owning stocks, mushroomed on Wall Street and contributed to the buying frenzy. Corporations with excess capital found that lending money to stockbrokers was a more profitable investment than plowing it back into their own plants.

The Crash

The tumbling of prices on the New York Stock Exchange ended the speculative mania. Though often portrayed as a one- or two-day catastrophe, the Wall Street Crash of 1929 was in reality a steep downward slide. The bull market peaked in early September, and prices drifted downward. On October 23 the Dow Jones industrials lost twenty-one points in one hour, and many large investors concluded the boom was over. The boom itself rested on expectations of continually rising prices; once those expectations began to melt, the market had to decline. On Monday, October 28, the Dow lost thirty-eight points, or 13 percent of its value. On October 29, "Black Tuesday," the bottom seemed to fall out. Over 16 million shares, more than double the previous record, were traded as panic selling took hold. For many stocks no buyers were available at any price.

The situation worsened. The market's fragile foundation of credit, based upon the debts incurred by margin accounts, quickly crumbled. Many investors with margin accounts had no choice but to sell when stock values fell. Since the shares themselves represented the security for their loans, more money had to be put up to cover the loans when prices declined. Never before had there been such a widespread dumping of stocks. By mid-November about $30 billion in the market price of stocks had been wiped out. Half the value of the stocks listed in the *New York Times* index was lost in ten weeks.

The nation's political and economic leaders

James Rosenberg, a lawyer and amateur artist, titled this grim sketch of the Wall Street stock market crash, *October 29, Dies Irae,* after a medieval Latin hymn describing the Day of Judgment. October 29 was the worst single day in the 112 year history of the New York Stock Exchange, as panic selling caused many stocks to lose half their value.

(James N. Rosenberg. Octo. 29, Dies Irae. 1929. Lithograph. Philadelphia Museum of Art.)

downplayed the impact of Wall Street's woes. "The fundamental business of the country," President Herbert Hoover told Americans in late October, "is on a sound and prosperous basis." Some analysts thought the crash a necessary correction to what one called "an orgy of reckless speculation." Secretary of the Treasury Andrew Mellon spoke for many in the financial world when he spoke of the benefits of the slump: "It will purge the rottenness out of the system. High costs of living and high living will come down. People will work harder, live a more moral life. Values will be adjusted, and enterprising people will pick up the wrecks from less competent people." At the end of 1929 hardly anyone was predicting that a depression would follow the stock market crash.

It would be too simplistic to say that the stock market crash "caused" the Great Depression. But like a person who catches a chill, the economy after the crash became less resistant to existing sources of disease. The resulting sickness revealed underlying economic weaknesses left over from the previous decade. First of all, workers and consumers by and large received too small a share of the enormous increases in labor productivity. In effect, the automobile of American capitalism had one foot pressed to the accelerator of production and another on the brake of consumption.

Better machinery and more efficient industrial organization had increased labor productivity enormously. But wages and salaries did not rise nearly as much. Between 1923 and 1929 manufacturing output per worker-hour increased by 32 percent. But wages during the same period rose only 8 percent, or one-quarter the rise in productivity. Moreover, the rise in productivity itself had encouraged overproduction in many industries. The farm sector had never been able to regain its prosperity of the World War I years. Farmers suffered under a triple burden of declining prices for their crops, a drop in exports, and larger debts incurred by wartime expansion.

The most important weakness in the economy was the extremely unequal distribution of income and wealth. In 1929, the top 0.1 percent of American families (24,000 families) had an aggregate income equal to that of the bottom 42 percent (11.5 million families). The top 5 percent of American families received 30 percent of the nation's income; the bottom 60 percent got only 26 percent. About 71 percent of American families had annual incomes below $2,500. Nearly 80 percent of the nation's families (21.5 million households) had no savings; the top 0.1 percent held 34 percent of all savings. The top 0.5 percent of Americans owned 32.4 percent of the net wealth of the entire population — the greatest such concentration of wealth in the nation's history.

The stock market crash undermined the confidence, investment, and spending of businesses and the well-to-do. Manufacturers decreased their production and began laying off workers, which brought further declines in consumer spending, and another round of production cutbacks. A spurt of consumer spending might have checked this downward spiral, but consumers had less to spend as industries laid off workers and reduced hours. With less of a market for products, businesses were

Distribution of Total Family Income among Various Segments of the Population, 1929–1944 (in Percentages)

Year	Poorest Fifth	Second Poorest Fifth	Middle Fifth	Second Wealthiest Fifth	Wealthiest Fifth	Wealthiest 5 Percent
1929		12.5	13.8	19.3	54.4	30.0
1935–1936	4.1	9.2	14.1	20.9	51.7	26.5
1941	4.1	9.5	15.3	22.3	48.8	24.0
1944	4.9	10.9	16.2	22.2	45.8	20.7

Source: Adapted from U.S. Bureau of the Census, *Historical Statistics of the United States, Colonial Times to 1970,* Bicentennial Edition (Washington, D.C.: U.S. Government Printing Office, 1975), p. 301.

hesitant to expand. A large proportion of the nation's banking funds were tied to the speculative bubble of Wall Street stock buying. Many banks began to fail as anxious depositors withdrew their funds, which were uninsured. Farmers suffered: While agricultural prices were plunging 86 percent from 1929 to 1933, production fell only 6 percent.

Mass Unemployment

The single most searing experience of the depression was unemployment. At a time when unemployment insurance did not exist and public relief was terribly inadequate, the loss of a job could mean economic catastrophe for workers and their families. Massive unemployment across America became the most powerful sign of a deepening depression. In 1930 the Department of Labor estimated that 4.2 million workers, or roughly 9 percent of the labor force, were out of work. These figures nearly doubled in 1931, and by 1933, 12.6 million workers — over one-quarter of the labor force — were without jobs. Other sources put the figure that year above 16 million, or nearly one out of every three workers. None of these statistics tells us how long people were unemployed or how many Americans found only part-time work. The United States Steel Corporation, which had a quarter million full-time employees in 1929, reported zero full-time workers in April 1933.

What did it mean to be unemployed and without hope in the early 1930s? Figures give us only an outline of the grim reality. Many Americans, raised believing that they were responsible for their own fate, blamed themselves for their failure to find work. A. S. Johnson, an Arkansas migrant farmer who relocated to California, told an interviewer:

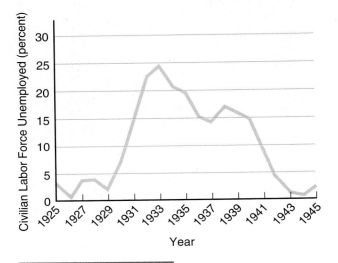

Unemployment, 1929–1945

In 1939, despite 6 years of New Deal programs, unemployment still hovered around 18 percent of the workforce. Only the onset of World War II ended the unemployment crisis.

(Source: *Historical Statistics of the United States from Colonial Times to 1970,* 1976, Part 1, p. 135.)

"Our sorrows and trials and tribulations are brought on by ourselves, more than anybody. Mine has. I'm a-judging everybody from myself. It's because I didn't do like I should've done." Contemporary journalists noted the common feelings of shame and guilt expressed by the unemployed.

Joblessness proved especially difficult for men between the ages of thirty-five and fifty-five, the period in their lives when family responsibilities were heaviest. Nathan Ackerman, a psychiatrist

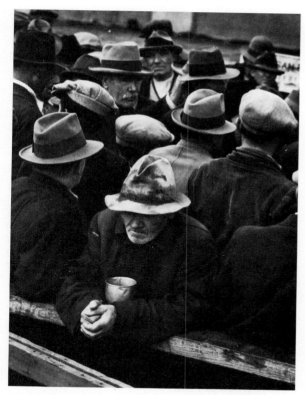

Dorothea Lange captured the lonely despair of unemployment in this photograph titled "White Angel Bread Line," San Francisco, 1933. During the 1920s Lange had specialized in taking portraits of wealthy families, but by 1932 she could no longer stand the contradiction between her portrait business and "what was going on in the street." She said of this photograph: "There are moments such as these when time stands still and all you can do is hold your breath and hope it will wait for you."

who went to Pennsylvania to observe the impact of prolonged unemployment upon coal miners, found an enormous sense of "internal distress":

> They hung around street corners and in groups. They gave each other solace. They were loath to go home because they were indicted, as if it were their fault for being unemployed. A jobless man was a lazy good-for-nothing. The women punished the men for not bringing home the bacon, by withholding themselves sexually. . . . These men suffered from depression. They felt despised, they were ashamed of themselves. They cringed, they comforted one another. They avoided home.

Women found it easier to hold onto jobs, as their labor was cheaper. Female clerks, secretaries, maids, and waitresses earned much less than male factory workers, but their jobs were more likely to survive hard times. Unemployment upset the psychological balance in many families by undermining the traditional authority of the male breadwinner. Male responses to unemployment varied: Some withdrew emotionally, others became angry or took to drinking. A few committed suicide over the shame of extended unemployment. Children also felt the sting of a father's failure. One Chicago social worker, writing about unemployment in 1934, summed up the strains she found in families: "Fathers feel they have lost their prestige in the home; there is much nagging, mothers nag at the fathers, parents nag at the children. Children of working age who earn meager salaries find it hard to turn over all their earnings and deny themselves even the greatest necessities and as a result leave home."

Pressures on those lucky enough to have a job increased as well. Anna Novak, a Chicago meatpacker, recalled the degrading harassment at the hands of foremen: "You could get along swell if you let the boss slap you on the behind and feel you up. God, I hate that stuff, you don't know!" Fear of unemployment and a deep desire for security marked the depression generation. "I mean there's a conditioning here by the Depression," a sanitation worker told an interviewer many years later. "I'm what I call a security cat. I don't dare switch [jobs]. 'Cause I got too much whiskers on it, seniority."

Hoover's Failure

The enormity of the depression overwhelmed traditional sources of relief. In most communities across America these sources were a patchwork of private agencies and local government units, such as towns, cities, or counties. They simply lacked the money, resources, and staff to deal with the worsening situation. In large urban centers like Detroit and Chicago, unemployment had approached 50 percent by 1932. Smaller communities could not cope either. One West Virginia coal mining county with 1,500 unemployed miners had only $9,000 to meet relief needs for that year. In Pennsylvania, many rural and urban families were getting only eight to twelve dollars a month for food. Unemployed transients, attracted by warm weather, posed a special problem for communities in California and Florida. By the end of 1931 Los Angeles had 70,000 nonresident jobless and homeless men; new arrivals numbered about 1,200 a day.

There was great irony, even tragedy, in President Hoover's failure to respond to human suffering. He had administered large-scale humanitarian efforts during World War I with great efficiency. Yet he seemed to most people a man with little personal warmth. Hoover made his reputation as an engineer and as one who believed in the importance of objective studies of social and economic problems, yet he failed to face the facts of the depression. He ignored all the mounting evidence to the contrary when he claimed in his 1931 State of the Union address, "Our people are providing against distress from unemployment in true American fashion by magnificent response to public appeal and by action of the local governments."

He resisted the growing calls from Congress and local communities for a greater federal role in relief efforts or public works projects. He worried, as he told Congress after vetoing one measure, about injuring "the initiative and enterprise of the American people." He feared "the negation of the ideals upon which our civilization has been based." The President's Emergency Committee for Unemployment, established in 1930, and its successor, the President's Organization for Unemployment Relief, created in 1931, did little more than encourage local groups to raise money to help the unemployed.

Hoover's plan for recovery centered in restoring business confidence. His administration's most important institutional response to the depression was the Reconstruction Finance Corporation, established in early 1932 and based upon the War Finance Corporation of the World War I years. The RFC was designed to make government credit available to ailing banks, railroads, insurance companies, and other businesses, thereby stimulating economic activity. The key assumption here was that the credit problem was one of supply (for businesses) rather than demand (from consumers). But given the public's low purchasing power, most businesses were not interested in obtaining loans for expansion. The RFC managed to save numerous banks and other businesses from going under, but its approach did not hasten recovery. Further, the Hoover administration's unwillingness to use the power of the federal purse to help out financially strapped cities and states in the same way it did the banks brought howls of protest.

Protest and the Election of 1932

Direct, at times violent, expressions of protest in 1932, widely covered in the press, reflected the desperate mood of many Americans. On March 7, several thousand Detroit auto workers and unemployed, led by Communist organizers, marched to the Ford River Rouge factory in nearby Dearborn.

When the demonstrators refused orders to turn back, Ford-controlled police fired tear gas and bullets, killing four and seriously wounding fifty others. Some 40,000 people attended a tense funeral service a few days later. Desperate farmers in Iowa organized the Farmers' Holiday Association, aimed at raising prices by refusing to sell produce. In August, some 1,500 farmers turned back cargo trucks outside Sioux City, Iowa, and made a point by dumping milk and other perishables into ditches.

That spring, the "Bonus Army" began descending upon Washington, D.C., to demand the cash bonuses that Congress had promised in 1924. By summer, around 20,000 of these World War I veterans and their families were camped out all over the capital city. Their lobbying convinced the House to pass a bill for immediate payment, but the Senate rejected the bill and most of the veterans left. At the end of July U.S. Army troops led by Chief of Staff General Douglas MacArthur forcibly evicted the remaining 2,000 veterans from their encampment. MacArthur exaggerated the menace of the peaceful demonstrators, insisting they were driven by "the essence of revolution." The spectacle of these unarmed and unemployed men, the heroes of 1918,

---

The Election of 1932

Democrats owed their overwhelming victory in 1932 to the popular identification of the Depression with the Hoover administration. Roosevelt's popular vote was about the same as Hoover's in 1928, and FDR's electoral college margin was even greater.

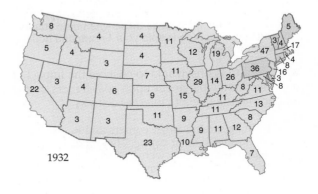

1932

Candidates (Party)	Electoral vote	Popular vote
Roosevelt (Democratic)	472 (89%)	22,821,857 (57%)
Hoover (Republican)	59 (11%)	15,761,841 (40%)
Minor parties	–	1,160,615 (3%)

The Presidential succession, 1932. A glum Herbert Hoover (left) avoids conversation with Franklin D. Roosevelt as the two ride from the White House to the Capitol for FDR's inauguration.

driven off by bayonets and bullets provided the most disturbing evidence yet of the failure of Hoover's administration.

The congressional elections of 1930 had already revealed a growing dissatisfaction with Hoover's approach. Democrats had won control of the House of Representatives for the first time since 1916, and gained eight seats in the Senate. The presidential election of 1932 showed just how disillusioned the public had become. In 1932, Democrats nominated Franklin D. Roosevelt, governor of New York, as their candidate. Roosevelt's acceptance speech stressed the need for reconstructing the nation's economy. "I pledge you, I pledge myself," he said, "to a new deal for the American people."

In the campaign, Roosevelt's plans for recovery were vague at best. He frequently attacked Hoover for reckless and extravagant spending, and accused him of trying to center too much power in Washington. He also spoke of the need for government to meet "the problem of underconsumption" and to help in "distributing wealth and products more equitably." Hoover bitterly condemned Roosevelt's ideas as a "radical departure" from the American way of life. But with the depression growing worse every day, probably any Democrat would have defeated Hoover. The Democratic victory was over-

whelming. Roosevelt carried forty-two states, taking the electoral college 472 to 59 and the popular vote by about 23 million to 16 million. Democrats won big majorities in both the House and the Senate. The stage was set for FDR's "new deal."

FDR AND THE FIRST NEW DEAL

FDR the Man

No president of this century had a greater impact on American life and politics than Franklin Delano Roosevelt. He was born in 1882 in Dutchess County, New York, where he grew up an only child, secure and confident, on his family's vast estate. Franklin's father, James, had made a fortune through railroad investments, but he was already in his fifties when Franklin was born, and it was his mother, Sara Delano, who was the dominant figure in his childhood. Roosevelt's education at Groton, Harvard, and Columbia Law School reinforced the aristocratic values of his family: a strong sense of civic duty, the importance of competitive athletics, and an attitude of noblesse oblige.

In 1905 he married his distant cousin, Anna Eleanor Roosevelt, niece of President Theodore Roosevelt; she would later emerge as an influential adviser and political force on her own. Young Franklin turned to politics as a career early on. He was elected as a Democrat to the New York State Senate in 1910, served as assistant navy secretary from 1913 to 1920, and was nominated for vice-president by the Democrats in the losing 1920 campaign.

A turning point came in the summer of 1921 when Roosevelt was stricken with polio at his summer home on Campobello Island, New Brunswick. The resulting paralysis left his legs permanently crippled; he was never to walk again without support. The disease strengthened his relationship with Eleanor, who encouraged him not only to fight his handicap but to continue with his political career. His patience and determination in fighting the disease transformed him. The wealthy aristocrat, for whom everything had come relatively easy, now personally understood the meaning of struggle and hardship. "Once I spent two years lying in bed trying to move my big toe," he recalled. "After that anything else seems easy."

Elected governor of New York in 1928, he served two terms and won a national reputation for reform. In Albany his achievements included unemployment insurance, improved child labor laws, farm tax relief, and old age pensions. As the depression hit the state he slowly increased public works and set up a Temporary Emergency Relief Administration. With his eye on the White House, he began assembling a group of key advisers, the "Brain Trust," who would follow him to Washington. The central figures were Columbia Law School professor and progressive Raymond Moley; two maverick economists, Rexford G. Tugwell and Adolf A. Berle; and attorneys Samuel Rosenman, Basil O'Connor, and Felix Frankfurter. They never met as a group after Roosevelt's inauguration, and they represented a variety of ideologies. But the "brain trusters" shared a faith in the power of organized intelligence to set the economy right, and a basic belief in government-business cooperation. They rejected the old progressive dream of re-creating an ideal society of small producers. Structural economic reform, they argued, must accept the modern reality of large corporate enterprise based on mass production and distribution.

Restoring Confidence

In the first days of his administration Roosevelt conveyed a sense of optimism and activism that helped restore the badly shaken confidence of the nation. "First of all," he told Americans in his inaugural address on March 4, 1933, "let me assert my firm belief that the only thing we have to fear is fear itself." The very next day he issued an executive order calling for a four-day "bank holiday" to shore up the country's ailing financial system. The nation's banks had been reeling from the twin blows of business decline and the melting of depositors' confidence. Contemporary investigations had revealed a disquieting pattern of stock manipulation, illegal loans to bank officials, and tax evasion that helped erode public confidence in the banking system. More than 1,300 banks failed in 1930, more than 2,000 in 1931. Between election day and the inauguration, the banking system had come alarmingly close to shutting down altogether due to widespread bank failures and the hoarding of currency.

Roosevelt therefore called for a special session of Congress to deal with the banking crisis, as well as unemployment aid and farm relief. On March 12 he broadcast his first "fireside chat" to explain the steps he had taken to meet the financial emergency. He consciously used the radio to project a warm, comforting image and to bring his considerable powers of persuasion to millions of households. These radio broadcasts became a standard part of

Roosevelt's political technique, and they proved enormously successful. They gave courage to ordinary Americans and communicated a genuine sense of compassion from the White House.

Congress immediately passed the Emergency Banking Act, which gave the president broad discretionary powers over all banking transactions and foreign exchange. By strengthening the Federal Reserve System, it created ways to aid banks in danger of failing and provided for the reopening of only those banks judged to be healthy. By the middle of March about half the country's banks, holding about 90 percent of the nation's deposits, were open for business again. Banks began to attract new currency from depositors who had held back. The bank crisis had passed.

The Hundred Days

From March to June of 1933 — the "Hundred Days" — FDR used the special congressional session to push through an extraordinary number of acts designed to combat various aspects of the depression. What came to be called the New Deal was no unified program to end the depression. There was no overall blueprint. Rather, as a master political broker, skilled at playing off diverse interests against one another, Roosevelt improvised a series of reform and relief measures, some of which seemed to contradict each other. He responded to pressures from Congress, from business, and from organized labor, but he also used his own considerable power over public opinion to get his way.

Five measures were particularly important and innovative. The Civilian Conservation Corps, established in March as an unemployment relief effort, provided work for jobless young men in protecting and conserving the nation's natural resources. Road construction, reforestation, flood control, and national park improvements were some of the major projects performed in work camps across the country. CCC workers received room and board and thirty dollars each month, up to twenty-five dollars of which had to be sent home to dependents. By the time the program was phased out in 1941, over 2.5 million youths had worked in some 1,500 CCC camps.

In May Congress authorized $500 million for the Federal Emergency Relief Administration. Half the money went as direct relief to the states; the balance was distributed on the basis of a dollar of federal aid for every three dollars of state and local funds spent for relief. This system of outright federal grants differed significantly from Hoover's approach, which provided only for loans. Establishment of work relief projects, however, was left to state and local governments. To direct the FERA Roosevelt turned to Harry Hopkins, an experienced reformer from the world of New York social work. A brilliant administrator with a special commitment to ending discrimination in relief work, Hopkins became the New Deal's most influential figure in relief policies and one of Roosevelt's most trusted advisers.

The Agricultural Adjustment Administration was set up to provide immediate relief to the nation's farmers. The AAA established a new federal role in agricultural planning and price setting. It established *parity prices* for seven basic farm commodities. The concept of parity pricing was based on the purchasing power that farmers had enjoyed during the prosperous years of 1909 to 1914. That period now became the benchmark for setting the prices of farm commodities. The AAA also incorporated the principle of *subsidy,* whereby farmers

received benefit payments in return for reducing acreage or otherwise cutting production where surpluses existed. The funds for these payments were to be raised from new taxes on food processing. The ideas behind the AAA actually dated back to reform proposals made by the Populists in the 1890s.

The AAA raised total farm income and was especially successful in pushing up the prices of wheat, cotton, and corn. But it had some troubling side effects as well. Landlords often failed to share their AAA payments with tenant farmers, and they frequently used benefits to buy tractors and other equipment that displaced sharecroppers. Many Americans were disturbed, too, by the sight of surplus crops, livestock, and milk being destroyed while millions went hungry.

The Tennessee Valley Authority proved to be one of the most unique and controversial projects of the New Deal era. It had its origins in the federal

The Tennessee Valley Authority

The TVA offered a prime example of how federally funded New Deal projects helped re-shape life in local communities. Beginning with the hydroelectric complex at Muscle Shoals, Alabama, the TVA eventually built five dams and improved twenty others along the Tennessee River. It brought electricity to rural areas, sold cheap fertilizers to farmers, engaged in flood control and soil conservation projects, and greatly improved river navigation.

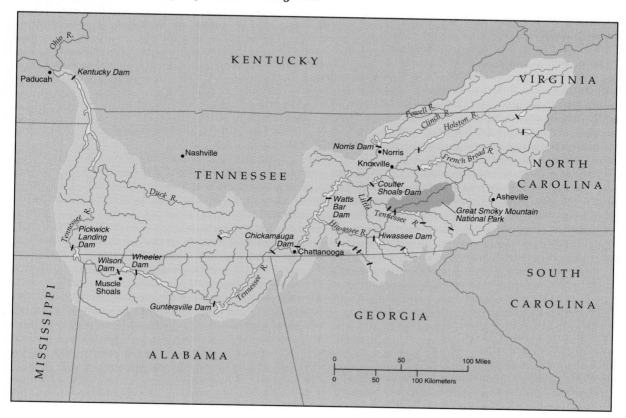

government's effort during World War I to build a large hydroelectric power complex and munitions plant on the Tennessee River at Muscle Shoals, Alabama. During the 1920s, Republican senator George W. Norris of Nebraska had led an unsuccessful fight to provide for permanent government operation of the Muscle Shoals facilities on behalf of the area's population. The TVA, an independent public corporation, built dams and power plants, produced cheap fertilizer for farmers, and, most significantly, brought cheap electricity for the first time to thousands of people in six southern states. Denounced by some as a dangerous step toward socialism, the TVA stood for decades as a model of how careful government planning could dramatically improve the social and economic welfare of an underdeveloped region.

On the very last of the Hundred Days, Congress passed the National Industrial Recovery Act, the closest attempt yet at a systematic plan for economic recovery. It had two main parts. The National Recovery Administration (NRA) looked to stimulate production and competition in business by means of industrial codes regulating prices, output, and trade practices. In theory, each industry would be self-governed by a code hammered out by representatives of business, labor, and the consuming public. Once approved by the NRA in Washington, led by General Hugh Johnson and symbolized by the distinctive Blue Eagle stamp, the codes would have the force of law. In practice, almost all the NRA codes were written by the largest firms in any given industry; labor and consumers got short shrift. The sheer administrative complexities involved with code writing and compliance made a great many people unhappy with the NRA's operation. Overall, the NRA looked to business and industry leaders to find a way to recovery.

The Public Works Administration, led by Secretary of the Interior Harold Ickes, authorized $3.3 billion for the construction of roads, public buildings, and other projects. The idea was to provide jobs and thus stimulate the economy through increased consumer spending. A favorite image for this kind of spending was "priming the pump." Just as a farmer had to work the pump handle for a while before water came up from the well, the government had to prime the economy with jobs for the unemployed. Eventually the PWA spent over $4.2 billion building roads, schools, post offices, bridges, courthouses, and other public buildings around the country. In thousands of communities today, these structures remain the most tangible remnants of the New Deal era.

Left Turn and the Second New Deal

The Hundred Days legislative package had tried to offer something for everybody. Certainly the active, can-do spirit in Washington brought reassurance that the nation was back on track. Yet the depression remained a stark reality for many millions. From the beginning, the New Deal had loud and powerful critics who complained bitterly that FDR had overstepped the traditional boundaries of government action. Others were angry that Roosevelt had not done nearly enough. These varied voices of protest helped shape the political debates of FDR's first term. Ultimately, they would contribute to a more radical direction for New Deal.

Roosevelt's Critics

On the right, conservative newspapers and the American Liberty League, organized in 1934, denounced Roosevelt and his advisers. They held the administration responsible for what they considered an attack on property rights, the growing welfare state, and the decline of personal liberty. Dominated by wealthy executives of Du Pont and General Motors, the league attracted support from a group of conservative Democrats, including Al Smith, who declared the New Deal's laws "socialistic." The league supported anti–New Dealers for Congress, but the 1934 election results suggested that Roosevelt's popularity was increasing. Democrats built up their majorities from 310 to 319 in the House and from 60 to 69 in the Senate — an unusually strong showing for the incumbent party in a midterm election.

More troublesome for Roosevelt and his allies were the vocal and popular movements on the left. These found the New Deal too timid in its measures. In California, well-known novelist and Socialist Upton Sinclair entered the 1934 Democratic primary for governor by running on a program he called EPIC, for End Poverty in California. He proposed a fifty-dollar-a-month pension for all poor people over age sixty. His campaign also emphasized a government-run system of "production for use" (rather than profit) workshops for the unemployed. Sinclair shocked local and national Democrats by winning the primary easily. He lost a close general election only because the Republican candidate received heavy financial and tactical support from wealthy Hollywood figures and frightened regular Democrats.

Another Californian, Francis E. Townsend, a retired doctor, created a large following among senior citizens with his Old Age Revolving Pension plan. He called for payments of $200 per month to all people over sixty, provided the money was spent within thirty days. The pensions would be financed by a national 2 percent tax on all commercial transactions. This plan managed to attract a nationwide following of over 3 million by 1936. But Townsend's plan was essentially regressive, since it proposed to tax all Americans equally, regardless of their income. In effect, it would have helped the aged at the expense of all working- and middle-class consumers.

Huey Long, Louisiana's flamboyant backcountry orator, posed the greatest potential threat to Roosevelt's leadership. Long had captured the state's governorship in 1928 by attacking the state's entrenched oil industry and calling for a radical redistribution of wealth. In office, he significantly

Senator Huey P. Long on the stump in 1932. Long was a mesmerizing speaker whose populist message struck a deep chord with Louisiana voters and millions of other Americans. He broke with Roosevelt's New Deal in 1934, claiming it was not radical enough to solve the nation's economic woes. His assassination in 1935 ended Long's threat to challenge FDR as a third party candidate for president.

improved public education, roads, medical care, and other public services, winning the loyalty of the state's poor farmers and industrial workers. Elected to the U.S. Senate in 1931, Long came to Washington with national ambitions. He at first supported Roosevelt, but in 1934 he began denouncing the New Deal as a failure.

Long organized the Share Our Wealth Society. Its purpose, he thundered, "was to break up the swollen fortunes of America and to spread the wealth among all our people." Limiting the size of large fortunes, Long promised, would mean a homestead worth $5,000 and a $2,500 annual income for everyone. Although Long's economics were fuzzy at best, he undoubtedly touched a deep nerve with his "Every Man a King" slogan. The Democratic National Committee was shocked when a secret poll in the summer of 1935 revealed that Long might attract 3 or 4 million votes. Only his assassination that September prevented Long's third-party candidacy, which might have proved disastrous for FDR.

In the nation's workplaces and streets, a rejuvenated and newly militant labor movement also loomed as a force to be reckoned with. In many industrial cities Unemployed Councils, organized largely by the Communist party, held large-scale marches and rallies demanding public works projects and relief payments. Section 7a of the National Industrial Recovery Act required that workers be allowed to bargain collectively with employers, through representatives of their own choosing. Though this provision of the NIRA was not enforced, it did help raise expectations and spark union organizing. Almost 1.5 million workers took part in some 1,800 strikes in 1934. But employers resisted unionization nearly everywhere, often with violence and the help of local and state police.

In Minneapolis, a local of the International Brotherhood of Teamsters won a bloody strike against the combined opposition of the union's national officials, vehemently antiunion employers, and a brutal city police force. Violence against strikers helped unite the city's working classes. The Minneapolis Central Labor Union was prepared to support a general strike, and the funeral of a striker shot by police drew 100,000 people. In San Francisco that year, a general strike in support of striking members of the International Longshoremen's Association effectively shut down the city. Employer use of strikebreakers and violent intimidation prompted an outpouring of support for the ILA from the city's working class, as well as many shopkeepers and middle-class professionals. When the ILA accepted government arbitration, it won on its main issue — control over the hiring halls on the waterfront. In both Minneapolis and San Francisco, workers had demonstrated the power of labor solidarity and mass protest.

The Second Hundred Days

Roosevelt knew it would be difficult to recover the support of conservative Democrats and alienated business leaders. The popularity of leaders like Sinclair, Townsend, and Long suggested Roosevelt might be losing electoral support among workers, farmers, the aged, and the unemployed. In early 1935 Roosevelt and his closest advisers responded by turning left and concentrating on a new program of social reform. They had three major goals: strengthening the national commitment to creating jobs; providing security against old age, unemployment, and illness; and improving housing conditions and cleaning slums. What came to be called the Second Hundred Days marked the high point of progressive lawmaking in the New Deal.

In April the administration pushed through the Emergency Relief Appropriation Act, which allocated $5 billion for large-scale public works programs for the jobless. New Deal economists, following the theories of Britain's John Maynard Keynes, argued that each government dollar spent had a *multiplier effect,* pumping two or three dollars into the depressed gross national product. The major responsible agency here was the Works Progress Administration, led by Harry Hopkins. Over the next seven years Hopkins oversaw the employment of over 8 million Americans on a vast array of construction projects: roads, bridges, dams, airports, and sewers. Among the most innovative WPA programs were community service projects that employed thousands of jobless artists, musicians, actors, and writers.

The landmark Social Security Act of 1935 provided for old-age pensions and unemployment insurance. A payroll tax on workers and their employers created a fund from which retirees received monthly pensions after age sixty-five. Payment size depended upon how much employees and their employers had contributed over the years. The unemployment compensation plan established a minimum weekly payment and a minimum number of weeks during which those who lost jobs could collect. The Social Security Board administered this complex system of federal-state cooperation. The original law had flaws. It failed to cover farm workers and domestics, many of whom were Latinos and African Americans. It also made no provisions for casual laborers or public employees. The old-age pensions were quite small at first, as little as ten dollars a month. And to collect unemployment, one had to have first lost a job. But the law, which has since been amended many times, established the crucial principle of federal responsibility for America's most vulnerable citizens.

Another 1935 law with far-reaching implications for American politics and the economy was the National Labor Relations Act (often called the Wagner Act for its chief sponsor, Democratic senator Robert F. Wagner of New York). For the first time, the federal government guaranteed the right of American workers to join or form independent labor unions and bargain collectively for improved wages, benefits, and working conditions. The National Labor Relations Board would conduct secret-ballot elections in shops and factories to determine which union, if any, workers desired as their sole bargaining agent. The law also defined and prohibited unfair labor practices by employers, including firing workers for union activity. The Wagner Act, described as "the Magna Carta for labor," quickly proved a boon to union growth, especially in previously unorganized industries such as automobiles, steel, and textiles.

Finally, the Resettlement Administration produced one of the most utopian New Deal programs, one designed to create new kinds of model communities. Established by executive order and led by key brain truster Rexford G. Tugwell, the RA helped destitute farm families relocate to more productive areas. It granted loans for purchasing land and equipment, and it directed reforestation and soil erosion projects, particularly in the hard-hit Southwest. Due to lack of funds and poor administration, however, only about 1 percent of the projected 500,000 families were actually moved.

Tugwell, one of the New Deal's most ardent believers in planning, was more successful in his efforts at creating model greenbelt communities combining the best of urban and rural environments. "My idea," he wrote, "is to go just outside centers of population, pick up cheap land, build a whole community and entice people into it." Though his vision was only partially fulfilled, several of these communities, such as Greenhills, near Cincinnati, and Greendale, near Milwaukee, still thrive, reminders of an idealistic effort to build carefully planned communities.

Labor's Upsurge: Rise of the CIO

In 1932 the American labor movement was nearly dead. Only 2.8 million workers were union members, a half million fewer than in 1929 and over 2 million less than in 1920. Yet by 1942, unions claimed over 10.5 million members, nearly a third of the total nonagricultural work force. This remarkable turnaround was one of the key events of the depression era. The growth in the size and power of the labor movement permanently changed the work lives and economic status of millions, as well as the national and local political landscapes.

At the core of this growth were a series of dramatic successes in the organization of workers in large-scale, mass production industries such as automobiles, steel, rubber, electrical goods, and textiles. Workers in these fields had largely been ignored by the conservative, craft-conscious unions that dominated the American Federation of Labor. At the 1935 AFL convention, a group of more militant union officials led by John L. Lewis (of the United Mine Workers) and Sidney Hillman (of the Amalgamated Clothing Workers) formed the Committee for Industrial Organization (CIO). Their goal was to organize mass production workers by industry, rather than by craft. They emphasized the need for opening the new unions to all, regardless of a worker's level of skill. And they differed from nearly all old-line AFL unions by calling for the inclusion of black and women workers.

Lewis was the key figure. The gruff son of a Welsh miner, Lewis was articulate, ruthless, and very ambitious. He saw the new legal protection given by the Wagner Act as a historic opportunity. "Why not make a contribution," he told the leaders of the AFL, "to the well being of those who are not fortunate enough to be members of your organizations? The labor movement is organized upon a principle that the strong shall help the weak." Despite the Wagner Act, whose constitutionality was unclear until 1937, Lewis knew that establishing permanent unions in the mass industries would be a bruising battle. He committed the substantial resources of the United Mine Workers to a series of organizing drives, focusing first on the steel and auto industries. Many CIO organizers were Communists or radicals of other persuasions, and their dedication, commitment, and willingness to work within disciplined organizations proved invaluable in the often dangerous task of creating industrial unions. Of the roughly 200 full-time organizers on the payroll of the Steel Workers Organizing Committee in 1937, almost a third were members of the Communist party.

Militant rank-and-file unionists were often

Philip Evergood, *American Tragedy* (1937). A classic example of the social realism characteristic of much Depression era art, this painting depicted the police violence against strikers at the Republic Steel Mill. Evergood was one of many contemporary artists who found work in the Federal Art Project painting murals in public buildings. (Philip Evergood. American Tragedy. 1937. Oil on canvas, 29½ × 39½ in. Private Collection. Terry D. Dintenfass Gallery.)

ahead of Lewis and other CIO leaders. The sit-down strike — refusing to work but staying in the factory to prevent "scab" workers from taking over — emerged as a popular tactic among rubber and auto workers. After the dramatic breakthrough in the Flint sit-down strike at General Motors, membership in CIO unions grew rapidly. In eight months membership in the United Automobile Workers alone soared from 88,000 to 400,000. CIO victories in the steel, rubber, and electrical industries followed, but often at a very high cost. One bloody example of the perils of union organizing was the 1937 Memorial Day Massacre in Chicago. In a field near the struck Republic Steel Mill in South Chicago, police fired into a crowd of union supporters, killing ten workers and wounding scores more.

Overall, the success of the CIO organizing drives was remarkable. In 1938 the CIO unions, now boasting nearly 4 million members, withdrew from the AFL and reorganized themselves as the Congress of Industrial Organizations. Ahead lay many hard battles organizing workers in such nonunion bastions as the Ford Motor Company and the textile plants of the South. But for the first time ever, the labor movement had gained a permanent place in the nation's mass production industries. It would also take its place as a key power broker in Roosevelt's New Deal and the national Democratic party. Frances Perkins, FDR's secretary of labor and the first woman Cabinet member, captured the close relationship between the new unionism and the New Deal: "Programs long thought of as merely labor welfare, such as shorter hours, higher wages, and a voice in the terms of conditions of work, are really essential economic factors for recovery."

The New Deal Coalition at High Tide

The 1936 presidential campaign shaped up as a clear national referendum. Did the American public support Roosevelt and his New Deal policies? Both major political parties looked forward to the elections, and the campaign itself was an exciting and hard-fought contest. Very few political observers predicted its lopsided result.

Republicans nominated Governor Alfred M. Landon of Kansas, who had gained attention by bucking the Democratic landslide of 1934. Landon, an easygoing, colorless man with little personal magnetism, emphasized a nostalgic appeal to traditional American values. The Republican platform did not call for repealing New Deal legislation. But Landon's campaign served as a lightning rod for all those, including many conservative Democrats, who were dissatisfied with Roosevelt and the direction he

had taken. Al Smith, the Democratic nominee in 1928, categorically denounced the New Deal as "socialism" and supported Landon. Kansas Republican William Allen White, editor of the *Emporia Gazette,* attacked the New Deal for its buildup of the federal government, for creating "a great political machine centered in Washington."

Roosevelt, easily renominated by the Democrats, attacked the "economic royalists" who denied that government "could do anything to protect the citizen in his right to work and his right to live." At the same time, FDR was careful to distance himself from radicalism. "It was this administration," he declared, "which saved the system of private profit and free enterprise after it had been dragged to the brink of ruin." As Roosevelt's campaign crossed the country, his advisers were heartened by huge and enthusiastic crowds, especially in large cities like Chicago and Pittsburgh. Still, the vast majority of the nation's newspapers endorsed Landon. And a widely touted "scientific" poll by the *Literary Digest* forecast a Republican victory in November.

Election Day erased all doubts. Roosevelt carried every state but Maine and Vermont, polling 61 percent of the popular vote. Democrats increased their substantial majorities in the House and Senate as well. The *Literary Digest* poll, it turned out, had been based upon telephone directories and car registration records. This provided a very unrepresentative sample, weighted toward wealthier Americans and those more likely to vote Republican. In 1936 the Democrats drew millions of new voters into the political process and at the same time forged a new coalition of voters that would dominate national politics for two generations.

The "New Deal coalition," as it came to be known, included traditional-minded white southern Democrats, big-city political machines, industrial workers of all races, trade unionists, and many depression-hit farmers. The Democrats' strong showing in the ethnic wards of America's large urban centers reinforced a trend that had begun with Al Smith's 1928 campaign. Roosevelt was especially popular among first- and second-generation immigrants of Catholic and Jewish descent. Organized labor, led by the CIO's Non-Partisan League, put an unprecedented amount of money and people power into Roosevelt's reelection. Black voters in the North and West, long affiliated with the party of Lincoln, went Democratic in record numbers. The depression was by no means over. But the New Deal's active response to the nation's misery, particularly the bold initiatives taken in 1935, had obviously struck a powerful chord with the American electorate.

THE NEW DEAL AND THE WEST

The New Deal had a more profound impact on the West than on any other region in the nation. Western citizens received more from the federal government in per capita payments for welfare, work relief, and loans than the people of any other section. But perhaps more important, New Deal programs, based on a philosophy of rational planning of resource use, transformed western agriculture, water and energy sources, and Indian policy. From Great Plains farming communities in Kansas and Oklahoma to Pacific Coast cities such as Los Angeles and Seattle, federal subsidy and management became an integral part of western life. In the process, the New Deal helped propel the West into the modern era. The region's economic development and politics would now be dominated by a combination of Washington-based bureaucracies, large-scale agriculture, and new industrial enterprises.

The Dust Bowl

An ecological and economic disaster of unprecedented proportions struck the southern Great Plains in the mid-1930s. The region had suffered several drought years in the early 1930s as rainfall fell far

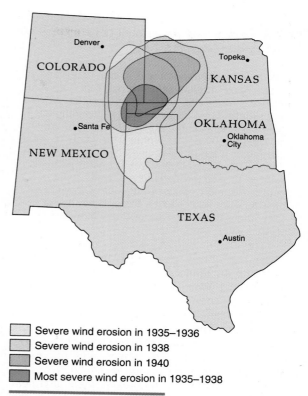

☐ Severe wind erosion in 1935–1936
☐ Severe wind erosion in 1938
▨ Severe wind erosion in 1940
▨ Most severe wind erosion in 1935–1938

The Dust Bowl, 1935–1940

Map shows the extent of the Dust Bowl on the southern Great Plains. Federal programs designed to improve soil conservation, water management, and farming practices could not prevent a mass exodus of hundreds of thousands out of the Great Plains region.

Approaching dust storm in Amarillo, Texas, April 1936. Arthur Rothstein's photograph, taken for the Farm Security Administration, captured the frightening power of one of the "black blizzards."

below normal levels. Such dry spells occurred regularly in roughly twenty-year cycles. But this time the parched earth became swept up in violent dust storms the likes of which had never been seen before. Black blizzards of dust a mile and a half high rolled across the landscape, darkening the sky and whipping the earth into great drifts that settled over hundreds of miles. Dust storms made it difficult for humans and livestock to breathe and destroyed crops and trees over vast areas. The hardest-hit regions were western Kansas, eastern Colorado, western Oklahoma, the Texas Panhandle, and eastern New Mexico. A Denver journalist coined the phrase "Dust Bowl" to describe the calamity he had witnessed on the southern plains.

Dust storms turned day into night, terrifying those caught in them. "Dust pneumonia" and other respiratory infections afflicted thousands, and many travelers found themselves stranded in automobiles and trains unable to move. The worst storms occurred in the early spring of 1935. A Garden City, Kansas, woman gave an account of her experience for the *Kansas City Times:*

> All we could do about it was just sit in our dusty chairs, gaze at each other through the fog that filled the room and watch that fog settle slowly and silently, covering everything — including ourselves — in a thick, brownish gray blanket. When we opened the door swirling whirlwinds of soil beat against us unmercifully. The door and windows were all shut tightly, yet those tiny particles seemed to seep through the very walls. It got into cupboards and clothes closets; our faces were as dirty as if we had rolled in the dirt; our hair was gray and stiff and we ground dirt between our teeth.

The dust storms were largely the result of years of stripping the landscape of its natural vegetation. During World War I, wheat fetched record-high prices on the world market, and for the next twenty years Great Plains farmers turned the region into a vast wheat factory. The wide flatlands of the Dust Bowl were especially suited to mechanized farming, and steam tractors, disk plows, and harvester-thresher combines increased productivity enormously. Back in 1830 it had taken some fifty-eight hours of labor to bring an acre of wheat to the granary; in much of the Great Plains a hundred years later it required less than three hours. As wheat prices fell in the 1920s, farmers broke still more land to make up the difference with increased production. Great Plains farmers had created an ecological time bomb that exploded when drought returned in the early 1930s. With native grasses destroyed for the sake of wheat growing, there was nothing left to prevent soil erosion. The dust storms blew away tens of millions of acres of rich topsoil, and thousands of farm families left the region. Those who stayed suffered deep economic and psychological losses from the calamity.

Several federal agencies intervened directly to relieve the distress. Many thousands of Great Plains farm families were given direct emergency relief by the Resettlement Administration. Other federal assistance included crop and seed loans, moratoriums on loan payments, and temporary jobs with the Works Progress Administration. In most Great Plains counties, from one-fifth to one-third of the families applied for relief; in the hardest-hit communities, as many as 90 percent of the families received direct government aid. The Agricultural Adjustment Administration paid wheat farmers millions of dollars not to grow what they could not sell and encour-

aged the diversion of acreage from soil-depleting crops like wheat to soil-enriching crops such as sorghum.

To reduce the pressure from grazing cattle on the remaining grasslands, the Drought Relief Service of the Department of Agriculture purchased over 8 million head of cattle in 1934 and 1935. For a brief time, the federal government was the largest cattle owner in the world. The DRS also loaned ranchers money to feed their remaining cattle. The Taylor Grazing Act of 1934 brought stock grazing on public domain lands under federal management.

The federal government also pursued longer-range policies designed to alter land-use patterns, reverse soil erosion, and nourish the return of grasslands. The Department of Agriculture, under Secretary Henry A. Wallace, sought to change farming practices. The spearhead for this effort was the Soil Conservation Service, which conducted research into controlling wind and water erosion, set up demonstration projects, and offered technical assistance, supplies, and equipment to farmers engaged in conservation work on farms and ranches. The SCS pumped additional federal funds into the Great Plains and created a new rural organization, the soil conservation district, which administered conservation regulations locally.

By 1940 the acreage subject to blowing in the Dust Bowl area of the southern plains had been reduced from roughly 50 million acres to less than 4 million acres. In the face of the Dust Bowl disaster New Deal farm policies had restricted market forces in agriculture. But the return of regular rainfall and the outbreak of World War II led many farmers to abandon the techniques that the SCS had taught them to accept. Wheat farming expanded and farms grew as farmers once again pursued commercial agriculture with little concern for its long-term effects on the land. While large landowners and ranchers reaped large benefits from AAA subsidies and other New Deal programs, tenant farmers and sharecroppers received very little. Many farmers used AAA cash payments to buy tractors and other machinery and evicted their tenants.

In the cotton lands of Texas, Oklahoma, Missouri, and Arkansas, thousands of tenant and share-cropper families were forced off the land. They became part of a stream of roughly 300,000 people, disparagingly called "Okies," who migrated to California in the 1930s. California migrants included victims of the Dust Bowl, but the majority were blue-collar workers and small businessmen looking to improve their economic lot. California suffered from the depression along with the rest of the nation, but it still offered more jobs, higher wages, and higher relief payments than the states of the southern plains. Most Okies could find work only as poorly paid agricultural laborers in the fertile San Joaquin and Imperial valley districts. There they faced discrimination and scorn as "poor white trash" as they struggled to create communities amidst the squalor of migrant labor camps. Only with the outbreak of World War II and the pressing demand for labor were migrants able to significantly improve their situation.

Water Policy

The New Deal ushered in the era of large-scale water projects constructed and controlled by the federal government. The long-range impact of these undertakings on western life would be difficult to overestimate. The key government agency in this realm was the Bureau of Reclamation of the Department of the Interior, established under the Reclamation Act of 1902. The bureau's original responsibility had been to construct dams and irrigation works and thereby encourage the growth of small farms throughout the arid regions of the West. Until the late 1920s the bureau had proved a relative failure in this regard, irrigating only a very small portion of the West. But its fortunes changed when it shifted its focus to building huge multipurpose dams designed to control entire river systems.

The first of these projects was the Boulder Dam (later renamed the Hoover Dam). The dam, actually begun during the Hoover administration, was designed to harness the Colorado River, wildest and most isolated of the major western rivers. The benefits would be flood prevention, irrigation of California's Imperial Valley, domestic water for Southern California, and cheap electricity for Los Angeles and southern Arizona. Hoover, however, had come out against the public power aspect of the project, arguing that the government ought not compete with private utility companies. Yet most westerners believed cheap public power was critical for development. Roosevelt's support for public power was a significant factor in his winning the political backing of the West in 1932 and subsequent election years.

Boulder Dam was completed in 1935 with the help of funds from the Public Works Administration. The total cost was $114 million; the sale of hydroelectric power generated by the dam would help repay construction costs. Los Angeles and neighboring cities built a 259-mile aqueduct, costing $220 million, to provide water for their growing popula-

tions. Lake Mead, created by construction of the dam, became the world's largest artificial lake, extending 115 miles up the canyon and providing a popular new recreation area. The dam's irrigation water helped make the Imperial Valley, covering over 500,000 acres, one of the most productive agricultural districts in the world.

The success of Boulder Dam transformed the Bureau of Reclamation into a major federal agency with huge resources at its disposal. The bureau supervised the construction and operation of several other massive water projects in the West. In 1938 it completed the All-American Canal—an 80-mile channel connecting the Colorado River to the Imperial Valley, with a 130-mile branch to the Coachella Valley. The canal cost $24 million to build and carried a flow of water equal to that of the Potomac River. Over a million acres of desert land were opened up to the cultivation of citrus fruits, melons, vegetables, and cotton. Irrigation districts receiving water promised to repay, without interest, the cost of the canal over a forty-year period. This interest-free loan was in effect a huge government subsidy to the private growers who benefited from the canal.

In 1935 the bureau began the giant Central Valley Project. The Central Valley, stretching through the California interior, is a 500-mile oblong watershed with an average width of 125 miles. The idea was to bring water from the Sacramento River in the north down to the arid lands of the larger San Joaquin Valley in the south. Completed in 1947, the CVP eventually cost $2.3 billion. Like other western New Deal water projects, it benefited from PWA grants and Civilian Conservation Corps labor. The CVP stored water and transferred it to the drier southern regions of the state. It also provided electricity, flood control, and municipal water. The federal government, local municipalities, and buyers of electric power paid most of the cost, and the project proved a boon to large-scale farmers in the Sacramento and San Joaquin River valleys.

The largest power and irrigation project of all was the Grand Coulee Dam, northwest of Spokane, Washington. Completed in 1941, it was designed to convert the power of the Columbia River into cheap electricity, irrigate previously uncultivated land, and thereby stimulate the economic development of the Pacific Northwest. The construction of Grand Coulee employed tens of thousands of workers and pumped millions of dollars into the region's badly depressed economy. Between 1933 and 1940 Washington State ranked first in per capita federal expenditures. In the longer run, Grand Coulee provided the cheapest electricity in the United States and helped attract new manufacturing to a region previously dependent on the export of raw materials, such as lumber and metals. The dam would eventually open up to irrigation and cultivation over a million acres of dry and largely unused land.

These technological marvels and the new economic development they stimulated were not without an environmental and human cost. The Grand Coulee and smaller dams nearby reduced the Columbia River, long a potent symbol of the western wilderness, to a series of lakes. Spawning salmon no longer ran the river above the dam. In California, the federal guarantee of river water made a relative handful of large farmers fabulously wealthy. But tens of thousands of farm workers, mostly of Mexican descent, labored in the newly fertile fields for very low wages, and their health suffered from contact with pesticides. The Colorado River, no longer emptying into the Pacific, began to build up salt deposits, making its water increasingly unfit for drinking or irrigation. By the 1950s Mexican farmers, who also use the Colorado for irrigation, found the water so salty they could not use it in their fields. Water pollution in the form of high salinity continues to be a problem along the 2,000-mile Colorado River to this day.

A New Deal for Indians

The New Deal brought important changes and limited improvements to the lives of Indians. In the aftermath of the Dawes Severalty Act of 1887, the Indian population on reservations had reached a low of 246,000 in the 1890s. That act had encouraged the dissolution of Indian tribes as legal entities, provided for the division of tribal lands among individual members, and promoted the assimilation of Indians into the larger culture (see Chapter 18). But by 1933 some 320,000 Indians, belonging to about 200 different tribes, lived on reservations. The largest numbers were to be found in Oklahoma, Arizona, New Mexico, and South Dakota.

But although their numbers were increasing again, their economic and social situation was desperate. Indians suffered from the worst poverty of any group in the nation, and an infant mortality rate twice that of the white population. The incidence of alcoholism and other diseases such as tuberculosis and measles was much higher on the reservation than off. Half of all Indians on reservations were landless, forced to rent or live with relatives. The Bureau of Indian Affairs, oldest of federal bureaucracies in the West, had a long history of corruption and mismanagement. The BIA had for years tried to assimilate Indians through education and had routinely interfered with Indian religious affairs and tribal customs. In 1928 the Meriam Report, prepared by the Brookings Institution, had offered a scathing and widely publicized critique of BIA mismanagement. But the Hoover administration made no effort to reform the agency.

In 1933 President Roosevelt appointed John Collier to bring change to the BIA. Collier had deep roots in Progressive era social work and community organizing in eastern big-city slums. During the 1920s he had become passionately interested in Indian affairs after spending time in Taos, New Mexico. He became involved with the struggle of the Pueblo Indians to hold onto their tribal lands, and he had served as executive secretary of the American Indian Defense Association. As the new BIA head, Collier pledged to "stop wronging the Indians and to rewrite the cruel and stupid laws that rob them and crush their family lives." Collier brought a reformer's zeal to his new job, and he quickly demonstrated his bureaucratic skills. He halted the sale of Indian lands, obtained emergency conservation work for 77,000 Indians under the CCC program, and secured millions of dollars in PWA funds to finance Indian day schools on the reservations. He also fired incompetent and corrupt BIA officials and insisted that those who remained respect tribal customs.

Most important, Collier became the driving force behind the Indian Reorganization Act (IRA) of 1934. The IRA repealed the allotment provisions of the Dawes Severalty Act, permitted the restoration of surplus reservation lands to tribal ownership, and allocated funds for the purchase of additional lands and for economic development. At its heart, the IRA sought to restore tribal structures by making the tribes instruments of the federal government. Any tribe that ratified the IRA could then elect a tribal council that would enjoy federal recognition as the legal tribal government. In this way, Collier argued, tribes would be "surrounded by the protective guardianship of the federal government and clothed with the authority of the federal government." He fought first to get the legislation through a reluctant Congress, which, uneasy with reversing the long-standing policy of Indian assimilation, insisted on many changes to Collier's original plan.

The more difficult battle involved winning approval by Indian peoples. Collier's efforts to win acceptance of the IRA met with mixed results on the reservations. Linguistic barriers made it nearly impossible for some tribes to fully assess the plan. The Papagos of southern Arizona, for example, had no words for "budget" and "representative." Their language made no distinction among the terms *law*, *rule*, *charter*, and *constitution*, and they used the same word for "president," "reservation agent," "king," and "Indian commissioner." The nation's largest tribe, the Navahos, rejected the IRA partly as a protest against BIA efforts to reduce Navaho livestock as part of a soil conservation program. In all, 192 tribes organized governments under the IRA, while 77 tribes rejected it.

Under Collier's tenure, the BIA became much more sensitive to Indian cultural and religious freedom. The number of Indians employed by the BIA itself increased from a few hundred in 1933 to more than 4,600 in 1940. Collier trumpeted the principle of Indian political autonomy, a radical idea for the day. But in practice, both the BIA and Congress regularly interfered with reservation governments, especially in money matters. Collier often dictated economic programs for tribes, which Congress usually underfunded. For the long run, Collier's most important legacy was the reassertion of the status of Indian tribes as semisovereign nations. In 1934 a Department of Interior lawyer, Nathan Margold, wrote a legal opinion that tribal governments retained all their original powers — their "internal sovereignty" — except when these were specifically limited by acts of Congress. In later years U.S. courts would uphold the Margold Opinion, leading to a significant restoration of tribal rights and land to Indian peoples of the West.

DEPRESSION–ERA CULTURE

American culture in the 1930s, like all other aspects of national life, was profoundly shaped by the Great Depression. Yet it would be a mistake to reduce the decade's cultural life to a mere reflection of economic hard times. The themes and images in various cultural forms frequently reflected Depression-related problems. Yet contradictory messages coexisted, sometimes within the same novel or movie. With American capitalism facing its worst crisis, radical expressions of protest and revolution were more common than ever. But there were also strong celebrations of individualism, nostalgia for a simpler, rural past, and searches for core American virtues. The 1930s also saw important shifts in the organization and production of culture. For a brief but significant moment, the federal government offered substantial and unprecedented support to artists and writers. In the realm of popular culture, Hollywood movies, network radio broadcasting, and big band jazz achieved a central place in the everyday lives of Americans.

A New Deal for the Arts

The depression hit America's writers, artists, and teachers just as hard as blue-collar workers. In 1935,

A Works Progress Administration (WPA) poster from 1938. The primary goal of federal relief projects, WPA officials stressed, was to rebuild the individual worker's confidence and self-respect. Typically, this poster uses only male laborers in its illustrations, reflecting a gender bias common in New Deal relief efforts.

the WPA allocated $300 million for the unemployed in these fields. Over the next four years, Federal Project No. 1, an umbrella agency covering writing, theater, music, and the visual arts, proved to be one of the most innovative and successful New Deal programs. "Federal One," as it was called, offered work to desperate artists and intellectuals, enriched the cultural lives of millions, and left a substantial legacy of artistic and cultural production. Nearly all of these works were informed by the spirit of documentary, a deep desire to record and communicate the experiences of ordinary Americans. Photographer Lewis Hine defined the documentary attitude simply and clearly when he said, "I wanted to show the things that had to be corrected. I wanted to show the things that had to be appreciated."

The Federal Writers Project employed 5,000 writers at its height on a variety of programs. Most notably, it produced a popular series of state and city guidebooks, each combining history, folklore, and tourism. The 150-volume Life in America series included valuable oral histories of former slaves, studies of ethnic cultures and Indians, and pioneering collections of American songs and folk tales. Work on the Writers Project helped many American writers to survive, hone their craft, and go on to great achievement and prominence. These included Ralph Ellison, Richard Wright, Margaret Walker, John Cheever, Saul Bellow, and Zora Neale Hurston. Novelist Anzia Yezierska recalled a strong spirit of camaraderie among the writers: "Each morning I walked to the Project as light hearted as if I were going to a party." For poet Muriel Rukeyser, the FWP embodied an essential part of the era: "The key to the 30s was the joy to awake and see life entire and tell the stories of real people."

Under the direction of the dynamic Hallie Flanagan of Vassar College, the Federal Theater Project reached as many as 30 million Americans with its productions. The FTP emphasized expanding the audience for theater beyond the regular patrons of the commercial stage. Tickets were cheap and a variety of dramatic forms were made available. Among the most successful were the "Living Newspaper" plays based on contemporary controversies and current events. *Power* concerned the public ownership of utilities; *Triple A Plowed Under* dealt with farm problems; *Injunction Granted* documented unionizing struggles. Other FTP productions brought classics as well as new plays to communities. Among the most successful productions were T. S. Eliot's *Murder in the Cathedral,* Maxwell Anderson's *Valley Forge,* and Orson Welles's version of *Macbeth,* set in Haiti with an all-black cast.

The FTP often came under attack from congressional critics who found it too radical. But Flanagan defended her vision of a theater that confronted political issues. If the plays were mixed with politics, she wrote, "it was because life in our country was mixed with politics. These Arts projects were coming up, through, and out of the people." The FTP supported scores of community-based theatrical units around the country, giving work and experience to actors, playwrights, directors, and set designers. It brought vital and exciting theater to millions who had never attended before.

Two smaller but similar programs were the Federal Music Project and the Federal Art Project. The FMP, under Nikolai Sokoloff of the Cleveland Symphony Orchestra, employed 15,000 musicians. It financed hundreds of thousands of low-priced public concerts by touring orchestras. The Composers' Forum Laboratory supported new works by American composers such as Aaron Copland and William Schuman.

Among the painters who received government assistance through the FAP were Willem de Kooning, Jackson Pollock, and Louise Nevelson. The FAP also employed painters and sculptors to teach studio skills and art history in schools, churches, and settlement houses. The *Index of American Design* was a comprehensive compilation of American folk art from colonial times. The FAP also commissioned artists to paint hundreds of murals on the walls of post offices, meeting halls, courthouses, and other government buildings. Many of these, done in the style of the revolutionary Mexican muralists Diego Rivera and José Clemente Orozco, emphasized political and social themes. All these projects, declared Holger Cahill, director of the FAP, were aimed at "raising a generation sensitive to their visual environment and capable of helping to improve it."

The Documentary Impulse

"You can right a lot of wrongs with 'pitiless publicity,'" Franklin Roosevelt once declared. Social change, he argued, "is a difficult thing in our civilization unless you have sentiment." During the 1930s an enormous number of artists, novelists, journalists, photographers, and filmmakers tried to document the devastation wrought by the depression in American communities. They also depicted people's struggles to cope with and reverse hard times. Some of these efforts were consciously linked to promoting political action, often as part of a radical commitment to overthrowing capitalism. Others were interested less in fomenting social

Sharecropper family, by Walker Evans, 1939. This photograph of the Bud and Ivy Woods family was first published in the 1941 book *Let Us Now Praise Famous Men,* with text by James Agee. Unlike some documentary photographers of the era, Evans' spare, direct pictures revealed his subjects to be not merely victims, but strong and complex individuals as well. Largely ignored in the 1930s, Evans' work enjoyed a critical revival during the 1960s.

change than in recording vanishing ways of life. Mainstream mass media, such as the photo essays found in *Life* magazine or Hollywood's *March of Time* newsreels, also adapted this stance.

Regardless of political agendas or the medium employed, what one historian calls "the documentary impulse" became a prominent style in 1930s cultural expression. At its core, the documentary impulse directly influenced its audience's intellect and feelings through documentary "evidence" of social problems and human suffering. The most direct and influential expression of the documentary style was the photograph. In 1935 Roy Stryker, chief of the Historical Section of the Resettlement Administration (later part of the Farm Security Administration), gathered a remarkable group of photographers to help document the work of the agency. Stryker encouraged them to photograph whatever caught their interest, even if the pictures had no direct connection with RA projects. These photographers, including Dorothea Lange, Walker Evans, Arthur Rothstein, Russell Lee, Ben Shahn, and Marion Post Walcott, left us the single most significant visual record of the Great Depression.

The photographers traveled through rural areas, small towns, and migrant labor camps, often not even stopping long enough to learn the names of their subjects. They produced powerful images of despair and resignation as well as hope and resilience. These photographs were reproduced in news-papers and magazines across America. Individual images could be interpreted in different ways, depending on context and captions. Stryker believed that the faces of the subjects were most memorable. "You could look at the people," he wrote, "and see fear and sadness and desperation. But you saw something else, too. A determination that not even the depression could kill. The photographers saw it — documented it."

That double vision, combining a frank portrayal of pain and suffering with a faith in the possibility of overcoming disaster, could be found in many other cultural works of the period. John Steinbeck's *The Grapes of Wrath* (1939) sympathetically portrayed the hardships of Oklahoma Dust Bowl migrants on their way to California. "We ain't gonna die out," Ma Joad asserts near the end of the book. "People is goin' on — changin' a little, maybe, but goin' right on." A similar, if more personal, ending could be found in Margaret Mitchell's 1936 best seller *Gone with the Wind.* Though this romantic novel was set in the Civil War–era South, many Americans identified with Scarlett O'Hara's determination to overcome the disaster of war and the loss of Rhett Butler. "With the spirit of her people who would not know defeat, even when it stared them in the face, she raised her chin. She could get Rhett back. She knew she could. There had never been a man she couldn't get, once she set her mind upon him."

Many writers interrupted their work to travel

around the country and discover the thoughts and feelings of ordinary people. "With real events looming larger than any imagined happenings," novelist Elizabeth Noble wrote, "documentary films and still photographs, reportage and the like have taken the place once held by the grand invention." Writers increasingly used documentary techniques to communicate the sense of upheaval around the nation. In *The American Jitters* (1932), Edmund Wilson rarely commented directly on what he saw in his travels. He relied instead on direct narration, observation, and description to evoke horror and anger in his readers. In *Puzzled America* (1935), Sherwood Anderson was struck by the psychological toll taken by unemployment. American men, especially, were losing "that sense of being some part of the moving world of activity, so essential to an American man's sense of his manhood — the loss of this essential something in the joblessness can never be measured in dollars." Yet writers also found a remarkable absence of bitterness and a great deal of faith. James Rorty, in *Where Life Is Better* (1936), was actually encouraged by his cross-country trip. "I had rediscovered for myself a most beautiful land, and a most vital, creative, and spiritually unsubdued people."

Waiting for Lefty

The appalling social and economic conditions of the 1930s shook the confidence of many artists and intellectuals. For some, the capitalist system itself, with its enormous disparities of private wealth amidst desperate poverty, was the culprit. Relatively few Americans became Communists or Socialists in the 1930s (at its height, the American Communist party had perhaps 100,000 members), and many of these remained active for only a brief time. Yet Marxist analysis, with its emphasis on class conflict and the failures of capitalism, had a wide influence on the era's thought and writing.

Some writers joined the Communist party as the best hope for political revolution. They saw in the Soviet Union an alternative to an American system that appeared mired in exploitation, racial inequality, and human misery. Communist writers, like the novelist Michael Gold and the poet Meridel LeSueur, sought to radicalize art and literature, and celebrated collective struggle over individual achievement. Gold's *Jews without Money* (1930) was one of the more successful attempts at a proletarian novel. It dramatized the sense of being locked into a system that could deliver only despair rather than prosperity. Granville Hicks, an editor of the Communist magazine *The New Masses,* flatly declared: "If

there is any other working interpretation of the apparent chaos than that which presents itself in terms of the class struggle, it has not been revealed."

A more common pattern for intellectuals, especially when they were young, was flirtation with communism. Many African American writers, attracted by the Communist party's militant opposition to lynching, job discrimination, and segregation, briefly joined the party or found their first supportive audiences there. These included Richard Wright, Ralph Ellison, and Langston Hughes. Many playwrights and actors associated with New York's influential Group Theater were part of the Communist party orbit in those years. That group's production of Clifford Odets's *Waiting for Lefty* (1935), depicted a union organizing drive among taxi drivers. At the play's climax, the audience was invited to join the actors in shouting "Strike!" A commercial and political success, it offered perhaps the most celebrated example of radical, politically engaged art.

Left-wing influence reached its height after 1935 during the "Popular Front" period. Alarmed by the rise of fascism in Europe, Communists around the world followed the Soviet line of uniting with liberals and all other anti-Fascists. The American Communist party adopted the slogan "Communism is Twentieth-Century Americanism." Communists became strong supporters of Roosevelt's New Deal, and their influence was especially strong within the various WPA arts projects. Some 3,200 Americans volunteered for the Communist-organized Abraham Lincoln Brigade, which fought in the Spanish civil war on the Republican side against the Fascists led by Francisco Franco. The Lincolns' sense of commitment and sacrifice appealed to millions of Americans sympathetic to the Republican cause. Communists and other radicals, known for their dedication and effectiveness, also played a leading role in the difficult CIO unionizing drives in the auto, steel, and electrical industries.

Hollywood in the 1930s

Commercial popular culture also boomed in the depression years. The coming of "talking pictures" right before the depression helped make movies the most popular entertainment form of the day. Over 60 percent of Americans attended one of the nation's 20,000 movie houses each week. Through fan magazines and gossip columns they followed the lives and careers of movie stars more avidly than ever. With so many movies being churned out by Hollywood studios for so many fans, it is difficult to generalize about the cultural impact of individual films. Moviegoing itself, usually enjoyed with friends, family, or a date, was perhaps the most significant development of all.

It is too easy to dismiss movies as mere escapism. The more interesting question is, What were people escaping to? Several film genres proved enormously popular during the 1930s. Gangster films did very well in the early depression years. *Little Caesar* (1930), starring Edward G. Robinson, and *The Public Enemy* (1931), with James Cagney, set the standard. They all depicted violent criminals brought to justice by society — but along the way audiences could vicariously enjoy the pleasures of wealth, power, and lawbreaking. Social disorder could also be treated comically, as in Marx Brothers films such as *Duck Soup* (1933) and *A Night at the*

Opera (1935). Mae West's popular comedies, such as *She Done Him Wrong* (1933) and *I'm No Angel* (1933), made people laugh by subverting expectations about sex roles. West was an independent woman, not afraid of pleasure. When Cary Grant asked her, "Haven't you ever met a man who could make you happy?" she replied, "Sure, lots of times."

Movie musicals offered audiences extravagant song-and-dance spectacles, as in Busby Berkeley's *Gold Diggers of 1933* and *42nd Street* (1933). "Screwball comedies" featured sophisticated, fast-paced humor and usually paired popular male and female stars: Clark Gable and Claudette Colbert in *It Happened One Night* (1934), Katharine Hepburn and Cary Grant in *Bringing Up Baby* (1938). A few movies, notably from the Warner Brothers studio, tried to offer a more "socially conscious" view of depres-

Reginald Marsh *Twenty Cent Movie*, 1936. Marsh documented the urban landscape of the 1930s with great empathy, capturing the city's contradictory mix of commercialism, optimism, energy, and degradation. The popularity of Hollywood films and their stars reached new heights during the Great Depression.
(Reginald Marsh. Twenty Cent Movie. *1936. Egg tempera on composition board. 40″ × 40″. Whitney Museum of American Art, New York.)*

sion-era life. These included *I Am a Fugitive from a Chain Gang* (1932), *Wild Boys of the Road* (1933), and *Black Legion* (1936). By and large, however, Hollywood avoided confronting controversial social or political issues.

Some 1930s filmmakers expressed highly personal visions of core American values. Two who succeeded in capturing both popular and critical acclaim were Walt Disney and Frank Capra. By the mid-1930s, Disney's animated cartoons had become moral tales that stressed keeping order and following the rules. The Mickey Mouse cartoons and the full-length features, such as *Snow White and the Seven Dwarfs* (1937), pulled back from the earlier cartoons' more fantastic possibilities of stretching time and space. Capra's comedies, such as *Mr. Deeds Goes to Town* (1936) and *You Can't Take It with You* (1938), idealized a small-town America with close families and comfortable homes. Although Capra's films dealt with contemporary problems more than most — unemployment, government corruption, economic monopoly — he made no critique of the social and economic system. Rather, he seemed to suggest that most of the country's ills could be solved if only the old-fashioned values of "common people" — kindness, loyalty, charity — could be learned by the false leaders at the top.

The Golden Age of Radio

Radio broadcasting became the most powerful medium of communication for the home, profoundly changing the rhythms and routines of everyday life. In 1930 roughly 12 million American homes, 40 percent of the total, had a radio set. By the end of the decade radio could be found in 90 percent of the nation's homes. Advertisers dominated the structure and content of American radio, forming a powerful alliance with the two large networks, the National Broadcasting Company (NBC) and the Columbia Broadcasting System (CBS). The Federal Communications Commission, established in 1934, continued long-standing policies that favored commercial broadcasting over other arrangements, such as municipal or university programing. By 1937 NBC and CBS controlled about 90 percent of the wattage in the American broadcasting industry. Nearly all network shows were produced by advertising agencies.

The depression actually helped radio expand. An influx of talent arrived from the weakened worlds of vaudeville, ethnic theater, and the recording industry. The well-financed networks offered an attractive outlet to advertisers seeking a national audience. Radio programming achieved a regularity

and professionalism absent in the 1920s, making it much easier for a listener to identify a show with its sponsor. Companies with national distribution paid thousands of dollars an hour to networks; by 1939 annual radio advertising revenues totaled $171 million.

Much of network radio was based on older cultural forms. The variety show, hosted by comedians and singers and based on the old vaudeville format, was the first important style. It featured stars like Eddie Cantor, Ed Wynn, Kate Smith, and Al Jolson, who constantly plugged the sponsor's product. The use of a studio audience re-created the human interaction so necessary in vaudeville. The popular comedy show "Amos 'n' Andy" adapted the minstrel "blackface" tradition to the new medium. White comedians Freeman Gosden and Charles Correll used only their two voices to invent a world of stereotyped African Americans for their millions of listeners.

The spectacular growth of the daytime serial, or soap opera, dominated radio drama. Aimed mainly at women working in the home, these serials alone constituted 60 percent of all daytime shows by 1940. Soaps such as "Ma Perkins," "Helen Trent," and "Clara Lou and Em" revolved around strong, warm female characters who provided advice and strength to weak, indecisive friends and relatives. Action counted very little; development of character and relationships was all-important. Contemporary studies found that the average soap opera fan regularly tuned in to six or more different series. Thrillers such as "Inner Sanctum" and "The Shadow" emphasized crime and suspense. Very popular on evening radio, they made great use of music and sound effects to sharpen their impact.

In the later 1930s serious drama bloomed briefly, independent of commercial sponsorship, over CBS's Columbia Workshop. Archibald MacLeish's *Fall of the City,* a parable about fascism, and Orson Welles's *War of the Worlds,* a superrealistic adaptation of the H. G. Wells classic, proved the power of radio to induce suspension of belief. Radio became a key factor in politics as well. President Roosevelt, in his famous fireside chats, had early on demonstrated radio's power to persuade. Individuals on the fringes of American politics also used radio to advantage. Charles Coughlin, the Detroit "Radio Priest," built a large following for his National Union for Social Justice through his weekly broadcasts. Father Coughlin's radio speeches mixed attacks on international bankers, Communists, labor unions, the New Deal, and Jews.

Finally, radio news arrived in the 1930s, showing the medium's potential for direct and immediate coverage of events. Network news and commentary shows multiplied rapidly over the decade. Complex political and economic issues and the impending European crisis fueled a news hunger among Americans. A 1939 survey found that 70 percent of Americans relied on the radio as their prime source of news. Yet commercial broadcasting, dominated by big sponsors and large radio manufacturers, failed to cover politically controversial events, such as labor struggles. The most powerful station in the country, WLW in Cincinnati, refused to even mention strikes on the air. NBC routinely canceled programs it feared might undermine "public confidence and faith."

The Swing Era

One measure of radio's cultural impact was its role in popularizing jazz. Before the 1930s, jazz was heard largely among African Americans and a small coterie of white fans and musicians. Regular broadcasts of live performances began to expose the music to a broader public. So did radio disc jockeys who played jazz records on their shows. Bands led by black artists such as Duke Ellington, Count Basie, and Benny Moten began to enjoy reputations outside of traditional jazz centers like Chicago, Kansas City, and New York.

Benny Goodman became the key figure in the "swing era," largely through radio exposure. Goodman, a white, classically trained clarinetist, had been inspired by African American bandleaders Fletcher Henderson and Don Redman. These men created arrangements for big bands that combined harmonic call-and-response patterns with breaks for improvised solos. Goodman purchased a series of arrangements from Henderson, smoothing out the sound but keeping the strong dance beat. His band's late Saturday night broadcasts began to attract attention.

In 1935, at the Palomar Ballroom in Los Angeles, Goodman made the breakthrough that established his enormous popularity. When the band started playing the Henderson arrangements, the young crowd, primed by the radio broadcasts, roared its approval and began to dance wildly. Goodman's music was perfect for doing the jitterbug or lindy hop, dances borrowed from African American culture. As the "King of Swing," Goodman helped make big-band jazz a hit with millions of teenagers and young adults from all backgrounds. In the late 1930s, big-band music by the likes of Goodman, Basie, Jimmie Lunceford, and Artie Shaw accounted for the majority of million-selling records.

Despite the depression, the mass culture industry expanded enormously during the 1930s. Millions of Americans no doubt used mass culture as a temporary escape from their problems, but the

The Benny Goodman band at the Meadowbrook Lounge, Cedar Grove, New Jersey, 1941. After his breakthrough into national prominence in 1935, Goodman became one of the first white bandleaders to hire and feature African American musicians. Although most in the audience were undoubtedly dancing to the "King of Swing," note the crowd of serious listeners gathered around the bandstand.

various meanings they drew from movies, radio, and popular music were by no means monolithic. In most communities, Americans, especially young people, identified more closely than ever with the national communities forged by modern media. If mass culture offered little in the way of direct responses to the economic and social problems of the day, it nonetheless played a more integral role than ever in shaping the rhythms and desires of the nation's everyday life.

THE LIMITS OF REFORM

In his second inaugural address Roosevelt emphasized that much remained to be done. Tens of millions of Americans were still denied the necessities for a decent life. "I see one third of a nation ill-housed, ill-clad, ill-nourished," the president said. With his stunning electoral victory, the future for further social reform seemed bright. Yet by 1937 the New Deal was in retreat. A rapid political turnaround over the next two years put the continuing social reform efforts on the defensive.

Court Packing

FDR and his advisers were frustrated by several Supreme Court rulings declaring important New Deal legislation unconstitutional. In May 1935, in *Schecter v. United States,* the Court found the National Recovery Administration unconstitutional in its entirety. Its ruling in *Butler v. United States* in early 1936 did the same for the Agricultural Adjustment Administration. The Court was composed mostly of Republican appointees, six of whom were over seventy. Roosevelt looked for a way to get more friendly judges on the high court.

In February 1937 FDR asked Congress for legislation that would expand the Supreme Court from nine to a maximum of fifteen justices. The president would be empowered to make a new appointment whenever an incumbent judge failed to retire upon reaching age seventy. Roosevelt argued that age prevented justices from keeping up with their workload, but not many really believed this logic. A bitter debate followed in the national press and Congress. Newspapers almost unanimously denounced FDR's "court-packing bill."

Even more damaging was the determined opposition from a coalition of conservatives and outraged New Dealers in the Congress, such as Democratic senator Burton K. Wheeler of Montana. The

president gamely fought on, maintaining that his purpose was simply to restore the balance of power among the three branches of the federal government. As the battle dragged on through the spring and summer, FDR's claims weakened. Conservative justice Willis Van Devanter announced plans to retire, giving Roosevelt the chance to make his first Court appointment.

More important, the Court upheld the constitutionality of some key laws from the second New Deal, including the Social Security Act and the National Labor Relations Act. At the end of August, FDR backed off from his plan and accepted a compromise bill that reformed lower court procedures but left the Supreme Court untouched. FDR lost the battle for his judiciary proposal, but he may have won the war for a more responsive Court. Still, the political price was very high. The Court fight badly weakened Roosevelt's relations with Congress. Many more conservative Democrats now felt free to oppose further New Deal measures. Roosevelt's controversial plan put a serious dent in his political power.

The Women's Network

The Depression and the New Deal did bring about some significant changes for women in American economics and politics. Most women continued to perform unpaid domestic labor within their homes. A growing minority also worked for wages and salaries outside the home; the female proportion of the work force rose from 22 to 25 percent. There was also an increase in the number of married working women, a result of hard times. Jobs where men predominated, such as construction and heavy industry, were hardest hit by the depression. By contrast, secretarial, sales, and other areas long associated with women's labor were less affected. But sexual stereotyping still routinely forced women into low-paying and low-status jobs.

The New Deal brought a measurable, if temporary, increase in women's political influence. For those women associated with social reform, the New Deal opened up possibilities to effect change. Historian Susan Ware has identified a "women's network," linked by personal friendships and professional connections, which made its presence felt in national politics and government. Most of the women in this network had long been active in movements promoting suffrage, labor law reform, and welfare programs. They agreed with Eleanor Roosevelt, the most influential figure among them, that women officials should measure their achievements through the social improvements they made, rather than by material gain.

Eleanor Roosevelt became a powerful political figure in her own right, actively using her prominence as First Lady to fight for the liberal causes she believed in. She revolutionized the role of the political wife by taking a position involving no institutional duties and turning it into a base for independent action. Privately, she enjoyed great influence with her husband, and her support for a cause could give it instant credibility. She worked behind the scenes with a wide network of women professionals and reformers whom she had come to know in the 1920s. She was a strong supporter of protective labor legislation for women, and her overall outlook owed much to the social reform tradition of the women's movement. "When all is said and done," she wrote in *It's Up to the Women* (1933), "women *are* different from men. They are equal in many ways, but they cannot refuse to acknowledge their differences. . . . Their physical functions in life are different and perhaps in the same way the contributions which they are to bring to the spiritual side of life are different."

One of her first public acts as First Lady was to convene a White House Conference on the Emergency Needs of Women, in November 1933. She helped Ellen Woodward, head of women's projects in the Federal Emergency Relief Administration, find jobs for 100,000 women, ranging from nursery school teaching to sewing. Roosevelt worked vigorously for antilynching legislation, compulsory health insurance, and child labor reform and fought racial discrimination in New Deal relief programs. She saw herself as the guardian of "human values" within the administration, a buffer between depression victims and government bureaucracy. She frequently testified before legislative committees, lobbied her husband privately and the Congress publicly, and wrote a widely syndicated newspaper column.

Eleanor Roosevelt's closest political ally was Molly Dewson. A long-time social worker and suffragist, Dewson wielded a good deal of political clout as director of the Women's Division of the national Democratic party. Under her leadership women for the first time played a central role in shaping the party platform and running election campaigns. Dewson proved a tireless organizer,

Eleanor Roosevelt on a campaign tour with her husband in Nebraska, 1935. Long active in women's organizations and Democratic Party circles, she used political activity both to maintain her independence and make herself a valuable ally to FDR. "The attitude of women toward change in society," she argued, "is going to determine to a great extent our future in this country."

traveling to cities and towns around the country and educating women about Democratic policies and candidates. Her success impressed the president, and he relied upon her judgment in recommending political appointments. Dewson placed more than a hundred women in New Deal positions.

Perhaps Dewson's most important success came in persuading FDR to appoint Frances Perkins secretary of labor — the first woman Cabinet member in U.S. history. As labor secretary, Perkins embodied the gains made by women in appointive offices. Her department was responsible for creating the Social Security Act and the Fair Labor Standards Act of 1938, both of which incorporated protective measures long advocated by women reformers. A graduate of Mount Holyoke College and a veteran of social welfare and reform activity, Perkins defined feminism as "the movement of women to participate in service to society." Yet despite the best efforts of the "women's network," women never constituted more than 19 percent of those employed by work relief programs, even though they made up 37 percent of the unemployed.

New Deal agencies opened up spaces for scores of women in the federal bureaucracy. These women were concentrated in Perkins's Labor Department, the FERA and WPA, and the Social Security Board. In addition, the social work profession, which remained roughly two-thirds female in the 1930s, grew enormously in response to the massive relief and welfare programs. Many new jobs opened up on the federal, state, and local levels for women trained in social work. In sum, although the 1930s saw no radical challenges to existing male and female roles, working-class women and professional women held their own and managed to make some gains.

A New Deal for Minorities?

"The Negro was born in Depression," recalled Clifford Burke. "It only became official when it hit the white man." Long near the bottom of the American economic ladder, African Americans suffered disproportionately through the difficult days of the thirties. The old saying among blacks that they were "last hired, first fired" was never more true than during times of high unemployment. With jobs made scarce by the depression, even traditional "Negro occupations" — domestic service, cooking, janitorial work, elevator operating — were coveted. One white clerk in Florida expressed a widely held view among white southerners when he defended a lynch mob attack on a store that employed blacks: "A nigger hasn't got no right to have a job when there are white men who can do the work and are out of work."

Overall, the Roosevelt administration made little overt effort to combat the racism and segregation entrenched in American life. FDR was especially worried about offending the powerful southern Democratic congressmen who were a key element in his political coalition. And local administration of many federal programs meant that most early New Deal programs routinely accepted discrimination. The CCC established separate camps for African Americans. The NRA labor codes tolerated lower wages for black workers doing the same jobs as whites. African Americans could not get jobs with the TVA. In Atlanta, relief payments for black clients averaged $19.29 per month, compared with $32.66 for whites. When local AAA committees in the South reduced acreage and production to boost prices, thousands of black sharecroppers and farm laborers were forced off the land. Racism was also embedded in the entitlement provisions of the Social Security Act. The act excluded domestics and casual laborers — workers whose ranks were disproportionately African Americans — from old-age insurance.

Yet some limited gains were made. President Roosevelt issued an executive order in 1935 banning discrimination in WPA projects. In the cities the WPA, paying minimum wages of twelve dollars a week, enabled thousands of African Americans to survive. Between 15 and 20 percent of all WPA employees were black, although African Americans made up less than 10 percent of the nation's population. The Public Works Administration, under Harold Ickes, constructed a number of integrated housing complexes and employed more than its fair share of black workers in construction.

FDR appointed a number of African Americans to second-level positions in his administration. This group became known as the "Black Cabinet." Mary McLeod Bethune, an educator who rose from a sharecropping background to found Bethune-Cookman College, proved a superb leader of the Office of Minority Affairs in the National Youth Administration. Her most successful programs substantially reduced black illiteracy. Harvard-trained Robert Weaver advised the president on economic affairs and in 1966 became the first black Cabinet member when he was appointed secretary of housing and urban development. Yet Roosevelt himself was diffident about advancing civil rights. Typically, he spoke out against lynching in the South, but unlike his wife, he refused to support legislation making it a federal crime. Nor would he risk alienating white southerners by working for long-denied voting rights for southern blacks.

In sum, the New Deal record on race was mixed at best. African Americans, especially in the cities, benefited from New Deal relief and work programs, though this assistance was not color-blind. Black industrial workers made inroads into labor unions affiliated with the CIO. The New Deal made no explicit attempt to attack the deeply rooted patterns of racism and discrimination in American life. Yet by 1936, for the first time ever, a majority of black voters had switched their political allegiance to the Democrats. This was the most concrete evidence that they supported the directions taken by FDR's New Deal.

The Roosevelt Recession

The nation's economy had improved significantly by 1937. Unemployment had declined to "only" 14 percent (9 million people), farm prices had improved to 1930 levels, and industrial production was slightly higher than the 1929 mark. Economic traditionalists, led by Secretary of the Treasury Henry Morgenthau, called for reducing the federal deficit, which had grown to over $4 billion in fiscal 1936. Roosevelt, always uneasy about the growing national debt, called for large reductions in federal spending, particularly in WPA and farm programs. Federal Reserve System officials, worried about inflation, tightened credit policies.

Rather than stimulating business, the retrenchment brought about a steep recession. The stock market collapsed in August 1937, and industrial output and farm prices plummeted. Most alarming was the big increase in unemployment. By March 1938 the jobless rate hovered around 20 percent, with over 13 million people looking for work. As conditions worsened, Roosevelt began to blame the "new depression" on a "strike of capital," claiming businessmen had refused to invest because they wanted to hurt his prestige. In truth, the administration's own severe spending cutbacks were more responsible for the decline.

The blunt reality was that even after five years the New Deal had not brought about economic recovery. Throughout 1937 and 1938 the administration drifted. Roosevelt received conflicting advice on the economy. Some advisers, suspicious of busi-

ness' reluctance to make new investment, urged a massive antitrust campaign against monopolies. Others urged a return to the Keynesian strategy of massive federal spending. Emergency spending bills in the spring of 1938 pumped new life into the WPA and the PWA. But Republican gains in the 1938 congressional elections (eighty-one seats in the House, eight in the Senate) made it harder than ever to get new reform measures through.

There were a couple of important exceptions. The 1938 Fair Labor Standards Act established the first federal minimum wage (twenty-five cents an hour) and set a maximum work week of forty-four hours for all employees engaged in interstate commerce. The National Housing Act of 1937, also known as the Wagner-Steagall Act, funded public housing construction and slum clearance and provided rent subsidies for low-income families. But by and large, by 1938 the reform whirlwind of the New Deal was complete.

CONCLUSION

Although American capitalism and democracy survived the cataclysm of the Great Depression, the New Deal failed in its central mission. It was never able to bring full economic recovery or end the scourge of mass unemployment. Only the economic boom that accompanied World War II would do that. Far from being the radical program its conservative critics charged, the New Deal did little to alter fundamental property relations or the distribution of wealth. Indeed, most of its programs largely failed to help the most powerless groups in America — migrant workers, tenant farmers and sharecroppers, African Americans and other minorities.

But the New Deal profoundly changed many areas of American life. Overall, it radically increased the role of the federal government in American lives and communities. Western and southern communities in particular were transformed through federal intervention in water, power, and agricultural policies. Relief programs and the Social Security system established at least the framework for a welfare state. For the first time in American history, the national government took responsibility for ensuring public assistance for its needy citizens. And also for the first time, the federal government guaranteed the rights of workers to join trade unions, and it set standards for minimum wages and maximum hours. In politics, the New Deal established the Democrats

CHRONOLOGY

1929	Stock market crash
1930	Democrats regain control of House of Representatives
1932	Reconstruction Finance Corporation established
	Bonus Army marches on Washington
	Franklin D. Roosevelt elected president
1933	Roughly 13 million workers unemployed
	First New Deal: National Recovery Administration; Public Works Administration; Agricultural Adjustment Administration; Tennessee Valley Authority; Federal Emergency Relief Administration; Civilian Conservation Corps
	Twenty-first Amendment repeals Prohibition (Eighteenth Amendment)
1934	Indian Reorganization Act
	Growing popularity of Father Coughlin and Huey Long
	General strike in San Francisco
1935	Second Hundred Days: National Labor Relations (Wagner) Act; Social Security Act; Works Progress Administration
	Committee for Industrial Organization (CIO) established
	Dust Bowl
	Boulder Dam completed
1936	Roosevelt defeats Alf Landon in reelection landslide
	Sit-down strike begins at Flint
1937	General Motors recognizes United Automobile Workers
	"Court-packing" plan
	Memorial Day Massacre in Chicago
	"Roosevelt recession" begins
1938	CIO unions withdraw from AFL to form Congress of Industrial Organizations
	Fair Labor Standards Act

as the majority party. Some version of the Roosevelt New Deal coalition would dominate the nation's political life for another three decades.

The New Deal's efforts to end racial and gender discrimination were modest at best. Some of the more ambitious programs, such as subsidizing the arts or building model communities, enjoyed only brief moments of success. Other reform proposals, such as national health insurance, never got off the ground. Conservative counterpressures, especially after 1937, limited what could be changed.

Still, the New Deal did more than strengthen the presence of the national government in people's lives. It also fed expectations that the federal presence would intensify. Washington became a much greater center of economic regulation and political power, and the federal bureaucracy grew in size and influence. With the coming of World War II, the direct role of national government in shaping American communities would expand beyond the dreams of even the most ardent New Dealer.

Additional Readings

Irving Bernstein, *Turbulent Years: A History of the American Worker, 1933–1941* (1969). Solid overview of the growth of the American labor movement during the 1930s, with excellent material on the workings of the NLRB.

John Braeman et al., eds., *The New Deal: The State and Local Levels* (1975). A useful collection of essays analyzing the workings of the New Deal in local communities throughout the nation.

Alan Brinkley, *Voices of Protest: Huey Long, Father Coughlin, and the Great Depression* (1982). Offers the best analysis of these two important New Deal critics and the sources of their popular appeal.

Lizabeth Cohen, *Making a New Deal* (1990). A brilliant study of industrial workers in Chicago during the 1920s and 1930s. Demonstrates the transformation of immigrant and African American workers into key actors in the creation of the CIO and in New Deal politics. Includes important material on the complex relationship between ethnic cultures and mass culture.

Paul K. Conkin, *The New Deal* (2nd ed., 1975). A well-written, concise history of the New Deal that emphasizes its limits and nonradical character.

Kenneth S. Davis, *FDR* (3 vols., 1972, 1985, 1986). The most comprehensive biography of FDR.

Melvyn Dubofsky and Warren Van Tine, *John L. Lewis* (1977). The standard biography of this key labor leader. Excellent on the development of the CIO.

Sidney Fine, *Sit-Down: The General Motors Strike of 1936–37* (1969). The standard account of this epochal strike.

Richard Lowitt, *The New Deal and the West* (1984). A comprehensive study of the New Deal's impact in the West, with special attention to water policy and agriculture.

Robert S. McElvaine, *The Great Depression: America, 1929–1941* (1984). The best one-volume overview of the depression. Especially good on the origins and early years of the worst economic calamity in American history.

Richard Pells, *Radical Visions and American Dreams* (1973). A useful survey of radical culture and social thought during the 1930s.

Lois Scharf, *To Work and to Wed* (1980). Examines female employment and feminism during the Great Depression.

Harvard Sitkoff, *A New Deal for Blacks* (1978). Focuses on the limited gains made by African Americans from New Deal programs, as well as the racism that pervaded most government programs.

William Stott, *Documentary Expression and Thirties America* (1973). An illuminating account of the documentary impulse and its relationship to the political and social upheavals of the 1930s.

Studs Terkel, *Hard Times* (1970). The best oral history of the Great Depression. Includes a very wide range of voices recalling life in the depression era.

Susan Ware, *Beyond Suffrage: Women in the New Deal* (1981). Examines the makeup and influence of the "women's network" within the Roosevelt administration.

25 WORLD WAR II

American Communities

● Los Angeles, California

On the night of June 4, 1943, while World War II raged overseas, 200 cars and taxis filled with white sailors roamed the streets of East Los Angeles in search of young Mexican Americans dressed in zoot suits. The sailors assaulted their victims at random, even chasing one youth into a movie theater and stripping him of his clothes while the audience cheered. Riots broke out for days.

Two communities had collided, with tragic results. The sailors had only recently been uprooted from their hometowns and regrouped under the strict discipline of boot camp. Now stationed in Southern California while awaiting departure overseas, they descended on Los Angeles by the thousands for weekend sprees and came face to face with the zoot-suiters. To the sailors, the Mexican Americans— many too young to be drafted but most old enough to volunteer— appeared not only self-indulgent but unpatriotic.

ZOOT— SUITERS DEFEND THEIR COMMUNITY

Military and civilian authorities contained the riots by ruling several sections of Los Angeles off-limits to military personnel— but only after the zoot-suiters had begun to fight back. The Los Angeles City Council passed legislation making the wearing of a zoot suit in public a criminal offense. A federal judge even issued a restraining order against a clothing store that specialized in the suits. Later, the Joint Finding Committee on Un-American Activities in California conducted hearings to determine if enemy agents had plotted the riots. Predictably, an FBI investigation turned up no evidence of subversion or political intent.

Why did a style of clothing cause so much excitement? The zoot suit, the "uniform" of young Mexican American men, contrasted sharply with the government-regulation clothing of sailors. It featured a wide-cut thigh-length jacket and pegged pants, full at the knees and narrow at the ankle. Zoot-suiters finished off the look with a pocket watch on a long chain and a large, floppy hat. Women put together their own version: long jacket, short, tight black skirt with fishnet stockings, pompadour hairdo, and heavy makeup. Originated by African Americans, the zoot suit had come to symbolize rebellion.

Zoot-suiters flaunted their difference from the white community as well as from their parents, the majority of whom worked in wartime factory jobs or served in the armed forces. These teenagers had become "twenty-four-hour orphans."

This Mexican American zoot-suiter wears the typical thigh-length, broad-lapel jacket with padded shoulders, baggy trousers pegged at the cuff, and a broad-brimmed felt hat. A dramatic contrast to the military uniforms of the day, the zoot soot symbolized cultural rebellion.

They skipped school and avoided work to hang out in the streets. Known locally as pachucos, they joined secret societies or gangs, whose members were distinguished by their tattoos and by the type of "ducktail" haircut they wore. Mexican poet and essayist Octavio Paz wrote at the time, "Their attitude reveals an obstinate, almost fanatical will to be, [although] this will affirms nothing specific except their determination not to be like those around them."

The parents of the zoot-suiters had left Mexico in search for work during the 1920s and had managed to survive the deportation programs instituted during the Great Depression that had sent many illegal immigrants back to their homeland. They reared their children from birth in Los Angeles, the city encompassing the largest community of Mexican Americans in the nation. Although the zoot-suiters grew up in a bilingual and bicultural environment, they were nevertheless at least one generation removed from their ancestral heritage. Teenagers during wartime, they set out — in their own fashion — to establish a unique identity.

The events of World War II broadened the horizons of many Mexican Americans, including the zoot-suiters who represented less than 10 percent of the community's youth. Over 300,000 of their peers served in the Armed Forces, in greater number than their proportion of the draft-age population and in the most hazardous branches, the paratrooper and marine corps. Others benefited from opportunities opened up by defense production and facilitated by federally legislated mandates against discrimination. The Spanish-Speaking People's Division in the Office of Inter-American Affairs developed programs to instill cultural pride and self-esteem among Mexican-American children. School districts in California and throughout the Southwest established extensive vocational training classes to channel their graduates into wartime industry. Mexican Americans managed to secure employment positions previously denied them, such as in Texas's burgeoning petroleum industry and in well-paying meat-packing plants.

As in Los Angeles, racial and ethnic conflict erupted in other localities during World War II. But the global configuration involving every major power in the world also pulled together large numbers of Americans. A new sense of national unity emerged in support of a common goal, if not necessarily a common lifestyle or outlook.

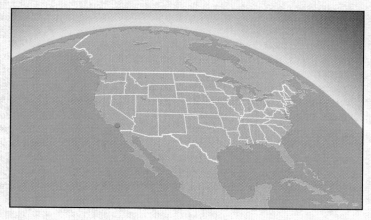

The massive mobilization of human and economic resources for war required an enormous change in the way most Americans lived. In addition to the 16 million men and women who left home for military service, nearly as many moved to take advantage of wartime jobs. Several states in the South and Southwest experienced huge surges in population. California, for example, grew by 2 million people, a large proportion of them from Mexico. Many broad social changes — such as massive economic expansion in the West, the erosion of farm tenancy among southern blacks and Appalachian whites, and the increased employment of married women — accelerated during wartime. Although reluctant to enter the war, the United States emerged not only from under the weight of the Great Depression but the leading super-power. The events of World War II, eroding old communities and creating new ones, transformed nearly all aspects of American society.

THE COMING OF WORLD WAR II

A majority of Americans feared entanglement in another world conflagration, but terrifying events overseas pulled the nation steadily toward military solutions. From the mid-1930s until the end of the decade, debate over U.S. policy heated up, with liberals and conservatives crisscrossing in unpredictable alignments for and against intervention. Franklin Roosevelt, drawing strength from the growing sympathy for war victims in Europe and Asia, maneuvered to consolidate the country behind his own strategies.

Isolationism

World War I had left a strong isolationist legacy in the United States. Best-selling novels such as Erich Maria Remarque's *All Quiet on the Western Front* (1930) and such popular films as *What Price Glory?* (1926) and *Submarine* (1928) vividly portrayed battle conditions, massacres of civilians, and officers' mistreatment of ordinary soldiers. Millions of Americans concluded that senseless slaughter was a centuries-old way of life in Europe, and not something for which the United States should sacrifice its own people.

These sentiments won strong support in Congress and the nation. Republican senator Gerald P. Nye of North Dakota headed a special subcommittee investigating supporters of the U.S. entry into World War I. The subcommittee identified munition makers and bankers and learned that they had pressured key diplomats and manipulated public opinion. College students, seeing themselves as future cannon fodder, were especially adamant in their rejection of war. In 1933, 39 percent of college students polled stated their unwillingness to fight in any war; 33 percent would fight only if the United States itself were attacked. Three years later, 500,000 boycotted classes nationwide to demonstrate their opposition to rearmament and other preparations for war. Among their professors, Charles Beard, the nation's most famous historian, attacked the nation's tendency to solve domestic troubles through foreign involvements. As late as 1937, nearly 70 percent of those responding to a Gallup poll concluded that American involvement in World War I had been a mistake.

Opposition to war spanned the political spectrum, left to right. Socialist leader Norman Thomas gathered leading liberals and trade unionists into the Keep America Out of War Congress in 1938, and the American League against War and Fascism claimed more than a million members. Meanwhile,

"Mr. Republican," Robert A. Taft, Ohio senator and son of former president William Howard Taft, argued that a new war would harm American democracy. The establishment of a huge, permanent military and a presidency with unprecedented executive power could only tighten the grip of the federal government upon its citizens.

To deter future U.S. entanglements, Congress passed several Neutrality Acts from 1935 to 1937. These measures authorized the president to deny American firms the right to sell or ship munitions to warring nations, and to allow trade only with those nations that could pay for goods in cash and carry them away in their own ships. Due to lobbying by the major oil, steel, and copper corporations, however, the ban did not cover the basic matériel of war, which the most aggressive nations rushed to buy.

The Drift Toward War

The rumblings of war and the threat of world conflict spread first across Asia. Determined to build its own empire, Japan wrested its former colony of Manchuria from the Soviet Union during the winter of 1931–32. Turning south, the Imperial forces invaded Shanghai, slaughtering thousands of Chinese civilians. Condemned by the League of Nations, Japan simply quit the organization in 1933, exposing the league's impotence. By 1937 Japan had overrun North China, and the extreme militarists in charge of the Tokyo government had placed the fate of all Asia and the Pacific in the balance.

Meanwhile, the rise of fascism in Italy and Germany had cast a shadow over the European continent. Demagogic mass movements arose out of popular resentments against the treaties imposed upon the governments defeated in World War I. Supported by powerful financial interests, Fascist parties seized power, violently crushed opponents, and plotted territorial expansion against weaker nations. Glorifying war as a test of virility, Italian Fascist leader Benito Mussolini declared, "We have buried the putrid corpse of liberty." In Germany, Adolf Hitler combined militaristic rhetoric with a doctrine of Aryan (Nordic) supremacy, identifying the blond-haired, blue-eyed peoples as biologically superior and describing nonwhites, including Jews, as "degenerate races." Backed by major industrialists such as the Krupp weapons-building family, Hitler took power as chancellor of Germany in 1933. With his brown-shirted storm troopers ruling the streets, he ordered the dissolution of the Reichstag (parliament), effectively making him dictator of the strongest nation in central Europe.

Initially, many American observers, including

Uniformed members of the National Socialist (Nazi) Party burn books in Germany. Nazis considered volumes by Jews and works about liberalism, Marxism, feminism, and modern art among other subjects to be decadent and dangerous. By burning books, Nazis insisted that they had helped "cleanse" the German nation and protect its citizens from subversive ideas.

the *New York Times,* regarded Hitler, like Mussolini, as merely an excessive nationalist and anti-Communist. But the Nazi leader proved them wrong. While ordering the books of liberals burned and thousands of dissidents arrested, he built up a vast industrial infrastructure and an army of half a million men poised to conquer Europe and then the world.

The prospect of war grew closer when Mussolini's troops bombarded the impoverished African nation of Ethiopia in 1935 and formally claimed it as a colony in May 1936. Nazi forces, meanwhile, advanced on central Europe. First they retook the Rhineland, German territory occupied by France for fifteen years after the close of World War I. Two years later, Hitler organized the Anschluss, forcibly unifying Germany and Austria, then pressed German claims to the Sudetenland, a part of Czechoslovakia bordering Germany. War suddenly seemed imminent, because the Soviet Union and France had pledged to assist the Czechs.

Hoping to avoid war through diplomacy, British prime minister Neville Chamberlain met with Hitler in Germany. At the Munich Conference of September 1938, England and France agreed to a German takeover of the Sudetenland. In return, Hitler promised to settle future disputes through diplomatic means. Five months later, Hitler seized the rest of Czechoslovakia.

During the Czech crisis more shocking details of Hitler's regime became known. After the Nazis passed the notorious Nuremburg Laws in 1935, denying Jews their rights as citizens of Germany, Hitler's campaign against them had become steadily more vicious. On November 10 of that year — *Kristallnacht,* the "Night of Broken Glass" — Nazi hoodlums rounded up German Jews, beating them mercilessly and burning Jewish shops, synagogues, hospitals, and orphanages. The Nazi government soon expropriated Jewish property and excluded Jews from all but the most menial forms of employment.

From Neutrality to Intervention

The news of Hitler's brutality against Jews and his conquest of central Europe prompted thousands of Americans to turn away from isolation and to mobilize against the spread of fascism. Diverse organizations called for boycotts of German-made products and raised money to aid Europeans fighting Hitler's forces. Celebrities helped publicize the cause. Horror film star Bela Lugosi joined refugee composer Béla Bartók in presiding over the Hungarian Democratic Federation against fascism. Other Hollywood notables, such as Paul Muni and Katherine Hepburn, endorsed the work of anti-Fascist organizations. The most dramatic aspect of the anti-Fascist campaign involved American volunteers fighting against Franco in the Spanish civil war (see Chapter 24). Famed novelist Ernest Hemingway and playwright Lillian Hellman, among others, joined the volunteers as combat journalists.

Step by step, the United States moved closer to war. On October 5, 1937, President Roosevelt called on all peace-loving nations to band together to "quarantine the aggressors." Public opinion at first appeared to side with the president. But a poll of congressional legislators revealed that two-thirds opposed economic sanctions, calling any such plan a "back door to war." Roosevelt drew back, but won from Congress $1 billion in appropriations to enlarge the U.S. Navy. In December 1937, the American patrol boat *Panay,* sailing on the Yangtze River in China, was sunk by the Japanese navy. Roosevelt denounced the attack, and Japan apologized. Isolationists pointed out, however, that the patrol boat had in fact been carrying Standard Oil products.

While Americans looked on anxiously, events in Europe prompted the president to ready himself for war. On September 1, 1939, Hitler invaded Poland. Committed by treaty to defend Poland, Great Britain and France immediately declared war on Germany. The Soviet Union just weeks earlier had stunned the world by signing a nonaggression pact with the Nazis, their avowed enemies. The Red Army entered Poland from the east, and the two great powers split the hapless nation between them. Then, as suddenly as it began, the fighting ceased, a final respite from all-out war.

Roosevelt invoked the Neutrality Acts, as required by law, banning the shipment of goods to combatants. But he also declared that "even a neutral cannot be asked to close his mind or his conscience." Opinion polls showed that the majority of Americans had changed their minds from opposing the sale of arms to Britain and France to supporting a repeal of the embargo. Roosevelt signaled his own intentions by calling Congress into special session in mid-September 1939 and obtaining revisions of the Neutrality Acts that allowed the sale of munitions to nations at war. Other revisions, forbidding American ships to sail into war zones or to unload cargoes in wartime ports, were designed to ease public fears.

Further developments in Europe added urgency to arguments for U.S. involvement. After pausing for the winter, Hitler struck Germany's northern neighbors in April 1940. Nazi armored divisions quickly occupied Denmark and Norway, then swept over Holland, Belgium, and Luxembourg. After sending Britain's forces into retreat across the English Channel, Hitler's army, joined by the Italians, easily conquered France in June 1940. Next, Hitler turned

---

Gallup Polls: European War and World War I, September, 1938–November, 1940

These three polls conducted by the American Institute of Public Opinion indicate the persistence of isolationist sentiment and popular criticism of U.S. involvement in World War I. Many respondents believed the United States, despite its commitments to European allies, should stay out of war. After 1940, in the aftermath of Nazi military victories in Europe, many Americans reconsidered their opposition, fearing a threat to democracy in their own nation.

OCTOBER 2
EUROPEAN WAR

If England and France go to war against Germany do you think the United States can stay out?

Yes	57%
No	43

By Region

	Yes	No
New England	46%	54%
Middle Atlantic	61	39
East Central	60	40
West Central	57	43
South	60	40
West	51	49

Interviewing Date 9/15–20/1938, Survey #132, Question #4

FEBRUARY 21
EUROPEAN WAR

If it appears that Germany is defeating England and France, should the United States declare war on Germany and send our army and navy to Europe to fight?

Yes	23%
No	77

7 percent expressed no opinion.

Interviewing Date 2/2–7/1940, Survey #183–K, Question #6

DECEMBER 16
EUROPEAN WAR

Do you think it was a mistake for the United States to enter the last World War?

Yes	39%
No	42
No opinion	19

By Political Affiliation
Democrats

Yes	33%
No	46
No opinion	21

Republicans

Yes	46%
No	38
No opinion	16

Interviewing Date 11/21–30/1940, Survey #244–K, Question #6

toward England. In the Battle of Britain, Nazi bombers pounded England while U-boats cut off incoming supplies.

Interventionists, highly placed in business and diplomatic services, pressed for U.S. entry into the war. The press joined the crusade. By June 1940, newspapers were ablaze with headlines such as "Declare War on Nazis, Notables Plead" and "American War Vote Demanded." Radio broadcasts and public rallies echoed similar sentiments.

Conservatives rushed to oppose intervention. The America First Committee, formed in September 1940 and chaired by top Sears executive Robert Wood, quickly gained publicity because of such prominent members as movie stars Robert Young and Lillian Gish, automobile manufacturer Henry Ford, and Charles A. Lindbergh, the beloved "Lindy," famous for his 1927 solo flight across the Atlantic. Another group of Americans actively supported Hitler. The German-American Bund, with a following of perhaps 25,000 and a core of some 8,000 uniformed storm troopers, condemned the "Jew Deal" of "Franklin D. Rosenfeld." Father Charles Coughlin of Royal Oak, Michigan (see Chapter 24), utilizing a newspaper read by a quarter million and a weekly radio show heard by 4 million, gave his blessing to local groups of right-wing, anti-Semitic "Christian Front" organizations. Public pro-Nazi activities peaked in 1939 with a German-American Bund rally of 50,000 in Madison Square Garden.

Roosevelt Readies for War

If the declarations of war between Germany and France and Great Britain made world war inevitable, U.S. leaders could not yet admit the certainty of American involvement — especially with an election year at hand. The "Roosevelt Recession" had caused a drop in the president's popularity, raising doubts about the possibility of his reelection to an unprecedented third term. Roosevelt waited until July 1940, the eve of the Democratic party convention, to announce that world events compelled him to accept a party "draft" for renomination. Democrats rallied behind him and his choice for vice-president, former secretary of agriculture Henry Wallace. Roosevelt campaigned promising voters not to "send your boys to any foreign wars."

Many political observers had expected the Republicans to recapture the White House by appealing to voter discontent with the economy and by playing upon isolationist feelings. But party leaders pushed aside isolationist Robert Taft for a candidate who had never before run for public office, Wendell Wilkie. A utilities executive and former Democrat, Wilkie ran a campaign attacking Roosevelt's "dictatorial" methods and effectively buried the war as a campaign issue. Wavering Democrats who dreaded intervention calculated the social benefits created by the New Deal and remained loyal to the chief executive. Roosevelt cruised to victory. Wilkie won 44 percent of the popular vote, doing better than 1936 Republican candidate Alf Landon but taking few states.

Within a short time of Roosevelt's reelection, the world crisis moved to a new stage. Hitler overwhelmed the Balkans and then set aside the expedient Nazi-Soviet Pact to resume his quest for all of Europe. In June 1941 Nazi troops invaded the Soviet Union, and by late fall they had nearly reached Moscow. All anti-Fascists now united against the Nazis, effectively limiting the American opponents of war to the far right and scattered pacifists.

Politically strengthened, Roosevelt secured the Selective Service and Training Act of 1940, the first peacetime draft in American history. The act initially brought 1,600,000 men into the army for a one-year tour of duty. The president also replaced his isolationist-minded secretaries of war and the navy with interventionist Republicans Henry Stimson and Henry Knox. In his annual message to Congress, he proposed a lend-lease policy, whereby the British would no longer pay cash for American munitions but instead return or replace them after the war. He also extended U.S. "defense" lines to Iceland and Greenland — nearly halfway across the ocean — and ordered the Coast Guard to seize any ships controlled or owned by Germany that entered an American port. During a series of incidents between U.S. ships and Nazi subs in 1941, Roosevelt declared an unlimited national emergency. He demanded that Germany and Italy close their U.S. consulates and ordered U.S. ships to shoot on sight any Nazi vessel. When Congress authorized the merchant marine to sail fully armed and to convey Lend-Lease supplies directly to Britain, a formal declaration of war seemed only a matter of time.

In August 1941, Roosevelt met at sea with British prime minister Winston Churchill to plan out "common principles." These principles, which became known as the Atlantic Charter, promised a "better future for the world." They included self-government and free trade for all nations, an end to territorial seizures, and the abandonment of war as a means of achieving ends. The Atlantic Charter pledged to all nations the right to self-determination.

The World Divided

Through 1940 and much of 1941 the United States had focused on the war in Europe. But anticipating danger to American interests in the Pacific, Roosevelt transferred the Pacific Fleet from its home base in San Diego to Pearl Harbor, Hawai'i, in May 1940. The next month, Congress forbade Americans to continue exporting war oil and scrap metal to Japan without licenses, effectively embargoing these items. By September, Roosevelt had extended the embargo to cover iron and steel scrap and had granted a large loan to China. Japan responded on September 27 by formally joining Germany and Italy as the Asian partner of the worldwide Axis.

While Hitler moved to establish a "New Order in Europe," Japan seized the moment to increase its prospects for a "Greater East Asia." Under the conditions of the alliance, Germany would support Japan's seizure of Dutch, British, or French colonial possessions in that region, and all three Axis powers would defend one another against aggression.

The United States and Japan each played for time in the Pacific. Roosevelt wanted to save his resources to fight against Germany, while Japan's leaders gambled that America's preoccupation with Europe might allow them to conquer Asia entirely. After Germany's invasion of France, Japan determined to swallow the French colonies in Indochina (Vietnam, Cambodia, and Laos). Roosevelt froze Japan's assets in the United States and added a total trade embargo of American-made goods to Japan.

Major Japanese troop movements were under way, and Roosevelt's advisers expected an imminent attack in the southern Pacific, British Malaya, or the Philippines. But Japan intended instead to knock out U.S. military strength in the Pacific with one blow. On Sunday, December 7, 1941, in one of the most successful strategic moves in twentieth-century military history, Japanese planes caught American forces completely off guard at Pearl Harbor. Japanese bombers destroyed most of the Pacific air force and sunk or badly damaged 18 ships. More than 2,300 American soldiers and sailors were killed, nearly 1,200 wounded. Historian Charles Beard and some conservatives later charged that Roosevelt had secretly anticipated the attack, needing a dramatic event to bring the nation into war. Official inquiries never determined why Americans had been so unsuspecting.

The next day Congress heard Roosevelt promise that "this day shall live in infamy." The president

President Franklin D. Roosevelt signs the Declaration of War with Japan, December 8, 1941, a day after the attack on Pearl Harbor. Congressional leaders, many of whom had earlier hoped to keep the United States out of war, here unite around the president and his policies.

asked for a declaration of war against Japan. With only one dissenting vote, Congress acceded. But the United States had not yet declared war on Japan's allies. Hitler obliged Roosevelt, appealing to the Reichstag on December 11 to support war against the "half Judaized and half Negrified" American nation. Mussolini joined him in the declaration, and the United States reciprocated the same day. Spain's Fascist government remained cautiously neutral.

THE WAR IN EUROPE AND ASIA

During the first year of declared war, the United States remained on the defensive. Hitler's forces held the European continent and pounded England by air, while driving a thousand miles into Russia and across northern Africa. Japan practically seized the Pacific. Roosevelt called the news "all bad," while his military experts predicted a long fight to victory.

But the Allies enjoyed several important advantages, including the coordinated military leadership of Britain and the United States, accelerating war production, determined fighting by anti-Fascist "partisan" forces, and the capacity of the USSR to endure immense losses. Slowly at first, but with quickening speed after 1941, these advantages made themselves felt.

Soviets Halt Nazi Drive

The burden of the war in Europe fell on the Soviet Union. In the summer and fall of 1941, Hitler's forces overtook the demoralized Red Army, capturing nearly one million soldiers and leaving thousands to die from exposure or starvation. In the battle of Stalingrad the Red Army lost more men than the Americans did during the entire war. The major Russian cities of Kiev and Leningrad as well as hundreds of small towns were destroyed. With an eye toward imminent victory, Hitler moved next on Moscow, directing his army to invade from three directions.

Russian civilians rallied, sending every available resource to the Red Army forces stationed just outside the capital city. Partisan units cut German supply lines, while the winter cold immobilized the German troops. For the first time, the Nazi war machine suffered a major setback, and on December 5 Soviet commanders ordered a counterattack. These stunning victories by the Red Army stalled the Nazi forces. Events at Stalingrad the following

winter would tip the balance of the war against the Germans.

Aid from the United States proved crucial. Initial proposals to help the Soviets provoked as much controversy among Americans as Lend-Lease to Britain had. Conservatives opposed assisting the Communist government, regardless of the circumstances. By 1940, when Roosevelt declared Lend-Lease for the Soviet Union, reports of Nazi atrocities had overcome such reservations. Once in place, the program operated efficiently, supplying (with help from England) 10 percent of the Russian tanks and aircraft, machine tools, railway equipment, and huge amounts of food. By the end of the war, 700,000 tons of American-produced flour and sugar and nearly as much canned meat had reached the USSR and the Red Army. By 1944, 2 percent of the total agricultural output of the United States was going to the Soviet Union.

Allied Offensive by Sea and Air

By the spring of 1942, Germany, Italy, and Japan commanded a territory ranging from southern France to the Pacific Ocean. They controlled central Europe and a large section of the Soviet Union as well as considerable parts of China and the southwestern Pacific. But the Allies outnumbered and could outproduce the Axis powers. These advantages increased over time.

Slowly and painfully, the Allies won control of the Atlantic, carefully patrolling in convoys to protect merchant ships and kill threatening submarines. Until this plan could be worked out, and even afterward, U.S. forces suffered huge casualties from German torpedoes. The U.S. Merchant Marine, which lost more men than the regular navy, managed to survive the carnage in large part because the United States could turn out new ships without letup.

Air power afforded more success at lower costs. Even by 1941, when victory appeared remote, Britain's aircraft production had surpassed Germany's. The Royal Air Force (RAF) seized the offensive and, joined by the U.S. Air Force in 1942, dodged antiaircraft fire to strike again and again at German targets.

Early hopes of winning the war through bombing alone, however, proved overly optimistic. Although Allied bombers inflicted heavy losses on transportation systems and fuel production, Germans managed to keep their factories sufficiently intact to produce large numbers of planes and submarines and a stockpile of rubber. There was no alternative to an Allied ground invasion. But the prospect of cutting through France, which was tightly controlled by the Germans, still appeared unlikely.

The Allies struck instead at Egypt. In October 1942, in Operation Torch, they landed at the Mediterranean port of El Alamein to fight General Erwin Rommel's famed Afrikan Korps. The Allied triumph there highlighted the role of the new Supreme Allied Commander, Dwight D. Eisenhower, who took charge of coordinating the three Allied armies (American, British, and Free French). Eisenhower followed the victory at El Alamein with naval landings in Algeria and Morocco. Driving eastward against German armies already under pressure from British forces, the Allied troops — British, Americans, Australians, and New Zealanders — surrounded a quarter of a million Germans and Italians in Tunisia, held them captive from March to May 1943, and compelled them to surrender. Africa had been saved from the Axis, and the Italians were thrown on the defensive once and for all.

Stalingrad and "Unconditional Surrender"

The next decisive blow fell in late 1942, again in the USSR. More through will than resources, the Soviet Union had regained much of its productive and agricultural capacity in regions still unconquered, thus enabling the civilian population and military forces to survive. German forces, joined by Romanians, Italians, and others, fought resolutely to hold Stalingrad against the returning Red Army. For five months the battle continued, until a Soviet counterattack encircled the German-led troops and virtually annihilated them. As the occupying armies starved and froze, their resistance steadily dwindled. At the end of January 1943, 200,000 German troops surrendered to the Red Army. Now the tide of the war had really turned, and the Red Army prepared to pursue the remaining German forces as they retreated.

The Nazis still held most of the territory they had seized, but less confidently. The most spectacular, if doomed, challenge to Nazi control was the heroic Jewish uprising in the Warsaw ghetto, in April 1943. Though easily crushed, this bold move by food-starved Jews, who briefly sealed off their quarter and killed collaborators, gave courage to other victims of nazism. Revolts followed in the Nazi labor camps, where prisoners of war and civilians were worked to death on starvation rations.

Partisan fighters now went on the offensive in many sections of eastern and western Europe. Irregular, often poorly equipped guerrilla forces issued anti-Fascist propaganda and prepared the way for future Allied offensives. As Axis forces grew weaker and began to withdraw, the partisans carried out their work more and more openly, punishing collaborators and arming citizens to fight for their own freedom.

Following the defeat of German troops at Stalingrad, Allied leaders at last caught sight of victory. Roosevelt and Churchill assured Stalin that they would send enough troops and supplies to retake the offensive in the Pacific. They further promised to begin the long-awaited "second front" in Europe, which would finally relieve the pressure on the depleted Red Army.

In a controversial diplomatic move, Churchill and Roosevelt met in Casablanca in January 1943 and formulated the terms of the peace proposal: unconditional surrender, with defeated Axis powers abandoning all claims to rule their own nations. Supporters of this policy underscored its ideological value — a promise to the world that the scourge of fascism would be totally banished. This approach satisfied Stalin, who still feared a British-American settlement with Hitler against the Soviets. For Roosevelt and his strategists, unconditional surrender represented a clear goal beyond simply an end to the war.

Critics charged that the demand for total capitulation would lengthen the war and add dramatically to the casualty list. Disillusioned factions of the governments in Germany and Japan, many diplomats believed, anticipated defeat and might negotiate a peace settlement if allowed minor concessions. Besides, the insistence on unconditional surrender would in effect penalize mainly civilians and soldiers rather than their leaders.

Allied aerial bombardment did shift increasingly from taking out strategic sites to terrorizing civilians. From the first weeks of 1943, U.S. and British planes poured bombs upon German cities. This operation cost hundreds of planes and some of the nations' best pilots. Worse, though, it turned the course of the main Allied air attack away from military targets, virtually the only kind that pilots had attacked during World War I. Hamburg was now practically leveled, with 60,000 people killed. But the worst raid of the war — 650,000 incendiary bombs on the city of Dresden, destroying eight square miles and killing 135,000 civilians — had no particular military value. Historians later concluded that such bombing, rather than weakening morale, actually hardened popular resistance by deflecting resentment from Nazi officials to the Allies.

Theaters of Conflict, 1943–1945
The Allies' successful counter-offensive against Germans and Italians stretched from the North Atlantic to Africa and the Middle East.

The Retaking of Europe

The British and American commanders had made several crucial strategic decisions even before the Soviet victories. They placed the Asian war on hold until Europe could be reconquered. They also deferred, despite Stalin's repeated appeals, any move for an early "second front" against the Germans' western flank. A direct assault through France was considered too risky and too expensive in human lives. Instead, the Allies set out to supply anti-Fascist resistance in all quarters and to create a more sustainable counteroffensive through southern Italy.

On the ground, the Allies moved determinedly

ahead. After attacking Sicily on July 10, 1943, Canadian, British, and American troops conquered the island in mid-August. King Vittorio Emmanuele dismissed Mussolini, and Italians celebrated in the streets, spitting at portraits of the former dictator and going on strike against employers who had supported the old regime. Hitler's troops saved Mussolini and provided him a smaller fighting force, which controlled parts of the nation. Outside Italy, most Italian troops surrendered or even joined partisan forces fighting the Nazis. Italy itself became a battleground of Nazi and Fascist armies against Allied forces and armed partisans. On September 8, 1943, the new Italian government signed an unconditional surrender and joined the Allies.

After capturing Naples, at the ankle of the nation's "boot," in September, however, the Allied forces still faced the tough German army. For nine long months, they failed to move the hundred miles northwest to Rome, and in the rugged northern Italian terrain they were still battling when the European war ended.

The Allies prepared to retake the continent with the decisive counterattack through France that Hitler had long anticipated. In early 1944, Americans and forces from a dozen other nations filled the southern half of England with military camps in preparation for Operation Overlord. Having canceled all leaves, armed U.S. military police (MPs) watched everywhere for trouble or for deserters. New weapons, such as flamethrowers and amphibious armored vehicles, were carefully camouflaged.

At last, Allied invasion plans went into action. On D-Day, June 6, 1944, tens of thousands of paratroopers landed in Normandy, France. The Germans, who had expected the landing elsewhere on the coast, quickly trained their deadly weaponry upon the paratroopers and shored up their lines for the inevitable amphibious assault. The Allied fleet brought more than 175,000 soldiers and more than 20,000 vehicles to shore under steady German fire — an accomplishment unimaginable in any previous war. At Omaha Beach, the American soldiers, their command shattered, were unable to escape; over one-third, some 2,500, fell dead or wounded. In the next six weeks, nearly one million more Allied soldiers came ashore. In July, after fierce fighting, they broke out of Normandy and prepared to march inland.

As the fighting continued, all eyes turned to Paris, the premier city of Europe. Allied bombers pounded factories producing German munitions on the outskirts of the French capital. Partisans assassinated the Vichy government's propaganda minister and unfurled the French flag at impromptu demonstrations on Bastille Day, July 14. On August 10, railway workers staged one of the first successful strikes against Nazi occupiers anywhere, and three days later the Paris police defected to the Resistance, which proclaimed in leaflets that the "hour of liberation has come." Conservative general Charles de Gaulle, accompanied by Allied troops, arrived in Paris on August 25 to become president of the reestablished French Republic.

D-Day Landing, June 6, 1944, marked the greatest amphibious maneuver in military history. Troop ships ferried Allied soldiers from England to Normandy beaches. Within a month, nearly one million men had assembled in France, ready to retake western and central Europe from German forces.

One former occupied European nation after another fell to the Allies. But for Allied troops, who had lost more than 200,000, the war had reached only a resting place between bloody battles.

The High Cost of European Victory

In September 1944, Allied commanders searched for a strategy to end the war quickly. Aiming to open the Netherlands for a thrust into Germany's industrial heartland, they ran into unexpectedly tough German resistance. Around Arnheim, Holland, poorly trained Allied units broke ranks and ran for their lives. By the end of the battle, the Germans had killed or wounded 17,000 Americans and captured thousands more.

A bloody seesaw of advances and retreats followed. In a final, desperate effort to reverse the Allied momentum, Hitler directed his last reserves, a quarter million men, at Allied lines in the French-Belgian Forest of Ardennes. After weeks of fighting, the Battle of the Bulge — named for the temporary dent in Allied lines — exhausted the German capacity for counterattack. The bloodiest single American battle since Gettysburg ended another phase of the European War as decisively as had Stalingrad two years earlier. By Christmas Day 1944, the Germans had fallen back to their own territory.

The end was now in sight. In March, the Allies rolled across the Rhine and took the Ruhr Valley with its precious industrial resources. The defense of Germany, now hopeless, had fallen into the hands of the only soldiers remaining, young teenagers and elderly men. When Germany surrendered on May 8, Hitler had already committed suicide in a Berlin bunker. The casualties of the Allied European campaign had been enormous: more than half a million killed, almost 80,000 captured or missing, and another 700,000 dead in nonbattle accidents or illness.

The War in the Pacific

The war that had begun with Pearl Harbor rapidly escalated into battles and strategic standoffs across a region of the world far larger than all of Europe, stretching from Southeast Asia to the Aleutian Islands. Japan followed up its early advantage by cutting Burma's supply routes to China, crushing the British navy, and seizing the Philippines, Hong Kong, Wake Island, British Malaya, and Thailand. After tenacious fighting at the Bataan Peninsula and on the island of Corregidor, the surviving U.S. troops retreated to Australia.

Japan pushed its advantage, sending a convoy to conquer the Pacific from the Aleutians to New Guinea. In May 1942 naval warfare broke out on the Coral Sea, off the eastern coast of Australia. But there was no direct contact between the enemy ships. Instead, aircraft carrier–based planes conducted spectacular dogfights. Japanese forces eventually turned back, after heavy losses on both sides. Japan next attempted to capture Midway Island and sever American lines of communication. Another huge naval battle, with fleets separated by 400 miles, raged on for three days in June 1942. Thanks in part to Operation Magic, in which specialists broke the Japanese secret code, U.S. officers knew when and from which direction the Japanese attack would come. They sunk four of Japan's vital aircraft carriers and eliminated the threat to Hawai'i. The United States now held the upper hand, although the war for the Pacific was far from over.

The Solomon Islands and Papua, on the island of New Guinea, had been chosen for the Allied counteroffensive. Americans and Australians fought together through the Papua jungle, while the marines prepared to attack the Japanese stronghold of Guadalcanal. After a two-month struggle, Guadalcanal was taken, and Japanese resources worn down significantly.

But the prospect of reconquering the Pacific island by island remained forbidding. Dozens of ships and thousands of troops could be tied down capturing tiny atolls from the well-armed Japanese forces. In the campaign for the tiny island of Tarawa in November 1943, one thousand marines died. As an alternative, General Douglas MacArthur developed the shrewd plan of island hopping. By avoiding a sustained battle for each Japanese island stronghold, MacArthur reduced casualties and opened a path to Japan through air power in 1943 and 1944.

The Battle of the Philippine Sea, fought in June 1944, marked Japan's final attempt to maintain the strategic periphery close to its own island home. Huge naval forces with thousands of men on both sides poured into combat. Under intense pressure, the Japanese retreated, and soon the United States held Guam, Saipan, and Tinian.

MacArthur now led a force of 250,000 to the Philippines in October 1944 for what was expected to be the largest naval battle in history. All that remained of the Japanese navy hurled itself at American transports in Leyte Gulf. After three days of battle, the United States virtually controlled the Pacific. Overcoming Japanese forces in the Philippines and the islands of Iwo Jima and Okinawa nevertheless proved extremely bloody, with more than 70,000 Americans lost in Japanese kamikaze

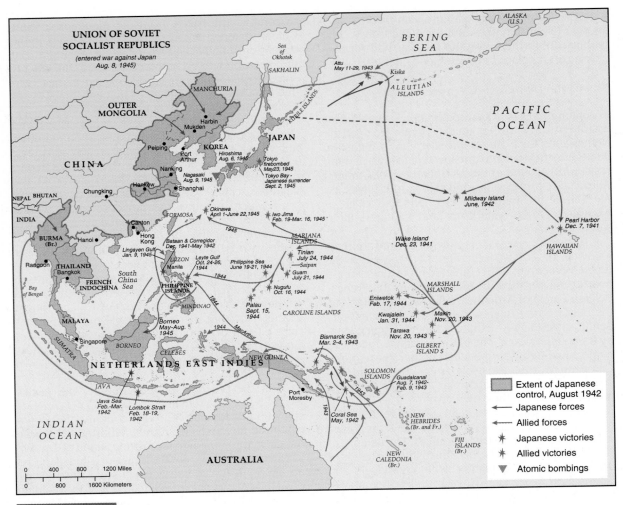

War in the Pacific

Across an ocean battlefield utterly unlike the European Theater, Allies battled Japanese troops near their homeland.

attacks on ships and in grueling hand-to-hand combat. In order to deceive Japanese intelligence, the marines had successfully used a Navaho Indian code.

Attacks on mainland Japan also began to take their toll. After Guam, land-based American bombers could reach Tokyo and other Japanese cities with devastating results. Trapped in houses and apartments built mostly of wood or bamboo, civilians faced terrifying fire bombings that burned thousands alive and left hundreds of thousands more homeless.

Japan could not hold out forever. Without a navy or air force, the government could not even transport the oil, tin, rubber, or grain needed to maintain a military force and feed the nation. The Allies pressed for an unconditional surrender. Great Britain and particularly the United States each had its own reasons to hurry. While formally linked to the Soviet Union, they looked beyond the war, determined to prevent the Red Army from taking any territories held by Japan. That motive, along with a profound desire to end the conflict, set the stage for a final, military ground assault on Japan itself — or the use of a secret weapon that American scientists had been preparing: the atomic bomb.

MEN AND WOMEN IN UNIFORM

During World War I, American soldiers served for a relatively brief period and in small numbers. A quarter century later, World War II mobilized 16.4 million Americans into the U.S. armed forces. Although only 34 percent of the men who served in the army saw combat — the majority during the final year of the war — the experience had a powerful impact on nearly everyone. Whether working in the steno pool at Great Lakes Naval Training Center in northern Illinois or slogging rifle in hand through mud in the Philippines, many men and women saw their lives reshaped in unpredictable ways. Uprooted from their communities, they found themselves among strangers, in unfamiliar surroundings, and under a severe military regimen.

Military Discipline

Before the European War broke out in 1939, the majority of the 200,000 men in the U.S. armed forces were employed as military police, patrolling the Mexican border, for example, or occupying colonial possessions, such as the Philippines. Neither the army nor the navy was prepared for the scale of combat necessitated by World War II. Only the Marine Corps, which had been planning since the 1920s to wrest control of the western Pacific from Japan, was poised to fight. Once mobilized for war, however, the U.S. armed forces became a first-rank military power.

The officer corps, drawn at the top from the U.S. Military Academy at West Point and the U.S. Naval Academy at Annapolis, tended to be highly professional, politically conservative, and personally autocratic. General Douglas MacArthur, supreme commander in the Pacific theater, was said to admire the discipline of the German army and often heard to disparage political democracy. "Old Blood and Guts," General George S. Patton, Jr., peppered his speeches with racist epithets (although he delivered a famous pep talk to African American troops preparing to fight the Germans). Mediocre as students at the military academies, many generals had excelled in athletic contests, and not a few derived their military strategies from sports. MacArthur got his from baseball: "Hit 'em where they ain't."

The democratic rhetoric of the war aims contrasted sharply with the arrogance of such commanding officers. Dwight D. Eisenhower, supreme

Wartime Army Camps, Naval Bases, and Airfields

Army camps: Devised for political as well as defense reasons, military facilities were rapidly constructed in every state. Although concentrated in the eastern states, these new installations also opened up large sections of the West and South to new populations and economic development.

Source: Clifford L. Lord and Elizabeth H. Lord, *Lord & Lord Historical Atlas of the United States*, rev. ed. (New York: Holt, 1953), p. 309.

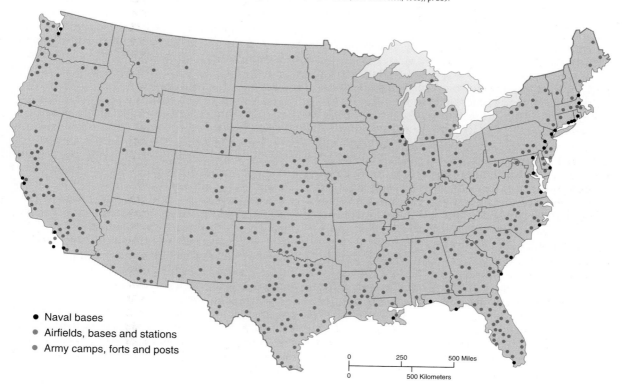

- ● Naval bases
- ● Airfields, bases and stations
- ● Army camps, forts and posts

commander of the Allied forces in Europe, was a different kind of leader. Mistrusted by MacArthur and many of the older brass, Eisenhower appeared to his officers and troops a model of fair play. Breaking with military tradition, he encouraged many young men to join the officer corps for idealistic more than career aspirations.

Most GIs (short for *government issue*), the vast majority draftees, ignored the officers at the higher command levels and instead forged bonds with the lower-ranked officers and men in their own combat divisions. "Everyone wants someone to look up to when he's scared," one GI explained. Most of all, soldiers depended on the solidarity of the group, the loyalty of their buddies, to pull them through the war.

The majority of GIs endured military discipline "to get the task done," as revealed in numerous polls. They longed foremost for peace. "In the magazines," wrote the popular war correspondent Ernie Pyle,

> war seemed romantic and exciting, full of heroics and vitality. . . . Certainly there were great tragedies, unbelievable heroism, even a constant undertone of comedy. But when I sat down to write, I saw instead men . . . suffering and wishing they were somewhere else . . . all of them desperately hungry for somebody to talk to besides themselves, no women to be heroes in front of, damned little wine to drink, precious little song, cold and fairly dirty, just toiling from day to day in a world full of insecurity, discomfort, homesickness and a dulled sense of danger.

Pledged to fight for democracy, most GIs hoped to return soon to their homes and families.

Despite the prolonged stress of combat, only a small proportion of GIs succumbed to "battle fatigue" or showed NP (neuropsychiatric) symptoms. In France, however, where soldiers spent up to 200 days in the field without a break from the fighting, thousands cracked, occasionally inflicting wounds upon themselves in order to be sent home. One who simply fled the battlefront, Private Eddie Slovak, was tried and executed for desertion — the first such execution since the Civil War. Slovak had been singled out as an example. Most deserters were sentenced to hard labor in military stockades. Only in 1944 did the army devise a rotation system to relieve exhausted soldiers.

Women Join the Armed Forces

Before World War II, women served in the armed forces mainly as nurses and clerical workers. The Army Nurse Corps, created in 1901, and the Navy Nurse Corps, formed in 1908, were scarcely military organizations. Recruits earned neither military pay nor rank and received scant public recognition for their services.

With the approach of World War II, Massachusetts Republican congresswoman Edith Nourse Rogers proposed legislation for the formation of a women's corps. The War Department instead drafted its own bill, which Rogers sponsored, creating in May 1942 the Women's Army Auxiliary Corps. Later changed to the Women's Auxiliary Corps (WAC), the organization enrolled women directly into the army. In 1942 and 1943, other bills established a women's division of the navy (the WAVES), the Women's Airforce Service Pilots, the Marine Corps Women's Reserve, expanded versions of the Army Nurse Corps and Navy Nurse Corps, and a women's division of the Coast Guard. Over all, more than 350,000 women served in World War II, two-thirds of them as WACs or WAVEs.

Although barred from combat, women were not necessarily protected from danger. Nurses accompanied the troops into combat in Africa, Italy, and France, treated men under fire, and dug and lived in their own foxholes. More than 1,000 women flew planes, though not on combat missions. The vast majority, however, remained far from battlefronts. Stationed mainly within the United States, they worked in administration, communications, and clerical or health care facilities.

The government feared the spread of "immorality" among women in the armed forces and closely monitored their conduct. While the secretary of war, as well as the president, vigorously denied widespread rumors of WAC and WAVE "wild behavior," they established strict rules. They advised women to avoid drinking in public and to abstain from sexually promiscuous behavior. The Marine Corps even used intelligence officers to ferret out suspected lesbians or those women who merely showed "homosexual tendencies." Homosexuality, whether in act or appearance, was cause for dishonorable discharge.

Some discriminatory practices eased, but only after women demanded fair treatment. High-ranking female officers, for example, argued for a repeal of military policy prohibiting women from supervising male workers, even in offices. The armed forces did not, however, lift its ban of women with children.

Racial segregation clung on tenaciously, despite government declarations of egalitarianism. Black women and white women ate in separate mess halls and slept in separate barracks. At the beginning of the war, black nurses were admitted to serve only black soldiers; the WAVEs refused all black women,

New recruits to the Women's Army Corps (WAC) pick up their clothing "issue" (allotment). These volunteers served in many capacities, from nursing men in combat to performing clerical and communications duties "state side" (within the U.S.). Approximately 140,000 women served in the WACs during World War II.

on the basis that the navy had no black airmen to attend to. Only in 1944 did Roosevelt order the Navy to incorporate black WAVEs, and fewer than a hundred ultimately served.

Old Practices and New Horizons

Many African Americans harbored suspicions of the government's intentions, viewing the war as a grand battle for white men's territorial expansion. Their fears were not allayed by the prevailing racial attitudes of white Americans, civilian or military. The army, for example, refused "to intermingle colored and white enlisted personnel in the same regimental organizations." Secretary of War Henry Stimson declined to challenge the policy of segregation, saying that the army could not operate effec-

tively as "a sociological laboratory." Meanwhile, the new government propaganda, patriotic animated cartoons, and popular songs alike caricatured the Japanese as devious, slant-eyed, yellow monkeys or rats; only the *leaders* of Germany and Italy were subjected to such ridicule.

Approximately one million African Americans nevertheless served in the armed forces during World War II, enlisting at a rate 60 percent above their proportion in the general population. The majority served in the Engineers and Quartermaster Corps, mainly in construction or stevedore work. In the army and navy, a small minority were permitted to rise above noncombatant roles to fighting status and lower officer ranks, but only toward the end of the war. An all-black tank squadron earned distinction in Germany. And despite the very small number of African Americans admitted to the air force, the 99th Pursuit Squadron gained high marks in action against the feared *Luftwaffe*. Even the marines and Coast Guard agreed to end their historic exclusion of African Americans, although they recruited and promoted only a small number.

For the ordinary black soldier, sailor, or marine, especially in the early part of the war, these changes in policy came too late. Serving in segregated, low-prestige units, they encountered discrimination at every point, from the USO to the religious chapel. Even the blood banks kept blood segregated by race (although a black physician, Charles Drew, had invented the process for storing plasma). Any protests, individual or group, were often met with brutal treatment by the MPs. Nor did the MPs protect off-duty black servicemen and women from harassment by civilians and local police.

The armed forces also grouped Japanese Americans into segregated units, sending most to fight in Italy, far from the Pacific theater. The Nisei 442d Infantry Regiment nevertheless became one of the most highly decorated units in history.

Despite segregationist military policy, the war pulled Americans of all races and ethnicities out of insular communities and introduced them to a broad spectrum of the population. Many Jews and other children of European immigrants, for example, described their stint in the military as an "Americanizing" experience. Large numbers of Indian peoples left reservations for the first time, approximately 25,000 serving in the armed forces. For many African Americans in particular, military service provided a bridge to postwar civil rights agitation. Amzie Moore, who later helped to organize the Mississippi Freedom Democratic party, traced his understanding that "people are just people" to his own experiences in the armed forces during World War II.

Many homosexuals also discovered a wider world, despite the implementation for the first time of a military policy disqualifying them. Although some homosexuals and lesbians were refused induction after examination by military psychiatrists, most slipped through public screenings without revealing their sexual orientation. Facing the risk of dishonorable discharge, homosexual soldiers nevertheless found themselves confronting their sexual identity in the rigidly sex-segregated organization of the military. The emotional pressures of wartime, including the fear of death, encouraged men to form close friendships, and homosexuals often found more room than in civilian life to express their sexual preferences openly. In Army canteens, for example, men often danced openly with one another, whereas in civilian settings they would have been subject to ridicule or even arrest for such activity. "The war is a tragedy to my mind and soul," one gay soldier confided, "but to my physical being, it's a memorable experience." On a smaller scale, lesbian WACs and WAVEs told similar tales of collective self-discovery.

Most soldiers looked back at the war, with all its dangers and discomforts, as the greatest experience they would ever know. As the *New Republic* predicted in 1943, they also met fellow Americans from every part of the country, and recognized for the first time in their lives "the bigness and wholeness of the United States." "Hughie was a Georgia cracker, so he knew something about moonshine," remembered one soldier. Another recalled fondly "this fellow from Wisconsin we called 'Moose.'" But rather than becoming more cosmopolitan, as many observers expected, GIs who served abroad more often developed a strong feeling of national pride that included contempt for the countries they had conquered or helped to save.

Overseas Occupation

As a liberating and occupying force, Americans stationed overseas had a mixed record. Children especially welcomed the American soldiers, who brought candy and chewing gum. But civilians in areas not actually invaded by the Axis powers sometimes resented the presence of American troops, whose demands for entertainment turned urban neighborhoods into red-light zones. Many Britishers, for example, viewed the American soldiers stationed in their country in 1942 and 1943 as a "friendly" occupation but troublesome nevertheless. American soldiers also caused trouble within their own ranks. Unprepared to see African Americans treated as equals by the British, white GIs rioted against black GIs, committing at least one castration and several murders. The British townsfolk found themselves in the middle.

The relationship between GIs and civilians grew worse on the Continent. At first, Italians and French welcomed the American troops of liberation. But when the Americans arrived in 1944, several million Europeans were without homes and nearly everyone lived on the brink of starvation. The GIs themselves were war-weary or war-crazed, and not a few committed petty robberies or rapes in towns and villages en route to Paris. "Intoxication," one study found, "was the largest contributing factor to crime in the European Theater of Operations."

In Belgium and southern Holland, however, where Nazi rule had been harsh, American soldiers were greeted as heroes. City restaurants were renamed "Cafe Texas" or "Cafe Alaska." Civilians cheered the Americans and eagerly shared — or traded sexual favors for — their supply of chewing gum, small cash, and cigarettes. Despite government-sponsored precautions, the rate of venereal disease ran at 42 per 1,000 soldiers.

Prisoners of War

Approximately 12,000 army personnel became prisoners of war (POWs). Captured mostly in Holland and Belgium by the Germans and taken back to work camps — *Olfags* for officers, *Stalags* for enlisted men — they sat out the war until Allied liberation. Individually registered by the Swiss Red Cross, they were able to receive packages from home and occasionally to join work brigades outside the camps for days at a time. Under these conditions, Americans and their fellow European captives generally survived. By contrast, Russian prisoners of war suffered starvation and sometimes murder in German camps.

Conditions for POWs in the Pacific were, however, worse than abysmal. Of the 20,000 captured in the surrender of the Philippines, only 40 percent survived Japanese captivity to return home in 1945. About 10,000 American and Filipino prisoners, beaten and denied food and water, died on the notorious "death march" through the jungles on the Bataan Peninsula in 1942. Sixteen thousand more American and Filipino prisoners perished in the first weeks at the former Camp O'Donnell in the Philippines.

Because the Japanese did not themselves believe in surrender (insisting their soldiers commit suicide instead), they considered American prisoners to be disgraced or subhuman. American POWs were guarded by misfits, allowed virtually no assistance from the International Red Cross, and permitted no mail deliveries from home. In a postwar survey, 90 percent of former POWs from the Pacific reported having been beaten. A sense of retribution, as well as racist attitudes, prompted GIs to treat Japanese prisoners far more brutally than enemy soldiers captured in Europe or Africa.

ARSENAL OF DEMOCRACY

Neither military power nor strategy, many observers agreed, was the decisive factor in the ultimate Allied victory. Heading Roosevelt's call to make the nation

Heavy industry surged forward from the depressed economic conditions of the late 1930s through wartime government incentives. Manufacturers rapidly converted plants previously devoted to manufacturing automobiles to factories producing air- and seacraft for military use.

"an arsenal of democracy," the United States won the war through production. Due to its large prewar industrial base, abundant natural resources (most of them free from interference by the war), and a civilian population sufficiently large to increase domestic labor without draining military energies, the nation rose to the challenge. The war inspired the most productive work force in the world, lifted the country out of the depression, and created the biggest economic boom in the history of any nation.

The speed with which wartime production accelerated could also be attributed to the massive reorientation and management of the economy by new government agencies. The power of the presidency and the federal government increased considerably, establishing precedents in executive authority that prevailed long after the war's end. The federal budget reflected this concentration of power and resources, growing ten times larger than the peacetime budget of the New Deal. The federal government spent twice as much during the war as in its entire prior history.

Government Revives Business

Going into the war, the United States enjoyed formidable advantages. Its annual steel output of 26.4 million tons easily surpassed that of the world's second largest producer, Germany, and American hard coal production of more than 350 million tons per year was twice that of Germany. These important assets did not, however, necessarily translate into readiness for military conflict. The American public stood firmly against rearmament until 1938, when expenditures for military purposes still amounted to only 1.5 percent of the federal budget.

In 1937 the "Roosevelt Recession" had brought unemployment and production back to the depression-era levels of 1932. Congressional conservatives, consistently unwilling to fund government projects for health and welfare, readily agreed to expand military projects. Offering high profits to companies and jobs for hundreds of voters in representatives' districts, such military spending proved irresistible to liberals as well. The American economy began to pick up as early as 1938, following a $50 million appropriation for naval expansion.

The 1939 repeal of the Neutrality Acts opened possibilities for huge sales of war materials to France and Britain; by 1940 such revenues amounted to almost $2.5 billion. Even before Pearl Harbor, military spending averaged $2 billion per month. Six months after the attack, the federal government had placed orders for equipment and supplies totaling more than $100 billion — more than American firms had produced in any previous single year. With war orders now too large to fill, U.S. industries and the economy were suddenly stronger than at any time since before the depression, and primed for all-out production.

Well before the United States officially entered the war, Roosevelt and his Cabinet had begun to plan a wartime marriage of business, government, and (if necessary) labor. The War Powers Act enabled Roosevelt to formulate and carry out plans for hundreds of special wartime agencies. The president announced a goal of 60,000 planes, 45,000 tanks, and 8 million tons of ships for 1942, and established an Office of Production Management (OPM) to replace the inefficient Advisory Commission within the Council for National Defense. In January 1942, the War Production Board (WPB) was directed to "exercise general responsibility" over the economy.

The leadership of the new Supply Priorities and Allocation Board (SPAB) accentuated the role of accounting and other methods of economic fine tuning. By precisely estimating costs, resources, and

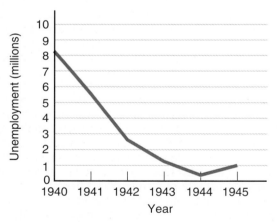

Effects of War Spending, 1940–1945

Wartime spending had a multiplier effect on the U.S. economy. Government contracts with industry rapidly increased the Gross National Product, and the sharp upswing in production utilized all available workers and sharply reduced unemployment.

Source: Robert L. Heilbroner, *The Economic Transformation of America* (New York: Harcourt, Brace, 1977), p. 205.

availability, SPAB leaders could effectively implement OPM programs. The SPAB's anti-inflation plan, covering more than 40 percent of war expenses with new taxes, helped control wartime production costs. A policy of deficit spending paid for the rest of the war costs, and the national debt rose rapidly.

An alphabet soup of other new agencies arose to fill the remaining production gaps. Working with the SPAB, the WPB allocated scarce materials, adjusting domestic consumption (even ending it for some products, such as automobiles) to war needs. It also had the weighty task of deciding which manufacturers received the lucrative war contracts. The Office of Price Administration supervised inflation directly, by imposing price controls. The War Manpower Commission directed the mobilization of military and civilian workers. And the National War Labor Board was directed to mediate disputes between labor and management, to smooth production by halting strikes, and to control inflation by limiting wage increases. The Office of War Mobilization, headed by former Supreme Court justice and close Roosevelt adviser James F. Byrnes, coordinated operations among all these agencies.

The immediate result of this activity, combined with the military mobilization, was to enlarge government many times over its New Deal size — which conservatives already considered far too big. Defense spending rose from $9 million to $98 million, and the Pentagon, one of the world's largest office buildings, housed as many as 35,000 personnel. The number of civilian employees in the federal government nearly quadrupled, from a little over a million in 1940 to nearly 4 million by the war's end.

GNP Victory

By any gauge, the plan to increase production succeeded gloriously. The gross national product (accounting for inflation) rose from $88.6 billion in 1939 to $198.7 billion five years later. Manufacturing of recently developed synthetic rubber and synthetic fabrics raced forward. Investment in new plants and equipment, much of it government-financed, made possible an increase in the economy's productive capacity by perhaps 50 percent. In turn, 17 million jobs were added. Factories that had operated forty hours a week now ran ninety hours, and labor productivity was said to have increased by 25 percent as a result of better equipment and more motivation. (American workers were twice as productive in terms of output per hour as the Germans, five times as productive as the Japanese.) The U.S. Army alone required 519.1 million pairs of socks and 229.4 pairs of pants. Production of airplanes, for American use only, increased from a few thousand to 18,000 per year. No wonder the physical volume of industrial production skyrocketed, increasing 15 percent annually between 1940 and 1944 — the most rapid rate in the nation's history. The value of manufactured goods increased by 300 percent. In all, war production increased from 2 percent of the 1939 total to 10 percent of the 1941 total and 40 percent of the 1943 total.

Businesses scored huge profits from military contracts. The government provided low-interest loans or even direct subsidies for the expansion of old plants or the construction of new factories. Other incentives, such as tax write-offs for retooling, allowed businesses to switch over from the production of consumer goods to that of defense materials with little risk. "If you are going to . . . go to war . . . in a capitalist country," Secretary of War Stimson explained, "you have to let business make money out of the process or business won't work." Because the departments of war and navy found it more convenient to contract with single firms, and because companies with large facilities were capable of filling the large orders, the biggest corporations took the lion's share of war profits. Antitrust legislation was suspended for the duration of the war, allowing monopolies to increase their range and influence. The 100 largest companies, which manufactured 30 percent of all goods in 1940, held 70 percent of all war and civilian contracts. In turn, many small businesses disappeared, a half million between 1941 and 1943 alone.

No section of the country felt the impact of war production more than the West. The federal government poured in nearly $40 billion to support both military and industrial expansion in this major staging area for the Pacific War. The allocation of such huge amounts of capital to produce the ships, planes, and other materials to wage war against Japan permanently reshaped the region's economy. The Pacific Coast states gained the most. California secured 10 percent of all federal funds disbursed during the war, and by 1944 Los Angeles had become the nation's second largest manufacturing center, a small step below Detroit.

The mostly rural, impoverished South also benefited from wartime spending by the federal government. The eleven former Confederate states received nearly $4.5 billion in defense contracts, less than the South's percentage of total population but more than its share of all prewar industry. This economic infusion lifted entire populations out of sharecropping and tenancy and into well-paid industrial jobs, and pumped unprecedented profits into southern business.

At first, farm output paled compared with the surge of industrial production. Because the New Deal had restricted production of certain crops in order to raise prices, reorganization of the agricultural economy for export proved difficult. The massive shift of capital and workers to the cities made the job doubly hard because it deprived farmers of precious resources. The farm population decreased by 17 percent during the war, as people left the countryside for the nation's industrial centers.

Only by the end of 1941, with the firm establishment of a Food for Freedom program, did production begin to increase significantly. Many communities organized Victory Gardens for their residents, and American farmers found themselves growing food not only for the British but for the Russians and even the Chinese. By 1943 and 1944, surpluses had disappeared and domestic shortages in milk, potatoes, fruits, and sugar were pinching civilians. The Department of Agriculture sought far higher production levels than farmers could reach, succeeding only in areas such as livestock (meat and milk), where skyrocketing wholesale prices encouraged the farmer.

The American farmer responded heroically to the challenge of production, but at a cost. War speeded the development of large-scale, mechanized production of crops, including the use of chemical fertilizers and pesticides. By 1945 farm income had doubled, but thousands of small farms had disappeared, never to return.

New Workers during Wartime

Wartime production brought an unprecedented number of new workers into the labor force. The *bracero* program, negotiated by the United States and Mexico in 1942, opened to Mexicans short-term employment in jobs previously closed to them, such as in shipbuilding on the Pacific Coast. Over 200,000 Mexican farm workers legally entered the United States to help harvest crops. Nearly 75,000 Indian people left the reservations for work in defense plants, mostly in the West. African Americans found new opportunities in industry, their number in the labor force rising from 2.9 million to 3.8 million.

The war most dramatically changed the wage-earning patterns of women. The female labor force grew by over 50 percent, to 19.5 million in 1945. The rate of growth proved especially high for white

Facing a shortage of workers and increased production demands, the War Manpower Commission and the Office of War Information conducted a campaign to recruit women into the labor force. Women were encouraged to "take a job for your husband/son/brother" and to "keep the world safe for your children." Higher wages also enticed many women to take jobs in factories producing aircraft, ships, and ordinance.

women over the age of thirty-five, as married women became for the first time the majority among female wage earners. The employment rate changed comparatively little for African American women, although many earned higher wages by shifting from domestic service to manufacturing. Of the black women employed at the close of the war, fully 90 percent had been in the labor force in 1940.

Despite this jump in employment rates, neither the government nor industry had rushed to hire women. Well into the summer of 1942, the Department of War advised businesses to hold back from hiring women "until all available male labor in the area had first been employed." Likewise, neither government nor industry expected women to stay in their jobs when the war ended. Recruitment campaigns addressed to "Mrs. Stay-at-Home" emphasized the patriotic yet temporary nature of women's wartime service. "Rosie the Riveter" thus represented the model female citizen, working in industry, but only "for the duration."

Recruitment advertisements used conventional gender stereotypes to portray female war workers, depicting their new industrial labors as simply a variation of their domestic talents. Where once housewives sewed curtains for their kitchens, they now produced silk parachutes for the U.S. Army. Their skills with a vacuum cleaner easily translated into riveting on huge ships. "Instead of cutting a cake," one newsreel explained, "this woman [factory worker] cuts the pattern of aircraft parts. Instead of baking a cake, this woman is cooking gears to reduce the tension in the gears after use. . . ."

In practice, however, many stereotypes broke down. Women employed in defense industries often found the work both unfamiliar and difficult. They mined coal, repaired aircraft engines, cut and welded sheet metal, and operated forklifts and drill presses. On the Pacific Coast, more than one-third of all workers in aircraft and shipbuilding were women. One black ship welder recalled: "There is nothing in the training to prepare you for the excruciating noise you get down in the ship. Any who were not heart-and-soul determined to stick it out would fade out right away. . . . And it isn't only your muscles that must harden. It's your nerve, too."

Compared with the Great Depression, when married women were barred from many jobs, World War II opened up new fields and radically altered public opinion on women's right to work. The number of women automobile workers, for example, jumped from 29,000 to 200,000, that of women electrical workers 100,000 to 374,000. Polled near the end of the war, the overwhelming majority — 75 percent — of women workers expressed a desire to keep working, preferably at the same job. One woman spoke for many in describing her wartime work as "thrilling" and "exciting," adding that it was also "something women have never been allowed to do before." Many also admitted candidly that the major inducement was the money. One woman reported that her assembly line job in the aircraft industry paid $1.15 per hour, a huge increase over the hourly wage she formerly earned as a waitress: $.20, with no tips allowed.

Although wartime employment changed the lives and raised the expectations of many new workers, the major advances proved to be only temporary. As early as 1943 some industries had begun to design plans for laying off women as war production wound down. With jobs reserved for returning veterans, women in industry saw their numbers rapidly diminish; as many as 4 million lost their jobs between 1944 and 1946. Although skyrocketing inflation propelled many married women to rejoin the labor force by the end of the decade, they had left behind the lucrative production jobs.

Wartime Strikes

The shadow of the enemy and the need to outproduce the Axis powers fostered a spirit of cooperation among wartime workers. Moreover, steady employment and wages much higher than in previous decades offset a load of resentments. Most workers envisioned themselves contributing to the defeat of Fascist tyrants and building a better world. But worker solidarity and rising expectations also came together to produce one of the most turbulent periods in American labor history.

Although 17 million new jobs were created during the war, the economic gains from increased production were unevenly distributed. Wages increased, up to 50 percent or more in some cases, but never as fast as profits or prices. Profits increased by 350 percent before taxes (but officially 120 percent after taxation). Prices went up an average of 20 percent, but shot up as much as 400 percent on individual food items, especially after 1942. This widely reported disparity prompted the largest strike wave in American history.

Only two weeks after the 1940 election, workers struck at the Vultee aircraft plant in Los Angeles. When the attorney general denounced the strikers as unpatriotic and the FBI began to harass participants, sympathy walkouts occurred throughout the area. In April 1941, the president himself intervened in a large strike near Milwaukee at Allis Chalmers,

Strikes and Lockouts in the United States, 1940–1945

Year	No. of Strikes	No. of Workers Involved	No. of Man-days Idle	Percent of Total Employed
1940	2,508	576,988	6,700,872	2.3
1941	4,288	2,362,620	23,047,556	8.4
1942	2,968	839,961	4,182,557	2.8
1943	3,752	1,981,279	13,500,529	6.9
1944	4,956	2,115,637	8,721,079	7.0
1945	4,750	3,467,000	38,025,000	12.2

Despite "no-strike" pledges, workers staged wildcat strikes in the war years. Union leaders negotiated shorter hours, higher wages, and seniority rules and helped to build union membership to a new height. When the war ended, nearly 30 percent of all nonagricultural workers were union members.
Source: "Work Stoppages Caused by Labor-Management Disputes in 1945," *Monthly Labor Review*, May 1946, p. 720; and Glaberman, *War Time Strikes*, (Detroit: Bewick, 1980), p. 36

threatening seizure of the plant and forcing a settlement after 75 days of work stoppage. Later that year Roosevelt ordered troops to break the North American Aviation strike at Inglewood, California.

More workers went on strike in 1941, before the U.S. entered the war, than in any previous year except 1919. Rising production orders and tightening labor markets made strikes feasible: jobs were plentiful, and business leaders, anticipating profits, had reason to settle peacefully. This climate prompted a militant union drive at Ford Motor Company's River Rouge plant in 1941, and the United Auto Workers (UAW) emerged as one of the most powerful labor organizations in the world.

Once the United States entered the war, the major unions readily agreed to no-strike pledges for its duration. The War Labor Board, with representatives from business and labor, encouraged employers to accept unions in their plants, and union-negotiated contracts won automatic dues checkoff, high wages, and new fringe benefits. Total union membership increased from 10.5 million to 14.7 million; women's share alone rose from 11 to 23 percent, to nearly 3 million. Unions also enrolled 1,250,000 African Americans, twice the prewar number.

Despite these agreements, rank-and-file union members staged illegal, "wildcat" strikes beginning in 1942. The most dramatic, a walkout of more than half a million coal miners in 1943 led by the rambunctious John L. Lewis, withstood the attacks of the government and the press. Roosevelt repeatedly ordered the mines seized, only to find, as Lewis retorted, that coal could not be mined with bayonets. The Democratic majority in Congress passed

the first antistrike bill, giving the president power to penalize strikers, even to draft them. And yet the strikes grew in size and number, involving nearly 13 million workers by war's end — more than in any other four-year period in U.S. history.

THE HOME FRONT

The sudden and dramatic changes in many aspects of American society reinforced major trends ongoing since the New Deal, such as the expansion of federal responsibility and the breakdown of regionalism. They set into motion styles of popular culture that brought people together in new ways. But wartime moods also reinforced an underlying conservatism, a retreat from the most politically far-reaching goals of the New Deal. As President Roosevelt proclaimed in 1942, "Dr. New Deal" had been replaced by "Dr. Win the War." The *economic* goals of the New Deal had in one sense been achieved: the United States had reached full employment and prosperity, although by virtue of military spending. But the *social* objectives for which many New Dealers had worked had all but vanished.

The 1942 elections, unseating many liberal Democrats, further weakened the New Deal coalition. The Republicans gained forty-six new members in the House of Representatives, nine in the Senate. The GOP now firmly opposed all proposals to extend the social programs instituted during the Great Depression. One of the most popular New Deal agencies, the Civilian Conservation Corps, secured funds from Congress, but only to cover its liquidation. In December 1942 the Works Progress Administration, which handled various forms of work relief, was given, in Roosevelt's words, a "wartime furlough"; a few months later Congress granted the agency an "honorable discharge." The major New Deal agencies were dismantled during 1943, never to be reinstated.

Marriage and Family

Despite the uncertainties of wartime, or perhaps because of them, men and women rushed into marriage. The surge in personal income caused by the wartime economic boom meant that many young couples could afford to set up their own households — something their counterparts in the 1930s had not been able to do. For others, the prospect of separation provided the incentive. The U.S. Census Bureau estimated that between 1940 and 1943 a million more people married than would have been expected had there been no war. After dropping a little during the initial stage of military mobilization, the marriage rate skyrocketed, peaking in 1946. The median age for first marriage for women dropped, moreover, to an unprecedented low of 20.3 years.

The circumstances of war placed unusual strains on marriage. Facing months or even years apart from their spouses, wives sometimes struck up casual romances, especially when they suspected their husbands of infidelity abroad. A surprisingly large number of servicemen's wives interviewed by the Women's Bureau revealed plans to divorce their returning men. Even those couples not separated by military service saw their relationships strained. Some husbands could not adjust to their wife's new work outside the home. Earning unusually high wages, many wives gained status in their family, occasionally challenging their husband's customary role as breadwinner. Work outside the home allowed wives to enlarge their circle of friends and to become less reliant on their husband for financial support and companionship. In 1946 the number of divorces set a new record.

Students at Officers' Training School at Northwestern University, who were not allowed to marry until they were commissioned as ensigns, apply for marriage licenses in Chicago, August 20, 1943, shortly before graduation. These young couples helped the marriage rate skyrocket during World War II.

The war also complicated household affairs. Housing shortages were acute and rents high, and families often doubled up. So scarce were apartments that taxi drivers became, for an extra fee, guides to up-to-the-minute vacancies. Able to set their own standards, landlords frequently discriminated against families with children and even more so against racial minorities. Supplying a household was scarcely less difficult. Although retailers extended hours into the evening and weekends, shopping had to be squeezed in between long hours in industry. Extra planning was necessary for purchasing government-rationed supplies of meat, flour, sugar, milk, and gasoline. Many women found it nearly impossible to manage both a demanding job and a household; this dual responsibility contributed to high turnover and absentee rates in factories. According to a 1943 survey, 40 percent of all women who left war plants did so for marital or household reasons rather than because of unsatisfactory wages or working conditions.

The care of small children proved a major problem. Husbands and wives often lived apart for the duration, leaving childcare in the hands of only one parent. But even when parents stayed together, both adults often worked long hours, sometimes on different shifts; little time was left for the family. Although the War Manpower Commission estimated that as many as 2 million children needed some form of day-care assistance, federally funded childcare centers served less than 10 percent of defense workers' children. Polls indicated that the majority of mothers would in any case refuse to send their youngsters to a public childcare center. In some areas, industries and municipal governments established limited facilities, but these could not keep up with the rapid increase in the number of "latchkey" children.

Juvenile delinquency became a major issue during the war. With employers often relaxing minimum age requirements for employment, many teenagers quit school for the high wages of factory jobs. Runaways drifted from city to city, finding temporary work at wartime plants or at military installations. Gangs formed in many areas, leading to automobile thefts for joy rides, brawling, or prostitution. Overall, however, with so many young men either employed or serving in the armed forces, the statistics for male juvenile crime indicated a decline. By contrast, complaints against girls, mainly for sexual offenses or for running away from home, increased significantly. In response, local officials created various youth agencies and changed them with developing more recreational and welfare programs.

In 1944 the U.S. Office of Education and the Children's Bureau inaugurated a back-to-school campaign. Local school boards appealed to employers to hire only older workers, and toward the war's end the dropout rate increased at a slower rate than during the years of mobilization. The public schools, meanwhile, expanded their curriculum to include information on nutrition, hygiene, first aid, and the political context of the war. Although many teachers had quit to take better-paying jobs in industry, those who remained often organized community salvage efforts, war bond drives, and letter-writing campaigns.

African Americans and Civil Rights

Throughout the war, African American activists conducted a "Double V" campaign, mobilizing not only for an Allied victory but for their own rights as citizens. "The army is about to take me to fight for democracy," one Detroit resident said, "but I would as leave fight for democracy right here." Black militants demanded, at a minimum, fair housing and equal employment opportunities. President Roosevelt responded only lukewarmly to these demands, supporting civil rights advances that did not, in his opinion, disrupt the war effort.

Before the United States entered the war, A. Philip Randolph, president of both the Brotherhood of Sleeping Car Porters and National Negro Congress, had organized the March on Washington movement. At a planning meeting in Chicago a black woman had proposed sending African Americans to Washington, D.C., "from all over the country, in jalopies, in trains, and any way they can get there until we get some action from the White House." At local rallies across the nation African Americans affirmed their determination to stage a "great rally" of no less than 100,000 people at the Lincoln Memorial. Eager to curtail the movement, President Roosevelt responded in June 1941 with Executive Order 8802, banning discrimination in defense industries and government and setting up the Fair Employment Practices Committee to enforce this policy. Randolph called off the march but did not disband his all-black March on Washington organization. He remained determined to "shake up white America."

New civil rights organizations formed during wartime to fight discrimination and especially Jim Crow practices, including segregation in the U.S. armed forces. The interracial Congress of Racial Equality (CORE), formed by pacifists in 1942, staged a sit-in at a Chicago restaurant that refused to serve African Americans. In several cities, including Detroit and Denver, CORE introduced nonviolent direct action as a means to end racial segregation in public facilities. Membership in the NAACP, which took a strong stand against discrimination in the military, grew from 50,000 in 1940 to 450,000 in 1946.

The struggle for equality took shape within local communities. Approximately 1.2 million African Americans left the rural South to take jobs in wartime industries. They encountered not only serious housing shortages but the determination of whites to keep them out of the best jobs and neighborhoods. New, integrated apartment projects, approved by the United States Housing Authority to meet the huge demand for housing, had generated controversy from the earliest planning stages. In February 1942, when twenty black families attempted to move into a new Detroit project built in a white neighborhood, a rampaging mob of 700 armed whites halted the moving vans. The police broke up the riot by arresting young blacks. Finally, two months later, 1,000 state troopers supervised the move of these families into the Sojourner Truth Homes, named after the famous abolitionist and former slave.

Racial violence reached its wartime peak during the summer of 1943, when 274 conflicts broke out in nearly fifty cities. In Detroit, a major center of wartime production, twenty-five blacks and nine whites were killed and hundreds more injured. After the riot one writer reported: "I thought that I had witnessed an experience peculiar to the Deep South. On the streets of Detroit I saw again the same horrible exhibition of uninhibited hate as they fought and killed one another — white against black — in a frenzy of homicidal mania, without rhyme or reason." Poet Langston Hughes, who supported U.S. involvement in the war, wrote:

Looky here, America
What you done done —
Let things drift
Until the riots come

— — —

Yet you say we're fightin
For democracy.
Then why don't democracy
Include me?

I ask you this question
Cause I want to know
How long I got to fight
BOTH HITLER — AND JIM CROW?

Other civil rights groups, such as the National Congress of American Indians, also organized during the war. Poet and educator Pauli Murray summed up the situation in a letter to President Roosevelt: "It is my conviction . . . that the problem of race, intensified by economic conflict and war nerves . . . will eventually . . . occupy a dominant position as a national domestic problem." Her words proved prescient.

The Internment of Japanese Americans

The government placed relatively few restrictions on the activities of enemy aliens, and Americans of Italian or German descent experienced little hostility from fellow citizens. The major exception was Japanese Americans. As early as December 8, 1941, the government froze the financial assets of the Issei (first-generation immigrants) and began to identify individuals suspected of loyalty to Japan. Politicians, patriotic organizations, and military officials, meanwhile, called for the removal of Japanese Americans from the West Coast, which was considered a vulnerable military area. Although a State Department intelligence report certified their loyalty, Japanese Americans, who constituted only .1 percent of the population, were nevertheless singled out for legal sanctions.

Charges of sedition masked long-standing racial attitudes. The press began to use the word *Jap* in headlines, while political cartoonists employed blatant racial stereotypes, reviving the "yellow peril" of earlier years. Popular songs appeared with titles like "You're a Sap, Mister Jap, to Make a Yankee Cranky." The head of the Western Defense Command, General John L. DeWitt, argued for relocation on the grounds that the Japanese constituted an "enemy race," no matter how many generations had apparently been "Americanized." An army report suggested, with twisted logic, "the very fact that no sabotage has taken place to date is a disturbing and confirming indication that action will be taken."

On February 19, 1942, President Roosevelt signed Executive Order 9066, suspending the civil rights of Japanese Americans and authorizing the removal to concentration camps of 120,000 men, women, and children from the Pacific states and southern Arizona. The government largely confiscated their personal property. Of those interned in the "relocation centers," two-thirds were Nisei (second-generation immigrants), citizens born in this country.

During the spring of 1942, families received one week's notice to close up their businesses and homes before being transported to one of the ten internment camps managed by the War Relocation Authority. The camps were located as far away as Arkansas, although the majority had been set up in

Government authorities move Japanese American families into one of ten inland internment camps in 1942. Deprived of their property and jobs and treated as potential enemies, about 120,000 Japanese Americans were incarcerated during World War II, some up to four years. Beginning in January 1945, they were allowed to return to the Pacific Coast.

desolate, arid districts of Utah, Colorado, Idaho, Arizona, Wyoming, and California. Karl G. Yoneda described his quarters at Manzanar in eastern California:

> There were no lights, stoves, or window panes. My two cousins and I, together with seven others, were crowded into a 25 × 30 foot room. We slept on army cots with our clothes on. The next morning we discovered that there were no toilets or washrooms. . . . We saw GIs manning machine guns in the watchtowers. The barbed wire fence which surrounded the camp was visible against the background of the snow-covered Sierra mountain range. "So this is the American-style concentration camp," someone remarked.

The Japanese American Citizens League charged that "racial animosity" rather than military necessity had dictated the policy of internment. Despite protests by the American Civil Liberties Union and several church groups against the abridgment of Japanese Americans' rights, the Supreme Court in *Korematsu v. U.S.* (1944), upheld the constitutionality of the relocation on the grounds of national security. By this time a program of gradual release was in place. Nevertheless, nearly 6,000 Nisei renounced their American citizenship. Japanese Americans had lost homes and businesses valued at $500 million in what many historians judge the worst violation of civil liberties in the United States during the war. Not until 1988 did the U.S. Congress vote reparations of $20,000 and public apologies to each of the 60,000 surviving victims.

V For Victory

Despite the massive influx of civilians into defense industries, World War II remained a foreign war for those Americans who stayed at home. Food shortages, long hours in the factories, and even missed loved ones did not diminish the significance of full employment and prosperity. For four years, Americans shaped their domestic culture around both patriotism and expectations of postwar abundance. The government thus sold war bonds to encourage "systematic savings" for postwar purchases as well as to "put bullets in the bellies of Hitler's hordes." Even during the war, Americans spent freely at vacation resorts, country clubs, racetracks, night-clubs, dance halls, and movie theaters. Sales of books skyrocketed, and spectator sports attracted huge audiences.

Popular culture, especially music, flourished during the war. For the first time, transplanted poor southerners, black and white, had money to spend on live music as well as on records. They also brought to northern cities musical styles to which they rapidly applied electronic amplification. "They'd made them steel guitars cry and whine," Ray Charles testified, "and it really attracted me." Played on jukeboxes in bars, bus stations, and cafes, country and rhythm-and-blues musics not only won over new audiences but also inspired musicians to adopt and interweave new styles. The International Sweethearts of Rhythm, an ethnically and racially diverse band, started playing in the Mississippi Delta but soon was pleasing audiences throughout the United States.

Many songs featured war themes. Irving Berlin's "White Christmas," the era's best-known tune, created a lyrical nostalgia of past celebrations with family and friends close by. The equally plaintive "A Rainbow at Midnight" by country singer Ernest Tubb expressed the hope of a "dogface" common soldier looking beyond the misery and horror of war to a brighter tomorrow. "Till Then," recorded by the harmonious black quartet the Mills Brothers, similarly offered the prospect of a romantic reunion when "the world will be free." On the lighter side, novelty artist Spike Jones made his name with the "razz," or "Bronx cheer," in "We're Going to Ffft in the Fuehrer's Face."

Hollywood artists, meanwhile, threw themselves into a perpetual round of fundraising or morale-boosting public events. Movie stars called on fans to buy war bonds and to support the troops. Numerous "war movies" made heroes of ordinary soldiers, often depicting GIs of different racial and ethnic backgrounds coming together in common cause. Movies with anti-Fascist themes, such as *Tender Comrade,* promoted friendship among Russians and Americans, while films like *Since You Went Away* portrayed the loyalty and resilience of families with servicemen stationed overseas.

The wartime spirit infected even the predominantly children's field of comic books. The nickel "books" featured superheroes such as the Flash, Hawkman, Green Lantern, Captain Marvel, and the more humorous Plastic Man, all of whom fought Axis villains. The most innovative series featured Wonder Woman, who shed her civilian clothes for a caped costume both to rescue the hapless army major Steve Trevor and to combat fascism.

The lines among propaganda, news, and entertainment blurred. The Office of War Information, established in June 1942, coordinated efforts among various federal agencies, the press, radio networks, and motion picture studios "to facilitate an understanding in the United States and abroad of the progress of the war effort and the policies, activities, and aims of the Government." Even Bugs Bunny put on a uniform and fought funny- or sinister-looking enemies. Film director Frank Capra, best remembered for his sentimental hit *It's a Wonderful Life,* created documentaries celebrating American democracy, such as the highly acclaimed *Why We Fight* and *The Negro Soldier.*

LAST STAGES OF THE WAR

From Pearl Harbor until mid-1943, foreign affairs were dominated by military strategy rather than long-term planning. But once the defeat of the Axis powers appeared in sight, high government officials began to reconsider their diplomatic objectives. President Roosevelt, who had focused on domestic problems during the Great Depression, worked with his long-time secretary of state Cordell Hull to map a new foreign policy. Roosevelt and Hull knew that they could not succeed without the cooperation of the other key leaders, Stalin and Churchill.

During 1943 and 1944 the "Big Three" — the United States, the Soviet Union, and Great Britain — met to hammer out the shape of the postwar world. Although none of these nations expected to reach a final agreement, neither did they anticipate the speed and enormity of global events still to come. It soon became clear that only the mission of destroying the Axis held the Allies together.

Revising the Atlantic Charter

In issuing the Atlantic Charter in 1941, Allied leaders outlined noble objectives for the world after the defeat of fascism. But the charter's high-sounding goals — national self-determination, no territorial aggrandizement, free access of all peoples to economic opportunities, freedom of the seas, disarmament, and "freedom from want and fear" — did not include a mandate for action. In January 1943,

Roosevelt again promised "a decent peace and a durable peace" but did not clarify what he meant.

By the fall of 1944 Roosevelt — now weak from heart trouble and exhaustion — realized that neither Great Britain nor the Soviet Union ever intended to abide by those principles of the Atlantic Charter that conflicted with its economic interests in other nations or in colonial territories. In October, Stalin and Churchill struck an agreement projecting their respective "spheres of influence" over the future central Europe. Only the disposition of Poland remained unresolved.

In February 1945 at Yalta, a Crimean resort on the Black Sea, Roosevelt held his last meeting with Churchill and Stalin. The president believed that prospects for postwar peace depended not only on cooperation but on compromise. Although diplomats avoided using the term *sphere of influence,* that principle guided all negotiations. Neither the United States nor Great Britain did more than protest the Soviet occupation of much of eastern Europe. In return, Stalin pledged to declare war on Japan. Stalin also approved plans for a future world organization, which Roosevelt strongly advocated. The Yalta agreements seemed to seal the arrangements by which the postwar world would be governed. Roosevelt announced to Congress that Yalta had been a "great success," while privately admitting that the Atlantic Charter had been nothing more than "a beautiful idea."

The death of Franklin Roosevelt of a stroke on April 12, 1945, cast a dark shadow over hopes for long-term, peaceful solutions to global problems. Stung by the Republican congressional comeback in 1942, Roosevelt had rebounded despite his failing health with an overwhelming electoral college victory (432 to 99) in 1944 against Republican New York governor Thomas E. Dewey. Loyal Democrats had linked their hopes for peace to Roosevelt's leadership. But now, as new and still greater challenges were appearing, the nation's great pragmatic idealist was gone.

The Holocaust

The European catastrophe — measured above all in the Nazi program of systematic extermination of Jews, Gypsies, homosexuals, and others of "inferior" races — brought into question the capacity of Americans ever to move past the terms of the war. The incredible inhumanity of the African slave trade and the decimation of Indian tribes had seemed to most Americans part of a receding past, a shameful but inevitable consequence of national development. Events in Germany, reputedly the most cultured and modern nation of Europe, showed that

Belsen Camp: The Compound for Women was painted by American artist Leslie Cole. This scene depicts the women's compound at Belsen as the Allied troops found it when they invaded Germany in 1945.

annihilistic hatred belonged to the present as well as the past.

Reports of Nazi death camps attracted surprisingly little attention when they first appeared in 1943. Liberal magazines such as *The Nation* and small committees of intellectuals pressed for more information, but important daily papers and major weeklies like the *New York Times* and *Time* magazine treated the reports as minor news items. As late as 1943, only 43 percent of Americans polled believed that Hitler had systematically murdered millions of Jews. An earlier generation of journalists had helped produce the climate of skepticism by reporting (or accepting from government sources) stories of German atrocity during World War I that proved in most cases to have been fabricated by the British.

Under the world's unbelieving eyes, Hitler had supported a plan for "a final solution to the Jewish question" and personally approved the construction of five extermination centers in central Europe. From the early 1940s, but with accelerating speed in 1943 and 1944, millions of people from Germany, Poland, Hungary, France, Lithuania, Romania, and Czechoslovakia died in these camps. Suspected by Americans but underreported for years, the Nazi extermination stands as the world's preeminent war crime.

When Jewish refugees pleaded for a military strike against the rail lines leading to the notorious Auschwitz camp in Poland, the War Department responded that it was "not contemplated that units of the armed forces will be employed for the purpose of rescuing victims of enemy oppression unless such rescues are the direct result of military operations conducted with the objective of defeating the armed forces of the enemy." In short, the government viewed civilian rescue as a diversion of precious resources. Roosevelt maintained that a speedy and total Allied victory would serve as the best means to rescue European Jews. Finally, in January 1944, Roosevelt signed an executive order that created the War Refugee Board, which set up refugee camps in Italy and North Africa.

Survivors of the death camps were discovered by Allied troops as they invaded Germany and liberated Poland. Nearly starved, they related the most horrible stories of inhumanity since the African slave trade centuries earlier. Perhaps 6 million Jews (a number since hotly debated, but considered by many experts as slightly high), one-quarter million Gypsies, and 60,000 homosexuals, among others, had perished.

The Bomb

The death of Roosevelt in April 1945 exposed the fragile foundations of the Big Three's Grand Alliance. Roosevelt's successor, Harry S. Truman, by background and training a Kansas City machine politician, Missouri judge, and U.S. senator, lacked diplomatic experience as well as the late president's personal finesse. Above all, he had no intention of making concessions to the war-devastated Russians. Within hours of becoming president, Truman said to his secretary of state, "We must stand up to the Russians at this point and not be easy with them."

In this light, negotiations at the Potsdam Conference, held just outside Berlin from July 17 to August 2, 1945, lacked the spirited cooperation characteristic of Roosevelt's leadership. The U.S. and Soviet delegations divided sharply over the postwar boundary between Poland and Germany as well as the question of reparations. Truman was determined to help Germany revive as a stabilizing factor in Europe and an ally against the Soviet Union, and he resisted the USSR's appeal for international controls guaranteeing a nonaggressive future for Germany. The final wartime meeting of the Big Three ensured a divided Germany and, in effect, a divided postwar Europe.

During the Potsdam meetings, Truman first learned about the successful test of an atomic bomb in New Mexico. Until this time, the United States had been seeking from the Soviet Union a declaration of war against Japan as a means to avoid a costly U.S. land invasion. But once Secretary of State Stimson received the cable reading "Babies satisfactorily born," U.S. diplomats concluded they no longer needed assistance from the Soviet Union to bring the war to an end.

Having broken Japan's secret diplomatic code before Pearl Harbor, Americans now learned that the emperor was prepared to end the fighting if the Allies would set aside the stipulation of unconditional surrender. At first, Truman considered accepting a slight modification of that policy, such as allowing the emperor to continue to occupy his traditional position as head of the Japanese nation. But he also went ahead with plans for using the bomb. As Truman later stated, the three bombs on hand had been developed specifically to be used, and he had no moral reservation about using them. Although some scientists proposed that one bomb be dropped upon a deserted island in order to threaten Japan, Truman had no intention of merely

On August 6, 1945, a U.S. B-29 fighter plane dropped "Little Boy," an atomic bomb, on Hiroshima, killing nearly 80,000 Japanese civilians and injuring another 70,000. Three days later, "Fat Man" destroyed Nagasaki, killing 40,000 and injuring 60,000 more. On August 14, the government of Japan surrendered, bringing an end to the war.

demonstrating destructive force as bargaining leverage.

From a purely scientific standpoint, the atomic experiments represented a remarkable breakthrough in physics. Reports about the production of atomic fission from uranium written by famed mathematician Albert Einstein — who regarded the development of atomic warfare as a perversion of his life's efforts — alerted the U.S. government to potential military uses. Top scientists working at the University of Chicago produced a small-scale atomic chain reaction in December 1942. Over the next three years, scientists involved in the Manhattan Project spent more than $2 billion in federal money in laboratories hidden in Tennessee, New Mexico, and elsewhere to create a vast chain reaction. Near Los Alamos, New Mexico, on July 16, 1945, they succeeded, and the first mushroom cloud formed above an explosion of unprecedented glare and destructiveness.

The American military command rapidly prepared the weapon for use, and Japan was offered only one last chance to surrender unconditionally.

Japanese officials wired their refusal on August 3, 1945. Three days later, the B-29 bomber *Enola Gay* changed the world. The bomb it dropped destroyed the Japanese city of Hiroshima, killing nearly 80,000 people. "I was greatly moved," Truman reported when he heard the news.

An editorialist wrote in the Japanese *Nippon Times,* "This is not war, this is not even murder; this is pure nihilism . . . a crime against God which strikes at the very basis of moral existence." In the United States, several leading religious publications mirrored this view. The *Christian Century* interpreted the use of the bomb as a "moral earthquake" that made the long-denounced use of poison gas by Germany in World War I utterly insignificant by comparison, and that defied any justification for the use of "forbidden" weapons.

Most Americans learned about the atomic bomb for the first time on August 7, when the news media reported the rampant destruction and death in Hiroshima. The surrender of the Japanese on August 14, after the dropping of the second bomb, on Nagasaki, was such welcome news that any implications other than those of military triumph dimmed.

The use of the bomb had many benefits for U.S. diplomacy. Although Truman recorded in his memoirs, written much later, that the decision to bomb Japan rested on the expectation of saving "a half a million American lives" in ground combat, no such official estimate existed. A recently declassified intelligence document of April 30, 1946, concluded that "the dropping of the bomb was the pretext seized upon by all leaders as the reason for ending the war, but [even if the bomb had not been used] the Japanese would have capitulated upon the entry of Russia into the war." The decision to use nuclear force reflected the belief that the bomb would bring a speedy end to the war and help determine the grounds for peace. Although State Department officials realized that the American atomic monopoly could not last, they hoped that in the meantime the United States could erect the structure of a new world order.

CONCLUSION

New weapons, such as massive air raids and the atomic bomb, had made warfare incomparably more deadly to both military and civilian popula-tions. Between 40 and 50 million people died in World War II — four times the number of deaths in World War I — and half the casualties were women and children. The American death toll exceeded 405,000, the number of wounded 670,000. Slight compared with the losses suffered by other Allied nations — over 20 million Russians died during the war — the human cost of World War II for Americans still was second only to that of the Civil War.

Coming at the end of two decades of resolutions to avoid military entanglements, the war pushed the nation's leaders to the center of global politics and into risky military and political alliances that would not outlive the war. The United States would emerge the strongest nation in the world, but it was a world where the prospects for lasting peace appeared increasingly remote.

If World War II raised the nation's international commitments to a new height, the impact on its citizens was not so easy to gauge. Many new communities formed as Americans migrated in mass numbers to regions booming in the wartime economy. Enjoying a rare moment of full-employment, many workers new to well-paying industrial jobs anticipated further advances against discrimination. Exuberant at the Allies' victory over Fascism and the return of the troops, the majority looked optimistically ahead.

CHRONOLOGY

1931	Japan occupies Manchuria
1933	Hitler seizes power in Germany U.S. recognizes USSR Japan quits League of Nations
1935	Italy invades Ethiopia
1935–37	Neutrality Acts
1937	Japan invades China *Panay* incident Roosevelt's quarantine speech
1938	Hitler and Chamberlain meet at Munich
1939	Germany annexes remainder of Czechoslovakia Nazi-Soviet Pact Germany invades Poland; World War II begins
1940	Soviet Union invades Finland Germany, Italy, and Japan form Axis powers America First Committee formed Selective Service and Training Act passed Franklin Roosevelt elected to unprecedented third term
1941	Lend-Lease Act A. Philip Randolph organizes March on Washington movement Fair Employment Practices Committee formed Germany invades Soviet Union Atlantic Charter Japanese attack Pearl Harbor; U.S. declares war on Japan, Italy, and Germany
1942	Internment of Japanese Americans National War Labor Board, War Production Board, and Supply Priorities and Allocation Board established Manhattan Project begun Battles of Coral Sea and Midway in Pacific U.S. invades Egypt; Operation Torch begins in North Africa
1943	Soviet victory over Germans at Stalingrad German Afrika Korps troops surrender in Tunisia Coal miners strike Summer of race riots Allied invasion of Italy Casablanca conference
1944	Operation Overlord and liberation of Paris Roosevelt elected to fourth term
1945	Yalta Conference renews American-Soviet alliance; Roosevelt dies in office; Harry Truman becomes president Germany surrenders Decisive Pacific battles; U.S. captures Iwo Jima and Okinawa Potsdam Conference U.S. bombing of Hiroshima and Nagasaki; Japan surrenders

Additional Readings

STEPHEN E. AMBROSE, *The Supreme Commander: The War Years of General Dwight D. Eisenhower* (1970). A popular account of the future president as military coordinator. Analyzes Eisenhower himself and the key decisions he made in coordinating the Allied forces and establishing a framework for world peace.

ALLAN BERUBE, *Coming Out under Fire: The History of Gay Men and Women in World War Two* (1991). A study of government policy toward homosexuals during the war and the formation of a gay community in the military. Offers many insights into the new opportunities offered homosexuals through travel and varied companionship, and the effects of sanctions against them.

JOHN MORTON BLUM, *V Was for Victory: Politics and American Culture during World War II* (1976). A colorful narration of American society and culture during wartime. Seeks to re-create the patriotic spirit that quelled potential conflict among diverse groups.

PAUL BOYER, *By the Bomb's Early Light: American Thought and Culture at the Dawn of the Atomic Age* (1985). An analysis of the intellectual and cultural assumptions underlying the development of atomic weaponry. Examines the development in President Truman and others of a political logic that made use of atomic weapons against the Japanese inevitable.

WAYNE S. COLE, *Roosevelt and the Isolationists, 1932–45* (1983). Shows the president and his critics sparring over foreign policy. Analyzes the complexities of liberal/conservative divisions over the war and offers insights into the logic of conservatives who feared the growth of a permanent bureaucratic, militarized state.

RICHARD M. DALFIUME, *Desegregation of the U.S. Armed Forces: Fighting on Two Fronts, 1939–1953* (1969). Analyzes wartime race relations in the military. By examining both the official mechanisms for ending discrimination in the armed forces and the patterns of racism that remained, Dalfiume reveals how changing attitudes from the top ran up against old assumptions among enlisted men and women.

ROGER DANIELS, *Concentration Camps USA: Japanese Americans and World War II* (1981). Perhaps the best account of Japanese American internment. Details the government internment programs, the experiences of detention and camp life, and the many long-run consequences of lost liberty.

SHERNA BERGER GLUCK, *Rosie the Riveter Revisited: Women, the War, and Social Change* (1987). An oral history–based study of women workers during World War II. The subjects reveal the diverse experiences and attitudes of women workers, but also their common feelings of accomplishment.

AKIRA IRIYE, *Power and Culture: The Japanese-American War, 1941–1945* (1981). Depicts the Pacific War from U.S. and Japanese perspectives. By showing the logic of both sides and analyzing a war rarely understood by the public, Iriye clarifies the military and political differences between the contesting powers.

RICHARD POLENBERG, *War and Society: The United States, 1941–1945* (1972). An overview of the home front. A useful survey of many issues, from government labor policies to cramped consumerism to domestic political controversies.

GORDON WRIGHT, *The Ordeal of Total War, 1939–1945* (1968). A standard account of the military mobilization. Gives a sense of the battles behind the war, the creation of firepower and supplies, and the vast casualties of actual warfare.

DAVID S. WYMAN, *The Abandonment of the Jews: America and the Holocaust, 1941–1945* (1984). A detailed examination of U.S. immigration policy and the American response to Hitler's program of genocide. Shows both the indifference of the Roosevelt administration to appeals for Allied protection of Jews, and the inclinations of leading American Jewish organizations to stress the future formation of a Jewish state above the protection of European Jewry.

Hasten the Homecoming

BUY VICTORY BONDS

In 1949 the Harvard Crimson, an undergraduate newspaper, discovered that the administration of Yale University was actively cooperating with FBI agents in spying on students and faculty. On May 25, the Crimson reported "eight or so agents" on campus who "wander in and out of Provost Edgar S. Furniss's office every day," and "several undercover agents and general informants" undermining freedom of expression. Untenured professors, the newspaper commented, worried that even speaking at public meetings might cost them their jobs. Candidates for unfilled positions never learned that their credentials had been screened by the FBI.

Students at many universities complained that FBI agents had infiltrated political, educational, and cultural groups—from folk music societies to civil rights organizations—and intimidated members by bringing them in for questioning by university security officials. Administrators also encouraged students to inform on their friends or roommates, an action that could result in the loss of scholarships and ruin future prospects.

STUDENTS AND FACULTY
FACE THE COLD WAR

What had provoked this near hysteria? Only the prospect of mutual destruction prevented the diplomatic conflict between the United States and the Soviet Union, the world's two most powerful nations, from developing into another world war. Instead of peace, a pattern of Cold War—icy relations between the two nations—prevailed. Uneasy allies during World War II, the United States and the Soviet Union now viewed each other as archenemies, and nearly all other nations lined up on one side or the other. Within the United States, the Cold War demanded pledges of absolute loyalty from citizens in every institution, from the university to trade unions and from the mass media to government itself.

If not for the outbreak of the Cold War, campuses would have experienced the most fruitful era in the history of higher education. The Servicemen's Readjustment Act, popularly known as the GI Bill of Rights, passed by Congress in 1944, offered stipends covering tuition and living expenses to veterans attending vocational schools or college. By the 1947–48 academic year, the federal government was subsidizing nearly half of all male college students. Many colleges doubled previous enrollments, and the student bodies of major univer-

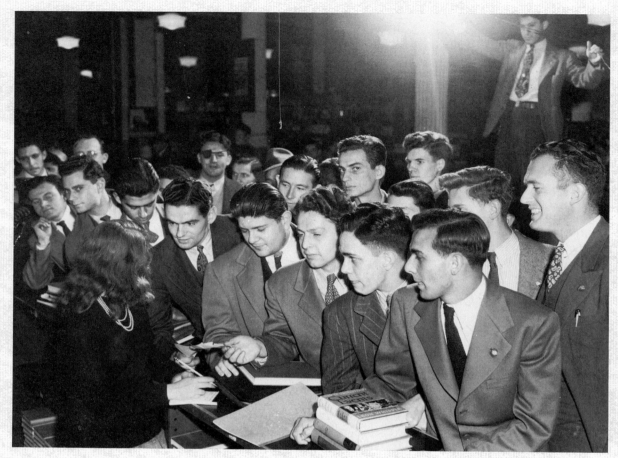

World War II veterans took advantage of the new entitlements furnished by the G.I. Bill of Rights passed in 1944. Using their benefits — up to $500 per academic year — to pay for college tuition and to purchase supplies, these former soldiers, all white and male, prepared themselves for upward mobility.

sities increased by as much as 75 percent. Between 1945 and 1950, 2.3 million students benefited from the GI Bill, at a cost of more than $10 billion. State legislatures and monied alumni likewise contributed large sums, allowing colleges and universities to construct new buildings for classrooms and dormitories and to hire droves of new instructors.

Even more impressive than the sheer numbers of students, teachers, and new buildings was the change of atmosphere. Veterans adapted quickly, transforming the campus from "the preserve of the relatively rich," as one university president described the prewar college, to the mecca of the average American who sincerely wanted a college education.

According to many observers, the spirit of community flourished among these war-weary undergraduates. One student at the University of Wisconsin recalled that "the majority of postwar GIs going to school were knowledgeable in the ways of the world and highly motivated." Often the first in their families to attend college, they studied hard. But they also joined other students in reform campaigns to improve the campus. Married, often fathers of young children, they expected university administrators to treat them as adults. They wanted less supervision of undergraduate social life, more affordable housing, and better cultural opportunities. On some campuses, film societies and student-run cooperatives vied with fraternities and sororities as centers of undergraduate social activity.

The Cold War put a damper on these community-building efforts. FBI director J. Edgar Hoover testified that the college campuses were centers of "red propaganda," full of teachers "tearing down respect for agencies of government, belittling tradition and moral custom and . . . creating doubts in the validity of the American way of life." Conservatives estimated there might be 3,500 professors alone who were outright Communists, "dupes," or espionage agents, and a Senate investigator totaled "more than 26,000 times" that these individuals had supposedly affiliated with a communistic organization. Due to communistic teachers and "communist-line textbooks," a senator lamented, thousands of parents sent "their sons and daughters to college as good Americans," only to see them return home "four years later as wild-eyed radicals."

These wild charges were never substantiated, and most complaints against "communistic" teachers and books turned out to old-fashioned outrage at racial integration, secularism, and iconoclasm. Conservatives who had long regarded the campus as a center of homosexuality and atheism leaped at the opportunity presented by the Cold War to take revenge on their enemies. Colorado, Texas, Pennsylvania, California, and other states enacted or revived "loyalty acts," by which those who refused to swear in writing their loyalty to the United States and their nonmembership in allegedly subversive organizations would be fired as teachers or released from scholarships. Approximately 200 faculty members were dismissed outright and many others denied tenure. Thousands simply left school, dropped out of organizations, or changed friends after "visits" from FBI agents or interviews with administrators. The main effect on campus was the restraint of free speech generally and fear of criticizing U.S. racial, military, or diplomatic policies in particular.

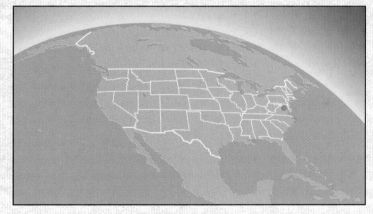

This gloomy mood seemed eons away from the raw optimism of only a few years earlier. (Victory over Japan) V–J Day had erupted into a two-day national holiday of wild celebrations, complete with ticker-tape parades, spontaneous dancing, and kisses for returned GIs. Americans, living in the richest and most powerful nation in the world, finally seemed to have gained the peace they had fought and sacrificed to win. But peace proved fragile and elusive.

GLOBAL INSECURITIES AT WAR'S END

The war that had engulfed the world from 1939 to 1945 created an international interdependence that no country could ignore. The legendary African American folk singer Leadbelly (Huddie Ledbetter) added a fresh lyric to an old spiritual melody: "We're in the same boat, brother. . . . And if you shake one end you're going to rock the other." Never before, not even at the end of World War I, had hopes risen so strong for a genuine "community of nations." But most Americans also recognized, a 1945 opinion poll revealed, that prospects for a durable peace rested on harmony among the Allies, especially between the Soviet Union and the United States.

Diplomatic conflict between these two competitors for world leadership had been the rule since the Russian Revolution of 1917. The threat of fascism had merely placed this conflict on hold. Each called for a retreat, if not an eradication, of the other's political system. Divergent interests and combative national leaders made a continued U.S.-Soviet alliance impossible, and almost destroyed prospects for a stable world order.

The "American Century"

In 1941 Henry Luce, publisher of *Time, Life,* and *Fortune* magazines, had forecast the dawn of the "American Century." Americans must, he wrote, "accept wholeheartedly our duty and our opportunity as the most powerful and vital nation in the world and in consequence to assert upon the world the full impact of our influence, for such means as we see fit." This bold pronouncement reflected the prevailing faith that, with the rest of the world in ruins, *only* American prestige and know-how could establish the principles of world order.

Americans had good reason to be confident about their prospects for setting the terms of peace. Compared with Great Britain and France, reduced to second-rate powers too weak to hold their once vast empires, the United States had not only escaped the ravishes of military conflict but had actually prospered. Between 1940 and 1944 industrial production rose by 90 percent, agricultural output by 20 percent. By June 1945 the capital assets of manufacturing had increased 65 percent over prewar levels, largely because of government subsidies, and was equal in value to approximately half the entire world's goods and services.

And yet the foundation of this vigorous economy appeared fragile. Above all, Americans feared the return of widespread unemployment. Memories of the Great Depression were still fresh, and many older Americans could recall the steep economic downturn that had followed World War I. Economists understood that it was the massive government spending associated with wartime industry, rather than New Deal programs, that had ended the nightmare of the 1930s. A great question loomed: What would happen when wartime production slowed and millions of troops returned home?

"We need markets — big markets — in which to buy and sell," answered Assistant Secretary of State for Economic Affairs Will Clayton. Just to maintain the current level of growth, the United States needed an estimated $14 billion in exports — an unprecedented amount. Many business leaders even looked to the Soviet Union as a potential trading partner. The president of the U.S. Chamber of Commerce testified that the USSR could become, "if not our biggest, at least our most eager consumer." With this prospect vanishing, Eastern European markets threatened, and large chunks of former colonial territories closed off, U.S. business and government leaders determined to secure Europe for American trade and investment.

During the final stages of the war, Roosevelt's advisers laid plans to secure U.S. primacy in the postwar global economy. In July 1944 representatives from forty-four Allied nations met at Bretton Woods, New Hampshire, and established the International Bank for Reconstruction and Development (World Bank) and the International Monetary Fund (IMF) to facilitate the rebuilding of war-torn Europe and to assist the nations of Asia, Latin America, and Africa. By centralizing world finances and ensuring open markets, the IMF would deter currency conflicts and trade wars — two maladies of the 1930s that were largely responsible for the political instability and national rivalries leading to World War II. The IMF was also seen as a means of foreclosing on any rivals to U.S. economic leadership.

As the principal supplier of funds for the IMF and the World Bank — over $7 billion to each — the United States could unilaterally shape the world economy by determining the allocation of loans. Its representatives could withhold funds from those nations that threatened to nationalize industry, for instance, while generously rewarding those that opened themselves to American investments. Foreign currencies were pegged to the U.S. dollar, a monetary policy that further enhanced the power of American bankers.

The Soviet Union interpreted the "American Century," and especially its aggressive economic programs, as a return to the policy that had guided international affairs since the Russian Revolution: U.S. determination to destroy communism. For this reason, the USSR simply refused to join either the World Bank or the IMF, regarding them as a concerted endeavor by the United States to remake the world in its own capitalist image. By spurning these financial institutions, the Soviet Union cut off the possibility of aid to its own people as well as to its Eastern European client states. Equally important, the USSR isolated itself economically.

Hopes for Collective Security

A thin hope remained amid the gloom of disunity. A month after the conference at Bretton Woods, Allied leaders met to lay plans for a system of collective security, the United Nations. The dream of international cooperation had been seeded earlier by President Roosevelt. Had Americans agreed to join the League of Nations — as President Woodrow Wilson had pleaded in 1919 — then perhaps, Roosevelt suggested, the second world war might have been averted. In late summer and fall 1944 at the Dumbarton Oaks Estate near Washington, D.C., and again in April 1945 in San Francisco, the Allies worked to shape the United Nations as an international agency that would arbitrate disputes among members as well as impede aggressors, by military force if necessary. Opinion polls showed that nearly 80 percent of Americans favored U.S. membership in the UN.

From its inception, the UN was plagued by an inability to act. The organization represented all member nations through its General Assembly, which met for the purpose of debate but not for adjudication. The "primary responsibility for the maintenance of international peace and security" lay exclusively with the Security Council, which comprised five permanent members (the United States, Great Britain, the Soviet Union, France, and Nationalist China) and six temporary members elected for two-year terms. Because each permanent member enjoyed absolute veto power, the Security Council could censure an act of aggression by any such member only if that nation abstained from the vote. This provision limited the UN's ability to carry out its peace-keeping mission.

The UN achieved its greatest success through its humanitarian programs for the victims of world war. Its relief agency provided the war-torn countries of Europe and Asia with billions of dollars for medical supplies, food, and clothing. The UN also dedicated itself to protecting human rights, and its high standards of human dignity owed much to the lobbying of Eleanor Roosevelt; the president's widow served as one of the first delegates from the United States. In December 1948 the UN adopted a document affirming the sacred and inalienable rights of all people.

The prospects for world cooperation appeared brightest when the International Court of Justice tried twenty-four top Nazi officials and found twenty-one of them guilty of "war crimes and atrocities." At the historic Nuremberg trials (1945–46), testimony revealed the ghastly details of organized cruelty, including the "final solution" applied to

Eleanor Roosevelt (1884–1962), along with Secretary of State George Marshall and future Secretary of State John Foster Dulles, listen to Soviet diplomats at a United Nations session in Paris, during 1948. Appointed to the U.N. delegation by President Truman in 1946, the former First Lady chaired the Commission on Human Rights.

Jews, Gypsies, homosexuals, and others. When the accused Nazis repeatedly claimed that they had only followed orders, the panel of judges solemnly declared the Nuremberg Principle: no soldier or civilian could be required, or should obey, an order — whatever its source — that conflicted with basic humanitarian tenets. Put forward by Robert Jackson, associate justice of the U.S. Supreme Court and chief U.S. prosecutor at the trials, this ruling was later affirmed by the United Nations. Tragically, the UN lacked the power and authority to enforce the ethics of war any more than the ideals of human rights.

The Division of Europe

The Atlantic Charter of 1941 had recognized the right of all nations to self-determination and renounced all claims to new territories as the spoils of war. Following a limited period of occupation, the Allies pledged to hold free, democratic elections in those areas taken from the Axis powers and then to relinquish control to the new governments. As polls revealed, however, most Americans were skeptical of this plan. The Allied leaders themselves, moreover, violated the charter's main points before the war had ended, dividing occupied Europe into spheres of influence (see Chapter 25).

So long as Franklin Roosevelt remained alive, this kind of realism in world politics had seemed reconcilable with world peace. Convinced of his ability to maneuver Stalin and the Soviets person to person and situation by situation, the president had balanced his own international idealism with his belief that the United States was entitled to extraordinary influence in Latin America and the Philippines, and that other great powers might have similar privileges or responsibilities elsewhere. "We shall have to take the responsibility for world collaboration," he said in a congressional address, "or we shall have to bear the responsibility for another world conflict."

Roosevelt also recognized the probable diplomatic consequences of the brutal European ground war, fought largely on Soviet territory: the Soviet Union's unnegotiable demand for territorial security along its European border. Russia lay in ruins, with 20 million dead, over 70,000 villages destroyed, and nearly 25 million people homeless; its steel and agricultural production was down to half of prewar levels. Roosevelt believed that by offering economic assistance he might ease Stalin's fears and loosen the Soviet grip on conquered nations. But by the time of the Potsdam Conference in July 1945, the USSR had already consolidated its influence over most of Eastern Europe and the little Baltic states. Only the Yugoslavians and Albanians, who had turned back fascist forces without the Red Army's assistance, could claim nominal independence from the Soviet Union.

Hopes for cooperation further unraveled in central Europe. France, Great Britain, the USSR, and the U.S. had divided Germany temporarily into four occupation zones, each governed by one of the Allied nations. But the Allies could not agree on long-term plans. Having borne the brunt of German aggression, France and the USSR both opposed reunification. The latter, in addition, demanded heavy reparations along with a limit on postwar reindustrialization. Roosevelt appeared to agree with the Soviets. "We have got to be tough with Germany, and I mean the German people not just the Nazis," he concluded. "We . . . have got to treat them in such a manner so they can't just go on reproducing people who want to continue the way they have in the past." But American business leaders, envisioning a new center for U.S. commerce, shared Churchill's hope of rebuilding Germany into a powerful counterforce against the Soviet Union.

The division of Germany forecast the shape of the new world order. West Germany became more and more "American," as the United States directed the reconstruction of its capitalist economy and canceled voters' mandates for government ownership of coal mines and major industries. While guiding liberal politicians into top government positions, U.S. advisers also "rehabilitated" a former Nazi elite that controlled large sectors of business and the civil service. Meanwhile, the Soviets dragged industrial equipment out of impoverished East Germany for their own domestic needs, and imposed a harsh discipline upon the inhabitants. Despite promising to deliver the economy over to German workers, the Soviets took no steps toward democracy in East Germany.

"The main prize of the victory" over the Axis powers was, a State Department document had noted in November 1945, a "limited and temporary power to establish the kind of world we want to live in." This power proved surprisingly elusive. Winston Churchill had himself parleyed with Stalin to establish spheres of influence and had sworn to preserve the British colonial empire. Yet he interpreted the expansion of Soviet control over unwilling Eastern European citizens as a uniquely dangerous sign of the times. In a speech delivered in Fulton, Missouri, in February 1946, he declared that "an iron curtain has descended upon the [European] continent." The dream of a community of nations had dissolved, but

Divided Europe

By the early days of the Cold War, Europe had been divided into opposing military alliances, the North American Treaty Organization (NATO) and the "Warsaw Pact" (Communist Bloc).

perhaps it had never been more than a fantasy contrived to maintain a fragile alliance amid the urgency of World War II.

THE POLICY OF CONTAINMENT

Many Americans believed that Franklin Roosevelt, had he lived, would have been able to stem the tide of tensions between the Soviet Union and the United States. Harry Truman sorely lacked FDR's talent for diplomacy. More comfortable with southern or conservative Democrats than with polished New Deal-

ers, the new president liked to talk tough and act defiantly. He did not hesitate to flaunt the U.S. monopoly of the atomic bomb. Just ten days after he took office, Truman complained that U.S.-Soviet negotiations had been a "one-way street." He vowed to "baby" them no longer, adding that if the Soviets didn't like it they could "go to hell."

Truman replaced Roosevelt's diplomatic advisers with a hard-line team. Drawing upon the advice of policy experts around him, he aimed to establish U.S. leadership in the world through a race for power that would exhaust Communist resources. In the short run, Truman determined to maintain U.S.

military superiority and prevent communism from spreading outside the USSR. *Containment,* a doctrine uniting military, economic, and diplomatic strategies, now became the linchpin of U.S. foreign policy.

The Truman Doctrine

Truman showed his cards early in 1947 when a crisis erupted in Turkey and civil war-torn Greece. Great Britain, which had considered both Mediterranean nations within its sphere of influence, announced on February 21 its plans to withdraw all economic and military aid. Stalin had refused to aid the Greek rebels who were fighting to overthrow the monarchist regime and instead urged negotiations. Truman nevertheless insisted that without U.S. intervention Greece and perhaps Turkey would fall under Soviet control.

Truman and the Department of State were determined to step in for the British. Such a commitment meant, however, something many Americans feared: an expenditure of hundreds of millions of dollars and the responsibility for controlling a region far outside the Western Hemisphere and the Pacific. To drum up support for his plan from a fiscally conservative Republican Congress, Truman enlisted his top-ranking advisers. Undersecretary of State (1945–47) and later Secretary of State (1949–53) Dean G. Acheson alerted congressional leaders that if Turkey and Greece fell into the Soviet sphere, Communist influence would spread rapidly across the Middle East, northern Africa, and southern Europe. These regions would become, he warned, "like apples in a barrel infected one by rotten one." But if Truman hoped to sway public opinion as well as secure votes in Congress, advised Republican senator Arthur H. Vandenberg of Michigan, chair of the Foreign Relations Committee, he would have to "scare hell out of the country."

In early March 1947 Truman swung into action. Speaking at Baylor University, he linked the survival of the American system of free enterprise to a capitalist world economy, and freedom to Western victory in Greece. A week later, on March 12, appearing before a joint session of Congress, the president argued: "At the present moment in world history, nearly every nation must choose between alternative ways of life. One way of life is based upon the will of the majority, and is distinguished by free institutions . . . and freedom from political oppression. The second way of life is based upon the will of a minority forcibly imposed on the majority . . . and the suppression of personal freedom." Never mentioning the Soviet Union by name, the president appealed for all-out resistance to a "certain ideology," wherever it appeared in the world. World peace and the welfare of all Americans depended, Truman insisted, on containing communism.

Truman won the day. Large bipartisan majorities in both houses of Congress approved his request to appropriate $400 million in economic and military aid to Greece and Turkey. The aid to Greece helped the monarchy and right-wing military crush the rebel movement. Truman's victory took the sting out of Republican criticisms and buoyed his popularity for the upcoming 1948 election. It also helped to turn Americans against their former Soviet allies and to generate popular support for a campaign against communism, both at home and abroad.

The significance of what became known as the Truman Doctrine far outlasted the events in the Mediterranean. One month before Churchill's dramatic Iron Curtain speech, George Kennan had sent an 8,000-word "long telegram" to the State Department insisting that Soviet fanaticism could be quelled only by ongoing military and diplomatic pressure. Four months after the Truman Doctrine address, Kennan, who now directed the State Department's policy-planning staff, reaffirmed his belief. Writing under the pseudonym "Mr. X" in *Foreign Affairs,* Kennan explained that the future depended on two possibilities: "either the break-up [of communism] or the gradual mellowing of Soviet power." Although critics such as Walter Lippmann described this position as a "strategic monstrosity," requiring an endless diffusion of resources for military operations around the world, containment served as the cornerstone of U.S. foreign policy for the next several decades.

The Marshall Plan

The Truman Doctrine directly inspired the European Recovery Program, commonly known as the Marshall Plan. Introduced in a commencement speech at Harvard University on June 5, 1947, by Secretary of State and former army chief of staff George C. Marshall, the plan aimed to reduce "hunger, poverty, desperation, and chaos" and to restore "the confidence of the European people in the economic future of their own countries and of Europe as a whole." In this region, the Truman administration did not fear a Soviet invasion as much as the possible political consequences of total disintegration of the region's economy. Indirectly, the Marshall Plan aimed to turn back Socialist and Communist bids for power in northern and western Europe.

The Marshall Plan in effect brought recipients of aid into a bilateral agreement with the United States. The Western European nations, seventeen in all, received nearly $13 billion between 1948 and 1951; more than half went to West Germany, France, and Great Britain. The seventeen nations formed the Organization for European Economic Cooperation (OEEC) to implement the plan, and ratified the General Agreement on Tariffs and Trades (GATT), which reduced commercial barriers among member nations and opened all to U.S. trade.

Considered by many historians the most successful postwar U.S. diplomatic venture, the Marshall Plan created the climate for a viable capitalist economy in Western Europe. Industrial production in that region rose by 200 percent between 1947 and 1952. Deflationary programs cut wages and increased unemployment, but profits soared and the standard of living improved significantly. Under U.S. leadership, the nations of Western Europe rallied as a center of American economic activity.

The Marshall Plan drove a further wedge between the United States and the Soviet Union. Stalin denounced it as an American scheme to dominate Europe and deprive Eastern European countries of desperately needed financial resources. The architects of the Marshall Plan, however, had never expected the Soviet Union to participate. As one planner noted, if the plan included funds to help the Communist nations recover, "the whole project would probably be unworkable." Although the Marshall Plan did not diminish Soviet control over Eastern Europe, it did help to create a stark contrast between the East and the West, between communism and capitalism. And this was intentional, the president readily acknowledged, describing the Truman Doctrine and the Marshall Plan as "two halves of the same walnut."

The Berlin Crisis and the Formation of NATO

Once the Marshall Plan was in place, the strategy of containment began to take clear shape in West Germany. The United States and Great Britain merged their occupation zones on January 1, 1947, brought Germans into the administration of these areas, and announced plans for political unification of all four Allied zones. Stalin perceived these policy changes as a violation of the Potsdam agreement and a threat to Soviet security. On June 24, 1948, he responded by cutting off rail and trucking access to West Berlin, formally controlled by Great Britain and the United States but situated deep within Soviet-occupied East Germany.

The Soviet mobilization created both a crisis for Truman and an opportunity for confrontation. Truman believed that not only the future of Germany but the stature of the Western powers was at stake. Although many of his advisers were reluctant to risk war by challenging Stalin militarily, the president threatened to use atomic weapons against the Soviets, and even sent two squadrons of B-29s to the U.S. military base in Great Britain. But this plan was quickly abandoned, and the United States instead began, with help from the Royal Air Force, an airlift of historic proportions — Operation Vittles, which delivered nearly 2 million tons of supplies to West Berliners. Finally, in May 1949, the Soviet Union conceded defeat and lifted the blockade. Within a few weeks, East Germany and West Germany were established as separate republics.

The Berlin crisis made a U.S.-led military alliance against the Soviets attractive to Western European nations. In April 1949 ten European nations, Canada, and the United States formed the North Atlantic Treaty Alliance (NATO), a mutual defense pact in which "an armed attack against one or more of them . . . shall be considered an attack against them all." NATO complemented the Marshall Plan, strengthening economic ties among the member nations by, according to one analyst, keeping "the Russians out, the Americans in, and the Germans down." It also deepened divisions between Eastern and Western Europe, making a permanent military mobilization on both sides almost inevitable.

By mid-1949 Truman and his advisers were basking in the glow of their victories. The U.S. Senate had ratified the first formal military treaty with a European nation since the Revolutionary War era — a giant step away from isolationism. Congress also approved $1.3 billion in military aid, which involved the creation of U.S. Army bases and the deployment of American troops abroad. Critics such as isolationist senator Robert A. Taft warned that the United States could not afford to police all of Europe without sidetracking domestic policies and undercutting the UN. But opinion polls revealed strong support for Truman's tough line against the Soviets.

Between 1947 and 1949, the Truman administration had defined the policies that would shape the Cold War for decades to come. The Truman Doctrine explained the ideological basis of containment; the Marshall Plan put into place its economic underpinnings in Western Europe; and NATO created the mechanisms for military enforcement. When the Soviet Union created a counterpart to NATO, the Warsaw Pact in 1955, the division of East and West was complete.

The Berlin Airlift. Laying deep within Communist East Germany, West Berlin had suddenly been cut off from Western supplies when Stalin blockaded all surface traffic in an attempt to take over the war-torn city. Between June 1948 and May 1949, British and U.S. pilots made 272,000 flights, dropping food and fuel to civilians. The Berlin Airlift successfully foiled the blockade, and the Soviet Union reopened borders on May 17.

The Cold War in Asia

Triumphant in Western Europe, Truman managed only a mixed record in Asia. In some areas, he proved that the United States could contain communism without massive displays of military strength. Elsewhere, the Truman Doctrine did not work, and the results were disastrous for the president.

The United States achieved its greatest success in occupied Japan. General Douglas MacArthur directed an interim government in a modest reconstruction program that included land reform, the creation of independent trade unions, abolition of contract marriages and granting of woman suffrage, sweeping demilitarization, and, eventually, a constitutional democracy that barred Communists from all posts. In return for its sovereignty, granted in 1952, Japan agreed to house huge U.S. military bases on its mainland and on the island of Okinawa, thus placing U.S. troops and weapons strategically close to the Soviet Union's Asian rim. U.S. advisers, meanwhile, prepared a new group of business leaders who were eager to build a capitalist economy in Japan and willing to quash anti-American dissent with a powerful national police. Economically, the United States took control, forbidding Japan to trade with the USSR and, later, the People's Republic of China.

Truman scored smaller but significant victories in both Indonesia and the Philippines. When a nationalist revolution in the Dutch East Indies began to threaten U.S. interests, the State Department forced Holland to grant independence to its colony, and the sovereign state of Indonesia was created in 1949. The United States had granted formal independence to the Philippines in 1946 but retained major naval bases as well as influence over Filipino foreign and domestic affairs. In response to a major uprising of peasants hungry for land, the United States directed massive amounts of aid to nationalist leader Ramón Magsaysay, who crushed the rebellion. General MacArthur proudly described the Philippines to Congress in 1950 as a "mighty bulwark of Christianity in the Far East."

The situation in China could not be handled so easily. After years of civil war, the pro-Western Nationalist government of Jiang Jeishi (Chiang Kaishek) collapsed. In 1947 Jiang sorely misjudged his resources and began a futile all-out offensive against his Communist adversaries. The Nationalist troops were forced to surrender in mid-1949 to the Communists, led by Mao Zedong. Mao and the Communists enjoyed the support of the Chinese countryside, where 85 percent of the population lived. By the end of the year the Nationalist government had withdrawn to the island of Formosa (Taiwan), leaving Mao the entire China mainland.

Since World War II, the United States had sent military and economic aid to Jiang despite his unpopularity in China. American officials warned him that without major reforms, the Nationalists were destined to lose the war. They tried, moreover, to convince Jiang to turn over the reins of government to a less corrupt group of moderates or to accept a coalition with Mao. But when Jiang insisted on fighting, the United States broke off relations. Secretary of State Acheson issued a 1,054-page "white paper" stating decisively that the situation in China was "beyond the control of the government of the United States" and blaming Jiang wholly for his own defeat.

The news of China's "fall" to communism created an uproar in the United States. The Asia First wing of the Republican party, which envisioned Asia rather than Europe as the site of economic expansion, blamed the Truman administration for "losing" China and began to refer to the Democrats as the "party of treason." They called Truman's explanation a "whitewash of a wishful, do-nothing policy." Large numbers of Americans agreed, although China was never America's to lose. The "China Lobby," its claims publicized broadly in Luce's *Time* magazine, had nevertheless trapped Truman in his own Cold War logic.

Shortly after the Communist victory, Acheson considered recognizing the People's Republic of China. But he backed down after the Communists arrested American citizens and seized American property in China. The Republicans, meanwhile, began to envision the day of Jiang's triumphant return to the mainland. The United States continued to regard Jiang's ministry in Taiwan as the legitimate government of China, going so far as to secure for Nationalist China a seat on the UN Security Council.

After Stalin signed a formal alliance with Mao in February 1950, the rhetoric of the Cold War became yet more pronounced. The perceived threat of "international communism" came to dominate American foreign policy for the next twenty years.

Atomic Diplomacy

The policy of containment depended on the ability of the United States to back up its commitments through military means, and Truman invested his faith in the U.S. monopoly of atomic weapons to pressure the Soviets to cooperate. On August 9, 1945, the day U.S. planes bombed Nagasaki, the president told Americans, "We must constitute ourselves trustees of this new force — to prevent its misuse, and to turn it into the channels of service to mankind." In a survey conducted one month later, 85 percent of the respondents wanted the United States to retain sole possession of the bomb for as long as possible. Many scientists nevertheless warned that once the bomb had been exploded, the "secret" could no longer be guarded. Secretary of War Henry L. Stimson tried to convince Truman that successful negotiations depended on trust, and that the U.S. could not maintain its relationship with the Soviet Union by "having this weapon ostentatiously on [its] hip."

After the war, many Americans favored control of atomic power by the United Nations. But a plan drafted by financier Bernard M. Baruch, U.S. ambassador to the UN Atomic Energy Commission, failed to win approval by the Soviet Union. When negotiations stalled, the United States quickly put aside all plans for international cooperation. In 1946 Congress passed the Atomic Energy Act, which granted the newly established Atomic Energy Commission control of all research and development under the strictest standards of national security.

As sole possessor of the "secret," the United States began to build atomic stockpiles and conducted further tests on the Bikini Islands in the Pacific. By 1949, just two years after the Joint Chiefs of Staff called for a substantial enlargement of the nuclear arsenal, the number of bombs had grown from thirteen to fifty. By 1950, as a scientific adviser subsequently observed, the United States "had a stockpile capable of somewhat more than reproducing World War II in a single day."

Despite warnings to the contrary by leading scientists, U.S. military analysts continued to play down Soviet nuclear capability. The Military Intelligence Division of the War Department estimated it would take the Soviet Union three to ten years to produce an atomic bomb. In August 1949, the Soviet Union proved the skeptics wrong by testing its own atomic bomb. "There is only one thing worse than one nation having the atomic bomb," Harold C. Urey, a Nobel Prize winner and atomic scientist, said; "that's two nations having it."

Within a few years, both the United States and the Soviet Union had tested hydrogen bombs a thousand times more powerful than the primitive weapons dropped on Hiroshima and Nagasaki in 1945. Both proceeded to stockpile bombs attached to missiles, inaugurating the fateful nuclear arms race that scientists had feared since 1945.

The United States and the Soviet Union were now firmly locked into the Cold War. The nuclear arms race imperiled their futures, diverted their economies, and fostered fears of impending doom. When he heard of the Soviet detonation of the bomb Senator Arthur Vandenberg remarked presciently, "This is now a different world." Prospects for global peace had dissipated, and despite the Allied victory in World War II, the world had again divided into hostile camps. The United States may have emerged the most powerful nation in the world, but uneasiness prevailed.

THE TRUMAN PRESIDENCY

Truman's aggressive, gusty personality suited the confrontational mood of the Cold War. He linked the Soviet threat in Europe to the need for a strong presidency. Meanwhile, he reached out to voters alarmed at Republican intentions to dismantle the New Deal. Pressed to establish his own political identity, "Give 'em Hell" Harry Truman successfully portrayed himself as a fierce fighter against all challengers, yet loyal to Roosevelt's legacy.

"To Err Is Truman"

In marked contrast with his illustrious predecessor, Harry Truman was a virtual unknown to most Americans. Within a year of assuming office, he rated lower in public approval than any twentieth-century president except Roosevelt's own predecessor, Herbert Hoover, who had been blamed for the Great Depression. The twin responsibilities of reestablishing peacetime conditions — demobilizing the troops and reconverting the economy — seemed to overwhelm the new president's administration. "To err is Truman," critics jeered.

Truman angered servicemen and -women eager to return home. Hundreds of thousands of combat veterans were surprised to find themselves shipped off to Pacific locations such as the Philippines, to put down labor and agrarian unrest. Members of Congress received bundles of protest letters, "Bring Daddy Home" clubs formed throughout the country, and in January 1946 demonstrations broke out in Manila. Spreading across the Pacific, the "Bring the Boys Home" movement so alarmed Truman that he reversed course and, in a dramatic radio address, promised a rapid demobilization. Under his orders the War Department gave in, but the president had already damaged his record.

At home, Truman did no better. In handling the enormous task of reconverting the economy to peacetime production, he appeared both inept and mean-spirited. The president faced millions of restless would-be consumers tired of rationing and eager to indulge themselves in shiny cars, new furniture, choice cuts of meat, and colorful clothing. The demand for consumer items rapidly outran supply, fueling inflation and creating a huge black market. When Congress proposed to extend wartime controls, Truman vetoed the bill and prices immediately began to skyrocket.

In 1945 and 1946, the country appeared ready to explode. While homemakers protested rising prices by boycotting neighborhood stores, industrial workers struck in unprecedented numbers. Employers, fearing a rapid decline to depression-level profits, determined to slash wages or at least hold them steady; workers wanted a bigger cut of the huge war profits they had heard about. As police and strikers clashed, citywide general strikes spread from transit workers to other laborers. In Oakland, Pittsburgh, and Rochester, the strikes halted all commerce for days and sometimes turned downtowns into virtual street festivals of strikers and their families. The spectacle of nearly 4.6 million workers on picket lines alarmed the new president.

Truman's strong-arm plan to bring order failed in Congress. In May 1946 he threatened to draft striking railroad workers and miners into the army. In a draft of an address to Congress, the president wrote, "Let's put transportation and production back to work, hang a few traitors and make our country safe for democracy." Although he toned down the final version of the speech, Truman insisted on his right as president to order strikers back to work in jobs he judged vital to the national welfare. The usually conservative Senate killed this plan.

Congress defeated most of Truman's proposals for reconversion. One week after Japan's surrender, the president introduced a twenty-one-point program that included greater unemployment compensation, higher minimum wages, and housing assistance. Later he added proposals for national health insurance and atomic energy legislation. Congress turned back the bulk of these bills, passing the Employment Act of 1946 only after substantial modification. The act created a new executive body, the Council of Economic Advisors, which would confer with the president and formulate policies for maintaining employment, production, and purchasing power. But the measure failed to grant the fiscal means to guarantee full employment, thus undermining Truman's chief effort to advance beyond the New Deal.

By 1946 Truman's popularity had dipped to 32 percent. Democrats, when asked what Roosevelt would do if still alive, often responded, "I wonder what Truman would do if he were alive." Republicans, sensing victory in the upcoming off-year elections, asked the voters, "Had enough?" Apparently

Police and strikers confront each other in Los Angeles during one of many postwar strikes in 1946. Employers desired to lower wages, and workers refused to give up the higher living standard achieved during the war.

the voters had. They repudiated Truman and the Democrats, giving Republicans majorities in both houses of Congress and in the state capitols. In office, the Republicans set out to turn back the New Deal. And in a symbolic repudiation of Roosevelt they passed an amendment limiting the presidency to two terms. Truman represented no danger of even reaching that goal.

The Republicans, dominant in Congress for the first time since 1928, prepared a full counteroffensive against the constituency most hated by business, organized labor. Unions had by this time reached a peak in size and prestige, with membership topping 15 million and encompassing nearly 40 percent of all wage earners. In the view of many conservatives, as well as many liberals, labor had already gone too far. In 1947 the Republican Eightieth Congress opportunely passed the Taft-Hartley bill.

The Labor-Management Relations Act, as the measure was officially known, outlawed many practices approved by the Wagner Act of 1935 (see Chapter 24), such as the closed shop, the secondary boycott, and the use of union dues for political activities. It also mandated an eighty-day cooling-off period in the case of strikes affecting national safety or health. Called the "slave labor bill" by union activists, Taft-Hartley furthermore required all union officials to swear under oath that they were not Communists — a Cold War mandate that abridged freedoms ordinarily guaranteed by the First Amendment. Those unions that refused to cooperate were denied access to the National Labor Relations Board, which arbitrated strikes and issued credentials to unions.

Truman regained some support from organized labor when he vetoed the Taft-Hartley Act, saying it would "conflict with important principles of our democratic society." Congress, however, overrode his veto, and Truman himself went on to invoke the act against strikers. Members of the president's own party now proposed that he resign, or sought to persuade General Dwight Eisenhower to accept the Democratic nomination for president in the upcoming national election.

The 1948 Election

Although lacking a strong candidate, Democrats gingerly approached the 1948 election — the first presidential contest since the inauguration of the Cold War — as an opportunity to campaign for their own post–New Deal agenda. In preparation, a group headed by Eleanor Roosevelt, labor leaders Philip Murray and Walter Reuther, and theologian Reinhold Niebuhr, among others, met on January 3, 1947, and formed Americans for Democratic Action (ADA). This body became the most important liberal lobby of the postwar era. Determined to defeat the Republicans, ADA moved to reorient the Democratic party itself, which appeared to be breaking up on the shoals of Cold War politics.

"As long as Franklin Roosevelt was President," wrote a journalist in the British *New Statesman* in 1948, "life was politically simple. . . . There was a place for [liberals] on the New Deal bandwagon, and until the driver died, some of them were permitted to sit on the front seat. . . ." The new president, however, had already divided the liberal community. He frankly considered some of Roosevelt's closest advisers to be "crackpots and the lunatic fringe." By late 1946 Truman had forced out the social planners who had staffed the Washington bureaus for over a decade, including one of the best-loved New Dealers, Secretary of the Interior Harold Ickes.

Truman had also fired his secretary of commerce, Henry Wallace, for advocating a more conciliatory policy toward the Soviet Union. Wallace, however, would not retreat and made plans to run for president as candidate of the newly formed Progressive party. Having served as Roosevelt's vice-president and secretary of agriculture, Wallace was well known as a long-time champion of New Deal liberalism. He avowed to expand New Deal programs dramatically at home and abroad, to move swiftly and boldly toward full employment, racial equality, and stronger trade unions, and to establish peace with the Soviet Union. As the election neared, Wallace appeared a viable third-party candidate.

The deepening Cold War soon quashed Wallace's chances. Encouraging Democrats to rally around the president, ADA denounced the Progressive party as a threat to national security. Truman himself, as well as many conservatives, accused Wallace of being a tool of Communists. These timely redbaiting attacks took a toll on the poorly organized and underfunded Wallace campaign, driving many liberals from its ranks, including future Democratic presidential candidate George McGovern.

Truman, meanwhile, deftly repositioned himself to discredit congressional Republicans. He called for government funds for education and new housing and a national program of medical insurance. Knowing the Republican Congress would kill all such proposals, Truman called back legislators into a fruitless special session in 1948 so that he could denounce the "do-nothing Congress" in his election bid. Truman warned voters that if Republicans won the White House, the United States would become "an economic colony of Wall Street."

A second tactic seemed to backfire. Pressed by ADA leaders to cut Wallace's lead on civil rights, Truman issued executive orders in July 1948 desegregating the armed forces and banning discrimination in the federal civil service. He also endorsed a plank on racial equality that he personally considered too strongly worded. In response, some 300 southern delegates bolted from the Democratic convention and formed a States' Rights ("Dixiecrat") ticket headed by Governor Strom Thurmond of

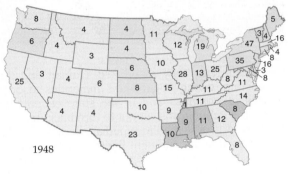

Candidates (Party)	Electoral vote	Popular vote
Harry S. Truman (Democratic)	303 (57%)	24,105,695 (49.5%)
Thomas E. Dewey (Republican)	189 (36%)	21,969,170 (45.1%)
Strom Thurmond (States' Rights)	39 (7%)	1,169,021 (2.4%)
Henry A. Wallace (Progressive)	–	1,156,103 (2.4%)
Other Candidates (Socialist, Prohibition, Socialist Labor, Socialist Workers)	–	272,713

Election of 1948

Harry Truman holds up a copy of the *Chicago Tribune* with headlines confidently and mistakenly predicting the victory of his opponent, Thomas E. Dewey. An unpopular candidate, Truman made a whistle-stop tour of the country by train to win 49.5 percent of the popular vote to Dewey's 45.1 percent.

South Carolina, known for his segregationist views. With the South as good as lost, and popular New York governor Thomas E. Dewey heading the Republican ticket, Truman appeared hopelessly far from victory.

Yet as the election neared, Truman managed to restore essential components of the New Deal coalition. Fear of the Republicans won back the bulk of organized labor, while the recognition of the new state of Israel in May 1948 helped prevent the defection of many liberal Jewish voters from Democratic ranks. By election time, Truman had deprived Henry Wallace of nearly all his liberal support. (Wallace still polled 1 million votes, mostly in New York and California.) Meanwhile, Dewey, who had run a hard-hitting campaign against Roosevelt in 1944, expected to coast to victory. By campaigning vigorously, Truman won back Democrats except in the South, where Thurmond took four states. The president carried most of the states and trounced Dewey 303 to 189 in the electoral college. Congressional Democrats returned to majorities in both houses. Truman's campaign had retained the loyalty of those Americans who feared a reversal of the New Deal. "Harry Truman won the election," concluded the New Republic, "because Franklin Roosevelt had worked so well."

The Fair Deal

President Truman laid out his domestic agenda before the new and solidly Democratic Congress in January 1949. "Every segment of our population and every individual has a right to expect from our Government a fair deal," he affirmed. Truman hoped that his election victory and the return of Democratic majorities in the House and Senate would allow him to translate campaign promises into concrete legislative achievements. But most of the president's plans were defeated in the new Congress by a powerful bloc of conservative southern Democrats and midwestern Republicans.

Truman could claim a few liberal victories. Congress passed a National Housing Act in 1949, promoting federally funded construction of low-income housing. It also raised the minimum wage from forty to seventy-five cents per hour and expanded the Social Security program to cover an additional 10 million people. Otherwise, Truman made little headway. He and congressional liberals introduced a variety of bills to weaken southern segregationism: making lynching a federal crime; outlawing the poll tax; prohibiting discrimination in interstate transportation. These measures were all defeated by southern-led filibusters. Proposals to create a national health insurance plan, provide federal aid for education, and repeal or modify Taft-Hartley remained bottled up in committees. Truman himself appeared to lose interest in the liberal agenda as his Cold War foreign policy increasingly took priority over domestic issues.

Truman managed best to articulate the basic principles of Cold War liberalism. Toning down the rhetoric of economic equality espoused by the visionary wing of the Roosevelt coalition, his Fair Deal exalted economic growth — not the reapportionment of wealth or political power — as the proper mechanism for ensuring social harmony and national welfare. The second Truman administration insisted, therefore, on an ambitious program of expanded foreign trade, while relying on the federal government to encourage high levels of productivity at home. Government expenditures for domestic and defense programs played an increasing role in the economy. Although federal expenditures dropped at the end of World War II, they remained at least seven times greater than they had been during the peak of the New Deal in the 1930s.

The Truman administration effectively used the threat of military confrontation between the United States and the Soviet Union to cut across conservative and liberal political lines. By the end of Truman's second term, defense allocations accounted for 10 percent of the gross national product, directly or indirectly employed hundreds of thousands of well-paid workers, and subsidized some of the nation's most profitable corporations. This vast financial outlay, guided through Congress by legislators who demanded economic benefits for their constituents, created a political base of support for the use of permanent, large-scale military spending as a basic stimulus to economic growth. A vigorous anti-Communist crusade at home strengthened the underpinnings of this ambitious Cold War program.

THE COLD WAR AT HOME

On June 21, 1946, Attorney General Tom C. Clark announced to the Chicago Bar Association that the United States had become the target of "a sinister and deep-seated plot on the part of Communists, ideologists, and small groups of radicals" to capture unions, cause strikes, and prevent lawful authorities from maintaining order. Four years later Republican senator Joseph R. McCarthy announced that he held lists of Communists serving secretly in government agencies. This, he declared, showed that the United States had already fallen prey to subversive influences. The specter of a prolonged Cold War with the USSR had encouraged many Americans, including the nation's leaders, to become obsessed with problems of national security, real or imagined, and to resort to extreme measures to solve them.

The National Security State

The climate of fear hastened the expansion of the federal government begun during World War II and diverted an increasingly large portion of its resources toward national defense. Shortly before the war, the federal work force totaled about 900,000 civilians, with about 10 percent engaged in security work; by war's end, the government employed nearly 4 million people, of whom 75 percent worked in national security agencies. The Pentagon, which had opened in 1942 as the largest office building in the world, housed the Joint Chiefs of Staff and 35,000 military personnel. Similarly, when the State Department consolidated its various divisions in 1961, it abandoned nearly thirty separate buildings that it had acquired during the 1950s to take over an eight-story structure covering an area the size of four city blocks. The ties between the armed forces and the State Department grew closer, as former military officers routinely began to fill positions in the State Department and diplomatic corps.

The National Security Act of 1947, passed by Congress with Truman's encouragement, laid the foundation for this expansion. Under its provisions, the War Department and Navy Department joined to form a mighty Department of Defense, and the National Security Council (NSC) was set up in the White House to coordinate the military services and to advise the president. The Central Intelligence Agency (CIA), with roots in the wartime Office of Strategic Services, was established as an independent agency. Although information about the CIA was classified — that is, not public — historians have estimated that the agency soon dwarfed the State Department in number of employees and size of budget. By late 1947, as Harrison Baldwin of the *New York Times* noted, there was an ominous trend toward "militarization of [the] government and of the American state of mind."

On March 21, 1947, Truman signed Executive Order 9835, establishing the Federal Employee Loyalty Program. The program barred members of the Communist party — as well as Fascists and anyone guilty of "sympathetic association" with either — from federal employment. It also outlined procedures for investigating current and prospective federal employees. Later amendments added "homosexuals" as potential security risks on the grounds that they might succumb to blackmail by enemy agents.

Many local governments enacted loyalty pro-

Full-Time White House Employees, 1934–1953

President	Fiscal Year	Total Salaried and Special Projects Employees	Detailed Employees*	Grand Total
Roosevelt	1939	45	112	157
	1940	63	114	177
	1941	62	117	179
	1942	47	137	184
	1943	46	148	194
	1944	47	145	192
	1945	48	167	215
Truman	1946	51	162	213
	1947	190	27	217
	1948	245	23	268
	1949	220	26	246
	1950	223	25	248
	1951	257	40	297
	1952	252	31	283
	1953	262	28	290

*Federal employees assigned to White House duty for a temporary period.
Source: Adapted from Stephen J. Wayne, *The Legislative Presidency* (New York: Harper & Row, 1978), appendix A, pp. 220–221.

grams and required state and city employees, including teachers at all levels, to sign loyalty oaths. In Detroit, the loyalty review board included city officials, FBI agents, and executives from the auto industry. Positions involving security clearances were closed off to many scientists and engineers. Scientists who had worked on the Manhattan Project were checked, and although no atomic spies turned up in the investigation, several project members lost their jobs. In all, nearly 10,000 people may have been fired as a result of loyalty programs.

Attorney General Clark aided this effort by publishing a list of hundreds of potentially subversive organizations selected by criteria so vague that any views "hostile or inimical to the American form of government" (as Clark's assistants noted in a memo) could make an organization liable for investigation and prosecution. There was, moreover, no right of appeal. Although designed primarily to screen federal employees, the attorney general's list effectively outlawed many political and social organizations. Church, civil rights, and musical groups, and even summer camps, all appeared on this list. Membership in a listed group became the rationale for firings at nearly every level of government. Fraternal and cultural institutions, especially popular among aging European immigrants, were among the largest groups destroyed. The state of New York, for example, legally dismantled the International Workers' Order, which had provided insurance to nearly 200,000 immigrants, after that fraternal organization appeared on the attorney general's list. Only a handful of organizations had the funds to challenge the listing legally; most simply closed their doors.

In 1950 Congress overrode the president's veto to pass a bill that Truman called "the greatest danger to freedom of press, speech, and assembly since the Sedition Act of 1798." The Internal Security (McCarran) Act required Communist organizations to register with the Subversive Activities Control Board and authorized the arrest of suspect persons during a national emergency. The Immigration and Nationality Act, sponsored by Republican senator Pat McCarran of Nevada and adopted in 1952, again over Truman's veto, barred people deemed "subversive" or "homosexual" from becoming citizens or even from visiting the United States. It also empowered the attorney general to deport immigrants who were members of Communist organizations, even if they had become citizens. Challenged repeatedly on constitutional grounds, the Subversive Activities Control Board remained in place until 1973, when it was terminated.

The Red Scare in Hollywood

Anti-Communist Democratic representative Martin Dies of Texas, who had chaired a congressional committee on "un-American activities" since 1938, told reporters at a press conference in Hollywood in 1944:

> Hollywood is the greatest source of revenue in this nation for the Communists and other subversive groups. . . . Two elements stand out in . . . the making of pictures which extoll foreign ideology — propaganda for a cause which seeks to spread its ideas to our people[,] and the "leftist" or radical screenwriters. . . . In my opinion, [motion picture executives] will do well to halt the propaganda pictures and eliminate every writer who has un-American ideas.

A few years later, Dies's successor, J. Parnell Thomas (later convicted and imprisoned for bribery) directed the committee to investigate supposed Communist infiltration of the movie industry.

Renamed and made a permanent standing committee in 1945, the House Un-American Activities Committee (HUAC) conducted one of the most spectacular domestic campaigns of the Cold War. HUAC had the power to subpoena witnesses to testify anywhere in the United States and to compel answers on threat of contempt of Congress charges. In well-publicized hearings held in Hollywood in October 1947, HUAC found ample evidence of leftist sympathies but none of the subversive activity it alleged. The committee heard, for example, the mother of actress Ginger Rogers explain that her daughter, duped into appearing in the pro-Russian wartime film *Tender Comrade*, "had been forced" to read the subversive line "Share and share alike, that's democracy." Conservative novelist Ayn Rand added that *The Song of Russia* (1944) had intentionally deceived the American public by showing Russians smiling!

In 1947 the studios announced that no writer, technician, or actor who refused to denounce communism would be employed again, and HUAC encouraged testimony by "friendly witnesses" such as Ronald Reagan, Gary Cooper, Adolphe Menjou, and Robert Montgomery. Barbara Stanwyck testified that her husband, Robert Taylor, another friendly witness, could not have been influenced by Communist ideas because he never read books; he even prepared gourmet meals solely "from the pictures" in cookbooks. The committee intimidated many who desperately feared the loss of their careers into naming suspect former friends and co-workers in order to be cleared for future work in Hollywood. Only a few former Communists, such as television superstar Lucille Ball, were too popular to be damaged by the bad publicity.

A small but prominent minority refused to cooperate with the investigators. By claiming the freedoms of speech and association guaranteed by the First and Sixth Amendments to the Constitution, they became known as "unfriendly witnesses." Many had worked in Hollywood films celebrating America's working people, a popular depression-era theme but now considered indicative of subversive intentions. During World War II, many of these same screenwriters and actors had teamed up on films attacking fascism. Among the most prominent "unfriendly witnesses" were actors Orson Welles, Zero Mostel, and Charlie Chaplin and Oscar-winning screenwriter Ring Lardner, Jr. Humphrey Bogart led a stars' delegation to "Defend the First Amendment" before Congress, but generated only headlines. A handful of dissenters served prison sentences for contempt of Congress. Meanwhile, a blacklist published as *Red Channels: The Report of Communist Influence in Radio and Television* (1950) persuaded advertisers to cancel their accounts with many programs considered friendly to the Soviet Union, the United Nations, and liberal causes. The blacklist remained in effect until the 1960s, effectively limiting the production of films dealing with social or political issues.

Hollywood studios themselves played into the mounting fears, releasing by 1954 over forty films with titles such as *I Married a Communist* (1950) and *The Red Menace* (1949). The television industry sponsored the dramatic series "The Hunter," featuring the adventures of an American businessman fighting Communist agents throughout the Free World. Few of these films or programs were popular, however.

Spy Cases

In August 1948, HUAC opened public hearings with a star witness: Whittaker Chambers, *Time* magazine editor and former Communist, who confessed to spying for the Soviet Union during the 1930s. Chambers named as a fellow Communist Alger Hiss, a veteran of Roosevelt's State Department, Roosevelt's adviser at Yalta, and at the time of the hearings president of the prestigious Carnegie Endowment for International Peace. After Hiss denied any affiliation with the Communist party and proceeded to sue his accuser for slander, Chambers dropped the claims in favor of another allegation: hidden away in a pumpkin patch near his farm were microfilms of secret documents passed to him by Hiss.

Republican representative Richard Nixon of California described this evidence as proof of "the most serious series of treasonable activities . . . in the history of America," but refused to allow anyone to examine the mysterious documents. (Many years later, the notorious "Pumpkin Papers" were revealed to be Bureau of Standards data, available in most public libraries.) Because a statute of limitations for espionage precluded a charge of treason, a federal grand jury in January 1950 convicted Hiss of perjury only (for denying he knew Chambers), and he received a five-year prison term.

Many Democrats, including Truman himself, at first dismissed the allegations against Hiss — conveniently publicized at the start of the 1948 election campaign — as a red herring, a Republican maneuver to convince the public that Democrats had allowed Communists to infiltrate the federal government. In 1952 Nixon circulated the pamphlet *The Hiss Case* to promote his candidacy for vice-president. Two years later, Hiss was released from prison, still claiming his innocence.

The most dramatic spy case of the era involved Julius Rosenberg, former government engineer, and his wife, Ethel, who were accused of stealing and conveying to Soviet agents the "secret" of the atomic bomb. The government's case against the Rosenbergs rested on the testimony of their supposed accomplices, some of them secretly coached by the FBI. Nevertheless, in March 1951 a jury found them guilty of conspiring to commit espionage. The American press showed no sympathy, but around the world the Rosenbergs were defended by citizens' committees and their convictions protested in large-scale demonstrations. Scientist Albert Einstein, the pope, and the president of France, among many prominent figures, all pleaded for clemency. The Rosenbergs maintained their innocence to the end, insisting they were being persecuted as Jews and for holding leftist political beliefs. They died in the electric chair on June 19, 1953.

McCarthyism

In a sensational Lincoln Day speech to the Republican Women's Club of Wheeling, West Virginia, on February 9, 1950, Republican senator Joseph R. McCarthy of Wisconsin announced that America had been betrayed by the "traitorous actions of those who have been treated so well by the nation." These "bright young men who have been born with silver spoons in their mouths" — such as Secretary of State Dean Acheson, whom McCarthy called a "pompous diplomat in striped pants, with a phony English accent"—were part of a conspiracy, he charged, of more than 200 Communists working in the State Department.

McCarthy refused to reveal names, however, and a few days later, after a drinking bout, he told persistent reporters: "I'm not going to tell you anything. I just want you to know I've got a pailful of shit, and I'm going to use it where it does me the most good." Although investigations uncovered not a single Communist in the State Department, McCarthy succeeded in making himself a major figure in the anti-Communist propaganda campaign by charging not only New Deal Democrats but the entire Truman administration with failing to defend the nation's security. Democrats were "soft" on communism, he repeatedly asserted; they had "lost" China. His name has provided the label for an era of fear and doubt: McCarthyism.

Behind the blitz of publicity—his staff assistant, lawyer Roy Cohn, called it *showbiz*—the previously obscure junior senator from Wisconsin had struck a chord. Communism seemed to many Americans to be much more than a military threat—indeed, nothing less than a demonic force capable of undermining basic values. It compelled vigorous patriots to proclaim themselves ready for atomic warfare: "Better Dead Than Red." McCarthy also had help from organizations like the American Legion and the Chamber of Commerce, prominent religious leaders such as the Catholic Francis Cardinal Spellman, and union leaders wishing to consolidate their power by eliminating dissenters. Many of McCarthy's fellow campaigners shared his deep resentment toward the eastern-born diplomatic elite that had come to power with the New Deal. McCarthyism, as a historian wrote at the time, was at least partly "the revenge of the noses that for 20 years of fancy parties were pressed against the outside window pane."

The targets of McCarthyism were often groups without much political clout, such as Jews and African Americans. Relying on familiar anti-Semitic stereotypes, conservative congressmen and the press frequently implied that Jews were not loyal to the nation. Civil rights organizations and black leaders faced the severest persecution since the 1920s. The Civil Rights Congress and the Negro Youth Council, for instance, were destroyed after frequent charges of red influence. W. E. B. Du Bois, the renowned black historian, and famed concert singer (and former All-American football hero) Paul Robeson had public appearances canceled and their right to travel abroad abridged.

In attacks on women's organizations and homosexual groups, meanwhile, anti-Communist rhetoric cloaked deep fears about changing sexual mores. HUAC published a pamphlet quoting a Columbia professor as saying that "girls' schools and

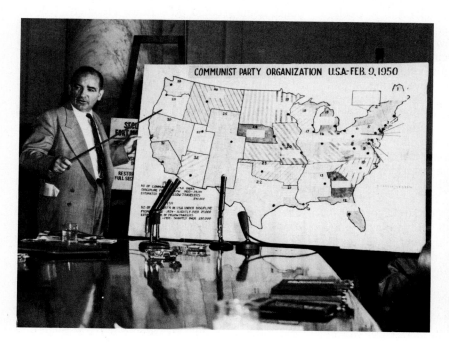

The tables turned on Senator Joseph McCarthy (1909–1957) after he instigated an investigation of the U.S. Army for harboring Communists. A Congressional committee then investigated McCarthy for attempting to make the Army grant special privileges to his staff aide, Private David Schine. During the televised hearings, Senator McCarthy discredited himself. In December 1954, the Senate voted to censure him.

women's colleges contain some of the most loyal disciples of Russia . . . often frustrated females. . . ." Guy Gabrielson, who chaired the Republican party, warned that "sexual perverts" who were possibly "as dangerous as actual Communists" had infiltrated the government. Aided by FBI reports, the federal government fired up to sixty homosexuals per month in the early 1950s. Undesirable discharges from the U.S. armed forces for homosexuality, an administrative procedure without appeal, also increased dramatically, to 2,000 per year. Even noted liberal historian Arthur Schlesinger, Jr., got into the act, accusing Henry Wallace's Progressive party supporters of wanting "something secret, sweaty and furtive like nothing so much . . . as homosexuals in a boys' school." Critics of the Cold War, Schlesinger suggested, were not "real" men, or, perhaps, "real" women either.

McCarthyism succeeded dramatically in its campaign of intimidation because McCarthy himself, as chair of the Permanent Subcommittee on Investigations of the Senate Government Operations Committee, went on making headlines and for a few years cowed potential opponents. He perfected the inquisitorial technique, asking directly, "Are you now, or have you ever been, a Communist?" By showing the press a blatantly doctored photo of Democratic senator Millard F. Tydings of Maryland talking with Soviet leaders, he helped defeat Tydings for reelection in 1950. When the distinguished liberal Republican Margaret Chase Smith of Maine appealed to fellow senators for support in a "Declaration of Conscience" against McCarthy's smear tactics, she secured only nine votes.

McCarthyism covered a circle far wider than Joseph McCarthy's reach, because many Americans had been terrified by global developments and because leading liberals and conservatives generally agreed on the chief cause of the crisis: Soviet aggression. The inflammatory rhetoric of the Truman Doctrine and accompanying political speeches comparing Communists to Satan or invasive bacteria promoted not only paranoia but hysteria. Attorney General J. Howard McGrath sounded the alarm in 1949: "Communists . . . are everywhere — in factories, offices, butcher shops, on street corners, in private businesses. . . . At this very moment [they are] busy at work — undermining your government, plotting to destroy the liberties of every citizen, and feverishly trying in whatever way they can, to aid the Soviet Union."

Joseph McCarthy and his fellow red-hunters eventually burned themselves out. During televised congressional hearings in 1954, not only did McCar-

thy fail to prove wild charges of Communist infiltration of the army, but in the glare of the television cameras he appeared deranged. Cowed for years, the Senate finally censured him for "conduct unbecoming a member." Other veteran purveyors of Communist-"conspiracy" charges, especially FBI director J. Edgar Hoover, continued to attack civil rights and peace organizations, and much repressive legislation remained in state and federal law. But the main energy of McCarthyism was spent.

AGE OF ANXIETY

At the end of World War II, while much of the world lay in rubble, the United States had begun the longest, steadiest period of economic growth and prosperity in its history. "We have about 50 percent of the world's wealth," George Kennan noted in 1948, "but only 3.6 percent of its population." Very large pockets of poverty remained, and all Americans did not share equally in the postwar abundance. Nonetheless, the continuous expansion of the economy and the improved living standards enjoyed by the majority stand as key domestic developments of the Cold War years.

Prosperity did not dispel an anxious mood. Many Americans feared an economic backslide. If war production had pushed aside the hardships of the Great Depression, how would the economy fare in peacetime? No one could say for sure. Above all, peace itself seemed precarious. President Truman himself suggested that World War III appeared inevitable, and his secretary of state, Dean Acheson, warned the nation to keep "on permanent alert." McCarthyism underscored the importance not only of distant enemies but of internal dangers. To ease their apprehensions, many Americans turned inward, abandoning politics for the security afforded by private life.

The Consumer Society

Shortages during World War II combined with high wages and full employment to produce a nation of eager consumers whose accumulated savings topped $150 billion. Once consumer goods reappeared, a spending spree of trailblazing proportions began. Consumers also enjoyed greater options in credit, which contributed to a rapid rise in personal debt. The Diner's Club, for example, established in 1950, pioneered a plan whereby cardholders "charged" their restaurant meals instead of paying in cash. The federal government abetted the post-

Energy Consumption, 1800–1951

Energy consumption, especially that dependent on fossil fuels, rises steadily from the early nineteenth century onward. As woodburning stoves disappeared, oil and natural gas (along with hydroelectric and atomic power) became the primary sources of energy.

Source: Jessie H. Ausubel and Robert Herman, eds., *Cities and Their Vital Systems* (Washington, D. C.: National Academy Press, 1980), fig. 8-16.

war surge by providing large-scale subsidies for housing, roads, and defense facilities. Whereas in 1929 federal expenditures represented just 1 percent of the GNP, within a decade after World War II they had reached 17 percent. Military spending accounted for the largest share of the growth.

The mix of government subsidies spawned sprawling, prosperous, mainly white and middle-class suburbs, such as those between San Diego and San Francisco. Homeownership defined a whole new way of living, impossible for previous generations. Whereas during the war no more than 300,000 new houses went up each year, more than four times that number were being built by the early 1950s. By the end of 1947, the GI Bill alone had underwritten mortgages for over 1 million veterans. Overall, homeownership rose from 43.6 percent in 1940 to a startling 55 percent in 1950. The majority of new homes were built in the suburbs, which absorbed nearly half of the increase in the nation's population. The construction of schools, churches, office buildings, shopping centers, and civic centers followed.

Automobiles, the heart of consumer-oriented production, made this pattern of growth possible. The quality of life meanwhile declined in the nation's major cities, which were deprived of govern-ment funds for low-cost housing comparable to the federal subsidies for suburban developments. The automobile allowed an easy commute between an urban job and a suburban home. By 1950 sales had hit 6.7 million units. Lower-priced models such as Chevrolets, Plymouths, and Fords were directed at blue-collar consumers.

"The year 1946," *Life* magazine claimed, "finds the U.S. on the threshold of marvels, ranging from runless stockings and shineless serge suits to jet-propelled airplanes that will flash across the country in just a little less than the speed of sound. . . ." For the first time, the majority of Americans could own consumer durables, such as automatic washers, and small appliances, from do-it-yourself power tools to cameras. The premier consumer item swept the nation: only 250,000 television sets were owned in 1949, but by the time Harry Truman left office two-thirds of all American households claimed at least one set.

The prosperity of the Cold War era also produced the nation's largest baby boom. Fertility rates had been dropping for well over a century before reaching an all-time low during the Great Depression. In 1933 the birth rate had bottomed out at 18.4 per 1,000 population. This trend reversed dramatically during World War II, when the birth rate climbed to nearly 23 per 1,000. A revived economy no doubt encouraged couples to marry younger and produce more children, as did insecurity about the fate of husbands going off to war. Demographers at the U.S. Census Bureau predicted that this wartime spurt would be temporary. To their surprise, the age of first marriage dropped even further while the birth rate continued to grow at a record pace, peaking at over 25 per 1,000 in 1957.

But something besides steady, higher wages facilitated this rush toward parenthood. As one writer noted, children represented a "defense — an impregnable bulwark" against the anxieties of the era.

The Two–Income Family

High rates of consumer spending and births encouraged an equally significant social development: the two-income family. During the first decade of the Cold War, women took jobs at a faster rate than men, providing half the total growth of the labor force. Despite this advance, women faced unprecedented pressure to devote themselves fulltime to their families and household affairs. Public opinion registered resounding disapproval — by 86 percent of those surveyed — of a married woman working if

This Cleveland family poses with a representation of the food they eat in an average year, including 300 pounds of beef and 350 pounds of sugar. The "American way of life," defined as a high standard of living, was one of the tangible fruits of U.S. victory in World War II.

jobs were scarce and her husband could support her. Commentators appealed for a return to an imaginary "traditional" family, where men alone were breadwinners and women stayed happily at home. And yet American women, including many who themselves shared this view, continued to enter the labor market. By 1952, 2 million more wives worked than at the peak of women's employment during World War II.

World War II had prepared many women for full-time employment, although reconversion to peacetime production forced the majority from their factory positions. Most women quickly returned, but not to high-paying, unionized jobs in manufacturing. Instead, they filled the expanding service sector: clerical work, health care and education, and restaurant, hotel, and retail services. Married women, especially mothers with children under the age of

eighteen, took most of these minimum wage jobs. "If it weren't for the children," one wife explained,

> I'd be tempted to try to get along on one salary, even if it meant skimping. But we need two incomes to enable us to have a house with a yard that the children can play in; to live in a neighborhood where I don't have to worry about their playmates; to provide a guitar for the musical one and dancing lessons for the one who needs to improve her muscular co-ordination — not to mention teeth-straightening and medical insurance and the bonds we are stowing away for their education.

Older women whose children were grown might work because they had enjoyed their wartime jobs and had come to value the experience of wage earning for its own sake. Young families, however, redefined the meaning of *economic necessity* to include a style of life demanding more than one income. Those women most likely to seek employment were white and married to men who earned between $6,000 and $10,000 — in short, members of the growing middle class.

Even though most women sought employment primarily to ensure their family's welfare, they ran up against popular opinion and expert advice urging them to return to their homes. Nervous writers noting that most Soviet women worked in industry, linked Communism to the destruction of the "traditional" family. To forestall this possibility, American men and women must play complementary but utterly different roles, they insisted. Just as the Marshall Plan and the Truman Doctrine responded to pitfalls abroad, the American family might "contain" dangers at home — if "restored" to its original form and function in the democratic nation.

This campaign began on a shrill note. Ferdinand Lundberg and Marynia Farnham, in their best-selling *Modern Woman: The Lost Sex* (1947), traced the "super-jittery age in which we live" to women's abandonment of the home to pursue careers. Like other Cold War liberals, they looked to the federal government to solve this problem. They proposed federally funded psychotherapy to readjust women to their housewifely roles and cash subsidies to encourage them to bear more children. They warned, too, that Red agents were at work in the United States encouraging American women to follow the Soviet example of equal rights in order to bring about the collapse of the American political system.

Articles in popular magazines, television shows, and high-profile experts chimed in with similar messages. Talcott Parsons, the distinguished Harvard sociologist, delineated the parameters of the "democratic" family: husbands served as breadwinners and links to the outside society, while

Wife and children of the typical white, middle-class family greet the breadwinning father arriving home from work. Such images, which appeared frequently in popular magazines, idealized the home as the safe haven from the tensions of the office and enshrined the family as the source of happiness and security.

wives — "the emotional hub of the family" — stayed home to care for their families. In the first edition of *Baby and Child Care* (1946), the child-rearing advice manual that soon outsold the Bible, Benjamin Spock similarly advised women to devote themselves full time, if financially possible, to their maternal responsibilities. "Women have many careers," another expert explained, "but only one vocation — motherhood."

The tension growing from the combination of wage earning and homemaking made many women anxious. As early as 1947 *Life* magazine registered this conflict in a thirteen-page feature, "American Woman's Dilemma." How could women comfortably take part in a world beyond the home and at the same time heed the advice of FBI director J. Edgar Hoover, who exalted the nation's "homemakers and mothers" to fulfill their unique role in fighting "the twin enemies of freedom — crime and communism"?

Religion and Education

Cold War uneasiness and the rampant fears of communism prompted a return to "old-time religion" in new settings. New fundamentalist churches arose, comprising mainly white Protestants who while moving from rural areas to cities and suburbs during World War II had changed their affiliations from mainstream denominations to Pentecostal or "born-again" Christian sects. The ideas of fundamentalism also spread quickly through the media as religious leaders adapted modern techniques of communication from consumer marketing.

Baptist Billy Graham emerged as the greatest of the Cold War evangelical ministers, star of the first major televised "crusades" for religious revival. Born in Charlotte, North Carolina, in 1918, Graham had grown up believing that all doubts in the literal truth of the Bible were traps set by Satan. He first became famous by giving a spiritual twist to Cold War anxieties, warning against the decline of "God-centered homes" and the increased number of wives who tried to "wear the trousers" of the family. Moral contagion, juvenile delinquency, liberalism, and communism could be halted only by what Graham called an "immediate decision for Christ." In 1950 he predicted the end of the world in "another year, maybe two years," and in 1952 he warned of catastrophe "unless this nation turns to Christ within the next few months." Yet even while he predicted imminent doom, Graham aligned himself with the Republican party and supported a large military budget. The United States, the last hope of Christianity, had to be protected.

Staunch anti-Communists such as Graham also looked suspiciously toward the nation's schools, long known for harboring liberal sympathies. In an era of higher education reshaped by the GI Bill, and of primary education reshaping itself to meet the postwar baby boom, the prestige and social importance of schooling reached new heights. According to guidelines set down by the Truman administration, teachers were to "strengthen national security through education," specifically redesigning their lesson plans to illustrate the superiority of the American democratic system over Soviet communism. In 1947 the federal Office of Education launched the "Zeal for Democracy" program for implementation by school boards nationwide.

Leading scholars demanded the same degree of political compliance from their colleagues. Samuel Eliot Morison insisted that fellow historians use their training and insight to mobilize young men for the impending conflict against the nation's foes. Richard Hofstadter's prize-winning 1948 volume *The American Political Tradition* insisted that the "rights of property, the philosophy of economic individualism, [and] the value of competition" constituted the uniquely American faith in "the economic virtues of capitalist culture as necessary qualities of man." Historians like Hofstadter portrayed earlier critics of this consensus, such as the Populists, as mentally unbalanced and dangerous to American democracy.

Hardening attitudes toward women's education reflected these conservative views. Women had made slight gains in higher education relative to men during World War II. When the GI Bill prompted a sudden upsurge in male enrollment, women lost ground. Some 40 percent of all college graduates in 1940, women represented only 25 percent a decade later. College administrators, disturbed by the trend toward women's wage earning and its social implications, called for a new curriculum that would prepare women for marriage and motherhood rather than careers. James Madison Wood, president of Stephens College, prescribed home economics as the basis of women's higher education, with such curriculum highlights as childcare and interior decoration. "The college years," he argued, "must be rehearsal periods for the major performance" — that is, the domestic performance — of women's lives.

Neither teachers nor students entirely accepted these prescriptions. A fearless minority of scholars pointed to the potential dangers of Cold War foreign policy. But the chilling atmosphere made their views at best unpopular.

The Cultural *Noir*

The postwar years, seen so optimistically in consumer terms, appeared to many observers a time of great psychic distress. The spirit of wartime unity had seemingly dissolved into rampant individualism, as newspaper headlines blasted the rapacity of war profiteers and selfish strikers. These Cold War anxieties soon surfaced in popular culture. For the returning veterans of the universally acclaimed film *The Best Years of Our Lives* (1946), the dreams of family life that had sustained them through years of fighting now somehow felt alien; their place in the household had become decidedly insecure. The feeling of community shared with wartime buddies dissipated, leaving only a profound sense of aloneness.

The genre of film *noir* (French for "black") brilliantly deepened this mood into an aesthetic. Movies like *Out of the Past, Deadline at Dawn,* and *They Live by Night* emphasized ruthless fate and betrayal. Their protagonists were strangers or loners falsely accused of crimes. High-contrast lighting emphasized life in the shadows and the difficulty of distinguishing friends from enemies. Feelings of frustration and loss of control seemed to come alive in characters played by tough, cynical Robert Mitchum. Many talented directors and writers of important *noir* films, however, were soon barred from Hollywood because of their association with radical causes.

Drama and novels described the contemporary alienation and anxiety in different terms. Playwright Arthur Miller sketched in *Death of a Salesman* (1949) an unforgettable portrait of self-destructive American individualism. Willy Loman, the play's hero, is a self-made man, a totally devoted salesman but a miserable failure. Worse, he has trained his sons in the arts of personal presentation and style — the very methods prescribed by standard American success manuals — making them both shallow and materialistic. J. D. Salinger's widely praised novel *Catcher in the Rye* (1951) focused on the confusion of youth and the rampant mistrust of the world of materialistic adults.

Cold War anxiety found its strangest manifestation in the flurry of Unidentified Flying Object (UFO, or flying saucer) sightings, the largest number since a similar wave in 1896. The U.S. Air Force closed its own investigations with a flat denial of any valid evidence, but a respected former Marine Corps major, Donald E. Keyhoe, attacked the official report as a cover-up in *The Flying Saucers Are Real* (1950). Dozens of private researchers and faddists claimed to have been contacted by aliens demanding that earthlings cease atomic testing. The popular film *The Day the Earth Stood Still* (1951) carried the same message, in the form of a godlike being who warns earthlings to abandon their weaponry. A very different genre of science fiction films, such as *The Thing* (1950), depicted space beings as akin to Communists, ruthless invaders to be met with military force and destroyed or driven from the planet.

The symbols of prosperity, such as large families, suburban homes, and automobiles, did not necessarily reflect a society at ease with its new-found wealth. To the contrary, many Americans believed the growing abundance of consumer goods would weaken the nation's moral fiber by encouraging acquisitive individualism. Equally important, material well-being could not in itself offset the domestic insecurity provoked by the Cold War. In 1950 the *New York Times* reported a chilling aspect of the boom in real estate: "country properties for this Atomic Age," located at least fifty miles outside major cities — the most likely targets, it was thought, of a Soviet nuclear attack. Meanwhile, schoolchildren were taught to prepare themselves for a surprise attack by ducking under their desks and closing their eyes against the blinding light of a nuclear bomb.

END OF THE DEMOCRATIC ERA

The Cold War created unresolvable dilemmas for Franklin Roosevelt's successor. Truman managed to project a vision of a strong, great nation and to rebuild the economy through an unprecedented buildup of peacetime military resources. To justify the escalation of arms and the abandonment of New Dealer reform visions, he felt compelled to portray communism as an intolerable threat to the nation's security. But Communist-run nations could not be conquered militarily, if at all, without the risk of another world war and a level of destruction unacceptable to American civilians.

As the Korean War showed, Truman had trapped himself within his own rhetoric. Asking Americans to sanction a limited war, one with significant casualties but no total victory in sight, meant probable political suicide. But the president had ruled out any escape. Amid the excitement and controversy of the war, Truman brought down the twenty-year Democratic lock on the presidency and ended the greatest era of reform in U.S. history.

The Korean War

On June 25, 1950, President Truman was called back to Washington, D.C., from a vacation at his home in Independence, Missouri. The State Department had just received a cablegram reporting a military attack on South Korea by Communist-controlled North Korea. Secretary of State Acheson immediately set up an emergency meeting of the UN Security Council to request action. Hoping to carve a niche in history by "being tough" on Communists, Truman now had to live up to his reputation.

Events in Korea underlined the major political tensions of the entire Cold War. Following the Axis defeat in 1945, the Allies agreed to occupy Korea, a colony of Japan since 1910, and divided the small peninsula at the thirty-eighth parallel. Although all parties hoped to reunite the nation under its own government, the line between north and south instead hardened. By 1950 the two superpowers had withdrawn their occupying forces, but in the South the United States backed the unpopular government of Syngman Rhee (the Republic of Korea), while the Soviet Union sponsored a rival government in North Korea under Kim Il Sung.

Truman considered the invasion not a civil war—as George Kennan rightly concluded at the time—but a major Soviet test of the U.S. policy of containment, an act of aggression that had to be met with force. "Korea is the Greece of the Far East," the president announced. "If we are tough enough now, if we stand up to them like we did in Greece three years ago, they won't take any next steps," he explained. The Soviets, on the other hand, regarded the invasion as "Kim Il Sung's affair." While supplying military equipment, they insisted they had neither ordered nor directed the attack. Having recently been accused of "selling out" Eastern Europe and "losing" China, Truman felt compelled to act. Three days after the invasion, the president sought approval from the UN Security Council to send in troops. Due to the absence of the Soviet delegate, who could have vetoed the decision, the Security Council agreed. Two-thirds of Americans polled approved the president's decision to send troops under the command of General Douglas MacArthur.

At first, military events confirmed the wisdom of the president's action. Seoul, the capital of South Korea, had fallen to North Korean troops within weeks of the invasion, and the Communist forces continued to push south until they had taken most of

American soldiers fought in Korea under the command of General Douglas MacArthur until President Truman named General Matthew Ridgway as his replacement in April 1951. Nearly 1.8 million Americans served in Korea.

The Korean War

The intensity of battles underscored the strategic importance of Korea in the Cold War.

the peninsula. The situation appeared grim until Truman authorized MacArthur to carry out an amphibious landing at Inchon. With tactical brilliance and good fortune, the general orchestrated a military campaign that succeeded on September 15, 1950, in halting the Communist drive. By October, UN troops had retaken South Korea.

Believing himself invincible, MacArthur now determined to "roll back" the invaders beyond the thirty-eighth parallel. Until this point, China had not been actively involved in the war. But it now warned that any attempt to cross the dividing line would be interpreted as a threat to its own national security. Kennan predicted China would retaliate. Opinion polls nevertheless showed most Americans opposed to anything less than total victory. Truman flew to Wake Island in the Pacific on October 15 for a conference with MacArthur, who assured the president that the chances of China or the Soviet Union joining the war were "very little." Moreover, he promised to have the UN troops "home by Christmas."

Overconfident, MacArthur had sorely miscalculated the effects of his UN forces driving across

Estimates of Total Cost of U.S. Wars (in millions of dollars, except percent)

War	Estimated Total War Costs	Original War Costs	Total Costs under Present Laws	Veterans' Benefits	
				Percent of Original War Costs	Total Costs to 1970
	849	850	851	852	853
Vietnam conflict	352,000	110,000	220,000	200	2,461
Korean conflict	164,000	54,000	99,000	184	15,016
World War II	664,000	288,000	290,000	100	87,445
World War I	112,000	26,000	75,000	290	45,585
Spanish-American War	6,460	400	6,000	1,505	5,436

Source: *Statistical Abstract of the United States,* 1991, p. 1140.

North Korea almost to the Chinese border. Zhou Enlai ordered Chinese troops to amass just above them, at the Yalu River. Suddenly, and without any air support, the Chinese attacked in human waves. After some of the fiercest fighting of the war, MacArthur's force was all but crushed. European allies warned against escalation, and White House officials debated deployment of the atomic bomb. The Chinese drove the UN troops back to South Korea, where they regrouped along the thirty-eighth parallel. By summer 1951, a stalemate had been reached very near the old border. Negotiations for a settlement went on for the next eighteen months amid heavy fighting.

"There is no substitute for victory," MacArthur insisted as he tried without success to convince Truman to prepare for a new invasion of Communist territory. Encouraged by strong support at home, he continued to provoke the president by speaking out against official policy, calling for bombing of supply lines in China and a naval blockade of the Chinese coast — actions certain to lead to a Chinese-American war. Finally, on April 12, 1951, Truman dismissed MacArthur for insubordination and other unauthorized activities, including off-the-record discussions with officials of Francisco Franco's Fascist government in Spain. As General Omar N. Bradley later remarked, MacArthur had proposed "the wrong war, at the wrong place and at the wrong time, and with the wrong enemy." He had also placed himself above the civilian commander in chief of the armed forces.

The Legacy of the "Sour Little War"

The Korean War had profound implications for the use of executive power. By instituting a peacetime draft in 1948 and then ordering American troops into Korea, Truman had bypassed congressional authority. Senators and representatives, like the rest of the nation, learned that the U.S. had already gone to war. Senator Robert Taft called the president's actions "a complete usurpation" of democratic checks and balances. Truman sidestepped such criticisms and their constitutional implications by carefully referring to the military deployment not as a U.S. war but as a UN-sanctioned "police action."

The president derived his authority from NSC-68, a paper adopted by the National Security Council in April 1950 that reinterpreted the basic policy of containment as well as decision making at the highest levels of government. Describing communism as "a new fanatic faith" that "seeks to impose its absolute authority over the rest of the world," NSC-68 pledged the United States not only to drive back Communist influence throughout the world but also to "foster the seeds of destruction within the Soviet Union." As Dean Acheson observed later, NSC-68 was the new "fundamental" paper of U.S. foreign policy. Its use demonstrated, as a prominent historian and former navy commander observed, a "centralization of power" in which the entire government "had literally been compressed or consolidated into the President and his like-minded appointees."

The Korean War, which permitted Truman to activate NSC-68, also provided the president the public rationale for a rapid and permanent military buildup, including the allocation of at least 20 percent of the GNP to national defense. Between 1950 and 1953, when the conflict subsided, military spending rose from $13 billion to over $50 billion annually. Over the summer of 1950 the size of the U.S. armed forces expanded from 630,000 to 1 million, and in 1951 the military began to draft young men eighteen and a half and older. By 1952 the U.S. Army had grown to 3.6 million, or six times its size at the beginning of the conflict. The war itself eventually cost the United States approximately $100 billion.

These policies provoked important critics to speak out. The military chiefs, especially Secretary of Defense Louis Johnson, worried that spending on this scale might seriously distort the economy and prove impossible to sustain. Columnist Walter Lippmann pointed out that a massive peacetime military buildup would inevitably give the president and his close advisers unprecedented power.

The outcome of the Korean War did nothing to improve Truman's case for rolling back communism. Negotiations and fighting proceeded in tandem until the summer of 1953, when a settlement was reached in which both North Korea and South Korea occupied almost the same territory as when the war began. American casualties topped 142,000; the North Koreans and Chinese lost well over 2 million people. The war devastated the civilian populations in both North and South, for the UN troops had used both carpet bombing and napalm, destroying most of the housing and food supplies in Korea. True to the emerging pattern of modern warfare, the majority of civilians killed were women and children. Nearly 1 million Koreans were left homeless.

For the United States, the Korean War extended the principle of containment far beyond Europe and enlarged the geographical range of the Cold War to include the Far East. The war also lined up the People's Republic of China and the United States as unwavering enemies for the next twenty years and heightened U.S. commitment to Southeast Asia. Now, as one historian commented, the "frontiers on every continent were going to remain frontiers in the traditional American meaning of a frontier — a region to penetrate and control and police and civilize."

The Korean War, moreover, did much to establish an ominous tradition of "unwinnable" conflicts that left many American soldiers and civilians skeptical of official policy. Truman and the State Department had initially rallied popular support for U.S. intervention by contrasting the Communist North with the "democratic" South, thus casting the conflict into the ideological terms of the Cold War. MacArthur's early victories had promised the liberation of North Korea and even the eventual disintegration of the Russian and Chinese regimes. But with the tactical stalemate came mass disillusionment.

In retrospect many Americans recognized that Truman, in fighting communism in Korea, had pledged the United States to defend a corrupt government and a brutal dictator. Decades later the Korean War inspired the dark comedy "M*A*S*H," adapted for television from the film written by Hollywood screenwriter Ring Lardner, Jr. Lardner, an "unfriendly witness" before HUAC, who was jailed during the Korean War for contempt of Congress. As late as 1990, members of Congress were still debating the terms of a Korean War memorial. "It ended on a sad note for Americans," one historian has concluded, "and the war and its memories drifted off into a void."

Truman's Downfall

There was only one burning issue during the election campaign of 1952: the Korean War. Opinion polls indicated widespread frustration with Truman's conduct of the war. Although respondents did not know what they wanted instead — an invasion of China, as MacArthur had planned, or an immediate withdrawal of U.S. troops — they were clearly angry at the leader who had created the bloody deadlock.

Truman's popularity had wavered continually since he took office in 1945, but it sank to an all-time low in the early 1950s shortly after he dismissed MacArthur as commander of the UN troops in Korea. The White House received thousands of letters and telegrams calling for Truman's impeachment. If Congress did not get rid of the Truman/Acheson team, McCarthy roared, "Asia, the Pacific and Europe may be lost to Communism" and "Red waters may lap at all of our shores." Effigies of the president were burned in California, and "Oust President Truman" bumper stickers could be seen. MacArthur, meanwhile, returned home a hero, welcomed by over 7 million fans in New York City alone.

A furious but short-lived MacArthur-for-president campaign began. On April 19, 1951, MacArthur gave an impassioned address to a joint session of the Congress. Legislators, many with tears in their eyes, gave him a standing ovation. But over the next two months, as the Senate Armed Services and Foreign Relations Committee conducted open hearings about MacArthur's role in Korea, the general's popularity rapidly fell.

While discrediting MacArthur, the hearings also revealed the extent of popular dissatisfaction with Truman. Newspapers reported that officials in his administration had been dealing in 5 percent kickbacks for government contracts, just the kind of corruption that critics had predicted when Truman replaced veteran New Dealers with his political cronies. Business and organized labor complained about the price and wage freezes imposed during the Korean War. A late-1951 Gallup poll showed the president's approval rating at 23 percent. In early 1952, Truman announced he would not run for reelection, a decision rare for a president eligible for another term.

In accepting political defeat and disgrace, Truman left the Democratic party in disarray. The Democrats' best hope for victory now lay in convincing Dwight Eisenhower to run on their ticket, although his reputation as a moderate conservative suggested no continuity with party traditions. When Eisenhower politely refused their offers, Democratic leaders turned to the popular but uncharismatic governor of Illinois, Adlai E. Stevenson, Jr.

Admired for his honesty and intelligence, Stevenson offered no solutions to the conflict in Korea, the accelerating arms race, or the Cold War generally. Accepting the Democratic nomination, Stevenson candidly admitted that "the ordeal of the twentieth century is far from over," a prospect that voters aching for peace were hardly eager to contemplate.

The Republicans made the most of the Democrats' dilemma. Without proposing any sweeping answers of their own, they pointed to all the obvious shortcomings of their opponents. The Korean stasis dovetailed with the "K_1C_2" — Korea, communism, and corruption — line of attack on the Democratic administration. Traditional Republican conservatives wanted to nominate Robert Taft, shrewd critic of Truman's "imperial" presidency and author of the antilabor Taft-Hartley Act. But when opinion polls showed that Dwight Eisenhower possessed an "unprecedented" 64 percent approval rating, and when

"Ike" allowed himself to be "drafted" for the Republican nomination, his triumph within the party was certain. Republicans had waited too long for a White House victory.

Eisenhower styled himself the moderate. He wisely avoided the negative impressions made by the unsuccessful 1948 Republican candidate, Thomas Dewey, who had seemed as aggressive as Truman on foreign policy and simultaneously eager to overturn the New Deal domestic legislation. Eisenhower knew better: voters wanted peace and government-assisted prosperity. He neither threatened to widen the war, as MacArthur had done, nor supported the stalemate created by Truman. He appeared firm but not confrontational. He promised to end the Korean War with "an early and honorable" peace, although he did not go into specifics. Whenever he was tempted to address questions of finance or the economy, his advisers warned him: "The chief reason that people want to vote for you is because they think you have more ability to keep us out of another war."

Meanwhile, Eisenhower's vice-presidential candidate, Richard Nixon, waged a relentless and defamatory attack on Stevenson, whom he called "Adlai the Appeaser." Nixon, who had made a name for himself charging the Truman administration with being "soft on communism," assaulted the "Ph.D. graduate of Dean Acheson's cowardly College of Communist Containment." Senator Joseph McCarthy chimed in, proclaiming that with club in hand he

Richard Nixon used the new media of television to convince American voters that he had not established an illegal slush fund in his campaign for the vice-presidency in 1952. Viewers responded enthusiastically to his melodramatic delivery and swamped the Republican campaign headquarters with telegrams endorsing his candidacy.

might be able to make "a good American" of Stevenson. A month before the election, McCarthy went on network television with his requisite "exhibits" and "documents," this time purportedly showing that the Democratic presidential candidate had promoted communism at home and abroad. Democrats had been as doggedly anti-Communist as Republicans, of course, and Stevenson held international views close to those of the confrontational Truman. But the political oratory helped to win over wavering Democrats and the outrageous charges kept the Stevenson campaign off balance.

The Republican campaign was itself not entirely free of scandal: Richard Nixon had been caught accepting personal gifts from wealthy benefactors. Nixon chose to plead his case on national television. Describing his wife Pat's "good Republican cloth coat" and their modest style of living, he contritely admitted that he had indeed accepted one gift, a puppy named Checkers that his daughters loved, and that he refused to give back. "The Poor Richard Show," as critics called the event, defused the scandal without answering the most important charges.

Eisenhower, meanwhile, continued to enchant the voters as a peace candidate, appealing especially to women. Ten days before the election he dramatically announced, "I shall go to Korea" to settle the war. Eisenhower received 55 percent of the vote and carried thirty-nine states, in part because he brought out an unusually large number of voters in normally Democratic areas. He won the popular vote in much of the South and in the northern cities of New York, Chicago, Boston, and Cleveland. He tallied 58.5 percent of the women's vote, to 52.5 percent of the men's. Riding his coattails, the Republicans regained control of Congress for the first time (except 1946–48) since before the New Deal. The Democratic coalition of ethnic and black voters, labor, northern liberals, and southern conservatives was no longer a majority.

CONCLUSION

Dwight Eisenhower's election diminished the intensity of the Cold War mood without actually halting the conflict. "The Eisenhower Movement," wrote Walter Lippmann, was a "mission in American politics" to restore a sense of community among the American people. In a larger sense, many of the issues of the immediate post–World War II years seemed to have been settled, or put off for a distant future. The international boundaries of communism were frozen with the Chinese Revolution, the Berlin Blockade, and now the Korean War. Meanwhile, at home Cold War defense spending had become a permanent part of the national budget, an undeniable drain on tax revenues but an important element in the government contribution to economic prosperity. If the nuclear arms race remained a cause for anxiety, joined by more personal worries about the changing patterns of family life, a sense of relative security nevertheless spread. Prospects for world peace had dimmed, but the worst nightmares of the 1940s had eased as well.

CHRONOLOGY

1941	Henry Luce's ''American Century''
1944	IMF and World Bank founded at Bretton Woods GI Bill
1945	Truman becomes president UN charter signed World War II ends Strike wave begins Truman proposes program of economic reforms
1946	Churchill's Iron Curtain speech Employment Act Atomic Energy Act Republicans win control of Congress Benjamin Spock, *Baby and Child Care*
1947	Americans for Democratic Action founded Truman Doctrine Taft-Hartley Act National Security Act Creation of attorney general's list of subversive organizations Federal Employee Loyalty Program established Marshall Plan HUAC hearings in Hollywood Lundberg and Farnham, *Modern Woman: The Lost Sex*
1948	State of Israel founded Berlin crisis Truman announces first peacetime draft and desegregates U.S. Army Henry Wallace runs for president on Progressive party ticket Truman wins election; Democrats sweep both houses of Congress
1949	Truman announces Fair Deal NATO created USSR explodes atomic bomb Communists take power in China
1950	Alger Hiss convicted of perjury Senator Joseph McCarthy begins anti-Communist crusade Adoption of NSC-68 Korean War begins Internal Security (McCarran) Act
1951	Truman dismisses MacArthur Armistice talks begin in Korea
1952	Hydrogen bomb exploded by U.S. Immigration and Nationality Act Eisenhower wins presidency; Richard Nixon becomes vice-president
1953	Julius and Ethel Rosenberg executed Armistice ends fighting in Korea
1954	Army-McCarthy Hearings

Additional Readings

Larry Ceplair and Steven Englund, *The Inquisition in Hollywood: Politics in the Film Community, 1930–1960* (1980). A study of the Hollywood blacklist of Communist filmmakers and actors and the effect of investigative hearings upon their community. Shows how the banning of important writers and actors changed the content of Hollywood films, in effect proscribing "social themes" for a decade.

Martin Bauml Duberman, *Paul Robeson* (1988). A biography of the renowned African American singer and actor who was driven from the stage for political reasons. Shows Robeson as a great artist but also a self-conscious representative of black rights who felt compelled to oppose U.S. foreign policy and suddenly lost his public career.

Lloyd C. Gardner, *Architects of Illusion: Men and Ideas in American Foreign Policy, 1941–1949* (1970). Biographical vignettes with critical interpretation of the major figures of U.S. international policy. Faults their efforts to control world policy making for drawing the country into an arms race and a mutually destructive Cold War.

Joyce and Gabriel Kolko, *The Limits of Power: The World and United States Foreign Policy, 1945–1954* (1972). A detailed commentary on U.S. efforts to dictate world conditions. Shows that the complexities of world politics, especially the rise of colonized nations toward independence, placed control outside American hands.

George Lipsitz, *Class and Culture in Cold War America: "A Rainbow at Midnight"* (1981). A vivid account of economic and cultural hopes, uneasiness, and disappointments after the war. Shows how struggles for economic democracy were defeated, and how popular culture — for example, country-and-western music and the roller derby — arose in blue-collar communities.

Elaine Tyler May, *Homeward Bound: American Families in the Cold War Era* (1988). A lively account of the effects on family life and women's roles of the national mood of "containment." Examines how government policy became part of a popular culture that firmed the Cold War era's "feminine mystique."

David G. McCullough, *Truman* (1992). An uncritical rendition of Truman's personal life and political career. Through personal correspondence and other documents, details Truman's view of himself and the generally favorable view of him by supporters of Cold War liberalism.

Victor S. Navasky, *Naming Names* (1980). A fascinating account of government informants, McCarthyism, and the blacklist. Especially interesting treatments of academic life, where blacklisting made only a slight impact, and Hollywood, where McCarthyism changed American popular culture.

David M. Oshinsky, *A Conspiracy So Immense: The World of Joe McCarthy* (1983). A study of McCarthyism and the driving personality within it. Presents a keen view of McCarthy as a product of his background and the political conditions of the time, a clever politician who found widespread support in the Republican party.

Walter and Miriam Schneir, *Invitation to an Inquest: A New Look at the Rosenberg-Sobell Case* (1983 ed.). An account of the "atom spy" case. Convinced of the defendants' innocence, the Schneirs examine the evidence, the questionable (perhaps illegal) methods used to gain conviction, and the significance of the death sentence that was handed down.

Daniel Yergin, *Shattered Peace: The Origins of the Cold War and the National Security State* (1977). Lucidly interprets the motives of the Americans and the Soviets that led to a full-scale arms race. Shows that each side misinterpreted the motives of the other and thereby lost the opportunity to attain world peace.

• ROCK-'N'-ROLL UNITES THE YOUNG

Inside the packed Cleveland Arena, a capacity audience of 11,000 young people stomped, whistled, and clapped rhythmically for the show to begin. Outside the building, a milling crowd of 6,000 ticket holders grew restless. Many had already paid $1.75 for their ticket to the Moondog Coronation Ball, yet it appeared they would not be allowed in. They had come from as far away as Toledo and Akron to hear a concert featuring several of the hottest rhythm-and-blues musical groups in the country. The musicians getting ready to perform were all African Americans, as were the majority of the impatient audience. A smattering of young white people were also in the crowd. A group of angry ticket holders suddenly took matters into their own hands. Pushing aside a small police guard, they broke down four outside doors and barreled into the arena. Amid the chaos inside, a police captain mounted the stage and announced the show was canceled. It took thirty policeman two hours to clear the hall and the streets, as thousands of young people reluctantly went home.

POPULAR MUSIC CREATES A NEW TEENAGE COMMUNITY

The ill-fated Cleveland Arena show in March 1952 was a flash point in the creation of a new teenage community. In the postwar years, a new popular music called rock-'n'-roll became the most important expression of the common identity of American young people. Rock-'n'-roll was an unprecedented cultural phenomenon, a music made largely for and by teens. The promoter of the Moondog Coronation Ball was Alan Freed, a local disk jockey who first popularized the term rock-'n'-roll. The phrase had long been a slang expression in African American speech and song, a shorthand for dancing and sexual intercourse. Freed had noticed that many young white listeners were dissatisfied with the bland, cloying pop records of the day. For dancing, driving, courting, and lovemaking, young whites increasingly turned to the rhythmic drive and emotional singing found in the best rhythm-and-blues records made by black artists.

Freed played this music regularly on his radio show, calling it rock-'n'-roll, and he began staging live shows that sold out in cities across the Midwest. The shows were advertised only on Freed's own radio program, which had developed a large and enthusiastic following throughout the region. By the mid-1950s rhythm-and-blues, once limited in sales appeal to the relatively small black market, had become very popular

(Tom Wesselmann. Still Life #30. 1963. Oil, enamel, and synthetic polymer paint on composition board with collage of printed advertisements, plastic artificial flowers, refrigerator door, plastic replicas of 7-Up bottles, glazed and framed color reproduction, and stamped metal. 48-1/2" × 66" × 4". The Museum of Modern Art, New York. Gift of Philip Johnson.)

Teenage fans began lining up before dawn at New York's Paramount Theater for Alan Freed's "Rock'n'Roll Revue," February 22, 1957. Concerts such as these signalled the arrival of the teenager as a new social force wielding considerable economic power in postwar America.

with white teenagers. "The present generation has not known the rhythmically exciting dance bands of the swing era," the music trade magazine Billboard noted. "It therefore satisfies its hunger for 'music with a beat' in modern r&b groups." Jukeboxes and radio broadcasts also reflected this trend, as white teenagers began buying the records of African American artists such as Chuck Berry, Fats Domino, Ruth Brown, Little Richard, and the Platters.

Structural changes in the postwar American mass media combined with this new teenage demand to reshape the nation's popular music. Television broadcasting rapidly replaced radio as the center of family entertainment. Locally produced radio shows, featuring music, news, and outrageous disk jockeys, replaced the old star-studded network programs. The production of portable transistor radios and car radios grew rapidly in the 1950s, as listeners increasingly tuned in as a diversion from or accompaniment to other activities. By 1956, 2,700 AM radio stations were on the air across the U.S., with about 70 percent of their broadcast time given to record shows. Popular disk jockeys achieved cultlike status among their invisible communities of listeners.

The existence of a separate and definable youth culture, embodied by middle-class white suburban teens, became an article of faith among journalists, social scientists, advertisers, and educators. Rock-'n'-roll was perhaps the most visible and lucrative aspect of this cultural phenomenon. In communities all over America, rock-'n'-roll brought teens together around jukeboxes, at sock hops, in cars, and at private parties. Rock-'n'-roll demonstrated the enormous consumer power of American teens: the dollar value of annual record sales nearly tripled between 1954 and 1959, from $213 million to $603 million. Teen-oriented movies, magazines, clothing stores, and advertising all revolved around the new musical craze.

By 1957 Alan Freed had moved to New York City, where he became the most popular radio personality in the country. On Washington's Birthday that year, he brought his live "Rock 'n' Roll Revue" to one of the pinnacles of American show business, the Paramount Theatre in Times Square. Like his first show in 1952 in Cleveland, this one featured African American performers exclusively. But the audience was now mostly white. Over 15,000 teenage fans broke records at the box office; the long lines snaked back through Times Square from 4 a.m. to midnight, tying up midtown traffic. Two hundred New York police kept order, and the performance went on continuously without a hitch. Fans sang along, stood on their seats, danced in the aisles, and shouted their love for Frankie Lymon and the Teenagers, Ruth Brown, the Platters, and the Cadillacs.

The day of the concert, a Columbia University psychiatrist denounced rock-'n'-roll as "a sign of depersonalization of the individual, of ecstatic veneration of mental decline and passivity." Interviewed by the New York Times, Alan Freed offered a different view: "It's the rhythm that gets the kids. They are starved for music they can dance to, after all those years of crooners. They are not bad kids, they are just enthusiastic." Thirteen-year-old Rosemary Samaritano

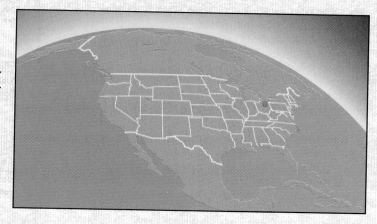

of Brooklyn agreed: "It's not true what they say about rock 'n' roll. Rock 'n' roll keeps kids off the street. They stay home and listen to it on the radio and phonograph."

In 1993, four decades after Alan Freed's historic Moondog Coronation Ball, a group of rock-'n'-roll performers and music business executives gathered in Cleveland to celebrate the ground-breaking of the Rock-'n'-Roll Hall of Fame.

AMERICAN SOCIETY AT MIDCENTURY

In his influential work *The Affluent Society* (1958), economist John Kenneth Galbraith observed that American capitalism had worked "quite brilliantly" in the years since World War II. The title of his book became a universally used description of postwar America, even for those who disagreed with Galbraith's larger argument—that Americans needed to spend less on personal consumption and devote more public funds to schools, medical care, cultural activities, and social services. But most Americans viewed the strong economic growth of the postwar period as the defining fact in the nation's life. In the years immediately following World War II, American culture reflected a fierce desire for consumer goods and "the good life." The deeply held popular assumption of a continuous expansion of the economy, along with a steady increase in the standard of living for most Americans, continued to shape social life and politics throughout the postwar era.

The Eisenhower Presidency

Dwight D. Eisenhower's landslide election victory in 1952 set the stage for the first full two-term Republican presidency since that of Ulysses S. Grant. During his eight-year administration, intellectuals and liberals found it easy to satirize and attack Eisenhower for his blandness, his frequent verbal gaffes, his vagueness, and his often contradictory pronouncements. But for Eisenhower, politics demanded conciliation and compromise more than devotion to principle and truth. He consciously adopted an evasive style in public. He was fond of the phrase "middle of the road." He told a news conference, "I feel pretty good when I'm attacked from both sides. It makes me more certain I'm on the right track." The majority of the American public evidently agreed with Eisenhower's easygoing approach to his office. "The public loves Ike," observed one journalist in 1959. "The less he does the more they love him. That, probably, is the secret. Here is a man who doesn't rock the boat."

Eisenhower's style owed something to his roots in turn-of-the-century Kansas and his socialization in the military. In the army he had risen through the command structure by playing it safe, keeping his own counsel, and allowing his subordinates to apprise him of his options. He once described his views on leadership to a critic: "It's persuasion—and conciliation—and patience. It's long, slow, tough work. That's the only kind of leadership I know or believe in—or will practice." By espousing a philosophy he called "dynamic conservatism," Eisenhower kept the two wings of his party united, and appealed to many Democrats and independents. "In all those things which deal with people, be liberal, be human. In all those things which deal with the people's money or their economy, or their form of government, be conservative."

In practice, this meant that Eisenhower wanted to run government in a businesslike manner while letting the states and corporate interests guide domestic policy and the economy. Eisenhower appointed nine businessmen to his first Cabinet, including three officials with ties to General Motors. Former GM chief Charles Wilson served as secretary of defense and epitomized the administration's economic views with his famous aphorism "What's good for General Motors business is good for America." In his appointments to the Federal Trade Commission, the Federal Communications Commission, and the Federal Power Commission, Eisenhower favored men congenial to the corporate interests they were charged with regulating. Eisenhower also secured passage of the Submerged Lands Act in 1953, which transferred $40 billion worth of disputed offshore oil lands from the federal government to the Gulf states. This insured a greater role for the states and private companies in the oil business, and cost the Treasury billions in lost revenues.

In the long run, the Eisenhower administration's lax approach to government regulation accelerated a trend toward the destruction of the natural environment. Oil exploration in Louisiana's bayous, for example, began the massive degradation of America's largest wetlands. Water diversion policies in Florida seriously damaged the biggest tropical forest in the United States. The increased use of toxic chemicals, begun during World War II and largely unregulated by law, placed warehouses of poisons in hundreds of sites, many abutting military installations. Virtually unregulated use and disposal of the pesticide DDT poisoned birds and other animals, and left permanent toxic scars in the environment. Eisenhower's atomic energy program, administered by the Atomic Energy Commission, exposed thousands of Nevada residents to radioactive contamination from nuclear tests. Weapons plants in communities such as Hanford, Washington, dumped radioactive wastes that poisoned surrounding farms and Indian reservations. Eisenhower's Atoms for Peace program launched the nuclear energy industry with promises of cheap electricity and power, thereby discouraging the search for renewable energy sources.

Distribution of Total Personal Income among Various Segments of the Population, 1947–1970 (in Percentages)

Year	Poorest Fifth	Second Poorest Fifth	Middle Fifth	Second Wealthiest Fifth	Wealthiest Fifth	Wealthiest 5 Percent
1947	3.5	10.6	16.7	23.6	45.6	18.7
1950	3.1	10.5	17.3	24.1	45.0	18.2
1960	3.2	10.6	17.6	24.7	44.0	17.0
1970	3.6	10.3	17.2	24.7	44.1	16.9

Note: Despite the general prosperity of the postwar era, unequal distribution of income remained essentially unchanged.
*Monetary income only.

Source: Adapted from U.S. Bureau of the Census, *Historical Statistics of the United States, Colonial Times to 1970,* Bicentennial Edition (Washington, D.C.: U.S. Government Printing Office, 1975), p. 292.

At the same time, Eisenhower accepted the New Deal legacy of greater federal responsibility for social welfare. He rejected calls from conservative Republicans, for example, to dismantle the Social Security system. His administration agreed to a modest expansion of Social Security and unemployment insurance and small increases in the minimum wage. Ike also created the Department of Health, Education, and Welfare, appointing Oveta Culp Hobby as only the second woman to hold a Cabinet post. In agriculture, Eisenhower continued the policy of parity payments designed to sustain farm prices. Between 1952 and 1960, Federal spending on agriculture jumped from about $1 billion to $7 billion.

Eisenhower proved hesitant to use fiscal policy to pump up the economy. After the Korean War ended in 1953, and again in 1958, when the unemployment rate reached 7.5 percent, the economy went into a recession. The administration refused to cut taxes or increase spending to stimulate growth. Eisenhower feared starting an inflationary spiral more than he worried about unemployment or poverty. By the time he left office, Eisenhower could proudly point out that real wages for an average family had risen 20 percent during his term. Combined with low inflation and steady, if modest, growth, the Eisenhower years meant greater prosperity for most Americans. Long after he retired from public life, Ike liked to remember his major achievement as having created "an atmosphere of greater serenity and mutual confidence."

Subsidizing Prosperity

During the Eisenhower years the federal government played a crucial role in subsidizing programs that helped millions of Americans achieve middle-class status. Federal aid helped people to buy homes, attend college and technical schools, and live in newly built suburbs. Much of this assistance expanded upon programs begun during the New Deal and World War II. For example, the Federal Housing Administration (FHA), established in 1934, extended the government's role in subsidizing the housing industry. Over the next half century, the FHA arguably had as great an impact on the lives of average Americans as any other federal agency. The FHA insured long-term mortgage loans made by private lenders for home building. By putting the full faith and credit of the federal government behind residential mortgages, the FHA attracted new private capital into home building and revolutionized the industry. A typical FHA mortgage required less than 10 percent for a down payment and spread low-interest monthly payments over thirty years.

Yet FHA policies also had longer-range negative effects. FHA insurance went overwhelmingly to new residential developments, usually on the fringes of urban areas, and this hastened the decline of older inner-city neighborhoods. A bias toward suburban, middle-class communities manifested itself in several ways: it was FHA policy to favor the construction of single-family projects while discouraging multi-unit housing; to refuse loans for the repair of older structures and rental units; and to require for any loan guarantee an "unbiased professional estimate" rating the property, the prospective borrower, and the neighborhood. In practice, these estimates resulted in blatant discrimination against communities that were racially mixed. The FHA's *Underwriting Manual* bluntly warned: "If a neighborhood is to retain stability, it is necessary that properties shall continue to be occupied by the same social and racial classes." FHA policies in effect inscribed the

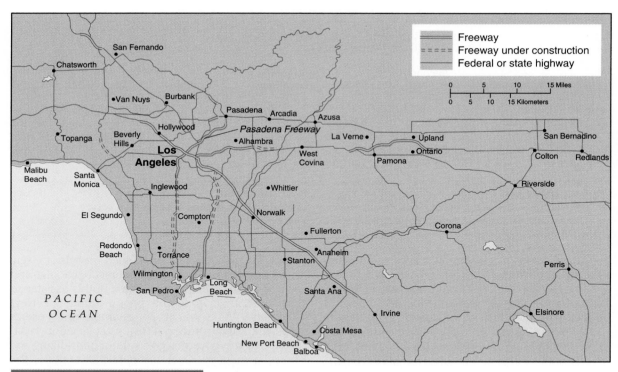

Los Angeles Road System, c. 1955

Map showing the growth of freeways and state supported highways in the Los Angeles area. Extensive road building, encouraged by the Interstate Highway Act, was crucial to the postwar expansion of suburbia. By 1960, L.A. County had 140 miles of freeway, which followed the pattern first set by streetcars earlier in the century.

racial and income segregation of suburbia in public policy.

In 1944 the Veterans Act, popularly known as the GI Bill of Rights, worked a minor revolution in American life (see Chapter 25). It provided educational grants, low-interest mortgages, and business loans for returning veterans. The GI Bill thus subsidized the postwar expansion of higher education and the growth of suburbs. By the 1947–48 academic year, the Veterans Administration (VA) was footing the bill for nearly half of all male college students. Through 1956, nearly 10 million veterans received tuition and training benefits under the act. VA-insured loans totaled more than $50 billion by 1962, providing assistance to millions of former GIs who started businesses. By 1961, one of every six owner-occupied houses in America, a total of over 5 million, had been financed through VA loans. For millions of American families, FHA and VA loans made it cheaper to buy a home than to rent one. The federal tax codes of the postwar years added a further inducement (and subsidy) to home owner-

ship by allowing mortgagors to deduct their interest payments from their income. By 1972, the FHA had helped some 11 million families to own houses and another 22 million to improve their property. Between 1934 and 1972, the percentage of Americans living in owner-occupied houses jumped from 44 percent to 63 percent.

The Federal Highway Act of 1956 gave another key boost to postwar growth, especially in the suburbs. It originally authorized $32 billion for the construction of a national system of highways. New taxes on gasoline, as well as on oil, tires, buses, and trucks, would finance this ambitious plan. These nondivertible revenues, held separately from general taxes in a Highway Trust Fund, proved the key to success. By 1972 the program had become the single largest public works program in American history; 41,000 miles of highway were built at a cost of $76 billion. Federal subsidy of the interstate highway system stimulated both the automobile industry and suburb building. But it also accelerated the decline of American mass transit and older cities. By 1970, the nation possessed both the world's best roads and one of its worst public transportation systems.

The shadow of the Cold War prompted the federal government to take new initiatives in aid for education. After the Soviet Union launched its first *Sputnik* satellite in the fall of 1957, American officials worried that the country might be lagging behind the Soviets in training scientists and engineers. The Eisenhower administration, with the bipartisan support of Congress, pledged to strengthen support for educating American students in mathematics, science, and technology. The National Defense Education Act (NDEA) of 1958 allocated $280 million in grants — tied to matching grants from the states — for state universities to upgrade their science facilities. The NDEA also created $300 million in low-interest loans for college students, who had to repay only half the amount if they went on to teach in elementary or secondary school after graduation. In addition, the NDEA provided fellowship support for graduate students planning to go into college and university teaching. The NDEA represented a new consensus on the importance of quality education to the national interest. It permanently shifted debate from whether or not there should be federal aid to education to what form that aid ought to take.

Building Suburban Communities

The suburb became the dominant pattern of community living in American society in the generation following the Second World War. Earlier spurts of suburban growth had been confined largely to

wealthy and upper-middle-class Americans able to afford alternatives to city living. But the postwar era, as we have seen, saw a tremendous increase in the percentage of American families able to own their homes. A single-family house in a suburb became the middle-class norm rather than the exclusive preserve of the rich. By 1960, as many Americans lived in suburbs as in cities. The cultural and political significance of this shift was central to the evolution of postwar society.

Many of the new postwar suburbs were planned communities, designed to be built with maximum efficiency and speed. The nation faced a severe housing shortage after the war, for there had been little new home construction in the depression and war years. Returning veterans and their families faced a tough time finding a place to live. Government policies making home ownership easier than ever, combined with the large demand for housing presented builders with a lucrative opportunity that they were quick to seize.

William Levitt, who described his firm as "the General Motors of the housing industry," was the first to bring mass production techniques to home building. The first Levittown opened in Hempstead, Long Island, in 1947, on 1,500 acres of former potato fields. It eventually encompassed over 17,000 houses and 82,000 people. Here Levitt perfected the techniques that radically changed the business. All building materials were precut and preassembled at a central factory, then brought to the site on a strict timetable. To make use of largely unskilled and cheaper nonunion labor, Levitt broke down each phase of construction into simple tasks. To avoid middlemen, he bought forests and sawmills to

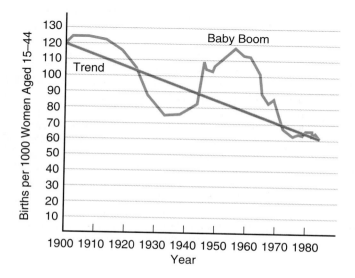

U.S. Birth Rate, 1930–1980
The bulge of the "baby boom," a leading demographic factor in the postwar economy, stands out for this fifty year period.

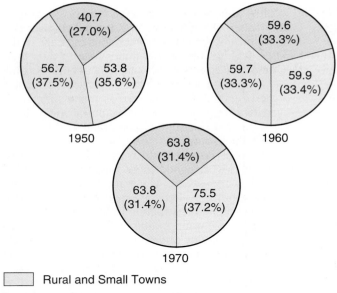

Numbers in Millions (% of total population)

1950
- 40.7 (27.0%)
- 56.7 (37.5%)
- 53.8 (35.6%)

1960
- 59.6 (33.3%)
- 59.7 (33.3%)
- 59.9 (33.4%)

1970
- 63.8 (31.4%)
- 63.8 (31.4%)
- 75.5 (37.2%)

☐ Rural and Small Towns

☐ Suburbs

☐ Central Cities

The Growth of the Suburbs, 1950–1970
Suburban growth, at the expense of older inner cities, was one of the key social trends in the 25 years following World War II. By 1970, more Americans lived in suburbs than in either inner cities or rural areas.

Source: Adapted from U.S. Bureau of the Census, *Current Censuses, 1930-1970* (Washington, D.C.: U.S. Government Printing Office).

---

provide lumber, a nail factory for hardware, and a supply company for electrical appliances.

In this way Levitt was able to put up hundreds of houses each week. Each house had the same four-room interior design, the same amount of floor space, and the same lot size. Levitt included a new refrigerator, stove, washer, and seven-inch television in the package. The 1947 version cost $7,990 and the demand for Levitt's houses far exceeded the supply. Other builders quickly adopted his methods. The early 1950s brought the most massive house-building boom in history. In 1950 alone, 1.4 million new units went up. By 1960, for the first time in history, more Americans owned their homes than rented.

In the Sunbelt, the abundance of space allowed for variations on design and lot size. The California-style ranch house featured a single, largely undifferentiated space including living, dining, kitchen, and recreation areas, along with bedrooms extending at right angles from a central corridor. These homes also included patios near the front and back doors, and a connected garage. In California's San Fernando Valley, Louis Boyar built the community of Lakewood Park: 70,000 residents living in 17,000 houses on 3,400 acres of former farmland. Around Los Angeles, over 900 square miles of agricultural land would eventually be converted into suburban developments.

California came to embody postwar suburban life. At the center of this lifestyle was the automobile. Cars were a necessity for commuting to work. California also led the nation in the development of drive-in facilities: motels, movies, shopping malls, fast-food restaurants, and banks. Over 500 miles of freeways would be constructed around Los Angeles alone. In Orange County, southeast of Los Angeles, the "centerless city" emerged as the dominant form of community. The experience of one woman resident was typical: "I live in Garden Grove, work in Irvine, shop in Santa Ana, go to the dentist in Anaheim, my husband works in Long Beach, and I used to be the president of the League of Women Voters in Fullerton."

Suburban Life

One of the most important characteristics of postwar suburbs was their racial and economic homogeneity. Certainly, racial discrimination was not new to the suburbs. But the newer communities often reinforced old patterns of exclusion through explicitly racist policies. The Levitt organization publicly and officially refused to sell houses to African Americans until forced to by the courts in the mid-1960s. In 1960 not one of the Long Island Levittown's 82,000 residents was African American. Suburban communities often used zoning regula-

A 1948 advertisement for homes in Levittown, New York. The text made a special appeal to veterans (no down payment required for two of the models); it also encouraged non-veterans to take advantage of the liberal mortgage policy of the Federal Housing Administration.

tions and land-use restrictions to keep out poor people, apartment houses, and industry as well. These practices helped speed the decline of many older urban areas. Cities were forced to provide economic facilities for a whole area and housing for those not admitted to suburbs.

The suburban boom strengthened the domestic ideal of the nuclear family as the model for American life. In particular, the picture of the perfect suburban wife — efficient, patient, always charming — became a dominant image in television, movies, and magazines. Suburban domesticity was usually presented as women's only path to happiness and fulfillment. This cultural image often masked a stifling existence defined by housework, childcare, and boredom. In the late 1950s Betty Friedan, a wife, mother, and journalist, began a systematic survey of her Smith College classmates. She found "a strange discrepancy between the reality of our lives as women and the image to which we were trying to conform." Friedan expanded her research and in 1963 published *The Feminine Mystique,* a landmark book that articulated the frustrations of suburban women and helped to launch the feminist movement.

The postwar rebirth of religious life was strongly associated with suburban living. In 1940 less than half the American population belonged to institutionalized churches; by the mid-1950s nearly three-quarters identified themselves as church members. A church-building boom was centered in the expanding suburbs. Best-selling religious authors such as Norman Vincent Peale and Bishop Fulton J. Sheen offered a shallow blend of reassurance and "the power of positive thinking." They stressed individual solutions to problems, and opposed social or political activism. Their emphasis on the importance of belonging, of fitting in, meshed well with suburban social life and the ideal of family-centered domesticity.

Contemporary journalists, novelists, and social scientists contributed to the popular image of suburban life as essentially dull, conformist, and peopled exclusively by the educated middle class. John Cheever, for example, won the National Book Award for *The Wapshot Chronicle* (1957), a novel set in fictional Remsen Park, "a community of four thousand identical homes." Psychiatrist Richard Gordon's *The Split Level Trap* (1960) focused on the emotional problems he observed among the suburban families of Bergen County, New Jersey. Yet these writers tended to obscure the real class and ethnic differences found among and between suburban communities. Many new suburbs had a distinctively blue collar cast. Milpitas, California, for example, grew up around a Ford auto plant about fifty miles outside San Jose. Its residents were blue collar assembly line workers and their families rather than salaried, college-educated, white-collar employees. Self segregation and zoning ordinances gave some new suburbs as distinctively Italian, Jewish, or Irish ethnic identities as older urban neighborhoods. For millions of new suburbanites, architectural and psychological conformity was an acceptable price to pay for the comforts of home ownership, a small plot of land, and a sense of security and status.

The Expansion of Higher Education

American higher education experienced rapid growth after the war. This expansion both reflected and reinforced other trends in postwar society. The number of students enrolled in colleges and universities climbed from 2.6 million in 1950 to 3.2 million in 1960. It then more than doubled — to 7.5 million — by 1970, as the baby boom generation came of age. Most of these new students attended greatly enlarged state university systems. Main campuses at state universities in Michigan, Wisconsin, California, and other states grew bigger than ever, enrolling as many as 40,000 students. Many states built branch campuses to accommodate the influx, such as the Riverside and San Diego branches of the University of California and the University of Illinois at Chicago campus. Many technical colleges and "normal schools" (designed originally for the training of teachers) were upgraded and expanded into full-fledged universities, as in the branches of the State University of New York, founded in 1948.

Several factors contributed to this explosion. A variety of new federal programs, including the GI Bill and the National Defense Education Act, helped subsidize college education for millions of new students. Government spending on research and development in universities, especially for defense-related projects, pumped further resources into higher education. Federal funds for R & D in universities grew from $160 million in 1954 to nearly $1 billion by 1964, and to $1.6 billion by 1970. Much of this money supported programs in graduate work, reflecting an important postwar shift in the priorities of American universities. Graduate education and faculty research now challenged traditional under-graduate teaching as the main locus of university activity and power.

Colleges and universities by and large accepted the values of postwar corporate culture. By the mid-1950s, 20 percent of all college graduates had majored in business or other commercial fields. The college degree was a gateway to the middle class. It became a requirement for a whole range of expanding white-collar occupations in banking, insurance, real estate, advertising and marketing, and other corporate enterprises. As much as educating young people, colleges trained them for careers in technical, professional, and management positions. Most administrators accommodated large business interests, which were well represented on university boards of trustees. Universities themselves were increasingly run like businesses, with administrators adopting the language of input-output, cost effectiveness, and quality control.

Researchers found that college students in the 1950s generally conformed to the conventions and attitudes associated with working in a corporate environment. A typical Iowa State student told one writer, "You have to be very careful not to associate with the wrong clan of people, an introvert that isn't socially acceptable, guys who dress in the fashion of ten years ago. These people are just not accepted — and, if you associate with them, you're not accepted either." The number of female college students increased markedly after the war, though not at the same rate as men. For women, the college degree did not ensure entry into a well-paying job or career, as it did for men. College enabled women to achieve upward mobility largely through marriage to successful, professional men. For white middle-class women in particular, college provided an entry to affluent domesticity.

Health and Medicine

Dramatic improvements in medical care allowed many Americans to enjoy longer and healthier lives. Like so many other technological advances of the era, these had their origins in World War II. During the war the federal government had poured unprecedented amounts of money into medical research and the diffusion of new techniques. The armed forces had immunized and treated millions of servicemen and -women for diseases ranging from syphilis to tuberculosis. New antibiotics such as penicillin and streptomycin were manufactured and distributed on a mass basis, and after the war they became widely available to the general population. Federal support for research continued after the war with the reorganization of the National Institutes of Health in 1948. Federal agencies, led by the National Institute of Mental Health, founded in 1949, also expanded research on and treatment of mental illness. This initiative grew out of the large number of veterans' hospital patients suffering from psychiatric disorders. Eighty percent of all psychiatric units in general hospitals were built after the war.

By 1960 many dreaded epidemic diseases, such as tuberculosis, diphtheria, whooping cough, and measles, had virtually disappeared from American life. Perhaps the most celebrated achievement of postwar medicine was the victory over poliomyelitis. Between 1947 and 1951 this disease, which usually crippled those it did not kill, struck an annual average of 39,000 Americans. In 1952, 58,000 cases, most of them children, were reported. Frightened parents warned children to stay away from crowded swimming pools and other gathering places. In 1955 Jonas Salk pioneered the first effective vaccine against the disease, using a preparation of dead polio virus. A nationwide program of polio vaccination, later supplemented by the oral Sabin vaccine, virtually eliminated polio by the 1960s.

Yet the benefits of "wonder drugs" and advanced medical techniques were not shared equally by all Americans. More sophisticated treatments

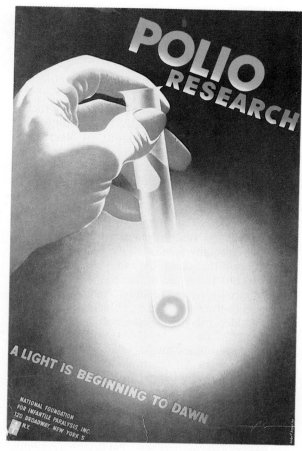

Polio Research, 1949. Lithograph poster designed to support the fight for a cure for polio, a disease that killed or crippled tens of thousands of children each year. Dr. Jonas Salk's 1955 scientific breakthrough of a killed-virus polio vaccine led to an array of viral vaccines to cure other diseases, such as hepatitis.
(Herbert Bayer. Polio Research. *1949. Offset lithography. 45 × 28-3/4 in (114 × 73 cm). Library of Congress, Washington, D.C.)*

and expensive new hospital facilities sharply increased the costs of health care. The very poor and many elderly Americans found themselves unable to afford modern medicine. Thousands of communities, especially in rural areas and small towns, lacked doctors or decent hospital facilities. Critics of the medical establishment charged that the proliferation of medical specialists and large hospital complexes had increased the number of unnecessary surgical operations, especially in the case of women and children. The decline of the general practitioner—the family doctor—meant fewer physicians made house calls; more and more people went to hospital emergency rooms or outpatient clinics for treatment. Unreasonable faith in sophisticated med-

ical technologies also contributed to the proliferation of iatrogenic ailments — sickness brought on by treatment for some other illness.

The American Medical Association (AMA), which certified medical schools, did nothing to increase the flow of new doctors. The number of physicians per 100,000 people actually declined between 1950 and 1960; the shortage was made up by doctors trained in other countries. The AMA also lobbied hard against efforts to expand government responsibility for the public's health. President Truman had advanced a plan for national health insurance, to be run along the lines of Social Security. President Eisenhower had proposed a program that would offer government assistance to private health insurance companies. The AMA denounced both proposals as "socialized medicine." It helped block direct federal involvement in health care until the passage of Medicare (for the elderly) and Medicaid (for the poor) in 1965.

YOUTH CULTURE

The term *teenager,* describing someone between thirteen and nineteen, entered standard usage only at the end of World War II. According to the *Dictionary of American Slang,* the U.S. is the only country with a word for this age group, and the only country to consider it "a separate entity whose influence, fads, and fashions are worthy of discussion apart from the adult world." The fifteen years following World War II saw an unprecedented amount of analysis and attention given to America's adolescents. Deep fears were expressed about everything from teenage sexuality and juvenile delinquency to young people's driving habits, hair styles, and choice of clothing. At the same time, advertisers and businesses pursued the disposable income of America's affluent youth with a vengeance. Teenagers often found themselves caught between their desire to carve out their own separate sphere and the pressure to become an adult as quickly as possible.

The Youth Market

Birth rates had accelerated gradually during the late 1930s and more rapidly during the war years. The children born in those years had by the late 1950s grown into the original teenagers, the older siblings of the celebrated baby boom of 1946–64. They came of age in a society that, compared with that of their parents and the rest of the world, was uniquely affluent. Together, the demographic growth of teens and the postwar economic expansion created a burgeoning youth market. Manufacturers and advertisers rushed to cash in on the special needs and desires of young consumers: cosmetics, clothing, radios and phonographs, and cars. Corporate giants such as R.J. Reynolds Tobacco, Pepsi, and Chevrolet began targeting teens in special promotional campaigns.

In 1959, *Life* summarized the new power of the youth market. "Counting only what is spent to satisfy their special teenage demands," the magazine reported, "the youngsters and their parents will shell out about $10 billion this year, a billion more than the total sales of GM." In addition, advertisers and market researchers found that teenagers often played a critical, if hard to measure, role as "secret persuaders" in a family's large purchases. Specialized market research organizations, such as Eugene Gilbert & Company and Teen-Age Survey Incorporated, sprang up to serve business clients eager to attract teen consumers and instill brand loyalty. Through the 1950s and into the 1960s, teenagers had a major, sometimes dominant, voice in setting America's cultural diet.

To many parents, the emerging youth culture was a dangerous threat to their authority. One mother summarized this fear in a revealing, if slightly hysterical, letter to *Modern Teen*:

> Don't you realize what you are doing? You are encouraging teenagers to write to each other, which keeps them from doing their school work and other chores. You are encouraging them to kiss and have physical contact before they're even engaged, which is morally wrong and you know it. You are encouraging them to have faith in the depraved individuals who make rock and roll records when it's common knowledge that ninety per cent of these rock and roll singers are people with no morals or sense of values.

The increasing uniformity of public school education also contributed to the public recognition of the special status of teenagers. In 1900, about one of every eight teenagers was in school; by the 1950s, the figure was six out of eight. Psychologists wrote guidebooks for parents, two prominent examples being Dorothy Baruch's *How to Live with Your Teenager* (1953) and Paul Landis's *Understanding Teenagers* (1955). Social scientists stressed the importance of peer pressure for understanding teen behavior. "The teenage group," Landis observed in *Understanding Teenagers*, "is self sufficient now as in no previous generation." The larger point here is that traditional sources of adult authority and social-

ization — the marketplace, schools, child-rearing manuals, the mass media — all reinforced the notion of teenagers as a special community, united by age, rank, and status.

"Hail! Hail! Rock-'n'-Roll!"

In the recording industry, small, independent record labels led the way in aggressively recording local rhythm-and-blues artists. Atlantic, in New York, developed the most influential galaxy of artists, including Ray Charles, Ruth Brown, the Drifters, Joe Turner, LaVerne Baker, and the Clovers. Chess, in Chicago, had the blues-based singer-songwriter-guitarists Chuck Berry and Bo Diddley, and the "doo-wop" group the Moonglows. In New Orleans, Imperial had the veteran pianist-singer Fats Domino, while Specialty unleashed the outrageous Little Richard upon the world. On radio, over jukeboxes, and in record stores, all of these African American artists "crossed over," adding millions of white teenagers to their solid base of black fans.

The older, more established record companies, such as RCA, Decca, M–G–M, and Capitol, had largely ignored black music, concentrating instead on popular music for the traditional adult market: pop ballads, novelty songs, and show tunes. Their response to the new trend was to offer slick, toned-down "cover" versions by white pop singers of r&b originals. Cover versions were invariably pallid imitations, artistically inferior to the originals. One has only to compare, say, Pat Boone's covers of Fats Domino's "Ain't That a Shame" or Little Richard's "Tutti Frutti" to hear how much was lost. While African American artists enjoyed new-found mass acceptance, there were limits to how closely white kids could identify with black performers. Racism, especially in so sexually charged an arena as musical performance, was still a powerful force in American life. Because of the superior promotional power of the major companies and the institutional racism in the music business, cover versions frequently outsold the originals.

The stage was thus set for the arrival of white rock-'n'-roll artists who could exploit the new sounds and styles. Elvis Presley burst upon the national scene and created as big a cultural convulsion as anyone in this century. He became the greatest rock-'n'-roll star and the ultimate teen idol. Born in Tupelo, Mississippi, in 1935, Elvis had moved with his family to a drab public housing project in Memphis. Reflecting his working-class southern heritage, his musical influences included country-and-western, blues, gospel, and contempo-

Elvis Presley on stage, c. 1955. In his early years Presley performed with only a trio of backup musicians. The sound was spare but hard driving. Both the music and Presley's stage moves owed a great deal to African American rhythm and blues artists.

rary pop. After graduating from high school, Elvis found himself driving a truck and dreaming of getting into the music business. In 1954 he caught the attention of Sam Phillips, owner of Sun Records. Phillips had been recording black r&b artists since 1950. He had often told friends that if he could find a white singer with the "Negro" sound and feel, he could make a fortune.

Presley's first records for Sun were regional hits, but no more. On songs like "That's Alright Mama," "Good Rockin' Tonight," and "Mystery Train," Presley and his small band created an utterly unique blend of black blues and white country that soon became known as *rockabilly*. But it was as a live performer, playing hundreds of small-town dances, school hops, and county fairs, that Elvis began attracting national attention. He sang and moved to the beat like a man possessed — hips gyrating, knees bending, voice pleading. With his carefully pomaded long hair, flashy outfits, and sexy sneer, Elvis was a big hit with young female fans and a nightmare for their parents. Sam Phillips had found his man.

But Sun Records was a small, regional outfit. Only when Phillips sold Presley's contract to RCA in 1956 did Elvis become a national star. Records such as "Heartbreak Hotel," "Don't Be Cruel," "Hound Dog," and "Jailhouse Rock" shot to the top of the charts and defined a new era in American music. Appearances on the network television shows of entertainment figures such as Milton Berle, Steve Allen, and Ed Sullivan added to his popularity. So did the movies he began making, beginning with *Love Me Tender* (1956). As a rock-'n'-roll performer and recording artist, Elvis reinvented American popular music. As a symbol of rebellious youth and as the embodiment of youthful sexuality, Elvis revitalized American popular culture.

Elvis opened the doors for a whole generation of white rock-'n'-rollers, who served up their own versions of rockabilly: Jerry Lee Lewis, Buddy Holly, the Everly Brothers, Roy Orbison. During this first golden age of rock-'n'-roll, the music had distinct regional accents, sounds that could be identified with specific cities and record labels. Yet teenagers across the country — black, white, and Latino — were united by a feeling that rock-'n'-roll was *their* music. But it was more than just a music — it was also an attitude, a way of walking and dancing, a celebration of being young, and a sense of having something that parents, and adult authority in general, could not understand or appreciate. Chuck Berry, the greatest songwriter and the most influential guitarist to emerge among the early rock-'n'-rollers, proved especially adept at capturing the teen spirit with humor, irony, and passion. He composed hits around the trials and tribulations of school ("School Days"), young love ("Memphis"), cars ("Maybellene"), and making it as a rock-'n'-roller ("Johnny B. Goode"). As much as anyone, Berry created music that defined what it meant to be young in postwar America.

Almost Grown

At least some of that sense of difference, of uniqueness, came from teens themselves. Teenage consumers remade the landscape of popular music into their own turf. The dollar value of annual record sales nearly tripled between 1954 and 1959, from $213 million to $603 million. New magazines aimed exclusively at teens flourished in the postwar years: *Seventeen, Modern Teen, Teen Digest,* and *Dig* were just a few. Most teen magazines, like rock-'n'-roll music, focused on the rituals, pleasures, and sorrows surrounding teenage courtship. These changes in popular culture both reflected and encouraged the declining age of the adolescent group. Paradoxically, behavior patterns among white middle-class teenagers in the 1950s and early 1960s exhibited both a new kind of youth orientation and a more pronounced identification with adults.

While large numbers of parents worried about the separate world inhabited by their teenage children, many teens seemed determined to become adults as quickly as possible. Postwar affluence multiplied the number of two-car families, making it easier for sixteen-year-olds to win driving privileges formerly reserved for eighteen-year-olds. Among girls, the continuing decline in the age of menarche, combined with the sharp drop in the age of marriage after World War II, contributed to earlier dating, wearing of brassieres and nylon stockings, and use of cosmetics. These activities often began at twelve or thirteen rather than fifteen or sixteen. Girls were encouraged by the precocious social climate of junior high schools, institutions that had become widespread only after 1945. The practice of going steady, derived from the college custom of fraternity and sorority pinning, became commonplace among high schoolers. By the late 1950s, eighteen had become the most common age at which American females married.

Teenagers often felt torn between their identification with youth culture and their desire to become adults as quickly as possible. Many young people juggled part-time jobs with school and very active social lives. Teen-oriented magazines, music, and movies routinely dispensed advice and sympathy regarding this dilemma. Rock-'n'-roll songs offered the most sympathetic treatments of the conflicts teens experienced over work ("Summertime Blues"), parental authority ("Yakety Yak"), and the desire to look adult ("Sweet Little Sixteen"). By 1960 sociologist James S. Coleman reflected a growing consensus when he noted that postwar society had given adolescents "many of the instruments which can make them a functioning community: cars, freedom in dating, continual contact with the opposite sex, money, and entertainment, like popular music and movies, designed especially for them."

Deviance and Delinquency

Many observers of the emerging youth culture were disturbed by the apparent decline of parental control. Certainly rock-'n'-roll received sharp and widespread denunciations from adults. A psychiatrist writing in the *New York Times* described rock as "a cannibalistic and tribalistic kind of a music" and "a communicable disease." Many clergymen and church leaders declared it "the devil's music." Much of the opposition to rock-'n'-roll, particularly in the South, played on long-standing racist fears that white females might be attracted to black music and black performers. The undercurrent beneath all this opposition was a deep anxiety over the more open expression of sexual feelings by both performers and audiences.

Paralleling the rise of rock-'n'-roll was a growing concern with an alleged increase in juvenile delinquency. An endless stream of magazine articles, books, and newspaper stories asserted that criminal behavior among the nation's young was chronic. Gang fights, drug and alcohol abuse, car theft, and sexual offenses received the most attention. The U.S. Senate established a special subcommittee on juvenile delinquency. Highly publicized hearings in 1955 and 1956 convinced much of the public that youthful criminals were terrorizing the country. Although crime statistics do suggest an increase in juvenile crime during the 1950s, particularly in the suburbs, the public perception of the severity of the problem was surely exaggerated.

In retrospect, the juvenile delinquency controversy tells us more about anxieties over family life and the erosion of adult authority. Teenagers seemed more defined by and loyal to their peer culture than their parents. A great deal of their music, speech, dress, and style was alien and threatening. The growing importance of the mass media in defining youth culture brought efforts to regulate or censor media forms believed to cause juvenile delinquency. For example, psychologist Fredric Wertham led a crusade that forced the comic book industry to adopt a code strictly limiting the portrayal of violence and crime.

Teens and their parents frequently interpreted mass media depictions of youthful deviance in very different ways. This was evident in reactions to two of the most influential "problem youth" movies of the postwar era. In *The Wild One* (1954), Marlon Brando played the crude, moody leader of a vicious motorcycle gang. Most adults thought of the film as a critique of mindless gang violence. But many teenagers identified with the Brando character, who, when asked, "What are you rebelling against?" coolly replied, "Whattaya got?" In *Rebel without a Cause* (1955), James Dean, Natalie Wood, and Sal Mineo played emotionally troubled youths in an affluent California suburb. The movie suggests that parents who fail to play the conventional roles may cause delinquency—Dean's father wears an apron and his mother is domineering. But on another level, the film suggests the possibilities of young people's forming their own families, without parents.

Brando and Dean, along with Elvis, were probably the most popular and widely imitated teen idols of the era. For most parents, they were vaguely threatening figures whose sexual energy and lack of discipline placed them outside the bounds of middle-class respectability. For teens, however, they offered an irresistible combination of rough exterior and sensitive core. They embodied, as well, the contradiction of individual rebellion versus the attractions of a community defined by youth.

Mass Culture and Its Discontents

No mass medium ever achieved such power and popularity as rapidly as television. The basic technology for combining visual images with sound had been developed by the late 1930s. Television demonstrations were among the most popular exhibits at the 1939 New York World's Fair. But World War II and corporate competition postponed television's introduction to the public until 1946. By 1960, nearly nine in ten American families owned at least one set, which was turned on an average of over five hours per day. Television reshaped leisure time and political life. It also helped create a new kind of national community defined by the buying and selling of consumer goods.

Important voices challenged the economic trends and cultural conformity of the postwar years. Academics, journalists, novelists, and poets offered a variety of works criticizing the overall direction of American life. These critics of what was dubbed "mass society" were troubled by the premium American culture put on conformity, status, and material consumption. Although a distinct minority, these critics were persistent. Many of their ideas and prescriptions would echo back during the political and cultural upheavals of the 1960s and 1970s.

Television: Tube of Plenty

Although television constituted a radical change from radio, its development as a mass medium was quicker and less chaotic. TV benefited from the broadcasting structure that had evolved between the two world wars. The three main television networks — NBC, CBS, ABC — grew directly from radio organizations. A short-lived fourth network, Dumont, grew from a television manufacturing business. The Federal Communications Commission oversaw the licensing of stations and set technical standards. The networks led the industry from the

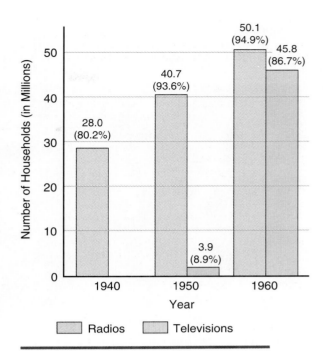

Radio and Television Ownership, 1940–1960

By 1960 nearly 90 percent of American households owned at least one television set, as TV replaced radio as the nation's dominant mass medium of entertainment. Radio ownership rose as well, but Americans increasingly listened to radio as an accompaniment to other activities, such as driving.

start, rather than following individual stations, as radio had done. Nearly all TV stations were affiliated with one or more of the networks; only a handful of independent stations could be found around the country.

Television not only depended upon advertising, it also transformed the advertising industry. The television business, like radio, was based upon the selling of time to advertisers who wanted to reach the mass audiences tuning into shows. Radio had offered entire shows produced by and for single sponsors, usually advertisers who wanted a close identification between their product and a star. But the higher costs of television production forced key changes. By the mid-1950s, it cost at least $150,000 to produce an hour of prime time. Sponsors left production of programs to the networks, independent producers, and Hollywood studios.

Sponsors now bought scattered time slots for spot advertisements, rather than bankrolling an entire show. Ad agencies switched their creative energy to producing slick thirty-second commercials rather than entertainment programs. A shift from

A Motorola television advertisement from *Woman's Home Companion*, 1951. Manufacturers designed TV sets as living room furniture and emphasized its role in fostering family togetherness.

broadcasting live shows to filming them opened up lucrative opportunities for reruns and foreign export. The total net revenue of the TV networks and their affiliated stations in 1947 was about $2 million; by 1957 it was nearly $1 billion. Advertisers spent $58 million on TV shows in 1949; ten years later the figure was almost $1.5 billion. Throughout the 1950s, Americans bought an average of 5 million television sets each year.

The staple of network radio, the comedy-variety show, was now produced with pictures. The first great national TV hit, *The Milton Berle Show*, followed this format when it premiered in 1948. Radio stars such as Jack Benny, Edgar Bergen, George Burns and Gracie Allen, and Eddie Cantor made the switch directly to television. Boxing, wrestling, roller derby, and other sporting events were also quite popular. For a brief time, original live drama flourished on writer-oriented shows such as *Goodyear Television Playhouse* and *Studio One*. In addition, early television featured an array of situation comedies with deep roots in radio and vaudeville.

Set largely among urban ethnic families, shows like *I Remember Mama, The Goldbergs, The Life of Riley, Life With Luigi,* and *The Honeymooners* often featured working-class families struggling with the dilemmas posed by consumer society. Most plots turned around comic tensions created and resolved by consumption: home ownership, going out on the

town, a move to the suburbs, buying on credit, purchasing a new car. Generational discord and the loss of ethnic identity were also common themes. To some degree, these early shows mirrored and spoke to the real dilemmas facing postwar families who had survived the Great Depression and the Second World War and were now finding their place in a prosperous consumer culture.

By the late 1950s all of the urban ethnic comedy shows were off the air. A new breed of situation comedies presented affluent suburban WASP middle-class families who had very little contact with the outside world. Shows like *Father Knows Best, Leave It to Beaver, Ozzie and Harriet,* and *The Donna Reed Show* epitomized the ideal suburban American family of the day. Most plots focused on ethical crises, usually brought on by children's mischief and resolved by wise, kind, and bland fathers. Politics, social issues, cities, white ethnic groups, African Americans, and Latinos were virtually nonexistent. In retrospect, what is most striking about these shows is what is absent.

Television cut deeply into the filmgoing habits of Americans. The audience for movies began a steep decline from the high point of 1948. Hollywood tried desperately to compete with its new rival by pushing spectacular new techniques such as Cinerama, CinemaScope, and 3-D. By the mid-1950s, studios had begun to sell off their valuable backlog of films to the networks; old movies thus became a staple of television programming. Many TV shows were produced on the same Hollywood back lots that had churned out "B" pictures in the 1930s and 1940s. Two of the most popular genres of television in these years were old movie stand-bys: Westerns (*Gunsmoke, Cheyenne, The Rifleman*) and crime dramas (*Dragnet, Highway Patrol, The Untouchables*).

Television also demonstrated a unique ability to create overnight fads and crazes across the nation. Successful television advertising campaigns made household names out of previously obscure products. A memorable example of TV's influence came in 1955 when Walt Disney produced a series of three one-hour shows on the life of frontier legend Davy Crockett. The tremendous success of the series instantly created a $300 million industry of Davy Crockett shirts, dolls, toys, and coonskin caps.

Television and Politics

Prime-time entertainment shows carefully avoided any references to political issues of the day. Network executives bowed to the conformist climate created by the domestic Cold War. Any hint of political controversy could scare off sponsors, who were extremely sensitive to public protest. Anti-Communist crusaders set themselves up as private watchdogs, warning of alleged subversive influence in the broadcasting industry. In 1951 one such group published *Red Channels* (see Chapter 26), a book branding 151 of the most well-known writers, directors, and actors in radio and television as Communists or Communist dupes. Television executives responded by effectively blacklisting many talented individuals.

As in Hollywood, the Cold War chill severely restricted the range of political discussion on television. Any honest treatment of the conflicts in American society threatened the consensus mentality at the heart of the television business. Even public affairs and documentary programs were largely devoid of substantial political debate. An important exception was Edward R. Murrow's *See It Now* series on CBS—but that show was off the air by 1955. Television news did not come into its own until 1963, with the beginning of half-hour nightly network newscasts. Only then did television's extraordinary power to rivet the nation on a current crisis become clear.

Still, some of the ways that TV would alter the nation's political life emerged in the 1950s. Television made Democratic senator Estes Kefauver of Tennessee a national political figure through live coverage of his 1951 Senate investigation into organized crime. It also contributed to the political downfall of Senator Joseph McCarthy in 1954 by showing his cruel bullying tactics during Senate hearings into alleged subversive influence in the army. In 1952, Republican vice-presidential candidate Richard M. Nixon effectively used an emotional, direct television appeal to voters—the "Checkers" speech—to counter charges of corruption (see Chapter 26).

The 1952 election also brought the first use of TV political advertising for presidential candidates. The Republican party hired a high-powered ad agency, Batten, Barton, Durstine & Osborn, to create a series of short, sophisticated advertisements touting Dwight D. Eisenhower. The Democrats were content to buy a few half-hour blocks of TV time for long speeches by their nominee, Adlai Stevenson. The BBD&O campaign saturated TV with twenty-second Eisenhower spots for two weeks before Election Day. Ever since then, television image making has been the single most important element in American electoral politics. Television has come to dominate political polling, fundraising, and issues. Indeed, for most Americans political life has been reduced to a television spectacle.

Lonely Crowds and Organization Men

Perhaps the most ambitious and controversial critique of postwar America was sociologist David Riesman's *The Lonely Crowd* (1950). Riesman argued that modern America had given birth to a new kind of character type, the "other-directed" man. America had previously been dominated by what Riesman called "inner-directed" people. These were self-reliant individualists who early on in life had internalized the self-discipline and moral standards that guided them through life. By contrast, the typical "other-directed" person of the modern era was peer-oriented. Morality, ideals, and goals came from the overarching desire to conform. Americans, Riesman thought, were now less likely to take risks or act independently. Their thinking and habits had come to be determined more by cues they received from the mass media.

Similarly, William H. Whyte's *The Organization Man* (1956), a study of the Chicago suburb of Park Forest, offered a picture of people obsessed with fitting in to their community and their job. In place of the old Protestant ethic of hard work, thrift, and competitive struggle, Whyte believed, middle-class suburbanites now strived mainly for a comfortable, secure niche in the system. They held to a new social ethic, he argued: "a belief in the group as the source of creativity; a belief in 'belongingness' as the ultimate need of the individual." Sloan Wilson's *The Man in the Grey Flannel Suit,* a 1955 best seller, featured a hero who rejects the top position at his firm. His boss sympathizes with this reluctance to sacrifice, telling him, "There are plenty of good positions where it's not necessary for a man to put in an unusual amount of work."

The most radical critic of mass society, and the one with the most enduring influence, was Texas-reared sociologist C. Wright Mills. In *White Collar* (1951), Mills analyzed the job culture that typified middle-class life: the salaried employee, the office worker, the bureaucrat. "When white collar people get jobs," he wrote, "they sell not only their time and energy, but their personalities as well. They sell by the week or month their smiles and their kindly gestures, and they must practice the prompt repression of resentment and aggression." In *The Power Elite* (1956), Mills argued that a small, interconnected group of corporate executives, military men, and political leaders had come to dominate American society. The arms race in particular, carried out in the name of Cold War policies, had given an unprecedented degree of power to the military-industrial complex.

Culture Critics

From both the left and the right, an assortment of writers expressed anger, fear, and plain disgust with the power of American mass culture. Traditional standards of beauty, truth, and quality, they believed, could not withstand the onslaught. Indeed, the urge to denounce the mass media for degrading the quality of American life tended to unite radical and conservative critics. Thus, Marxist writer Dwight MacDonald sounded an old conservative warning when he described mass culture as "a parasite, a cancerous growth on High Culture." Society's most urgent problem, MacDonald claimed, was a "tepid, flaccid Middlebrow Culture that threatens to engulf everything in its spreading ooze."

Critics of mass culture argued that the audiences for the mass media were atomized, anonymous, and detached. The media themselves had become omnipotent, capable of manipulating the attitudes and behavior of the isolated individuals in the mass. These critics undoubtedly overestimated the power of the media. They ignored the preponderance of research suggesting that most people watched and responded to mass media in family, peer group, and other social settings. The critics also

Fred McDarrah

Pop artist Andy Warhol at a gallery exhibit featuring his Brillo soap pads, 1964. Warhol's provocative work wryly challenged the pretensions of the art world by unapologetically celebrating mass culture. Early sixties Pop artists like Warhol found beauty in mass produced objects and images, and they were preoccupied with the fleeting nature of modern celebrity. "In the future," Warhol predicted, "everyone will be famous for fifteen minutes."

missed the genuine vitality and creative brilliance to be found within mass culture: African American music; the films of Nicholas Ray, Elia Kazan, and Howard Hawks; the television of Ernie Kovacs; the satire of *Mad* magazine.

Many of these critics achieved great popularity themselves, which suggested that the public was deeply ambivalent about mass culture. One of the best-selling authors of the day was Vance Packard, whose 1957 exposé *The Hidden Persuaders* showed how advertisers exploited motivational research into the irrational side of human behavior. Paul Goodman won a wide audience for his *Growing Up Absurd* (1960), which charged that America made it very difficult for young people to find meaningful work, sexual fulfillment, or a true sense of community. Goodman was only one of the thinkers at the end of the decade whose work pointed toward the coming youth rebellion in culture and politics.

The Beats

One of the sharpest dissents from the cultural conformity of the day came from a group of writers known collectively as the Beats. Led by the novelist Jack Kerouac and the poet Allen Ginsberg, the Beats were a loose collection of writers who shared a distrust of the American virtues of progress, power, and material gain. Kerouac, born and raised in a working-class French Canadian family in Lowell, Massachusetts, coined the term *beat* in 1948. It meant for him a "weariness with all the forms of the modern industrial state" — conformity, militarism, blind faith in technological progress. The Beat sensibility celebrated spontaneity, friendship, jazz, open sexuality, drug use, and the outcasts of American society.

Kerouac's novel *On the Road* became the Beat manifesto. Originally written in 1951, the novel was not published until 1957. It chronicled the tumultuous adventures of Kerouac's circle of friends as they traveled by car back and forth across America. The main character, Dean Moriarty, became a potent symbol of freedom and rebellion, "mad to live, mad to talk, mad to be saved, desirous of everything at the same time." Many readers mistook Dean for Kerouac, a sensitive and complex artist. The instant celebrity brought by the book ultimately drove Kerouac to alcoholism and an early death.

Allen Ginsberg had grown up in New Jersey in an immigrant Jewish family. His father was a poet and teacher, and his mother had a history of mental problems. After being expelled from Columbia University, Ginsberg grew close to Kerouac and another writer, William Burroughs. At a 1955 poetry reading in San Francisco, Ginsberg introduced his epic poem *Howl* to a wildly enthusiastic audience:

> "I saw the best minds of my generation destroyed
> by madness, starving hysterical naked,
> dragging themselves through the negro streets at
> dawn looking for an angry fix,
> angelheaded hipsters burning for the ancient
> heavenly connection to the starry dynamo in the
> machinery of night . . ."

Howl was published in 1956 and was quickly confiscated by police as "obscene and indecent." A highly publicized trial led to a landmark legal decision that the poem was literature, not pornography. *Howl* became one of the best-selling poetry books in the history of publishing, and it established Ginsberg as an important new voice in American literature.

Beat writers received a largely antagonistic, even virulent reception from the literary establishment. But millions of young Americans read their work and became intrigued by their alternative visions. The mass media soon managed to trivialize the Beats. A San Francisco journalist coined the term *beatnik,* and by the late 1950s the Beat image was little more than an affected pose by men and women dressed in black, wearing sunglasses and berets, and acting rebellious and alienated. *Life* did a highly negative photo portrayal of beatniks, hiring models for the spread. On television, "The Many Loves of Dobie Gillis" even featured a comic beatnik character, Maynard G. Krebs. But Beat writers like Kerouac, Ginsberg, Burroughs, Diane DiPrima, Gary Snyder, and others continued to produce serious work that challenged America's official culture. They foreshadowed the mass youth rebellion and counterculture to come.

THE COLD WAR CONTINUED

Eisenhower's experience in foreign affairs had been one of his most attractive assets as a presidential candidate. His success as supreme commander of the Allied forces in World War II owed as much to diplomatic skill as to military prowess. As president, Eisenhower sustained the anti-Communist rhetoric of Cold War diplomacy, and his administration persuaded Americans to accept the Cold War stalemate as a more or less permanent fact. Eisenhower developed new strategies for containment and for the support of United States power abroad, including a greater reliance on nuclear weapons, aggressive use of covert action, sharp increases in foreign military aid, and a greater reliance on collective security arrangements. Yet Eisenhower also resolved to do everything he could to forestall an all-out nuclear conflict. He recognized the limits of raw military power. He accepted a less than victorious end to the Korean War and he avoided a full military involvement in Indochina. By the time he left office, Eisenhower felt compelled to warn the nation of the growing danger of its military-industrial complex.

The "New Look" in Foreign Affairs

Secretary of State John Foster Dulles gave shape to the "new look" in American foreign policy in the 1950s. Raised a devout Presbyterian and trained as a lawyer, Dulles had been involved in diplomatic affairs since World War I. He brought a strong sense of righteousness to his job, a nearly missionary belief in America's responsibility to preserve the "free world" from godless, immoral communism. He was by far the most influential of Eisenhower's advisers, enjoying constant, direct access to the president. As one foreign diplomat put it: "We felt that Dulles was the United States and the United States was Dulles. He gave this feeling to the whole world."

Dulles articulated a more assertive policy toward the Communist threat by calling not simply for containment but for a "rollback." The key would be greater reliance upon America's nuclear superiority. This appealed to Republicans, who had been frustrated by the restriction of UN forces to conventional arms during the Korean War. As Vice-President Richard Nixon explained the shift: "Rather than let the communists nibble us to death all over the world in little wars, we will rely in the future on massive mobile retaliatory powers." The emphasis on massive retaliation, the administration claimed, would also facilitate cuts in the military budget. As Secretary of Defense Charles Wilson said, the goal was to "get more bang for the buck." Following the successful test of a huge hydrogen bomb in the Pacific in 1954, Dulles was all the more certain that the United States could reduce its defense commitments, which were spread around the world. The nation could now take advantage of the "great capacity to retaliate by means and at places of our own choosing."

The "new look" conflicted, however, with Eisenhower's own sense of caution, especially during moments of crisis in Eastern Europe and potential military confrontation with the Soviet Union. The limits of a policy based on nuclear strategy became painfully clear when American leaders faced tense situations with no clear alternative means of pressure. An uprising of East Berliners against the Soviets in 1953 offered, to Cold War hardliners, the long-awaited opportunity for rollback. But precisely how could the United States intervene? The public bitterness over the Korean conflict merged with Eisenhower's sense of restraint. Apart from angry denunciations, the United States did nothing to prevent the Soviets from crushing the rebellion. U.S. leaders faced the same dilemma on a grander scale during the Hungarian revolt in the fall of 1956. Hungarians staged a general strike against their Soviet-dominated Communist rulers, taking over the streets and factories in Budapest and other cities. Amid urgent appeals for American action, Eisenhower recognized that the Soviets would defend their own borders, and all of Eastern Europe as well, by all-out military force if necessary. The U.S. opened its gates to thousands of Hungarian refugees, but it refused to intervene when Soviet tanks and troops crushed the revolt.

The death of Joseph Stalin in 1953, and the worldwide condemnation of his crimes, revealed by his successor, Nikita Khrushchev, in 1956, gave Eisenhower fresh hope for a new spirit of détente

Soviet Premier Nikita S. Khrushchev toured an Iowa farm in 1959 as part of a goodwill visit to the U.S. Simultaneously treated as a buffoon and a demon by the U.S. press, Khrushchev made the first halting efforts to turn the Soviet economy toward producing more for consumers. A planned reciprocal visit to the Soviet Union by President Eisenhower was cancelled due to the U-2 spy plane crisis of early 1960.

between the two superpowers. Khrushchev, in a gesture of goodwill, withdrew Soviet troops from Austria. The first real rollback had been achieved by negotiations and a spirit of common hope, not threats or force. In 1958 Khrushchev, probing American intentions and hoping to redirect the Soviet economy toward the production of more consumer goods, unilaterally suspended nuclear testing. Tensions rose again that year when the Soviet leader, threatened by a revived West Germany, announced that the Western Allies had six months to get out of Berlin. But after Khrushchev made a twelve-day trip to America in 1959, he suspended the deadline and relations warmed. Khrushchev visited an Iowa farm, went sightseeing in Hollywood, and spent time with Eisenhower at Camp David, Maryland.

The two leaders achieved nothing concrete, but with summit diplomacy seeming to offer at least a psychological thaw in the Cold War, the press began referring to the "spirit of Camp David." In early 1960 Khrushchev called for another summit in Paris, to discuss German reunification and nuclear disarmament. Eisenhower, meanwhile, planned his own friendship tour of the Soviet Union. But in May 1960 the Soviets shot down an American U-2 spy plane gathering intelligence on Soviet military installations. A deeply embarrassed Eisenhower at first denied the existence of U-2 flights, but the Soviets produced the pilot, Francis Gary Powers, who readily confessed. The summit collapsed when Khrushchev's demands for an apology and an end to the spy flights were refused by Eisenhower.

The U-2 incident demonstrated the limits of personal diplomacy in resolving the deep structural rivalry between the superpowers. Although Eisenhower knew from earlier U-2 flights that the Soviet Union had undertaken no major military buildup, he had agreed with Congress to a hike of $2.5 billion in military spending in 1957. The launching of the first space-orbiting satellite by the Soviets in October 1957 provided a new incentive for expanded defense spending. *Sputnik* demonstrated Russian technological prowess and upset Americans' precarious sense of security. Urged to sponsor the building of "fallout shelters" for the entire population in case of nuclear attack, Eisenhower rejected what he called the "negative stuff." He supported instead a program of more federal funds for science education, as provided in the National Defense Education Act of 1958. Yet in Congress, a bipartisan majority voted to increase the military budget by another $8 billion in 1958, thereby accelerating the arms race and helping to prop up the growing defense sector of the economy.

Covert Action

While the U.S. moderated its stance toward the Soviet Union and its Eastern European satellites, it hardened its policies in the Third World. The need for anti-Communist tactics short of all-out military conflict pushed the Eisenhower administration to develop new means of fighting the Cold War. Under President Truman, the Psychological Strategy Board had created the idea of "psywars" (psychological wars) against communism. The premise rested on encouraging confusion or rivalry within the Communist sphere, and on destabilizing or destroying anticapitalist movements around the world. As one Eisenhower adviser put it, "the three big ingredients of psychological warfare are 1) money, 2) no holds barred, and 3) no questions asked."

The Central Intelligence Agency, created in 1947, was perfectly designed for this task. For CIA director Eisenhower named Allen Dulles, brother of the secretary of state and a former leader in the CIA's World War II precursor, the Office of Strategic Services (OSS). Mandated to collect and analyze information, the CIA did much more under Dulles's command. Thousands of covert agents stationed all over the world carried out a wide range of political activities. Some agents arranged large, secret financial payments to friendly political parties, such as the conservative Christian Democrats in Italy and Latin America, or to foreign trade unions opposed to Socialist policies. Other agents secretly funded and guided intellectuals in, for instance, the Congress of Cultural Freedom, a prestigious group of liberal writers in Europe and the United States. The CIA also secretly paid members of the National Student Association and similar college-student organizations abroad to support U.S. policies and spy on other students' political activities.

CIA-sponsored covert paramilitary operations became a key facet of American foreign policy in the Eisenhower years. These actions were particularly effective in the former colonial areas of Asia, Africa, and the Caribbean. Eisenhower increasingly relied upon the CIA to destabilize emerging Third World governments deemed too radical or too friendly with the Soviets. Covert actions also proved vital for propping up more conservative regimes under siege by indigenous revolutionaries. The Soviet Union tried to win influence in these regions by appealing to a shared "anti-imperialism" and by offering modest amounts of foreign aid.

In most cases, Communists played only small roles in Third World independence movements. But the issue of race, and the popular desire to recover national resources from foreign investors, inflamed already widespread anti-European and anti-American feelings. The State Department countered with offers of financial aid, mostly in the form of credits for purchasing U.S. products and military equipment. But when new nations or familiar allies threatened to interfere with U.S. regional security arrangements, or to expropriate the property of American businesses, the Eisenhower administration turned to covert action and military intervention.

Intervening around the World

The CIA marked a swift, major victory in Iran in 1953. The popular prime minister, Mohammed Mossadegh, had nationalized Britain's Anglo-Iranian Oil Company. The State Department worried that this precedent might encourage a trend toward nationalization throughout the oil-rich Middle East. Kermit Roosevelt, CIA chief in Iran, organized and financed an opposition to Mossadegh within the Iranian army and on the streets of Teheran. This CIA-led movement forced Mossadegh out of office and replaced him with Riza Shah Pahlavi. The Shah proved his loyalty to his American sponsors by renegotiating oil contracts so as to assure American companies of 40 percent of Iran's oil concessions.

The continued rivalry of Israelis and Arabs complicated U.S. policy in the rest of the Middle East. Following American and Soviet recognition of Israel's independence in 1948, Arab states had launched an all-out attack, which the Israelis repulsed. Driving thousands of Palestinians from their homes and occupying territory that hundreds of thousands of others had fearfully fled, the Israelis seized lands far in excess of the terms of a United Nations–sponsored armistice of 1949. Enduring peace did not appear on the horizon. The Arab states refused to recognize Israel's right to exist, and they put into place a damaging economic boycott. Meanwhile, hundreds of thousands of Palestinians languished in refugee camps. Eisenhower believed that Truman had perhaps been too hasty in encouraging the Israelis. Yet most Americans supported the new Jewish state as a refuge for a people who had suffered so much persecution.

Israel stood as a reliable U.S. ally in an unstable region. Arab nationalism continued to vex American policy makers, culminating in the Suez crisis of 1956. Egyptian president Gamal Abdel Nasser, a leading voice of Arab nationalism, looked for American and British economic aid. He had long dreamed of building the Aswan High Dam on the Nile in order to create more arable land and provide cheap electric power. When negotiations broke down, Nasser announced he would nationalize the strategically sensitive Suez Canal and he turned toward the Soviet Union for aid. Eisenhower refused European appeals for U.S. help in seizing the Suez Canal and returning it to the British. When British, French, and Israeli forces attacked Egypt in October 1956, the U.S. sponsored a UN resolution calling for a cease-fire and a withdrawal of foreign forces. Yielding to this pressure, along with Soviet threats to intervene, the British and French withdrew, and eventually so did the Israelis. Eisenhower had won a major diplomatic battle through patience and pressure, but he did not succeed in bringing lasting peace to the troubled region.

The most publicized CIA intervention of the Eisenhower years took place in Guatemala, where a fragile democracy had taken root in 1944. President Jacobo Arbenz Guzmán, elected in 1950, aggressively pursued land reform and encouraged the formation of trade unions. At the time, 2 percent of the Guatemalan population owned 72 percent of all farmland. Arbenz also challenged the long-standing dominance of the United Fruit Company by threatening to expropriate hundreds of thousands of acres that United Fruit was not cultivating. The company had powerful friends in the administration (CIA director Dulles had sat on its board of trustees), and it began intensive lobbying for U.S. intervention. United Fruit linked the land reform program to the evils of international communism, and the CIA spent $7 million training antigovernment dissidents based in Honduras.

The American navy stopped ships bound for Guatemala and seized their cargo, and on June 14, 1954, a U.S.-sponsored military invasion began. Guatemalan citizens resisted by seizing United Fruit buildings, but U.S. Air Force bombing saved the invasion effort. Guatemalans appealed in vain to the United Nations for help. Meanwhile, President Eisenhower publicly denied any knowledge of CIA activities. The newly appointed military leader, Carlos Castillo Armas, flew to the Guatemalan capital in a U.S. embassy plane. Widespread terror followed, unions were outlawed, and thousands arrested. United Fruit circulated photos of Guatemalans murdered by the invaders, labeling them "victims of communism." In 1957 Castillo Armas was assassinated, and a decades-long civil war ensued between military factions and peasant guerrillas.

American intervention in Guatemala increased suspicion of and resentment against American foreign policy throughout Central and Latin America. Vice-President Nixon declared that the new Guatemalan government had earned "the overwhelming

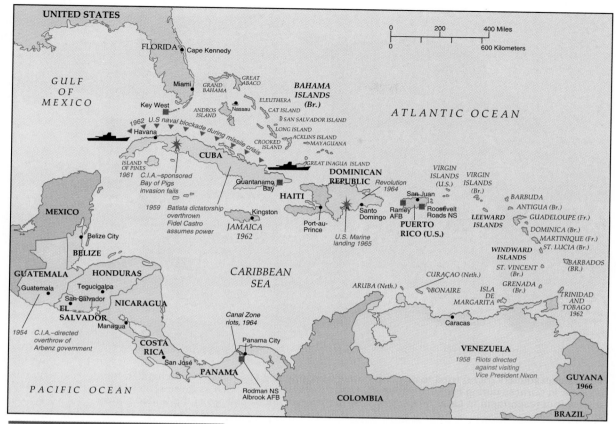

The U.S. in the Caribbean, 1948–1966

U.S. military intervention and economic presence grew steadily in the Caribbean following World War II. After 1960 opposition to the Cuban Revolution dominated U.S. Caribbean policies.

support of the Guatemalan people." But in 1958, while making a "goodwill" tour of Latin America, Nixon was stoned by angry mobs in Caracas, Venezuela, suggesting that U.S. actions in the region had invited an anti-American backlash.

In Indochina, the United States provided France with massive military aid and CIA cooperation in its desperate struggle to maintain a colonial regime in Vietnam. From 1950 to 1954 America poured $2.6 billion (about three-quarters of the total French costs) into the fight against the nationalist Vietminh movement, led by Communist Ho Chi Minh. When Vietminh forces surrounded 25,000 French troops at Dien Bien Phu in March 1954, France pleaded with the U.S. to intervene directly. Secretary of State Dulles and Vice-President Nixon, among others, recommended the use of tactical nuclear weapons and a commitment of ground troops. But Eisenhower, recalling the difficulties of the Korean conflict, rejected this call. "I can conceive of no greater

tragedy," he said, "than for the United States to become engaged in all-out war in Indochina."

At the same time, Eisenhower wanted to contain communism in Asia, and he offered the so-called domino theory to illustrate his point. "You have a row of dominoes set up, and you knock over the first one and what will happen to the last one is the certainty that it will go over quickly." The "loss" of Vietnam would threaten other Southeast Asian nations, such as Laos, Thailand, the Philippines, and perhaps even India and Australia. After the French surrender at Dien Bien Phu, a Geneva convention established a cease-fire and a temporary division of Vietnam along the seventeenth parallel into northern and southern sectors. The Geneva agreement called for reunification and national elections in 1956. The U.S. attended these sessions, along with the Soviet Union and China, but it refused to sign the accord. In response to the Vietnam situation the Eisenhower administration had created the South-

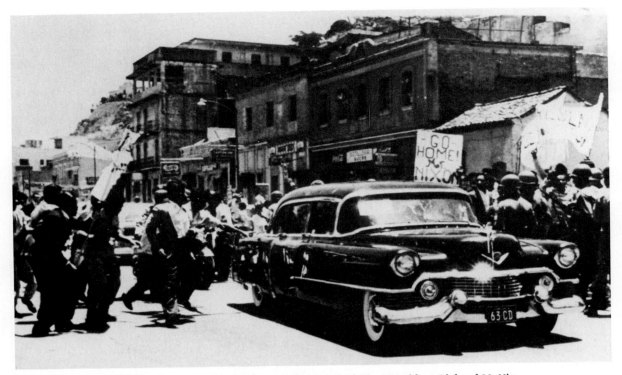

Venezuelan soldiers (right) tried to disperse rioters who attacked Vice-President Richard M. Nixon's car in Caracas during his 1958 "goodwill tour." Demonstrations such as these showed a reservoir of resentment in Latin America against the interventionist policies of the United States in the region.

east Asia Treaty Organization (SEATO) in 1954. This NATO-like security pact was dominated by the U.S. and ultimately included South Vietnam, Laos, Cambodia, Thailand, and the Philippines.

South Vietnamese leader Ngo Dinh Diem, a former Japanese collaborator and a Catholic in a country that was 90 percent Buddhist, quickly alienated many peasants with his corruption and repressive policies. American economic and military aid, along with continuing covert CIA activity, was crucial in keeping the increasingly isolated Diem in power. Both Diem and Eisenhower refused to permit the 1956 elections stipulated in Geneva, because they knew popular hero Ho Chi Minh would easily win. By 1959 Diem's harsh and unpopular government in Saigon faced a civil war; thousands of peasants had joined guerrilla forces determined to drive him out. Eisenhower's commitment of advisers and economic aid to South Vietnam, based on firm belief in Cold War assumptions, laid the foundation for the full-scale commitment of American ground troops in the early 1960s.

The Military-Industrial Complex

Throughout the 1950s small numbers of peace advocates in the United States had pointed to the ultimate illogic of the "new look" in foreign policy. The increasing reliance on nuclear weapons, they argued, did not strengthen national security but rather threatened the entire planet with extinction. They demonstrated at military camps, atomic test sites, and missile launching ranges, often getting arrested to make their point. Reports of radioactive fallout around the world rallied a larger group of scientists and prominent intellectuals against further nuclear testing. Mirroring the large Ban the Bomb movement in Europe, the National Committee for a Sane Nuclear Policy (SANE) claimed 25,000 members by 1958. The Women's International

League for Peace and Freedom collected petitions calling for a test ban. The Student Peace Union, founded in 1959, established itself on many campuses. Small but well-publicized actions against civil defense drills took place in several big cities: protesters marched on the streets rather than entering bomb shelters.

As he neared retirement, President Eisenhower came to share some of the protesters' anxiety and doubts about the arms race. He chose to devote his farewell address, delivered in January 1961, to warning the nation about the dangers of what he termed the *military-industrial complex*. Its total influence, he cautioned, "economic, political, even spiritual — is felt in every city, every statehouse, every office of the Federal government." The conjunction of a large military establishment and a large arms industry, Eisenhower noted, was new in American history. "The potential for the disastrous rise of misplaced power exists and will persist. We must never let the weight of this combination endanger our liberties or democratic processes."

The old soldier understood perhaps better than most the dangers of raw military force. Eisenhower's public posture of restraint and caution in foreign affairs accompanied an enormous expansion of American economic, diplomatic, and military strength. Yet the Eisenhower years also demonstrated the limits of power and intervention in a world that did not always conform to the simple dualistic assumptions of Cold War ideology.

John F. Kennedy and the New Frontier

No one could have resembled Dwight Eisenhower less in personality, temperament, and public image than John Fitzgerald Kennedy. The handsome son of a prominent, wealthy Irish American diplomat, husband of a fashionable, trend-setting heiress, forty-two-year-old JFK embodied youth, excitement, and sophistication. As the first Catholic candidate for president since Al Smith in 1928, Kennedy ran under the banner of the New Frontier. His liberalism inspired idealism and hope in millions of young people at home and abroad. In foreign affairs, Kennedy generally followed, and in some respects deepened, the Cold War precepts that dominated postwar policy making. But by the time of his assassination in 1963, Kennedy may have been veering away from the hardline anti-Communist ideology he had embraced. What a second term might have brought remains debatable, but his death ended a unique moment in American public life.

The Election of 1960

John F. Kennedy's political career had begun in Massachusetts, which elected him to the House in 1946 and then the Senate in 1952. Kennedy won the Democratic nomination after a bruising series of primaries in which he defeated party stalwarts

Studio television set for one of the four Kennedy-Nixon presidential debates, October, 1960. Howard K. Smith of CBS News was the moderator. Eighty-five million viewers watched at least one of the debates, which both reflected and increased the power of television in the electoral process.

Hubert Humphrey of Minnesota and Lyndon B. Johnson of Texas. Unlike Humphrey and Johnson, Kennedy had not been part of the powerful group of insiders who dominated the Senate. But he drew strength and financial support from a loyal coterie of friends and family, including his father, Joseph P. Kennedy, Jr., and his younger brother Robert. Vice-President Richard M. Nixon, the Republican nominee, had faithfully served the Eisenhower administration for eight years, and was far better known than his younger opponent. The Kennedy campaign stressed its candidate's youth and his image as a war hero. During his World War II tour of duty in the Pacific, Kennedy had bravely rescued one of his crew after their PT boat had been sunk. Kennedy's supporters also pointed to his intellectual ability. JFK had won the Pulitzer Prize in 1957 for his book *Profiles in Courage*, which in fact had been written largely by aides.

The election featured the first televised presidential debates. Nixon appeared unshaven and nervous through the camera, while Kennedy's confident manner and good looks added to his stature. Both candidates emphasized foreign policy. Nixon defended the Republican record and stressed his own maturity and experience. Kennedy hammered away at the "missile gap" with the Soviet Union and promised more vigorous executive leadership. He promised to keep church and state separate, dampening the anti-Catholic prejudice of evangelical Protestants. Political analysts have long argued over the precise impact of the four debates. But all agree that the 1960 election moved television to the center of presidential politics, making image and appearance more critical than ever.

Kennedy squeaked to victory in the closest election since 1884. He won by a little over 100,000 votes out of nearly 69 million cast. He ran poorly in the South, but won the Catholic vote so overwhelmingly that he carried most of the Northeast and Midwest. Though the margin of victory was tiny, Kennedy was a glorious winner. Surrounded by prestigious Ivy League academics, Hollywood movie stars, and talented artists and writers, he imbued the presidency with an aura of celebrity. The inauguration brought out a bevy of poets, musicians, and fashionably dressed politicians from around the world. The new administration promised to be exciting and stylish, a modern-day Camelot peopled by heroic young men and beautiful women. The new president's ringing inaugural address ("Ask not what your country can do for you — ask what you can do for your country.") had special resonance for a whole generation of young Americans.

Election of 1960

Kennedy's popular vote margin over Nixon was only a little over 100,000, making this one of the closest elections in American history.

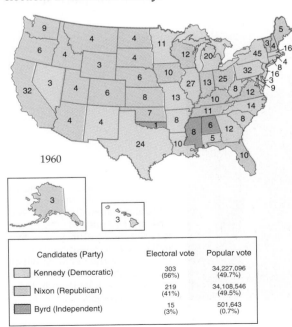

1960

Candidates (Party)	Electoral vote	Popular vote
Kennedy (Democratic)	303 (56%)	34,227,096 (49.7%)
Nixon (Republican)	219 (41%)	34,108,546 (49.5%)
Byrd (Independent)	15 (3%)	501,643 (0.7%)

New Frontier Liberalism

Kennedy promised to revive the long-stalled liberal domestic agenda. His New Frontier advocated such liberal programs as a higher minimum wage, greater federal aid for education, increased Social Security benefits, medical care for the elderly, support for public housing, and various antipoverty measures. Yet the thin margin of his victory and the stubborn opposition of conservative southern Democrats in Congress made it difficult to achieve these goals. Congress refused, for example, to enact the administration's attempt to extend Social Security and unemployment benefits to millions of uncovered workers. Congress also failed to enact administration proposals for aid to public schools, mass transit subsidies, and medical insurance for retired workers over sixty-five.

There were a few New Frontier victories. Congress did approve a modest increase in the minimum wage (to $1.25 per hour), agreed to a less ambitious improvement in Social Security, and appropriated $5 billion for public housing. It also passed the Manpower Retraining Act, appropriating $435 million to train the unemployed. The Area

Redevelopment Act provided federal funds for rural, depressed Appalachia. The Higher Education Act of 1963 offered aid to colleges for constructing buildings and upgrading libraries. One of the best-publicized New Frontier programs was the Peace Corps, in which thousands of mostly young men and women traveled overseas for two-year stints in underdeveloped countries. There they provided technical and educational assistance in setting up health care programs and improving agricultural efficiency. As a force for change, the Peace Corps produced modest results. But as a vehicle for young people, the Peace Corps epitomized Kennedy's promise to direct the idealism of a new generation.

Kennedy helped revive the issue of women's rights with his Presidential Commission on the Status of Women, led by Eleanor Roosevelt. The commission's 1963 report was the most comprehensive study of women's lives ever produced by the federal government. It documented the ongoing discrimination faced by American women in the workplace and in the legal system, as well as the inadequacy of social services such as day care. It called for federally supported day-care programs, continuing-education programs for women, and an end to sex bias in Social Security and unemployment benefits. The commission also insisted that more women be appointed to policy-making positions in government. One concrete legislative result, the Equal Pay Act of 1963, made it illegal for employers to pay men and women different wages for the same job. The law did not do much to improve women's economic status, since most working women were employed in job categories that included no men. But the issue of economic inequality had at least been put on the public agenda. President Kennedy also directed executive agencies to prohibit sex discrimination in hiring and promotion. The work of the commission led to similar studies by states and contributed to a new generation of women's rights activism.

Kennedy took a more aggressive stance on stimulating economic growth and creating new jobs than had Eisenhower. Kennedy relied heavily upon Walter Heller, chair of the Council of Economic Advisers (CEA). Heller emphasized the goal of full employment, which he believed could be attained through deficit spending, encouragement of economic growth, and targeted tax cuts. The administration thus pushed lower business taxes through Congress, even at the cost of a higher federal deficit. The Revenue Act of 1962 encouraged new investment and plant renovation by easing tax depreciation schedules for business. Kennedy also gained approval for lower U.S. tariffs as a way to increase foreign trade. To help keep inflation down, Kennedy intervened in the steel industry in 1961 and 1962, pressuring labor to keep its wage demands low and management to curb price increases.

Kennedy also increased the federal commitment to a wholly new realm of government spending: the space program. The National Aeronautics and Space Administration (NASA) had been established under Eisenhower in response to the Soviet

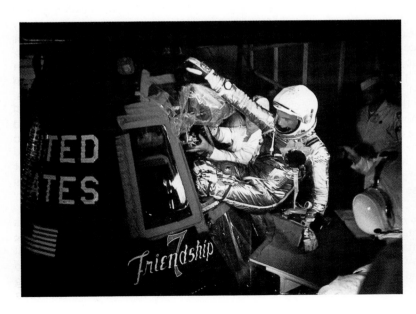

Astronaut John H. Glenn as he prepared for the first American manned space orbit of the earth. The space program of the early 1960s emphasized the technical training and courage of astronauts, consciously creating a set of public heroes as a way to ensure popular support and Congressional funding.

success with *Sputnik.* NASA had originally focused on launching and maintaining spy satellites. In 1961 Kennedy won approval for a greatly expanded space program with the goal of landing an American on the moon by the end of the decade. NASA eventually spent $33 billion before reaching this goal in 1969. This program of manned space flight — the *Apollo* missions — appealed to the public, acquiring a science fiction aura. In space, if not on earth, the New Frontier might actually be reached.

Overall, Kennedy's most long-lasting achievement as president may have been his strengthening of the executive branch itself. He insisted on direct presidential control of details that Eisenhower had left to advisers and appointees. Moreover, under Kennedy the White House staff assumed many of the decision-making and advisory functions previously held by Cabinet members. This increased Kennedy's authority, since these appointees, unlike Cabinet secretaries, escaped congressional oversight and confirmation proceedings. White House aides also lacked an independent constituency; their power and authority derived solely from their ties to the president. Kennedy's aides, "the best and the brightest," as he called them, dominated policy making. With men such as McGeorge Bundy directing foreign affairs and Theodore Sorensen coordinating domestic issues, Kennedy began a pattern whereby American presidents increasingly governed through small groups of fiercely loyal aides often acting in secret.

Kennedy and the Cold War

During Kennedy's three years in office his approach to foreign policy shifted between aggressive containment and efforts to ease U.S.-Soviet tensions. Certainly when he first entered office, Kennedy and his chief aides considered it their main task to confront the Communist threat. In his first State of the Union address, in January 1961, Kennedy told Congress that America must seize the initiative in the Cold War. The nation must "move outside the home fortress, and . . . challenge the enemy in fields of our own choosing." To head the State Department Kennedy chose Dean Rusk, a conservative former assistant to Truman's secretary of state, Dean Acheson. Secretary of Defense Robert McNamara, a Republican and Ford Motor Company executive, was determined to streamline military procedures and weapons buying. McNamara typified the technical, cost-efficient, superrational approach to policy making. Allen Dulles, Eisenhower's CIA director, remained at his post. These and other officials

believed with Kennedy that Eisenhower had timidly accepted stalemate when the Cold War could have been won.

Kennedy built up American nuclear and conventional weapons systems. Between 1960 and 1962 defense appropriations increased by nearly a third, from $43 billion to $56 billion. He expanded Eisenhower's policy of covert operations, creating the elite Special Forces ("Green Berets") as a supplement to CIA covert operations in counterinsurgency battles against Third World guerrillas. These soldiers, fighting under the direct orders of the president, could provide "rapid response" to "brush-fire" conflicts where Soviet influence threatened American interests. The Special Forces reflected Kennedy's desire as president to acquire greater flexibility, secrecy, and independence in the conduct of foreign policy.

The limits of the Special Forces and covert action became apparent in Southeast Asia. In Laos, where the U.S. had ignored the 1954 Geneva agreement and installed a friendly military regime, the CIA-backed government could not defeat Soviet-backed Pathet Lao guerrillas. The president had to arrange with the Soviets to neutralize Laos. In neighboring Vietnam, the situation proved more difficult. When Viet Cong guerrillas launched a civil war in South Vietnam against the U.S.-supported government in Saigon, Kennedy began sending hundreds of Green Berets and other military advisers to support the rule of Ngo Dinh Diem. In May 1961, in response to North Vietnamese aid to the Viet Cong, Kennedy ordered a covert action against Ho Chi Minh's government that included sabotage and intelligence gathering.

Kennedy accepted the analysis of two aides, General Maxwell Taylor and Walt Rostow, who saw the situation in Vietnam through purely Cold War eyes. "The Communists are pursuing a clear and systematic strategy in Southeast Asia," they concluded, ignoring the inefficiency, corruption, and unpopularity of the Diem government. By 1963, with Diem's army unable to contain the Viet Cong rebellion, Kennedy had sent nearly 16,000 support and combat troops to South Vietnam. By then, a wide spectrum of South Vietnamese society had joined the revolt against the hated Diem, including highly respected Buddhist monks and their students. Americans watched in horror as television news reports showed footage of Buddhists burning themselves to death on the streets of Saigon — the ultimate protest against Diem's repressive rule. American press and television also reported the mounting casualty lists of U.S. forces in Vietnam. The South Vietnamese army, bloated by U.S. aid and weakened by corruption, continued to disintegrate. In the fall of 1963, American military officers and CIA operatives watched with approval as a group of Vietnamese generals removed President Diem, killing him and his top advisers. It was the first of many coups that racked the South Vietnamese government over the next few years.

In Latin America, Kennedy looked for ways to forestall various revolutionary movements that were gaining ground. The erosion of peasant landholdings had accelerated rapidly after 1950. Huge expanses of fertile land long devoted to subsistence farming were converted to business-dominated agriculture that grew staple crops for export (bananas, coffee, sugar). Millions of impoverished peasants were forced to relocate to already overcrowded cities. In 1961 Kennedy unveiled the Alliance for Progress, a ten-year, $100 billion plan to spur economic development in Latin America. The U.S. committed $20 billion to the project, with the Latin nations responsible for the rest. The main goals included greater industrial growth and agricultural productivity, more equitable distribution of income, and improved health and housing. Kennedy intended the program as a kind of Marshall Plan that would benefit the poor and middle classes of the continent. The alliance did help raise growth rates in Latin American economies. But the expansion in export crops and in consumption by the tiny upper class did little to aid the poor or encourage democracy. The U.S. hesitated to challenge the power of dictators and extreme conservatives who were staunch anti-Communist allies. Thus, the alliance soon degenerated into just another foreign-aid program, incapable of generating genuine social change.

The Cuban Revolution and the Bay of Pigs

The direct impetus for the Alliance for Progress was the Cuban Revolution of 1959, which loomed over Latin America. The U.S. economic domination of Cuba had continued through the 1950s. American-owned business controlled all of Cuba's oil production, 90 percent of its mines, and roughly half of its railroads and sugar and cattle industries. Havana, the island's capital, was an attractive tourist center for Americans, and U.S. crime syndicates shared control of the island's lucrative gambling, prostitution, and drug trade with dictator Fulgencio Batista. In the early 1950s a peasant-based revolutionary movement, led by Fidel Castro, began gaining strength in the rural districts and mountains outside Havana.

On New Year's Day 1959, after years of military defeat, the rebels entered Havana and seized power amid great public rejoicing. For a brief time, Castro seemed a hero to many North Americans as well. The New York Times had conducted sympathetic interviews with Castro in 1958, while he was still in the mountains. Many young people visited the island and returned with enthusiastic reports. Famous writers such as James Baldwin and Ernest Hemingway embraced Castro. The CIA and President Eisenhower, however, shared none of this exuberance. Castro's land reform program, involving the seizure of acreage from the tiny minority that controlled much of the fertile land, threatened to set an example for other Latin American countries. Although Castro had not joined the Cuban Communist party, he turned to the Soviet Union after the U.S. withdrew economic aid. He began to sell sugar to the Soviets and soon nationalized American-owned oil companies and other enterprises. Eisenhower established an economic boycott of Cuba in 1960, then severed diplomatic relations.

Kennedy inherited from Eisenhower plans for a U.S. invasion of Cuba, including the secret arming and training of Cuban exiles. The CIA drafted the invasion plan, which was based on the assumption that a U.S.-led invasion would trigger a popular uprising of the Cuban people and bring down Castro. Kennedy went along with the plan, but at the last moment decided not to supply an Air Force cover for the operation. On April 17, 1961, a ragtag army of 1,400 counterrevolutionaries led by CIA operatives landed at the Bay of Pigs, on Cuba's south coast. Castro's efficient and loyal army easily subdued them. At the United Nations Ambassador Adlai Stevenson, deceived by presidential aides, flatly denied any U.S. involvement, only to learn the truth later.

The debacle revealed that the CIA, blinded by Cold War assumptions, had failed to understand the Cuban Revolution. There was no popular uprising against Castro. Instead, the invasion strengthened Castro's standing among the urban poor and peasants, already attracted by his programs of universal literacy and medical care. As his government stifled internal opposition, many Cuban intellectuals and professionals fled to the U.S. An embarrassed Kennedy reluctantly took the blame for the abortive invasion, and his administration was censured time and again by Third World delegates to the United

President Kennedy and exploding Cuban cigar, April, 1961. This cartoon by Leslie Illingworth satirized the political backfire brought on by the failed Bay of Pigs invasion. Kennedy took responsibility for the debacle, but mutual political suspicions between Cuba and the United States continued for decades.

Nations. American liberals criticized Kennedy for plotting Castro's overthrow while conservatives blamed him for failing to carry out the plan. Despite the failure, Kennedy remained committed to getting rid of Castro and keeping up the economic boycott. The CIA continued to support anti-Castro operations and launched at least eight attempts to assassinate the Cuban leader.

The Missile Crisis

The aftermath of the Bay of Pigs led to the most serious confrontation of the Cold War: the Cuban missile crisis of October 1962. Frightened by U.S. belligerency, Castro asked Soviet premier Khrushchev for military help. Khrushchev responded in the summer of 1962 by shipping Cuba a large amount of sophisticated weaponry, including intermediate-range nuclear missiles. In early October U.S. reconnaissance planes found camouflaged missile silos dotting the island. For the first time, American cities and military bases were potential targets for Soviet nuclear bombs, sited a mere ninety miles from Florida. Several Kennedy aides demanded an immediate bombing of Cuban bases, arguing that the missiles had decisively changed the strategic global advantage the U.S. had previously enjoyed.

Instead, Kennedy went on national television on October 22. He announced the discovery of the missile sites, demanded the removal of all missiles, and ordered a strict naval blockade of all offensive military equipment shipped to Cuba. He also requested an emergency meeting of the UN Security Council and promised that any missiles launched from Cuba would bring "a full retaliatory response upon the Soviet Union." For a tense week, the American public wondered if nuclear Armageddon was imminent. Eyeball to eyeball, the two superpowers waited for each other to blink. On October 28 Khrushchev yielded, ordering twenty-five Soviet ships off their course to Cuba, thus avoiding a challenge to the American blockade. Khrushchev offered to remove all the missiles in return for a pledge from the United States not to invade Cuba. Khrushchev later added a demand for removal of American weapons from Turkey, equally close to the Soviet Union. On November 20, after weeks of delicate negotiations, Kennedy publicly announced the withdrawal of Soviet missiles and bombers from Cuba, pledged to respect Cuban sovereignty, and promised that U.S. forces would not invade the island.

The crisis had passed. The Soviets, determined not to be intimidated again, engaged in the largest weapons buildup in their history. For his part Kennedy, perhaps chastened by this flirtation with nuclear disaster, made important gestures toward détente with the Soviets. In a June 1963 address at American University, Kennedy called for a rethinking of Cold War diplomacy. Both sides, he said, had been "caught up in a vicious cycle in which suspicion on one side breeds suspicion on the other, and new weapons beget counter-weapons." It was important "not to see only a distorted and desperate view of the other side. . . . No government or social system is so evil that its people must be considered as lacking in virtue." Shortly after, Washington and

Moscow set up a hot line — a direct phone connection to facilitate instant communication during times of crisis. More substantial was the Limited Nuclear Test Ban Treaty, signed in August by the U.S., the USSR, and Great Britain. The treaty prohibited above-ground, outer space, and underwater nuclear weapons tests. Underground testing continued to accelerate for years. But the limited test ban represented an important landmark in arms control, as well as a psychological breakthrough in East-West relations.

CONCLUSION

The assassination of John F. Kennedy on November 22, 1963, sent the entire nation into shock and mourning. Tens of millions watched his funeral on television, trying to make sense of the brutal murder. Although a special commission found the killing to be the work of a lone assassin, Lee Harvey Oswald, many Americans still doubt this conclusion. Kennedy's death gave rise to a host of conspiracy theories, none of which seems provable. We will never know, of course, what Kennedy might have achieved in a second term. But in his 1,000 days as

Vice-President Lyndon B. Johnson took the oath of office as President aboard Air Force One after the assassination of John F. Kennedy, November 22, 1963. Onlookers included the grief stricken Jacqueline Kennedy (right) and Lady Bird Johnson (left). This haunting photo captured both the shock of Kennedy's assassination and the orderly succession of power that followed.

CHRONOLOGY

1944	Veterans Act (GI Bill of Rights)
1950	David Riesman, *The Lonely Crowd*
1952	Dwight Eisenhower elected president
1953	CIA installs Riza Shah Pahlavi as leader of Iran
1954	U.S. explodes first hydrogen bomb
	CIA overthrows Arbenz government in Guatemala
	Vietminh force French surrender at Dien Bien Phu
1955	Salk pioneers vaccine for polio
	James Dean stars in the movie *Rebel without a Cause*
1956	Federal Highway Act
	Elvis Presley signs with RCA
	Eisenhower reelected
	Allen Ginsberg, *Howl*
1957	*Sputnik* launched
	Jack Kerouac, *On the Road*
1958	National Defense Education Act
1960	John F. Kennedy elected president
	Over 90 percent of American homes have television
1961	President Kennedy creates Special Forces ("Green Berets")
	Bay of Pigs invasion
1962	Cuban missile crisis
1963	Report by the Presidential Commission on the Status of Women
	President Kennedy assassinated

president, he demonstrated a capacity to change and grow in office. Having gone to the brink at the missile crisis, he had then managed to launch new initiatives toward détente. At the time of his death, relations between the U.S. and the Soviet Union were more amicable than at any time since the end of World War II.

If Kennedy had not realized his dream of transforming the world, he had not destroyed it either. Much of the domestic liberal agenda of the New Frontier would be finally implemented by his successor, Lyndon B. Johnson, who dreamed of creating a Great Society. But Johnson would have to contend with a new threat to American "national security." Growing domestic opposition to American involvement in Vietnam, along with the radicalization of African Americans and many white young people, posed a challenge perhaps more profound than the "Communist menace" that shaped so much postwar foreign and domestic policy.

Additional Readings

STEPHEN AMBROSE, *Eisenhower* (2 vols., 1983, 1984). The most comprehensive scholarly biography of the general and president.

ERIK BARNOUW, *Tube of Plenty* (1982). The best one-volume history of television, with excellent material on the new medium's impact upon cultural and political life.

JOHN PATRICK DIGGINS, *The Proud Decades: America in War and Peace, 1941–1960* (1988). A unique, well-written synthesis of the political, cultural, and diplomatic history of this era.

HERBERT GANS, *The Levittowners* (1967). A classic study of postwar suburban life, arguing that suburban communities were far more diverse and less conformist than pictured in popular accounts of the 1950s.

JAMES B. GILBERT, *A Cycle of Outrage* (1986). An insightful analysis of juvenile delinquency and its treatment by social scientists and the mass media during the 1950s.

CHARLIE GILLETT, *The Sound of the City* (rev. ed., 1983). A detailed, pioneering history of rock-'n'-roll, with special emphasis on its urban roots.

KENNETH T. JACKSON, *Crabgrass Frontier* (1985). The most comprehensive overview of the history of American suburbs. Provides a broad historical context for understanding postwar suburbanization, and offers an excellent analysis of the impact of government agencies, such as the Federal Housing Administration.

GEORGE LIPSITZ, *Time Passages* (1990). An illuminating set of essays charting developments in American popular culture. Especially strong analysis of music and early television.

GREIL MARCUS, *Mystery Train* (1976). A provocative set of essays on rock-'n'-roll and its connections with older forms of American culture. Includes a brilliant analysis of Elvis Presley's career and impact.

ELAINE TYLER MAY, *Homeward Bound: American Families in the Cold War* (1988). A thoughtful social history linking family life of the 1950s with the political shadow of the Cold War.

DOUGLAS T. MILLER AND MARION NOVAK, *The Fifties: The Way We Really Were* (1977). A very useful critical appraisal of the decade's cultural life and social trends.

GERALD NICOSIA, *Memory Babe: A Critical Biography of Jack Kerouac* (1983). Both the best biography of this key Beat writer and the best analysis of the Beat Generation.

HERBERT PARMET, *JFK* (1983). A solid, balanced analysis of the Kennedy presidency.

RICHARD POLENBERG, *One Nation Divisible* (1980). A concise overview of American society from World War II to the 1970s, with special attention to the persistence of class, racial, and ethnic divisions.

RICHARD WALTON, *Cold War and Counterrevolution* (1972). A useful critical overview of U.S. interventions in Third World revolutions and their connections with Cold War policies.

PETER WYDEN, *Bay of Pigs* (1980). An excellent account that includes good material on the government's efforts to control media coverage of this crucial foreign policy crisis.

28 CIVIL RIGHTS AND THE GREAT SOCIETY, 1945–1966

AMERICAN COMMUNITIES

● THE MONTGOMERY BUS BOYCOTT

A steady stream of cars and pedestrians jammed the streets around the Holt Street Baptist Church in Montgomery, Alabama. By early evening a patient, orderly, and determined crowd of over 5,000 African Americans had packed the church and spilled over onto the sidewalks. Loudspeakers had to be set up for the thousands who could not squeeze inside. After a brief prayer and a reading from the Scripture, all attention focused on the twenty-six-year-old minister who was to address the gathering. "We are here this evening," he began slowly, "for serious business. We are here in a general sense because first and foremost we are American citizens, and we are determined to apply our citizenship to the fullness of its means."

Sensing the expectant mood of the crowd, the minister got down to specifics. Rosa Parks, a seamstress and well-known activist in Montgomery's African American com-

AN AFRICAN AMERICAN COMMUNITY CHALLENGES SEGREGATION

munity, had been taken from a bus, arrested, and put in jail for refusing to give up her seat to a white passenger on December 1, 1955. Composing roughly half the city's 100,000 people, Montgomery's black community had long endured the humiliation of a strictly segregated bus system. Drivers could order a whole row of black passengers to vacate their seats for one white person. And black people had to pay their fares at the front of the bus and then step back outside and reenter through the rear door. The day of the mass meeting, over 30,000 African Americans had answered a hastily organized call to boycott the city's buses in protest of Mrs. Parks's arrest. As the minister quickened his cadence and drew shouts of encouragement, he seemed to draw strength and confidence from the crowd. "You know, my friends, there comes a time when people get tired of being trampled over by the iron feet of oppression. There comes a time, my friends, when people get tired of being flung across the abyss of humiliation when they experience the bleakness of nagging despair."

Even before he concluded his speech, it was clear to all present that the bus boycott would continue for more than just a day. The minister laid out the key principles that would guide the boycott — nonviolence, Christian love, unity. By the time he finished his brief but stirring address, the minister had created a powerful sense of communion. "If we are wrong, justice is a

Rev. Dr. Martin Luther King, Jr. addressing a packed mass meeting at the First Baptist Church during the Montgomery bus boycott. Regular gatherings in the city's African American churches were crucial to maintaining community solidarity.

lie," he told the clapping and shouting throng. "And we are determined here in Montgomery to work and fight until justice runs down like water and righteousness like a mighty stream." Historians would look back at Montgomery, he noted, and have to say: " 'There lived a race of people, black people, fleecy locks and black complexion, of people who had the moral courage to stand up for their rights.' And thereby they injected a new meaning into the veins of history and of civilization."

The Reverend Dr. Martin Luther King, Jr., made his way out of the church amid waves of applause and rows of hands reaching out to touch him. His speech catapulted him into leadership of the Montgomery bus boycott, and it also proved him to be a prophet. But he had not started the movement. When Rosa Parks was arrested local activists with deep roots in the black protest tradition galvanized the community with the idea of a boycott. Mrs. Parks herself had served for twelve years as secretary of the local NAACP chapter. She was a committed opponent of segregation and was thoroughly respected in the city's African American community. E. D. Nixon, president of the Alabama NAACP and head of the local Brotherhood of Sleeping Car Porters union, saw Mrs. Parks's arrest as the right case on which to make a stand. On December 5, Nixon brought together Montgomery's black ministers to coordinate a boycott of city buses. They formed the Montgomery Improvement Association (MIA) and chose Dr. King as their leader.

While Nixon organized black ministers, Jo Ann Robinson, an English teacher at Alabama State College, played a key role in spreading the word to the larger black community. Robinson led the Women's Political Council (WPC), an organization of black professional women founded in 1949. With her WPC allies, Robinson wrote, mimeographed, and distributed 50,000 copies of a leaflet telling the story of Mrs. Parks's arrest and urging all African Americans to stay off city buses on December 5. Buoyed by the success of that protest, the MIA now faced the more difficult task of keeping the boycott going. Success depended upon providing alternate transportation for the 30,000 to 40,000 maids, cooks, janitors, and other black working people who needed to get to work.

The MIA coordinated an elaborate system of car pools, using hundreds of private autos and volunteer drivers to provide as many as 20,000 rides each day. Local authorities, shocked by the discipline and sense of purpose shown by Montgomery's African American community, refused to engage in serious negotiations. With the aid of the NAACP, the MIA brought suit in federal court against bus segregation in Montgomery. Police harassed boycotters with traffic tickets and arrests. White racists exploded bombs in the homes of Dr. King and E. D. Nixon. The days turned into weeks, then months, but still the boycott continued. All along, mass meetings in Montgomery's African American churches helped boost morale. People drew inspiration and renewal from singing, praying, and hearing stories of individual sacrifice. One elderly woman, refusing all suggestions that she drop out of the boycott on account of her age, made a spontaneous remark that became a classic refrain of the movement: "My feets is tired, but my soul is rested."

The boycott reduced the bus company's revenues by two-thirds. In February 1956 city officials obtained indictments against King, Nixon, and 113 other boycotters under an old law forbidding hindrance to business without "just cause or legal excuse." A month later King went on trial as the first of the indicted defendants. A growing contingent of newspaper reporters and TV crews from around the country watched as the judge found King guilty, fined him $1,000, and released him on bond pending appeal. But on June 4, a panel of three federal judges struck down Montgomery's bus segregation ordinances as unconstitutional. Attorneys for Montgomery and the state of Alabama immediately appealed to the U.S. Supreme Court. On November 13 the Court affirmed the district court ruling. After eleven hard months and against all odds, the boycotters had won.

The struggle to end legal segregation took root in scores of southern cities and towns. African American communities led these fights, developing a variety of tactics, leaders, and ideologies. With white allies, they engaged in direct-action protests such as boycotts, sit-ins, and mass civil disobedience, as well as strategic legal battles in state and federal courts. The movement was not without

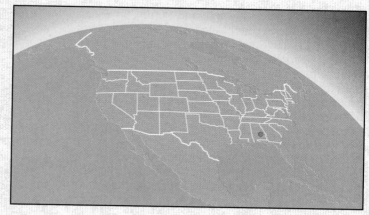

its inner conflicts. Tensions between local movements and national civil rights organizations flared up regularly. Within African American communities, long-simmering distrust between the working classes and rural folk on the one hand and middle-class ministers, teachers, and business people on the other sometimes threatened to destroy political unity. There were generational conflicts between African American student activists and their elders. But overall, the civil rights movement created new social identities for African Americans and profoundly changed American society as a whole.

ORIGINS OF THE MOVEMENT

The experiences of African Americans during World War II and immediately thereafter laid the foundation for the civil rights struggle of the 1950s and 1960s. Nearly 1 million black men and women had served in the armed forces. The contradictions of fighting totalitarianism abroad while enduring segregation and other racist practices in the military embittered many combat veterans and their families. Between 1939 and 1945 nearly 2 million African Americans gained employment in defense plants and another 200,000 entered the federal civil service. Black union membership doubled, reaching over 1.2 million. But the wartime stress on national unity and consensus largely muted political protests. With the war's end, African Americans and their white allies determined to push ahead for full political and social equality.

Civil Rights after World War II

The boom in wartime production spurred a mass migration of nearly a million black southerners to northern cities. Forty-three northern and western cities saw their black population double during the 1940s. Although racial discrimination in housing and employment was by no means absent in northern cities, greater economic opportunities and political freedom continued to attract rural African Americans after the war. Black people gained significant influence in local political machines in such cities as New York, Chicago, and Detroit. In industrial unions such as the United Automobile Workers and the United Steel Workers, white and black workers learned the power of biracial unity in fighting for better wages and working conditions. Harlem congressman Adam Clayton Powell, Jr., captured the new mood of 1945 when he wrote that black people were eager "to make the dream of America become flesh and blood, bread and butter, freedom and equality."

After the war, civil rights issues returned to the national political stage for the first time since Reconstruction. Black voters had already begun to switch their allegiance from the Republicans to the Democrats during the New Deal. A series of symbolic and substantial acts by the Truman administration solidified that shift. In 1946 Truman created a Presidential Committee on Civil Rights. Its report, *To Secure These Rights,* set out an ambitious program to end racial inequality. Recommendations included a permanent civil rights division in the Justice Department, voting rights protection, antilynching legisla-

tion, and a legal attack on segregated housing. Yet, although he publicly endorsed nearly all the proposals of the new committee, Truman introduced no legislation to make them law.

Truman and his advisers walked a political tightrope on civil rights. They understood that black voters in several key northern states would be pivotal in the 1948 election. At the same time, they worried about the loyalty of white southern Democrats adamantly opposed to changing the racial status quo. In July of 1948 the president made his boldest move on behalf of civil rights, issuing an executive order barring segregation in the armed forces. When liberals forced the Democratic National Convention to adopt a strong civil rights plank that summer, a group of outraged southerners walked out and nominated Governor Strom Thurmond of South Carolina for president on a States Rights ticket. Thurmond carried four southern states in the election. But with the help of over 70 percent of the northern black vote, Truman barely managed to defeat Republican Thomas E. Dewey in November. The deep split over race issues would continue to rack the national Democratic party for a generation.

Electoral politics was not the only arena for civil rights work. During the war, membership in the National Association for the Advancement of Colored People had mushroomed from 50,000 to 500,000. Working- and middle-class urban black people provided the backbone of this new membership. The NAACP conducted voter registration drives and lobbied against discrimination in housing and employment. Its Legal Defense and Education Fund, vigorously led by Thurgood Marshall, mounted several significant legal challenges to segregation laws. In *Morgan v. Virginia* (1946), the Supreme Court declared that segregation on interstate buses was an undue burden on interstate commerce. Other decisions struck down all-white election primaries, racially restrictive housing covenants, and the exclusion of blacks from law and graduate schools.

The NAACP's legal work demonstrated the potential for using federal courts in attacking segregation. Courts were one place where black people, using the constitutional language of rights, could make forceful arguments that could not be voiced in Congress or at political conventions. But federal enforcement of court decisions was often lacking. In 1947 a group of black and white activists tested compliance with the *Morgan* decision by traveling on a bus through the Upper South. This "Freedom Ride" was cosponsored by the Christian pacifist Fellowship of Reconciliation (FOR) and its recent

Charlie Parker (alto sax) and Miles Davis (trumpet) with their group in 1947, at the Three Deuces Club in New York City. Parker and Davis were two creative leaders of the "be bop" movement of the 1940s. Working in Northern cities, boppers re-shaped jazz music and created a distinct language and style that was widely imitated by young people. They challenged older stereotypes of African American musicians by insisting that they be treated as serious artists.

neered the development of swing and earlier jazz styles, white bandleaders and musicians had reaped most of the recognition and money from the public. Artists such as Charlie Parker, Dizzy Gillespie, Thelonius Monk, Bud Powell, and Miles Davis revolted against the standard big band format of swing, preferring small groups and extended jam sessions to express their musical visions. The new music, dubbed *bebop* by critics and fans, demanded a much more sophisticated knowledge of harmony and melody and featured more complex rhythms and extended improvisation.

In urban black communities the "boppers" consciously created a music that, unlike swing, white popularizers found difficult to copy or sweeten. These black artists insisted on independence from the white-defined norms of show business. Serious about both their music and the way it was presented, they refused to cater to white expectations of grinning, easygoing black performers. Although most boppers had roots in the South, they preferred the relative freedom they found in northern urban black communities. A significant number of northern black (and white) youths identified with the distinctive music, language, and dress of the boppers. In both their music and their public image, these musicians presented a rebellious alternative to the traditional image of the African American entertainer.

The Segregated South

In the postwar South, still home to over half the nation's 15 million African Americans, the racial situation remained largely unchanged. The 1896 Supreme Court ruling in *Plessy v. Ferguson* (discussed in Chapter 19) had sanctioned the principle of "separate but equal" in southern life. In practice, segregation meant separate and unequal. A tight web of state and local ordinances enforced strict separation of the races in schools, restaurants, movie theaters, libraries, restrooms, even cemeteries. Fifty years of legal segregation meant inferior public schools, health care, and public lodging for the region's black people. There were no black policemen in the Deep South and only a handful of black lawyers. "A white man," one scholar observed, "can steal from or maltreat a Negro in almost any way without fear of reprisal, because the Negro cannot claim the protection of the police or courts."

In the late 1940s only about 10 percent of eligible southern black people voted, most of these

offshoot, the Congress of Racial Equality (CORE), which was devoted to interracial, nonviolent direct action. The riders met stiff resistance in North Carolina. A number were arrested and sentenced to thirty days on a chain gang for refusing to leave the bus.

Two symbolic "firsts" raised black expectations and inspired pride. In 1947 Jackie Robinson broke the color barrier in major league baseball, winning rookie-of-the-year-honors with the Brooklyn Dodgers. Robinson's courage in the face of fan and player hostility paved the way for the other black ballplayers who soon followed him to the big leagues. In 1950 United Nations diplomat Ralph Bunche won the Nobel Peace Prize for arranging a Middle East armistice. However, Bunche later declined an appointment as undersecretary of state because he did not want to subject his family to the humiliating segregation laws of Washington, D.C.

Cultural change could have political implications as well. In the 1940s, African American musicians created a new form of jazz that revolutionized American music and asserted a militant black consciousness. Although black musicians had pio-

Signs designating "White" and "Colored" rest rooms, waiting rooms, entrances, benches, and even water fountains were a common sight in the segregated South. They were a constant reminder that legal separation of the races in public spaces was the law of the land.

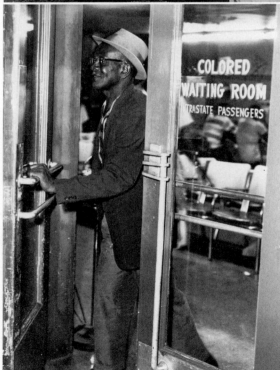

in urban areas. A combination of legal and extralegal measures kept all but the most determined black people disenfranchised. Poll taxes, all-white primaries, and discriminatory registration procedures reinforced the belief that voting was "the white man's business." African Americans who insisted on exercising their right to vote, especially in remote rural areas, faced physical violence — beatings, shootings, lynchings. A former president of the Alabama Bar Association expressed a commonly held view when he declared, "No Negro is good enough and no Negro will ever be good enough to participate in making the law under which the white people of Alabama have to live."

Outsiders often noted the irony of Jim Crow laws (discussed in Chapter 21) coexisting with the most intimate contact between blacks and whites. The mass of black southerners worked on white-owned plantations and in white households. One black preacher neatly summarized the nation's regional differences this way: "In the South, they don't care how close you get as long as you don't get too big; in the North, they don't care how big you get as long as you don't get too close." The South's racial code forced African Americans to accept, at least outwardly, social conventions that reinforced their low standing with whites. A black person did not shake hands with a white person, or enter a white home through the front door, or address a white person except formally.

In these circumstances, survival and self-respect depended to a great degree upon patience and stoicism. Black people learned to endure humiliation by keeping their thoughts and feelings hidden from white people. Paul Laurence Dunbar, an African American poet, captured this bitter truth in his turn-of-the-century poem "We Wear the Mask."

We wear the mask that grins and lies,
It hides our cheeks and shades our eyes,
This debt we pay to human guile;
With torn and bleeding hearts we smile,
And mouth with myriad subtleties.

Why should the world be over-wise,
In counting all our tears and sighs?
Nay, let them only see us, while
We wear the mask.

Brown v. Board of Education

Since the late 1930s, the NAACP had chipped away at the legal foundations of segregation. Rather than making a frontal assault on the *Plessy* separate-but-equal rule, civil rights attorneys launched a series of suits seeking complete equality in segregated facilities. The aim of this strategy was to make segregation so prohibitively expensive that the South would be forced to dismantle it. In the 1939 case *Missouri v. ex.rel. Gaines,* the Supreme Court ruled that the University of Missouri law school must either admit African Americans or build another, fully equal law school for them. NAACP lawyers pushed their arguments further, asserting that equality could not be measured simply by money or physical plant. In *McLaurin v. Oklahoma State Regents* (1950), the Court agreed. Thurgood Marshall successfully argued that regulations forcing a black law student to sit, eat, and study in areas apart from white students inevitably created a "badge of inferiority."

By 1951, Marshall had begun coordinating the NAACP's legal resources for a direct attack on the separate-but-equal doctrine. The goal was to overturn *Plessy* and the constitutionality of segregation itself. For a test case, Marshall combined five lawsuits challenging segregation in public schools. One of these suits argued the case of Oliver Brown of Topeka, Kansas, who sought to overturn a state law permitting cities to maintain segregated schools. The law forced Brown's eight-year-old daughter Linda to travel by bus to a black school even though she lived only three blocks from an all-white elementary school. The Supreme Court heard initial arguments on the cases, grouped together as *Brown v. Board of Education,* in December 1952.

In his argument before the Court, Thurgood Marshall tried to establish that separate facilities, by definition, denied black people their full rights as American citizens. He used evidence from psychologists and sociologists demonstrating that black children educated in segregated schools developed a negative self-image and low self-esteem. When Chief Justice Fred Vinson died suddenly in 1953, President Dwight Eisenhower appointed California Governor Earl Warren to fill the post. After hearing further arguments, the Court remained divided on the issue of overturning *Plessy.* Warren, eager for a unanimous decision, patiently worked at convincing two holdouts. Using his political skills to persuade and achieve compromise, Warren urged his colleagues to affirm a simple principle as the basis for the decision.

On May 17, 1954, Warren read the Court's unanimous decision aloud. "Does segregation of

Attorneys for the NAACP in front of the Supreme Court in Washington, after winning their landmark legal victory in the 1954 *Brown v. Board of Education* school desegregation case. From l. to r.: George E. C. Hayes, Thurgood Marshall, and James Nabrit, Jr. In 1967, after a long career fighting segregation and serving as a judge in the federal judiciary, Marshall became the first African American to sit on the Supreme Court when President Lyndon B. Johnson appointed him an Associate Justice.

children in public schools solely on the basis of race . . . deprive the children of the minority group of equal educational opportunities?" The chief justice paused. "We believe that it does." Warren made a point of citing several of the psychological studies of segregation's effects. He ended by directly addressing the constitutional issue. Segregation deprived the plaintiffs of the equal protection of the laws guaranteed by the Fourteenth Amendment. "We conclude that in the field of public education the doctrine of 'separate but equal' has no place. Separate educational facilities are inherently unequal. . . . Any language in *Plessy v. Ferguson* contrary to these findings is rejected."

African Americans and their liberal allies around the country hailed the decision and the legal genius of Thurgood Marshall. Marshall himself predicted that all segregated schools would be abolished within five years. Black newspapers were full of stories on the imminent dismantling of segregation. The *Chicago Defender* called the decision "a second emancipation proclamation." But the issue of enforcement soon dampened this enthusiasm. To gain a unanimous decision, Warren had to agree to let the Court delay for one year its ruling on how to implement desegregation. This second *Brown* ruling, handed down in May 1955, assigned responsibility for desegregation plans to local school boards. The Court left it to federal district judges to monitor compliance, requiring only that desegregation proceed "with all deliberate speed." Thus, although the Court had made a momentous and clear constitutional ruling, the need for compromise dictated gradual enforcement by unspecified means.

Crisis in Little Rock

Resistance to *Brown* took many forms. Most states passed laws transferring authority for pupil assignment to local school boards. This prevented the NAACP from bringing statewide suits against segregated school systems. Counties and towns created layers of administrative delays designed to stop implementation of *Brown*. Some school boards transferred public school property to new, all-white private "academies." State legislatures in Virginia, Alabama, Mississippi, and Georgia resurrected the nineteenth-century doctrines of "interposition" and "nullification" in an effort to resist federal authority. They passed resolutions declaring their right to "interpose" themselves between the people and the federal government. In 1956, 101 congressmen from the former Confederate states signed the Southern Manifesto, urging their states to refuse compliance with desegregation. President Eisenhower declined to publicly endorse *Brown,* contributing to the spirit of southern resistance. "I don't believe you can change the hearts of men with laws or decisions," he said. Privately, the president opposed the *Brown* decision, and he later called his appointment of Earl Warren as chief justice "the biggest damn fool mistake I ever made."

In Little Rock, Arkansas, the tense controversy over school integration became a test case of state versus federal power. A federal court ordered public schools to begin desegregation in September 1957, and the local school board made plans to comply. But Governor Orval Faubus, facing a tough reelection fight, decided to make a campaign issue out of defying the court order. He dispatched Arkansas National Guard troops to Central High School to prevent nine black students from entering. For three weeks, armed troops stood guard at the school. Screaming crowds, encouraged by Faubus, menaced the black students, beat up two black reporters, and chanted "two, four, six, eight, we ain't going to integrate."

At first, President Eisenhower tried to intervene quietly, gaining Faubus's assurance that he would protect the nine black children. But when Faubus suddenly withdrew his troops, leaving the black students at the mercy of the white mob, Eisenhower had to move. On September 24 he placed the Arkansas National Guard under federal control and ordered a thousand paratroopers to Little Rock. The nine black students arrived in a U.S. Army car. With fixed bayonets, the soldiers protected the students as they finally integrated Little Rock High School. Eisenhower, the veteran military commander, justified his actions on the basis of upholding federal authority and enforcing the law. He made no endorsement of desegregation. But as the first president since Reconstruction to use armed federal troops in support of black rights, Eisenhower demonstrated that the federal government could, indeed, protect civil rights. Unfazed, Governor Faubus kept Little Rock high schools closed during the 1958–59 academic year to prevent what he called "violence and disorder."

No Easy Road
to Freedom, 1958–62

The legal breakthrough represented by the *Brown* decision heartened opponents of segregation everywhere. Most important, *Brown* demonstrated the potential for using the federal court system as a weapon against discrimination and as a means of protecting the full rights of citizenship. Yet the widespread opposition to *Brown* and its implications showed the limits of pursuing a strictly legal strategy. In Little Rock, the ugly face of white racism received wide coverage in the mass media and quickly sobered the more optimistic champions of integration. However welcome Eisenhower's intervention, his reluctance to endorse desegregation suggested that civil rights activists could still not rely upon federal help. As the Montgomery bus boycott had proved, black communities would have to help themselves first.

Martin Luther King and the SCLC

The 381-day Montgomery bus boycott made Martin Luther King a prominent national figure. In January 1957 *Time* magazine put King on its cover. The *New York Times Magazine* published a detailed history of the bus boycott, focusing on King's role. NBC's "Meet the Press" invited him to become only the second African American ever to appear on that program. Speaking invitations poured in from universities and organizations around the country. King himself was an extraordinary and complex man. Born in 1929 in Atlanta, he enjoyed a middle-class upbringing as the son of a prominent Baptist minister. After graduating from prestigious Morehouse College, an all-black school, King earned a divinity degree at Crozer Theological Seminary in Pennsylvania and a Ph.D. in theology from Boston University.

In graduate school King explored a very diverse range of philosophers and political thinkers—the ancient Greeks, French Enlightenment thinkers, the German idealists, and Karl Marx. He was drawn to the social Christianity of American theologian Walter Rauschenbusch, who insisted on connecting religious faith with struggles for social justice. Above all King admired Mohandas Gandhi, a lawyer turned ascetic who had led a successful nonviolent resistance movement against British colonial rule in India. Gandhi taught his followers to confront authorities with a readiness to suffer, in order to expose injustice and force those in power to end it. This tactic of nonviolent civil disobedience required discipline and sacrifice from its followers, who were sometimes called upon to lay their lives on the line against armed police and military forces.

Like Gandhi and many of the Christian saints he had studied, King grappled with inner doubts about his faith and true mission. Since childhood he had suffered from extreme mood swings. He was charming and popular, but also self-restrained and dignified. Even after becoming pastor of Montgomery's Dexter Baptist Church in 1954, King often agonized over his inner emotions, including his religious faith. The rigorous discipline required by the philosophy of nonviolence helped King to master his inner turmoil. A unique blend of traditional African American folk preacher and erudite intellectual, King used his passion and intelligence to help transform a community's pain into a powerful moral force for change.

In a December 1956 address celebrating the bus boycott victory, King laid out six key lessons from the year-long struggle. "(1) We have discovered that we can stick together for a common cause; (2) our leaders do not have to sell out; (3) threats and violence do not necessarily intimidate those who are sufficiently aroused and non-violent; (4) our church is becoming militant, stressing a social gospel as well as a gospel of personal salvation; (5) we have gained a new sense of dignity and destiny; (6) we have discovered a new and powerful weapon—non-violent resistance." The influence of two visiting northern pacifists, Bayard Rustin of the War Resisters' League and Glenn Smiley of the Fellowship of Reconciliation, had helped deepen King's own commitment to the Gandhian philosophy.

King recognized the need to exploit the momentum of the Montgomery movement. In early 1957, with the help of Rustin and other aides, he brought together nearly 100 black ministers to found the Southern Christian Leadership Conference (SCLC). The clergymen elected King president and his close friend, the Reverend Ralph Abernathy, treasurer. The SCLC called upon black people "to understand that nonviolence is not a symbol of weakness or cowardice, but as Jesus demonstrated, nonviolent resistance transforms weakness into strength and breeds courage in the face of danger."

Previously, the struggle for racial equality had been dominated by a northern elite focusing on legal action. The SCLC now envisioned the southern black church, preaching massive nonviolent protest, as leading the fight. The SCLC gained support among black ministers, and King vigorously spread his message in speeches and writings. But the organization failed to spark the kind of mass, direct-action movement that had made history in Montgomery. Instead, the next great spark to light the fire of protest came from what seemed at the time a most unlikely source: black college students.

Sit-Ins: Greensboro, Nashville, Atlanta

On Monday, February 1, 1960, four black freshmen from North Carolina Agricultural and Technical College in Greensboro sat down at the whites-only lunch counter in Woolworth's. They politely ordered coffee and doughnuts. As the students had anticipated while planning the action in their dorm rooms, they were refused service. Although they could buy pencils or toothpaste, black people were not allowed to eat in Woolworth's. But the four students stayed at the counter until closing time. Word of their actions spread quickly, and the next day they returned with over two dozen supporters. On the third day, students occupied sixty-three of the sixty-six lunch counter seats. By Thursday they had been joined by three white students from the Women's College of the University of North Carolina in Greensboro. Scores of sympathizers overflowed Woolworth's and started a sit-in down the street in S. H. Kress. On Friday hundreds of black students and a few whites jammed the lunch counters.

The week's events made Greensboro national news. City officials, looking to end the protest, offered to negotiate in exchange for an end to demonstrations. But white business leaders and politicians proved unwilling to change the racial status quo, and the sit-ins resumed on April 1. In response to the April 21 arrest of forty-five students for trespassing, an outraged African American com-

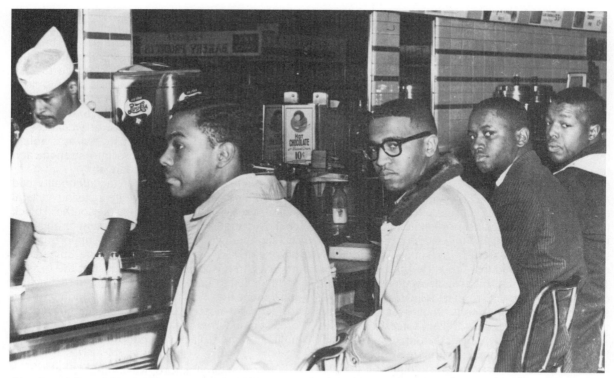

The second day of the "sit-in" at the Greensboro, North Carolina Woolworth's lunch counter, February 2, 1960. From l. to r.: Joseph McNeil, Franklin McCain, Billy Smith, and Clarence Henderson. The Greensboro protest sparked a wave of sit-ins across the South, mostly by college students, demanding an end to segregation in restaurants and other public places.

munity organized an economic boycott of targeted stores. The boycott cut deeply into merchants' profits, and Greensboro's leaders reluctantly acceded. On July 25, 1960, the first African American ate a meal at Woolworth's.

The Greensboro sit-in sent a shock wave throughout the South. During the next eighteen months 70,000 people — most of them black students, a few of them white allies — participated in sit-ins against segregation in dozens of communities. Over 3,000 were arrested. African Americans had discovered a new form of direct-action protest, dignified and powerful, which white people could not ignore. The sit-in movement also transformed participants' self-image, empowering them psychologically and emotionally. Franklin McCain, one of the original four Greensboro students, later recalled a great feeling of soul cleansing: "I probably felt better on that day than I've ever felt in my life. Seems like a lot of feelings of guilt or what-have-you suddenly left me, and I felt as though I had gained my manhood, so to speak, and not only gained it, but had developed quite a lot of respect for it."

In Nashville, Rev. James Lawson, a northern-born black minister, had led workshops in nonviolent resistance since 1958. Lawson had served a jail term as a conscientious objector during the Korean War and become active in the Fellowship of Reconciliation. He had also spent three years as a missionary in India, where he learned close up the Gandhian methods of promoting social change. Lawson gathered around him a group of deeply committed black students from Fisk, Vanderbilt, and other Nashville colleges. Young activists there talked not only of ending segregation but also of creating a "Beloved Community" based on Christian idealism and Gandhian principles.

In the spring of 1960 more than 150 Nashville students were arrested in disciplined sit-ins aimed at desegregating downtown lunch counters. Lawson, who preached the need for sacrifice in the cause of justice, found himself expelled from the divinity school at Vanderbilt. Lawson and other veterans of the Nashville sit-ins, such as John Lewis, Diane Nash, and Marion Barry, would go on to play influential roles in the national civil rights movement. The Nashville group developed rules of conduct that became a model for protesters elsewhere: "Don't strike back or curse if abused. . . . Show yourself courteous and friendly at all times. . . . Report all serious incidents to your leader in a polite manner. Remember love and nonviolence."

The most ambitious sit-in campaign developed in Atlanta, the South's largest and richest city, home to the region's most powerful and prestigious black community. Students from Morehouse, Spelman, and the other all-black schools that made up Atlanta University took the lead. On March 15, 1960, 200 young black people staged a well-coordinated sit-in at restaurants in City Hall, the State Capitol, and other government offices. Police arrested and jailed seventy-six demonstrators that day, but the experience only strengthened the activists' resolve. Led by Julian Bond, the students formed the Committee on an Appeal for Human Rights. In full-page advertisements in Atlanta newspapers the students demanded an end to segregation, as well as jobs, equal housing and education, and better health services for the city's black people. "[We will] use every legal and non-violent means at our disposal to secure full citizenship rights as members of this great democracy of ours," the students promised. Over the summer they planned a fall campaign of large-scale sit-ins at major Atlanta department stores and a boycott of downtown merchants. Their slogan became "Close out your charge account with segregation, open up your account with freedom." In October 1960 Martin Luther King and thirty-six students were arrested when they sat down in the all-white Magnolia Room restaurant in Rich's Department Store. As in Greensboro and Montgomery, the larger African American community in Atlanta supported the continuing sit-ins, picketing, and boycotts. The campaign stretched on for months, and hundreds of protesters went to jail. The city's business leaders finally relented in September 1961, and desegregation came to Atlanta.

SNCC and the "Beloved Community"

The sit-in movement pumped new energy into the civil rights cause, creating a new generation of activists and leaders. Mass arrests, beatings, and vilification in the southern white press only strengthened the resolve of those in the movement. Students also had to deal with the fears of their families, many of whom had made great sacrifices to send them off to college. John Lewis, a seminary student in Nashville, remembered his mother in rural Alabama pleading with him to "get out of that mess, before you get hurt." Lewis wrote to his parents that he

acted out of his Christian conscience: "My soul will not be satisfied until freedom, justice, and fair play become a reality for all people."

The new student militancy also caused discord within black communities. The authority of local African American elites had traditionally depended upon influence and cooperation with the white establishment. Black lawyers, schoolteachers, principals, and businessmen had to maintain regular and cordial relations with white judges, school boards, and politicians. Student calls for freedom disturbed many community leaders worried about upsetting traditional patronage networks. Some black college presidents, pressured by trustees and state legislators, sought to moderate or stop the movement altogether. The president of Southern University in Baton Rouge, the largest black college in the nation, suspended eighteen sit-in leaders in 1960 and forced the entire student body of 5,000 to reapply to the college so that agitators could be screened out.

An April 1960 conference of 120 black student activists in Raleigh, North Carolina, underlined the generational and radical aspects of the new movement. The meeting had been called by Ella Baker, executive director of the SCLC, to help the students assess their experiences and plan future actions. Fifty-five at the time, Baker had for years played an important behind-the-scenes role in the civil rights cause, serving as a community organizer and field secretary for the NAACP before heading the staff of the SCLC. She understood the psychological importance of the students' remaining independent of adult control. She counseled them to resist affiliating with any of the national civil rights organizations. Baker also encouraged the trend toward group-centered leadership among the students. She later commented that social movements needed "the development of people who are interested not in being leaders as much as in developing leadership among other people."

With Baker's encouragement, the conference voted to establish a new group, the Student Nonviolent Coordinating Committee (SNCC). The strong influence of the Nashville students, led by James Lawson, could be found in the SNCC statement of purpose:

> We affirm the philosophical or religious ideal of nonviolence as the foundation of our purpose, the presupposition of our faith, and the manner of our action. Nonviolence as it grows from Judaic-Christian tradition seeks a social order of justice permeated by love. Integration of human endeavor represents the crucial first step towards such a society.

By appealing to conscience and standing on the moral nature of human existence, nonviolence nurtures the atmosphere in which reconciliation and justice become actual possibilities.

In the fall of 1960 SNCC established an organizational structure, a set of principles, and a new style of civil rights protest. The emphasis was on fighting segregation through direct confrontation, mass action, and civil disobedience. SNCC field workers initiated and supported local, community-based activity. Three-quarters of the first field workers were less than twenty-two years old. Leadership was vested in a nonhierarchical Coordinating Committee, but local groups were free to determine their own direction. SNCC people distrusted bureaucracy and structure; they stressed spontaneity and improvisation. Bob Moses, a former Harvard graduate student and New York City schoolteacher, best expressed the freewheeling SNCC attitude: "Go where the spirit say go and do what the spirit say do." Over the next few years SNCC was at the forefront of nearly every major civil rights battle.

The Election of 1960 and Civil Rights

The issue of race relations was kept from center stage during the very close presidential campaign of 1960. As vice-president, Richard Nixon had been a leading Republican voice for stronger civil rights legislation. In contrast, Democratic nominee Senator John F. Kennedy had played virtually no role in the congressional battles over civil rights during the 1950s. But during the campaign, their roles reversed. Kennedy praised the sit-in movement as part of a revival of national reform spirit. He declared, "It is in the American tradition to stand up for one's rights—even if the new way is to sit down." While the Republican platform contained a strong civil rights plank, Nixon minimized his own identification with the movement. In October, when Martin Luther King was jailed after leading a demonstration in Atlanta, Kennedy telephoned Coretta Scott King to reassure her and express his personal support. Kennedy's brother Robert telephoned the judge in the case and angrily warned him that he had violated King's civil rights, as well as endangering the national Democratic ticket. The judge released King soon afterward.

News of this intervention did not gain wide attention in the white South, much to the relief of the Kennedys. The race was tight, and they knew they could not afford to alienate traditional white southern Democrats. But the campaign effectively played up the story among black voters all over the country.

On election day, Kennedy squeaked by Nixon with a plurality of only 100,000 votes out of 69 million cast. He won 70 percent of the black vote, which helped put him over the top in such critical states as Illinois, Texas, Michigan, and Pennsylvania. Many civil rights activists optimistically looked forward to a new president who would have to acknowledge his political debt to the black vote.

But the very closeness of his victory constrained Kennedy on the race question. Democrats had also lost ground in the House and Senate, and Kennedy had to worry about alienating conservative southern Democrats who chaired key congressional committees. Passage of major civil rights legislation would be virtually impossible. The new president told leaders such as Roy Wilkins of the NAACP that a strategy of "minimum legislation, maximum executive action" offered the best road to change. The president did appoint some forty African Americans to high federal positions, including Thurgood Marshall to the federal appellate court. He established a Committee on Equal Employment Opportunity, chaired by Vice-President Lyndon B. Johnson, to fight discrimination in the federal civil service and in corporations that received government contracts.

Most significant, the Kennedy administration sought to invigorate the Civil Rights Division of the Justice Department. That division had been created by the Civil Rights Act of 1957, which authorized the attorney general to seek court injunctions to protect people denied their right to vote. But the Eisenhower administration had made little use of this new power. Robert Kennedy, the new attorney general, began assembling a staff of brilliant and committed attorneys, headed by Burke Marshall. He encouraged them to get out of Washington and get into the field wherever racial troubles arose. In early 1961, when Louisiana school officials balked at a school desegregation order, Robert Kennedy warned them that he would ask the federal court to hold them in contempt. When Burke Marshall started court proceedings, the state officials gave in. But the new, more aggressive mood at Justice could not solve the central political dilemma: how to move forward on civil rights without alienating southern Democrats. Pressure from the newly energized southern civil rights movement soon revealed the true difficulty of that problem.

Freedom Rides

In the spring of 1961 James Farmer, national director of CORE, announced plans for an interracial Freedom Ride through the South. The goal was to test

A Freedom Riders' bus burns after being hit by a firebomb in Anniston, Alabama, May 14, 1961. Black and white riders aboard a second bus that day were beaten by a racist mob in Birmingham. Violent scenes like this one received extensive publicity in the mass media and helped compel the Justice Department to enforce court rulings banning segregation on interstate bus lines.

compliance with court orders banning segregation in interstate travel and terminal accommodations. CORE had just recently made Farmer its leader in an effort to revitalize the organization. One of the founders of CORE in 1942, Farmer had worked for various pacifist and socialist groups and served as program director for the NAACP. He designed the Freedom Ride to induce a crisis, in the spirit of the sit-ins. "Our intention," Farmer declared, "was to provoke the southern authorities into arresting us and thereby prod the Justice Department into enforcing the law of the land." CORE received financial and tactical support from the SCLC and several NAACP branches. It also informed the Justice Department and the FBI of its plans, but received no reply.

On May 4 seven blacks and six whites split into two interracial groups and left Washington on buses bound for Alabama and Mississippi. As the two buses made their way south, incidents of harassment and violence were isolated. But when one bus entered Anniston, Alabama, on May 14 an angry mob surrounded it, smashing windows and

slashing tires. Six miles out of town, the tires went flat. A firebomb tossed through a window forced the passengers outside. The mob then beat the Freedom Riders with blackjacks, iron bars, and clubs, and the bus burst into flames. A caravan of cars organized by the Birmingham office of the SCLC rescued the wounded. Another mob attacked the second bus in Anniston, leaving one Freedom Rider close to death and permanently brain-damaged.

The violence escalated. In Birmingham, a mob of forty whites waited on the loading platform and attacked the bus that managed to get out of Anniston. Although police had been warned to expect trouble, they did nothing to stop the mob from beating the Freedom Riders with pipes and fists. Nor did the police make any arrests. FBI agents observed and took notes but did nothing. The remaining Freedom Riders decided to travel as a single group on the next lap, from Birmingham to Montgomery, but no bus would take them. Stranded and frightened, they reluctantly boarded a special flight to New Orleans arranged by the Justice Department.

On May 17 the CORE-sponsored Freedom Ride disbanded.

But that was not the end of the Freedom Rides. SNCC leaders in Atlanta and Nashville assembled a fresh group of volunteers to continue the trip. On May 20 twenty-one Freedom Riders left Birmingham for Montgomery. The bus station in the Alabama capital was eerily quiet and deserted as they pulled in. But when the passengers left the bus a mob of several hundred whites rushed them, yelling "Get those niggers!" and clubbing people to the ground. James Zwerg, a white Freedom Rider from the University of Wisconsin, had his spinal cord severed. John Lewis, veteran of the Nashville sit-in movement, suffered a brain concussion. As he lay in a pool of blood, a policeman handed him a state court injunction forbidding interracial travel in Alabama. The mob indiscriminately beat journalists and clubbed John Siegenthaler, a Justice Department attorney sent to observe the scene. It took police over an hour to halt the rioting. Montgomery's police commissioner later said, "We have no intention of standing guard for a bunch of troublemakers coming into our city."

The mob violence and the indifference of Alabama officials made the Freedom Ride page-one news around the country and throughout the world. Newspapers in Europe, Africa, and Asia denounced the hypocrisy of the federal government. The Kennedy administration, preparing for the president's first summit meeting with Soviet premier Nikita Khrushchev, saw the situation as a threat to its international prestige. On May 21, an angry mob threatened to invade a support rally at Montgomery's First Baptist Church. A hastily assembled group of 400 U.S. marshals, sent by Robert Kennedy, barely managed to keep the peace. The attorney general called for a cooling-off period, but Martin Luther King, James Farmer, and the SNCC leaders announced that the Freedom Ride would continue. When Robert Kennedy warned that the racial turmoil would embarrass the president in his meeting with Khrushchev, Ralph Abernathy of the SCLC replied, "Doesn't the Attorney General know that we've been embarrassed all our lives?"

A bandaged but spirited group of twenty-seven Freedom Riders prepared to leave Montgomery for Jackson, Mississippi, on May 24. To avoid further violence Robert Kennedy arranged a compromise through Mississippi senator James Eastland. In exchange for a guarantee of safe passage through Mississippi, the federal government promised not to interfere with the arrest of the Freedom Riders in Jackson. This Freedom Ride and several that fol-lowed thus escaped violence. But more than 300 people were arrested that summer in Jackson on charges of traveling "for the avowed purpose of inflaming public opinion." Sticking to a policy of "jail, no bail," Freedom Riders clogged the prisons and faced harsh treatment that went largely unreported in the press. Their jail experiences turned most of them into committed leaders who formed the core of the student movement.

The Justice Department eventually petitioned the Interstate Commerce Commission to issue clear rules prohibiting segregation on interstate carriers. At the end of 1962 CORE proclaimed victory in the battle against Jim Crow interstate travel. By creating a crisis, the Freedom Rides had forced the Kennedy administration to act. But they also revealed the unwillingness of the federal government to fully enforce the law of the land. The Freedom Rides exposed the ugly face of southern racism to the world. At the same time, they reinforced white resistance to desegregation. The jailings and brutality experienced by Freedom Riders made it clearer than ever to the civil rights community that moral suasion on its own went only so far.

The Albany Movement: The Limits of Protest

Where the federal government chose not to enforce the constitutional rights of black people, segregationist forces tenaciously held their ground. This was especially true in the more remote areas of the Deep South. In Albany, a small city in southwest Georgia, activists from SNCC, the NAACP, and other local groups formed a coalition known as the Albany Movement. Starting in October 1961 and continuing for over a year, thousands of Albany's black citizens marched, sat in, and boycotted as part of a citywide campaign to integrate public facilities and win voting rights. Over a thousand people spent time in jail. In December, the arrival of Martin Luther King and the SCLC transformed Albany into a national symbol of the struggle.

But the gains at Albany proved minimal. Infighting among the various civil rights organizations hurt the cause. Local SNCC workers opposed the more cautious approach of NAACP officials, even though the more established organization paid many of the campaign's expenses. The arrival of King guaranteed national news coverage, but local activists worried that his presence might undermine the community focus and their own influence. Most important, Albany police chief Laurie Pritchett shrewdly deprived the movement of the kind of national sympathy won by the Freedom Riders.

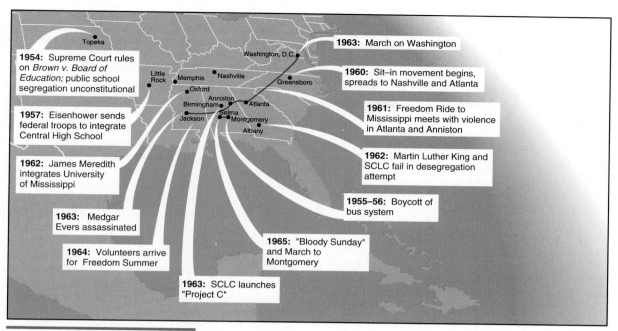

Map of the Civil Rights Movement
Key battlegrounds in the struggle for racial justice in communities across the South.

Pritchett filled the jails with black demonstrators, kept their mistreatment to a minimum, and prevented white mobs from running wild. "We met 'nonviolence' with 'nonviolence,'" he boasted.

King himself was twice arrested in the summer of 1962, but Albany officials quickly freed him to avoid negative publicity. The Kennedy administration kept clear of the developments in Albany, hoping to help the gubernatorial campaign of "moderate" Democrat Carl Sanders. By late 1962 the Albany Movement had collapsed, and Pritchett proudly declared the city "as segregated as ever." One activist summed up the losing campaign: "We were naive enough to think we could fill up the jails. Pritchett was hep to the fact that we couldn't. We ran out of people before he ran out of jails." Albany showed that mass protest without violent white protest and direct federal intervention could not end Jim Crow.

Events at the University of Mississippi drove home this realization among civil rights leaders. In the fall of 1962 James Meredith, an Air Force veteran, tried to register as the first black student at the university. Governor Ross Barnett defied a federal court order and personally blocked Meredith's path at the admissions office. When Barnett refused to assure Robert Kennedy that Meredith would be protected, the attorney general dispatched 500 federal marshals to the campus. Over the radio, Barnett encouraged resistance to the "oppressive power of the United States," and an angry mob of several thousand whites, many of them armed, laid siege to the campus on September 30. A night of violence left 2 people dead and 160 marshals wounded, 28 from gunfire. President Kennedy ordered 5,000 army troops onto the campus to stop the riot. A federal guard remained to protect Meredith, who graduated the following summer. In contrast with Albany, the successful battle to integrate the University of Mississippi again demonstrated the unique power of the federal government in guaranteeing civil rights to African Americans.

THE MOVEMENT AT HIGH TIDE,
1963–65

The tumultuous events of 1960–62 convinced civil rights strategists that segregation could not be dismantled merely through orderly protest and moral persuasion. Only comprehensive civil rights legislation, backed by the power of the federal government, could guarantee full citizenship rights for African Americans. To build the national consensus needed for new laws, civil rights activists looked for ways to gain broader support for their cause. By 1963, their sense of urgency had led them to plan dramatic confrontations that would expose the violence and terror routinely faced by southern blacks. With the whole country — indeed, the whole world — watching, the movement reached the peak of its political and moral power.

Birmingham

At the end of 1962, Martin Luther King and his SCLC allies decided to launch a new campaign against segregation in Birmingham, Alabama. After the failure in Albany, King and his aides looked for a way to shore up his leadership and inject new momentum into the freedom struggle. They needed a major victory. Birmingham was the most segregated big city in America, and it had a deep history of racial violence. African Americans endured total segregation in schools, restaurants, city parks, and department store dressing rooms. Although black people composed over 40 percent of the city's population, fewer than 10,000 of Birmingham's 80,000 registered voters were black. The city's prosperous steel industry relegated black workers to menial jobs.

Working closely with local civil rights groups led by longtime Birmingham activist Rev. Fred Shuttlesworth, the SCLC carefully planned its campaign. The strategy was to fill the city jails with protesters, boycott downtown department stores, and enrage Public Safety Commissioner Eugene "Bull" Connor. In April, King arrived with a manifesto demanding an end to racist hiring practices and segregated public accommodations and the creation of a biracial committee to oversee desegregation. "Here in Birmingham," King told reporters, "we have reached the point of no return." Connor's police began jailing hundreds of demonstrators, including King himself, who defied a state court injunction against further protests.

Held in solitary confinement for several days, King managed to write a response to a group of Birmingham clergy who had deplored the protests. King's *Letter from Birmingham Jail* was soon widely reprinted and circulated as a pamphlet. It set out the key moral issues at stake, and scoffed at those who claimed the campaign was illegal and ill timed. King wrote:

> We know through painful experience that freedom is never voluntarily given by the oppressor; it must be demanded by the oppressed. Frankly I have never yet engaged in a direct action movement that was "well timed," according to the

timetable of those who have not suffered unduly from the disease of segregation. For years now I have heard the word "Wait!" It rings in the ear of every Negro with a piercing familiarity. This "wait" has almost always meant "never."

After King's release on bail, the campaign intensified. The SCLC kept up the pressure by recruiting thousands of Birmingham's young students for a "children's crusade." In early May, Bull Connor's forces began using high-powered water cannons, billy clubs, and snarling police dogs to break up demonstrations. Millions of Americans reacted with horror to the violent scenes from Birmingham shown on national television. Many younger black people, especially from the city's poor and working-class districts, began to fight back, hurling bottles and bricks at police. On May 10, mediators from the Justice Department negotiated an uneasy truce. The SCLC agreed to an immediate end to the protests. In exchange, businesses would desegregate and begin hiring African Americans over the next three months, and a biracial city committee would oversee desegregation of public facilities.

King claimed "the most magnificent victory for justice we've ever seen in the Deep South." But whites such as Bull Connor and Governor George Wallace denounced the agreement. A few days after the announcement, more than a thousand robed Ku Klux Klansmen burned a cross in a park on the outskirts of Birmingham. When bombs rocked SCLC headquarters and the home of King's brother, a Birmingham minister, enraged blacks took to the streets and pelted police and firefighters with stones and bottles. President Kennedy ordered 3,000 army troops into the city and prepared to nationalize the Alabama Guard. The violence receded, and white city business people and politicians began to carry out the agreed-upon pact. But in September a bomb killed four black girls in a Birmingham Baptist church, reminding the city and the world that racial harmony was still a long way off.

The Birmingham campaign and the other protests it sparked over the next seven months engaged over 100,000 people and led to nearly 15,000 arrests. The civil rights community now drew support from millions of Americans, black and white, who were inspired by the protesters and repelled by the face of southern bigotry. At the same time, Birmingham changed the nature of black protest. The black unemployed and working poor who joined in the struggle brought a different perspective from that of the students, professionals, and members of the religious middle class who had dominated the movement before Birmingham. They cared less

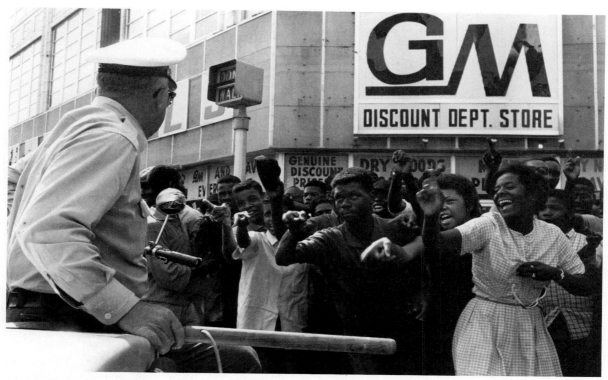

Birmingham, Alabama, elementary and high school students taunting city police during demonstrations against segregation, May 2, 1963. These students were part of the "children's crusade" organized by SCLC as part of its campaign to fill the city's jails with protesters. Over 900 Birmingham school children went to jail that day.

about the philosophy of nonviolence and more about immediate gains in employment and housing and an end to police brutality. The urgent cries for "Freedom now!" were more than simply a demand to end legal segregation.

JFK and the March on Washington

The growth of black activism and white support convinced President Kennedy the moment had come to press for sweeping civil rights legislation. Continuing white resistance in the South also made clearer than ever the need for federal action. In June of 1963, Alabama governor George Wallace threatened to personally block the admission of two black students to the state university. Only the deployment of National Guard troops, placed under federal control by the president, insured the students' safety and their peaceful admission into the University of Alabama.

It was a defining moment for Kennedy. On June 11 the president went on national television and offered his personal endorsement of the civil rights activism. Reviewing the racial situation, Kennedy told his audience that America would not be fully free until all its citizens were free. "We face . . . a moral crisis as a country and a people. It cannot be met by repressive police action. It cannot be left to increased demonstrations in the streets. It cannot be quieted by token moves or talk. It is a time to act in the Congress, in your state and local legislative body, and, above all, in all our daily lives." The next week Kennedy asked Congress for a broad law that would insure voting rights, outlaw segregation in public facilities, and bolster federal authority to deny funds for programs that discriminated. Knowing they would face a stiff fight from congressional conservatives, administration officials began an intense lobbying effort. After three years of fence-sitting, Kennedy finally committed his office and his political future to the civil rights cause.

Movement leaders lauded the president's initiative. Yet they understood that racial hatred still haunted the nation. Only a few hours after Kennedy's television speech, a gunman murdered Medgar Evers, leader of the Mississippi NAACP,

Part of the huge throng that made the historic March on Washington for "jobs and freedom," August 28, 1963. The size of the crowd, the stirring oratory and song, and the live network television coverage produced one of the most memorable political events in the nation's history.

outside his home in Jackson. To pressure Congress and demonstrate the urgency of their cause, a broad coalition of civil rights groups planned a massive, nonviolent March on Washington. The idea had deep roots in black protest. A. Philip Randolph, head of the Brotherhood of Sleeping Car Porters, had originally proposed such a march in 1941 to protest discrimination against blacks in the wartime defense industries. Now Randolph, along with his aide Bayard Rustin, revived the concept and convinced leaders of the major civil rights groups to support it.

The Kennedy administration originally opposed the march, fearing it would jeopardize support for the president's civil rights bill in Congress. But as plans for the rally solidified, Kennedy reluctantly gave his approval. Leaders from the SCLC, the NAACP, SNCC, the Urban League, and CORE — the leading organizations in the civil rights community — put aside their tactical differences to forge a

broad consensus for the event. John Lewis, the young head of SNCC who had endured numerous brutal assaults, planned a speech that denounced the Kennedys as hypocrites. Lewis's speech enraged Walter Reuther, the white liberal leader of the United Auto Workers union, which had helped finance the march. Reuther threatened to turn off the loudspeakers he was paying for, believing Lewis's speech would embarrass the Kennedys. Randolph, the acknowledged elder statesman of the movement, convinced Lewis at the last moment to tone down his remarks. "We've come this far," he implored. "For the sake of unity, change it."

On August 28, 1963, over a quarter of a million people, including 50,000 whites, gathered at the Lincoln Memorial to rally for "jobs and freedom." Union members, students, teachers, clergy, professionals, musicians, actors — Americans from all walks of life joined the largest political assembly in the nation's history. The sight of all those people holding hands and singing "We Shall Overcome," led by the white folk singer Joan Baez, would not be easily forgotten. At the end of a long, exhilarating day of speeches and freedom songs, Martin Luther King provided an emotional climax. Combining the democratic promise of the Declaration of Independence with the religious fervor of his Baptist heritage, King stirred the crowd with his dream for America:

> I have a dream today that one day this nation will rise up and live out the true meaning of its creed: "We hold these truths to be self-evident — that all men are created equal.". . . When we let freedom ring, when we let it ring from every village and every hamlet, from every state and every city, we will be able to speed up that day when all of God's children, black men and white men, Jews and Gentiles, Protestants and Catholics, will be able to join hands and sing in the words of the old Negro spiritual, "Free at last! Free at last! Thank God almighty, we are free at last!"

LBJ and the Civil Rights Act of 1964

An extraordinary demonstration of interracial unity, the March on Washington stood as the high-water mark in the struggle for civil rights. It buoyed the spirits of movement leaders, as well as the liberals pushing the new civil rights bill through Congress. But the assassination of John F. Kennedy on November 22, 1963, in Dallas threw an ominous cloud over the whole nation and the civil rights movement in particular. In the Deep South, many ardent segregationists welcomed the president's death because of his support for civil rights. Most African Americans probably shared the feelings of Coretta Scott King, who recalled her family's vigil: "We felt that President Kennedy had been a friend of the Cause and that with him as President we could continue to move forward. We watched and prayed for him."

Lyndon Baines Johnson, Kennedy's successor, had never been much of a friend to civil rights. As a senator from Texas (1948 to 1960, including six years as majority leader), Johnson had built a career as one of the shrewdest and most powerful Democrats in Congress. Throughout the 1950s he had obstructed civil rights legislation and helped water down enforcement provisions — though as vice-president he had ably chaired Kennedy's working group on equal employment. Johnson reassured a grieving nation that "the ideas and the ideals which [Kennedy] so nobly represented must and will be translated into effective action." Even so, civil rights activists looked upon Johnson warily as he took over the Oval Office.

As president, Johnson realized that he faced a new political reality, one created by the civil rights movement. Eager to unite the Democratic Party and prove himself as a national leader, he seized upon civil rights as a golden political opportunity. "I knew that if I didn't get out in front on this issue," he later recalled, "they [the liberals] would get me. They'd throw up my background against me, they'd use it to prove that I was incapable of bringing unity to the land I loved so much. . . . I had to produce a civil rights bill that was even stronger than the one they'd have gotten if Kennedy had lived." Throughout the early months of 1964, the new president let it be known publicly and privately that he would brook no compromise on civil rights.

Johnson exploited all his skills as a political insider. He cajoled, flattered, and threatened key members of the House and Senate. Working with the president, the fifteen-year-old Leadership Conference on Civil Rights coordinated a sophisticated lobbying effort in Congress. Groups such as the NAACP, the AFL–CIO, the National Council of Churches, and the American Jewish Congress made the case for a strong civil rights bill. The House passed the bill in February by a 290–130 vote. The more difficult fight would be in the Senate, where a southern filibuster promised to block the bill or weaken it. But by June, Johnson's persistence had paid off and the southern filibuster had collapsed.

On July 2, 1964, Johnson signed the Civil Rights Act of 1964. Every major provision had survived intact. This landmark law represented the most significant civil rights legislation since Reconstruction. It prohibited discrimination in most places of public accommodation; outlawed discrimination in employment on the basis of race, color, religion, sex, or national origin; outlawed bias in federally assisted programs; authorized the Justice Department to institute suits to desegregate public schools and other facilities; created the Equal Employment Opportunity Commission; and provided technical and financial aid to communities desegregating their schools.

Mississippi Freedom Summer

While President Johnson and his liberal allies won the congressional battle for the new civil rights bill, activists in Mississippi mounted a far more radical and dangerous campaign. In the spring of 1964 a coalition of workers led by SNCC launched the Freedom Summer project, an ambitious effort to register black voters and directly challenge the iron rule of segregation. Mississippi stood as the toughest test for the civil rights movement, racially and economically. It was the poorest, most backward state in the nation, and had remained largely untouched by the freedom struggle. African Americans constituted 42 percent of the state's population, but fewer than 5 percent could register to vote. Median black family income was under $1,500 a year, roughly one-third that of white families. A small white planter elite controlled most of the state's wealth, and a long tradition of terror against black people had maintained the racial caste system.

Bob Moses of SNCC and Dave Dennis of CORE planned Freedom Summer as a way of opening up this closed society to the glare of national publicity. The project recruited over 900 volunteers, mostly white college students, to aid in voter registration, teach in "freedom schools," and help build a "freedom party" as an alternative to the all-white party of Mississippi Democrats. Organizers expected violence, which was precisely why they wanted white volunteers. Dave Dennis later explained their reasoning: "The death of a white college student would bring on more attention to what was going on than for a black college student getting it. That's cold, but that was also in another sense speaking the language of this country." Mississippi authorities prepared for the civil rights workers as if expecting a foreign army, beefing up state highway patrols and local police forces.

The predictions of violence proved accurate. On June 21, while most project volunteers were still undergoing training in Ohio, word arrived that three activists had disappeared in Neshoba County, Mississippi. Two white activists, Michael Schwerner and Andrew Goodman, and a local black activist, James Chaney, had gone to investigate the burning of a black church that was supposed to serve as a freedom school. Six weeks later, after a massive search belatedly ordered by President Johnson, FBI agents discovered the bodies of the three, buried in an earthen dam. Goodman and Schwerner had been shot once; Chaney had been severely beaten before being shot three times. Over the summer, at least three other civil rights workers died violently. Project workers suffered 1,000 arrests, 80 beatings, 35 shooting incidents, and 30 bombings in homes, churches, and schools.

Within the project, simmering problems tested the ideal of the "beloved community." Many black veterans of SNCC resented the affluent white volunteers, many of whom had not come to terms with their own racial prejudices. White volunteers, staying only a short time in the state, often found it difficult to communicate with African Americans in the local communities, who were wary of breaking old codes of deference. Sexual tensions between black male and white female volunteers also strained relations. A number of black and white women, led by Ruby Doris Robinson, Mary King, and Casey Hayden, began to raise the issue of women's equality as a companion goal to racial equality. The day-to-day reality of violent reprisals, police harassment, and constant fear took a hard toll on everyone.

The project did manage to rivet national attention on Mississippi racism, and it won enormous sympathy from northern liberals. Among their concrete accomplishments, the volunteers could point with pride to over forty freedom schools that brought classes in reading, arithmetic, politics, and African American history to thousands of black children. Some 60,000 black voters signed up to join the Mississippi Freedom Democratic party (MFDP). In August 1964 the MFDP sent a slate of delegates to the Democratic Convention looking to challenge the credentials of the all-white regular state delegation.

In Atlantic City, the idealism of Freedom Summer ran into the more cynical needs of the national Democratic Party. Lyndon Johnson opposed the seating of the MFDP because he wanted to avoid a divisive floor fight. He was already concerned that Republicans might carry a number of southern states in November. But MFDP leaders and sympathizers gave dramatic testimony before the convention, detailing the racism and brutality in Mississippi

After they were barred from the floor of the August 1964 National Democratic convention, Fanny Lou Hamer led members of the Mississippi Freedom Democratic Party in a song-filled protest outside the hotel.

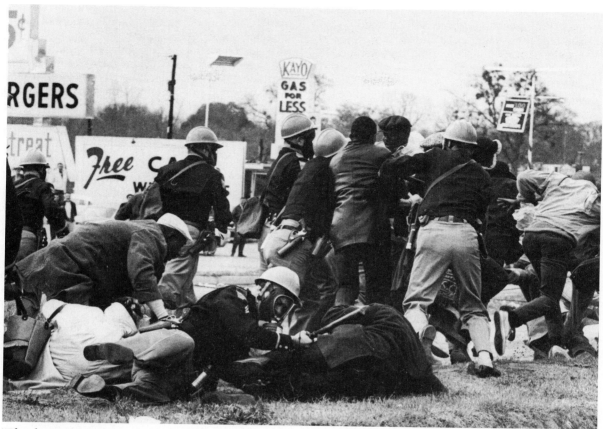

"Bloody Sunday" on the Edmund Pettus Bridge, Selma, Alabama, March 7, 1965. State troopers and local police attacked 600 civil rights marchers who were beginning a 54 mile trek to the state capitol in Montgomery to demonstrate for voting rights. Televised scenes of the police brutality shocked the nation and helped create a political consensus that led to the Voting Rights Act of 1965.

politics. "Is this America," asked Fannie Lou Hamer, "the land of the free and the home of the brave, where we are threatened daily because we want to live as decent human beings?" Led by vice-presidential nominee Senator Hubert Humphrey, Johnson's forces offered a compromise that would have given the MFDP a token two seats on the floor. Bitter over what they saw as a betrayal, the MFDP delegates turned the offer down. Within SNCC, the defeat of the MFDP intensified disillusion with the Democrats and the liberal establishment.

Selma and the Voting Rights Act of 1965

Lyndon Johnson won reelection in 1964 by a landslide, capturing 61 percent of the popular vote. Of the 6 million black people who voted in the election,

2 million more than in 1960, an overwhelming 94 percent went for Johnson. Republican candidate Senator Barry Goldwater managed to carry only his home state of Arizona and five Deep South states, where fewer than 45 percent of eligible black people could vote. With Democrats in firm control of both the Senate and the House, civil rights leaders believed the time was ripe for further legislative gains. Johnson and his staff began drafting a tough voting rights bill in late 1964, partly with an eye toward countering Republican gains in the Deep South with newly registered black and Democratic voters. Martin Luther King and the SCLC shared this goal of passing a strong voting rights law that would provide southern black people with direct federal protection of their right to vote.

Once again, movement leaders plotted to create

a crisis that would arouse national indignation, pressure Congress, and force federal action. King and his aides chose Selma, Alabama, as the target of their campaign. Selma, a city of 27,000 some fifty miles west of Montgomery, had a notorious record of preventing black voting. Of the 15,000 eligible black voters in Dallas County, registered voters numbered only in the hundreds. In 1963, local activists Amelia Boynton and Rev. Fred Reese had invited SNCC workers to aid voter registration efforts in the community. But they had met a violent reception from county sheriff Jim Clark. Sensing that Clark might be another Bull Connor, King arrived in Selma in January 1965, just after accepting the Nobel Peace Prize in Oslo. "We are not asking, we are demanding the ballot," he declared. King, the SCLC staff, and SNCC workers led daily marches on the Dallas County Courthouse, where hundreds of black citizens tried to get their names added to voter lists. By early February, Clark had imprisoned over 3,000 protesters.

Despite the brutal beating of Rev. James Bevel, a key SCLC strategist, and the killing of Jimmie Lee Jackson, a young black demonstrator in nearby Marion, the SCLC failed to gain the national indignation it sought. Consequently, in early March SCLC staffers called on black activists to march from Selma to Montgomery, where they planned to deliver a list of grievances to Governor Wallace. On Sunday, March 7, while King preached to his church in Atlanta, a group of 600 marchers crossed the Pettus Bridge on the Alabama River, on their way to Montgomery. A group of mounted, heavily armed county and state lawmen blocked their path and ordered them to turn back. When the marchers did not move, the lawmen attacked with billy clubs and tear gas, driving the protesters back over the bridge in a bloody rout. Over fifty marchers had to be treated in local hospitals.

The dramatic "Bloody Sunday" attack received extensive coverage on network television, prompting a national uproar. Demands for federal intervention poured into the White House from all over the country. King issued a public call for civil rights supporters to come to Selma for a second march on Montgomery. But a federal court temporarily en-

---

Impact of the Voting Rights Act of 1965
Shows increased voter registration among African Americans in the South between 1960 and 1971.

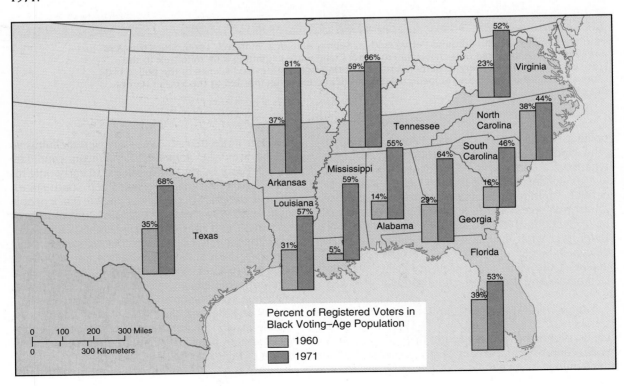

joined the SCLC from proceeding with the march. King found himself trapped. He reluctantly accepted a face-saving compromise: in return for a promise from Alabama authorities not to harm marchers, King would lead his followers across the Pettus Bridge, stop, pray briefly, and then turn back. This plan outraged the more militant SNCC activists and sharpened their distrust of King and the SCLC.

But just when it seemed the Selma movement might die, white racist violence revived it. A gang of white toughs attacked four white Unitarian ministers who had come to Selma to participate in the march. One of them, Rev. James J. Reeb of Boston, died of multiple skull fractures. His death brought new calls for federal action. On March 15, President Johnson delivered a televised address to a joint session of Congress to request passage of a voting rights bill. In a stirring speech, the president fused the political power of his office with the moral power of the movement. "Their cause must be our cause, too. Because it is not just Negroes, but really all of us who must overcome the crippling legacy of bigotry and injustice. And," he concluded firmly, invoking the movement's slogan, "we *shall* overcome." Johnson also prevailed upon federal judge Frank Johnson to issue a ruling allowing the march to proceed, and he warned Governor Wallace not to interfere.

On March 21 Martin Luther King led a group of more than 3,000 black and white marchers out of Selma on the road to Montgomery. Four days later they arrived at the Alabama statehouse. Their ranks had been swelled by more than 30,000 supporters, including hundreds of prominent politicians, entertainers, and black leaders. "I know some of you are asking today," King told the crowd, " 'How long will it take?' " He went on in a rousing, rhythmic cadence:

> I come to say to you this afternoon, however difficult the moment, however frustrating the hour, it will not be long because truth pressed to earth will rise again. How long? Not long, because no lie can live forever. How long? Not long, because you will reap what you sow. How long? Not long, because the arc of the moral universe is long but it bends toward justice. How long? Not long, because mine eyes have seen the glory of the coming of the Lord!

In August 1965 President Johnson signed the Voting Rights Act into law. It authorized federal supervision of registration in states and counties where fewer than half of voting-age residents were registered. It also outlawed literacy and other dis-criminatory tests that had kept blacks disenfran-chised. Between 1964 and 1968, black registrants in Mississippi leaped from 7 percent to 59 percent of the statewide black population; in Alabama, from 24 percent to 57 percent. In those years the number of southern black voters grew from 1 million to 3.1 million. For the first time in their lives, black southerners in hundreds of small towns and rural communities could enjoy full participation in American politics. Ten years after the Montgomery bus boycott, the civil rights movement had reached a peak of national influence and interracial unity.

FORGOTTEN MINORITIES, 1945–65

The civil rights movement revolved around the aspirations and community strength of African Americans. The historic injustices of slavery, racism, and segregation gave a moral and political urgency to the black struggle for full citizenship rights. Yet other minorities as well had long been denied their claim to civil rights. After World War II, Latinos, Indian peoples, and Asian Americans began making their own halting efforts to improve their political, legal, and economic status. They faced strong opposition from institutional racism and various economic interests that benefited from keeping these groups in a subordinate position. By the late 1960s, the success of the black civil rights movement had inspired these minority groups to adopt more militant strategies of their own.

Mexican Americans

Mexican Americans in the West and Southwest included immigrants from Mexico who did not seek American citizenship and long-time citizens who found that white authorities did not recognize their rights. After World War II, several Mexican American political organizations began to stress their own sense of American identity in the belief that this would help guarantee the Mexican American community equal rights and equal opportunity. The most important of these groups were the League of United Latin American Citizens (LULAC), founded in Texas in 1928, and the GI Forum, founded in Texas in 1948 by Mexican American veterans of World War II. Both emphasized the learning of English, assimilation into American society, improved education, and the promotion of political power through voting. LULAC successfully pursued two important legal cases that anticipated *Brown v. Board of Education.* In *Mendez v. Westminster,* a 1947 California case, and in the 1948

Delegates to the 1948 National Convention of the League of United Latin American Citizens met in Kingsville, Texas. After World War II LULAC grew to about 15,000 members active in two hundred local councils, mostly in Texas and California.

Delgado case in Texas, the Supreme Court upheld lower-court rulings that declared segregation of Mexican Americans unconstitutional. Like *Brown,* these two decisions did not immediately end segregation, but they offered pathbreaking legal and psychological victories to Mexican American activists. LULAC won another significant legal battle in the 1954 *Hernandez* decision, in which the Supreme Court ended the exclusion of Mexican Americans from Texas jury lists.

Mexican migration to the United States increased dramatically during and after World War II. During the war, the U.S. and Mexican governments created the *bracero* program, through which some 300,000 Mexicans entered the U.S. as temporary agricultural and railroad laborers. The program continued after the war as American agribusiness came to depend upon hundreds of thousands of Mexicans as a key source of cheap farm labor. Most braceros endured harsh work, poor food, and substandard housing in the camps in which they lived. Some migrated into the newly emerging *barrio* neighborhoods in cities such as San Antonio, Los Angeles, El Paso, and Denver. Many braceros and their children became American citizens, but most returned to Mexico. Another stream of postwar Mexican immigrants were the *mojados,* or "wetbacks," so called because many swam across the Rio Grande River to enter the U.S. illegally.

In 1954 the Eisenhower administration launched the massive "Operation Wetback," in which Immigration Service agents tried to curb the flow of undocumented immigrants from Mexico. Over the next three years some 3.7 million allegedly illegal migrants were rounded up and sent back over the border. Immigration agents made little distinction between so-called illegals on the one hand and braceros and Mexican American citizens on the other. Many families were broken up, and thousands who had lived in the U.S. for a decade or more found themselves deported. Many deportees were denied basic civil liberties, such as due process, and suffered physical abuse and intimidation. Most Mexican Americans had ambivalent feelings about *mojados* and Operation Wetback. The deportations tended to improve job opportunities and wages for those who remained. Yet the so-called illegals were considered members of *la raza,* the larger Mexican American community, and family ties between these groups were common. LULAC and the Asociación Nacional Mexico-Americana, founded in 1950, tried in vain to curb abuses against aliens and Mexican Americans. Among Mexican Americans, Operation Wetback left a bitter legacy of deep mistrust and estrangement from Anglo culture and politics.

Puerto Ricans

The U.S. took possession of the island of Puerto Rico in 1898, during the final stages of the Spanish-American War. The Jones Act of 1917 made the island an unincorporated territory of the United States and granted U.S. citizenship to all Puerto Ricans. Over the next several decades, Puerto Rico's economic base shifted from a diversified, subsistence-oriented agriculture to one dominated by sugar grown for export. U.S. absentee owners dominated the sugar industry, absorbing most of the island's arable land, previously tilled by small farmers growing crops for local consumption. Puerto Rico's sugar industry grew enormously profitable, but few island residents benefited from this expansion. By the 1930s, unemployment and poverty were widespread and the island was forced to import its foodstuffs.

Small communities of Puerto Rican migrants had begun to form in New York City during the 1920s. The largest was on the upper east side of Manhattan—*el barrio* in East Harlem. During World War II, labor shortages led the federal government to sponsor the recruitment of Puerto Rican workers for industrial jobs in New Jersey, Philadelphia, and Chicago. But the "great migration" took place from 1945 to 1964. During these two decades the number of Puerto Ricans living on the mainland jumped from less than 100,000 to roughly 1 million. Economic opportunity was the chief impetus for this migration, for the island suffered from high unemployment rates and low wages.

The advent of direct air service between Puerto Rico and New York in 1945 made the city easily accessible. The Puerto Rican community in East (or Spanish) Harlem mushroomed, and new communities in the South Bronx and Brooklyn began to emerge. By 1970 there were about 800,000 Puerto Ricans in New York—more than 10 percent of the city's population. New Puerto Rican communities also took root in Connecticut, Massachusetts, New Jersey, and the Midwest. Puerto Ricans frequently circulated between the island and the mainland, often returning home when economic conditions on the mainland were less favorable.

The experience of Puerto Rican migrants both resembled and differed from that of other immigrant groups in significant ways. Puerto Ricans were foreign in language, culture, and experience, yet they entered the United States as citizens. Many Puerto Ricans were also African Americans. Racial and ethnic discrimination came as a double shock, since Puerto Ricans, as citizens, entered the U.S. with a sense of entitlement. In New York, Puerto Ricans found themselves barred from most craft unions, excluded from certain neighborhoods, and forced to take jobs largely in the low-paying garment industry and service trades. Puerto Rican children were not well served by a public school system insensitive to language differences and too willing to track Spanish-speaking students into obsolete vocational programs.

By the early 1970s, Puerto Rican families were substantially poorer on average than the total population of the country, and they had the lowest median income of any Latino groups. The steep decline in manufacturing jobs and the garment industry in New York during the 1960s and 1970s hit the Puerto Rican community especially hard. So did the city's fiscal crisis, which brought sharp cuts in funding for schools, health care, libraries, government jobs, and other public services traditionally available to immigrant groups. The structural shift in the U.S. economy away from manufacturing and toward service and high-technology jobs reinforced the Puerto Rican community's goal of improving educational opportunities for its members. The struggle to establish and improve bilingual education in schools became an important part of this effort. Most Puerto Ricans, especially those who had succeeded in school and achieved middle-class status, continued to identify strongly with their Puerto Rican heritage and the Spanish language.

Indian Peoples

The postwar years also brought significant changes in the status and lives of Indian peoples. Congress reversed the policies pursued under the New Deal, which had stressed Indian sovereignty and cultural independence. Responding to a variety of pressure groups, including mining and other economic interests wishing to exploit the resources on Indian reservations, Congress adopted a policy known as "termination" designed to cancel Indian treaties and terminate sovereignty rights. In 1953 it passed House Concurrent Resolution No. 108, which allowed Congress to terminate a tribe as a political entity by passing legislation specific to that tribe. The leader of the termination forces, Senator Arthur Watkins of Utah, declared the new law meant that "the concept that the Indian people exist within the United States as independent nations has been rejected." Between 1954 and 1962, Congress passed twelve termination bills covering more than sixty tribes, nearly all in the West.

Even when tribes consented to their own termi-

George Gillette (left foreground), chairman of the Fort Berthold Indian Council, wept as Secretary of Interior J. A. Krug signed a contract buying 155,000 acres of the tribe's best land in North Dakota for a reservoir project, May 20, 1948. "The members of the tribal council sign this contract with heavy hearts," Gillette said.

principal of "unique and limited" sovereignty. The Court recognized tribal independence except where limited by treaty or Congress.

Since the 1920s the Indian population had begun growing again, but most reservations had trouble making room for a new generation. They suffered increased rates of poverty, chronic unemployment, alcoholism, and poor health. The average Indian family in the early 1960s earned only one-third of the average family income in the United States. Many Indians left the reservations voluntarily, and the Bureau of Indian Affairs encouraged relocation with a program to place reservation Indians in urban jobs. For some, relocation meant assimilation, intermarriage with whites, and the loss of tribal identity. Others, as many as one-third, returned to the reservations, and still others traveled back and forth.

Those who remained in the cities usually became "ethnic Indians," identifying themselves more as Indians than as members of specific tribes. By the late 1960s ethnic Indians had begun emphasizing civil rights over tribal rights, making common cause with black people and other minorities. The National Indian Youth Council (NIYC), founded in 1960, tried to unite the two causes of equality for individual Indians and special status for tribes. But the organization foundered on the contradictions between a common Indian identity, emphasizing Indians as a single ethnic group, and tribal identity, stressing the citizenship of Indians in separate nations.

Asian Americans

The harsh relocation program of World War II devastated the Japanese American community on the West Coast (see Chapter 25). But the war against nazism also helped weaken older notions of white superiority and racism. During the war the state of California had aggressively enforced an alien land law by confiscating property declared illegally held by Japanese. In November 1946 a proposition supporting the law appeared on the state ballot. But, thanks in part to a campaign by the Japanese American Citizens League (JACL) reminding voters of the wartime contributions of Nisei (second-generation) soldiers, voters overwelmingly rejected the referendum. One JACL leader hailed the vote as proof that "the people of California will not approve discriminatory and prejudiced treatment of persons of Japanese ancestry." Two years later the Supreme Court declared the law unconstitutional, calling it "nothing more than outright racial discrimination."

The 1952 McCarran-Walter Act removed the old ban against Japanese immigration, and also made

nation, they discovered that dissolution brought unforeseen problems. For example, members of the Klamaths of Oregon and the Paiutes of Utah received large cash payments from the division of tribal assets. But after these one-time payments were spent, members had to take poorly paid, unskilled jobs to survive. Many Indian peoples became dependent upon state social services, and slipped into poverty and alcoholism. In the early 1960s opposition to termination grew as Indians came to see the policy as geared mainly to exploiting resources on Indian lands. The National Congress of American Indians condemned it, calling for a review of federal policies and a return to self-determination. When the termination policy ended in the early 1960s, it had affected only about 3 percent of federally recognized Indian peoples.

But the scars left by termination helped mobilize a new movement to defend Indian sovereignty. Taking their cue from the civil rights movement, Indian activists used the court system to reassert sovereign rights. Indian and white liberal lawyers, many with experience in civil rights cases, worked through the Native American Rights Fund, which became a powerful force in western politics. Much of this legal work was financed by the Indian Claims Commission, established in 1946 to help settle treaty disputes. A series of Supreme Court decisions, culminating in *U.S. v. Wheeler* (1978), reasserted the

Issei (first-generation Japanese Americans) eligible for naturalized citizenship. Japanese Americans, who lobbied hard for the new law, greeted it with elation. "It gave the Japanese equality with all other immigrants," said JACL leader Harry Takagi, and that was the principle we had been struggling for from the very beginning." By 1965 some 46,000 immigrant Japanese, most of them elderly Issei, had taken their citizenship oaths. One of these wrote a poem to celebrate the achievement:

> Going steadily to study English,
> Even through the rain at night,
> I thus attain,
> Late in life,
> American citizenship.

The McCarran-Walter Act allowed immigration from the "Asian-Pacific Triangle." It was nonetheless racially discriminatory, in that each country in Asia was permitted only 100 immigrants a year. In addition, the act continued the national-origins quotas of 1924 for European countries. The civil rights struggle helped spur a movement to reform immigration policies. "Everywhere else in our national life, we have eliminated discrimination based on national origins," Attorney General Robert Kennedy told Congress in 1964. "Yet, this system is still the foundation of our immigration law." In 1965 Congress passed the Immigration and Nationality Act, abolishing the national-origins quotas and providing for the admission each year of 170,000 immigrants from the Eastern Hemisphere and 120,000 from the Western Hemisphere. The new law set a limit of 20,000 per country from the Eastern Hemisphere — these immigrants to be admitted on a first-come, first-served basis — and established preference categories for professional and highly skilled immigrants.

The 1965 act would have a profound effect on Asian American communities, opening the way for a new wave of immigration. In the twenty years following the act the number of Asian Americans soared from 1 million to 5 million. Four times as many Asians settled in the U.S. in this period as in the entire previous history of the nation. This new wave also brought a strikingly different group of Asian immigrants. In 1960 the Asian American population was 52 percent Japanese, 27 percent Chinese, and 20 percent Filipino. In 1985, the composition was 21 percent Chinese, 21 percent Filipino, 15 percent Japanese, 12 percent Vietnamese, 11 percent Korean, 10 percent Asian Indian, 4 percent Laotian, and 3 percent Cambodian. These newcomers included significant numbers of highly educated professionals and city dwellers, a sharp contrast with the farmers and rural peoples of the past.

THE GREAT SOCIETY

As soon as he succeeded to the presidency, Lyndon Johnson looked for ways to establish a unique identity for his new administration. To be sure, Johnson hoped to fulfill the legacy of John F. Kennedy's New Frontier. And he had always identified with the reform achievements of Franklin D. Roosevelt's New Deal. In early 1964, eager to express his own vision and carve his place in history, Johnson began invoking the promise of a "Great Society." He argued that America now had a special opportunity to enrich and elevate the quality of national life. The foundation for the Great Society, he said, "rests on abundance and liberty for all. It demands an end to poverty and racial injustice, to which we are totally committed in our time." The Johnson administration did make significant strides toward these ambitious goals. But the widening war in Vietnam, the persistence of racial strife, and the collapse of a national political consensus all helped thwart the Great Society Johnson envisioned.

The Other America

During the Kennedy administration, civil rights activism spurred a new awareness of and concern with poverty in America. As poor African Americans from both the rural South and the urban North got involved in political protests, they added the issues of unemployment, low wages, and slum housing to the demands for desegregation and voting rights. In particular, the movement exposed the chronic rural poverty of the Deep South to the nation. It also revealed the close links between racial discrimination and economic want. What good was winning the right to sit at a lunch counter if one could not afford to buy a hamburger? African Americans asked.

A series of new sociological and historical studies challenged the complacent belief that America was an "affluent society." The most passionate and influential of these books was Michael Harrington's *The Other America* (1962). Harrington argued that one-fifth of the nation — as many as 40 to 50 million people — still suffered from bad housing, malnutrition, poor medical care, and the other deprivations of poverty. He documented the miseries of what he called the "invisible land of the other Americans," the rejects of society who simply did

Comparative Figures on Life Expectancy at Birth by Race and Sex, 1950–1970.

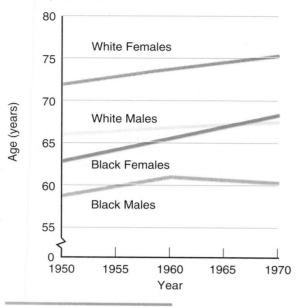

Comparative Figures on Infant Mortality by Race, 1940–1970.

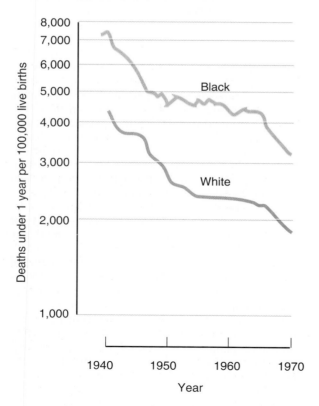

not exist for middle-class suburbanites or the mass media. The other America, Harrington wrote, "is populated by failures, by those driven from the land and bewildered by the city, by old people suddenly confronted with the torments of loneliness and poverty, and by minorities facing a wall of prejudice."

Poverty was by no means limited to black people. Many white Appalachian Mountain communities, for example, were among the poorest in the nation. But African Americans suffered a disproportionate level of poverty. They had not shared equally in the post–World War II economic boom. In the early 1960s, over 40 percent of all black families fell into the poverty bracket, earning less than $3,000 per year. Average black income was only a little over half the average white income. The unemployment rate among blacks was double that of whites. Fewer than 40 percent of black teenagers finished high school, and their unemployment rate was double that of black adults.

The War on Poverty

President Kennedy had begun to formulate a national campaign against poverty. Like many liberals, he read Harrington's book, as well as other accounts of the problem. In 1963 Kennedy directed Walter Heller, chairman of his Council of Economic Advisers, to take a serious look at the problem. Heller's staff conducted statistical studies that showed an increase in the percentage of poor who were aged, members of female-headed families, or minorities. Heller told Kennedy in May 1963 that there was "a dramatic slowdown in the rate at which the economy is taking people out of poverty." But the Kennedy administration's economic policy focused on cutting taxes as a way to stimulate investment and economic growth. The president put a lid on domestic spending for the coming fiscal year. Thus, there would be no money available for the sort of poverty programs suggested by Harrington and others.

Lyndon Johnson sought to expand Kennedy's initial moves into a substantial government program. He saw the poverty issue as a way to prove himself a national reform leader in the tradition of his political hero, Franklin Roosevelt. Johnson also thought that racial divisions at heart turned on economics. If African Americans could get better jobs and higher incomes, he believed, they would also earn more respect from whites and racial

Persons Below Poverty Level: 1959 to 1969

Year	Number below Poverty Level (In Millions)			Percent below Poverty Level		
	Total	White	Black and Other Races	Total	White	Black and Other Races
1969	24.3	16.7	7.6	12	10	31
1968	25.4	17.4	8.0	13	10	33
1967	27.8	19.0	8.8	14	11	37
1966	28.5	19.3	9.2	15	11	37
1965	33.2	22.5	10.7	17	13	47
1964	36.1	25.0	11.1	19	15	50
1963	36.4	25.2	11.2	19	15	51
1962	38.6	26.7	12.0	21	16	56
1961	39.6	27.9	11.7	22	17	56
1960	39.9	28.3	11.5	22	18	56
1959	39.5	28.5	11.0	22	18	56

Note: The poverty threshold for a nonfarm family of four was $3,743 in 1969 and $2,973 in 1959.
Source: Congressional Quarterly, Civil Rights: A Progress Report, 1971, p. 46

tensions would ease. On a more personal level, Johnson had vivid memories of his own experience teaching school to poor Mexican Americans in the 1920s. "Somehow you never forget what poverty and hatred can do when you see its scars on the hopeful face of a young child," he told Congress while urging passage of the Voting Rights Bill in 1965. "I want to be the President who educated young children . . . who helped to feed the hungry . . . who helped the poor to find their own way."

Johnson called for "an unconditional war on poverty" in his State of the Union message in 1964. Over the next two years, Johnson used the political momentum of the civil rights movement and the overwhelming Democratic majorities in the House and Senate to push through the most ambitious reform program since the New Deal. In August 1964 the Economic Opportunity Act launched the War on Poverty. It established an Office of Economic Opportunity (OEO), which coordinated a network of federal programs designed to increase opportunities in employment and education. To lead the OEO, Johnson chose Sargent Shriver, John F. Kennedy's brother-in-law and an enthusiastic liberal who had headed the Peace Corps. Subsequent legislation focused on improving medical care and urban housing.

The Office of Economic Opportunity

From the start, the OEO suffered from bureaucratic infighting, confusion over goals, and underfunding. It directly operated some programs, while others were administered by the Department of Labor and the Department of Health, Education and Welfare. Both of the latter were hostile toward the new agency. Shriver, though bright and energetic, proved a poor administrator. Most crucial was the relatively small amount of money allocated to the OEO. Congress had granted an original appropriation of less than $1 billion in 1965, and some of this came from existing programs. Between 1965 and 1970, the OEO received appropriations averaging $1.7 billion annually. These amounted to around 1.5 percent of the total federal budget, or one-third of 1 percent of the gross national product. If all the OEO money had gone directly to poor people as income, each poor person in America would have received about fifty to seventy dollars per year.

The programs themselves had mixed results. The Job Corps provided vocational training mostly for urban black youth considered unemployable. Housed in dreary barrack-like camps far from home, trainees often found themselves learning factory skills that were already obsolete. The dropout rate was very high. The Neighborhood Youth Corps

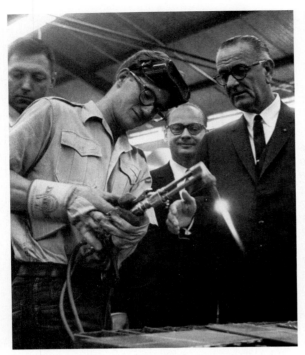

President Lyndon B. Johnson posing with a Job Corps welding student in San Marcos, Texas, where Johnson himself attended college. One of the most highly touted programs of the War on Poverty, the Job Corps suffered from underfunding and a tendency to teach young trainees obsolete technical skills.

managed to provide work to about 2 million young people aged sixteen to twenty-one. But nearly all of these were low-paying, make-work jobs. Educational programs proved more successful. VISTA (Volunteers in Service to America) was a kind of domestic Peace Corps that brought several thousand idealistic teachers into poor school districts.

Conceptual confusion about the nature and causes of poverty hampered the OEO from the start. On the one hand, the program's supporters understood that America's overall economic growth was not enough to pull all people out of poverty. Poor people needed direct transfer payments to improve their lot. But the OEO emphasized improving opportunities in the labor market as the way to end poverty. Even most liberals resisted costly programs that might sustain a large class of people dependent upon government handouts. Yet the rhetoric and

idealism surrounding the OEO did raise expectations, especially among poor urban blacks. In ways unanticipated by its planners, the War on Poverty helped arouse anger, frustration, and a new militancy.

The Community Action Program

The most innovative and controversial element of the OEO was the Community Action Program (CAP). This program invited local communities to establish community action agencies (CAAs), to be funded through the OEO. The Economic Opportunity Act included language requiring these agencies to be "developed, conducted, and administered with the maximum feasible participation of residents of the areas and members of the groups served." In theory, community action would empower the poor by giving them a direct say in mobilizing resources to attack poverty. Three major strategies for "maximum feasible participation" emerged: direct representation of poor people on the governing boards of CAAs; employing the poor as "paraprofessionals" in schools, hospitals, and welfare agencies; hiring community activists to organize poor people into local pressure groups.

By 1966 the OEO was funding over 1,000 CAAs, mostly in black neighborhoods in big cities. The traditional powers in the cities — mayors, business elites, and political machines — generally resisted the CAP's promotion of institutional change. They looked at CAAs as merely another way to dispense services and patronage, with the federal government picking up the tab. A continual tug-of-war over who should control funding and decision making plagued the CAP in most cities. In some cities, CAAs threatened to become a new and independent political force, sparking intense power struggles that helped to cripple the antipoverty effort.

In Syracuse, one CAA trained a group of community organizers in the techniques of the radical activist Saul Alinsky. They soon began directing the formation of tenant unions in public housing projects, using public funds to bail out protesting welfare mothers, and conducting voter registration drives with the aim of defeating Republican mayor William Walsh. In San Francisco, local civil rights leaders won control of a CAA in the black Western Addition neighborhood and used federal funds to create their own political machine. "This is not a poverty program," one black leader remarked. "It is a civil rights program and anybody who thinks differently is mistaken." In Atlanta, a wealthy white businessman, Bo Jones, ran a top-down poverty program called Economic Opportunity, Atlanta. He excluded poor people from its board of directors and placed strict limits on the political activities of neighborhood service centers.

Despite its political problems, the CAP did make strides in improving services to the urban poor. Its most successful and popular offshoots were the so-called national-emphasis programs, designed in Washington and administered according to federal guidelines. The Legal Services Program, staffed by attorneys, helped millions of poor people in legal battles with housing authorities, welfare departments, police, and slumlords. Head Start and Follow Through reached over 2 million poor children and significantly improved the long-range educational achievement of participants. Comprehensive Community Health Centers — one-stop clinics — provided basic medical services to poor patients who could not afford to see doctors. Upward Bound helped low-income teenagers develop the skills and confidence needed for college. Birth control programs dispensed contraceptive supplies and information to hundreds of thousands of poor women.

But the root causes of poverty lay in unequal income distribution. The Johnson administration never really committed itself to the redistribution of income or wealth. Spending on social welfare jumped from 7.7 percent of the GNP in 1960 to 16 percent in 1974. But roughly three-quarters of social welfare payments went to the nonpoor. The largest sums went to Medicare, established by Congress in 1965 to provide basic health care for the aged, and to expanded Social Security payments and unemployment compensation. The major surge in federal spending on poor people resulted from the explosive growth of Aid to Families with Dependent Children (AFDC), a program begun during the New Deal. The number of people on AFDC went from 3.1 million in 1960 to 10.8 million in 1974. But the total cost of AFDC in the mid-1970s was only about $5 billion per year, compared with $65 billion annually for the roughly 30 million Americans receiving Social Security payments.

The civil rights movement had helped create a climate of rising expectations and a sense of entitlement among the poor. In the late 1960s, its influence continued within a new and militant welfare rights movement. But the War on Poverty, like the Great Society itself, became a forgotten dream. "More than five years after the passage of the Economic Opportunity Act," a 1970 study concluded, "the war on poverty has barely scratched the surface. Most poor people have had no contact with it, except perhaps to hear the promises of a better life to come." The OEO finally expired in 1974. Probably no government program in modern American history promised so much more than it delivered. In the end, the War on Poverty was declared but never fought.

CONCLUSION

The mass movement for civil rights, it could be argued, was the most important domestic event of the twentieth century. The struggle that began in Montgomery in December 1955 ultimately transformed race relations in thousands of American communities. By the early 1960s this community-based movement had placed civil rights at the very center of national political life. It achieved its greatest successes by invoking the law of the land to destroy legal segregation and win individual freedom for African Americans. The Civil Rights Act of 1964 and the Voting Rights Act of 1965 testified to the power of an African American and white liberal coalition. Yet the persistence of racism, poverty, and ghetto slums challenged a central assumption of liberalism: that equal protection of constitutional rights would give all Americans equal opportunities in life. By the mid-1960s, many black people had begun to question the core values of liberalism, the benefits of alliance with whites, and the philosophy of nonviolence. At the same time, a conservative white backlash against the gains made by African Americans further weakened the liberal political consensus.

In challenging the persistence of widespread poverty and institutional racism, the civil rights movement called for deep structural changes in American life. By 1967, Martin Luther King was articulating a broad and radical vision linking the struggle against racial injustice to other defects in American society. "The black revolution," he argued, "is much more than a struggle for the rights of Negroes. It is forcing America to face all its interrelated flaws — racism, poverty, militarism, and materialism. It is exposing evils that are deeply rooted in the whole structure of our society." Curing these ills would prove far more difficult than ending legal segregation.

CHRONOLOGY

1941   Executive Order 8802 forbids racial discrimination in defense industries and government.

1946   In *Morgan v. Virginia,* U.S. Supreme Court rules that segregation on interstate buses is unconstitutional.

President Truman creates the Committee on Civil Rights.

1947   Jackie Robinson integrates major league baseball.

1948   President Truman issues executive order desegregating the armed forces.

1954   In *Brown v. Board of Education of Topeka,* Supreme Court rules segregated schools inherently unequal.

The first White Citizens Council is organized in Mississippi.

1955   U.S. Supreme Court rules that school desegregation must proceed "with all deliberate speed."

Montgomery Bus Boycott begins.

1956   Montgomery Bus Boycott ends in victory.

1957   Southern Christian Leadership Conference (SCLC) is founded.

President Eisenhower sends in federal troops in Little Rock, Arkansas.

1960   Sit-in movement throughout the South.

Student Nonviolent Coordinating Committee (SNCC) founded.

1961   Freedom Rides begin.

1962   James Meredith integrates the University of Mississippi.

The Albany Movement fails to end segregation in Albany, Georgia.

1963   SCLC's campaign to desegregate Birmingham, Alabama.

Medgar Evers is assassinated.

March on Washington. Martin Luther King, Jr., delivers his historic "I Have a Dream" speech.

1964   President Johnson calls for "an unconditional war on poverty" in his State of the Union message. The Economic Opportunity Act establishes the Office of Economic Opportunity (OEO).

Mississippi Freedom Summer Project.

Michael Schwerner, James Chaney, and Andrew Goodman are found buried in Philadelphia, Mississippi.

Mississippi Freedom Democratic Party (MFDP) denied seats at the 1964 Democratic Presidential Convention.

Civil Rights Act of 1964.

1965   SCLC and SNCC begin voter registration campaign in Selma, Alabama.

Marchers walk from Selma to Montgomery.

Voting Rights Act of 1965.

Additional Readings

MICHAEL R. BELKNAP, *Federal Law and Southern Order: Racial Violence and Constitutional Conflict in the Post-Brown South* (1987). The best overview of the evolution of Federal policy toward controlling anti-civil rights violence.

TAYLOR BRANCH, *Parting the Waters: America in the King Years, 1954–1963* (1988). A deeply researched and monumental narrative history of the Southern civil rights movement organized around the life and influence of Rev. Martin Luther King, Jr.

CLAYBORNE CARSON, *In Struggle: SNCC and the Black Awakening of the 1960s* (1981). The most comprehensive history of the Student Nonviolent Coordinating Committee, arguably the most important civil rights organization. Carson stresses the evolution of SNCC's radicalism during the course of the decade.

WILLIAM CHAFE, *Civilities and Civil Rights: Greensboro, North Carolina and the Black Struggle for Equality* (1980). Examines the community of Greensboro from 1945–1975. Chafe focuses on the "etiquette of civility" and its complex relationship with the promise of racial justice, along with black protest movements and relations between the city's blacks and whites.

ROBERT A. DIVINE, ed., *Exploring the Johnson Years* (1981). Includes several good essays on the War on Poverty and its relationship to the civil rights movement.

SARA EVANS, *Personal Politics: The Roots of Women's Liberation in the Civil Rights Movement and the New Left* (1979). A pathbreaking study showing the important connections between the struggle for black rights and the rebirth of feminism.

DAVID J. GARROW, *Bearing the Cross: Martin Luther King, Jr. and the Southern Christian Leadership Conference* (1986). An exhaustively researched biography of King that effectively ties together King's student days, his understanding of Gandhi, and his economic views. Garrow makes excellent use of FBI files and other government documents.

MICHAEL B. KATZ, *In the Shadow of the Poorhouse: A Social History of Welfare in America* (1986). Offers an important historical perspective on the expansion of public assistance in the 1960s and 1970s. Katz is especially good on demonstrating how the great increase in federal entitlement spending went largely to the middle class, not the poor.

RICHARD KLUGER, *Simple Justice* (1977). Explores the politics of civil rights at the national level through a close examination of the landmark *Brown v. Board of Education* ruling.

ALLEN J. MATUSOW, *The Unraveling of America: A History of Liberalism in the 1960s* (1984). Offers a useful overview of the promises and failures of the Great Society.

ALDON D. MORRIS, *The Origins of the Civil Rights Movement: Black Communities Organizing for Change* (1984). An important study combining history and social theory. Morris emphasizes the key role of ordinary black people, acting through their churches and other community organizations before 1960.

JAMES T. PATTERSON, *America's Struggle Against Poverty, 1900–1985* (1986). Provides a critical analysis of the War on Poverty in the historical context of other 20th century efforts to end poverty.

HOWELL RAINES, *My Soul Is Rested: Movement Days in the Deep South Remembered* (1977). The best oral history of the Movement, drawing from a wide range of participants and points of view. It is brilliantly edited by Raines, who covered the events as a journalist.

ARMSTEAD ROBINSON and PATRICIA SULLIVAN, eds., *New Directions in Civil Rights Studies* (1991). A solid collection of essays reflecting the latest scholarship on the subject.

JO ANN GIBSON ROBINSON, *The Montgomery Bus Boycott and the Women Who Started It,* ed. David J. Garrow (1987). An important memoir by one of the key behind-the-scenes players in the Montgomery bus boycott. Robinson stresses the role of middle and working class black women in the struggle.

HARVARD SITKOFF, *The Struggle for Black Equality, 1954–1980* (1981). A brief, well-researched, narrative history of the Movement, with good material on the complex relationship between racial justice and economic issues.

ROBERT WEISBROT, *Freedom Bound: A History of America's Civil Rights Movement* (1990). Offers one of the best single volume syntheses of the Movement. Weisbrot is especially strong on the often turbulent relations between black activists and white liberals, and the relationship between civil rights and broader currents of American reform.

29

WAR ABROAD, WAR AT HOME, 1965–1974

Lyndon Baines Johnson believed that through his presidential program he could fulfill the promise of the New Deal and place a stamp on American history equal to that of Franklin D. Roosevelt. Johnson stressed repeatedly that the Great Society stood for more than the end to poverty and racial inequality. In May 1964 at the University of Michigan the president described his vision of a society "where every child can find knowledge to enrich his mind and to enlarge his talents," where "leisure is a welcome chance to build and reflect, not a feared cause of boredom and restlessness," and where "the city of man serves not only the needs of the body and the demands of commerce but the desire for beauty and the hunger for community."

Just two years earlier, in June 1962 at nearby Port Huron, Michigan, founding members of the Students for a Democratic Society (SDS) issued a remarkably similar statement, drafted mainly by graduate student Tom Hayden. "We are people of this generation, bred in at least modern comfort, housed now in universities," the Port Huron Statement began, "looking uncomfortably to the world we inherit." Like President Johnson later, the students recognized not only the dire effects of poverty and social injustice but a deeper ailment in the body of American politics. Everyone, including Americans like themselves with few material wants, suffered from a sense of "loneliness, estrangement, and alienation." Life in the United States had become "inauthentic," yet few people questioned the false values that had come to govern their existence.

YOUNG ADULTS SEEK TO REVIVE THE SPIRIT OF COMMUNITY

Like Johnson, SDSers deplored this prevailing lack of community. "Human relationships should involve fraternity and honesty," they insisted, as a "condition of future survival" in a world of powerful weaponry and impersonal bureaucracies. SDS envisioned itself a new kind of political movement that would bring people "out of isolation and into community." Through "participatory democracy," Americans would remake their institutions and overcome their sense of "powerlessness [and hence] resignation before the enormity of events."

SDS grew out of campus civil rights movements and other kinds of political activism. The organization soon caught the attention of liberal students, encouraging them to realize their political potential as the nation's largest college population to

Most early members of SDS (Students for a Democratic Society) attended major state universities or prestigious private colleges. They majored mainly in the liberal arts and avoided sororities and fraternities. This photograph, taken in Bloomington, Indiana in September 1963, shows members of the SDS national council. By the end of the decade between 60,000 and 100,000 young people participated in local chapters of SDS.

date. By its peak in 1968, SDS had spawned 350 chapters, enlisted an estimated 100,000 members, and won a following of a million or more students.

During the summers of 1964 and 1965, SDS decided to take its commitment to community into the nation's cities. SDS sent small groups to live in ten urban poor districts, where its members created the Economic Research and Action Project (ERAP). Modeled on the civil rights movement, ERAP encouraged neighborhood residents to take control of their own communities and to demand from their government improved facilities and services.

The most tenacious of these projects, Jobs or Income Now (JOIN) in Chicago, focused on Uptown, a one-mile-square section five miles north of the city center. The residents, perhaps as many as half only recently transplanted from the poverty of the Appalachian South, lived in crowded apartment buildings, some of them elegant mansions at one time but now subdivided into tiny, run-down dwellings. On just one street running four blocks lived 4,000 people, 20 percent of them on welfare. Chicago civic authorities had recently designated this neighborhood a Conservation Area, and with federal funds provided by the Urban Renewal Act they hoped to clear out the current residents and upgrade the housing for middle-income families.

JOIN organizers, who moved to Uptown in August 1965, made friends in the neighborhood and worked with them to fight the city's plans. They then helped residents develop scores of other programs. They campaigned against Mayor Richard Daley's policy of "police omnipresence," the fleet of squad cars and paddy wagons that continually patrolled the neighborhood. They protested police harassment and demanded civilian review boards. They also helped community members establish new social clubs, a food-buying cooperative, a community theater, and a health clinic. Within a few years, Uptown street kids had formed the Young Patriots organization, put out a community newspaper, **Rising Up Angry**, and staffed free breakfast programs.

Most other ERAP projects, such as one carried out on the Near West Side of Cleveland, achieved less. Organizers learned quickly that major objectives like more and higher-paying jobs could not be won at the local level and that struggles for limited goals like better garbage collection did not necessarily build a solid movement. Nevertheless, organizers had succeeded in bringing many neighborhood residents "out of isolation and into community," as the founders of SDS had intended. They also set a style of politics that would gain in momentum, although headed in a direction entirely different from the one imagined in the early 1960s.

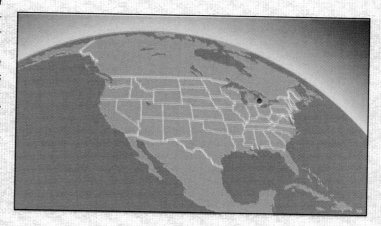

By 1967 the escalation of the war in Vietnam had upset the domestic agendas of both SDS and the Johnson administration. If SDSers had once believed they could work with liberal Democrats to reduce poverty in the United States, they now interpreted social injustice at home as the inevitable consequence of dangerous and destructive foreign policies pursued by liberals and conservatives alike. SDS broke ranks with the Democratic party and threw its energies into the antiwar movement. President Johnson, meanwhile, directed a foreign policy that would swallow up the War on Poverty and precipitate a very different war at home, Americans against Americans. The dream of community did not vanish, but consensus appeared increasingly remote as the United States fought — and eventually lost — the longest war in its history.

VIETNAM: AMERICA'S LONGEST WAR

The origins of American involvement in Vietnam can be traced to the foreign policy inaugurated by the Truman administration and grounded in the principle of containing communism [See Chapter 26]. Following World War II, the United States endeavored to help France preserve its colonial rule in Indochina against the ardent Vietnamese nationalists led by communist Ho Chi Minh. When France was defeated in 1954, an armistice signed at Geneva, Switzerland, created two nations, the Communist-ruled North Vietnam and noncommunist South Vietnam, and required free elections to determine the type of government that would oversee a reunited nation. When South Vietnamese officials refused to comply, insurgents allied themselves with North Vietnam. Determined to defeat the rebels, the United States meanwhile deepened its commitments in Southeast Asia. During the Kennedy administration, the number of military advisers and personnel assigned to South Vietnam grew from less than 700 to more than 16,000. In 1964 American combat troops finally became directly involved in a major air and ground war against the Communist-led guerrilla forces.

The Vietnam War created a huge rift in American society as hawks and doves lined up opposite each other. The political and emotional fallout was both heated and long-lasting. President Johnson himself eventually saw that the "bitch of a war" in Asia placed in jeopardy "the only woman I really loved—the Great Society." Yet Johnson remained wedded to a military policy that ended all prospects for the community he had once envisioned.

Johnson's War

Although President Kennedy had prepared the way, it was Lyndon B. Johnson who made the decision to engage the United States in a major war. Johnson took office only three weeks after the overthrow of the repressive Diem government in South Vietnam. This event, as General Maxwell Taylor reflected, caused "a sequence of crisis, political and military," that forced the new president "to choose between accepting defeat or introducing American combat forces."

Determined to avoid the fate of President Truman, who had bogged down politically by "losing" China to communism and producing a stalemate in Korea (see Chapter 26), Johnson feared the consequences of inaction. "I am not going to lose Vietnam," he declared. "I am not going to be the President who saw Southeast Asia go the way China

went." Johnson also believed that the United States must honor its international commitments. "We are [in Vietnam]," he once explained, "because we have a promise to keep."

While the president continued to assure Americans that he would never "send American boys nine or ten thousand miles away from home to do what Asian boys ought to be doing for themselves," he and his advisers responded to the worsening situation in Vietnam by developing plans to deepen U.S. involvement. They found their pretext on August 1, 1964, when two North Vietnamese patrol boats fired torpedoes at U.S. Navy ships sailing provocatively close to North Vietnam in the Gulf of Tonkin.

President Johnson announced in a special televised address on August 4 that he had ordered retaliatory measures. He next appealed to Congress for the authority to use military force in Vietnam. Secretly drafted six weeks prior to the attack, the Tonkin Gulf resolution passed the Senate with only two dissenting votes and moved unanimously through the House. It served, in Undersecretary of State Nicholas Katzenbach's words, as the "functional equivalent" of a declaration of war.

Although Johnson's actions helped him win the presidential election in November, he now faced a harder decision. The limited bombing raids against North Vietnam did little to quell the civil war. The Communist-led Vietcong forces continued to spread across the countryside and pressure the government in Saigon, the capital of South Vietnam. Johnson had to choose between a Communist victory or massive U.S. involvement. Although adviser George Ball warned Johnson that no amount of U.S. troops could defeat the Vietcong, General William Westmoreland and the Joint Chiefs, convinced they would win, demanded and won another 150,000 U.S. troops.

The U.S. involvement had reached this second turning point for several related reasons. Nguyen Cao Ky, a colorful air marshal known for political intrigue, took over the South Vietnamese government with a collaborator, General Nguyen Van Thieu, in May 1965. Regarded by U.S. diplomats as "absolutely the bottom of the barrel," these leaders seriously undermined hopes for a viable government in South Vietnam, just as the massive desertions from the South Vietnamese army undermined hopes for a military force independent of American troops. Under these conditions, an increase in U.S. military and financial aid constituted an open-ended commitment. Secretary of Defense McNamara warned that any later attempt to withdraw might be "even more difficult and costly than would be the case today."

Deeper Into the Quagmire

Unable to prevent the Vietcong from making further inroads in South Vietnam, the Johnson administration determined to cut off their source of supplies and encouragement in the North. Johnson himself and some of his advisers hesitated, fearing an all-out military attack on North Vietnam would bring China or the USSR into the war. But State Department analyst Walt W. Rostow insisted that victory could be achieved merely by bombing North Vietnamese industrial sites into rubble.

In early February 1965, Johnson found a rationale to justify massive bombing of the North. The Vietcong stormed the U.S. military base at Pleiku, killing 8 and wounding over 100 Americans. Waving the list of casualties, Johnson rushed into an emergency meeting of the National Security Council, announcing that the time had passed for keeping "our guns over the mantle and our shells in the cupboard." Johnson pleaded, "I can't ask our American soldiers out there to continue to fight with one hand behind their backs." He ordered immediate reprisal bombing of North Vietnam, and one week later authorized Operation Rolling Thunder, a campaign of gradually intensifying air attacks. To the North Vietnamese ambassador to the United States, Rolling Thunder meant that "the occasion was lost to end the war."

Johnson settled on what he considered a moderate course, combining saturation bombing in hapless South Vietnam with selective bombing in the North. In response to critics who charged that the bombing of the North had a minimal impact on the civil war in the South, Johnson argued that the only alternative was retreat. Even members of his own administration did not fully realize that a major shift in U.S. policy had taken place.

Once Rolling Thunder had begun, the Johnson administration found it increasingly difficult to hold the line against further escalations, or to speak frankly with the American public about the course of the war. The president initially announced no expansion in ground troops except for two additional battalions of marines requested by General Westmoreland, head of the U.S. military mission in South Vietnam, to protect the Danang air base, where the bombing runs began. Six weeks later 50,000 U.S. troops had been shipped to Vietnam, and Johnson secretly promised Westmoreland another 50,000 by the end of the year. By 1968, the total figure had exceeded 500,000.

Several advisers urged Johnson to take these decisions to the American people, even to declare a state of national emergency and call for higher

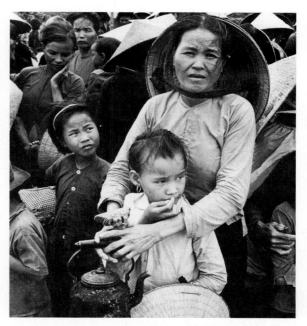

Refugees, Binh Dinh Province, 1967. The massive bombing and ground combat broke apart the farming communities of South Vietnam, creating huge numbers of civilian casualties and driving millions into quickly constructed refugee camps or into already overcrowded cities. Approximately 25 percent of the South Vietnamese population fled their native villages, many never to return.

taxes. But Johnson feared he would lose momentum on domestic reforms if he drew attention to the war. Seeking to avoid "undue excitement in the Congress and in domestic public opinion," he embarked on a course of intentional deceit. He promised congressional leaders that he would push foremost for a diplomatic settlement, not revealing his determination never to accept the terms offered by the North Vietnamese.

The strategy pursued by the Johnson administration and outlined by General Westmoreland — a war of attrition — was based on the premise that continued bombing would eventually exhaust the North Vietnamese. Meanwhile, U.S. forces would inflict such heavy losses in the South that the Vietcong would succumb to both moral and military defeat as its soldiers defected and its supporters scattered. In practice, U.S. initiatives introduced havoc in South Vietnamese culture and society and wrought ecological devastation. U.S. ground troops conducted search-and-destroy missions throughout the rural villages of South Vietnam, intending to locate and eradicate the support network of the Vietcong. They attacked villagers, burned their straw huts, and in ferreting out Vietcong sympathizers inflicted numerous casualties on civilians, mainly women and children, and turned hundreds of thousands of them into refugees. By late 1967, more munitions had been dropped on Vietnam than the Allies had delivered during all of World War II. The millions of gallons of herbicides used to defoliate suspected Vietcong camps and supply routes constituted the most destructive chemical warfare in all history. Yet victory was still nowhere in sight.

The Credibility Gap

Johnson's popularity had surged at the time of the Tonkin Gulf resolution, skyrocketing in one day from 42 to 72 percent, according to a Louis Harris poll. But afterwards it waned rapidly. Despite Westmoreland's optimistic reading, the war dragged on. Every night network television news publicized the latest American body count. No president had worked so hard to control the news media. But Johnson found himself cornered at press conferences in 1965 and 1966 by charges of a credibility gap. Enraged, he lashed out at one reporter, "Why do you come and ask me, the leader of the Western world, a chickenshit question like that?"

Scenes of human suffering and devastation recorded by newspaper and network television cameras increasingly undermined the administration's moral claims. Until 1965, network news had tended either to ignore Vietnam or to deliver strong patriotic support. But in 1966 veteran CBS commentator Eric Sevareid journeyed to Vietnam and came back with a dismal half-hour report. By 1967, according to a noted media observer, "every subject tended to become Vietnam." CBS reporter Morley Safer, watching marines come upon the village of Cam Ne, himself attempted unsuccessfully to persuade the civilians (who were warned but understood no English) to leave their homes so they would not be killed. Official army reports described this operation as the destruction of "fortified Vietcong bunkers." The bunkers existed, Safer noted to the television audience, only because American troops had built them. Other televised news reports told of new varieties of American cluster bombs, which released up to 180,000 fiberglass shards, and showed the nightmarish effects of the defoliants used on forests in South Vietnam to uncover enemy strongholds.

A similarly critical development took place in the press. As early as 1965, *Look* magazine carried the sensational revelation that diplomat and former presidential candidate Adlai Stevenson, just before he died, had wanted to protest the Johnson administration's sabotaging of peace negotiations conducted by UN secretary-general U Thant. By 1967, independent news teams were putting aside the government's official releases. Harrison Salisbury, Pulitzer Prize–winning *New York Times* reporter, questioned the Department of Defense's claims of precision bombing, charging that U.S. planes had bombed the population center of Hanoi, capital of North Vietnam, and intentionally ravaged villages in the South. As American military deaths climbed over 800 per month during the first half of 1967, newspaper coverage of the war became skeptical; noted liberal newspapers were downright hostile.

The most vocal congressional critic of Johnson's war policy was Democratic senator J. William Fulbright of Arkansas, who chaired the Senate Foreign Relations Committee and who had personally speeded the passage of the Tonkin Gulf resolution. A strong supporter of the Cold War, Fulbright had decided that the war in Vietnam was unwinnable and destructive to domestic reform. At first he stood alone: in October 1966, only 15 percent of Congress favored a negotiated settlement. Fulbright's *The Arrogance of Power* (1966), which proposed a negotiated withdrawal from a neutralized Southeast Asia, became a best seller. Fulbright encouraged prominent Democrats in Congress, such as Frank Church, Mike Mansfield, and George McGovern, to put aside their personal loyalty to Johnson and oppose his conduct of the war. In 1967 the Congress passed a nonbinding resolution appealing to the United Nations to help negotiate an end to the war.

By mid-1967 opponents were urging the Johnson administration to negotiate a settlement. Even some of the nation's most trusted European allies called for restraint. The UN's U Thant charged publicly that the United States government had been withholding crucial facts from its own citizens.

The impact of the war, which cost Americans $21 billion per year, was also felt at home. Johnson encouraged Congress to levy a 10 percent surcharge on individual and corporate taxes. Later adjustments in the national budget tapped the Social Security fund, heretofore safe from interference. Inflation raced upward, fed by spending on the war. Enduring this double financial squeeze and unavoidably aware of the body bags bringing home dead GIs, a sizable number of Americans began to question the administration's handling of the war.

A Generation in Conflict

As the war in Vietnam escalated, a movement grew to end U.S. involvement. Millions of Americans from all walks of life eventually took part in this effort, which stretched from informal neighborhood meetings to congressional debates and eventually won over a near majority. But during its years of peak activity, between 1965 and 1971, the peace movement conveyed a distinct generational quality. Young adults, most of them college students, took the most militant and visible stand against the war, demanding the immediate and unconditional withdrawal of U.S. troops from Vietnam.

The baby boomers, whose numbers increased from 16.5 million in 1960 to 24.7 million in 1970, also made a decisive impact on American society. Through music, dress, and even hair style, a large number expressed a deep estrangement from the values and aspirations of their parents' generation. By 1967, when opposition to the war began to mount, "flower children" were putting daisies in the rifle barrels of troops stationed to quell campus protests, providing a seemingly innocent counterpoint to the grim news of war abroad. Such young people believed they represented the "culture of life," versus the "culture of death" rampant in a militarized society.

The Culture of Protest

The free speech movement (FSM) at the University of California at Berkeley in 1964 was the first sign of a new kind of protest. Civil rights activists had returned to the campus from Freedom Summer in Mississippi to picket segregated stores in the Bay Area and to recruit students at Berkeley. When the university administration moved to prevent student groups from setting up literature and information tables on campus, eighteen groups protested, including Students for Goldwater, claiming that their right to free speech had been abridged. The administration sent police to arrest participants in a protest rally, but students spontaneously surrounded the squad car, refusing to release it for thirty hours. A few weeks later, FSM supporters occupied university buildings and set up informal classes in subjects from law to music, the latter led by folk singer Joan Baez. Among those students subsequently arrested were twenty Phi Beta Kappas, eight Woodrow Wilson scholars, and fifty-three National Merit scholars.

Mario Savio, a civil rights activist, spoke for many when he complained that the university had become a faceless bureaucratic machine rather than a community of learning. Treating students as children while preparing them for colorless lives as corporation clerks, the university made them "so sick at heart" that they had decided to put their "bodies against the gears . . . and make it stop until [they were] free." A popular slogan comparing students to computer data-input cards read "Please Don't Bend, Fold, Spindle, or Mutilate Me." The FSM eventually won a majority of students to its position, and in the spring of 1965 university administrators acceded to its earlier demands.

Across the bay in San Francisco, other young people in school and out developed alternatives to what they perceived as a bureaucratic, militaristic, and flavorless society. The Haight-Ashbury district, destined to be the most famous counterculture zone in the United States, drew 75,000 young people during the 1967 "Summer of Love." Public displays of rebellion took the form of "be-ins," staged in city parks and adjoining college campuses across the country. But the most spectacular gatherings that summer occurred at San Francisco's beautiful Golden Gate Park. Masses of long-haired young men and women dressed in colorful but often inexpensive clothes congregated for no other purpose but to listen to music, take drugs, and "be" with each other. "If you're going to San Francisco," a popular rock group sang, "be sure to wear some flowers in your hair . . . you're going to meet some gentle people there."

These young people dramatized a generational revolt that took many forms. The 1960s, for instance, witnessed a revolution in sexual behavior, a massive change that triggered many quarrels between parents and their maturing children over matters having nothing to do with Vietnam. During the 1960s more teenagers experienced premarital sex — by the decade's end barely a quarter of college seniors had never engaged in sexual intercourse — and far more talked about it openly than in previous eras. With lessening social pressure for early marriage and with birth control methods widely available, many young couples chose to set up their own households in preparation or even as a substitute for marriage. The slogan "Make Love, Not War," popularized by John Lennon of the Beatles, linked generational rebellion and opposition to the U.S. invasion of Vietnam.

The new communities of young people often

came together around the use of psychedelic and other hallucinogenic drugs. LSD (lysergic acid diethylamide) gained popularity in large part because of the enthusiasm and public relations genius of Harvard professor Timothy Leary. Urging young people to "turn on, tune in, drop out," Leary advocated the mass production and distribution of LSD, which was not criminalized until 1966. Marijuana, long used by jazz musicians, was illegal yet readily available and relatively inexpensive.

One interpreter, Charles Reich, whose *The Greening of America* (1970) became a best seller, saw the counterculture as a generation's attempt to create "a form of community in which love, respect, and a mutual search for wisdom replace the competition and separation of the past. . . ." At a farm near Woodstock, New York, over 400,000 people gathered in August, 1969 for a three-day rock concert and to give witness to these ideals. Thousands took drugs while security officials and local police stood by, some stripped off their clothes to dance or swim, and a few even made love in the grass. The headlining rock group Crosby, Stills, Nash and Young called everyone back to "the Garden" of Eden. The Woodstock Generation, as it was quickly dubbed by the media, did not actually represent the sentiments of most younger Americans. But its attitudes and styles, especially its efforts to create a new community, or counterculture, did speak for the growing number who ur-gently sought a peaceful alternative to the intensifying climate of war.

From Campus Protest to Mass Mobilization

On campuses across the United States, an antiwar movement grew with the escalation of American involvement in Vietnam. Three weeks after the announcement of Operation Rolling Thunder, activists called for a day-long boycott of classes so that students and faculty might meet to discuss the war. At the University of Michigan in Ann Arbor, forty-nine faculty members sponsored the first teach-in. Though held at night because university administrators and state legislators refused to cancel classes, over 3,000 students showed up, including many women who had received special permission to stay out of their dorms overnight. During the following weeks, teach-ins spread across the United States and as far away as Europe and Japan.

Students felt a personal obligation to protest because of the universities' role in the war and because the burden of fighting fell so hard upon their own age group. The expansion of the university system in the 1960s depended largely on federally funded programs, including war-related research on counterinsurgency tactics and new chemical weapons. The opponents of the war aimed to stop such research, or at least to remove it from the campus. Meanwhile, the implementation in 1965 of the

An anti-war demonstrator places a flower, a symbol of peace, in the rifle barrel of troops during the March on the Pentagon in October 1967. Nearly 100,000 opponents of the Vietnam War gathered in Washington, D.C. Hundreds were arrested as they attempted to storm the entrance to the Pentagon.

Anti-War Protests on College and University Campuses, 1967–1969

Campus-based protests against the war in Vietnam, at first centered on the East Coast and in California, spread to nearly every region by the decade's end.

Selective Service Act — the draft — threatened male students. Although educational deferments protected most undergraduates until 1970, when the policy was changed, academic failure or expulsion often resulted in an automatic draft call.

Protests against war-related research did not slow university pursuit of lucrative government contracts, as students soon learned. By the fall semester of 1967, war protesters had turned to more militant tactics. In October the Dow Chemical Company, makers of napalm, sent job recruiters to the University of Wisconsin at Madison despite warnings that a group of students would try to prevent them from conducting interviews. A few hundred students staged a sit-in at the building where the recruitment interviews were scheduled, and a crowd of several hundred more gathered outside. Ordered

by university administrators to disperse the crowd, the city's police broke glass doors, dragged students through the debris, and clubbed those who refused to move. Suddenly the campus erupted. Thousands rushed to the scene, and police attempted to disperse them with tear gas and Mace. Although faculty members pleaded for deliberation and discussion, undergraduate students and their teaching assistants went on strike for a week. During the next three years, hundreds of similar strikes took place on campuses in every region of the country.

Many student strikes merged opposition to the war with other campus and community issues. At Columbia University, students struck in 1968 against the administration's plans to evict Harlem residents in order to erect new campus buildings. In the Southwest, Mexican American students demonstrated against the use for military projects of funds that might otherwise be allocated to antipoverty and educational programs.

By the late 1960s the peace movement had spread well beyond the campus and commanded a diverse following. While some protesters marched, others held vigils, staged art fairs, distributed leaflets door to door, or simply engaged friends and neighbors in conversation about the war in Vietnam. Vietnam Veterans against the War organized returning soldiers and sailors, encouraging them to cast off the medals and ribbons they had won in battle. In April 1967 the largest demonstration in American history to this time featured celebrities including Benjamin Spock, the famous "baby doctor." At Sheep's Meadow in Manhattan's Central Park, 500,000 people attended the day-long rally.

The steadily increasing size of antiwar demonstrations provoked conservatives and prowar liberals to take a stronger stand in support of the war. On the weekend following the huge turn-out in Central Park, the Veterans of Foreign Wars staged a "Loyalty Day" parade in New York City under the banner "One Country, One Flag, Love It or Leave It." Although only 7,500 people participated, the event signaled the hardening of opposition to the peace movement. Several newspaper and magazine editorialists called for the arrest of antiwar leaders on charges of treason. Secretary of State Rusk, appearing on NBC's "Meet the Press," expressed his concern that "authorities in Hanoi" might conclude, incorrectly, that the majority of Americans did not back their president and that "the net effect of these demonstrations will be to prolong the war, not to shorten it."

Many demonstrators themselves concluded that mass mobilizations alone made little impact on U.S. policy. Some sought to serve as moral witness. Despite a congressional act of 1965 providing for a five-year jail term and a $10,000 fine for destroying a draft card, thousands of cards were burned or delivered to the Justice Department in Washington, D.C. Two priests, Daniel and Philip Berrigan, raided the offices of local draft boards, pouring a mixture of human and duck blood over records. A few protesters even doused their clothes with gasoline and set fire to themselves, as Buddhist monks protesting the war had done in Vietnam. Other activists determined to "bring the war home." An estimated 40,000 bombing incidents or bomb threats took place from January 1969 to April 1970; over $21 million of property was damaged, and forty-three persons were killed. The majority of the perpetrators never became known.

Observers at the time noted a similarity between the violence in Vietnam and the violence in the United States. Parallel wars were now being fought, one between two systems of government in Vietnam, another between the American government and masses of its citizens. Those Americans sent to Vietnam were caught in between.

Teenage Soldiers

The Vietnam War era witnessed not only a generation gap but a fissure *within* the generation of young adults. Overall, college graduates constituted only 12 percent of the soldiers and 9 percent of those in combat. Working-class young men, disproportionately African American and Latino, bore the brunt of the combat. Whereas the average age of the World War II soldier was twenty-six, the age of those who fought in Vietnam hovered around nineteen. High school dropouts were the most likely to be sent to Vietnam, and by far the most likely to die there. This disparity forced a rupture that would last well past the actual war.

By virtue of their age, GIs in significant numbers smoked marijuana, listened to rock music, and considered themselves part of the sexual revolution. But most resented the protests at home as the voice of privileged peers who did not have to fight. Only a small number spoke out against the war. Yet soldiers increasingly showed their frustration, their eagerness to get home alive rather than win the war, and a desperate desire to escape psychologically. Flagrantly imbibing drugs while on duty or off, many simply refused to enter battle, and hundreds "fragged" (threw grenades at) hated officers. Some African American soldiers sported helmets emblazoned with slogans like "No Gook Ever Called Me Nigger," paraphrasing boxing champion Muhammad Ali, who said, "No Vietcong ever called me 'Nigger.' "

The nature of the war fed these feelings. U.S. troops entering South Vietnam expected a welcome from the populations whose homeland they had been sent to defend. Instead, they faced anti-American demonstrations and placards with messages like "End Foreign Dominance of Our Country." Worse, civilians of all types willingly risked their lives to help drive the invaders out. American soldiers chased elusive enemies through deep swamps, crawled through dense jungles, found themselves covered with leeches and fire ants, and stumbled across deadly mine fields and booby traps. Patently false U.S. government press releases heralding glorious victories and grateful civilians not

African American troops in Vietnam, 1970. Serving on the front lines in disproportionate numbers, many black soldiers echoed the growing racial militancy in the United States and increasingly viewed the military conflict in Southeast Asia as a "white man's war."

only fooled no one, but deepened the bitterness on the front lines.

Vietnam veterans returned to civilian life quietly and without fanfare, denied the glory earned by the soldiers of previous wars. They reentered a society badly divided over the cause for which they had risked their lives. Tens of thousands suffered debilitating physical injuries. Many more came home with drug dependencies or posttraumatic stress disorder, which made regular employment problematic. Still others lacked skills to cope with a shrinking industrial economy. Many veterans, perhaps a majority, felt betrayed either by fellow members of their generation or by their government.

BLACK POWER

A generational divide also marked the civil rights movement. When the Great Society programs failed to diminish poverty among African Americans and black men began to die in disproportionate numbers in Vietnam, faith in the old ways lapsed. After months of marching and holding meetings for integrated housing and schools in 1966, Martin Luther King, Jr., admitted defeat. "I have never seen such hate," he remarked, "not in Mississippi, or Alabama, as I see here in Chicago." Impatience with King's strategy prompted many younger civil rights workers to spurn nonviolence for direct action and self-defense. They greeted veteran orators like King with chants of "Black Power!"

Popularized in 1966 by Stokely Carmichael, who chaired the Student Nonviolent Coordinating Committee, Black Power expressed a growing aspiration among African Americans to gain control of their own communities. Self-determination and self-sufficiency were key tenets in this political idea, which derived from a century-long tradition of black nationalism. The phrase also expressed racial pride and affirmed the unique history and heritage of African peoples.

Malcolm X

In life and in death, Malcolm X was the clearest symbol of Black Power. In 1963 he outlined its basic assumptions in a dramatic speech, predicting "the end of 'Whitism' . . . white supremacy, the end of the evil white man's rule." He delivered this message for the Nation of Islam (NOI), a religious sect founded in Detroit in 1931. Like the followers of Marcus Garvey in the 1920s (see Chapter 23), the NOI aspired to create a self-reliant, highly disciplined, and proud community—a separate "nation." Especially well organized in New York City, Detroit, and Chicago, the NOI reached deep into many black communities, operating hundreds of schools, restaurants, and retail stores. Son of the Reverend Earl Little, a Garveyite and Baptist preacher, Malcolm X converted to the NOI while serving a six-year prison term for burglary.

Malcolm X left behind a youthful life of petty crime to become a dynamic and popular orator for the Black Muslims. He spoke frequently on college campuses but won his largest following among

Born Malcolm Little, Malcolm X (1925–1965) took the name "X" as a symbol of the stolen identity of African slaves. He emerged in the early 1960s as the foremost advocate of racial unity and black nationalism. The black power movement, initiated in 1966 by SNCC members, was largely influenced by Malcolm X.

urban African Americans. He encouraged his audiences to take pride in their African heritage, to consider armed self-defense rather than relying solely nonviolence — in short, to break free of white domination "by any means necessary." In his best-selling *Autobiography of Malcolm X* (1965), he admitted that his position was extremist. "The black race here in North America is in extremely bad condition. You show me a black man who isn't an extremist," he argued, "and I'll show you one who needs psychiatric attention."

After breaking with the Nation of Islam, Malcolm X made a pilgrimage to Mecca, the holy city of Islamic religion, where he met Islamic peoples of all colors and underwent a "radical alteration in my whole outlook about 'white' men." He returned to the United States as El-Hajj Malik El-Shabazz, aban-

doned his black separatist views, and moved in the direction of socialism. In June 1964, he founded the Organization of Afro-American Unity.

On February 21, 1965, Malcolm X was assassinated, possibly by members of a New Jersey NOI branch infiltrated by the FBI, during a speech at Harlem's Audubon Ballroom. In his death he became a martyr for the idea of Black Power. "More than any other person," remarked black author Julius Lester, "Malcolm X was responsible for the new militancy that entered The Movement in 1965. . . . He was not concerned with stirring the moral conscience of America, because he knew — America had no moral conscience."

Urban Uprisings

Malcolm X articulated the sense of frustration that many African Americans felt about urban life. By the mid-1960s African Americans had become near majorities in the nation's decaying inner cities. Large numbers had fled rural poverty only to find themselves earning minimum wages at best and living in miserable, racially segregated neighborhoods. The exodus of whites to the suburbs had reduced the tax base for public services of all kinds, especially schools and recreational facilities. Slumlords became notorious for allowing their urban properties to deteriorate while collecting high rents; some even hired arsonists to burn their buildings for insurance money. City leaders, the majority of whom were white, meanwhile fought for federal funds for "urban renewal" — projects that more often than not sliced apart poor neighborhoods with new highways or demolished them in favor of expensive new office complexes.

Urban pressures reached a boiling point, producing over 100 uprisings during the "long, hot summers" between 1964 and 1968. As poet Amiri Baraka noted, these incidents were spontaneous rebellions against authority. Unlike the race riots of the 1920s and 1940s, when angry whites assaulted blacks, masses of African Americans now took revenge for the white domination of their communities and for police abuse, destroying white-owned commercial property. Waves of turbulence rippled through the black neighborhoods of Harlem, Rochester, and Philadelphia in 1964, previewing the summers ahead.

The first major uprising erupted in mid-August 1965 in the Watts section of Los Angeles. Here, in just six years, median income had fallen by 8 percent; the male unemployment rate hovered around 30 percent. Watts lacked health care facili-

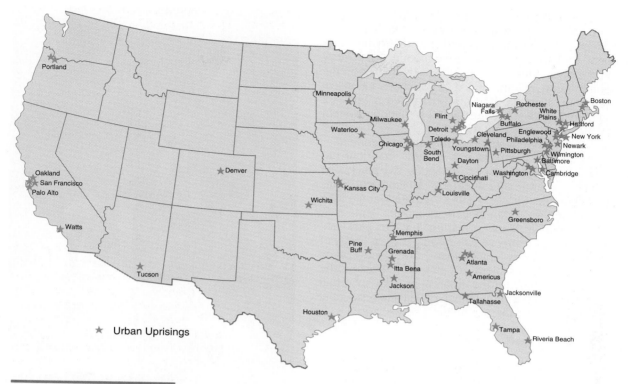

Urban Uprisings, 1965–1968

After World War II urban uprisings precipitated by racial conflict increasingly took place *within* African American communities. In Watts in 1965 and in Detroit and Newark in 1967 rioters struck out at symbols of white control of their communities, such as white-owned businesses and residential properties.

ties — the nearest hospital was twelve miles away — and although fewer than one-fifth of its residents owned cars, the city offered little public transportation. It took only a minor arrest to set off the uprising, which quickly spread fifty miles. Throwing rocks and bottles through store windows, participants reportedly shouted, "This is for Selma! This is for Birmingham!" and "Burn, baby, burn!" Nearly 50,000 people turned out, and 20,000 National Guard troops were sent in. Stores were looted, and 200 of them burned. Property damage estimates topped $200 million. After six days, 34 people lay dead, 900 were injured, and 4,000 more had been arrested. Los Angeles chief of police William H. Parker blamed civil rights workers, the mayor accused Communists, and both feigned ignorance when the media reported that white police assigned to the Watts district had for years referred to their nightsticks as "nigger knockers."

The following summer, large-scale uprisings occurred in San Francisco, Milwaukee, Dayton, and Cleveland. On July 13, 1967, in Newark, New Jersey, a city with severe housing shortages and the nation's highest black unemployment rate, the beating and arrest of a black taxi driver by a white police officer provoked a wide-scale protest. Five days of looting and burning of white-owned buildings ended with twenty-five people killed by the bullets of police and the National Guard. One week later the Detroit "Great Rebellion" began. *Time* magazine reported, "Detroit became the scene of the bloodiest uprising in a half century and the costliest in terms of property damage in U.S. history." Army tanks and paratroopers eventually quelled the massive disturbance, which left 34 people dead and 7,000 under arrest.

The uprisings seemed at first to prompt badly needed reforms. After Watts, President Johnson set up a task force headed by Deputy Attorney General Ramsey Clark, and allocated funds for a range of antipoverty programs. Several years later the Kerner Commission, headed by Governor Otto Kerner of Illinois, studied the riots and indicted "white racism" for creating an "explosive mixture" of poverty and police brutality. Appointed by Johnson, the commission recommended a yet more extensive program of public housing, integrated schools, 2 million new jobs, and funding for a "national system of income supplementation."

But Congress ignored both the recommendations and the commission's warning that "our nation is moving toward two societies, one black, one white — separate and unequal." As President Johnson admitted, the costs of the Vietnam War left little federal money for antipoverty programs. Moreover, many political leaders, fearing a white backlash, backed away from even discussing the possibility of bias in local law enforcement. The ghetto, once known as the problem of cities, now became the solution, walling off the urban poor from suburban whites through a combination of de facto residential segregation and intense political surveillance.

"Power to the People"

In 1966 African Americans in Oakland formed the Black Panther Party for Self-Defense to monitor police activities in black neighborhoods, a practice they referred to as "patrolling the pigs." The Panthers' paramilitary style — the black leather jackets and black berets and the open display of weapons — infuriated local authorities. But it instilled racial pride in many of the youngsters nationwide who sold the *Black Panther,* a popular weekly newspaper. The Panthers also ran free breakfast programs for schoolchildren, a service often accompanied by African flags and nationalist cultural messages.

By the late 1960s programs designed to foster economic self-sufficiency had appeared in several cities. The Reverend Jesse Jackson rallied African Americans in Chicago to boycott the A&P supermarket chain until the firm hired 700 black workers. A dynamic speaker and skillful organizer, Jackson encouraged African Americans to support their own businesses and services. "We are going to see to it," he explained in 1969, "that the resources of the ghetto are not siphoned off by outside groups. . . . If a building goes up in the black community, we're going to build it." His program, Operation Breadbasket, strengthened community control. By 1970 it had spread beyond Chicago to fifteen other cities.

These programs marked a major shift in direction for the civil rights movement. Under King's leadership, civil rights activists had focused on

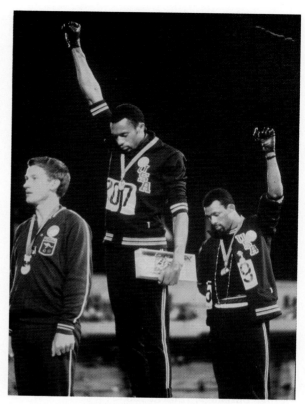

Tommie Smith and John Carlos lift their fists in the **black power salute before they received their medals at the 1968 Olympic Games in Mexico City. The International Olympic Committee responded by threatening to evict all U.S. athletes from the event unless the two demonstrators were disciplined.**

eliminating racial segregation and securing voting rights in the South. As the urban uprisings of the mid-1960s began to highlight the problems of northern blacks, younger civil rights leaders revived long-standing traditions of black self-sufficiency and asserted the right to retaliate against violence. National conferences on Black Power, held annually beginning in 1966, adopted separatist resolutions, even endorsing a plan to partition the United States into black and white nations, and called upon African Americans to boycott the draft.

These ideas came together in the politics of Trinidad-born Stokely Carmichael, who as chairman of SNCC had helped turn it into an all-black organization. "Black power!" he exclaimed. "Move over, or we'll move on over you!" "Stokely was the nightmare America had been dreading," an admiring activist exalted, "the black man . . . strong, tough and dangerous." Many veteran civil rights leaders disapproved of this change in strategy. King warned that it was "no solution." Some women opposed the equation of racial pride and manliness, and a contingent walked out of the 1967 Black Power Conference in Newark when it passed an anti–birth control resolution. But the strongest censure of Black Power came from white authorities. Chicago police gunned down unarmed Black Panther leader Fred Hampton, and the FBI targeted hundreds of Panthers for arrest, prosecution, and long jail sentences, effectively destroying the organization.

Black Power nevertheless continued to grow during the late 1960s and became a multifaceted movement for racial pride. Advocate Charles V. Hamilton urged African Americans "to assert their own definitions, to reclaim their history, their culture; to create their own sense of community and togetherness." Thousands of college students called for more scholarships and for the creation of black studies programs. Strikes for these demands broke out on several campuses. Meanwhile, fashion trend setters put aside Western dress for African-style dashikis and hairdos, and black parents gave their children African names. Luminaries such as Imamu Amiri Baraka (formerly Le Roi Jones), Muhammad Ali (formerly Cassius Clay), and Kwame Touré (formerly Stokely Carmichael) rejected their "slave names." This deepening sense of racial identity and solidarity was summed up in the popular slogan "Black Is Beautiful."

1968

The summer of 1967 was the apex of the most drawn-out violence in the United States since the Civil War. The following winter brought a change of venue, but no respite, in the violence. On January 30, 1968, the North Vietnamese launched the Tet offensive (named for the Vietnamese lunar new year holiday), stunning the U.S. military command in South Vietnam. Occupying the courtyard around the U.S. embassy in Saigon, a suicide squad set the pace for a coordinated attack on major cities and provincial capitals in the South. It took over three weeks for U.S. troops to regain control. In the process, American soldiers killed more than 30,000 North Vietnamese and Vietcong and inflicted casualties on hundreds of thousands of civilians. As many as 1 million South Vietnamese were reduced to refugees, their villages totally ruined. The beautiful, ancient city of Hue was devastated almost beyond recogni-

tion. Americans at home grasped U.S. policy from a casual remark by a U.S. officer about a village that had to be "destroyed" in order to be "saved."

American casualties were comparatively modest — 1,600 dead, 8,000 wounded — and military leaders quickly claimed a decisive victory over the Vietcong. But the drama of the Tet Offensive had shattered the credibility of American officials, who had repeatedly predicted a quick victory over an unpopular enemy. For the first time, polls showed strong opposition to the war, 49 percent concluding that the entire operation in Vietnam was a mistake. Network television commentators who had earlier radiated optimism now began to urge a negotiated settlement and withdrawal of U.S. troops. In Rome, Berlin, Paris, and London, students and others turned out in huge demonstrations to protest U.S. involvement in Vietnam.

The Tet Offensive also opened a year of political drama at home. President Johnson, facing the 1968 election campaign, knew the odds were piling up against him, and on March 31 he announced he would not seek the Democratic party's nomination. He also declared a bombing halt over North Vietnam and called Hanoi to peace talks, which began in Paris in May. Like Truman almost thirty years earlier, Johnson had lost his presidency in Asia.

King, the War, and the Assassination

By 1968 both the civil rights and Black Power movements stood in opposition to the war, and Martin Luther King, Jr., had reached a turning point in his life. Although pursued by the FBI through tapped telephones and malicious rumors — bureau chief J. Edgar Hoover swore to "destroy the burrhead" — King abandoned his customary caution in criticizing U.S. policy in Vietnam. In the fall of 1965 he began to connect domestic unrest with the war abroad, calling the U.S. government the "greatest purveyor of violence in the world today." Only by understanding that the roots of warmaking lay in "racism, poverty, militarism and materialism," he concluded, could American society come to terms with its flaws and take a giant step toward democracy. In taking this stand, King lost the support of liberals and labor leaders who remained loyal to Johnson. King refused to compromise.

In the spring of 1968 King chose Memphis, Tennessee, home of striking sanitation workers, as the place to inaugurate a Poor People's Campaign for peace and justice. Noting that the United States was "much, much sicker" than when he had begun working in 1955, he refused to grieve and instead delivered a message of hope. In his last speech, King prophesied:

> We've got some difficult days ahead [*yeah! oh yes!.*, the audience responded]. Like anybody I would like to live a long life. Longevity has its place. But I'm not concerned about that now. I just want to do God's will. And He's allowed me to go up to the mountain [*go ahead*]. And I've looked over [*yes, doctor*]. And I've seen the Promised Land [applause, cries, *go ahead, go ahead*]. So I'm happy tonight. I'm not worried about anything. I'm not fearing any man. Mine eyes have seen the glory of the coming of the Lord [cries, applause]. I have a dream this afternoon that the brotherhood of man will become a reality. With this faith, I will go out and carve a tunnel of hope from a mountain of despair.

As he stepped out on the balcony of his motel the next evening, April 4, 1968, King was shot in the head by a lone assassin, James Earl Ray.

Throughout the world crowds turned out to mourn King's death. The *New York Times* declared King's murder "a national disaster." Cheers, however, rang through the regional FBI office. President Johnson, who had ordered the investigation of King, declined to attend the funeral, sending in his place Attorney General Ramsey Clark. Black Power leader Stokely Carmichael stormed, "When white America killed Dr. King, she declared war on us." He advised African Americans to buy guns.

Riots occurred in more than 100 cities. Chicago Mayor Richard Daley ordered his police to shoot to kill. In Washington, D.C., U.S. Army units set up machine guns outside the Capitol and the White House. By week's end, nearly 27,000 African Americans had been jailed. The physical scars of these riots remained for years, as banks redlined black neighborhoods and refused funds for rebuilding. The psychic scars survived even longer. With King's death, his vision of humanity as a "beloved community" faded.

The Democratic Campaign

The dramatic events of the first part of the year had a direct impact on the presidential campaign. For those liberals dissatisfied with Johnson's conduct of the war, and for African Americans suffering the loss of their greatest national leader, New York senator Robert F. Kennedy emerged as the candidate of choice. Kennedy had been moved by King's assassination to take up more aggressively the cause of impoverished Americans, and, like King, he had begun to interpret the war as a mirror of injustice at home. Kennedy insisted during the Tet Offensive

Following his victory speech during the California Democratic primary campaign, Senator Robert F. Kennedy (1925–1968) was assassinated in June, 1968. Pulitzer prize-winning author John Hersey later wrote that the year of violence led Americans "to feel that all our paragons must die by the gun, as Martin Luther King and Bobby Kennedy did." Not long before his death, Kennedy had become one of the most vocal opponents of the war in Vietnam and had campaigned for the presidency on a peace platform.

that "our nation must be told the truth about this war, in all its terrible reality." On this premise he began to build a campaign for the Democratic nomination.

Ironically, Kennedy faced an opponent who agreed with him, Minnesota senator Eugene McCarthy. The race for the Democratic nomination positioned McCarthy, the witty philosopher, against Kennedy, the charismatic campaigner. McCarthy briefly garnered support on college campuses, so much so that his effort became known as the "children's crusade." Kennedy reached out successfully to African Americans, Mexican Americans, working-class whites, and liberal Democrats in states ranging politically from Indiana to California, and won all but the Oregon primary.

Adroitly planning to unify the various wings of the Democratic party behind him, Kennedy appeared unbeatable as June 5, the day of the California primary, dawned. But as the final tabulation of his victory came into his Los Angeles campaign headquarters that evening, Robert Kennedy was struck down by the bullet of an assassin, Jordanian Sirhan Sirhan.

Vice-President Hubert H. Humphrey, a long-time presidential hopeful, was now the sole Democrat with the credentials to succeed Johnson. But his reputation as a Truman or Cold War Democrat had become a liability. In the 1950s Humphrey had delivered stirring addresses for civil rights and antipoverty legislation, yet sponsored repressive Cold War legislation and supported huge defense appropriations that diverted needed funds from domestic programs. He fully supported the Vietnam War and had publicly scorned peace activists as cowardly and un-American. Incongruously calling his campaign the Politics of Joy, Humphrey simultaneously courted Democrats who grimly supported the war and the King-Kennedy wing, which was sickened by it.

Humphrey skillfully cultivated the Democratic power brokers. Without entering a single state primary, he lined up delegates loyal to city bosses, labor leaders, and conservative southern Democrats. Humphrey secured his party's nomination and promised a sweeping peace proposal, including a cease-fire. This struck liberal Democrats as hypocritical, and in their eyes proved Humphrey's lack of character. Even before the convention began, the power brokers had settled on him as the candidate least likely to rock the party's boat.

August 1968: "The Whole World Is Watching"

The events surrounding the Democratic convention of August 21–26 showed the world, through satellite television, how deep the divisions within the United States had become. Antiwar activists had called for a massive demonstration at the delegates' hotel and at the convention center. The media focused, however, on the plans announced by the "Yippies," or Youth International party, a largely imaginary organization of politicized hippies led by jokester and counterculture guru Abbie Hoffman. Yippies called

The "police riot" in Chicago, August, 1968, during the Democratic National Convention capped a spring and summer of violence. Mayor Richard Daley had prepared his city for the anticipated protest against the war by assembling more than 20,000 law enforcement officials, including police, National Guard, and U.S. Army troops carrying flame throwers and bazookas. Television cameras and photographers recorded the massive clubbing and tear-gassing of demonstrators as well as bystanders and news reporters.

for a Festival of Life, including a nude-in on Lake Michigan beaches and the release of greased pigs (one crowned King "Pigasus") throughout the city. Still reeling from the riots following King's assassination, Chicago mayor Richard Daley refused to issue parade permits. According to later accounts, he sent hundreds of undercover police into the crowds to encourage rock throwing and generally incite violence in order to make retaliation appear necessary and reasonable.

Daley's strategy boomeranged when his officers staged what a presidential commission later termed a police riot, randomly assaulting demonstrators, casual passers-by, and television crews filming the events. For one of the few times in American history, the media appeared to join a protest against civil authorities. Enraged at the embarrassing publicity, Daley's forces raided Eugene McCarthy's campaign headquarters, where Democrats opposed to the war had gathered.

Inside the convention hall, a raging debate over a peace resolution underscored the depth of this division. Representative Wayne Hays of Ohio lashed out at those who substituted "beards for brains . . . (and) pot (for) patriotism." When the resolution failed, McCarthy delegates put on black armbands and followed folk singer Theodore Bikel in singing "We Shall Overcome." Later, as tear gas used against the demonstrators outside turned the amphitheater air acrid, delegates heard the beaming Humphrey praise Mayor Daley and Johnson's conduct of the Vietnam War. When Senator Abraham Ribicoff of Connecticut addressed the convention and protested the "Gestapo tactics" of the police, television cameras focused on Mayor Daley saying, "You Jew son of a bitch, you lousy motherfucker, go home!" The crowd outside chanted, "The whole world is watching! The whole world is watching!" Indeed it was.

Well beyond Chicago, the events of 1968 appeared equally unsettling. Across the United States the antiwar movement picked up steam. In Paris, students took over their campuses and workers occupied factories. Young people scrawled on the walls such humorous and half-serious slogans as "Be Realistic, Demand the Impossible!" Similar protests against authority occurred in Eastern Europe. In Prague, Czechoslovakia, students wearing blue jeans and quoting lyrics from Beatles songs threw rocks at Soviet tanks. Meanwhile, demonstrations in Japan, Italy, Ireland, Germany, and England all brought young people into the streets to demand democratic reforms in their own countries and an end to the war in Vietnam.

THE POLITICS OF IDENTITY

While war raged in Vietnam, groups consisting mainly of young adults formed to express and promote their own sense of collective identity. Gay liberation and women's liberation movements emerged with great media fanfare in the late 1960s. By the early 1970s Latinos, Asian Americans, and Indian peoples had drawn their own lessons from the Black Power movement, and "Brown Power" and "Yellow Power" joined the era's popular political slogans. These movements constituted distinctly new communities of protest.

Gay Liberation

The gay community had been generations in the making but gained visibility during World War II (see Chapter 25). By the mid-1950s two pioneering homophile organizations, the Mattachine Society and the Daughters of Bilitis, were campaigning openly to reduce discrimination against homosexuals in employment, the military, and all areas of social and cultural life. Other groups, such as the Society for Individual Rights, rooted themselves in the bar scene of New York's Greenwich Village, San Francisco's North Beach, and other centers of gay night life. But it was during the tumultuous 1960s that gay and lesbian movements aroused many men and women to proclaim publicly their sexual identity: "Say It Loud, Gay Is Proud."

The major event prompting gays to organize grew out of repeated police raids of gay bars and harassment of their patrons. In February 1966 New York City's popular liberal mayor John Lindsay announced a crackdown against "promenading perverts" and assigned police to patrol the bars between Times Square and Washington Square. The American Civil Liberties Union responded by pointing out that the mayor was "confusing deviant social behavior with criminal activity." Lindsay's police commissioner soon announced the end of the entrapment policy by which undercover police had been luring homosexuals into breaking the law, but various forms of individual harassment continued. Finally, on Friday, June 27, 1969, New York police raided a well-known gay bar in Greenwich Village and provoked an uprising of angry homosexuals that lasted the entire night. The next day, "Gay Power" graffiti appeared on buildings and sidewalks throughout the neighborhood.

The Stonewall Riot, as it was called, sparked a new sense of collective identity among many gays and lesbians and touched off a new movement for both civil rights and liberation. Gay men and women in New York City formed the Gay Liberation Front (GLF), announcing themselves as "a revolutionary homosexual group of men and women formed with the realization that complete sexual liberation for all people cannot come about unless existing social institutions are abolished. We reject society's attempt to impose sexual roles and definitions of our nature. We are stepping outside these roles and simplistic myths. We are going to be who we are." The GLF also took a stand against the war in Vietnam and supported the Black Panthers. It quickly adopted the forms of public protest, such as street demonstrations and sit-ins, developed by the civil rights movement and given new direction by antiwar protesters.

Changes in public opinion and policies followed. As early as 1967 a group of Episcopal priests had urged church leaders to avoid taking a moral position against same-sex relationships. The San Francisco–based Council on Religion and Homosexuality established a network for clergy sympathetic to gay and lesbian parishioners. In 1971 the American Psychological Association, which had long viewed homosexuality as a treatable mental illness, reclassified it as a normal sexual preference. Meanwhile, there began a slow process of decriminalization of homosexual acts between consenting adults. In 1975 the U.S. Civil Service Commission ended its ban on the employment of homosexuals.

The founders of gay liberation encouraged not only legal changes and the establishment of supporting institutions but self-pride. "Gay Is Good" (like "Black Is Beautiful") expressed the aspiration of a large hidden minority (estimated at 10 million or more people) to "come out" and demand public acceptance of their sexual identity. The Gay Activist Alliance, founded in 1970, demanded "freedom of expression of our dignity and value as human beings. . . ." By the mid-1970s Gay Pride marches held simultaneously in several cities were drawing nearly 500,000 participants.

Sisterhood Is Powerful

The report issued by President Kennedy's Commission on the Status of Women signaled a growing political awareness among women during the early 1960s (see Chapter 27). Betty Friedan's best-selling *The Feminine Mystique* (1963) swelled feelings of discontent among many middle-class white women and sparked the formation of the National Organization for Women (NOW) in 1966. Members spearheaded numerous legal and economic reforms, addressing primarily issues of women's civil rights and demanding equal opportunities in all areas of American society.

The second half of the decade produced a distinct movement styled on the era's major protest movements: women's liberation. Comprising mainly young women who had been active in civil rights, the New Left, and campus antiwar movements, the women's liberation movement endorsed many of the same principles promoted by NOW but set out primarily to create a new sense of gender identity. Groups of white women, following the example of black women in SNCC, began to object to their secondary status in the protest movements of the late 1960s. Women must come to understand, one activist wrote, that "they are not inferior — nor chicks, nor bunnies, nor quail, nor cows, nor bitches, nor ass, nor meat," but agents of their own destiny.

In 1967 small groups of women broke off from male-led protest movements. Proclaiming "Sisterhood is powerful," they sought in one another's company new ways of changing the world. They viewed the enemy as patriarchy — that is, the power of men to dominate all institutions, from the family to business to the military to protest movements themselves. Patriarchy, they argued, was the prime cause of exploitation, racism, and war. Outraged and sometimes outrageous, radical feminists, as they called themselves, conducted "guerrilla theater" at the 1968 Miss American Beauty Pageant in Atlantic City, crowning a live sheep queen and throwing implements of female torture (bras, girdles, curlers, and copies of the *Ladies Home Journal*) into a "freedom trash can."

The media focused on the audacious acts and brazen pronouncements of radical feminists, who were mainly college-age women. But the majority involved in the women's liberation movement were women in young adulthood trying to come to terms with their domestic responsibilities and the demands of full-time employment. They joined together primarily to form a community distinct from their families, to discuss their relationships with men at home and at work, and to realize their own aspirations. These consciousness-raising (CR) groups multiplied by the thousands in the late 1960s and early 1970s. They established the constituency for the movement's most important belief, expressed in the aphorism "The personal is political." Believing that no aspect of life lacked a political dimension, women in these groups explored the power dynamics of the institutions of family and marriage as well as the work force and government.

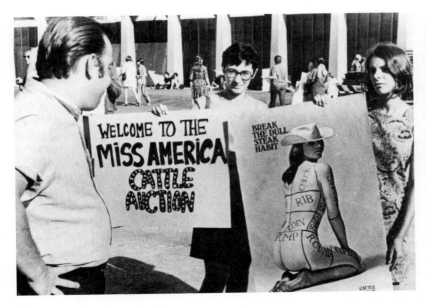

Members in the early women's liberation movement staged the first major protest publicized widely by the mass media in Atlantic City in 1968. Contrary to the myth created by a hostile press, no bras were burned. These women did protest the presentation of beauty contestants as sex-objects. They also criticized the pageant's support of the Vietnam War by sending Miss America to entertain U.S. troops.

"The small group has served as a place where thousands of us have learned to support each other," one participant reported, "where we have gained new feelings of self-respect and learned to speak about what we are thinking and to respect other women."

Participants in the women's liberation movement engaged in a wide range of activities. Some staged sit-ins at *Newsweek* to protest demeaning media depictions of women. Others established health clinics, day-care centers, rape crisis centers, and shelters for women fleeing abusive husbands or lovers. The women's liberation movement also had a significant educational impact. Feminist bookstores and publishing companies, such as the Feminist Press, reached out to eager readers. Scholarly books such as Kate Millett's *Sexual Politics* found a wide popular audience. By the early 1970s the first women's studies programs had appeared on college campuses; there followed a flowering of scholarship across the disciplines.

The women's liberation movement remained, however, a bastion of white middle-class women. The appeal to sisterhood did not unite women across race or class or even sexual orientation. Lesbians, who charged the early leaders of NOW with homophobia, found large pockets of "heterosexism" in the women's liberation movement and broke off to form their own organizations. Although some African American women were outraged at the posturing of Black Power leaders like Stokely Carmichael, who joked that "the only position for women in SNCC is prone," the majority remained wary of white women's appeals to sisterhood. African American women formed their own "womanist" movement to address their distinct cultural and political concerns. Similarly, by 1970 a Latina feminist movement had begun to address issues uniquely relevant to women of color in an Anglo-dominated society.

By the early 1970s the women's liberation movement had fostered a sense of community that provided support and solidarity to many women. But its emphasis on gender identity did not dispel ethnic and racial conflict.

La Raza

A movement for Mexican American liberation gained steam in the mid-1960s from a well-publicized strike of agricultural workers in California led by the charismatic César Chavez. Inspired by the civil rights movements of the 1950s, Chavez broadened the struggle for better wages and union recognition into a dramatic campaign for dignity. He formed the United Farm Workers (UFW) in California's San Joaquin Valley in 1962, and he set out goals for the Mexican American community drawn from its religious and national traditions. A UFW-inspired nationwide boycott of grapes, the main crop of the valley, won support from an estimated 17 million Americans. The union leader quickly became a political celebrity, his picture appearing on the cover of *Time* magazine. Chavez's reputation among Mexican Americans soon rivaled that of Martin Luther King among African Americans.

By the mid-1960s young Mexican Americans had created, according to one historian, *a moral community* founded on collectivist principles and a determination to resist Anglo domination. Mainly high school and college students, they adopted the slang term *Chicano,* in preference to Mexican American, to express a militant ethnic nationalism. Chicano militants demanded not only equality with white people but cultural and political self-determination. Tracing their roots to the heroic Aztecs, they identified *la raza* (the race or people) as the source of a common language, religion, and heritage.

Between 1965 and 1969 the Chicano movement reached its peak of activism. Students staged blowouts or strikes in East Los Angeles high schools to demand educational reform and a curricular emphasis on the history and literature of Mexican Americans. In 1967 a group of students formed the Brown Berets, modeled on the Black Panthers, to address such community issues as housing and employment and generally to encourage teenagers to express *Chicanismo,* or pride in their Mexican American identity and heritage. By 1972 the Brown Berets had organized 20 chapters, published a newspaper, *La Causa,* and run a successful health clinic. From college campuses spread a wider cultural movement that spawned literary journals in "Spanglish" (a mixture of English and Spanish), theatrical companies and music groups, and murals illustrating ethnic themes on buildings in Los Angeles and elsewhere.

Chicano nationalism inspired a variety of regional political movements in the late 1960s. Several organizations, such as Corky Gonzales's Crusade for Justice, formed in 1965 to protest the failure of the Great Society's antipoverty programs. Former boxer and popular poet, Gonzales was especially popular among barrio youth and college students. He led important campaigns for greater job opportunities and land reform throughout the Southwest well into the 1970s. In Colorado and New Mexico, the Alianza Federal de Mercedes, formed in 1963 by Reies López Tijerina, fought to reclaim land fraudulently appropriated by white settlers. The Texas-based La Raza Unida Party (LRUP), meanwhile, increased Mexican American representation in local government and established social and cultural programs. The student-led Mexican American Youth Organization (MAYO) worked closely with the LRUP to help Mexican Americans take political power in Crystal City, Texas. The two organizations registered voters, ran candidates for office, and staged a massive boycott of Anglo-owned businesses.

Mexican American activists, even those who won local office, soon discovered that economic power remained out of community hands. The grape boycott failed to secure a firm basis for the United Farm Workers, whose organization dwindled. Stifled by poverty, ordinary Mexican Americans had less confidence in the political process, and many fell back into apathy after early hopes of great, sudden

Cesar Chavez leading a march of striking United Farm Workers in Delano, California, during the summer of 1965. To dramatize the plight of grape pickers and other migrant workers, Chavez drew on the tactics of the civil rights movement. He emphasized the principle of nonviolence and the importance of attracting outside help from religious groups, well-known politicians, students, and civil rights organizations.

change. Despite these setbacks, a sense of identity had been forged among many young people, and Mexican American content had been added to many school curriculums.

Red Power

Having battled government programs to terminate their tribal status (see Chapter 28), Indian peoples entered the 1960s determined to reassert themselves. The Civil Rights Act passed in 1968 restored the legitimacy of tribal laws on the reservations, and Lyndon Johnson personally promised a "new goal" that "erases old attitudes of paternalism." Although economic and social reforms were limited by a shortage of antipoverty and educational funds, a movement to build a sense of Indian identity spread widely among young people. In the 1970 census, many of the 800,000 respondents who identified themselves as Indians did so for the first time.

The American Indian Movement (AIM), founded in 1968 by Chippewas George Mitchell and Dennis Banks, challenged the Bureau of Indian Affairs' guidance over Indian life. Affirming Indian dignity while calling for greater economic opportunities and an end to police harassment, AIM quickly inspired a plethora of new Indian publications and local organizations. In 1969 AIM created national headlines when militant activists occupied Alcatraz Island in San Francisco Bay and demanded government funds for an Indian cultural center and university.

The most dramatic event of the Red Power movement began in November 1972, when members of the once powerful but now greatly reduced Sioux tribe occupied the headquarters of the Bureau of Indian affairs for nearly a week. Three months later, AIM Sioux and members of other tribes took over the site of the 1890 massacres at Wounded Knee, South Dakota, swearing to hold their position by force if necessary. Occupiers asked only that the federal government honor treaty rights. Instead, dozens of FBI agents invaded under Director J. Edgar Hoover's shoot-to-kill orders, leaving two Indians dead and one federal marshall wounded.

Major Indian Reservations, 1976

Although sizable areas, designated Indian reservations represented only a small portion of territory occupied in earlier times.

Members of the American Indian Movement (AIM) guard the door to the Bureau of Indian Affairs in Washington, D.C., during a week-long occupation in November, 1972, meant to dramatize their grievances. Formed in 1968 to work for equal rights and better living conditions, AIM had led a march of Indian peoples along the "Trail of Broken Treaties" before occupying the BIA offices.

Several tribes won in court, by legislation, or by administrative fiat small parts of what had earlier been taken from them. President Nixon returned the sacred Blue Lake to the Pueblo Indians in Taos and backed Congress in granting Alaskan natives legal title to 40 million acres (and compensation of almost $1 billion). The Native American Rights Fund (NARF), established in 1971, gained additional thousands of acres in Atlantic Coast states. Despite these victories, tribal lands continued to suffer from industrial and government dumping and other commercial uses. On reservations and in urban areas with heavy Indian concentrations, alcohol abuse and ill health remained serious problems.

The 1960s also marked the beginning of an "Indian Renaissance." New books like Vine Deloria, Jr.'s *Custer Died for Your Sins* (1969) Dee Brown's *Bury My Heart at Wounded Knee* (1971) and the classic *Black Elk Speaks* (1961), reprinted from the 1930s, reached millions of readers inside and outside Indian communities. A wide variety of Indian novelists, historians, and essayists, such as Jamake Highwater and Leslie Silko, followed up these successes, and fiction and nonfiction works about Indian life and lore continued to attract a large audience.

Asian American Activism

In the late 1960s, Chinatowns in San Francisco and New York were flooded with new immigrants, many from the island nation of Hong Kong. New Chinese-language daily newspapers appeared, some friendly to the People's Republic of China. Groups formed to protest the Vietnam War and the increasing poverty of the community. Some young activists in San Francisco and New York created political organizations inspired by the thought of Mao Zedong, the Communist leader of China. The Chinatown Red Guards, closely modeled on the Black Panthers, organized street gangs (made up mostly of first-generation immigrant teenagers), preached Asian racial pride, monitored local police, and urged armed self-defense. At their high point, the Red Guards led a community-wide struggle to save San Francisco's International Hotel, a low-income residential facility threatened with destruction.

Inspired by the Red Guards, activists ranging from college teachers to neighborhood artists worked in a variety of campaigns to heighten public awareness. Trade union organizers attempted to raise the low wages in the garment industry which employed many recent immigrants. Other campaigns reflected the growing diversity of the Asian population, which included Koreans, Thais, and large numbers of Pacific Islanders. Filipinos, for instance, organized to educate themselves and other Americans about the destructive role of U.S.-backed Philippine dictator Ferdinand Marcos. Students from South Korea similarly formed solidarity circles in which they denounced their own repressive homeland government. Samoans sought to publicize the damage caused by nuclear testing in the Pacific Islands.

Like the Black Power and Latino movements, Asian American organizations embraced a nationalism that emphasized ethnic pride and cultural survival. Groups such as the Asian American Students Union, founded in 1971, fostered collective identity. Lane Nishikawa, actor, writer, and director in the Asian American Theatre Company, pleaded:

> Asian American
> is in the heart
> search for it
> in your soul

Artists, writers, documentary filmmakers, oral historians, and anthropologists sought to recover the Asian American past. They encouraged young writers like Frank Chin and Maxine Hong Kingston, whose works of fiction found large audiences both inside and outside the Asian American community. After generations of discrimination, these activists had begun to forge a transnational identity with roots in the many homelands and varied cultures of Asia.

The groups organized for the purpose of collective pride had spotlighted the nation's cultural diversity as a source of energy and political potential. They initiated a movement that would continue to grow through the next two decades of mainly conservative rule, broadening the content of films, television programs, and popular music. In the 1980s, the politics of multiculturalism would prevail, for example, in reviews of educational curriculum at all levels and in all regions of the country.

The politics of identity also had its limitations, which its numerous critics were quick to underscore. *Chicanismo,* for instance, celebrated distinctly masculine themes in the culture of Mexican Americans, provoking Chicana feminists to invoke alternative myths and to create their own voice within the larger Chicano movement. The appeal to Asian American identity likewise blurred the differences among individual ethnic groups, such as Koreans, Chinese, Japanese, and Filipinos.

Almost immediately, the movement, especially the actions of those groups organized for women's and gay liberation, generated a major political backlash expressed vividly at the polls in 1968. The Republican presidential contender, Richard Milhous Nixon, deftly built on voter hostility toward the young militants. His community, he insisted, represented the "Silent Majority."

THE NIXON PRESIDENCY

The silent majority, according to Republican strategists, comprised those Americans who worked, paid taxes, and did not protest. The campaign therefore targeted those voters tired of domestic unrest and eager to see order restored. Yet Richard Nixon himself proved far less conservative than his challengers for the party's presidential nomination, Arizona senator Barry Goldwater and new California governor Ronald Reagan. In order to achieve peace at home, Nixon reasoned that he would have to accede to some of the protesters' demands.

As president, Nixon ordered unprecedented illegal government action against private citizens, while agreeing with Congress to enhance several welfare programs and improve environmental protection. He widened and intensified the war in Vietnam, yet made stunning moves toward detente with the People's Republic of China. An architect of the Cold War, Nixon became the first president to foresee its end. In several ways, he disappointed the silent majority, finding a middle course — until he brought himself down.

The Nixon Consensus

In a carefully staged event during the 1968 Republican campaign, a young woman held up to television cameras a sign greeting candidate Nixon: "Bring Us Together." Recovering from defeats for the presidency in 1960 and the governorship of California in 1962, Nixon declared himself the one leader who could restore order and stability to the nation. Republican leaders also recognized the growing electoral importance of the Sunbelt, where populations grew with the rise of high-tech industries and retirement colonies. A powerful conservatism dominated this region, home to a large number of military bases, defense plants, and an increasingly influential Protestant evangelism. Making it Republican presidential country, (even when voters continued to elect local Democrats) would overcome the advantages the Democrats had held since the New Deal.

Nixon the Californian selected as his running mate Maryland governor Spiro Agnew, considered tough on crime and popular in the South. Agnew treated dissent as near treason. He attacked intellectual critics as "an effect corps of impudent snobs" and blasted liberal newscasters as "nattering nabobs of negativism."

The 1968 campaign underscored the antiliberal sentiment of the voting public. The most dramatic example was the relative success of Governor George Wallace's third-party bid for the presidency. Wallace took state office in 1963 promising white Alabamans "segregation now . . . segregation tomorrow . . . segregation forever." In 1968 he waged a national campaign around a conservative hate list that included school busing, antiwar demonstrations, and the urban uprisings. His running mate in the American Independent party, retired air force general Curtis LeMay, proposed the use of nuclear weapons in Vietnam. Winning only five southern states, Wallace nevertheless captured 13.5 percent of the popular vote and gave voice to the growing backlash against dissent.

Democrat Hubert Humphrey not only gave up the South to Wallace and Nixon but also the white northern voters who had become disenchanted with the party of FDR, Truman, and Kennedy. Rallying toward the end of the campaign by promising a cease-fire in Vietnam, Humphrey still lost more than 15 million voters from the Democratic rolls of 1964.

1968

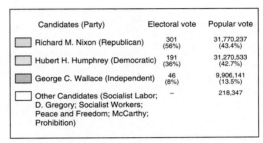

Candidates (Party)	Electoral vote	Popular vote
Richard M. Nixon (Republican)	301 (56%)	31,770,237 (43.4%)
Hubert H. Humphrey (Democratic)	191 (36%)	31,270,533 (42.7%)
George C. Wallace (Independent)	46 (8%)	9,906,141 (13.5%)
Other Candidates (Socialist Labor; D. Gregory; Socialist Workers; Peace and Freedom; McCarthy; Prohibition)	–	218,347

Election of 1968
Although the Republican Nixon-Agnew team won the popular vote by only a small margin, the Democrats lost in most of the northern states that had voted Democratic since the days of FDR. Segregationist Governor George Wallace of Alabama polled over 9 million votes.

The Nixon-Agnew team squeaked to victory, capturing the popular vote by the slim margin of 43.4 percent to Humphrey and Maine senator Edmund Muskie's 42.7 percent but taking nearly all the West's electoral votes. Bitterly divided by the campaign, the Democrats would remain out of presidential contention for decades, except when the Republicans suffered scandal and disgrace. United by victory, Republicans began their era of triumph under "King Richard," as critics called the new president.

Nixon's War

During his campaign, Nixon told journalists he hoped the Soviet Union would help him negotiate with North Vietnam; if not, he had a secret plan that

The Southeast Asian War

The Indo-Chinese sub-continent, home to long-standing regional conflict, became the center of a prolonged war with the United States.

was bound to bring "peace with honor." Despite this pledge, the war raged for four more years before a peace settlement was reached.

Much of the responsibility for the prolonged conflict rested with Henry A. Kissinger. A dominating personality on the National Security Council, Kissinger insisted that the United States could not retain its global leadership by appearing weak to either allies or enemies. "However we got into Vietnam," he wrote in 1969, the United States "cannot accept a military defeat, or a change in the political structure of South Vietnam brought about by external military forces. . . ." Brilliant and ruthless, the secretary of state overpowered Cabinet members who had concluded that Nixon could not continue to rally support for the unpopular war.

In public Nixon followed a plan of "phased withdrawal" of American troops, announcing on May 14, 1969, a program of "Vietnamization." At a time soon "approaching," the president promised, "South Vietnamese forces will be able to take over some of the fighting fronts now being manned by Americans." But after several months of Vietnamization, the ability of the South Vietnamese to hold their own against the North remained in question. In private, with Kissinger's guidance, Nixon mulled over the option of a "knockout blow" to Hanoi.

On April 30, 1970, Nixon made one of the most controversial decisions of his presidency. Adding Cambodia to the war zone, he ordered U.S. military personnel to bomb and invade the tiny nation. Within a few days American troops had ravaged large jungle areas, turning them into almost lifeless deserts. Nixon had hoped in this way to end North Vietnamese infiltration into the South, but he had also decided to live up to what he privately called his "wild man" or "mad bomber" reputation. The enemy would be unable to anticipate the location or severity of the next U.S. strike, Nixon reasoned, and would thus feel compelled to negotiate.

Nixon could not have predicted the outpouring of protest that followed the invasion of Cambodia. The largest series of demonstrations and police-student confrontations in the nation's history filled campuses and city streets. At Kent State University in Ohio, twenty-eight National Guardsmen apparently panicked. Shooting into an unarmed crowd, they killed four and injured nine more. Ten days later, on May 14, at Jackson State University, a black school in Mississippi, state troopers entered a campus dormitory and began shooting wildly, killing two students and wounding nine others.

The nation was shocked. Thirty-seven college and university presidents signed a letter calling

In view of the developments since we entered the fighting in Vietnam, do you think the United States made a mistake sending troops to fight in Vietnam?

Yes	52%
No	39
No opinion	9

Interviewing Date 1/22–28/1969, Survey #774–K, Question #6/Index #45

Public Opinion on the War in Vietnam
By 1969 Americans were sharply divided in their assessments of the progress of the war and peace negotiations. The American Institute of Public Opinion, founded in 1935 by George Gallup, charted a growing dissatisfaction with the war in Vietnam.

Source: *The Gallup Poll: Public Opinion, 1935–1974* (New York. Random House, 1974), p. 2189.

upon the president to end the war. A few weeks later the Senate adopted a bipartisan resolution outlawing the use of funds for U.S. military operations in Cambodia, starting July 1, 1970. Although the House rejected the resolution, Nixon saw the writing on the wall. He had planned to demand a simultaneous withdrawal of North Vietnamese and U.S. troops, but could no longer afford to hold out for this condition. Domestic pressure for an end to the war grew well beyond its 1968 level. Finally, on November 3, 1970, Nixon announced plans for a gradual withdrawal of U.S. ground troops.

The president, still goaded by Kissinger, did not accept defeat easily. In February 1971, Nixon directed the South Vietnamese army to invade Laos and cut guerrilla supply lines, but the demoralized invading force suffered a quick and humiliating defeat. Faced with enemy occupation of more and more territory during a major offensive in April 1972, Nixon ordered the mining of North Vietnamese harbors and directed B-52s on massively destructive bombing missions in Cambodia and North Vietnam.

Nixon also sent Kissinger to Paris for secret negotiations with delegates from North Vietnam. They agreed to a cease-fire specifying the withdrawal of all U.S. troops and the return of all U.S. prisoners of war. Knowing these terms ensured defeat, South Vietnam's president refused to sign the agreement. On Christmas Day 1972, hoping for a better negotiating position, Nixon ordered one final wave of bomb attacks on North Vietnam's cities. To secure a halt to the bombing, the North Vietnamese offered to resume negotiations. But the terms of the Paris Peace Agreement, signed by North Vietnam

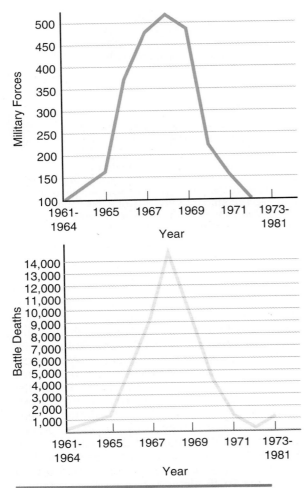

U.S. Military Forces in Vietnam and Casualties, 1961–1981

The United States government estimated battle deaths between 1969–1973 for South Vietnamese troops at 107,504 and North Vietnamese and Viet Cong at more than a half million. Although the United States suffered fewer deaths, the cost was enormous.

Source: U.S. Dept. of Defense, *Selected Manpower Statistics*, annual, and unpublished data; beginning 1981, National Archives and Records Service, "Combat Area Casualty File," (3–330–80–3).

and the United States in January 1973, differed little from the settlement Nixon could have procured in 1969. Moreover, the future political status of South Vietnam, the question for which the war had been fought, was no longer in doubt. The government of South Vietnam had no future.

In April 1975 North Vietnamese troops took over Saigon, and the Communist-led Democratic Republic of Vietnam soon united the small nation. The war was finally over. It had cost the U.S. 58,000 lives and $150 billion. The United States had not only failed to achieve its stated war goal but had lost an important post in Southeast Asia. Equally important, the policy of containment introduced by Truman had proved impossible to sustain.

While Nixon was maneuvering to bring about "peace with honor," the chilling crimes of war had already begun to haunt Americans. In 1971 the army court-martialed a young lieutenant, William L. Calley, Jr., for the murder of "at least" twenty-two Vietnamese civilians during a March 1968 search-and-destroy mission subsequently known as the My Lai Massacre. Calley's platoon had destroyed a village and slaughtered more than 350 unarmed South Vietnamese, raping and beating many of the women before killing them. "My Lai was not an isolated incident," one veteran attested, but "only a minor step beyond the standard official United States policy in Indochina." Commander of the platoon at My Lai, Calley was first sentenced to life imprisonment before given a reduced term of ten years. The secretary of the army paroled Calley after he served three years in house arrest in his apartment.

The "China Card"

Apart from Vietnam, Nixon's foreign policy defied the expectations of liberals and conservatives alike. Actually, he followed traditions of previous Republican moderates such as Herbert Hoover and Dwight Eisenhower, who had so effectively "proved" their anticommunism that they could conciliate international foes without denting their popularity at home. He added a new page, however, with the Nixon Doctrine, a policy of détente that replaced U.S.-Soviet bipolarity with multilateral relations. Nixon could cultivate relations with the People's Republic of China, a rising world power more rigidly Communist than the Soviet Union, to form an alliance against the USSR. And he could easily persuade the Soviet Union to cooperate on trade agreements, thus limiting the two nation's ruthless competition to control governments in Asia, Africa, and the Middle East. Opponents of the Vietnam War accused Nixon of double dealing, while conservatives howled at any compromise with Communist governments. But Nixon persisted in his plans, anticipating an end to the Cold War on American terms.

Playing the "China card" was the most dramatic

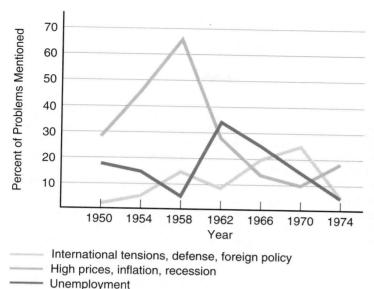

International tensions, defense, foreign policy

High prices, inflation, recession

Unemployment

Public Perceptions of the Most Important Problems Facing the United States, 1948–1989

The tensions surrounding the war in Vietnam superseded concerns for domestic issues, especially the economy. Following the end of the war and decline in military spending, Americans would once again turn their attention to economic issues, especially the high cost of living.

Source: Theodore Caplow, et al., *Recent Social Trends in the United States, 1960–1990* (Frankfurt: Campus Verlag, 1991), p. 541.

of Nixon's moves. Early in his political career he had avidly supported the arch-conservative China lobby. But as president he considered the People's Republic of China too important to be isolated by the West and too obviously hostile to the Soviet Union to be discounted as a potential ally. "If there is anything I want to do before I die," he confided to a *Time* magazine reporter, "it is to go to China."

"Ping pong diplomacy" began in April 1971, when the Chinese hosted a table tennis team from the United States. Henry Kissinger embarked on a secret mission a few months later. Finally, in February 1972 Richard and Pat Nixon flew to Beijing, where they were greeted by foreign minister Zhou Enlai and a band playing "The Star-Spangled Banner."

It was a momentous event, one that marked a new era in East-West diplomacy. The move increased diplomatic pressure on the Soviets, but did not halt their support of North Vietnam. The Nationalist Chinese government in Taiwan, so long supported by Nixon's Californian sponsors, slipped into virtual diplomatic obscurity.

Next the president arrived in Moscow to negotiate with Soviet leader Leonid Brezhnev, who was anxious about U.S. involvement with China and eager for economic assistance. Declaring, "There must be room in this world for two great nations with different systems to live together and work

together," Nixon offered to sell $1 billion of grain to the Soviets. Winning the favor of American wheat farmers, this deal simultaneously relieved U.S. trade deficits and crop surpluses. Afterward, the Soviet leader became visibly more cautious about supporting revolutions in the Third World. Nixon also negotiated the Strategic Arms Limitation Treaty (SALT, known later as SALT I). A measure that controlled the pace or direction of arms spending rather than reducing production, SALT I represented either a small move toward disarmament or a public relations victory for the leaders of the two superpowers.

Nixon's last major diplomatic foray proved far less effective. The president sent Kissinger on a two-year mission of "shuttle diplomacy" to mediate Israeli-Arab disputes, to ensure the continued flow of oil, and to increase lucrative U.S. arms sales to Arab countries. The Egyptians and Israelies agreed to a cease-fire to their October 1973 Yom Kippur War, but little progress toward peace in the area was achieved.

Domestic Policy

Nixon deeply desired to restore order in American society. "We live in a deeply troubled and profoundly unsettled time," he noted. "Drugs, crime, campus revolts, racial discord, draft resistance — on every hand we find old standards violated, old values discarded." Despite his philosophical hostility to liberalism, however, Nixon had some surprises for conservatives. Determined to win reelection in 1972, he supported new Social Security benefits and subsidized housing for the poor and oversaw the creation of the Environmental Protection Agency and the Occupational Safety and Health Administration. Most notable was his 1969 Family Assistance Plan, guided by Democratic adviser Daniel P. Moynihan, which proposed a minimal income (as little as $1,600) for the poor in place of welfare benefits. Nixon was spurred by a Democratic-dominated House and Senate but appeared genuinely willing to ease social tensions through government assistance programs. Conservatives judged Nixon's proposals for the Family Assistance Plan (FAP) too generous while liberals found them inadequate, and the bill died a bipartisan death.

After seeing his attempts to pursue conservative monetary policy lead to a severe recession, Nixon lunged toward fiscal liberalism. Early in 1971 he accepted the idea of deficit spending. Later that year he ordered a first: the dollar's value would float on the world market rather than being tied to the value of gold. His ninety-day freeze on wages, rents, and prices, designed to halt the inflation caused by massive spending on the Vietnam War, also closely resembled Democratic policies. Finally, Nixon's support of "black capitalism" — adjustments or quotas favoring minority contractors in construction projects — created an explosive precedent for set-aside programs later blamed on liberals.

Nixon lined up with conservatives, however, on most civil rights and civil libertarian issues. He accepted the principle of school integration but bitterly rejected the busing programs required to implement racial balance. His nominees to the Supreme Court, far more conservative than Eisenhower's, were known for their support of police authority. Warren Burger, whom the president appointed to replace Chief Justice Earl Warren, steered the Court away from the liberal direction it had taken since the 1950s.

One of the most noteworthy events of the Nixon years had little to do with domestic or foreign policy: it was interplanetary. The distant result of President Kennedy's determination to outshine the Soviets in outer space (see Chapter 27) climaxed on July 21, 1969, when the lunar module of *Apollo 11* descended to the moon's Sea of Tranquility. As millions watched on television, Neil Armstrong stepped onto the surface and with fellow astronaut Buzz Aldrin placed an American flag bearing the message "We came in peace for all mankind."

WATERGATE

At times Richard Nixon expressed his yearning for the consensus associated with the Eisenhower era in strange ways. The weekend following the bombing of Cambodia in May 1970, he wandered out of the White House alone at 5 a.m. to talk to antiwar demonstrators. He tried to engage them in small talk about football and pleaded, "I know that probably most of you think I'm an SOB, but I want you to know I understand just how you feel." According to H. R. Haldeman, one of his closest advisers, the killings at Kent State had pushed the president over the edge.

Yet only a few months later Nixon ordered illegal wiretaps of news professionals. He also reaffirmed his support of CIA surveillance of US citizens and organizations — a policy specifically forbidden by the CIA charter — and encouraged members of his administration to spy on Democrats planning for the 1972 election campaign. When news of these extralegal activities surfaced, one of the most canny politicians in American history found himself the first president since Andrew Johnson to face the likelihood of impeachment proceedings. The inner secrets of a clique at the center of the world's greatest power became headline stories for months on end.

Foreign Policy as Conspiracy

Although Nixon welcomed the publicity surrounding his historic moves toward détente with the Soviet Union and normalized relations with China, he continued to conduct the bulk of the nation's foreign affairs in surreptitious fashion. But as dissent over the Vietnam War spread from campuses into Congress, he began to face mounting opposition to long-standing procedures. By 1970 congressional liberals, Republican as well as Democrat, were challenging covert operations in foreign countries. In response, the president, the Department of State, and the CIA developed plans to tighten security even further. Nixon issued a tough mandate against all leaks of information by government personnel, news specialists, or politicians.

At the time, apart from the highly publicized

tour to China, Nixon revealed little about his policy for other parts of the globe. Unknown to most Americans, he accelerated arms supplies to foreign dictators, including the shah of Iran, Ferdinand Marcos of the Philippines, and the Botha regime of South Africa. His CIA assistants trained and aided SAVAK, the Iranian secret police force notorious for torturing political dissidents. They also stood behind the South African government in its effort to curtail the activities of the antiapartheid African National Congress. In Latin American, Nixon provided financial assistance and military aid to repressive regimes such as that of Anastazio Somoza of Nicaragua, notorious for its blatant corruption and repeated violations of human rights.

Still more controversial was Nixon's plan to overthrow the legally elected Socialist government of Salvador Allende in Chile. With the assistance of nongovernment agencies, such as the AFL–CIO's American Institute for Free Labor Development, the CIA destabilized the regime by funding right-wing parties, launching demonstrations, and preparing the Chilean army for a coup. In September 1973, a military junta killed President Allende and captured, tortured, or murdered thousands of his supporters. Nixon and Kissinger warmly welcomed the new ruler, Augusto Pinochet, granting him financial assistance to restabilize the country.

Toward the end of Nixon's term, members of Congress who had been briefed on these policies began to break silence, and reports of clandestine operations flooded the media. Several former CIA agents issued anguished confessions of their activities in other countries. More troubling to Nixon, in spite of all his efforts the United States continued to lose ground as a superpower.

The Age of Dirty Tricks

As Nixon approached the 1972 re-election campaign, he tightened his inner circle of White House staff who assisted him in withholding information from the public, discrediting critics, and engaging in assorted "dirty tricks." Circle members solicited illegal contributions for the campaign and laundered the money through Mexican bank accounts. They also formed a secret squad, "the plumbers," to halt the troublesome leaks of information. This team, headed by former CIA agent E. Howard Hunt and former FBI agent G. Gordon Liddy, assisted in conspiracy at the highest levels of government.

The first person on the squad's "hit list" was

Daniel Ellsburg, a former researcher with the Department of Defense who in 1971 had turned over to the press secret documents outlining the military history of American involvement in Vietnam. The so-called *Pentagon Papers* exposed the role of presidents and military leaders in deceiving the public and Congress about the conduct of the United States in Southeast Asia. Nixon sought to bar publication by the *New York Times,* but the Supreme Court ruled in favor of the newspaper on the basis of the First Amendment. Within weeks, a complete version of the *Pentagon Papers* became a best-selling book, and in 1972 the *New York Times* won a Pulitzer Prize for the series of articles. Frustrated in his attempt to suppress the report, Nixon directed the Department of Justice to prosecute Ellsberg on charges of conspiracy, espionage, and theft. Meanwhile, Hunt and Liddy, seeking to discredit Ellsberg, broke into the office of his former psychiatrist. They found nothing that would make their target less heroic in the eyes of an increasingly skeptical public, and by 1973 the charges against Ellsberg were dropped after the Nixon administration itself stood guilty of misconduct.

The next undercover operation took place against the background of the 1972 presidential campaign. Nixon ran a skillful negative campaign charging George McGovern, the liberal Democrat who had won his party's nomination on the first ballot, with supporting "abortion, acid [LSD] and amnesty [for those who had resisted the draft or deserted the armed forces]." The Republicans also informed the news media that McGovern's running mate, Senator Thomas Eagleton, had once undergone electric shock therapy for depression, thus forcing his resignation from the Democratic team. Voter turnout fell to an all-time low, and McGovern lost every state but one. It was only later that bumper stickers read, "Don't Blame me, I'm from Massachusetts."

The Committee to Re-Elect the President (CREEP) enjoyed a huge war chest and spent a good portion on dirty tricks designed to divide the Democrats and discredit them in the eyes of the voting public. The most ambitious plan — wiretapping the Democratic National Committee headquarters — backfired.

On June 17, 1972, a security team had trippd up a group of intruders hired by CREEP to install listening devices in the Washington, D.C., Watergate apartment and office complex where the Democrats were headquartered. The police arrested five men, who were later found guilty of conspiracy and burglary. Although Nixon disclaimed any knowledge of the plan, two Washington Post reporters, Bob Woodward and Carl Bernstein, assiduously followed a trail of evidence back to the nation's highest office.

Televised Senate hearings opened to public view more than a pattern of presidential wrongdoing: an attempt to impede investigations of the Watergate case. Testifying before the committee, a former Nixon aide revealed the existence of secret tape recordings of conversations held in the Oval Office. After special prosecutor Archibald Cox refused to allow Nixon to claim executive privilege and withhold the tapes, the president ordered Cox's firing. This "Saturday Night Massacre," as it came to be called, further tarnished Nixon's reputation and swelled curiosity about the tapes. On June 24, 1974, the Supreme Court voted unanimously that Nixon had to release the tapes to a new special prosecutor, Leon Jaworski.

The Fall of the Executive

The case against the president had solidified. Although incomplete, the Watergate tapes proved sufficiently damning. The surviving portions documented Nixon's ravings against his enemies, including anti-Semitic slurs, and his conniving efforts to harass private citizens through federal agencies. The tapes also proved that Nixon had not only known about plans to cover-up the Watergate break-in but had ordered it. The news media enjoyed a field day with the revelations. In July, 1974, the House Judiciary Committee adopted three articles of impeachment, charging Nixon with obstructing justice.

Charges of executive criminality had clouded

Richard Nixon bid a final farewell to his White House staff as he left Washington, D.C., in August, 1974. The first president to resign from office, Nixon had become so entangled in the Watergate scandal that his impeachment appeared certain. He was succeeded by Vice-President Gerald Ford, who appears in the foreground.

the Nixon administration since his vice-president had resigned in disgrace. In 1972 Spiro Agnew had admitted accepting large kick-backs while governor of Maryland. Pleading no contest to this and to charges of federal income tax evasion, Agnew resigned from office in October, 1973. Gerald Ford, a moderate Republican representative from Michigan, had replaced him, and now stood in the wings while the president himself faced final judgment.

Facing certain impeachment by the House of Representatives, Richard Nixon became, on August 9, 1974, the first president to resign from office.

Conclusion

The resignations of Richard Nixon and Spiro Agnew brought little relief to the feeling of national exhaustion that attended the Vietnam War. Although the war officially ended in 1975, the accompanying mood did not dissipate but merely changed form. Bitterness lingered over the unprecedented — and, for many, humiliating — defeat. Moreover, confidence in the government's highest office was severely shaken. The dream of community that had inspired Johnson, King, and a generation of student activists could not be revived. No other vision took its place.

In 1968 seven prominent antiwar protesters had been brought to trial for allegedly conspiring to disrupt the Democratic National Convention in Chicago. Just a few years later, the majority of Americans had concluded that presidents Johnson and Nixon had conspired to do far worse. They had intentionally deceived the public about the nature and fortunes of the war. This moral failure signaled a collapse at the center of the American political system. Since Dwight Eisenhower left office warning of the potential danger imbedded in the "military-industrial complex," no elected president had finished a term with his dignity intact. Watergate, then, appeared to cap the post-Eisenhower era, its revelations imparting a legacy of futility and cynicism.

CHRONOLOGY

1964	Tonkin Gulf resolution passes Congress Johnson elected president Free speech movement at University of California at Berkeley
1965	Malcolm X assassinated Johnson authorizes Operation Rolling Thunder First teach-ins held on college campuses First major march on Washington for peace Watts uprising César Chavez leads strike of farm workers in San Joaquin Valley
1966	J. William Fulbright, *The Arrogance of Power* Uprisings in several cities Black Panthers formed National Organization for Women (NOW) formed
1967	486,000 U.S. ground troops in Vietnam Antiwar rally in New York City draws 500,000 Vietnam Veterans against the War formed Uprisings in Newark, Detroit, and other cities "Summer of Love" U.S. supports Israel in Six-Day War against Egypt
1968	Tet offensive in Vietnam, followed by international protests against U.S. policies Martin Luther King, Jr., Robert Kennedy assassinated Democratic National Convention, held in Chicago, nominates Hubert Humphrey Vietnam peace talks begin in Paris Richard Nixon elected president American Indian Movement (AIM) founded
1969	Woodstock music festival Stonewall Riot in Greenwich Village U.S. moon landing
1970	U.S. incursion into Cambodia brings campus demonstrations; students killed at Kent State and Jackson State universities
1971	*Pentagon Papers* published Court-martial of Lieutenant William Calley, Jr.
1972	President Nixon visits China and Soviet Union Watergate break-in during successful Nixon reelection campaign FBI seizes Indian occupants of Wounded Knee, South Dakota Christmas Day bombing of North Vietnam
1973	Vice-President Spiro Agnew resigns Watergate burglars on trial; congressional hearings on Watergate Elected Chilean government overthrown Vietnam cease-fire signed
1974	House Judiciary Committee votes to impeach Nixon Nixon resigns

Additional Readings

Loren Baritz, *Backfire: A History of How American Culture Led Us into Vietnam and Made Us Fight the Way We Did* (1985). A keen study of U.S. military policies and dissent within the military during the Vietnam War. Shows how decisions for aggressive military policies in Vietnam divided poorer young men from their middle- and upper-class counterparts by sending to war those who did not or could not manage deferments. Analyzes the increasing bitterness toward the government and the military by the men who fought the war.

Morris Dickstein, *Gates of Eden: American Culture in the Sixties* (1977). An overview of the rise and fall of the counterculture. Examines the intersection of culture and politics in the youth movements of the 1960s.

Sara Evans, *Personal Politics: The Roots of Women's Liberation in the Civil Rights Movement and the New left* (1979). Traces the origins of the women's liberation movement to protests by African American women involved in the civil rights movement of the early 1960s. Examines the formation of feminist politics within the New Left and the move by radical women to form their own organizations in the late 1960s. Based on personal interviews with participants.

Todd Gitlin, *The Sixties: Years of Hope, Days of Rage* (1987). A political view of the protest movements. Outlines the sharp difference between the peaceful antiwar movement of the middle 1960s and the destructive turn of the student movements at the end of that decade.

George C. Herring, *America's Longest War: The United States and Vietnam, 1950–1975* (2d ed., 1986). A narrative account, including a chapter on the legacy of the war. Attempts to demonstrate that diplomatic policy was based on flawed assumptions that made the war unwinnable at a moral or material cost most Americans could accept.

Neil Sheehan, *A Bright Shining Lie: John Paul Vann and America in Vietnam* (1988). A study of U.S. government deception of the public, perpetrated with greater and greater intensity as the Vietnam War grew worse. Emphasizes the ways in which prowar messages played upon false images of a noble and committed South Vietnamese government and a military force always on the verge of defeating an unpopular enemy.

Athan Theoharis, *Spying on Americans* (1978). A sweeping view of 1960s and early-1970s FBI and CIA investigations and dirty tricks against dissidents. Shows that the application of illegal spy methods against Americans was not an aberrant policy of lower-level government, but a decision made at the very top levels.

William L. Van Deburg, *New Day in Babylon: The Black Power Movement and American Culture, 1965–1975* (1992). A lively, well-researched study of the transformation of racial consciousness among African Americans.

Bob Woodward and Carl Bernstein, *The Final Days* (1976). Journalistic accounts of the Watergate cover-up by the news team that broke the first stories. Traces the series of events that led to the resignation of President Nixon.

Marilyn B. Young, *The Vietnam Wars, 1945–1990* (1991). An excellent overview of French and American military and diplomatic involvement in Vietnam from the 1910s to 1975, and of the various movements against them. Highlights the nationalism of the Vietnamese as ultimately more powerful than the troops and weaponry of their opponents.

30 THE OVEREXTENDED SOCIETY, 1974–1980

American Communities

• Three Mile Island, Pennsylvania

On Wednesday, March 28, 1979, a series of mechanical problems and judgment errors at the nuclear generating facility at Three Mile Island (TMI), near Harrisburg, Pennsylvania, caused the loss of a reactor's protective blanket of water. As much as two-thirds of the nuclear core was uncovered, causing the formation of a dangerous hydrogen bubble and a massive release of radioactive gas into the atmosphere. The plant director declared a site emergency and reported a "slight problem" to the governor at 7:40 a.m. By 9:00 a.m. President Jimmy Carter had been notified. The Associated Press issued a national news bulletin announcing a general emergency but stating that no radiation had been released. On Wednesday and Thursday Metropolitan Edison, which ran the TMI facility, denied the existence of any danger.

A COMMUNITY RESPONDS TO A NEAR DISASTER

At 8:00 a.m. on Friday, when a higher-than-anticipated radiation level above a vent was recorded, staff at the Nuclear Regulatory Commission suggested an evacuation of people living near the plant. Fearing panic, the governor urged residents within ten miles of TMI to stay indoors with their windows shut. Pregnant women and preschool children within five miles of the facility were advised to leave the area. Federal officials ordered massive doses of potassium iodide — which, taken orally, saturates the thyroid gland and inhibits the absorption of radiation — shipped to Pennsylvania. The mayor of nearby Middletown later recalled:

> Friday was the day. . . . A lot of the kids thought about dying and wrote their last wills and testaments. Fifth and sixth grade kids! People were concerned. You could tell they were afraid because a lot of people who left town left their doors wide open, unlocked. They just put anything in the car and took off. . . . I had a bus set up in front of City Hall for pregnant women. But heck, most of the people who were in that condition left themselves.

Meanwhile, national television transformed the local event into an international drama. The world watched, as one newscaster put it, while "the danger faced by man for tampering with natural forces, a theme familiar from the myth of Prometheus to the story of Frankenstein, moved closer to fact from fantasy." To show their personal concern, the governor of Pennsylvania, President Carter, and Rosalynn Carter all bravely visited the site.

Radioactive gases released by an accident at the Three Mile Island nuclear generating plant in 1979 prompted residents of nearby Goldsboro, Pennsylvania, to mind the governor's warnings to stay indoors. The plant's cooling towers loom over the seemingly deserted community. Although the Nuclear Regulatory Commission, after investigating the incident, concluded that the amount of radioactivity released posed no health threat, antinuclear power activists and many residents denied this claim.

On Monday, April 9, ten days after recommending evacuation, Pennsylvania governor Richard Thornburgh announced that the danger of a meltdown had passed. The Nuclear Regulatory Commission, equally eager to end the crisis, reported that the size of the hydrogen bubble had decreased. The next day the NRC described the situation as stable, the danger of explosion over.

What had seemed an isolated event in one community grew quickly into a regional phenomenon with national repercussions. During the crisis, millions of people living downwind in the eastern states stayed glued to their televisions or radios, anxiously awaiting further developments. Ten days after the near meltdown, elevated levels of radioactivity were found in milk supplies as far away as New York City. People throughout the mid-Atlantic area worried for months about the wholesomeness of dairy products, meat, vegetables, and even jams or jellies coming from the central Pennsylvania agricultural region. Closer to TMI, more than 1,000 people became involved in legal claims of mental or physical harm. Protests and lawsuits against the plant's reopening continued for years, and its owner, General Public Utilities, teetered toward bankruptcy. Although steadfast proponents of nuclear energy argued that the events at TMI demonstrated that safety had prevailed even at the moment of the worst potential crisis, the scales had been tipped in favor of those who opposed it.

The events at Three Mile Island capped a wave of community-style political mobilization against nuclear power. Several years earlier, when a less serious accident at Brown's Ferry, Alabama, raised serious questions about safety, public support of nuclear generating plants began to dwindle. Broad coalitions, ranging from conservatives to liberals, from rural landowners to urban renters, formed to keep their communities safe from danger. Labeled NIMBYs (Not in My Backyard), community groups defeated referendums to fund new facilities or rallied around candidates sworn to shut down existing ones. If fewer communities wanted nuclear generating plants, fewer still were eager to accept the radioactive wastes created by the process of making electricity.

The economy itself helped slow the development of new plants. At the time of the TMI crisis, over seventy generating plants had been built, producing altogether about 13 percent of the nation's electrical energy. Of the ninety-six still under construction and the thirty more planned, only a handful would ever be completed. The Shoreham plant, built on Long Island, New York, was never put into operation. New York City and regional authorities blocked its testing and courts agreed to mothball the project. News of faulty construction and building-cost overruns sometimes topping 1,000 percent, or hundreds of millions of dollars, made local governments hesitant to back new projects.

Many Americans woke from the dream of unlimited, inexpensive, and safe nuclear energy and lowered their expectations. To its promoters during the 1950s, nuclear energy had promised a supply of power so cheap that utility companies could "turn off the meter" on costs. Communities would bask in prosperity, advancing as quickly and dramatically as towns and cities had grown with the introduction of electricity seventy-five years earlier. Unguardedly optimistic as late as 1974, President Nixon predicted that by 1980 the United States would be totally free of its dependence on foreign energy sources. But life in the United States during the 1970s disappointed experts and ordinary citizens alike, shattering these dreams of unsurpassed abundance. Now faced with diminished financial assets, environmental disasters, discredited political leaders, and international defeats, many Americans uneasily and uncomfortably experienced the contraction of a society that had grown too large for its own resources. As the Cold War wound down, the battle for energy sources became the new national passion.

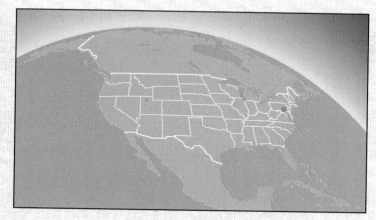

Americans in the 1970s faced an unfamiliar combination of skyrocketing prices, rising unemployment, and low economic growth. Economists termed this novel condition *stagflation*. Annual economic growth sunk almost one-quarter from its robust 3.2 percent average of the 1950s. By 1975 unemployment had reached nearly 9 percent, the highest since the Great Depression, and it remained close to 7 percent for most of the rest of the decade. Inflation, meanwhile, reached double-digit numbers.

The United States had reached a turning point in its economic history. Emerging from World War II as the strongest nation in the world and retaining this status through the 1960s, the country suddenly found itself falling behind Western Europe and Japan. The standard of living in the United States dropped to fifth place worldwide (below that of Denmark, West Germany, Sweden, and Switzerland). Polls at the end of the 1970s revealed that a majority of Americans believed conditions would worsen. Faith in progress and prosperity, hallmark of the "American Century," wore thin.

In October 1973, American motorists were hit with a big surprise at the gas pumps. Gasoline prices nearly doubled, in some regions jumping from forty to nearly seventy cents per gallon. Worse, many dealers suddenly ran out of supplies. In New Jersey, gas lines ran four miles long. Fistfights broke out among frustrated motorists. Gas tank locks enjoyed brisk sales after thieves began to siphon fuel out of parked autos. Several states introduced rationing programs.

Although the energy crisis began suddenly, it had been decades in the making. Until the late 1950s, the United States, which used about 70 percent of all oil produced in the world, had found sufficient sources at home. The rising demand for oil, however, soon began to deplete national reserves and require more expensive methods of extracting oil. Even as domestic oil production peaked in 1968, the huge reserves beneath the sands of the Middle East were yielding to new, inexpensive technologies. Within five years the United States had become dependent on foreign oil, imports of which tripled to 36 percent of annual consumption.

O.P.E.C., 1973

In the 1950s Americans produced all the oil they needed. By 1973 the United States purchased one of every three barrels used at home from Arab or Venezuelan producers.

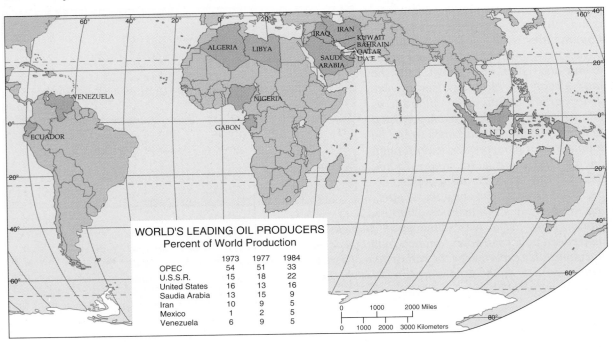

WORLD'S LEADING OIL PRODUCERS
Percent of World Production

	1973	1977	1984
OPEC	54	51	33
U.S.S.R.	15	18	22
United States	16	13	16
Saudia Arabia	13	15	9
Iran	10	9	5
Mexico	1	2	5
Venezuela	6	9	5

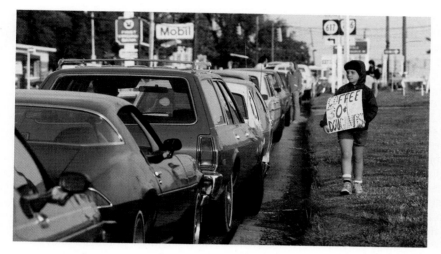

Motorists line up for gas during the oil crisis of 1973. On October 17. O.P.E.C. declared an embargo on the shipment of oil to nations that had allied with Israel during the Yom Kippur War. The embargo demonstrated the dependence of the United States on foreign oil and caused gas rationing, long lines at gas stations, and a sharp increase in consumer prices. Many motorists installed gas-cap locks for the first time in an attempt to thwart thieves who siphoned the precious fuel for themselves.

Prices nevertheless remained fairly stable until the escalation of political and military conflicts in the Middle East. Following the Six-Day War of 1967, Arabs became increasingly embittered at the United States and other Western nations that had assisted Israel. Finally the Organization of Petroleum Exporting Countries (OPEC), a cartel of mainly Arab oil producers that served as a bargaining agency for oil-rich nations, for the first time unilaterally declared an increase in world oil prices. The American-owned companies that extracted the bulk of Middle Eastern oil readily agreed to this price hike for their own reasons: their profits skyrocketed, despite higher export fees imposed by the Arab governments.

Then came the Yom Kippur War of 1973, so named because the Arab attack on Israel began at the start of the Jewish holy days. Renewed U.S. assistance to Israel, which broke a near stalemate between Israel and Arab military forces, humiliated and enraged Arab leaders. They quickly announced an embargo on shipments of oil to Israel's allies, mainly the United States, Europe, and Japan.

The embargo which extended from October 17, 1973, to March 18, 1974, sent a shock wave through the United States. American experts at first believed that Arab resolve would soon collapse and oil would once again flow freely. But only a few weeks later President Nixon delivered a dramatic televised address in which he announced "a very stark fact: We are heading toward the most acute shortage of energy since World War II." A newspaper headline declared, "Things Will Get Worse before They Get Worse." A crisis had emerged on the level of the threat of communism and the arms race.

Enraged American motorists usually blamed Arabs for skyrocketing prices at the gas pump, but they also looked suspiciously at their own energy companies. By 1978 almost 50 percent of those polled believed they were "just being told" a shortage existed as a pretext for raising prices. Skepticism grew as a congressional committee reported that Texaco Oil was withholding natural gas from the market, and that Gulf Oil had overstated its crude oil costs by $79.1 million, charging consumers wildly inflated prices. Whatever the cause, whoever the scapegoat, the energy crisis was the cataclysmic event of the decade.

The Bill Comes Due

President Nixon quickly responded to the embargo. He appointed William Simon "energy czar," paving the way for the creation of the Department of Energy in 1977. Nixon also claimed executive power to impose emergency energy conservation measures. He ordered air travel cut by 10 percent and appealed to Congress to lower speed limits on state highways to fifty-five miles per hour and to extend daylight-saving time into the winter months. State governments complied, turning down the thermostats in public buildings to sixty-eight degrees, reducing nonessential lighting, and restricting hours of service. Colleges and universities canceled midwinter sessions, and some factories voluntarily shortened the workday.

These conservation measures produced one unintended, positive result: a 23 percent reduction in highway deaths between 1973 and 1974 due to the lower speed limit. But children, meanwhile, returned home from school in the dark, workers shivered in their offices, and the poor and elderly succumbed to hypothermia in cold apartments.

Virtually all energy prices rose following the Arab oil embargo, reversing a century-old trend. Since its advent on the consumer market, electricity, for example, had fallen in relation to the overall cost of living nearly every decade. The low-cost days came to a sudden end, and electricity bills grew much higher for business and residential users alike.

With the cost of gasoline, oil, and electricity up, many other prices also rose, from apartment rents to telephone bills to restaurant checks. Inflation rose to 11 percent and assumed first place in a list of common worries, according to a 1974 poll; by 1980 it stood at 13.5 percent. The middle-class lifestyle that schoolteachers, secretaries, factory workers, and others had managed to create for themselves and their families on relatively modest incomes became harder to maintain; for young families it was often impossible to achieve. A San Francisco home-maker told a reporter, "I used to keep a budget, but it got so discouraging. I gave it up. The whole economic picture scares me. It's so unreal."

Falling Productivity

Many Americans had experienced the recessions of the 1950s, millions even remembered the Great Depression, but few were prepared to witness the death of entire sectors of basic industry. In Pennsylvania's Monongahela Valley, center of the U.S. steel industry since the 1880s, economic and psychological depression spread during the 1970s to blue-collar workers and managers alike. "The way they made steel was crummy," said a former U.S. Steel superintendent, "the way they operated was crummy, and the way they handled labor relations was crummy."

The problem, according to many experts, was not simply a result of dependence on foreign oil reserves. It had deeper roots — in the failure of American manufacturers to keep up with the rising industrial efficiency of Western Europe and Japan. As long as U.S. steelmakers faced scant competition from abroad, they had little incentive to update their machinery or to establish management techniques that fully utilized the skills of younger, more educated managers and workers. American companies could meet increased demands by producing more steel, but they could not fabricate *good* steel.

Japanese, Latin American, and European manufacturers offered consumers cheaper and better alternatives. Whereas the United States produced 60 percent of the world's steel in 1947, by 1975 American firms accounted for only 16 percent. Similar trends developed in related industries. Sales of foreign automobiles in the U.S., negligible in 1960, topped 15 percent in the early 1970s. Meanwhile, sales of American-made autos dropped by 11 million in 1973 and another 8 million in 1974. In 1977 more American cars were recalled for defects than were produced. By the end of the decade foreign manufacturers had also shattered the near monopoly the United States once enjoyed in the production of precision machine tools. In high-tech electronics, the United States scarcely competed against German- and especially Japanese-produced televisions, radios, tape players, cameras, and computers.

By the mid-1970s major American corporations had begun to devise their own strategies to combat falling profits. Rather than copy the new, highly automated General Motors plant in Lordstown, Ohio, which was designed to produce competitively priced small cars, other automakers turned to Mexico, Taiwan, South Korea, and the Philippines for cheaper labor. Growing percentages of automobiles were "outsourced" — that is, made from parts produced abroad and imported into the United States as semifinished materials (which were subject to a lower tariff than finished goods).

A few American corporations tried to improve their production capacities by adopting the model of labor-management relations developed by their foremost competitors. In giant Japanese firms a system of benefits and rewards gave employees a sense of security and offered them incentives for helping to improve the quality and speed of production. "Quality work life" circles — American versions of Japanese factory teams — experienced distinctly less success, however. Older workers interpreted new management programs as an attempt to replace unions, and few new workers believed they would derive significant material benefits from the system.

American industrial productivity continued to lag, increasing 1.4 percent between 1971 and 1975 and only 0.2 percent in the last half of the decade. The balance of trade tipped sharply toward the foreign countries that manufactured and exported better and cheaper products than U.S. firms. An AFL–CIO leader complained that the United States was becoming "a nation of hamburger stands. . . .

a country stripped of industrial capacity and meaningful work . . . a service economy . . . a nation of citizens busily buying and selling cheeseburgers and root beer floats.''

In agriculture, the situation was equally grim. Ironically, a shortage of grain in the Soviet Union, Egypt, and the Third World during the 1970s hiked agricultural prices and encouraged American farmers to raise their productivity sharply. But the huge increase in oil prices translated into higher gasoline and fertilizer costs, forcing farmers to borrow heavily from banks. Soon, the high rates on borrowed money caught many farmers in a downward-spiraling debt cycle.

When overseas sales declined at the end of the 1970s, tens of thousands of farmers defaulted on loans and lost their farms to banks and credit companies. These failures often ended a way of life generations in the making. A near majority of the remaining family farmers survived only through part-time jobs in town. They considered themselves fortunate if they could retire on the price offered by land developers who turned their farms into suburban housing. Continuing soil erosion, high costs, and unstable prices offered a gloomy prospect for all but the leaders in corporate-style agribusiness, the 12 percent of farmers who made 90 percent of all farm income.

Blue-Collar Blues

In past decades, labor unions had typically responded to inflation by negotiating new contracts or, if necessary, striking for higher pay. When successful, these actions elevated living standards for millions of additional workers, as nonunion employers often felt compelled to raise wages competitively. But by the 1970s new legislation and legal decisions had changed labor-management relations. The National Labor Relations Board, created during the 1930s to facilitate fair elections for union representation, increasingly ruled in favor of management, making the formation of new union locals far more difficult. Between 1970 and 1982 the AFL–CIO lost nearly 30 percent of its membership, and its political influence dipped accordingly. Labor-backed measures now routinely failed in Congress, despite the Democratic majority.

The only real growth in organized labor took place among public employees, including teachers, civil service workers, and health professionals. Their gains were, however, often less than expected.

During the 1970s local and state budgets sagged, due to rising costs, lower revenues from business, and most of all a growing unwillingness of voters to shoulder a bigger tax burden. Government workers themselves demanded higher wages and then voted against the tax hikes that would be levied on their own houses and automobiles.

The number of wage-earning women continued to grow during the 1970s, but without any significant improvement in their economic status. By 1980 more than half of all married women and nearly 60 percent of mothers with children between the ages of six and seventeen were in the labor force. Employment for women had become the norm, and most households depended on two wages. Yet despite these statistical changes, women had lost ground relative to men. In 1955 women earned 64 percent of the average wages paid to men; in 1980 they earned only 59 percent. The reason for this dip lay in the increasing concentration of women in a few, mostly nonunionized occupations. Over 80 percent of employed women worked in only 20 of the 420 occupations compiled by the U.S. Census Bureau. The great majority were clustered in the clerical and service trades (among women professionals, teaching and nursing), where the lowest wages prevailed.

African American women made some gains. Through Title VII of the Civil Rights Act, outlawing discrimination by sex or race, and the establishment of the Equal Employment Opportunity Commission to enforce it, they managed to climb the lower levels of the job ladder. By 1980 northern black women's median earnings were about 95 percent of white women's earnings. Proportionately, slightly more black women than white were gainfully employed in technical, sales, and administrative jobs.

In contrast, Hispanic women, whose labor force participation leaped by 80 percent over the decade, were restricted to a very few, poorly paid occupations. Puerto Ricans found jobs in the garment industry of the Northeast; Mexican Americans more typically worked as domestics or agricultural laborers in the Southwest. Neither group earned much more than the minimum wage.

Several local organizations formed in the 1970s to push for equality in the workplace. The most successful addressed office workers. In 1973 Boston's Nine to Five drew up an Office Workers' Bill of Rights calling for equal pay, maternity benefits, and promotion opportunities. California's WAGE (Women Act to Gain Equality) and Chicago's WU

(Women United) pressured government agencies for stricter enforcement of antidiscrimination laws. Unenthusiastically supported by the AFL–CIO, whose leaders continued to regard women as poor prospects for unionization, these organizations drew media attention but rarely achieved better pay or working conditions.

Sunbelt/Snowbelt

While the economic woes of the 1970s affected all sections of the country, regional differences became more pronounced. The Midwest and Northeast lost status and political influence as their economies slumped. The Sunbelt of the South, Southwest, and Far West, meanwhile, witnessed the largest land rush in American history. Economic growth in this region was three times that of the rest of the nation.

By the 1970s the Sunbelt boasted a gross prod-uct greater than almost any country in the world and more cars, television sets, houses, and even miles of paved roads than the rest of the United States. Large influxes from Latin America, the Caribbean, and Asia combined with the population shift of North Americans in search of warmer climates. From 56 million people in 1940, the region had more than doubled, to 118 million, just forty years later. Boca Raton, formerly a small town twenty-three miles north of Miami, constructed more buildings in 1972 than the whole state of Vermont.

The Sunbelt states gained enormously from defense spending, both on military bases and on weapons production. But the region gained nearly as greatly from the allocation of Social Security funds. The number of those over the age of sixty-five increased by 30 percent during the 1970s, reaching 26 million by 1980. Armed with benefit packages won decades earlier, huge "golden age" migrations

These newly-built houses in Phoenix, Arizona, a popular retirement community as well as the state capitol, accompanied a fifty-five percent rise in the city's population between 1970 and 1980. Like other burgeoning cities of the Mountain West, Phoenix experienced many urban tensions during this decade, including racial conflict, antagonism between affluent suburbs and decaying downtowns, air pollution, traffic congestion, and strained water supplies.

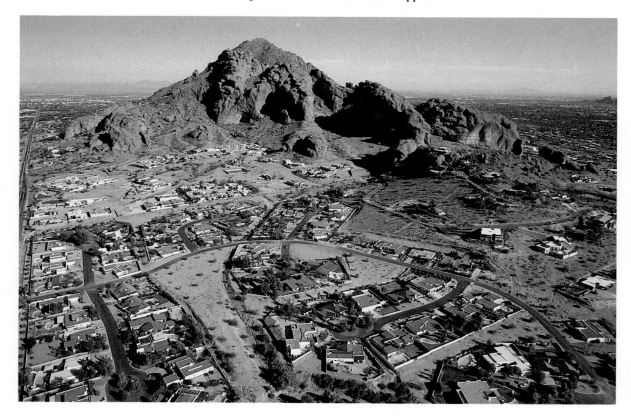

created new communities in Florida, Arizona, and Southern California, pumping $8 billion per year into the Florida economy alone. Always economically significant, seasonal tourism paled before the waves of new permanent residents.

The South experienced some of the most dramatic changes in demographic and economic patterns. High-profit agribusiness leaped to meet the taste of Americans for more poultry, beef, and frozen foods. By the 1970s billion-dollar processing plants like Perdue, Inc., of Salisbury, Maryland, were marketing 1 to 2 million broilers each week through a high-technology mix of computerized feedings, growth hormones, conveyor-belt packaging, and aggressive advertising. Meanwhile, southern cities reversed the century-long trend of migration among African Americans. In 1978 *Ebony* magazine listed the "ten best cities for Blacks"; five were the southern cities of Atlanta, Dallas, Houston, Baltimore, and Washington, all of them rigidly segregated only a few years earlier. For the first time, African Americans in large numbers returned south.

The Southwest and West, large parts of which had traditionally been considered unsuitable for large populations, changed yet more dramatically. Through migration, air conditioning, water diversions, public improvements, and sheer building mania, California became the nation's most populous state; Texas was third, behind New York. Former farm towns and deserts turned almost overnight into huge metropolitan areas dominated by automobile traffic and suburbs. Phoenix grew from 664,000 in 1960 to 1,509,000 in 1980, Las Vegas from 127,000 to 463,000. Meanwhile, agribusiness giants turned entire California valleys to the production of a single crop or several crops of fruit or vegetables, such as strawberries or lima beans.

West Coast firms at the heart of the information revolution, meanwhile, led the way in research and development in high-technology fields. The rapidly growing computer industry created California's Silicon Valley (named for the production of silicon chips), south of San Francisco, adding more than half a million jobs and billions of dollars of profit during the 1970s in Santa Clara County alone. Even when the number of lucrative defense contracts dropped off after the end of the Vietnam War, military outlays increased in high technology, with spin-offs in research and development centered in the Los Angeles area. Virtually guaranteed profits by government contracts, high-tech, defense-based industries weathered the recession very well.

On the down side, much of the Sunbelt wealth tended to be temporary, producing a boom-and-bust economy. Corporate office buildings in cities like

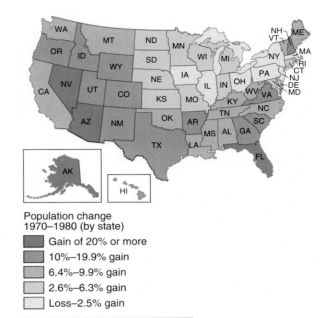

Population change
1970–1980 (by state)

- Gain of 20% or more
- 10%–19.9% gain
- 6.4%–9.9% gain
- 2.6%–6.3% gain
- Loss–2.5% gain

Population Shifts, 1970–1980

Industrial decline in the Northeast coincided with an economic boom in the Sunbelt, encouraging millions of Americans to head for warmer climes and better jobs.

Houston emptied almost as fast as they filled. Likewise, textile and similarly labor-intensive industries that had earlier moved to the South for lower wages now relocated to Mexico, the Caribbean, or Asia. Even microchip processing, considered virtually a native Californian industry, gradually moved to Pacific islands and the Far East.

The Sunbelt's economic assets were also distributed very unevenly. Older Mexican American populations made only modest gains, while recent Mexican immigrants and Indian peoples suffered low incomes and poor public services. Whereas eastern and midwestern states traditionally dependent on urban political machines and liberal voters spent significantly on public housing, education, and mass transit, the conservative Sunbelt states concentrated their tax and federal monies on strengthening police forces, improving roads or sanitation systems for expanding suburbs, and creating budget surpluses. Even liberal Californians complained of a two-tier society, an upper middle class and growing lower class, each locked firmly in place.

The Snowbelt (or "Rustbelt"), as the Northeast and Upper Midwest came to be called, meanwhile suffered sudden population losses along with factory closings and a general decline in industry and manufacturing. Of the nineteen metropolitan areas that lost population during the 1970s, all were old manufacturing centers — topped by New York, Cleveland, Pittsburgh, Boston, Philadelphia, and Buffalo. Reduced federal outlays compounded municipal budget crises, accentuating a feeling of defeat that prevailed in these areas.

Philadelphia, once the most important manufacturing center in the nation, was a case in point. From 1969 to 1981, the city lost 14 percent of its residents and 20 percent of its jobs, including 42 percent of its factory jobs. Only service employment grew, but in relatively small numbers (35,000 jobs gained versus more than 130,000 total lost). The restoration of certain downtown neighborhoods with lovely eighteenth-century cobblestone streets stood alongside widespread decay, a crime rate rising nearly 200 percent, a huge city debt ($167 million), and the closing of the only municipally owned hospital. Ranked fifty-seventh in terms of prosperity and service in a survey of sixty-five American cities, Philadelphia had nearly hit bottom.

New York City offered a still more spectacular example. A fiscal crisis in 1975 forced liberal mayor Abraham Beame to choose between wage freezes for city employees and devastating cuts and layoffs. Eventually, with the municipal government teetering on the brink of bankruptcy, he took both. In response to cutbacks in mass transit and the deterioration of the city's public health system as well as municipal services generally, a large sector of the middle class left. At the same time, the number of poor in the city's population rose from 15 percent in 1969 to nearly 25 percent only fourteen years later.

"Lean Years" Presidents

Gerald R. Ford and Jimmy Carter presided over a depressed economy and a nation of disillusioned citizens. Neither came up with a viable program to stimulate the economy. Carter admitted publicly that he doubted the government could solve this pressing problem, thus swelling the tide of voter apathy.

During the 1970s many Americans viewed electoral politics, especially at the federal level, as irrelevant to their lives. After the 1968 election, voter participation began a two-decade decline. A little over half of eligible voters turned out for presidential elections. By the end of Carter's administration, a majority of those polled agreed that the "people running the country don't really care what happens to you."

"I'm a Ford, Not a Lincoln"

Gerald Ford, described by a childhood friend as "a rich boy — but a regular guy," was a former college football star and a Yale Law School graduate. Elected to Congress from Michigan in 1948, he built a reputation for honesty and was elected House minority leader in 1965. When Vice-President Spiro T. Agnew was forced to resign, Nixon chose Ford, a conservative Republican, as his replacement. Following Nixon's own resignation in August 1974, an overwhelming majority of Americans reported that they supported the new president. But after reassuring the public that "our long national nightmare is over," Ford turned around and, just one month later, pardoned Nixon for all the federal crimes he may have committed as president. Amid cries of protest and allegations that a deal had been struck, Ford irrevocably lost the nation's trust.

As president, Ford lacked a clear program and offered few initiatives to put the economy on the road to recovery. At best, he hoped to encourage a slow but steady growth of the economy by keeping interest rates stable, raising taxes to reduce federal deficits, and above all restraining federal spending. His voluntary anti-inflation program, Whip Inflation Now, publicized by big red and white lapel buttons marked *WIN,* failed to restore public confidence. Even his own staff dubbed this meager program a "lick-your-plate-clean" approach to a national emergency.

As inflation and unemployment continued to sail upward, the midterm elections in 1974 added fifty-two Democrats to the House and four to the Senate, further eroding Ford's congressional support. Although Ford issued more vetoes of major bills than any other president in the twentieth century, Congress overrode most of them. Ford nevertheless swore to hold fast even against popular measures such as emergency job bills and education, health, and child nutrition programs. When New York City faced bankruptcy, Ford promised "to veto any bill that had as its purpose a federal bail-out." The *New York Daily News* followed with the now famous headline "FORD TO CITY: DROP DEAD." The president relented when both houses of Congress united against him. Ironically, Ford insisted that his "motto toward Congress is communication, conciliation, compromise, and cooperation."

The image that Ford conveyed as president was that of a pleasant person of modest ability. The press often caught him stumbling or mixing up his ideas. In a televised debate with Carter during the 1976 presidential campaign, he astonished Americans by saying "there is no Soviet domination" of Eastern Europe. Another time he said that "things are more like they are now than they have ever been." Lyndon B. Johnson once quipped: "The trouble with Jerry Ford is that he used to play football without a helmet."

First Lady Betty Ford, on the other hand, won the admiration of many Americans. A former student of modern dancer Martha Graham, she broke ranks with other Republicans to champion the Equal Rights Amendment. She once told a television reporter that she supported abortion rights, would not scold her adult daughter for having premarital sex, and probably would have tried marijuana herself if it had been in vogue when she was growing up. She also won praise for her courage in discussing her mastectomy for breast cancer and her voluntary entry into a substance abuse clinic for a drinking problem.

The Election of 1976

Despite his flagging popularity, Ford banked on his incumbency and put himself forward in 1976 as the Republican candidate for president. His chief Republican opponent was Ronald Reagan, a film and television actor and a former governor of California known widely for his conservative views. Most Republicans feared, however, that a Reagan candidacy would push the party too far to the right and result in a landslide victory for the Democrats. Under these circumstances the party, which in the aftermath of Watergate claimed only 18 percent of registered voters, unenthusiastically nominated Ford and Senator Robert Dole of Kansas as his running mate.

On the Democratic side, the public's alienation from government was the most important factor in the selection of a presidential candidate. Jimmy Carter, a former one-term governor of Georgia, depicted himself as an antipolitician, an outsider, and someone who was independent of the Washington establishment. (When Carter told his mother he was running for president, she reportedly asked, "President of what?") Carter's personal integrity was his chief qualification for the nation's highest office. Promising to apply the "Golden Rule . . . in all public matters," he further pledged, "I will never lie to you."

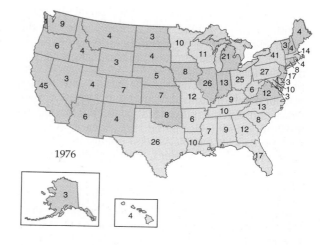

1976

Candidates (Party)	Electoral vote	Popular vote
Jimmy Carter (Democratic)	297 (55%)	40,828,587 (50.0%)
Gerald R. Ford (Republican)	240 (45%)	39,147,613 (47.9%)
Ronald Reagan (Independent)	1	
Other Candidates (McCarthy (Independent); Libertarian)	–	1,575,459 (2.1%)

Election of 1976

Incumbent Gerald Ford could not prevail over the disgrace brought to the Republican party by Richard Nixon. The lingering pall of the Watergate scandal, especially Ford's pardon of Nixon, worked to the advantage of Jimmy Carter, who campaigned as an outsider to national politics. Although Carter and Mondale won by only a narrow margin, the Democrats gained control of both the White House and Congress.

A moderate Democrat, Carter appealed to conservative and southern voters by playing up his status as a born-again Christian. But he also made fairly liberal statements on domestic policy, including civil rights, and favored a strong national defense. Although Ford retorted that it was "not enough for anyone to say, 'Trust me,' " Carter capitalized on the Nixon pardon. His pointed references to the "Nixon-Ford Administration," as well as the sagging economy, encouraged voters to try their luck with a Democrat. He entered the campaign with a 30 percent lead over Ford.

Carter and his running mate, Senator Walter Mondale of Minnesota, won the election with just under 50 percent of the popular vote, 40.8 million to Ford's 39.1 million, and secured a 297-to-241 margin in the electoral college. Carter swept the Deep South and everywhere won a majority among the lower classes. Ford carried a majority of educated, well-to-do suburbanites and did surprisingly well for a Republican among Jews and Italians. Carter won more than 90 percent of the black vote, which provided his margin of victory in Pennsylvania, Ohio, and seven southern states. Apathy proved the most important factor in the 1976 election. A record 46.7 percent of eligible voters, mainly the nation's poor, did not even bother to cast ballots.

The Carter Presidency

Jimmy Carter, the first president to come of age since World War II, remained an enigma to most political analysts. As a professed outsider, he never gained the confidence of congressional Democrats, let alone Republicans, and could never command their votes. To the contrary, he appeared uncertain and hesitant, a mirror image of the uneasiness that spread across the country in the late 1970s. Lacking an overarching political vision, Carter gradually shifted to the right, so much so that critics called him a "Democrat who often talks and thinks like a Republican."

The stalled economy resisted his best efforts, but Carter made his own mistakes. When he took office, he admitted that the nation's problems might require truly novel solutions but offered only a lackluster legislative program. His tax reform measure of 1977 did little to help the middle classes; his energy bill, enacted in 1978, appeared to benefit the

oil companies as much as the consumer; and the health reform measures promised during his campaign failed altogether.

Carter's style reflected his managerial outlook as well as his lack of experience as a politician. He generally abstained from the customary bargaining with legislators. Instead, Carter stated his position and waited for Congress to respond. Lacking leadership qualities, he tended to seek technical solutions to the country's enormous social problems. On occasion he got caught up in trivial detail, such as planning a players' schedule for the White House tennis courts. Overall, Carter relied on a small circle of advisers, mainly close friends from Georgia, and kept an unusually low profile for the nation's chief executive.

Carter's decisions nevertheless reflected his sense of political reality. Although he appointed a higher percentage of women, African Americans, and Latinos to full-time federal appointments than any previous president and created a "superfund" to clean up abandoned toxic waste sites, he broke step with liberal Democrats. Carter believed the nation faced problems that could not be solved by the redistribution of power and wealth that Democrats since FDR had advocated. Like many southerners, Carter sought to reduce the scale of federal government as well as to lessen its control over the marketplace. He deregulated airlines, bringing fares down for millions of business and vacation travelers. He also removed the banks from congressional control, a policy change that inadvertently encouraged fraud, the granting of questionable loans, and

When Jimmy Carter took the oath of office in January, 1977, he inherited an office dishonored by the Nixon-Ford administration. Hoping to dispel the political cynicism that had settled over the nation, he smiled broadly as he left the inaugural platform, bypassed his armored limousine, and walked hand-in-hand with Rosalynn Carter. Spectators cheered along the Pennsylvania Avenue parade route, greeting the new president's gesture as the symbolic end of an unhappy era.

eventually a round of disastrous bank failures. He "campaigns liberal but he governs conservative," complained former Carter fundraiser Bert Lance.

Carter made no effort to renew the social welfare initiatives of his Democratic predecessor, Lyndon B. Johnson. Under Carter's administration, inner-city schools and health and social services declined. The federal funds that might have gone to poverty programs instead bolstered military spending. Although Carter had promised to reduce defense expenditures, once in office he promptly proposed an additional $10 billion for the Pentagon's budget (while dropping a $25 million program for poor children's school meals). The press, aided by whistle blowers working inside defense goods factories, found military spending loaded with fraud and abuse. Exposés of screwdrivers costing taxpayers fifty dollars each made Carter appear, despite his campaign promises, unable or unwilling to challenge corruption in government.

Inflation and the energy crisis proved Carter's worst enemies. By 1978 inflation hit 10 percent, and at times it rose as high as 18 percent. As older Americans could recognize, half of all the inflation since 1940 had occurred in just ten years. Mortgages for new homes became at best difficult to procure, rents in many locations doubled, sales of automobiles and other consumer products slumped, and many small businesses went under. Tuition costs skyrocketed along with unemployment, and millions of young men and women who could neither afford to go to college nor find a job moved back home. Carter could not deliver on his promise to turn the economy around.

THE NEW POVERTY

Despite the diversion of federal funds to military spending during the Vietnam War, President Johnson's Great Society had brought a higher standard of living to many Americans. The disparity between the incomes of black and white Americans — and between the incomes of men and women — lessened during the 1960s; segregation in schools, housing, and public facilities declined as well. By the mid-1970s, however, it had become clear that many of these gains were short-lived. A contracting economy and persistent racism actually reversed these trends. Michael Harrington, author of the highly influential *The Other America* (1962) (see Chapter 28), observed that nearly twenty years "after the President of the United States declared an 'unconditional' war on poverty, . . . we must deal

. . . with a new poverty much more tenacious than the old."

A Two–Tiered Society

During the 1970s Americans were healthier and lived longer than at any time in history. Life expectancy rose from sixty years in 1930 to seventy-three years, and gains were even greater for those Americans who survived past the age of seventy-five. The majority of Americans also enjoyed greater wealth. Real personal income had doubled since the late 1930s, and by 1977 median family income had reached $15,000.

The distribution of wealth, however, had not changed. The wealthiest 20 percent of American families received about 40 percent of all income, while the poorest 20 percent received only about 5 percent. Nearly 26 million Americans — about 12 percent of the population — lived in poverty. Another 12 percent squeaked over the line of $6,000 per family of four only because of welfare assistance. By 1980 over 11 million families were receiving welfare assistance from Aid to Families with Dependent Children (AFDC).

The widening gap between rich and poor was sharply defined by race. Although poor whites outnumbered poor blacks by a ratio of two to one, a disproportionate number of African Americans lived below the poverty line. Whereas 8.7 percent of whites lived in poverty in 1978, 30.6 of blacks and 21.6 percent of Hispanics did (the rate was especially high among Puerto Ricans, low among Cuban Americans). The gains achieved by the civil rights movement and Great Society programs steadily eroded over the 1970s. By most indicators, the status of African Americans returned to levels observed in 1954, the year of the *Brown v. Board of Education* decision. In that year black families had earned about 53 percent of the income of white families. This figure rose to 60 percent in 1969 and peaked at 62 percent in 1975. By 1979 black family income had fallen back to about 57 percent of white family income. At the same time, residential segregation rose in most American cities.

As the gap in living standards between black and white Americans widened during the 1970s, so too did differences *among* African Americans become more pronounced. The number of African Americans attending college peaked in 1976 at 9.3 percent of the black population, a 500 percent increase over the 1960 average. Implementing affirmative action mandates, major corporations began to recruit black college graduates, and a sizable number of African Americans found places in the professional, clerical, managerial, and technical realm. By the late 1970s one-third of all black workers had found white-collar employment.

But although 35 to 45 percent of African American families achieved middle-class status, others fell into poverty in nearly the same proportion. Sociologist William Julius Wilson confirmed "a deepening economic schism . . . in the black community." While middle-class blacks were joining whites in the professional workplace and integrated suburbs, the poor stayed behind in increasingly segregated urban neighborhoods and in jobs that did not pay a living wage.

This trend dramatically affected the black community. Until the 1970s the majority of African Americans had held to common residential neighborhoods, institutions, and political outlooks. The growing income and residential disparity, which widened faster among blacks than among whites, eventually produced sharp differences among African Americans on social, economic, and political issues.

In reviewing these developments, Wilson concluded that "class has become more important than race in determining black life-chances." Other scholars disagreed. They pointed out that even middle-class blacks owned little property compared with whites and therefore had less chance to pass on their good fortune to their children. African Americans as a group were still far behind whites, historian Manning Marable countered, and "no amount of statistical doubletalk will obscure this fundamental fact."

Toward the end of the decade, opportunities for advancement into the middle class dwindled. A major setback for young African Americans had taken place in the nation's public schools. By 1980 fewer black students attended integrated schools than in 1954, except in the South, where about half the black students did. The turnabout resulted in part from increasing opposition by white parents to court-ordered school busing, which had served since *Brown v. Board of Education* as the principal means of achieving racial balance in urban school systems. In 1975 a major clash between local white residents and black children occurred in Boston when a federally mandated busing plan was put into operation. By the end of the decade the busing controversy had nearly disappeared, because federal judges hesitated to mandate busing programs. But more important was the change in the racial composition of American cities. By 1980 big-city school systems served mainly African American and Latino children, making the issue of integration

moot. By this time, the dropout rate of black teenagers had reached 50 percent in inner-city schools.

New legal rulings closed off important routes to employment in the professions. In 1978 the U.S. Supreme Court issued a sharp blow to affirmative action programs. To ensure acceptance of a minimum number of minority students, the University of California–Davis Medical School had established a quota system. In 1973 and 1974 the school denied admission to Allan Bakke, a white student. Bakke sued the university for "reverse discrimination," claiming his academic record surpassed that of the sixteen minority students who were admitted. The California Supreme Court ruled in his favor in 1976, and after an appeal by the University of California the U.S. Supreme Court handed down a five-to-four decision on June 18, 1978, stating that the use of an "explicit racial classification" in situations where no earlier discrimination had been demonstrated violated the equal protection clause of the Fourteenth Amendment. The Court ordered the University of California to admit Bakke to its medical school. Affirmative action programs could now operate only when "a legacy of unequal treatment" could be proved.

Feminization of Poverty

Women as a group lost economic ground during the 1970s despite a growing rate of labor force participation. There were some notable exceptions to this trend, particularly in the professions. During the 1970s, the number of women lawyers rose from 4 to 14 percent, the number of women doctors from 9 to 22 percent. Although still a minority, a sizable number of women now held executive positions in the country's most prestigious corporations and legal firms. The majority of gainfully employed women, however, did not earn a living wage.

Divorce or separation therefore struck a serious blow at most women's economic well-being. Although professionally employed women benefited from the new no-fault divorce laws, which lowered or eradicated alimony, wage-earning women and homemakers suffered major financial losses. In the mid-1970s, when marriages had only a fifty-fifty chance of survival, the majority of men defaulted on child-support payments within one year of separation. At the same time, divorced men enjoyed an average 42 percent increase in their standard of living, whereas divorced women saw theirs drop by 73 percent. Approximately one-quarter of all working women who headed households with children earned incomes below the poverty level.

Poverty among women thus grew in tandem

with the 72 percent rise in the number of female-headed households during the 1970s. The number of poor families headed by women increased nearly 40 percent during the 1970s, while the number of poor families headed by a man declined by 25 percent. This trend was even more pronounced among African Americans and Puerto Ricans.

In the black community, a sharp rise in teenage pregnancy reinforced this pattern. In the 1970s over half of all African American babies were born to women without husbands, whereas in 1940 only an estimated 15 percent were. Many of these mothers were too young to have gained either the education or skills to secure jobs that would pay enough to support themselves and their children. By 1980 two-thirds of black families living in poverty were headed by women. Even with AFDC payments and food stamps, it was impossible for a single mother to keep her family above the poverty level. And with rising inflation, the real income of welfare recipients dropped in many states by almost one-half from its level in 1970.

Welfare was becoming an issue of relevance primarily to women and children. By 1980 women received 90 percent of Social Security benefits; constituted 60 percent of Medicare enrollees; received 70 percent of food stamps; and headed 80 percent of all households receiving AFDC money.

In 1978 sociologist Diana Pearce described these trends as the "feminization of poverty." Women constituted nearly 70 percent of the adult poor. Poverty was also a condition of life for a greater proportion of children in the United States than in eleven other industrialized countries. The National Advisory Council on Economic Opportunity issued a report in 1982 predicting that by the turn of the century, if these trends persisted, female heads of households and their children would account for all the poor in the United States.

"A Permanent Underclass"

In 1978 Senator Edward Kennedy identified one of the greatest problems facing Americans as "the growth, rapid and insidious, of a group in our midst, perhaps more dangerous, more bereft of hope, more difficult to confront, than any for which our history has prepared us. It is a group that threatens to become what America has never known — a permanent underclass in our society." Kennedy's designation for the urban poor stuck. Although the majority of poor Americans lived in rural areas and small towns, with Missouri, South Dakota, and Texas accounting for the nation's largest pockets of poverty, experts and the news media alike focused on the inner cities. Poverty, in their discussions, became synonymous not only with unemployment but drug and alcohol abuse and violent street crime.

The majority of poor African Americans, six out of ten, did live in central cities with high unemployment rates. The economic boom of the late 1960s, and the expansion of public programs with the Great Society, had built huge municipal payrolls, enabling African Americans to secure jobs in the public

Until World War II, the South had been the nation's poorest region. With the growth of Sunbelt prosperity and the migration of poor southerners to other parts of the country, the gap between the South and other regions began to close. In the 1970s and 1980s, policy makers and politicians focused mainly on urban poverty. Nevertheless, large pockets of rural poverty, such as neighborhoods in Yellville, Arkansas, photographed here, remained.

sector. With the drastic cutbacks of the 1970s, especially acute in the realm of city services, these particular groups of workers saw their gains erode. Large numbers of municipal workers, which now included many African Americans and Puerto Ricans, were laid off. Jobs became as scarce as at any time since the Great Depression. One unemployed worker in Kansas City commented that despite the advances brought about by the civil rights movement, conditions appeared no better: "The truth is that black people ain't no closer to catching up with white than they were before" the depression. For the first time, the economy spurred a reverse migration, with many blacks leaving the economically stagnant northern cities for the South, and Puerto Ricans fleeing New York's depressed economy for the island.

The bleak prospects took a toll especially on young African Americans. A black child was twice as likely to die before reaching the first birthday than a white child and four times more likely to be killed between the ages of one and four. Among black teenagers, the unemployment rate topped 40 percent and the jobs open to them were among the lowest-paid occupations. Despite the paucity of jobs for teenagers, the high school dropout rate skyrocketed during the 1970s. Illiteracy, frequent arrests, alcohol and drug abuse, and long-term public welfare became commonplace in their lives. AFDC saw its case load increase by nearly 500 percent, as over 3 million families appealed for assistance.

"We're going to slowly disappear — get doped up or put in jail or shot," a black youth in Detroit announced. "Something's going' to happen to all of us, 'cause, see, for us right now all the stuff in the street — dope, guns, fast money — we see people makin' tops doin' that every day. We're gonna want a piece of the rock, too. Nobody wants to walk around poor."

Sociologists associated the rising crime rate with the growth of teenage poverty. Violent crimes, such as aggravated assault, robbery, rape, or murder, increased dramatically in all poor neighborhoods throughout the country and changed in character. Murder, for example, mainly a crime of passion involving neighbors or relatives, increasingly became a killing of strangers or result of random violence. The number of serious crimes, such as burglary, car theft, and murder, perpetrated by children between the ages of ten and seventeen increased at an alarming rate during the 1970s.

The poorest and most disadvantaged of all racial or ethnic groups remained Indian peoples. Ironically, the 1970s saw Indian populations grow faster than the population at large, mainly because increasing numbers designated themselves as "Indians" rather than as members of specific tribes to U.S. Census takers. Yet Indian peoples suffered from an excessive death rate — six times the national average from tuberculosis, and 22 times the rate of non-Indians from alcohol-related causes. Efforts at self-determination advanced but were considerably slowed by neighboring whites who filed competing land and mineral claims. The Supreme Court, in *United States v. Wheeler,* ruled in 1978 that tribal sovereignty existed "only at the sufferance of Congress." Another case in the same year, *Oliphant v. Suquamish Indian Tribe,* added that tribes had no authority to arrest or punish trespassers who violated their laws. Meanwhile the federal government did little to help integrate Indian peoples who lived off the reservations, slightly less than half of their total population.

COMMUNITIES AND GRASS-ROOTS POLITICS

With the winding down of the Vietnam War, the mass demonstrations of the 1960s gave way to a different style of political mobilization centered squarely in communities. Unlike national elections, which registered increasing voter apathy, local campaigns brought lots of people to the voting booth and into voluntary associations. "I didn't care so much about my neighborhood until I had children," one East Coast city dweller told a sociologist. "I wasn't aware of the various facets of the community. Then came a lot of other things that I began to do as the parent of a child in this neighborhood. We became committed to this area."

Community residents divided along the familiar Democratic and Republican or liberal and conservative lines. Rent-control advocates and environmentalists, for instance, sought restrictions on the public uses of private property. The same groups usually wanted better training of local police, especially in racially mixed neighborhoods, and government subsidies for day-care centers. Conservatives assailed school busing as an attack on parents' rights and regarded most environmental regulations as unwarranted interference. They also wanted stricter law enforcement and fought all legislative proposals that they believed might weaken the family.

But on several issues, communities often pulled together. New Englanders, for example, attributed the high cost of their energy bills to the federal subsidies allotted to southwestern oil-producing states. Alaskan leaders fought environmentalist legislation that might slow economic growth in their state. Problems of illegal drugs and juvenile crime or unwanted "urban renewal" projects likewise crossed party lines at the local level. During the 1970s numerous groups formed to save neighborhoods from the threat of destruction or to revitalize the entire community.

Urban Coalitions

Although voters greeted presidential campaigns with apathy if not cynicism, they responded more enthusiastically to local initiatives. In many areas of the country, new coalitions formed to improve municipal or state services, their leaders shifting gears from the mass mobilizations of the 1960s and allying with liberal Democrats. In Berkeley, California, Madison, Wisconsin, Ann Arbor, Michigan, and Eugene, Oregon, among other college towns touched by 1960s activism, these coalitions secured seats for their candidates on city councils.

With similar backing, African American candidates scored impressive victories during the 1970s. The newly elected African American mayor of Atlanta, Maynard Johnson, concluded that "politics is the civil rights movement of the 1970s." Indeed, by the 1976 election, 46 percent of black southerners (compared with 57 percent of white southerners) voted regularly. By 1978, 2,733 African Americans held elected offices in the South, ten times the number a decade earlier. Mississippi, the state that had produced violent opposition to the civil rights movement, had more African American elected officials by 1980 than any other state in the union. Voters had elected African American mayors in the South's premier cities, New Orleans and Atlanta. In other parts of the country, black mayors, such as Coleman Young in Detroit, Richard Hatcher in Gary, and Tom Bradley in Los Angeles, held power along with many minor black officials.

Other racial or ethnic groups advanced more slowly, rarely in proportion to their actual numbers in the population. Mexican Americans had already won offices in little Crystal City, Texas, and in 1978 took control for the first time of a major city council, in San Antonio. They also scored electoral victories in other parts of Texas and in New Mexico and developed strong neighborhood or ward organizations in southern California. Puerto Ricans elected a handful of local officials in New York, mostly in the Bronx. Asian Americans advanced in similar fashion in parts of Hawai'i.

Members of these groups also advanced into such previously all-white municipal jobs as fire fighters, police, and civil servants. Cities with black mayors spent more than other municipalities of similar size on education and social services. In all these cities, officials elected by the new urban coalitions acted to improve community health services, to ensure equity in government employment, and to protect the environment.

The fiscal crises of the 1970s nevertheless foiled their best plans. Most of these new officials found themselves unable to make the sweeping changes they had promised during their campaigns. In tackling the problem of youth unemployment, they discovered that temporary job programs could not counteract the effects of factory shutdowns and the disappearance of industrial jobs. Moreover, affirmative action programs aroused cries of "reverse discrimination" from angered whites who felt that progress had been registered at their expense. But although their support frequently dissipated when the cycle of poverty and violence could not be slowed, community-based mobilizations remained the political touchstone of the decade.

The City and the Neighborhood

The nation's cities inspired a range of responses from those residents who chose to resist the pull of the suburbs and the majority who simply couldn't afford to leave. For them, the city's hospitals, public libraries, symphony orchestras, museums, and art galleries became anchoring institutions demanding public support. Changes in federal policies also encouraged local initiative. The Community Development Act of 1974, signed by President Ford, combined federal grant programs for cities into a single program and put mayors and city managers directly in charge of spending. With grants totaling $8.4 billion over three years, city governments could allocate funds as they saw fit to public works, law enforcement, residential redevelopment, or even to salaries for public employees. These community development block grants encouraged citizens to take part in local planning efforts. Communities Organized for Public Service (COPS) in San Antonio, Texas, and the Association of Community Organizations for Reform Now (ACORN) in Little Rock, Arkansas, formed to advise public officials. In other cities, Save the City campaigns engaged residents in defining problems important to the community, such as traffic, sewerage, or stray dogs.

Groups of preservationists organized to save historical buildings and public spaces and formed land trusts to take over and refurbish old houses or

Geronimo, 1981, by Victor Orozco Ochoa. During the 1970s public murals appeared in many cities, often giving distinctive expression to a community's racial or ethnic identity. The murals painted in the mid-1970s on the outside of the Centro Cultural de la Raza, in San Diego, were among the most striking. After vandals ruined one section, Ochoa, whose grandmother was Yanqui, replaced it with this enormous representation of Geronimo, surrounded by figures of contemporary Chicano cultural life.

to turn vacant lots into neighborhood parks. The Providence (Rhode Island) Preservation Society, for instance, worked with city planners and individual donors to restore hundreds of houses, organized festival tours of neighborhoods to lure prospective buyers, and spurred the formation of similar societies in nearby towns.

Local and national foundations joined federal agencies in funding Community Development Corporations (CDCs) through a series of antipoverty agencies. By the end of the 1970s some 700 community-based economic development groups had formed to infuse more capital into neighborhood businesses and housing. These community groups promoted "development banks" that would facilitate "sweat equity," that is, the granting of low-interest mortgage loans to buyers willing to rebuild or refurbish dilapidated housing themselves. They also acted to prevent local banks from closing when a neighborhood became mainly black.

Otherwise ordinary people, who became known as "local heroes," guided neighborhood campaigns. They usually insisted that tensions between old and new neighborhood residents, problems of housing and schools, could be solved face to face and

cooperatively with the resources available to them. In San Francisco during the early 1970s, a law professor, Ray Schonholtz, launched "Community Boards," neighborhood arbitration centers which he described as "a new justice model . . . a neighborhood stabilization program . . . a volunteer service delivery system" with a "new philosophy about conflict, viewing it positively instead of negatively." Federal assistance proved crucial in maintaining most programs, however, especially in the late 1970s when cities faced major fiscal crises.

In 1979 President Carter's National Commission on Neighborhoods compiled 200 specific recommendations to broaden and speed the development of local institutions. The long-range goal of such efforts, the Commission suggested, should be "to reorganize our society . . . to a new democratic system of grassroots involvement." But local advocacy groups were often caught up creating the kinds of projects that foundations and federal agencies desired. As a leader of *Los Sures* in the Bronx concluded, he and his fellow activists were "diverted from organizing" and "seen — rightly — as part of the establishment" when they found themselves administering large-scale, well-funded projects that they had not originally intended. And even when local preservationists succeeded in re-creating entire urban districts to look much as they had a century or more earlier, "gentrification" often followed restoration, with poor residents displaced for "Yuppies" (Young Upwardly Mobile Professionals) who craved the increasingly fashionable old homes.

The Endangered Environment

The discovery of high rates of cancer and birth defects in Love Canal, near Buffalo, New York, offered compelling evidence of a growing danger to many American communities. Here, toxic wastes dumped by the Hooker Chemical Laboratory had oozed into basements and backyards, and home-maker Lois Gibbs organized a vigorous publicity campaign to draw attention to the grim situation and demanded evacuation of the immediate area. Meanwhile, outraged Florida residents realized that the damming of the Everglades for cotton produc-tion and housing developments, undertaken by the Army Corps of Engineers decades earlier, had de-graded thousands of acres of wildlife, eliminating natural filtration systems and killing millions of birds and other species.

Even before the energy crisis, many Americans had begun to reassess their priorities and even to make changes in their own ways of living. Many families began to save glass bottles and newspapers for reuse. Some began to reduce or eliminate the consumption of beef, which was far more costly to produce than the grains fed to cattle. Backyard vegetable gardens became popular, as did grocers who stocked organic foods, which were grown without pesticides or chemical fertilizers.

These efforts enlarged the audience for the "small is beautiful" movement that had begun in the 1960s. Nutritionist Frances Moore Lappe's popular *Diet for a Small Planet* (1971) had argued that a logic of excess could no longer prevail in the minds of Americans who already used one-third of the world's energy resources. Barry Commoner's *The Closing Circle* (1971) also helped to popularize the term *ecology* (Greek for "home," in reference to the earth as home) to represent the balance required to maintain life on the planet.

The environmentalist movement grew stronger in a handful of long-standing organizations, such as the Audubon Society and the Wilderness Society. The Sierra Club, formed in 1892 as a small society of Western mountain hikers, grew to 100,000 members in 1970 and a half million over the next decade. New

Since the 1950s environmentalists have urged both government and industry to take action to curb water and air pollution, and in the 1970s expanded their fight to include toxic chemical and radioactive wastes. In the 1970s environmentalists began to enlist the aid of long-standing nature organizations such as the Wil-derness Society and the National Audubon Society to lobby the government for legislative reform. They also campaigned among Americans at large to shape new values and attitudes about public resources.

groups sprang up in response to the energy crisis, often devoted to developing renewable energy sources such as solar power. Some, like Green-peace, sponsored direct action campaigns to bring to a halt practices that potentially caused harm to the environment.

Cutting across nearly all population groups and regions, environmentalists reached such tradition-ally conservative areas as the Deep South (where bumper stickers read "Don't Dump It in Dixie!") with warnings of toxic wastes, destruction of wet-lands, and ruin of fishing industries. Sometimes campaigns succeeded in blocking massive construc-tion projects, such as nuclear energy plants; more often they halted small-scale destruction of a nature habitat or historic urban district. Most important, all these campaigns made the public more aware of the consequences of private and government decisions about the environment. Responding to organized pressure groups, Congress passed scores of bills designed to protect endangered species, reduce pollution caused by automobile emissions, limit and ban the use of some pesticides, and control strip mining practices. The Environmental Protection Agency (EPA), established in 1970, grew to become the federal government's largest regulatory agency, the employer of over 10,000 people by decade's end.

Environmentalists enjoyed only limited success in bringing large-scale changes in policy, however. Clean-air mandates passed by Congress for cities to deal with pollution problems were usually avoided. Despite the introduction of lead-free gasoline, the air in major metropolitan areas grew worse because automobile traffic increased at a very fast pace. Environmentalists lost an important campaign when Nixon's secretary of the interior, former Alaska governor Walter Hickel, chose Earth Day to announce the approval of the Alaska Pipeline, 800 miles of pipe connecting oil fields with refining facilities. Despite predictions of environmental destruction from leaks and other catastrophes, pipeline construction began in 1973. White House advisor John Ehrlichman explained, "Conservation is not in the Republican ethic."

Small-Town America

A host of unresolved problems, ranging from air pollution to rising crime rates to higher taxes, encouraged a massive exodus from the nation's cities. Between 1970 and 1975, for every 100 people relocating to metropolitan areas, 138 moved out. Newer residential communities in small towns and in semirural or formerly rural areas grew at a fast pace, attracting retirees and others seeking solace or security. In 1971 alone, according to the National Association of Home Builders, 90,000 "second" homes were constructed, most in a typically American fashion with individual lawns, garages, and gardens.

Government programs such as mortgage guarantees and low-interest financing on individual homes promoted these large "low-density" developments of single-family houses. In many regions, the countryside gradually disappeared into "exurbia," a trend that population experts Peter A. Morison and Judith P. Wheeler attributed to the American "wish to love one's neighbor but keep him at arm's length." In opinion polls, respondents reported that they desired to live in a small town that was not a suburb but was still no more than thirty miles from a major city.

Soon even small towns developed their own suburbs, usually moderate-income tracts of ranch houses squeezed between the older wood-frame colonial or Victorian styles. Federal subsidies for the construction of sewage and water lines, originally intended to aid rural communities, now became springboards for further development. Ironically, shopping malls on former farmland now drained commercial activity from the small town centers, channeling to the chain stores rather than local merchants the economic boost that development had been expected to bring.

Sometimes the new residents became staunch opponents of further development and organized to stop the construction of new highways, nuclear energy generating plants, and toxic dumps. In Vermont, "hippies" and "back-to-the-landers" joined traditionally conservative landowners to defeat a 1974 gubernatorial plan to attract developers. "From coast to coast," the New York Times concluded, "environmental, economic and social pressures have impelled hundreds of cities and towns to adopt limitations on the size and character of their populations." To encourage public discussion of land-use issues, such as the utilization of open space or farms for commercial development, President Carter created the Small Community and Rural Development Policy group.

Little towns without mild climates or proximity to cities suffered the down side of this ex-urban expansion. In parts of Kansas, Iowa, and the Dakotas, where family farms failed at a high rate, other businesses also closed. The New York Times reported a "snowball effect" of rundown schools, inadequate medical care, and abandoned movie theaters and grocery stores. Only nursing homes and funeral parlors continued to thrive. An elderly woman told a journalist that the graveyard was "the friendliest place in town. There are so many people I have known and loved . . . that I don't [expect to] feel a bit lonely."

THE NEW CONSERVATISM

While many Americans in the 1970s concentrated their political energies in their communities, others organized to turn back the liberal programs enacted under the Great Society. Sizable numbers of taxpayers resented the hikes required to fund government programs in behalf of minorities or to provide expanded social services for the poor. By 1978 California voters staged a "taxpayers' revolt," approving Proposition 13, which cut property taxes and government revenues for social programs and education. In other, mainly economically hard-pressed urban areas, white voters who resented the gains made by African Americans or Latinos formed a powerful backlash movement. Poles in Chicago, Irish in Boston, and Italians and Jews in Brooklyn, for example, organized to consolidate their political influence. By the end of the decade, the only substantial increase in voter participation was among conservatives.

Archie Bunker (Carroll O'Connor) and Edith Bunker (Jean Stapleton) endowed television with a social and political complexity that previous situation comedies had scrupulously avoided. First broadcast in 1971, *All in the Family* featured a working-class family living in Queens, New York, trying to sort out their differences with Archie, the highly bigoted but lovable center of the household. Producer Norman Lear explained that the show "holds a mirror up to our prejudices. . . . We laugh now, swallowing just the littlest bit of truth about ourselves, and it sits there for the unconscious to toss about later."

The New Right

The political surge rightward in the 1970s united traditional conservatives aligned with business interests and Republicans with disgruntled white ethnic voters. It gained intellectual steam from neoconservatives, former liberals who now placed the blame for the declining power of the United States on the social movements of the 1960s. The American Enterprise Institute and the Heritage Foundation, richly funded by major corporations, provided numerous fellowships and grants to neoconservative scholars and access to positions in government agencies. These foundations also funded numerous right-wing student newspapers and magazines.

The biggest boost came, however, from the new religious right, mainly evangelical Protestants but also numerous Catholics and Jews, who wanted to revive what they believed to be traditional moral virtues. By decade's end over 50 million Americans had joined the ranks of evangelical Christians, and Southern Baptists had become the nation's largest Protestant denomination. One year after Billy Graham published his fast-selling *How to Be Born Again* (1977), 40 percent of all Americans, including the nation's president, reported that they were indeed "born again." These evangelical Christians became the backbone of key organizations such as the National Conservative Political Action Committee and, most especially, the Moral Majority.

The New Right used sophisticated marketing techniques to build its constituency. Conservatives were among the first political groups to employ direct mail. In the 1970s, approximately 100 conservative organizations each created lists of potential donors, traded or sold these lists, and kept in circulation millions of personally addressed letters requesting financial contributions in return for monthly newsletters, insignia buttons, bumper stickers, or even embossed Bibles.

Greater success came from the work of "televangelists." Beginning as local programming in the early days of television and moving to syndication by the late 1960s, televangelists such as Pat Robertson and Jim Bakker frequently mixed conservative political messages with appeals to prayer. The *Old Time Gospel Hour,* featuring the Reverend Jerry Falwell, was broadcast on over 200 television stations and 300 radio stations each week. Falwell told his listeners that Christians were morally compelled to support issues and candidates that punish "the enemies of God," designated as communists, abortion advocates, and the "secular humanist" opponents of prayer in public schools. Christian broadcasters generally endorsed Falwell's faith that "the free-enterprise system is clearly outlined in the Book of Proverbs of the Bible." By the end of the decade more than 1,400 radio stations and 30 TV stations specialized in religious broadcasts and reached an audience of perhaps 20 million weekly.

Urging Americans to repent their sins and acknowledge God's authority or suffer terrible wrath,

Falwell formed the Moral Majority as a political lobbying group to urge the rightful "place for biblical moral law in public policy." The Moral Majority advocated tough laws against homosexuality and pornography, a reduction of government services, especially welfare payments to poor families, but a stronger national defense. The Moral Majority promised campaign funds and votes for, as Falwell put it, "the mighty man . . . that man of war, that judge, that prophet, that preacher who is willing to call sin by its right name."

Jesse Helms was the first major politician to appeal directly to the New Right and to build his own impressive fundraising empire with its help. A North Carolina journalist who had fought the integration of public schools and defended the Ku Klux Klan, he had often attacked Martin Luther King, Jr., as a Communist-influenced demagogue. Helms entered national politics as a Goldwater supporter in 1964 and ran for the Senate in 1972. Carried to victory with Nixon's success in North Carolina, Helms immediately promoted a host of conservative bills. He introduced legislation to allow automobile owners

or dealers to disconnect mandatory antipollution devices. He also defended the Watergate break-ins as necessary to offset the "traitorous conduct" of antiwar activists. By 1978, he raised $8.1 million, the largest amount ever, for his successful re-election campaign. Helms won few victories in the Senate but built a powerful, loyal, and wealthy following.

Anti–ERA, Antiabortion

The New Right sponsored several important campaigns during the 1970s. They rallied support for a balanced budget amendment to the Constitution, sought unsuccessfully to return prayers to public schools, and endorsed the Supreme Court's approval of the death penalty in 1977. The New Right's most ardent campaign, however, centered on the restoration of "traditional family values." Appalled by the rising divorce rate and number of single parents, the New Right traced these problems to the women's liberation movement.

The defeat of the Equal Rights Amendment (ERA) stood at the top of the New Right agenda.

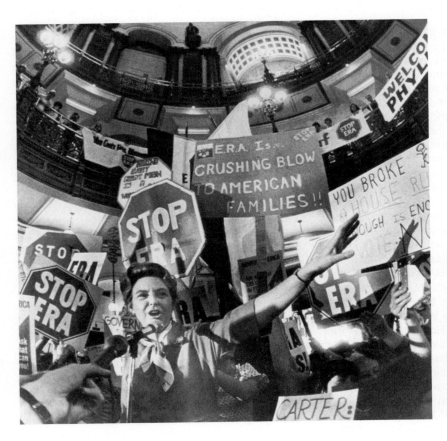

Phyllis Schlafly led the campaign to defeat the ratification of the Equal Rights Amendment. She wrote widely and delivered speeches throughout the country denouncing women's liberation as a threat to the family. The Alton, Illinois homemaker appears here with her STOP-ERA forces in the rotunda of the Illinois State Capital, where the house was voting on the proposed amendment in 1978.

Gallup Polls on Abortion: 1969, 1975

During the 1960s, numbers of American women began to demand control over their own reproductive processes and to demand the repeal of legislation in place in all fifty states rendering abortion illegal. The American Institute of Public Opinion surveyed Americans in 1969, when abortion was still illegal, and again in 1975, two years after the passage of *Roe v. Wade,* which struck down all state laws prohibiting abortion during the first three months of pregnancy.

Source: *The Gallop Poll: Public Opinion, 1935-1974* (New York: Random House, 1974).

Gallup Poll on Equal Rights Amendment, 1975

By 1973 thirty of the thirty-eight states required to ratify the ERA had done so. Although the amendment ultimately failed to achieve ratification and died in June 1982, public support was strong. In the 1976 presidential campaign, the platforms of both Democrats and Republicans included planks favoring its passage.

Source: *The Gallop Poll: Public Opinion, 1935-1974* (New York: Random House, 1974).

Approved by Congress in March 1972, fifty years after its original introduction (see Chapter 22), the ERA stated "equality of rights under the law shall not be denied or abridged by the United States or by any State on account of sex." Approved by both House and Senate, the amendment appeared likely to be ratified by the individual states. Nearly all mainstream women's organizations, including the Girl Scouts of America, endorsed the ERA, as had first ladies Lady Bird Johnson, Betty Ford, and Rosalynn Carter. Even the AFL–CIO retracted its long-standing opposition and endorsed the amendment.

Cued by this ground swell in favor of the ERA, the New Right swung into action. Phyllis Schlafly, a self-described suburban housewife and popular conservative lecturer, headed the STOP ERA campaign, describing the amendment's supporters as "a bunch of bitter women seeking a constitutional cure for their personal problems." She warned that the ERA would deprive women of their true rights "such

as the right of a wife to be supported by her husband" and bring about unisex public toilets and homosexual marriages. As one woman wrote her senator, "Forced busing, forced mixing, forced housing. Now forced women. No thank you!" Conservatives mounted large, expensive campaigns in each swing state and overwhelmed pro-ERA resources. Although thirty-five states had ratified the ERA by 1979, the amendment remained three votes short of passage. Despite a three-year extension, the ERA died in 1982.

Although STOP–ERA garnered enthusiastic support from Catholics as well as evangelical Protestants, "Right to Life" surpassed it as the New Right's principal "profamily" campaign. This facet of the movement took shape in the aftermath of the Supreme Court's 1973 ruling of *Roe v. Wade* that state laws decreeing abortion a crime during the first two trimesters of pregnancy constituted a violation of a woman's right of privacy. Well-organized opponents of abortion rallied for a Constitutional amendment of their own, defining the beginning of life with conception and arguing that the "rights of the unborn" superseded a woman's right to control her own body. The Catholic Church organized the first antiabortion demonstrations in the aftermath the Supreme Court's decision and sponsored the formation of the National Right to Life Committee, which claimed 11 million members by 1980.

Abortion foes rallied behind the conservative Representative from Illinois, Henry Hyde, who sponsored a legislative bill that severely restricted the use of Medicare funds for abortions. Upheld by the Supreme Court in 1980, the Hyde Amendment affected mainly poor women. Antiabortion groups also picketed Planned Parenthood counseling centers, intimidating potential clients. They rallied against government-subsidized day-care centers and against sex education programs in public schools. A small minority turned to more extreme actions, bombing dozens of abortion clinics.

The "Me Decade"

The shift in the political winds of the 1970s registered not only the rise of the New Right but the disengagement of millions of Americans from politics altogether. In 1976 novelist Tom Wolfe coined the phrase the "me-decade" to describe an era obsessed with personal well-being, happiness, and emotional security. Health foods and diet crazes, a mania for physical fitness, and a quest for happiness through therapy involved millions of middle-class Americans. Historian Christopher Lasch provided his own label for this enterprise in the title of his best-selling book *The Culture of Narcissism: American Life in an Age of Diminishing Expectations* (1978). "After the political turmoil of the sixties," he explained, "Americans have returned to purely personal preoccupations."

The rise of the "human potential movement" provided a vivid example of this trend. The most successful was Erhard Seminars Training (EST), a self-help program blending insights from psychology and mysticism. Founded by Werner Erhard (born Jack Rosenberg, a former door-to-door encyclopedia salesperson), the institute taught individuals to form images of themselves as successful and satisfied. Through 60 hours of intensive training involving play acting and humiliation, participants learned one major lesson: "You are the one and only source of your experience. You created it." In addition to emphasizing self-esteem, the seminars taught the value of "power relationships," that is, the importance of selecting friends or business colleagues compatible with one's own goals and ambitions.

Priced at $400 for a series of two weekend sessions, EST peaked at 6,000 participants per month, grossing $25 million in revenue in 1980. In the San Francisco Bay Area, where Erhard had established his headquarters, one of every nine college graduates took part. Typically white, single, middle-class, and between the ages of twenty and forty-five, EST clientele appeared to find in therapy what previous generations and other contemporaries found in religion.

Alongside EST, other popular therapies encouraged clients to value living in the present and being in touch with one's body signals rather than laying abstract plans for the future. The record-breaking best seller *Open Marriage,* for example, urged husbands and wives to stress "personal growth" and to search for "the true ME." Transcendental Meditation (TM) promised a shortcut to mental tranquility and found numerous advocates among Wall Street brokers, Pentagon officials, and star athletes. Techniques of TM were taught in more than 200 special teaching centers and practiced by a reputed 350,000 devotees.

Religious cults also formed in relatively large numbers during the 1970s. The Unification Church, founded by the Korean Reverend Sun Myung Moon, extracted intense personal loyalty from its youthful disciples. Many parents, however, were horrified by the mass marriage ceremonies of couples selected for pairing by church leaders. The most desperate hired private detectives to "kidnap" their own children from the Moonies. According to a 1977 Gallup survey, the Reverend Moon "elicited one of the most overwhelmingly negative responses ever reported by a major national poll." Moon's financial empire, which included hundreds of retail businesses and the *Washington Times,* a conservative daily newspaper, nevertheless proved very lucrative and kept his church solvent despite numerous lawsuits. By contrast, Jim Jones's People's Temple, a liberal interracial movement organized in the California Bay Area, ended in a mass murder and suicide when Jones induced over 900 of his followers to take cyanide with him in Guyana in 1978.

Popular music expressed and reinforced these trends. The songs of community and hope common in the late 1960s gave way to songs of dispair or nihilism. Bruce Springsteen, whose lyrics lamented the disappearance of the white working class, became the decade's most popular new rock artist. At the same time, heavy metal bands such as KISS as well as "punk" and "new wave" artists underscored themes of decadence and drew crowds of mainly white young men to their concerts. At the other end of the popular music scale, Country & Western music hit its peak with best-selling "crossover" hits, charismatic stars, and numerous new all-C&W radio stations. Willie Nelson, invited to perform at the White House by President Carter, sang melodic refrains reeking of loneliness or nostalgia and appealing to older, white, working-class Americans.

ADJUSTING TO A NEW WORLD

The Communist takeover of Saigon (renamed Ho Chi Minh City) on May 1, 1975, meant that, as President Ford remarked, the Vietnam War was "finished as far as America is concerned." The final U.S. military action in Indochina actually took place a few weeks later, when the new Communist Khmer Rouge government in Cambodia seized the American merchant ship *Mayaguez*. Forty-one Marines died and fifty more were wounded in a misguided attempt to save the thirty-nine crew members who had already been released. The tragic incident underscored for many Americans the futility of the entire war, and for many years afterward, the "Vietnam syndrome" hung like a pall over the nation. "After our war. . . ." wrote poet John Balaban, "the dismembered bits/— all those . . . eyes, ear slivers/jaw splinters, gouged lips, odd tibias, skin flaps, and toes — /came squinting, wobbling, jabbering back."

A new realism entered U.S. foreign policy deliberations in the late 1970s. Presidents Ford and Carter as well as their chief advisors acknowledged that U.S. power in the world had been declining since 1950 and too often had been used in the wrong causes. The "realists" shared with dissatisfied nationalists a single goal, "No More Vietnams."

A Thaw in the Cold War

The military defeat in Vietnam forced the makers of U.S. foreign policy to reassess priorities. The United States must continue to defend its "vital interests," Ford's secretary of state Henry Kissinger declared, but must also understand that "Soviet-American relations are not designed for tests of manhood." Both nations had experienced a relative decline of power in world affairs. And both were suffering from the already enormous and relentlessly escalating costs of sustaining a prolonged Cold War.

At the close of World War II, the United States could afford to allocate huge portions of its ample economic resources to maintaining and enlarging its global interests. Soon, however, military and defense expenses began to grow at a pace much faster than the economy itself. Whereas the Korean

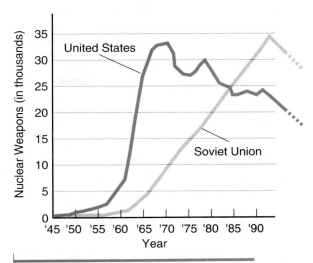

Nuclear Arsenals, the United States, and the Soviet Union

During the Cold War, both superpowers built up huge stockpiles of nuclear weapons, including sea and land missiles. President Lyndon Johnson began negotiations with the Soviet Union in an attempt to slow down the perilous nuclear arms race. In 1972, the Strategic Arms Limitation Talks (SALT) set limits on offensive intercontinental ballistic missiles. SALT II, negotiated by President Carter in 1979, called for further reductions but failed to win approval in the U.S. Senate.

Source: Sterngold, "Milestones of the Nuclear Era," *The New York Times*, Dec. 1, 1992, p. C10. Copyright © *The New York Times Company*; Illustrations by Rebecca Perry and Martha Hernandez; and The Bulletin of the Atomic Scientists.

War cost around $69.5 billion, the Vietnam War cost $172.2 billion. But expense of military conflicts accounted for only one portion of the defense budget. Clandestine operations, alliance building, and weapons production accounted for trillions of dollars more. The Voice of America's network of radio stations which broadcast anti-Communist propaganda abroad cost $640 million in the 1970s alone.

Military spending at this level eventually took its toll on the American economy, especially as the federal government increasingly relied on deficit spending in an attempt to cover the bill. The federal debt, which stood at $257 billion in 1950, had jumped to $908 billion in 1980, and increasingly large parts of the federal budget went to paying just the interest on this debt. At the same time, military spending diverted funds away from programs that could have strengthened the economy. The results were disastrous. While the United States endured falling productivity levels and rate of personal savings, rising high school drop out rates and a disappearing skilled work force, other nations rushed ahead. In the 1970s, when Japan and West Germany had emerged as potent economic competitors, *Business Week* noted that the American "colossus" was "clearly facing a crisis of the decay of power."

Western European nations acted to nudge U.S. foreign policy away from its Cold War premises. In 1975 representatives of 35 nations meeting in Helsinki, Finland, approved the national boundaries drawn in Eastern and Western Europe after World War II, and in return the Soviet Union agreed to enact a more liberal human rights policy that included few restrictions on the emigration of Soviet Jews. Recognizing that the Soviet Union no longer posed a military threat to their national sovereignty — if indeed it ever had — Western leaders also sought to strengthen economic relations between the two major blocs.

The Soviet Union, whose economy suffered even greater setbacks from defense spending, joined the United States in moving toward detente. Relations between the two superpowers had improved following the 1962 Cuban missile crisis but deteriorated again during the Vietnam war. But the signing of SALT I during Nixon's administration, followed by the U.S. withdrawal from Vietnam, encouraged new efforts to negotiate on strategic arms control. In November 1974 Ford and Brezhnev met in Vladivostok to set the terms of SALT II, and Carter secured the final agreement in 1979. The treaty failed, however, to win confirmation from the Senate when the Soviet Union invaded Afghanistan in December.

Although repeated conflicts in the Third World continued to slow the pace toward detente, leaders in both the United States and the Soviet Union recognized that their economic well-being depended on a reduction in defense spending. However haltingly, steps toward reconciliation had to be taken. Many Americans, including business leaders, welcomed or accepted this change in policy as inevitable. "If you think you can run the world and then you find out you can't," the aged journalist Walter Lippmann explained, "you withdraw to what you can run."

Foreign Policy and "Moral Principles"

Historian Gaddis Smith has argued that "the four years of the Carter Administration were among the most significant in the history of American foreign policy in the twentieth century" because the whole legacy of a century of diplomatic relations came to bear on each major decision. For the first time since 1945 diplomacy tilted away from the Cold War and toward global conflict over energy sources.

In 1977, when Carter took office, he happily admitted his lack of experience in foreign affairs as an asset. "We've seen a loss of morality," he noted, "and we're ashamed." His policy would demonstrate "the decency and generosity and common sense of our own people," its "soul" an "absolute" commitment to human rights. Carter condemned those policies that allowed the United States to support "right-wing monarchs and military dictators" in the name of anticommunism. In 1976 a powerful human rights lobby had pressured Congress to pass a bill that required the secretary of state to report annually on the status of human rights in all countries receiving aid from the United States, and to cut off assistance to any country with a record of "gross violations." Carter's secretary of state, Cyrus R. Vance, and the assistant secretary for human rights and humanitarian affairs, Pat Derrian, worked effectively to punish or at least to sanction repressive military regimes in Brazil, Argentina, and Chile. For the first time, leading U.S. diplomats spoke out against the South African Apartheid regime.

But toward nations considered vital to U.S. interests, such as South Korea, the Philippines, and El Salvador, Carter put aside his principles to stabilize repressive regimes and dictatorships against threats from Communist revolutionaries. In restoring formal diplomatic relations with the People's Republic of China in January 1979, Carter likewise overlooked the regular imprisonment of dissidents. "The real problem" a U.S. diplomat observed, was that human rights was "not a policy but an attitude." The Soviet Union dismissed it as mere propaganda.

Carter did try, however, to clean up the CIA, particularly to prevent intelligence agents from intervening directly in the affairs of foreign governments. He appointed Admiral Stanfield Turner, a Rhodes scholar, as director and ordered a purge of the "rogue elephants" who had pursued covert operations in Southeast Asia during the Vietnam war. "The CIA must operate within the law," Carter insisted, and restrict its activities to intelligence gathering. Under Turner, however, these reforms remained incomplete; they later proved temporary.

Carter scored his biggest moral victory in foreign affairs by paving the way for Panama to assume the ownership, operation, and defense of the Panama Canal Zone. Negotiations with Panama had begun during Johnson's administration, following riots by Panamanians against U.S. territorial rule in their country. Carter pressured the Senate to ratify new treaties in 1978 (by a vote of sixty-eight to thirty-two) that turned the Panama Canal over to Panama by the year 2000. Some foreign policy experts judged Carter's success in U.S.-Latin American relations the greatest since FDR's Good Neighbor policies of the 1930s.

The Camp David Accords

Carter nearly triumphed in the Middle East. Following the Israeli victory in the Yom Kippur War of 1973, Henry Kissinger devoted two years to "shuttle diplomacy" but could not resolve regional problems. Before taking over the presidency, Carter had little knowledge of the Middle East, although as a born-

again Christian he had strong feelings about the "Holy Land." Early in his administration, Carter met privately with Israeli prime minister Menachem Begin to encourage conciliation with Egypt. When negotiations between the two countries stalled in 1978, Carter brought Begin together with Egyptian president Anwar el-Sadat for a thirteen-day retreat at Camp David, Maryland.

The Camp David Accords set the terms for peace in the region. Egypt became the first Arab country to recognize Israel's right to exist and in exchange regained control of the Sinai Peninsula, including important oil fields. By signing this agreement, in March 1979, Israel secured a virtual guarantee of future U.S. assistance.

Carter's greatest disappointment concerned the fate of Palestine. An extremely adept negotiator,

President Carter signs Mideast Peace treaty with Egyptian President Anwar Sadat and Israeli Prime Minister Menachem Begin, in Washington, D.C., in March 1979. President Carter had invited both leaders to Camp David, the presidential retreat in Maryland, where for two weeks he mediated between the two leaders on territorial rights to the West Bank and Gaza Strip. Considered Carter's greatest achievement in foreign policy, the negotiations resulted not only in the historic peace treaty but the Nobel Peace Prize for Begin and Sadat.

Begin had refused to agree even to a cessation of new settlements in the territories. The final document, which formally recognized "the legitimate rights of the Palestine people," nevertheless did not clarify their status — or that of Jerusalem which, according to many Christians and Muslims, should be an autonomous holy city, free from any direct governmental control.

Carter himself believed the Camp David Agreement constituted an important step in the ongoing process for Middle East peace. It was the first time since 1948, when Israel was declared an independent state, that normal diplomatic relations existed between Egypt and Israel. Later in 1979 the Nobel Prize for Peace was awarded jointly to Begin and Sadat. But by the end of the year, the Israelis had announced plans for more settlements on the West Bank. Sadat, unable to resolve this difference even with U.S. help, meanwhile felt isolated within the Arab world; and in 1981 he was assassinated by disgruntled Islamic fundamentalists. Meanwhile, a new war threatened in Lebanon, where tens of thousands of Palestinian refugees had relocated. Although Carter had demonstrated his sincerity — devoting more attention to the Middle East than any previous American president — his triumph proved short-lived.

CARTER'S CRISIS OF CONFIDENCE

Carter's modest victories in Middle East negotiations, as it turned out, marked the final high point of his presidency. By 1979 it was clear that his domestic program for economic recovery had failed. To reassess his priorities, Carter withdrew with his staff to Camp David in July and emerged ten days later with a series of new energy proposals that Congress later rejected. But in his first public speech after the retreat, the president struck a nerve. The nation was experiencing a "crisis of confidence," he complained, and a feeling of "paralysis and stagnation and drift" hung like a dark cloud over the land. He called upon the people to change their attitude, to stop wallowing in personal problems, and to show more faith in their leaders.

Carter's "malaise" speech, as it was called, backfired. His public approval rating hardly rose again from a trough of 26 percent. While many Americans resented the president for heaping blame on the public instead of taking responsibility for his own failures, the press responded in full force. News

analysts attacked Carter with zeal, breaking stories of minor scandals in his administration and ridiculing the president in various ways. Jokes about Carter's bumbling brother Billy, who had endorsed "Billy Beer," and even the president's own painful hemorrhoids got television laughs on the "Johnny Carson Show" and "Saturday Night Live." Far from pleasing the public, Carter could not even hold their respect.

Carter's prospects for reelection appeared, therefore, to hang on the balance of international affairs. If he could only put his human rights policy on a firm ground, move toward lasting peace in the Middle East, or strike a bargain with the Soviets on arms limitation, he might restore voter confidence. If not, his presidency would end after one term.

(Mis)Handling the Unexpected

As Carter's first term came to a close, multiple crises suddenly cut loose in foreign affairs, and long-standing divisions within the State Department drew Carter first one way and then the other. His secretary of state Cyrus Vance recommended well-planned negotiations to soothe Soviet-U.S. relations and resolve disagreements with Third World nations. National security advisor Zbigniew Brzezinski, a bitterly anti-Communist Polish exile, adhered to Cold War policies and interpreted events in even remote sections of Africa or South America as plays in a zero-sum game: wherever the United States lost influence, the Soviet Union gained, and vice-versa. Often disoriented by contradictory advice, the president found himself mired in problems inherited from his predecessors and unable to move.

In 1979, the overthrow of the brutal Nicaraguan dictatorship of Anastasio Somoza, long-time ally of the United States, left Carter without a moderate successor to support. When the new Sandinista revolutionary government pleaded for help, Congress turned down Carter's request for $75 million in aid to Nicaragua. The Sandinistas aligned with Cuba and the Soviet Union and began to assist a revolutionary movement in El Salvador. The Carter administration continued to back the government in San Salvador even after the assassination of Oscar Romero, the Catholic archbishop who supported the revolutionaries. Following the rape and murder of four U.S. Catholic church women, apparently by the ultraright Salvadoran Armed Forces trained in the United States, peace activists and other Americans pleaded with Carter to withhold further military aid.

Conservatives meanwhile demanded yet more funds to bolster the repressive anticommunist regime.

Africa posed similarly perplexing problems. Emerging from colonial rule, African nations vacillated between allying with the United States and courting the Soviet Union. In this tricky political territory, UN Ambassador (and former civil rights leader) Andrew Young, the first major African American diplomat assigned to Africa, scored an important victory in encouraging oil-rich Nigeria to resume economic relations with the United States. But Young could not persuade Carter to recognize the antiapartheid government of Angola, which had invited 20,000 Cuban troops to help in their fight against South Africa. Nor did Carter's and Young's criticisms of the South African regime, unaccompanied by any economic sanctions, satisfy black Africans. After Carter fired Young for having met secretly with the Palestine Liberation Organization (PLO), the president proved even less effective in negotiating with antiapartheid leaders.

Carter had once advised Americans to put their "inordinate fear of Communism" behind them in order to focus more clearly on the pressing problems of the Third World. By 1979, events in Central America and in Africa gave the fear of communism a new twist and caused relations between the United States and Soviet Union, which backed these revolutionary movements, to slide backward.

The Soviet invasion of neighboring Afghanistan produced a major stalemate. Two Afghan military coups during the 1970s had troubled the Soviets, who feared that the United States might forge an alliance with a new right-wing government and create yet another border fortified with U.S. missiles. After widespread rioting broke out, 30,000 Soviet troops entered Afghan territory in December, 1979, precipitating a civil war quickly labeled by the American press the "Russian Vietnam." The Soviets possessed high-technology weapons, but the Islamic fundamentalists, who received arms from the United States, knew their territory. The war quickly bogged down, and Americans heard familiar stories, this time of Soviet soldiers using drugs and expressing disillusionment with their government. And this time, it was the United States that called for an immediate withdrawal of troops.

President Carter responded to these events with his own corollary to the Monroe Doctrine. The so-called Carter Doctrine asserted the determination of the United States to protect its interests in yet another area of the world, the Persian Gulf. Carter acted on the advice of Brzezinski who believed the Soviet Union would soon try to secure for itself a warm-water port on the Gulf, an area rich in oil and now vital to U.S. interests. The president backed up his policy by halting exports of grain and high technology to the Soviet Union, asking American athletes to boycott the 1980 Olympic Games in Moscow, and reinstituting registration for the military draft in the United States, and the massive U.S. arms build-up of the 1980s was already under way.

By the end of Carter's first term, the Cold War had once again heated up. In his State of the Union address in January, 1980, Carter pledged that "the United States will remain the strongest of all nations." With the economy still hurting from the effects of Cold War spending, Carter called for yet another increase in the military budget. He also signed Presidential Directive 59 guaranteeing the arms alleged necessary to win a prolonged nuclear war. The prospect of peace and detente dried up.

The Iran Hostage Crisis

On November 4, 1979, Iranian revolutionaries seized the U.S. embassy in Tehran, and held fifty-two employees hostage for 444 days. This event made President Carter's previous problems small by comparison. "I–R–A–N," wrote Rosalynn Carter. "Those four letters had become a curse to me."

For decades, U.S. foreign policy in the Middle East had depended on a friendly government in Iran. After the CIA had helped to overthrow a nationalist regime and installed the Pahlavi family in 1953, millions of U.S. dollars poured into the Iranian economy and the shah's armed forces. By the late 1970s, Iran had become the most Westernized society in the Arab world. President Carter toasted the shah in 1978 for "the admiration and love which your people give you" while he overlooked the rampant corruption in the shah's government and a well-organized opposition. By early 1979 a revolution led by the Islamic fundamentalist Ayatollah Ruholla Khomeini had overthrown the shah.

When Carter allowed Mohammad Reza Pahlavi, the deposed shah, to enter the United States for treatment for cancer in November, a group of radical students retaliated, storming the U.S. embassy and taking the staff as hostages. Islamic fundamentalists paraded in the streets of Tehran waving placards with anti-American and anti-Carter slogans and calling the United States the "Great Satan."

Iranians demonstrate against the United States, burning an American flag and waving signs declaring "the U.S. is our enemy." The Iran hostage crisis, which began November 4, 1979 when a mob of Iranians seized the U.S. embassy in Teheran, contributed to Carter's defeat at the polls the following year. Despite a dramatic but failed helicopter rescue mission, fifty-two embassy employees were held hostage for 444 days.

Cyrus Vance assured Carter that only negotiations could free the Americans. Caught up in a reelection campaign and lobbied by Brzezinski for decisive action, Carter directed U.S. military forces to stage a nighttime helicopter rescue mission. But a sandstorm caused the aircraft to crash and burn, leaving eight Americans dead, their burned corpses displayed by the enraged Iranians. Short of all-out armed attack, which surely would have resulted in the hostages' death, the United States had used up its options.

The political and economic fallout was heavy. Cyrus Vance resigned, the first Secretary of State in sixty-five years to leave office over a political difference with a president. The price of oil rose by 60 percent, nearly doubling inflation to 13 percent. Carter had failed in the one area he had proclaimed central to the future of the United States — energy. He had also violated his own human rights policy, which was to be his distinctive mark on American foreign affairs. At the close of his term, the United States was more dependent on foreign oil yet less influential in the Middle East than at any time in the twentieth century.

Election 1980

Jimmy Carter began his campaign for renomination and reelection in what seemed the worst possible light. The *Wall Street Journal* commented in August 1980 that "one continues to look in vain for anything beyond his own reflection that he wants to accomplish with the power of his office, for any consistent purpose or vision." Carter had no significant accomplishments to stand on, not even a program for the future. His Democratic rival from 1976, Washington Senator Henry Jackson, described Carter as "washed up."

One more surprise dogged Carter. During May, Fidel Castro invited thousands of Cubans, including political prisoners and petty criminals, to leave the island. Dubbed the "Marielitos," these Cuban refugees landed in Florida and demanded asylum. Unable to convince them to leave and unwilling to deport them, Carter established camps that were, inmates charged, inhumane. "We ought to be thankful we have a country that people want to come to," Carter insisted, while many Americans did not welcome the Cuban "boat people."

Carter's bid for renomination depended more on his incumbency than his popularity. Delegates at the Democratic convention unenthusiastically endorsed Carter, along with running mate Walter Mondale, a similarly uninspiring campaigner. On the Republican side, former California governor Ronald Reagan had been building his campaign since his near nomination in 1976. Former CIA director and Texas oil executive George Bush, more moderate than Reagan, became the Republican candidate for vice-president. The Moral Majority, led by Reverend Jerry Falwell, placed itself squarely in his camp, promising a ''Conservative Revolution'' to end legal abortion, reinstate school prayer, and bear down on world Communism. Senator Jesse Helms's Congressional Club contributed $4.6 million to the Reagan campaign and funded strident ''negative'' campaigns against noted Senatorial liberals.

The Republican campaign made the most of Carter's mismanagement of both domestic and foreign affairs. Reagan repeatedly asked voters ''Are you better off now than you were four years ago?'' Although critics questioned Reagan's competence, the attractive, soft-spoken actor shrugged off criticisms while spotlighting the many problems besetting the country.

The Republican ticket cruised to victory. Carter won only 41 percent of the popular vote to Reagan's 50.7 percent, 49 votes in the electoral college to Reagan's 489. Liberal Republican John Anderson, running as an independent, won nearly six million votes, or 6.6 percent of the popular vote. The Republicans won control of the Senate, for the first time since 1952 and with the largest majority since 1928. Still, most Americans remained apathetic toward the electoral process. Barely half of the eligible voters had turned out in the 1980 election, bringing Ronald Reagan into office with a mandate of a thin 25 percent.

CONCLUSION

An era of quavering liberalism, but also of moderate conservatism, had come to an end. Gerald Ford's failure to set a new course either domestically or internationally had completed the Republican debacle of Richard Nixon's administration. Jimmy Carter, elected to office promising to restore public confidence in government, suffered repeated embarrassments and political defeats. Hopeful signs appeared mainly in local communities, in the form of campaigns for better schools, neighborhoods, and protection from toxic wastes. Grass-roots activism cut across political lines but stopped short of developing into a national movement.

As Carter's tenure in office came to a close, the economic problems that concerned most Americans continued to be exacerbated by military spending and dependence on foreign oil. The focus of U.S. foreign policy had begun to shift from the Soviet Union to the Middle East, where diplomatic conflict brought neither national security nor a fresh supply of lost-cost crude oil. The erosion of America's industrial base meanwhile mirrored the nation's decline from unquestioned superpower status. Like the Soviet Union, the United States had paid too much for the Cold War.

CHRONOLOGY

1973   Arab oil embargo
Roe v. Wade legalizes abortion;
Construction begins of Alaska Oil Pipeline

1974   OPEC oil prices increase
Richard Nixon resigns presidency;
Gerald Ford takes office with Nelson Rockefeller as vice-president
Ford pardons Nixon
Ford introduces WIN

1975   Fall of South Vietnamese government
Mayaguez incident
Antibusing protests

1976   Percentage of African Americans attending college (9.3 percent) peaks
Hyde Amendment on abortions;
Tom Wolfe declares "Me Decade"
Jimmy Carter elected president

1977   President Carter announces human rights policy

1978   *Bakke v. University of California*
Camp David Peace Accords signed;
Panama Canal Treaties;
Proposition 13 passes in California referendum;
Inflation reaches 10 percent

1979   Three Mile Island nuclear accident
Moral Majority formed;
Nicaraguan Revolution;
SALT II treaty negotiated;
Soviets invade Afghanistan;
Iranian Revolution and hostage crisis

1980   U.S. boycotts Olympic Games in Moscow
Ronald Reagan elected president

Additional Readings

PETER CARROLL, *It Seemed Like Nothing Happened* (1983). A delightful collection of anecdotes about the 1970s. Captures the everyday lives of Americans, especially their frustrations to achieve according to their expectations. Finds a bitter comedy in the blunders of the era's mediocre political leaders.

DANIEL F. FORD, *Three Mile Island: Thirty Minutes to Meltdown* (1982). A journalistic account of the crisis at the time of the nuclear accident.

SUSAN HARTMANN, *From Margin to Mainstream: American Women and Politics Since 1960* (1989). An interpretation of women's growing role in American politics. Analyzes the important developments of the 1970s, most pointedly women's influence on the Democratic party. Also looks at the forces that pushed the Equal Rights Amendment through Congress but failed to see it ratified in the states.

JEROME L. HIMMELSTEIN, *To the Right: The Transformation of American Conservatism* (1990). The story of the decline of "Old Right" fiscal conservatives, isolationists, and Republican "centrists" during the 1970s and the rise of the "New Right" based in evangelical Protestantism. Analyzes the New Right's ability to rally support for Cold War foreign policy and the rollback of social welfare programs at both federal and state levels of government.

JOHN P. HOERR, *And the Wolf Finally Came: The Decline of the American Steel Industry* (1988). A personal and journalistic view of Pittsburgh's eclipse as a steel-producing center. Details the decline in productivity since the complacently prosperous years of the 1950s and the failure of plant managers, as well as unions, to adjust to the more competitive methods of steel production abroad.

WILLIAM QUANDT, *Camp David* (1986). An insider's story of Jimmy Carter's greatest triumph. Analyzes the Middle Eastern diplomacy as the centerpiece of Carter's otherwise unsuccessful program of world peace through negotiations and better understanding.

EDWIN SCHUR, *The Awareness Trap: Self Absorption Instead of Social Change* (1976). A description of the various contemporary "awareness" movements. Schur gives detailed examples of how programs of self-improvement and religious mysticism appealed to people disoriented by social change and willing to pay money to find "meaning" in their lives.

JAMES I. SUNDQUIST, *The Decline and Resurgence of Congress* (1981). A close political study of changing relations between two key branches of government. Sundquist underlines the revival of congressional strength after President Johnson's successful broadening of executive powers, and the bipartisan tug of war that took place between Congress and its 1970s counterparts: the often haughty Nixon, the congressional-style "weak" president Gerald Ford, and the distant Jimmy Carter.

CYRUS VANCE, *Hard Choices* (1983). A former secretary of state's day-to-day recollections of his time in office during the Carter years. Vance, a career diplomat, reviewed the crucial policy decisions concerning Afghanistan and the Middle East, as well as the factors that caused him to resign from the Carter administration.

WILLIAM JULIUS WILSON, *The Declining Significance of Race: Blacks and Changing American Institutions* (rev. ed., 1980). A controversial book on the distinctions between racial and class differences affecting poor African Americans. Wilson argues that with integration of communities and businesses race has become less important than class.-

31 THE CONSERVATIVE ASCENDANCY, 1980–1992

● MASHANTUCKET PEQUOTS BUILD A CASINO

Slow Turtle, an Indian medicine man, burned a thanksgiving offering of herbs and bark to the Great Spirit. He presided over dedication ceremonies at the new $58 million Foxwoods High Stakes Bingo and Casino on the Mashantucket Pequot reservation in Ledyard, Connecticut. Several days later, 15,000 people swarmed through Foxwoods, eager to try their luck at blackjack, roulette, poker, and craps. Hundreds of cheerful employees were on hand to serve their needs, the men dressed in Indian-style blouses trimmed with beads and the women in skimpy fringed tunics. The atmosphere inside was soft and understated, with Indian patterns and designs leading the eye to the casino's most unusual feature: large bay windows looking out upon wooded hills. Unlike Las Vegas and Atlantic City, the players here would know night from day.

GAMBLING RESHAPES THE ECONOMY OF A CONNECTICUT COMMUNITY

Foxwoods represented a return to economic power for the Mashantucket Pequots and it promised to reshape the economic landscape of surrounding Connecticut communities as well. In the early seventeenth century the Pequot Indians had fifteen villages along the southeastern Connecticut coast and along its rivers. They were expanding their territory and trade networks at the time of the initial European settlements in the region. The bloody Pequot War of 1636–37 was the first serious conflict between colonizers and the indigenous populations in New England. Puritan militiamen shot and burned as many as 700 Pequot men, women, and children in one battle alone at Mystic Fort. This massacre established English control over the Indians of southern New England and began a long downward spiral for the Pequots.

Colonial authorities split the survivors into two groups, granting the Mashantucket (western) Pequots some 2,000 to 3,000 acres of land. But over the years this land was slowly stripped away. By the early 1970s, the tribe's numbers had dwindled to about fifty, only two of whom lived on a reservation that had shrunk to 214 acres. Revival began in 1983 when the tribe won federal recognition and received a $900,000 trust fund to buy 2,500 acres of ancestral lands. Various business ventures — a restaurant, a hog farm, maple syrup production, a greenhouse — all failed, with one exception: a high-stakes bingo hall. After a long legal battle with the state of Connecticut, decided by the U.S. Supreme Court in 1991, the tribe won

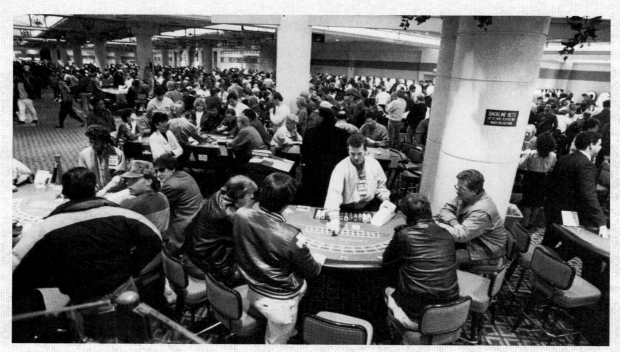

Gamblers crowded around card games and dice tables at the Foxwoods High Stakes Bingo and Casino, on the Ledyard, Connecticut reservation of the Mashantucket Pequots, 1993. The success of Foxwoods made it one of the biggest employers in southeast Connecticut. It also spurred a host of Indian nations and municipalities across the nation, all eager to rake in profits and create new jobs, to propose plans for more gambling casinos.

the right to convert their bingo operation into a full-scale gambling casino, excluding slot machines.

To build Foxwoods, the Mashantuckets borrowed $55 million from a Malaysian company that operated hotels and casinos in Asia. Under an agreement between Connecticut and the tribe, state agencies regulate the casino. All profits remain with the tribe, after it reimburses the state for money spent on regulation. The Mashantuckets paid no taxes to the state or federal governments. Some in the adjacent community of Ledyard, a traditional New England village of 15,000 people, worried about traffic congestion, pollution, and crime. Others expressed concern over the human tragedies caused by compulsive gambling. But the potential for Foxwoods to reverse southeastern Connecticut's disastrous economic decline dominated all discussion. A 1990 state study estimated that New London County stood to lose anywhere from 13,000 to 27,000 jobs over the next five years due to cutbacks in military spending. Out of 110,000 jobs in the county, 66,000 depended directly on the Pentagon. The Electric Boat division of General Dynamics employed 23,000 people alone building Seawolf submarines, a program scheduled for cancelation. Forty percent of all households in Ledyard had at least one person in a military-related job. No wonder, then, that over 25,000 people applied for the 2,300 job openings at Foxwoods. At $3.75 an hour plus tips, dealers and cocktail waitresses would earn as much as $30,000 a year.

For the Mashantucket Pequots, conflicts would continue between ancient tribal traditions and hard-nosed profit making. When they discovered that the water line to the casino went through ancient tribal encampments, they had it rerouted. Indians worried about the forests that had to be destroyed to clear the building site. To help allay these concerns, tribe members personally tagged every tree in the area. The original motif for the casino, a beaded Pequot wampum belt, was considered too close in design to a belt found in a tribal grave, and the design was changed to avoid offending the spirit of a long-dead ancestor. "I think in terms of quarterly profits and annual results," noted Albert Luciani, an Atlantic City veteran hired by the tribe to run the business. "And they really think in terms of the millennium."

By 1993 Foxwoods was the single most profitable gambling casino in the United States, turning an estimated annual profit of over $200 million on gross revenues of over $400 million. In exchange for permission to install slot machines and a promise not to legalize gambling off the reservation, the Pequots began contributing $100 million per year to the state of Connecticut. The tribe could now guarantee college tuition for all its children, world travel for its elders, and new homes for its 250 members. It hired its own archeologist to help recover lost tribal history. Plans for expansion included a second casino, two hotels, a golf course, as well as an Indian museum and conference center. The number of jobs at the Foxwoods complex was expected to climb to over 10,000.

Foxwoods' success inspired other Indian peoples across the nation: some 52 tribes in 17 states operated more than 100 casinos and bingo sites, creating a $6 billion per year industry. Reid A. Walker, an executive with the National Indian Gaming Association, explained that reservation gambling had "brought us new hope. It's a renaissance for Indian country, giving us power to start our own programs in health care, infrastructure, education and more." In California the once impoverished Cabayan Mission Indians, who had built the first reservation casino in the early 1980s, constructed a 950 unit housing development, a new power plant, and guaranteed universal employment, health care, and education for its members. In New Mexico the 600 year old Sandia tribe renewed its culture with $16 million in annual gambling profits and helped revive the economy in Albuquerque. In upstate New York the 1000 member Oneida Nation made plans to build a new $10 million casino that promised 2000 new jobs and an end to the chronic unemployment rate on its reservation.

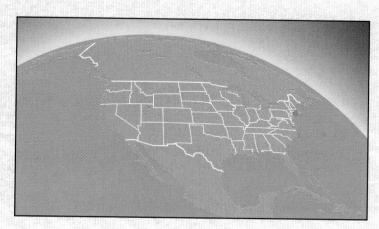

The creation of the Foxwoods Casino brought about a dramatic change in the economic life of Ledyard and nearby Connecticut towns. During the 1980s, many American communities experienced a conversion from an economy based on industry and manufacturing to one organized around services and information. The move to a postindustrial base — in this case gambling and tourism — brought wrenching dislocations for Ledyard workers, including stiff pay cuts for most. But as in many communities throughout the nation, the new service-based economy symbolized by the Foxwoods Casino was the only game in town.

THE REAGAN REVOLUTION

No other twentieth-century president except Franklin D. Roosevelt left as deep a personal imprint on American politics as Ronald Reagan. Ironically, Reagan himself began his political life as an ardent New Deal Democrat. Even after his transformation into a conservative Republican, Reagan regularly invoked the words and deeds of FDR. Reagan admired Roosevelt as an inspirational leader who led the nation through depression and war. But by the time he entered the White House in 1981, Reagan had rejected the activist welfare state legacy of the New Deal era. With his overwhelming electoral victories in 1980 and 1984, Reagan and his conservative allies tried to radically reshape the political and social landscape of the nation.

The Great Communicator

Ronald Reagan was born in 1911 and raised in the small town of Dixon, Illinois. Reagan's father was a salesman and an alcoholic who had a tough time

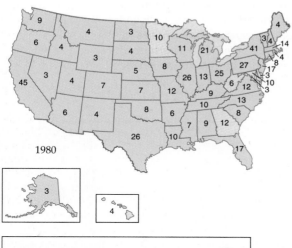

1980

Candidates (Party)	Electoral vote	Popular vote
Ronald Reagan (Republican)	489 (91%)	43,901,812 (50.7%)
Jimmy Carter (Democratic)	49 (9%)	35,483,820 (41.0%)
John B. Anderson (Independent)	–	5,719,722 (6.6%)
Other Candidates (Libertarian)	–	921,299 (1.1%)

The Election of 1980
Ronald Reagan won a landslide victory over incumbent Jimmy Carter, who managed to carry only 5 states. Reagan attracted millions of traditionally Democratic voters to the Republican camp.

holding a job. His strong-willed mother was a fundamentalist Christian who kept the family together amidst frequent moves. A WPA job for the father helped the Reagans survive the hard times of the Great Depression. As a child, Reagan learned to disconnect himself from the difficult scenes at home, withdrawing into himself. He took refuge in his own world of imaginary stories and plays. He identified with real-life sports heroes like Babe Ruth and Jack Dempsey, as well as fictional figures, heroes of the Wild West. Encouraged by his mother, Reagan began acting in church plays and in productions of Eureka College, from which he graduated in 1932.

In 1937 Reagan made a successful screen test with the Warner Brothers studio in Hollywood, and he began a movie acting career that lasted for a quarter century. He was never a big star, appearing in scores of mostly "B" movies. But Reagan became a skilled actor. On screen, he was tall, handsome, and affable, and his characters usually projected an optimistic and sunny personality. In later years, Reagan cheerfully credited his acting experience with his political success. He told one interviewer: "An actor knows two important things—to be honest in what he's doing and to be in touch with the audience. That's not bad advice for a politician either. My actor's instincts simply told me to speak the truth as I saw it and felt it."

While in Hollywood Reagan became active in union affairs. While serving as president of the Screen Actors Guild from 1947 to 1952, Reagan became a leader of the anti-Communist forces in Hollywood. He then began to distance himself from New Deal liberalism. In 1954 Reagan became host of a new national television program, "General Electric Theater," and began a long stint as a national spokesman for GE. Reagan toured GE plants and surrounding communities across the country, publicizing the TV show and giving political speeches on behalf of the company. These talks celebrated the achievements of corporate America and emphasized the dangers of big government, excessive liberalism, and radical trade unions. Reagan's GE experience made him a significant public figure and allowed him to perfect a political style and a conservative message.

He switched his party affiliation to Republican and became a popular fundraiser and speaker for the California GOP. Reagan took a leading role in conservative Republican Barry Goldwater's 1964 presidential campaign. A televised address on Goldwater's behalf thrust Reagan himself into national political prominence. By this time, Reagan had formulated a standard speech that hammered home

Ronald and Nancy Reagan at the Inaugural Ball, January 20, 1981. The Reagans, supported by a circle of wealthy conservative friends from the business world and Hollywood, brought a lavish style to the White House that helped define the culture of the 1980s.

his conservative message: antitax, anticommunism, antigovernment. The attack on big government was at the core of the Reagan message. He lashed out at growing bureaucracy and celebrated the achievements of entrepreneurs unfettered by government regulation or aid. He invoked the Founding Fathers, who knew, he claimed, "that outside of its legitimate functions, government does nothing as well or as economically as the private sector of the economy."

A group of wealthy, conservative Southern Californians encouraged Reagan to run for office himself. These backers, most of whom had made fortunes in California real estate and the oil business, saw themselves as self-made men and shared a basic distrust of government intervention in the economy. With their financial and political support, Reagan defeated Democratic governor Edmund G. Brown in 1966 and won reelection in 1970. As governor, Reagan cut the state welfare rolls, placed limits on the increase of state employees, and

funneled a large share of state tax revenues back to local governments. He vigorously attacked student protesters and black militants, thereby tapping into the conservative backlash against 1960s activism.

As governor, Reagan also perfected a laid-back style of governing that left most of the actual work to his aides and allowed him to concentrate on speech-making and fundraising. Reagan became the Republican candidate for president in 1980 after failing to win the nomination in 1968 and 1976. Exploiting his strengths as an actor and salesman, he became an extremely likable and effective campaigner. The conservative message that had been consigned to the fringes of American politics in 1964 now re-emerged as the mainstream. Jimmy Carter's political weakness also helped the Republicans to carry the Senate for the first time since 1954. As Reagan entered the White House in January 1981, his supporters confidently predicted that the "Reagan revolution" would usher in a new age in American political life.

Reaganomics

In the 1980 election Republicans successfully exploited popular discontent over stagflation — an unprecedented combination of recession, high inflation, and steep interest rates. The last two years of the Carter administration saw prices rising between 10 and 18 percent a year. Interest rates of 20 percent were the highest in American history. During the Reagan presidency, supply-side economists dominated the administration's thinking and helped redirect American economic policy. Since the mid-1970s, supply-side theorists had urged a sharp break with the Keynesian policies that had been dominant since the New Deal era. Keynesians traditionally favored moderate tax cuts and increases in government spending to stimulate the economy and reduce unemployment during recessions. By putting more money in people's pockets, they argued, greater consumer demand would lead to economic expansion.

By contrast, supply-siders called for simultaneous tax cuts and reductions in public spending. This combination, they claimed, would give private entrepreneurs and investors greater incentives to start businesses, take risks, invest capital — and thereby create new wealth and jobs. Whatever revenues were lost in lower tax rates would be more than made up by the new growth. At the same time, spending cuts would keep the federal deficit under control and thereby keep interest rates down. George Gilder, conservative author of the best-selling *Wealth and Poverty* (1981), summarized the supply-side view when he wrote, "a successful economy depends on the proliferation of the rich"; entrepreneurs were the heroes of the American economy. "To help the poor and middle classes," Gilder declared, "one must cut the taxes of the rich." On the political level, supply-siders looked to reward the most loyal Republican constituencies: the affluent and the business community. At the same time, they hoped to reduce the flow of federal dollars received by two core Democratic constituencies: the recipients and professional providers of health and welfare programs.

Reagan quickly won approval for two key pieces of legislation based on these ideas. The Economic Recovery Tax Act of 1981, passed by a very willing Congress, cut income and corporate taxes by $747 billion over five years. For individuals, the act cut taxes across the board by 5 percent in 1981, then 10 percent in 1982 and another 10 percent in 1983. It also reduced the maximum tax on all income from 70 percent to 50 percent, lowered the maximum capital gains tax from 28 percent to 20 percent, and eliminated the distinction between earned and unearned income. This last measure proved a boon to the small and richest fraction of the population, which derives most of its income from rent, dividends, and interest.

With the help of conservative southern and western Democrats in the House, the administration also pushed through a comprehensive program of spending cuts awkwardly known as the Omnibus Reconciliation Act of 1981. This bill mandated reduced federal spending of $136 billion for the period 1982–84, covering over 200 social and cultural programs. The hardest-hit areas included federal appropriations for education, the environment, synthetic fuels research, health, housing, urban aid, food stamps, and the arts. The conservative coalition in the House allowed only one vote on the entire package of spending cuts. This strategy allowed conservatives to slash appropriations for a wide variety of domestic programs in one fell swoop. One leading House liberal, Democrat Leon Panetta of California, lamented: "We are dealing with over 250 programs with no committee consideration, no committee hearings, no debate and no opportunity to offer amendments."

Reagan appointed conservatives to head the Environmental Protection Agency (EPA), the Occupational Safety and Health Administration (OSHA), and the Consumer Product Safety Commission (CPSC). These individuals abolished or weakened hundreds of rules governing business activity in the environment, workplace safety, and consumer protection, all in the name of efficiency and productivity. The deregulatory fever dominated Cabinet departments as well. Secretary of the Interior James Watt typified the administration's desire to privatize the federal government, opening up formerly protected wilderness areas and wetlands to private developers. Secretary of Transportation Drew Lewis eliminated regulations passed in the 1970s aimed at reducing air pollution and improving fuel efficiency in cars and trucks.

The Reagan administration aggressively curbed the regulatory authority of the federal government in the business sphere as well. Following the tenets of supply-side economics, Reagan weakened the Antitrust Division of the Justice Department, the Securities and Exchange Commission, and the Federal Home Loan Bank Board. Large corporations, Wall Street stock brokerages, investment banking houses, and the savings and loan banking industry were all allowed to operate with a much freer hand than ever before. By the late 1980s, the unfortunate consequences of this freedom would become apparent in a series of unprecedented scandals in the nation's financial markets and banking industry.

Military Buildup

During the 1980 election campaign, Reagan argued that American military capability had weakened seriously since the Vietnam War. His calls to "restore America's defenses" helped reinforce the public perception that President Carter had dealt ineffectively with the Iranian hostage crisis. For Reagan, there was no contradiction between his campaign vows to cut the cost of government and the need to beef up defense spending. Along with reduced government spending and lowered tax rates, a stronger military posture was part of the ideological core of Reagan's world view. Military strength symbolized the power of the nation rather than the authority of government.

The Reagan administration greatly accelerated a trend already under way during the last two years of the Carter presidency: a sharp increase in defense spending. The Pentagon's annual budget expanded from $171 billion in 1981 to over $300 billion by 1985. Secretary of Defense Caspar Weinberger and Secretary of State Alexander Haig persistently lobbied the Congress, emphasizing the need for a stronger nuclear weapons capability. This included the MX missile, based mostly in western states, and the deployment of Cruise and Pershing missiles in Western Europe. In 1983, President Reagan pro-

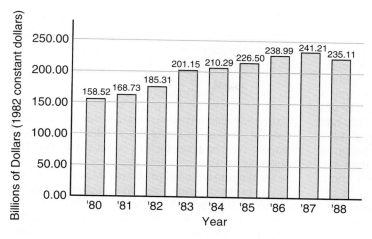

U.S. Military Spending, 1980–1990

Measured in constant dollars, American military spending grew nearly 50 percent between 1981 and 1987.

Source: From Robert Griffith, ed., *Major Problems in American History Since 1945* (D.C. Heath, 1992), p. 694. Statistics compiled by David Murphy.

claimed his Strategic Defense Initiative (SDI) popularly called Star Wars. He claimed, though few scientists agreed, that this enormously expensive project could use satellites and lasers to provide an impregnable shield against nuclear attack. Overall, the Reagan budgets for military spending totaled $1.6 trillion over five years.

Defense contracts meant the difference between prosperity and recession for blue- and white-collar workers, merchants, developers, and bankers in scores of communities. Most of these were located in the Pacific, Atlantic, and Gulf states. In 1983, California led all states with over $26 billion in military contracts, followed by New York ($9.6 billion), Texas ($8.2 billion), and Virginia ($7.1 billion). The military buildup of the 1980s reflected a significant shift in federal budget priorities. In 1980, 28 percent of federal spending went to what the Office of Management and Budget calls "human resources" (excluding Social Security and Medicare): housing, education, urban, and social services. By 1987, federal outlays for human resources totaled only 22 percent. In the same period, defense spending rose from 23 to 28 percent of the federal budget.

Recession, Recovery, Fiscal Crisis

The Reagan administration's economic policies had very mixed results. A severe recession, the worst since the 1930s, gripped the nation in 1982. The official unemployment rate reached nearly 11 percent by the end of that year, over 11.5 million people. Another 3 million had been out of work so long they no longer actively looked for jobs, and therefore were not counted in official statistics. Many communities, particularly in the industrial Midwest and Northeast, experienced depression-

like conditions. In January 1983, 20,000 people lined up for hours in subfreezing weather to apply for 200 jobs at a Milwaukee auto-frame factory. American steelmakers operated at only about one-third of capacity.

By the middle of 1983 the economy had begun to recover. That year unemployment dropped to about 8 percent, and inflation was below 5 percent. The economy as a whole grew 3.6 percent, the biggest increase since the mid-1970s. Unemployment remained relatively low, and the stock market boomed, pushing the Dow Jones industrial average from 776 in August 1982 to an all-time high of 2,722 in August 1987. Inflation averaged just over 3 percent from 1982 to 1986. Administration spokesmen took credit for the turnaround, hailing the supply-side fiscal policies that had drastically cut taxes and domestic spending. But critics pointed to other factors: the Federal Reserve Board's tight-money policies, the drastic drop in oil prices due to a worldwide energy glut, and the large military buildup that pumped hundreds of billions into defense spending.

The economic recovery of the early and mid-1980s spread unevenly across the nation's regions, industries, and classes. It produced over 13 million new jobs between 1981 and 1986. But half of these paid less than $11,661, the federally defined poverty level for a family of four. Real family income rose nearly 11 percent from 1982 to 1986. But with average hourly earnings stagnant, most of this gain resulted from the addition of a second paycheck from a wife or child. While certain industries and the communities they supported boomed — computers, electronics, real estate, financial services — others experienced painful shrinkage — automobiles, steel, rubber, machine tools, and textiles.

The supply-side formula also intensified an

ominous fiscal crisis. Although President Reagan had promised to balance the budget, his policies brought on the exact opposite. The effect of the 1982 tax cuts, which shrank the government's revenue base, along with the massive increase in military spending, brought chronic budget deficits and a mushrooming federal debt. Before the 1980s the largest single-year budget deficit in U.S. history had been $66 billion; in 1986 the deficit reached $221 billion. The national debt grew from $907 billion in 1980 to over $2 trillion in 1986, more than the federal government had accumulated in its entire previous history. Expenditures for paying just the interest on the national debt reached 14 percent of the annual budget in 1988, double the percentage set aside in 1974.

Deficit spending and a large national debt had existed long before the 1980s, but in the Reagan years the fiscal crisis became a structural problem with newly disturbing and perhaps permanent implications for the American economy. Big deficits kept interest rates high, as the government drove up the cost of borrowing the money it needed to pay its own bills. Foreign investors, attracted by high interest rates on government securities, pushed up the value of the dollar in relation to foreign currencies. The overvalued dollar made it more difficult for foreigners to buy American products, while making overseas goods cheaper to American consumers. Basic American industries — steel, autos, textiles — thus found it more difficult to compete abroad and at home. In 1980, the U.S. still enjoyed a trade surplus

of $166 billion. By 1987 the nation had an indebtedness to foreigners of $340 billion. Since World War I, America had been the world's leading creditor; in the mid-1980s it became its biggest debtor.

The Election of 1984

As the 1984 election approached, several Democrats vied for the opportunity to challenge President Reagan. They believed he was politically vulnerable, especially on the economic issues of recession and the weakening of social programs. Many Americans also expressed fears over the nuclear weapons buildup of the early 1980s. Many worried that such arms spending not only fueled deficits but also made a nuclear confrontation more likely. Polls showed that over 70 percent of Americans favored a nuclear freeze with the Soviet Union. In June 1982, three-quarters of a million people — the largest political rally in American history — demonstrated in New York City for a halt to spending on and deployment of nuclear weapons.

By early 1984, Walter Mondale had emerged as the leading candidate for the Democratic nomination. As a senator from Minnesota and Jimmy Carter's vice-president, Mondale had close ties with the party's liberal establishment.

Mondale's strength within the party establishment helped win him the nomination. At the Democratic convention, Mondale named Representative Geraldine Ferraro of New York as his running mate, a first for women in American politics. Charismatic

The Reverend Jesse Jackson, a dynamic disciple of the Martin Luther King, Jr., won wide support from black voters and poor people in the 1984 and 1988 Democratic presidential primaries. His Rainbow Coalition registered thousands of new voters in the South and the inner cities. Jackson's inspiring oratory emphasized the "common ground" shared by Americans of all races and classes.

speakers such as the Reverend Jesse Jackson, a dynamic disciple of Martin Luther King, Jr., and Governor Mario Cuomo of New York stirred the convention, and many watching on television, with their appeals to compassion, fairness, and brotherhood. Opinion polls showed Mondale running even with Reagan. But the president's enormous personal popularity, along with the booming economy, overwhelmed the Democratic ticket. While Mondale emphasized the growing deficit and called attention to those Americans left out of prosperity, Reagan cruised above it all. It was "morning again in America," his campaign ads claimed. The nation was strong, united, and prosperous, a far cry from the dark years of the Carter administration.

As *Newsweek* put it, Reagan embodied "America as it imagined itself to be — the bearer of the traditional Main Street values of family and neighborhood, of thrift, industry, and charity instead of government intervention where self-reliance failed." Reagan, despite his close association with the rich and powerful, remained what one journalist called a "cultural democrat," effectively reprising his Hollywood persona as the affable, friendly, neighborly citizen. Mondale's effort to revive the New Deal coalition failed, as Reagan won 59 percent of the popular vote and carried every state but Minnesota. In one of the biggest landslides in American history, Reagan won a quarter of registered Democrats, over 60 percent of independents, and a majority of the blue-collar vote. Despite Ferraro's presence, he took 54 percent of the women's vote. Small wonder that Republicans believed they now had a chance to replace the Democrats as the nation's majority party.

REAGAN'S FOREIGN POLICY

Against the stark imagery of the Iranian hostage crisis, Ronald Reagan campaigned to restore American leadership in world affairs. As president, he revived Cold War patriotism and championed American interventionism in the Third World, especially the Caribbean. The unprecedented military buildup during the Reagan years would have enormous consequences for the domestic economy as well as for America's international stance. Yet along with its hardline exhortations against the Soviet Union and international terrorism, the Reagan administration also pursued a less ideological, more pragmatic approach in key foreign policy decisions. Most important, sweeping and unanticipated internal changes within the Soviet Union made the entire Cold War framework of American foreign policy largely irrelevant by the late 1980s.

The Evil Empire

Part of Reagan's success in the 1980 campaign lay in appeals to restoring America's will to assert itself in the post-Vietnam era. In the early 1980s the Reagan administration made vigorous anti-Communist rhetoric the centerpiece of its foreign policy. A sharp turn from President Carter's focus on human rights and President Nixon's pursuit of détente, the Reagan approach brought a return to the Cold War mode of the 1950s and early 1960s. In a March 1983 speech to the National Association of Evangelicals, Reagan described the Soviet Union as "an evil empire . . . the focus of evil in the modern world." The president denounced the growing movement for a nuclear freeze, arguing that "we must find peace through strength."

Administration officials argued that the nation's military strength had fallen dangerously behind that of the Soviet Union during the 1970s. Critics disputed this, pointing out that the Soviet advantage in intercontinental ballistic missiles (ICBMs) was offset by American superiority in submarine-based forces and strategic aircraft. When asked at a congressional hearing whether he would exchange forces with his Soviet counterpart, General John Vessey, chairman of the Joint Chiefs of Staff, replied, "Not on your life." Nonetheless, the administration proceeded with plans designed to enlarge America's nuclear strike force. These included placing multiple-warhead MX missiles in hardened, fixed silos in the American heartland; deploying Cruise and Pershing II missiles in Western Europe, a short distance from the Soviet Union; and pressing for 100 new B-1 long-range bombers.

The call for the Strategic Defense Initiative introduced an unsettling new element into superpower relations. The administration pushed the concept of a space-based "Star Wars" missile defense system. Reagan himself was SDI's most ardent proponent, and it eventually grew into a $17 billion research and development program. Many scientists expressed deep skepticism about the technical feasibility of the project, likening it to a science fiction fantasy. From the Soviet perspective, SDI looked rather like a potentially offensive weapon that enhanced America's first-strike capability. Not only Soviets but millions of Europeans and Americans worried about the administration's routine acceptance of the possibility of nuclear war. A National Security Council directive outlined how the U.S.

might "prevail" in a "protracted" nuclear conflict. The Federal Emergency Management Agency published detailed plans for the evacuation of major cities in the event of such a war.

Attempts at meaningful arms control stalled in this atmosphere, and U.S.-Soviet relations deteriorated. In the fall of 1983, the Soviets shot down a Korean airliner that had strayed over Soviet airspace, killing 269 people. Soviet military officials, believing the plane to be on a spy mission, acted at best in a confused and incompetent manner. President Reagan immediately denounced the act as a deliberate "crime against humanity," and a wave of anti-USSR sentiment swept the country. The Soviet Union and its Eastern European allies boycotted the 1984 Olympics in Los Angeles, partly in response to the American boycott of the 1980 Moscow games. Reagan transformed images of enthusiastic Americans chanting "USA! USA!" and "We're number one!" into an effective backdrop for his reelection campaign. But the American-Soviet relationship seemed to have fallen to a new low.

Central America

Declaring the "Vietnam syndrome" over, the president confidently reasserted America's right to intervene anywhere in the world to fight Communist insurgency. The Reagan Doctrine, as this declaration was later called, offered a corollary to the notion of the "evil empire." It assumed that social revolution anywhere must be directed and controlled by the Soviet Union and its allies. The Reagan Doctrine found its most important expression in Central America, where the U.S. hoped to reestablish its historical control over the Caribbean basin. In early 1981 the U.S. ambassador to the United Nations, Jeanne Kirkpatrick warned, "Central America is the most important place in the world for the United States today."

On the economic front, the Caribbean Basin Initiative (CBI) promised to revitalize friendly nations through $350 million in U.S. aid and what Reagan called "the magic of the marketplace." The idea was to stimulate the Caribbean economy by encouraging the growth of business corporations and a freer flow of capital. Yet the Congress refused to play by the rules of free trade, placing stiff tariffs and import quotas on shoes, leather goods, and sugar competing with U.S. products. Many Latin American businessmen opposed key parts of CBI, such as generous tax breaks for foreign investors. They feared that once large multinational corporations entered their markets, CBI would strengthen the kind of chronic economic dependency that had

shaped so much of the region's past. In fact, indigenous history, internal political struggles, and the grinding poverty endured by the overwhelming majority of Central Americans counted for little in the administration's understanding of the region.

The administration preferred an essentially military solution to the region's problems, which, National Security Adviser Richard Allen argued, stemmed from "Fidel Castro's Soviet directed, armed, and financed marauders." Between 1980 and 1983 the U.S. poured more military aid into Central America than during the previous thirty years. In October 1983, American marines landed on the tiny island of Grenada, population 110,000, and quickly ousted an anti-American Marxist regime. The administration claimed that Grenada had become a base for the Cuban military and therefore posed a dangerous threat to the hemisphere. The easy triumph proved popular with most Grenadans and Americans. But in the larger and more complicated nations of El Salvador and Nicaragua, this sort of unilateral military action proved politically and strategically more difficult.

In El Salvador, the U.S. encouraged a repressive regime dominated by the military and a handful of wealthy landowners to pursue a military victory over a coalition of rebel groups fighting for social revolution. Salvadoran soldiers received special training in North American camps and from U.S. advisers sent to El Salvador. Military aid jumped from $6 million in 1980 to $82 million in 1982, and El Salvador received more U.S. economic assistance than any other Latin American country. By 1983 right-wing death squads, encouraged by military elements within the regime, had tortured and assassinated thousands of opposition leaders, including the Roman Catholic archbishop Oscar Romero. The election in 1984 of centrist president Jose Napoleon Duarte failed to end the bloody civil war. Some 53,000 Salvadorans, more than one out of every hundred, lost their lives in the conflict. As many as 300,000 Salvadoran refugees illegally entered the United States between 1979 and 1985.

In Nicaragua, the Reagan administration claimed that the Sandinista regime posed "an unusual and extraordinary threat to the national security." In 1979 the Sandinistas had successfully overthrown the Somoza family dictatorship, which had ruled Nicaragua with U.S. support since the 1930s. They took their name from Augusto Sandino, a popular leader who had led the resistance against U.S. occupation forces in the 1920s and 1930s (see Chapter 22). U.S. officials accused the Sandinistas of shipping arms to antigovernment rebels in El Salvador. In December 1981 Reagan approved a $19

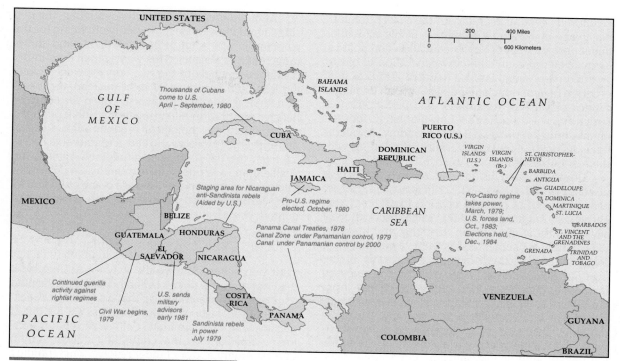

The U.S. in Central America, 1978–1990

U.S. intervention in Central America reached a new level of intensity with the so-called Reagan Doctrine. The bulk of U.S. aid came in the form of military support for the government of El Salvador and the "contra" rebels in Nicaragua.

million CIA plan arming and organizing Nicaraguan exiles, known as Contras, to fight against the Sandinista government. Reagan described the Contras, made up mostly of ex-*Somocista* National Guardsmen, as "freedom fighters" and "the moral equivalent of the Founding Fathers." As Reagan escalated this undeclared war, the aim became not merely the cutting of Nicaraguan aid to Salvadoran rebels but the overthrow of the regime itself.

Toward this end the CIA used neighboring Honduras as a sanctuary and training base for the Contras. In 1984 the CIA secretly mined Nicaraguan harbors. When Nicaragua won a judgment against the U.S. in the World Court over this violation of its sovereignty, the Reagan administration refused to recognize the court's jurisdiction in the case and ignored the verdict. Predictably, the U.S. covert war pushed the Sandinistas closer to Cuba and the Soviet bloc. Meanwhile, U.S. grass-roots opposition to Contra aid grew more vocal and widespread. A number of U.S. communities set up sister city projects offering humanitarian and technical assistance to Nicaraguan communities. Scores of U.S. churches offered sanctuary to political refugees from Central America.

In 1984 Congress reined in the covert war by passing the Boland Amendment, forbidding government agencies from supporting "directly or indirectly military or paramilitary operations" in Nicaragua. Denied funding by Congress, President Reagan now turned to the National Security Council to find a way to keep the Contra war going. Between 1984 and 1986 the NSC staff secretly ran the Contra assistance effort, raising $37 million in aid from foreign countries and private contributors. In 1987, the revelation of this unconstitutional scheme exploded before the public as part of the Iran-Contra affair. As we will soon see, this was the most damaging political scandal of the Reagan years.

Glasnost and Arms Control

Meanwhile, momentous political changes within the Soviet Union set in motion a reduction in East-West tensions and ultimately the end of the Cold War itself. Soviet premier Leonid Brezhnev, in power since 1964, died at the end of 1982. His successors, Yuri Andropov and Konstantin Chernenko, both died after brief terms in office. But in 1985 a new, reform-minded leader, Mikhail Gorbachev, won election as general secretary of the Soviet Communist party. A lifelong Communist in his mid-fifties and a pure product of Soviet education and politics, Gorbachev represented a new generation of disenchanted party members. He initiated a radical new program of economic and political reform under the rubrics of *glasnost* (openness) and *perestroika* (restructuring). Gorbachev's "new thinking" focused on modernizing the rigid Soviet economy, democratizing its politics, and transforming its relations with the rest of the world.

Gorbachev and his advisers opened up political discussion and encouraged criticism of the Soviet economy and its political culture. Inefficiency and chronic shortages plagued the Soviet production of such staples as meat, grain, clothing, and housing. Even when consumer goods were available, high prices often put them beyond the means of the average Soviet family. The government released long-time dissidents like Andrei Sakharov from prison and took the first halting steps toward profit-based, private initiatives in the economy. The "new thinking" inspired an unprecedented wave of diverse, critical perspectives in Soviet art, literature, journalism, and scholarship. In Gorbachev's view, improving the economic performance of the Soviet system depended first upon halting the arms race. Over 10 percent of the Soviet GNP went to defense spending, while the majority of its citizens still struggled to find even the most basic consumer items in shops. Gorbachev thus took the lead in negotiating a halt to the arms race with the United States.

The historical ironies were stunning. Reagan had made militant anticommunism the centerpiece of his political life. He staunchly resisted arms control initiatives and presided over the greatest military buildup in American history. But between 1985 and 1988 Reagan had four separate summit meetings with the new Soviet leader. In October 1986 Reagan and Gorbachev met in Reykjavík, Iceland. Gorbachev proposed a startling 50 percent cut in all strategic nuclear weapons. He also suggested "zero option" for intermediate nuclear forces (INF), with the Soviets giving up their predominance in missiles in the European theater in exchange for American removal of Pershing missiles. But the Iceland summit bogged down over the issue of SDI. Reagan refused to abandon his plan for a space-based defensive umbrella. Gorbachev insisted that the plan violated the 1972 Anti-Ballistic Missile Treaty, and that SDI might eventually allow the U.S. to make an all-out attack.

After another year of tough negotiating, the two sides agreed to a modest INF treaty providing for the elimination of a total of 2611 medium- and short-range nuclear missiles. This was a small dent in the combined arsenals of the two superpowers, covering less than 4 percent of total nuclear warheads. Nonetheless, the INF treaty also called for comprehensive, mutual, on-site inspections, and it provided an important psychological breakthrough. Reagan himself visited Moscow in 1988, a remarkable reversal from the days when he thundered against the "evil empire." At one of the summits a Soviet leader humorously announced, "We are going to do something terrible to you Americans — we are going to deprive you of an enemy."

The Iran-Contra Scandal

With Gorbachev clearing the way for scaling back the Cold War, the Soviet Union no longer presented itself as the overarching foe that had shaped American foreign policy over four decades. Yet the gift of glasnost did not eliminate Cold War thinking entirely, especially in the continuing covert war in Central America. Nor could it resolve long-standing and complex international disputes in regions like the Middle East. In 1987 the revelations of the Iran-Contra affair laid bare the continuing contradictions and difficulties attending America's role in world affairs. The affair also demonstrated how overzealous and secretive government officials subverted the Constitution and compromised presidential authority under the guise of patriotism.

The Middle East presented the Reagan administration with its most frustrating foreign policy dilemmas. In Afghanistan, it expanded the military aid, begun under President Carter, to the *mujahedeen* forces resisting the Soviet-backed regime. In June 1982 Israel invaded Lebanon in an attempt to destroy the Palestine Liberation Organization (PLO). President Reagan dispatched marines to Beirut, hoping they might protect a weak Lebanese government overwhelmed by a brutal civil war. In October 1983 a terrorist bombing in the marine barracks killed 241 American servicemen, and the administration shied away from a long-term commitment of U.S. forces in the region.

Terrorist acts, including the seizing of Western hostages and the bombing of commercial airplanes and cruise ships, redefined the politics of the region. These were desperate attempts by small, essentially powerless sects, many of them splinter groups associated with the Palestinian cause or Islamic

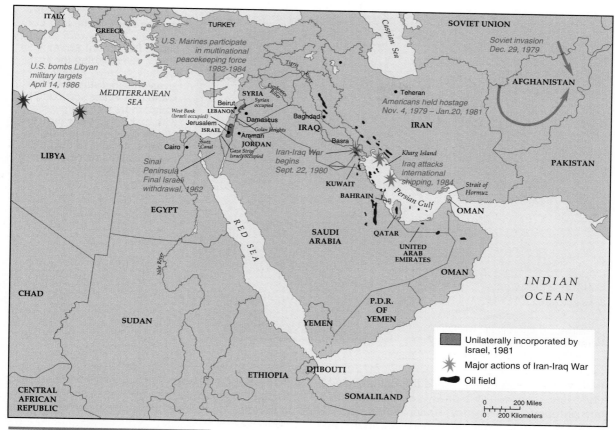

The U.S. in the Mideast in the 1980s

The volatile combination of ancient religious and ethnic rivalries, oil, and emerging Islamic fundamentalism made peace and stability elusive in the Mideast.

fundamentalism. In trying to force the Western world to pay attention to their grievances, they succeeded mostly in provoking outrage and anger. The Reagan administration insisted that behind international terrorism lay the sinister influence and money of the Soviet bloc, the Ayatollah Khomeini of Iran, and Libyan leader Muammar Qaddafi. In the spring of 1986 the president, eager to demonstrate his antiterrorist resolve, ordered the bombing of Tripoli in a failed effort to kill Qaddafi.

While administration officials railed against "state sponsored terrorism," they had little luck in capturing terrorists or gaining the release of Western hostages. With the escalation of the fierce Iran-Iraq War, the administration tilted publicly toward a pro-Iraqi stance designed to please the Arab states around the Persian Gulf. But in 1986 the administration began secret negotiations with the revolutionary Iranian government. In exchange for help in securing the release of Americans held hostage by radical Islamic groups in Lebanon, the U.S. offered to supply Iran with sophisticated weapons for use against Iraq. A Lebanese magazine first broke the story of the arms-for-hostages deal in November 1986, bringing a fire storm of criticism in the press and Congress. On its face, it looked as if the president had broken his repeated promises that he would "never negotiate with terrorists."

Subsequent disclosures elevated the story into a major scandal. Some of the money from the arms deal had been secretly diverted into covert aid for the Nicaraguan Contras. The American public soon learned the sordid details from investigative journalists and through televised congressional hearings in the summer of 1987. In order to escape congressional oversight of the CIA, Reagan and CIA director

Marine Lt. Col. Oliver North, the key figure in the Iran-Contra affair, being sworn to testify before the special Senate committee investigating the scandal, July 7, 1987. A joint congressional investigation later found that when North and his compatriots were threatened with exposure, "they destroyed official documents and lied to Cabinet officials, to the public, and to elected representatives in Congress."

William Casey essentially turned the National Security Council, previously a policy-coordinating body, into an operational agency. Under the direction of National Security Advisers Robert McFarlane and later Admiral John Poindexter, the NSC sold TOW and HAWK missiles to the Iranians, using Israel as a go-between. Millions of dollars from these sales were then given to the Contras in blatant and illegal disregard of the Boland Amendment.

In the televised congressional hearings, NSC staffer and marine lieutenant colonel Oliver North emerged as the figure running what he euphemistically referred to as "the Enterprise." North defiantly defended his actions in the name of patriotism. Some Americans saw the handsome and dashing North as a hero. But most were appalled by his and Poindexter's blithe admissions. They had lied to Congress, shredded evidence, and refused to inform the president of details in order to guarantee his "plausible deniability." A blue-ribbon commission led by former senator John Tower concluded that Reagan himself "did not seem to be aware" of the policy or its consequences. But the Tower Report offered a stunning portrait of a president at best confused and far removed from critical policy-making responsibilities. The joint congressional committee investigating what it termed the "profoundly sad" story concluded: "The common ingre-dients of the Iran and Contra policies were secrecy, deception, and disdain for the law. A small group of senior officials believed that they alone knew what was right."

Ultimately, the Iran-Contra investigation raised more questions than it answered. The full role of CIA director Casey, who died in 1987, particularly his relationships with North and the president, remained murky. The role of Vice-President George Bush remained mysterious as well, and it would return as an issue in the 1992 presidential election. Both North and Poindexter were convicted of felonies, including lying to Congress and falsifying official documents, but their convictions were overturned by higher courts on technical grounds. Like Watergate, the scandal had mesmerized a national television audience. But Iran-Contra produced no equivalent movement for impeachment. Unlike Richard Nixon, Ronald Reagan did not defiantly stonewall congressional investigators. Instead, he pleaded ignorance. When pressed on what happened, he repeatedly claimed, "I'm still trying to find out." The scandal damaged the Reagan administration politically, but the genial president remained personally popular and protected by his reputation for *not* being in charge.

In December of 1992, six years after the scandal broke, President George Bush granted pardons to six key players in the Iran-Contra affair. Among those pardoned was former secretary of defense Caspar Weinberger, who was scheduled to be tried on four felony counts, including perjury. Bush asserted that the officials had been motivated by "patriotism," and he attacked Special Prosecutor Lawrence Walsh for the "criminalization of policy differences." Yet critics argued that the Bush pardons suggested that government officials might violate the law as long as they believed their actions were good for the country. The Bush pardons made it unlikely that the full truth about the arms-for-hostages affair would ever be known.

Best of Times, Worst of Times

During the 1980s, American communities experienced economic and social change in profoundly diverse ways. However one judged the economic policies of the Reagan era, all could agree that the reality of recession and recovery varied enormously across the nation's regions, cities, and industries. On a deeper structural level, the decade witnessed the rapid expansion of relatively new industries such as microelectronics, biotechnology, robotics, and computers. Simultaneously, old standbys such as steel and auto manufacturing declined more quickly than many could have imagined. Communities long dependent on industry and manufacturing for their livelihood now struggled to remake their job base around newer service- and information-based enterprises.

As the nation faced competition from a tougher, more dynamic global economy, citizens, politicians, and business leaders had to rethink some of their most basic assumptions about the American way of life. American society became more stratified along lines of race and income. Now immigrant groups, especially from Asia and Latin America, changed the face of the nation's neighborhoods, schools, and workplaces. New epidemics and spreading poverty threatened the public health of whole communities. New media technologies made cultural life more accessible and more homogenized, and made the manipulation of image more crucial than ever in politics and entertainment.

The very notion of community itself, once defined entirely in terms of space, increasingly became a function of demographic categories. The proliferation of computer-based communications technologies made it easier to create communities based on these demographic categories, such as income, profession, hobbies, and consumption preferences.

During the 1980s the mass media, advertisers and marketers, and political professionals all intensified their reliance upon sophisticated marketing and polling techniques. Thus, American culture defined and addressed its citizens less as whole human beings and more as merely the sums of statistical characteristics.

Silicon Valley

In the early 1980s, a thirty-by-ten-mile strip of Santa Clara County, California, emerged as both the real and symbolic capital of the most important new industry in America. Silicon Valley achieved a special place in the American economy and imagination as the center of the microelectronics industry. As recently as the 1950s, the valley had consisted largely of uninhabited range land and fruit orchards. Now two dozen cities, each with about 100,000 people, formed a continuous suburban sprawl between San Francisco and San Jose. None of the cities had real centers, unless shopping malls could be considered the heart of a community. Silicon Valley was a suburb of nowhere.

The name referred to the semiconductor chips, made of silicon, that provided the foundation for local high-technology firms. Semiconductors, containing complex integrated circuits, formed the brains of modern electronics and the basic building blocks of modern electronics. The nucleus for Silicon Valley began in Stanford Research Park in Palo Alto. In the 1950s, Stanford University started leasing space to electronics firms as a way to earn money from unused land. Electronics firms such as Hewlett-Packard and Fairchild Semiconductor wanted the advantages of being close to a major research university. Military contracts played a crucial role in the business during the 1950s and 1960s. In the 1970s a consumer electronics revolution fueled an explosive new wave of growth. Silicon Valley firms gave birth to pocket calculators, video games, home computers, cordless telephones, digital watches, and almost every other new development in electronics.

Silicon Valley flourished amidst this unique combination of research facilities, investment capital, attractive environment, and a large pool of highly educated people. By 1980 some 1,700 high-tech firms engaged in gathering, processing, or distributing information, or in manufacturing information technology. Companies like Atari, Apple, and Intel achieved enormous international success and became familiar household names. Silicon Valley boasted the greatest concentration of new

A silicon microchip, with imprinted circuit, on a finger. These tiny chips provided the basic building blocks for the rapid development of the computer industry. An aerial view of Santa Clara and Sunnyvale showed semiconductor plants and other microelectronic facilities in the heart of "Silicon Valley."

wealth in the U.S., and it attracted widespread coverage in trade magazines, business periodicals, and the popular press. These media documented the amazing success stories of a young entrepreneurial elite, such as Steve Jobs of Apple and Nolan Bushnell of Atari. These tales reinforced one of the most powerful images of the decade. Silicon Valley represented a unique culture mixing youth, inventiveness, and entrepreneurship and producing fortunes by exploiting technological breakthroughs.

Silicon Valley became increasingly divided along geographic and class lines. The nearly all-white, all-male affluent managers and engineers tended to live in North County communities, such as Palo Alto, Mountain View, and Sunnyvale. Manual workers on assembly lines and in low-paying service jobs clustered in San Jose and Gilroy. Most of these were Latino, black, Vietnamese, Chinese, and Filipino men and women. The majority of Silicon Valley workers did not see or enjoy the affluent lifestyle publicized in the mass media; they constituted a cheap, nonunionized labor pool with an extremely high turnover rate. Public services in South County — schools, welfare, police and fire protection — were poor; among Latino public school students in Santa Clara County, the dropout rate reached 50 percent in the mid-1980s.

By the early 1990s the Silicon Valley economy had matured, slowing growth and the infusion of venture capital. Stiff competition from computer companies in Japan, Korea, and Malaysia made it much more difficult for young entrepreneurs to start successful new companies. And the leap from small, start-up company to large corporation was becoming more and more difficult. The center of the world

for the computer industry had shifted to the Pacific Rim, of which Silicon Valley was only one part. The crowds, traffic jams, and inflated cost of living led many companies and individuals to move out of the area. The mature Silicon Valley was so well developed and dense that it still had a critical mass of technological and business talent. But the boom-town atmosphere of the early years had faded.

Monongahela Valley

Across the continent, in western Pennsylvania, a different kind of economic transformation reshaped the industrial cities along the Monongahela River valley. Since the late nineteenth century, the "Mon Valley" had proudly stood as the steelmaking center of the nation and much of the world. The very way of life in cities like Pittsburgh, Homestead, and Clairton revolved around manufacturing jobs at companies like U.S. Steel, Bethlehem, and smaller firms in the area. In the 1980s the American steel industry suffered dramatic losses as the overvalued dollar hurt U.S. producers in two ways. They lost sales directly to imported steel, and indirectly, as their domestic customers in steel-intensive industries (automobiles, machine tools) also lost sales to imports.

But much of the problem stemmed from the long-term failure to big steel companies to invest in modernizing their operations. Instead they redirected profits into buying chemical firms, shopping malls, and oil companies. In 1984 U.S. Steel's sales from steel accounted for just 34 percent of all revenues and only 9 percent of total operating income. It paid $6 billion to acquire Marathon Oil of Ohio. At the same time, U.S. Steel increased its investments in overseas mining and mineral processing companies, some of which worked closely with foreign steelmakers. This policy of *disinvestment* had a devastating impact on the people and communities who had helped build the nation's basic production industries.

Overall employment in the American steel industry dropped from 400,000 in 1980 to 167,000 in 1987. In Mon Valley, U.S. Steel employed 26,500 people in 1979, but just 4,000 by 1990. The company's steelmaking capacity plunged from 8.5 million tons to 2.3 million tons a year in that period. Its Homestead Steel Works, where 15,000 people once made the steel for the Empire State Building, the Golden Gate Bridge, and the Sears Tower, closed for good in 1986. During the 1980s the valley lost 30,000 people, or 10 percent of its population. Those who stayed behind were often middle-aged steelworkers unable to find jobs or sell their homes. A survey of nearly 30,000 laid-off workers found a majority of those over forty remained either unemployed or underemployed in part-time, low-paying jobs. Men-

Demolished blast furnaces at Pittsburgh's Jones and Laughlin Steel Company testified to the decline of the American steel industry. The permanent loss of high paying jobs in the manufacturing sector devastated scores of American communities in the 1980s.

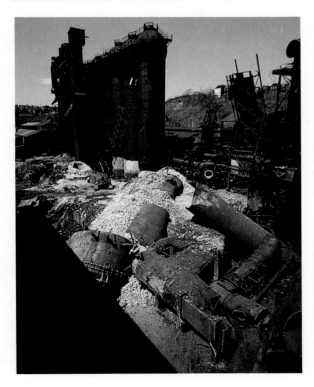

tal and physical problems, and an overall sense of resignation, haunted many of them.

On a hill about fifteen miles south of Pittsburgh sits Clairton, a small city of about 20,000. Clairton was once a bustling city of immigrants, with active Slavic, Italian, and Irish communities. At the end of World War II Clairton's coke works were the largest in the world, and its by-products division made components for thousands of different products, including fertilizer, resin, and dyes. By the mid-1980s Clairton was suffering a permanent unemployment rate of about 35 percent and an indefinite state of municipal bankruptcy. The taxes once paid by U.S. Steel to the city dropped from $805,000 in 1980 to $331,000 in 1985. The entire thirteen-member police force had to be laid off. A state-appointed trustee still handles Clairton's financial affairs. Several thousand have moved out since 1980; others remain trapped and dependent upon charity and food banks.

Some Mon Valley communities have made strides toward rebuilding around "postindustrial" enterprises. One plan called for demolishing mills to make way for the area's first interstate highway. Another project would turn the valley's steelmaking past into a tourist attraction, transforming the remnants of the Homestead Works into a museum run by the National Park Service. In Pittsburgh, on the former site of Jones & Laughlin Steel, state government, business, and local universities pooled resources to create a high-tech industrial park. Commercial tenants include ventures born of university research into biotechnology, robotics, and computer software. UPARC (University of Pittsburgh Applied Research Center) has also attracted industrial and academic tenants. Pittsburgh's assets now include the world's largest robotics institute and the biggest research program on the industrial uses of artificial intelligence. This modest boom may point the way to a future in which the old steelmaking center becomes a knowledge-based community.

An Electronic Culture

Important technological developments helped reconfigure American cultural life during the 1980s. Revolutions in computers and telecommunications merged telephones, televisions, computers, cable, and satellites into a single differentiated system. The new information technologies of the 1980s changed the way people worked and played. They made the nation's cultural life more homogenous, and they played a greater role than ever in shaping politics. The new world of *compunications* (referring to the merging of computer and communications technologies) speeded the growth of what many analysts call postindustrial society. In this view, the creation, processing, and sale of information, and services have replaced the manufacturing and distribution of material goods as the most important and dynamic wealth-producing activities of the society.

The twin arrivals of cable and the videocassette recorder (VCR) expanded and redefined the power of television. By the end of the 1980s pay cable services and VCRs had penetrated roughly two-thirds of American homes. Cable offered television viewers scores of new programming choices, especially sports events and movies. For the first time ever, the mass audience for traditional network programming declined as *narrowcasting*— the targeting of more specialized audiences— competed with broadcasting. The VCR revolutionized the way people used their sets, allowing them to organize program

Madonna, one of the biggest music stars of the 1980s, pioneered the new cultural form of music video. Madonna shrewdly developed an ambiguous persona that allowed audiences to identify with her variously as vulnerable romantic, a hard edged ''material girl,'' a thoughtful feminist, or a self-described ''boy toy.''

watching around their own schedules. People also used VCRs for playing video games and viewing Hollywood movies. Indeed, tape rental and sale for home viewing quickly replaced theater tickets as the main profit source for filmmakers. The VCR thus radically changed the economics of the entire entertainment business.

The intensification of television's power could be measured in many ways. A new cable channel called MTV (for Music Television) began in 1981 as a means of boosting record sales; music videos, featuring popular music stars, soon became a new art form in themselves. MTV redefined popular music by placing as much emphasis on image as on sound, and it revived dance as a popular performance art as well. Artists who best exploited music video, such as Madonna and Michael Jackson, achieved international superstar status. MTV also transformed smaller, cult musics, such as rap and heavy metal, into giant mass market phenomena. MTV pioneered an imaginative visual style, featuring rapid cutting, animation, and the sophisticated fusion of sound and image. Television producers, filmmakers, advertisers, and political consultants quickly adapted MTV techniques to just about every kind of image making.

More than ever, television drove the key strategies and tactics defining American political life. Politicians and their advisers focused on shaping a candidate's television image, producing slick campaign commercials, and raising the enormous amounts of money needed get them on TV. Issues, positions, and debate all paled alongside the key question: how did it look on TV? Even Ronald Reagan's harshest critics conceded that the former actor had mastered the art of television-based politics. Fewer citizens voted or took an active role in campaigns, and most relied upon television coverage to make their choices. Thus, creating effective television ''character'' emerged as perhaps the most crucial form of political discourse. Television could also be used to make money and gain political power by appealing to religious faith. ''Televangelists'' like Pat Robertson, Jimmy Swaggart, and Jim and Tammy Bakker, attracted large audiences and built lucrative empires by preaching versions of fundamentalist Protestantism over cable networks.

The dominant themes in popular culture were money, status, and power— the values embraced by the Reagan administration. The newly elected president himself set the tone when he responded to a reporter's question asking him what was best about America. ''What I want to see above all,'' Reagan replied, ''is that this remains a country where someone can always get rich." Certainly there were many thousands of Americans who made fortunes in the expansive and lucrative sectors of the economy: stock trading, real estate, business services, defense contracting, and high-tech industries. A step below the new rich were the *yuppies* (young upwardly mobile professionals). The term, coined in 1984, gained influence as a tool for the advertising and marketing worlds, a shorthand description of those people most likely to define themselves by their upscale consumer behavior. Yuppies ate gourmet foods, wore designer clothes, drove expensive automobiles, and lived in "gentrified" neighborhoods. They were not necessarily rich, but they patterned their lifestyle after that of the wealthy.

Popular culture reflected and reinforced an obsession with getting rich and living well. Novelist Tom Wolfe called this phenomenon *plutography*— "graphic depictions of the acts of the rich." Hit TV series like *Dallas* and *Dynasty* (and their imitators) focused on the family wars and business intrigues of oil tycoons and fashion queens. Shows such as *Lifestyles of the Rich and Famous* and *Entertainment Tonight* offered vicarious pleasures by taking viewers into the homes and on the shopping sprees of wealthy celebrities. Movies that reveled in money-making and the entrepreneurial spirit attracted huge audiences: *Risky Business, Ghostbusters, Working Girl.* So, too, did films that combined spectacular special effects and science fiction with the comforting verities of so-called traditional family values: *ET: The Extraterrestrial, Return of the Jedi,* and *Back to the Future.*

The marketing of marketing drove American culture, as exposure through the mass media became more crucial than ever for business success. Tie-ins proliferated among films, television shows, advertising, newspapers and magazines, popular music, and politicians. A growing concentration of ownership among television networks, movie studios, publishers, and cable companies accelerated this trend. New media forms intensified the national culture of celebrity: the newspaper *USA Today,* the news channel Cable News Network, the weekly magazine *People.* On a deeper level, demographic analysis created the most important "communities" in American life — communities of consumer choice. Polls, graphs, and charts increasingly located and divided Americans by race, gender, ethnicity, education, income, and religion so that advertisers, manufacturers, book publishers, moviemakers, television producers, political candidates — anyone looking to sell a product or provide a service — could define and target the right demographic community.

Epidemics: Drugs, AIDS, Homelessness

The scourge of drug addiction and drug trafficking took on frightening new dimensions in the early 1980s. The arrival of crack, a cheap, smokable, and highly addictive form of cocaine, made that drug affordable to the urban poor. As crack addiction spread, the drug trade assumed alarming new proportions both domestically and internationally. Crack ruined hundreds of thousands of lives and led to a dramatic increase in crime. Studies showed that over half the men arrested in the nation's largest cities tested positive for cocaine. The crack trade spawned a new generation of young drug dealers willing to risk jail and death for enormous profits. In city after city, drug wars over turf took the lives of dealers and innocents, both caught in the escalating violence. Many ghetto youths looked at the drug trade as the only real business enterprise open to them.

Well-financed and carefully organized groups like the Medellin cartel in Colombia linked coca plant farmers in Bolivia, money launderers in Panama, and smugglers in Mexico and the United States. Drug money corrupted large numbers of public officials in all these countries. By the end of the 1980s, opinion polls were revealing that Americans identified drugs as the nation's number one problem. The Reagan administration declared a highly publicized "war on drugs" to bring the traffic under control. This multi-billion-dollar campaign focuses on stopping the flow of illegal drugs into the U.S., destroying cocaine-producing labs in Bolivia, and stiffening the penalties for those convicted of violating federal drug statutes. Critics charged that the war on drugs focused on supply from abroad when it needed to look at demand here at home. They urged more federal money for drug education, treatment, and rehabilitation. Drug addiction and drug use, they argued, were primarily health problems, not law enforcement issues.

In 1981 doctors in Los Angeles, San Francisco, and New York began encountering a puzzling new medical phenomenon. Young homosexual men were dying suddenly from rare types of pneumonia and cancer. Researchers at the Centers for Disease Control (CDC) in Atlanta named the mysterious disease Acquired Immune Deficiency Syndrome (AIDS). AIDS destroyed the body's natural defenses against illness, making its victims susceptible to a host of opportunistic infections. The virus was transmitted through semen or blood, but full-blown AIDS might not appear for years after initial exposure to the virus. Thus, one could infect others without even knowing one had the disease. Although tests could determine whether one carried the AIDS virus, there was no cure. The preponderance of early AIDS victims were homosexual men infected through sexual contact. Many Americans thus perceived AIDS as a disease of homosexuals. But other victims became infected through intravenous drug use, blood transfusions, or birth to AIDS-carrying mothers.

As more and more gay men fell victim to the disease, AIDS provoked fear, anguish, and anger. It also brought an upsurge of organization and political involvement. The Gay Men's Health Crisis, formed in New York in 1981, drew thousands of volunteers to care for the sick, raised millions of dollars for education and research, and lobbied vigorously for federal research money toward finding a cure. In city after city, the gay community responded to the AIDS crisis with energy and determination. Most gay men changed their sexual habits, practicing "safe sex" to lessen the chances of infection. The Reagan administration, playing to antihomosexual prejudices, largely ignored the epidemic. One important exception was Surgeon General C. Everett Koop, who urged a comprehensive sex education program in the nation's schools, including information about condoms. Individual American communities became bitterly divided over whether school boards and other local agencies ought to take responsibility for sex education and the distribution of condoms.

By the end of the 1980s the AIDS epidemic had spread far beyond gay men. The fastest-growing group of AIDS victims were intravenous drug users, their sex partners, and their babies. The AIDS epidemic spread rapidly among African Americans and Latinos as well. By 1990 the CDC had confirmed almost 100,000 AIDS cases and over 57,000 deaths from the disease. As many as 1.5 million Americans could be infected with the virus. The revelations of AIDS infection in such well-known public figures as actor Rock Hudson and athletes Magic Johnson and Arthur Ashe helped remove some of the stigma and aided AIDS awareness. More important were the continuing political and educational efforts mounted by groups like the AIDS Coalition to Unleash Power (ACT–UP), Women's Health Action Mobilization (WHAM), and the AIDS Quilt Project, which stitched together a moving tribute to AIDS victims out of thousands of individual memorial quilts.

Another chronic social problem plagued America during the 1980s. In cities all around the country citizens could not help noticing the disturbing pres-

The AIDS Quilt in Washington, D.C., October, 1992. The quilt project united thousands of individual memorials to AIDS victims into one powerful statement expressing the national sense of loss from the disease. Mourners were thus able to transcend their personal grief and connect with the larger movement to fight AIDS.

ence of homeless people. Often disoriented, shoeless, and forlorn, growing numbers of street people slept over heating grates, on subways, and in parks. Homeless people wandered city sidewalks panhandling and struggling to find scraps of food. Winters proved especially difficult. In the early 1980s, the Department of Housing and Urban Development placed the number of the nation's homeless at 250,000–350,000. But homeless advocates estimated that the number was as high as 3 million.

Who were the homeless? Analysts agreed that at least a third were mental patients who had been discharged from hospitals amidst the deinstitutionalization trend of the 1970s. Many more were alcoholics and drug addicts unable to hold jobs. But the ranks of the homeless also included female-headed families, battered women, Vietnam veterans, AIDS victims, and elderly people with no place to go. Some communities made strong efforts to place their homeless in city-run shelters. But the shelters themselves scared away many homeless, who feared the violence and theft common to them. Some critics pointed to the decline in decent housing for poor people and the deterioration of the nation's health care system. No matter how large and what its components, the permanent class of American homeless reflected the desperate situation of America's poor.

Economic Woes

Congress sought to check burgeoning deficits, which had topped $200 billion in the annual budget for 1984. In late 1985, amidst great fanfare, Congress enacted the Balanced Budget and Emergency Deficit Control Act, more popularly known by the names of its principal authors, Senators Phil Gramm and Warren Rudman. It mandated automatic spending cuts if the government failed to meet fixed deficit reduction goals. Under the plan, congressional and presidential budget officials would forecast whether target reductions would be met. If not, the General Accounting Office would compile a list of across-the-board reductions, evenly divided between domestic and military programs. Gramm-Rudman targeted a deficit of $172 billion for 1986, with further reductions leading to a balanced budget by 1991.

But the deficit for 1986 reached $238 billion, some $66 billion over the target. In fact, the actual deficit was $283 billion. But Congress and the president took the $45 billion surplus from Social Security and other trust funds and spent it on government programs, thereby masking the true size of the deficit. This tactic of diverting trust funds to reduce the deficit became standard during the 1980s. Congress revised the Gramm-Rudman targets in 1987, but once again the numbers did not add up. The 1989 deficit wound up at $153 billion instead of the promised $136 billion. The 1991 deficit set an all-time record at $269 billion; if the Social Security surplus was subtracted from government spending books, the real deficit totaled $321 billion.

On Wall Street, the bull market of the 1980s ended abruptly in the fall of 1987. The Dow-Jones average of thirty leading industrial stocks had reached an all-time high of 2,722 at the end of August. There followed a gradual slide over the next few weeks and then a resounding crash. On October 19, the Dow lost an incredible 508 points in one day, almost 23 percent of its value. Analysts blamed the decline on computerized program trading, which automatically instructed money managers to sell stock-index futures when prices on the New York Stock Exchange fell below certain levels. The panic on the trading floors reminded many of the pandemonium set off by the Great Crash of 1929. Millions of Americans now feared that the 1987 crash would signal the onset of a great recession or even a depression.

But the Wall Street of the 1980s differed substantially from that of the 1920s. In late 1986, the Securities and Exchange Commission (SEC) uncovered the biggest stock scandal in history, in the process revealing the inner workings of high finance in the 1980s. Ivan Boesky, one of the nation's biggest stock speculators, admitted to using confidential information about upcoming corporate takeovers to trade stocks illegally. Just two years earlier the dapper Boesky had made more than $100 million on two deals. "Greed is all right," he told a cheering University of California Business School audience in 1985. "Everybody should be a little bit greedy. . . . You shouldn't feel guilty."

Now, Boesky agreed to pay the U.S. government 100 million dollars to settle civil charges, and he cooperated with SEC investigators. The biggest fish caught in their net was Michael Milken, a Boesky ally and the most successful businessman of the era. An investment banker for Drexel Burnham Lambert, Milken perfected the art of corporate raiding through creative manipulation of debt. He showed how enormous profits could be earned from weak firms that were tempting targets for takeovers and mergers. Their debt could be used as tax write-offs, less efficient individual corporate parts could be sold off piecemeal, and more profitable units could be retained, merged, or sold again to form new entities. Instead of borrowing from banks, Milken financed his deals by underwriting high-yield junk bonds for companies rated below investment grade. Investors in turn reaped huge profits by selling these junk bonds to hostile-takeover dealers.

Milken and other corporate raiders reshaped the financial world, setting off the greatest wave of buying and selling in American business history. During the 1980s corporate America undertook 25,000 mergers, takeovers, and restructuring deals, cumulatively valued at over $2 trillion. Between 1984 and 1987, there were twenty-one such deals for over a billion dollars each. Milken himself made a staggering *$550 million* in one year alone. Just before filing for bankruptcy in 1990, Drexel Burnham Lambert paid its executives $350 million in bonuses—almost as much as it owed its creditors. Milken was eventually convicted of insider trading and stock fraud and sent to prison. Critics both within and outside the Wall Street world questioned the economic benefits of this "paper entrepreneurialism." Many American businesses enjoyed rising profits and cash flow, but these depended as much upon debt manipulation and corporate restructuring as upon investment in research and development or the creation of new products.

Growing Inequality

The celebration of wealth, moneymaking, and entrepreneurship dominated much of 1980s popular culture, politics, and intellectual life. But grimmer realities lay under the surface. A variety of measures strongly suggested that the nation had moved toward greater inequality, that the middle class was shrinking, and that poverty was on the rise. Analysts disagreed over the causes of these trends. No doubt some trends reflected structural changes in the American economy and a rapidly changing global marketplace. After eight years of tax cuts, defense buildup, growing budget deficits, and record trade imbalances, the economic future looked uncertain at best. Two of the most cherished basic assumptions about America—that life would improve for most people and their children, and that a comfortable middle-class existence was available to all who worked for it—looked shaky by the early 1990s. The following tables illustrate several of the key trends in wealth, income, and poverty during the 1980s.

The very wealthy did extremely well during the 1980s. In 1989 the richest 1 percent of American households accounted for 37 percent of the nation's private wealth—up from 31 percent in 1983, a jump of almost 20 percent. This top 1 percent, 834,000 households with about $5.7 trillion of net worth, owned more than the bottom 90 percent of Americans, 84 million households with about $4.8 trillion in net worth. The top 1 percent owned a dispropor-

tionate share of many types of assets: 78 percent of bonds and trusts, 62 percent of business assets, 49 percent of publicly held stock, and 45 percent of nonresidential real estate. The average wealth of the Forbes 400 (the wealthiest individuals in America) jumped from $230 million in 1982 to $682 million in 1990. The total net worth of this group rose from $92 billion to $273 billion over the same period, and the number of billionaires jumped from thirteen to sixty-six.

The most affluent Americans made the biggest gains in family income as well. In 1980 the top 5 percent of families earned 15.3 percent of the nation's total income. By 1990 their share had grown to 17.4 percent, an increase of about 14 percent; their average income was $148,000 a year. In 1980 the top 20 percent of families earned 41.6 percent of the nation's total. By 1990 their share had

---

Percentage Share of Aggregate Family Income, 1980–1990

	1980	1990
Top 5 Percent	15.3%	17.4%
Highest Fifth	41.6	44.3
Fourth Fifth	24.3	23.8
Third Fifth	17.5	16.6
Second Fifth	11.6	10.8
Lowest Fifth	5.1	4.6

Source: U.S. Bureau of the Census, Current Population Reports: Consumer Incomes, Series P-60, No. 167, and 174, 1990, 1991. U.S. federal data compiled by Ed Royce, Rollins College.

Share of Total Net Worth of American Families

	1983	1989
Richest 1% of families	31%	37%
Next richest 9%	35	31
Remaining 90%	33	32

Source: *New York Times*, April 21, 1992, from Federal Reserve Survey of Consumer Finances.

Measures of Average Earnings, 1960–1989 (in 1990 dollars)

Year	Average Weekly Earnings	Average Hourly Earnings
1980	$367.93	$10.42
1985	358.02	10.26
1989	347.18	10.03

Source: U.S. House of Representatives, Committee on Ways and Means, *Overview of Entitlement Programs* (Washington, D.C.: GPO, 1991), table 34, p. 552. U.S. federal data compiled by Ed Royce, Rollins College.

Net New Job Creation by Wage Level, 1979–1987

	Number of Net New Jobs Created	Percentage of Net New Jobs Created
Low-Wage Jobs (less than $11,661)	5,955,000	50.4%
Middle-Wage Jobs ($11,612 to $46,444)	4,448,000	31.7%
High-Wage Jobs ($46,445 and above)	1,405,000	11.9%

Source: Committee on the Budget, United States Senate, *Wages of American Workers in the 1980s* (Washington, D.C.: GPO, 1988). U.S. federal data compiled by Ed Royce, Rollins College.

Number of Poor, Rate of Poverty, and Poverty Line, 1979–1990

	1979	1990
Millions of Poor	26.1	33.6
Rate of Poverty	11.7%	13.5%
Poverty Line (Family of Four)	$7,412	$13,359

Source: U.S. Bureau of the Census, Current Population Reports: Consumer Income, Series P-60, Nos. 161 and 175, 1988, 1991. U.S. federal data compiled by Ed Royce, Rollins College.

grown to 44.3 percent, an increase of about 6.5 percent, with an average income of $94,000 a year. In contrast, the bottom 40 percent of families in 1980 had 16.7 percent of aggregate income. By 1990 their share had declined to 15.4 percent, a drop of nearly 8 percent, with an average income of about $16,500 a year.

Average weekly earnings for American workers declined from $368 in 1980 to $347 in 1989, and average hourly wages dropped from $10.42 to $10.03 (in 1990 dollars). Both these figures reflected the fact that most of the new jobs created during the 1980s were in low-paying service and manufacturing sectors.

Of the roughly 12 million (net) new jobs created between 1979 and 1987, 50.4 percent paid less than the poverty-level income for a family of four: $11,611. Only 12 percent were high-wage jobs, paying over $46,445. Millions of families now needed two wage earners to maintain middle-class status where formerly one would have sufficed.

The number and percentage of Americans in poverty grew alarmingly during the decade. The government classified about 26.1 million people as poor in 1979, 11.7 percent of the total population. By 1990 the number of poor had reached 33.6 million, or 13.5 percent of the country. This represented an increase of more than 15 percent in the nation's poverty rate. Over 20 percent of all American children under eighteen lived in poverty, including 45 percent of all black children and 38 percent of all Hispanic children. Thirty-two percent of all African Americans lived in poverty, as did 28 percent of Hispanics. Female-headed households, comprising 12.6 million people, made up nearly 38 percent of the poor.

END OF AN ERA

As Americans approached the end of the twentieth century, they faced dramatic changes around the world and at home. The fall of world communism promised to reshape the fundamental premises of the nation's foreign policy. Economic competition with the nations of the Pacific Rim and Europe would replace the ideological rivalry with Marxism-Leninism as the defining premise of the nation's stance in the world. Global economic struggles forced a reassessment of the core beliefs in growth and abundance that had dominated the nation's post–World War II political and cultural life. The limits of military power to solve complex political and economic disputes became clear in the aftermath of victory in the Persian Gulf War. Economic inequality and racial divisions continued to plague many American communities. Democrats recaptured the White House for the first time since 1976,

Year	All Races	White	Black	Hispanic
1980	$33,346	$34,743	$20,103 (.58)	$23,342 (.67)
1985	33,689	35,410	20,390 (.58)	23,112 (.65)
1990	35,353	36,915	21,423 (.58)	23,431 (.63)

Source: U.S. Bureau of the Census, Current Population Reports, Series P-60, No. 174, 1991. U.S. federal data compiled by Ed Royce, Rollins College.

riding a wave of desire for change. But the depth and degree of that change remained quite uncertain.

The Election of 1988

For the 1988 campaign, Republicans nominated Vice-President George Bush. He embodied the eastern WASP establishment, with a few twists. Son of an investment banker and senator from Connecticut, educated at Yale, he moved to Texas after serving in World War II as a fighter pilot. Bush made money in the oil business and entered Texas Republican politics. His detractors dismissed him as a "wimp" and "the resume candidate." He had held a string of appointive offices under three presidents: head of the National Republican Committee, UN ambassador, envoy to China, director of the CIA, and, finally, vice-president. Bush promised to carry forward the policies of his patron, Ronald Reagan.

The Democratic nominee, Governor Michael Dukakis of Massachusetts, stressed competence over ideology and took credit for his state's economic boom. With Reagan retiring, Democrats believed they had a good chance to recapture the White House in 1988. At first, Dukakis led Bush in the polls. But Bush aggressively staked out his differences with Dukakis. Republican strategists, led by Lee Atwater and Roger Ailes, created and ran a cynical and effective negative campaign that painted Dukakis as outside the mainstream of "American values." They attacked Dukakis for vetoing a law requiring students to pledge allegiance to the flag; for opposing the death penalty and mandatory school prayer; for being a "card-carrying member" of the American Civil Liberties Union. Most damaging was an ad campaign accusing Dukakis of being soft on crime by authorizing weekend furloughs for some Massachusetts prison inmates. One spot showed a black man named Willie Horton, serving time for rape and assault, who escaped and committed another rape. The gut appeal to racist stereotypes was shocking and potent. "If I can make Willie Horton a household name," said Lee Atwater, "we'll win the election."

The Bush campaign succeeded in raising a negative image of Dukakis, especially among undecided voters. While Bush excoriated liberalism, wrapped himself in the flag, and made thinly veiled appeals to racism and nativism, Dukakis distanced himself from the campaign and the Democratic party's liberal tradition. The 1988 election intensified the importance of image over substance in the nation's politics. The creation of daily sound bites and spin control by campaign aides seemed far more crucial than debate over issues. Even during televised debates, the candidates appeared unwilling and incapable of discussing such pressing concerns as the political upheaval in the USSR, the environmental crisis, the de-skilling of the American work force, and the globalization of the world economy. Bush and his running mate, Dan Quayle, won the popular vote by 54 to 46 percent and carried the electoral votes of forty out of fifty states. Above all, the election of 1988 signaled that more sophisticated levels of media manipulation and image making were the keys to success in presidential politics.

The New Immigration

Figures from the 1990 census confirmed what many Americans had observed over the previous decade in their communities and workplaces. The face of the nation was perceptibly changing. The Census Bureau estimated that 6 million legal and 2 million undocumented immigrants entered the country during the 1980s, second only to the 8.8 million foreign immigrants that arrived between 1900 and 1910. More than a third of the nation's population growth over the decade — from 227 million to 248 million — came from immigration. This proportion of increase caused by foreign migrants was greater than any since the decade between 1910 and 1920, when immigration accounted for 40 percent of population

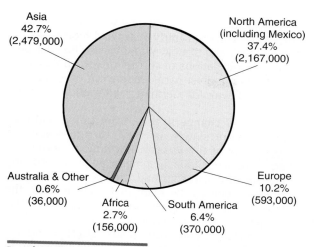

Immigration, 1981–1989   Total: 5,802,000

During the 1980s, more immigrants arrived from Asia than from any other continent. The vast majority from North America were from Mexico and the Central American nations.

growth. Seven states, headed by California, New York, Texas, and Florida, received 75 percent of the newcomers.

Hispanics and Asians led the accelerated trend toward cultural diversity. The Hispanic population increased by more than 50 percent, from 14.6 million to 22.4 million. One out of every five immigrants living in the U.S. was Mexican-born, and Mexican Americans overall composed more than 60 percent of the Hispanic population identified in the 1990 census. Hispanics formed over a third of the population of New Mexico, a quarter of the population of Texas, and over 10 percent of the populations of California, Arizona, and Colorado. Nearly a million Mexican Americans lived in Los Angeles alone. Large Hispanic communities, including Cuban, Puerto Rican, Dominican, and Salvadoran Americans, also grew in New York City, Miami, and Chicago. Demographers predicted that by the middle of the next century Hispanics would replace African Americans as the largest minority group in the nation.

The decline of world oil prices had a devastating impact on the Mexican economy, worsening poverty and unemployment and spurring more people to seek a better life in North America. Most Mexican Americans struggled in low-paying jobs and fought to hold onto their distinctive cultural heritage. They worked on farms, in garment sweatshops and high-tech assembly plants, and as gardeners and domestics. Through education and business success, a significant number achieved middle-class status and wealth. But almost 20 percent of Mexican Americans lived below the poverty line.

The number of Asian Americans more than doubled, from 3.5 million to 7.3 million. Nearly two out of every five Asian Americans lived in California. The population of Koreatown in Los Angeles approached 300,000 and the area seemed a world unto itself. Like earlier immigrant groups, new Americans from Korea, Vietnam, and the Philippines tended to cluster in their own communities and maintain a durable group identity. As a whole, Asian Americans made mobility through education a priority, along with pooling family capital and labor to support small businesses. Newcomers selected communities with job opportunities or where families and friends had settled. This social network, for example, explained the large numbers of Hmongs, a tribal group from Laos, drawn to Minneapolis and St. Paul. The stream of Hmongs began with church-sponsored refugee programs, then gained momentum as more and more family members followed. Minnesota's total Asian population tripled, from 26,000 to 78,000, during the 1980s.

The Immigration Reform Act of 1965 had eliminated quotas based on national origin. It also gave preferential treatment to highly educated foreigners seeking professional opportunities in the U.S. The 1965 act set limits of 120,000 immigrants per year from the Western Hemisphere and 170,000 from countries outside the Western Hemisphere. By the mid-1980s, growing concern over "illegal aliens" had become a hotly debated political issue, particularly in the Southwest. The Immigration Reform and Control Act of 1987 addressed the concerns of Anglos worried about "illegals" and the increasingly influential Mexican American community. It required employers for the first time to vouch for the legal status of their employees. At the same time, it offered an amnesty to all undocumented workers who had entered the country before 1982. The law, critics charged, led to discrimination in hiring. And no matter what Congress did, the desperate economic realities in Mexico and Central America continued to encourage the flow of illegal immigration.

The Collapse of Communism

In the Soviet Union, the political reforms initiated by Mikhail Gorbachev in the mid-1980s ultimately led to the dissolution of the Soviet state. By calling for a greater openness and a new spirit of democracy, Gorbachev had boldly challenged the Communist party establishment that had dominated Soviet life for three-quarters of a century. He had also inspired open opposition to Communist rule throughout Eastern Europe. The outright revolt against Commu-

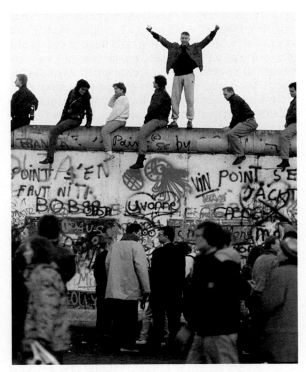

German demonstrators defiantly tearing down the Berlin Wall, November, 1989. For three decades the Wall dividing East and West Berlin had embodied the political divisions of the Cold War. Images such as these underscored the passing of an era.

nist rule gathered strength first in Eastern European nations, then hit home in Moscow with stunning swiftness.

In June of 1989 Poland held its first free elections since the Communists took power following World War II, bringing an overwhelming victory for the Solidarity movement. Solidarity leader Tadeusz Mazowieicki became prime minister, forming a government that shared power with, but was no longer dominated by, Communists. In Hungary, the Communist party changed its name and called for a multi-party system, which in 1990 resulted in the election of a center-right government. In the fall of 1989 angry prodemocracy demonstrations forced out long-time Communist party leaders in Czechoslovakia, Bulgaria, and Romania. Most dramatic of all were the events in East Germany. Hungary opened its border with Austria, allowing the exit of East Germans gathered at the West German Embassy in Budapest. Huge protests broke out during official celebrations of East Germany's fortieth anniversary and thousands of refugees flooded routes to the West. The Berlin Wall had suddenly been ren-

dered irrelevant. East Germany was forced to open the Wall, which for thirty years had loomed as the ultimate symbol of Cold War division. Popular protests and revelations of corruption forced East Germany's Communist party leaders out of power and paved the way for German reunification the next year.

Political change in the Soviet Union had progressed more slowly. In 1987, on the seventieth anniversary of the Russian Revolution, Gorbachev had denounced Stalin, helping to legitimize growing criticism of censorship and organs of political repression, such as the KGB. In March of 1989, the Soviet Union held its first free elections since 1917, as a new Congress of People's Deputies replaced the old Communist party–dominated Supreme Soviet. Hundreds of party officials went down to defeat. In early 1990, over the fierce objections of hardliners, the Central Committee agreed to Gorbachev's plan to end the Communist party's constitutional monopoly of power. In elections held in March of 1990, prodemocracy groups in Russia, Ukraine, and Byelorussia achieved major gains, and the Communist party lost control of the local governments in Moscow, Leningrad, and other cities. By the middle of 1991, most of the fifteen republics that constituted the Soviet Union had announced plans to break away from Moscow's control.

The party's hardliners made one final attempt to prevent the dissolution of the USSR. In August of 1991, they attempted a coup by placing Gorbachev under house arrest at his vacation home in the Crimea, reasserting control of the press, and banning street demonstrations. Boris Yeltsin, president of the Russian Republic, denounced Gorbachev's removal and urged thousands of Muscovites gathered outside the Parliament building to resist. The coup failed when Soviet Army troops refused orders to attack the Russian parliament building. Upon his return from the Crimea, Gorbachev resigned as head of the Communist party and then banned it. As leader of Russia, the largest of the republics, Yeltsin now emerged as the most powerful political leader. At the end of 1991 Russia proclaimed its independence and, along with Ukraine and Byelorussia (now Belarus), formed the Commonwealth of Independent States, in a final rejection of the Soviet structure. Eight more republics quickly joined the new commonwealth, and on Christmas Day 1991 a weary and bitter Gorbachev resigned as president of the USSR and recognized the Commonwealth of Independent States. The Soviet Union had dissolved.

In the end, Gorbachev's zeal to reform politics had outrun his ability to reform the economy. As one sympathetic editorial in *Pravda* put it: "Gorbachev was unable to change the living standards of the people, but he changed the people." Attempts to move toward a more open free-market economy had been stymied by resistance from much of the entrenched and privileged Communist party *apparatchiks*. A severe shortage of capital had also hampered plans to shift the economy toward greater production of consumer goods. Promises of economic investment and technical aid from the United States and the European Economic Community ran far behind the actual delivery of assistance. Violent ethnic conflict and a weak economy threatened the future of the new commonwealth. The sticky question of who controlled the enormous nuclear and military might of the former USSR remained unresolved. Gorbachev and the movement he had inspired had wrought revolutionary changes. But the 280 million people of the former Soviet Union faced a very uncertain future.

The Persian Gulf War

Like most Americans, President George Bush greeted the momentous changes in the Soviet Union and Eastern Europe with a sense of hope. A consensus emerged among the nation's citizens and elected officials that the Cold War was over. The collapse of the Soviet Union meant the end of the great superpower rivalry that had shaped post–World War II American foreign policy and domestic politics. What, if anything, would take its place? Bush spoke optimistically of an emerging "new world order" for the post–Cold War era: "freer from the threat of terror, stronger in the pursuit of justice, and more secure in the quest for peace, an era in which the nations of the world, East and West, North and South, can prosper and live in harmony." But the first great post–Cold War international crisis demonstrated how new kinds of conflicts might now define global politics. Economic competition, ethnic hatreds, and regional struggles for power seemed to replace the old ideological divide between the U.S. and the USSR as the fulcrum of international conflict.

On August 2, 1990, 120,000 Iraqi troops backed by 850 tanks swept into neighboring Kuwait and quickly seized control of that tiny country. The invasion motives of Saddam Hussein, Iraq's military dictator, were mixed. Like most Iraqis, Saddam believed that oil-rich Kuwait was actually an ancient province of Iraq, illegally carved away by British imperial agents in the 1920s as part of the dismemberment of the Ottoman Empire. Control of Kuwait would give Saddam control of its huge oil reserves, as well as Persian Gulf ports for his landlocked

country. Oil rivalry within the Organization of Petroleum Exporting Countries (OPEC) was a factor as well. Iraq, which had just ended an exhausting and inconclusive eight-year war with Iran, bitterly resented Kuwait's production of oil beyond OPEC quotas, which had helped send the world price of oil plummeting.

The U.S. responded swiftly to news of the invasion. Its first concern was that Saddam might attack Saudi Arabia as well, which as far back as 1943 the U.S. had defined as vital to its interests. On August 15, President Bush quickly ordered U.S. forces to Saudi Arabia and the Persian Gulf, calling it Operation Desert Shield. The president stressed the importance of oil as his rationale. "Our jobs, our way of life, our own freedom, and the freedom of friendly countries around the world will suffer if control of the world's great oil reserves fall in the hands of that one man, Saddam Hussein." The U.S. also led a broad coalition in the United Nations that condemned the Iraqi invasion of Kuwait and declared strict economic sanctions against Iraq if it did not withdraw. By the middle of October, some 230,000 American troops had been sent to the Persian Gulf.

In early November, President Bush announced a change in policy to what he called "an offensive military option," and the U.S. troop deployment quickly doubled to over 400,000, reaching 580,000 by January of 1991. The president also shifted to the moral high ground in justifying the biggest U.S. troop buildup since the Vietnam War. "The fight isn't about oil," he insisted. "The fight is about naked aggression that will not stand." Bush administration officials now demonized Saddam as another Hitler, and warned that he controlled a formidable fighting machine of over a million men. The UN sanctions failed to budge Saddam from Kuwait, and the drift to war now looked inevitable. In January, the Senate and the House vigorously debated a joint resolution authorizing the use of military force. Opponents urged the president to give the economic sanctions more time to force Iraq out, and they warned of the bloody cost of a drawn-out ground war against Saddam. They also pointed out that the U.S. had only recently supported Saddam (with economic aid, wheat exports, and arms sales) in his war with Iran. Supporters argued that if war came, it would be both morally just and in the nation's strategic economic interest. The resolution passed narrowly in the Senate (52 to 47), and more comfortably in the House (250 to 183).

A last-minute UN peace mission failed to break the deadlock. On January 16, 1991, President Bush announced the start of Operation Desert Storm. U.S.

U.S. Marines swept into Kuwait City, March, 1991. After six weeks of intensive bombing and less than five days after the start of a massive ground offensive, U.S. and allied forces overwhelmed the Iraqi army and ended Saddam Hussein's occupation of Kuwait.

and Allied air forces began forty-two days of massive bombing of Iraqi positions in Kuwait, as well as Baghdad and other Iraqi cities. They dropped 142,000 tons of bombs on Iraq and Kuwait, roughly six times the equivalent of the atomic bomb dropped on Nagasaki in World War II. The ground war began on February 24, and it took only 100 hours to force Saddam out of Kuwait. Iraqi troops, most of whom were poor conscripts reluctant to fight, surrendered in droves. Saddam's vaunted military machine turned out to be far weaker than advertised. U.S. forces lost only 184 dead, compared with nearly 100,000 Iraqi deaths, mostly from bombing.

At home, the vast majority of Americans supported Operation Desert Storm; the scattered antiwar protests around the nation received scant media coverage. Almost every community in the country had sent men and women to the Gulf as part of regular armed forces units and support personnel. Millions placed yellow ribbons outside their doors as a show of support for American forces. Unlike the coverage of Vietnam, Americans saw virtually no blood or death on their television screens. The Pentagon required that all reporters be accompanied by "military escorts," giving army commanders unprecedented control over the press. The Pentagon carefully controlled the release of silent film footage

documenting precision bombing runs. On television these looked more like video games than bombing attacks. American military officials insisted that the bombing had been limited to Iraqi military targets. But subsequent investigations revealed the devastation of Iraq's electrical and communications systems, waterways, bridges, factories, and highways — in short, the nation's entire infrastructure.

Politically, the Persian Gulf War marked the high point of President Bush's popularity. Along with General Norman Schwartzkopf and Colin Powell, chairman of the Joint Chiefs of Staff, Bush enjoyed enormous acclaim in the afterglow of the swift victory. To most Americans, the war seemed a welcome reassertion of the nation's military prowess and world leadership. Bush received a hero's welcome from a joint session of Congress in March. His approval rating with the public reached nearly 90 percent, higher than President Roosevelt's during World War II.

Yet nagging questions remained unanswered. Saddam himself survived, and the U.S. abandoned Iraqi opposition forces and Kurds after encouraging them to rebel. The U.S. had succeeded in restoring the government of Kuwait to power, but that government itself was an undemocratic feudal monarchy. The ecological damage in the Gulf region, mainly from Saddam's torching of Kuwaiti oil wells, will take years to assess. The massive bombing of Iraq led to a severe public health crisis and destroyed its economy. Human rights groups reported an appalling toll among innocent Iraqis. Democratic representative Jim McDermott of Washington, who visited Iraq the summer following the war, testified before a House committee on the misery he saw and the ethical dilemma posed by American policy. "The Iraqi people did not vote for Saddam Hussein, yet hundreds of thousands of Iraqis, most of them children, are hungry, sick, and dying because of Saddam's intransigence and our commitment to oust Hussein at all cost." The war brought an intense spirit of triumph to the people of the United States. But for the 18 million people of Iraq, heavily bombed and left with Saddam in power, the war produced the worst possible outcome.

Multicultural Riot in Los Angeles

In the spring of 1992 a devastating riot in Los Angeles offered the starkest evidence of how racial tensions and desperate poverty continued to plague many American communities. The spark that ignited the worst riot of the century was black outrage over police brutality. Rodney King, a black motorist, had been severely beaten by four white police officers after being stopped and pulled from his vehicle. What made the King case so unique was an amateur videotape of the incident, made by an onlooker. The video received wide exposure on television news shows, and it seemed to confirm long-standing charges by minority groups that many L.A. police engaged in a persistent pattern of racist behavior. But the trial of the four white officers, held in the white middle-class suburb of Simi Valley, resulted in an acquittal on all but one charge.

For three days, rioters swept through South Central Los Angeles and nearby Koreatown, looting and burning businesses. Fifty-one people were killed, more than $750 million in damage was reported, and about 500 buildings were destroyed before L.A. police and National Guard troops managed to restore order. Over 12,000 people were arrested for looting, arson, and violations of curfew. Journalists were quick to make comparisons with the Watts riot of 1965, in which thirty-four people

died. But the 1992 riot was different. Not only was it more deadly and more destructive, it was also more complex. The riot was not simply a black-versus-white affair. It was a multicultural riot that involved the large Korean and Latino populations of Los Angeles as well.

A Sheriff's Department analysis of riot-related arrests revealed that 45 percent were Latino, 41 percent African American, and 12 percent Anglo. Sixty percent lacked prior criminal records. They included a large number of poor, non-English-speaking recent immigrants from Mexico, El Salvador, and Nicaragua, many of whom were undocumented. These rioters represented the most desperate and marginal population in Los Angeles. They were generally confined to minimum wage jobs as laborers, busboys, domestics, and factory workers, and their unemployment rate had tripled during two years of economic recession. Thousands lived in homeless colonies near the MacArthur Park neighborhood and in the concrete bed of the Los Angeles River. Those who engaged in looting ap-

Looters struggled to make off with their booty during the Los Angeles riots of April, 1992. Most of the 12,000 people arrested during the riots were from the most economically marginal elements of the L.A. population, including a large number of recent immigrants from Central America and Mexico.

peared more interested in clothing and food than in televisions or other consumer durables.

The city's large Korean community suffered enormous economic and psychological damage in the riot. Almost 2,000 Korean businesses, mostly liquor stores, groceries, and discount "swap meets," were destroyed. Korean businessmen angrily accused the police of making no effort to defend their stores, and many hired armed guards to patrol their property. Animosity between Korean store owners and African American customers ran deep. Blacks had been outraged by the recent acquittal of a Korean grocer who had shot and killed an African American girl she thought was stealing a bottle of orange juice. Blacks also complained about the large number of Korean-owned liquor stores in South Central. They resented Korean business success within black neighborhoods, where very few Koreans lived. The Korean community, generally ambitious and hardworking, questioned why it had been singled out for attack and wondered if the American dream remained attainable.

For most African Americans, the situation in Los Angeles seemed more desperate than ever, reflecting many of the larger trends in American society over the previous decade. The poverty rate in the south Los Angeles area was 30.3 percent, three times the national average. Unemployment for adult black males hovered around 40 percent and a quarter of the population was on welfare. Los Angeles had lost 100,000 manufacturing jobs in the three years before the riot. In 1976, the passage of the statewide Proposition 13 tax cut began a sharp reduction in public investment in the inner-city educational system. Drug dealing and gang warfare had escalated, reflecting the sense of despair among young people. The riot exposed the festering ethnic and racial divisions within Los Angeles. "We are all quite isolated in our own communities," a resident of Westwood, a mostly white middle-class neighborhood, explained. "We don't know and don't care about the problems in the inner cities. Driving to work every day most of us don't even know where South Central is — except many of us saw the fires from that direction when we were stuck in traffic."

The Election of 1992

As President Bush's popularity soared following the Persian Gulf War, most political analysts believe he would win reelection easily. But as the glow of military victory faded, so too did Bush's political fortunes. A harsh and lingering recession in 1991 and 1992 dominated the presidential election campaign. The recession was different from other post–World War II slumps in several ways. Although interest rates were low and theoretically should have encouraged investment, business continued to shrink rather than expand. The nation's manufacturers faced stiffer competition than ever, especially from Japan, Korea, and the industrialized nations of Europe. As unemployment climbed above 8 percent, consumer confidence and retail sales plummeted. The recession was unique in producing a large number of highly educated, white-collar unemployed, thrown out of work by declining real estate, financial, and computer industries.

The paradoxes of the Reagan-Bush years became apparent. Conservatives took credit for forcing the fall of communism and reviving America's military strength. Yet the fundamental international problem facing the country seemed to be the erosion of American economic competitiveness and the decline in real wages. In communities devastated by the loss of key industries, millions wondered whether the structural changes transforming the world economy meant an irreversible decline in the American standard of living. Conservatives had made cutting government spending a central premise of their appeal. But after twelve years of Republican rule the national debt stood at an astronomical $4 trillion and threatened to undermine the nation's economic future. Perhaps the clearest success for Reagan and Bush came in remaking the courts, as their appointees constituted 65 percent of all federal judges and a majority of the Supreme Court. Conservative courts rewrote criminal procedure and allowed states to limit women's access to abortion.

President Bush faced a primary challenge from his right with the insurgent candidacy of conservative commentator Patrick Buchanan. A former aide to Presidents Nixon and Reagan, Buchanan espoused a conservatism that emphasized "traditional values": opposition to abortion and gay rights; celebration of the nuclear family above all others; attacks on government social programs, welfare recipients, and the poor; and a tough-on-crime stance. Buchanan failed to win any primaries against Bush, but his campaign forced the president to shore up his conservative flank. At the Republican National Convention Buchanan and the Reverend Pat Robertson, a conservative fundamentalist, tried to frame the upcoming election as a "cultural war," and in the process alienated many moderate voters.

After a vigorous primary season the Democrats

Republican President George Bush, Democrat Bill Clinton, and independent H. Ross Perot debated the issues on television three times during the 1992 presidential campaign. Bush emphasized the "character" issue by hammering away at Clinton's failure to serve during the Vietnam War. Clinton focused on the plight of the "forgotten middle class," many of whom had deserted the Democratic Party. Perot made the national debt the centerpiece of his campaign, and he appealed to voter frustration with the two major parties.

nominated Governor Bill Clinton of Arkansas. Clinton had begun his political life as a liberal, anti–Vietnam War Democrat. But after suffering defeat after his first term as Arkansas governor, he had remade himself politically as a centrist. Clinton's campaign for the nomination effectively adopted many of the conservative themes that had proved so popular for Republicans over the past twelve years. He called for "responsibility" from the recipients of social programs, spoke of the importance of stable families, promised to be tough on crime and bureaucracy, and stressed the need for encouraging private investment to create new jobs.

A wild-card element in the 1992 election was the independent campaign of Texas billionaire H. Ross Perot. Perot had made a fortune with a data-processing company that had computerized Social Security and Medicare records in the 1960s and 1970s. He promoted his candidacy through appearances on television talk shows, hoping to bypass traditional media outlets and directly reach voters. With his folksy, East Texas twang, Perot appealed to the deep distrust and anger that millions felt toward the two major parties. He made the national debt his central issue, and he argued that a successful businessman like himself was more qualified to solve the nation's economic woes than Washington insiders. Perot spent millions of dollars of his own money funding "volunteer" organizations in the fifty states. In July, with polls showing him running nearly even with Bush and Clinton, he abruptly announced that he was quitting the race.

His reasoning was unclear. Two months later, in an effort to restore his damaged reputation, he was back in.

The campaign featured sophisticated new media strategies by all the candidates. Clinton, Bush, and Perot all appeared frequently on call-in television and radio talk shows in an effort to circumvent the power of professional journalists and connect more directly with voters. Perot spent millions on half-hour "infomercials" broadcast over the major networks. Clinton made a special effort to reach younger voters by appearing on MTV and youth-oriented programs. As the first baby boomer candidate, the forty-six-year-old Clinton stressed the theme of generational change.

On Election Day, Democrats recaptured the White House after twelve years of Republican control. Clinton won big, beating Bush 43 percent to 38 percent in the popular vote and 370 to 168 in the electoral vote. Although he carried no states, Perot garnered 19 percent of the popular vote, the strongest showing by a third-party candidate since Theodore Roosevelt in 1912. Clinton ran especially strong in the Northeast, the industrial Midwest, and the Far West, where he became the first Democratic presidential candidate to capture California since Lyndon Johnson in 1964. Clinton won back many of the Reagan Democrats he had courted, and his campaign also broke the long Republican grip on the states of the trans-Mississippi West. Women made historic gains with the election of four new Democratic senators. Carol Moseley Braun of Illinois became the first African American woman elected to the Senate; Diane Feinstein and Barbara Boxer won election in California and Patty Murray in Washington. With a solidly Democratic House and Senate, President Clinton called for an "American renewal" as he began his term.

Changing American Communities: Metropolitan Areas and Suburban Cities

The 1990 census showed that for the first time in U.S. history a majority of the populace lived within a large metropolitan area. The census defined *metropolitan area* as "one or more countries including a large population nucleus and nearby communities that have a high degree of interaction." The census divided these metropolitan areas into two groups: those above 1 million population and those below. It revealed that nearly 125 million people out of a total population of 249 million lived within the thirty-nine

large (over 1 million) metropolitan centers. Greater New York City, with more than 18 million people, was the largest of these areas, followed by Greater Los Angeles, with 14.5 million residents. The nation's fastest-growing large metropolitan areas were all in the West and South. These included Orlando, which grew by 53 percent in the 1980s, Phoenix (40 percent), Sacramento (34 percent), San Diego (34 percent), Dallas-Ft. Worth (32 percent), Atlanta (32 percent), and Los Angeles (26 percent).

This historic statistical shift to metropolitan areas stemmed directly from the expansion of the economy's service sector. The nation's postindustrial economy relied heavily on the growth of management, research and development, marketing, and distribution activities. These required the critical mass of educated people and services that could be found only in metropolitan areas. The proportion of the population with at least a college degree grew disproportionately in metro areas, to 22.5 percent, compared with 13 percent in nonmetro areas.

An enormous range of differences could be found both between and within metropolitan area communities. Recent immigrants brought a striking new multiculturalism to many coastal and Sunbelt cities, the "port of entry" communities. But many smaller communities in the Midwest remained relatively unchanged. In Greater Los Angeles, for example, half the population was Hispanic, black, or Asian, and 27 percent of the residents were foreign-born. But the community many demographers called typical was Indianapolis, where less than 15 percent of the population was Hispanic, black, or Asian, and less than 2 percent of the residents were foreign-born. A larger percentage of people lived in bigger and bigger metropolitan areas, but a larger proportion of metropolitan people lived in the suburbs. Metropolitan expansion created huge semiurban sprawls, which erased older lines of demarcation between many towns. Population and job growth were concentrated at the geographic edges of metropolitan areas.

The suburban city of Plano, Texas, offered a harbinger of the future for many American communities. Part of the Dallas–Forth Worth metropolitan area, Plano's population jumped from 72,000 to 128,000 during the 1980s, an increase of 78 percent. Plano was one of five suburban cities with over 100,000 population in the Dallas-Forth Worth area. The others included Arlington, Garland, Irving, and Mesquite. Altogether, these five suburban cities grew almost twice as much as Dallas and Fort Worth during the 1980s. Whereas the traditional American city was built around a central business district, newer suburban cities grew up around a principal business or economic activity: a collection of computer companies, a large regional medical center, or a sports complex. Plano's economic life revolved around Legacy Park, a huge office development housing one of the world's largest data-processing centers, along with the headquarters of five major corporations. Two large fiber optic communications stations kept Legacy Park plugged into the global economy. A nearby complex of telecommunications manufacturing plants provided another new source of jobs.

Every rush hour, traffic moved in both directions as commuters drove to and from Plano for jobs in office buildings, factories, warehouses, and shopping malls. During the 1980s, Plano began to display many attributes associated with large urban centers. Thai, Chinese, and other ethnic restaurants sprang up. A quaint downtown featured antique and crafts shops in storefronts where cotton farmers used to buy supplies. The city boasted its own small chamber music ensemble. Yet the rapid growth of suburban cities like Plano also exposed and reinforced the deepening economic and racial divisions in American society. Plano had a very small immigrant and minority population, and nearly 90 percent of its public school students were white. In Dallas, by contrast, the 1990 census showed that for the first time a majority of the city's population was African American or Latino.

Suburban cities have become even more specialized economically than the industrial centers of the nineteenth century. Yet their gains often meant losses for older cities. As core cities like Fort Worth lost jobs and part of their tax base to suburban cities like Plano, it became more difficult to pay the central city's costs of maintaining infrastructure and caring for the elderly, poor, and sick. While suburban cities like Plano often suffered from labor shortages, unemployment simultaneously rose in the core cities, especially among African Americans and Latinos. Lack of adequate transportation and low-cost housing made it difficult for central-city residents to take advantage of new job opportunities in the suburban city.

CONCLUSION

During the 1980s the very notion of community itself, once defined entirely in terms of space, increasingly became a function of demographic categories. The proliferation of computer-based communication technologies made it easier to create communities based on these demographic categories, such as income, profession, education level, and consumption preferences. The mass media, advertisers, and political professionals all intensified their reliance upon sophisticated marketing and polling techniques. Thus American culture defined and addressed its citizens less as whole human beings and more as merely the sums of statistical characteristics. Yet people still live and work in local places. As American communities continue to evolve in response to a more global, service-oriented, and high-tech economy, they will no doubt be forced to seek regional solutions to the problems posed by the twenty-first century.

CHRONOLOGY

1980   Ronald Reagan elected president

1981   Major cuts in taxes and domestic spending
Beginning of military buildup
Discovery of AIDS
MTV and CNN start broadcasting as cable channels

1982   Economic recession
Nuclear freeze rally attracts 750,000 in New York City

1983   Strategic Defense Initiative ("Star Wars") begins
241 Marines killed in Beirut terrorist bombing

1984   Reagan reelected

1985   Mikhail Gorbachev begins glasnost and perestroika

1986   Immigration Reform and Control Act
Democrats regain control of Senate

1987   Iran-Contra hearings before Congress
Stock market crash

1988   Reagan and Gorbachev sign INF treaty
George Bush elected president

1989   Collapse of Communist authority in Eastern Europe

1990   Iraqi invasion of Kuwait leads to massive U.S. military presence in the Persian Gulf

1991   Operation Desert Storm
Soviet Union dissolves into Commonwealth of Independent States

1992   Rodney King verdict sparks rioting in Los Angeles
Bill Clinton elected president

Additional Readings

Donald Barlett and James B. Steele, *America: What Went Wrong* (1992). An expansion of the authors' series in the *Philadelphia Inquirer,* this book offers a mass of interesting data documenting the declining fortunes of the American middle class in the 1980s.

Barry Bluestone and Bennett Harrison, *The Deindustrialization of America* (1982). A pathbreaking analysis showing how corporate strategy and government policy combined to weaken America's industrial base after the late 1960s.

Sidney Blumenthal and Thomas B. Edsall, eds., *The Reagan Legacy* (1988). A collection of critical essays assessing the impact of Reagan's presidency on American society and culture.

Barbara Ehrenreich, *Fear of Falling* (1989). A thoughtful and well-argued book that examines the cultural and economic insecurities of the American middle class in recent years.

Haynes Johnson, *Sleepingwalking through History* (1991). A readable, journalistic narrative of the Reagan presidency.

Michael T. Klare and Peter Kornbluh, eds., *Low Intensity Warfare* (1988). A valuable set of essays offering case studies of counterinsurgency and antiterrorist tactics during the 1980s.

Robert Lekachman, *Visions and Nightmares* (1987). An economist's view of Reagan's legacy, emphasizing the long-range impact of military spending, tax cuts, and the shrinking of social programs.

Michael Mandlebaum, *Reagan and Gorbachev* (1987). Solid overview of the two superpower leaders and what they accomplished in arms control.

Nicolaus Mills, *Culture in an Age of Money* (1990). An acerbic account of the impact of corporate power and big money on the cultural life of the nation during the 1980s.

Kevin Phillips, *The Politics of Rich and Poor* (1990). A fascinating, superbly documented, and often brilliant analysis of the growth in economic inequality that characterized the 1980s. Phillips, a prominent Republican strategist, makes historical comparisons with the 1920s and the late nineteenth century to bolster his argument.

Everett M. Rogers and Judith K. Larsen, *Silicon Valley Fever* (1984). Useful account of the rise of the computer industry in Silicon Valley with special emphasis on the development of Apple and Hewlett-Packard.

Randy Shilts, *And the Band Played On* (1986). The best history of the AIDS epidemic and the politics surrounding AIDS research and treatment.

William Serrin, *Homestead* (1991). A study of Homestead, Pennsylvania, and the decline of the American steel industry.

Micah L. Sifry and Christopher Cerf, eds., *The Gulf War Reader* (1991). An excellent collection of historical essays, government documents, and political addresses that provides a comprehensive overview of the Persian Gulf War.

James B. Stewart, *Den of Thieves* (1991). A well-documented inside look at the people and events at the center of Wall Street's insider trader scandal. Offers a detailed account of the shady financial practices of the 1980s.

Garry Wills, *Reagan's America* (1987). A thoughtful meditation that analyzes Reagan's popularity largely as a function of the nation's nostalgia for a more "innocent" time.

Appendix

The Declaration of Independence

When in the course of human events it becomes necessary for one people to dissolve the political bands which have connected them with another and to assume, among the powers of the earth, the separate and equal station to which the laws of nature and of nature's God entitle them, a decent respect to the opinions of mankind requires that they should declare the causes which impel them to the separation.

We hold these truths to be self-evident, that all men are created equal; that they are endowed by their Creator with certain unalienable rights; that among these are life, liberty, and the pursuit of happiness. That, to secure these rights, governments are instituted among men, deriving their just powers from the consent of the governed; that, whenever any form of government becomes destructive of these ends, it is the right of the people to alter or to abolish it, and to institute a new government, laying its foundation on such principles, and organizing its powers in such form, as to them shall seem most likely to effect their safety and happiness. Prudence, indeed, will dictate that governments long established should not be changed for light and transient causes; and, accordingly, all experience hath shown that mankind are more disposed to suffer, while evils are sufferable, than to right themselves by abolishing the forms to which they are accustomed. But when a long train of abuses and usurpations, pursuing invariably the same object, evinces a design to reduce them under absolute despotism, it is their right, it is their duty, to throw off such government and to provide new guards for their future security. Such has been the patient sufferance of these colonies, and such is now the necessity which constrains them to alter their former systems of government. The history of the present King of Great Britain is a history of repeated injuries and usurpations, all having, in direct object, the establishment of an absolute tyranny over these States. To prove this, let facts be submitted to a candid world:

He has refused his assent to laws the most wholesome and necessary for the public good.

He has forbidden his governors to pass laws of immediate and pressing importance, unless suspended in their operation till his assent should be obtained; and, when so suspended, he has utterly neglected to attend to them.

He has refused to pass other laws for the accommodation of large districts of people, unless those people would relinquish the right of representation in the legislature; a right inestimable to them and formidable to tyrants only.

He has called together legislative bodies at places unusual, uncomfortable, and distant from the depository of their public records, for the sole purpose of fatiguing them into compliance with his measures.

He has dissolved representative houses, repeatedly for opposing, with manly firmness, his invasions on the rights of the people.

He has refused, for a long time after such dissolutions, to cause others to be elected; whereby the legislative powers, incapable of annihilation, have returned to the people at large for their exercise; the state remaining, in the meantime, exposed to all the danger of invasion from without and convulsions within.

He has endeavored to prevent the population of these States; for that purpose, obstructing the laws for naturalization of foreigners, refusing to pass others to encourage their migration hither, and raising the conditions of new appropriations of lands.

He has obstructed the administration of justice by refusing his assent to laws for establishing judiciary powers.

He has made judges dependent on his will alone for the tenure of their offices and the amount and payment of their salaries.

He has erected a multitude of new offices and sent hither swarms of officers to harass our people and eat out their substance.

He has kept among us, in time of peace, standing armies, without the consent of our legislatures.

He has affected to render the military independent of, and superior to, the civil power.

He has combined with others to subject us to a jurisdiction foreign to our Constitution and unacknowledged by our laws, giving his assent to their acts of pretended legislation —

For quartering large bodies of armed troops among us;

For protecting them by a mock trial from punishment for any murders which they should commit on the inhabitants of these States;

For cutting off our trade with all parts of the world;

For imposing taxes on us without our consent;

For depriving us, in many cases, of the benefit of trial by jury;

For transporting us beyond seas to be tried for pretended offences;

For abolishing the free system of English laws in a neighboring province, establishing therein an arbitrary government, and enlarging its boundaries, so as to render it at once an example and fit instrument for introducing the same absolute rule into these colonies;

For taking away our charters, abolishing our most valuable laws, and altering, fundamentally, the powers of our governments;

For suspending our own legislatures and declaring themselves invested with power to legislate for us in all cases whatsoever.

He has abdicated government here by declaring us out of his protection and waging war against us.

He has plundered our seas, ravaged our coasts, burnt our towns, and destroyed the lives of our people.

He is, at this time, transporting large armies of foreign mercenaries to complete the works of death, desolation, and tyranny already begun with circumstances of cruelty and perfidy scarcely paralleled in the most barbarous ages, and totally unworthy the head of a civilized nation.

He has constrained our fellow citizens, taken captive on the high seas, to bear arms against their country, to become the executioners of their friends and brethren, or to fall themselves by their hands.

He has excited domestic insurrections amongst us and has endeavored to bring on the inhabitants of our frontiers, the merciless Indian savages, whose known rule of warfare is an undistinguished destruction of all ages, sexes, and conditions.

In every stage of these oppressions, we have petitioned for redress in the most humble terms; our repeated petitions have been answered only by repeated injury. A prince whose character is thus marked by every act which may define a tyrant is unfit to be the ruler of a free people.

Nor have we been wanting in attention to our British brethren. We have warned them, from time to time, of attempts made by their legislature to extend an unwarrantable jurisdiction over us. We have reminded them of the circumstances of our emigration and settlement here. We have appealed to their native justice and magnanimity, and we have conjured them, by the ties of our common kindred,

to disavow these usurpations, which would inevitably interrupt our connections and correspondence. They, too, have been deaf to the voice of justice and consanguinity. We must, therefore, acquiesce in the necessity which denounces our separation, and hold them, as we hold the rest of mankind, enemies in war, in peace, friends.

We, therefore, the representatives of the United States of America, in general Congress assembled, appealing to the Supreme Judge of the world for the rectitude of our intentions, do, in the name and by the authority of the good people of these colonies, solemnly publish and declare, that these united colonies are, and of right ought to be, free and independent states: that they are absolved from all allegiance to the British Crown, and that all political connection between them and the state of Great Britain is, and ought to be, totally dissolved; and that, as free and independent states, they have full power to levy war, conclude peace, contract alliances, establish commerce, and to do all other acts and things which independent states may of right do. And, for the support of this declaration, with a firm reliance on the protection of Divine Providence, we mutually pledge to each other our lives, our fortunes, and our sacred honor.

The Constitution of the United States of America

We the people of the United States, in order to form a more perfect union, establish justice, insure domestic tranquillity, provide for the common defense, promote the general welfare, and secure the blessings of liberty to ourselves and our posterity, do ordain and establish this Constitution for the United States of America.

Article I

Section 1. All legislative powers herein granted shall be vested in a Congress of the United States, which shall consist of a Senate and House of Representatives.

Section 2. 1. The House of Representatives shall be composed of members chosen every second year by the people of the several States, and the electors in each State shall have the qualifications requisite for electors of the most numerous branch of the State legislature.

2. No person shall be a representative who shall not have attained to the age of twenty-five years, and been seven years a citizen of the United States, and who shall not, when elected, be an inhabitant of that State in which he shall be chosen.

3. Representatives and direct taxes[1] shall be apportioned among the several States which may be included within this Union, according to their respective numbers, which shall be determined by adding to the whole number of free persons, including those bound to service for a term of years, and excluding Indians not taxed, three fifths of all other persons.[2] The actual enumeration shall be made within three years after the first meeting of the Congress of the United States, and within every subsequent term of ten years, in such manner as they shall by law direct. The number of representatives shall not exceed one for every thirty thousand, but each State shall have at least one

representative; and until such enumeration shall be made, the State of New Hampshire shall be entitled to choose three, Massachusetts eight, Rhode Island and Providence Plantations one, Connecticut five, New York six, New Jersey four, Pennsylvania eight, Delaware one, Maryland six, Virginia ten, North Carolina five, South Carolina five, and Georgia three.

4. When vacancies happen in the representation from any State, the executive authority thereof shall issue writs of election to fill such vacancies.

5. The House of Representatives shall choose their speaker and other officers; and shall have the sole power of impeachment.

Section 3. 1. The Senate of the United States shall be composed of two senators from each State, chosen by the legislature thereof,[3] for six years; and each senator shall have one vote.

2. Immediately after they shall be assembled in consequence of the first election, they shall be divided as equally as may be into three classes. The seats of the senators of the first class shall be vacated at the expiration of the second year, of the second class at the expiration of the fourth year, and of the third class at the expiration of the sixth year, so that one third may be chosen every second year; and if vacancies happen by resignation, or otherwise, during the recess of the legislature of any State, the executive thereof may make temporary appointments until the next meeting of the legislature, which shall then fill such vacancies.[4]

3. No person shall be a senator who shall not have attained to the age of thirty years, and been nine years a citizen of the United States, and who shall not, when elected, be an inhabitant of that State for which he shall be chosen.

---

[1]See the Sixteenth Amendment.
[2]See the Fourteenth Amendment.

[3]See the Seventeenth Amendment.
[4]See the Seventeenth Amendment.

4. The Vice President of the United States shall be President of the Senate, but shall have no vote, unless they be equally divided.

5. The Senate shall choose their other officers, and also a president pro tempore, in the absence of the Vice President, or when he shall exercise the office of the President of the United States.

6. The Senate shall have the sole power to try all impeachments. When sitting for that purpose, they shall be on oath or affirmation. When the President of the United States is tried, the chief justice shall preside: and no person shall be convicted without the concurrence of two thirds of the members present.

7. Judgment in cases of impeachment shall not extend further than to removal from office, and disqualification to hold and enjoy any office of honor, trust or profit under the United States: but the party convicted shall nevertheless be liable and subject to indictment, trial, judgment and punishment, according to law.

SECTION 4. 1. The times, places, and manner of holding elections for senators and representatives, shall be prescribed in each State by the legislature thereof; but the Congress may at any time by law make or alter such regulations, except as to the places of choosing senators.

2. The Congress shall assemble at least once in every year, and such meeting shall be on the first Monday in December, unless they shall by law appoint a different day.

SECTION 5. 1. Each House shall be the judge of the elections, returns and qualifications of its own members, and a majority of each shall constitute a quorum to do business; but a smaller number may adjourn from day to day, and may be authorized to compel the attendance of absent members, in such manner, and under such penalties as each House may provide.

2. Each House may determine the rules of its proceedings, punish its members for disorderly behavior, and, with the concurrence of two thirds, expel a member.

3. Each House shall keep a journal of its proceedings, and from time to time publish the same, excepting such parts as may in their judgment require secrecy; and the yeas and nays of the members of either House on any question shall, at the desire of one fifth of those present, be entered on the journal.

4. Neither House, during the session of Congress, shall, without the consent of the other, adjourn for more than three days, nor to any other place than that in which the two Houses shall be sitting.

SECTION 6. 1. The senators and representatives shall receive a compensation for their services, to be ascertained by law, and paid out of the Treasury of the United States. They shall in all cases, except treason, felony, and breach of the peace, be privileged from arrest during their attendance at the session of their respective Houses, and in going to and returning from the same; and for any speech or debate in either House, they shall not be questioned in any other place.

2. No senator or representative shall, during the time for which he was elected, be appointed to any civil office under the authority of the United States, which shall have been created, or the emoluments whereof shall have been increased, during such time; and no person holding any office under the United States shall be a member of either House during his continuance in office.

SECTION 7. 1. All bills for raising revenue shall originate in the House of Representatives; but the Senate may propose or concur with amendments as on other bills.

2. Every bill which shall have passed the House of Representatives and the Senate, shall, before it become a law, be presented to the President of the United States; If he approves he shall sign it, but if not he shall return it, with his objections, to that House in which it shall have originated, who shall enter the objections at large on their journal, and proceed to reconsider it. If after such reconsideration two thirds of that House shall agree to pass the bill, it shall be sent, together with the objections, to the other House, by which it shall likewise be reconsidered, and if approved by two thirds of that House, it shall become a law. But in all such cases the votes of both Houses shall be determined by yeas and nays, and the names of the persons voting for and against the bill shall be entered on the journal of each House respectively. If any bill shall not be returned by the President within ten days (Sundays excepted) after it shall have been presented to him, the same shall be a law, in like manner as if he had signed it, unless the Congress by their adjournment prevent its return, in which case it shall not be a law.

3. Every order, resolution, or vote to which the concurrence of the Senate and the House of Representatives may be necessary (except on a question of adjournment) shall be presented to the President of the United States; and before the same shall take effect, shall be approved by him, or being disapproved by him, shall be repassed by two thirds of the Senate and House of Representatives, according to the rules and limitations prescribed in the case of a bill.

SECTION 8. The Congress shall have the power

1. To lay and collect taxes, duties, imposts, and excises, to pay the debts and provide for the common defense and general welfare of the United States; but all duties, imposts, and excises shall be uniform throughout the United States;

2. To borrow money on the credit of the United States;

3. To regulate commerce with foreign nations, and among the several States, and with the Indian tribes;

4. To establish a uniform rule of naturalization, and uniform laws on the subject of bankruptcies throughout the United States;

5. To coin money, regulate the value thereof, and of foreign coin, and fix the standard of weights and measures;

6. To provide for the punishment of counterfeiting the securities and current coin of the United States;

7. To establish post offices and post roads;

8. To promote the progress of science and useful arts, by securing for limited times to authors and inventors the exclusive right to their respective writings and discoveries;

9. To constitute tribunals inferior to the Supreme Court;

10. To define and punish piracies and felonies committed on the high seas, and offenses against the law of nations;

11. To declare war, grant letters of marque and reprisal, and make rules concerning captures on land and water;

12. To raise and support armies, but no appropriation of money to that use shall be for a longer term than two years;

13. To provide and maintain a navy;

14. To make rules for the government and regulation of the land and naval forces;

15. To provide for calling forth the militia to execute the laws of the Union, suppress insurrections and repel invasions;

16. To provide for organizing, arming, and disciplining the militia, and for governing such part of them as may be employed in the service of the United States, reserving to the States respectively, the appointment of the officers, and the authority of training the militia according to the discipline prescribed by Congress;

17. To exercise exclusive legislation in all cases whatsoever, over such district (not exceeding ten miles square) as may, by cession of particular States, and the acceptance of Congress, become the seat of the government of the United States, and to exercise like authority over all places purchased by the consent of the legislature of the State in which the same shall be, for the erection of forts, magazines, arsenals, dockyards, and other needful buildings; and

18. To make all laws which shall be necessary and proper for carrying into execution the foregoing powers, and all other powers vested by this Constitution in the government of the United States, or any department or officer thereof.

Section 9. 1. The migration or importation of such persons as any of the States now existing shall think proper to admit, shall not be prohibited by the Congress prior to the year one thousand eight hundred and eight, but a tax or duty may be imposed on such importation, not exceeding ten dollars for each person.

2. The privilege of the writ of habeas corpus shall not be suspended, unless when in cases of rebellion or invasion the public safety may require it.

3. No bill of attainder or ex post facto law shall be passed.

4. No capitation, or other direct, tax shall be laid, unless in proportion to the census or enumeration hereinbefore directed to be taken.[5]

5. No tax or duty shall be laid on articles exported from any State.

6. No preference shall be given by any regulation of commerce or revenue to the ports of one State over those of another: nor shall vessels bound to, or from, one State be obliged to enter, clear, or pay duties in another.

7. No money shall be drawn from the treasury, but in consequence of appropriations made by law; and a regular statement and account of the receipts and expenditures of all public money shall be published from time to time.

8. No title of nobility shall be granted by the United States: and no person holding any office of profit or trust under them, shall, without the consent of the Congress, accept of any present, emolument, office, or title, of any kind whatever, from any king, prince, or foreign State.

Section 10. 1. No State shall enter into any treaty, alliance, or confederation; grant letters of marque and reprisal; coin money; emit bills of credit; make any thing but gold and silver coin a tender in payment of debts; pass any bill of attainder, ex post facto law, or law impairing the obligation of contracts, or grant any title of nobility.

2. No State shall, without the consent of the Congress, lay any imposts or duties on imports or exports, except what may be absolutely necessary for executing its inspection laws: and the net produce of all duties and imposts laid by any State on imports or exports, shall be for the use of the treasury of the United States; and all such laws shall be subject to the revision and control of the Congress.

3. No State shall, without the consent of the Congress, lay any duty of tonnage, keep troops, or ships of war in time of peace, enter into any agreement or compact with another State, or with a foreign power, or engage in war, unless actually invaded, or in such imminent danger as will not admit of delay.

Article II

Section 1. 1. The executive power shall be vested in a President of the United States of America. He shall hold his office during the term of four years, and, together with the Vice President, chosen for the same term, be elected, as follows:

2. Each State shall appoint, in such manner as the legislature thereof may direct, a number of electors, equal to the whole number of senators and representatives to which the State may be entitled in the Congress: but no senator or representative, or person holding any office of trust or profit under the United States, shall be appointed an elector.

The electors shall meet in their respective States, and vote by ballot for two persons, of whom one at least shall not be an inhabitant of the same State with themselves. And they shall make a list of all the persons voted for, and of the number of votes for each; which list they shall sign and certify, and transmit sealed to the seat of the government of the United States, directed to the president of the Senate. The president of the Senate shall, in the presence of the Senate and House of Representatives, open all the certificates, and the votes shall then be counted. The person having the greatest number of votes shall be the President, if such number be a majority of the whole number of electors appointed; and if there be more than one who have such majority, and have an equal number of votes, then the House of Representatives shall immediately choose by ballot one of them for President; and if no person have a majority, then from the five highest on the list the said House shall in like manner choose the President. But in choosing the President, the votes shall be taken by States, the representation from each State having one vote; a quorum for this purpose shall consist of a member or members from two thirds of the States, and a majority of all the States shall be necessary to a choice. In every case after the choice of the President, the person having the greatest number of votes of the electors shall be the Vice President. But if there should remain two or more who have equal votes, the Senate shall chose from them by ballot the Vice President.[6]

3. The Congress may determine the time of choosing the electors, and the day on which they shall give their votes; which day shall be the same throughout the United States.

4. No person except a natural born citizen, or a citizen of the United States, at the time of the adoption of this Constitution, shall be eligible to the office of President; neither shall any person be eligible to the office who shall not have attained to the age of thirty-five years, and been fourteen years a resident within the United States.

5. In case of the removal of the President from office, or of his death, resignation, or inability to discharge the powers and duties of the said office, the same shall devolve on the Vice President, and the Congress may by law provide for the case of removal, death, resignation or inability, both

---

[5]See the Sixteenth Amendment.

[6]Superseded by the Twelfth Amendment.

of the President and Vice President, declaring what officer shall then act as President, and such officer shall act accordingly until the disability be removed, or a President shall be elected.

6. The President shall, at stated times, receive for his services a compensation which shall neither be increased nor diminished during the period for which he shall have been elected, and he shall not receive within that period any other emolument from the United States, or any of them.

7. Before he enter on the execution of his office, he shall take the following oath or affirmation:— ''I do solemnly swear (or affirm) that I will faithfully execute the office of President of the United States, and will to the best of my ability, preserve, protect and defend the Constitution of the United States.''

Section 2. 1. The President shall be commander in chief of the army and navy of the United States, and of the militia of the several States, when called into the actual service of the United States; he may require the opinion in writing, of the principal officer in each of the executive departments, upon any subject relating to the duties of their respective offices, and he shall have power to grant reprieves and pardons for offenses against the United States, except in cases of impeachment.

2. He shall have power, by and with the advice and consent of the Senate, to make treaties, provided two thirds of the senators present concur; and he shall nominate, and by and with the advice and consent of the Senate, shall appoint ambassadors, other public ministers and consuls, judges of the Supreme Court, and all other officers of the United States, whose appointments are not herein otherwise provided for, and which shall be established by law; but the Congress may by law vest the appointment of such inferior officers, as they think proper, in the President alone, in the courts of laws, or in the heads of departments.

3. The President shall have power to fill up all vacancies that may happen during the recess of the Senate, by granting commissions which shall expire at the end of their next session.

Section 3. He shall from time to time give to the Congress information of the state of the Union, and recommend to their consideration such measures as he shall judge necessary and expedient; he may, on extraordinary occasions, convene both Houses, or either of them, and in case of disagreement between them with respect to the time of adjournment, he may adjourn them to such time as he shall think proper; he shall receive ambassadors and other public ministers; he shall take care that the laws be faithfully executed, and shall commission all the officers of the United States.

Section 4. The President, Vice President, and all civil officers of the United States, shall be removed from office on impeachment for, and conviction of, treason, bribery, or other high crimes and misdemeanors.

Article III

Section 1. The judicial power of the United States shall be vested in one Supreme Court, and in such inferior courts as the Congress may from time to time ordain and establish. The judges, both of the Supreme and inferior courts, shall hold their offices during good behavior, and shall, at stated times, receive for their services, a compensation, which shall not be diminished during their continuance in office.

Section 2. 1. The judicial power shall extend to all cases, in law and equity, arising under this Constitution, the laws of the United States, and treaties made, or which shall be made, under their authority;— to all cases affecting ambassadors, other public ministers and consuls;— to all cases of admiralty and maritime jurisdiction;— to controversies to which the United States shall be a party;[7]— to controversies between two or more States; — between a State and citizens of another State;— between citizens of different States;— between citizens of the same State claiming lands under grants of different States, and between a State, or the citizens thereof, and foreign States, citizens or subjects.

2. In all cases affecting ambassadors, other public ministers and consuls, and those in which a State shall be party, the Supreme Court shall have original jurisdiction. In all the other cases before mentioned, the Supreme Court shall have appellate jurisdiction, both as to law and fact, with such exceptions, and under such regulations as the Congress shall make.

3. The trial of all crimes, except in cases of impeachment, shall be by jury; and such trial shall be held in the State where the said crimes shall have been committed; but when not committed within any State, the trial shall be at such place or places as the Congress may by law have directed.

Section 3. 1. Treason against the United States shall consist only in levying war against them, or in adhering to their enemies, giving them aid and comfort. No person shall be convicted of treason unless on the testimony of two witnesses to the same overt act, or on confession in open court.

2. The Congress shall have power to declare the punishment of treason, but no attainder of treason shall work corruption of blood, or forfeiture except during the life of the person attainted.

Article IV

Section 1. Full faith and credit shall be given in each State to the public acts, records, and judicial proceedings of every other State. And the Congress may by general laws prescribe the manner in which such acts, records and proceedings shall be proved, and the effect thereof.

Section 2. 1. The citizens of each State shall be entitled to all privileges and immunities of citizens in the several States.[8]

2. A person charged in any State with treason, felony, or other crime, who shall flee from justice, and be found in another State, shall on demand of the executive authority of the State from which he fled, be delivered up to be removed to the State having jurisdiction of the crime.

3. No person held to service or labor in one State under the laws thereof, escaping into another, shall, in consequence of any law or regulation therein, be discharged from such service or labor, but shall be delivered up on claim of the party to whom such service or labor may be due.[9]

Section 3. 1. New States may be admitted by the Congress into this Union; but no new State shall be formed or erected within the jurisdiction of any other State; nor any State be formed by the junction of two or more States, or

---

[7]See the Eleventh Amendment.
[8]See the Fourteenth Amendment, Sec. 1.
[9]See the Thirteenth Amendment.

parts of States, without the consent of the legislatures of the States concerned as well as of the Congress.

2. The Congress shall have power to dispose of and make all needful rules and regulations respecting the territory or other property belonging to the United States; and nothing in this Constitution shall be so construed as to prejudice any claims of the United States, or of any particular State.

SECTION 4. The United States shall guarantee to every State in this Union a republican form of government, and shall protect each of them against invasion; and on application of the legislature, or of the executive (when the legislature cannot be convened) against domestic violence.

Article V

The Congress, whenever two thirds of both Houses shall deem it necessary, shall propose amendments to this Constitution, or, on the application of the legislatures of two thirds of the several States, shall call a convention for proposing amendments, which in either case, shall be valid to all intents and purposes, as part of this Constitution, when ratified by the legislatures of three fourths of the several States, or by conventions in three fourths thereof, as the one or the other mode of ratification may be proposed by the Congress; Provided that no amendment which may be made prior to the year one thousand eight hundred and eight shall in any manner affect the first and fourth clauses in the ninth section of the first article; and that no State, without its consent, shall be deprived of its equal suffrage in the Senate.

Article VI

1. All debts contracted and engagements entered into, before the adoption of this Constitution, shall be as valid against the United States under this Constitution, as under the Confederation.[10]

2. This Constitution, and the laws of the United States which shall be made in pursuance thereof; and all treaties made, or which shall be made, under the authority of the United States, shall be the supreme law of the land; and the judges in every State shall be bound thereby, any thing in the Constitution or laws of any State to the contrary notwithstanding.

3. The senators and representatives before mentioned, and the members of the several State legislatures, and all executive and judicial officers, both of the United States and of the several States, shall be bound by oath or affirmation to support this Constitution; but no religious test shall ever be required as a qualification to any office or public trust under the United States.

Article VII

The ratification of the conventions of nine States shall be sufficient for the establishment of this Constitution between the States so ratifying the same.

Done in Convention by the unanimous consent of the States present the seventeenth day of September in the year of our Lord one thousand seven hundred and eighty-seven, and of the independence of the United States of

America the twelfth. In witness whereof we have hereunto subscribed our names.

[Names omitted]

* * *

Articles in addition to, and amendment of, the Constitution of the United States of America, proposed by Congress, and ratified by the legislatures of the several States, pursuant to the fifth article of the original Constitution.

Amendment I [First ten amendments ratified December 15, 1791]

Congress shall make no law respecting an establishment of religion, or prohibiting the free exercise thereof; or abridging the freedom of speech, or of the press; or the right of the people peaceably to assemble, and to petition the government for a redress of grievances.

Amendment II

A well regulated militia, being necessary to the security of a free State, the right of the people to keep and bear arms, shall not be infringed.

Amendment III

No soldier shall, in time of peace be quartered in any house, without the consent of the owner, nor in time of war, but in a manner to be prescribed by law.

Amendment IV

The right of the people to be secure in their persons, houses, papers, and effects, against unreasonable searches and seizures, shall not be violated, and no warrants shall issue, but upon probable cause, supported by oath or affirmation, and particularly describing the place to be searched, and the persons or things to be seized.

Amendment V

No person shall be held to answer for a capital or otherwise infamous crime, unless on a presentment or indictment of a grand jury, except in cases arising in the land or naval forces, or in the militia, when in actual service in time of war or public danger; nor shall any person be subject for the same offense to be twice put in jeopardy of life or limb; nor shall be compelled in any criminal case to be a witness against himself, nor be deprived of life, liberty, or property, without due process of law; nor shall private property be taken for public use, without just compensation.

Amendment VI

In all criminal prosecutions, the accused shall enjoy the right to a speedy and public trial, by an impartial jury of the State and district wherein the crime shall have been committed, which district shall have been previously ascertained by law, and to be informed of the nature and cause of the accusation; to be confronted with the witnesses against him; to have compulsory process for obtaining

---

[10]See the Fourteenth Amendment, Sec. 4.

witnesses in his favor, and to have the assistance of counsel for his defense.

Amendment VII

In suits at common law, where the value in controversy shall exceed twenty dollars, the right of trial by jury shall be preserved, and no fact tried by a jury shall be otherwise reexamined in any court of the United States, than according to the rules of the common law.

Amendment VIII

Excessive bail shall not be required, nor excessive fines imposed, nor cruel and unusual punishments inflicted.

Amendment IX

The enumeration in the Constitution of certain rights shall not be construed to deny or disparage others retained by the people.

Amendment X

The powers not delegated to the United States by the Constitution, nor prohibited by it to the States, are reserved to the States respectively, or to the people.

Amendment XI [January 8, 1798]

The judicial power of the United States shall not be construed to extend to any suit in law or equity, commenced or prosecuted against one of the United States by citizens of another State, or by citizens or subjects of any foreign State.

Amendment XII [September 25, 1804]

The electors shall meet in their respective States, and vote by ballot for President and Vice President, one of whom, at least, shall not be an inhabitant of the same State with themselves; they shall name in their ballots the person voted for as President, and in distinct ballots, the person voted for as Vice President, and they shall make distinct lists of all persons voted for as President and of all persons voted for as Vice President, and of the number of votes for each, which lists they shall sign and certify, and transmit sealed to the seat of the government of the United States, directed to the President of the Senate;— The President of the Senate shall, in the presence of the Senate and House of Representatives, open all the certificates and the votes shall then be counted;— The person having the greatest number of votes for President, shall be the President, if such number be a majority of the whole number of electors appointed; and if no person have such majority, then from the persons having the highest numbers not exceeding three on the list of those voted for as President, the House of Representatives shall choose immediately, by ballot, the President. But in choosing the President, the votes shall be taken by States, the representation from each State having one vote; a quorum for this purpose shall consist of a member or members from two thirds of the States, and a majority of all the States shall be necessary to a choice. And if the House of Representatives shall not choose a President whenever

the right of choice shall devolve upon them, before the fourth day of March next following, then the Vice President shall act as President, as in the case of the death or other constitutional disability of the President. The person having the greatest number of votes as Vice President shall be the Vice President, if such number be a majority of the whole number of electors appointed, and if no person have a majority, then from the two highest numbers on the list, the Senate shall choose the Vice President; a quorum for the purpose shall consist of two thirds of the whole number of Senators, and a majority of the whole number shall be necessary to a choice. But no person constitutionally ineligible to the office of President shall be eligible to that of Vice President of the United States.

Amendment XIII [December 18, 1865]

Section 1. Neither slavery nor involuntary servitude, except as a punishment for crime whereof the party shall have been duly convicted, shall exist within the United States, or any place subject to their jurisdiction.
Section 2. Congress shall have power to enforce this article by appropriate legislation.

Amendment XIV [July 28, 1868]

Section 1. All persons born or naturalized in the United States, and subject to the jurisdiction thereof, are citizens of the United States and of the State wherein they reside. No State shall make or enforce any law which shall abridge the privileges or immunities of citizens of the United States; nor shall any State deprive any person of life, liberty, or property, without due process of law; nor deny to any person within its jurisdiction the equal protection of the laws.
Section 2. Representatives shall be apportioned among the several States according to their respective numbers, counting the whole number of persons in each State, excluding Indians not taxed. But when the right to vote at any election for the choice of electors for President and Vice President of the United States, representatives in Congress, the executive and judicial officers of a State, or the members of the legislature thereof, is denied to any of the male inhabitants of such State, being twenty-one years of age, and citizens of the United States, or in any way abridged, except for participating in rebellion, or other crime, the basis of representation therein shall be reduced in the proportion which the number of such male citizens shall bear to the whole number of male citizens twenty-one years of age in such State.
Section 3. No person shall be a senator or representative in Congress, or elector of President and Vice President, or hold any office, civil or military, under the United States, or under any State, who having previously taken an oath, as a member of Congress, or as an officer of the United States, or as a member of any State legislature, or as an executive or judicial officer of any State, to support the Constitution of the United States, shall have engaged in insurrection or rebellion against the same, or given aid or comfort to the enemies thereof. But Congress may by a vote of two thirds of each House, remove such disability.
Section 4. The validity of the public debt of the United States, authorized by law, including debts incurred for payment of pensions and bounties for services in suppressing insurrection or rebellion; shall not be questioned. But

neither the United States nor any State shall assume or pay any debt or obligation incurred in aid of insurrection or rebellion against the United States, or any claim for the loss or emancipation of any slave; but all such debts, obligations, and claims shall be held illegal and void.

Section 5. The Congress shall have the power to enforce, by appropriate legislation, the provisions of this article.

Amendment XV [March 30, 1870]

Section 1. The right of citizens of the United States to vote shall not be denied or abridged by the United States or by any State on account of race, color, or previous condition of servitude.

Section 2. The Congress shall have power to enforce this article by appropriate legislation.

Amendment XVI [February 25, 1913]

The Congress shall have power to lay and collect taxes on incomes, from whatever source derived, without apportionment among the several States, and without regard to any census or enumeration.

Amendment XVII [May 31, 1913]

The Senate of the United States shall be composed of two senators from each State, elected by the people thereof, for six years; and each senator shall have one vote. The electors in each State shall have the qualifications requisite for electors of the most numerous branch of the State legislature.

When vacancies happen in the representation of any State in the Senate, the executive authority of such State shall issue writs of election to fill such vacancies: *Provided,* That the legislature of any State may empower the executive thereof to make temporary appointments until the people fill the vacancies by election as the legislature may direct.

This amendment shall not be so construed as to affect the election or term of any senator chosen before it becomes valid as part of the Constitution.

Amendment XVIII[11] [January 29, 1919]

After one year from the ratification of this article, the manufacture, sale, or transportation of intoxicating liquors within, the importation thereof into, or the exportation thereof from the United States and all territory subject to the jurisdiction thereof for beverage purposes is thereby prohibited.

The Congress and the several States shall have concurrent power to enforce this article by appropriate legislation.

This article shall be inoperative unless it shall have been ratified as an amendment to the Constitution by the legislatures of the several States, as provided in the Constitution, within seven years from the date of the submission hereof to the States by Congress.

---

[11]Repealed by the Twenty-first Amendment.

Amendment XIX [August 26, 1920]

The right of citizens of the United States to vote shall not be denied or abridged by the United States or by any State on account of sex.

Congress shall have the power to enforce this article by appropriate legislation.

Amendment XX [January 23, 1933]

Section 1. The terms of the President and Vice President shall end at noon on the 20th day of January and the terms of Senators and Representatives at noon on the 3d day of January, of the years in which such terms would have ended if this article had not been ratified; and the terms of their successors shall then begin.

Section 2. The Congress shall assemble at least once in every year, and such meeting shall begin at noon on the 3d day of January, unless they shall by law appoint a different day.

Section 3. If, at the time fixed for the beginning of the term of President, the President-elect shall have died, the Vice President-elect shall become President. If a President shall not have been chosen before the time fixed for the beginning of his term, or if the President-elect shall have failed to qualify, then the Vice President-elect shall act as President until a President shall have qualified; and the Congress may by law provide for the case wherein neither a President-elect nor a Vice President-elect shall have qualified, declaring who shall then act as President, or the manner in which one who is to act shall be selected, and such person shall act accordingly until a President or Vice President shall have qualified.

Section 4. The Congress may by law provide for the case of the death of any of the persons from whom the House of Representatives may choose a President whenever the right of choice shall have devolved upon them, and for the case of the death of any of the persons from whom the Senate may choose a Vice President whenever the right of choice shall have devolved upon them.

Section 5. Sections 1 and 2 shall take effect on the 15th day of October following the ratification of this article.

Section 6. This article shall be inoperative unless it shall have been ratified as an amendment to the Constitution by the legislatures of three-fourths of the several States within seven years from the date of its submission.

Amendment XXI [December 5, 1933]

Section 1. The Eighteenth Article of amendment to the Constitution of the United States is hereby repealed.

Section 2. The transportation or importation into any State, Territory, or possession of the United States for delivery or use therein of intoxicating liquors in violation of the laws thereof, is hereby prohibited.

Section 3. This article shall be inoperative unless it shall have been ratified as an amendment to the Constitution by conventions in the several States, as provided in the Constitution, within seven years from the date of the submission thereof to the States by the Congress.

Amendment XXII [March 1, 1951]

No person shall be elected to the office of the President more than twice, and no person who has held the office of President, or acted as President, for more than two years of a term to which some other person was elected President shall be elected to the office of the President more than once.

But this article shall not apply to any person holding the office of President when this article was proposed by the Congress, and shall not prevent any person who may be holding the office of President, or acting as President, during the term within which this article becomes operative from holding the office of President or acting as President during the remainder of such term.

This article shall be inoperative unless it shall have been ratified as an amendment to the Constitution by the legislatures of three-fourths of the several States within seven years from the date of its submission to the States by the Congress.

Amendment XXIII [March 29, 1961]

SECTION 1. The District constituting the seat of Government of the United States shall appoint in such manner as the Congress may direct.

A number of electors of President and Vice President equal to the whole number of Senators and Representatives in Congress to which the District would be entitled if it were a State, but in no event more than the least populous State; they shall be in addition to those appointed by the States, but they shall be considered, for the purposes of the election of President and Vice President, to be electors appointed by a State; and they shall meet in the District and perform such duties as provided by the twelfth article of amendment.

SECTION 2. The Congress shall have power to enforce this article by appropriate legislation.

Amendment XXIV [January 23, 1964]

SECTION 1. The right of citizens of the United States to vote in any primary or other election for President or Vice President, for electors for President or Vice President, or for Senator or Representative in Congress, shall not be denied or abridged by the United States or any State by reason of failure to pay any poll tax or other tax.

SECTION 2. The Congress shall have power to enforce this article by appropriate legislation.

Amendment XXV [February 10, 1967]

SECTION 1. In case of the removal of the President from office or of his death or resignation, the Vice President shall become President.

SECTION 2. Whenever there is a vacancy in the office of the Vice President, the President shall nominate a Vice President who shall take office upon confirmation by a majority of both Houses of Congress.

SECTION 3. Whenever the President transmits to the President pro tempore of the Senate and the Speaker of the House of Representatives his written declaration that he is unable to discharge the powers and duties of his office, and until he transmits to them a written declaration to the contrary, such powers and duties shall be discharged by the Vice President as Acting President.

SECTION 4. Whenever the Vice President and a majority of either the principal officers of the executive departments or of such other body as Congress may by law provide, transmit to the President pro tempore of the Senate and the Speaker of the House of Representatives their written declaration that the President is unable to discharge the powers and duties of his office, the Vice President shall immediately assume the powers and duties of the office as Acting President.

Thereafter, when the President transmits to the President pro tempore of the Senate and the Speaker of the House of Representatives his written declaration that no inability exists, he shall resume the powers and duties of his office unless the Vice President and a majority of either the principal officers of the executive departments or of such other body as Congress may by law provide, transmit within four days to the President pro tempore of the Senate and the Speaker of the House of Representatives their written declaration that the President is unable to discharge the powers and duties of his office. Thereupon Congress shall decide the issue, assembling within forty-eight hours for that purpose if not in session. If the Congress, within twenty-one days after receipt of the latter written declaration, or, if Congress is not in session, within twenty-one days after Congress is required to assemble, determines by two-thirds vote of both Houses that the President is unable to discharge the powers and duties of his office, the Vice President shall continue to discharge the same as Acting President; otherwise, the President shall resume the powers and duties of his office.

Amendment XXVI [June 30, 1971]

SECTION 1. The right of citizens of the United States who are eighteen years of age or older to vote shall not be denied or abridged by the United States or by any State on account of age.

SECTION 2. The Congress shall have power to enforce this article by appropriate legislation.

Presidents, Vice Presidents, and Cabinet Members

PRESIDENT AND VICE PRESIDENT	SECRETARY OF STATE	SECRETARY OF TREASURY	SECRETARY OF WAR	SECRETARY OF NAVY	POSTMASTER GENERAL	ATTORNEY GENERAL	SECRETARY OF INTERIOR
1. George Washington (1789) John Adams (1789)	Thomas Jefferson (1789) Edmund Randolph (1794) Timothy Pickering (1795)	Alexander Hamilton (1789) Oliver Wolcott (1795)	Henry Knox (1789) Timothy Pickering (1795) James McHenry (1796)		Samuel Osgood (1789) Timothy Pickering (1791) Joseph Habersham (1795)	Edmund Randolph (1789) William Bradford (1794) Charles Lee (1795)	
2. John Adams (1797) Thomas Jefferson (1797)	Timothy Pickering (1797) John Marshall (1800)	Oliver Wolcott (1797) Samuel Dexter (1801)	James McHenry (1797) John Marshall (1800) Samuel Dexter (1800) Roger Griswold (1801)	Benjamin Stoddert (1798)	Joseph Habersham (1797)	Charles Lee (1797) Theophilus Parsons (1801)	
3. Thomas Jefferson (1801) Aaron Burr (1801) George Clinton (1805)	James Madison (1801)	Samuel Dexter (1801) Albert Gallatin (1801)	Henry Dearborn (1801)	Benjamin Stoddert (1801) Robert Smith (1801) J. Crowninshield (1805)	Joseph Habersham (1801) Gideon Granger (1801)	Levi Lincoln (1801) Robert Smith (1805) John Breckinridge (1805) Caesar Rodney (1807)	
4. James Madison (1809) George Clinton (1809) Elbridge Gerry (1813)	Robert Smith (1809) James Monroe (1811)	Albert Gallatin (1809) George Campbell (1814) Alexander Dallas (1814) William Crawford (1816)	William Eustis (1809) John Armstrong (1813) James Monroe (1814) William Crawford (1815)	Paul Hamilton (1809) William Jones (1813) Benjamin Crowninshield (1814)	Gideon Granger (1809) Return Meigs (1814)	Caesar Rodney (1809) William Pinckney (1811) Richard Rush (1814)	
5. James Monroe (1817) Daniel D. Thompkins (1817)	John Quincy Adams (1817)	William Crawford (1817)	Isaac Shelby (1817) George Graham (1817) John C. Calhoun (1817)	Benjamin Crowninshield (1817) Smith Thompson (1818) Samuel Southard (1823)	Return Meigs (1817) John McLean (1823)	Richard Rush (1817) William Wirt (1817)	
6. John Quincy Adams (1825) John C. Calhoun (1825)	Henry Clay (1825)	Richard Rush (1825)	James Barbour (1825) Peter B. Porter (1828)	Samuel Southard (1825)	John McLean (1825)	William Wirt (1825)	

PRESIDENT AND VICE PRESIDENT	SECRETARY OF STATE	SECRETARY OF TREASURY	SECRETARY OF WAR	SECRETARY OF NAVY	POSTMASTER GENERAL	ATTORNEY GENERAL	SECRETARY OF INTERIOR
7. Andrew Jackson (1829) John C. Calhoun (1829) Martin Van Buren (1833)	Martin Van Buren (1829) Edward Livingston (1831) Louis McLane (1833) John Forsyth (1834)	Samuel Ingham (1829) Louis McLane (1831) William Duane (1833) Roger B. Taney (1833) Levi Woodbury (1834)	John H. Eaton (1829) Lewis Cass (1831) Benjamin Butler (1837)	John Branch (1829) Levi Woodbury (1831) Mahlon Dickerson (1834)	William Barry (1829) Amos Kendall (1835)	John M. Berrien (1829) Roger B. Taney (1831) Benjamin Butler (1833)	
8. Martin Van Buren (1837) Richard M. Johnson (1837)	John Forsyth (1837)	Levi Woodbury (1837)	Joel R. Poinsett (1837)	Mahlon Dickerson (1837) James K. Paulding (1838)	Amos Kendall (1837) John M. Niles (1840)	Benjamin Butler (1837) Felix Grundy (1838) Henry D. Gilpin (1840)	
9. William H. Harrison (1841) John Tyler (1841)	Daniel Webster (1841)	Thomas Ewing (1841)	John Bell (1841)	George E. Badger (1841)	Francis Granger (1841)	John J. Crittenden (1841)	
10. John Tyler (1841)	Daniel Webster (1841) Hugh S. Legaré (1843) Abel P. Upshur (1843) John C. Calhoun (1844)	Thomas Ewing (1841) Walter Forward (1841) John C. Spencer (1843) George M. Bibb (1844)	John Bell (1841) John McLean (1841) John C. Spencer (1841) James M. Porter (1843) William Wilkins (1844)	George E. Badger (1841) Abel P. Upshur (1841) David Henshaw (1843) Thomas Gilmer (1844) John Y. Mason (1844)	Francis Granger (1841) Charles A. Wickliffe (1841)	John J. Crittenden (1841) Hugh S. Legaré (1841) John Nelson (1843)	
11. James K. Polk (1845) George M. Dallas (1845)	James Buchanan (1845)	Robert J. Walker (1845)	William L. Marcy (1845)	George Bancroft (1845) John Y. Mason (1846)	Cave Johnson (1845)	John Y. Mason (1845) Nathan Clifford (1846) Isaac Toucey (1848)	
12. Zachary Taylor (1849) Millard Fillmore (1849)	John M. Clayton (1849)	William M. Meredith (1849)	George W. Crawford (1849)	William B. Preston (1849)	Jacob Collamer (1849)	Reverdy Johnson (1849)	Thomas Ewing (1849)
13. Millard Fillmore (1850)	Daniel Webster (1850) Edward Everett (1852)	Thomas Corwin (1850)	Charles M. Conrad (1850)	William A. Graham (1850) John P. Kennedy (1852)	Nathan K. Hall (1850) Sam D. Hubbard (1852)	John J. Crittenden (1850)	Thomas McKennan (1850) A. H. H. Stuart (1850)
14. Franklin Pierce (1853) William R. King (1853)	William L. Marcy (1853)	James Guthrie (1853)	Jefferson Davis (1853)	James C. Dobbin (1853)	James Campbell (1853)	Caleb Cushing (1853)	Robert McClelland (1853)

PRESIDENT AND VICE PRESIDENT	SECRETARY OF STATE	SECRETARY OF TREASURY	SECRETARY OF WAR	SECRETARY OF NAVY	POSTMASTER GENERAL	ATTORNEY GENERAL	SECRETARY OF INTERIOR
15. James Buchanan (1857) John C. Breckinridge (1857)	Lewis Cass (1857) Jeremiah S. Black (1860)	Howell Cobb (1857) Philip F. Thomas (1860) John A. Dix (1861)	John B. Floyd (1857) Joseph Holt (1861)	Isaac Toucey (1857)	Aaron V. Brown (1857) Joseph Holt (1859)	Jeremiah S. Black (1857) Edwin M. Stanton (1860)	Jacob Thompson (1857)
16. Abraham Lincoln (1861) Hannibal Hamlin (1861) Andrew Johnson (1865)	William H. Seward (1861)	Salmon P. Chase (1861) William P. Fessenden (1864) Hugh McCulloch (1865)	Simon Cameron (1861) Edwin M. Stanton (1862)	Gideon Welles (1861)	Horatio King (1861) Montgomery Blair (1861) William Dennison (1864)	Edward Bates (1861) Titian J. Coffey (1863) James Speed (1864)	Caleb B. Smith (1861) John P. Usher (1863)
17. Andrew Johnson (1865)	William H. Seward (1865)	Hugh McCulloch (1865)	Edwin M. Stanton (1865) Ulysses S. Grant (1867) Lorenzo Thomas (1868) John M. Schofield (1868)	Gideon Welles (1865)	William Dennison (1865) Alexander Randall (1866)	James Speed (1865) Henry Stanbery (1866) William M. Evarts (1868)	John P. Usher (1865) James Harlan (1865) O. H. Browning (1866)
18. Ulysses S. Grant (1869) Schuyler Colfax (1869) Henry Wilson (1873)	Elihu B. Washburne (1869) Hamilton Fish (1869)	George S. Boutwell (1869) William A. Richardson (1873) Benjamin H. Bristow (1874) Lot M. Morrill (1876)	John A. Rawlins (1869) William T. Sherman (1869) William W. Belknap (1869) Alphonso Taft (1876) James Cameron (1876)	Adolph E. Borie (1869) George M. Robeson (1869)	John A. J. Creswell (1869) James W. Marshall (1874) Marshall Jewell (1874) James N. Tyner (1876)	Ebenezer R. Hoar (1869) Amos T. Akerman (1870) G. H. Williams (1871) Edwards Pierrepont (1875) Alphonso Taft (1876)	Jacob D. Cox (1869) Columbus Delano (1870) Zachariah Chandler (1875)
19. Rutherford B. Hayes (1877) William A. Wheeler (1877)	William M. Evarts (1877)	John Sherman (1877)	George W. McCrary (1877) Alexander Ramsey (1879)	R. W. Thompson (1877) Nathan Golf, Jr. (1881)	David M. Key (1877) Horace Maynard (1880)	Charles Devens (1877)	Carl Schurz (1877)
20. James A. Garfield (1881) Chester A. Arthur (1881)	James G. Blaine (1881)	William Windom (1881)	Robert T. Lincoln (1881)	William H. Hunt (1881)	Thomas I. James (1881)	Wayne MacVeagh (1881)	S. I. Kirkwood (1881)
21. Chester A. Arthur (1881)	F. T. Frelinghuysen (1881)	Charles J. Folger (1881) Walter Q. Gresham (1884) Hugh McCulloch (1884)	Robert T. Lincoln (1881)	William E. Chandler (1881)	Timothy O. Howe (1881) Walter Q. Gresham (1883) Frank Hatton (1884)	B. H. Brewster (1881)	Henry M. Teller (1881)
22. Grover Cleveland (1885) T. A. Hendricks (1885)	Thomas F. Bayard (1885)	Daniel Manning (1885) Charles S. Fairchild (1887)	William C. Endicott (1885)	William C. Whitney (1885)	William F. Vilas (1885) Don M. Dickinson (1888)	A. H. Garland (1885)	L. Q. C. Lamar (1885) William F. Vilas (1888)

PRESIDENT AND VICE PRESIDENT	SECRETARY OF STATE	SECRETARY OF TREASURY	SECRETARY OF WAR	SECRETARY OF NAVY	POSTMASTER GENERAL	ATTORNEY GENERAL	SECRETARY OF INTERIOR
23. Benjamin Harrison (1889) Levi P. Morgan (1889)	James G. Blaine (1889) John W. Foster (1892)	William Windom (1889) Charles Foster (1891)	Redfield Procter (1889) Stephen B. Elkins (1891)	Benjamin F. Tracy (1889)	John Wanamaker (1889)	W. H. H. Miller (1889)	Jon W. Noble (1889)
24. Grover Cleveland (1893) Adlai E. Stevenson (1893)	Walter Q. Gresham (1893) Richard Olney (1895)	John G. Carlisle (1893)	Daniel S. Lamont (1893)	Hilary A. Herbert (1893)	Wilson S. Bissel (1893) William L. Wilson (1895)	Richard Olney (1893) Judson Harmon (1895)	Hoke Smith (1893) David R. Francis (1896)
25. William McKinley (1897) Garret A. Hobart (1897) Theodore Roosevelt (1901)	John Sherman (1897) William R. Day (1897) John Hay (1898)	Lyman J. Gage (1897)	Russell A. Alger (1897) Elihu Root (1899)	John D. Long (1897)	James A. Gary (1897) Charles E. Smith (1898)	Joseph McKenna (1897) John W. Griggs (1897) Philander C. Knox (1901)	Cornelius N. Bliss (1897) E. A. Hitchcock (1899)
26. Theodore Roosevelt (1901) Charles Fairbanks (1905)	John Hay (1901) Elihu Root (1905) Robert Bacon (1909)	Lyman J. Gage (1901) Leslie M. Shaw (1902) George B. Cortelyou (1907)	Elihu Root (1901) William H. Taft (1904) Luke E. Wright (1908)	John D. Long (1901) William H. Moody (1902) Paul Morton (1904) Charles J. Bonaparte (1905) V. H. Metcalf (1906) T. H. Newberry (1908)	Charles E. Smith (1901) Henry Payne (1902) Robert J. Wynne (1904) George B. Cortelyou (1905) George von L. Meyer (1907)	Philander C. Knox (1901) William H. Moody (1904) Charles J. Bonaparte (1907)	E. A. Hitchcock (1901) James R. Garfield (1907)
27. William H. Taft (1909) James S. Sherman (1909)	Philander C. Knox (1909)	Franklin MacVeagh (1909)	Jacob M. Dickinson (1909) Henry Stimson (1911)	George von L. Meyer (1909)	Frank H. Hitchcock (1909)	G. W. Wickersham (1909)	R. A. Ballinger (1909) Walter L. Fisher (1911)
28. Woodrow Wilson (1913) Thomas R. Marshall (1913)	William J. Bryan (1913) Robert Lansing (1915) Bainbridge Colby (1920)	William G. McAdoo (1913) Carter Glass (1918) David F. Houston (1920)	Lindley M. Garrison (1913) Newton D. Baker (1916)	Josephus Daniels (1913)	Albert S. Burleson (1913)	J. C. McReynolds (1913) T. W. Gregory (1914) A. Mitchell Palmer (1919)	Franklin K. Lane (1913) John B. Payne (1920)
29. Warren G. Harding (1921) Calvin Coolidge (1921)	Charles E. Hughes (1912)	Andrew W. Mellon (1921)	John W. Weeks (1921)	Edwin Denby (1921)	Will H. Hays (1921) Hubert Work (1922) Harry S. New (1923)	H. M. Daugherty (1921)	Albert B. Fall (1921) Hubert Work (1923)
30. Calvin Coolidge (1923) Charles G. Dawes (1925)	Charles E. Hughes (1923) Frank B. Kellogg (1925)	Andrew W. Mellon (1923)	John W. Weeks (1923) Dwight F. Davis (1925)	Edwin Denby (1923) Curtis D. Wilbur (1924)	Harry S. New (1923)	H. M. Daugherty (1923) Harlan F. Stone (1924) John G. Sargent (1925)	Hubert Work (1923) Roy O. West (1928)

PRESIDENT AND VICE PRESIDENT	SECRETARY OF STATE	SECRETARY OF TREASURY	SECRETARY OF WAR	SECRETARY OF NAVY	POSTMASTER GENERAL	ATTORNEY GENERAL	SECRETARY OF INTERIOR
31. Herbert C. Hoover (1929) Charles Curtis (1929)	Henry L. Stimson (1929)	Andrew W. Mellon (1929) Ogden L. Mills (1932)	James W. Good (1929) Patrick J. Hurley (1929)	Charles F. Adams (1929)	Walter F. Brown (1929)	W. D. Mitchell (1929)	Ray L. Wilbur (1929)
32. Franklin D. Roosevelt (1933) John Nance Garner (1933) Henry A. Wallace (1941) Harry S. Truman (1945)	Cordell Hull (1933) E. R. Stettinius, Jr. (1944)	William H. Woodin (1933) Henry Morgenthau, Jr. (1934)	George H. Dern (1933) Harry H. Woodring (1936) Henry L. Stimson (1940)	Claude A. Swanson (1933) Charles Edison (1940) Frank Knox (1940) James V. Forrestal (1944)	James A. Farley (1933) Frank C. Walker (1940)	H. S. Cummings (1933) Frank Murphy (1939) Robert Jackson (1940) Francis Biddle (1941)	Harold L. Ickes (1933)
33. Harry S. Truman (1945) Alben W. Barkley (1949)	James F. Byrnes (1945) George C. Marshall (1947) Dean G. Acheson (1949)	Fred M. Vinson (1945) John W. Snyder (1946)	Robert P. Patterson (1945) Kenneth C. Royal (1947) *Secretary of Defense* James V. Forrestal (1947) Louis A. Johnson (1949) George C. Marshall (1950) Robert A. Lovett (1951)	James V. Forrestal (1945)	R. E. Hannegan (1945) Jesse M. Donaldson (1947)	Tom C. Clark (1945) J. H. McGrath (1949) James P. McGranery (1952)	Harold L. Ickes (1945) Julis A. Krug (1946) Oscar L. Chapman (1949)
34. Dwight D. Eisenhower (1953) Richard M. Nixon (1953)	John Foster Dulles (1953) Christian A. Herter (1959)	George M. Humphrey (1953) Robert B. Anderson (1957)	Charles E. Wilson (1953) Neil H. McElroy (1957) Thomas S. Gates (1959)		A. E. Summerfield (1953)	H. Brownell, Jr. (1953) William P. Rogers (1957)	Douglas McKay (1953) Fred Seaton (1956)
35. John F. Kennedy (1961) Lyndon B. Johnson (1961)	Dean Rusk (1961)	C. Douglas Dillon (1961)	Robert S. McNamara (1961)		J. Edward Day (1961) John A. Gronouski (1963)	Robert F. Kennedy (1961)	Stewart L. Udall (1961)
36. Lyndon B. Johnson (1963) Hubert H. Humphrey (1965)	Dean Rusk (1963)	C. Douglas Dillon (1963) Henry H. Fowler (1965) Joseph W. Barr (1968)	Robert S. McNamara (1963) Clark M. Clifford (1968)		John A. Gronouski (1963) Lawrence F. O'Brien (1965) W. Marvin Watson (1968)	Robert F. Kennedy (1963) N. deB. Katzenbach (1965) Ramsey Clark (1967)	Stewart L. Udall (1963)
37. Richard M. Nixon (1969) Spiro T. Agnew (1969) Gerald R. Ford (1973)	William P. Rogers (1969) Henry A. Kissinger (1973)	David M. Kennedy (1969) John B. Connally (1970) George P. Schultz (1972) William E. Simon (1974)	Melvin R. Laird (1969) Elliot L. Richardson (1973) James R. Schlesinger (1973)		Winton M. Blount (1969)	John M. Mitchell (1969) Richard G. Kleindienst (1972) Elliot L. Richardson (1973) William B. Saxbe (1974)	Walter J. Hickel (1969) Rogers C. B. Morton (1971)

PRESIDENT AND VICE PRESIDENT	SECRETARY OF STATE	SECRETARY OF TREASURY	SECRETARY OF DEFENSE	SECRETARY OF NAVY	POSTMASTER GENERAL	ATTORNEY GENERAL	SECRETARY OF INTERIOR
38. Gerald R. Ford (1974) Nelson A. Rockefeller (1974)	Henry A. Kissinger (1974)	William E. Simon (1974)	James R. Schlesinger (1974) Donald H. Runsfeld (1975)			William B. Saxbe (1974) Edward H. Levi (1975)	Rogers C. B. Morton (1974) Stanley K. Hathaway (1975) Thomas D. Kleppe (1975)
39. James E. Carter, Jr. (1977) Walter F. Mondale (1977)	Cyrus R. Vance (1977) Edmund S. Muskie (1980)	W. Michael Blumenthal (1977) G. William Miller (1979)	Harold Brown (1977)			Griffin B. Bell (1977) Benjamin R. Civiletti (1979)	Cecil D. Andrus (1977)
40. Ronald W. Reagan (1981) George H. Bush (1981)	Alexander M. Haig, Jr. (1981) George P. Schultz (1982)	Donald T. Regan (1981)	Caspar W. Weinberger (1981)			William French Smith (1981)	James G. Watt (1981) William Clark (1983)
41. Ronald W. Reagan (1985) George H. Bush (1985)	George P. Schultz (1985)	James A. Baker III (1985)	Caspar W. Weinberger (1985)			Edwin Meese III (1985)	Donald P. Hodel (1985)
42. George H. Bush (1989) James D. Quayle III (1989)	James A. Baker III (1989)	Nicholas Brady (1989)	Richard B. Cheney (1989)			Richard L. Thornburgh (1989)	Manuel Lujan, Jr. (1989)
43. William J. B. Clinton (1993) Albert Gore (1993)	Warren Christopher (1993)	Lloyd Bentsen (1993)	Les Aspin (1993)			Janet Reno (1993)	Bruce Babbit (1993)

Presidential Elections

YEAR	NUMBER OF STATES	CANDIDATES	PARTY	POPULAR VOTE*	ELEC-TORAL VOTE†	PERCENT-AGE OF POPULAR VOTE
1789	11	GEORGE WASHINGTON	No party designations		69	
		John Adams			34	
		Other Candidates			35	
1792	15	GEORGE WASHINGTON	No party designations		132	
		John Adams			77	
		George Clinton			50	
		Other Candidates			5	
1796	16	JOHN ADAMS	Federalist		71	
		Thomas Jefferson	Democratic-Republican		68	
		Thomas Pinckney	Federalist		59	
		Aaron Burr	Democratic-Republican		30	
		Other Candidates			48	
1800	16	THOMAS JEFFERSON	Democratic-Republican		73	
		Aaron Burr	Democratic-Republican		73	
		John Adams	Federalist		65	
		Charles C. Pinckney	Federalist		64	
		John Jay	Federalist		1	
1804	17	THOMAS JEFFERSON	Democratic-Republican		162	
		Charles C. Pinckney	Federalist		14	
1808	17	JAMES MADISON	Democratic-Republican		122	
		Charles C. Pinckney	Federalist		47	
		George Clinton	Democratic-Republican		6	
1812	18	JAMES MADISON	Democratic-Republican		128	
		DeWitt Clinton	Federalist		89	
1816	19	JAMES MONROE	Democratic-Republican		183	
		Rufus King	Federalist		34	
1820	24	JAMES MONROE	Democratic-Republican		231	
		John Quincy Adams	Independent Republican		1	
1824	24	JOHN QUINCY ADAMS		108,740	84	30.5
		Andrew Jackson		153,544	99	43.1
		William H. Crawford		46,618	41	13.1
		Henry Clay		47,136	37	13.2
1828	24	ANDREW JACKSON	Democrat	647,286	178	56.0
		John Quincy Adams	National Republican	508,064	83	44.0
1832	24	ANDREW JACKSON	Democrat	687,502	219	55.0
		Henry Clay	National Republican	530,189	49	42.4
		William Wirt	Anti-Masonic	33,108	7	2.6
		John Floyd	National Republican		11	
1836	26	MARTIN VAN BUREN	Democrat	765,483	170	50.9
		William H. Harrison	Whig		73	
		Hugh L. White	Whig	739,795	26	49.1
		Daniel Webster	Whig		14	
		W. P. Mangum	Whig		11	
1840	26	WILLIAM H. HARRISON	Whig	1,274,624	234	53.1
		Martin Van Buren	Democrat	1,127,781	60	46.9
1844	26	JAMES K. POLK	Democrat	1,338,464	170	49.6
		Henry Clay	Whig	1,300,097	105	48.1
		James G. Birney	Liberty	62,300		2.3
1848	30	ZACHARY TAYLOR	Whig	1,360,967	163	47.4
		Lewis Cass	Democrat	1,222,342	127	42.5
		Martin Van Buren	Free Soil	291,263		10.1
1852	31	FRANKLIN PIERCE	Democrat	1,601,117	254	50.9
		Winfield Scott	Whig	1,385,453	42	44.1
		John P. Hale	Free Soil	155,825		5.0
1856	31	JAMES BUCHANAN	Democrat	1,832,955	174	45.3
		John C. Frémont	Republican	1,339,932	114	33.1
		Millard Fillmore	American	871,731	8	21.6

*Percentage of popular vote given for any election year may not total 100 percent because candidates receiving less than 1 percent of the popular vote have been omitted.

†Prior to the passage of the Twelfth Amendment in 1904, the electoral college voted for two presidential candidates; the runner-up became Vice-President. Data from *Historical Statistics of the United States, Colonial Times to 1957* (1961), pp. 682–683, and *The World Almanac*.

Presidential Elections (*continued*)

YEAR	NUMBER OF STATES	CANDIDATES	PARTY	POPULAR VOTE*	ELEC- TORAL VOTE†	PERCENT- AGE OF POPULAR VOTE
1860	33	ABRAHAM LINCOLN	Republican	1,865,593	180	39.8
		Stephen A. Douglas	Democrat	1,382,713	12	29.5
		John C. Breckinridge	Democrat	848,356	72	18.1
		John Bell	Constitutional Union	592,906	39	12.6
1864	36	ABRAHAM LINCOLN	Republican	2,206,938	212	55.0
		George B. McClellan	Democrat	1,803,787	21	45.0
1868	37	ULYSSES S. GRANT	Republican	3,013,421	214	52.7
		Horatio Seymour	Democrat	2,706,829	80	47.3
1872	37	ULYSSES S. GRANT	Republican	3,596,745	286	55.6
		Horace Greeley	Democrat	2,843,446	*	43.9
1876	38	RUTHERFORD B. HAYES	Republican	4,036,572	185	48.0
		Samuel J. Tilden	Democrat	4,284,020	184	51.0
1880	38	JAMES A. GARFIELD	Republican	4,453,295	214	48.5
		Winfield S. Hancock	Democrat	4,414,082	155	48.1
		James B. Weaver	Greenback-Labor	308,578		3.4
1884	38	GROVER CLEVELAND	Democrat	4,879,507	219	48.5
		James G. Blaine	Republican	4,850,293	182	48.2
		Benjamin F. Butler	Greenback-Labor	175,370		1.8
		John P. St. John	Prohibition	150,369		1.5
1888	38	BENJAMIN HARRISON	Republican	5,447,129	233	47.9
		Grover Cleveland	Democrat	5,537,857	168	48.6
		Clinton B. Fisk	Prohibition	249,506		2.2
		Anson J. Streeter	Union Labor	146,935		1.3
1892	44	GROVER CLEVELAND	Democrat	5,555,426	277	46.1
		Benjamin Harrison	Republican	5,182,690	145	43.0
		James B. Weaver	People's	1,029,846	22	8.5
		John Bidwell	Prohibition	264,133		2.2
1896	45	WILLIAM MCKINLEY	Republican	7,102,246	271	51.1
		William J. Bryan	Democrat	6,492,559	176	47.7
1900	45	WILLIAM MCKINLEY	Republican	7,218,491	292	51.7
		William J. Bryan	Democrat; Populist	6,356,734	155	45.5
		John C. Woolley	Prohibition	208,914		1.5
1904	45	THEODORE ROOSEVELT	Republican	7,628,461	336	57.4
		Alton B. Parker	Democrat	5,084,223	140	37.6
		Eugene V. Debs	Socialist	402,283		3.0
		Silas C. Swallow	Prohibition	258,536		1.9
1908	46	WILLIAM H. TAFT	Republican	7,675,320	321	51.6
		William J. Bryan	Democrat	6,412,294	162	43.1
		Eugene V. Debs	Socialist	420,793		2.8
		Eugene W. Chafin	Prohibition	253,840		1.7
1912	48	WOODROW WILSON	Democrat	6,296,547	435	41.9
		Theodore Roosevelt	Progressive	4,118,571	88	27.4
		William H. Taft	Republican	3,486,720	8	23.2
		Eugene V. Debs	Socialist	900,672		6.0
		Eugene W. Chafin	Prohibition	206,275		1.4
1916	48	WOODROW WILSON	Democrat	9,127,695	277	49.4
		Charles E. Hughes	Republican	8,533,507	254	46.2
		A. L. Benson	Socialist	585,113		3.2
		J. Frank Hanly	Prohibition	220,506		1.2
1920	48	WARREN G. HARDING	Republican	16,143,407	404	60.4
		James M. Cox	Democrat	9,130,328	127	34.2
		Eugene V. Debs	Socialist	919,799		3.4
		P. P. Christensen	Farmer-Labor	265,411		1.0

*Because of the death of Greeley, Democratic electors scattered their votes.

Presidential Elections (*continued*)

YEAR	NUMBER OF STATES	CANDIDATES	PARTY	POPULAR VOTE*	ELEC-TORAL VOTE†	PERCENT-AGE OF POPULAR VOTE
1924	48	CALVIN COOLIDGE	Republican	15,718,211	382	54.0
		John W. Davis	Democrat	8,385,283	136	28.8
		Robert M. La Follette	Progressive	4,831,289	13	16.6
1928	48	HERBERT C. HOOVER	Republican	21,391,993	444	58.2
		Alfred E. Smith	Democrat	15,016,169	87	40.9
1932	48	FRANKLIN D. ROOSEVELT	Democrat	22,809,638	472	57.4
		Herbert C. Hoover	Republican	15,758,901	59	39.7
		Norman Thomas	Socialist	881,951		2.2
1936	48	FRANKLIN D. ROOSEVELT	Democrat	27,752,869	523	60.8
		Alfred M. Landon	Republican	16,674,665	8	36.5
		William Lemke	Union	882,479		1.9
1940	48	FRANKLIN D. ROOSEVELT	Democrat	27,307,819	449	54.8
		Wendell L. Willkie	Republican	22,321,018	82	44.8
1944	48	FRANKLIN D. ROOSEVELT	Democrat	25,606,585	432	53.5
		Thomas E. Dewey	Republican	22,014,745	99	46.0
1948	48	HARRY S. TRUMAN	Democrat	24,105,812	303	49.5
		Thomas E. Dewey	Republican	21,970,065	189	45.1
		J. Strom Thurmond	States' Rights	1,169,063	39	2.4
		Henry A. Wallace	Progressive	1,157,172		2.4
1952	48	DWIGHT D. EISENHOWER	Republican	33,936,234	442	55.1
		Adlai E. Stevenson	Democrat	27,314,992	89	44.4
1956	48	DWIGHT D. EISENHOWER	Republican	35,590,472	457†	57.6
		Adlai E. Stevenson	Democrat	26,022,752	73	42.1
1960	50	JOHN F. KENNEDY	Democrat	34,227,096	303‡	49.9
		Richard M. Nixon	Republican	34,108,546	219	49.6
1964	50	LYNDON B. JOHNSON	Democrat	42,676,220	486	61.3
		Barry M. Goldwater	Republican	26,860,314	52	38.5
1968	50	RICHARD M. NIXON	Republican	31,785,480	301	43.4
		Hubert H. Humphrey	Democrat	31,275,165	191	42.7
		George C. Wallace	American Independent	9,906,473	46	13.5
1972	50	RICHARD M. NIXON*	Republican	47,165,234	520	60.6
		George S. McGovern	Democrat	29,168,110	17	37.5
1976	50	JIMMY CARTER	Democrat	40,828,929	297	50.1
		Gerald R. Ford	Republican	39,148,940	240	47.9
		Eugene McCarthy	Independent	739,256		
1980	50	RONALD REAGAN	Republican	43,201,220	489	50.9
		Jimmy Carter	Democrat	34,913,332	49	41.2
		John B. Anderson	Independent	5,581,379		
1984	50	RONALD REAGAN	Republican	53,428,357	525	59.0
		Walter F. Mondale	Democrat	36,930,923	13	41.0
1988	50	GEORGE BUSH	Republican	48,901,046	426	53.4
		Michael Dukakis	Democrat	41,809,030	111	45.6
1992	50	BILL CLINTON	Democrat	43,728,275	370	43.2
		George Bush	Republican	38,167,416	168	37.7
		H. Ross Perot	United We Stand, America	19,237,247		19.0

†Walter B. Jones received 1 electoral vote.‡ Harry F. Byrd received 15 electoral votes.
*Resigned August 9, 1974: Vice President Gerald R. Ford became President.

Supreme Court Justices

Name	Service	Appointed by
John Jay	1789–1795	Washington
James Wilson	1789–1798	Washington
John Blair	1789–1796	Washington
John Rutledge	1790–1791	Washington
William Cushing	1790–1810	Washington
James Iredell	1790–1799	Washington
Thomas Johnson	1791–1793	Washington
William Paterson	1793–1806	Washington
John Rutledge*	1795	Washington
Samuel Chase	1796–1811	Washington
Oliver Ellsworth	1796–1799	Washington
Bushrod Washington	1798–1829	J. Adams
Alfred Moore	1799–1804	J. Adams
John Marshall	1801–1835	J. Adams
William Johnson	1804–1834	Jefferson
Henry B. Livingston	1806–1823	Jefferson
Thomas Todd	1807–1826	Jefferson
Gabriel Duval	1811–1836	Madison
Joseph Story	1811–1845	Madison
Smith Thompson	1823–1843	Monroe
Robert Trimble	1826–1828	J. Q. Adams
John McLean	1829–1861	Jackson
Henry Baldwin	1830–1844	Jackson
James M. Wayne	1835–1867	Jackson
Roger B. Taney	1836–1864	Jackson
Philip P. Barbour	1836–1841	Jackson
John Catron	1837–1865	Van Buren
John McKinley	1837–1852	Van Buren
Peter V. Daniel	1841–1860	Van Buren
Samuel Nelson	1845–1872	Tyler
Levi Woodbury	1845–1851	Polk
Robert C. Grier	1846–1870	Polk
Benjamin R. Curtis	1851–1857	Fillmore
John A. Campbell	1853–1861	Pierce
Nathan Clifford	1858–1881	Buchanan
Noah H. Swayne	1862–1881	Lincoln
Samuel F. Miller	1862–1890	Lincoln
David Davis	1862–1877	Lincoln
Stephen J. Field	1863–1897	Lincoln
Salmon P. Chase	1864–1873	Lincoln
William Strong	1870–1880	Grant
Joseph P. Bradley	1870–1892	Grant
Ward Hunt	1873–1882	Grant
Morrison R. Waite	1874–1888	Grant
John M. Harlan	1877–1911	Hayes
William B. Woods	1880–1887	Hayes
Stanley Matthews	1881–1889	Garfield
Horace Gray	1882–1902	Arthur
Samuel Blatchford	1882–1893	Arthur
Lucius Q. C. Lamar	1888–1893	Cleveland
Melville W. Fuller	1888–1910	Cleveland
David J. Brewer	1889–1910	B. Harrison
Henry B. Brown	1890–1906	B. Harrison
George Shiras	1892–1903	B. Harrison
Howell E. Jackson	1893–1895	B. Harrison
Edward D. White	1894–1910	Cleveland
Rufus W. Peckham	1896–1909	Cleveland

Name	Service	Appointed by
Joseph McKenna	1898–1925	McKinley
Oliver W. Holmes	1902–1932	T. Roosevelt
William R. Day	1903–1922	T. Roosevelt
William H. Moody	1906–1910	T. Roosevelt
Horace H. Lurton	1910–1914	Taft
Charles E. Hughes	1910–1916	Taft
Willis Van Devanter	1910–1937	Taft
Joseph R. Lamar	1911–1916	Taft
Edward D. White	1910–1921	Taft
Mahlon Pitney	1912–1922	Taft
James C. McReynolds	1914–1941	Wilson
Louis D. Brandeis	1916–1939	Wilson
John H. Clarke	1916–1922	Wilson
William H. Taft	1921–1930	Harding
George Sutherland	1922–1938	Harding
Pierce Butler	1923–1939	Harding
Edward T. Sanford	1923–1930	Harding
Harlan F. Stone	1925–1941	Coolidge
Charles E. Hughes	1930–1941	Hoover
Owen J. Roberts	1930–1945	Hoover
Benjamin N. Cardozo	1932–1938	Hoover
Hugo L. Black	1937–1971	F. Roosevelt
Stanley F. Reed	1938–1957	F. Roosevelt
Felix Frankfurter	1939–1962	F. Roosevelt
William O. Douglas	1939–1975	F. Roosevelt
Frank Murphy	1940–1949	F. Roosevelt
Harlan F. Stone	1941–1946	F. Roosevelt
James F. Byrnes	1941–1942	F. Roosevelt
Robert H. Jackson	1941–1954	F. Roosevelt
Wiley B. Rutledge	1943–1949	F. Roosevelt
Harold H. Burton	1945–1958	Truman
Frederick M. Vinson	1946–1953	Truman
Tom C. Clark	1949–1967	Truman
Sherman Minton	1949–1956	Truman
Earl Warren	1953–1969	Eisenhower
John Marshall Harlan	1955–1971	Eisenhower
William J. Brennan, Jr.	1956–	Eisenhower
Charles E. Whittaker	1957–1962	Eisenhower
Potter Stewart	1958–1981	Eisenhower
Byron R. White	1962–1993	Kennedy
Arthur J. Goldberg	1962–1965	Kennedy
Abe Fortas	1965–1969	Johnson
Thurgood Marshall	1967–1991	Johnson
Warren E. Burger	1969–1986	Nixon
Harry A. Blackmun	1970–	Nixon
Lewis F. Powell, Jr.	1972–1988	Nixon
William H. Rehnquist	1972–1986	Nixon
John Paul Stevens	1975–	Ford
Sandra Day O'Connor	1981–	Reagan
William H. Rehnquist	1986–	Reagan
Antonin Scalia	1986–	Reagan
Anthony Kennedy	1988–	Reagan
David Souter	1990–	Bush
Clarence Thomas	1991–	Bush
Ruth Bader Ginsburg	1993–	Clinton

Note: **Chief Justices appear in bold type.**
*Acting Chief Justice; Senate refused to confirm appointment.

Admission of States into the Union

State	Date of Admission
1. Delaware	December 7, 1787
2. Pennsylvania	December 12, 1787
3. New Jersey	December 18, 1787
4. Georgia	January 2, 1788
5. Connecticut	January 9, 1788
6. Massachusetts	February 6, 1788
7. Maryland	April 28, 1788
8. South Carolina	May 23, 1788
9. New Hampshire	June 21, 1788
10. Virginia	June 25, 1788
11. New York	July 26, 1788
12. North Carolina	November 21, 1789
13. Rhode Island	May 29, 1790
14. Vermont	March 4, 1791
15. Kentucky	June 1, 1792
16. Tennessee	June 1, 1796
17. Ohio	March 1, 1803
18. Louisiana	April 30, 1812
19. Indiana	December 11, 1816
20. Mississippi	December 10, 1817
21. Illinois	December 3, 1818
22. Alabama	December 14, 1819
23. Maine	March 15, 1820
24. Missouri	August 10, 1821
25. Arkansas	June 15, 1836

State	Date of Admission
26. Michigan	January 26, 1837
27. Florida	March 3, 1845
28. Texas	December 29, 1845
29. Iowa	December 28, 1846
30. Wisconsin	May 29, 1848
31. California	September 9, 1850
32. Minnesota	May 11, 1858
33. Oregon	February 14, 1859
34. Kansas	January 29, 1861
35. West Virginia	June 20, 1863
36. Nevada	October 31, 1864
37. Nebraska	March 1, 1867
38. Colorado	August 1, 1876
39. North Dakota	November 2, 1889
40. South Dakota	November 2, 1889
41. Montana	November 8, 1889
42. Washington	November 11, 1889
43. Idaho	July 3, 1890
44. Wyoming	July 10, 1890
45. Utah	January 4, 1896
46. Oklahoma	November 16, 1907
47. New Mexico	January 6, 1912
48. Arizona	February 14, 1912
49. Alaska	January 3, 1959
50. Hawaii	August 21, 1959

BIBLIOGRAPHY

Chapter 1

Settling the Continent

Larry D. Agenbroad, et al., eds. *Megafauna and Man* (1990)
John Bierhorst, ed., *The Red Swan: Myths and Tales of the American Indians* (1976)
Warwick M. Bray, et al., *The New World: The Making of the Past* (1977)
Mark Nathan Cohen, *The Food Crisis in Prehistory: Overpopulation and the Origins of Agriculture* (1977)
Henry F. Dobyns, *Native American Historical Demography: A Critical Bibliography* (1976)
Richard Erdoes and Alfonso Ortiz, eds., *American Indian Myths and Legends* (1984)
Jonathon E. Ericson, et al., eds., *Peopling of the New World* (1982)
Brian M. Fagan, *Ancient North America* (1991)
Stuart J. Fiedel, *Prehistory of the Americas* (1987)
Jeffrey Goodman, *American Genesis: The American Indian and the Origins of Modern Man* (1981)
Lee Eldridge Huddleston, *Origins of the American Indians: European Concepts, 1492–1729* (1967)
Jesse D. Jennings, ed., *Ancient North Americans* (1983)
William S. Laughlin and Albert B. Harper, eds., *The First Americans: Origins, Affinities, and Adaptations* (1979)
Kenneth MacGowan and J. A. Hester, Jr., *Early Man in the New World* (1950)
James L. Phillips and James A. Brown, eds., *Archaic Hunters and Gatherers in the American Midwest* (1983)
Paul Shao, *The Origin of Ancient American Cultures* (1983)
Richard Shutler, Jr., ed., *Early Man in the New World* (1983)
Waldo R. Wedel, *Prehistoric Man on the Great Plains* (1961)
Gordon R. Willey, *An Introduction to American Archaeology* (1966)

The Beginning of Regional Cultures

Frances R. Berdan, *The Aztecs of Central Mexico* (1982)
David S. Brose, et al., *Ancient Art of the American Woodland Indians* (1985)
David S. Brose and N'omi Greber, eds., *Hopewell Archaeology* (1979)
Michael D. Coe, *Mexico* (1967)
Linda S. Cordell, *Prehistory of the Southwest* (1984)
Munro Edmondson, ed., *Sixteenth-Century Mexico: The Works of Sahagun* (1974)
Richard I. Ford, ed., *Prehistoric Food Production in North America* (1985)
Melvin L. Fowler, *Perspectives in Cahokia Archeology* (1975)
Emil W. Haury, *The Hohokam* (1976)
William F. Keegan, ed., *Emergent Horticultural Economies of the Eastern Woodlands* (1987)
A. L. Kroeber, *Cultural and Natural Areas of Native North America* (1939)
Eric Wolf, *Sons of the Shaking Earth* (1959)
W. H. Wills, *Early Prehistoric Agriculture* (1988)
Clark Wissler, [North American Indians of the Plains] (1941)

The Eve of Colonization

James Axtell, ed., *The Indian Peoples of Eastern America: A Documentary History of the Sexes* (1981)
Lyle Campbell and Marianne Mithun, eds., *The Languages of Native America* (1979)
Olive P. Dickason, *Canada's First Nations: A History of Founding Peoples* (1992)
Edward P. Dozier, *The Pueblo Indians of North America* (1970)
Harold E. Driver, *Indians of North America* (1961)
James A. Ford, *A Comparison of Formative Cultures in the Americas* (1969)
Charles Hudson, *The Southeastern Indians* (1976)
Alvin Josephy, Jr., *The Indian Heritage of America* (1968)
Clyde Kluckhohn and Dorothea Leighton, *The Navaho* (1962)
Alfonso Ortiz, ed., *New Perspectives on the Pueblos* (1972)
Howard S. Russell, *Indian New England Before the Mayflower* (1980)
Frank G. Speck, *Penobscot Man* (1940)
Robert F. Spencer and Jesse D. Jennings, et al., *The Native Americans: Ethnology and Backgrounds of the North American Indians* (1977)
John R. Swanton, *The Indians of the Southeastern United States* (1946)
Bruce Trigger, *The Children of Aaeaentsic: A History of the Huron People to 1660* (1976)
Wilcomb E. Washburn, *The Indian in America* (1975)
J. Leitch Wright, Jr., *The Only Land They Knew* (1981)

Chapter 2

The Expansion of Europe

Fernand Braudel, *The Mediterranean and the Mediterranean World in the Age of Philip II* (1972)
Fernand Braudel, *Civilization and Capitalism, 15th-18th Centuries* 3 vols. (1981)
Carol Cipolla, *Before the Industrial Revolution: European Society and Economy, 1100–1700* (1976)
Patrick Collinson, *The Religion of Protestants: The Church in English Society, 1559–1625* (1982)
Ralph Davis, *The Rise of Atlantic Economies* (1973)
W. H. McNeill, *The Rise of the West* (1963)
J. H. Parry, *The Age of Reconnaissance* (1963)
J. H. Parry, *The Establishment of the European Hegemony: Trade and Expansion in the Age of the Renaissance* (1966)
J. H. Parry, *Europe and the New World, 1415–1715* (1949)

The Spanish in the Americas

Fredi Chiapelli, ed., *First Images of America* (1976)
Alfred Crosby, *The Columbian Exchange: Biological and Cultural Consequences of 1492* (1972)
Warner Bowden, *American Indians and Christian Missions* (1982)
Henry F. Dobyns, *Their Number Become Thinned* (1983)
J. H. Elliott, *Imperial Spain, 1469–1716* (1963)
J. H. Elliott, *The Old World and the New, 1492–1650* (1970)
Charles Gibson, *Spain in America* (1966)
Lewis Hanke, *The Spanish Struggle for Justice in the Conquest of America* (1965)
C. H. Harwig, *The Spanish Empire in America* (1947)
Hugh Honour, *New Golden Land* (1975)
Peter Iverson, *The Navaho Nation* (1981)
Elizabeth A. H. John, *Storms Brewed in Other Men's Worlds* (1975)
James Lang, *Conquest and Commerce: Spain and England in the Americas* (1975)
James Lockhart and Stuart B. Schwartz, *Early Latin America: A History of Colonial Spanish America and Brazil* (1983)
Jerald T. Milanich, *Hernando de Soto and the Indians of Florida* (1993)

Samuel Eliot Morison, *The European Discovery of America: The Southern Voyages* (1974)
James Howlett O'Donnell, III, *Southeastern Frontiers: Europeans, Africans, and American Indians, 1513–1840: A Critical Bibliography* (1982)
Edmundo O'Gorman, *The Invention of America* (1961)
J. H. Parry, *The Spanish Seaborne Empire* (1966)
Carl O. Sauer, *Sixteenth Century North America* (1971)

Northern Explorations and Encounters

Alfred Goldsworthy Bailey, *The Conflict of European and Eastern Algonkian Cultures, 1504–1700* (1969)
Carl Bridenbaugh, *Vexed and Troubled Englishmen, 1590–1642* (1968)
Samuel Eliot Morison, *The European Discovery of America: The Northern Voyages* (1971)
Peter Clark and Paul Slack, *English Towns in Transition, 1500–1700* (1976)
Patrick Collinson, *The Elizabethan Puritan Movement* (1967)
A. G. Dickens, *The English Reformation* (1964)
G. R. Elton, *England Under the Tudors* (1974)
C. H. George and Katherine George, *The Protestant Mind of the English Reformation* (1961)
Karen Ordahl Kupperman, *Settling with the Indians: The Meeting of English and Indian Cultures in America, 1580–1640* (1980)
Karen Ordahl Kupperman, *Roanoke: The Abandoned Colony* (1984)
Peter Laslett, *The World We Have Lost* (1965)
E. B. Leacock and N. O. Laurie, eds., *North American Indians in Historical Perspective* (1971)
Wallace Notestein, *The English People on the Eve of Colonization, 1603–1630* (1954)
David B. Quinn, *North America from Earliest Discovery to First Settlements* (1977)
David B. Quinn, *The Roanoke Voyages, 1584–1590* 2 vols. (1955)
E. E. Rich, *The Fur Trade and the Northwest to 1857* (1967)
Lewis O. Saum, *The Fur Trader and the Indian* (1965)
Bernard W. Sheehan, *Savagism and Civility* (1980)
Marcel Trudel, *The Beginnings of New France, 1524–1663* (1973)
Michael Walzer, *The Revolution of the Saints* (1965)
Penry Williams, *The Tudor Regime* (1979)
Peter H. Wood, et al., eds., *Powhatan's Mantle* (1989)
Keith Wrightson, *English Society, 1580–1680* (1982)

Biography

Morris Bishop, *Champlain, The Life of Fortitude* (1948)
Samuel E. Morison, *Admiral of the Ocean Sea: A Life of Christopher Columbus* (1942)
J. E. Neale, *Queen Elizabeth I* (1934)
A. L. Rowse, *Sir Walter Raleigh* (1962)
John Ure, *Prince Henry the Navigator* (1977)
Henry Raup Wagner, *The Life and Writings of Bartolome de las Casas* (1967)
Jon E. M. White, *Cortes and the Downfall of the Aztec Empire* (1971)

Chapter 3

The Spanish and French in North America

James Axtell, *The Invasion Within: The Contest of Culture in Colonial North America* (1985)
James Axtell, *The European and the Indian: Essays in the Ethnohistory of Colonial North America* (1981)
W. J. Eccles, *The Canadian Frontier, 1534–1760* (1969)
W. J. Eccles, *France in America* (1972)

Virginia

Warren M. Billings, ed., *The Old Dominion in the Seventeenth Century: A Documentary History of Virginia, 1606–1689* (1975)
Wesley F. Craven, *The Dissolution of the Virginia Company* (1932)
Wesley F. Craven, *The Southern Colonies in the Seventeenth Century* (1949)
Wesley F. Craven, *White, Red, and Black: The Seventeenth Century Virginian* (1971)
Carville Earle, *The Evolution of a Tidewater Settlement Pattern: All Hallow's Parish, Maryland, 1650–1783* (1975)
Jack P. Greene and J. R. Poole, eds., *Colonial British America: Essays in the New History of the Early Modern Era* (1984)
J. A. Leo Lemay, *Did Pocahontas Save Captain John Smith?* (1992)
Gloria L. Main, *Tobacco Colony: Life in Early Maryland, 1650–1720* (1982)
Richard L. Morton, *Colonial Virginia* 2 vols. (1960)
John E. Pomfret and F. M. Shumway, *Founding the American Colonies, 1583–1660* (1970)
David B. Quinn, ed., *Early Maryland in a Wider World* (1982)
Thad W. Tate and David L. Ammerman, eds., *The Chesapeake in the Seventeenth Century* (1979)
Clarence L. Ver Steeg, *The Formative Years, 1607–1763* (1964)
Alden T. Vaughn, *American Genesis* (1975)

New England

David Grayson Allen, *In English Ways: The Movement of Societies and the Transferal of English Local Law and Custom* (1981)
Bernard Bailyn, *The New England Merchants in the Seventeenth Century* (1955)
Emery Battis, *Saints and Sectaries* (1962)
Theodore Dwight Bozeman, *To Live Ancient Lives: The Primitivist Dimension in Puritanism* (1988)
William Bradford, *Of Plymouth Plantation,* edited by Samuel E. Morison (1952)
T. H. Breen, *Character of the Good Ruler* (1970)
Carl Bridenbaugh, *Fat Mutton and Liberty of Conscience* (1974)
Charles L. Cohen, *God's Caress: The Psychology of Puritan Religious Experience* (1986)
David Cressy, *Coming Over: Migration and Communication Between England and New England in the Seventeenth Century* (1987)
William Cronon, *Changes in the Land* (1983)
John Demos, *A Little Commonwealth: Family Life in Plymouth Colony* (1970)
M. Etienne and E. Leacock, eds., *Women and Colonization* (1980)
Stephen Foster, *Their Solitary Way: The Puritan Social Ethic in the First Century of Settlement in New England* (1971)
Philip Greven, Jr., *Four Generations: Population, Land, and Family in Colonial Andover* (1970)
David D. Hall, *The Faithful Shepherd: A History of the New England Ministry in the Seventeenth Century* (1972)
Christopher Hill, *The World Turned Upside Down* (1972)
Stephen Innes, *Labor in a New Land* (1983)
Sydney V. James, *Colonial Rhode Island* (1975)
Francis Jennings, *The Invasion of America: Indians, Colonialism, and the Cant of Conquest* (1975)
David T. Konig, *Law and Society in Puritan Massachusetts* (1979)
Amy Scrager Lang, *Prophetic Women: Anne Hutchinson and the Problem of Dissent in the Literature of New England* (1987)
George D. Langdon, Jr., *Pilgrim Colony* (1966)
Kenneth A. Lockridge, *A New England Town: The First Hundred Years* (1970)
Paul R. Lucas, *Valley of Discord* (1976)
Samuel Eliot Morison, *Builders of the Bay Colony* (1930)
Darrett Rutman, *Husbandmen of Plymouth: Farms and Villages in the Old Colony, 1620–1649* (1967)
Darrett Rutman, *Winthrop's Boston* (1965)
Neal Salisbury, *Manitou and Providence: Indians, Europeans and the Making of New England* (1982)
Alan Simpson, *Puritanism in Old and New England* (1955)

Alden T. Vaughn, *New England Frontier: Puritans and Indians* (1965)

R. E. Wall, *Massachusetts Bay: The Crucial Decade, 1640–1650* (1972)

John Winthrop, *History of New England,* edited by James Kendall Hosmer, 2 vols. (1908)

Restoration Colonies

Thomas J. Condon, *New York Beginnings: Commercial Origins of the New Netherlands* (1968)

Wesley F. Craven, *The Southern Colonies in the Seventeenth Century, 1607–1689* (1949)

Melvin B. Endy, Jr., *William Penn and Early Quakerism* (1973)

Michael Kammen, *Colonial New York* (1975)

Sung Bok Kim, *Landlord and Tenant in Colonial New York: Manorial Society, 1664–1775* (1978)

H. T. Merrens, *Colonial North Carolina* (1964)

Gary B. Nash, *Quakers and Politics: Pennsylvania, 1681–1726* (1968)

John E. Pomfret, *The Province of East New Jersey, 1609–1702: The Rebellious Province* (1962)

John E. Pomfret, *The Province of West New Jersey, 1609–1702: A History of the Origins of an American Colony* (1956)

Oliver Rink, *Holland on the Hudson: An Economic and Social History of Dutch New York* (1986)

Robert C. Ritchie, *The Duke's Province* (1977)

M. Eugene Sirmans, *Colonial South Carolina: A Political History, 1663–1763* (1966)

George L. Smith, *Religion and Trade in New Netherland* (1973)

Jack M. Sosin, *English America and the Restoration Monarchy of Charles II: Transatlantic Politics, Commerce, and Kinship* (1980)

Clarence L. Ver Steeg, *Origins of a Southern Mosaic* (1975)

Frederick B. Tolles, *Quakers and the Atlantic Culture* (1960)

Robert Weir, *Colonial South Carolina* (1983)

Conflict and War

Thomas J. Archdeacon, *New York City, 1664–1710* (1976)

Richard R. Johnson, *Adjustment to Empire: The New England Colonies, 1675–1715* (1981)

D. W. Jordan, *Maryland's Revolution of Government* (1974)

Yusuhide Kawashima, *Puritan Justice and the Indian: White Man's Law in Massachusetts, 1630–1763* (1986)

Douglas Leach, *Flintlock and Tomahawk* (1958)

David S. Lovejoy, *The Glorious Revolution in America* (1972)

Michael J. Publisi, *Puritans Besieged: The Legacies of King Philip's War in the Massachusetts Bay Colony* (1991)

Jack M. Sosin, *English America and the Revolution of 1688* (1982)

Wilcomb E. Washburn, *The Governor and the Rebel: A History of Bacon's Rebellion in Virginia* (1957)

Stephen S. Webb, *1676: The End of American Independence* (1980)

Thomas J. Wertenbaker, *Torchbearer of the Revolution* (1940)

Biography

Philip L. Barbour, *The Three Worlds of Captain John Smith* (1964)

Edwin B. Bronner, *William Penn's ''Holy Experiment''* (1962)

Mary M. Dunn, *William Penn, Politics and Conscience* (1967)

Edmund S. Morgan, *Puritan Dilemma: The Story of John Winthrop* (1958)

Edmund S. Morgan, *Roger Williams: The Church and the State* (1967)

Josephine K. Piercy, *Anne Bradstreet* (1965)

Marc Simmons, *The Last Conquistador: Juan de Onate and the Settling of the Far Southwest* (1991)

Bradford Smith, *Captain John Smith* (1953)

George Leon Walker, *Thomas Hooker, Preacher, Founder, Democrat* (1969)

Alvin Gardner Weeks, *Massasoit of the Wampanoags* (1919)

Perry D. Westbrook, *William Bradford* (1978)

Selma R. Williams, *Divine Rebel: The Life of Anne Marbury Hutchinson* (1981)

Chapter 4

The African Slave Trade

Paul Bohannan and Philip Curtin, *Africa and the Africans* (1971)

G. E. Brooks, *Yankee Traders, Old Coasters, and African Middlemen* (1970)

Jay Coughtry, *The Notorious Triangle: Rhode Island and the African Slave Trade, 1799–1807* (1981)

Philip D. Curtin, *The Atlantic Slave Trade: A Census* (1969)

Philip D. Curtin, *Economic Change in Precolonial Africa: Senegambia in the Era of the Slave Trade* (1975)

Basin Davidson, *Black Mother: The Years of the African Slave Trade* (1961)

Kenneth G. Davies, *The Royal African Company* (1957)

Elizabeth Donnan, ed., *Documents Illustrative of the History of the Slave Trade to America* 4 vols. (1930–35)

J. S. Fage, *A History of Africa* (1978)

Herbert S. Klein, *The Middle Passage: Comparative Studies in the Atlantic Slave Trade* (1978)

Suzanne Miers and I. Kopytoff, eds., *Slavery in Africa: Historical and Anthropological Perspectives* (1977)

Richard Olaniyan, *African History and Culture* (1982)

J. A. Rawley, *The Transatlantic Slave Trade* (1981)

Edward Reynolds, *Stand the Storm: A History of the Atlantic Slave Trade* (1985)

A. C. De C. M. Saunders, *A Social History of Black Slaves and Freemen in Portugal, 1441–1555* (1982)

Jon Vogt, *Portuguese Rule on the Gold Coast, 1469–1682* (1979)

The Development of North American Slave Societies

L. R. Bailey, *Indian Slave Trade in the Southwest* (1966)

T. H. Breen and Stephen Innes, *''Myne Owne Ground'': Race and Freedom on Virginia's Eastern Shore* (1980)

Kenneth Coleman, *Colonial Georgia: A History* (1976)

Verner W. Crane, *The Southern Frontier, 1670–1732* (1929)

Richard S. Dunn, *Sugar and Slaves: The Rise of the Planter Class in the English West Indies, 1624–1713* (1972)

Stanley Engerman and Eugene D. Genovese, eds., *Race and Slavery in the Western Hemisphere: Quantitative Studies* (1975)

Laura Foner and Eugene D. Genovese, eds., *Slavery in the New World: A Reader in Comparative History* (1969)

Charles Joyner, *Down By the Riverside: A South Carolina Slave Community* (1984)

Alan Kulikoff, *Tobacco and Slaves: The Development of Southern Cultures in the Chesapeake, 1680–1800* (1986)

Daniel Littlefield, *Rice and Slaves: Ethnicity and the Slave Trade in Colonial South Carolina* (1981)

Paul E. Lovejoy, *Transformations in Slavery: A History of Slavery in Africa* (1983)

Edgar J. McManus, *Black Bondage in the North* (1973)

Gary B. Nash, *Red, White, and Black* (1982)

Julia Floyd Smith, *Slavery and Rice Culture in Low Country Georgia, 1750–1860* (1985)

Thad W. Tate, *The Negro in Eighteenth-Century Williamsburg* (1966)

Betty Wood, *Slavery in Colonial Georgia, 1730–1775* (1984)

Peter Wood, *Black Majority: Negroes in Colonial South Carolina from 1670 through the Stono Rebellion* (1974)

Becoming African American

Roger Bastide, *African Civilizations in the New World,* translated by Peter Green (1972)

John W. Blassingame, *The Slave Community: Plantation Life in the Antebellum South* (revised ed., 1979)

John B. Boles, *Black Southerners, 1619–1869* (1984)

John B. Boles, ed., *Masters and Slaves in the House of the Lord: Race and Religion in the American South, 1740–1870* (1988)
Eugene Genovese, *From Rebellion to Revolution* (1979)
Joseph E. Harris, ed., *Global Dimensions of the African Diaspora* (1982)
Melville J. Herskovits, *The Myth of the Negro Past* (1958)
Sidney W. Mintz and Richard Price, *An Anthropological Approach to the Afro-American Past: A Caribbean Perspective* (1976)
G. W. Mullin, *Flight and Rebellion: Slave Resistance in Eighteenth-Century Virginia* (1972)
Orlando Patterson, *Slavery and Social Death* (1982)
Willie Lee Rose, ed., *Documentary History of Slavery in North America* (1976)
V. B. Thompson, *The Making of the African Diaspora in the Americas, 1441–1900* (1984)
Joel Williamson, *New People: Miscegenation and Mulattoes in the United States* (1980)

The Structure of Empire

Charles M. Andrews, *The Colonial Period of American History* 4 vols. (1934–38)
Joyce O. Appleby, *Economic Thought and Ideology in Seventeenth-Century England* (1978)
Bernard Bailyn, *The New England Merchants* (1965)
Eugene Genovese and Elizabeth Fox-Genovese, *Fruits of Merchant Capital* (1983)
M. G. Hall, *Edward Randolph and the American Colonies* (1960)
Lawrence Harper, *The English Navigation Laws* (1939)
James Henretta, *Salutary Neglect* (1972)
E. J. Hobsbawn, *Industry and Empire* (1968)
Michael Kammen, *Empire and Interest: The American Colonies and the Politics of Mercantilism* (1970)
John J. McCusker and Russell R. Menard, *The Economy of British America, 1607–1787* (1985)
Edwin J. Perkins, *The Economy of Colonial America* (1988)
Jacob M. Price, *Capital and Credit in British Overseas Trade* (1980)
I. K. Steele, *The Politics of Colonial Policy* (1968)
Immanuel Wallerstein, *The Modern World System: Capitalist Agriculture and the Origins of the European World-Economy in the Sixteenth Century* (1974)
Gary M. Walton and James F. Shepherd, *The Economic Rise of Early America* (1979)
Eric Williams, *Capitalism and Slavery* (1944)
Stephen S. Webb, *The Governors-General: The English Army and the Definition of Empire* (1979)

Slavery and Freedom

David Brion Davis, *The Problem of Slavery in Western Culture* (1966)
Carl N. Degler, *Neither Black Nor White: Slavery and Race Relations in Brazil and the United States* (1971)
Winthrop D. Jordan, *White Over Black: American Attitudes Toward the Negro, 1550–1812* (1968)
Edmund S. Morgan, *American Slavery, American Freedom: The Ordeal of Colonial Virginia* (1975)
Magnus Morner, *Race Mixture in the History of Latin America* (1967)

Biography

Philip D. Curtin, ed., *Africa Remembered: Narratives of West Africans from the Era of the Slave Trade* (1967)
Paul Edwards, ed., *Interesting Narrative of the Life of Olaudah Equiano, or Gustavus Vassa, the African, written by himself* (1987)
James B. Hedges, *The Browns of Providence Plantation* (1952)
Kenneth A. Lockridge, *The Diary and Life of William Byrd II of Virginia, 1674–1744* (1987)
Phinizy Spalding, *Oglethorpe in America* (1977)
Janet Whitman, *John Woolman, American Quaker* (1942)

Chapter 5

Population Growth and Immigration

Bernard Bailyn, *The Peopling of British North America: An Introduction* (1986)
Bernard Bailyn, *Voyages to the West: A Passage in the Peopling of America on the Eve of the Revolution* (1986)
R. J. Dickson, *Ulster Immigration to the United States* (1966)
Albert B. Faust, *The German Element in the United States* 2 vols. (1909)
C. C. Graham, *Colonists from Scotland: Emigration to North America, 1707–1783* (1956)
Marcus Hanson, *The Atlantic Migration, 1607–1860* (1940)
James G. Leyburn, *The Scotch-Irish: A Social History* (1962)
James Kettner, *The Development of American Citizenship* (1978)
Frederic Klees, *The Pennsylvania Dutch* (1950)
Robert V. Wells, *The Population of the British Colonies in America Before 1776* (1975)

The Spanish Borderlands and New France

John Francis Bannon, *The Spanish Borderlands Frontier, 1513–1821* (1970)
Sherburne F. Cook, *The Conflict Between the California Indian and White Civilization* (1976)
W. J. Eccles, *The Canadian Frontier, 1534–1760* (1969)
W. J. Eccles, *France in America* (1972)
Robert F. Heizer, *The Destruction of California Indians* (1974)
Charles Edwards O'Neill, *Church and State in French Colonial Louisiana: Policy and Politics to 1732* (1966)
David J. Weber, ed., *New Spain's Far Western Frontier: Essays on Spain in the American West* (1979)

New England

James Axtell, *The School Upon a Hill: Education and Society in Colonial New England* (1974)
Sacvan Bercovitch, *The American Jerimiad* (1978)
Sacvan Bercovitch, *The Puritan Origins of the American Self* (1975)
Richard L. Bushman, *From Puritan to Yankee: Character and the Social Order in Connecticut, 1690–1765* (1967)
Charles E. Hambrick-Stowe, *The Practice of Piety: Puritan Devotional Disciplines in Seventeenth-Century New England* (1982)
Christine Leigh Hyrman, *Commerce and Culture: The Maritime Communities of Colonial Massachusetts* (1984)
Lyle Kohler, *A Search For Power: "The Weaker Sex" in Seventeenth-Century New England, 1650–1750* (1982)
Kenneth Lockridge, *Literacy in Colonial New England* (1974)
Perry Miller, *Errand into the Wilderness* (1956)
Perry Miller, *The New England Mind: From Colony to Province* (1953)
Perry Miller, *The New England Mind: The Seventeenth Century* (1939)
Edmund S. Morgan, *The Puritan Family* (1966)
Edmund S. Morgan, *Visible Saints* (1963)
Marylynn Salmon, *Women and the Law of Property in Early America* (1986)
Roger Thompson, *Women in Stuart England and America: A Comparative Study* (1974)
Laurel T. Ulrich, *Good Wives: Image and Reality in the Lives of Women in Northern New England, 1650–1750* (1982)
Larzer Ziff, *Puritanism in America* (1973)

Middle Colonies

Carl Bridenbaugh, *Cities in the Wilderness* (1938)
William Frost, *The Quaker Family in Colonial America* (1972)
Gary B. Nash, *The Urban Crucible* (1979)
Sally Schwartz, *A Mixed Multitude: The Struggle for Toleration in Colonial Pennsylvania* (1987)

Stephanie G. Wolf, *Urban Village: Population, Community, and Family Structure in Germantown, Pennsylvania* (1977)

The Backcountry

John P. Garber, *The Valley of the Delaware and Its Place in American History* (1934)
Joseph W. Glass, *The Pennsylvania Culture Region: A View from the Barn* (1986)
Henry Glassie, *Pattern in the Material Folk Culture of the Eastern United States* (1968)
Bernard Herman, *Architecture and Rural Life in Central Delaware, 1700–1900* (1987)
Donald A. Hutslar, *The Architecture of Migration: Log Construction in the Ohio Country, 1750–1850* (1986)
Terry G. Jordan and Matti Kaups, *The American Backwoods Frontier: An Ethnic and Ecological Interpretation* (1988)
James T. Lemmon, *The Best Poor Man's Country: A Geographical Study of Early Southeastern Pennsylvania* (1972)
Kenneth E. Lewis, *The American Frontier: An Archaeological Study of Settlement Pattern and Process* (1984)
W. Lynwood Montell and Michael Morse, *Kentucky Folk Architecture* (1976)
Harold R. Shurtleff, *The Log Cabin Myth: A Study of the Early Dwellings of the English Colonists in North America* (1939)

The South

T. H. Breen, *Puritans and Adventurers: Change and Persistence in Early America* (1980)
Carl Bridenbaugh, *Myths and Realities: Societies in the Colonial South* (1952)
Rhys Isaac, *The Transformation of Virginia, 1740–1790* (1983)
A. C. Land, et al., eds., *Law, Society, and Politics in Early Maryland* (1977)
Edmund S. Morgan, *Virginians at Home* (1952)
Darrett B. Rutman and Anita H. Rutman, *A Place in Time: Middlesex County, Virginia, 1650–1750* (1984)
Daniel Blake Smith, *Inside the Great House: Planter Family Life in Eighteenth-Century Chesapeake Society* (1980)

Indian America

Patricia Albers and Beatrice Medicine, eds., *The Hidden Half* (1983)
John C. Ewers, *The Horse in Blackfoot Indian Culture* (1955)
Joseph Jablow, *The Cheyenne in Plains Indian Trade Relations, 1795–1840* (1951)
Francis Jennings, *The Ambiguous Iroquois Empire* (1984)
James H. Merrell, *The Indians' New World: Catawbas and their Neighbors from European Contact Through the Era of Removal* (1989)
Jacqueline Peterson and Jennifer S. H. Brown, eds., *The New Peoples: Being and Becoming Metis in North America* (1985)
Daniel K. Richter, *The Ordeal of the Longhouse: The Peoples of the Iroquois League in the Era of European Colonization* (1992)
Daniel K. Richter and James H. Merrell, eds., *Beyond the Covenant Chain: The Iroquois and Their Neighbors in Indian North America, 1600–1800* (1987)
William S. Simmons, *Spirit of the New England Tribes: Indian History and Folklore, 1620–1984* (1986)
Edward H. Spicer, *Cycles of Conquest: The Impact of Spain, Mexico, and the United States on the Indians of the Southwest, 1533–1960* (1962)
Edward H. Spicer, *Perspectives in American Indian Culture Change* (1961)
Helen Horbeck Tanner, ed., *Atlas of Great Lakes Indian History* (1987)
Daniel H. Usner, Jr., *Indians, Settlers, and Slaves in a Frontier Exchange Economy: The Lower Mississippi Valley Before 1783* (1992)

Indentured Servitude

A. Roger Ekirch, *Bound for America: The Transportation of British Convicts to the Colonies, 1718–1775* (1987)
David W. Galenson, *White Servitude in Colonial America: An Economic Analysis* (1981)
Sharon V. Salinger, *"To Serve Well and Faithfully": Labor and Indentured Servants in Pennsylvania, 1682–1800* (1987)
A. E. Smith, *Colonists in Bondage: White Servitude and Convict Labor in America, 1607–1776* (1947)

Colonial Government

Bernard Bailyn, *The Origins of American Politics* (1968)
Patricia Bonomi, *A Factious People: Politics and Society in Colonial New York* (1977)
Robert E. Brown, *Middle-Class Democracy and the Revolution in Massachusetts, 1691–1780* (1955)
Richard L. Bushman, *King and People in Provincial Massachusetts* (1985)
Bruce C. Daniels, ed., *Power and Status: Essays on Officeholding in Colonial America* (1986)
Robert J. Dinkin, *Voting in Provincial America: A Study of Elections in the Thirteen Colonies, 1689–1776* (1977)
A. Roger Ekirch, *"Poor Carolina," Politics and Society in Colonial North Carolina, 1729–1776* (1981)
Gerald W. Gawalt, *The Promise of Power: The Emergence of the Legal Profession in Massachusetts, 1760–1840* (1979)
Jack P. Green, *The Quest for Power* (1963)
Leonard W. Labaree, *Royal Government in America* (1930)
Thomas L. Purvis, *Proprietors, Patronage, and Paper Money: Legislative Politics in New Jersey, 1703–1776* (1986)
A. G. Roeber, *Faithful Magistrates and Republican Lawyers: Creators of Virginia Legal Culture, 1680–1810* (1981)
Robert Zemsky, *Merchants, Farmers, and River Gods* (1971)

Tradition and Change

Paul Boyer and Stephen Nissenbaum, *Salem Possessed* (1974)
Henry Steele Commager, *The Empire of Reason: How Europe Imagined and America Realized the Enlightenment* (1977)
John Demos, *Entertaining Satan: Witchcraft and the Culture of Early New England* (1982)
Carol F. Karlsen, *The Devil in the Shape of a Woman: Witchcraft in Colonial New England* (1987)
Jackson Maine, *The Social Structure of Revolutionary America* (1965)
Henry F. May, *The Enlightenment in America* (1976)
Louis B. Wright, *The Cultural Life of the American Colonies* (1957)

The Great Awakening

Sidney E. Ahlstrom, *Religious History of the American People* (1972)
Patricia U. Bonomi, *Under the Cope of Heaven: Religion, Society, and Politics in Colonial America* (1986)
J. M. Bumsted and John E. Van de Wetering, *What Must I Do to Be Saved? The Great Awakening in Colonial America* (1976)
Edwin S. Gaustad, *The Great Awakening in New England* (1957)
Alan Heimert, *Religion and the American Mind* (1966)
Alan Heimert and Perry Miller, eds., *The Great Awakening* (1967)
Sidney Mead, *The Lively Experiment: The Shaping of Christianity in America* (1963)
W. W. Sweet, *Religion in Colonial America* (1942)

Biography

Milton J. Coalter, *Gilbert Tennent, Son of Thunder* (1986)
Verner W. Crane, *Benjamin Franklin and a Rising People* (1952)
Harry Kelsey, *Juan Rodriguez Cabrillo* (1986)

H. Leventhal, *In the Shadow of Enlightenment* (1976)
Robert Middlekauff, *The Mathers* (1971)
Perry Miller, *Jonathan Edwards* (1949)
Martin J. Morgado, *Junipero Serra's Legacy* (1987)
Kenneth Silverman, *The Life and Times of Cotton Mather* (1984)
Harry S. Stout, *The Divine Dramatist: George Whitefield and the Rise of Modern Evangelicalism* (1991)
Patricia Tracy, *Jonathan Edwards: Pastor* (1980)
Laurel Ulrich, *A Midwife's Tale: The Life of Martha Ballard, Based on her Diary, 1785–1812* (1990)

Chapter 6

The Great War for Empire

John R. Alden, *John Stuart and the Southern Colonial Frontier* (1944)
Fred Anderson, *A People's Army: Massachusetts Soldiers and Society in the Seven Years' War* (1984)
Sylvia R. Frey, *The British Soldier in America: A Social History of Military Life in the Colonial Period* (1981)
Lawrence H. Gipson, *The British Empire Before the American Revolution* 8 vols. (1936–49)
Dougles E. Leach, *Arms for Empire: A Military History of the British Colonies in North America, 1607–1763* (1973)
Richard Middleton, *The Bells of Victory: The Pitt-Newcastle Ministry and the Conduct of the Seven Years' War, 1757–1762* (1985)
Robert C. Newbold, *The Albany Congress and Plan of Union of 1754* (1955)
Howard H. Peckham, *The Colonial Wars, 1689–1762* (1964)
Howard H. Peckham, *Pontiac and the Indian Uprising* (1947)
William Pencak, *War, Politics, and Revolution in Provincial Massachusetts* (1981)
Alan Rogers, *Empire and Liberty* (1974)
Jack M. Sosin, *Whitehall and the Wilderness* (1961)

Imperial Crisis in British North America

Thomas C. Barrow, *Trade and Empire: The British Customs Service in Colonial America* (1967)
John Brewer, *Party Ideology and Popular Politics at the Accession of George III* (1976)
Oliver M. Dickinson, *The Navigation Acts and the American Revolution* (1951)
Joseph Ernst, *Money and Politics in America, 1755–1775* (1973)
Alice Hanson Jones, *The Wealth of a Nation to Be* (1980)
L. B. Namier, *The Structure of Politics at the Accession of George III* (1929)
J. G. A. Pocock, *The Machiavellian Moment: Florentine Political Thought and the Atlantic Republican Tradition* (1975)
Caroline Robbins, *The Eighteenth-Century Commonwealthman* (1959)
Arthur M. Schlesinger, *The Colonial Merchants and the American Revolution* (1917)
W. A. Speck, *Stability and Strife: England, 1714–1760* (1977)
John W. Tyler, *Smugglers and Patriots: Boston Merchants and the Advent of the American Revolution* (1966)
Carl Ubbelohde, *The Vice-Admiralty Courts and the American Revolution* (1960)

From Resistance to Rebellion

David Ammerman, *In the Common Cause: American Response to the Coercive Acts of 1774* (1974)
Bernard Bailyn, *The Ideological Origins of the American Revolution* (1967)
Carl Becker, *The Declaration of Independence* (1922)
T. H. Breen, *Tobacco Culture: The Mentality of the Great Tidewater Planters on the Eve of Revolution* (1985)
Richard D. Brown, *Revolutionary Politics in Massachusetts: The Boston Committee of Correspondence and the Towns, 1772–1774* (1970)

Richard L. Bushman, *King and People in Provincial Massachusetts* (1985)
H. Trevor Colbourn, *The Lamp of Experience: Whig History and the Intellectual Origins of the American Revolution* (1965)
Edward Countryman, *A People in Revolution: The American Revolution and Political Society in New York, 1760–1790* (1982)
Oliver M. Dickerson, *The Navigation Acts and the American Revolution* (1951)
Bernard Donoughue, *British Politics and the American Revolution: The Path to War, 1773–1775* (1964)
Dirk Hoerder, *Crowd Action in Revolutionary Massachusetts* (1977)
Benjamin W. Labaree, *The Boston Tea Party* (1974)
Pauline Maier, *From Resistance to Revolution: Colonial Radicals and the Development of American Opposition to Britain, 1765–1776* (1972)
Edmund S. Morgan and Helen M. Morgan, *The Stamp Act Crisis* (1953)
Edmund S. Morgan, *The Birth of the Republic, 1763–1789* (1956)
John Shy, *Toward Lexington: The Role of the British Army in the Coming of the American Revolution* (1965)
Morton White, *The Philosophy of the American Revolution* (1978)
Gary Wills, *Inventing America* (1978)
Hiller B. Zobel, *The Boston Massacre* (1970)

Biography

Bernard Bailyn, *The Ordeal of Thomas Hutchinson* (1974)
Richard R. Beeman, *Patrick Henry: A Biography* (1974)
Jeremy Black, *Pitt the Elder* (1992)
John Brooke, *King George III* (1974)
John E. Ferling, *The Loyalist Mind: Joseph Galloway and the American Revolution* (1977)
Milton E. Flower, *John Dickinson: Conservative Revolutionary* (1983)
Eric Foner, *Tom Paine and Revolutionary America* (1976)
Esther Forbes, *Paul Revere and the World He Lived In* (1942)
William M. Fowler, Jr., *The Baron of Beacon Hill: A Biography of John Hancock* (1979)
David A. McCants, *Patrick Henry, the Orator* (1990)
John C. Miller, *Sam Adams: Pioneer in Propaganda* (1936)
J. H. Plumb, *Sir Robert Walpole* 2 vols. (1956–60)
Peter Shaw, *The Character of John Adams* (1976)
Peter D. G. Thomas, *Lord North* (1974)

Chapter 7

The War for Independence

Thomas P. Abernathy, *Western Lands and the American Revolution* (1937)
G. W. Allen, *Naval History of the American Revolution* 2 vols. (1913)
Richard Buel, Jr., *Dear Liberty: Connecticut's Mobilization for the Revolutionary War* (1980)
George A. Billias, ed., *George Washington's Generals* (1964)
Edward Countryman, *The American Revolution* (1985)
Lawrence D. Cress, *Citizens in Arms: The Army and the Militia in American Society to the War of 1812* (1982)
William M. Fowler, *Rebels Under Sail: The American Navy During the Revolution* (1976)
Ira D. Gruber, *The Howe Brothers and the American Revolution* (1972)
Don Higginbotham, *The War of American Independence* (1971)
Ronald Hoffman and Peter J. Albert, eds., *Arms and Independence: The Military Character of the American Revolution* (1984)
Ronald Hoffman and Thad W. Tate, eds., *An Uncivil War: The Southern Backcountry During the American Revolution* (1985)
Piers Mackesy, *The War for America, 1775–1783* (1964)
James K. Martin and Mark E. Lender, *A Respectable Army: The Military Origins of the Republic, 1763–1789* (1982)
Robert Middlekauff, *The Glorious Cause: The American Revolution, 1763–1789* (1982)

Howard W. Peckham, *The Toll of Independence: Engagements and Battle Casualties of the American Revolution* (1974)
Howard H. Peckham, *The War for Independence: A Military History* (1956)
Paul H. Smith, *Loyalists and Redcoats: A Study in British Revolutionary Policy* (1964)
Jack M. Sosin, *The Revolutionary Frontier, 1763–1783* (1967)
Willard Wallace, *Appeal to Arms* (1950)
Christopher Ward, *The War of the Revolution* 2 vols. (1952)

The Outsiders and the Revolution

Richard Buel, Jr., *The Way of Duty: A Woman and Her Family in Revolutionary America* (1984)
Wallace Brown, *The King's Friends: The Composition and Motives of the American Loyalist Claimants* (1965)
Ira Berlin, *Slaves Without Masters: The Free Negro in the Antebellum South* (1974)
Ira Berlin and Ronald Hoffman, eds., *Slavery and Freedom in the Age of the American Revolution* (1983)
Robert M. Calhoon, *The Loyalists in Revolutionary America, 1760–1781* (1973)
Linda Grant DePauw, *Founding Mothers: Women in America in the Revolutionary Era* (1975)
Barbara Graymont, *The Iroquois in the American Revolution* (1972)
Duncan MacLeod, *Slavery, Race, and the American Revolution* (1974)
Paul C. Nagel, *The Adams Women: Abigail and Louise Adams, Their Sisters and Daughters* (1987)
William H. Nelson, *The American Tory* (1961)
Mary Beth Norton, *The British Americans: The Loyalist Exiles in England, 1774–1789* (1972)
Mary Beth Norton, *Liberty's Daughters: The Revolutionary Experience of American Women, 1750–1800* (1980)
James O'Donnell, *Southern Indians in the American Revolution* (1973)
Benjamin Quarles, *The Negro in the American Revolution* (1961)
Donald L. Robinson, *Slavery in the Structure of American Politics, 1765–1820* (1971)
Alfred F. Young, ed., *The American Revolution: Explorations in American Radicalism* (1976)
James W. St. G. Walker, *The Black Loyalists* (1976)
Anthony F. C. Wallace, *The Death and Rebirth of the Seneca* (1970)
Arthur Zilversmit, *The First Emancipation* (1961)

The United States in Congress Assembled

Robert A. Becker, *Revolution, Reform and the Politics of American Taxation, 1763–1783* (1980)
Richard Beeman, et al., eds., *Beyond Confederation: Origins of the Constitution and American National Identity* (1987)
Samuel F. Bemis, *The Diplomacy of the American Revolution* (1935)
E. Wayne Carp, *To Starve the Army at Pleasure: Continental Army Administration and American Political Culture, 1774–1783* (1984)
Jack Eblen, *The First and Second United States Empires* (1968)
E. J. Ferguson, *The Power of the Purse: A History of American Public Finance, 1776–1790* (1960)
H. J. Henderson, *Party Politics in the Continental Congress* (1974)
Merrill Jensen, *The Articles of Confederation* (1959)
Merrill Jensen, *The New Nation, A History of the United States During the Confederation, 1781–1789* (1950)
L. S. Kaplan, *Colonies into Nation: American Diplomacy, 1763–1801* (1972)
Richard H. Kohn, *Eagle and Sword: The Federalists and the Creation of the Military Establishment in America* (1975)
Forrest McDonald, *E Pluribus Unum: The Formation of the American Republic, 1776–1790* (1965)
Jackson Turner Main, *Political Parties Before the Constitution* (1973)
Richard B. Morris, *The Peacemakers: The Great Powers and American Independence* (1965)

Jack N. Rakove, *The Beginnings of National Politics: An Interpretive History of the Continental Congress* (1979)
Gerald Sourzh, *Benjamin Franklin and American Foreign Policy* (1969)
Gordon S. Wood, *The Creation of the American Republic, 1776–1787* (1969)

Revolutionary Politics in the States

Willi Paul Adams, *The First American Constitutions: Republican Ideology and the Making of the State Constitutions* (1980)
J. Franklin Jameson, *The American Revolution Considered as a Social Movement* (1926)
Donald S. Lutz, *Popular Consent and Popular Control: Whig Political Theory in the Early State Constitutions* (1980)
Jackson Turner Main, *The Sovereign States, 1775–1789* (1973)
Anne M. Ousterhout, *A State Divided: Opposition in Pennsylvania to the American Revolution* (1987)
J. R. Pole, *Political Representation in England and the Origins of the American Republic* (1960)
David P. Szatmary, *Shay's Rebellion: The Making of an Agrarian Insurrection* (1980)
Chilton Williamson, *American Suffrage from Property to Democracy, 1760–1860* (1960)

Biography

Silvio A. Bedini, *The Life of Benjamin Banneker* (1972)
John Mack Faragher, *Daniel Boone: The Life and Legend of An American Pioneer* (1992)
James T. Flexner, *Washington: The Indispensable Man* (1974)
Douglas Southall Freeman, *George Washington* 7 vols. (1948–57)
Edith Belle Gelles, *Portia: The World of Abigail Adams* (1992)
Lowell Hayes Harrison, *George Rogers Clark and the War in the West* (1976)
Isabel Thompson Kelsay, *Joseph Brant, 1743–1807: Man of Two Worlds* (1984)
Samuel Eliot Morison, *John Paul Jones: A Sailor's Biography* (1959)
Willard Sterne Randall, *Benedict Arnold: Patriot and Traitor* (1990)
William Henry Robinson, *Phillis Wheatley and Her Writings* (1984)
Charles Royster, *Light-Horse Harry Lee and the Legacy of the American Revolution* (1981)
Clarence L. Ver Steeg, *Robert Morris: Revolutionary Financier* (1954)

Chapter 8

The Constitution

Douglass Adair, *Fame and the Founding Fathers*, edited by Trevor Colbourn (1974)
Charles A. Beard, *An Economic Interpretation of the Constitution of the United States* (1913)
Richard Buel, Jr., *Securing the Revolution: Ideology in American Politics, 1789–1815* (1972)
J. E. Cooke, ed., *The Federalist* (1961)
Linda Grant DePauw, *The Eleventh Pillar: New York State and the Federal Constitution* (1966)
Jonathan Elliot, ed., *The Debates in the Several State Conventions on the Adoption of the Federal Constitution* 5 vols. (1876)
Max Farrand, *The Framing of the Constitution of the United States* (1913)
Max Farrand, ed., *Records of the Federal Convention of 1787* 4 vols (1911–37)
John P. Kaminski and Gaspare J. Saladino, eds., *The Documentary History of the Ratification of the Constitution* (1982)
Staughton Lynd, *Class Conflict, Slavery, and the United States Constitution* (1968)
Forrest McDonald, *We the People: The Economic Origins of the Constitution* (1958)

Forrest McDonald, *Novus Ordo Seclorum: The Intellectual Origins of the Constitution* (1985)
Jackson Turner Main, *The Anti-Federalists, Critics of the Constitution, 1781–1788* (1961)
Alpheus T. Mason, *The States-Rights Debate* (1964)
Richard B. Morris, *Witnesses at the Creation: Hamilton, Madison, Jay and the Constitution* (1985)
Peter Onuf, *Origins of the Federal Republic* (1983)
Clinton Rossiter, *1787: The Grand Convention* (1965)
Herbert J. Storing, ed., *The Complete Anti-Federalist* 7 vols. (1981)
Garry Wills, *Explaining America: The Federalist* (1981)

The New Nation

Harry Ammon, *The Genet Mission* (1973)
Steven R. Boyd, ed., *The Whiskey Rebellion: Past and Present Perspectives* (1985)
Collin G. Calloway, *Crown and Calumet: British-Indian Relations, 1783–1815* (1987)
Gerald A. Combs, *The Jay Treaty: Political Battleground of the Founding Fathers* (1970)
Alexander De Conde, *Entangling Alliance: Politics and Diplomacy Under George Washington* (1956)
Felix Gilbert, *To the Farewell Address* (1961)
Reginald Horsman, *The Frontier in the Formative Years, 1783–1815* (1970)
Ralph Ketcham, *Presidents Above Party: The First American Presidency, 1789–1829* (1984)
John C. Miller, *The Federalist Era, 1789–1801* (1960)
Forrest McDonald, *The Presidency of George Washington* (1974)
Charles R. Ritcheson, *Aftermath of Revolution: British Policy Toward the United States, 1783–1795* (1969)
Thomas P. Slaughter, *The Whiskey Rebellion: Frontier Epilogue to the American Revolution* (1986)
Wiley Sword, *President Washington's Indian War: The Struggle for the Old Northwest, 1790–1795* (1985)
J. Leitch Wright, *Britain and the American Frontier, 1783–1815* (1975)

Federalists and Republicans

Joyce Appleby, *Capitalism and a New Social Order: The Republican Vision of the 1790s* (1984)
Lance Banning, *The Jeffersonian Persuasion: Evolution of a Party Ideology* (1978)
Albert H. Bowman, *The Struggle for Neutrality: Franco-American Diplomacy during the Federalist Era* (1974)
Ralph Adams Brown, *The Presidency of John Adams* (1975)
Richard Buel, Jr., *Securing the Revolution: Ideology in American Politics, 1789–1815* (1972)
William N. Chambers, *Political Parties in a New Nation: The American Experience, 1776–1809* (1963)
Joseph Charles, *The Origins of the American Party System* (1956)
Nobel E. Cunningham, Jr., *The Jeffersonian Republicans: The Formation of Party Organization, 1789–1801* (1957)
Manning J. Dauer, *The Adams Federalists* (1953)
Alexander De Conde, *The Quasi-War: Politics and Diplomacy of the Undeclared War with France, 1797–1801* (1966)
Richard Hofstadter, *The Idea of a Party System: The Rise of Legitimate Opposition in the United States, 1780–1840* (1969)
Stephen G. Kurtz, *The Presidency of John Adams: The Collapse of Federalism, 1795–1800* (1957)
Leonard Levy, *Legacy of Suppression: Freedom of Speech and Press in Early American History* (1960)
Drew McCoy, *The Elusive Republic: Political Economy in Jeffersonian America* (1980)
James Morton Smith, *Freedom's Fetters: The Alien and Sedition Laws and American Civil Liberties* (1956)
Alfred F. Young, *The Democratic Republicans of New York: The Origins, 1763–1797* (1967)
William Stinchcombe, *The XYZ Affair* (1970)

"The Rising Glory of America"

Joseph J. Ellis, *After the Revolution: Profiles of Early American Culture* (1979)
Emory Elliott, *Revolutionary Writers: Literature and Authority in the New Republic* (1982)
Michael Kammen, *A Season of Youth: The American Revolution and the Historical Imagination* (1978)
Linda Kerber, *Women of the Republic: Intellect and Ideology in Revolutionary America* (1980)
Russel B. Nye, *The Cultural Life of the New Nation* (1960)
Kenneth Silverman, *A Cultural History of the American Revolution* (1976)

Biography

Robert C. Alberts, *Benjamin West: A Biography* (1978)
John R. Alden, *George Washington: A Biography* (1984)
Gay Wilson Allen, *St. John de Crevecoeur: The Life of an American Farmer* (1987)
Aleine Austin, *Matthew Lyon, "New Man" of the Democratic Revolution, 1749–1822* (1981)
Harvey Lewis Carter, *The Life and Times of Little Turtle: First Sagamore of the Wabash* (1987)
Jacob Ernest Cooke, *Alexander Hamilton* (1982)
Helen A. Cooper, *John Trumbull: The Hand and Spirit of a Painter* (1982)
Marcus Cunliffe, *George Washington: Man and Monument* (1958)
Herbert Alan Johnson, *John Jay, Colonial Lawyer* (1989)
Ralph Ketcham, *James Madison: A Biography* (1971)
Adrianne Koch, *Jefferson and Madison: The Great Collaboration* (1950)
Milton Lomask, *Aaron Burr* 2 vols. (1979–82)
Dumas Malone, *Jefferson and His Time* 6 vols (1948–81)
Daniel Marder, *Hugh Henry Brackenridge* (1967)
David Nelson, *Anthony Wayne, Soldier of the Early Republic* (1985)
Merrill D. Peterson, *Thomas Jefferson and the New Nation: A Biography* (1970)
Jules David Prown, *John Singleton Copley* (1966)
Edgar P. Richardson, et al., *Charles Willson Peale and His World* (1983)
Donald A. Ringe, *Charles Brockden Brown* (1991)
Page Smith, *John Adams* (1962)
K. Alan Synder, *Defining Noah Webster: Mind and Morals in the Early Republic* (1990)
Mason Locke Weems, *The Life of Washington* edited by Marcus Cunliffe (1962)

Chapter 9

European Communities from Coast to Coast

Eccles, W.J., *France in America* (1972)
Gibson, James, *Imperial Russia in Frontier America* (1976)
Giraud, Marcel, *A History of French Louisiana, 1698–1715* (1974)
Kushner, Howard, *Conflict on the Northwest Coast: American-Russian Rivalry in the Pacific Northwest, 1790–1867* (1975)
McWilliams, Carey, *North From Mexico: The Spanish-Speaking People of the United States* (1948)
Monroy, Douglas, *Thrown Among Strangers: The Making of Mexican Culture in Frontier California* (1990)
Smith, Barbara Sweetland and Redmond Barnett, eds., *Russian America* (1990)
Weber, David, *The Spanish Frontier in North America* (1993)

Shipping and the National Economy

Brownlee, W. Eliot, *Dynamics of Ascent: A History of the American Economy* (1979)
Bruchey, Stuart, *The Roots of American Economic Growth, 1607–1861* (1965)

Lindstrom, Diane, *Economic Development in the Philadelphia Region, 1810–1860* (1983)

North, Douglass C., *The Economic Growth of the United States, 1790–1860* (1961)

Morison, S.E., *Maritime History of Massachusetts: 1783–1860* (1921)

Albion, R.G., *The Rise of New York Port, 1815–1860* (1939)

Cutler, C.C., *Greyhounds of the Sea* (1930)

The Jeffersonians

Abernathy, Thomas P., *The Burr Conspiracy* (1954)

Adams, Henry, *The United States in 1800* (1955)

Ammon, Harry, *James Monroe: The Quest for National Identity* (1971)

Appleby, Joyce, *Capitalism and the New Social Order: The Republican Vision of the 1790s* (1984)

Baker, Leonard, *John Marshall: A Life in Law* (1974)

Brant, Irving, *James Madison*, vols. 4–6 (1953–1961)

Cunningham, Noble E. *The Jeffersonian Republicans and Power: Party Operations, 1801–1809* (1963)

Dangerfield, George, *The Era of Good Feelings* (1952)

Dangerfield, George, *The Awakening of American Nationalism, 1815–1828* (1965)

Ellis, Richard E., *The Jeffersonian Crisis: Courts and Politics in the Young Republic* (1971)

Fischer, David Hackett, *The Revolution of American Conservatism: The Federalist Party in the Era of Jeffersonian Democracy* (1965)

Haines, Charles G., *The Role of the Supreme Court in American Government and Politics, 1789–1835* (1944)

Horsman, Reginald, *The Causes of the War of 1812* (1962)

Johnstone, Robert M., Jr., *Jefferson and the Presidency: Leadership in the Young Republic* (1978)

Kerber, Linda K., *Federalists in Dissent: Imagery and Ideology in Jeffersonian America* (1970)

LaFeber, Walter, ed., *John Quincy Adams and the American Continental Empire* (1965)

Livermore, Shaw, *The Twilight of Federalism: The Disintegration of the Federalist Party, 1815–1830* (1962)

Malone, Dumas, *Jefferson the President: First Term, 1801–1805* (1970)

Malone, Dumas, *Jefferson the President: Second Term, 1805–1809* (1974)

May, Ernest R. *The Making of the Monroe Doctrine* (1975)

McCoy, Drew R., *The Last of the Fathers: James Madison and the Republican Legacy* (1989)

McDonald, Forrest, *The Presidency of Thomas Jefferson* (1976)

Risjard, Norman, *Jefferson's America* (1991)

Sisson, Daniel, *The Revolution of 1800* (1974)

Spivak, Burton, *Jefferson's English Crisis: Commerce, Embargo, and the Republican Revolution* (1979)

Watts, Steven, *The Republic Reborn: War and the Making of Liberal America, 1790–1820* (1987)

White, G. Edward, *The Marshall Court and Cultural Change, 1815–1835*, abridged edition (1991)

Wiebe, Robert H., *The Opening of American Society: From the Adoption of the Constitution to the Eve of Disunion* (1984)

Young, James S., *The Washington Community: 1800–1828* (1966)

Indian Relations

Berkhofer, Robert, *The White Man's Indian* (1973)

Berkhofer, Robert F., Jr., *Salvation and Savage: An Analysis of Protestant Missions and American Indian Response, 1787–1862* (1965)

Bowden, Henry Warner, *American Indians and Christian Missions: Studies in Cultural Conflict* (1981)

Dowd, Gregory Evans, *A Spirited Resistance: The North American Indian Struggle for Unity, 1745–1815*

Fitzhugh, William W., ed., *Cultures in Contact* (1985)

Horsman, Reginald, *Expansion and American Indian Policy, 1783–1812* (1967)

Jones, Dorothy, *License for Empire: Colonialism by Treaty in Early America* (1982)

Prucha, Francis Paul, *American Indian Policy in the Formative Years: The Indian Trade and Intercourse Acts, 1790–1834* (1962)

Prucha, Francis Paul, *The Great Father: The United States Government and the American Indians*, 2 volumes (1984)

Sheehan, Bernard, *Seeds of Extinction: Jeffersonian Philanthropy and the American Indian* (1973)

Trans-Appalachia

Cayton, Andrew, *The Frontier Republic: Ideology and Politics in the Ohio Country, 1789–1812* (1986)

Goodstein, Anita Shafer, *Nashville, 1780–1860: From Frontier to City* (1989)

Hatcher, Harlan, *The Western Reserve: The Story of New Connecticut in Ohio* (1991)

Horsman, Reginald, *The Frontier in the Formative Years, 1783–1815* (1970)

Rohrbough, Malcolm J., *The Land Office Business* (1968)

Rohrbough, Malcolm J., *The Transappalachian Frontier: Peoples, Societies, and Institutions, 1775–1850* (1958)

Rose, William Ganson, *Cleveland: The Making of a City* (1990)

Slotkin, Richad, *Regeneration Through Violence: The Mythology of the American Frontier* (1973)

Wade, Richard C., *The Urban Frontier: The Rise of Western Cities, 1790–1850* (1973)

Religion and Culture

Boles, John B., *Religion in Antebellum Kentucky* (1976)

Brooke, John L., *Knowledge is Power: The Diffusion of Information in Early America, 1700–1865* (1989)

Butler, Jon, *Awash in a Sea of Faith* (1989)

Conkin, Paul K., *Cane Ridge: America's Pentecost* (1990)

Davidson, Cathy N., *Revolution and the Word: The Rise of the Novel in America* (1986)

Davidson, Cathy N., ed., *Reading in America: Literature and Social History* (1989)

Elliott, Emory, *Revolutionary Writers: Literature and Authority in the New Republic, 1725–1810* (1985)

Ellis, Joseph, *After the Revolution: Profiles of Early American Culture* (1979)

Gilmore, William J. *Reading Becomes a Necessity of Life: Material and Cultural Life in Rural New England, 1780–1835* (1989)

Harris, Neil, *The Artist in American Society: The Formative Years, 1790–1860* (1966)

Hatch, Nathan O., *The Democratization of American Christianity* (1989)

Hedges, William L., *Washington Irving: An American Study, 1802–1832* (1965)

Johnson, C.A., *The Frontier Camp Meeting* (1955)

Mathews, Donald G., *Religion of the Old South* (1977)

McLoughlin, William G., *Revivals, Awakenings, and Reform: An Essay on Religion and Social Change in America, 1607–1977*

McLoughlin, William G., *Modern Revivalism* (1959)

Miller, Perry, *The Life and Mind in America: From the Revolution to the Civil War* (1966)

Seldes, Gilbert, *The Stammering Century* (1928)

Simpson, David, *The Politics of American English* (1986)

Smith, Barbara, *After the Revolution: The Smithsonian History of Everyday Life in the Eighteenth Century* (1985)

Von Frank, Albert, *The Sacred Game: Provincialism and Frontier Consciousness in American Literature, 1630–1860* (1985)

Weisberger, R., *They Gathered at the River* (1958)

Chapter 10

Jacksonian Politics

Ashworth, John, *Agrarians and Aristocrats: Party Ideology in the United States, 1837–1846* (1983)

Bartlett, Irving H., *Daniel Webster* (1978)

Coit, Margaret, *John P. Calhoun: American Portrait* (1950)

Current, Richard, *Daniel Webster and the Rise of National Conservatism* (1955)

Current, Richard N., *John C. Calhoun* (1963)

Ellis, Richard E., *The Union at Risk* (1987)

Goodman, Paul, *Towards a Christian Republic: Antimasonry and the Great Tradition in New England, 1826–1836* (1988)

Gunderson, R.G., *The Log Cabin Campaign* (1957)

Hammond, Bray, *Banks and Politics in America* (1957)

Hofstadter, Richard, *The Idea of a Party System: The Rise of Legitimate Opposition in the United States, 1780–1840* (1969)

Howe, Daniel W., *The Political Culture of the American Whigs* (1980)

Kohl, Lawrence F., *The Politics of Individualism: Parties and the American Character in the Jacksonian Era* (1989)

McCormick, Richard P., *The Second American Party System: Party Formation in the Jacksonian Era* (1966)

Morgan, Robert J., *A Whig Embattled* (1954)

Remini, Robert V., *Henry Clay: Statesman for the Union* (1991)

Richards, Leonard L., *The Life and Times of Congressman John Quincy Adams* (1986)

Schlesinger, Arthur M., Jr., *The Age of Jackson* (1945)

Shade, William G., *Banks or No Banks: The Money Question in Western Politics* (1972)

Sharp, James Roger, *The Jacksonians Versus the Banks: Politics in the United States After the Panic of 1837* (1970)

Silbey, Joel H., *The Partisan Imperative: The Dynamics of American Politics before the Civil War* (1985)

Ward, John, *Andrew Jackson: Symbol for an Age* (1955)

Watson, Harry L., *Jacksonian Politics and Community Conflict: The Emergence of the Second American Party System in Cumberland County, North Carolina* (1981)

Williamson, Chilton, *American Suffrage: From Property to Democracy, 1760–1860* (1960)

Wilson, Major L., *The Presidency of Martin Van Buren* (1984)

Wiltse, C.M., *John C. Calhoun: Nullifier, 1829–1839* (1949)

Transportation Revolution

Bogue, Allan G., *From Prairie to Corn Belt: Farming on the Illinois and Iowa Frontier* (1968)

Bourne, Russell, *Floating West: The Erie and Other American Canals* (1992)

Danhof, Clarence, *Changes in Agriculture: The Northern United States, 1820–1870* (1969)

Dodd, E.M., *American Business Corporations Until 1860* (1954)

Fishlow, Albert, *American Railroads and the Transformation of the Ante-Bellum Economy* (1965)

Fogel, Robert W., *Railroads and American Economic Growth: Essays in Econometric History* (1964)

Goodrich, Carter, *Government Promotion of American Canals and Railroads, 1800–1890* (1960)

Haeger, John Denis, *The Investment Frontier: New York Businessmen and the Economic Development of the Old Northwest* (1981)

Handlin, Oscar and Mary, *Commonwealth: A Study of the Role of Government in the American Economy: Massachusetts, 1774–1861* (1947)

Hartz, Louis, *Economic Policy and Democratic Thought: Pennsylvania, 1776–1860* (1948)

Hiates, Erik F., James Mak, and Gary M. Walton, *Western River Transportation: The Era of Early Internal Development, 1800–1860* (1975)

Horwitz, Morton J., *The Transformation of American Law, 1780–1860* (1977)

Jordan, Philip, *The National Road* (1948)

Scheiber, Harry N., *The Ohio Canal Era: A Case Study of Government and the Economy, 1820–1861* (1969)

Shaw, Ronald E., *Canals for a Nation: The Canal Era in the United States, 1790–1860* (1990)

Shaw, Ronald, *Erie Water West: History of the Erie Canal* (1966)

Temin, Peter, *The Jacksonian Economy* (1965)

Temin, Peter, *Iron and Steel in Nineteenth-Century America* (1964)

Arts and Letters

Allen, Gay Wilson, *Waldo Emerson: A Biography* (1981)

Allen, Gay Wilson, *The Solitary Singer: A Critical Biography of Walt Whitman* (1955)

Arvin, Newton, *Herman Melville* (1950)

Bardes, Barbara A. and Suzanne Gossett, *Declarations of Independence: Women and Political Power in Nineteenth-American Fiction* (1990)

Baym, Nina, *Woman's Fiction: A Guide to Novels By and About Women in America* (1978)

Baym, Nina, *Feminism and American Literary History* (1992)

Blanchard, Paul, *Margaret Fuller: From Transcendentalism to Revolution* (1978)

Boller, Paul F., *American Transcendentalism, 1830–1860* (1974)

Carby, Hazel, *Reconstructing Womanhood: The Emergence of the Afro-American Woman Novelist* (1987)

Davis, Daniel Brion, *Antebellum American Culture: An Interpretive Anthology* (1979)

Harding, Walter, *Thoreau: Man of Concord* (1960)

Kaplan, Harold, *Democratic Humanism and American Literature* (1972)

Kasson, Joy S., *Marble Queens and Captives: Women in Nineteenth-Century American Sculpture* (1990)

Kelley, Mary, *Private Women, Public Stage: Literary Domesticity in Nineteenth-Century America* (1984)

Matthiessen, F.O., *American Renaissance* (1941)

Mellow, J.R., *Nathaniel Hawthorne in His Time* (1980)

Michaels, Walter Benn and Donald E. Pease, eds., *The American Renaissance Reconsidered* (1985)

Miller, E.H., *Salem Is My Dwelling Place: A Life of Nathaniel Hawthorne* (1992)

Miller, Perry, ed., *The Transcendentalists* (1950)

Neufeldt, Leonard, *The Economist: Henry Thoreau and Enterprise* (1989)

Novak, Barbara, *Nature and Culture: American Landscape Painting, 1825–1875* (1982)

Nye, Russell, *Society and Culture in America, 1830–1860* (1974)

Perry, Lewis, *Intellectual Life in America* (1984)

Porte, Joel, *Representative Man: Ralph Waldo Emerson in His Time* (1979)

Richardson, R.D., Jr., *Henry Thoreau: A Life of the Mind* (1986)

Rose, Ann, *Transcendentalism as a Social Movement* (1981)

Rusk, R.L., *The Life of Ralph Waldo Emerson* (1949)

Samuels, Shirley, ed., *The Culture of Sentiment: Race, Gender, and Sentimentality in Nineteenth-Century America* (1992)

Turner, Arlin, *Nathaniel Hawthorne: A Biography* (1980)

Van Doren, Mark, *Nathaniel Hawthorne* (1949)

Wallace, Robert K., *Melville and Turner: Spheres of Love and Fright* (1992)

Walker, Cheryl, *The Nightingale's Burden: Women Poets and American Culture Before 1900* (1982)

Warren, Joyce W., *The (Other) American Traditions: Nineteenth-Century Women Writers* (1993)

Wilmerding, John, ed., *American Light: The Luminist Movement, 1850–1875* (1980)

Wright, Gwendolyn, *Building the Dream: A Social History of Housing in America* (1981)

Ziff, Larzar, *Literary Democracy, The Declaration of Cultural Independence in America* (1981)

Indian Removal

Anderson, William L., *Cherokee Removal: Before and After* (1991)

Cotterill, Ralph S., *The Southern Indians* (1954)

Ehle, John, *Trail of Tears* (1988)

Forman, Grant, *Indian Removal* (1953)

Green, Michael D., *The Politics of Indian Removal* (1982)

Maddox, Lucy, *Removals: Nineteenth-Century American Literature and the Politics of Indian Affairs* (1991)

Rogin, Michael, *Fathers and Children: Andrew Jackson and the Destruction of American Indians* (1975)

Satz, Ronald N., *American Indian Policy in the Jacksonian Era* (1975)

Chapter 11

Economy

Coclanis, Peter A., *The Shadow of a Dream: Economic Life and Death in the South Carolina Low Country, 1670–1920* (1989)
Fogel, Robert W. and Stanley Engerman, *Time on the Cross: The Economics of American Negro Slavery* (1974)
Russel, R.R., *Economic Aspects of Southern Sectionalism, 1840–1861* (1924)
Woodman, Harold D., *Slavery and the Southern Economy* (1966)
Wright, Gavin, *The Political Economy of the Cotton South: Households, Markets, and Wealth in the Nineteenth Century* (1978)
Wright, Gavin, *The Political Economy of the Cotton South* (1978)

Indians

Finger, John R., *The Eastern Band of Cherokees, 1819–1900* (1984)
Green, Michael D., *The Politics of Indian Removal: Creek Government and Society in Crisis* (1982)
Martin, Joel W., *Sacred Revolt: The Muskogees' Struggle for a New World* (1991)
McLoughlin, William G., *Cherokee Renascence in the New Republic* (1986)
McLoughlin, William G., *Cherokees and Missionaries, 1789–1839* (1984)
Usner, Daniel, *Indians, Settlers, and Slaves in a Frontier Exchange Economy . . . before 1763* (1992)
Wright, J. Leitch, Jr., *Creeks and Seminoles: The Destruction and Regeneration of the Muscogulge People* (1986)

White South

Bailey, David T., *Shadow on the Church: Southwestern Evangelical Religion and the Issue of Slavery, 1783–1860* (1985)
Bleser, Carol, ed., *In Joy and in Sorrow: Women, Family, and Marriage in the Victorian South, 1830–1900* (1991)
Bruce, Dickson D., *Violence and Culture in the Antebellum South* (1979)
Cash, Wilbur J., *The Mind of the South* (1941)
Cashin, Joan, *A Family Venture: Men and Women on the Southern Frontier* (1991)
Censer, Jane T., *North Carolina Planters and Their Children, 1800–1860* (1984)
Collins, Bruce, *White Society in the Antebellum South* (1985)
Cooper, William J., *The South and the Politics of Slavery, 1829–1856* (1978)
Cooper, William J., *Liberty and Slavery: Southern Politics to 1860* (1983)
Eaton, Clement, *The Freedom of Thought Struggle in the Old South* (1964)
Eaton, Clement, *The Growth of Southern Civilization, 1790–1860* (1961)
Fox-Genevese, Elizabeth, *Within the Plantation Household* (1988)
Franklin, John Hope, *The Militant South 1800–1861* (1956)
Frederickson, George M., *White Supremacy: A Comparative Study in American and South African History* (1981)
Frederickson, George M., *The Black Image in the White Mind: The Debate on Afro-American Character and Destiny, 1817–1914* (1971)
Friedman, Jean, *The Enclosed Garden: Women and Community in the Evangelical South, 1830–1900* (1985)
Hahn, Steven, *The Roots of Southern Populism: Yeomen Farmers and the Transformation of the Georgia Upcountry, 1850–1890* (1983)
Harris, J. William, *Plain Folk and Gentry in a Slave Society: White Liberty and Black Slavery in Augusta's Hinterlands* (1985)

Jenkins, W.S., *Pro-Slavery Thought in the Old South* (1935)
Lebsock, Suzanne, *The Free Women of Petersburg: Status Culture in a Southern Town, 1784–1860* (1984)
Mathews, Donald G., *Religion in the Old South* (1977)
McCardell, John, *The Idea of a Southern Nation: Southern Nationalists and Southern Nationalism, 1830–1860* (1979)
Oakes, James, *Slavery and Freedom: An Interpretation of the Old South* (1990)
Owsley, Frank, *Plain Folk in the South* (1949)
Scott, Anne F., *The Southern Lady, From Pedestal to Politics, 1830–1930* (1970)
Stowe, Steven, *Intimacy and Power in the Old South: Ritual in the Lives of the Planters* (1987)
Wyatt-Brown, Bertram, *Southern Honor: Ethics and Behavior in the Old South* (1982)

Black Communities/Slavery

Blassingame, John, *The Slave Community*, revised edition (1979)
Campbell, Randolph B., *An Empire for Slavery: The Peculiar Institution in Texas, 1821–1865* (1989)
Cooper, William J., *Liberty and Slavery: Southern Politics to 1860* (1983)
Davis, Charles T. and Henry Louis Gates, Jr., eds., *The Slave's Narrative* (1985)
Degler, Carl N., *Neither White Nor Black: Slavery and Race Relations in Brazil and the United States* (1971)
Dillon, Merton L., *Slavery Attacked: Southern Slaves and Their Allies, 1619–1865* (1990)
Douglass, Frederick, *The Narrative of the Life of Frederick Douglass* (1845)
Escott, Paul D., *Slavery Remembered: A Record of 20th-Century Slave Narratives* (1979)
Field, Barbara, *Slavery on the Middle Ground: Maryland During the Nineteenth Century* (1985)
Genovese, Eugene D., *From Rebellion to Revolution: Afro-American Slave Revolts in the Making of the Modern World* (1979)
Goldin, Claudia D., *Urban Slavery in the American South, 1820–1860* (1976)
Huggins, Nathan, *Slave and Citizen: The Life of Frederick Douglass* (1980)
Huggins, Nathan I., *Black Odyssey: The Afro-American Ordeal in Slavery* (1977)
Johnson, Michael P. and James L. Roark, *Black Masters: A Free Family of Color in the Old South* (1984)
Johnson, Michael P. and James L. Roark, *No Chariot Down: Charleston's Free People of Color on the Eve of the Civil War* (1984)
Jones, Jacqueline, *Labor of Love, Labor of Sorrow: Black Women, Work, and the Family from Slavery to the Present* (1985)
Joyner, Charles, *Down by the Riverside: A South Carolina Slave Community* (1984)
Levine, Lawrence W., *Black Culture and Black Consciousness: Afro-American Folk Thought from Slavery to Freedom* (1977)
Oates, Stephen B., *The Fires of Jubilee: Nat Turner's Fierce Rebellion* (1975)
Owens, Leslie H., *This Species of Property: Slave Life and Slave Culture in the Old South* (1976)
Raboteau, Albert, *Slave Religion: The "Invisible Institution" in the Antebellum South* (1978)
Rawick, George P., *From Sundown to Sunup: The Making of a Black Community* (1972)
Rose, Willie Lee, *A Documentary History of Slavery in North America* (1976)
Stampp, Kenneth, *The Peculiar Institution* (1956)
Starobin, Robert, *Industrial Slavery in the Old South* (1970)
Stuckey, Sterling, *Slave Culture: Nationalist Theory and the Foundation of Black America* (1987)
Tadman, Michael, *Speculators and Slaves: Masters, Traders, and Slaves in the Old South* (1989)
Webber, Thomas L., *Deep Like Rivers: Education in the Slave Quarters, 1831–1865* (1978)
White, Deborah Gray, *Arn't I a Woman?* (1985)

Chapter 12

Industrialization

Clemens, Paul G.E., *The Atlantic Economy and Colonial Maryland's Eastern Shore: From Tobacco to Grain* (1980)

Cochran, Thomas C., *Frontiers of Change: Early Industrialism in America* (1981)

Cochran, T.C. and William Miller, *The Age of Enterprise* (1942)

Coolidge, John, *Mill and Mansion: Architecture and Society in Lowell, Massachusetts, 1820–1860* (1942)

Dalzell, Robert F., Jr., *Enterprising Elite: The Boston Associates and the World They Made* (1987)

Douglass, E.P., *The Coming of Age of American Business* (1971)

Ferguson, Eugene, *Oliver Evans: Inventive Genius of the American Industrial Revolution* (1980)

Hunter, L.C., *A History of Industrial Power in the United States, 1780–1930, Vol. I, Waterpower in the Century of the Steam Engine* (1979)

Jeremy, David J., *Transatlantic Industrial Revolution: The Diffusion of Textile Technology Between Britain and America* (1981)

Labaree, Benjamin W., *The Merchants of Newburyport, 1764–1815* (1962)

Linstrom, Diane, *Economic Development in the Philadelphia Region, 1810–1850* (1978)

Rosenberg, Nathan, *Technology and American Economic Growth* (1972)

Smith, Merritt R., *Harpers Ferry Armory and the New Technology* (1977)

Tucker, Barbara, *Samuel Slater and the Origins of the American Textile Industry, 1790–1860* (1984)

Ware, Caroline F., *Early New England Cotton Manufacturing* (1931)

Workers

Blewett, Mary H., *Men, Women, and Work: Class, Gender, and Protest in the New England Shoe Industry, 1780–1910* (1988)

Brooke, John L., *The Heart of the Commonwealth: Society and Political Culture in Worcester County, Massachusetts, 1713–1861* (1989)

Doherty, Robert, *Society and Power: Five New England Towns, 1800–1860* (1977)

Faler, Paul G., *Mechanics and Manufacturers in the Early Industrial Revolution: Lynn, Massachusetts* (1981)

Frisch, Michael H., *Town into City: Springfield, Massachusetts and the Meaning of Community, 1840–1880* (1972)

Glickstein, Jonathan A., *Concepts of Free Labor in Antebellum America* (1991)

Hirsch, Susan E., *Roots of the American Working Class: The Industrialization of Crafts in Newark, 1800–1860* (1978)

Innes, Stephen, ed., *Work and Labor in Early America* (1988)

Jensen, Joan M., *Loosening the Bonds: Mid-Atlantic Farm Women, 1750–1850* (1986)

Larkin, Jack, *The Reshaping of Everyday Life, 1790–1840* (1988)

Laurie, Bruce, *Working People of Philadelphia, 1800–1850* (1980)

Rock, Howard, *Artisans of the New Republic: Tradesmen of New York City in the Age of Jefferson* (1979)

Rorabaugh, W.J., *The Craft Apprentice: From Franklin to the Machine Age in America* (1986)

Steffan, Charles G., *The Mechanics of Baltimore: Workers and Politics in the Age of Revolution, 1763–1812* (1984)

Middle Class

Boydston, Jeanne, *Home and Work* (1990)

Cott, Nancy E., *The Bonds of Womanhood: 'Woman's Sphere' in New England, 1780–1835* (1977)

Doyle, Don H., *The Social Order of the Frontier Community: Jacksonville, Illinois, 1825–1870* (1978)

Gordon, Linda, *Woman's Body, Woman's Rights: A Social History of Birth Control in America* (1976)

Griffen, Clyde and Sally Griffen, *Natives and Newcomers: The Ordering of Opportunity in Mid-Nineteenth-Century Poughkeepsie* (1978)

Halttunen, Karen, *Confidence Men and Painted Women: A Study of Middle-Class Culture in America, 1830–1870* (1982)

Kasson, John F., *Civilizing the Machine: Technology and Republican Values in America, 1776–1900* (1977)

Mohr, James C., *Abortion in America: The Origins and Evolution of National Policy, 1800–1900* (1978)

Pease, William and Jane, *The Web of Progress: Private Values and Public Styles in Boston and Charleston, 1828–1843* (1985)

Pessen, Edward, *Riches, Class, and Power Before the Civil War* (1973)

Reed, James, *From Private Vice to Public Virtue: The Birth Control Movement and American Society since 1830* (1978)

Rodgers, Daniel T., *The Work Ethic in Industrial America, 1850–1920* (1978)

Wallace, Anthony F.C., *Rockdale: The Growth of an American Village in the Early Industrial Revolution* (1977)

Chapter 13

Urban and Labor

Boyer, Paul, *Urban Masses and Moral Order in America, 1820–1920* (1978)

Bremner, R.H., *From the Depths* (1956)

Feldberg, Michael, *The Philadelphia Riots of 1844: A Study of Ethnic Conflict* (1975)

Gilje, Paul A., *The Road to Mobocracy: Popular Disorder in New York City, 1763–1834* (1987)

Gutman, Herbert G., *Work, Culture, and Society in Industrializing America: Essays in American Working-Class History* (1976)

Haeger, John Denis, *John Jacob Astor: Business and Finance in the Early Republic* (1991)

Horton, James Oliver and Lois E. Horton, *Black Bostonians: Family Life and Community Struggle in the Antebellum North* (1979)

Kasson, John F., *Rudeness and Civility: Manners in Nineteenth-Century America* (1990)

Kessler-Harris, Alice, *Out to Work: A History of Wage-Earning Women in the United States* (1982)

Knights, Peter, *The Plain People of Boston, 1830–1860* (1971)

Lott, Eric, *Love and Theft: Blackface Minstrelsy and the American Working Class* (1993)

Nash, Gary B., *Forging Freedom: Philadelphia's Black Community, 1720–1840* (1988)

Pelling, H.M., *American Labor* (1960)

Pessen, Edward, *Most Uncommon Jacksonians: The Radical Leaders of the Early Labor Movement* (1967)

Rayback, J.G., *History of American Labor* (1959)

Tyrrell, Ian, *Sobering Up: From Temperance to Prohibition in Antebellum America* (1979)

Warner, Sam Bass, *The Private City: Philadelphia in Three Periods of Its Growth* (1968)

Immigrants

Berthoff, Rowland, *British Immigrants in Industrial America* (1953)

Conzen, Kathleen Neils, *Immigrant Milwaukee, 1836–1860* (1976)

Diner, Hasia, *Erin's Daughters in America* (1983)

Dolan, Jay P., *The Immigrant Church: New York's Irish and German Catholics, 1815–1865* (1975)

Ernst, Robert, *Immigrant Life in New York City, 1825–1863* (1949)

Handlin, Oscar, *The Uprooted* (1951, second edition, 1973)

Hansen, Marcus L., *The Atlantic Migration, 1607–1860* (1940)

Hueston, Robert F., *The Catholic Press and Nativism, 1840–1860* (1976)

Jones, Maldwyn Allen, *American Immigration* (1960)

Miller, Kerby A., *Emigrants and Exiles: Ireland and the Irish Exodus to North America* (1985)

Nadel, Stanley, *Little Germany: Ethnicity, Religion, and Class in New York City, 1845–1880* (1990)

Rippley, LaVern J., *The German-Americans* (1976)

Ryan, Dennis P., *Beyond the Ballot Box: A Social History of the Boston Irish, 1845–1917* (1989)

Shannon, William V., *The American Irish: A Political and Social Portrait* (1989)

Taylor, Philip, *The Distant Magnet: European Emigration to the United States of America* (1971)

Wittke, Carl, *The Irish in America* (1956)

Wittke, Carl, *Refugees of Revolution: The German Forty-Eighters in America* (1952)

Religion, Reform, and Utopianism

Binder, F.M., *The Age of the Common School* (1974)

Brodie, Fawn, *No Man Knows My History: The Life of Joseph Smith, Mormon Prophet* (1945)

Carden, Maren Lockwood, *Oneida: Utopian Community to Modern Corporation* (1969)

Cremin, Lawrence, *American Education: The National Experience, 1783–1861* (1981)

Cross, Whitney R., *The Burned-Over District, The Social and Intellectual History of Enthusiastic Religion in Western New York, 1800–1850* (1950)

Dannenbaum, Jed, *Drink and Disorder: Temperance Reform in Cincinnati from the Washingtonian Revival to the WCTU* (1984)

Epstein, Barbara, *The Politics of Domesticity: Women, Evangelism, and Temperance in Nineteenth Century America* (1981)

Fellman, Michael, *The Unbounded Frame: Freedom and Community in Nineteenth-Century America Utopianism* (1973)

Ginzberg, Lori D., *Women and the Work of Benevolence: Morality, Politics, and Class in the 19th-Century United States* (1990)

Griffin, Clifford S., *Their Brothers' Keepers: Moral Stewardship in the United States* (1960)

Griffin, C.S., *The Ferment of Reform* (1967)

Grob, Gerald W., *Mental Institutions in America: Social Policy to 1875* (1973)

Hansen, Klaus J., *Mormonism and the American Experience* (1981)

Harrison, J.F.C., *Quest for the New Moral World: Robert Owen and the Owenites in Britain and America* (1969)

Kaestle, Carl F., *Pillars of the Republic: Common Schools and American Society, 1780–1860* (1983)

Katz, Michael, *The Irony of Early School Reform* (1968)

Kern, Louis J., *An Ordered Love: Sex Roles and Sexuality in Victorian Utopias — The Shakers, the Mormons, and the Oneida Community* (1981)

Kolmerten, Carol, *Women in Utopia* (1990)

Lender, M.E. and J.K. Martin, *Drinking in America: A History* (1982)

Lewis, W. David, *From Newgate to Dannemora: The Rise of the Penitentiary* (1965)

Mennel, Robert, *Thorns and Thistles* (1973)

O'Dea, Thomas F., *The Mormons* (1957)

Perry, Lewis, *Childhood, Marriage, and Reform: Henry Clark Wright, 1797–1870* (1980)

Rose, Ann C., *Transcendentalism as a Social Movement, 1830–1850* (1981)

Schultz, Stanley K., *The Culture Factory: Boston Public Schools, 1789–1860* (1973)

Smith, Timothy L., *Revivalism and Social Reform: American Protestantism on the Eve of the Civil War* (1980)

Soltow, Lee and Edward Stevens, *The Rise of Literacy and the Common School in the United States* (1981)

Stegner, Wallace, *The Gathering of Zion: The Story of the Mormon Trial* (1964)

Stewart, James B., *Holy Warriors: The Abolitionists and American Slavery* (1976)

Tyler, Alice F., *Freedom's Ferment: Phases of American Social History to 1860* (1944)

Tyrrell, I.R., *Sobering Up: From Temperance to Prohibition in Antebellum America, 1800–1860* (1979)

Abolitionism

Abzug, Robert H., *Passionate Liberator, Theodore Dwight Weld and the Dilemma of Reform* (1980)

Barnes, Gilbert H., *The Antislavery Impulse, 1830–1844* (1933)

Blackett, R.J.M., *Building an Antislavery Wall: Black Americans in the Abolitionist Movement, 1830–1860* (1983)

Davis, David Brion, *The Problems of Slavery in the Age of Revolution, 1770–1823* (1975)

Dillon, M.L., *The Abolitionists: The Growth of a Dissenting Minority* (1974)

Douglass, Frederick, *The Narrative of the Life of Frederick Douglass, An American Slave* (1845)

Douglass, Frederick, *My Bondage and My Freedom* (1855)

Filler, Louis, *The Crusade Against Slavery, 1830–1860* (1960)

Friedman, Lawrence J., *Gregarious Saints: Self and Community in American Abolitionism, 1830–1870* (1982)

Fuller, Edmund, *Prudence Crandall: An Incident of Racism in Nineteenth-Century America* (1978)

Gerteis, Louis, *Morality and Utility in American Antislavery Reform* (1987)

Hersh, Blanche, *The Slavery of Sex: Female Abolitionists in Nineteenth-Century America* (1978)

Huggins, Nathan I., *Slave and Citizen: The Life of Frederick Douglass* (1980)

Lerner, Gerda, *The Grimke Sisters from South Carolina: Pioneers for Women's Rights and Abolition* (1967)

Lutz, Alma, *Crusade for Freedom: Women of the Antislavery Movement* (1968)

Mabee, Carleton, *Black Freedom: The Nonviolent Abolitionists from 1830 through the Civil War* (1970)

Martin, Waldo E., *The Mind of Frederick Douglass* (1985)

Matthews, D.G., *Slavery and Methodism* (1965)

McFeely, William S., *Frederick Douglass* (1991)

McKivigan, J.R., *The War Against Proslavery Religion: Abolitionism and the Northern Churches* (1984)

Pease, Jane A. and William H. Pease, *They Who Would be Free: Blacks' Search for Freedom, 1830–1861* (1974)

Perry, Lewis, *Radical Abolitionism: Anarchy and the Government of God in Antislavery Thought* (1973)

Quarles, Benjamin, *Black Abolitionists* (1969)

Richards, Leonard L., *"Gentlemen of Property and Standing": Anti-Abolition Mobs in Jacksonian America* (1970)

Sorin, Gerald, *Abolitionism: A New Perspective* (1972)

Stewart, James B., *Holy Warriors: The Abolitionists and American Slavery* (1976)

Thomas, John L., *The Liberator: William Lloyd Garrison* (1963)

Walters, Ronald G., *The Antislavery Appeal: American Abolitionists After 1830* (1976)

Wyatt-Brown, Bertram, *Lewis Tappan and the Evangelical War Against Slavery* (1959)

Yellin, Jean Fagan, *Women & Sisters: The Antislavery Feminists in American Culture* (1989)

Zilversmit, Arthur, *The First Emancipation* (1967)

Women's Rights

Banner, Lois, *Elizabeth Cady Stanton* (1980)

Berg, Barbara J., *The Remembered Gate — Women and the City, 1800–1860* (1978)

Boydston, Jeanne et al., eds., *The Limits of Sisterhood: The Beecher Sisters on Women's Rights and Woman's Sphere* (1988)

Degler, Carl N., *At Odds: Women and the Family in America from the Revolution to the Present* (1980)

Dubois, Ellen C., *Feminism and Suffrage: The Emergence of an Independent Women's Movement in America, 1848–1869* (1978)

Griffith, Elisabeth, *In Her Own Right: The Life of Elizabeth Cady Stanton* (1984)

Melder, K.E., *Beginnings of Sisterhood: The American Women's Rights Movement, 1800–1850* (1977)

Weber, Sandra S., *Special History Study, Women's Rights National Historical Park, Seneca Falls, New York* (1985)

Chapter 14

Exploration, the Fur Trade, and Expansion

Brown, Jennifer S.H., *Strangers in Blood: Fur Trade Company Families in Indian Country* (1980)

Goetzmann, William H., *Exploration and Empire: The Explorer and the Scientist in the Winning of the American West* (1966)

Goetzmann, William H., *Army Exploration in the American West, 1803–1863* (1959)

Goetzmann, William H. and William N. Goetzmann, *The West of the Imagination* (1986)

Hafen, LeRoy R., ed., *The Mountain Men and the Fur Trade of the Far West,* 10 vols., (1968–1972)

Horsman, Reginald, *Race and Manifest Destiny* (1981)

Jeffrey, Julie Roy, *Frontier Women: The Trans-Mississippi West, 1840–1860* (1979)

Karaminski, Theodore J., *Fur Trade and Exploration: Opening of the Far Northwest, 1821–1852* (1983)

Limerick, Patricia Nelson, *The Legacy of Conquest: The Unbroken Past of the Unbroken West* (1987)

Merk, Frederick, *Manifest Destiny and Mission in American History: A Reinterpretation* (1963)

Merk, Frederick, *History of the Westward Movement* (1978)

Morgan, Dale, *Jedediah Smith and the Opening of the West* (1982)

Nabakov, Peter, ed., *Native American Testimony: An Anthology of Indian and White Relations* (1978)

Ronda, James P., *Astoria and Empire* (1990)

Smith, Henry Nash, *Virgin Land: The American West as Symbol and Myth* (1950)

Spicer, Edward H., *Cycles of Conquest: The Impact of Spain, Mexico, and the United States on the Indians of the Southwest, 1533–1960* (1981)

Trennert, Robert A., *Alternative to Extinction: Federal Indian Policy and the Beginnings of the Reservation System, 1846–1851* (1975)

Unruh, John I., Jr., *The Plains Across: Overland Emigrants and the Trans-Mississippi West, 1840–1860* (1979)

Van Kirk, Sylvia, "Many Tender Ties": Women in Fur Trade Society in Western Canada, 1670–1870 (1980)

Weinberg, Albert K., *Manifest Destiny: A Study of Nationalist Expansionism in American History* (1957)

Wiley, Peter Booth with Korogi Ichiro, *Yankees in the Land of the Gods: Commodore Perry and the Opening of Japan* (1990)

Wishart, David J., *The Fur Trade of the American West, 1807–1840: A Geographic Synthesis* (1979)

California and Oregon

Caughey, John W., *The California Gold Rush* (1975)

Clark, Malcolm, Jr., *Eden Seekers: The Settlement of Oregon, 1818–1862* (1981)

Daniels, Douglas H., *Pioneer Urbanites: A Social and Cultural History of Black San Francisco* (1980)

Gibson, James R., *Farming the Frontier: The Agricultural Opening of Oregon Country, 1786–1846* (1985)

Hurtado, Albert L., *Indian Survival on the California Frontier* (1988)

Johnson, David, *Founding the Far West: California, Oregon, and Nevada, 1840–1890* (1992)

Josephy, Alvin, *The Nez Perce and the Opening of the Northwest* (1965)

Paul, Rodman W., *California Gold: The Beginning of Mining in the Far West* (1974)

Pitt, Leonard, *The Decline of the Californios: A Social History of the Spanish-Speaking Californians, 1846–1890* (1966)

Rawls, James J., *Indians of California: The Changing Image* (1984)

Starr, Kevin, *Americans and the California Dream, 1850–1915* (1973)

Texas and the Mexican-American War

Bauer, K. Jack, *The Mexican War, 1846–1848* (1974)

Binkley, William C., *The Texas Revolution* (1952)

Brack, Gene M., *Mexico Views Manifest Destiny* (1976)

Conner, Seymour and Odie Faulk, *North America Divided: The Mexican War, 1846–1848* (1971)

De Leon, Arnoldo, *They Called Them Greasers: Anglo Attitudes Toward Mexicans in Texas, 1821–1900* (1983)

DeVoto, Bernard, *The Year of Decision, 1846* (1943)

Graebner, Norman A., *Empire on the Pacific: A Study in American Continental Expansion* (1955)

Harlow, Neil, *California Conquered: War and Peace on the Pacific, 1846–1850* (1982)

Horsman, Reginald, *Race and Manifest Destiny: The Origins of American Racial Anglo-Saxonism* (1981)

James, Marquis, *The Raven: The Story of Sam Houston* (1929)

Lander, Ernest McPherson, Jr., *Reluctant Imperialist: Calhoun, South Carolina, and the Mexican War* (1980)

Merk, Frederick, *Slavery and the Annexation of Texas* (1972)

Montejano, David, *Anglos and Mexicans in the Making of Texas, 1836–1986* (1987)

Morrison, Chaplain W., *Democratic Politics and Sectionalism: The Wilmot Proviso Controversy* (1967)

Pletcher, David, *The Diplomacy of Annexation: Texas, Oregon, and the Mexican War* (1973)

Rayback, Joseph G., *Free Soil: The Election of 1848* (1970)

Reichstein, Andreas V., *Rise of the Lone Star: The Making of Texas* (1989)

Schroeder, John H., *Mr. Polk's War: American Opposition and Dissent, 1846–1848* (1971)

Sellers, Charles G., *James K. Polk: Continentalist, 1843–1846* (1966)

Sellers, Charles G., *James K. Polk: Jacksonian, 1795–1843* (1957)

Silbey, Joel H., *The Shrine of Party: Congressional Voting Behavior, 1841–1852* (1967)

Singletary, Otis A., *The Mexican War* (1960).

Chapter 15

The Controversy Over Slavery

Abbott, Richard H., *Cotton and Capital: Boston Businessmen and Antislavery Reform, 1854–1868* (1991)

Berwanger, Eugene, *The Frontier Against Slavery: Western Anti-Negro Prejudice and the Slavery Extension Controversy* (1967)

Campbell, Stanley W., *The Slave Catchers* (1970)

Davis, D.B., *The Slave Power Conspiracy and the Paranoid Style* (1969)

Ehrlich, W., *They Have No Rights: Dred Scott's Struggle for Freedom* (1979)

Finkelman, P., *An Imperfect Union: Slavery, Freedom, and Comity* (1981)

Goen, C.C., *Broken Churches, Broken Nation* (1985)

Grossett, Thomas F., *Uncle Tom's Cabin and American Culture* (1985)

Herring, Joseph, *The Enduring Indians of Kansas: A Century and a Half of Acculturation* (1990)

McKivigan, J.R., *The War Against Proslavery Religion* (1984)

Miner, H. Craig and William E. Unrau, *The End of Indian Kansas* (1978)

Nevins, Allan, *The Ordeal of the Union,* vols. 1–2 (1947)

Nichols, Roy, *The Disruption of American Democracy* (1948)

Morris, Thomas D., *Free Men All: The Personal Liberty Laws of the North, 1780–1861* (1974)

Oates, Stephen, *To Purge This Land with Blood: A Biography of John Brown* (1970)

Rayback, Joseph G., *Free Soil: The Election of 1848* (1970)

Rossbach, J., *Ambivalent Conspirators: John Brown, the Secret Six, and a Theory of Black Political Violence* (1982)

Slaughter, Thomas P., *Bloody Dawn: The Christiana Riots and Racial Violence in the Antebellum North* (1991)

Stampp, Kenneth, *The Causes of the Civil War,* revised edition (1974)

Stratton, Joanna L., *Pioneer Women: Voices from the Kansas Frontier* (1981)

Wolff, Gerald W., *The Kansas-Nebraska Bill: Party, Section, and the Coming of the Civil War* (1977)
Wyatt-Brown, B., *Yankee Saints and Southern Sinners* (1985)

Political Realignment

Alexander, Thomas B., *Sectional Stress and Party Strength* (1967)
Anbinder, Tyler, *Nativism and Slavery: The Northern Know-Nothings and the Politics of the 1850's* (1992)
Baker, J.H., *Affairs of Party: The Political Culture of Northern Democrats in the Mid-Nineteenth-Century* (1983)
Bauer, K.J., *Zachary Taylor: Soldier, Planter, Statesman of the Old Southwest* (1985)
Blue, F.J., *The Free Soilers: Third Party Politics* (1973)
Donald, D.H., *Charles Sumner and the Coming of the Civil War* (1960)
Fehrenbacher, Don E., *Prelude to Greatness: Lincoln in the 1850's* (1962)
Forgie, G.B., *Patricide in the House Divided* (1981)
Formisano, Ronald, *The Birth of Mass Political Parties: Michigan, 1827–1861* (1971)
Gienapp, William E., *The Origins of the Republican Party, 1852–1856* (1987)
Holt, Michael, *Forging a Majority: The Formation of the Republican Party in Pittsburgh, 1848–1860* (1969)
Holt, Michael F., *The Political Crisis of the 1850's* (1978)
Jennings, Thelma, *The Nashville Convention* (1980)
Johannsen, Robert W., *Stephen A. Douglas* (1973)
Johannsen, R.W., *The Lincoln-Douglas Debates* (1965)
Kleppner, Paul, *The Third Electoral System, 1853–1892: Parties, Voters, and Political Cultures* (1979)
Mayfield, John, *Rehearsal for Republicanism: Free Soil and the Politics of Antislavery* (1980)
Oates, Stephen, *Without Malice Toward None: A Life of Abraham Lincoln* (1977)
Sewell, Richard, *Ballots for Freedom: Antislavery Politics in the United States, 1837–1865* (1976)

South

Brown, Charles H., *Agents of Manifest Destiny: The Lives and Times of the Filibusters* (1980)
Cooper, William J., *The South and the Politics of Slavery* (1978)
Craven, Avery O., *The Growth of Southern Nationalism, 1848–1861* (1953)
Donald, David, *Charles Sumner and the Coming of the Civil War* (1960)
Franklin, John Hope, *A Southern Odyssey: Travelers in the Antebellum North* (1976)
Franklin, John Hope, *The Militant South, 1800–1861* (1956)
Freehling, William W., *The Road to Disunion: Vol. I: Secessionists at Bay, 1776–1854* (1991)
Goetzmann, William H., *When the Eagle Screamed: The Romantic Horizon in American Diplomacy, 1800–1860* (1966)
Johnson, Michael P. and James L. Roark, eds., *No Chariot Let Down: Charleston's Free People of Color on the Eve of the Civil War* (1984)
May, Robert E., *The Southern Dream of a Caribbean Empire, 1854–1861* (1973)
McCardell, John, *The Idea of a Southern Nation: Southern Nationalists and Southern Nationalism, 1830–1861* (1979)
Osterweis, Rollin G., *Romanticism and Nationalism in the Old South* (1949)
Potter, D.M., *The South and the Sectional Conflict* (1968)
Rauch, Basil, *American Interest in Cuba* (1948)
Scroggs, William O., *Filibusters and Financiers: The Story of William Walker and His Associates* (1960)
Stout, Joe A., *The Liberators: Filibustering Expeditions into Mexico, 1848–1862, and the Last Thrust of Manifest Destiny* (1973)
Takaki, Ronald L., *A Proslavery Crusade: The Agitation to Reopen the African Slave Trade* (1971)
Thornton, J. Mills, *Politics and Power in a Slave Society* (1978)

Woodward, C. Vann, *American Counterpoint: Slavery and Racism in the North-South Dialogue* (1971)

Secession

Barney, W.L., *The Road to Secession* (1972)
Channing, Steven A., *Crisis of Fear: Secession in South Carolina* (1970)
Johnson, Michael P., *Toward a Patriarchal Republic: The Secession of Georgia* (1977)
Johnson, Michael, *Secession and Conservatism in the Lower South: The Social and Ideological Bases of Secession in Georgia, 1860–1861* (1983)
Potter, D.M., *Lincoln and His Party in the Secession Crisis* (1942)
Stampp, K.M., *And the War Came: The North and the Secession Crisis, 1860–61* (1950)
Wooster, R.A., *The Secession Conventions of the South* (1962)

Chapter 16

General

Davis, William C., *Jefferson Davis: The Man and His Hour* (1991)
Davis, Cullom, *The Public and Private Lincoln: Contemporary Perspectives* (1979)
Donald, David, *Liberty and Union* (1978)
Donald, David, ed., *Why the North Won the Civil War* (1960)
Foner, Eric, *Politics and Ideology in the Age of the Civil War* (1980)
McPhersen, James M., *Abraham Lincoln and the Second American Revolution* (1990)
Neely, Mark E., *The Fate of Liberty: Abraham Lincoln and Civil Liberties* (1991)
Parrish, Peter J., *The American Civil War* (1985)
Parrish, William E., *Turbulent Partnership: Missouri and the Union, 1861–1865* (1963)
Randall, James G. and David Donald, *The Civil War and Reconstruction,* second edition (1961)
Royster, Charles, *The Destructive War: William Tecumseh Sherman, Stonewall Jackson, and the Americans* (1991)
Thomas, John L., ed., *Abraham Lincoln and the American Political Tradition* (1986)
Vinovskis, Maris A., ed., *Toward a Social History of the American Civil War: Exploratory Essays* (1990)
Wills, Gary, *Lincoln at Gettysburg: Words that Remade America* (1992)

Military

Barton, Michael, *Good Men: The Character of Civil War Soldiers* (1981)
Beringer, Richard G. et al, *Why The South Lost the Civil War* (1986)
Berlin, Ira et al., eds., *Freedom, A Documentary History of Emancipation, 1861–1867, Series II, The Black Military Experience* (1982)
Burns, Ken, *The Civil War* (1990)
Catton, Bruce, *A Stillness at Appomattox* (1953)
Catton, Bruce, *Glory Road* (1952)
Catton, Bruce, *Mr. Lincoln's Army* (1951)
Cornish, Dudley, *The Sable Arm: Negro Troops in the Union Army, 1861–1865* (1956)
Foote, Shelby, *The Civil War: A Narrative,* 3 vols. (1958–1974)
Glatthaar, Joseph T., *Forged in Battle: The Civil War Alliance of Black Soldiers and White Officers* (1990)
Glatthaar, Joseph T., *The March to the Sea and Beyond: Sherman's Troops in the Savannah and Carolinas Campaign* (1985)
Hagerman, Edward, *The American Civil War and the Origins of Modern Warfare* (1988)
Hattaway, Herman and Archer Jones, *How the North Won: A Military History of the Civil War* (1984)
Hesseltine, William B., *Civil War Prisons: A Study in War Psychology* (1930)
Hyman, Harold, *A More Perfect Union* (1975)

Linderman, Gerald F., *Embattled Courage: The Experience of Combat in the American Civil War* (1987)

McPhersen, James M., *Ordeal By Fire* (1982)

Mitchell, Reid, *Civil War Soldiers* (1988)

Nevins, Allan, *The War for the Union*, 4 vols. (1959–1971)

Redkey, Edwin S., ed., *A Grand Army of Black Men: Letters from African-American Soldiers in the Union Army, 1861–1865* (1992)

Sears, Stephen W., *Landscape Turned Red: The Battle of Antietam* (1983)

Simpson, Lewis P., *Mind and the American Civil War* (1989)

Williams, T. Harry, *The History of American Wars* (1981)

Williams, T. Harry, *Lincoln and His Generals* (1952)

Black Experience

Belz, Herman, *A New Birth of Freedom: The Republican Party and Freedmen's Rights, 1861–1866* (1976)

Berlin, Ira et al., eds., *Freedom, A Documentary History of Emancipation, 1861–1867, Series I, Volume I: The Destruction of Slavery* (1985)

Berlin, Ira et al., eds., *Freedom, A Documentary History of Emancipation, 1861–1867, Series I, Volume III: The Wartime Genesis of Free Labor: The Lower South* (1990)

Berlin, Ira et al., *Slaves No More: Three Essays on Emancipation and the Civil War* (1992)

Franklin, John Hope, *The Emancipation Proclamation* (1963)

Gerteis, Louis S., *From Contraband to Freedom: Federal Policy Toward Southern Blacks, 1861–1865* (1973)

Hesseltine, William B., *Lincoln's Plan of Reconstruction* (1960)

Litwack, Leon, *Been in the Storm So Long: The Aftermath of Slavery* (1979)

McPherson, James M., *The Struggle for Equality: Abolitionists and the Negro in the Civil War and Reconstruction* (1964)

Quarles, Benjamin, *The Negro in the Civil War* (1953)

Rose, Willie Lee, *Rehearsal for Reconstruction: The Port Royal Experiment* (1964)

Wiley, B., *Southern Negroes, 1861–1865* (1938)

South

Crofts, Daniel W., *Reluctant Confederates: Upper South Unionists in the Secession Crisis* (1989)

Dew, C.B., *Ironmaker to the Confederacy* (1966)

Durden, R.F., *The Gray and the Black* (1972)

Eaton, Clement, *A History of the Southern Confederacy* (1954)

Faust, Drew Gilpin, *The Creation of Confederate Nationalism* (1988)

Myers, Robert M., ed., *The Children of Pride: A True Story of Georgia and the Civil War* (1972)

Paludan, Philip S., *Victims: A True History of the Civil War* (1981)

Rable, George C., *Civil Wars: Women and the Crisis of Southern Nationalism* (1989)

Ramsdell, Charles W., *Behind the Lines in the Southern Confederacy* (1944)

Roark, James L., *Masters Without Slaves: Southern Planters in the Civil War and Reconstruction* (1978)

Thomas, Emory M., *The Confederate Nation, 1861–1865* (1979)

Wiley, Bell I., *Road to Appomattox* (1956)

Wiley, Bell I., *The Plain People of the Confederacy* (1943)

North

Bensel, Richard Franklin, *Yankee Leviathan: The Origins of Central State Authority in America, 1859–1877* (1991)

Fite, E.D., *Social and Industrial Conditions in the North During the Civil War* (1910)

Frederickson, George M., *The Inner Civil War: Northern Intellectuals and the Crisis of the Union* (1965)

Gates, P.W., *Agriculture and the Civil War* (1965)

Klement, Frank L., *The Copperheads of the Middle West* (1960)

Rawley, James, *The Politics of Union: Northern Politics During the Civil War* (1974)

Sibley, Joel, *A Respectable Minority: The Democratic Party in the Civil War Era, 1860–1868* (1977)

Smith, George W. and Charles Judah, eds., *Life in the North During the Civil War* (1952)

Trefousse, Hans L., *The Radical Republicans* (1968)

Personal Narratives

Blue, Frederick J., *Salmon P. Chase: A Life in Politics* (1987)

Donald, David, *Charles Summer and the Rights of Man* (1970)

Donald, David, ed., *Inside Lincoln's Cabinet: The Civil War Diaries of Samuel P. Chase* (1959)

Evans, Eli N., *Judah P. Benjamin, The Jewish Confederate* (1988)

Freeman, Douglas S., *R.E. Lee: A Biography*, 4 vols. (1934–1935)

Grant, Ulysses S., *Memoirs and Selected Letters* (1990)

Higginson, T.W., *Army Life in a Black Regiment* (1867)

Schott, Thomas E., *Alexander H. Stephens of Georgia: A Biography* (1988)

Sears, Stephen W., *George B. McClellan: The Young Napoleon* (1988)

Sherman, W.T., *Memoirs* (1990)

Wiley, Bell I., *The Life of Johnny Reb* (1943)

Wiley, Bell I., *The Life of Billy Yank* (1952)

Chapter 17

General Studies

John Hope Franklin, *Reconstruction After the Civil War* (1961)

James McPherson, *Ordeal By Fire: The Civil War and Reconstruction* (1982)

Kenneth M. Stampp, *The Era of Reconstruction, 1865–1877* (1965)

National Politics and Constitutional Issues

Richard H. Abbott, *The Republican Party and the South, 1855–1877* (1986)

Herman Belz, *Emancipation and Equal Rights* (1978)

Michael Les Benedict, *A Compromise of Principle: Congressional Republicans and Reconstruction* (1974)

Fawn M. Brodie, *Thaddeus Stevens* (1959)

John Cox and LaWanda Cox, *Politics, Principles, and Prejudice* (1963)

Michael Kent Curtis, *No State Shall Abridge: The Fourteenth Amendment and the Bill of Rights* (1990)

David Donald, *Charles Sumner and the Rights of Man* (1970)

Eric Foner, *Politics and Ideology in the Age of the Civil War* (1980)

Harold M. Hyman, *A More Perfect Union* (1973)

Robert Kaczorowski, *The Politics of Judicial Interpretation* (1985)

Stanley I. Kutler, *Judicial Power and Reconstruction Politics* (1968)

Peyton McCrary, *Abraham Lincoln and Reconstruction* (1978)

Eric L. McKitrick, *Andrew Johnson and Reconstruction* (1960)

James M. McPherson, *The Struggle For Equality* (1964)

Earl M. Maltz, *Civil Rights, the Constitution, and Congress, 1863–1869* (1990)

William E. Nelson, *The Fourteenth Amendment* (1988)

Hans L. Trefousse, *Andrew Johnson* (1989)

———, *The Radical Republicans* (1969)

African Americans After Slavery

James D. Anderson, *The Education of Blacks in the South* (1989)

Ira Berlin, et al., eds., *Freedom: A Documentary History*, 3 vols. (1985–91)

John Blassingame, *Black New Orleans, 1860–1880* (1973)

Norman L. Crockett, *The Black Towns* (1979)

W.E.B. DuBois, *Black Reconstruction* (1935)

Barbara J. Fields, *Slavery and Freedom on the Middle Ground* (1985)

Eric Foner, *Nothing But Freedom* (1983)

Louis S. Gerteis, *From Contraband to Freedman* (1973)
Herbert G. Gutman, *The Black Family in Slavery and Freedom* (1976)
Thomas Holt, *Black Over White: Negro Political Leadership in South Carolina During Reconstruction* (1977)
Peter Kolchin, *First Freedom* (1972)
William S. McFeely, *Frederick Douglass* (1989)
Lynda J. Morgan, *Emancipation in Virginia's Tobacco Belt* (1992)
Nell Irvin Painter, *Exodusters* (1977)
Howard N. Rabinowitz, ed., *Southern Black Leaders in Reconstruction* (1982)
Joel Williamson, *After Slavery* (1965)

Postwar South

Roberta S. Alexander, *North Carolina Faces the Freedmen* (1985)
George Bentley, *A History of the Freedmen's Bureau* (1955)
Dan T. Carter, *When the War Was Over* (1985)
Richard N. Current, *Those Terrible Carpetbaggers* (1988)
Paul M. Gaston, *The New South Creed* (1970)
William C. Harris, *The Day of the Carpetbagger* (1979)
Elizabeth Jancoway, *Yankee Missionaries in the South* (1979)
Jacqueline Jones, *Soldiers of Light and Love: Northern Teachers and Georgia Blacks, 1865–1873* (1980)
William S. McFeely, *Yankee Stepfather: General O.O. Howard and the Freedmen* (1968)
Michael S. Perman, *Reunion Without Compromise* (1973)
——— , *The Road to Redemption* (1984)
Lawrence N. Powell, *New Masters: Northern Planters During the Civil War and Reconstruction* (1984)
George C. Rable, *But There Was No Peace: The Role of Violence in the Politics of Reconstruction* (1984)
Peter J. Rachleff, *Black Labor in the South: Richmond, Virginia, 1865–1890* (1984)
Roger L. Ransom and Richard Sutch, *One Kind of Freedom: The Economic Consequences of Emancipation* (1977)
James Roark, *Masters Without Slaves* (1977)
Laurence Shore, *Southern Capitalists* (1986)
Ted Tunnell, *Crucible of Reconstruction* (1984)
Michael Wayne, *The Reshaping of Plantation Society* (1983)
Jonathan M. Wiener, *Social Origins of the New South* (1978)
Sarah W. Wiggins, *The Scalawag in Alabama Politics* (1977)

The Northern Scene and the End of Reconstruction

Steven Buechler, *The Transformation of the Woman Suffrage Movement* (1986)
Phyllis F. Field, *The Politics of Race in New York* (1982)
William Gillette, *Retreat from Reconstruction, 1869–1879* (1979)
——— , *The Right to Vote* (1969)
Ari Hoogenboom, *Outlawing the Spoils* (1961)
Morton Keller, *Affairs of State* (1977)
James C. Mohr, ed., *Radical Republicans in the North* (1976)
David Montgomery, *Beyond Equality: Labor and the Radical Republicans, 1862–1872* (1967)
Keith Ian Polakoff, *The Politics of Inertia* (1973)
John C. Sproat, *"The Best Men": Liberal Reformers in the Gilded Age* (1968)
Margaret S. Thompson, *The "Spider Web": Congress and Lobbying in the Age of Grant* (1985)
Irwin Unger, *The Greenback Era* (1964)
C. Vann Woodward, *Reunion and Reaction: The Compromise of 1877 and the End of Reconstruction* (1956)

Chapter 18

Settlement and Farming

Arrington, Leonard J. and Davis Bitton, *The Mormon Experience*, 2d ed. (1992)
Billington, Monroe Lee, *Buffalo Soldiers, 1866–1900* (1991)
Billington, Ray Allen and Martin Ridge, *Westward Expansion*, 5th ed. (1982)
Fite, Gilbert C., *The Farmer's Frontier, 1865–1900* (1963)
Goetzmann, William H., *Exploration and Empire* (1966)
Hardy, B. Carmon, *Solemn Covenant: The Mormon Polygamous Passage* (1992)
Hine, Robert V., *The American West*, 2d ed. (1984)
Hine, Robert V., *Community on the American Frontier* (1980)
Hoig, Stan, *The Oklahoma Land Rush of 1889* (1984)
McMurry, Sally, *Families and Farmhouses in Nineteenth-Century America* (1988)
McQuillan, D. Aidan, *Prevailing Over Time: Ethnic Adjustment on the Kansas Prairies, 1875–1925* (1990)
Merk, Frederick, *History of the Westward Movement* (1978)
Paul, Rodman W., *The Far West: the Great Plains in Transition, 1859–1900* (1988)
Pisani, Donald J., *From Family Farm to Agribusiness* (1984)
Salamon, Sonya, *Prairie Patrimony: Family, Farming, and Community in the Midwest* (1992)
Williams, John Hoyt, *The Great & Shining Road: The Epic Story of the Transcontinental Railroad* (1988)
Winther, Oscar Osborn, *The Transportation Frontier: Trans-Mississippi West, 1865–1890* (1964)

Mining

Emmons, David M., *The Butte Irish: Class and Ethnicity in an American Mining Town, 1875–1925* (1989)
Goldman, Marion S., *Gold Diggers & Silver Miners: Prostitution and Social Life on the Comstock* (1981)
Lingenfelter, Richard E., *The Hardrock Miners* (1974)
Paul, Rodman, *Mining Frontiers of the Far West, 1848–1880* (1963)
Rohrbough, Malcolm J., *Aspen: The History of a Silver-Mining Town, 1879–1893* (1986)
Rowe, John, *Hard-Rock Men: Cornish Immigrants and the North American Mining Frontier* (1974)
Smith, Duane A., *Rocky Mountain Mining Camps* (1974)
Wyman, Mark, *Hard Rock Epic* (1979)

Cattle Industry

Allmendinger, Blake, *The Cowboy* (1992)
Dale, Edward Everett, *The Range Cattle Industry*, rev. ed. (1969)
Drago, Harry Sinclair, *The Great Range Wars* (1985)
Durham, Philip and Everett L. Jones, *The Negro Cowboys* (1965)
Dykstra, Robert R., *The Cattle Towns* (1968)
Erickson, John R., *Panhandle Cowboy* (1980)
Gordon, Terry G., *Trails to Texas: Southern Roots of Western Cattle Ranching* (1981)
Haywood, C. Robert, *Victorian West: Class and Culture in Kansas Cattle Towns* (1991)
Slatta, Richard, W., *Cowboys of the Americas* (1990)
Walker, Don D., *Clio's Cowboys: Studies in the Historiography of the Cattle Trade* (1981)
Wellman, Paul I., *The Trampling Herd: The Story of the Cattle Range in America* (1988)
Worcester, Don, *The Chisholm Trail* (1980)

Women Settlers

Armitage, Susan, Ruth B. Moynihan, and Christiane Fischer Dichamp, eds., *So Much to Be Done: Women Settlers on the Mining and Ranching Frontier* (1990)
Cordier, Mary Hulrbut, *Schoolwomen of the Prairie and Plains* (1993)
Fink, Deborah, *Agrarian Women: Wives and Mothers in Rural Nebraska, 1880–1940* (1992)
Hampsten, Elizabeth, *Read This Only to Yourself: The Private Writings of Midwestern Women, 1880–1910* (1982)
Jeffrey, Julie Roy, *Frontier Women* (1979)
Jensen, Joan M., *With These Hands: Women Working on the Land* (1981)

Juster, Norton, *So Sweet to Labor: Rural Women in America, 1865–1895* (1979)

Leckie, Shirley A., *Elizabeth Bacon Custer and the Making of a Myth* (1993)

Myres, Sandra L., *Westering Women and the Frontier Experience, 1800–1915* (1882)

Riley, Glenda, *Frontierswomen, The Iowa Experience* (1981)

Schlissel, Lillian, *Women's Diaries of the Westward Journey* (1982)

Schlissel, Lillian, and Vicki L. Ruiz and Janice Monk, eds. *Western Women* (1988)

Stratton, Joanna L., *Pioneer Women: Voices from the Kansas Frontier* (1981)

Indian Peoples and Indian-White Relations

Albers, Patricia and Beatrice Medicine, *The Hidden Half: Studies of Plains Indian Women* (1983)

Bender, Norman J., *"New Hope for the Indians": The Grant Peace Policy and the Navahos in the 1870s* (1989)

Blaine, Martha Royce, *Pawnee Passage: 1870–1975* (1990)

Coleman, Michael C., *American Indian Children at School, 1850–1930*

Dinnerstein, Leonard, Roger L. Nichols and David M. Reimers, *Natives and Strangers: Blacks, Indians and Immigrants in America*, 2d ed. (1990)

Drinnon, Richard, *Facing West: The Metaphysics of Indian-Hating and Empire Building* (1990)

Foster, Morris W., *Being Comanche: A Social History of an American Indian Community* (1991)

Fowler, Loretta, *Shared Symbols, Contested Meanings: Gros Ventre Culture and History, 1778–1984* (1987)

Grinnell, George Bird, *The Cheyenne Indians* (1962)

Hedren, Paul L., *First Scalp for Custer* (1980)

Hoxie, Frederick E., *A Final Promise: The Campaign to Assimilate the Indians, 1880–1920* (1984)

Hurtado, Albert L., *Indian Survival on the California Frontier* (1988)

Keller, Robert H., Jr., *American Protestantism and United States Indian Policy, 1869–82* (1984)

Mathes, Valerie Sherer, *Helen Hunt Jackson and her Indian Reform Legacy* (1990)

McDonnell, Janet A., *The Dispossession of the American Indian, 1887–1934* (1991)

Mihesuah, Deveon A., *Cultivating the Rosebud: The Education of Women at the Cherokee Female Seminary, 1851–1909* (1992)

Prucha, Francis P. *American Indian Policy in Crisis: Christian Reformers and the Indian* (1976)

Prucha, Francis Paul, *The Great Father: The United States Government and the American Indians* (2 vols., 1984)

Riley, Glenda, *Women and Indians on the Frontier, 1825–1915* (1984)

Utley, Robert M., *The Indian Frontier of the American West, 1846–1890* (1984)

Washburn, Wilcomb E., *The Indian in America* (1975)

White, Richard, *The Roots of Dependency: Subsistence, Environment, and Social Change among the Choctaws, Pawnees, and Navajos* (1983)

Wooster, Robert, *The Military and United States Indian Policy, 1865–1902* (1988)

Mexican-Americans

Barrera, Mario, *Race and Class in the Southwest* (1979)

Camarillo, Albert, *Chicanos in a Changing Society* (1979)

De Leon, Arnoldo, *They Called Them Greasers: Anglo Attitudes Toward Mexicans in Texas, 1821–1900* (1983)

Deutsch, Sarah, *No Separate Refuge: Culture, Class and Gender on an Anglo-Hispanic Frontier in the American Southwest, 1880–1940* (1987)

Griswold del Castillo, Richard, *La Familia: Chicano Families in the Urban Southeast, 1848 to the Present* (1984)

Griswold del Castillo, Richard, *The Los Angeles Barrio, 1850–1890* (1979)

Monroy, Douglas, *Thrown Among Strangers: The Making of Mexican Culture in Frontier California* (1993)

Montejano, David, *Anglos and Mexicans in the Making of Texas, 1836–1986* (1987)

Ortiz, Roxanne Dunbar, *Roots of Resistance: Land Tenure in New Mexico, 1680–1980* (1980)

Rosenbaum, Robert J., *Mexicano Resistance in the Southwest* (1981)

The West, The Land, and the Imagination

Berkhofer, Robert F., Jr., *The White Man's Indian: Images of the American Indian from Columbus to the Present* (1978)

Bold, Christine, *Selling the West: Popular Western Fiction, 1860–1960* (1987)

Emmons, David M., *Garden in the Grasslands: Boomer Literature of the Great Central Plains* (1971)

Goetzmann, William H. and William N. Goetzmann, *The West of the Imagination* (1986)

Logsdon, Guy, ed., *"The Whorehouse Bells Were Ringing" and Others Songs Cowboys Sing* (1989)

Malone, Michael P., ed. *Historians and the American West* (1983)

Marx, Leo, *The Machine in the Garden: Technology and the Pastoral Ideal in America* (1964)

Nash, Roderick, *Wilderness and the American Mind*, 3d ed., (1982)

Orsi, Richard J., Afred Runte, and Marlene Smith-Barazini, eds., *Yosemite and Sequoia: A Century of California National Parks* (1993)

Pisani, Donald J., *To Reclaim a Divided West: Water, Law, and Public Policy, 1848–1901* (1993)

Rock, Roger O., *The Native American in American Literature: A Selectively Annotated Bibliography* (1985)

Savage, William W., ed., *Cowboy Life: Reconstructing an American Myth* (1975)

Slotkin, Richard, *The Fatal Environment: The Myth of the Frontier in the Age of Industrialization, 1800–1890* (1985)

——— , *Gunfighter Nation: The Myth of the Frontier in 20th-Century America* (1992)

Smith, Henry Nash, *Virgin Land: The American West as Symbol and Myth* (1950)

Steadman, Raymond William, *Shadows of the Indian: Stereotypes in American Culture* (1982)

Trenton, Patricia and Peter H. Hassrick, *The Rocky Mountains: A Vision for Artists in the Nineteenth Century* (1983)

Chapter 19

Science, Technology, and Industry

Bruce, Robert V., *Alexander Graham Bell and the Conquest of Solitude* (1973)

Carlson, W. Bernard, *Innovation as a Social Process: Elihu Thomson and the Rise of General Electric, 1870–1900* (1991)

Hounshell, David A., *From the American System to Mass Production, 1800–1932* (1984)

Landes, David, *The Unbound Prometheus: Technological Change and Industrial Development* (1969)

McGaw, Judith A., *Most Wonderful Machine: Mechanization and Social Change in Berkshire Paper Making, 1801–1885* (1987)

Millard, A.J., *Edison and the Business of Innovation* (1990)

Reich, Leonard S., *The Making of American Industrial Research: Science and Business at G.E. and Bell, 1876–1926* (1985)

Segal, Howard, *Technological Utopianism in American Culture* (1985)

Business and the Economy

Bowman, John R., *Capitalist Collective Action: Competition, Cooperation, and Conflict in the Coal Industry* (1989)

Higgs, Robert, *The Transformation of the American Economy, 1865–1914* (1971)

———, *Competition and the Economy: Blacks in the American Economy, 1865–1914* (1977)

Hoogenboom, Ari and **Olive Hoogenboom,** *A History of the ICC* (1976)

Horwitz, Howard, *By the Law of Nature: Form and Value in Nineteenth Century America* (1990)

Ingham, John, *Iron Barons, A Social Analysis of an Urban Elite* (1978)

Klein, Maury, *The Life and Legend of Jay Gould* (1986)

Lamoreaux, Naomi R., *The Great Merger Movement in American Business, 1895–1904* (1985)

Leyendecker, Liston Edgington, *Palace Car Prince: A Biography of George Mortimer Pullman* (1992)

Livesay, Harold C., *Andrew Carnegie and the Rise of Big Business* (1975)

———, *American Made: Men Who Shaped the American Economy* (1979)

Nelson, Daniel, *Managers and Workers: Origins of the Factory System in the United States, 1880–1920* (1975)

Smith, George David, *From Monopoly to Competition, The Transformation of Alcoa, 1888–1986* (1988)

Watts, Sarah Lyons, *Order Against Chaos: Business Culture and Labor Ideology in America, 1800–1915* (1991)

Whitten, David O., *The Emergence of Giant Enterprise, 1860–1914* (1983)

Wyllie, Irvin G., *The Self-Made Man in America* (1954)

Working Class and Labor

Arnesen, Eric, *Waterfront Workers of New Orleans: Race, Class, and Politics, 1863–1923* (1991)

Avrich, Paul, *The Haymarket Tragedy* (1984)

Cumbler, John T., *Working-Class Community in Industrial America* (1979)

Fine, Lisa M., *The Souls of the Skyscraper: Female Clerical Workers in Chicago, 1870–1930* (1990)

Fink, Leon, *Workingmen's Democracy: The Knights of Labor and American Politics* (1983)

Hattam, Victoria C., *Labor Visions and State Power* (1993)

Katzman, David M., *Seven Days a Week: Women and Domestic Service in Industrializing America* (1978)

Livesay, Harold C., *Samuel Gompers and Organized Labor in America* (1978)

Montgomery, David., *The Fall of the House of Labor: The Workplace, the State, and American Labor Activism, 1865–1925* (1987)

Nelson, Bruce C., *Beyond the Martyrs: A Social History of Chicago's Anarchists, 1870–1900* (1988)

Oestreicher, Richard J., *Solidarity and Fragmentation: Working People and Class Consciousness in Detroit, 1875–1900* (1986)

Pacyga, Dominic A., *Polish Immigrants and Industrial Chicago* (1991)

Rodgers, Daniel T., *The Work Ethic in Industrial America, 1850–1920* (1978)

Ross, Stephen J. *Workers on the Edge: Work, Leisure, and Politics in Industrializing Cincinnati, 1788–1890* (1985)

Turbin, Carole, *Working Women of Collar City* (1992)

The Industrial City

Barth, Gunther Paul, *City People: The Rise of Modern City Culture in Nineteenth Century America* (1980)

Fried, Lewis F., *Makers of the City* (1990)

Garner, John S., ed., *The Midwest in American Architecture* (1991)

Gilbert, James, *Perfect Cities: Chicago's Utopias of 1893* (1991)

Hayden, Dolores, *The Grand Domestic Revolution: A History of Feminist Designs for American Homes, Neighborhoods, and Cities* (1981)

Hendrickson, Robert, *The Grand Emporiums: The Illustrated History of America's Great Department Stores* (1979)

Rosenzweig, Roy, and Elizabeth Blackmar, *The Park and the People: A History of Central Park*

Schuyler, David, *The New Urban Landscape* (1986)

Stilgoe, John R., *Borderland: Origins of the American Suburb, 1820–1939* (1988)

Twombly, Robert C., *Louis Sullivan* (1986)

Ward, David, *Cities and Immigrants* (1971)

———, *Poverty, Ethnicity, and the American City, 1840–1925* (1989)

The New South

Ayers, Edward L. *The Promise of the New South* (1992)

Bleser, Carol, ed., *In Joy and Sorrow: Women, Family, and Marriage in the Victorian South, 1830–1900* (1991)

Coclanis, Peter A., *The Shadow of a Dream: Economic Life and Death in the South Carolina Low Country, 1670–1920* (1989)

Doyle, Don H., *New Men, New Cities, New South* (1990)

Hall, Jacquelyn D., et al, *Like a Family: The Making of a Southern Cotton Mill World* (1987)

Jaynes, Gerald D., *Branches Without Roots: Genesis of the Black Working Class in the American South, 1862–1882* (1986)

Kane, Nancy Frances, *Textile in Transition* (1988)

Larsen, Lawrence H., *The Urban South* (1990)

McHugh, Cathy, *Mill Family: The Labor System in the Southern Textile Industry, 1880–1915* (1988)

McLaurin, Melton Alonza, *The Knights of Labor in the South* (1978)

Tullos, Allen, *Habits of Industry: White Culture and the Transformation of the Carolina Piedmont* (1989)

Wallenstein, Peter, *From Slave South to New South* (1987)

Wiener, Jonathan M., *Social Origins of the New South: Alabama, 1860–1885* (1978)

Woodward, C. Vann, *Origins of the New South, 1877–1913* (1966)

Wright, Gavin, *Old South, New South* (1986)

Society and Culture

Abelson, Elaine S., *When Ladies Go A-Thieving* (1989)

Barth, Gunther Paul, *Fleeting Moments: Nature and Culture in American History* (1990)

Blumin, Stuart, *The Emergence of the Middle Class* (1989)

Bushman, Richard L., *The Refinement of America* (1992)

Carnes, Mark C., *Secret Ritual and Manhood in Victorian America* (1989)

Clark, Clifford E., Jr., *The American Family Home, 1800–1960* (1986)

Cootkin, George, *Reluctant Modernism: American Thought and Culture, 1880–1900* (1992)

Duis, Perry, *The Saloon: Public Drinking in Chicago and Boston, 1880–1920* (1983)

Green, Harvey, *Fit For America: Health, Fitness, Sport, and American Society* (1986)

Hardy, Stephen, *How Boston Played: Sport, Recreation, and Community, 1865–1915* (1982)

Kasson, John F., *Rudeness and Civility: Manners in Nineteenth-Century Urban America* (1992)

Levine, Lawrence W., *Black Culture and Black Consciousness* (1977)

Levine, Peter, *A.G. Spalding and the Rise of Baseball* (1985)

McCarthy, Kathleen D., *Women's Culture: American Philanthropy and Art, 1830–1939* (1991)

Marks, Patricia, *Bicycle, Bangs, and Bloomers: The New Woman in the Popular Press* (1990)

Mintz, Steven, *A Prison of Expectations: The Family in Victorian Culture* (1983)

Novak, Barbara, *Nature and Culture: American Landscape Painting, 1825–1875* (1980)

Riess, Steven A., *City Games: The Evolution of American Urban Society and the Rise of Sports* (1989)

Schlereth, Thomas J., *Victorian America* (1991)

Solomon, Barbara M., *In the Company of Educated Women: A History of Women and Higher Education in America* (1985)

Stevenson, Louise L., *The Victorian Homefront: American Thought and Culture, 1860–1880* (1991)

Strasser, Susan, *Never Done: A History of American Housework* (1982)

Sutherland, Daniel E., *The Expansion of Everyday Life, 1860–1876* (1989)

Tyack, David B., *The One Best System: A History of American Urban Education* (1974)

Chapter 20

The Nation and Politics

Aron, Cindy Sondik, *Ladies and Gentlemen of the Civil Service* (1987)

Baker, Paula C., *The Moral Frameworks of Public Life: Gender, Politics, and the State in Rural New York, 1870–1930* (1991)

Gould, Lewis L., *The Presidency of William McKinley* (1981)

Hoffmann, Charles, *The Depression of the Nineties* (1970)

Hoogenboom, Ari A., *Outlawing the Spoils: History of the Civil Service Reform Movement, 1865–1883* (1961)

Keller, Morton, *Affairs of the State: Public Life in Late Nineteenth Century America* (1977)

Kleppner, Paul, *The Third Electoral System, 1853–1892* (1979)

Kousser, J. Morgan, *The Shaping of Southern Politics: Suffrage Restriction and the Establishment of a One-Party South* (1974)

Leech, Margaret and **Harry J. Brown,** *The Garfield Orbit* (1978)

McSeveney, Samuel T., *The Politics of Depression: Political Behavior in the Northeast, 1893–1896* (1972)

Mink, Gwendolyn, *Old Labor and New Immigrants in American Political Development* (1986)

Peskin, Allan, *Garfield: A Biography* (1978)

Rothman, David J., *Politics and Power: The United States Senate, 1869–1901* (1966)

Socolofsky, Homer E. and **Allan B. Spetter,** *The Presidency of Benjamin Harrison* (1987)

Terrill, Tom E., *The Tariff, Politics, and American Foreign Policy, 1874–1901* (1973)

Welch, Richard E., Jr., *The Presidencies of Grover Cleveland* (1988)

Populism

Argersinger, Peter H., *Populism and Politics: William Alfred Peffer and the People's Party* (1974)

Durden, Robert, *The Climax of Populism* (1965)

Hackney, Sheldon, *Populism to Progressivism in Alabama* (1969)

Hahn, Steven, *The Roots of Southern Populism* (1983)

Hicks, John D., *The Populist Revolt* (1961, c. 1931)

Martin, Donald B., *Women of the Grange* (1991)

McMath, Robert C., *Populist Vanguard: A History of the Southern Farmers' Alliance* (1975)

——— , *American Populism: A Social History* (1993)

McNall, Scott G., *The Road to Rebellion: Class Formation and Kansas Populism, 1865–1900* (1988)

Mitchell, Theodore R., *Political Education in the Southern Farmers Alliance, 1887–1900* (1987)

Nelson, Jane Taylor, ed., *A Prairie Populist: The Memoirs of Luna Kellie* (1992)

Nugent, Walter T.K., *The Tolerant Populists* (1963)

Parsons, Stanley B., *The Populist Context* (1973)

Pollack, Norman, *The Populist Response to Industrial America* (1962)

——— , *The Humane Economy: Populism, Capitalism, and Democracy* (1990)

Ridge, Martin, *Ignatius Donnelly* (1962)

Woodward, C. Vann, *Tom Watson* (1963)

Wright, James Edward, *The Politics of Populism: Dissent in Colorado* (1974)

Protest and Reform Movements

Beeton, Beverly, *Women Vote in the West: The Suffrage Movement, 1869–1896* (1986)

Bordin, Ruth, *Frances Willard: A Biography* (1986)

Bruce, Robert V., *1877: Year of Violence* (1959).

Buhle, Mari Jo and **Paul Buhle,** eds., *The Concise History of Woman Suffrage* (1978)

Curtis, Susan, *A Consuming Faith: The Social Gospel and Modern American Culture* (1991)

Epstein, Barbara Leslie, *The Politics of Domesticity: Women, Evangelism, and Temperance in Nineteenth-Century America* (1981)

Fogarty, Robert S., *All Things New: American Communes and Utopian Movements, 1860–1914* (1990)

Foner, Philip S., *The Great Labor Uprisings of 1877* (1977)

Frederick, Peter J., *Knights of the Golden Rule: The Intellectual as Christian Social Reformer in the 1890s* (1976)

Krause, Paul, *The Battle for Homestead, 1880–1892* (1992)

Luker, Ralph E., *The Social Gospel in Black and White* (1991)

Mann, Arthur, *Yankee Reformers in an Urban Age: Social Reform in Boston, 1880–1900* (1954)

Patai, Daphne, ed., *Looking Backward, 1988–1888: Essays on Edward Bellamy* (1988)

Roberts, Jon R., *Darwinism and the Divine in America: Protestant Intellectuals and Organic Evolution, 1859–1900* (1988)

Rooney, Charles, *Dreams and Visions: A Study of American Utopias, 1865–1912* (1985)

Salvatore, Nick, *Eugene V. Debs* (1982)

Schwantes, Carlos A., *Coxey's Army* (1985)

Sproat, John, *"The Best Men": Liberal Reformers in the Gilded Age* (1982, c. 1968)

Stromquist, Shelton, *A Generation of Boomers: The Pattern of Railroad Labor Conflict in Nineteenth Century America* (1987)

Thomas, John L., *Alternative America: Henry George, Edward Bellamy, Henrey Demarest Lloyd and the Adversary Tradition* (1983)

Imperialism & Empire

Beisner, Robert L., *Twelve Against Empire: The Anti-Imperialists, 1898–1900* (1968)

——— , *From Old Diplomacy to the New, 1865–1900* (1975)

Brands, H.W., *Bound to Empire: The United States and Empire* (1992)

Campbell, Charles S., *The Transformation of American Foreign Relations, 1865–1900* (1976)

Chauduri, Nupur, and **Margaret Strobel,** eds., *Western Women and Imperialism* (1992)

Dallek, Robert, *The American Style of Foreign Policy* (1983)

Dobson, John, *Reticent Expansionism: The Foreign Policy of William McKinley* (1988)

Gatewood, Willard B., Jr., *Black Americans and the White Man's Burden* (1975)

Healy, David, *United States Expansionism* (1970)

——— , *Drive to Hegemony: The United States in the Caribbean, 1888–1917* (1988)

Hill, Patricia, *The World Their Household: The American Woman's Foreign Mission Movement and Cultural Transformation, 1870–1920* (1985)

Hunter, Jane, *The Gospel of Gentility: American Women Missionaries in Turn-of-the-Century China* (1984)

Jensen, Ronald J., *The Alaska Purchase and Russian American Relations* (1975)

Marchand, C. Roland, *The American Peace Movement and Social Reform, 1898–1918* (1973)

Osborne, Thomas J., *"Empire Can Wait": American Opposition to Hawaiian Annexation, 1893–1898* (1981)

Ridge, Martin, ed., *History, Frontier, and Section: Three Essays by Frederick Jackson Turner* (1993)

Rydell, Robert W., *All the World's A Fair: Vision of Empire at American International Expositions, 1876–1916* (1984)

Weston, Rubin F., *Racism in American Imperialism* (1972)

Young, Marilyn Blatt, *American Expansionism* (1973)

Zwiep, Mary, *Pilgrim Path: The First Company of Women Missionaries to Hawaii* (1991)

Spanish-American War & the Philippines

Brands, H.W., *Bound to Empire: The United States and the Philippines* (1992)

Clymer, Kenton J., *Protestant Missionaries in the Philippines, 1898–1916* (1986)

Cosmas, Graham A., *An Army for Empire* (1971)

Gates, John M., *Schoolbooks and Krags: The United States Army in the Philippines, 1898–1902* (1973)

Healy, David, *The Drive to Hegemony: The United States in the Caribbean, 1898–1917* (1988)

Karnow, Stanley, *In Our Image: America's Empire in the Philippines* (1989)

Linderman, Gerald F., *The Mirror of War: American Society and the Spanish-American War* (1974)

Linn, Brian M., *The U.S. Army and Counterinsurgency in the Philippine War, 1898–1902* (1989)

May, Glenn Anthony, *Battle for Batangas: A Philippine Province at War* (1991)

——— , *Social Engineering in the Philippines: The Aims, Execution, and Impact of American Colonial Policy, 1900–1913* (1980)

Miller, Stuart Creighton, *"Benevolent Assimilation": The American Conquest of the Philippines, 1899–1903* (1982)

Offner, John L., *An Unwanted War: The Diplomacy of the United States and Spain over Cuba, 1895–1898* (1992)

Pomeroy, William J., *Philippines: Colonialism, Collaboration, Resistance* (1992)

Thompson, Winfred Lee, *The Introduction of American Law in the Philippines and Puerto Rico, 1889–1905* (1989)

Trask, David F., *The War with Spain in 1898* (1981)

Welch, Richard E., *Response to Imperialism: The United States and the Philippine-American War* (1979)

Chapter 21

General Studies

John D. Buenker, John C. Burnham, and **Robert M. Crunden,** *Progressivism* (1977)

John W. Chambers, *The Tyranny of Change: America in the Progressive Era* (1980)

Richard Hofstadter, *The Age of Reform: From Bryan to FDR* (1955)

Gabriel Kolko, *The Triumph of Conservatism* (1963)

Nell Irvin Painter, *Standing At Armageddon: The United States, 1877–1919* (1987)

Robert Wiebe, *The Search For Order* (1967)

Social Progressivism

Jane Addams, *Twenty Years at Hull House* (1910)

Mina Carson, *Settlement Folk* (1990)

Ruth H. Crocker, *Social Work and Social Order* (1991)

Robert M. Crunden, *Ministers of Reform* (1982)

Allen F. Davis, *American Heroine: The Life and Legend of Jane Addams* (1973)

William R. Hutchinson, *The Modernist Impulse in American Protestantism* (1982)

Roy Lubove, *The Progressives and the Slums* (1962)

Lillian Wald, *The House on Henry Street* (1931)

Urban and State Reform

John Allswang, *Bosses, Machines, and Urban Voters* (1977)

James B. Crooks, *Politics and Progress: The Rise of Urban Progressivism in Baltimore* (1968)

Dewey Grantham, *Southern Progressivism* (1983)

J. Joseph Huthmacher, *Senator Robert F. Wagner and the Rise of Urban Liberalism* (1971)

Richard L. McCormick, *From Realignment to Reform: Political Change in New York State, 1893–1910* (1981)

Zane L. Miller, *Boss Cox's Cincinnati* (1968)

George Mowry, *California Progressives* (1951)

Bradley Rice, *Progressive Cities* (1977)

Martin J. Schiesl, *The Politics of Efficiency* (1977)

Jon C. Teaford, *The Unheralded Triumph: City Government in America, 1870–1900* (1984)

David P. Thelen, *The New Citizenship: Origins of Progressivism in Wisconsin* (1972)

Immigration and Labor

John Bodnar, *Immigration and Industrialization* (1977)

——— , *The Transplanted* (1985)

Roger Daniels, *Coming to America* (1990)

Melvyn Dubofsky, *We Shall Be All: A History of the Industrial Workers of the World* (1969)

——— , *Industrialism and the American Worker* (1985)

Alice Kessler-Harris, *Out to Work: A History of Wage Earning Women in the United States* (1982)

Michael Kazin, *Barons of Labor* (1981)

John Laslett, *Labor and the Left* (1974)

Matt S. Meier and **Feliciano Rivera,** *The Chicanos* (1972)

David Montgomery, *The Fall of the House of Labor* (1987)

Moses Rischin, *The Promised City: New York's Jews, 1870–1914* (1962)

Roy Rosenzweig, *Eight Hours for What We Will* (1983)

Nick Salvatore, *Eugene V. Debs* (1982)

Maxine Schwartz Seller, *Immigrant Women* (1981)

Leon Stein, *The Triangle Fire* (1962)

Ronald Takaki, *Strangers From A Different Shore: A History of Asian Americans* (1989)

James Weinstein, *The Decline of Socialism in America, 1912–1925* (1967)

Progressive Thought and Culture

Burton Bledstein, *The Culture of Professionalism* (1976)

Kathleen Brady, *Ida Tarbell* (1984)

Arthur W. Ekrich, *Progressivism in America* (1974)

Louis Filler, *The Muckrakers* (rev. ed., 1980)

Leslie Fishbein, *Rebels in Bohemia* (1982)

Charles Forcey, *The Crossroads of Liberalism* (1961)

Lynn D. Gordon, *Gender and Higher Education in the Progressive Era* (1990)

Leon Harris, *Upton Sinclair* (1975)

Thomas L. Haskell, *The Emergence of Professional Social Science* (1977)

Justin Kaplan, *Lincoln Steffens* (1974)

T.J. Jackson Lears, *No Place of Grace* (1981)

David W. Noble, *The Progressive Mind* (rev. ed., 1981)

Daniel T. Rodgers, *The Work Ethic in Industrial America* (1978)

Robert Westbrook, *John Dewey and American Democracy* (1991)

Rebecca Zurier, *Art for the Masses* (1988)

Social Control

Norman H. Clark, *Deliver Us From Evil: An Interpretation of American Prohibition* (1976)

Marc T. Connelly, *The Response to Prostitution in the Progressive Era* (1980)

Samuel Haber, *Efficiency and Uplift* (1964)

John Higham, *Strangers in the Land: Patterns of American Nativism, 1860–1925* (1955)

David Pivar, *Purity Crusade* (1973)

Ruth Rosen, *The Lost Sisterhood: Prostitutes in America, 1900–1918* (1982)

James T. Timberlake, *Prohibition and the Progressive Movement* (1963)

David Tyack and **Elizabeth Hansot,** *Managers of Virtue: Public School Leadership in America, 1820–1980* (1982)

Women

Paula Baker, *The Moral Frameworks of Public Life* (1991)
Karen Blair, *The Clubwoman as Feminist* (1980)
Mari Jo Buhle, *Women and American Socialism* (1983)
Nancy Cott, *The Grounding of Modern Feminism* (1987)
Nancy Shrom Dye, *As Equal As Sisters* (1981)
Linda Gordon, *Woman's Body, Woman's Right: A Social History of Birth Control* (1976)
David M. Kennedy, *Birth Control in America: The Career of Margaret Sanger* (1970)
Ellen C. Lagemann, *A Generation of Women* (1979)
Elaine Tyler May, *Great Expectations: Marriage and Divorce in Post Victorian America* (1980)
William O'Neill, *Divorce in the Progressive Era* (1967)
Rosalind Rosenberg, *Beyond Separate Spheres* (1982)
Elyce J. Rotella, *From Home to Office* (1981)

African Americans

George Fredrickson, *The Black Image in the White Mind* (1971)
Louis R. Harlan, *Booker T. Washington* (1983)
———— , *Separate and Unequal* (1968)
Charles F. Kellogg, *NAACP* (1967)
J. Morgan Kousser, *The Shaping of Southern Politics* (1974)
James McPherson, *The Abolitionist Legacy* (1975)
W. Manning Marable, *W.E.B. DuBois* (1986)
Donald Spivey, *Schooling for the New Slavery* (1978)
Joel Williamson, *The Crucible of Race* (1985)

National Progressivism

John M. Blum, *The Progressive Presidents* (1980)
John M. Cooper, Jr., *The Warrior and the Priest: Theodore Roosevelt and Woodrow Wilson* (1983)
Lewis Gould, *Reform and Regulation* (1978)
Samuel Hays, *Conservation and the Gospel of Efficiency* (1959)
Arthur S. Link, *Woodrow Wilson and the Progressive Era* (1963)
Thomas K. McCraw, *Prophets of Regulation* (1984)
Michael McGerr, *The Decline of Popular Politics* (1986)
Edmund Morris, *The Rise of Theodore Roosevelt* (1979)
James Penick, Jr., *Progressive Politics and Conservation* (1968)
Melvin I. Urofsky, *Louis D, Brandeis and the Progressive Tradition* (1981)
Robert Wiebe, *Businessmen and Reform* (1962)

Chapter 22

A New World Power

James R. Anderson, *William Howard Taft* (1973)
Richard H. Collin, *Theodore Roosevelt's Caribbean* (1990)
John Dobson, *America's Ascent* (1978)
Akira Iriye, *Pacific Estrangement* (1972)
Burton I. Kaufman, *Efficiency and Expansion* (1974)
Walter LaFeber, *The Panama Canal* (1978)
Lester E. Langley, *The Banana Wars* (1983)
Frederick W. Marks, *Velvet on Iron: The Diplomacy of Theodore Roosevelt* (1979)
David McCullough, *The Path Between the Seas* (1977)
Dana G. Munro, *Intervention and Dollar Diplomacy in the Caribbean, 1900–1921* (1964)
Emily Rosenberg, *Spreading the American Dream* (1982)
Robert F. Smith, *The United States and Revolutionary Nationalism in Mexico* (1972)
William A. Williams, *The Roots of the Modern American Empire* (1969)

The War Abroad

Arthur Barbeau and **Florette Henri,** *The Unknown Soldiers: Black American Troops in World War I* (1974)
John W. Chambers, *To Raise an Army* (1987)
John Coogan, *The End of Neutrality* (1981)
John M. Cooper, Jr., *The Vanity of Power: American Isolation and the First World War* (1969)
Patrick Devlin, *Too Proud to Fight* (1974)
Lloyd Gardner, *Safe for Democracy* (1984)
Ross Gregory, *The Origins of American Intervention in the First World War* (1977)
Robert Jackson, *At War With the Bolshevik: The Allied Intervention Into Russia, 1917–1920* (1972)
N. Gordon Levin, Jr., *Woodrow Wilson and World Politics* (1968)
Ernest R. May, *The World War and American Isolation, 1914–1917* (1966)
Jeffrey Safford, *Wilsonian Maritime Diplomacy* (1977)
Donald Smythe, *Pershing* (1986)
Laurence Stallings, *The Doughboys* (1963)

The Home Front

Daniel R. Beaver, *Newton D. Baker and the American War Effort, 1917–1918* (1966)
Allen Brandt, *No Magic Bullet* (1985)
William J. Breen, *Uncle Sam at Home* (1984)
Norman H. Clark, *Deliver Us From Evil: An Interpretation of American Prohibition* (1976)
John Clifford, *Citizen Soldiers* (1972)
Valerie J. Conner, *The National War Labor Board* (1983)
Robert D. Cuff, *The War Industries Board* (1973)
John P. Finnegan, *Against the Specter of the Dragon: The Campaign for American Military Preparedness* (1974)
Charles Gilbert, *American Financing of World War I* (1970)
Carol S. Guber, *Mars and Minerva: World War I and the Uses of Higher Learning in America* (1975)
Frank L. Grubbs, Jr., *Samuel Gompers and the Great War* (1982)
Michael T. Isenberg, *War on Film* (1981)
Aileen Kraditor, *Ideas of the Woman Suffrage Movement* (1965)
Harold Lasswell, *Propaganda Technique in the World War* (1938)
John F. McClymer, *War and Welfare* (1980)
David Morgan, *Suffragists and Democrats* (1972)
Harold C. Peterson, *Propaganda for War* (1968)
Jordan Schwarz, *The Speculator: Bernard M. Baruch in Washington, 1917–1965* (1981)
Barbara Steinson, *American Women's Activism in World War I* (1982)
James Timberlake, *Prohibition and the Progressive Movement* (1970)
Stephen Vaughn, *Holding Fast the Inner Lines: Democracy, Nationalism, and the Committee on Public Information* (1979)

Dissent and Repression

Zechariah Chafee, Jr., *Free Speech in the United States* (1941)
Frederick C. Luebke, *Bonds of Loyalty: German Americans and World War I* (1974)
Roland Marchand, *The American Peace Movement and Social Reform* (1973)
Paul Murphy, *World War I and the Origins of Civil Liberties* (1979)
Gerald Patton, *War and Race: The Black Officer in the American Military* (1981)
Harold C. Peterson and **Gilbert Fite,** *Opponents of War, 1917–1918* (1968)
Richard Polenberg, *Fighting Faiths: The Abrams Case, the Supreme Court, and Free Speech* (1987)
William Preston, Jr., *Aliens and Dissenters* (1966)
Anne Wiltsher, *Most Dangerous Women: Feminist Peace Campaigners of the Great War* (1985)

Race Relations and Red Scare

David Brody, *Labor in Crisis: The Steel Strike of 1919* (1965)
Stanley Coben, *A. Mitchell Palmer* (1963)
Robert L. Friedheim, *The Seattle General Strike* (1965)
James P. Grossman, *Land of Hope: Chicago, Black Southerners, and the Great Migration* (1989)
Robert Haynes, *A Night of Violence: The Houston Riot of 1917* (1976)
Florette Henri, *Black Migration* (1975)
Robert K. Murray, *Red Scare* (1955)
Elliott M. Rudwick, *Race Riot at East St. Louis* (1964)
Francis Russell, *A City in Terror* (1975)
Emmett J. Scott, *Negro Migration During the War* (1920)
Alan Spear, *Black Chicago* (1967)
Judith Stein, *The World of Marcus Garvey* (1986)
William M. Tuttle, Jr., *Race Riot: Chicago in the Red Summer of 1919* (1970)
Theodore Vincent, *Black Power and the Garvey Movement* (1971)

Peace and the Aftermath of War

Lloyd Ambrosius, *Woodrow Wilson and the American Diplomatic Tradition* (1987)
Wesley M. Bagby, *The Road to Normalcy: The Presidential Campaign and Election of 1920* (1962)
Kendrick Clements, *The Presidency of Woodrow Wilson* (1992)
Robert Ferrell, *Woodrow Wilson and World War I* (1985)
Paul Fussell, *The Great War and Modern Memory* (1975)
Arthur S. Link, *Woodrow Wilson: War, Revolution, and Peace* (1979)
Arno Mayer, *Politics and Diplomacy of Peacemaking* (1965)
Charles Mee, Jr., *The End of Order, Versailles, 1919* (1980)
Burl Noggle, *Into the Twenties* (1974)
Stuart Rochester, *American Liberal Disillusionment in the Wake of World War I* (1977)
Ralph A. Stone, *The Irreconcilables* (1970)
Arthur Walworth, *America's Moment: American Diplomacy at the End of World War I* (1977)
Stephen R. Ward, ed., *The War Generation: Veterans of the First World War* (1975)
William C. Widenor, *Henry Cabot Lodge and the Search for an American Foreign Policy* (1980)

Chapter 23

General Studies

Paul A. Carter, *Another Part of the Twenties* (1977)
William Leuchtenberg, *The Perils of Prosperity* (1958)
Geoffrey Perrett, *America in the Twenties* (1982)
David Shannon, *Between the Wars* (1979)

The State and Business

Guy Alchon, *The Invisible Hand of Planning* (1985)
Louis Galambos and **Joseph Pratt,** *The Rise of the Corporate Commonwealth* (1988)
James Gilbert, *Designing the Industrial State* (1972)
Ellis W. Hawley, *Herbert Hoover as Secretary of Commerce* (1974)
John D. Hicks, *Republican Ascendancy* (1960)
Donald R. McCoy, *Calvin Coolidge* (1967)
Robert K. Murray, *The Politics of Normalcy* (1973)
Eugene Trani and **David Wilson,** *The Presidency of Warren G. Harding* (1977)
Mira Wilkins, *The Maturing of Multinational Enterprise* (1974)
Joan Hoff Wilson, *American Business and Foreign Policy* (1971)
——— , *Herbert Hoover* (1975)
Robert Zieger, *Republicans and Labor* (1969)

The Price of Prosperity

Adolph A. Berle and **Gardiner F. Means,** *The Modern Corporation and Private Property* (rev. ed., 1969)
Irving Bernstein, *The Lean Years: A History of the American Worker, 1920–1933* (1960)
Alfred D. Chandler, *Strategy and Structure* (1962)
Lizabeth Cohen, *Making A New Deal: Industrial Workers in Chicago, 1919–1939* (1990)
Ronald Edsforth, *Class Conflict and Cultural Consensus* (1987)
Gilbert C. Fite, *American Farmers* (1981)
Stephen Meyer, *The Five Dollar Day* (1981)
John Rae, *The Road and the Car in American Life* (1971)
Gerald Zahavi, *Workers, Managers and Welfare Capitalism* (1988)
Ronald W. Schatz, *The Electrical Workers* (1983)
Gwendolyn Wright, *Building the American Dream* (1981)

The New Mass Culture

Tino Balio, ed., *The American Film Industry* (rev. ed., 1985)
Robert Creamer, *Babe* (1974)
Daniel J. Czitrom, *Media and the American Mind* (1982)
Edwin and **Michael Emery,** *The Press in America* (rev. ed., 1976)
John D'Emilio and **Estelle B. Freedman,** *Intimate Matters: A History of Sexuality in America* (1988)
Susan J. Douglas, *Inventing American Broadcasting* (1987)
Stuart Ewen, *Captains of Consciousness* (1976)
Stephen Fox, *The Mirror Makers* (1984)
Neal Gabler, *An Empire of Their Own: How the Jews Invented Hollywood* (1988)
Roland Gelatt, *The Fabulous Phonograph* (rev. ed., 1977)
J. Fred MacDonald, *Don't Touch That Dial* (1979)
Lary May, *Screening Out the Past: The Birth of Mass Culture and the Motion Picture Industry* (1980)
Randy Roberts, *Jack Dempsey* (1979)
David Robinson, *Chaplin* (1985)
Philip T. Rosen, *The Modern Stentors: Radio Broadcasting and the Federal Government, 1920–1933* (1980)

Resistance to Modernity

Loren Baritz, ed., *The Culture of the Twenties* (1970)
David Chalmers, *Hooded Americanism* (1965)
Robert Divine, *American Immigration Policy* (1957)
Joseph Gusfeld, *Symbolic Crusade* (1963)
John Higham, *Strangers in the Land* (1955)
Kenneth T. Jackson, *The Ku Klux Klan in the City* (1967)
K. Austin Kerr, *Organized for Prohibition* (1985)
Lawrence W. Levine, *Defender of the Faith, William Jennings Bryan* (1965)
George M. Marsden, *Fundamentalism and American Culture* (1980)
Andrew Sinclair, *Prohibition* (1962)

Promises Postponed

Jervis Anderson, *This Was Harlem* (1982)
Carlos Baker, *Ernest Hemingway* (1969)
Mary Campbell, *Harlem Renaissance: Art of Black America* (1987)
Ruth Schwartz Cowan, *More Work for Mother* (1983)
Robert Crunden, *From Self to Society* (1972)
Paula Fass, *The Damned and the Beautiful* (1977)
David L. Lewis, *When Harlem Was in Vogue* (1981)
George H. Douglas, *H.L. Mencken* (1978)
Mark Reisler, *By the Sweat of Their Brow: Mexican Immigrant Labor in the U.S., 1900–1940* (1976)
Sheila Rothman, *Woman's Proper Place* (1978)
Lois Scharf, *To Work and To Wed* (1980)
Joe Trotter, *Black Milwaukee* (1985)

Kenneth M. Wheller and **Virginia L. Lussier,** eds., *Women and the Arts and the 1920s in Paris and New York* (1982)
Edmund Wilson, *The Twenties* (1975)

The Election of 1928

Kristi Anderson, *The Creation of a Democratic Majority, 1928–1936* (1979)
Paula Elder, *Governor Alfred E. Smith: The Politician as Reformer* (1983)
Matthew and **Hannah Josephson,** *Al Smith* (1970)
Allan J. Lichtman, *Prejudice and the Old Politics* (1979)
Elisabeth Perry, *Belle Moskowitz: Feminine Politics and the Exercise of Power in the Age of Alfred E. Smith* (1987)

Chapter 24

The Great Depression and Its Impact

James Agee, *Let Us Now Praise Famous Men* (1941)
Ann Banks, *First Person America* (1980)
Michael A. Bernstein, *The Great Depression* (1988)
Peter Fearon, *War, Prosperity, and Depression* (1987)
John K. Galbraith, *The Great Crash, 1929* (1961)
James M. Gregory, *American Exodus: The Dust Bowl Migration and Okie Culture in California* (1989)
Federal Writers Project, *These Are Our Lives* (1939)
Susan Kennedy, *The Banking Crisis of 1933* (1973)
Charles Kindleberger, *The World in Depression, 1929–1939* (1973)
Robert S. McElvaine, ed., *Down and Out in the Great Depression* (1983)
Janet Poppendieck, *Breadlines Knee-Deep in Wheat* (1986)
Tom E. Terrill and **Jerrold Hirsch,** eds., *Such as Us: Southern Voices of the Thirties* (1978)

FDR and the New Deal

Bernard Bellush, *The Failure of the NRA* (1975)
Lyle Dorsett, *Franklin D. Roosevelt and the City Bosses* (1977)
Steve Fraser and **Gary Gerstle,** eds., *The Rise and Fall of the New Deal Order* (1988)
Frank Freidel, *Franklin D. Roosevelt,* 4 vols. (1952–73)
Ellis W. Hawley, *The New Deal and the Problem of Monopoly* (1965)
Norris Hundley, Jr., *The Great Thirst: California and Water, 1770s–1990s* (1992)
J. Joseph Huthmacher, *Robert F. Wagner and the Rise of Urban Liberalism* (1968)
Joseph Lash, *Dealers and Dreamers* (1988)
William Leuchtenberg, *In the Shadow of FDR* (1983)
Roy Lubove, *The Struggle for Social Security* (1968)
Thomas McCraw, *TVA and the Public Power Fight* (1970)
George McJimsey, *Harry Hopkins* (1987)
Paul Mertz, *The New Deal and Southern Rural Poverty* (1978)
Ted Morgan, *FDR: A Biography* (1985)
James S. Olson, *Saving Capitalism* (1988)
James Patterson, *Congressional Conservatives and the New Deal* (1967)
——— , *The New Deal and the States* (1969)
——— , *America's Struggle Against Poverty* (1981)
Frances Perkins, *The Roosevelt I Knew* (1946)
Van L. Perkins, *Crisis in Agriculture* (1969)
Albert Romasco, *The Politics of Recovery* (1983)
John Salmond, *The Civilian Conservation Corps* (1967)
Theodore M. Saloutos, *The American Farmer and the New Deal* (1982)
Geoffrey Ward, *A First Class Temperament: The Emergence of Franklin Roosevelt* (1989)
Donald Worster, *Dust Bowl* (1979)

Protest and Dissent

David H. Bennett, *Demagogues in the Depression* (1969)
Alan Brinkley, *Voices of Protest: Huey Long, Father Coughlin, and the Great Depression* (1982)
Abraham Holzman, *The Townsend Movement* (1963)
Leo Ribuffo, *The Old Christian Right* (1983)
T. Harry Williams, *Huey Long* (1969)

Labor and the Left

John Barnard, *Walter Reuther and the Rise of the Auto Workers* (1983)
Irving Bernstein, *The Turbulent Years* (1970)
——— , *A Caring Society: The New Deal, the Worker, and the Great Depression* (1985)
Bert Cochran, *Labor and Communism* (1977)
Steven Fraser, *Labor Will Rule: Sidney Hillman and the Rise of American Labor* (1991)
Joshua B. Freeman, *In Transit: The Transport Workers Union in New York City, 1933–1966* (1989)
Peter Friedlander, *The Emergence of a UAW Local* (1975)
Gary Gerstle, *Working Class Americanism* (1989)
Robin D.G. Kelley, *Hammer and Hoe: Alabama Communists During the Great Depression* (1990)
Harvey Klehr, *The Heyday of American Communism* (1984)
Alice and Staughton Lynd, eds., *Rank and File* (1973)
Mark Naison, *Communists in Harlem During the Depression* (1983)
Bruce Nelson, *Workers on the Waterfront* (1988)
Robert Rosenstone, *Crusade of the Left: The Lincoln Battalion in the Spanish Civil War* (1969)
Ronald Schatz, *The Electrical Workers* (1983)
Robert H. Zieger, *John L. Lewis* (1988)

Depression Era Culture

Andrew Bergman, *We're In the Money: Depression America and Its Films* (1971)
Stanley Dance, *The World of Swing* (1974)
Richard McKinzie, *The New Deal for Artists* (1973)
Jere Mangione, *The Dream and the Deal: The Federal Writers' Project, 1935–1943* (1972)
Jane deHart Matthews, *The Federal Theater* (1967)
Francis O'Connor, ed., *Art for the Millions* (1973)
Karen Becker Orhn, *Dorothea Lange and the Documentary Tradition* (1980)
Marlene Park and **Gerald Markowitz,** *Democratic Vistas: Post Offices and Public Art in the New Deal* (1984)
David P. Peeler, *Hope Among Us Yet* (1987)
Richard Pells, *Radical Visions and American Dreams* (1973)
Thomas Schatz, *The Genius of the System: Hollywood Filmmaking in the Studio Era* (1988)
Richard Schickel, *The Disney Version* (1968)
Gunther Schuller, *The Swing Era* (1989)
Warren Susman, *Culture As History* (1984)

Minorities

Francisco E. Balerman, *In Defense of LaRaza* (1982)
Sarah Deutsch, *No Separate Refuge* (1987)
Abraham Hoffman, *Unwanted Mexican Americans in the Great Depression* (1974)
Laurence Kelly, *The Assault on Assimilation: John Collier and the Origins of Indian Policy Reform, 1920–1954* (1983)
John B. Kirby, *Black Americans in the Roosevelt Era* (1980)
August Meier and **Elliott Rudwick,** *Black Detroit and the Rise of the UAW* (1979)
Donald L. Parman, *The Navajos and the New Deal* (1975)
Kenneth Philp, *John Collier's Crusade for Indian Reform, 1920–1954* (1977)

Graham D. Taylor, *The New Deal and American Indian Tribalism* (1980)

Nancy J. Weiss, *Farewell to the Party of Lincoln: Black Politics in the Age of FDR* (1983)

Robert L. Zangrando, *The NAACP Crusade Against Lynching* (1980)

Women

Julia Kirk Blackwelder, *Women of the Depression* (1984)

Blanche Wiesen Cook, *Eleanor Roosevelt* (1992)

George Martin, *Madame Secretary: Frances Perkins* (1976)

Lois Scharf, *To Work and Wed* (1980)

——— , *Eleanor Roosevelt* (1987)

Winifred Wandersee, *Women's Work and Family Values, 1920–1940* (1981)

Susan Ware, *Holding Their Own: American Women in the 1930s* (1982)

——— , *Partner and I: Molly Dewson, Feminism, and New Deal Politics* (1987)

Jeane Westin, *Making Do: How Women Survived the '30s* (1976)

Chapter 25

Entry Into War

Clausen, Henry C. and Bruce Lee, *Pearl Harbor: Final Judgment* (1992)

Cole, Wayne S., *Roosevelt and the Isolationists, 1932–1945* (1983)

Dallek, Robert, *Franklin D. Roosevelt and American Foreign Policy* (1979)

Divine, Robert A., *The Reluctant Belligerent* (1979)

Ellet, Cynthia, *Conscientious Objectors and the Second World War* (1991)

Heinrichs, Waldo H., *Threshold of War* (1988)

Iriye, Akira, *The Origins of the Second World War in Asia and the Pacific* (1988)

Lipstadt, Deborah, *Beyond Belief: The American Press and the Coming of the Holocaust, 1933–1945* (1992)

Mintz, Frank P. *Revisionism and the Origins of Pearl Harbor* (1985)

Murray, Williamson, and Alla R. Millett, eds., *Calculations: Net Assessment and the Coming of World War II* (1992)

Prange, Gordon W. et. al., *December 7, 1941* (1988)

Schneider, James C., *Should America Go to War?*

Smith, Geoffrey S., *To Save a Nation* (1992)

The Military Front

Ambrose, Stephen E. E Company, *Band of Brothers: 506th Regiment, 101st Airborne From Normandy to Hitler's Eagle's Nest* (1992)

Baldwin, Hanson, *Battles Lost and Won* (1966)

Buchanan, Russell A., *The United States and World War II* (1964, 2 vols)

——— , *Black Americans in World War II* (1977)

Cole, Jean H., *Women Pilots of World War II* (1992)

Crane, Conrad C., *Bombs, Cities, and Civilians* (1993)

Dower, John W., *War Without Mercy* (1986)

Eisenhower, John S.D., *Allies: Pearl Harbor to D-Day* (1982)

Keegan, John, *Six Armies in Normandy* (1982)

——— , *Soldiers: A History of Men in Battle* (1987)

Leckie, Robert, *Delivered From Evil* (1987)

MacDonald, Charles B., *The Mighty Endeavor* (1986)

Maddox, Robert James, *The United States and World War II* (1992)

Perret, Geoffrey, *There's a War to Be Won* (1991)

Renzi, William A., and Mark D. Roehrs, *Never Look Back* (1991)

Schaffer, Ronald, *Wings of Judgment: American Bombing in World War II* (1985)

Spector, Ronald H., *Eagle Against the Sun: The American War with Japan* (1985)

Stoler, Mark A., *The Politics of the Second Front* (1977)

Toland, John, *The Rising Sun: The Decline and Fall of the Japanese Empire* (1970)

Weigley, Russell P., *Eisenhower's Lieutenants: The Campaign for France and Germany 1944–1945* (1981)

Willmott, H.P., *The Great Crusade* (1989)

Y'Blood, William T., *Red Sun Setting: The Battle of the Philippine Sea* (1981)

Diplomacy

Cashman, Sean Dennis, *America, Roosevelt, and World War II* (1989)

Clemens, Diana S., *Yalta* (1970)

Dallek, Robert, *Diplomacy and World War II* (1970, 1978)

Divine, Robert A., *Second Chance: The Triumph of Internationalism in America During World War II* (1967)

Gardner, Lloyd C., *Architects of Illusion* (1970)

Kimball, Warren F., *The Juggler: Franklin Roosevelt as Wartime Statesman* (1991)

Kolko, Gabriel, *Politics of War* (1968, 1990)

Neu, Charles E., *The Troubled Encounter: The United States and Japan* (1975, 1979)

Sainsbury, Keith, *The Turning Point: Roosevelt, Stalin, Churchill, and Chiang-Kai-Shek, 1943* (1985)

Shewmaker, Kenneth E., *Americans and Chinese Communists, 1927–1945* (1971).

Thorne, Christopher, *Allies of a Kind: The United States, Britain and the War Against Japan, 1941–1945* (1979)

Varg, Paul, *The Closing of the Door: Sino-American Relations, 1936–1946* (1973)

Mobilization and the Home Front

Anderson, Karen, *Wartime Women* (1981)

Bailey, Beth and David Farber, *The First Strange Place: The Alchemy of Race and Sex in World War II Hawaii* (1993)

Bernstein, Alison, R., *American Indians and World War II* (1991)

Casdorph, Paul D., *Let the Good Times Roll: Life at Home in America During World War II* (1989)

Capeci, Dominic J., and Martha Wilkerson, *Layered Violence: The Detroit Rioters of 1943* (1991)

Clive, Alan, *State of War: Michigan in World War II* (1979)

Daniels, Roger, *Prisoners Without Trial: Japanese Americans in World War II* (1993)

Flynn, George Q., *The Mess in Washington: Manpower Mobilization in World War II* (1979)

Glenn, Evelyn Nakano, *Issei, Nisei, War Bride* (1986)

Graebner, William, *The Age of Doubt: American Thought and Culture in the 1940s* (1991)

Hartmann, Susan, *The Homefront and Beyond: American Women in the 1940s* (1982)

Hubbard, Preston John, *Apocalypse Undone: My Survival of Japanese Imprisonment During World War II* (1990)

Isserman, Maurice, *Which Side Were You On? The American Communist Party During World War II* (1982)

Kesselman, Amy, *Fleeting Opportunities: Women Shipyard Workers in Portland and Vancouver during World War II* (1990)

Lichtenstein, Nelson, *Labor's War At Home: The CIO in World War II* (1982)

Litoff, Judy Barrett and David C. Smith, eds., *Since You Went Away: World War II Letters from American Women on the Home Front* (1991)

Milkman, Ruth, *Gender at Work: The Dynamics of Job Segregation by Sex During World War II* (1987)

Milward, Alan S., *War, Economy and Society, 1939–1945* (1977).

Neal, Steve, *Dark Horse: A Biography of Wendell Willkie* (1984)

Perrett, Geoffrey, *Days of Sadness, Years of Triumph: The American People, 1939–1945* (1974)

Pfeffer, Paula F. *A. Philip Randolph* (1990)

Roeder, George H., *The Censored War: American Visual Experience During World War II* (1993)

Scaffer, Ronald, *America in the Great War: The Rise of the War Welfare State* (1991)

Shulman, Holly Cowan, *The Voice of America: Propaganda and Democracy, 1941–1945* (1990)

Smith, Bradley, F., *The Shadow Warriors: The OSS and the Origins of the CIA* (1983)

Vatter, Harold, *The U.S. Economy in World War II* (1985)

Winkler, Allan M. *The Politics of Propaganda: The Office of War Information, 1942–1945* (1978)

———— , *Homefront, U.S.A.* (1986)

Atomic Bomb

Alperovitz, Gar, *Atomic Diplomacy* (1965, 1985)

Bernstein, Barton J., ed., *The Atomic Bomb* (1976)

Feifer, George, *Tennozan: The Battle of Okinawa and the Atomic Bomb* (1992)

Feis, Herbert, *Japan Subdued: The Atomic Bomb and the End of World War II* (1966)

Hersey, John, *Hiroshima* (1946)

Sherry, Michael S., *The Rise of American Air Power* (1987)

Sherwin, Martin J., *A World Destroyed: The Atomic Bomb and the Grand Alliance* (1975)

Stoff, Michael B., and **Jonathan F. Fanton,** eds., *The Manhattan Project:* (1991)

Chapter 26

Foreign Policy

Ambrose, Stephen E., *Rise to Globalism* (5th ed., 1988)

Anderson, Terry H., *The United States, Great Britain, and the Cold War, 1944–1947* (1981)

Barnet, Richard J., *The Alliance: America, Europe, Japan* (1983)

Brands, H.W. Jr., *Cold Warriors: Eisenhower's Generation and American Foreign Policy* (1988)

———— , *Inside the Cold War* (1991)

Clawson, Robert W., and **Lawrence S. Kaplan,** eds., *The Warsaw Pact* (1982)

Frazier, Robert, *Anglo-American Relations with Greece: The Coming of the Cold War, 1942–47* (1991)

Gaddis, John Lewis, *Strategies of Containment* (1982)

Gaddis, John Lewis, *The United States and the Origins of the Cold War, 1941–1947* (1972)

Gormly, James L., *The Collapse of the Grand Alliance, 1945–1948* (1987)

———— , *From Potsdam to the Cold War: Big Three Diplomacy, 1945–1947* (1990)

Herken, Gregg, *The Winning Weapon: The Atomic Bomb in the Cold War, 1945–1950* (1980)

Hersh, Burton, *The Old Boys: The American Elite and the Origins of the CIA* (1992)

Hogan, Michael J., *The Marshall Plan* (1987)

Ireland, Timothy P. *Creating the Entangling Alliance: The Origins of NATO* (1981)

Jones, Howard, *"A New Kind of War"* (1989)

Killebrew, Robert B., *Conventional Defense and Total Deterrence: Assessing NATO's Strategic Options* (1986)

Kuniholm, Bruce R., *The Origins of the Cold War in the Near East* (1980)

Larson, Deborah W., *Origins of Containment* (1985)

LaFeber, Walter, *America, Russia, and the Cold War, 1945–1980,* 7th ed. (1993)

May, Ernest R., *American Cold War Strategy: Interpreting NSC 68* (1993)

Messer, Robert L., *The End of an Alliance: James F. Byrnes, Roosevelt, Truman, and the Origins of the Cold War* (1982)

Milward, Alan S., *The Reconstruction of Western Europe, 1945–1951* (1984)

Miscamble, Wilson D., *George F. Kennan and the Making of American Foreign Policy, 1947–1950* (1992)

Newman, Robert P., *Owen Lattimore and the "Loss" of China* (1992)

Paterson, Thomas G., *Meeting the Communist Threat* (1988)

Schaller, Michael, *American Occupation of Japan: The Origins of the Cold War in Asia* (1985)

Taubman, William, *Stalin's American Policy* (1982)

Taylore, Telford, *The Anatomy of the Nuremberg Trials: A Personal Memoir* (1992)

Wexler, Imanuel, *The Marshall Plan Revisited* (1983)

The Truman Administration

Ballard, Jack, *Shock of Peace* (1983)

Donovan, Robert J., *Tumultuous Years: The Presidency of Harry S. Truman* (1982)

Dunar, Andrew J., *The Truman Scandals and the Politics of Morality* (1984)

Ferrell, Robert H., *Harry S. Truman and the Modern American Presidency* (1983)

Leffler, Melvyn P. *A Preponderance of Power: National Security, the Truman Administration, and the Cold War* (1992)

McCoy, Donald, *The Presidency of Harry S. Truman* (1984)

Maddox, Robert James, *From War to Cold War: The Education of Harry S. Truman* (1988)

Pemberton, William E., *Harry S. Truman* (1989)

Reichard, Gary W., *Politics as Usual* (1988)

Truman, Harry S., *Memoirs,* 2 vol. (1955, 1956)

———— , *Dear Bess: The Letters from Harry to Bess Truman, 1910–1959,* edited by Robert H. Ferrell (1983)

McCarthyism

Belknap, Michal R., *Cold War Political Justice: The Smith Act, the Communist Party, and American Civil Liberties* (1977)

Callahan, David, *Dangerous Capabilities: Paul Nitze and the Cold War* (1990)

Diamond, Sigmund, *Compromised Campus: The Collaboration of Universities with the Intelligence Communities, 1945–1955* (1992)

Fowler, Robert Booth, *Believing Skeptics: American Political Intellectuals, 1945–1964* (1978)

Fried, Richard M., *Nightmare in Red* (1990)

Freeland, Richard M., *The Truman Doctrine and the Origins of McCarthyism* (1972, 1985)

Gentry, Curt J., *Edgar Hoover: The Man and the Secrets* (1991)

Griffith, Robert, *The Politics of Fear: Joseph R. McCarthy and the Senate,* 2d ed., (1987)

Kutler, Stanley I., *The American Inquisition* (1982)

McAuliffe, Mary Sperling, *Crisis on the Left: Cold War Politics and American Liberals, 1947–1954* (1978)

O'Neill, William L., *A Better World: Stalinism and American Intellectuals* (1983)

O'Reilly, Kenneth, *Hoover and the Un-Americans: The FBI, HUAC, and the Red Menace* (1983)

Philipson, Ilene, *Ethel Rosenberg* (1988, 1993)

Powers, Richard G., *Secrecy and Power: The Life of J. Edgar Hoover* (1987)

Reeves, Thomas C., *The Life and Times of Joe McCarthy* (1981)

Schrecker, Ellen W., *No Ivory Tower: McCarthyism in the Universities* (1988)

Steinberg, Peter L., *The Great "Red Menace": United States Prosecution of American Communists, 1947–1952* (1984)

Theoharis, Athan, and **Johnn Stuart Cox,** *The Boss: J. Edgar Hoover and the Great American Inquisition* (1988)

Society and Culture During the Cold War

Barson, Michael, *"Better Dead than Red!" A Nostalgic Look at the Golden Years of Russiaphobia, Red-Baiting, and other Commie Madness* (1992)

Boyer, Paul, *By the Bomb's Early Light: American Thought and Culture at the Dawn of the Atomic Age* (1985)

Cottrell, Robert D., *Izzy: A Biography of I.F. Stone*

Fast, Howard, *Being Red* (1990)
Gilbert, James B., *Another Chance: Postwar America, 1945–1985,* 2d ed. (1986)
Ginger, Ann Fagan, and **David Christiano,** eds., *The Cold War Against Labor: An Anthology* (1987)
Green, Gil, *Cold War Fugitive: A Personal Story of the McCarthy Years* (1984)
Inglis, Fred, *The Cruel Peace: Everyday Life in the Cold War* (1991)
Jezer, Marty, *The Dark Ages: Life in the United States, 1945–1960* (1982)
Leslie, Stuart W., *The Cold War and American Science* (1993)
Lynn, Susan, *Progressive Women in Conservative Times*
MacDonald, J. Fred., *Television and the Red Menace* (1985)
May, Lary, ed., *Recasting America: Culture and Politics in the Age of the Cold War* (1989)
Powers, Richard G., *G-Men: Hoover's FBI in American Popular Culture* (1983)
Preis, Art, *Labor's Giant Step, Twenty Years of the CIO* (1964)
Ross, Andrews, *No Respect: Intellectuals and Popular Culture* (1989)
Rupp, Leila, and **Verta Taylor,** *Survival in the Doldrums: The American Women's Rights Movement, 1945 to the 1960s* (1987)
Sayre, Nora, *Running Time: Films of the Cold War* (1982)
Schaub, Thomas, *American Fiction in the Cold War* (1991)
Siebers, Tobin, *Cold War Criticism and the Politics of Skepticism* (1993)
Skolnick, Arlene, *Embattled Paradise: The American Family in an Age of Uncertainty* (1991)
Whitfield, Stephen J., *The Culture of the Cold War* (1991)
Winkler, Allan M., *Life Under a Cloud: American Anxiety about the Atom* (1993)

Korean War

Brady, James, *The Coldest War: A Memoir* (1987)
Cowdrey, Albert, *The Medics' War* (1987)
Cumings, Bruce, *The Origins of the Korean War* (1981)
Dobbs, Charles M., *The Unwanted Symbol: American Foreign Policy, the Cold War, and Korea, 1945–1950* (1981)
Foot, Rosemary, *The Wrong War* (1985)
Goulden, Joseph C., *Korea* (1982)
Hackworth, David H., and **Julie Sherman,** *About Face* (1989)
Halliday, Jon, and **Bruce Cumings,** *Korea* (1988)
Kaufman, Burton I., *The Korean War* (1986)
James, D. Clayton, *Refighting the Last War: Command and Crisis in Korea, 1950–1953* (1992)
Lowe, Peter, *The Origins of the Korean War* (1986)
Schaller, Michael, *Douglas MacArthur* (1989)
Stueck, William W., Jr., *The Road to Confrontation* (1981)
Toland, John, *In Mortal Combat: Korea, 1950–1953* (1992)

Chapter 27

Eisenhower Presidency

Charles Alexander, *Holding the Line* (1975)
Piers Brandon, *Ike* (1986)
Robert F. Burk, *Dwight D. Eisenhower* (1986)
Blanche W. Cooke, *The Declassified Eisenhower* (1981)
Robert A. Divine, *Blowing in the Wind: The Nuclear Test Ban Debate, 1954–1960* (1978)
Burton Kaufman, *Trade and Aid* (1982)
Peter Lyons, *Eisenhower: Portrait of the Hero* (1974)
Richard A. Melanson and **David A. Mayers,** eds., *Reevaluating Eisenhower* (1986)
Richard Nixon, *Six Crises* (1962)
Herbert Parmet, *Eisenhower and the American Crusades* (1972)
William L. O'Neill, *American High: The Years of Confidence, 1945–1960* (1986)
I.F. Stone, *The Haunted 50s* (1963)

Affluent Society

Daniel Bell, *The End of Ideology* (1960)
Richard M. Bernard and **Bradley R. Rice,** eds., *Sunbelt Cities* (1983)
David P. Calleo, *The Imperious Economy* (1982)
Barbara B. Clowse, *Brainpower for the Cold War* (1981)
Robert Fishman, *Bourgeois Utopias* (1987)
John K. Galbraith, *The Affluent Society* (1963)
——— , *The New Industrial State* (1967)
Mark I. Gelfand, *A Nation of Cities* (1975)
Dolores Hayden, *Redesigning the American Dream* (1984)
Will Herberg, *Protestant-Catholic-Jew* (1960)
Godfrey Hodgson, *America in Our Time* (1976)
Marty Jezer, *The Dark Ages* (1982)
Landon Y. Jones, *Great Expectations: America and the Baby Boom Generation* (1980)
Zane L. Miller, *Suburb* (1982)
C. Wright Mills, *The Power Elite* (1956)
——— , *White Collar* (1960)
Kenneth W. Olson, *The GI Bill, the Veterans, and the Colleges* (1974)
John B. Rae, *The Road and the Car in American Life* (1971)
Mark H. Rose, *Interstate* (1979)
Joel Spring, *The Sorting Machine: National Education Policy Since 1945* (1976)
Robert Wuthnow, *The Restructuring of American Religion* (1988)

Popular Culture

Beth Bailey, *From Front Porch to Back Seat: Courtship in Twentieth Century America* (1988)
James L. Baughman, *The Republic of Mass Culture* (1992)
Chuck Berry, *Chuck Berry* (1987)
Peter Biskind, *Seeing is Believing* (1983)
William Boddy, *Fifties Television* (1990)
Paul A. Carter, *Another Part of the Fifties* (1983)
Ann Charters, *Kerouac* (1973)
Edgar Z. Freidenberg, *The Vanishing Adolescent* (1959)
Albert Goldman, *Elvis* (1981)
George Lipsitz, *Class and Culture in Cold War America* (1981)
J. Fred MacDonald, *Television and the Red Menace* (1985)
David Marc, *Demographic Vistas* (1984)
Stephen J. Whitfield, *The Culture of the Cold War* (1991)
Michael Wood, *America in Movies* (1975)
John Tytell, *Naked Angels* (1976)

The Cold War Continued

Richard A. Aliano, *American Defense Policy from Eisenhower to Kennedy* (1975)
Stephen Ambrose, *Ike's Spies* (1981)
Douglas S. Blaufarb, *The Counterinsurgency Era* (1977)
Robert Divine, *Eisenhower and the Cold War* (1981)
Townsend Hoopes, *The Devil and John Foster Dulles* (1973)
Richard Immerman, *The CIA in Guatemala* (1982)
Rhodri Jeffreys-Jones, *The CIA and American Democracy* (1989)
Madeline Kalb, *The Congo Cables: The Cold War in Africa from Eisenhower to Kennedy* (1982)
Walter LaFeber, *Inevitable Revolutions* (1983)
John Ranelagh, *The Agency: The Rise and Decline of the CIA* (1986)
Stephen Schlesinger and **Steven Kinzer,** *Bitter Fruit* (1981)
Richard Welch, Jr., *Response to Revolution: The United States and the Cuban Revolution, 1954–1961* (1985)
Marilyn B. Young, *The Vietnam Wars* (1990)

Women and the Family

Ruth Schwartz Cowan, *More Work for Mother* (1983)
Benita Eisler, *Private Lives: Men and Women of the Fifties* (1983)
Betty Friedan, *The Feminine Mystique* (1963)

Cynthia Harrison, *On Account of Sex: The Politics of Women's Issues, 1945–1968* (1988)
Eugenia Kaledin, *Mothers and More* (1984)
Glenna Matthews, ''*Just a Housewife*'' (1987)
Leila J. Rupp and **Verta Taylor,** *Survival in the Doldrums: The American Women's Rights Movement, 1945 to the 1960s* (1987)

Kennedy Presidency

Michael Beschloss, *The Crisis Years: Kennedy and Khruschev, 1961–1963* (1991)
Thomas Brown, *JFK: The History of an Image* (1988)
David Burner, *John F. Kennedy and a New Generation* (1988)
Herbert Dinerstein, *The Making of a Missile Crisis* (1976)
Henry Fairlie, *The Kennedy Promise* (1973)
James N. Giglio, *The Presidency of John F. Kennedy* (1991)
Trumbull Higgins, *The Perfect Failure: Kennedy, Eisenhower, and the CIA at the Bay of Pigs* (1987)
Henry Hurt, *Reasonable Doubt: An Investigation into the Assassination of John F. Kennedy* (1985)
Robert Kennedy, *Thirteen Days* (1969)
Richard D. Mahoney, *JFK: Ordeal in Africa* (1983)
Bruce Miroff, *Pragmatic Illusions* (1976)
Thomas G. Patterson, ed., *Kennedy's Quest for Victory* (1989)
Gerald D. Rice, *The Bold Experiment: JFK's Peace Corps* (1985)
Garry Wills, *The Kennedy Imprisonment* (1982)
——— , *Nixon Agonistes* (1970)

Chapter 28

Origins of the Movement

William C. Berman, *The Politics of Civil Rights in the Truman Administration* (1970)
A. Russell Buchanan, *Black Americans in World War II* (1977)
Robert F. Burk, *The Eisenhower Administration and Black Civil Rights* (1984)
Richard M. Dalfiume, *Desegregation of the U.S. Armed Forces* (1969)
Herbert Garfinkel, *When Negroes March* (1969)
Dizzy Gillespie, *To Be or Not to Bop* (1979)
Ira Gitler, *Swing to Bop* (1985)
Elizabeth Huckaby, *Crisis at Central High* (1980)
V.O. Key, Jr., *Southern Politics in State and Nation* (1949)
Martin Luther King, Jr., *Stride Toward Freedom* (1958)
Donald R. McCoy and **Richard T. Ruetten,** *Quest and Response: Minority Rights and the Truman Administration* (1973)
August Meier and Elliot Rudwick, *CORE* (1975)
Henry Lee Moon, *Balance of Power: The Negro Vote* (1948)
Paula F. Pfeffer, *A. Philip Randolph* (1990)
Bernard Schwartz, *Inside the Warren Court* (1987)
Arnold Shaw, *Black Popular Music in America* (1986)
Mark Tushnet, *The NAACP's Legal Strategy Against Segregated Education* (1987)
Jules Tygiel, *Baseball's Great Experiment: Jackie Robinson and His Legacy* (1983)
C. Vann Woodward, *The Strange Career of Jim Crow* (3rd ed., 1974)
Neil A. Wynn, *The Afro-American and the Second World War* (1976)

No Easy Road to Freedom

Russell H. Barrett, *Integration at Ole Miss* (1965)
Numan V. Bartley, *The Rise of Massive Resistance* (1969)
Jack Bloom, *Class, Race, and the Civil Rights Movement* (1987)
James Farmer, *Lay Bare the Heart* (1985)
James Forman, *The Making of Black Revolutionaries* (1985)
David J. Garrow, *The FBI and Martin Luther King, Jr.* (1983)
David L. Lewis, *King: A Critical Biography* (1970)
W. Manning Marable, *Race, Reform, and Rebellion* (1984)
James Meredith, *Three Years in Mississippi* (1966)
Ann Moody, *Coming of Age in Mississippi* (1970)

Benjamin Muse, *Virginia's Massive Resistance* (1961)
Robert J. Norvell, *Reaping the Whirlwind: The Civil Rights Movement in Tuskegee* (1985)
Stephen B. Oates, *Let the Trumpet Sound: The Life of Martin Luther King, Jr.* (1982)
Cleveland Sellers with **Robert Terrell,** *The River of No Return* (1973)
Miles Wolff, *Lunch at the Five and Ten* (1970)
Pat Watters, *Down to Now* (1971)
Harris Wofford, *Of Kennedys and Kings* (1980)
Howard Zinn, *Albany: A Study in National Responsibility* (1962)
——— , *SNCC: The New Abolitionists* (1965)

The Movement at High Tide

Carl Brauer, *John F. Kennedy and the Second Reconstruction* (1977)
Seth Cagin and **Philip Dray,** *We Are Not Afraid* (1988)
Charles Fager, *Selma 1965* (1974)
David J. Garrow, *Protest at Selma* (1978)
Henry Hampton and **Steve Fayer,** *Voices of Freedom* (1990)
Len Holt, *The Summer That Didn't End* (1965)
Mary King, *Freedom Song* (1987)
Martin Luther King, Jr., *Why We Can't Wait* (1964)
Stephen Lawson, *Black Ballots* (1976)
Burke Marshall, *Federalism and Civil Rights* (1964)
Charles Morgan, Jr. *A Time To Speak* (1964)
Victor Navasky, *Kennedy Justice* (1971)
Mary Aickin Rothschild, *A Case of Black and White* (1982)
Sheyann Webb and **Rachel West Nelson,** *Selma, Lord, Selma* (1980)
Charles and **Barbara Whalen,** *The Longest Debate: A Legislative History of the 1964 Civil Rights Act* (1985)
Roy Wilkins with **Tom Matthews,** *Standing Fast* (1982)
Juan Williams, *Eyes on the Prize* (1987)

Forgotten Minorities

Rodolfo Acuna, *Occupied America* (3rd ed., 1981)
Mario Barerra, *Race and Class in the Southwest* (1979)
Frank T. Bean and **Marta Tienda,** *The Hispanic Population of the United States* (1988)
Larry Burt, *Tribalism in Crisis: Federal Indian Policy, 1953–1961* (1982)
Don Fixico, *Termination and Relocation: Federal Indian Policy, 1945–1960* (1986)
Mario T. Garcia, *Mexican Americans* (1989)
Virginia Sanchez Korrol, *From Colonia to Community* (1983)
Benjamin Marquez, *LULAC* (1993)
Darcy McNickle, *Native American Tribalism* (1973)
Joan Moore and **Harry Pachon,** *Hispanics in the United States* (1985)
Ronald Takaki, *Strangers From A Different Shore: A History of Asian Americans* (1989)
——— , *A Different Mirror: A History of Multicultural America* (1993)
Karl Wagenheim, *Puerto Rico: A Profile* (1975)

The Great Society

Vaughn D. Bornet, *The Presidency of Lyndon B. Johnson* (1983)
Paul K. Conkin, *Big Daddy from the Pedernales: Lyndon Baines Johnson* (1986)
Ronnie Dugger, *The Politician* (1982)
Greg J. Duncan, *Years of Poverty, Years of Plenty* (1984)
J. Wayne Flint, *Dixie's Forgotten People* (1979)
Hugh Davis Graham, *Uncertain Trumpet* (1984)
Michael Harrington, *The Other America* (rev. ed., 1981)
Robert H. Haveman, ed., *A Decade of Federal Antipoverty Programs* (1977)
Doris Kearns, *Lyndon Johnson and the American Dream* (1976)
Sar Levitan, *The Great Society's Poor Law* (1969)

Sar Levitan and **Robert Taggart,** *The Promise of Greatness* (1976)
Charles Murray, *Losing Ground: American Social Policy, 1950–1980* (1983)
Frances Fox Piven and **Richard Cloward,** *Regulating the Poor* (1971)
Stephen M. Rose, *The Betrayal of the Poor* (1972)
David S. Walls and **John B. Stephenson,** eds., *Appalachia in the Sixties* (1972)

Chapter 29

General: The 1960s

Chalmers, David, *And the Crooked Places Made Straight: The Struggle for Social Change in the 1960s* (1991)
Goodwin, Richard N., *Remembering America* (1988)
Morgan, Edward P., *The 60s Experience* (1991)
Morris, Charles R., *A Time of Passion: America, 1960–1980* (1984)
O'Neill, William L., *Coming Apart* (1971)
Tischler, Barbara L., ed., *Sights on the Sixties* (1992)
Viorst, Milton, *Fire in the Streets* (1979)
Wiener, Jon, *Come Together: John Lennon and His Time* (1984, 1991)

Vietnam Conflict

Anderson, David L., *Shadow on the White House: Presidents and the Vietnam War, 1945–1975* (1993)
Appy, Christian G., *Working-Class War: American Combat Soldiers in Vietnam* (1993)
Bergerud, Eric, *Red Thunder, Tropic Lightning: The World of a Combat Division in Vietnam* (1993)
Berman, Larry, *Lyndon Johnson's War* (1989)
Berman, William C., *William Fulbright and the Vietnam War* (1988)
Clarke, Jeffrey J., *Advice and Support: the Final Years, 1965–1973* (1988)
DiLeo, David L., *George Ball, Vietnam, and the Rethinking of Containment* (1991)
Elwood-Akers, Virginia, *Women War Correspondents in the Vietnam War, 1961–1975* (1988)
FitzGerald, Frances, *Fire in the Lake* (1972)
Halberstam, David, *The Best and the Brightest* (1972, 1992)
Hallin, Daniel C., *The "Uncensored War"* (1989)
Herring, George C., ed., *The Pentagon Papers,* Abridged Edition (1993)
Hess, Martha, *Then the Americans Came: Voices from Vietnam* (1993)
Isaacs, Arnold R., *Without Honor* (1983)
Jamieson, Neil L., *Understanding Vietnam* (1993)
Karnow, Stanley, *Vietnam, A History* (1983, 1991)
Shilts, Randy, *Conduct Unbecoming: Lesbians and Gays in the U.S. Military, Vietnam to the Persian Gulf* (1993)
Sim, Kevin, and **Micahel Bilton,** *Four Hours in My Lai: The Soldiers of Charlie Company* (1992)
Spector, Ronald H., *After Tet* (1993)
Turner, Kathleen J., *Lyndon Johnson's Dual War: Vietnam and the Press* (1981)
VanDeMark, Brian, *Into the Quagmire* (1990)
Wilson, James R., *Landing Zones: Southern Veterans Remember Vietnam* (1990)
Wirtz, James J., *The Tet Offensive: Intelligence Failure in War* (1991)
Wyatt, Clarence R., *Paper Soldiers: The American Press and the Vietnam War* (1993)

Black, Red, and Power Movements

Brown, Elaine, *A Taste of Power* (1993)
Button, James, *Black Violence: Political Impact of the 1960s Riots* (1978)
Carmichael, Stokely, and **V. Charles Hamilton,** *Black Power* (1967, 1992)

Campisi, Jack, *The Mashpee Indians* (1991)
Carson, Clayborne, *Malcolm X: The F.B.I. File* (1991)
Cone, James H., *Martin & Malcolm & America* (1991)
Hilliard, David and **Lewis Cole,** *This Side of Glory: The Autobiography of David Hilliard and the Story of the Black Panther Party* (1993)
Malcolm X and **Alex Haley,** *The Autobiography of Malcolm X* (1965, 1992)
Marable, Manning, *Race, Reform, and Rebellion* (1984)
Marin, Marguerite V., *Social Protest in an Urban Barrio: A Study of the Chicano Movement, 1966–1972* (1991)
Matthiessen, Peter, *In the Spirit of Crazy Horse* (1991)
Perry, Bruce, *Malcolm* (1991)

Counter Culture, Anti-War, and Student Movements

Breines, Wini, *Community and Organization in the New Left* (1982)
DeBeneditti, Charles, *An American Ordeal: The Antiwar Movement of the Vietnam Era* (1990)
Dellinger, David T., *From Yale to Jail: A Memoir* (1993)
Fraser, Ronald, et al., *1968: A Student Generation in Revolt* (1988)
Gitlin, Todd, *The Whole World Is Watching* (1980)
Gottlieb, Sherry, *Hell No, We Won't Go* (1991)
Heineman, Kenneth, *Campus Wars: The Peace Movement at American State Universities in the Vietnam Era* (1993)
Hoffman, Abbie, *The Best of Abbie Hoffman* (1989)
Isserman, Maurice, *If I Had a Hammer: The Death of the Old Left and the Birth of the New Left* (1987)
Jezer, Marty, *Abbie Hoffman* (1992)
Meyers, R. David, *Toward a History of the New Left* (1989)
Miller, Jim, *"Democracy Is in the Streets"* (1987)
Miller, Timothy, *The Hippies and American Values* (1991)
Powers, Thomas, *The War at Home* (1973)
Rorabaugh, W.J., *Berkeley at War: The 1960s* (1989)
Sayres, Sohnya, et al., ed., *The 60s Without Apology* (1984)
Zaroulis, Nancy and **Gerald Sullivan,** *Who Spoke Up? American Protest Against the War in Vietnam, 1963–1975* (1984)

Rebirth of Feminism and Gay Liberation

Adam, Barry D., *The Rise of a Gay and Lesbian Movement* (1987)
Bambara, Toni Cade, ed., *The Black Woman* (1972)
Bardwick, Judith M., *In Transition: How Feminism, Sexual Liberation, and the Search for Fulfillment Have Altered Our Lives* (1979)
Chafe, William H., *The Paradox of Change: American Women in the 20th Century* (1991)
Cruikshank, Margaret, *The Gay and Lesbian Liberation Movement* (1992)
D'Emilio, John, *Making Trouble: Essays on Gay History, Politics, and the University* (1992)
Duberman, Martin, *Stonewall* (1993)
Freeman, Jo, *The Politics of Women's Liberation* (1979)
Hooks, Bell, *Ain't I a Woman: Black Women and Feminism* (1981)
Levine, Ellen and **Judith Hole,** *Rebirth of Feminism* (1971)
Linden-Ward, Blanche, *American Women in the 1960s* (1992)
Marcus, Eric, *Making History: The Struggle for Gay and Lesbian Equal Rights, 1945–1990: An Oral History* (1992)
Millett, Kate, *Sexual Politics* (1970, 1990)
Morgan, Robin, ed., *Sisterhood Is Powerful* (1970)
Polatnick, M. Rivka, *Strategies for Women's Liberation: A Study of a Black and White Group of the 1960s* (1987)
Yates, Gayle Graham, *What Women Want* (1975)

Presidential Elections and Administrations

Ambrose, Stephen E., *Nixon,* 3 vol. (1987–1991)
Bernstein, Carl and **Bob Woodward,** *All the President's Men* (1974)
Brodie, Fawn, *Richard Nixon* (1981)
Carlson, Jody, *George C. Wallace and the Politics of Powerlessness* (1981)
Ehrlichman, John, *Witness to Power* (1982)

Farber, David, *Chicago '68* (1988)
Gould, Lewis L., *1968: The Election That Changed America* (1993)
Hougan, Jim, *Secret Agenda: Watergate, Deep Throat, and the CIA* (1984)
Morns, Roger, *Richard Milhous Nixon* (1990)
Nixon, Richard, *RN: The Memoirs of Richard Nixon* (1978)
Parmet, Herbert S., *Richard Nixon and His America* (1990)
Schandler, Herbert, *The Unmaking of a President: Lyndon Johnson and Vietnam* (1977)
Schlesinger, Arthur M., Jr., *Robert Kennedy and His Times* (1974)
Schudson, Michael, *Watergate in American History* (1992)
Wicker, Tom, *One of Us: Richard Nixon and the American Dream* (1991)

Chapter 30

Energy and Stagflation

Bell, Daniel, *The Coming of the Post-Industrial Society* (1973, 1976)
Calleo, David P., *The Imperious Economy* (1982)
Clark, Gordon L., *Unions and Communities Under Siege* (1989)
Evans, Sara M. and Barbara J. Nelson, *Wage Justice: Comparable Worth and the Paradox of Technocratic Reform* (1989)
Goldin, Claudia, *Understanding the Gender Gap: An Economic History of American Women* (1990)
Kapstein, Ethan B., *The Insecure Alliance: Energy Crises and Western Politics Since 1944* (1990)
Leppzer, Robert, *Voices from Three Mile Island* (1980)
Maurer, Harry, *Not Working: An Oral History of the Unemployed* (1979)
Rothschild, Emma, *Paradise Lost: The Decline of the Auto-Industrial Age* (1973)
Schulman, Bruce J., *From Cotton Belt to Sun Belt* (1990)
Sherrill, Robert, *The Oil Follies of 1970–1980* 1983)
Teaford, Jon, *Cities of the Heartland: The Rise and Fall of the Industrial Midwest* (1993)
Tugwell, Franklin, *The Energy Crisis and the American Political Economy* (1988)

Ford and Carter Presidencies

Barnet, Richard J., *The Lean Years* (1980)
Carter, Jimmy, *Keeping Faith* (1982)
———, *Turning Point* (1992)
Carter, Rosalynn, *First Lady From Plains* (1984)
Edwards, George C. III, *At the Margins: Presidential Leadership of Congress* (1989)
Ford, Gerald R., *Time to Heal* (1979)
Hargrove, Erwin C., *Jimmy Carter As President* (1989)
Isaacson, Walter, *Kissinger* (1992)
Jones, Charles O., *The Trusteeship Presidency: Jimmy Carter and the United States Congress* (1988)
Kaufman, Burton I., *The Presidency of James Earl Carter, Jr.*
Lamis, Alexander P. *The Two-Party South* 2d ed (1990)
McLellan, David S., *Cyrus Vance* (1985)
Reichley, A. James, *Conservatives in an Age of Change* (1981)
Rozell, Mark J., *The Press and the Carter Presidency* (1989)
———, *The Press and the Ford Presidency* (1992)
Sick, Gary, *October Surprise* (1991)
Ware, Alan, *The Breakdown of the Democratic Party Organization, 1940–1980* (1985)
Wattenberg, Martin P., *The Decline of American Political Parties, 1952–1988* (1990)

Foreign Policy

Bill, James A., *The Eagle and the Lion* (1988)
Christopher, Warren, et al., *American Hostages in Iran* (1985)
LaFeber, Walter, *The Panama Canal* (1978, 1989)
Lake, Anthony, *Somoza Falling* (1989)
Moens, Alexander, *Foreign Policy Under Carter* (1990)

Mower, A. Glenn, Jr., *Human Rights and American Foreign Policy* (1987)
Newell, Nancy Peabody and Richard S. Newell, *The Struggle for Afghanistan* (1981)
Pastor, Robert A., *Condemned to Repetition* (1987)
Schoultz, Lars, *Human Rights and U.S. Policy Toward Latin America* (1981)
Smith, Gaddis, *Morality, Reason, and Power* (1986)
Spencer, Donald S., *The Carter Implosion: Jimmy Carter and the Amateur Style of Diplomacy* (1988)
Vogelgesang, Sandy, *American Dream, Global Nightmare* (1980)

The Vietnam Legacy

Holsti, Ole R. and James N. Rosenau, *American Leadership in World Affairs: Vietnam and the Breakdown of Consensus* (1984)
Capps, Walter H., *The Unfinished War*, 2d ed. (1990)
Charlton, Michael and Anthony Moncrieff, *Many Reasons Why* (1978)
Hellman, John, *American Myth and the Legacy of Vietnam* (1986)
Jeffords, Susan, *The Remasculinization of America: Gender and the Vietnam War* (1989)
McCloud, Bill, *What Should We Tell Our Children about Vietnam?* (1989)
MacPherson, Myra, *Long Time Passing: Vietnam and the Haunted Generation* (1984)
Podhoretz, Norman, *Why We Were in Vietnam* (1982)
Ravenal, Earl C., *Never Again* (1978)
Salisbury, Harrison E., ed., *Vietnam Reconsidered* (1984)
Thompson, W. Scott and Donaldson D. Frizzill, eds., *The Lessons of Vietnam* (1977)

Race and the New Ethnicity

Auletta, Ken, *The Underclass* (1982).
Blauner, Bob, *Black Lives, White Lives: Three Decades of Race Relations in America* (1990)
Caplan, Nathan, et. al., *The Boat People and Achievement in America* (1989)
Cockcroft, James D., *Outlaws in the Promised Land: Mexican Immigrant Workers and America's Future* (1986)
Farley, Reynolds and Walter R. Allen, *The Color Line and Quality of Life in America* (1987, 1989)
Glasgow, Douglas, *The Black Underclass* (1980)
Gomez-Quinones, Juan, *Chicano Politics: Reality and Promise, 1940–1990* (1990)
Henry, Charles P., *Culture and African American Politics* (1990)
Jones, Fausine Childress, *The Changing Mood in America* (1977)
Jones, Jacqueline, *The Dispossessed: America's Underclasses from the Civil War to the Present* (1992)
Katz, Michael B., ed., *The "Underclass" Debate* (1993)
Sollors, Werner, ed., *The Invention of Ethnicity* (1989)
Spickard, Paul R., *Mixed Blood: Intermarriage and Ethnic Identity in Twentieth-Century America* (1989)
Stack, Carol B., *All Our Kin: Strategies for Survival in a Black Community* (1975)
Wilkinson, J. Harvie, III, *From Brown to Bakke: The Supreme Court and School Integration, 1954–1978* (1979)

Grassroots Politics & the New Conservatism

Abbott, Carl, *The New Urban America: Growth and Politics in the Sunbelt Cities* (1987)
Bedford, Henry F., *Seabrook Station: Citizens' Politics and Nuclear Power* (1990)
Belasco, Warren J., *Appetite for Change: How the Counterculture Took on the Food Industry* (1989)
Boyer, Paul S., *When Time Shall Be No More: Prophecy Belief in Modern American Culture* (1992)
Bruce, Steve, *The Rise and Fall of the New Christian Right* (1988)
Clecak, Peter, *America's Quest for the Ideal Self* (1983).

Entman, Robert M., *Democracy Without Citizens: Media and the Decay of American Politics* (1989)
Faux, Marian, *Roe v. Wade* (1988)
Furguson, Ernest B., *Hard Right: The Rise of Jesse Helms* (1986)
Garment, Suzanne, *Scandal: The Crisis of Mistrust in American Politics* (1991)
Gordon, Linda, ed., *Women, the State, and Welfare* (1990)
Hill, Samuel S. and Owen, Dennis E., *The New Religious Right in America* (1982)
Hillis, Bryan V., *Can Two Walk Together Unless They Be Agreed? American Religious Schisms in the 1970s* (1991)
Hoff-Wilson, Joan, ed., *Rights of Passage: The Past and Future of the ERA* (1986)
Hollander, Paul, *Anti-Americanism: Critiques at Home and Abroad, 1965–1990* (1992)
Klatch, Rebecca, *Women of the New Right* (1987)
MacDonald, Michael C.D., *America's Cities: A Report on the Myth of the Urban Renaissance* (1984)
Rae, Nicol C., *The Decline and Fall of the Liberal Republicans* (1989)
Schlozman, Kay Lehman and Sidney Verba, *Injury to Insult: Unemployment, Class and Political Response* (1979)
Staggenborg, Suzanne, *The Pro-Choice Movement: Organization and Activism in the Abortion Conflict* (1991)
Thorne, Melvin J., *American Conservative Thought Since World War II* (1990)
Tipton, Steven M., *Getting Saved from the Sixties* (1982)
Wilcox, William Clyde, *God's Warriors: The Christian Right in Twentieth-Century America* (1992)
Wuthnow, Robert, *The Restructuring of American Religion* (1988)

Chapter 31

The Reagan Revolution

Frank Ackerman, *Reaganomics* (1982)
Ryan J. Barrilleaux, *The Post-Modern Presidency* (1988)
Sidney Blumenthal, *Our Long National Daydream* (1988)
Michael Boskin, *Too Many Promises* (1986)
Lou Cannon, *President Reagan: The Role of A Lifetime* (1991)
Joan Claybrook, *Retreat From Safety: Reagan's Attack on American Health* (1984)
Robert Dallek, *Ronald Reagan: The Politics of Symbolism*
Ronnie Dugger, *On Reagan* (1983)
Rowland Evans and Robert Novak, *The Reagan Revolution* (1981)
William Greider, *Secrets of the Temple* (1987)
Dilys Hill, et. al., *The Reagan Presidency* (1990)
James J. Horgan and Joseph A. Cernik, eds., *The Reagan Years* (1988)
Kitty Kelley, *Nancy Reagan* (1991)
Robert Kuttner, *The Economic Illusion* (1984)
Robert Lekachman, *Greed Is Not Enough* (1983)
Jane Mayer and Doyle McManus, *Landslide: The Unmaking of the President, 1984–1988* (1988)
Roger E. Meiners and Bruce Yandle, *Regulation and the Reagan Era* (1989)
Michael Rogin, *Ronald Reagan* (1987)
C. Brant Short, *Ronald Reagan and the Public Lands* (1989)
Dennis Swann, *The Retreat of State* (1988)
David Stockman, *The Triumph of Politics* (1986)
Susan and Martin Tolchin, *Dismantling America: The Rush to Deregulate* (1983)
Elder Witt, *A Different Justice: Reagan and the Supreme Court* (1986)

Foreign Policy

Raymond Bonner, *Weakness and Deceit: U.S. Policy and El Salvador* (1984)
William E. Brock and Robert D. Hormats, eds., *The Global Economy* (1990)
Bradford Burns, *At War With Nicaragua* (1987)
David Calleo, *Beyond American Hegemony* (1987)
Leslie Cockburn, *Out of Control* (1987)
Theodore Draper, *A Very Thin Line: The Iran-Contra Affairs* (1991)
Stephen R. Graubard, *Mr. Bush's War* (1992)
Roy Gutman, *Banana Diplomacy* (1988)
Jerry Hough, *The Struggle for the Third World* (1986)
Bruce Jentelson, *Pipeline Politics* (1986)
Michael T. Klare and Peter Kornbluh, eds., *Low Intensity Warfare* (1988)
Jonathan Kwitny, *Endless Enemies* (1984)
Walter LaFeber, *Inevitable Revolutions* (2nd ed., 1984)
Robert S. Leiken and Barry M. Rubin, eds., *The Central American Crisis Reader* (1987)
Michael Mandelbaum, *Reagan and Gorbachev* (1987)
Morris H. Morley, *Crisis and Confrontation* (1988)
Kenneth Oye, et. al., eds., *Eagle Resurgent?* (1987)
Jonathan Schell, *The Fate of the Earth* (1982)
Micah L. Sifry and Christopher Cerf, eds., *The Gulf War Reader* (1991)
Strobe Talbot, *Deadly Gambits* (1984)
Sanford Ungar, *Africa* (1986)
Thomas Walker, ed., *Reagan Versus the Sandinistas* (1987)
Bob Woodward, *Veil: The Secret Wars of the CIA* (1987)

Social and Political Trends

David Bensman and Roberta Lynch, *Rusted Dreams: Hard Times in a Steel Community* (1987)
Mike Davis, *City of Quartz: Excavating the Future in Los Angeles* (1990)
Marian Wright Edelman, *Families in Peril* (1987)
Thomas Edsall, *The New Politics of Inequality* (1984)
Barbara Ehrenreich, *The Worst Years of Our Lives* (1990)
Thomas Ferguson and Joel Rogers, *Right Turn* (1986)
Barbara Garson, *The Electronic Sweatshop* (1988)
Todd Gitlin, *Inside Prime Time* (1986)
Andrew Hacker, *Two Nations: Black and White, Separate, Hostile, Unequal* (1992)
Bennet Harrison and Barry Bluestone, *The Great U-Turn: Corporate Restructuring and the Polarizing of America* (1988)
J. Hoberman, *Vulgar Modernism: Writing on Movies and Other Media* (1991)
Paul Kling, et. al., eds., *Postsuburban California* (1991)
Peter Kwong, *The New Chinatown* (1987)
John Langone, *AIDS: The Facts* (1988)
Frank Levy, *Dollars and Dreams: The Changing American Income Distribution* (1987)
Robert McElvaine, *The End of the Conservative Era* (1987)
Luciano Mangiafico, *Contemporary American Immigrants* (1988)
Jane Mansbridge, *Why We Lost the ERA* (1986)
Kim Moody, *An Injury to All: The Decline of American Unionism* (1988)
Adolph L. Reed, Jr., *The Jesse Jackson Phenomenon* (1986)
David Reimers, *Still The Golden Door* (1985)
Harrell R. Rodgers, Jr., *Poor Women, Poor Families* (1986)
Al Santoli, *New Americans* (1988)
Hilda Scott, *Working Your Way to the Bottom: The Feminization of Poverty* (1985)
Ruth Sidel, *Women and Children Last* (1986)
Robert Spitzer, *The Right to Life Movement and Third Party Politics* (1987)
Studs Terkel, *The Great Divide* (1988)
E. Fuller Torrey, *Nowhere to Go: The Tragic Odyssey of the Homeless Mentally Ill* (1988)
William Julius Wilson, *The Truly Disadvantaged* (1987)

PHOTO CREDITS

Chapter 1
David Muench, xxxii; Jerry Jacka/Arizona State Museum, University of Arizona, 6; Denver Museum of Natural History, 8; Peabody Museum, Harvard University, 11; National Museum of the American Indian, 14; Arizona State Museum, University of Arizona, 14; David Muench, 15; George Gerster/Comstock, 16; Ohio Historical Society, 17; William H. Jackson/Museum of New Mexico, 21.

Chapter 2
Diego Duran/Biblioteca Nacional/Oronoz, Madrid, 26; Bridgeman Art Library, 28; Art Resource, 30; British Library, 32; James L. Stanfield/National Geographic Society, 34; Frey Bernardino de Sahagun/Peabody Museum, Harvard University, 37; Lopez de Gomara, 40; Jim Tuten/Southern Stock, 43; Thomas Gilcrease Institute of History and Art, Tulsa, OK, 45; Bridgeman Art Library, 46, 47.

Chapter 3
Colonial Williamsburg Foundation, 50; Terrence Moore, 52; New York Public Library, 55; Library of Congress, 57; Yale University Art Gallery, 59 (left); Board of Regents, Gunnerston Hall, Lorton, VA, 59 (right); John Carter Brown Library, Brown University, 63; Worcester Art Museum, 65; New York Historical Society, 69; Historical Society of Pennsylvania, 70; American Antiquarian Society, 71.

Chapter 4
Abby Aldrich Rockefeller Folk Art Center, 76; Harper's Weekly, 78; Biblioteque Nationale, Paris, 81; National Museum of American History, Smithsonian Institution, 84; Bridgeman Art Library, 85; Musees du Chanteau des Ducs, Nantes, 86 (top); National Maritime Museum, Greenwich, England, 86 (bottom); American Antiquarian Society, 88; Maryland Historical Society, 91; Gibbes Museum of Art, 94; Ferrum College, Blue Ridge Institute, 96; Philbrook Museum of Art, Tulsa, OK, 98; Saint Louis Art Museum, 100; Virginia Museum of Fine Arts, 106.

Chapter 5
Massachusetts Historical Society, 110; Paul Rocheleau, 112; Jack W. Dykinga, 116; United States Geological Survey EROS Data Center, 118; William Johnson/Stock, Boston, 121; Henry Glassie, 125; Metropolitan Museum of Art, 128; Historical Society of Pennsylvania, 128; American Anitquarian Society, 130 (left); Library of Congress, 130 (right); New York Public Library, 134; John Carter Brown Library, Brown University.

Chapter 6
Library of Congress, 141, 142; Anne S.K. Brown Military Collection, Brown University Library, 147; National Museum of the American Indian, Smithsonian Institution, 149; Massachusetts Historical Society, 151; Library of Congress, 153; Library Company of Philadelphia, 156; Library of Congress, 157, 159, 161; Connecticut Historical Society, 165; Yale University Art Gallery, 167; Library of Congress, 169.

Chapter 7
Library of Congress, 172; New York Historical Society, 174; Anne S.K. Brown Military Collection, Brown University Library, 177; Library of Congress, 178, 181; Bostonian Society/Old State House, 184; Library of Congress, 188; New York Historical Association, Cooperstown, 189; Library of Congress, 193; Bettmann, 197; National Portrait Gallery, Smithsonian Institution, 201.

Chapter 8
Colonial Williamsburg, 204; Atwater Kent Museum, 206; Metropolitan Museum of Art, 209; New York Historical Society, 211; Brooklyn Museum, 213; Museum of the American Indian, 217; Henry Francis du Pont Winterthur Museum, 218; New York Historical Society, 222; Independence National Historical Park Collection, Philadelphia, 225; Library of Congress, 226; American Antiquarian Society, 229 (top); Metropolitan Museum of Art, 229 (bottom); Library Company of Philadelphia, 230.

Chapter 9
Metropolitan Museum of Art, Rogers Fund, 234; Art Resource, 236; Historical Society of Pennsylvania, Philadelphia, 241; Peabody & Essex Museum, Salem, 244; Independence National Historic Park, 245 (top); Blerancourt Museum, 245 (bottom); Library of Congress, 246; Mark Sexton, 251; Thomas Gilcrease Museum, Tulsa, OK, 253; Field Museum of Natural History, 256; Yale University Art Gallery, 260; National Gallery of Art, 263; New Bedford Whaling Museum, 265.

Chapter 10
Toledo Museum of Art, Ohio, 270; Library of Congress, 272; Walters Art Gallery, Baltimore, 277; Library of Congress, 280; Gibbes Museum of Art/Carolina Art Association, 285; The New York Public Library, Astor, Lenox and Tilden Foundations, 288; Museum of the City of New York, 291; Chicago Historical Society, 295; Library of Congress, 297; New York Historical Society, 299; Houghton Library, Harvard University, 303; The New York Public Library, 305.

Chapter 11
Historic New Orleans Collection, 308; Mississippi Department of Archives and History, 310; Library of Congress, 312; Philadelphia Museum of Art, 318 (left); Library of Congress, 318 (right); Daughters of the Republic of Texas, Library at the Alamo, 319; The Image Bank, 323; National Archives, 325; Chicago Historical Society, 327; Library of Congress, 331; Historic New Orleans Collection, 333; Smith College Archives, Smith College, 334; American Numismatic Society, 335; Library of Congress, 336; Smithsonian Institution, 338.

Chapter 12
Yale University Art Gallery, 342; Museum of American Textile History, 344; Abby Aldrich Rockefeller Folk Art Center, Williamsburg, VA, 346; Museum of Fine Arts, Boston, 348; Metropolitan Museum of Art, 349; Rhode Island Historical Society, 354; National Geographic Society, 358; New York Public Library, 363; Museum of Fine Arts, Boston, 364; Historical Pictures Collection/Stock Montage, 366; Brown Brothers, 368.

Chapter 13
Museum of the City of New York, 372; Lynn Historical Society, 374; Metropolitan Museum of Art, 378; Brown Brothers, 382; International Museum of Photography, Rochester, 384; Henry Francis du Pont Winterthur Museum, 386; Library of Congress, 388; Radcliffe College, Schlesinger Library, 390; Library of Congress, 392; Michael Melford, 395; Library of Congress, 398; Smith College Archives, Smith College, 400.

Chapter 14
Art Resource, 404; San Antonio Museum Association, 406; Walters Art Gallery, Baltimore, 409; Nebraska State Historical Society, 415; American Antiquarian Society, 418; Art Resource, 419; Walters Art Gallery, Baltimore, 421; Franklin Delano Roosevelt Library, 426; National Academy of Design, 428; Smithsonian Institution, 431; California State Library Picture Collection, 432; Museum of Fine Arts, Boston, 433; Museum of American Political Life, University of Hartford, 435.

Chapter 15
Bettmann, 438; Kansas State Historical Society, Topeka, 440; American Antiquarian Society, 445; Library of Congress, 446; Stowe-Day Foundation, Hartford, CT, 450; Bettmann, 451; Maryland Historical Society, 455; Library of Congress, 457, 459; Museum of the City of New York, 460; Library of Congress, 461, 463, 464; Lincoln Museum, Fort Wayne, Indiana, 469.

Chapter 16
Metropolitan Museum of Art, 472; The Picture Bank, 474; Burton Historical Collection of the Detroit Public Library, 477; Lincoln Museum, Fort Wayne, Indiana, 482; Library of Congress, 484; Valentine Museum, Cook Collection, 485 (top); Richmond Dispatch, 485 (bottom); Chicago Historical Society, 491; United States Army Military History Institute, 494; Culver Pictures, 497; National Archives, 501; Library of Congress, 504; National Museum of Health and Medicine, 505.

Chapter 17
Metropolitan Museum of Art, 508; Library of Congress, 510; National Archives, 512; Chicago Historical Society, 514; Library of Congress, 517; Radcliffe College, Schlesinger Library, 521; Harper's Weekly, 522; Library of Congress, 529; New York Historical Society, 531; University of North Carolina, Chapel Hill, 534 (left); Rutherford B. Hayes Memorial Library, 534 (right); Library of Congress, 537; The Picture Bank, 539.

Chapter 18
Amon Carter Museum, Fort Worth, TX, 544; Mitchell and DeGroff/University of Oklahoma Library, 546; Nebraska Historical Society, 548; Arizona Historical Society, Tucson, 556; Marlon Koogler McNay Art Institute, San Antonio, TX 559; Iowa State Historical Society, 561; Library of Congress, 562; Harper's Weekly, 564; Library of Congress, 567, 568; Idaho State University Press, Pocatello, Idaho, 572; Metropolitan Museum of Art, 574.

Chapter 19
Museum of the City of New York, 580; Historical Pictures Service/Stock Montage, 582; Edison National Historic Site, 584; Chicago Historical Society, 587; Library of Congress, 589; Denver Public Library, Western History Department, 591; Bruce Henstell, Venice, CA, 598; Harper's Weekly, 600; National Archives, 601; Chicago Historical Society, 604; New York State Historical Association, 605; Jacof A. Riis/Museum of the City of New York, 608; Rhode Island School of Design Museum of Art, 611.

Chapter 20
Chicago Historical Society, 614; Hunting Library, San Marino, CA, 616 (top); Alice Dehay/National Icarian Heritage Society, 616 (bottom); Museum of American Political Life, University of Hartford, 619; Library of Congress, 622; Library of Congress, 625, 627; Sally Anderson-Bruce/Museum of American Political Life, University of Hartford, 633; Theater Collection/Museum of the City of New York, 637; Bettmann, 641; Life Magazine, 643; Library of Congress, 645.

Chapter 21
National Gallery of Art, Washington, DC, 648; Chicago Historical Society, 650; International Museum of Photography at George Eastman House, 652; Henry Street Settlement, 654; Jacob A. Riis Collection/Museum of the City of New York, 657; Culver Pictures, 660; Toledo Museum of Art, 662; M. Barton Collection, 664; National Archives, 666; Western History Department/Denver Public Library, 667; Yale University Art Gallery, 671; Planned Parenthood Federation, New York, 673; Schomburg Center for Research in Black Culture/New York Public Library, 675; Library of Congress, 676; National Museum of American Art/Art Resource, 678.

Chapter 22
Whitney Museum of American Art, 684; Brown Brothers, 686; Library of Congress, 688; Culver Pictures, 691; Library of Congress, 695; Museum of the City of New York, 696; National Archives, 698; National Archives, 699; War Memorial Museum, Newport News, VA, 704; Library of Congress, 705; Historical Picture Service/Stock Montage, 708; Pemco Webster & Stevens Collection/Museum of History and Industry, Seattle, 710; White House Historical Association, 713.

INDEX

A

Abenaki, 70
Abernathy, Ralph, 904
Abolitionism, 93, 221, 268, 338–339, 434
  African American, 397, 399–400
  colonization and, 397
  Garrison's leadership of, 397–398, 399, 400
  opposition to, 399
  Quakers and, 397, 399
  rescue of fugitive slaves, 449
  women and, 520
  writings and speeches of, 398–399, 449–450, 456
Abortion, 983–984
  in nineteenth century, 367
Abraham Lincoln Brigade, 776
Abrams v. *United States,* 707
Acadia, 102, 117, 144
Acheson, Dean G., 830, 833, 841, 847, 850, 852, 884
Ackerman, Nathan, 758–759
Acoma, 55, 411
Acosta, Joseph de, 4
Acquired Immune Deficiency Syndrome (AIDS), 1013–1014
Acres of Diamonds (Conwell), 588
Adams, Abigail, 141, 186, 187, 199–200
Adams, Charles Francis, 466
Adams, Charles Francis, Jr., 538
Adams, Henry, 238
Adams, John, 119, 155, 180, 186, 192, 208, 213, 227
  at Continental Congress, 141, 142, 163, 166
  Declaration of Independence and, 169
  election of 1800, 224
  presidency of, 221–225, 248
Adams, John Quincy, 261
  election of 1824, 278
  election of 1828, 279
  opposition to gag rule, 399
  opposition to Texas annexation, 423
  presidency of, 278
  as secretary of state, 264–265
Adams, Samuel, 154, 158, 159, 162, 163, 211
Adams-Onis Treaty, 265
Addams, Jane, 649–650, 653, 694, 697
Adena tradition, 16–17

Advertising, 587, 733–734, 737, 871–872, 873
Affirmative action, 973, 974, 977
Afghanistan, Soviet invasion of, 989
Africa:
  agriculture in, 81–82
  communities of West Africa, 81
  effects of slave trade on, 88
  Portuguese trade in, 80
  slave trade in, 80, 82–88
African Americans
  abolitionists, 397, 399–400
  accommodation philosophy and, 674
  in armed forces, 699, 710, 802–804, 934, 935
  in baseball, 612, 895
  cowboys, 565
  culture of, 95–97
  discrimination against, 384, 513, 516–517, 532, 634–635, 656, 673, 864–865
  education of, 527–528, 532, 610, 674, 939, 973, 974
  family of, 523–524, 709
  free blacks, 107, 188, 334–335, 383–385, 397
  in Harlem, 745–747
  Ku Klux Klan and, 511, 520, 533, 741
  in labor force, 525–526, 591, 592, 602, 709, 967, 973–974
  in labor unions, 783, 810
  and land ownership, 524–525
  lynching of, 673, 674, 709, 710, 837
  and McCarthyism, 841
  middle class, 974
  in military service, 491–493
  mulattoes, 107, 309
  music of, 608, 610, 747, 868
  and New Deal, 782–783
  and Niagara movement, 675
  political participation of, 528–529, 530, 977
  in poverty, 973, 974, 975
  in race riots, 709–710, 813, 936–938, 940, 1022–1024
  race riots and, 453
  racial stereotypes of, 673–674
  during Reconstruction, 509–511, 516–518, 521–529
  reverse migration of, 969
  riots and, 384–385
  sharecroppers, 526–527
  and teenage pregnancy, 975

  underclass, 975–976
  urban migration of, 596, 708–710, 744–745, 894
  urban population of, 383–384
  voting rights and, 276, 518, 535, 634–635, 636, 656, 673, 896
  during World War I, 699, 708–710
  women, 674, 709, 967
  writers, 746, 776
  See also Civil rights movement; Slaves and slave trade
African Methodist Episcopal (AME) Church, 264, 333, 336, 384
Age of Reason, The (Paine), 228
Agnew, Spiro, 949, 957, 970
Agrarianism, Republican, 246–247
Agrarian Tradition, 13
Agricultural Adjustment Administration (AAA), 763, 770, 780, 782
Agriculture:
  agribusiness, 570–571, 969
  colonial, 130–131
  commercialization of, 294–295
  continental exchange and, 38–39
  debt, 732, 967
  dry farming technique, 549
  farmers' organizations, 621–623, 625, 626
  foreclosures, 266, 550, 967
  during Great Depression, 547, 757, 760, 769–771
  income, 732
  of Indians, 1–3, 10–19, 21, 22, 43, 53, 55, 563
  indigo, 91
  land purchase, 294
  market production and, 570
  in Medieval Europe, 30
  migrant workers, 547, 555
  Mormon, 554
  nature and, 547, 570
  and New Deal programs, 763, 770
  in New France, 56
  Plains communities, 571–573
  prices, 731–732, 757, 763, 861, 967
  range wars, 566
  rice, 77, 90
  rural life in North, 346–347
  sharecropping, 526–527, 536, 545–547
  in Southwest, 555, 556, 743–744
  strikes, 944–945
  subsidy, 763

K

Kachinas, 21
Kansas, 548, 552
  Bleeding Kansas, 439–441, 454
  Indian removal, 410–412
  Lecompton constitution, 457, 460
  opened for white settlement,
    452–453, 454
  populist movement in, 632
  raid on Lawrence, 489
  suffrage in, 520–521
  territory, 411
Kansas City (Kansas), 564, 744
Kansas-Nebraska Act, 444, 452–453
Kaskaskia, 146, 184, 411
Katzenbach, Nicholas, 928
Kearny, Stephen, 426
Keckley, Elizabeth, 474
Kefauver, Estes, 873
Kelley, Florence, 651, 653, 669, 697
Kellogg-Briand Pact, 725
Kemble, Fanny, 326, 327, 328
Kendall, Mary, 324
Kendall, Nicanor, 356
Kenna, Michael, 619
Kennan, George, 830, 842, 848
Kennedy, Edward, 975
Kennedy, John F.:
  assassination of, 887, 909
  and civil rights, 902, 904, 905,
    906, 907, 908, 909
  domestic policy of, 882–884, 918
  election of 1960, 881–882, 902
  foreign policy of, 884–887
  and Vietnam War, 884–885, 928
Kennedy, Joseph P., 882
Kennedy, Patrick Joseph, 378
Kennedy, Robert, 882, 902, 904,
  905, 917, 940–941
Kent, Elizabeth, 712
Kentucky, 123, 194, 316, 467
  in Civil War, 478–479, 481
  in Indian wars, 317
  statehood, 240
Kerensky, Alexander, 714
Kerner Commission, 938
Kerner, Otto, 938
Kerouac, Jack, 875
Keyhoe, Donald E., 847
Keynes, Maynard, 766
Khlebnikov, Kyrill, 429
Khomeini, Ayatollah Ruholla, 989,
  1007
Khrushchev, Nikita, 876, 877,
  886–887, 904
Kickapoo, 24, 411
Kim Il Sung, 848
King, Coretta Scott, 909
King George's War, 102, 144
King, Martin Luther, Jr., 901, 904,
  905, 911, 912, 935, 982, 1003
  assassination of, 940
  background of, 898–899
  ''I have a dream'' speech of, 909
  in jail, 902, 906
  in Montgomery bus boycott,
    891–892, 893

  in Montgomery march, 913
  and nonviolence, 899
  Poor People's Campaign of,
    939–940
King, Mary, 910
King Philip's War, 71–72, 121, 135
King, Rodney, 1023
King, Rufus, 261
King William's War, 73, 101, 128,
  129
Kino, Eusebio, 115
Kiowa, 411, 557, 558, 559, 560
Kipling, Rudyard, 638
Kissinger, Henry A., 951, 953, 955,
  985, 987
Kitchin, Claude, 694
Klamath, 916
Knights of Labor, 593, 594, 595,
  602, 624–625, 626
Know-Nothing party, 455
Knox, Henry, 193, 213, 793
Knox, Philander C., 689, 690
Kodiak Island, 239
Koop, C. Everett, 1014
Korean Americans, 948, 1019, 1024
Korean War, 847–851, 852, 928
Korematsu v. U.S., 814
Kossuth, Lajos, 432
Kristallnacht, 791
Krutch, Joseph Wood, 748
Ku Klux Klan, 511, 520, 533, 740–
  741, 906, 982
Kuwait, 1021, 1022
Ky, Nguyen Cao, 928

L

Labor:
  African American, 525–526,
    591, 592, 602, 709, 967,
    973–974
  benefits, 727, 729–730
  bound, 129–130
  child, 354, 360, 602, 652
  civil service, 618
  convict, 602
  discrimination, 602
  domestic, 347
  early strikes and, 362
  economic uncertainty and, 369
  free, 362
  gospel of work, 590
  immigrant, 376, 590–591, 592,
    664–668
  indentured servants, 59–60, 89,
    129
  length of work day, 361, 387,
    593–595, 703
  mobility of, 369–370
  populist movement of, 623–624
  productivity, 757
  safety conditions for, 666, 668–
    669, 728
  size of work force, 663
  wage, 361–362
  wage system, 590, 663
  white-collar, 365
  women's, 591–592, 593, 703–

    704, 743, 759, 780, 809,
    843–846, 883, 967–968
  working conditions for, 591,
    592–593, 727
  in World War I, 702–704
  in World War II, 808–810
  See also Artisans; Factories;
    Industrial Revolution; Slaves
    and slave trade;
    Unemployment
Labor Department, 618, 703, 782,
  919
Labor-Management Relations Act
  of 1947 (Taft-Hartley Act),
  835
Labor party, 624
Labor unions, 663–664
  African Americans in, 783, 810
  bohemians and, 671
  boycotts of, 669
  during Civil War, 496
  company, 728–729
  cowboys in, 565
  decline of, 729, 967
  early, 362, 386–387, 593–595
  formation of AFL, 595
  growth of, 703, 767, 835
  Industrial Workers of the World
    (IWW), 670, 673, 703, 708,
    711
  judicial decisions against, 669
  Knights of Labor, 593, 594, 595,
    602, 624–625, 626
  mining, 554
  precursors to, 385–386
  of public employees, 967
  racial discrimination in, 602, 635
  regulation of, 766, 835
  rise of CIO, 767–768
  violence and, 670, 768
  women in, 594, 624–625, 668,
    704
  See also Strikes
Labrador, 44
La Follette, Robert M., 656, 659,
  714, 723
Lake Erie, 146
Lake Mead, 771
Lake Tulare, 576
Lakota, 4
Land:
  claims, 545
  government territories, 552–553
  homesteading, 548–550
  Indian, 127, 128, 129, 144, 150,
    196, 218, 219, 252, 254, 255,
    545, 561, 772, 916, 976
  public, 196, 266, 294, 298, 538
  redistribution among former
    slaves, 503, 514, 515, 524
  sales, 550, 552
  speculation, 150, 266, 298, 546,
    550
  survey of, 410
Landis, Paul, 868
Landon, Alfred M., election of
  1936, 768
Land Ordinance of 1785, 195–196

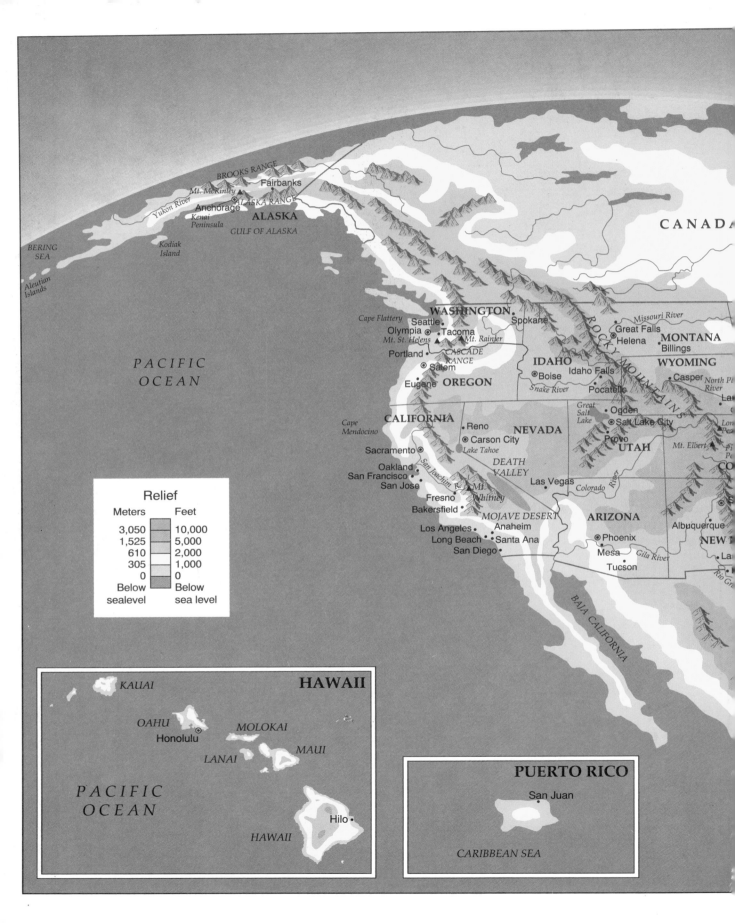

BROOKS RANGE

Fairbanks

Mt. McKinley ▲

ALASKA RANGE

Anchorage

Yukon River

Kenai
Peninsula

ALASKA

GULF OF ALASKA

BERING
SEA

Kodiak
Island

Aleutian
Islands

CANADA

PACIFIC
OCEAN

Cape Flattery

WASHINGTON

Seattle

Spokane

Missouri River

Great Falls

Olympia

Tacoma

Mt. St. Helens ▲

Mt. Rainier ▲

MONTANA

Helena

Billings

Portland

CASCADE
RANGE

IDAHO

WYOMING

Salem

Boise

Idaho Falls

Casper

North Pla
River

Eugene

OREGON

Snake River

Pocatello

La

Cape
Mendocino

CALIFORNIA

Reno

NEVADA

Great
Salt
Lake

Ogden

Salt Lake City

Lon
Pea

Carson City

Provo

UTAH

Mt. Elbert ▲

Sacramento

Lake Tahoe

DEATH
VALLEY

CO

San Joaquin R.

S

Oakland

San Francisco

San Jose

Mt.
Whitney ▲

Las Vegas

Colorado River

P

Fresno

Bakersfield

MOJAVE DESERT

ARIZONA

Albuquerque

Los Angeles

Anaheim

Phoenix

NEW

Long Beach

Santa Ana

Mesa

Gila River

La

San Diego

Tucson

Rio Gra

BAJA CALIFORNIA

Relief

Meters	Feet
3,050	10,000
1,525	5,000
610	2,000
305	1,000
0	0
Below sealevel	Below sea level

HAWAII

KAUAI

OAHU

MOLOKAI

Honolulu

LANAI

MAUI

PACIFIC
OCEAN

Hilo

HAWAII

PUERTO RICO

San Juan

CARIBBEAN SEA